GW00838430

WICHMANN'S

POCKET DICTIONARY
OF THE
GERMAN AND ENGLISH
LANGUAGES

(WITH RULES AS TO PRONUNCIATION)

ENTIRELY REVISED

By L. BORINSKI, Ph.D.

AND H. B. BUSSMANN, Ph.D.

ROUTLEDGE & KEGAN PAUL

LONDON, HENLEY AND BOSTON

Revised Edition published in 1952
by Routledge & Kegan Paul Limited
39 Store Street
London WC1E 7DD,
Broadway House, Newtown Road
Henley-on-Thames
Oxon RG9 1EN and
9 Park Street
Boston, Mass. 02108, USA
Printed in Great Britain by
Redwood Burn Limited
Trowbridge & Esher
Reprinted 1958, 1961, 1963, 1966, 1972 and 1978

ISBN 0 7100 2290 5

CONTENTS

INHALT

SOME REMARKS ON GERMAN PRONUNCIATION

As very few German sounds are exactly like the corresponding English sounds the English equivalents given below represent in most cases only approximately the sounds of the German vowels and consonants.

A. Vowels

Simple vowels are either long or short in German.

They are always long when doubled or followed by *h*, and mostly long when followed by a single consonant.

They are, as a rule, short when followed by a group of consonants.

All long vowels are simple sounds in German, e.g. long *e* in *Fee* is like the first part of the English *a* in *mane*, but does not shift to *i*; long *o* is like the English *o* in *no*, without shifting to *u*.

Short *i* is like *i* in *it*, e.g. *mit*.
Long *i* ,, ,, *i* in *machine*, e.g. *dir*.
Short *e* ,, ,, *e* in *let*, e.g. *fett*.
Long *e* ,, ,, *a* in *late*, e.g. *Fee*.
Long *a* ,, ,, *a* in *alms*, e.g. *Tal*.
Short *o* ,, ,, *o* in *not*, e.g. *flott*.
Long *o* ,, ,, *o* in *no*, e.g. *rot*.
Short *u* ,, ,, *u* in *put*, e.g. *und*.
Long *u* ,, ,, *u* in *rude*, e.g. *Mut*.
Short *ä* ,, ,, *e* in *fell*, e.g. *fällt*.
Long *ä* ,, ,, *a* in *mare*, e.g. *fährt*.

The letters *ie* always represent the long English *ee* sound as in *field*, e.g. *sie*.

ö is pronounced like German *e* with rounded and protruded lips.

ü is pronounced like German *i* with rounded and protruded lips.

Final *e* is always pronounced in German words, e.g. *fette* like English *fetter* (without the *r*-sound).

B. Diphthongs

äu and *eu* resemble the *oi*-sound in *boy*, e.g. *Mäuse, Heu*.

ei⎱ are like ⎰*ei* in height⎱ e.g. *Ei*.
ai⎰ ⎱*ai* in aisle ⎰ *Mai*.

au is like *ow* in *how*, e.g. *lau*.

C. Consonants

b, d=English *b, d* at the beginning of a word or syllable, e.g. *Boden*.

b, d=English *p, t* in all other cases, e.g. *Lob, Abt, und*.

ch=(1) Scotch *ch* in 'loch' after *a, o, u*, e.g. *ach, doch, Tuch*.
 =(2) first sound of 'hew' after the remaining vowels, and consonants, e.g. *ich, echt, Mächte, reich, euch, Gretchen*.
 =(3) *k* before 's', e.g. *Fuchs, wachsen, Ochs*, and in some words of Greek origin, e.g. *Christ, Chor, Charakter*.

ck=*k*, e.g. *Lack, wecken*.

g=(1) English *g* at the beginning of a word or syllable, e.g. *gar, legen*.
 =(2) *ch* (1) or (2) in all other cases, e.g. *zag, selig, lugte, Berg*. This *g* may also be pronounced like English *g* or *k*, except after *i* and *n*.

ng=English *ng* in *long*, e.g. *lang, singen*.

j=English *y* in *yes*, e.g. *ja, jeder*.

r=Scotch *r* in *girl*, e.g. *roh, Herr*.

s=(1) English *z*, at the beginning of a word or syllable, e.g. *so, Rose*.
 =(2) English voiceless *s* in *hiss*, in all other cases, e.g. *es, ist*.

ss=English voiceless *s* in *hiss*, e.g. *lassen, Fuss, grösser*.

sp, st=English *shp, sht*, at the beginning of a word, e.g. *spät, Stuhl*; in all other cases like English *sp, st*.

th=English *t*, e.g. *Theater*.

v=English *f*, e.g. *vor, Vetter*; in words of Latin origin like English *v*, e.g. *Viktoria*.

w=English *v*, e.g. *wer, wir, Löwe*.

x=English *ks* (never like *gs*), e.g. *Max*.

y=mostly like *ü*, e.g. *Symphonie*, sometimes like *i*.

z, tz=English *ts*, e.g. *zu, Reiz, Sitz, Katze*.

-tion=*-tsyon*, e.g. *Nation*.

Stress

The principal stress in German words rests on the root syllable which is usually the first syllable, e.g. *ságen, élterlich.*

Exceptions are *Forélle, Holúnder, Wachélder, lebóndig*, nouns ending in *-ei*, like *Bettelei*, and verbs ending in *-ieren*, e.g. *spazieren.*

The prefixes *be-, ge-, er-, ver-, ent-, zer-*, are unstressed.

The prefix *ant-* has always, and the prefix *un-* has usually the principal stress, e.g. *ántworten, únruhig.*

Exceptions are *unmöglich, unéndlich.*

Words borrowed from foreign languages retain their original stress, e.g. *Natúr, Dóktor, Doktóren, Universität.*

Compound adverbs have their principal stress on the second part, e.g. *hervór, dahín, zusámmen.*

BEMERKUNGEN ZUR AUSSPRACHE DES ENGLISCHEN

Die Aussprache des Englischen unterscheidet sich von der deutschen hauptsächlich dadurch, dass der Engländer beim Sprechen die Zunge senkt und zurückzieht, sodass sie flacher im Munde liegt. Der Unterkiefer wird ein wenig nach vorn geschoben und die Lippen werden viel weniger gebraucht, vor allem nicht vorgestülpt, höchstens mässig gerundet.

Lautzeichen und Lautwerte decken sich im Englischen noch viel weniger als im Deutschen. Derselbe Laut kann durch ganz verschiedene Buchstaben wiedergegeben werden und derselbe Buchstabe kann ganz verschiedene Laute bezeichnen. Die Schreibweise ist also durchaus kein Führer für die Aussprache. Dennoch dürften einige allgemeine Hinweise nützlich sein.

A. Vokale

Langes *a* ist wie im deutschen *kam*, z.B. *car, alms*.

Kurzes *a* liegt zwischen deutschem *a* und *ä*, doch ist der Raum zwischen Zunge und Gaumen grösser als beim deutschen *a*, z.B. *rat, can*.

Ausserdem gibt es ein kurzes dunkles *a*, wobei die zurückgezogene Zunge sich gegen den weichen Gaumen hebt, z.B. *but, some*.

Langes *e* ist ein Diphthong, der mit *e* beginnt und nach *i* hin ausklingt, z.B. *may=mee-i*.

Langes halboffenes *o* ist ein Diphthong, der mit *o* beginnt und nach *u* hin ausklingt, z.B. *no=noo-u*.

Langes offenes *o* liegt zwischen *a* und *o* (der Laut des *o* in *Gott* verlängert), z.B. *all, or*.

Kurzes offenes *o* klingt nach *a* hin, z.B. *not, god*.

Langes offenes ö in Wörtern wie *fir, girl, learn*. Die Zunge bleibt flach in mittlerer Lage und der Unterkiefer wird gesenkt.

Auslautendes *e* ist immer stumm im Englischen.

B. Konsonanten

b, d, und *g* werden auch am Ende einer Silbe stimmhaft, d.h. wie am Anfang gesprochen, z.B. *bib, dead, gag.*

j ist ein stimmhaftes *sch* wie in *Genie,* mit einem *d* davor, z.B. *Jew;* derselbe Laut wird oft durch *g* bezeichnet, z.B. *gin.*

r vor Vokalen wird mit der Zungenspitze hervorgebracht, aber nicht gerollt, z.B. *rid, proud.* Im Auslaut verschwindet es fast ganz, z.B. *far.*

s im Anlaut ist immer stimmlos wie im deutschen *ist,* z.B. *so.* Zwischen Vokalen wird es stimmhaft, z.B. *rose,* wie im deutschen *Rose.*

sp und *st* sind niemals wie deutsches *schp* und *scht* zu sprechen.

th ist ein Reibelaut (wie *s*), bei dem sich die Zunge an die oberen Schneidezähne legt. Es ist entweder stimmlos, z.B. *thick,* oder stimmhaft, z.B. *them.*

w ist ein mit den Lippen gebildetes deutsches *w* mit der Zungenstellung für *u.*

z ist immer der stimmhafte s-Laut (wie im deutschen *sie*), z.B. *zest, lazy.*

LIST OF ABBREVIATIONS USED IN THE DICTIONARY
VERZEICHNIS DER IM WÖRTERBUCH GEBRAUCHTEN ABKÜRZUNGEN

a. = adjective, Adjektiv.
adv. = adverb, Adverb, Umstandswort.
Am. = Americanism, Amerikanismus.
ar. = arithmetic, Arithmetik.
arch. = architecture, Baukunst.
art. = article, Artikel, Geschlechtswort.
avi. = aviation, Flugwesen.
c. = conjunction, Konjunktion, Bindewort.
com. = commercial, Handel.
cp. = compare, vergleiche.
def. = defective, defektiv.
elek. = electricity, Elektrizität.
f. = feminine, weiblich.
fam. = familiarly, familiär.
fig. = figuratively, figürlich.
geom. = geometry, Geometrie.
gram. = grammar, Grammatik.
her. = heraldry, Heraldik.
hist. = history, Geschichte.
hunt. = hunting, Jagdwesen.
i. = interjection, Empfindungswort.
ir. = irregular, unregelmässig.
lit. = literally, wörtlich.
m. = masculine, männlich.
math. = mathematics, Mathematik.
mech. = mechanics, Maschinenwesen.
med. = medicine, Medizin.
met. = metallurgy, Hüttenwesen.
mil. = military, Heerwesen.
min. = mining, Bergbau.
mot. = motoring, Kraftfahrwesen.

mus. = music, Musik.
   n. = neuter, sächlich.
nav. = navigation, Seewesen.
obs. = obsolete, veraltet.
opt. = optics, Optik.
   p. = participle, Partizipium.
phot. = photography, Photographie.
phys. = physics, Physik.
  pl. = plural, Mehrzahl.
 pn. = pronoun, Fürwort.
 pr. = preposition, Verhältniswort.
print. = printing, Druckereibetrieb.
   r. = regular, regelmässig.
rail. = railway, Eisenbahn.
  s. = substantive, Hauptwort.
 sl. = slang, Slang.
 st. = strong, stark.
subj. = subjunctive, Konjunktiv.
theat. = theatre, Theater.
 tel. = telegraphy, Telegraphie.
 tel. = telephone, Fernsprechwesen.
 typ. = typography, Buchdruck.
 v.i. = intransitive verb, intransitives Zeitwort.
v.refl. = reflexive verb, rückbezügliches Zeitwort.
 v.t. = transitive verb, transitives Zeitwort.
vulg. = vulgar, gemein.
Zus. = Zusammensetzung(en), compound word(s).

NOTES ON SIGNS

0   Indicates that a German noun has no plural form.

(-,) Indicates that a German noun remains unaltered in the
      genitive or plural.

(s) Indicates that the German verb is conjugated with *sein*.

(h, s) Indicates that the German verb is conjugated with either
        haben or *sein*. (Where neither of these is mentioned, the
        verb is conjugated with *haben*.)

~   Indicates the main word at the beginning of each separate
     entry.

BEMERKUNGEN ZU DEN ZEICHEN

0   Anzeige, dass ein deutsches Substantiv keine Pluralform
     hat.

(-,) Anzeige, dass ein deutsches Substantiv im Genitiv oder
      Plural unverändert bleibt.

(s) Anzeige, dass das deutsche Zeitwort mit '*sein*' verbunden
     wird.

(h, s) Anzeige, dass beide Hilfszeitwörter (*haben* und *sein*)
        zulässig sind. (Wo eine Angabe fehlt, versteht sich die
        Verbindung mit *haben* von selbst.)

~   Zeigt das Stichwort an derSpitze des betreffenden Artikels
     an.

GERMAN AND ENGLISH

A

Aal *m.* (-[e]s, -e) eel.

Aas *n.* (-es, Äser) carcass, carrion.

Aasgeier *m.* carrion-kite.

ab *adv.* off; down; (away) from; ~ *und zu,* from time to time; to and fro; occasionally; *auf und* ~, up and down; *Hut* ~! hats off!

abändern *v.t.* to alter; (*Gesetz*) to amend.

Abänderung *f.* (-, -en) alteration; (*Gesetz*) amendment.

abarbeiten (sich) *v.refl.* to overwork oneself.

Abart *f.* (-, -en) variety.

Abbau *m.* (-[e]s, 0) working (of a mine); retrenchment; *Preis* ~, reduction of prices.

abbauen *v.t.* to work (a mine); *Stellen* ~, to abolish; *Beamte* ~, to dismiss.

abbehalten *v.t.st.* **den Hut** ~, to remain uncovered.

abbeissen *v.t.st.* to bite off.

abbekommen *v.t.st.* to get a share in.

abberufen *v.t.st.* to call back, to recall.

Abberufung *f.* (-, -en) recall.

abbestellen *v.t.* to countermand.

abbezahlen *v.t.* to pay off, to pay up.

abbiegen *v.t. & i.st.* to bend off; to turn off, to branch off.

Abbild *n.* (-[e]s, -er) copy, image.

abbilden *v.t.* to copy, to portray; *nach dem Leben* ~, to draw from the life.

Abbildung *f.* (-, -en) picture, illustration.

Abbitte *f.* (-, -en) apology; ~ *leisten,* ~ *tun,* to apologize.

abbitten *v.t.st.* to apologize for; to deprecate.

abblasen *v.t.st.* to blow off; to sound (a retreat).

abblenden *v.t.* (*mot.*) to dim.

abblühen *v.i.* (*h, s*) to cease flowering; to wither.

abbrechen *v.t.st.* to break off, to pluck off; to demolish, to pull down (*Häuser etc.*); *kurz* ~, to cut short; ~ *v.i.st.* to break off, to leave off; to drop a subject.

abbrennen *v.t.ir.* to burn off (away, down); (*Feuerwerk*) to let off; ~ *v.i.ir.* (*s*) to be burnt down; to lose one's property by fire.

abbringen *v.t.ir.* to dissuade; to divert.

abbröckeln *v.t. & i.* (*s*) to crumble away.

Abbruch *m.* (-[e]s, -brüche) breaking off; pulling down; damage, injury, detriment.

abbürsten *v.t.* to brush off, to brush.

abbüssen *v.t.* to atone for, to expiate; to serve (*Strafe*).

abdachen *v.refl.* to slope of.

abdämmen *v.t.* to dam up; to embank.

abdanken *v.i.* to resign, to abdicate.

Abdankung *f.* (-, -en) abdication.

abdecken *v.t.* to uncover; to unroof; to flay; (*den Tisch*) to clear.

Abdecker *m.* (-s, -) knacker.

abdienen *v.t.* to pay off by service, to work off; to serve one's time.

abdrängen *v.t.* to force (one) away.

abdrehen *v.t.* (*Gas*) to turn off; (*el. Licht, Radio*) to switch off.

abdringen *v.t.st.* to extort from.

abdrosseln *v.t.* to throttle.

Abdruck *m.* (-[e]s, -drücke) impression; copy; (*phot.*) print; cast (*Abguss*), stamp, mark.

abdrucken *v.t.* to take a copy, to print off.

abdrücken *v.t.* to pull the trigger, to fire.

Abend *m.* (-s, -e) evening, night; (*Himmelsgegend*) West *m.*; *gestern* ~, last night; *heute* ~, to-night.

Abendanzug *m.* (-[e]s, -züge), **Abendkleid** *n.* (-[e]s, -er) evening dress.

Abend: ~**blatt** *n.* evening paper; ~**brot** *n.* supper; ~**dämmerung** *f.* twilight, dusk; ~**essen,** supper; ~**land** *n.* West, Occident.

abendländisch *a.* western.

abendlich *a.* evening...

Abendmahl *n.* *das heilige* ~, the Lord's Supper; *das* ~ *empfangen,* to take the sacrament.

Abendrot *n.* sunset glow.

abends *adv.* in the evening.

Abendstern *m.* evening star, Hesperus.

Abenteuer *n.* (-s, -) adventure.

abenteuerlich *a.* adventurous; strange.

Abenteurer *m.* (-s, -) adventurer.

aber *c.* but; ~ *doch,* but yet; ~ *adv.* however.

Aberglaube *m.* (-ns, 0) superstition.

abergläubig, abergläubisch *a.* superstitious.

aberkennen *v.t.ir.* to deprive of or disallow, by legal verdict.

1

abermalig *a.* reiterated, repeated.
abermals *adv.* again, once more.
abernten *v.t.* to reap (a field).
Aberwitz *m.* (-es, 0): craziness.
abfahren *v.t.st.* to cart away; ~ *v.i.ir.* (s) to depart, to start, to leave.
Abfahrt *f.* (-, -en) departure, start; (*Schiff*) sailing.
Abfall *m.* (-[e]s, -fälle) falling off; waste, offal, refuse; apostasy; defection.
abfallen *v.i.st.* to fall off; to slope; to desert, to apostatise; *es fällt dabei etwas für mich ab*, I profit by it.
abfällig *a.* derogatory.
abfangen *v.t.st.* to catch; to intercept.
abfärben *v.i.* to lose colour, to come off (of colours); to stain.
abfassen *v.t.* to compose, to draw up, to draft.
Abfassung *f.* (-, -en) composing, wording.
abfegen *v.t.* to wipe, to sweep (off).
abfeilen *v.t.* to file off.
abfertigen *v.t.* to dispatch, to send off; *kurz* ~, to snub, to put down.
Abfertigung *f.* (-, -en) dispatch; clearance.
abfeuern *v.t.* to fire off, to discharge.
abfinden *v.t.st.* to satisfy, to pay off; (sich) ~ (*mit*), *v.refl.* to put up with.
Abfindung *f.* (-, -en) indemnity.
Abfindungssumme *f.* composition.
abfliegen *v.i.st.* (avi.) to take off.
abfliessen *v.i.st.* (s) to flow off.
Abflug *m.* (-[e]s, -flüge) take-off.
Abfluss *m.* (-flusses, -flüsse) flowing off; discharge; gutter, drain, waste-pipe.
abfordern *v.t.* to call away; to demand.
abfragen *v.t.* to inquire of, to get (a thing) out of (one); *eine Lektion* ~, to hear a lesson.
Abfuhr *f.* (-, -en) removal; rebuff.
abführen *v.t.* to carry away; (med.) to purge; (*Schuld*) to discharge.
abführend *a.* (med.) aperient.
Abführmittel *n.* purgative.
abfüllen *v.t.* to decant, to bottle.
abfüttern *v.t.* to feed.
Abgabe *f.* (-, -en) delivery, surrender; tax, duty.
Abgang *m.* (-[e]s, -gänge) departure; loss, waste; (com.) deficiency, tare; diminution; (von Waren) sale; (theat.) exit.
Abgangsprüfung *f.* leaving examination.
Abgangszeugnis *n.* leaving certificate.
Abgas *n.* (-es, -e) waste gas, exhaust gas.
abgeben *v.t.st.* to deliver up, to give up, to turn in; *sich* ~ *mit*, to concern oneself about a thing, to keep company with a person.
abgebrannt *a.* (fig.) stony broke.
abgebrüht *a.* hardened.
abgedroschen *p. & a.* trite, hackneyed.
abgefeimt *a.* cunning, arch.

abgegriffen *p. & a.* well-thumbed.
abgehen *v.i.st.* (s) to go off, to depart; (*Schiff*) to sail; to come off; *es geht mir ab*, I lack; *sich* ~ *lassen*, to deny oneself.
abgehend *a.* outgoing.
abgeklärt *a.* (fig.) detached.
abgelebt *a.* decrepit.
Abgelebtheit *f.* (-, 0) decrepitude.
abgelegen *a.* remote, outlying.
abgemacht *a.* settled; ~! done! agreed!
abgemessen *a.* measured; formal.
abgeneigt *a.* disinclined.
Abgeneigtheit *f.* (-, 0) disinclination, aversion.
abgenutzt *a.* worn out, used up; threadbare.
Abgeordnete(r) *m.* (-n, -n) deputy, representative; Member of Parliament.
Abgeordnetenhaus *n.*, Abgeordnetenkammer *f.* House of Commons; (*Am.*) House of Representatives.
abgerechnet *p.* not counting, exclusive (of), deducting.
abgerissen *p. & a.* ragged; (fig.) abrupt.
abgesagt *a.* declared, sworn.
Abgesandte(r) *m.* (-n, -n) messenger.
abgeschieden *a.* secluded; retired; deceased.
abgeschmackt *a.* tasteless; absurd.
abgesehen *p.* ~ *von*, apart from; ~ *auf*, aimed at.
abgespannt *a.* (fig.) exhausted, run down.
abgestanden *p. & a.* stale, flat.
abgestorben *a.* dead.
abgestumpft *a.* blunted; (fig.) dull.
Abgestumpftheit *f.* (-, 0) dullness.
abgetan *a.* done with, settled; dispatched.
abgetragen *a.* (*Kleider*) threadbare, worn out.
abgewinnen *v.t.st.* to win from; *Geschmack* ~, to get a taste for.
abgewöhnen *v.t.* to wean from; *sich etwas* ~, *v.refl.* to give up.
abgiessen *v.t.ir.* to pour off, to decant.
Abglanz *m.* (-es, 0) reflection, image.
Abgott *m.* (-[e]s, -götter) idol.
Abgötterei *f.* (-, 0) idolatry.
abgöttisch *a.* idolatrous.
abgraben *v.t.st.* to drain off.
abgrämen (sich) *v.refl.* to pine away.
abgrasen *v.t.* to graze.
abgrenzen *v.t.* to delimit(ate).
Abgrund *m.* (-[e]s, -gründe) abyss; precipice.
abgucken *v.t.* to learn through observation.
Abguss *m.* (-gusses, -güsse) cast, copy.
abhacken *v.t.* to chop off.
abhaken *v.t.* to unhook.
abhalftern *v.t.* to undo the halter.
abhalten *v.t.st.* to detain; to prevent; to keep off; (*Versammlung*) to hold.

Abhaltung f. (-, -en) detention, prevention, hindrance.

abhandeln v.t. (*vom Preise*) to beat down; to discuss, to treat of.

abhanden adv. not at hand; ~ kommen, to be missing, to get lost.

Abhandlung f. (-, -en) treatise, paper.

Abhang m. (-[e]s, Abhänge) declivity, slope.

abhängen v.t. & i. to take down; to depend.

abhängig a. dependent; ~ von, subject to.

Abhängigkeit f. (-, 0) dependence.

abhärmen (sich) v.refl. to pine away, to grieve.

abhärten v.t. to harden; to inure.

abhaspeln v.t. to reel off.

abhauen v.t. to chop off, to cut off.

abhäuten v.t. to skin.

abheben v.t.st. (*Karten*) to cut; (*Geld*) to withdraw; (*sich*) ~, to stand out (against).

abhelfen v.t.st. to remedy, to redress.

abhetzen v.t. to run down.

Abhilfe f. (-, 0) redress, remedy, relief.

abhold a. averse, ill-disposed (towards).

abholen v.t. to fetch, to go for, to call for; *einen vom Bahnhof* ~, to meet a person at the station; ~ lassen, to send for.

Abholung f. (-, -en) collection.

abholzen v.t. to clear a wood.

abhören v.t. to listen in, to monitor.

Abhülfe, s. Abhilfe.

abirren v.i. (s) to deviate, to stray.

Abirrung f. (-, -en) deviation, aberration.

Abitur n. (-s, 0) leaving examination.

Abiturient m. (-en, -en) candidate for the leaving examination of a secondary school.

abjagen v.t. to retrieve; to override, overdrive (a horse).

abkanten v.t. to bevel.

abkanzeln v.t.(*fig.*) to rebuke.

abkarten v.t. to prearrange; *abgekartete Sache*, put-up job, plot, collusion.

abkaufen v.t. to buy from.

Abkehr f. (-, 0) falling away, desertion.

abkehren (sich), v.refl. to fall away, to desert.

Abklatsch m. (-es, -e) cast, impression; poor imitation.

abklopfen v.t. to tap.

abknabbern v.t. to nibble off.

abkneifen v.t.ir. to pinch (off), to nip (off).

abknöpfen v.t. to unbutton; (*fam.*) to do a person out of a thing.

abkochen v.t. to cook a meal in camp.

abkommandieren v.t. to detach.

abkommen v.i.st. (s) to deviate; to fall into disuse; *ich kann nicht* ~, I am busy.

Abkommen n. (-s, -) agreement.

Abkömmling m. (-s, -e) descendant.

abkonterfeien v.t. to take a person's likeness.

abkratzen v.t. to scrape off, to scratch off.

abkriegen v.t. to get (a share of); *etwas* ~, to come in for a wigging.

abkühlen v.t. to cool; (sich) ~ v.refl. to cool down, to get cool.

Abkühlung f. (-, -en) cooling; (*chem.*) refrigeration.

Abkunft f. (-, 0) descent, origin; *von guter* ~, of good family.

abkürzen v.t. to shorten, to abridge, to abbreviate; (*math.*) to reduce.

Abkürzung f. (-, -en) abbreviation.

Abkürzungsweg m. short cut.

abküssen v.t. to kiss and hug.

abladen v.t.st. to unload, to dump.

ablagern v.t. to deposit.

Ablagerung f. (-, -en) sediment; (*geol.*) deposit.

Ablass m. (-lasses, -lässe) indulgence; *vollkommener* ~, plenary indulgence.

ablassen v.t.st. (*vom Preise etwas*) to abate, to come off; (*einen Teich*) to drain; ~ v.i.st. to cease, to leave off.

Ablativ m. (-[e]s, -e) ablative.

Ablauf m. (-[e]s, 0) lapse, expiration.

ablaufen v.i.st. (s) to flow down; to end, to expire; to become due; ~ v.t.ir. to wear off by walking; (*den Rang*) ~, to outdo; ~ lassen, to snub; *schlecht* ~, to end ill.

ablauschen v.t. to overhear.

Ableben n. (-s, 0) decease, death.

ablecken v.t. to lick off.

ablegen v.t. to lay aside; to take off, to put down; (*einen Eid*) to take (an oath); (*ein Kleid*) to take off, to cease wearing; (*Rechenschaft*) to account for; *Zeugnis* ~, to bear witness.

Ableger m. (-s, -) layer, slip, shoot.

ablehnen v.t. to decline, to refuse, to turn down; (*Richter, Geschworene*) to challenge.

Ablehnung f. (-, -en) refusal; (*Richter, Geschworene*) challenge.

ableisten v.t. to perform duly.

ableiten v.t. to divert; to derive.

Ableitung f. (-, -en) derivation; diversion.

ablenken v.t. to avert, to divert, to turn off; (*phys.*) to deflect.

ablernen v.t. to learn from.

ablesen v.t.st. to read off.

Ablesung f. (-, -en) reading.

ableugnen v.t. to deny, to disown.

Ableugnung f. (-, -en) denial, abnegation.

abliefern v.t. to deliver.

Ablieferung f. (-, -en) delivery.

abliegen v.i.st. (s) to lie away from.

ablocken v.t. to get by coaxing.

ablöschen v.t. to wipe off.

ablösen v.t. to loosen; (*die Wache*) to discharge, to redeem; (*die Wache*) to

relieve; (sich) ~ *v.refl.* to peel off; to relieve one another, to alternate.
Ablösung *f.* (-, -en) loosening; redemption; relief.
abmachen *v.t.* to undo, to loosen; to arrange, to stipulate.
Abmachung *f.* (-, -en) arrangement, stipulation.
abmagern *v.i.* (*s*) to fall away, to grow lean, thin.
abmahnen *v.t.* to dissuade from.
abmalen *v.t.* to paint, to portray; to depict.
Abmarsch *m.* (-[e]s, -märsche) marching off.
abmarschieren *v.i.* (*s*) to march off.
abmartern *v.t.* to torture; to vex; to worry.
abmatten *v.t.* to fatigue, to tire out.
abmelden (sich) *v.t.* & *refl.* to report out, to report a person's departure.
abmessen *v.t.st.* to measure off, to survey.
Abmessung *f.* (-, -en) measurement; proportion.
abmieten *v.t.* to rent (from); to hire.
abmontieren *v.t.* (*mech.*) to dismantle.
abmühen (sich) *v.refl.* to exert oneself.
abnagen *v.t.* to gnaw, to nibble.
Abnahme *f.* (-, -n), decrease; (*einer Maschine*) acceptance.
abnehmen *v.t.st.* to take off *or* away; ~ *v.i.ir.* to decrease, to diminish.
Abnehmer *m.* (-s, -) buyer.
Abneigung *f.* (-, -en) disinclination, aversion, dislike.
abnötigen *v.t.* to force (from), to extort (from).
abnutzen *v.t.* to wear out; (sich)~, *v.refl.* to wear off.
Abnutzung *f.* (-, -en) wear and tear.
Abonnement *n.* (-s, -s) subscription; *Jahres* ~, annual subscription; *Monats* ~, monthly subscription; *sein* ~ *aufgeben*, to discontinue one's subscription.
Abonnent *m.* (-en, -en) subscriber.
abonnieren *v.i.* to subscribe to (*auf*).
abordnen, *v.t.* to delegate; (*mil.*) to detail.
Abordnung *f.* (-, -en) delegacy, delegation, deputation.
Abort *m.* (-[e]s, -e) water-closet (W.C.), lavatory; (*Am.*) toilet.
abpachten *v.t.* to rent, to farm (from).
abpassen *v.t.* to watch for; to choose a fitting time, to time.
abpflücken *v.t.* to pluck off; to pick.
abplacken, abplagen (sich) *v.refl.* to tire oneself out, to drudge.
abplatten *v.t.* to flatten.
abprallen *v.i.* (*s*) to rebound; to ricochet.
Abpraller *m.* (-s, -) ricochet.
abprotzen *v.t.* to unlimber.
abputzen *v.t.* to clean, to polish.
abquälen *v.t.* to torment, to worry.

abrackern (sich) *v.refl.* to slave, to toil.
abrahmen *v.t.* to skim (milk).
abraten *v.t.st.* to dissuade (from), to warn (against).
abräumen *v.t.* to clear, to take away, to remove.
abrechnen *v.t.* to deduct; ~ *v.i.* to settle (accounts).
Abrechnung *f.* (-, -en) settlement; *auf* ~, on account.
Abrechnungstag *m.* (*Börse*) settling day.
Abrede *f.* (-, -n) agreement; *in* ~ *stellen*, to deny, to dispute.
abreden *v.t.* to dissuade from.
abreiben *v.t.st.* to rub off, to rub down; to grind (colours).
Abreise *f.* (-, -n) departure.
abreisen *v.i.* (*s*) to depart, to set out, to start.
abreissen *v.t.st.* to tear off; (*Häuser*) pull down; ~ *v.i.st.* to break (off), to snap off.
abrichten *v.t.* (*Pferd*) to break (in); (*Hund*) to train.
abriegeln *v.t.* to bolt.
abringen *v.t.st.* to twist off; (*fig.*) to wrest (a thing) from.
abrinnen *v.i.st.* (*s*) to flow down.
Abriss *m.* (risses, -risse) sketch, abstract; digest.
abrollen *v.i.* (*s*) to roll off; ~ *v.t.* to unroll.
abrücken *v.t.* & *i.* to move away, to move off.
Abruf *m.* (-[e]s, -e) recall; *auf* ~ (*com.*) on call.
abrufen *v.t.st.* to call away *or* off.
abrunden *v.t.* (*Zahlen*) to correct, to round off.
abrupfen *v.t.* to pluck off.
abrüsten *v.t.* to disarm.
Abrüstung *f.* (-, -en), disarmament.
abrutschen *v.i.* to glide down.
Absage *f.* (-, -n) refusal.
absagen *v.t.* & *i.* to cancel (one's engagement).
absatteln *v.t.* to unsaddle.
Absatz *m.* (-es, -sätze) (*Treppen*~) landing; (*Waren*~) sale, market; (*Stiefel*~) heel; (*im Druck*) paragraph; *schnellen* ~ *finden*, to have a ready sale.
Absatz: ~**bewegung** (*mil.*) disengagement; ~**genossenschaft,** marketing association; ~**markt,** outlet, market.
abschaben *v.t.* to scrape off.
abschaffen *v.t.* to abolish, to remove.
Abschaffung *f.* (-, -en) abolition.
abschälen *v.t.* to peel, to pare.
abschatten *v.t.* to shade.
abschätzen *v.t.* to value; to assess, to estimate.
Abschätzung *f.* (-, -en) estimate, valuation.
Abschaum *m.* (-[e]s, -schäume) scum; dross; (*fig.*) dregs, *pl.*

abschäumen v.t. to scum, to skim.
abscheiden v.t.st. to separate, to part; ~ v.i. (s) to die.
Abscheu m. (-[e]s, 0) abhorrence, horror.
abscheulich a. abominable, detestable.
abschicken v.t. to send off, to despatch.
abschieben v.t.st. to shove off; (fam.) to move off.
Abschied m. (-[e]s, -e) discharge; departure, leave; ~ nehmen, to bid farewell, to take leave; einem den ~ geben, to dismiss someone.
Abschiedsgesuch n. resignation.
abschiessen v.t.st. to shoot off; to fire, to discharge; (avi.) to shoot down.
abschildern v.t. to depict; to describe.
abschinden v.t.st. to flay, to skin; (sich) v.refl. to fag oneself to death.
abschirren v.t. to unharness.
abschlachten v.t. to slaughter, to butcher.
Abschlag m. (-[e]s, -schläge); (im Preise) decline; auf ~, on account, in part-payment; ~zahlung, payment on account.
abschlagen v.t.st. to refuse, to deny; (den Feind) to repel; (sein Wasser) to make water.
abschlägig a. negative, refusing; ~e Antwort f. refusal, denial.
abschläglich a. on account.
abschleifen v.t.st. to grind off, to polish.
abschleppen v.t. to drag off; (sich) ~ v.refl. to exert oneself in carrying.
abschliessen v.t.st. to close, to lock; (einen Handel) to conclude (or strike) a bargain.
abschliessend a. definitive, final.
Abschluss m. (-schlusses, -schlüsse) close, settlement, conclusion.
abschnallen v.t. to unbuckle.
abschnappen v.i. to snap off; to stop short.
abschneiden v.t.st. to cut off, to clip; to pare; gut ~ v.i. to come off well.
abschnellen v.t. to let fly with a jerk; ~ v.i. (s) to fly off with a jerk.
Abschnitt m. (-[e]s, -e) cut; section; division; chapter, part, (geom.) segment.
abschnittweise adv. in paragraphs, piece by piece.
abschnüren v.t. to cut off.
abschöpfen v.t. to skim.
abschrägen v.t. (mech.) to bevel.
abschrauben v.t. to unscrew.
abschrecken v.t. to frighten, to deter.
Abschreckungsmittel n. (-s, -) deterrent, determent.
abschreiben v.t. to transcribe, to copy; to write off; ~ v.t. to cancel an engagement in writing.
Abschreiber m. (-s, -) copyist; plagiarist.
Abschreibung f. (-en) depreciation.

abschreiten v.t.st. to measure by steps; (mil.) to review.
Abschrift f. (-, -en) copy, transcript; die Richtigkeit der ~ wird bezeugt, certified true copy.
abschriftlich adv. in a copy.
abschuppen v.t. to scale.
abschüssig a. steep, precipitous.
abschütteln v.t. to shake off.
abschwächen v.t. to weaken.
abschwatzen v.t. to talk (one) out of (a thing).
abschweifen v.i. (s) to stray; to digress.
Abschweifung f. (-, -en) digression.
abschwenken v.i. (s) to wheel, to turn aside.
abschwindeln v.t. to swindle (a person) out of.
abschwören v.t.st. to abjure, to forswear.
absegeln v.i. (s) to set sail, to put to sea.
absehbar a. within sight; (fig.) measurable.
absehen v.t.st. to learn by observation; ~ auf, to aim at; ~ von, to leave out of account, to disregard.
abseits adv. aside, apart.
absenden v.t.ir. to send away, to dispatch.
Absender m. (-s, -) sender, consignor.
Absendung f. (-, -en) sending, dispatch.
absetzen v.t. to depose; to cashier; (Waren) to sell; (sich) ~, v.refl. (mil.) to disengage.
Absetzung f. (-, -en) removal, deposition.
Absicht f. (-, -en) view, intention, purpose; mit der ~, with a view (to).
absichtlich a. intentional, designed; ~ adv. on purpose.
absichtslos adv. unintentionally.
absingen v.t.st. to sing, to chant.
absitzen v.i.st. (s) to dismount, to alight; ~ v.t. to sit out (a given time).
absolut a. absolute, positive; ~ adv. absolutely, perfectly.
Absolutismus m. (-, 0) absolutism.
absolvieren v.t. (Schule) to graduate from.
absonderlich a. particular; singular, odd.
absondern v.t. to separate, to set apart; (med.) to secrete; (sich) ~ v.refl. to seclude oneself, to withdraw; to dissolve partnership.
Absonderung f. (-, -en) separation; seclusion, retirement; (med.) secretion.
absorbieren v.t. to absorb.
abspalten v.t. to split off.
Abspannung f. (-, 0) fatigue.
absparen v.t. sich ~, to pinch oneself.
abspeisen v.t. to feed; (fig.) to put off, to fob off.
abspenstig a. ~ machen, to alienate (from); ~ werden, to fall off from.
absperren v.t. to shut off, to cut off; to block; polizeilich ~, to cordon off.

Absperrung f. (-, -en) isolation; blockage, closure.
abspiegeln v.t. to reflect, to mirror.
abspielen v.refl. to take place, to come off; to wear out by playing.
absplittern v.t. to splinter; ~ v.i. to come off in splinters.
absprechen v.t. to deny; ~ v.i. to criticize rashly.
absprechend a. adverse.
abspringen v.i.st. (s) to leap off, to jump off; to rebound; (fig.) to shift, to digress.
Absprung m. (-[e]s, -sprünge) (downward) leap, jump.
abspulen v.t. to wind off, to unwind.
abspülen v.t. to wash up.
abstammen v.i. (s) to descend; to be derived.
Abstammung f. (-, -en) descent; derivation.
Abstand m. (-[e]s, -stände) distance; ~ nehmen, to desist from.
Abstandsgeld n., **Abstandssumme** f. compensation.
abstatten v.t. to render; (Besuch) to pay.
abstäuben v.t. to dust.
abstechen v.t.st. to stab; to kill; ~ v.i. (h, s) to contrast (with).
Abstecher m. (-s, -) excursion, trip.
abstecken v.t. to mark out, to plot (the course).
abstehen v.i.st. to stand off; to desist from, to give up; (schal werden) to get stale.
absteigen v.i.st. (s) (vom Pferd) to dismount; (vom Wagen) to alight; (im Gasthof) to put up at, to stop at.
Absteigequartier, n. (-s, -e) temporary lodging.
abstellen v.t. to stop (machine); to turn off (gas); to redress, to abolish, to do away with.
abstempeln v.t. to stamp.
absterben v.i.st. (s) to die away, out; (med.) to mortify; to fade.
Absterben n. (-s, 0) death, demise, decease.
Abstieg m. (-[e]s, -e) descent.
abstimmen v.i. to vote, to divide; ~ lassen über etwas, to put a thing to the vote; ~ v.t. to tune.
Abstimmung f. (-, -en) voting, division.
Abstinenz f. total abstinence.
Abstinenzler m. (-s, -) total abstainer, teetotaller.
abstossen v.t.st. to knock off, to thrust off; (fig.) to repel.
abstossend a. revolting, repulsive.
Abstossung f. (-, -en) repulsion.
abstrahieren v.t. to abstract.
abstrakt a. abstract.
abstrapazieren v.t. to knock up.

abstreichen v.t. to mark off; to strop (a razor).
abstreifen v.t. to strip off, to slip off.
abstreiten v.t.st. to dispute.
Abstrich m. (-[e]s, -e) deduction.
abstufen v.t. to grade, to graduate.
Abstufung f. (-, -en) gradation.
abstumpfen v.t. to blunt; (sich) ~ v.refl. to grow blunt or dulled.
Absturz m. (-es, -stürze) precipice; (avi.) crash.
abstürzen v.i. to fall;.(avi.) to crash.
absuchen v.t. to search, to beat (a field).
Absud m. (-[e]s, -e) decoction.
absurd a. absurd; ~ adv. absurdly.
Abt m. (-[e]s, Äbte) abbot.
abtakeln v.t. to lay up, dismantle.
Abtei f. (-, -en) abbey.
Abteil n. or m. (-es, -e) compartment.
abteilen v.t. to divide off; to partition off.
Abteilung f. (-, -en) division; partition; compartment; department; (Soldaten) detachment.
abtelegraphieren v.i. to cancel one's engagement by wire.
abteufen v.t. to sink (a shaft).
Äbtissin f. (-, -nen) abbess.
abtönen v.t. to shade (Farbe, Ton).
abtöten v.t. to mortify; to destroy.
abtragen v.t.st. (Kleider) to wear out; (Gebäude) to demolish, to pull down; (Hügel) to level; (Schuld) to pay; den Tisch ~, to clear away.
abträglich a. prejudicial, derogatory.
abtreiben v.t.st. to drive off; (med.) to procure abortion; ~ v.i. to drift off.
Abtreibung f. (-, -en) abortion.
abtrennen v.t. to separate; to rip, to unstitch.
abtreten v.t.st. to cede, to make over; ~ v.i. (s) to retire.
abtretend a. outgoing.
Abtretung f. (-, -en) abdication, cession.
Abtritt m. (-[e]s, -e) exit; (Abort) water-closet, urinal.
abtrocknen v.t. to dry.
abtröpfeln v.i. (s) to drip off.
abtrotzen v.t. to bully (someone) out of.
abtrünnig a. rebellious, apostate.
Abtrünnig(er) m.(-n,-n) deserter, renegade.
abtun v.t.st. to take off; to settle, to finish; to kill.
aburteilen v.i. to criticize rashly.
abverlangen v.t. to ask someone to give (a thing) up, to demand (from).
abvermieten v.t. to sublet.
abwägen v.t.st. to weigh, to weigh out.
abwälzen v.t. to shift; (Schuld) to exculpate onself.
abwandeln v.t. (gram.) to decline, to conjugate.
Abwandlung f. (-, -en) (gram.) declension, conjugation.

abwarten v.t. to await, to wait for.
abwärts adv. downward(s).
abwaschen v.t.st. to wash off.
Abwasser n. (-s, -) waste-water.
abwechseln v.t. to alternate; to vary; ~ v.i. to come or go by turns.
abwechselnd a. & adv. alternate; by turns, in rotation.
Abwechslung f. (-, -en) change; variation; zur ~, for a change.
Abweg m. (-e[s], -e) wrong way; auf ~e geraten, to go astray.
Abwehr f. (-, 0) defence; (mil.) counter-intelligence.
abwehren v.t. to ward off; to avert.
abweichen v.i.st. (s) to deviate, to differ; (phys.) to decline.
abweichend a. anomalous, different, divergent; ~e Meinung, (law) dissenting opinion.
Abweichung f. (-, -en) deviation; deflection; divergence; zugelassene ~ (mech.) tolerance.
abweisen v.t.st. to refuse; to reject; to dismiss; to repel.
Abweisung f. (-, -en) refusal, rejection; (law) nonsuit.
abwelken v.i. (s) to wither, to fade away.
abwenden v.t.ir. to turn away (off); to prevent; to avert; (sich) ~ v.refl.ir. to turn away (from), to abandon.
abwendig a. ~ machen, to alienate (from).
abwerfbar a. (avi.) jettisonable.
abwerfen v.t.st. to throw off, to cast off; (Gewinn) to yield a profit; (Bomben) to release.
abwerten v.t. to devalue.
Abwertung f. (-, -en) devaluation.
abwesend a. absent; ~ ohne Urlaub (mil.) absent without leave.
Abwesender m. (bes. von der Arbeit) absentee.
Abwesenheit f. (-, -en) absence.
abwetzen v.t. to blunt off, to rub off.
abwickeln v.t. to unwind; (Geschäfte) to wind up.
abwiegen v.t.st. to weigh out.
abwinken v.t. to stop with a hint.
abwirtschaften v.i. to come to grief.
abwischen v.t. to wipe (off).
abwracken v.t. to break up, to scrap.
Abwurf m. (-[e]s, -würfe) (avi.) (Bomben) release.
abwürgen v.t. to strangle.
abzahlen v.t. to pay off.
abzählen v.t. to tell; to count out.
Abzahlung f. (-, -en) hire purchase; instalment.
abzapfen v.t. to tap; Blut ~, to draw blood.
abzäumen, v.t. to unbridle.
abzehren v.i. to pine away, to waste away.
Abzeichen n. (-s, -n) badge; ~ pl. insignia.

abzeichnen v.t. to mark (out); to draw; to copy a drawing.
Abziehbild n. (-[e]s, -er) transfer-picture.
abziehen v.t.st. to draw off; to deduct; to subtract; (phot.) to print; (die Aufmerksamkeit) to divert; to sharpen; to skin; ~ v.i.st. (s) to march off.
abzielen v.i. to aim at.
abzirkeln v.t. to measure with compasses.
Abzug m. (-[e]s, -züge) departure; discount, deduction; (phot.) print; (typ.) proof.
Abzugsgraben m. drain, conduit.
abzwacken v.t. to pinch off.
abzwecken v.i. to aim at, to tend towards.
abzweigen v.i. (s) to branch off; (sich) ~ v.refl. to branch off, to turn off.
abzwicken v.t. to nip off.
abzwingen v.t.st. to extort (from).
ach! i. alas! ah!
Achat m. (-[e]s, -e) agate.
Achse f. (-, -n) axle, axle-tree; axis.
Achsel f. (-, -n) shoulder; die ~n zucken, to shrug one's shoulders.
Achselhöhle f. arm-pit.
Achselklappe f. shoulder-strap.
Achselträger m. double-dealer, time-server.
acht a. eight; ~ Tage, a week.
Acht f. (-, 0) ban, outlawry; attention, care; sich in acht nehmen, to be careful; achtgeben, to pay attention.
achtbar a. respectable.
achteckig a. octagonal.
Achtel n. (-s, -) eighth part, eighth.
Achtelnote f. quaver.
achten v.t. & i. to mind; to attend to; to consider; to esteem.
ächten v.t. to outlaw, to proscribe.
achtenswert a. estimable.
achter adv. aft.
Achterdeck n. (nav.) quarterdeck.
achtfach a. eightfold.
achtlos a. careless, negligent.
achtsam a. attentive, mindful.
Achtstundentag m. eight-hour day.
achttägig a. for eight days; weekly.
Achtung f. (-, 0) attention; esteem, regard.
Ächtung f. (-, -en) ostracism, proscription.
achtungswert a. estimable, respectable.
achtzehn a. eighteen.
achtzig a. eighty.
Achtziger m. (-s, -) octogenarian.
ächzen v.i. to groan.
Acker m. (-s, Äcker) field, soil.
Acker: ~bau m. agriculture; ~land n. arable land.
ackern v.t. to plough, to till.
addieren v.t. to sum up, to add up.
Addition f. (-, -en) addition; ~szeichen n. sign of addition.

ade! *i.* adieu! good-bye! farewell!

Adel *m.* (-s, 0) nobility, peerage; (*fig.*) nobleness.

adelig *a.* titled.

adeln *v.t.* to ennoble.

Ader *f.* (-, -n) vein; artery; grain, streak; *zur ~ lassen,* to bleed.

Aderlass *m.* (-lasses, -lässe) bleeding, blood-letting, phlebotomy.

adieu *adv.* adieu; *~ sagen,* to bid farewell.

Adjektiv *n.* (-s, -e), adjective.

Adjutant *m.* (-en, -en) adjutant, aide-de-camp.

Adler *m.* (-s, -) eagle.

Adlernase *f.* aquiline *or* hooked nose.

adlig *a.* noble; die Adligen *m.pl.* the nobles, the nobility.

Admiral *m.* (-[e]s, -e) admiral.

Admiralität *f.* (-, -en) Board of Admiralty.

adoptieren *v.t.* to adopt.

Adoptivkind *n.* (-[e]s, -er) adopted child.

Adressat *m.* (-en, -en) drawee, addressee.

Adressbuch *n.* (-[e]s, -bücher) directory.

Adresse *f.* (-, -n) address, direction; *per ~ care of (c/o).*

adressieren *v.t.* to address, to direct.

adrett *a.* smart.

Adverb *n.* (-s, -ien) adverb.

Advokat *m.* (-en, -en) lawyer, counsel.

Aeroplan *m.* (-s, -e) aeroplane.

Affe *m.* (-n, -n) ape, monkey.

Affekt *m.* (-s, -e) passion; affection.

affektieren *v.t.* to affect.

affektiert *a.* conceited, affected.

Affenliebe *f.* blind fondness.

Affenschande *f.* (-, 0) great shame.

Afferei *f.* (-, -en) apish behaviour; mimicry, mockery.

Äffin *f.* (-, -nen) she-ape.

affizieren *v.t.* to affect, to influence.

After *m.* (-s, -) anus, backside.

After: ~miete *f.* sub-tenure; ~weisheit *f.* pretended wisdom.

Agende *f.* (-, -n) agenda, liturgy, prayer-book; memorandum-book.

Agent *m.* (-en, -en) representative, agent.

Agentur *f.* (-, -en) agency.

Ägide *f.* (-, 0) ægis; auspices *pl.*

Agio *n.* (-s, 0) agio, premium.

agitieren *v.i.* to agitate.

Agonie *f.* (-, -n) agony.

Agraffe *f.* (-, -n) clasp, brooch.

Agrarier *m.* (-s, -) agrarian.

Agrarpolitik *f.* (-, 0) agricultural policy.

ah! *i.* ah! ha!

Ahle *f.* (-, -n) awl.

Ahn *m.* (-s, -en) ancestor, forefather.

ahnden *v.t.* to punish; to avenge.

Ahne *f.* (-, -n) ancestress.

ähneln *v.i.* to resemble.

ahnen *v.t.* to have a presentiment; to have an inkling.

Ahnherr *m.* ancestor.

ähnlich *a.* resembling, similar, alike.

Ähnlichkeit *f.* (-, -en) resemblance, likeness.

Ahnung *f.* (-, -en) foreboding, presentiment, suspicion, inkling; *keine ~,* not the slightest idea.

ahnungslos *a.* unsuspecting.

ahnungsvoll *a.* ominous, awe-inspiring.

Ahorn *m.* (-s, -e) maple.

Ähre *f.* (-, -n) ear; *~n lesen,* to glean.

Akademie *f.* (-, -en) (*Kunst.*) Academy.

Akademiker *m.* (-s, -) university man; academician.

akademisch *a.* academic.

Akazie *f.* (-, -n) acacia.

akklimatisieren *v.t.* to acclimatize.

Akkord *m.* (-[e]s, -e) (*mus.*) chord, accord; contract, agreement.

Akkordarbeit *f.* piece work; *in Akkord arbeiten,* to do piecework; Akkordlohn *m.* piece(work) rates.

akkordieren *v.t.* to agree, to compound.

akkreditieren *v.t.* to accredit.

Akkumulator *m.* (-s, -en) accumulator, storage battery; (*Am.*) battery.

Akkusativ *m.* (-s, -e) accusative.

Akt *m.* (-[e]s, -e) act; deed; the nude; (*Aktenbündel*) file.

Akten *pl.* acts, deeds, instruments, official documents, dossier.

Akten: ~deckel *m.* file; (*Am.*) folder; ~klammer *f.* paper-clip; ~tasche *f.* brief-case; ~stück *n.* document; ~zeichen *n.*, -nummer *f.* file-number, reference-number.

Aktie *f.* (-, -n) share.

Aktien: ~gesellschaft *f.* joint-stock company; ~kapital share capital.

Aktion *f.* (-, -en) drive, project.

Aktionär *m.* (-[e]s, -e) shareholder.

aktiv *a.* active; *~er Teilhaber* (*com.*) working partner.

Aktiv *n.* (-s, -e) (*gram.*) active voice.

Aktiva *n.pl.* assets.

Akustik *f.* (-, 0) acoustics, *pl.*

akustisch *a.* acoustic.

Akzent *m.* (-s, -e) stress, accent.

akzentuieren *v.t.* to stress, to accentuate.

Akzept *n.* (-[e]s, -e) (*com.*) acceptance.

akzeptieren *v.t.* to accept, to honour.

Alabaster *m.* (-s, 0) alabaster.

Alarm *m.* (-s, 0) alarm.

alarmieren *v.t.* to sound the alarm.

Alaun *m.* (-[e]s, -e) alum.

albern *a.* silly, foolish.

Alchimie *f.* (-, 0) alchemy.

Alexandriner *m.* (-s, -) (*poet.*) Alexandrine.

Alge *f.* (-, -n) seaweed.

Algebra *f.* (-, 0) algebra.

Alibi *n.* (*law*) alibi; *sein ~ nachweisen,* to prove one's alibi.

Alimente *n.pl.* alimony; *(Scheidungs-)* ~, separation allowance.

alkalisch *a.* alkaline.

Alkohol *m.* (-s, -e) alcohol.

alkoholische Getränke *n.pl.* strong drinks; *(Am.)* hard drinks.

alkoholfrei *a.* non-alcoholic.

Alkoven *m.* (-s, -) alcove; recess.

all(er), alle, alles *a.* all; whole; every.

All *n.* (-s, 0) the universe.

allbekannt *a.* notorious.

alle *adv.* ~ *sein,* to be gone, to be spent.

Allee *f.* (-, -[e]n) avenue.

Allegorie *f.* (-, -[e]n) allegory.

allein *a.* alone; single; ~ *c.* only, but.

Alleinvertreter *m.* sole agent.

alleinig *a.* sole, exclusive.

alleinstehend *a.* detached, isolated; unmarried.

allemal *adv.* always, every time; *ein für* ~, once for all.

allenfalls *adv.* if need be; perhaps.

allenthalben *adv.* everywhere.

allerdings *adv.* indeed, to be sure, however, I admit.

allererst, zu allererst *adv.* first of all.

allerhand *a.* of all kinds.

Allerheiligen(fest) *n.* (-festes, -feste) All-Hallows, All Saints' day.

allerlei *a.* of all kinds.

allerletzt *a.* last of all.

allerliebst *a.* charming, exquisite.

allermeist *a. & adv.* most, most of all; chiefly, mostly.

Allerseelentag *m.* All Souls' Day.

allerseits *adv.* on every side, everywhere.

allerwärts *adv.* everywhere.

Allerweltskerl *m.* (-s, -e) devil of a fellow.

allesamt *adv.* one and all.

allezeit *adv.* always; (at) any time.

Allgebrauchs... general purpose, general utility.

Allgegenwart *f.* (-, 0) omnipresence.

allgegenwärtig *a.* omnipresent, ubiquitous.

allgemach *adv.* by degrees.

allgemein *a.* universal, general, common; *im* ~*en,* in general; ~ *adv.* generally.

Allgemeinheit *f.* (-, -en) universality, generality; general public.

Allgewalt *f.* (-, 0) omnipotence.

Allheilmittel *n.* panacea.

Allianz *f.* (-, -en) alliance.

alljährlich *a.* yearly, annual; ~ *adv.* yearly, annually.

Allmacht *f.* (-, 0) omnipotence.

allmächtig *a.* omnipotent, almighty.

allmählich *a.* gradual.

Allotria *pl.* tomfoolery.

allseitig *a.* in all respects; universal, versatile; ~ *adv.* on all hands.

alltäglich *a.* daily; *(fig.)* trite, everyday, commonplace.

allwissend *a.* omniscient, all-knowing.

allzu *adv.* too, much too.

Alm *f.* (-, -en) Alpine meadow.

Almanach *m.* (-[e]s, -e) almanac.

Almosen *n.* (-s, -) alms, charity.

Alp *m.* (-[e]s, -e), **Alpdrücken** *n.* nightmare, incubus.

Alphabet *n.* (-[e]s, -e) alphabet.

alphabetisch *a. & adv.* alphabetic(al); ~**anordnen** *v.t.* to alphabetize.

Alraun *m.* (-[e]s, -e), **Alraune** *f.* mandrake.

als *c.* than; as; like; when; but; *sowohl* ~ *auch,* as well as; ~ *ob,* as if.

alsbald *adv.* forthwith, directly.

alsdann *adv.* then.

also *adv.* thus, so; ~ *c.* consequently.

alt *a.* old, ancient; aged; stale.

Alt *m.* (-[e]s, -e) contralto.

Altan *m.* (-[e]s, -e) balcony.

Altar *m.* (-[e]s, -, Altäre) altar.

Altarbild *n.* altar-piece.

altbacken *a.* stale.

Alte[r] *m.* (-n, -n) *die* ~*n,* the ancients.

Alter *n.* (-s, 0) age; old age; antiquity; *vor alters,* of old, in olden days.

altern *v.i.* (*h, s*) to grow old; to age.

Alters: ~**grenze** *f.* age limit; ~**heim** *n.* home for the aged; ~**klasse** *(mil.)* age class, age group; ~**rente** *f.* old-age pension; ~**schwäche** *f.* decrepitude; ~**versicherung** *f.* old-age insurance.

Altertum *n.* (-s, -tümer) antiquity.

altertümlich *a.* old-fashioned; antique.

Altistin *f.* (-, -nen) alto-singer.

altklug *a.* precocious.

ältlich *a.* elderly, oldish.

altmodisch *a.* old-fashioned.

Altstadt *f.* city.

Altvordern *pl.* ancestors, progenitors, forbears.

Altweibersommer *m.* Indian summer.

Aluminium *n.* (-s, 0) aluminium; *(Am.)* aluminum.

am *(statt:* an dem), at the.

amalgamieren *v.t.* to amalgamate.

Amazone *f.* (-, -n) Amazon.

Amboss *m.* (-bosses, -bosse) anvil.

ambulanter Kranker *m.* outpatient.

Ameise *f.* (-, -n) ant.

Ameisen: ~**haufen** *m.* ant-hill; ~**säure** *f.* formic acid.

Amme *f.* (-, -n) wet-nurse.

Ammen: ~**märchen** *n.* nursery tale; ~**stube** *f.* nursery.

Ammer *f. & m.* (-, -n) yellow-hammer, bunting.

Ammoniak *n.* (-s, 0) ammonia.

Amnestie *f.* (-, -[e]n) amnesty.

amortisieren *v.t.* to pay off, to redeem (a debt).

Ampel *f.* (-, -n) hanging-lamp.

Ampère: ~**meter** *m.* *(el.)* ammeter; ~**stunde** *f.* ampere-hour.

Amphibie f. (-, -n), amphibium.

Amphitheater n. (-s, -) amphitheatre.

amputieren v.t. to amputate.

Amsel f. (-, -n) blackbird.

Amt n. (-[e]s, Ämter) charge, employment; board; office; court.

amtieren v.i. to officiate.

amtlich a. official.

Amtmann m. (-s, -männer) bailiff, rural magistrate.

Amts: ~anmassung f. assumption of authority; ~eid m. oath of office; ~enthebung f. discharge from office; ~führung f. administration; ~geheimnis n. official secret; ~gericht n. local court; ~gewalt f. official authority; ~inhaber m. office-holder; ~pflicht f. official duty; ~richter m. district-judge; ~stunden f.pl. office hours; ~zeit f. term of office.

amtswegen adv. von ~, officially, ex officio.

amüsieren v.t. to amuse; sich ~, to enjoy oneself.

an pr. on, by, near, of, against, about, at.

analog a. analogous.

Analphabet m. (-en, -en) illiterate.

Analphabetentum n. illiteracy.

Analyse f. (-, -n) analysis.

analysieren v.t. to analyse.

Anaemie f. (-, -n) anaemia.

Ananas f. (-, - u. -nasse) pine-apple.

Anarchie f. (-, -n) anarchy.

Anatom m. (-en, -en) anatomist.

Anatomie f. (-, -[e]n) anatomy; dissecting-room.

anatomisch a. anatomical.

anbahnen v.t. to pave the way for.

Anbau m. (-[e]s, -e) cultivation, culture; out-building, wing.

anbauen v.t. to cultivate; to add.

Anbeginn m. (-s, 0) beginning, outset.

anbehalten v.t.st. to keep on.

anbei adv. herewith, enclosed, attached.

anbeissen v.t. & i.st. to bite.

anbelangen v.t. was mich anbelangt, for my part.

anbequemen v.t. (& refl. sich) to accommodate (oneself to), to put up with.

anberaumen v.t. to appoint, to fix (a day).

anbeten v.t. to adore, to worship.

Anbetracht m. in ~, considering, seeing.

anbetteln v.t. to ask alms of, to importune.

Anbetung f. (-, -en) adoration, worship.

anbieten v.t.st. to offer.

anbinden v.t.st. to tie, to bind, to fasten; ~ v.i. (mit einem) to pick a quarrel (with one); kurz angebunden sein, to be short with one.

anblasen v.t.st. to blow (the fire).

Anblick m. (-[e]s, -e) view, aspect, sight beim ersten ~, at first sight.

anblicken v.t. to look at.

anbohren v.t. to bore, to pierce.

anbrechen v.t.st. to break, to begin to cut off; ~ v.i. (s) to break, to begin, to appear.

anbrennen v.i.ir. to burn; angebrannt schmecken, to taste of burning.

anbringen v.t.ir. to apply, to fix; to sell; to dispose of; to lodge (a complaint).

Anbruch m. (-[e]s, -brüche) beginning, ~ der Nacht, night-fall.

anbrüllen v.t. to roar at.

Anciennität f. seniority.

Andacht f. (-, -en) devotion, prayers, pl.

andächtig a. devout, attentive.

andauern v.i. to last.

andauernd a. constant, continual, continuous.

Andenken n. (-s, -) souvenir; memory.

ander a. other, second; next.

ändern v.t., sich ändern v.refl. to alter, to change; ich kann es nicht ~, I cannot help it.

andernfalls adv. otherwise, else.

anders adv. otherwise; else.

anderseits adv. on the other side or hand.

anderswo adv. elsewhere.

anderthalb a. one and a half.

Änderung f. (-, -en) change, alteration.

anderweitig a. & adv. other; in another way.

andeuten v.t. to signify, to hint; to intimate.

Andeutung f. (-, -en) intimation, suggestion, hint.

andichten v.t. to impute falsely.

Andrang m. (-[e]s, 0) throng, rush.

andringen v.i.st. (s) to press forward.

androhen v.t. to threaten, to menace.

andrücken v.t. to press towards or against.

aneignen (sich) v.refl. to appropriate.

aneinander adv. together.

Anekdote f. (-, -n) anecdote.

anekeln v.t. to disgust.

Anerbieten n. (-s, -) offer, tender.

anerkennen v.t.ir. to acknowledge, to recognize; Schuld nicht ~, to repudiate a debt.

anerkennenswert a. commendable.

Anerkennung f. (-, -en) acknowledgement, recognition; appreciation.

anfachen v.t. to blow into a flame; (fig.) to kindle.

anfahren v.t. to convey, to carry; (fig. einen) to snub.

Anfahrt f. (-, -en) approach (to a building).

Anfall m. (-[e]s, -fälle) fit, seizure.

anfallen v.t.st. to attack; to accrue; ~de Zinsen pl. accrued interest.

Anfang m. (-[e]s, -fänge) commencement, beginning, opening.

anfangen v.t.st. to begin, to commence; ~ v.i. to begin; to open.

Anfänger m. (-s, -) beginner; tyro.

anfänglich a. & adv. initial, incipient; at first, at the outset, originally.

anfangs adv. in the beginning.

Anfangs: ~buchstabe m. initial (letter); ~gründe m.pl. elements, rudiments.

anfassen v.t. to take hold of, to seize.

anfaulen v.t. to begin to rot, to go bad; **angefault** a. half-decayed.

anfechtbar a. open to criticism.

anfechten v.t.st. to contest; to challenge; to tempt; to trouble.

Anfechtung f. (-, -en) temptation.

anfeinden v.t. to attack, to persecute.

anfertigen v.t. to manufacture, to make.

anfeuchten v.t. to moisten.

anfeuern v.t. to inflame.

anflehen v.t. to implore.

Anflug m. (-[e]s, -flüge) blush, flush; tinge, smattering.

anfordern v.t. (mil.) to requisition.

Anforderung f. (-, -en) demand; (mil.) requisition.

Anfrage f. (-, -n) inquiry, application.

anfragen v.t. to inquire, to call for.

anfressen v.t.st. to gnaw; to corrode; to eat into.

anfreunden v.refl. to become friends.

anfügen v.t. to join to; to annex, to subjoin.

anfühlen v.t. to touch, to handle.

Anfuhr f. (-, -en) conveying; supply.

anführen v.t. to lead, to conduct, to command; to impose upon, to dupe; to cite, to quote.

Anführer m. (-s, -) leader, commander.

Anführung f. (-, 0) leadership; command; quotation.

Anführungszeichen n. quotation mark, inverted commas; in ~ setzen, to inclose in inverted commas.

anfüllen v.t. to fill; to replenish.

Angabe f. (-, -n) declaration, statement; instruction; (com.) entry.

angängig a. feasible, practicable.

angeben v.t.st. to specify; to suggest; to declare, to assert; to denounce; den Ton ~, (fig.) to set the fashion.

Angeber m. (-s, -) informer.

angeblich a. pretended, purported, alleged.

angeboren a. innate, inborn.

Angebot n. (-[e]s, -e) offer; bid; supply; (com.) tender; ~ und Nachfrage, supply and demand.

angebracht a. proper, appropriate.

angedeihen (lassen) v.i.st. to bestow upon.

angegriffen a. (Gesundheit) delicate.

angeheiratet a. by marriage.

angeheitert a. tipsy.

angehen v.t.st. to apply to; to have to do

with, to concern; (einen um etwas) to solicit; ~ v.i.st. to begin; to be tolerable; to be practicable; es geht nicht an, it won't do.

angehend a. incipient, young.

angehören v.i. to belong to.

Angehörige m.pl. relations; abhängige~ pl. dependents.

Angeklagte[r] m. (-n, -n) defendant, accused.

Angel f. (-, -n) fishing-hook; (archaic) angle; hinge.

angelegen, sich ~ sein lassen, to make a point of.

Angelegenheit f. (-, -en) affair, matter; kümmere dich um deine eigenen ~en, mind your own business.

angelegentlich a. pressing, urgent; ~ adv. earnestly, instantly.

angeln v.t. to fish, to angle; (fig.) to fish for.

Angel: ~punkt m. pivot; ~rute f. fishing-rod; ~schnur f. fishing-line.

angemessen a. suitable, fit, adequate.

angenehm a. agreeable, pleasant, acceptable.

angenommen c. ~ dass, supposing that, assuming that.

angesehen a. distinguished, respected.

angesessen a. settled, resident.

Angesicht n. (-[e]s, -er) face, countenance; von ~, by sight.

angesichts pr. in the face of, considering.

angestammt a. hereditary, ancestral.

Angestellte[r] m. (-n, -n) employee.

angetrunken a. tipsy.

angewandt a. applied.

angewiesen (auf) a. dependent (on).

angewöhnen v.t. to accustom, to inure.

Angewohnheit f. (-, -en) habit, custom.

angleichen v.t.st. to assimilate.

angliedern v.t. to attach.

angreifen v.t.st. to attack; to undertake (fig.) to fatigue, to tell upon, to affect

Angreifer m. (-s, -) aggressor.

angrenzen v.i. to border (up)on.

angrenzend a. adjacent, contiguous.

Angriff m. (-[e]s, -e) attack, assault, aggression; in ~ nehmen, to start (on).

Angriffskrieg m. war of aggression.

Angst f. (-, Ängste) anxiety, anguish, fright, fear.

ängstigen v.t. to alarm, to torment; (sich) ~ v.refl. to feel uneasy, to feel alarmed.

ängstlich a. & adv. anxious, uneasy; anxiously; scrupulously.

angucken v.t. to look at, to peep at.

angstvoll a. anxious.

anhaben v.t.st. to have on, to wear; er kann ihm nichts ~, he cannot find anything against him.

anhaken v.t. to hook (on).

Anhalt m. (-[e]s, -e) support, hold; clue.

anhalten *v.t.st.* to stop, to arrest; ~ *v.i.st.* to last; ~ *um*, to propose (to), to ask in marriage; to pull up, to draw up.

Anhaltspunkt *m.* evidence, clue.

Anhang *m.* (-[e]s, -hänge) appendix; supplement; adherents.

anhangen, *v.i.st.* to hang on; to adhere to.

anhängen *v.t.* to hang on; to join, to annex, to affix.

Anhänger *m.* (-s, -) adherent, follower.

Anhängewagen (Anhänger) *m.* trailer.

anhängig *a.* (*Prozess*) pendent, pending; ~machen, to bring (an action against).

anhänglich *a.* attached (to).

Anhängsel *n.* (-s, -) attachment.

anhäufen *v.t. & r.* (*sich*) to heap up; to accumulate.

Anhäufung *f.* (-, -en) accumulation.

anheben *v.t. & i.st.* to begin.

anheften *v.t.* to fasten to; to stitch to.

anheimeln *v.t.* to remind one of home.

anheimfallen *v.i.st.* (*s*) to fall to.

anheimstellen *v.t.* to leave, to submit (to).

anheischig *a. sich ~ machen*, to pledge oneself, to undertake.

anheizen *v.t.* to make a fire.

Anhöhe *f.* (-, -n) rising ground, hill.

anhören *v.t.* to listen to, to attend; *sich ~*, to sound.

Anilin *n.* (-s, 0) aniline.

animieren *v.t.* to encourage.

Animosität *f.* (-, -en) animosity.

Anis *m.* (-es, -e) anise, aniseed.

ankämpfen (gegen) *v.i.* to struggle against.

Ankauf *m.* (-[e]s, -käufe) purchase.

ankaufen *v.t.* to purchase, to buy; (*sich*) ~ *v.refl.* to buy land, to settle at a place.

Anker *m.* (-s, -) anchor; (*el.*) armature; *vor ~ gehen*, to cast anchor; *~ lichten*, to weigh anchor.

ankern *v.t.* to anchor.

Anker: ~platz *m.* anchorage; ~winde *f.* windlass, capstan.

anketten *v.t.* to chain (to).

Anklage *f.* (-, -n) accusation, charge; *öffentliche ~* (*law*), arraignment; *unter ~ stehen* (*law*), to be on trial, to stand trial (for).

Anklagebehörde *f.* prosecution.

anklagen *v.t.* to accuse, to impeach.

Anklagepunkt *m.* count (of the indictment).

Anklageschrift *f.* indictment.

Anklagevertreter *m.* counsel for the prosecution.

anklammern (sich) *v.refl.* to cling (to).

Anklang *m.* (-[e]s, -klänge)(*fig.*) approval, kind reception; *Anklänge* (*an etwas*) reminiscences (of), *pl.*

ankleben *v.t. & i.* to paste on; to stick up; to stick to, to adhere.

ankleiden *v.t.* to dress, to attire.

Ankleidezimmer *n.* dressing-room.

anklingen *v.i.st.* (*fig.*) to remind one (of).

anklingeln *v.t.* to ring up.

anklopfen *v.i.* to knock (at the door).

anknüpfen *v.t.* (*ein Gespräch*) to enter (into a conversation); *Bekanntschaft ~*, to make one's acquaintance.

Anknüpfungspunkt *m.* point of contact, starting-point.

ankommen *v.i.st.* (*s*) to arrive; *auf etwas ~*, to depend upon; *es darauf ~ lassen*, to take a chance; *es nicht darauf ~ lassen*, to take no chances; *es kommt nicht darauf an*, it does not matter.

Ankömmling *m.* (-s, -e) new-comer.

ankreiden *v.t.* to chalk up; to score (an account); to make someone pay.

ankündigen *v.t.* to announce.

Ankündigung *f.* (-, -en) announcement.

Ankunft *f.* (-, 0) arrival.

ankurbeln *v.t.* to put into gear, to crank up; (*fig.*) to start.

Anlage *f.* (-, -n) (*von Kapital*) investment; (*von Strassen, Gärten*) layout; (*Park*) park, grounds, *pl.*; (*fig.*) talent, disposition; (*Fabrik*) plant; (*in Brief*) enclosure.

anlangen *v.i.* (*s*) to arrive; ~ *v.t.* to concern.

Anlass *m.* (-lasses, -lässe) occasion.

anlassen *v.t.st.* to keep on; to start, to turn on; (sich) ~ *v.refl.* to promise.

Anlasser *m.* (-s, -) starter.

Anlauf *m.* (-[e]s, -läufe) run, start, rush.

anlaufen *v.i.st.* (*s*) to run against; (*sich trüben*) to tarnish.

Anlegehafen *m.* port of call.

anlegen *v.t.* (*Kleider, etc.*) to put on; (*Gewehr*) to take aim; to found, to establish; (*Kapital*) to invest; (*Garten*) to lay out; (*Hand*) to set to work; ~ *v.i.* (*nav.*) to land.

Anlegestelle *f.* landing-place.

anlehnen *v.t.* to lean on *or* upon; (*Tür*) to leave ajar.

Anleihe *f.* (-, -n) loan; *eine ~ auflegen*, to float a loan; *eine ~ machen*, to raise a loan.

anleiten *v.t.* to guide, to instruct (in).

Anleitung *f.* (-, -en) guidance.

anlernen *v.t.* to break in.

Anliegen *n.* (-s, -) concern, request.

anliegend *a.* adjacent, tight-fitting.

anlocken *v.t.* to allure.

anmachen *v.t.* to fasten to; (*Feuer*) to light; (*Salat*) to dress.

Anmarsch *m.* (-[e]s, -märsche) approach (of an army).

anmassen (sich) *v.refl.* to assume, to arrogate, to usurp; to pretend to.

anmassend *a.* arrogant.

Anmassung *f.* (-, -en) assumption, usurpation, arrogance.

anmelden v.t. to announce; (sich) ~ v.refl. (polizeilich) to register; to notify.

anmerken v.t. to remark, to note.

Anmerkung f. (-, -en) note, footnote.

anmessen v.t. to take a person's measurements.

Anmut f. (-, 0) sweetness, charm, grace.

anmuten v.t. to give the impression.

anmutig a. graceful, charming.

annageln v.t. to nail to.

annähen v.t. to sew on.

annähern (sich) v.refl. to approach.

annähernd a. approximate.

Annäherung f. (-, -en) approach.

Annahme f. (-, -n) acceptance; (an Kindes Statt) adoption; (Meinung) assumption.

Annahmestelle f. receiving office.

Annalen pl. annals.

annehmbar a. admissible, plausible.

annehmen v.t.st. to accept; to assume; (als ausgemacht) to take for granted; (sich) ~ v.refl. to take care of, to befriend.

Annehmlichkeit f. (-, -en) comfort, amenity.

annektieren v.t. to annex.

Annexion f. (-, -en) annexation.

Annonce f. (-, -n) advertisement.

annoncieren v.t. to advertise.

annullieren v.t. to annul; (law) to set aside.

Anode f. (-, -n) anode.

anonym a. anonymous.

Anonymität f. (-, -en) anonymity.

anordnen v.t. to order, to dispose, to arrange.

Anordnung f. (-, -en) order; arrangement; disposition, alignment.

anorganisch a. inorganic.

anpacken v.t. to grasp, to seize.

anpassen v.t. to fit to; to try on; to adapt, to accommodate.

Anpassung f. (-, 0) adaptation.

Anpassungsfähigkeit f. adaptability.

anpflanzen v.t. to plant.

anpochen v.i. to knock (at the door).

Anprall m. (-[e]s, 0) impact; (mil.) shock.

anprallen v.i. (s) to bound against.

anprangern v.t. to denounce (publicly).

anpreisen v.t. to commend, to extol.

Anprobe f. (-, -en) fitting.

anproben, anprobieren v.t. to try on, to fit on.

anpumpen v.t. to borrow money of.

anraten v.t.st. to advise.

anrechnen v.t. to charge; to rate; to impute; ~ gegen, to set off against.

Anrecht n. (-[e]s, -e) claim, title.

Anrede f. (-, -n) address; (Brief) salutation.

anreden v.t. to address, to accost.

anregen v.t. to suggest; to stimulate; to mention.

Anregung f. (-, -en) incitement, stimulation; suggestion.

anreihen (sich) v.refl. to join.

Anreisser m. (-s, -) tout.

anreizen v.t. to incite, to instigate.

Anreiz m. (-s, -e) incitement; stimulus.

anrempeln v.t. to jostle against.

anrennen v.i.st. (s) to run against.

Anrichte f. (-, -n) dresser, sideboard.

anrichten v.t. to prepare; to serve up, to dish up; (fig.) to cause, to occasion.

anrüchig a. disreputable.

anrücken v.i. to approach, to move up.

anrufen v.t.st. to call (to); (tel.) to ring up; (Am.) to call up.

Anrufung f. (-, -en) invocation.

anrühren v.t. to touch, to handle.

ans = an das.

ansagen v.t. to announce; (Kartenspiel) to bid.

Ansager m. (-s, -) announcer.

ansammeln (sich) v.refl. to gather, to collect.

ansässig a. settled, domiciled; ~e Briten, British residents.

Ansatz m. (-es, -sätze) start.

anschaffen v.t. to provide, to procure, to buy.

Anschaffung f. (-, -en) procurement; purchase.

anschauen v.t. to look at, to view; to contemplate; (sich) ~ v.refl. to look over.

anschaulich a. intuitive; evident; graphic, lucid.

Anschauung f. (-, -en) view.

Anschein m. (-s, 0) appearance, semblance.

anscheinend a. apparent, seeming.

anschicken (sich) v.refl. to prepare; to set about.

anschirren v.t. to harness.

Anschlag m. (-[e]s, -schläge) (Mauer~) poster; (Schätzung) estimate; (Komplott) plot; (auf das Leben) attempt.

anschlagen v.t.st. to affix; (Zettel) to post; (Saite) to strike; ~ v.i. to prove effectual.

anschliessen v.t.st. to annex; to fasten with a lock; (sich) ~ v.refl.st. to join (a company).

Anschluss m. (-schlusses, -schlüsse) (rail., el.) connection; ~ dose, f. connection-box.

anschmiegen (sich) v.refl. to cling to.

anschmieren v.t. to smear, to daub; (vulg.) to cheat.

anschnallen v.t. to buckle on.

anschnauzen v.t. to tell off.

anschneiden v.t.st. to cut; to raise (Frage).

Anschnitt m. (-[e]s, -e) first cut.

anschreiben v.t.st. to write (down); to score up; gut angeschrieben, favourably known.

Anschrift f. (-, -en) address.

Anschuldigung f. (-, -en) accusation, charge.

anschwärzen v.t. to blacken; (fig.) to slander.

anschwellen v.i.st. (s) to swell.

anschwemmen v.t. to deposit.

Anschwemmung f. (-, -en) deposit (of flood).

ansehen v.t.st. to look at (upon); to consider; to regard.

Ansehen n. (-s, 0) appearance; (Achtung) esteem, credit, reputation, authority; von ~, by sight.

ansehnlich a. considerable, siz(e)able; good-looking.

Ansehung f. (-, 0) in ~, with regard (to).

ansetzen v.t. to put to; (Preis) to fix; (schätzen) to rate, to estimate; (Blätter) to put forth.

Ansicht f. (-, -en) sight, view; inspection; (Meinung) opinion; zur ~, on approval.

Ansichts(post)karte f. picture (post)card, view (post)card.

ansiedeln (sich) v.t. & refl. to settle.

Ansied(e)lung f. (-, -en) settlement.

Ansiedler m. (-s, -) settler, colonist.

Ansinnen n. (-s, -) demand.

anspannen v.t. to stretch; (Pferde) to put to; (fig.) to exert, to strain.

Anspannung f. (-, -en) exertion, strain.

anspielen v.i. to hint at, to allude to.

Anspielung f. (-, -en) allusion, hint.

anspinnen, sich ~, to begin.

Ansporn m. (-s, 0) incentive.

anspornen v.t. to spur; (fig.) to incite.

Ansprache f. (-, -n) address, speech.

ansprechen v.t.st. to address, to accost; to please, to appeal to.

Anspruch m. (-[e]s, -sprüche) claim, pretension, title.

anspruchslos a. unassuming.

anspruchsvoll a. exacting, fastidious.

anspucken v.t. to spit at.

anspülen v.t. to wash ashore, to deposit.

anstacheln v.t. to prick, to goad.

Anstalt f. (-, -en) institution, establishment; ~en treffen, machen, to make arrangements; to arrange (for).

Anstand m. (-[e]s, -stände) decorum, decency, polite manners; (Beanstandung) objection.

anständig a. becoming, proper; (pers.) respectable, decent.

Anständigkeit f. (-, -en) propriety, decency.

Anstandsdame f. chaperon.

anstandslos adv. without hesitation.

anstarren v.t. to stare at.

anstatt pr. instead of; ~dass c. instead of.

anstaunen v.t. to gaze at.

anstechen v.t.st. to prick; (ein Fass) to broach.

anstecken v.t. to stick on; to pin; (mit Krankheit) to infect; (Licht) to light; (Feuer) to make fire.

ansteckend a. contagious, catching; infectious; communicable.

Ansteckung f. (-, -en) contagion, infection.

anstehen v.i.st. to queue up; to suit.

ansteigen v.i.st. (s) to ascend, to rise.

anstellen v.t. to appoint; to arrange; (Versuch) to make; (sich) ~ v.re,l. to behave; to feign, to make believe.

anstellig a. handy, skilful.

Anstellung f. (-, -en) appointment; (Stelle) place, situation.

Anstieg m. (-[e]s, -e) rise, increase.

anstiften v.t. to contrive, to cause; to instigate, to set on.

anstimmen v.t. to sing, to strike up.

Anstoss m. (-es, -stösse) impulse; (fig.) offence; (Fussball) kick-off; Stein des ~es m. stumbling-block.

anstossen v.t.st. to push or strike against; ~ v.i.st. to stumble; to give offence; (mit den Gläsern) clink glasses; (mit der Zunge) to lisp.

anstössig a. scandalous, shocking.

anstreben v.t. & i. to aspire to.

anstreichen v.t.st. to paint, to stain.

Anstreicher m. (-s, -) house-painter.

anstrengen v.t. to strain; to exert; (Klage) to bring an action; (sich) ~ v.refl. to exert oneself.

anstrengend a. trying, fatiguing.

Anstrengung f. (-, -en) exertion, effort.

Anstrich m. (-[e]s, -e) colour, painting; (fig.) appearance, tinge, air.

Ansturm m. (-s, -stürme) rush, onrush.

anstürmen v.i. (s) to storm at, to rush upon.

ansuchen v.t. to apply for, to petition for.

Ansuchen n. (-s, -) request, application.

Antagonismus m. (-, -men) antagonism.

antarktisch a. antarctic.

antasten v.t. to touch, to handle.

Anteil m. (-[e]s, -e) share, portion; contribution; lot; (fig.) interest; ~ nehmen, to sympathize with.

antelephonieren v.t. to ring up.

Antenne f. (-, -n) (radio) aerial, antenna.

Antezedentien f.pl. antecedents.

Anthrazit m. (-s, 0) anthracite.

Anthropolog m. (-en, -en) anthropologist.

antik a. antique.

Antilope f. (-, -n) antelope.

Antimon n. (-s, 0) antimony.

Antipathie f. (-, -n) antipathy.

antippen v.t. to touch lightly, to tap.

Antiqua f. (-, 0) (printing) Roman type.

Antiquar m. (-[e]s, -e) antiquary; second-hand bookseller.

Antiquariat n. (-s, -e) second-hand bookshop.

antiquarisch a. & adv. second-hand.

asozial *a.* antisocial.
Asphalt *m.* (-[e]s, -e) asphalt.
asphaltieren *v.t.* to asphalt.
Aspirant *m.* (-en, -en) candidate.
Assekuranz *f.* (-, -en) insurance.
assekurieren *v.t.* to insure, to assure.
Assessor *m.* (-s, -en) assessor; assistant judge.
assimilieren *v.t.* to assimilate.
assoziieren (sich) *v.refl.* to enter into partnership (with).
Assistent *m.* (-en, -en) assistant.
Ast *m.* (-es, Äste) bough, branch; (*im Holze*) knot.
Aster *f.* (-, -n) aster.
Ästhetik *f.* (-, 0) æsthetics *pl.*
ästhetisch *a.* æsthetic.
Asthma *n.* (-s, 0) asthma.
Astloch *n.* knot-hole.
Astrolog *m.* (-en, -en) astrologer.
Astrologie *f.* (-, 0) astrology.
Astronom *m.* (-en, -en) astronomer.
Astronomie *f.* (-, 0) astronomy.
astronomisch *a.* astronomical.
Asyl *n.* (-[e]s, -e) asylum.
Atelier *n.* (-s, -s) (artist's) studio.
Atem *m.* (-s, 0) breath, breathing; *ausser* ~, out of breath; *den* ~ *anhalten*, to hold one's breath.
atemlos *a.* breathless.
Atem: ~not *f.* shortness of breath; ~pause *f.* breathing space; ~zug *m.* breath.
Äther *m.* (-s, 0) ether.
Atheismus *m.* (0) atheism.
Atheist *m.* (-en, -en) atheist.
ätherisch *a.* ethereal, aerial.
Athlet *m.* (-en, -en) athlete.
Athletik *f.* (-, 0) athletics.
Atlas *m.* (- *u.* -lasses, -lanten) atlas.
Atlas *m.* (- *u.* -lasses, -lasse) (*Stoff*) satin.
atmen *v.t. & i.* to breathe, to respire.
Atmosphäre *f.* (-, -n) atmosphere.
atmosphärisch *a.* atmospheric.
Atmung *f.* (-, 0) respiration.
Atom *n.* (-[e]s, -e) atom; particle.
Atom... atomic.
Attaché *m.* (-s, -s) attaché.
Attentat *n.* (-[e]s, -e) assault, outrage; attempt against one's life.
Attentäter *m.* (-s, -) criminal, assailant.
Attest *n.* (-[e]s, -e) certificate.
attestieren *v.t.* to certify.
Attrappe *f.* (-, -n) fancy box; sham things.
Attribut *n.* (-[e]s, -e) attribute.
ätzen *v.t.* (*ärztlich*) to cauterize; (*Kunst*) to etch; to feed.
ätzend *a.* corrosive; (*fig.*) caustic.
Ätzmittel *n.* corrosive; (*med.*) cautery.
au! *i.* oh!
auch *c.* also, too, even, likewise; ~ *nicht*, neither, nor; *sowohl...als* ~, as well... as..., both...and.

Audienz *f.* (-, -en) audience.
Auerhahn *m.* capercailzie.
Auerochs *m.* bison, aurochs.
auf *pro.* on, upon, in, at, to, up, into, after; ~ *adv.* up, upwards; ~! *i.* arise; ~ *dass*, in order that; ~ *und ab*, up and down; ~ *einmal*, at once.
aufarbeiten *v.t.* to work up.
aufatmen *v.i.* to breathe again.
aufbahren *v.t.* to lay out.
Aufbahrung *f.* (-, 0) lying in state.
Aufbau *m.* (-[e]s, -e) erection, structure, construction; organization.
aufbauen *v.t.* to erect, to build up.
aufbäumen (sich) *v.refl.* to prance.
aufbauschen *v.t. & i.* to puff, to swell up.
aufbegehren *v.i.* to rise or revolt against.
aufbehalten *v.t.st.* to keep on.
aufbessern *v.t.* (*Gehalt*) to raise.
aufbewahren *v.t.* to preserve, to keep, to take charge of.
Aufbewahrung *f.* (-, 0) preservation.
aufbieten *v.t.st.* to raise, to summon; (*fig.*) to exert oneself; (*Verlobte*) to publish banns of marriage.
aufbinden *v.t.st.* to untie, to loosen.
aufblähen *v.t.* to puff up; to inflate.
aufblasen *v.t.st.* to blow up, to inflate.
aufbleiben *v.i.st.* (s) to sit up; to remain open.
aufblicken *v.i.* to look up.
aufbrauchen *v.t.* to consume, to use up.
aufbrausen *v.i.* (s) to roar; to effervesce; (*fig.*) to fly out.
aufbrechen *v.t.st.* to break open; ~ *v.i.st.* (s) to burst open; to set out.
aufbringen *v.t.ir.* (*Truppen, Geld*) to raise; (*erzürnen*) to provoke; (*Kosten*) to defray.
Aufbruch *m.* (-[e]s, 0) departure.
aufbügeln *v.t.* to iron, to do up.
aufbürden *v.t.* to burden with.
aufdecken *v.t.* to uncover; to disclose.
aufdrängen *v.t.* to thrust upon; sich ~, *v.refl.* to obtrude oneself (upon).
aufdrehen *v.t.* to turn on.
aufdringen *v.t.st.* to force upon.
aufdringlich *a.* obtrusive, officious.
aufdrücken *v.t.* to impress.
aufeinander *adv.* one after another, one upon another.
Aufenthalt *m.* (-[e]s, -e) stay; abode; (*Verzögerung*) delay; (*rail.*) stop.
Aufenthaltsort *m.* place of residence.
auferlegen *v.t.* to impose (upon).
auferstehen *v.i.st.* (s) to rise from the dead.
Auferstehung *f.* (-, 0) resurrection.
auferwecken *v.t.* to raise from the dead, to resuscitate.
aufessen *v.t.st.* to eat (up), to finish.
auffahren *v.i.st.* (s) to ascend; to start (up).
Auffahrt *f.* (-, -en) (*vor Palästen*) drive, approach.

auffallen *v.i.st.* (*s*) (*einem*) to strike (*fig.*)
auffallend, auffällig *a.* striking.
auffangen *v.t.st.* to catch.
Auffanglinie *f.* (*mil.*) holding-line.
auffassen *v.t.* to understand, to take in, to conceive; to interpret (*Rolle*).
Auffassung *f.* (-, -en) comprehension, perception.
auffindbar *a.* traceable.
auffinden *v.t.st.* to find.
aufflammen *v.i.* (*s*) to flame up, to blaze.
auffordern *v.t.* to ask, to invite, to request.
Aufforderung *f.* (-, -en) summons; invitation.
aufforsten *v.t.* to reafforest.
auffressen *v.t.st.* to eat up, to devour.
auffrischen *v.t.* to refresh, to touch up.
Auffrischung *f.* (*mil.*) rehabilitation.
aufführen *v.t.* to erect; to perform; to represent (*Einzelnes*) to list, to specify; (*sich*) ~, *v.refl.* to behave.
Aufführung *f.* (-, -en) performance, representation; behaviour.
auffüllen *v.t.* to fill up.
Aufgabe *f.* (-, -n) delivery; (*Brief~*) posting; (*Schul.*) lesson; task, problem; giving up, resignation.
Aufgang *m.* (-[e]s, -gänge) ascent.
aufgeben *v.t.st.* to give up, to deliver; (*Brief*) to post; (*Gepäck*) to book; (*Frage, Rätsel*) to propose; (*Plan, Stelle*) to abandon, to resign, to give up.
aufgeblasen *a.* puffed up.
Aufgebot *n.* (-[e]s, -e) (*mil.*) levy; banns of marriage *pl.*
aufgebracht *a.* angry, provoked (at).
aufgedunsen *a.* bloated, swollen, sodden.
aufgehen *v.i.st.* (*Sonne*) to rise; (*Blüten*) to open; (*Knoten*) to get loose, to come undone; (*Fenster*, etc.) to come open; (*Genähtes*) to give way; (*math.*) to leave no remainder.
aufgeklärt *a.* enlightened; explained.
aufgelegt *a.* disposed (for), minded.
aufgeräumt *a.* merry, in good humour.
aufgeregt *a.* excited, flurried.
aufgeweckt *a.* bright, clever.
Aufguss *m.* (-gusses, -güsse) infusion.
aufhaben *v.t.* to have on.
aufhaken *v.t.* to unhook, to unclasp.
aufhalsen *v.t.* to saddle (with).
aufhalten *v.t.st.* to hold up; to delay, to detain; (*sich*) ~ *v.refl.st.* to reside, to stay; (*über etwas*) to find fault with.
aufhängen *v.t.* to hang up; to hang upon; (*sich*) ~ *v.refl.* to hang oneself.
aufhäufen *v.t.* to heap up, to pile; (*sich*) ~ *v.refl.* to accumulate.
Aufhäufung *f.* (-, -en) accumulation.
aufheben *v.t.st.* to pick up; (*bewahren*) to keep, to preserve; (*sparen*) to save; (*Gesetz*) to abrogate; (*Belagerung*) to raise.

Aufheben *n.* (-s, 0) *viel ~s machen*, tc make a great fuss (about).
Aufhebung *f.* (-, -en) (*eines Gesetzes*) repeal, rescission.
aufheitern *v.t.* to clear up; to cheer up; (*sich*) ~ *v.refl.* to clear up; (*fig.*) to grow cheerful.
Aufheiterung *f.* (-, -en) clearing up.
aufhelfen *v.t.st.* to help up.
aufhellen *v.t.* to brighten; (*sich*) ~ *v.refl.* to clear up.
aufhetzen *v.t.* to stir up.
aufholen *v.i.* to catch up (with).
aufhorchen *v.i.* to listen.
aufhören *v.i.* to cease, to leave off, to stop; *da hört alles auf*, that's the limit.
aufjauchzen *v.i.* to shout with joy.
aufkaufen *v.t.* to buy up.
Aufkäufer *m.* (-s, -) forestaller.
aufklären *v.t.* to clear up; (*fig.*) to explain; (*einen*) to enlighten; (*mil.*) to reconnoitre.
Aufklärung *f.* (-, -en) clearing up; enlightenment; explanation; reconnoitring.
aufkleben *v.t.* to paste upon.
aufknöpfen *v.t.* to unbutton.
aufknüpfen *v.t.* to untie; (*einen*) to hang.
aufkommen *v.i.st.* (*s*) to come into use. (*für etwas*) to be responsible (for); to prevail against.
aufkündigen *v.t.* to renounce; (*Kapital*) to recall.
aufladen *v.t.st.* to load; (*fig.*) to impose, to saddle (with).
Auflage *f.* (-, -n) impost, duty, tax; (*eines Buches*) edition; (*einer Zeitung*) circulation.
auflassen *v.t.st.* to leave open.
auflauern *v.i.* to lie in wait for, to waylay.
Auflauf *m.* (-[e]s, -läufe) crowd; tumult, riot; (*Speise*) soufflé.
auflaufen *v.i.st.* (*s*) (*mar.*) to run aground; (*anwachsen*) to accumulate; *aufgelaufene Summe*, aggregate amount.
aufleben *v.i.* (*s*) to revive.
auflegen *v.t.* to impose.
Auflegen *n.* (-s, 0) (*einer Anleihe*) flotation (of a loan).
auflehnen (*sich*) *v.refl.* (*gegen*) to rebel against, to oppose.
Auflehnung *f.* (-, -en) insurrection, mutiny.
auflesen *v.t.st.* to pick up, to glean.
aufliegen *v.i.st.* to be laid out; (*sich*) ~ *v.refl.st.* to become bed-sore.
auflockern *v.t.* to loosen (soil).
auflodern *v.i.* (*s*) to blaze up.
auflösbar *a.* soluble.
auflösen *v.t.* to loosen, to untie; to dissolve, to melt; (*Rätsel*) to solve; (*Brüche*) to reduce; (*mil. Einheiten*) to disband; (*sich*) ~ *v.refl.* to dissolve, to break up.

Auflösung f. (-, -en) solution; (mil.) disbandment, deactivation.

aufmachen v.t. to open; to unpack; (sich) ~ v. refl. to set out (for).

Aufmachung f. (-, -en) style; make-up.

Aufmarsch m. (-es, -märsche) (mil.) review; deployment.

aufmarschieren v.i. (s) to march up, to deploy.

aufmerken v.i. to attend to.

aufmerksam a. attentive; ~ machen auf, to draw a person's attention to.

Aufmerksamkeit f. (-, -en) attention, attentiveness.

aufmuntern v.t. to encourage, to cheer.

Aufmunterung f. (-, -en) encouragement.

Aufnahme f. (-, -n) reception, admission, survey; photo, snap-shot.

Aufnahme: ~gebühr f. entrance fee; ~prüfung f. entrance examination.

aufnehmen v.t.st. to take up; to receive; to admit; (abbilden) to photograph; (messen) to survey; (Geld) to borrow; (Gäste) to take; es mit einem ~, to try conclusions with someone.

aufnötigen v.t. to force upon.

aufopfern v.t. to sacrifice.

Aufopferung f. (-, -en) sacrifice.

aufpassen v.i. to attend, to look out, to take notice of.

Aufpasser m. (-s, -) spy, watch.

aufpflanzen v.t. (Seitengewehr) to fix.

aufpfropfen v.t. to graft on.

aufpflügen v.t. to plough up.

aufpumpen v.t. to pump up.

Aufputz m. (-es, -e) finery, dress.

aufraffen (sich) v.refl. to recover; (fig.) to pluck up courage.

aufräumen v.t. to remove, to set in order; to clear (a shop); mit etwas ~, to make a clean sweep of.

aufrecht a. & adv. upright, erect; ~ erhalten, to maintain.

Aufrechthaltung f. (-, 0) maintenance.

aufrechtstehend a. on end, on edge.

aufregen v.t. to stir up, to rouse; to incite to excite; (nervös) to flutter.

Aufregung f. (-, -en) excitement, stir.

aufreiben v.t.st. to rub open, to gall; (fig.) to worry; (vertilgen) to destroy.

aufreihen v.t. to string.

aufreissen v.t.st. to tear open; (Tür) to fling open; ~ v.i.st. to burst, to split.

aufreizen v.t. to rouse, to excite.

aufreizend a. inflammatory.

Aufreizung f. (-, -en) provocation; incitement.

aufrichten v.t. to set up; to erect; to straighten up; (fig.) to comfort; (sich) ~ v.refl. to sit up.

aufrichtig a. sincere, frank.

Aufrichtigkeit f. (-, 0) sincerity.

aufriegeln v.t. to unbolt.

Aufriss m. (-risses, -risse) sketch, elevation.

aufrollen v.t. to roll up; to unroll.

Aufruf m. (-[e]s, -e) call, summons.

aufrufen v.t.st. to call up, to summon.

Aufruhr m. (-[e]s, -e) uproar, insurrection, rebellion.

aufrühren v.t. to stir up; (fig.) to rake up.

Aufrührer m. (-s, -) rebel, mutineer.

aufrührerisch a. rebellious.

aufrüsten v.i. & t. to rearm.

Aufrüstung f. (-, 0) rearmament.

aufrütteln v.t. to shake up, to rouse.

aufs = auf das.

aufsagen v.t. to recite.

aufsässig a. refractory, adverse.

Aufsatz m. (-es, sätze) top; (Tafel~) centre-piece; essay, paper.

aufsaugen v.t.st. to suck up; to absorb.

aufschauen v.i. to look up.

aufscheuchen v.t. to frighten; to scare.

aufschichten v.t. to pile up, to stack.

aufschieben v.t.st. to delay, to defer, to put off; to adjourn.

Aufschlag m. (-[e]s, -schläge) (Rock~) cuff, facings; (Preis~) rise, advance; plussage; (mil. Geschoss) impact.

aufschlagen v.t.st. (die Augen) to cast up; (Gerüst) to put up; (Buch) to open; (Wort) to look up; (Zelt) to pitch; ~ v.i. (s) (im Preise) to rise (in price); (tennis) to serve.

aufschliessen v.t.st. to unlock.

aufschlitzen v.t. to slit, to rip up.

Aufschluss m. (-schlusses, -schlüsse) (fig.) explanation.

aufschnallen v.t. to buckle upon; to unbuckle.

aufschnappen v.t. to pick up.

aufschneiden v.t.st. to cut open; (Buch) to cut; ~ v.i.st. to swagger, to brag.

Aufschneider m. (-s, -) swaggerer, braggart.

Aufschnitt m. (-[e]s, -e) kalter ~, slices of cold meat.

aufschnüren v.t. to unlace.

aufschrauben v.t. to unscrew; to screw on.

aufschrecken v.t. to startle; ~ v.i. (s) to start, to jump.

Aufschrei m. (-[e]s, -e) scream, shriek, outcry.

aufschreiben v.t.st. to write down, to take down, to put down.

aufschreien v.i.st. to cry out, to scream.

Aufschrift f. (-, -en) inscription; direction, address.

Aufschub m. (-[e]s, 0) delay, adjournment.

aufschürzen v.t. to tuck up.

aufschütteln v.t. to shake up, to rouse.

aufschütten v.t. to heap up; to pour upon.

aufschwingen (sich) v.refl.st. to soar, to rise.

G.D.

Aufschwung *m.* (-[e]s, -schwünge) rise, progress.

Aufsehen *n.* (-s, 0) looking up; (*fig.*) stir, sensation.

Aufseher *m.* (-s, -) inspector.

auf sein *v.i.ir.* (*s*) to be up (out of bed); to be open.

aufsetzen *v.t.* (*Hut, Miene*) to put on; (*schriftlich*) to draw up; (sich) ~ *v.refl.* to sit up.

Aufsicht *f.* (-, 0) inspection, supervision, superintendence, charge.

Aufsichts... supervisory; ~**behörde** *f.* inspectorate; ~**rat** *m.* board of directors.

aufsitzen *v.i.st.* (*s*) to sit up; to mount (a horse).

aufspalten *v.t.* & *i.st.* to split, to cleave.

aufspannen *v.t.* (*Schirm*) to put up; (*Segel*) to spread; (*Saiten* ~, to string.

aufsparen *v.t.* to save, to lay up.

aufspeichern *v.t.* to store up.

aufsperren *v.t.* to open wide, to throw wide; (*Schlösser*) to pick; (*das Maul*) to gape.

aufspielen (sich) *v.refl.* to swagger; to set up for.

aufspiessen *v.t.* to spit, to pierce; to impale.

aufsprengen *v.t.* to burst open.

aufspringen *v.i.st.* (*s*) to leap up; to crack; (*Hände*) to chap.

aufspüren *v.t.* to trace out, to track.

aufstacheln *v.t.* to goad, to incite.

aufstampfen *v.i.* to stamp (on the ground).

Aufstand *m.* (-[e]s, -stände) insurrection, uproar, sedition.

aufständisch *a.* rebellious, seditious.

aufstapeln *v.t.* to pile up.

aufstechen *v.t.st.* to pick open; (*Geschwür*) to lance.

aufstehen *v.i.st.*(*s*) to get up, to rise; (*aufrecht*) to stand up.

aufsteigen *v.i.st.* (*s*) to rise.

aufsteigend *a.* ascending.

aufstellen *v.t.* to set up, to put up, to erect; (*mil. Einheit*) to activate; (*Behauptung*) to make (an assertion); (*Grundsatz*) to lay down; (*Kandidaten*) to nominate.

Aufstellung *f.* (-, -en) (*mil.*) disposition; (*eines Kandidaten*) nomination.

Aufstieg *m.* (-[e]s, -e) ascent, rise.

aufstöbern *v.t.* (*fig.*) to ferret out.

aufstören *v.t.* to stir, to disturb, to rouse.

aufstossen *v.t.st.* to push open; ~ *v.i.st.* (*s*) to occur to, to meet with; (*Speisen*) to rise up.

aufstreichen *v.t.st.* to lay on, to spread.

aufstülpen *v.t.* to turn up, to cock.

aufstützen *v.t.* to prop up; ~ *v.i.* to lean (upon).

aufsuchen *v.t.* to seek out, to look up.

auftakeln *v.t.* to rig out.

Auftakt *m.* (-es, -e) anacrusis; (*fig.*) prelude, preliminaries *pl.*

auftauchen *v.t.* to emerge, to appear.

auftauen *v.t.* & *i.* to thaw.

aufteilen *v.t.* to parcel out, to dismember.

Aufteilung *f.* (-, -en) dismemberment.

auftischen *v.t.* to serve up.

Auftrag *m.* (-[e]s, -träge) commission, order, mandate; (*mil.*) assignment, mission; *Aufträge annehmen* (*com.*) to accept orders.

auftragen *v.t.st.* to carry up; (*Speise*) to serve up; (*einem etwas*) to charge someone with; (*Farbe*) to lay on; (*Kleider*) to wear out.

Auftraggeber *m.* customer (who gives an order).

auftreiben *v.t.st.* (*Geld*) to raise; (*finden*) to hunt up.

auftrennen *v.t.* to rip up; to undo.

auftreten *v.i.st.* (*s*) to appear, to come forth; to behave.

Auftrieb *m.* (-[e]s, -e) buoyancy.

Auftritt *m.* (-[e]s, -e) (*Theater*) scene.

auftrocknen *v.t.* & *i.* to dry up.

auftrumpfen *v.i.*(*fig.*) to fight back.

auftürmen *v.t.* to pile up; (sich) ~ *v.refl.* to tower.

aufwachen *v.i.* (*s*) to wake up.

aufwachsen *v.i.st.* (*s*) to grow up.

Aufwallung *f.* (-, -en) bubbling; ebullition; (*fig.*) emotion, transport.

Aufwand *m.* (-[e]s, 0) expense, display.

aufwärmen *v.t.* to warm up.

Aufwartefrau *f.* (-, -en) charwoman.

aufwarten *v.t.* to wait on; to serve; to visit; ~ *mit*, to offer.

Aufwärter *m.* (-s, -) attendant, steward.

aufwärts *adv.* upward, upwards.

Aufwartung *f.* (-, -en) (*Bedienung*) attendance; *seine* ~ *machen*, to pay a visit to somebody.

aufwaschen *v.t.st.* to wash up.

aufwecken *v.t.* to wake up.

aufweichen *v.t.* to moisten, to soak.

aufweisen *v.t.st.* to show, to produce, to exhibit.

aufwenden *v.t.* to spend (upon).

aufwerfen *v.t.st.* (*Frage*) to raise; *sich* ~ *zu*, to set up for.

aufwerten *v.t.* to revalue, to revalorize.

Aufwertung *f.* (-, -en) revaluation, revalorization.

aufwickeln *v.t.* to wind up.

aufwiegeln *v.t.* to incite (to mutiny), to stir up.

aufwiegen *v.t.st.* to outweigh; to counterbalance.

aufwinden *v.t.st.* to wind up, to hoist.

aufwischen *v.t.* to wipe up.

aufwühlen *v.t.* to agitate.

aufzählen *v.t.* to enumerate.

aufzäumen v.t. to bridle.

aufzehren v.t. to consume.

aufzeichnen v.t. to record.

Aufzeichnung f. (-, -en) note, record.

aufziehen v.t.st. to draw up, to pull up; (Uhr) to wind up; (Vorhang) to draw; (Kinder) to rear, to bring up; (Pflanzen) to cultivate, to grow, to rear; (foppen) to rally, to chaff; ~ v.i. (s) to march up.

Aufzug m. (-[e]s, -züge) hoist; (Fahrstuhl) lift, (Am.) elevator; (Theater) act; Gewand) attire.

aufzwingen v.t.st. to force upon.

Augapfel m. eyeball; (fig.) apple of one's eye, darling.

Auge n. (-s, -n) eye; unter vier ⁓n, between ourselves, in private; aus dem ⁓ verlieren, to lose sight of; (mil.) ⁓n geradeaus, eyes front; ⁓n rechts, eyes right.

Augen..., **augenärztlich** a. ophthalmic.

Augen: ~arzt m. oculist; ~blick m. moment, twinkling.

augenblicklich a. instantaneous, momentary; ~ adv. instantly.

Augen: ~braue f. eye-brow; ~brauenstift m. eyebrow-pencil.

augenfällig = augenscheinlich.

Augen: ~glas n. eye-glass; (des Fernrohrs) eye-piece; ~höhle f. socket, orbit; ~licht n. eye-sight; ~lid n. eye-lid; ~mass n. correct eye, estimate; ~merk n. attention; ~nerv m. optic nerve; ~schein m. appearance; view, inspection.

augenscheinlich a. evident, apparent.

Augen: ~spiegel m. ophthalmoscope; ~wimper f. eye-lash; ~zeuge m. eye-witness.

August m. (-[e]s, -e) (Monat) August.

Auktion f. (-, -en) public sale, auction.

Auktionator m. (-s, -en) auctioneer.

Aula f. (-, -s) (large) hall.

aus pr. out of, from, through, about, on, upon, in, by; ~ adv. out, over, up, finished, consumed.

ausarbeiten v.t. to elaborate, to perfect, to compose.

ausarten v.i. (s) to degenerate.

ausatmen v.t. to breathe out, to exhale.

ausbaden v.t. (fig.) to suffer for.

Ausbau m. (-es, 0) extension, completion.

ausbauen v.t. to finish; (fig.) to improve.

ausbedingen v.t.st. to stipulate, to reserve.

ausbessern v.t. to mend, to repair.

Ausbesserung f. (-, -en) repair, reparation.

Ausbeute f. (-, 0) gain, profit.

ausbeuten v.t. to exploit.

Ausbeutung f. (-, 0) exploitation.

ausbezahlen v.t. to pay down.

ausbilden v.t. to form; to school, to train, to cultivate; (sich) ~ v.refl. to improve one's mind.

Ausbildung f. (-, 0) cultivation; training; in der ~ sein, to be in training, under training; ~sstelle f. training centre.

ausbitten v.t.st. to request, to beg for; sich ⁓, to insist on.

ausblasen v.t.st. to blow out.

ausbleiben v.i.st. (s) to stay away, to fail to appear.

Ausbleiben n. (-s, 0) absence.

Ausblick m. (-[e]s, -e) view, prospect.

ausbrechen v.t.st. to break out; ~ v.i.st. (s) to break out.

ausbreiten v.t. to spread, to extend; to propagate; (sich) ~ v.refl. to gain ground.

Ausbreitung f. (-, -en) spreading, propagation.

Ausbruch m. (-[e]s, -brüche) outbreak; (Vulkan) eruption; outburst.

ausbrüten v.t. to hatch; (fig.) to breed; to plot.

Ausbund m. (-[e]s, -bünde) best, paragon.

Ausbürgerung f. (-, -en) expatriation.

ausbürsten v.t. to brush.

Ausdauer f.(-, 0) perseverance, endurance.

ausdauern v.i. to last to the end, to hold out.

ausdehnbar a. expansible, extensible.

ausdehnen v.t. to extend, to stretch; (fig.) to prolong.

Ausdehnung f. (-, -en) extension, expansion, extent; dimension.

ausdenken v.t.ir. to contrive, to devise; to imagine.

ausdeuten v.t. to interpret, to explain.

Ausdeutung f. (-, -en) interpretation.

ausdienen v.i. ausgedient haben, to be used up.

ausdörren v.t. to parch; to dry up.

ausdrehen v.t. (das Gas) to turn off; (elektr. Licht) to switch off.

Ausdruck m. (-[e]s, -drücke) expression; term.

ausdrücken v.t. to express; (sich) ~ v.refl. to express oneself.

ausdrücklich a. express, explicit.

ausdruckslos a. blank, vacant.

ausdrucksvoll a. expressive, significant.

Ausdrucksweise f. mode of expression.

ausdunsten, **ausdünsten** v.i. & t. to evaporate; (schwitzen) to perspire.

Ausdünstung f. (-, -en) evaporation; exhalation; (Schweiss) perspiration.

auseinander adv. asunder; separately.

auseinandernehmen v.t. to take to pieces.

Auseinandersetzung f. (-, -en) explanation; arrangement; discussion.

auserkoren a. chosen, elect.

auserlesen v.t.st. to choose, to select; ~ a. select, choice; exquisite.

ausersehen v.t.st. to single out.

ausfahren v.t.st. (Flotte) to put out, to put to sea.

Ausfahrt f. (-, -en) drive; (*Tor*) gateway.

Ausfall m. (-[e]s, -fälle) falling out; deficiency; (*Ergebnis*) result; (*mil.*) sally; (*im Fechten*) thrust, pass.

ausfallen v.i.st (s) (*gut oder schlecht*) to turn out; (*Haar*) to come off; not to take place; (*mil.*) to make a sally; (*im Fechten*) to lunge.

ausfallend a. aggressive.

ausfechten v.t.st. to fight out.

ausfegen v.t. to sweep (out).

ausfertigen v.t. to dispatch; (*Rechnung*) to make out; (*Urkunde*) to execute.

Ausfertigung f. (-, -en) dispatch; execution.

ausfindig machen v.t. to find out.

Ausflucht f. (-, -flüchte) evasion, subterfuge, poor excuse.

Ausflug m. (-[e]s, flüge) trip, excursion.

Ausfluss m. (-flusses, -flüsse) flowing out; (*Loch etc.*) outlet; (*Mündung*) mouth; (*med.*) discharge; (*phys.*) emanation.

ausfolgen v.t. to deliver, to hand over.

ausforschen v.t. to search out.

ausfragen v.t. to examine.

ausfransen v.t. to fray out.

Ausfuhr f. (-, -en) exportation, export.

ausführbar a. practicable, feasible.

ausführen v.t. (*Waren*) to export; (*vollenden*) to perform, to execute; to set forth.

Ausfuhrhandel m. export trade.

ausführlich a. detailed, ample, full; ~ adv. in detail, fully.

Ausfuhr: ~**stelle** f. export control office; ~**zoll** m. export duty.

Ausführung f. (-, -en) (*fig.*) execution; statement.

Ausführungsbestimmung f. (executive) regulation.

ausfüllen v.t. to fill out; (*Formular*) to complete, to fill up.

Ausgabe f. (-, -n) (*eines Buchs*) edition; (*Kosten*) expense; (*Papiergeld*) issue.

Ausgang m. (-[e]s, -gänge) going out; (*Ergebnis*) issue, event; (*Ende*) end, conclusion; (*Tür*) way out, exit.

Ausgangspunkt m. starting-point.

ausgeben v.t.st. (*Buch*) to publish, to edit; (*Geld*) to spend; (*Papiergeld*) to issue; *sich* ~ *für*, to pass oneself off for...

ausgebrannt a. gutted.

ausgebreitet a. extensive.

Ausgeburt f. (-, -en) product, creature.

ausgedient a. superannuated.

ausgehen v.i.st. (s) to go out; ~ *von*, to originate with; (*Haare, Farbe*) to come out or off, to fade; (*zu Ende gehen*) to run out; *es ist uns ausgegangen*, we are run out of it *or* short of it.

Ausgehverbot n. curfew; ~ *aufheben*, to lift the curfew.

ausgelassen a. frisky, exuberant; boisterous.

ausgemacht a. downright; ~*e Sache*, foregone conclusion.

ausgenommen pr. & adv. except, save.

ausgeprägt a. clear-cut, decided.

ausgeschnitten a. low-necked.

ausgesprochen a. marked, decided.

ausgestreckt a. outstretched.

ausgesucht a. choice, exquisite; (*com.*) picked.

ausgewachsen a. full-grown.

ausgezeichnet a. excellent, first-rate.

ausgiebig a. abundant.

ausgiessen v.t.st. to pour out.

Ausgleich m. (-[e]s, -e) settlement; (*el.*) compensation.

ausgleichen v.t.st. to equalize, to compensate; to offset; to balance; (*Streit*) to make up.

ausgleiten v.t.st. (s) to slip.

ausgraben v.t.st. to dig out; (*Leichnam*) to exhume.

Ausgrabung f. (-, -en) excavation; exhumation.

Ausguss m. (-gusses, -güsse) sink; gutter; (*Tülle*) spout.

aushalten v.t.st. to hold out; to last; (*pers.*) to hold out, to persevere; ~ v.t.st. to endure, to bear, to stand.

aushändigen v.t. to hand over.

aushängen v.t. to hang out; to unhinge.

Aushängeschild n. sign-board.

ausharren v.i. to persevere, to hold out.

aushauchen v.i. & t. to breathe out, to expire; to exhale.

ausheben v.t.st. to lift out; (*Tür*) to unhinge; (*mil.*) to levy (troops).

Aushebung f. (-, -en) draft of soldiers, levy.

aushecken v.t. to hatch; (*fig.*) to devise.

ausheilen v.t. to heal thoroughly.

aushelfen v.i.st. to help out; to aid.

Aushilfe f. (-, -n) help, assistance, aid; (*Notbehelf*) makeshift, expedient.

aushöhlen v.t. to hollow out, to excavate.

ausholen v.t. (*einen*) to sound; ~ v.i. to strike out; (*fig.*) to go far back.

aushorchen v.t. to sound, to pump.

aushören v.t. to hear the end.

Aushülfe = Aushilfe.

aushungern v.t. to starve, to famish.

auskämmen v.t. to comb (out).

auskämpfen v.t. to fight out.

auskehren v.t. to sweep (out), to brush.

auskennen (sich) v.refl. to be at home in.

auskernen v.t. (*Früchte*) to stone.

auskleiden v.t. to undress; (sich) ~ v.refl. to undress.

ausklingen v.i.st. to die away (of sound).

ausklopfen v.t. to beat.

ausklügeln v.t. to puzzle out.

auskneifen v.i.st. (s) (*fam.*) to make oneself scarce.

auskochen v.t. to boil sufficiently; to extract by boiling.

auskommen *v.i.st.* (*s*) (*Feuer*) to break out; (*mit etwas*) to make both ends meet; (*mit einem*) to get on well.

Auskommen *n.* (-s, 0) competency.

auskömmlich *a.* sufficient.

auskramen *v.t.* to display (for sale).

auskratzen *v.t.* to scratch out.

auskriechen *v.i.st.* (*s*) to creep forth.

auskundschaften *v.t.* to explore, to reconnoitre.

Auskunft *f.* (-, -künfte) information.

Auskunftei, *f.* (-, -en) inquiry office.

Auskunfts: ~**bureau** *n.* private inquiry office; ~**mittel** *n.* expedient.

auslachen *v.t.* to laugh at, to make fun of.

Ausladebahnhof *m.* railhead.

ausladen *v.t.* to unload, to discharge; (*Truppen*) to detrain.

Auslage *f.* (-, -n) disbursement; (*Kosten*) outlay; (*Schaufenster*) window.

Auslagerung *f.* (-, -en) dispersal of industry.

Ausland *n.* (-[e]s, 0) foreign country; *im* ~, *ins* ~, abroad.

Ausländer *m.* (-s, -), **Ausländerin** *f.* (-, -nen) foreigner; alien; *feindliche* ~, enemy alien.

ausländisch *a.* foreign.

Auslands: ~**gespräch** *n.* (*tel.*) international call; ~**wechsel** *m.* (*com.*) foreign bill.

auslangen *v.i.* to suffice, to last.

auslassen *v.t.st.* to omit; to melt; (*Wut*) to give vent; (*sich*) ~ *v.refl.st.* to speak one's mind.

Auslassung *f.* (-, -en) omission.

auslaufen *v.i.st.* (*s*) to run out; to leak; (*nav.*) to put to sea.

Ausläufer *m.* (-s, -) offshoot.

ausleeren *v.t.* to empty, to clear.

auslegen *v.t.* to lay out; (*erklären*) to interpret; (*Geld*) to disburse, to advance.

Auslegung *f.* (-, -en) interpretation.

ausleihen *v.t.st.* to lend out.

Auslese *f.* (-, -n) selection.

auslesen *v.t.* to select; (*Buch*) to read through.

ausliefern *v.t.* to deliver, to give up.

Auslieferung *f.* (-, -en) delivery; (*von Verbrechern*) extradition.

ausliegen *v.i.st.* (*Zeitungen*) to display.

auslöschen *v.t.* to extinguish, to quench; to efface; ~ *v.i.* to go out.

auslosen *v.t.* to draw lots for; to draw.

auslösen *v.t.* to redeem, to ransom.

Auslöser *m.* (-s, -) (*phot.*) release.

Auslösung *f.* (-, -en) ransom; redemption; (*phot.*) release.

auslüften *v.t.* to air, to ventilate.

ausmachen *v.t.* (*Feuer*) to put out; (*betragen*) to come to, to constitute; *es macht nichts aus*, it does not matter.

ausmalen *v.t.* to paint; to illuminate.

ausmarschieren *v.i.* (*s*) to march out.

Ausmass *n.* (-es, e) extent; measurement.

ausmauern *v.t.* to line with brickwork *or* masonry.

ausmergeln *v.t.* to emaciate.

ausmerzen *v.t.* to expunge, to eliminate.

ausmessen *v.t.st.* to measure.

ausmieten *v.t.* to job.

ausmustern *v.t.* to reject; to discharge.

Ausnahme *f.* (-, -n) exception; *keine* ~ *zulassen*, to admit of no exception; ~**gesetz**, *n.* emergency law.

ausnahmsweise *adv.* by way of exception.

ausnehmen *v.t.st.* to take out; (*Geflügel*) to draw; (*fig.*) to except, to exclude; (*sich*) ~ *v.refl.st.* to show, to look.

ausnehmend *adv.* exceedingly.

ausnutzen *v.t.* to utilize fully; to use up.

auspacken *v.t.* to unpack, to open.

auspeitschen *v.t.* to whip.

auspfeifen *v.t.* to hiss.

ausplaudern *v.t.* to blab out, to let out.

ausplündern *v.t.* to plunder, to pillage, to sack.

auspolstern *v.t.* to stuff.

ausposaunen *v.t.* to trumpet forth, to cry up.

auspressen *v.t.* to press out, to squeeze.

ausproben *v.t.* to test.

ausprügeln *v.t.* to cudgel thoroughly.

Auspuff *m.* (-s, -püffe) exhaust.

Auspuff: ~**klappe** *f.* exhaust valve; ~**rohr** *n.* exhaust pipe.

auspumpen *v.t.* to pump (out).

ausputzen *v.t.* to clean; to prune; (*schmücken*) to trim out, to deck out.

ausquartieren *v.t.* to dislodge.

ausquetschen *v.t.* to squeeze (out).

ausradieren *v.t.* to erase.

ausrasen *v.i.* to cease raging, to subside.

ausrasten (**sich**) *v.refl.* to have a rest.

ausrauben *v.t.* to despoil, to spoliate.

ausräuchern *v.t.* to fumigate, to perfu_ _e.

ausraufen *v.t.* to pluck out.

ausräumen *v.t.* to remove, to clear away.

ausrechnen *v.t.* to reckon, to compute.

Ausrechnung *f.* (-, -en) calculation, computation.

Ausrede *f.* (-, -n) subterfuge, evasion.

ausreden *v.t.* & *i.* to finish speaking; (*einem etwas*) to dissuade someone from; (*sich*) ~ *v.refl.* to shuffle, to beat about the bush.

ausreiben *v.t.st.* to rub out.

ausreichen *v.i.* to suffice.

Ausreise *f.* (-, -n) departure to a foreign country; ~**erlaubnis** *f.* exit permit.

ausreisen *v.i.* to leave the country.

ausreissen *v.t.st.* to tear out, to pull out; ~ *v.i.st.* (*fig.*) to run away, to decamp; to desert.

Ausreisser *m.* (-s, -) runaway, deserter.

ausreiten *v.i.st.* (*s*) to ride out, to go for a ride.

ausrenken v.t. to dislocate.
ausrichten v.t. to achieve; (mil.) to dress; *eine Botschaft* ~, to give a message; *etwas* ~ *lassen*, to leave a message.
ausrotten v.i.st. to root out or up; (fig.) to exterminate, to extirpate.
Ausrottung f. (-, -en) extirpation, extermination.
ausrücken v.i. to march out; to decamp.
Ausruf m. (-[e]s, -e) cry, exclamation; proclamation.
ausrufen v.i.st. to cry out, to call out; ~ v.t.st. to proclaim.
Ausrufungszeichen n. mark of exclamation.
ausruhen v.i. to rest, to repose.
ausrupfen v.t. to pluck out.
ausrüsten v.t. to equip; to furnish; to fit out.
Ausrüstung f. (-, -en) outfit; equipment.
ausrutschen v.i. to slip; to skid.
Aussaat f. (-, -en) sowing; seed-corn.
aussäen v.t. to sow; to disseminate.
Aussage f. (-, -n) declaration, statement; deposition; (gram.) predicate.
aussagen v.t. to say, to declare; (als Zeuge) to depose, to give evidence.
Aussatz m. (-es, 0) leprosy; scab.
aussätzig a. leprous.
Aussätzige[r] m. (-n, -n) leper.
aussaugen v.t.st. or weak to suck out; (fig.) to exhaust, to impoverish.
Aussauger m. (-s, -) blood-sucker, extortioner.
ausschachten v.i. to sink.
ausschalten v.t. to switch off; to eliminate.
Ausschank m. (-[e]s, 0) retail licence.
ausschauen v.i. to look out; to look.
ausscheiden v.t.st. to separate; to secrete; ~ v.i.st. (s) to withdraw.
ausscheidend a. outgoing.
ausschenken v.t. to pour out; to retail.
ausschliessen v.t. to rule out, to exclude.
ausschiffen v.t. & i. to disembark, to land.
ausschimpfen v.t. to abuse, to revile.
ausschlachten v.t. to exploit.
ausschlafen v.i.st. to have one's sleep out.
Ausschlag m. (-[e]s, -schläge) (der Waage) turn of the scales; (Krankheit) rash; (Entscheidung) decision.
ausschlagen v.t.st. (mit etwas) to line; (Geschenk) to decline, to refuse; ~ v.i. (s) (von Pferden) to kick; (Knospen) to bud, to shoot; (gut, schlecht) to turn out, to prove.
ausschlaggebend a. decisive, deciding.
ausschliesslich a. exclusive.
Ausschluss m. (-schlusses, -schlüsse) exclusion, exemption.
ausschmücken v.t. to adorn, to decorate.
ausschneiden v.t.st. to cut out.
Ausschnitt m. (-[e]s, -e) cutting out; cut; low neck; (math.) sector.

ausschrauben v.t. to unscrew.
ausschreiben v.t.st. to write out, to spell out; (Landtag, etc.) to convene, to summon; (Steuern) to impose; (Stelle) to advertise.
Ausschreitung f. (-, -en) excess.
Ausschuss m. (-schusses, -schüsse) damaged goods pl.; (Komitee) committee, board, panel; *dem* ~ *angehören*, to be on the committee.
ausschütteln v.t. to shake out.
ausschütten v.t. to pour out; (fig.) to unburden (one's heart); to pay (dividend).
ausschwärmen v.i. (s) to swarm out; (mil.) to extend.
ausschwatzen v.t. to blab; to talk of.
ausschweifend a. dissolute, licentious.
Ausschweifung f. (-, -en) debauchery.
ausschwenken v.t. to rinse.
ausschwitzen v.t. to exude.
aussehen v.i.st. to look; (nach) to look out (for).
Aussehen n. (-s, 0) appearance, look.
aus sein v.i.ir. (s) to be out; to be over.
aussen adv. on the outside, without; *nach* ~, outward.
Aussenbordmotor m. outboard motor.
aussenden v.t.ir. to send out.
Aussenhandel m. foreign trade.
Aussenpolitik f. (-, 0) foreign politics, foreign policy.
Aussenseite f. outside, exterior.
Aussenseiter m. outsider.
Aussenstände m.pl. outstanding debts.
Aussenwelt f. outer world.
ausser pr. without, out of; except; besides; but; ~ c. unless, except that, but that.
ausseramtlich a. unofficial.
ausserdem adv. besides, moreover.
Ausserdienststunden f.pl. off-duty hours.
äussere a. outer, exterior, external.
Äussere n. (-n, 0) external appearance; *Minister des Äussern*, Minister of Foreign Affairs.
aussergerichtlich adv. out of court.
aussergewöhnlich a. extraordinary.
ausserhalb adv. outside, outwardly.
äusserlich a. external, outward; ~ adv. (med.) for external use only!
Äusserlichkeit f. (-, -en) formality.
äussern v.t. to utter, to express; (sich) ~ v.refl. to express oneself.
ausserordentlich a. extraordinary; ~er *Professor*, assistant (associate) professor.
äusserst a. outermost; extreme, utmost; ~ adv. extremely.
ausserstande a. unable.
Äusserung f. (-, -en) utterance, pronouncement.
aussetzen v.t. (Kind) to expose; (Belohnung) to promise; (Summe) to settle; (Tätigkeit) to suspend; (rügen) to find

fault (with); ~ v.i. to intermit; (*mit etwas*) to discontinue.

Aussetzung f. (-, -en) suspension; intermission; censure; (*Summe*) settlement.

Aussicht f. (-, -en) view, prospect.

aussichtslos a. without prospects.

Aussichtsturm m. watch-tower.

aussinnen v.t.t. to contrive.

aussöhnen v.t. to reconcile; (sich) ~ v.refl. to become reconciled (to).

Aussöhnung f. (-, -en) reconciliation.

aussondern v.t. to single out.

aussortieren v.t. to assort, to sort (out).

ausspähen v.t. to spy out; v.i. to look out (for).

ausspannen v.t. to stretch, to extend; (*Pferd*) to unharness; ~ v.i. to take a rest.

ausspeien v.t.st. to spit (out).

aussperren v.t. to shut out; to lock out.

Aussperrung f. (-, -en) lock-out.

ausspielen (gegen) v.t. to play off against.

ausspionieren v.t. to spy out.

Aussprache f. (-, -n) pronunciation, accent; talk.

aussprechen v.t.st. to pronounce; (*äussern*) to declare, to utter; (sich) ~ v.refl. to speak one's mind.

aussprengen v.t. (*fig.*) to divulge, to report.

Ausspruch m. (-[e]s, -sprüche) utterance; sentence, verdict.

ausspucken v.t. to spit out.

ausspülen v.t. to rinse.

ausstatten v.t. to equip, to fit out; to dress up, to rig out.

Ausstand m. (-[e]s, -stände) outstanding debts, arrears pl.; (*von Arbeitern*) strike.

ausständig a. outstanding; (*Arbeiter*) on strike.

ausstatten v.t. to endow; to provide with; (*Töchter*) to portion off.

Ausstattung f. (-, -en) outfit; marriage-portion; (*von Büchern*) get-up.

ausstäuben v.t. to beat (carpets), to dust.

ausstechen v.t.st. to cut out; (*Augen*) to put out; (*fig.*) to supplant.

ausstehen v.t.st. to endure, to undergo.

aussteigen v.i.st. (s) to get out, to get off, to alight; (*vom Schiffe*) to disembark.

ausstellen v.t. (*auf einer Ausstellung*) to exhibit; (*Wechsel*) to draw; (*tadeln*) to find fault (with).

Aussteller m. (-s, -) (*Wechsel*) drawer; (*Industrie*) exhibitor.

Ausstellung f. (-, -en) (*Industrie*) exhibition; (*Tadel*) objection.

Ausstellungsraum m. (-[e]s, -räume) showroom.

aussterben v.i.st. (s) to die out; to become extinct.

Aussteuer f. (-, -n) dowry, portion, trousseau.

aussteuern v.t. to portion, to endow.

ausstopfen v.t. to stuff.

ausstossen v.t.st. to drive out; (*Schrei*) to utter.

ausstrahlen v.t. & i. (s) to radiate.

ausstrecken v.t. to stretch (out).

ausstreichen v.t.st. to strike out.

ausstreuen v.t. to scatter, to spread.

ausströmen v.i. to stream forth; to escape; to emanate.

Ausströmen (*von Gas*) n. (-s, 0) escape of gas.

aussuchen v.t. to select; to pick out.

Austausch m. (-[e]s, -e) exchange, barter.

austauschen v.t. to exchange, to barter; (*Am.*) to trade.

austeilen v.t. to distribute, to issue; (*Gnaden*) administer.

Auster f. (-, -n) oyster.

austilgen v.t. to extirpate; to obliterate.

Austilgung f. (-, -en) extirpation.

Austrag m. (-[e]s, -träge) decision; issue.

austragen v.t.st. to carry out; (*Briefe*) to deliver; (*Streit*) to fight out.

austreiben v.t.st. to drive out, to expel.

Austreibung f. expulsion.

austreten v.t. to stamp out; ~ v.i.st. (s) (*Fluss*) to overflow; (*verlassen*) to retire.

austrinken v.t.st. to drink up.

Austritt m. (-[e]s, -e) stepping out; retirement, leaving.

austrocknen v.t. & i. (s) to dry up; to drain.

ausüben v.t. to exercise, to practise.

Ausübung f. (-, 0) exercise, practice.

Ausverkauf m. (-[e]s, -käufe) (clearance) sale, selling off.

ausverkauft a. sold out.

auswägen v.t.st. to weigh (out).

Auswahl f. (-, -en) choice, selection; *eine* ~ *treffen*, to make a choice.

auswählen v.t. to choose, to select.

auswalzen v.t. to roll out.

Auswanderer m. (-s, -) emigrant.

auswandern v.i. (s) to emigrate.

Auswanderung f. (-, -en) emigration.

auswärtig a. foreign; ~e Beziehungen pl. international relations pl.

Auswärtige Amt n. Foreign Office.

auswärts adv. outward, outwards; abroad.

auswaschen v.t.st. to wash (out).

auswechselbar a. interchangeable.

auswechseln v.t. to exchange.

Ausweg m. (-[e]s, -e) way out; outlet; (*fig.*) expedient.

ausweichen v.i.st. (s) to make way for; to avoid, to evade; to turn aside (*von Wagen*).

ausweichend a. evasive.

ausweiden v.t. to eviscerate, to draw.

Ausweis *m.* (-es, -e) identification; ~*papier,* identity paper, certificate of identity.

ausweisen *v.t.st.* to expel, to banish; (*erweisen*) to prove; *sich* ~, to prove one's identity.

Ausweisung *f.* (-, -en) expulsion, banishment.

ausweiten *v.t.* to widen, to stretch.

auswendig *a.* outer, exterior; ~ *adv.* by heart.

auswerfen *v.t.st.* (*Gehalt*) to appoint.

auswerten *v.t.* to make full use of.

auswirken *v.t. sich* ~, to operate.

auswischen *v.t.* to wipe out.

Auswuchs *m.* (-wuchses, -wüchse) excrescence; abuse.

Auswurf *m.* (-[e]s, -würfe) excretion, expectoration; (*fig.*) refuse, dregs *pl.*

auszahlen *v.t.* to pay (down).

Auszahlung *f.* (-, -en) payment.

Auszehrung *f.* (-, -en) consumption.

auszeichnen *v.t.* to mark (out), to distinguish.

Auszeichnung *f.* (-, -en) distinction.

ausziehen *v.t.st.* to draw *or* pull out; (*chem.*) to extract; (*dehnen*) to stretch, to extend; (*Kleider*) to take off; ~ *v.i.st.* to move, to remove; (*mil.*) to march out; *sich* ~, to undress.

Ausziehtisch *m.* extending table.

Auszug *m.* (-[e]s, -züge) (*Wohnungs*~) removal; (*aus einem Buche*) abstract; (*fig.*) extract, summary, digest.

Autarkie *f.* (-, 0) self-sufficiency.

authentisch *a.* (& *adv.*) authentic(ally).

Auto *n.* (-s, -s) motor car.

Autobahn *f.* (-, -en) motor highway.

Autodidakt *m.* (-en, -en) self-taught person.

Autogramm *n.* (-[e]s, -e) autograph.

Autohaltestelle *f.* cab rank, taxi stand.

Automat *m.* (-en, -en) automaton.

automatisch *a.* (& *adv.*) automatic(ally).

Automobil *n.* (-s, -e) motor car; (*Am.*) automobile.

Auto: ~**droschke** *f.* taxi-cab; ~**mobilist** *m.* motorist; ~**omnibus** *m.* motor bus; ~**strasse** *f.* motor road.

autonom *a.* autonomous.

Autopsie *f.* (-, -[e]n) coroner's inquest.

Autor *m.* (-s, -en) author, writer.

autorisieren *v.t.* to authorize.

Autorität *f.* (-, -en) authority.

Autorschaft *f.* (-, 0) authorship.

Autowinker *m.* traffic indicator.

avancieren *v.i.* to rise, to get promotion.

avisieren *v.t.* to advise, to inform.

Avitaminose *f.* (-, -n) (*med.*) avitaminosis.

Axt *f.* (-, Äxte) axe, hatchet.

Azalie *f.* (-, -n) azalea.

Azetylen *n.* (-s, 0) acetylene.

azurblau, azurn *a.* azure.

B

Bach *m.* (-[e]s, Bäche) brook, rivulet.

Bachstelze *f.* (-, -n) wag-tail.

Back *f.* (-[e]s, -e) forecastle; mess.

back *a.* abaft; larboard...

Backbord *n.* larboard, port.

Backe *f.* (-, -n) cheek; jaw; (*mech.*) jaw.

backen *v.t.* to bake; (*Fische*) to fry; (*Ziegel*) to burn.

Backen: ~**bart** *m.* whiskers *pl.*; beard; ~**knochen** *m.* cheek-bone.

Bäcker *m.* (-s, -) baker.

Bäcker: ~**bursche** *m.* baker's boy; ~**gesell** *m.* baker's man.

Bäckerei *f.* (-, -en) bakery.

Back: ~**fisch** *m.* girl in her teens, flapper; ~**obst** *n.* dried fruit; ~**ofen** *m.* baking oven; ~**pfanne** *f.* drying pan; ~**pulver** *n.* baking powder; ~**stein** *m.* brick.

Backpulvermehl *n.* self-raising flour.

Bad *n.* (-es, Bäder) bath; (*Ort*) watering-place, spa; (*Handlung*) bathe.

Bade: ~**anstalt** *f.* baths *pl.*; bathing-establishment; ~**anzug** *m.* bathing-suit; ~**kur** *f.* course of mineral waters; ~**mantel** *m.* dressing-gown, (*Am.*) bath-robe.

baden *v.t. & i.* to bathe.

Bade: ~**ofen** *m.* geyser; ~**ort** *m.* watering-place, spa.

Bade: ~**wanne** *f.* bath, (*Am.*) bath-tub; ~**tuch** *n.* bath sheet; ~**zimmer** *n.* bathroom.

Bäffchen *n.pl.* bands.

Bagage (-, 0) *f.* (*fig.*) rabble, slut.

Bagger *m.* (-s, -) ~ **maschine** *f.* dredger, dredging-machine.

baggern *v.t.* to dredge.

Bahn *f.* (-, -en) road, path; course; (*Eisen*~) railway, (*Am.*) railroad; (*fig.*) career; *mit der* ~, by rail.

bahnbrechend *a.* epoch-making.

Bahnbrecher *m.* (-s, -) pioneer.

bahnen *v.t.* (*Weg*) to open a way; (*fig.*) to pave the way for.

Bahn: ~**hof** *m.* railway-station; ~**hofsvorsteher** *m.* stationmaster; ~**linie** *f.* line (of railway); ~**steig** *m.* platform; ~**steigkarte** *f.* platform ticket; (*schienengleicher*) **Bahnübergang** *m.* level crossing.

Bahre *f.* (-, -n) stretcher, bier.

Bai *f.* (-, -en) bay.

Baisse *frz.f.* fall in prices, slump; *auf* ~ *spekulieren,* to bear.

Baissier *m.* (-s, -s) (*Börse*) bear.

Bajonett *n.* (-[e]s, -e) bayonet.

Bakelit *n.* bakelite.

Bakterie *f.* (-, -n) bacterium.

Bakterien. . . bacteriological.

balancieren *v.t. & i.* to balance.

bald *adv.* soon, shortly; nearly, almost; ~..., ~..., now..., now...
Baldachin *m.* (-[e]s, -e) canopy.
in Bälde soon.
baldig *a.* quick, speedy, early.
Baldrian *m.* (-s, 0) valerian.
Balg *m.* (-[e]s, Bälge) skin; (*fig.*) brat.
balgen (sich) *v.refl.* to romp, to scuffle.
Balgerei *f.* (-, -en) scuffle.
Balken *m.* (-s, -) beam; rafter.
Balkon *m.* (-s, -e *u.* -s) balcony.
Ball *m.* (-[e]s, Bälle) ball; globe.
Ballade *f.* (-, -n) ballad.
Ballast *m.* (-es, -e) ballast.
ballen *v.t.* die Faust ~, to clench; (sich) ~ *v.refl.* to cluster; to gather.
Ballen *m.* (-s, -) bale, pack; (*Fuss*) ball, bunion.
Ballett *n.* (-[e]s, -e) ballet.
Ballon *m.* (-s, -s) balloon.
Ballsaal *m.* ballroom; ~spiel *n.* ball-game.
Balsam *m.* (-s, -e) balm, balsam.
balsamich *a.* balmy.
Balz *f.* (-, -n) (*Auerhahn*) coupling-time, coupling-place.
Bambusrohr *n.* bamboo.
banal *a.* hackneyed, trite.
Banane *f.* (-, -n) banana.
Band *n.* (-[e]s, Bänder *u.* [*fig.*] Bande) band; (*Seiden~*) ribbon; (*Zwirn~*) tape; (*anat.*) ligament; (*fig.*) tie, bond.
Band *m.* (-es, Bände) (*Buch*) volume; (*Einband*) binding.
Bandage *f.* (-, -n) bandage, truss.
Bande *f.* (-, -n) band, gang.
Bande *n.pl.* fetters, chains; ties *pl.*
Banderole *f.* (-, -n) revenue stamp.
bändigen *v.t* to tame; (*Pferd*) to break (in); (*fig.*) to subdue.
Bandit *m.* (-en, -en) bandit.
Bandwurm *m.* tape-worm.
bange *a.* afraid, alarmed, uneasy.
bangen *v.imp.* to be afraid of; (*nach*) to long for.
Bangigkeit *f.* (-, -en) anxiety.
Bank *f.* (-, Bänke) bench; (*Schul~*) form; auf die lange ~ schieben, to put off; durch die ~, without exception.
Bank *f.* (-, Banken) (*Geld~*) bank.
bank(e)rott *a.* bankrupt.
Bank(e)rott *m.* (-[e]s, -e) bankruptcy; be-trügerische ~, fraudulent bankruptcy.
Bank(e)rottierer *m.* (-s, -) bankrupt.
Bankett *n.* (-s, -e) banquet.
Bank: ~konto *n.* banking account; ~note *f.* banknote, (*Am.*) bank bill.
Bankier *m.* (-s, -s) banker.
Bann *m.* (-[e]s, 0) ban, excommunication.
bannen *v.t.* to banish; (*Geister*) to exorcise.
Banner *n.* (-s, -) banner.
bar *a.* bare; cash, ready-money; gegen ~ for cash; ~bezahlen, to pay cash.

Bär *m.* (-en, -en) bear; der Grosse ~ Charles's Wain.
Baracke *f.* (-, -n) shed, hut.
Barbar *m.* (-en, -en) barbarian.
Barbarei *f.* (-, -en) barbarity; vandalism.
barbarisch *a.* barbarous.
bärbeissig *a.* grumpy.
Barbier *m.* (-[e]s, -e) barber, hair-dresser.
barbieren *v.t.* to shave; to cheat.
Barchent *m.* (-[e]s, -e) cotton flannel.
Barde *m.* (-n, -n) bard.
Bärenhaut *f.* bearskin; auf der ~ liegen to be idle.
Barett *n.* (-s, -e) cap.
barfuss, barfüssig *a.* & *adv.* barefoot.
Bargeld *n.* ready money, cash.
barhäuptig *a.* bareheaded.
Bariton *m.* (-s, -e) barytone.
Barkasse *f.* (-, -n) launch.
Barke *f.* (-, -n) barge.
barmherzig *a.* merciful, compassionate; ~e Schwester, sister of mercy.
Barmherzigkeit *f.* (-, 0) mercy, compassion.
Barock *m.* & *a.* baroque.
Barometer *n.* & *m.* (-s, -) barometer; das ~ steigt, the glass is going up.
Baron *m.* (-[e]s, -e) baron.
Baronin *f.* (-, -nen) baroness.
Barren *m.* (-s, -n) (*Metall*) pig, ingot; (*Turnen*) parallel bars.
Barriere *f.* (-, -n) barrier.
Barrikade *f.* (-, -n) barricade.
Barsch *m.* (-es, -e *u.* Bärsche) perch.
barsch *a.* harsh, rude, abrupt.
Barschaft *f.* (-, -en) cash, ready-money.
Bart *m.* (-[e]s, Bärte) beard.
bärtig *a.* bearded.
bartlos *a.* beardless.
Barzahlung *f.* cash-payment.
Basalt *m.* (-[e]s, -e) basalt.
Basar *m.* (-s, -e) bazaar.
Base *f.* (-, -n) (female) cousin; (*chem.*) base.
basieren *v.i.* to be based on.
Basis *f.* (-, 0) basis.
Baskenmütze *f.* (-, -n) beret.
Bass *m.* (Basses, Basse) bass; bass-viol.
Bassgeige *f.* bass-viol.
Bassist *m.* (-en) bass-singer, basso.
Bast *m.* (-es, -e) bast, inner bark of trees.
Bastard *m.* (-[e]s, -e) bastard.
basteln *v.i.* to pursue a mechanical hobby.
Bataillon *n.* (-s, -e) battalion.
Batate *f.* (-, -n) sweet potato.
Batist *m.* (-[e]s, -e) cambric.
Batterie *f.* (-, -[e]n) battery.
Bau *m.* (-es, -e) building, structure; edifice; (*Körper*) build, frame; cultivation; (*von Tieren*) den, earth; im ~, under construction.
Bau: ~amt *n.* Board of Works; ~bataillon *n.* (*mil.*) construction battalion.

Bauch *m.* (-[e]s, Bäuche) belly; (*Schiffs~*) bottom; (*vulgar*) stomach.

Bauch: ~fell *n.* peritoneum; ~fellentzündung *f.* peritonitis.

bauchig *a.* bellied, bulgy.

Bauchlandung *f.* (*air.*) pancake landing.

Bauch: ~redner *m.* ventriloquist; ~weh *n.* colic, stomach-ache.

bauen *v.t.* to build; to till; (*Getreide*) to grow; (*Pflanzen*) to cultivate; *auf jemand ~,* to rely on one.

Bauer *m.* (-n *or* -s, -n) peasant, farmer, husbandman; (*im Schach*) pawn; (*Karte*) knave.

Bauer *m. & n.* (-s, -) cage.

Bäuerin *f.* (-, -nen) peasant *or* countrywoman.

bäu(e)risch *a.* rustic; (*fig.*) clownish, boorish.

Bauern: ~hof *m.* farmhouse; ~fänger *m.* confidence trickster.

Baufach *n.* (-[e]s, 0) architecture.

baufällig *a.* out of repair, tumble-down.

Baufälligkeit *f.* (-, 0) disrepair.

Bau: ~führer *m.* overseer (at building works); ~gerüst *n.* scaffolding; ~holz *n.* timber; ~kasten *m.* box of bricks; ~kunst *f.* architecture.

baulich *a.* architectural.

Baum *m.* (-[e]s, Bäume) tree; (*nav.*) boom.

Baumast *m.* knot.

Baumeister *m.* architect; master builder.

baumeln *v.i.* to dangle, to bob.

bäumen (sich) *v.refl.* to prance, to rear.

Baum: ~schere *f.* pruning-shears *pl.*; ~schule *f.* nursery; ~stamm *m.* trunk.

Baumwolle *f.* cotton.

baumwollen *a.* (made of) cotton.

Baumwollgarn *n.* cotton-yarn.

Baumwollspinnerei *f.* cotton-mill.

Bau: ~platz *m.* building-lot; ~polizei *f.* building department; ~rat *m.* government surveyor (of works).

Bausch *m.* (-es, Bäusche) bolster, pad; compress; *in ~ und Bogen,* in the lump.

bauschen *v.i.* to bag; to bulge, to swell out.

bauschig *a.* baggy, puffed out; swollen.

Bau: ~sparkasse *f.* building society; ~stein *m.* building-stone; ~stelle *f.* building-plot; ~stelle! men working!

Bauten *f.pl.* buildings *pl.*

Bauunternehmer *m.* builder.

Bauxit *m.* (-[e]s, -e) bauxite.

Bazillus *m.* (-, Bazillen) bacillus.

beabsichtigen *v.t.* to intend.

beachten *v.t.* to pay attention to.

beachtenswert *a.* noteworthy.

beachtlich *a.* worth notice.

Beamte[r] *m.* (-en, -en) official; civil servant; *höherer ~,* senior official.

beängstigen *v.t.* to alarm.

beanspruchen *v.t.* to claim, to demand.

Beanspruchung *f.* (-, -en) *starke ~,* hard wear.

beanstanden *v.t.* to object to.

beantragen *v.t.* to move, to propose.

beantworten *v.t.* to answer, to reply to.

Beantwortung *f.* (-, -en) reply, answer.

bearbeiten *v.t.* to work; to process; (*Angelegenheit*) to attend to, to deal with; (*fig. einen*) to influence.

Bearbeitung *f.* (-, -en) working; revision; treatment.

beaufsichtigen *v.t.* to superintend, to control.

beauftragen *v.t.* to charge.

bebauen *v.t.* to build over; to cultivate.

bebaut *a.* built-up.

beben *v.i.* to quake, to shiver.

Becher *m.* (-s, -) cup, goblet; (*ohne Fuss*) tumbler; (*Würfel*) box.

Becken *n.* (-s, -) basin; (*mus.*) cymbal; (*anat.*) pelvis.

Bedacht *m.* (-[e]s, 0) consideration; *mit ~,* deliberately.

bedacht *a.* (*auf*) intention.

bedächtig *a.* considerate, advised, prudent.

Bedächtigkeit *f.* (-, 0) caution, circumspection.

bedachtsam *a.* circumspect.

Bedachung *f.* (-, -en) roofing.

bedanken (sich) *v.refl.* to thank; to decline.

Bedarf *m.* (-[e]s, 0) need, want.

Bedarfsartikel *m.pl.* requisites *pl.*

bedauerlich *a.* deplorable.

bedauern *v.t.* to pity; to regret.

bedauernswert *a.* deplorable, pitiable.

bedecken *v.t.* to cover; (sich) ~ *v.refl.* to put on one's hat.

Bedeckung *f.* (-, -en) covering; (*mil.*) escort, convoy.

bedenken *v.t.ir.* to consider, to mind, to reflect upon; (*im Testament*) to remember; (sich) ~ *v.refl.ir.* to deliberate; *sich anders ~,* to change one's mind.

Bedenken *n.* (-s, -) consideration, hesitation, scruple; misgiving.

bedenklich *a.* doubtful, risky; scrupulous.

Bedenkzeit *f.* time for reflection.

bedeuten *v.t.* to signify, to mean; to indicate; *es hat nichts zu ~,* it is of no consequence.

bedeutend *a.* important, considerate.

bedeutsam *a.* significant.

Bedeutung *f.* (-, -en) meaning, sense; consequence, importance.

bedeutungslos *a.* insignificant.

bedienen *v.t.* to serve, to attend; (*Maschinen*) to operate; (sich) ~ *v.refl.* to make use of; (*bei Tische*) to help oneself.

Bedienstete[r] *m.* (-n, -n) employee.

Bediente[r] *m.* (-en, -en) servant, attendant, man.

Bedienung f. (-, -en) service, attendance.

Bedienungsmannschaft f. gunners.

bedingen v.t. to stipulate, to involve.

bedingt (durch) a. conditional (on).

Bedingung f. (-, -en) condition; stipulation; terms pl.

bedingungslos a. unconditional.

bedingungsweise adv. conditionally.

bedrängen v.t. to press hard; to oppress, to afflict.

Bedrängnis f. (-, -nisse) oppression; affliction; distress.

bedrohen v.t. to threaten, to menace.

bedrohlich a. threatening.

Bedrohung f. (-, -en) threat, menace.

bedrücken v.t. to oppress.

Beduine m. (-n, -n) Bedouin.

bedünken v.imp. to seem.

bedürfen v.t. & i.ir. to need, to want.

Bedürfnis n. (-nisses, nisse) want, need; **Bedürfnisse** pl. necessaries pl.

Bedürfnisanstalt f. public convenience.

bedürftig a. needy, indigent.

beehren v.t. to honour.

beeilen (sich) v.refl. to hurry up, to make haste.

beeinflussen v.t. to influence.

beeinträchtigen v.t. to impair.

beenden, beendigen v.t. to finish, to terminate.

Beendigung f. (-, -en) conclusion.

beengen v.t. to narrow, to cramp.

beerben v.t. (einen) to succeed to a person.

beerdigen v.t. to inter, to bury.

Beerdigung f. (-, -en) funeral, burial.

Beere f. (-, -en) berry.

Beet n. (-[e]s, -e) bed, border.

befähigen v.t. to enable, to qualify.

Befähigung f. (-, -en) qualification; capacity; (Am.) caliber.

befahren v.t.st. to pass over.

befallen v.t.st. to befall; to attack.

befangen a. biased; self-conscious.

Befangenheit f. (-, -en) prejudice; self-consciousness.

befassen (sich) v.refl. to occupy oneself with, to engage in.

befehden v.t. to make war upon.

Befehl m. (-[e]s, -e) command, order; auf ~ von, by order of.

befehlen v.t.st. to command, to order; to commit.

befehligen v.t. to command.

Befehls: ~ausgabe f. (mil.) briefing; ~haber m. (-s, -) commanding officer; ~weg m. chain of command.

befestigen v.t. to fasten, to fortify.

Befestigung f. (-, -en) consolidation; fortification.

Beffchen f.npl. (-s, -) bands.

befinden v.t.st. to find; to deem; (sich) ~ v.refl. to be; wie ~ Sie sich? how are

you?; für tauglich befunden werden, to be passed as fit.

Befinden n. (-s, 0) health; opinion.

befindlich a. being; contained.

beflaggen v.t. to deck with flags.

beflecken v.t. to stain, to spot; (fig.) to pollute.

befleissigen (sich) v.refl. to bestow pains upon; to apply oneself to.

beflissen a. studious, intent (upon).

befolgen v.t. to follow, to obey; (Gesetz) to abide by, to comply with.

Befolgung f. (-, 0) observance of; adherence to.

Beförderer m. (-s, -) promoter, patron.

befördern v.t. to further, to promote, to advance; (Am.) to upgrade; (verschicken) to forward, to dispatch; to convey.

Beförderung f. (-, -en) furtherance, promotion, advancement; forwarding.

Beförderungsmittel n. means of transport.

befragen v.t. to question, to examine.

befreien v.t. to free, to deliver, to liberate, to release; vom Erscheinen befreit, excused from appearing.

Befreier m. (-s, -) liberator.

Befreiung f. (-, -en) deliverance; exemption.

befremden v.t. to appear strange (to), to surprise.

befremdlich a. strange, odd, surprising.

befreunden (sich) v.refl. to make friends.

befriedigen v.t. to content, to satisfy.

befriedigend a. satisfactory.

Befriedigung f. (-, -en) satisfaction.

befristet a. limited in time.

befruchten v.t. to impregnate.

Befruchtung f. (-, -en) impregnation, fecundation.

Befugnis f. (-, -nisse) authority.

befugt a. authorised, competent.

Befund m. (-[e]s, Befunde) finding.

befürchten v.t. to fear, to apprehend.

Befürchtung f. (-, -en) fear, apprehension.

befürworten v.t. to recommend.

begabt a. gifted, talented.

Begabung f. (-, -en) endowment, gift, talent.

begatten (sich) v.refl. to pair, to copulate.

Begattung f. (-, -en) coition, copulation.

begeben v.t.st. (Wechsel) to negotiate; (sich) ~ v.refl.st. to proceed to; (geschehen) to come to pass, to happen.

Begebenheit f. (-, -en) event, occurrence.

begegnen v.i. (s) to meet (with); to happen (to), to befall.

Begegnung f. (-, -en) meeting.

begehen v.t.st. (feiern) to celebrate; (verüben) to commit.

Begehren n. (-s, 0) desire, wish.

begehren v.t. to desire; to request.

begehrlich a. desirous, covetous.

Begehung *f.* (-, -en) perpetration; (*Feier*) celebration.

begeistern *v.t.* to inspire.

Begeisterung *f.* (-, -en) enthusiasm.

Begier, Begierde *f.* (-, Begierden) desire, appetite.

begierig *a.* desirous; eager.

begiessen *v.t.st.* to water; to baste.

Beginn *m.* (-[e]s, 0) beginning, origin.

beginnen *v.t. & i.st.* to begin; to undertake.

beglaubigen *v.t.* to attest, to confirm, to authenticate; to accredit.

Beglaubigung *f.* (-, -en) attestation.

Beglaubigungsschreiben *n.* credentials *pl.*

begleichen *v.t.* to settle; to pay.

Begleit... (*mil.*) escort.

Begleit: ~brief *m.* cover(ing) letter; ~erscheinung *f.* concomitant.

begleiten *v.t.* to accompany, to attend.

Begleiter *m.* (-s,-) companion, attendant.

Begleitung *f.* (-, -en) company, attendants; (*mil.*) escort; retinue; (*mus.*) accompaniment.

beglücken *v.t.* to bless, to make happy.

beglückwünschen *v.t.* to congratulate.

begnadigen *v.t.* to pardon.

Begnadigung *f.* (-, -en) pardon; amnesty.

begnügen (sich) *v.refl.* to be satisfied (with), to acquiesce (in).

begraben *v.t.st.* to bury, to inter.

Begräbnis *n.* (-nisses, -nisse) burial, funeral; tomb, grave.

begreifen *v.t.st.* to include, to contain, to comprise; (*fig.*) to understand, to conceive, to comprehend.

begreiflich *a.* conceivable, intelligible.

begrenzen *v.t.* to bound, to border; to limit.

Begrenztheit *f.* (-, 0) limitation.

Begrenzung *f.* (-, -en) delimitation.

Begriff *m.* (-[e]s, -e) idea, notion, concept, conception; *im ~*, about to, on the point of.

begrifflich *a.* conceptual.

Begriffsbestimmung *f.* definition.

begründen *v.t.* to found, to establish; to confirm, to prove.

begrüssen *v.t.* to greet, to salute.

begucken *v.t.* to peep at.

begünstigen *v.t.* to favour, to patronize.

Begünstiger *m.* (-s, -) (*law*) accessory after the fact.

Begünstigung *f.* (-, -en) encouragement, patronage; advantage, privilege.

begutachten *v.t.* to give an opinion on.

begütert *a.* wealthy, well-to-do.

behaart *a.* hairy; hirsute; pilose.

behäbig *a.* easy, well-to-do; stout.

behaftet *a.* affected (with), infected (with).

behagen *v.imp.* to please, to suit.

Behagen *n.* (-s, 0) pleasure, comfort.

behaglich *a.* comfortable, pleasing, snug.

behalten *v.t.st.* to keep; to retain.

Behälter *m.* (-s, -) container, receptacle.

behandeln *v.t.* to handle; to deal with; to treat; (*Arzt*) to attend; (*chem.*) to process.

Behandlung *f.* (-, -en) management, treatment.

behängen *v.t.* to hang with.

beharren (bei) *v.i.* to persist in, to stick to.

beharrlich *a.* constant, steady, persevering.

behaupten *v.t.* to assert, to maintain; (sich) ~ *v.refl.* to keep one's ground.

Behauptung *f.* (-, -en) assertion, statement.

Behausung *f.* (-, -en) lodging, habitation.

beheben *v.t.* to clear away.

Behelf *m.* (-[e]s, -e) expedient, shift.

behelfen (sich) *v.refl.st.* to make shift (with); (*ohne etwas*) to do without.

behelligen *v.t.* to trouble, to importune.

behend(e) *a.* quick, agile, nimble.

Behendigkeit *f.* (-, 0) agility, nimbleness.

beherbergen *v.t.* to lodge, to shelter.

beherrschen *v.t.* to reign over, to rule over; to govern; (*Sprache*) to master; (sich) ~ *v.refl.* to control oneself.

Beherrschung *f.* (-, 0) domination, rule, sway; mastery.

beherzigen *v.t.* to take to heart, to mind.

beherzt *a.* courageous, bold.

behilflich *a.* helpful, serviceable.

Behörde *f.* (-, -n) authority.

Behördeneigentum *n.* government property.

Behuf *m.* (-[e]s, 0) *zu diesem ~*, for this purpose.

behufs *pr.* for the purpose of.

behüten *v.t.* to guard, to preserve; *Gott behüte!* God forbid!

behutsam *a.* cautious, wary.

bei *pr.* at, by, about, near; beside, with, to, in, upon, on.

beibehalten *v.t.st.* to keep, to retain.

beibringen *v.t.ir.* to bring forward; (*Verluste*) to inflict upon; *einem etwas ~*, to teach something to one.

Beichte *f.* (-, -n) confession; ~ *hören*, to confess (one).

beichten *v.t.* to confess.

Beicht: ~kind *n.* penitent; ~stuhl *m.* confessional; ~vater *m.* father-confessor.

beide *a.* both, either.

beiderlei *a.* both, of both sorts.

beiderseits *adv.* on both sides.

Beifall *m.* (-[e]s, 0) approbation, applause; ~ *klatschen*, to applaud.

beifällig *a.* approving, favourable.

beifolgend *a.* annexed, enclosed.

beifügen *v.t.* to add, to enclose.

beigeben *v.t.st.* to add; to climb down.

Beigeschmack *m.* (-[e]s, -geschmäcke) tang, savour, flavour.

Beihilfe *f.* (-, 0) aid, assistance; subsidy; ~ *leisten* (*law*) to aid and abet.

beikommen *v.i.st.*(*s*) (*fig.*) to match, to come up to.

Beil *n.* (-[e]s, -) hatchet.

Beilage *f.* (-, -n) addition; (*eines Briefes*) enclosure; (*Gemüse*) vegetables *pl.*; (*einer Zeitung*) supplement.

beiläufig *a.* incidental; ~ *adv.* by the way, incidentally.

beilegen *v.t.* to add, to enclose; (*Streit etc.*) to settle, to make up; (*zuschreiben*) to attribute.

Beilegung *f.* (-, -en) settlement.

beileibe nicht not for the world.

Beileid *n.* (-[e]s, 0) **Beileidsbezeigung** *f.* condolence.

beiliegen *v.i.st.* to be enclosed.

beiliegend *a.* enclosed, attached.

beimessen *v.t.st.* to impute, to attribute.

beimischen *v.t.* to mix with.

Beimischung *f.* (-, -en) admixture.

Bein *n.* (-[e]s, -e) leg; (*Knochen*) bone; *zweibeinig, dreibeinig,* etc., two-legged, three-legged.

beinahe *adv.* almost, nearly.

Beiname *m.* (-ns, -n) surname.

Beinbruch *m.* fracture (of a leg).

beinern *a.* made of bone, bony.

Beinkleider *n.pl.* trousers *pl.*

Beinschiene *f.* splint.

beiordnen *v.t.* to adjoin; to co-ordinate.

beipflichten *v.t.* to agree (with).

Beirat *m.* (-[e]s, -räte) adviser; advisory board.

beirren *v.t.* to confuse; to divert from.

beisammen *adv.* together.

Beischlaf *m.* (-[e]s, 0) cohabitation.

Beisein *n.* (-s, 0) presence.

beiseite, beiseits *adv.* aside, apart.

beisetzen *v.t.* (*Leiche*) to bury.

Beisitzer *m.* (-s, -) assessor; assistant judge or magistrate.

Beispiel *n.* (-[e]s, -e) *n.* example; *zum* ~, for instance.

beispiellos *a.* unparalleled, unexampled.

beispringen *v.i.st.* (*s*) to assist, to succour.

beissen *v.t. & i.st.* to bite.

beissend *a.* pungent, hot; mordant.

Beisszange *f.* nippers *pl.*

Beistand *m.* (-[e]s, -stände) assistance.

beistehen *v.i.st.* to stand by; to assist, to support.

Beisteuer *f.* (-, -n) contribution.

beisteuern *v.t.* to contribute (to).

beistimmen *v.i.* to agree with.

Beitrag *m.* (-[e]s, -träge) contribution, subscription; share.

beitragen *v.t.st.* to contribute (to), to conduce (to).

beitreiben *v.t.st.* (*mil.*) to requisition.

beitreten *v.i.st.* (*s*) to accede, to assent; (*einer Gesellschaft*) to join.

Beitritt *m.* (-[e]s, 0) accession; joining.

Beiwagen *m.* (-s, -) side-car.

Beiwerk *n.* (-[e]s, -e) accessories *pl.*

beiwohnen *v.i.* to be present at, to attend; to cohabit.

Beize *f.* (-, -n) (*Mittel*) caustic.

beizeiten *adv.* betimes, in time.

beizen *v.t.* (*chem.*) to corrode; (*Fleisch*) to pickle; (*Holz*) to stain; (*med.*) to cauterize.

bejahen *v.t.* to answer in the affirmative.

bejahend *a.* affirmative.

bejahrt *a.* aged, elderly.

Bejahung *f.* (-, -en) affirmation; acceptance.

bejammern *v.t.* to bemoan, to bewail.

bejammernswert *a.* lamentable, deplorable.

bekämpfen *v.t.* to combat.

bekannt *a.* well-known; acquainted (with).

Bekannte[r] *m. & f.* (-en, -en) acquaintance.

bekanntlich *adv.* as is well-known.

Bekanntmachung *f.* (-, -en) notice.

Bekanntschaft *f.* (-, -en) acquaintance.

bekehren *v.t.* to convert.

Bekehrte[r] *m. & f.* (-en, -en) convert.

Bekehrung *f.* (-, -en) conversion.

bekennen *v.t.st.* to confess, to own; (sich) ~ *v.refl.st.* to profess; to acknowledge.

Bekenntnis *n.* (-nisses, -nisse) confession, avowal; creed.

Bekenntnisschule *f.* denominational school.

beklagen *v.t.* to lament, to deplore, to pity; (sich) ~ *v.refl.* to complain (of).

beklagenswert *a.* lamentable, pitiable.

Beklagte[r] *m. & f.* (-en, -en) defendant.

bekleben *v.t.* to paste upon.

bekleiden *v.t.* to clothe, to attire; (*fig.*) to invest (with); (*Amt, Stelle*) to hold, to fill.

Bekleidung *f.* (-, -en) clothing, clothes *pl*; (*fig.*) investiture.

Beklemmung *f.* (-, -en) (*der Brust*) oppression (of the chest); (*fig.*) anguish.

beklommen *a.* oppressed, anxious.

bekommen *v.t.st.* to obtain, to get, to receive; (~ *v.i.st.* (*s*) (*einem wohl*) to agree with; *nicht gut* ~, to disagree with.

bekömmlich *a.* beneficial; digestible.

beköstigen *v.t.* to board, to feed.

bekräftigen *v.t.* to confirm, to corroborate.

bekränzen *v.t.* to wreathe, to crown.

bekreuzen, bekreuzigen *v.t.* (sich) ~ *v.refl.* to make the sign of the cross, to cross oneself.

bekümmern *v.t.* to afflict; (sich) ~ *v.refl.* to concern oneself with.

Bekümmernis *f.* (-, -nisse) affliction.

bekunden *v.t.* to depose; to manifest.

belächeln *v.t.* to smile at.

beladen *v.t.st.* to load; (*fig.*) to burden, to charge.

Belag *m.* (-[e]s, -läge) (*Zunge*) fur.

belagern *v.t.* to besiege, to beleaguer.

Belagerung *f.* (-, -en) siege.

Belang *m.* (-[e]s, -e) interest.

belangen *v.t.* to concern, to relate to; (*vor Gericht*) to sue.

belanglos *a.* unimportant, trifling.

Belangung *f.* (-, -en) prosecution.

belassen *v.t.st.* to let be.

belasten *v.t.* to load, to charge; (*com.*) to debit; *erblich belastet,* tainted by hereditary disease.

belastend *a.* incriminating.

belästigen *v.t.* to trouble, to bother.

Belästigung *f.* (-, -en) molestation.

Belastung *f.* (-, -en) charge, load; debit; strain; (*el.*) load.

Belastungszeuge *m.* witness for the prosecution.

belaufen (sich) *v.refl.st.* to amount to, to run to.

belauschen *v.t.* to watch, to overhear.

beleben *v.t.* to animate; to enliven.

belebt *a.* lively, animated; crowded.

Belebung *f.* (-, -en) animation, revival.

belecken *v.a.* to lick.

Beleg *m.* (-[e]s, -e) voucher, proof.

belegen *v.t.* to lay on or over; (*Platz*) to reserve, to secure; (*mit Beweisen*) to prove.

Belegschaft *f.* (-, -en) total of men employed.

belegt *a.* (*Zunge*) furred, coated; ~e Brötchen *n.* sandwich.

belehnen *v.t.* to invest; to enfeoff.

belehren *v.t.* to inform, to instruct.

belehrend *a.* instructive.

Belehrung *f.* (-, -en) instruction.

beleibt *a.* corpulent, stout.

beleidigen *v.t.* to offend, to insult.

Beleidigte[r] *m.* (*law*) offended party.

Beleidigung *f.* (-, -en) offence, insult; *tätliche* ~ (*law*), assault; *schwere tätliche* ~, assault and battery.

belesen *a.* well-read.

beleuchten *v.t.* to illumine, to illuminate, to light; (*fig.*) to illustrate.

Beleuchtung *f.* (-, -en) lighting, illumination.

Beleuchtungskörper *m.* light fixture.

belichten *v.t.* (*phot.*) to expose.

Belichtung *f.* (-, -en) (*phot.*) exposure; ~smesser *m.* exposure meter.

belieben *v.t.* to like; ~ *v.i.* to please.

Belieben *n.* (-s, 0) pleasure, liking.

beliebig *a.* (with *ein*) any.

beliebt *a.* popular.

beliefern *v.t.* to supply.

bellen *v.i.* to bark.

belohnen *v.t.* to reward, to recompense.

Belohnung *f.* (-, -en) reward, recompense.

belustigen *v.t.* to amuse, to divert.

Belustigung *f.* (-, -en) amusement, diversion.

bemächtigen (sich) *v.refl.* to take possession of, to seize.

bemalen *v.t.* to paint (over).

bemängeln *v.t.* to find fault with.

bemannen *v.t.* to man, to equip.

Bemannung *f.* (-, -en) crew.

bemänteln *v.t.* to cloak; (*fig.*) to palliate.

bemeistern (sich) *v.refl.* to master, to get into one's power.

bemerken *v.t.* to remark, to observe; to perceive, to note.

bemerkenswert *a.* remarkable.

Bemerkung *f.* (-, -en) remark, observation, comment.

bemitleiden *v.t.* to pity, to commiserate.

bemittelt *a.* well-off, independent.

bemühen *v.t.* to trouble; (*sich*) *v.refl.* to take pains, to endeavour; to apply (for).

Bemühung *f.* (-, -en) trouble, pains *pl.*; effort.

benachbart *a.* neighbouring.

benachrichtigen *v.t.* to inform, to advise, to let a person know.

Benachrichtigung *f.* (-, -en) information, advice.

Benachteiligung *f.* (-, -en) prejudice, detriment.

benebeln *v.t.* to fog, to dim, to cloud.

benehmen (sich) *v.refl.st.* to behave.

Benehmen *n.* (-s, 0) behaviour, conduct.

beneiden *v.t.* to envy, to grudge.

beneidenswert *a.* enviable.

benennen *v.t.ir.* to name, to denominate.

Benennung *f.* (-, -en) name, appellation.

benetzen *v.t.* to moisten, to wet.

Bengel *m.* (-s, -) urchin.

benommen *a.* benumbed.

benötigen *v.t.* to be in want of, to want.

benutzen *v.t.* to make use of, to take advantage of.

Benzin *n.* (-s, -e) benzine; petrol; (*Am.*) gasoline; ~stelle *f.* petrol station, gasoline station.

Benzol *n.* (-s, -e) benzol(e).

beobachten *v.t.* to observe, to watch; to keep, to perform.

Beobachter *m.* (-s, -) observer.

Beobachtung *f.* (-, -en) observation; observance.

beordern *v.t.* to order, to command.

bepacken *v.t.* to load, to charge.

bepflanzen *v.t.* to plant.

bequem *a.* convenient; apt, fit, commodious, comfortable; easy going.

bequemen (sich) *v.refl.* to comply with, to submit.

Bequemlichkeit *f.* (-, -en) convenience, comfort, ease; indolence.

beraten *v.t.st.* to advise; (sich) ~ *v.refl.st.* to consult with, to deliberate.

beratschlagen (sich) *v.i. & refl.* to deliberate, to take counsel.

Beratung *f.* (-, -en) council, conference; consultation.

Beratungstelle *f.* advice bureau.

berauben *v.t.* to rob.

berauschen *v.t.* to intoxicate; (sich) ~ *v.refl.* to get drunk; ~de Getränke *n.pl.* intoxicating liquors.

berechenbar *a.* calculable.

berechnen *v.t.* to compute, to calculate; (*anschreiben*) to charge; *der Kaffee wird besonders berechnet*, coffee will be extra.

Berechnung *f.* (-, -en) computation, calculation.

berechtigen *v.t.* to entitle, to authorize.

Berechtigung *f.* (-, -en) right; authorization; qualification.

Beredsamkeit *f.* (-, 0) eloquence.

beredt *a.* eloquent.

Bereich *m. & n.* (-[e]s, -e) reach, range; sphere, orbit.

bereichern *v.t.* to enrich; (*fig.*) to enlarge.

bereifen *v.t.* (*Fass*) to hoop; (*mot.*) to tyre.

bereinigen *v.t.* to settle.

bereit *a.* ready, prepared, prompt.

bereiten *v.t.* to prepare, to dress.

bereits *adv.* already.

Bereitschaft *f.* (-, -en) readiness, preparedness; flying squad (*Polizei*).

Bereitung *f.* (-, -en) preparation.

bereitwillig *a.* ready, willing; ~ *adv.* willingly.

bereuen *v.t.* to repent; to regret.

Berg *m.* (-[e]s, -e) mountain, hill; *hinter dem ~e halten*, to hold in reserve; *zu Berge stehn*, to stand on end (*Haar*).

bergab *adv.* down-hill.

bergan, bergauf *adv.* up-hill.

Berg: ~akademie *f.* mining academy; ~amt *n.* mining bureau; ~bau *m.* mining.

bergen *v.t.st.* to save; to salvage; to conceal ,to contain.

bergig *a.* mountainous, hilly.

Berg: ~kette *f.* mountain-chain *or* range; ~mann *m.* miner; ~predigt *f.* (Christ's) sermon on the Mount; ~steiger *m.* mountaineer, alpinist; ~werk *n.* mine.

Bericht *m.* (-[e]s, -e) report, account.

berichten *v.t.* to inform, to send word, to report.

Berichterstatter *m.* reporter.

berichtigen *v.t.* to set right, to correct; (*Rechnung*) to settle.

Berichtigung *f.* (-, -en) correction.

beritten *a.* mounted.

Bernstein *m.* (-[e]s, 0) amber.

bersten *v.i.st.* (*s*) to burst, to crack.

berüchtigt *a.* notorious, ill-reputed.

berücken *v.t.* to fascinate.

berücksichtigen *v.t.* to regard, to respect, to allow for, to consider.

Berücksichtigung *f.* (-, -en) regard, consideration.

Beruf *m.* (-[e]s, -e *u.* Berufsarten) vocation; calling, trade, profession.

berufen *v.t.st.* to call; to appoint to an office; (*zusammenrufen*) to convene, to convoke; (sich) ~ *v.refl.* to refer to, to invoke.

Berufs... occupational, professional.

Berufs: ~beratung *f.* vocational guidance; ~diplomat *m.* career diplomat; ~spieler *m.* professional.

Berufung *f.* (-, -en) appeal; ~einlegen, to lodge an appeal; *einer ~ stattgeben*, to allow an appeal; *eine ~ zurückweisen*, to dismiss an appeal; ~sgericht *n.* court of appeal, appellate court.

beruhen *v.i.* to rest upon; to depend upon *or* on.

beruhigen *v.t.* to quiet, to calm; (sich) ~ *v.refl.* to compose oneself.

Beruhigung *f.* (-, -en) reassurance.

berühmt *a.* famous, celebrated.

Berühmtheit *f.* (-, -en) celebrity; renown.

berühren *v.t.* to touch, to handle.

Berührung *f.* (-, -en) contact, touch.

besagen *v.t.* to mean, to signify.

besänftigen *v.t.* to soften, to soothe; to mitigate; to placate.

Besatz *m.* (-es, -sätze) trimming.

Besatzung *f.* (-, -en) garrison, crew; occupation; ~szone *f.* zone of occupation.

Besatzungs... occupation—.

besaufen (sich) *v.refl.st.* to get drunk.

beschädigen *v.t.* to hurt, to damage.

Beschädigung *f.* (-, -en) damage, hurt.

beschaffen *a.* constituted, conditioned; ~ *v.t.* to procure.

Beschaffenheit *f.* (-, -en) condition, quality, constitution.

beschäftigen *v.t.* to employ, to occupy.

beschäftigt *a.* occupied, busy.

Beschäftigung *f.* (-, -en) occupation, employment.

beschälen *v.t.* to horse (a mare).

beschämen *v.t.* to shame.

beschatten *v.t.* to shade.

beschauen *v.t.* to look at, to view, to inspect.

beschaulich *a.* contemplative.

Beschauung *f.* (-, -en) contemplation.

Bescheid *m.* (-[e]s, -e) decision; information; answer; ~ *wissen*, to know.

bescheiden *v.t.st.* (*zu sich*) to send for; (sich) ~ *v.refl.st.* to acquiesce (in).

bescheiden *a.* modest, unassuming.

Bescheidenheit *f.* (-, 0) modesty, discretion.

bescheinigen *v.t.* to attest, to certify.

Bescheinigung *f.* (-, -en) certificate.

beschenken *v.t.* to present with.

bescheren *v.t.* to give, to confer.
Bescherung *f.* (-, -en) distribution of presents; *eine schöne* ~, a nice mess.
beschicken *v.t.* to send to.
beschiessen *v.t.st.* to fire upon.
Beschiessung *f.* (-, -en) bombardment.
beschimpfen *v.t.* to insult, to disgrace.
beschirmen *v.t.* to protect, to defend.
beschlafen *v.t.st.* (*eine Sache*) to sleep upon.
Beschlag *m.* (-[e]s, -schläge) (*metal*) mounting; (*gerichtlicher*) sequestration, seizure, confiscation; (*eines Pferdes*) shoeing; *in* ~ *nehmen, mit* ~ *belegen,* to seize, to sequestrate.
beschlagen *v.t.* to mount; (*Pferde*) to shoe; (*mit Nägeln*) to nail, to stud.
beschlagen *a.* (*fig.*) versed, skilled.
Beschlagnahme *f.* (-, -en) seizure, sequestration; (*nav.*) embargo; ~ *aufheben,* to derequisition.
beschlagnahmen *v.t.* to impound, to seize.
beschleunigen *v.t.* to hasten, to accelerate, to speed up.
beschliessen *v.t.st.* to resolve (upon), to determine.
Beschluss *m.* (-schlusses, -schlüsse) resolution; decree.
beschlussfähig *a. das Haus war* ~, there was a quorum of the House.
beschmutzen *v.t.* to dirty, to soil.
beschneiden *v.t.st.* to cut, to clip; (*Juden*) to circumcise; (*Bäume*) to lop; (*fig.*) to curtail.
Beschneidung *f.* (-, -en) circumcision; (*der Bäume*) lopping.
beschönigen *v.t.* to palliate, to gloss over.
beschränken *v.t.* to circumscribe; to limit; to reduce to.
beschränkt *a.* narrow; dull; half-witted.
Beschränktheit *f.* (-, 0) narrowness; (*fig.*) narrow-mindedness.
Beschränkung *f.* (-, -en) limitation, restriction.
beschreiben *v.t.st.* to describe.
Beschreibung *f.* (-, -en) description.
beschreiten *v.t.st.* to step over.
beschuldigen *v.t.* to charge with, to accuse of.
Beschuldigung *f.* (-, -en) charge, accusation; impeachment.
beschummeln *v.t.* (*fam.*) to cheat.
beschützen *v.t.* to protect, to defend.
Beschützer *m.* (-s, -) protector, patron.
Beschwerde *f.* (-, -n) trouble; (*Mühe*) hardship; (*Klage*) grievance, complaint; (*Leiden*) complaint; ~ *einlegen,* to lodge a complaint; ~ *führen,* to complain (of).
Beschwerdeführer *m.* complainant.
beschweren *v.t.* to burden, to charge; (*sich*) ~ *v.refl.* to complain (of).
beschwerlich *a.* laborious, troublesome; ~ *fallen,* to molest, to importune.

Beschwerlichkeit *f.* (-, -en) trouble, inconvenience.
beschwichtigen *v.t.* to soothe, to allay.
beschwindeln *v.t.* to cheat, to swindle.
beschwören *a.* sworn (to).
beschwören *v.t.st.* to confirm by oath; (*bitten*) to entreat; to conjure; (*bannen*) to exorcise.
Beschwörer *m.* (-s, -) conjuror; exorcist.
Beschwörung *f.* (-, -en) confirmation by oath; (*Geister* ~) exorcism.
beseelen *v.t.* to animate, to inspirit.
besehen *v.t.st.* to look at, to view.
beseitigen *v.t.* to eliminate, to remove.
beseligen *v.t.* to bless, to enrapture.
Besen *m.* (-s, -) broom, besom.
Besenstiel *m.* broom-stick.
besessen *a.* possessed.
besetzen *v.t.* to occupy; to garrison; (*Stelle*) to fill; (*Platz*) to engage; (*mit Spitzen etc.*) to trim, to border.
besetzt *a. die Leitung ist besetzt,* (*tel.*) the line is busy *or* engaged.
Besetzung *f.* (-, -en) (*von Stellen*) appointment; occupation.
besichtigen *v.t.* to view, to inspect.
Besichtigung *f.* (-, -en) inspection.
besiedeln *v.t.* to settle in, to colonize.
besiegeln *v.t.* to seal.
besiegen *v.t.* to vanquish, to conquer.
besingen *v.t.st.* to celebrate, to sing.
besinnen (sich) *v.refl.st.* to recollect, to call to mind; to consider, to reflect.
Besinnung *f.* (-, 0) reflection.
besinnungslos *a.* insensible, unconscious.
Besitz *m.* (-es, 0) possession, property; *in* ~ *haben,* to be in possession of.
besitzen *v.t.st.* to possess, to own.
Besitzer *m.* (-s, -) proprietor, owner.
Besitzergreifung, Besitznahme *f.* occupation.
Besitzstörungsklage *f.* action of trespass.
Besitzung *f.* (-, -en) possession, estate.
Besitzurkunde *f.* title deed.
besoffen *a.* tipsy, drunk.
besohlen *v.t.* to sole.
besolden *v.t.* to pay.
besoldet *a.* salaried.
Besoldung *f.* (-, -en) salary; pay, stipend.
besonder *a.* (*abgesondert*) separate; peculiar, particular, special.
besonders *adv.* particularly, specially.
besonnen *a.* cautious, discreet.
besorgen *v.t.* to provide; (*befürchten*) to fear.
Besorgnis *f.* (-, -nisse) care; apprehension.
besorgniserregend *a.* alarming.
besorgt *a.* apprehensive, anxious.
Besorgung *f.* (-, -en) commission.
bespannen *v.t.* to put (horses) to; to string.
bespötteln *v.t.* to rally, to ridicule.

besprechen *v.t.st.* to discuss, to talk over; (*bösen Geist*) to conjure; (sich) ~ *v.refl.st.* to confer with.
Besprechung *f.* (-, -en) discussion, conference; review.
besprengen *f.* to besprinkle, to water.
besser *a. & adv.* better; *umso* ~, so much the better.
bessern *v.t.* to better; to improve, to mend, to repair.
Besserung *f.* (-, -en) improvement; amendment; recovery.
Besserungsanstalt *f.* remand home.
best *a.* best; *der erste* ~*e*, the first comer; *zum* ~*en*, for the benefit; *aufs* ~*e*, in the best manner; *einen zum* ~*en haben*, to make fun of one.
Bestallung *f.* (-, -en) appointment.
Bestand *m.* (-[e]s, -stände) continuance; (*Belauf*) amount, number.
Bestandaufnahme *f.* stocktaking.
beständig *a.* constant, continual; steady.
Bestandteil *m.* constituent (part).
bestärken *v.t.* to confirm.
bestätigen *v.t.* to confirm; to ratify, to sanction; (*Empfang*) to acknowledge; (sich) ~ *v.refl.* to be confirmed.
Bestätigung *f.* (-, -en) confirmation; acknowledgment.
bestatten *v.t.* to bury, to inter.
Bestattung *f.* (-, -en) burial.
bestechen *v.t.st.* to corrupt, to bribe.
bestechend *a.* specious.
bestechlich *a.* corrupt.
Bestechung *f.* (-, -en) corruption, bribery.
Besteck *n.* (-[e]s, -e) (*Tisch*~) fork, knife, and spoon; case of instruments; (*nav.*) *das* ~ *machen*, to prick the chart.
bestehen *v.i.st.* (*aus etwas*) to consist of; (*auf etwas*) to insist on; (*dauern*) to continue, to last; ~ *v.t.st.* to undergo, to endure, to stand; *die Prüfung* ~, to pass; *nicht* ~, to fail, to be ploughed.
bestehlen *v.t.st.* to rob, to steal from.
besteigen *v.t.st.* to step upon; to ascend; to mount (a horse).
bestellen *v.t.* to order; (*Briefe*) to deliver; (*Plätze*) to book; (*das Feld*) to till; (*einen*) to send for; (*Zeitung*) to take in a paper; (*ernennen*) to appoint.
Bestellschein *m.* order form.
Bestellung *f.* (-, -en) order, command; (*des Feldes*) tillage; *auf* ~, to order; *eine* ~ *aufnehmen*, to take an order.
bestenfalls *adv.* in the best possible case.
bestens *adv.* in the best manner.
besteuern *v.a.* to tax.
Besteuerung *f.* (-, -en) taxation.
Bestie *f.* (-, -n) beast, brute.
bestimmen *v.t.* to determine; to appoint; to define; to destine (for).
bestimmt *a.* appointed, fixed; (*entschlossen*) decided; (*gewiss*) certain, positive.

Bestimmung *f.* (-, -en) destination; destiny; regulation, provision; definition.
bestmöglich *a.* best possible.
bestrafen *v.t.* to punish; to chastise.
Bestrafung *f.* (-, -en) punishment.
bestrahlen *v.t.* to irradiate; (*med.*) to treat with X-rays.
Bestrahlung *f.* (-, -en) exposure to rays; (*med.*) X-ray treatment.
bestreben (sich) *v.refl.* to endeavour.
Bestreben *n.* (-s, 0), Bestrebung *f.* (-, -en) endeavour, exertion.
bestreichen *v.t.ir.* to spread over; (*mil.*) to rake.
bestreiten *v.t.st.* to contest, to dispute; *die Kosten* ~, to defray the expenses.
bestreuen *v.t.* to strew, to sprinkle.
bestricken *v.t.* to charm.
bestürmen *v.t.* to storm, to assail; (*fig.*) to importune.
bestürzen *v.t.* to perplex, to confound.
bestürzt *a.* dismayed.
Bestürzung *f.* (-, 0) dismay.
Besuch *m.* (-[e]s, -e) visit; (*pers.*) company, visitors *pl.*
besuchen *v.t.* to call upon, to pay a visit; (*Lokale etc.*) to frequent, to attend.
Besucher *m.* (-s, -) visitor.
besudeln *v.t.* to soil, to dirty.
betagt *a.* aged, elderly.
betasten *v.t.* to touch, to handle, to finger.
betätigen *v.t.* to practise; to manifest; *sich* ~, to take an active part in.
betäuben *v.t.* to stun; (*med.*) to narcotize.
Betäubung *f.* (-, -en) (*fig.*) stupor, bewilderment.
Betäubungsmittel *n.* anæsthetic.
beteiligen *v.t.* to give one his share; *beteiligt sein*, to have a share in; *die Beteiligten*, those concerned; (sich) ~ *v.refl.* to participate in; to have an interest in.
beten *v.i.* to pray; to say one's prayers.
beteuern *v.t.* to assert; to protest.
betiteln *v.t.* to give a title, to style.
Beton *(frz.) m.* (-s, -s) concrete.
betonen *v.t.* to stress; (*fig.*) to emphasize.
Betonung *f.* (-, -en) stress; accentuation.
betören *v.t.* to fool, to infatuate.
Betracht *m.* (-[e]s, 0) consideration, regard; *in* ~ *ziehen*, to take into consideration *or* account.
betrachten *v.t.* to look at; to consider.
beträchtlich *a.* considerable, important.
Betrachtung *f.* (-, -en) contemplation.
Betrag *m.* (-[e]s, -träge) amount.
betragen *v.t.st.* to amount to; (sich) ~ *v.refl.st.* to behave.
Betragen *n.* (-s, 0) behaviour, conduct.
betrauen *v.t.* to entrust.
betrauern *v.t.* to mourn for.
Betreff *m.* (-[e]s, 0) subject, re; *in betreff*, with regard to.

betreffen *v.t.st.* to concern; *was das' betrifft*, as far as that is concerned.
betreffend *a.* concerning.
betreffs *p.* with respect to, concerning.
betreiben *v.t.st.* to urge; (*Geschäft*) to manage, to carry on, to run; (*Beruf*) to pursue.
betreten *v.t.st.* to step upon, to enter.
betreten *a.* disconcerted.
betreuen *v.t.* to look after, to take care of.
Betreuung *f.* (-, 0) care.
Betrieb *m.* (-[e]s, -e) management; establishment, works; (*öffentlicher*) service; *in ~ sein*, to operate; *ausser ~ setzen*, to put out of action.
betriebsam *a.* industrious, active.
Betriebs: ~kapital *n.* working capital; ~kosten *pl.* working expenses; ~leiter *m.* works manager; ~rat *m.* shop steward, works council; ~vorrat *m.* stock-in-trade.
betrinken (sich) *v.refl.st.* to get drunk.
betroffen *a.* struck, perplexed.
betrüben *v.t.* to afflict; (sich) ~ *v.refl.* to grieve (at).
Betrug *m.* (-[e]s, 0) fraud, deceit.
betrügen *v.t.st.* to cheat, to deceive; to defraud; (*Am.*) to doublecross.
Betrüger *m.* (-s, -) sharper; deceiver.
betrügerisch *a.* fraudulent; deceitful.
betrunken *a.* drunk, tipsy, intoxicated.
Betrunkenheit *f.* (-, 0) drunkenness.
Bett *n.* (-[e]s, -en) bed.
Bettbelag *m.* bedspread.
Bettdecke *f.* counterpane; quilt.
Bettelei *f.* (-, -en) begging; solicitation.
bettelhaft *a.* beggarly.
betteln *v.i.* to ask alms, to beg.
Bettjacke *f.* bed-jacket.
bettlägerig *a.* bed-ridden.
Bettler *m.* (-s, -) beggar.
Bett: ~stelle *f.* bedstead; ~tuch, *n.* sheet; ~überzug *m.* bed-slip; ~wäsche *f.* bed-linen; ~zeug *n.* bed-clothes *pl.*
beugen *v.t.* to bend, to bow; (*fig.*) to humble; (*gram.*) to inflect.
Beugung *f.* (-, -en) inflexion.
Beule *f.* (-, -en) bump, bruise.
Beulenpest *f.* bubonic plague.
beunruhigen *v.t.* to disquiet, to harass.
beurkunden *v.t.* to authenticate, to prove.
beurlauben *n. v.t.* to grant *or* to give leave of absence; (sich) ~ *v.refl.* to take leave.
beurteilen *v.t.* to judge; to criticize.
Beurteilung *f.* (-, -en) judgment; appraisal; (*mil.*) efficiency rating.
Beute *f.* (-, 0) booty, spoil, prey.
Beutel *m.* (-s, -) bag, pouch; purse.
beuteln *v.t.* (*Mehl*) to bolt, to sift.
bevölkern *v.t.* to people, to populate.
Bevölkerung *f.* (-, -en) population.
bevollmächtigen *v.t.* to authorize.

Bevollmächtigte[r] *m.* (-en, -en) attorney, deputy; (*Gesandte*) plenipotentiary.
bevor *c.* before.
bevormunden *v.t.* to patronize.
bevorstehen *v.i.st.* to impend, to be imminent.
bevorstehend *a.* imminent, coming.
bevorzugen *v.t.* to favour, to privilege.
bewachen *v.t.* to watch over, to guard.
Bewachung *f.* (-, -en) escort, guard.
bewachsen *a.* overgrown.
bewaffnen *v.t.* to arm.
Bewaffnung *f.* (-, -en) arming, armament.
bewahren *v.t.* to preserve; to guard, to keep; *Gott bewahre!* God forbid!
bewähren (sich) *v.refl.* to stand the test.
bewahrheiten *v.t.* (*sich*) to prove true.
bewährt *a.* approved, tried.
Bewährung *f.* (-, 0) proof, verification.
Bewährungsfrist *f.* period of probation; *eine ~ von zwei Jahren erhalten*, to be bound over for two years.
bewaldet *a.* woody.
bewältigen *v.t.* to overcome, to master.
bewandert *a.* versed, skilled, experienced.
Bewandtnis *f.* (-, -nisse) condition, state.
bewässern *v.t.* to irrigate.
Bewässerung *f.* (-, -en) irrigation.
bewegen *v.t. & st.* to move; to stir; to induce; sich ~ *v.refl.* to move .
Beweggrund *m.* (-[e]s, -gründe) motive.
beweglich *a.* mobile; movable; versatile; ~es *Vermögen*, movables, movable property, personal estate.
Bewegung *f.* (-, -en) motion; movement; commotion; exercise; emotion.
beweinen *v.t.* to weep for, to deplore.
Beweis *m.* (-weises, -weise) proof; evidence; argument; *zum ~ von*, in proof of; ~ *antreten*, to produce evidence; ~ *liefern*, to furnish proof; *als ~ zulassen*, to admit in evidence.
beweisen *v.t.st.* to prove; to demonstrate.
Beweis: ~grund *m.* argument; ~last *f.* burden of proof.
beweisbar *a.* demonstrable.
bewenden *v.ir. es dabei ~ lassen*, to let the matter rest there.
bewerben (sich) *v.refl.st.* to apply for.
Bewerber *m.* (-s, -) applicant.
Bewerbung *f.* (-, -en) application.
bewerkstelligen *v.t.* to effect.
bewerten *v.t.* to estimate, to value .
bewilligen *v.t.* to consent to, to grant, to concede; bewilligte Mittel *pl.* appropriated funds, appropriations (for).
Bewilligung *f.* (-, -en) concession; grant; consent; (*von Geldern*) appropriation of funds.
bewillkommnen *v.t.* to welcome.
bewirken *v.t.* to effect, to cause, to bring about.
bewirten *v.t.* to entertain, to treat.

bewohnbar *a.* habitable.
bewohnen *v.t.* to inhabit.
Bewohner *m.* (-s, -) inhabitant; (*eines Hauses*) resident, inmate.
bewölken (sich) *v.refl.* to become overcast.
bewundern *v.t.* to admire.
bewundernswert, bewundernswürdig, *a.* admirable.
Bewunderung *f.* (-, 0) admiration.
Bewurf *m.* (-[e]s, 0) plaster, rough-cast.
bewusst *a.* conscious (of); in question.
bewusstlos *a.* unconscious.
Bewusstsein *n.* (-s, 0) consciousness.
bezahlen *v.t.* to pay, to discharge; (*Wechsel*) to honour.
Bezahlung *f.* (-, 0) payment, pay; *gegen* ~, against payment.
bezähmen *v.t.* to tame; (*fig.*) to restrain, to subdue.
bezaubern *v.t.* to bewitch, to charm.
bezeichnen *v.t.* to mark, to denote; to signify; ~*d,* characteristic.
Bezeichnung *f.* (-, -en) note, mark, designation.
bezeigen *v.t.* to show, to manifest.
bezeugen *v.t.* to testify.
bezichtigen *v.t.* to charge with, to accuse of.
beziehen *v.t.st.* to cover; (*Instrument*) to string; (*Geld*) to draw; (*Waren*) to obtain; (*Zeitung*) to take; (*Wohnung*) to move into; (*Hochschule*) to enter; (*sich*) ~, to refer to; to relate to; (*Himmel*) to become cloudy.
Bezieher *m.* (-s, -) subscriber.
Beziehung *f.* (-, -en) relation, connection; respect; *mit guten* ~*en,* well connected.
beziehungsweise *adv.* respectively.
beziffern (sich) *v.refl.* to amount to (to).
Bezirk *m.* (-[e]s, -e) district, area.
Bezogene[r] *m.* (-n, -n) drawee.
Bezug *m.* (-[e]s, -züge) case; (*Waren*) supply; reference; *in* ~ *auf,* with respect to.
bezüglich, *a.* respecting, referring to.
Bezugnahme *f.* (-, -n) reference.
Bezugs: ~**bedingungen** *f.pl.* terms of delivery; ~**quelle** *f.* source of supply.
bezwecken *v.t.* to aim at.
bezweifeln *v.t.* to doubt (of).
bezwingen *v.t.st.* to subdue, to vanquish.
Bibel *f.* (-, -n) Bible, Scripture.
Bibelspruch *m.* Scripture text.
Biber *m.* (-s, -) beaver.
Bibliograph *m.* (-en, -en) bibliographer.
Bibliothek *f.* (-, -en) library.
Bibliothekar *m.* (-s, -e) librarian.
biblisch *a.* biblical, scriptural.
bieder *a.* honest, straightforward.
biegen *v.t.* & *i.st.* to bend, to bow; to curve; to turn; *sich* ~, to bend, to warp.
biegsam *a.* flexible; supple, pliant.
Biegung *f.* (-, -en) bend, curve.

Biene *f.* (-, -n) bee.
Bienen: ~**königin** *f.* queen-bee; ~**korb,** *m.* beehive; ~**schwarm** *m.* swarm of bees; ~**stock** *m.* beehive; ~**wachs** *n.* beeswax; ~**zucht** *f.* bee-keeping, apiculture.
Bier *n.* (-[e]s, -e) *n.* beer; (*englisches*) ale.
bieten *v.t.st.* to bid; to offer.
Bigamie *f.* (-, -n) bigamy.
Bigamist *m.* (-en, -en) bigamist.
bigott *a.* bigoted.
Bilanz, *f.* balance-sheet.
Bild *n.* (-[e]s, -er) image; picture.
bilden *v.t.* to form; to shape, to model, to cultivate, to improve; to constitute; (*fig.*) to improve one's mind.
bildend *a.* instructive; (*Kunst*) plastic.
Bilder: ~**galerie** *f.* picture-gallery; ~**rahmen** *m.* picture-frame; ~**stürmer** *m.* iconoclast.
Bildhauer *m.* (-s, -) sculptor, statuary.
Bildhauerkunst *f.* sculpture.
bildlich *a.* figurative; ~*e Darstellung,* pictorial representation.
Bildnis *n.* (-nisses, -nisse) portrait.
bildsam *a.* plastic.
Bildsäule *f.* statue.
Bildschnitzer *m.* wood-carver.
bildschön *a.* very beautiful, dazzling.
Bildung *f.* (-, -en) formation; constitution; culture; training, education.
billard *n.* (-s, -s) billiards *pl.*; billiard-table.
Billett *n.* (-[e]s, -e *or* -s) (*Fahrkarte*) ticket; *ein* ~ *lösen,* to take a ticket.
billig *a.* equitable, just, fair, reasonable; (*im Preise*) cheap.
billigen *v.t.* to approve (of).
Billigkeit *f.* (-, 0) fairness; cheapness.
Billigung *f.* (-, 0) sanction, approval.
Bimsstein *n.* pumice-stone.
Binde *f.* (-, -n) band; fillet; (neck) tie; bandage, sling.
Binde: ~**glied** *n.* connecting link; ~**haut** *f.* conjunctiva; ~**hautentzündung** *f.* conjunctivitis.
binden *v.t.st.* to bind; to tie, to fasten; (*mil.*) to tie down, to contain; (*fig.*) to engage; (*sich*) ~, *v.refl.* to commit oneself.
Bindestrich *m.* (*gram.*) hyphen.
Bindfaden *m.* string, packthread, twine.
Bindung *f.* (-, -en) binding; (*mus.*) ligature; (*fig.*) obligation; restriction.
binnen *pr.* within.
Binnen: ~**hafen** *m.* inland harbour, inland port; basin (of a port); ~**handel** *m.* home trade; ~**land** *n.* inland, interior.
Binse *f.* (-, -n) rush.
Biochemie, *f.* biochemistry.
Biograph *m.* (-en, -en) biographer.
Biographie *f.* (-, -en) biography.
Biolog *m.* (-en, -en) biologist.

Biologie f. (-, -n) biology.
Birke f. (-, -n) birch, birch-tree.
Birnbaum m. pear-tree.
Birne f. (-, -n) pear; (el.) (light-)bulb; ~nkontakt m. lampholder.
bis pr. to, up to, as far as, till, until; ~ c. till, until; ~ dahin, ~ jetzt, so far.
Bisam m. (-[e]s, -e) musk.
Bischof m. (-[e]s, -schöfe) bishop.
bischöflich a. episcopal.
Bischofs: ~mütze f. mitre; ~sitz m. see; ~stab m. crosier.
bisher adv. hitherto, till now.
bisherig a. hitherto existing.
Biskuit m. or n. (-s, -s u. -e) biscuit; sponge cake.
Biss m. (Bisses, Bisse) bite, sting.
Bisschen n. (-s, -) ein ~, a little.
Bissen m. (-s, -) morsel.
bissig a. biting; (Hund) snappish; sarcastic.
Bistum n. (-[e]s, -tümer) bishopric.
bisweilen adv. sometimes, now and then.
Bitte f. (-, -n) request, entreaty, prayer.
bitten v.t.i.st. to beg, to request; to pray; to invite; bitte, please.
bitter a. bitter; stinging.
bitterböse a. very wicked; extremely angry.
Bitterkeit f. (-, -en) bitterness.
Bittersalz n. Epsom salt.
Bitt: ~schrift f. petition, supplication; ~steller m. petitioner, supplicant.
Biwak n. (-s, -e) bivouac.
bizarr a. strange, odd.
blähen v.t. to inflate, to cause flatulency.
blähend a. flatulent.
Blähung f. (-, -en) flatulence.
Blamage f. (frz.) (-, -n) exposure to ridicule, disgrace.
blamieren v.t. to expose to ridicule; (sich)~, to make a fool of oneself.
blank a. blank; smooth, polished, bright.
blanko a. blank (Scheck).
Blase f. (-, -n) bladder; pimple; bubble; blister; flaw (in glass).
Blasebalg m. bellows pl.
blasen v.t. & i.st. to blow; to sound.
blasiert a. blasé, cloyed.
Blasinstrument n. wind-instrument.
blass a. pale, wan, pallid.
Blässe f. (-, 0) paleness, pallor.
Blatt n. (-[e]s, Blätter) leaf; sheet; blade; newspaper; vom ~, at sight; das ~ wendet sich, the tide turns.
Blatter f. (-, -n) blister, pustule; ~n pl. smallpox.
blättern v.i. to turn over the leaves.
Blatternarbe f. pock-mark.
blau a. Blau n. (-s, 0) blue; ins Blaue, at random.
Blaubeere f (-, -en) blueberry.
bläulich a. bluish.

Blaupause f. (mech.) blueprint.
Blau: ~säure f. Prussic acid; ~strumpf, m. blue-stocking.
Blaustift m. blue pencil.
Blech n. (-[e]s, -e) sheet-metal; tin-plate, tin; (fam.) stuff, nonsense.
Blechmusik f. brass band.
Blei n. (-s, -e) lead.
bleiben v.i.st. (s) to remain, to stay; to rest; to continue, to keep; ~ lassen, to let alone.
bleibend p. & a. lasting, permanent.
bleich a. pale, wan; faint.
Bleiche f. (-, -n) bleaching-(ground).
bleichen v.t. to bleach, to whiten; ~ v.i. to get bleached.
Bleichsucht f. anæmia, chlorosis.
bleichsüchtig a. anæmic, chlorotic.
bleiern a. leaden; (fig.) heavy, dull.
Blei: ~stift m. pencil; ~stiftspitzer m. pencil sharpener; ~weiss n. white lead.
Blende f. (-, -n) blind, folding-screen; shutter; (Pferde~) blinker; (nav.) deadlights pl.; (opt.) diaphragm.
blenden v.t. to blind, to blindfold; to make blind; (fig.) to dazzle.
Blend: ~laterne f. dark-lantern; ~leder n. blinkers pl.
Blendwerk n. delusion, illusion.
Blick m. (-[e]s, -e) glance, look; view; auf den ersten ~, at first sight.
blicken v.i. to glance, to look.
Blickfeld n. range of vision.
blind a. blind; dull; ~er Alarm, false alarm; ~ machen (Granate) to render harmless.
Blinddarm m. appendix; ~entzündung f. appendicitis.
Blindekuh f. blindman's buff.
Blindgänger m. dud.
Blindheit f. (-, 0) blindness.
blindlings adv. blindly, blindfold.
Blindschleiche f. (-, -n) blind-worm.
blinken v.i. to glitter, to gleam, to twinkle.
Blinkfeuer m. intermittent light.
blinzeln, blinzen v.i. to blink; to wink; to twinkle.
Blitz m. (-es, -e) lightning; wie ein ~ aus heiterem Himmel, out of the blue.
Blitzableiter m. lightning conductor; (Am.) lightning rod.
blitzen v.i. to flash, to sparkle.
Blitz: ~krieg m. lightning war; ~licht n. flashlight.
blitzschnell a. swift as lightning.
Block m. (-[e]s, Blöcke) block; log.
Blockade f. (-, -n) blockade; die ~ brechen, to run the blockade; ~brecher m. blockade-runner.
Blockhaus n. log-cabin.
blockieren v.t. to block up, to blockade.
blöde a. shy, bashful; imbecile.
Blödsinn m. nonsense, trash.

blöken v.i. to bleat; (von Kühen) to low.
blond a. fair, blonde.
Blondine f. (-, -n) blonde.
bloss a. naked, bare; uncovered; mere; ~ adv. merely, only; ~ stellen, to expose.
Blösse f. (-, -n) nakedness, bareness; weak side.
blühen v.i. to bloom, to flower, to blossom; (fig.) to flourish.
Blume f. (-, -n) flower; (Wein~) bouquet; durch die ~, figuratively, allusively.
Blumen: ~ausstellung f. flower-show; ~beet n. flower-bed; ~blatt n. petal; ~händler m. florist; ~kohl m. cauliflower; ~spende f. floral tribute; ~stock m. pot-flower; ~strauss m. bunch of flowers, nosegay, posy; ~topf m. flower-pot; ~zucht f. floriculture; ~zwiebel f. bulb.
blumig a. flowery; (fig.) florid.
Bluse f. (-, -n) blouse, (Am.) waist (Damenbluse).
Blut n. (-[e]s, 0) blood.
Blutader f. vein; blood-vessel.
blutarm a. anæmic; poor as Job.
Blutarmut f. anæmia.
Blut: ~buche f. copper-beech, bronze-beech; ~druck m. blood pressure.
blutdürstig a. bloodthirsty.
Blüte f. (-, -n) blossom, bloom; (fig.) prime, heyday.
Blutegel m. leech.
bluten v.i. to bleed.
Blütenstaub m. pollen.
Blütezeit f. prime, golden age.
Blut: ~erguss m. hæmorrhage; ~erkrankheit f. hæmophilia; ~gefäss n. blood-vessel.
blutgierig a. sanguinary, bloodthirsty.
Blutgruppe f. blood group.
blutig a. bloody; sanguinary.
blutjung a. very young.
Blutkörperchen n. (blood-)corpuscle.
blutleer, blutlos a. bloodless.
Blutprobe f. blood test.
Blutrache f. vendetta.
blutrünstig a. bloody.
Blut: ~sauger m. vampire; (fig.) extortioner, skinflint; ~schande f. incest.
blutschänderisch a. incestuous.
Blutschuld f. blood-guilt; capital crime.
Blut: ~spender m. blood donor; ~stillend a. hæmostatic, styptic; ~sturz m., Blutung f. hæmorrhage; ~übertragung f. blood-transfusion; ~unterlaufen a. bloodshot; ~vergiftung f. blood-poisoning; ~vergiessen n. bloodshed; ~sverwandt a. consanguineous; ~sverwandter m. blood-relationship; ~sverwandtschaft f. consanguinity, blood-relationship.
Blutwurst f. black-pudding.[1]
Bö f. (-, -en) sudden squall, white squall.

Bock m. (-[e]s, Böcke) ram; (anderer Tiere) buck; trestle; high stool; einenr~ schiessen, to make a blunder.
bockbeinig a. stubborn.
Bockgestell n. trestle.
bockig a. pig-headed.
Bockleder n. buckskin.
Bockshorn n. einen ins ~ jagen, to intimidate one.
Boden m. (-s, - u. Böden) ground; soil; bottom; garret, loft; (eines Fasses etc.) head; floor.
Boden: ~fenster n. dormer-window; ~kammer f. garret.
Bodenkreditbank f. mortgage-credit bank.
bodenlos a. bottomless.
Boden: ~rente f. ground-rent; ~ständig, indigenous; ~satz m. sediment, dregs pl.; ~schätze m.pl. mineral resources.
Bodmerei f. (-, -en) bottomry.
Bogen m. (-s, -) arch, vault; bow; (math.) arc; (Geigen~) fiddle-stick; sheet (Papier); in Bausch und ~, in the lump.
Bogen: ~gang m. arcade; ~lampe f. arc-lamp; ~schütze m. archer.
Bohème f. Bohemia.
Bohèmien m. Bohemian.
Bohle f. (-, -n) board, plank.
bohlen v.t. to board, to plank.
böhmisch a. Bohemian; das sind mir ~e Dörfer, that is Greek to me.
Bohne f. (-, -n) bean; dicke ~n, broad beans; grüne ~n, French beans, runner beans.
bohnern v.t. to wax.
Bohnenstange f. bean-stick.
bohren v.t. to bore, to drill; in den Grund ~, to sink (a ship).
Bohrer m. (-s, -) drill.
Bohr: ~lehre, ~schablone f. jig; ~maschine f. boring machine, drilling machine.
Boje f. (-, -n) buoy.
Böller m. (-s, -) small mortar.
Bollwerk n. bastion, bulwark.
Bolzen m. (-s, -) bolt; arrow.
Bombardement n. (-s, -s) bombardment.
bombardieren v.t. to bombard, to shell, to pound.
Bombast m. (-es, 0) bombast.
bombastisch a. bombastic, inflated.
Bombe f. (-, -n) bomb, shell.
Bomben: ~flugzeug n. bomber; ~punktwurf m. pinpoint bombing; ~schacht m. bomb-rack; ~sicher a. bombproof; ~zielgerät n. bomb-sight.
Bonbon (frz.) n. (-s, -s) sweet.
Boot n. (-[e]s, -e) boat.
Bootsmann m. boatswain.
Bord m. (-[e]s, -e) board; an ~, aboard; über ~, overboard.
Bordell n. (-[e]s, -e) brothel.
Bordfunker m. (avi.) radio operator.

Borg *m.* (-[e]s, 0) credit; tick.
borgen *v.t.* to borrow; to lend.
Borke *f.* (-, -n) bark.
borniert *a.* narrowminded.
Börse *f.* (-, -n) purse; stock-exchange.
Börsen: ~**bericht** *m.* market report; ~**kurs** *m.* quotation; ~**makler** *m.* stockbroker.
Borste *f.* (-, -n) bristle.
borstig *a.* bristly.
Borte *f.* (-, -n) lace-braid.
bösartig *a.* malignant; malicious.
Böschung *f.* (-, -en) scarp, slope.
böse *a.* bad; evil, ill, wicked; angry.
Bösewicht *m.* (-[e]s, -e[r]) villain.
boshaft *a.* spiteful, malicious.
Bosheit *f.* (-, -en) malice, spite.
böswillig *a.* malevolent, wicked.
Botanik *f.* (-, 0) botany.
Botaniker *m.* (-s, -) botanist.
botanisch *a.* botanic(al).
botanisieren *v.i.* to botanize.
Bote *m.* (-n -n) messenger; ~**ngang** m. errand.
Botschaft *f.* (-, -en) message; news; embassy.
Botschafter *m.* (-s, -) ambassador.
Böttcher *m.* (-s, -) cooper.
Bottich *m.* (-[e]s, -e) vat, coop, tub.
Bouillon *f.* (meat) broth; ~**würfel** *m.* bouillon-cube.
Bowle *f.* (-, -n) tureen; (*Getränk*) spiced wine, claret-cup, iced cup.
boxen *v.i.* to box.
Boxer *m.* (-s, -) boxer, pugilist, prize-fighter.
boykottieren *v.t.* to boycott.
brach *a.* fallow, unploughed.
Brachfeld *n.* fallow (ground).
brackig *a.* brackish.
Bramarbas *m.* (-ses, -basse) braggart, swaggerer.
bramarbasieren *v.i.* to swagger, to bully.
Bramsegel *n.* topsail.
Branche *f.* (-, -n) branch, line (of business).
Brand *m.* (-[e]s, Brände) combustion; fire, conflagration; (*med.*) gangrene; fuel; fire-brand; (*bot.*) blight, mildew; in ~ *stecken,* to set on fire.
Brand: ~**brief** *m.* urgent letter; ~**bombe** *f.* incendiary bomb.
branden *v.i.* to surge, to break.
brandig *a.* blighted, blasted; (*med.*) gangrenous; smelling as if burnt.
Brandlegung *f.* (-, -en) incendiarism.
Brandmal *n.* (-[e]s, -e) stigma.
brandmarken *v.t.* to brand.
Brand: ~**mauer** *f.* fire-proof wall; ~**schaden** *m.* damage by fire.
brandschatzen *v.t.* to plunder.
Brand: ~**stifter** *m.* incendiary; ~**stiftung** *f.* arson, incendiarism.

Brandung *f.* (-, -en) breakers *pl.*; surf, surge.
Brandwunde *f.* burn, scald.
Branntwein *m.* (-[e]s, -e) spirits *pl.*
Branntweinbrenner *m.* distiller.
braten *v.t.st.* to roast; to broil, to grill; (*in der Pfanne*) to fry.
Braten *m.* (-s, -) roast-meat.
Bratenfett *n.* dripping.
Brat: ~**kartoffel** *f.* fried potato; ~**ofen** *m.* roasting-oven; ~**pfanne** *f.* frying-pan; ~**rost** *m.* gridiron, grill.
Bratsche *f.* (-, -n) viola, bass-viol.
Brat: ~**spiess** *m.* spit; ~**wurst** *f.* sausage.
Brauch *m.* (-[e]s, Bräuche) usage, custom.
brauchbar *a.* useful, serviceable.
brauchen *v.t.* to use, to employ; to need, to want.
brauen *v.t.* to brew.
Brauer *m.* (-s, -) brewer.
Brauerei *f.* (-, -en) brewery.
braun *a.* brown, tawny; (*Pferd*) bay; **Braune** *m.* bay-horse.
Bräune *f.* (-, 0) (*med.*) quinsy; croup.
bräunen *v.t.* to make brown.
Braunkohle *f.* lignite.
Braunsche Röhre *f.* cathode-ray tube.
Braus *m.* in Saus und ~ leben, to revel and riot.
Brausebad *n.* shower-bath.
brausen *v.i.* to roar; to buzz; to effervesce.
Brausepulver *n.* effervescent powder.
Braut *f.* (-, Bräute) fiancée; (*am Hochzeitstage*) bride.
Braut: ~**aussteuer** *f.* trousseau; ~**führer** *m.* bestman.
Bräutigam *m.* (-s, -e) fiancé; (*am Hochzeitstage*) bridegroom.
Braut: ~**jungfer** *f.* bridesmaid; ~**kleid** *n.* wedding-dress; ~**kranz** *m.* bridal wreath.
Braut: ~**nacht** *f.* wedding-night; ~**paar** *n.* couple.
brav *a.* honest, good, brave, courageous.
bravo! *i.* bravo! well done!
Brecheisen *n.* crowbar.
brechen *v.st.* to break; (*Knochen*) to fracture; (*Lichtstrahlen*) to be refracted.
Brech: ~**mittel** *n.* emetic; ~**reiz** *m.* retching; nausea.
Brechung *f.* (-, -en) (*opt.*) refraction.
Brei *m.* (-[e]s, -e) pap; porridge; pulp.
breit *a.* broad; wide, large; weit und ~, far and wide; ~ schlagen, to persuade.
Breite *f.* (-, -n) breadth; width; (*geographische*) latitude.
Breitengrad *m.* degree of latitude.
breitspurig *a.* bumptious.
Bremse *f.* (-, -n) gadfly; brake.
bremsen *v.t.* to apply the brake.
brennbar *a.* combustible.
brennen *v.t.ir.* to burn, to scorch; (*med.*) to cauterize; (*Kaffee*) to roast; (*Kohlen*)

to char; (*Branntwein*) to distil; (*Ziegel*) to bake; ~ *v.i.st.* to burn, to be on fire; (*Wunde*) to smart; (*Nessel*) to sting.

Brennerei *f.* (-, -en) distillery.

Brenn: ~**holz** *n.* fire-wood; ~**material** *n.* fuel; ~**nessel** *f.* stinging nettle; ~**punkt** *m.* focus; ~**stoff** *m.* fuel; ~**spiegel** *m.* burning-mirror.

brenzlich *a.* dangerous, risky.

Bresche *f.* (-, -n) breach; gap.

Brett *n.* (-[e]s, -er) board; plank; *mit Brettern verschlagen*, to board up.

Brevier *n.* (-s, -e) breviary.

Brezel *f.* (-, -n) bretzel.

Brief *m.* (-[e]s, -e) letter, epistle; *unter ~ und Siegel*, under hand and seal.

Brief: ~**beschwerer** *m.* paper-weight; ~**bote** *m.* postman.

Briefkasten *m.* letter-box; pillar-box.

brieflich *a. & adv.* by letter.

Brief: ~**marke** *f.* (postage) stamp; ~**markensammler** *m.* stamp collector; ~**papier** *n.* note-paper; ~**porto** *n.* postage.

Briefschaften *f.pl.* letters, papers, documents *pl.*

Brief: ~**steller** *m.* model letter-writer; ~**tasche** *f.* wallet; ~**taube** *f.* carrier-pigeon; ~**telegramm** *n.* nightletter telegram; ~**träger** *m.* postman; ~**umschlag** *m.* envelope; ~**waage** *f.* letter-balance; ~**wechsel** *m.* correspondence.

Brigade *f.* (-, -n) brigade.

Brigg *f.* (-, -s) brig.

Brikett *n.* (-s, -s) briquette.

Brillant *m.* (-en, -en) brilliant.

Brille *f.* (-, -n) (pair of) spectacles *pl.*; glasses *pl.*; goggles *pl.*

Brillen: ~**futteral** *n.* spectacle-case; ~**gestell** *n.* spectacle-frame; ~**schlange** *f.* cobra.

brillieren *v.i.* to shine.

bringen *v.t.ir.* to bring; to carry; to take; to convey; to conduct; to give, to present; *in Gang ~*, to set going; *zustand(e) ~*, to bring about; *es weit ~*, to get on in the world; *um etwas ~*, to deprive; *ums Leben ~*, to kill, to murder; *ein Opfer ~*, to make a sacrifice.

Brise *f.* (-, -n) breeze.

bröck[e]lig *a.* crumbling.

bröckeln *v.t. & i.* to crumble.

Brocken *m.* (-s, -) fragment; morsel; crumb.

brodeln *v.i.* to bubble.

Brodem *m.* (-s, 0) steam, exhalation.

Brokat *m.* (-[e]s, -e) brocade.

Brom *m.* (-s, 0) bromine.

Brombeere *f.* blackberry.

Brombeerstrauch *m.* bramble.

Bronchialkatarrh *m.* bronchitis.

Bronze,I *f.* (-, -n) bronze, brass.

Brosame *f.* (-, -n) crumb.

Brosche *f.* (-, -n) brooch.

broschiert *a.* paper-bound.

Broschüre *f.* (-, -n) pamphlet.

Brösel *m.* (-s, -) crumb.

Brot *n.* (-[e]s, -e) bread; loaf.

Brot: ~**aufstrich** *m.* sandwich spread; ~**beutel** *m.* haversack.

Brötchen *n.* (-s, -) roll.

brotlos *a.* unprofitable.

Bruch *m.* (-[e]s, Brüche) breach, rupture; (*Bein~*) fracture; (*med.*) rupture, hernia; (*ar.*) fraction; *gemeiner ~*, vulgar or common fraction; *in die Brüche gehen*, to come to naught.

Bruchband *n.* truss.

brüchig *a.* full of cracks, brittle.

Bruch: ~**landung** *f.* (*avi.*) crash-landing; ~**strich** *m.* fraction line; ~**stück** *n.* fragment; ~**teil** *m.* fraction.

Brücke *f.* (-, -n) bridge.

Brücken: ~**kopf** *m.* bridge-head; ~**pfeiler** *m.* pier.

Bruder *m.* (-s, Brüder) brother; (*Mönch*) friar.

brüderlich *a. & adv.* fraternal.

Brudermord *m.* fratricide.

Brüderschaft *f.* (-, -en) brotherhood.

Brühe *f.* (-, -n) broth, gravy, sauce.

brühen *v.t.* to scald.

brühheiss, brühwarm *a.* boiling-hot.

brüllen *v.i.* to roar; to bellow, to low.

brummen *v.i.* to growl, to grumble; to hum; to mumble.

Brünette *f.* (-, -n) brunette.

Brunft *f.* (-, 0) rut, rutting-time.

Brunnen *m.* (-s, -) spring, well; fountain; mineral waters *pl.*

Brunst *f.* (-, 0) rut, sexual desire.

brünstig *a.* ardent, fervent; in heat.

brüsk *a.* brusque; **brüskieren** *v.t.* to snub.

Brust *f.* (-, Brüste) breast; bosom, chest.

Brustbild *n.* half-length portrait.

brüsten (sich) *v.refl.* to plume oneself.

Brust: ~**fellentzündung** *f.* pleurisy; ~**kasten**, ~**korb** *m.* chest, thorax.

Brustschwimmen *n.* breast-stroke.

Brüstung *f.* (-, -en) parapet, breast-work.

Brust: ~**warze** *f.* nipple; ~**wehr** *f.* parapet.

Brut *f.* (-, -en) brood, hatch; (*Fische*) fry; (*Vögel*) covey; (*fig.*) set, pack.

brutal *a.* brutish, brutal.

brüten *v.t.* to brood, to hatch; to sit (on eggs).

Brutapparat *m.* incubator.

Bruthenne *f.* (-, -n) sitting hen.

Brutstätte *f.* breeding place; hot bed.

Bruttogewicht *n.* (-[e]s, -e) gross weight.

bst! *i.* hush! hist!

Bube *m.* (-n, -n) boy, lad; knave, rogue; (*in der Karte*) Knave.

Bubenstreich *m.* knavish trick.

Bubikopf *m.* bobbed hair.

Buch n. (-[e]s, Bücher) book; (~ Papier) quire; die Bücher führen, to keep the books.

Buch: ~binder m. bookbinder; ~drucker m. printer.

Buche f. (-, -n) beech, beech-tree.

Buchecker f. (-, -n) beechnut.

buchen v.t. to book, to enter.

Bücher: ~brett n. book-shelf; ~ei f. library; ~revisor m. auditor; beeidigter Bücherrevisor, chartered accountant; ~schrank m. book-case.

Buch: ~führung f. book-keeping; ~halter m. book-keeper; ~handel m. book-trade; ~händler m. bookseller; ~handlung f., ~laden m. bookseller's shop; ~macher m. bookmaker.

Buchsbaum m. (-[e]s, -bäume) box-tree.

Buchschuld f. (-, -en) book-debt.

Büchse f. (-, -n) box, case; tin; (Flinte) rifle.

Büchsen: ~fleisch n. tinned meat; ~öffner m. tin-opener.

Buchstabe m. (-n[s], -n) letter, character; type.

buchstabieren v.t. to spell.

buchstäblich a. literal, verbatim; ~ adv. literally.

Bucht f. (-, -en) creek, bay, inlet, cove.

Buchung f. (-, -en) entry.

Buchweizen m. (-s, 0) buck-wheat.

Buckel m. (-s, -) humpback, hump.

bücken (sich) v.refl. to stoop, to bow.

Bücking, Bückling m. (-s, -e) (smoked) herring.

Bude f. (-, -n) booth, stall.

Budget n. (-s, -s) budget.

Büffet n. (-s, -s) sideboard; bar.

Büffel m. (-s, -) buffalo.

büffeln v.i. to cram, to grind.

Bug m. (-[e]s, -e) bow.

Bügel m. (-s, -) hoop, bow.

Bügeleisen n. iron.

Bügelfalte f. crease.

bügeln v.i. to iron, to smoothe.

bugsieren v.t. to tow, to take in tow.

Bugspriet n. (-[e]s -e) bowsprit.

Buhle m. (-n, -n) & f. (-, -n) lover.

buhlen v.i. to court.

Bühne f. (-, -n) stage; scaffold; platform; zur ~ gehen, to go on the stage.

Bühnen: ~anweisung f. stage-direction; ~leiter, m. stage-manager.

Bukett n. (-s, -s) bouquet, bunch of flowers.

Bulette f. (-, -n) Vienna steak, meatball.

Bulle m. (-en, -en) bull f. (-, -n).

Bummel m. (-s, -) stroll.

Bummelei f. (-, -en) carelessness.

bummeln v.i. to loaf.

Bund m. (-[e]s, Bünde) band, tie; league, alliance, confederacy; covenant.

Bund n. (-[e]s, -e) bundle, bunch, truss.

Bündel n. (-s, -) bundle, bunch, truss, wisp (of straw).

Bundes... federal.

Bundes: ~genosse m. confederate, ally; ~lade f. ark of the covenant; ~staat m. Federal state; ~tag m. Federal Diet.

bündig a. concise, terse; convincing.

Bündnis n. (-nisses, -nisse) alliance.

Bunker m. (-s, -) pillbox; bunker.

bunt a. variegated; motley, parti-coloured, spotted; das ist zu ~, it goes too far.

Buntdruck m. (-[e]s, -e) colour-printing.

buntscheckig a. checkered.

Bürde f. (-, -n) burden, load.

Bureau n. (-s, -u -x) office.

Burg f. (-, -en) castle, stronghold.

Bureaukratie f. bureaucracy.

Bürge m. (-n, -n) bail, guarantee, surety.

bürgen v.i. to bail, to answer for, to warrant.

Bürger m. (-s, -) citizen, townsman.

Bürgerkrieg m. civil war.

bürgerlich a. civil, civic; ~es Gesetzbuch n. code of Civil Law.

Bürgerliche[r] m. (-n, -n) commoner.

Bürger: ~meister m. burgomaster, mayor; ~recht n. civic rights pl.; freedom (of a city); ~schule f. higher elementary school.

Bürger: ~stand m. middle class(es); ~steig m. pavement, sidewalk.

Bürgertum n. (-[e]s, 0) middle class.

Bürgschaft f. (-, -en) bail, surety, security; guarantee, (Am.) guaranty; gegen ~ freilassen, to release on bail; ~ leisten, to go bail; ~ zulassen, to admit to bail.

Büro n. (-s, -s) office.

Büro: ~arbeit f. paper work; ~artikel m.pl. office appliances pl.; ~personal n. clerical staff.

Bursch(e) m. (-en, -en) fellow, lad.

burschikos a. student-like, free-and-easy.

Bürste f. (-, -n) brush.

bürsten v.t. to brush.

Bürstenabzug m. brush proof.

Bürstenbinder m. brushmaker.

Busch m. (-[e]s, Büsche) bush; thicket.

Büschel m. (-s, -) tuft; bunch; aigrette.

Busen m. (-s, -) bosom; breast; heart.

Busennadel f. breast-pin, brooch.

Bussard m. (-s, -e) buzzard.

Busse f. (-, -n) penance, penitence; (Geld~) fine, penalty.

büssen v.t. to atone for; ~ v.i. to suffer, to expiate.

Büsser m. (-s, -) penitent.

bussfertig a. penitent, repentant.

Busstag m. day of penance.

Büste f. (-, -n) bust.

Büstenhalter m. (-s, -) brassiere.

Bütte f. (-, -n) tub, coop.

Büttel m. (-s, -) beadle, verger.

Büttenpapier n. hand-made paper.
Butter f. (-, 0) butter.
Butter: ~**blume** f. butter-cup; ~**fass** n. churn.
Butterbrotpapier n. greaseproof paper.
Buttermilch f. butter-milk.
buttern v.t. to churn.
Buttersemmel f. roll and butter.
Butzenscheibe f. bull's eye window-pane.

C

(See also under K, Sch, and Z)

Café n. (-s, -s) coffee-house, café.
Cellist m. (-en, -en) violoncellist.
Cello n. (-[s], -s) violoncello.
Ces n. (-, 0) (mus.) C flat.
Chamäleon n. (-s, -s) chameleon.
Champagner m. (-s, -) champagne.
Champignon m. (-s, -s) champignon, mushroom.
Chance f. (-, -n) chance.
Chaos n. (-, 0) chaos.
chaotisch a. chaotic.
Charakter m. (-s, **Charaktere**) character.
charakterfest a. firm.
charakterisieren v.t. to characterize.
Charakteristik f. (-, -en) characteristic.
charakteristisch a. characteristic.
charakterlos a. unprincipled.
Charakterzug m. (~es, züge) characteristic.
Chassis n. chassis.
Chauffeur (frz.) m. (-s, -e) chauffeur.
Chaussee f. (-, -n) highroad.
Chauvinismus m. (-, 0) jingoism.
Chef m. (-s, -s) head, principal, boss.
Chefarzt m. head physician.
Chemie f. (-, 0) chemistry.
Chemikalien n.pl. chemicals pl.
Chemiker m. (-s, -) (analytical) chemist.
chemisch a. & adv. chemical; ~**e Reinigung** f. dry cleaning; ~**e Wirkung** f. chemical action.
Cherub m. (~s, ~rubim) cherub.
Chiffre f. (-, -n) cipher.
Chiffretelegramm n. code telegram, cipher.
chiffrieren v.t. to cipher, to code.
Chinarinde f. Peruvian bark.
Chinin n. (-s, 0) quinine.
Chirurg m. (-en, -en) surgeon.
Chirurgie f. (-, 0) surgery.
chirurgisch a. surgical.
Chlor n. (-[e]s, 0) chlorine.
Chlor: ~**kalium** n. potassium chloride; ~**kalk** m. chloride of lime; ~**kalzium** n. calcium chloride.
chloroformieren v.t. to chloroform.
Cholera f. (-, 0) cholera.
cholerisch a. choleric.

Chor m. (-s, **Chöre**) chorus; ~ n. choir.
Choral m. (-[e]s, **Choräle**) chorale.
Chor: ~**hemd** n. surplice, albe; ~**stuhl** m. (cathedral) stall.
Christ(in) m. (& f.) (-en, -en) (f. - -nen) Christian.
Christbaum m. Christmas-tree.
Christenheit f. (-, 0) Christendom.
Christentum n. (-s, 0) Christianity.
Christkind n. infant Jesus.
christlich a. Christian.
Christliche Wissenschaft f. (-,) Christian Science.
Christ: ~**mette** f. ~**nacht** f. Christmas-night.
Chrom n. (-s, 0) chromium, chrome.
chromatisch a. chromatic.
Chronik f. (-, -en) chronicle.
chronisch a. chronic.
Chronist m. (-en, -en) chronicler.
Chronologie f. (-, -[e]n) chronology.
chronologisch a. chronological.
circa (zirka) adv. about, nearly.
Cis n. (-, 0) (mus.) C sharp.
Coupé n. (-s, -s) compartment.
Couplet (frz.) n. (-s, -s) comic song.
Coupon m. (-s, -s) coupon, interest warrant.
Cour f. (-, -en) reception at Court; Court; levee; die ~ machen, to pay court (to), to court.
Cousine f. (-, -n) (female) cousin.
Crême (frz.) (-, 0) f. & m. cream.
Cut m. (-s, -s) morning-coat.

D

da adv. there; then; ~ c. when; because, as, since; wer ~? who goes there?
dabei adv. thereby, near it; on this occasion; ~ bleibt es, that is agreed; was ist ~? what harm is there in that?
dabeistehen v.i.st. to stand by.
dableiben v.i.st. (s) to stay, to remain.
da capo i. encore.
Dach n. (-[e]s, **Dächer**) roof.
Dach: ~**balken** m. rafters pl.; ~**boden** m. loft, garret; ~**decker** m. slater, tiler; ~**garten** m. roof-garden; ~**kammer** f. garret, attic; ~**pappe** f. roofing, roofing-felt; ~**rinne** f. gutter.
Dachs m. (**Dachses**, **Dachse** u. **Dachse**) badger.
Dachshund m. dachshund.
Dach: ~**stuhl** m. framework of a roof; ~**ziegel** m. tile.
dadurch adv. thereby.
dafür adv. for that, for it; instead; ich kann nichts dafür, I cannot help it.
Dafürhalten n., nach meinem ~, in my opinion.

dagegen adv. against that, in return, on the other hand.

daheim adv. at home.

daher adv. thence; therefore; along.

dahin adv. thither, to that place; *dahin, gone; lost.

dahinbringen v.t.ir. to manage to, to persuade, to prevail upon.

dahinkommen v.i.st. (s) to come so far.

dahinstellen v.t. *dahingestellt sein lassen*, to leave undecided.

dahinten adv. behind.

dahinter adv. behind that, after it; *es steckt nichts* ~, there is nothing in it.

damalig a. then, of that time.

damals adv. then, at that time.

Damast m. (-es, -e) damask.

Dame f. (-, -n) lady, gentlewoman; (*im Kartenspiel*) Queen; (*beim Tanzen*) partner; draughts.

Damen: ~abteil n. ladies' compartment; ~brett n. draught-board; ~sattel m. side-saddle; ~schneider m. ladies' tailor.

damit adv. & c. with that; in order that; ~ *nicht*, lest.

dämlich a. (*vulg.*) foolish.

Damm m. (-[e]s, Dämme) dam, dike; mole; causeway; (*rail.*) embankment; (*fig.*) barrier.

Dammbruch m. bursting of a dike; rupture of the perineum.

dämmen v.t. to dam.

dämmern v.i. to grow dusky, to dawn.

Dämmerung f. (-, -en) twilight, dawn.

Dämon m. (-s, Dämonen) demon.

dämonisch a. demoniac(al).

Dampf m. (-[e]s, Dämpfe) vapour; steam; fume.

Dampfdruckmesser m. steam-pressure gauge.

dampfen v.i. to smoke, to steam.

dämpfen v.t. to damp; (*fig.*) to quell; (*Speisen*) to stew.

Dampfer m. (-s, -) steamer.

Dämpfer m. (-s, -) damper.

Dampf: ~kessel m. boiler; ~maschine f. steam-engine; ~schiff n. steam-vessel, steamer; ~schiffahrt f. steam-navigation.

Dampfwalze f. steam-roller.

Damwild n. (-es, 0) fallow deer.

danach adv. after that; accordingly; ~ *aussehn*, to look like it.

daneben adv. near it; besides.

danieder adv. on the ground; down; ~*liegen* v.i. to lie prostrate, to be depressed.

Dank m. (-es, 0) thanks pl.; acknowledgment; gratitude; vote of thanks.

dankbar a. thankful, grateful; profitable.

Dankbarkeit f. (-, 0) gratitude.

danke! thank you; ~ *nein*, no, thanks.

danken v.i. to thank; ~ v.t. (*einem etwas*) to be indebted to one for a thing.

dankenswert a. deserving of thanks.

Dankfest n. thanksgiving-day.

Danksagung f. (-, -en) thanksgiving.

Dankschreiben n. letter of acknowledgment.

dann adv. then; ~ *und wann*, now and then.

daran adv. thereon, thereat; by, of, about it; *es ist nichts* ~, it is not true; *er ist* ~, it is his turn.

darankommen v.i.st. *ich komme daran*, it is my turn.

darauf adv. thereupon, thereon; on that; after that.

daraus adv. out of that, therefrom; thence; *es wird nichts* ~, it won't come to anything.

darben v.i. to suffer want; to starve.

darbieten v.t.st. to offer, to present.

darbringen v.t.ir. to tender, to render, to offer up.

darein adv. into it, therein.

darf s. **dürfen**.

darin(nen) adv. therein; in it, in this.

darlegen v.t. (*fig.*) to explain, to prove.

Darlehen n. (-s, -) loan.

Darlehnskasse f. loan bank.

Darm m. (-[e]s, Därme) gut; bowels, intestines pl.

Darm... enteric.

Darmsaite f. catgut.

darnach s. **danach**.

Darre f. (-, -n) (*med.*) atrophy.

darreichen v.t. to reach, to hand, to present.

darstellen v.t. to exhibit; to represent; to personate, to act; (*chem.*) to produce.

Darsteller m. (-s, -) performer.

Darstellung f. (-, -en) presentation, representation, exhibition.

dartun v.t.st. to demonstrate.

darüber adv. over it, about it; concerning that; above, upwards.

darum adv. around that; therefore, for that reason; ~ *kommen*, to lose.

darunter adv. under that, beneath it; below that; among them, between them.

das art. pn. the; that; which.

dasein v.i.ir. (s) to be present; to exist.

Dasein n. (-, 0) existence; presence.

daselbst adv. there, in that place.

dass c. that; ~ *nicht*, lest.

datieren v.t. to date.

Dativ m. (-[e]s, -e) dative (case).

Dattel f. (-, -n) date.

Datum n. (-[s], Daten) date; *ohne* ~, undated.

Daube f. (-, -n) stave.

Dauer f. (-, 0) duration; continuance; *auf die* ~, in the long run.

dauerhaft a. durable, lasting.

Dauerkarte f. season ticket.
dauern v.i. to last, to continue; to abide; *er dauert mich*, I pity him; *es dauert mich*, I regret it.
Dauerwelle f. permanent wave.
Daumen m. (-s, -) thumb.
Daumschraube f. thumbscrew.
Daune f. (-, -n) down.
Daunendecke f. (-, -n) eiderdown.
davon adv. thereof, therefrom, of that; off, away; ~*kommen*, to get away; ~*tragen*, to obtain, to win.
davor adv. before that; for that.
dawider adv. against that, against it; *ich habe nichts* ~, I have no objection.
dazu adv. thereto, to that, to it; in addition to that; for that purpose; ~ *kommen*, to find time for.
dazwischen adv. between them, among them.
Dazwischenkunft f. (-, 0) intervention.
Debatte f. (-, -n) debate.
debattieren v.i. to debate.
Debet n. (-s, -s) (*com.*) debit.
Debüt n. (-s, -s) first appearance.
dechiffrieren v.t. to decipher; to decode.
Deck n. (-[e]s, -e) deck.
Deck: ~*adresse* f. cover address; ~*blatt* n. (Zigarren) wrapper.
Decke f. (-, -n) cover; blanket, coverlet, quilt; (*eines Zimmers*) ceiling; *unter einer* ~ *stecken*, to conspire together.
Deckel m. (-s, -) cover; lid.
decken v.t. to cover, to roof; (*com.*) to reimburse, to refund; *den Tisch* ~, to lay the table.
Deckengemälde n. ceiling-piece.
Deck: ~*mantel* m. cloak; ~*name* m. pseudonym; ~*offizier* m. warrant officer.
Deckung f. (-, -en) (*com.*) reimbursement; (*mil.*) cover; Golddeckung f. gold-backing; *Zahlungsmittel mit Dollardeckung*, dollar-backed instruments.
Deckwort n. codeword.
dedizieren v.t. to dedicate, to inscribe.
deduktiv a. deductive.
Defaitist m. (-en, -en) defeatist.
Defekt m. (-[e]s, -e) defect, deficiency; ~ a. defective, incomplete.
Defensive f. (-, 0) defensive; *in die* ~ *gehen*, to go over to the defensive.
defilieren v.i. (s) to march past.
definieren v.t. to define.
definitiv a. final.
Defizit n. (-s, -s) deficit, deficiency.
Degen m. (-s, -) sword.
degradieren v.t. (*Am.*) to downgrade; to demote; *zum Gemeinen* ~, to reduce to the ranks.
dehnbar a. elastic; (*Begriff*) vague.
dehnen v.t. to stretch, to extend.
Deich m. (-[e]s, -e) dike, dam.

Deichsel f. (-, -n) pole, shaft.
dein pn. thy; your.
deinesgleichen, the like of you.
deinetwegen, **deinethalben** adv. on your account, for thy sake.
dekadent a. decadent.
Dekan m. (-s, -e) dean.
Deklamation f. (-, -en) declamation.
deklamieren v.t. to recite, to declaim.
deklarieren v.t. to declare.
Deklination f. (- -en) declension.
deklinieren v.t. to decline.
dekolletiert s. low (-necked).
Dekoration f. (-, -en) decoration.
dekorieren v.t. to decorate; *neu* ~, to redecorate.
Dekret n. (-[e]s, -e) decree.
dekretieren v.t. to decree.
delegieren v.t. to delegate.
delikat a. delicious, delicate.
Delikatessen f.pl. delicatessen.
Delikt n. (-[e]s, -e) crime, offence.
Delphin m. (-[e]s, -e) dolphin.
Delta n. (-s, -s) delta.
Demagog[e] m. (-en, -en) demagogue.
demagogisch a. demagogic(al).
Demarkationslinie f. demarcation line.
demaskieren v.t. to unmask.
dementieren v.t. to deny.
Dementi n. (-s, -s) denial.
dementsprechend adv. accordingly.
demgegenüber adv. held against this.
demgemäss adv. accordingly.
demnach c. therefore, consequently.
demnächst adv. soon after.
demobilisieren v.t. u. v.i. to demobilize.
Demokrat m. (-en, -en) democrat.
Demokratie f. (-, 0) democracy.
demokratisch a. democratic.
demolieren v.t. to demolish.
Demonstration f. (-, -en) demonstration.
demonstrieren v.t. to demonstrate.
Demontage n. (-, -n) dismantling.
demontieren v.t. to dismantle.
demoralisieren v.t. to demoralize.
Demut f. (-, 0) humility, meekness.
demütig a. humble; submissive.
demütigen v.t. to humble, to humiliate.
Demütigung f. (-, -en) humiliation.
demzufolge adv. consequently.
dengeln v.t. to sharpen (a scythe) by hammering.
denkbar a. conceivable, imaginable.
denken v.i.st. to think (of).
Denkmal n. (-[e]s, -mäler) monument.
Denk: ~*münze* f. medal; ~*schrift* f. memorial; memoir.
denkwürdig a. memorable.
Denkwürdigkeiten f.pl. memoirs.
Denkzettel m. refresher, reminder.
denn c. & adv. for; then; than.
dennoch c. yet, nevertheless.
Denunziant m. (-en, -en) informer.

denunzieren *v.t.* to denounce, to inform against.

Depesche *f.* (-, -n) dispatch, telegram, wire.

depeschieren *v.t. & i.* to wire, to cable.

deponieren *v.t.* to deposit, to depose.

deportieren *v.t.* to deport.

Deportierter *m.* deportee.

Depositen *n.pl.* deposits; **~kasse** *f.* (*Bank*) branch office.

deprimieren *v.t.* to depress.

Deputierte[r] *m.* (-en, -en) deputy.

der, die, das, *art.* the; **der, die, das,** *pn.* that, who, which.

derartig *a.* such, of the kind.

derb *a.* compact; coarse.

derenthalben, derentwegen, derentwillen *adv.* on their (her, whose) account.

dergestalt *adv.* in such a manner, thus.

dergleichen *adv.* such, such like.

Derivat *n.* (-[e]s, -e) (*chem.*) derivative.

derjenige, diejenige, dasjenige *pn.* that, this, he.

derlei *a.* of that kind.

dermassen *adv.* in such a degree *or* manner, so much.

derselbe, dieselbe, dasselbe *pn.* the same; he, she, it; that.

Derwisch *m.* (-[e]s, -e) dervish.

derzeitig *a.* for the time being.

Des *n.* (*mus.*) D flat.

desavouieren *v.t.* to disavow.

Deserteur *m.* (-[e]s, -e) deserter.

desertieren *v.i.* (*s*) to desert.

deshalb *c.* therefore.

desinfizieren *v.t.* to disinfect.

Despot *m.* (-en, -en) despot, tyrant.

Despotie *f.* (-, -n) despotism.

despotisch *a.* despotic.

Despotismus *m.* (-, 0) Despotie.

dessentwegen, dessentwillen *adv.* on that account.

dessenungeachtet *adv.* notwithstanding.

destillieren *v.t.* to distil.

desto *adv.* the; **~ besser,** so much the better.

deswegen *adv. & c.* therefore.

Detail *n.* (-s, -s) detail, particulars *pl.*; **~handel** *m.* retail trade.

detaillieren *v.t.* to detail, to itemize; to retail.

Detaillist *m.* (-en, -en) retailer, retail dealer.

Detektiv *m.* (-s, -e) detective.

Detektor *m.* (-s, -en) detector.

Deut *m.* (-[e]s, -e) doit; farthing.

deuteln *v.t & i.* to subtilize, to twist the meaning.

deuten *v.i.* to point (at *or* to); **~** *v.t.* to interpret, to explain.

deutlich *a.* clear, distinct; evident, plain.

Deutschtum *n.* (-s, 0) German nationality; German manners.

Deutung *f.* (-, -en) interpretation.

Devise *f.* (-, -n) motto; foreign exchange; **~nzwangswirtschaft,** *f.* foreign exchange control.

devot *a.* humble.

Dezember *m.* (-s, -) December.

Dezernat *n.* (-[e]s, -e) government department.

Dezernent *m.* (-en, -en) head of a government department.

dezimal *a.* decimal.

Diadem *n.* (-s, -e) diadem, tiara.

Diagnose *f.* (-, -n) diagnosis.

diagnostizieren *v.t.* to diagnose.

Diagonale *f.* (-, -n) diagonal.

Diakon *m.* (-s, -e) deacon.

Diakonissin *f.* (-, -nen) deaconess.

Dialekt *m.* (-[e]s, -e) dialect.

Dialog *m.* (-[e]s, -e) dialogue.

Diamant *m.* (-en, -en) diamond.

Diamantschleifer *m.* diamond-cutter.

Diarrhöe *f.* (-, -n) diarrhœa.

Diät *f.* (-, 0) special diet.

Diäten *f.pl.* daily allowance.

Diätetik *f.* dietetics.

Diätköchin *f.* (-, -nen) dietician.

dicht *a.* dense, solid, compact, close; tight.

dichten *v.t.* to make watertight, to caulk.

dichten *v.t. & i.* to write poetry.

Dichter *m.* (-s, -) poet.

Dichterin *f.* (-, -nen) poetess.

dichterisch *a.* poetic(al).

Dichterling *m.* (-s, -e) poetaster.

Dichtkunst *f.* poetry.

Dichtung *f.* (-, -en) poetry; (*mech.*) gasket.

Dichtungsring *m.* washer.

dick *a.* thick; stout; large, bulky; (*Milch*) curdled.

Dicke *f.* (-, 0) thickness, bigness, bulk.

Dickdarm *m.* large intestine, great gut.

dickflüssig *a.* sticky.

dickhäutig *a.* thick-skinned, callous, dull.

Dickicht *n.* (-[e]s, -e) thicket.

Dickkopf *m.* pig-headed person.

dickköpfig *a.* obstinate.

Dieb *m.* (-[e]s, -e) thief.

diebisch *a.* thievish; (*Freude*) devilish.

Diebs (Diebes): ~bande *f.* gang of thieves.

Diebstahl *m.* (-[e]s, -stähle) theft, robbery.

Diele *f.* (-, -n) board, plank, deal; hall.

dielen *v.t.* to board, to floor.

dienen *v.i.* to serve; to be serviceable.

Diener *m.* (-s, -), **Dienerin** *f.* (-, -nen) servant.

Dienerschaft *f.* (-, -en) servants, domestics *pl.*

dienlich *a.* serviceable, useful.

Dienst *m.* (-[e]s, -e) service; employment, office; *im* **~,** on duty; *ausser* **~,** off duty, retired; **~ leisten,** to render service.

Dienstag *m.* (-[e]s, -e) Tuesday.

Dienstalter *n.* seniority.

dienstälter *a.* senior.

Dienstantritt *m.* assumption of duty.
dienstbar *a.* subject; subservient; tributary.
Dienst: ~**bote** *m.* domestic servant; ~**eid** *m.* oath of office.
diensteifrig *a.* officious, eager to serve.
dienstfrei *a.* exempt from service; off duty.
Dienst: ~**gebrauch** *m. nur für Dienstgebrauch,* restricted, *a.;* ~**grad** *m.* (*nav.*) rating; ~**liste** *f.* (*mil.*) roster.
dienstlich *a.* (*amtlich*) official.
Dienst: ~**mädchen** *n.* servant-girl, maidservant; ~**mann** *m.* porter; ~**pflicht** *f.* compulsory military service.
dienstpflichtig *a.* liable to service.
Dienstreise *f.* official tour, official journey.
Dienstsache *f.* official matter; On His Majesty's Service.
Dienst: ~**stelle** *f.* agency; ~**stunden** *f.pl.* duty hours; ~**tauglich** *a.* fit for service; ~**tuend** *a.* on duty; ~**turnus** *m.* rota.
Dienst: frankierter Dienstumschlag *m.* penalty envelope.
dienstunfähig *a.* disabled, invalid.
Dienst: ~**wohnung** *f.* official residence; ~**zeit** *f.* time spent in service, term.
dies *s.* dieser.
dieser, diese, dieses *pn.* this; the latter.
diesbezüglich *a.* referring to this.
diesjährig *a.* of this year, this year's.
diesmal *adv.* this time, for this once.
dies: ~**malig** *a.* present; ~**seitig** *a.* on this side.
diesseits *adv.* (on) this side.
Diesseits *n.* (-, 0) this world.
Dietrich *m.* (-[e]s, -e) pick-lock, skeleton-key.
Differentialrechnung *f.* differential calculus.
Differenz *f.* (-, -en) difference.
Diktat *n.* (-s, -e) dictation.
diktatorisch *a.* dictatorial.
Diktatur *f.* (-, -en) dictatorship.
diktieren *v.t.* to dictate.
Dilettant *m.* (-en, -en) amateur.
Dill *m.* (-[e]s, -e) (*bot.*) dill.
Ding *n.* (-[e]s, -e[r]) thing, matter; creature; *guter* ~*e sein,* to be in high spirits.
dingfest *a.,* ~ *machen,* to arrest.
dinglich *a.* (*law*) real.
Dinkel *m.* (-s, 0) spelt.
Diözese *f.* (-, -n) diocese.
Diphtheritis *f.* (-, 0) diphtheria.
Diphthong *m.* (-s, -e) diphthong.
Diplom *n.* (-[e]s, -e) diploma, patent.
Diplomat *m.* (-n, -en) diplomatist.
Diplomatenmappe *f.* diplomatic pouch *or* bag.
Diplomatie *f.* (-, 0) diplomacy.
diplomatisch *a.* diplomatic.
direkt *a.* direct.

Direktion *f.* (-, -en) direction, management; board of directors.
Direktive *f.* (-, -n) directive.
Direktor *m.* (-s, -en) director, manager; head-master.
Direktrice *f.* (-, -n) manageress.
Dirigent *m.* (-en, -en) (*mus.*) conductor.
dirigieren *v.t.* to direct; (*mus.*) to conduct.
Dirne *f.* (-, -n) maid, lass, prostitute.
Dis *n.* (-, 0) (*mus.*) D sharp.
Disharmonie *f.* (-, -[e]n) disharmony.
Diskant *m.* (-[e]s, -e) treble, soprano.
Diskont, Diskonto *m.* (-s, -s *u.* -i) discount.
diskontieren *v.t.* to discount.
diskreditieren *v.t.* to bring into disrepute.
diskret *a. & adv.* discreet; discreetly.
Diskretion *f.* (-, 0) discretion.
diskutieren *v.t.* to debate, to discuss.
Dispens *m.* (-es, -e) dispensation, licence.
dispensieren *v.t.* to dispense (of), to excuse, to exempt (from).
Disponent *m.* (-en, -en) manager.
disponieren *v.i.* to dispose (of).
Disposition *f.* (-, -en) arrangement, disposition.
Disput *m.* (-[e]s, -e) dispute.
disputieren *v.i.* to dispute; to argue.
Dissertation *f.* (-, -en) thesis, dissertation.
Dissident *m.* (-en, -en) dissenter.
Dissonanz *f.* (-, -en) dissonance, discord.
Distanz *f.* (-, -en) distance.
distanzieren (sich) *v.refl.* to dissociate oneself from.
Distel *f.* (-, -n) thistle.
distinguiert *a.* distinguished, distinguished-looking.
Distrikt *m.* (-[e]s, -e) district.
Disziplin *f.* (-, -en) discipline.
Disziplinar... disciplinary; ~**gewalt** *f.* disciplinary power; ~**verfahren** *n.* disciplinary action *or* proceedings.
Dividende *f.* (-, -n) dividend.
dividieren *v.t.* to divide.
Division *f.* (-, -en) (*auch mil.*) division.
Diwan *m.* (-s, -s) divan, sofa.
doch, *c.* yet; however; but, nevertheless; *ja* ~! yes, to be sure!; *nicht* ~! certainly not! don't!; yes (after negat. clause).
Docht *m.* (-[e]s, -e) wick.
Dock *n.* (-s, -s *u.* -e) dock, dock-yard.
Docke *f.* (-, -n) (*mech.*) mandrel.
Dogge *f.* (-, -n) bull-dog, mastiff.
Dohle *f.* (-, -n) jackdaw.
Doktor *m.* (-s, -en) doctor; physician.
Doktor: ~**würde** *f.* doctorate.
Doktrinär *m.* (-s, -e) doctrinaire, theorist.
Dokument *n.* (-[e]s, -e) *n.* document.
dokumentieren *v.t.* to prove by documentary evidence.
Dolch *m.* (-[e]s, -e) dagger, poniard, dirk.
dolmetschen *v.t.* to interpret.
Dolmetscher *m.* (-s, -) interpreter.

Dom *m.* (-[e]s, -e) cathedral.
Domäne *f.* (-, -n) domain, crown-land.
Domherr *m.* canon, prebendary.
dominieren *v.i.* to domineer (over).
Domino: ~spiel *n.* dominoes *pl.*; ~stein *m.* domino.
Domkapitel *n.* chapter.
Donner *m.* (-s, -) thunder; *vom* ~ *gerührt*, thunderstruck.
donnern *v.i.* to thunder.
Donnerschlag, *m.* thunder-clap.
Donnerstag *m.* (-[e]s, -e) Thursday.
Donnerwetter *n.*, ~! *i.* confound it!
Doppel *n.* (-s, -) duplicate.
Doppel: ~decker *m.* biplane; ~fenster *n.* double-window; ~flinte *f.* double- barrelled gun; ~gänger *m.* double.
doppelkohlensauer *a.* ~es Natron bicarbonate of soda.
doppelläufig *a.* double-barrelled.
Doppelpunkt *m.* colon.
doppelseitige Lungenentzündung *f.* double pneumonia.
doppelsinnig *a.* ambiguous.
Doppelspiel *n.* (tennis) doubles; (*fig.*) double game.
doppelt *a.* double, twofold; ~e *Buchführung*, book-keeping by double entry.
Doppeltür *f.* folding-doors *pl.*
Doppelzüngigkeit *f.* (-, -en) duplicity.
Dorf *n.* (-[e]s, Dörfer) village.
Dorn *m.* (-[e]s, -en *u.* -e) thorn, prickle.
dornenvoll *a.* (*fig.*) thorny.
Dörrobst *n.* (-[e]s, 0) dried fruit.
Dorsch *m.* (-es, -e) torsk, codling.
dort *adv.* there, yonder.
dorther *adv.* from there, thence.
dorthin *adv.* thither, that way.
dortig *a.* of that place; residing there.
Dose *f.* (-, -n) box; snuff-box.
dosieren *v.t.* to dose.
Dosis *f.* (-, Dosen) dose; *zu starke* ~, overdose.
Dotation *f.* (-, -en) donation.
dotieren *v.t.* to endow.
Dotter *m. or n.* (-s, -) yolk.
Dotterblume *f.* marsh-marigold.
Dozent *m.* (-en, -en) university teacher.
Drache *m.* (-n, -n) dragon; (paper) kite; (*Weib*) termigant.
Dragoner *m.* (-[e]s, -) dragoon.
Draht *m.* (-[e]s, Drähte) wire.
Drahtbürste *f.* wirebrush.
drahten *v.t.* to wire.
Draht: ~geflecht *n.* wire netting; ~los *a.* wireless; ~seil *n.* wire-rope; ~seilbahn *f.* funicular railway; ~verhau *n.* wire entanglements; ~zange *f.* pliers *pl.*; ~zieher *m.* wire-puller.
drahtlich *adv.* by telegraph.
Drama *n.* (-[e]s, Dramen) drama.
Dramatiker *m.* (-s, -) dramatist, playwright.

dramatisch *a.* dramatic.
dran=daran.
Dränage *f.* (-, -n) drainage.
Drang *m.* (-[e]s, 0) pressure; impulse.
drängen *v.t.* to throng, to press; to urge.
Drangsal *n.* (-[e]s, -e *u. f.* -, -e) oppression; distress, misery.
drangsalieren *v.t.* to worry, to torment.
dränieren *v.t.* to drain.
drastisch *a.* drastic; strong.
drauf *adv.*=darauf.
draussen *adv.* out of doors; without.
Drechselbank *f.* turner's lathe.
drechseln *v.t.* to turn (on a lathe).
Drechsler *m.* (-s, -) turner.
Drechslerarbeit, Drechslerei *f.* turnery.
Dreck *m.* (-[e]s, 0) dirt, filth.
dreckig *a.* dirty, muddy.
Dreh: ~bank *f.* (turner's) lathe; ~buch *n.* (Film) script, scenario; ~brücke *f.* swing-bridge.
drehen *v.t.* to turn; (Film) to shoot; (sich) ~ *v.refl.* to turn, to rotate, to revolve; *sich drehen um*, to pivot round.
Dreher *m.* (-s, -) (*mech.*) turner.
Dreh: ~kreuz *n.* turnstile; ~orgel *f.* barrel-organ; ~punkt *m.* pivot; ~schalter *m.* (*el.*) rotary switch; ~scheibe *f.* potter's wheel; (*rail.*) turntable; ~strom *m.* three-phase current; ~tür *f.* swinging door; ~stuhl *m.* swivel chair.
Drehung *f.* (-, -en) turn; revolution.
drei *a.* three.
Dreiachteltakt *m.* (-[e]s, -e) (*mus.*) three-eighth time.
dreibeinig *a.* three-legged.
Dreieck *n.* (-[e]s, -e) triangle.
dreieckig *a.* triangular, three-cornered.
dreierlei *a.* of three kinds.
dreifach *a.* threefold, treble; ~e *Ausfertigung*, triplicate.
Dreifaltigkeit *f.* (-, 0) Trinity.
Dreifuss *m.* (-es, -füsse) tripod; trivet.
dreijährig *a.* three years old; triennial.
Dreiklang *m.* (-[e]s, 0) (*mus.*) triad.
Dreikönigsfest *n.* Twelfth Night; Epiphany.
Dreimächte... tripartite.
dreimal *adv.* three times, thrice.
drein=darein.
Dreirad *n.* (-[e]s, -räder) tricycle.
dreissig *a.* thirty.
Dreissiger *m.* (-s, -) man of thirty years.
dreist *a.* bold, confident.
Dreistigkeit *f.* (-, -en) boldness, confidence.
Dreivierteltakt *m.* (-[e]s, 0) (*mus.*) triple time *or* measure.
Dreizack *m.* (-[e]s, -e) trident.
dreizehn *a.* thirteen.
Drell *m.* (-[e]s, -e) tickling, drill(ing).
dreschen *v.t.st.* to thrash.

Dresch: ~flegel *m.* flail; ~tenne *f.* thresh-ing-floor.

dressieren *v.t.* to break in (horses); to train dogs, etc.

Dressur *f.* (-, -en) breaking in; training.

Drillbohrer *m.* drill.

drillen *v.t.* to drill.

Drillich *m.* (-[e]s, -e) ticking.

Drillichanzug *m.* fatigue-dress.

Drilling *m.* (-[e]s, -e) triplet; lantern-wheel; three-barrelled gun.

drin=darin.

dringen *v.t. & i.st.* to urge; to penetrate.

dringlich *a.* urgent, pressing.

drinnen *adv.* within.

dritte *a.* third; ~ *Person* (*law*) third party.

Drittel *n.* (-s, -) third part, third.

drittens *adv.* thirdly.

drittletzt *a.* last but two, antepenultimate.

droben *adv.* above, on high, overhead.

Drogen *pl.* drugs *pl.*

Drogerie *f.* (-, -n) chemist's shop.

Drogist *m.* (-en, -en) druggist.

Drohbrief *m.* threatening letter.

drohen *v.i.* to threaten, to menace.

Drohne *f.* (-, -n) drone.

dröhnen *v.i.* to boom, to roar.

Drohung *f.* (- ,-en) threat, menace.

drollig *a.* droll, odd, funny.

Droschke *f.* (-, -n) cab; hansom.

Drossel *f.* (-, -n) thrush.

drosseln *v.t.* to throttle.

drüben, da drüben *adv.* yonder; over there.

drüber=darüber.

Druck *m.* (-[e]s, -e *u.* Drücke) pressure, compression; oppression; print, impression; ~ *auf einen ausüben,* to put pressure on someone

Druckbogen *m.* proof (sheet).

Drückeberger *m.* (-s, -) shirker.

drücken *v.t.* to press, to squeeze; (*Schuhe*) to pinch; (*Preise*) to bring down; (sich) ~ *v.refl.* to shirk work.

drucken *v.t.* to print.

Drücker *m.* (-s, -) trigger; latch.

Drucker *m.* (-s, -) printer.

Druckerei (-, -en) *f.* printing-office.

Drucker: ~presse *f.* printing-press; ~schwärze *f.* printer's ink.

Druckfehler *m.* misprint.

druckfertig *a.* ready for the press.

Druck: ~knopf *m.* patent fastener; ~sache *f.* printed matter; ~schrift, print.

drum=darum.

drunten *adv.* there below.

drunter und drüber, upside down.

Drüse *f.* (-, -n) gland.

Dschungel *m.* (-s, -) jungle.

du *pn.* thou; you.

Dublette *f.* (-, -n) duplicate.

ducken *v.t.* to duck; to humble; (*sich*) ~, to submit, to stoop.

Duckmäuser (-s, -) *m.* sneak, shuffler.

Dudelsack *m.* (-[e]s, -säcke) bagpipes.

Dudelsackpfeifer *m.* bagpiper.

Duell *n.* (-[e]s, -e) duel.

duellieren (sich) *v.refl.* to fight a duel.

Duett *n.* (-[e]s, -e) duet.

Duft *m.* (-[e]s, Düfte) scent, fragrance.

duften *v.i.* to smell sweet.

dulden *v.t.* to endure; to tolerate.

dumm *a.* dull, stupid.

Dummheit *f.* (-, -en) stupidity; blunder.

Dummkopf *m.* (-[e]s, -köpfe) block-head.

dumpf *a.* hollow, dull; close, musty, damp; ~ig *a.* musty, damp; dull.

Düne *f.* (-, -n) sandhill, dune.

düngen *v.t.* to manure.

Dünger *m.* (-s, -) dung, manure; fertilizer.

Dünkel *m.* (-s, 0) conceit, arrogance.

dünkelhaft *a.* arrogant, conceited.

dunkel *a.* dark, dusky, gloomy; obscure; mysterious.

Dunkelheit *f.* (-, -en) darkness; obscurity.

Dunkelkammer *m.* (*phot.*) dark room.

dünken *v.t.imp.* to seem, to appear; to think.

dünn *a.* thin, fine, slender; (*Getränk*) weak; (*Luft*) rare.

Dünndruckpapier *n.* (-s, -e) India paper.

Dünne *f.* (-, 0) thinness; sparseness.

Dunst *m.* (-es, Dünste) vapour; steam; fume (of wine).

dünsten *v.t.* to stew.

dunstig *a.* vaporous; hazy, dank.

Dur *n.* (*mus.*) major.

Duodez *n.* (-es, 0) duodecimo.

düpieren *v.t.* to dupe.

Duplikat *n.* ([e]s, -e) duplicate.

durch *pr.* through, by; ~ *a.* well-done; ~ *und* ~, thoroughly; ~ *und* ~ *nass,* wet through.

durcharbeiten *v.t.* to work through.

durchaus *adv.* by all means, absolutely; ~ *nicht,* by no means.

durchbeissen (sich) ~ *v.refl.st.* (*fig.*) to fight one's way through.

durchbilden *v.t.* to give a thorough edu-cation.

durchblättern *v.t.* to skim (a book).

Durchblick *m.* vista, peep.

durchblicken: ~ *lassen,* to give to under-stand.

durchbohren *v.t.* to pierce; to perforate.

durchbrechen *v.t. & i.st.* (*s*) to break through.

durchbrennen *v.i.ir.* (*s*) (*el.*) to blow, to fuse; (*fig.*) to abscond.

durchbringen *v.t.ir.* to squander.

durchbrochen *a.* open (pierced) work.

Durchbruch *m.* (-[e]s, -brüche) breach; (*mil.*) breakthrough.

durchdenken *v.t.ir.* to think over.

durchdrängen (sich) *v.refl.* to elbow one's way (through the crowd).

durchdringen *v.t.st.* to penetrate; ~ *v.i.st.* (s) (*fig.*) to prevail.
durchdringend *a.* penetrating, sharp.
durcheinander *adv.* pell-mell.
Durcheinander *n.* (-s, 0) muddle.
durchfahren *v.i.st.* (s) to pass through.
Durchfahrt *f.* (-, -en) passage, thoroughfare, gateway; transit.
Durchfall *m.* (-[e]s, -fälle) diarrhœa.
durchfallen *v.i.st.* (s) to fall through; to fail; to be ploughed (at an examination).
durchfinden *v.t.st.* (*sich*) to find one's way.
durchfliessen *v.i.st.* (s) u. *v.t.st.* to flow through.
durchforschen *v.t.* to explore.
Durchforschung *f.* (-, -en) exploration.
durchfragen (sich) *v. refl.* to ask one's way through.
durchfressen *v.t.st.* to corrode.
Durchfuhr *f.* (-, 0) transit.
durchführen *v.t.* to accomplish, to implement, to carry through.
durchfurchen *v.t.* to furrow, to wrinkle; to plough (the sea).
Durchgang *m.* (-[e]s, ~gänge) passage, transit; ~sverkehr *m.* transit traffic; ~szoll *m.* transit duty.
durchgängig *a.* general, common; ~ *adv.* in all cases.
durchgehen *v.t.st.* to peruse, to go through; ~ *v.i.st.* (s) to abscond; to bolt.
durchgehend *a.* (*Zug, Fahrkarte*) through.
durchgehends *a.* generally, universally.
durchgeistigen *v.t.* to spiritualize.
durchgreifen *v.i.st.* to take energetic action.
durchgreifend *a.* determined, energetic.
durchhalten *v.t.* to see through; ~ *v.i.* to stick it out.
durchhauen *v.t.ir.* to cut through; to flog.
durchhecheln *v.t.* to criticize.
durchhelfen *v.i.st.* to support; (sich) ~ *v.refl.* to make shift.
durchkämpfen *v.t.* to fight out.
durchkommen *v.i.st.* (s) to get through; (*Prüfung*) to pass; to succeed; to recover.
durchkönnen *v.i.ir.* to be able to pass.
durchkreuzen *v.t.* to cross; to thwart.
durchlassen *v.t.st.* to let pass, to let through.
durchlässig *a.* previous.
Durchlaucht *f.* (-, -en) Serene Highness.
durchlaufen *v.i.st.* (s) to run through; ~ *v.t.st.* to wear out (shoes); to run over (a book).
durchleben *v.t.* to live through.
durchlesen *v.t.st.* to read through.
durchleuchten *v.t.* to X-ray.
durchlöchern *v.t.* to perforate; to riddle.
durchmachen *v.t.* to go through.
Durchmarsch *m.* (-es, -märsche) (troops) transit.

durchmessen *v.t.st.* to traverse.
Durchmesser *m.* (-s, -) diameter.
durchmüssen *v.i.ir.* to have to pass through.
durchmustern *v.t.* to scan, to review.
durchnässen *v.t.* to soak, to wet through.
durchnehmen *v.t.st.* to go over, to explain.
durchpausen *v.t.* to trace.
durchprügeln *v.t.* to cudgel, to thrash.
durchqueren *v.t.* to cross.
durchrechnen *v.t.* to reckon over, to examine.
durchreiben *v.t.st.* to rub a hole in.
Durchreise *f.* (-, -n) passage.
durchreisen *v.i.* (s) to travel through.
durchreissen *v.t.st.* to tear asunder.
durchsäuern *v.t.* to leaven thoroughly.
durchschauen *v.i.* to look through; ~ *v.t.* (*fig.*) to see through.
durchschauern *v.t.* to fill with awe.
durchscheinen *v.i.st.* (s) to shine through; to be transparent.
durchscheuern *v.t.* to rub through.
durchschiessen *v.t.st.* to interleave (a book); (*im Drucke*) to lead, to interline.
Durchschlag *m.* (-[e]s, -schläge) (carbon) copy.
durchschlagen *v.i.st.* to penetrate; (*fig.*) to tell, to have effect; (sich) ~ *v.refl.st.* to rough it.
durchschlüpfen *v.i.* (s) to slip through.
durchschneiden (sich) *v.refl.st.* to intersect.
Durchschnitt *m.* (-[e]s, -e) cut; intersection; profile; average.
durchschnittlich *a. & adv.* average; on an average.
durchschreiten *v.t.st.* to stride through.
Durchschuss *m.* (-schusses, -schüsse) (*Druck*) leads *pl.*, space-line; (*Gewebe*) weft.
durchschwitzen *v.t.* to soak with sweat.
durchsehen *v.t.st.* to revise, to look over.
durchseihen *v.t.* to filter, to strain.
durchsein *v.i.ir.* (s) to be done with.
durchsetzen *v.t.* (*fig.*) to carry through; to mix with.
durchsetzt (mit) *a.* honeycombed with.
Durchsicht *f.* (-, -en) revision, perusal.
durchsichtig *a.* transparent.
durchsickern *v.i.* (s) to trickle through, to ooze through; (*fig.*) to transpire.
durchsieben *v.t.* to sift, to bolt.
durchspielen *v.t.* to go through (a piece of music).
durchsprechen *v.t.st.* to talk (a thing) over.
Durchstecherei *f.* (-, -en) intrigue, collusion.
Durchstich *m.* (-[e]s, -e) (*rail.*) cutting, excavation.
durchstöbern *v.t.* to rummage, to ransack.
durchstossen *v.t.st.* to break by thrusting; to pierce, to run through the body.

durchstreichen *v.t.st.* to strike out, to cancel; to roam through, to scour (the country).
durchstreifen *v.t.* to rove through, to range.
durchsuchen *v.t.* to search, to ransack.
Durchsuchung *f.* (-, -en) search.
durchtränken *v.t.* to soak with.
durchtrieben *a.* arrant, cunning.
durchwachsen *a.* (*vom Fleisch*) streaked, streaky.
durchwärmen *v.t.* to warm thoroughly.
durchweg *adv.* throughout.
durchweichen *v.t.* to soak thoroughly, to drench; ~ *v.i.* (s) to become soft.
durchwinden *v.t.st.* to entwine; (sich) ~ *v.refl.st.* to struggle through.
durchwischen *v.i.* (s) to slip away.
durchwühlen *v.t.* to root up; (*fig.*) to ransack.
durchzählen *v.t.* to count over.
Durchzug *m.* (-[e]s, -züge) passage, march through.
dürfen *v.i.ir.* to be allowed; *darf ich?* may I?; *du darfst nicht*, you must not.
dürftig *a.* needy, indigent; scanty, insufficient.
dürr *a.* dry, arid; withered; barren; lean; ~*e Worte*, plain language.
Dürre *f.* (-, -n) drought.
Durst *m.* (-es, 0) thirst.
dursten, dürsten *v.i.* to thirst, to be thirsty; to long for.
durstig *a.* thirsty.
Dusche *f.* (-, -n) douche; shower-bath.
Düse *f.* (-, -n) nozzle.
Düsenjäger *m.* (*avi.*) jet-fighter.
duselig *a.* dizzy, drowsy.
düster *a.* gloomy, dismal.
Dutzend *n.* (-s, -e) dozen.
dutzendweise *adv.* by the dozen.
duzen *v.t.* to thee and thou; *sich* ~, to thou each other.
Dynamik *f.* (-, 0) dynamics *pl.*
Dynamit *m.* (-s, 0) dynamite.
Dynamomaschine *f.* dynamo.
Dynastie *f.* (-, -en) dynasty.
dynastisch *a.* dynastic(al).
D-Zug *m.* (-[e]s, -züge) corridor train.

E

Ebbe *f.* (-, -n) ebb, low water.
ebben *v.i.* to ebb.
eben *a.* even, level; flat; (*math.*) plane; ~ *adv.* just; precisely; ~ *erst*, just now; *ebenso*, just so, quite as.
Ebenbild *n.* (-[e]s, -er) image; likeness.
ebenbürtig *a.* of equal birth.
Ebene *f.* (-, -n) plain; (*math.*) plane.
ebenfalls *adv.* likewise, too, also.

G.D.

Ebenholz *n.* (-es, 0) ebony.
Ebenmass *n.* (-es, -e) symmetry.
Eber *m.* (-s, -) boar.
Eberesche *f.* mountain-ash, roan-tree.
ebnen *v.t.* to level, to smoothe.
Echo *n.* (-s, -s) echo.
echt *a.* genuine; true; (*Farben*) fast; (*Perle, Diamant*) real.
Ecke *f.* (-, -n) corner, nook; *an allen* ~*n und Enden*, everywhere; *um die* ~ *gehen*, (*fig.*) to go west.
Ecker *f.* (-, -n) acorn.
Eckhaus *n.* corner-house.
eckig *a.* angular; (*fig.*) awkward.
Eck: ~platz *m.* corner-seat; ~stein *m.* corner-stone.
edel *a.* noble; well-born; generous; precious; *die edlen Teile*, the vital parts.
Edelmann *m.* nobleman.
Edelmetall *n.* rare metal, precious metal.
Edelmut *n.* (-[e]s, 0) generosity.
edelmütig *a.* generous.
Edel: ~stein *m.* precious stone; ~tanne *f.* silver-fir, pitch-pine.
Edikt *n.* (-[e]s, -e) edict.
Efeu *m.* (-s, 0) ivy.
Effekten *m.pl.* (*com.*) securities.
effektiv *a.* effective; real.
egal *a.* equal; all one, the same.
Egge *f.* (-, -n) harrow.
eggen *v.t.* to harrow.
Egoismus *m.* (-, 0) selfishness, egotism.
Egoist *m.* (-en, -en) selfish person, egotist.
egoistisch *a.* selfish.
ehe *c.* before.
Ehe *f.* (-, -n) marriage, wedlock; matrimony; *aus erster* ~, of his first marriage; *wilde* ~, concubinage.
ehebrechen *v.i.st.* to commit adultery.
Ehebrecher *m.* (-s, -) adulterer.
Ehebrecherin *f.* (-, -nen) adulteress.
ehebrecherisch *a.* adulterous.
Ehebruch *m.* adultery; (*law*) misconduct.
ehedem *adv.* formerly.
Ehe: ~frau *f.* wife, consort; ~gatte *m.* husband; spouse; ~gattin *f.* wife, consort.
Ehe: ~hälfte *f.* (*fam.*) better half, spouse; ~hindernis *n.* (*marriage*) impediment; ~leute *pl.* married people, spouses.
ehelich *a.* matrimonial; legitimate.
ehelichen *v.t.* to marry.
ehelos *a.* unmarried, single.
Ehelosigkeit *f.* (-, 0) celibacy, unmarried state.
ehemalig *a.* former; late.
ehemals *adv.* formerly.
Ehe: ~mann *m.* husband; ~paar *n.* married couple.
eher *adv.* sooner; rather.
Eherecht *n.* matrimonial law.
ehern *a.* brazen.
Ehescheidung *f.* divorce.

Ehe: ~stand *m.* married state, wedlock; ~vertrag *m.* marriage-settlement; ~trennung *f.* separation; ~weib *n.* spouse, wife.
Ehrabschneider *m.* slanderer.
ehrbar *a.* respectable; honourable.
Ehre *f.* (-, -n) honour, reputation.
ehren *v.t.* to honour, to respect.
Ehren: ~amt *n.* post of honour; ~amtlich *a.* unpaid; ~bürger *m.* (honorary) freeman; ~bürgerrecht *n.* freedom of the city; ~gericht *n.* court of honour.
ehrenhaft *a.* honourable.
ehrenhalber *adv.* for honour's sake.
Ehren: ~handel *m.* affair of honour; ~kränkung *f.* affront, libel, defamation; ~mann *m.* man of honour; ~mitglied *n.* honorary member.
ehrenrührig *a.* defamatory, calumnious.
ehrenvoll *a.* honourable, creditable.
Ehrenwache *f.* guard of honour.
ehrenwert *a.* respectable.
Ehrenwort *n.* word of honour.
ehrerbietig *a.* respectful, reverential.
Ehrerbietung *f.* (-, 0) reverence.
Ehrfurcht *f.* (-, 0) reverence, awe.
Ehr: ~gefühl *n.* sense of honour; ~geiz *m.* ambition.
ehrgeizig *a.* ambitious.
ehrlich *a.* honest, fair, faithful.
Ehrlichkeit *f.* (-, 0) honesty, faithfulness.
ehrlos *a.* dishonourable, infamous.
Ehrlosigkeit *f.* (-, 0) infamy.
ehrwürdig *a.* venerable, reverend.
Ei *n.* (-[e]s, -er) egg; *gekochtes* ~, boiled egg (*hartgekocht*, hardboiled, *weichgekocht*, softboiled); *frischgelegtes* ~, newlaid egg.
ei! *i.* ah! why; indeed!
Eibe *f.* (-, -n) yew(-tree).
Eichamt *n.* (-s, -ämter) gauging office.
Eiche *f.* (-, -n) oak.
Eichel *f.* (-, -n) acorn; glans; (*Karten*) club.
eichelförmig *a.* acorn-shaped.
eichen *v.t.* to gauge.
eichen *a.* oaken, oak.
Eichenlaub *n.* oak-leaves *pl.*
Eich: ~hörnchen, ~kätzchen *n.* (-s, -) squirrel; ~mass *n.* standard.
Eid *m.* (-es, -e) oath; *einen* ~ *leisten*, to take an oath; *unter* ~, on oath; *an Eides statt, eidesstattlich*, in lieu of an oath.
eidbrüchig *a.* perjured, forsworn.
Eidechse *f.* (-, -n) lizard.
Eiderdaunen *f.pl.* eider-down.
Eidesformel *f.* formula of an oath.
eidesstattliche Erklärung *f.* statutory declaration.
eidlich *a.* by oath, upon oath, sworn; ~e Versicherung *f.* affidavit; *eine* ~*e Versicherung abgeben*, to make an affidavit.
Eidotter *m.* or *n.* yolk.

Eier: ~becher *m.* egg-cup; ~kuchen *m.* omelet.
eierlegend *a.* oviparous.
Eier: ~schale *f.* egg-shell; ~stock *m.* ovary.
Eifer *m.* (-s, 0) zeal, ardour; passion.
eifern *v.i.* to be zealous.
Eifersucht *f.* (-, 0) jealousy.
Eifersüchtelei *f.* (-, -en) petty jealousy.
eifersüchtig *a.* jealous.
eifrig *a.* zealous; ardent, eager.
Eigelb *n.* yolk.
eigen *a.* own; singular, strange, odd.
Eigenart *f.* peculiarity; originality.
eigenartig *a.* original, peculiar.
Eigenbrödler *m.* (-s, -) crank.
Eigendünkel *m.* (-s, 0) self-conceit.
eigenhändig *a.* with one's own hand.
Eigenheit *f.* (-, -en) peculiarity, singularity; idiosyncrasy.
eigenmächtig *a.* arbitrary, autocratic.
Eigenname *m.* (-ns, -n) proper name.
Eigennutz *m.* (-es, 0) self-interest.
eigennützig *a.* self-seeking, selfish.
eigens *adv.* particularly, expressly.
Eigenschaft *f.* (-, -en) quality, property; attribute; (*chem.*) property; *in seiner Eigenschaft als . . .*, in his capacity of.
Eigenschaftswort *n.* adjective.
Eigensinn *m.* (-[e]s, 0) obstinacy.
eigentlich *a.* proper; real; peculiar; true; ~ *adv.* properly; exactly.
Eigentum *n.* (-[e]s, -tümer) property.
Eigentümer *m.* (-s, -) owner, proprietor.
eigentümlich *a.* peculiar; proper.
Eigentümlichkeit *f.* (-, -en) peculiarity.
Eigentumsrecht *n.* right of possession; copyright.
eigenwillig *a.* self-willed.
eignen (sich) *v.refl.* to suit, to be fit, to be adapted for.
Eilbestellung *f.* express delivery.
Eilbote *m.* courier, express messenger.
Eilbrief *m.* express letter.
Eile *f.* (-, 0) haste, speed, hurry.
eilen *v.i.* to hasten, to make haste; *die Sache eilt (nicht)*, the matter requires despatch; there is no hurry.
eilend, eilends *i.* & *adv.* speedy; hastily.
eilfertig *a.* hasty, precipitate, speedy.
Eilgut *n.* express goods; *als* ~ or *mit Eilboten schicken*, to send express.
eilig *a.* hasty, speedy; *ich hab es sehr* ~, I am pressed for time.
Eil: ~marsch *m.* forced march; ~zug *m.* fast train.
Eimer *m.* (-s, -) pail, bucket.
ein *adv.* in; *ich weiss nicht wo* ~ *und aus*, I am at my wits' end.
ein, eine, ein *art.* a, an; *unser* ~er, people like you and me; ~er nach dem andern, one by one; ~s, one; *in* ~em zu, continuously.

einander *a.* one another, each other; *nach* ~, in succession, one after another.

einarbeiten (sich) *v.refl.* to familiarize oneself (with), to get used to a job.

einarmig *a.* one-armed.

einäschern *v.t.* to cremate.

einatmen *v.t.* to inhale, to breathe.

einäugig *a.* one-eyed.

Einbahnstrasse *f.* one-way street.

Einbahnverkehr *m.* one-way traffic.

einbalsamieren *v.t.* to embalm.

Einband *m.* (-[e]s, -bände) binding; *in Leinwand* ~, clothbound; *in Leder* ~, leatherbound.

einbändig *a.* in one volume.

einbedingen *v.t.st.* to include in the bargain.

einbegreifen *v.t.st.* to include.

einbehalten *v.t.st.* to keep back.

einberufen *v.t.st.* to convene (a meeting); (*mil.*) to call up.

einbettiges Zimmer *n.* single room.

einbeziehen *v.t.* to include.

Einbeziehung *f.* (-, -en) inclusion.

einbiegen *v.t.* to bend inward; ~ *v.i.* to turn into.

einbilden (sich) *v.refl.* to imagine, to fancy; *sich etwas (viel)* ~, to think a good deal of oneself.

Einbildung *f.* (-, -en) imagination, fancy; conceit.

einbinden *v.t.st.* to bind (a book).

Einblick *m.* (-s, -e) insight.

einbrechen *v.i.st.* (s) to break into; to set in.

Einbrecher *m.* (-s, -) burglar.

einbrennen *v.t.ir.* to burn in; to brand.

einbringen *v.t.ir.* to bring in; to yield; *wieder* ~, to recoup.

Einbruch *m.* (-[e]s, -brüche) burglary; (*mil.*) penetration; ~ *der Nacht*, nightfall.

Einbuchtung *f.* (-, -en) recess.

einbürgern *v.t.* to naturalize.

Einbusse *f.* (-, -n) loss.

einbüssen *v.t.* to suffer loss; to lose.

eindämmen *v.t.* to dam up, to embank.

eindecken (sich) (mit) *v.refl.* to lay in.

Eindecker *m.* (-s, -) monoplane.

eindeutig *a.* unambiguous, univocal.

eindringen *v.i.st.* (s) to penetrate.

eindringlich *a.* impressive.

Eindringling *m.* (-s, -e) intruder.

Eindruck *m.* (-[e]s, -drücke) impression.

Einehe *f.* monogamy.

einengen *v.t.* to confine; to cramp.

Einer *m.* (-s, -) (*ar.*) unit; single number, digit.

einerlei *a.* of the same kind, the same; *es ist mir* ~, it's all one to me.

Einerlei *n.* sameness, identity.

einerseits *adv.* on the one hand.

einfach *a.* single, simple; plain; ~e Buch-

führung *f.* book-keeping by single entry.

Einfachheit *f.* (-, 0) simplicity.

einfädeln *v.t.* to thread; (*fig.*) to contrive, to scheme.

einfahren *v.i.* (s) to enter; to descend (into a mine).

Einfahrt *f.* (-, -en) entrance.

Einfall *m.* (-[e]s, -fälle) invasion; idea, whim, fancy.

einfallen *v.i.st.* (s) to fall in; to interrupt; to invade; to occur (to one's mind); *es will mir nicht* ~, I can't think of it; (*das*) *fällt mir gar nicht ein!* catch me doing that!

Einfalt *f.* (-, 0) simplicity; silliness.

einfältig *a.* simple; silly.

Einfamilienhaus *n.* one-family cottage.

einfangen *v.t.st.* to seize.

einfarbig *a.* of one colour; plain.

einfassen *v.t.* to set; to mount.

Einfassung *f.* (-, -en) setting; foil.

einfetten *v.t.* to oil, to grease; to lubricate.

einfinden (sich) *v.refl.st.* to turn up.

einflechten *v.t.st.* to mention casually.

einfliessen *v.i.st.* (*eine Bemerkung, ein Wort*) ~ *lassen*, to put in (a word, a remark).

einflössen *v.t.* to imbue, to inspire with.

Einfluss *m.* (-flusses, -flüsse) influence.

einflussreich *a.* influential.

einflüstern *v.t.* to whisper to, to suggest.

einfordern *v.t.* to call in.

einförmig *a.* uniform; monotonous.

Einförmigkeit *f.* (-, -en) uniformity, monotony.

einfrieden *v.i.* to enclose.

einfriedigen *v.t.* to enclose.

einfrieren *v.t.st.* (s) to freeze in.

einfügen *v.t.* to insert.

Einfuhr *f.* (-, -en) importation, import.

einführen *v.t.* to import; to introduce.

Einführung *f.* (-, -en) introduction.

Einführungsbesprechung *f.* general orientation.

Einfuhrzoll *m.* import-duty.

einfüllen *v.t.* to fill into.

Eingabe *f.* (-, -n) petition; memorial.

Eingang *m.* (-[e]s, -gänge) entrance, entry; way in; preamble.

eingeben *v.t.st.* to administer; to prompt.

ein: ~*gebildet a.* imaginary; conceited; ~*geboren a.* native.

Eingebung *f.* (-, -en) inspiration.

eingedenk *a.* mindful of.

eingefleischt *a.* inveterate.

eingehen *v.i.st.* (s) (*Brief*)to come to hand; (*Ehe*) to contract; *eine Wette* ~, to make a bet; to consent to; to decay; to shrink.

eingehend *a.* thorough, exhaustive; (*Post etc.*) incoming.

eingeklemmt *a.* trapped.

Eingemachte[s] *n.* (-n, 0) preserves *pl*; (*in Essig*) pickles *pl*.
eingemeinden *v.t.* to incorporate.
eingeschneit *a.* snowed up.
eingeschränkt *a.* restrained, limited.
eingestandenermassen *adv.* avowedly.
Eingeständnis *n.* (-nisses, -nisse) avowal.
eingestehen *v.t.st.* to confess, to avow.
Eingeweide *n.* (-s, -) entrails, intestines, bowels *pl*.
eingewöhnen (sich) *v.refl.* to accustom oneself to.
eingewurzelt *a.* inveterate, deep-rooted.
eingezogen *a.* retired, solitary; quiet.
eingiessen *v.t.st.* to pour in; (*ein Glas*) to pour out.
eingleisig *a.* single-track.
eingraben *v.t.st.* to engrave; (sich) ~ *v.refl.* (*mil.*) to entrench.
eingreifen *v.i.st.* (*von Zahnrädern*) to interlock; to interfere.
Eingriff *m.* (-[e]s, -e) interference; (*med.*) operation; (*mech.*) mesh.
Einhalt *m.* (-[e]s, 0) check.
einhalten *v.t.st.* to observe.
einhandeln *v.t.* to purchase, to buy.
einhändig *a.* one-handed, single-handed.
einhändigen *v.t.* to hand (over).
Einhändigung *f.* (-, 0) delivery.
einhängen *v.t.* to hang (up).
einhauchen *v.t.* to inspire (with).
einhegen *v.t.* to enclose.
einheimisch *a.* indigenous.
einheimsen *v.t.* to garner, to house.
einheiraten *v.i.* to marry into.
Einheit *f.* (-, -en) unity; (*ar.*) unit.
Einheits: ~preis *m.* uniform price; ~staat *m.* unitary state; ~tarif *m.* flat rate.
einheitlich *a.* uniform, homogeneous.
einheizen *v.t.* to light a fire.
einhellig *a.* unanimous.
einher *adv.* forth, along, on.
einholen *v.t.* to catch up with; to collect, to get.
Einhorn *n.* (-[e]s, -hörner) unicorn.
einhüllen *v.t.* to envelop.
einig *a.* united.
einigen *v.t.* to unite; (sich) ~ *v.refl.* to come to terms (with).
einige[r] *pron.* einiges *pn.* some, any; einige *pl.* some, a few; *einige hundert*, a hundred odd.
einigermassen *adv.* to a certain extent.
Einigkeit *f.* (-, 0) union, unanimity, concord.
Einigung *f.* (-, -en) agreement, union.
einimpfen *v.t.* to inoculate.
einjagen *v.t. einem einen Schrecken* ~, to frighten someone.
einjährig *a.* one year old.
einkassieren *v.t.* to cash.
Einkauf *m.* (-[e]s, -käufe) purchase; *Einkäufe machen*, to go shopping.

einkaufen *v.t.* to buy, to purchase; to shop.
Einkaufspreis *m.* cost-price, prime-cost.
einkehren *v.i.* (s) to stop *or* to put up at an hotel.
einkerben *v.t.* to notch.
einkerkern *v.t.* to imprison.
einklagen *v.t.* to sue for.
einklammern *v.t.* to put in brackets.
Einklang *m.* (-[e]s, 0) unison, harmony; *im* ~ *stehen*, to be in unison, to agree.
einkleiden *v.t.* to put into uniform; (*Gedanken*) to put into words.
einklemmen *v.t.* to squeeze in, to jam, to wedge in.
einkochen *v.t.* (*Frucht*) to bottle.
einkommen *v.i.st.* (s) to apply to a person for a thing.
Einkommen *n.* (-s, -) income, revenue.
Einkommensteuer *f.* income tax; ~erklärung *f.* income tax return.
einkreisen *v.t.* to encircle; (*mil.*) to envelop.
Einkreisung *f.* (-, -en) encirclement.
Einkünfte *f.pl.* income, revenue, rent.
einladen *v.t.st.* to invite, to bid; (*Güter*) to load.
Einladung *f.* (-, -en) invitation.
Einlage *f.* (-, -n) (*Brief*) enclosure; (*Bank*) deposit; (*Schuh*) arch-support; (*Zahn*) filling; (*Schneiderei*) wadding.
einlagern *v.t.* to store, to warehouse.
Einlass *m.* (-lasses, 0) admission; inlet.
einlassen *v.t.st.* to let in; to admit; (sich) ~ *v.refl.* to engage in.
Einlasskarte *f.* ticket of admission.
Einlauf *m.* (-s, -läufe) enema.
einlaufen *v.i.st.* (s) to shrink; (*Schiff*) to make *or* enter a port; (*Briefe, Gelder*) to come to hand; *nicht einlaufend a.* unshrinkable.
einleben (sich) *v.refl.* to accustom oneself.
Einlegearbeit *f.* inlaid work, intarsia.
einlegen *v.t.* to lay in, to put in; to inlay; to deposit; (*Früchte etc.*) to preserve, to pickle; (*Berufung*) to lodge; *ein Wort für einen* ~, to intercede for someone.
einleiten *v.t.* to introduce; (*Massnahmen*) to initiate.
einleitend *a.* introductory.
Einleitung *f.* (-, -en) introduction.
einlenken *v.i.* to come round.
einlernen *v.t.* to get by heart; to teach, to drill.
einleuchten *v.i.* to be evident.
einliefern *v.t.* to deliver up.
einliegend *a.* enclosed, herewith.
einlösen *v.t.* to redeem (a pledge); (*Wechsel*) to honour, to take up; (*Scheck*) to cash.
Einlösung *f.* (-, -en) redemption.
einlullen *v.t.* to lull to sleep.
einmachen *v.t.* to pickle, to preserve.

einmal *adv.* once; *auf* ~, all at once, on a sudden; *nicht* ~, not even.

Einmaleins *n.* (-, -) multiplication table.

einmalig *a.* non-recurring.

Einmarsch *m.* (-[e]s, -märsche) entry.

einmarschieren *v.i.* (*s*) to march in.

einmauern *v.t.* to wall in.

einmengen (sich) *v.refl.* to meddle (with), to interfere (in).

einmieten (sich) *v.refl.* to take lodgings.

einmischen (sich) *v.refl.* to interfere (in), to meddle (with).

Einmischung *f.* (-, -en) intervention, interference.

einmonatlich *a.* one month's.

einmünden *v.i.* to flow into, to debouch.

einmütig *a.* unanimous.

Einmütigkeit *f.* (-, 0) concord, unanimity.

einnähen *v.t.* to sew in.

Einnahme *f.* (-, -n) receipt, income, revenue; capture, taking; *Einnahmen und Ausgaben*, revenue and expenditure.

einnehmen *v.t.st.* to take; (*fig.*) to charm, to captivate; (*den Kopf*) to disturb.

einnehmend *a.* engaging, charming.

Einnehmer *m.* (-s, -) receiver, collector.

einnicken *v.i.* (*s*) to nod off.

einnisten (sich) *v.refl.* to get a footing.

Einöde *f.* (-, -n) desert, solitude.

einölen *v.t.* to oil, to grease.

einordnen *v.t.* to classify; to file.

einpacken *v.t.* to pack up.

einpauken *v.t.* (*Studenten*) to coach, to cram.

einpferchen *v.t.* to huddle together.

einpflanzen *v.t.* to inculcate.

einpökeln *v.t.* to salt, to pickle.

einprägen *v.t.* to impress.

einquartieren *v.t.* to quarter, to billet.

Einquartierung *f.* (-, -en) soldiers quartered *pl.*

einquetschen *v.t.* to squeeze in.

einrahmen *v.t.* to frame.

einräumen *v.t.* to clear away; to concede.

einrechnen *v.t.* to include (in an account).

Einrede *f.* (-, -n) objection, exception; (*law*) plea.

einreden *v.t.* to talk into; ~ *v.i.* to remonstrate.

einreiben *v.t.st.* to rub into.

einreichen *v.t.* to hand in, to tender; *ein Gesuch* ~, to file *or* present a petition.

einreihen *v.t.* to range, to enroll.

einreihig *a.* (*Rock*) single-breasted.

Einreise *f.* (-, -n) entry; ~*erlaubnis f.* entry permit.

einreissen *v.t.st.* to pull down, to tear, to rend; ~ *v.i.st.* (*s*) to gain ground.

einrenken *v.t.* to set (a bone); to arrange.

einrennen *v.t.st.* to force open by running against.

einrichten *v.t.* to arrange, to settle; (*Wohnung*) to furnish.

Einrichtung *f.* (-, -en) contrivance; arrangement, institution; furniture.

Einrichtungsgegenstände *m.pl.* furnishings.

einrosten *v.i.* (*s*) to get rusty.

einrücken *v.i.* (*s*) to march in(to); to enter; ~ *v.t.* to insert.

Eins *f.* (-, Einsen) one.

einsagen *v.t.* to prompt.

einsalzen *v.t.st.* to salt, to cure.

einsam *a.* lonely, solitary.

Einsamkeit *f.* (-, 0) solitude.

einsammeln *v.t.* to gather in, to collect.

Einsatz *m.* (-es, -sätze) stake, pool; (*mil.*) commitment, employment.

einsaugen *v.t.st.* to suck in; to absorb.

einsäumen *v.t.* to hem; to border.

einschalten *v.t.* to insert; (*el.*) to switch on; (*anderen Gang*) to put in another gear.

einschärfen *v.t.* (*fig.*) to impress.

einschätzen *v.t.* to assess; to estimate.

einschenken *v.t.* to pour out, to fill; *einem reinen Wein* ~, to tell one the plain truth.

einschicken *v.t.* to send in.

einschieben *v.t.st.* to interpolate.

einschiessen (sich) *v.refl.st.* (*mil.*) to get the range.

einschiffen *v.t.* & *v.refl.* to embark.

Einschiffung *f.* (-, -en) embarkation.

einschlafen *v.i.st.* (*s*) to go to sleep, to fall asleep.

einschläfern *v.t.* to lull to sleep.

einschläfernd *a.* soporific; narcotic.

Einschlag *m.* (-[e]s, -schläge) woof, weft; tuck; touch.

einschlagen *v.t.st.* to beat in; to break; to wrap up; *einen Weg* ~, to take a road; ~ *v.i.st.* (*Blitz*) to strike.

einschlägig *a.* pertinent.

einschleichen (sich) *v.refl.st.* to creep in.

einschleppen *v.t.* (*Krankheit*) to introduce.

einschliessen *v.t.st.* to lock up; to enclose; (*fig.*) to include.

einschliesslich *a.* inclusive.

Einschluss *m.* (-schlusses, -schlüsse) inclusion; *mit* ~ *von*, inclusive of, including.

einschmeicheln (sich) *v.refl.* to ingratiate oneself.

einschmelzen *v.t.st.* to melt down.

einschmieren *v.t.* to grease, to oil.

einschmuggeln *v.t.* to smuggle.

einschneiden *v.t.st.,* ~**d** *a.* incisive, thorough.

einschneien *v.t.* to snow up.

Einschnitt *m.* (-[e]s, -e) incision; notch.

einschränken *v.t.* to confine; to restrain; (sich) ~ *v.refl.* to retrench.

Einschränkung *f.* (-, -en) limitation, restriction; retrenchment.

Einschreibe: ~**brief** *m.* registered letter; ~**gebühr** *f.* registration-fee.

einschreiben *v.t.st.* to register; (sich) ~ *v.refl.st.* to enter one's name.

einschreiten *v.i.st.* (*s*) to intervene.
einschrumpfen *v.i.*(*s*) to shrink up.
Einschub *m.* (-[e]s, -schübe) interpolation.
einschüchtern *v.t.* to intimidate.
einschwärzen *v.t.* to smuggle in.
einschwenken *v.i.* (*mil.*) to wheel in.
einsegnen *v.t.* to consecrate; to confirm.
Einsegnung *f.* (-, -en) consecration, blessing; confirmation.
einsehen *v.t.st.* to look into, to look over; to understand, to see.
Einsehen *n.* (-s, 0) *ein ~ haben*, to be reasonable.
einseifen *v.t.* to soap; (*den Bart*) to lather; (*fig.*) to take in.
einseitig *a.* unilateral; partial, one-sided.
einsenden *v.t.ir.* to send in.
Einsenkung *f.* (-, -en) depression.
einsetzen *v.t.* (*mil.*) to commit, to employ; (*Pflanze*) to set up; to insert; (*Geld*) to stake; (*Kraft*) to use; (*einen*) to appoint, to instal; *einen zum Erben ~*, to make one one's heir; *~ v.i.* to begin, to set in; (*sich*) *~ v.refl.* (*für*) to work hard (for).
Einsicht *f.* (-, -en) insight; intelligence.
einsichtig *a.* sensible, well-advised.
Einsiedler *m.* (-s, -) hermit, anchorite.
einsilbig *a.* monosyllabic; (*fig.*) taciturn.
einsinken *v.i.st.* (*s*) to sink in, to fall in.
einsitzig *a.* single-seated.
einspannen *v.t.* (*Pferde*) to harness to.
einspännig *a.* drawn by one horse.
einsparen *v.t.* to save, to economize.
einsperren *v.t.* to lock up; to imprison.
einspringen *v.i.* (*s*) *helfend ~*, to lend a hand; *als Stellvertreter ~*, to step in for someone.
einspritzen *v.t.* to inject.
Einspritzung *f.* (-, -en) injection.
Einspruch *m.* protest, objection.
einst *adv.* once.
einstampfen *v.t.* to pulp.
einstecken *v.t.* to pocket.
einstehen *v.i.st.* to answer for, to guarantee.
einsteigen *v.i.st.* (*s*) to get in; to get into, to enter (a carriage); *~! i.* take your seats!
einstellbar *a.* (*mech.*) adjustable.
einstellen *v.t.* (*mech.*) to adjust; (*mil.*) to enlist; (*Radio*) to tune; (*Zahlungen*) to stop; *die Arbeit ~*, to strike; (*sich*) *~ v.refl.* to appear, to turn up.
Einstellung *f.* (-, -en) (*der Feindseligkeiten*) cessation; *~ der Arbeit*, strike; enlistment; (*Zahlungen*) suspension; attitude, mentality.
·instig *a.* future; ancient, former.
einstimmig *a.* unanimous.
Einstimmigkeit *f.* (-, 0) unanimity.
einstmals *adv.* once, formerly.
einstöckig *a.* one-storied.
einstossen *v.t.st.* (*Tür*) to smash.

einstreichen *v.t.st.* to pocket.
einstreuen *v.t.* to intersperse.
einströmen *v.i.* to pour into.
einstudieren *v.t.* (*Theater*) to produce, to rehearse.
einstürmen *v.t.* (*auf*) to assail.
Einsturz *m.* (-es, -stürze) downfall.
einstürzen *v.i.* (*s*) to fall in.
einstweilen *adv.* for the present.
einstweilig *a.* provisional, temporary.
eintägig *a.* lasting one day.
Eintänzer *m.* (-s, -) gigolo.
eintauchen *v.t.* to immerse, to dip, to steep; *~ v.i.* to dive.
Eintausch *m.* (-es, 0) exchange.
eintauschen *v.a.* to receive in exchange.
einteilen *v.t.* to divide, to distribute.
Einteilung *f.* (-, -en) division; distribution; classification.
eintönig *a.* monotonous.
Eintracht *f.* (-, 0) concord, union.
einträchtig *a.* harmonious.
Eintrag *m.* (-[e]s, -träge) prejudice, detriment; entry.
eintragen *v.t.st.* to enter, to yield.
einträglich *a.* profitable, lucrative.
Eintragung *f.* (-, -en) entry, registration.
eintreffen *v.i.st.* (*s*) to arrive; to happen.
eintreiben *v.t.st.* (*Geld*) to call in, to collect.
eintreten *v.i.st.* (*s*) to enter, to join; (*für einen*) to intercede; (*Hindernisse*) to arise, to crop up.
Eintritt *m.* (-[e]s, 0) entry, entrance; beginning, setting in; *freier ~*, free admission.
Eintritts: **~geld** *n.* admission-fee; **~karte** *f.* ticket.
eintrocknen *v.i.* (*s*) to dry up, to shrivel.
eintunken *v.t.* to dip, to steep.
einüben *v.t.* to practise, to drill, to train.
einverleiben *v.t.* to incorporate.
Einverleibung *f.* (-, -en) annexation.
Einvernehmen *n.* (-s, 0) understanding; *im besten ~ mit einem*, on the best of terms with one.
einverstanden *a.* agreed; *mit etwas ~ sein*, to agree to.
Einverständnis *n.* (-nisses, -nisse) agreement, understanding.
Einwand *m.* (-[e]s, -wände) objection.
Einwanderer *m.* (-s, -) immigrant.
einwandern *v.i.* (*s*) to immigrate.
Einwanderung *f.* (-, -en) immigration.
einwandfrei *a.* unobjectionable; *~ adv.* beyond doubt.
einwärts *adv.* inward, inwards.
einwechseln *v.t.* to change.
einweichen *v.t.* to soak.
einweihen *v.t.* to inaugurate, to consecrate; to initiate.
einwenden *v.t.ir.* to object; to reply.

einwerfen *v.t.st.* (*Scheiben*) to smash, **to break;** (*fig.*) to object.
einwickeln *v.t.* to wrap up, to envelop.
einwilligen *v.t.* to consent, to agree.
Einwilligung *f.* (-, -en) consent, assent.
einwirken *v.t.* to influence.
Einwohner *m.* (-s, -) inhabitant.
Einwurf *m.* (-[e]s, -würfe) objection; (*des Briefkastens*) slit, slot.
einwurzeln *v.i.* (*s*) to take root.
Einzahl *f.* (-, 0) singular (number).
einzahlen *v.t.* to pay in.
Einzahlung *f.* (-, -en) payment.
einzäunen *v.t.* to fence in.
Einzäunung *f.* (-, -en) enclosure, fence.
einzeichnen *v.t.* to mark.
Einzelhaft *f.* (-, 0) solitary confinement.
Einzelhandel *m.* retail trade.
Einzelheit *f.* (-, -en) detail; particulars *pl.*
einzeln *a.* odd; single; individual; isolated.
Einzelverkauf *m.* (-[e]s, -verkäufe) selling by retail.
Einzelwesen *n.* (-s, -) individual.
einziehen *v.t.st.* to draw in; (*zur Strafe*) to confiscate; (*Münzen etc.*) to call in, to withdraw; (*Erkundigungen*) to make (inquiries); ~ *v.i.st.* (*s*) to march in; (*Haus*) to move into.
Einziehung *f.* (-, -en) confiscation; collection.
einzig *a.* only; single; sole; ~ *in seiner Art,* unique.
Einzug *m.* (-[e]s, -züge) entry, entrance; moving in.
einzwängen *v.t.* to squeeze in.
Eis, *n.* (Eises, 0) ice; *Frucht* ~, ice-cream.
Eis: ~bahn *f.* skating-rink; ~bär *m.* polar bear; ~bein *n.* pig's knuckles *pl.*; ~berg *m.* iceberg; ~brecher *m.* ice-breaker.
Eisdiele *f.* (-, -n) ice-cream parlour.
Eisen *n.* (-s, -) iron.
Eisen: ~bahn *f.* railway, railroad; ~bahndamm *m.* embankment; ~bahnendpunkt *m.* railhead; ~bahnnetz *n.* railway network; ~bahnwagen *m.* railway carriage; ~bahnwerkstätte *f.* railway workshop.
Eisenbeton *m.* ferro-concrete, reinforced concrete.
Eisenerz *n.* iron ore.
Eisengiesserei *f.* iron-foundry.
Eisenkonstruktion *f.* steel frame.
eisern *a.* iron, of iron; ~er Vorhang *m.* safety curtain, iron curtain.
Eisgang *m.* breaking up and floating of the ice.
eisig *a.* icy, glacial; chilly.
eiskalt *a.* icy cold.
Eis: ~ lauf *m.* skating; ~schrank *m.* refrigerator; ~zapfen *m.* icicle.
eitel *a.* & *adv.* vain.
Eitelkeit *f.* (-, -en) vanity.
Eiter *m.* (-s, 0) matter, pus.

eiterig *a.* purulent.
eitern *v.i.* to suppurate.
Eiweiss *n.* (-es, 0) white of an egg, albumen; ~haltig *a.* albuminous.
Ekel *m.* (-s, 0) disgust.
ekelhaft *a.* loathsome, disgusting.
ekeln (sich) *v.refl.* to feel disgusted.
Ekstase *f.* (-, -n) ecstasy.
Ekzem *n.* (-[e]s, -e) eczema.
elastisch *a.* elastic.
Elch *m.* (-e[s], -e) elk.
Elefant *m.* (-en, -en) elephant.
elegant *a.* elegant, smart.
Eleganz *f.* (-, 0) elegance.
Elegie *f.* (-, -n) elegy.
elegisch *a.* elegiac; mournful.
elektrifizieren *v.t.* to electrify.
Elektriker *m.* (-s, -) electrician.
elektrisch *a.* electrical; ~er Installateur *m.* electrical contractor.
elektrisieren *v.t.* to electrify.
Elektrizität *f.* (-, 0) electricity.
Elektrode *f.* (-, -n) electrode.
Elektron *n.* (-s, -en) electron.
Elektro: ~lyse *f.* electrolysis; ~lyt *m.* electrolyte; ~technik *f.* electrical engineering; ~techniker *m.* electrical engineer.
Element *n.* (-[e]s, -e) element; rudiment; (*el.*) cell.
elementar *a.* elementary; primary.
Elend *n.* (-[e]s, 0) misery; affliction.
elend *a.* miserable, wretched.
elf *a.* eleven.
Elfe *f.* (-, -n) elf, fairy.
Elfenbein *n.* (-[e]s, 0) ivory.
elftens *adv.* in the eleventh place.
Elitetruppen *f.pl.* (*mil.*) crack troops.
Ellbogen *m.* (-s, -) elbow.
Elle *f.* (-, -n) German ell (abt. ⅔ yard).
Ellipse *f.* (-, -n) ellipse; ellipsis.
Elster *f.* (-, -n) magpie.
elterlich *a.* parental.
Eltern *pl.* parents *pl.*
Email *n.* (-s, 0) enamel.
emaillieren *v.t.* to enamel.
emanzipieren *v.t.* to emancipate.
Emission *f.* (-, -en) (*Finanz*) issue.
Empfang *m.* (-[e]s, -pfänge) reception, receipt.
empfangen *v.t.st.* to receive; ~ *v.i.st.* to conceive.
Empfänger *m.* (-s, -) receiver, recipient; addressee; consignee.
empfänglich *a.* susceptible.
Empfängnis *f.* (-, 0) conception.
Empfängnisverhütung *f.* contraception; empfängnisverhütendes Mittel *n.* contraceptive.
Empfangs: ~dame *f.* receptionist; ~schein *m.* receipt; ~zimmer *n.* reception-room, drawing-room.
empfehlen *v.t.st.* to recommend; (sich) ~ *v.re l.st.* to take leave; ~ *Sie mich Ihrem*

Herrn Vater, please remember me to your father.

empfehlenswert *a.* commendable.

Empfehlung *f.* (-, -en) recommendation.

Empfehlungsbrief *m.* ~**schreiben** *n.* letter of introduction.

empfinden *v.t.st.* to feel, to perceive, to be sensible (of).

empfindlich *a.* sensible; sensitive, touchy; delicate; painful, grievous.

empfindsam *a.* sentimental; sensitive.

Empfindung *f.* (-, -en) perception, sensation, feeling.

empfindungslos *a.* insensible, unfeeling.

emphatisch *a.* emphatic(al).

empirisch *a.* empirical.

empor *adv.* upwards, on high, up, aloft.

emporarbeiten (sich) *v.refl.* to work one's way up.

empören *v.t* to revolt, to shock; (sich) ~ *v.refl.* to rebel.

Empörer *m.* (-s, -) insurgent, rebel.

emporkommen *v.i.st.* to rise in the world.

Emporkömmling *m.* (-[e]s, -e) upstart.

emporragen *v.i.* to tower.

Empörung *f.* (-, -en) rebellion, revolt; indignation.

emsig *a.* assiduous, industrious, busy.

Ende *n.* (-s, -n) end; close, conclusion; *zu* ~ *gehen*, to draw to an end.

endemisch *a.* endemic.

enden *v.i. & refl.* (*sich*) to end, to finish, to terminate, to conclude.

Endergebnis *n.* (-nisses, -nisse) final result.

Endesunterzeichnete[r] *m.* (-n, -n) (the) undersigned.

Endgeschwindigkeit *f.* (-, -en) terminal velocity.

endgültig *a.* definitive, final.

endigen *v.t.* to end, to finish.

Endivie *f.* (-, -n) endive.

endlich *a.* finite; final, ultimate; ~ *adv.* at last, finally.

endlos *a.* endless, infinite.

End: ~**punkt** *m.* final point; terminus; ~**station** *f.* terminus.

Endung *f.* (-, -en) ending, termination.

Endzweck *m.* design, aim.

Energie *f.* (-, -n) energy.

energisch *a.* energetic, vigorous.

eng *a.* narrow, tight, strait; strict.

engagieren *v.t.* to engage.

Enge *f.* (-, -n) narrowness, tightness; *in die* ~ *treiben*, to drive into a corner.

Engel *m.* (-s, -) angel.

engherzig *a.* narrow-minded, illiberal.

Engländer *m.* (-s, -) (*mech.*) adjustable spanner. (See also Table of Geogr. Names.)

englisch *a.* English; angelic; ~*e Krankheit*, rickets *pl.*

Engpass *m.* (-es, -pässe) defile (*fig.*) bottleneck.

en gros (*frz.*) *adv.* wholesale.

Engrospreis *m.* trade price.

Enkel *m.* (-s, -) grandson, grandchild.

Enkelin *f.* (-, -nen) grand-daughter.

Enklave *f.* (-, -n) enclave.

enorm *a.* enormous, immense, huge.

entarten *v.i.* (*s*) to degenerate.

entartet *p. & a.* degenerate.

Entartung *f.* (-, -en) degeneration, degeneracy.

entäussern (sich) *v.refl.* to part with, to give up.

entbehren *v.t.* to lack, to be without; to want, to miss; to do without.

entbehrlich *a.* unnecessary, dispensable.

Entbehrung *f.* (-, -en) privation.

entbinden *v.t.st.* to deliver (a woman); to disengage; (*fig.*) to release.

Entbindung *f.* (-, -en) childbirth delivery, confinement; disengagement.

Entbindungsanstalt *f.* maternity home.

entblössen *v.t.* to denude, to uncover.

entdecken *v.t.* to discover, to detect.

Entdeckung *f.* (-, -en) discovery.

Ente *f.* (-, -n) duck; (*Zeitungs-*) canard.

entehren *v.t.* to dishonour; to violate.

entehrend *a.* disgraceful, degrading.

enteignen *v.t.* to expropriate.

Enteignung *f.* (-, -en) expropriation.

Entenbraten *m.* roast duck.

enterben *v.t.* to disinherit.

Enterich *m.* (-s, -e) drake.

entern *v.t.* to board, to grapple.

entfachen *v.t.* to kindle.

entfahren *v.i.st.* (*s*) to escape.

entfallen *v.i.st.* (*s*) ~ *auf*, to fall to one's share; *es ist mir* ~, I cannot remember.

entfalten *v.t.* to unfold; to develop; (sich) ~ *v.refl.* to open, to expand.

entfärben (sich) *v.refl.* to lose colour.

entfernen *v.t.* to remove; (sich) ~ *v.refl.* to withdraw.

entfernt *a.* remote, distant; far from.

Entfernung *f.* (-, -en) removal; distance.

Entfernungsmesser *m.* (*phot.*) rangefinder.

entfesseln *v.t.* to unchain, to let loose.

entflammen *v.t.* to inflame, to kindle.

entfliehen *v.i.st.* (*s*) to run away; to escape.

entfremden *v.t.* to estrange, to alienate.

Entfremdung *f.* (-, -en) estrangement.

entführen *v.t.* to carry off; to abduct; to elope with; (*Kinder*) to kidnap; *sich* ~ *lassen*, to elope (with a man).

entgegen *pr.* against, contrary to, in opposition to.

entgegenarbeiten *v.t.* to counteract.

entgegengehen *v.i.st.* (*s*) to go to meet.

entgegengesetzt *a.* opposite, contrary.

entgegenhalten *v.t.* to object.

entgegenkommen *v.i.st.* (*s*) to come to meet; (*fig.*) to meet (half-way).

entgegenkommend *a.* accommodating.

Entgegennahme *f.* (-, 0) receipt.

entgegennehmen *v.t.st.* to accept, to receive.

entgegensehen *v.i.st.* to look forward to.

entgegensetzen *v.t.* to oppose, to contrast.

entgegenstehen *v.i.st.* to be opposed.

entgegenstellen *v.t.* to oppose.

entgegentreten *v.i.st.* (*s*) (*fig.*) to oppose.

entgegenwirken *v.i.* to counteract.

entgegnen *v.i.* to reply, to rejoin.

Entgegnung *f.* (-, -en) rejoinder, retort.

entgehen *v.i.st.* (*s*) to escape, to get off.

Entgelt *n.* (-[e]s, 0) remuneration.

entgelten *v.t.st.* to atone for.

entgleisen *v.i.* (*s*) to run off the rails; (*fig.*) to make a slip.

Entgleisung *f.* (-, -en) derailment; slip.

entgleiten *v.i.st.* (*s*) to slip from.

entgräten *v.t.* to bone.

enthalten *v.t.st.* to contain; (sich) ~ *v.refl.st.* to abstain (from), to forbear.

enthaltsam *a.* abstemious.

Enthaltsamkeit *f.* (-, 0) abstinence.

enthaupten *v.t.* to behead, to decapitate.

entheben *v.t.st.* to remove (from office).

enthüllen *v.t.* to unveil; to reveal.

Enthüllung *f.* (-, -en) unveiling (of a statue); (*fig.*) exposure, revelation.

enthusiastisch *a.* enthusiastic.

entkleiden *v.t.* to undress.

entkommen *v.i.st.* (*s*) to escape.

entkorken *v.t.* to uncork, to open.

entkräften *v.t.* to enfeeble, to weaken.

entladen (sich) *v.refl.* to go off, to burst.

entlang *adv.* along.

entlarven *v.t.* to unmask.

entlassen *v.t.st.* to dismiss, to discharge.

Entlassung *f.* (-, -en) dismissal; *seine ~ nehmen,* to resign (one's office); *seine ~ beantragen,* to tender one's resignation.

entlasten *v.t.* to unburden, to exonerate, to discharge; to credit.

Entlastung *f.* (-, -en) exoneration.

Entlastungszeuge *m.* witness for the defence.

entlaufen *v.i.st.* (*s*) to run away.

entledigen (sich) *v.refl.* to get rid (of); to acquit oneself (of one's duty).

entleeren *v.t.* to empty.

entlegen *a.* remote.

entlehnen *v.t.* to borrow.

entleihen *v.t.st.* to borrow (of, from).

entlocken *v.t.* to elicit, to draw from.

entlohnen *v.t.* to pay off.

entmenscht *a.* inhuman, brutish.

entmündigen *v.t.* to put (an adult) under tutelage.

entmutigen *v.t.* to discourage.

entnehmen *v.t.st.* to take from; to gather (from); (*com.*) to draw upon.

entnerven *v.t.* to enervate.

entpuppen (sich) *v.refl.* (*als*) to turn out to be.

enträtseln *v.t.* to unriddle, to make out.

entreissen *v.t.st.* to snatch away (from).

entrichten *v.t.* to pay.

entrinnen *v.i.st.* (*s*) to escape; *knapp ~,* to have a narrow escape.

entrollen *v.t.* to unroll, to unfurl.

entrüsten *v.t.* to provoke, to exasperate; (sich) ~ *v.refl.* to get indignant, to get angry.

Entrüstung *f.* (-, 0) indignation.

entsagen *v.i.* to renounce, to waive.

Entsagung *f.* (-, -en) renunciation.

Entsatz *m.* (-es, 0) relief, succour.

entschädigen *v.t.* to indemnify, to compensate; to make up for (*fig.*).

Entschädigung *f.* (-, -en) compensation; indemnity; ~ *leisten,* to make compensation for.

entscheiden *v.t.st.* to decide; (sich) ~ *v.refl.st.* to come to a decision.

entscheidend *a.* decisive.

Entscheidung *f.* (-, -en) decision; *zur ~ bringen,* to bring to a head.

entschieden, decided; resolute; definite.

Entschiedenheit *f.* (-, 0) determination.

entschliessen (sich) *v.refl.st.* to resolve, to make up one's mind.

Entschliessung *f.* (-, -en) resolution.

entschlossen *a.* resolute, determined.

entschlüpfen *v.i.* (*s*) to escape.

Entschluss *m.* (-schlusses, -schlüsse) resolution.

entschuldigen *v.t.* to excuse; (sich) ~ *v.refl.* to apologize.

Entschuldigung *f.* (-, -en) excuse, apology; *um ~ bitten,* to beg pardon.

entsenden *v.t.ir.* to send off, to despatch.

entsetzen *v.t.* to depose; to relieve, to raise the siege of; (sich) ~ *v.refl.* to be shocked.

Entsetzen *n.* (-s, 0) terror, horror.

entsetzlich *a.* horrible, terrible, dreadful.

entsiegeln *v.t.* to open, to unseal.

entsinnen (sich) *v.refl.st.* to recall to mind.

entspannen (sich) *v.i. or refl.* to relax.

Entspannung *f.* (-, 0) relaxation.

entspinnen (sich) *v.refl.st.* to begin.

entsprechen *v.i.st.* to correspond to; to answer, to suit (a purpose).

entsprechend *a.* corresponding; suitable.

entspringen *v.i.st.* (*s*) to escape; to arise, to rise.

entstammen *v.i.* (*s*) to descend from.

entstehen *v.i.st.* (*s*) to begin, to originate, to arise; to result, to spring (from).

Entstehung *f.* (-, -en) origin, rise.

entstellen *v.t.* to disfigure, to deface; to misrepresent.

Entstellung *f.* (-, -en) distortion.

enttäuschen *v.t.* to disappoint.

Enttäuschung *f.* (-, -en) disappointment.

entthronen *v.t.* to dethrone.

entvölkern *v.t.* to depopulate.

entwachsen *v.i.st.* (*s*) to outgrow.
entwaffnen *v.t.* to disarm.
Entwarnung *f.* (-, -en) (*Luftschutz*) 'all-clear' signal.
entwässern *v.t.* to drain.
entweder *c.* either.
entweichen *v.i.st.* (*s*) to escape.
entweihen *v.t.* to profane, to desecrate.
entwenden *v.t.* to purloin, to embezzle.
entwerfen *v.t.st.* to sketch, to design.
entwerten *v.t.* to depreciate.
Entwertung *f.* (-, -en) depreciation.
entwickeln *v.t.* to develop.
Entwick[e]lung *f.* (-, -en) development; evolution; (*phot.*) developing.
entwirren *v.t.* to unravel, to disentangle.
entwischen *v.i.* (*s*) to escape.
entwöhnen *v.t.* to disaccustom; to wean (a child).
entwölken (sich) *v.refl.* to clear up.
entwürdigen *v.t.* to disgrace, to degrade.
Entwurf *m.* (-[e]s, -würfe) sketch, draft, blueprint; *erster* ~, rough draft.
entwurzeln *v.t.* to uproot.
entziehen *v.t.st.* to deprive of; (sich) ~ *v.refl.* to withdraw.
entziffern *v.t.* to decipher.
entzücken *v.t.* to enrapture, to charm.
Entzückung *f.* (-, -en) transport.
entzünden *v.t.* to kindle, to set on fire; (*fig.*) to inflame; (sich) ~ *v.refl.* to catch fire.
Entzündung *f.* (-, -en) inflammation.
entzwei *adv.* in two, asunder; broken.
entzweien *v.t.* to disunite, to set at variance; (sich) ~ *v.refl.* to fall out.
Enzian *m.* (-[e]s, -e) (*bot.*) gentian.
Epaulett *n.* (-s, -s) epaulet.
Epheu = Efeu.
Epidemie *f.* (-, -[e]n) epidemic.
epidemisch *a.* epidemic.
Epigramm *n.* (-s, -e) epigram.
Epilepsie *f.* (-) epilepsy.
epileptisch *a.* epileptic.
Epilog *m.* (-[e]s, -e) epilogue.
episch *a.* epic.
Episode *f.* (-, -n) episode.
Epistel *f.* (-, -n) epistle.
Epoche *f.* (-, -n) epoch.
Epos *n.* (-, Epen) epic poem.
Equipage *f.* (-, -n) carriage.
er *pn.* he; ~ *selbst*, he himself.
erachten *v.t.* to think, to be of opinion.
Erachten *n.* (-s, 0) opinion; *meines* ~s, in my opinion, for all I know.
erarbeiten *v.t.* to obtain by labour.
erbarmen (sich) *v.refl.* to pity.
Erbarmen *n.* (-s, 0) mercy, commiseration, pity.
erbarmenswert, erbarmenswürdig *a.* pitiable.
erbärmlich *a.* miserable, pitiful.
erbarmungslos *a.* pitiless, remorseless.

erbauen *v.t.* to build, to erect; (*fig.*) to edify; (sich) ~ *v.refl.* to be edified.
Erbauer *m.* (-s, -) builder, founder.
erbaulich *a.* edifying.
Erbe *m.* (-n, -n) heir; *gesetzlicher*~, heir-at-law; *mutmasslicher*~, heir presumptive; ~n. (-s, 0) inheritance; heritage.
erben *v.t.* to inherit, to succeed to.
erbetteln *v.t.* to get by begging.
erbeuten *v.t.* to capture.
Erbfall *m.* case of succession, heritage.
Erbfolge *f.* hereditary succession.
erbieten (sich) *v.refl.st.* to volunteer.
Erbin *f.* (-, -nen) heiress.
erbitten *v.t.st.* to request, to solicit.
erbittern *v.t.* to exasperate, to provoke.
Erbitterung *f.* (-, -en) exasperation.
Erbkrankheit *f.* hereditary disease.
erblassen *v.i.* (*s*) to turn pale, to pale.
Erblasser *m.* (-s, -) testator.
erbleichen *v.i.st.* (*s*) to pale; to die.
erblich *a.* hereditary.
erblicken *v.t.* to see, to discover.
erblinden *v.i.* (*s*) to grow blind.
erblühen *v.i.* (*s*) to open, to bud out.
erborgen *v.t.* to borrow.
erbost *a.* angry.
erbrechen *v.t.st.* to break open; (sich) ~ *v.refl.* to vomit.
Erbrechen *n.* (-s, 0) vomiting.
erbringen *v.t.ir.* to produce.
Erbrecht *n.* law of inheritance.
Erbschaft *f.* (-, -en) inheritance.
Erbschleicher *m.* legacy-hunter.
Erbse *f.* (-, -n) pea.
Erb: ~stück *n.* heirloom; ~sünde *f.* original sin.
Erbteil *n.* portion (of an inheritance).
Erd: ~apfel *m.* potato; ~ball *m.* globe; ~beben *n.* earthquake; ~beere *f.* strawberry; ~boden m. ground, soil; earth.
Erde *f.* (-, -n) earth; world; ground, soil; (*fam.*) floor; (*fig.*) dust, clay; (*el.*) earth, (*Am.*) ground.
erden *v.t.* to earth, to ground.
erdenken *v.t.ir.* to imagine, to contrive.
erdenklich *a.* imaginable, conceivable.
Erdgeschoss *n.* ground-floor.
erdichten *v.t.* to invent, to feign.
Erd: ~kreis m. ~kugel *f.* globe; ~kunde *f.* geography; ~leitung *f.* earth; ~nuss, *f.* groundnut; ~öl *n.* petroleum.
erdolchen *v.t.* to stab.
Erdreich *n.* earth; soil.
erdreisten (sich) *v.refl.* to make bold.
erdrosseln *v.t.* to strangle, to throttle.
erdrücken *v.t.* to crush; to overwhelm.
Erd: ~rutsch *m.* land-slip; ~teil *m.* continent.
Erdtruppen *f.pl.* ground forces.
erdulden *v.t.* to suffer, to endure.
ereifern (sich) *v.refl.* to grow excited.

ereignen (sich) *v.refl.* to happen, to come to pass.

Ereignis *n.* (-nisses, -nisse) occurrence, event.

ereilen *v.t.* to overtake.

Eremit *m.* (-en, -en) hermit.

ererben *v.t.* to inherit.

erfahren *v.t.st.* to experience, to suffer; to learn, to hear; ~ *a.* experienced, expert; conversant (with).

Erfahrung *f.* (-, -en) experience; knowledge; practice; *in ~ bringen*, to learn, to be informed, to find out.

erfassen *v.t.* to comprehend.

erfinden *v.t.st.* to invent; to contrive.

Erfinder *m.* (-s, -) inventor.

erfinderisch *a.* inventive.

Erfindung *f.* (-, -en) invention.

erflehen *v.i.* (*s*) to obtain by entreaty.

Erfolg *m.* .(-[e]s, -e) result, effect, success.

erfolgen *v.i.* (*s*) to result, to ensue.

erfolg: ~**los** *a.* unsuccessful, vain; ~**reich** *a.* successful.

erforderlich *a.* necessary, requisite.

erfordern *v.t.* to demand, to require.

Erfordernis *n.* (-nisses, -nisse) requirement, requisite; necessaries *pl.*

erforschen *v.t.* to explore, to investigate.

Erforschung *f.* (-, -en) exploration.

erfragen *v.t.* to ascertain by inquiry.

erfreuen *v.t. & refl.* (*sich*) to rejoice; to cheer, to please.

erfreulich *a.* gratifying; encouraging.

erfrieren *v.i.st.* (*s*) to freeze (to death).

erfrischen *v.t.* to refresh.

Erfrischung *f.* (-, -en) refreshment.

erfüllen *v.t.* to fulfil; to accomplish; *seine Pflicht ~*, to do one's duty; *ein Versprechen ~*, to keep a promise.

Erfüllung *f.* (-, 0) fulfilment, accomplishment; *in ~ gehen*, to come true.

Erfüllungsort *m.* settling place.

ergänzen *v.t.* to complete, to supply.

ergänzend *a.* supplementary.

Ergänzung *f.* (-, -en) supplement; supplementation.

ergeben *v.t.st.* to yield, to produce; (sich) ~ *v.refl.* to surrender; to result; to devote onself.

ergeben *a.* devoted, addicted; obedient.

ergebenst *adv.* very truly yours.

Ergebnis *n.* (-nisses, -nisse) result.

ergebnislos *a.* without result.

Ergebung *f.* (-, 0) surrender; submission, resignation.

ergehen *v.i.st. es wird ihm schlimm ~*, he will suffer for it; ~ *lassen*, to issue, to promulgate; *über sich ~ lassen*, to submit to.

ergiebig *a.* productive.

ergiessen (sich) *v.refl.st.* to fall (into).

ergötzen *v.t.* to amuse, to delight; (sich) ~ *v.refl.* to enjoy oneself.

ergötzlich *a.* delightful, amusing.

ergreifen *v.t.st.* to seize, to take up; (*Flucht*) to take to flight; (*Partei*) to side with; to affect.

ergriffen *a.* struck, affected.

ergründen *v.t.* to get to the bottom of.

Erguss *m.* (-gusses, -güsse) (*fig.*) effusion.

erhaben *a.* raised, elevated; sublime.

erhalten *v.t.st.* to maintain; to sustain; to preserve; to receive, to get; to obtain; (sich) ~ *v.refl.* to live *or* subsist on.

erhältlich *a.* obtainable.

Erhaltung *f.* (-, 0) preservation, conservation; maintenance.

erhandeln *v.t.* to buy.

erhängen (sich) *v.refl.* to hang oneself.

erhärten *v.t.* to substantiate.

erhaschen *v.t.* to catch, to seize.

erheben *v.t.st.* to lift up; to elevate, to raise; to extol, to praise; (sich) ~ *v.refl.st.* to rise; *ein Geschrei ~*, to set up a cry; *die Frage ~*, to start the question; *Geld ~*, to raise money; *ins Quadrat ~*, to square.

erheblich *a.* considerable.

Erheblichkeit *f.* (-, 0) relevance.

Erhebung *f.* (-, -en) elevation; promotion; (*Steuer*) levy; (*Nachforschung*) inquest; (*Aufstand*) insurrection.

erheitern *v.t.* to cheer, to exhilarate.

Erheiterung *f.* (-, -en) amusement, diversion.

erhellen *v.t.* to light up, to clear up; ~ *v.i.* to become evident.

erheucheln *v.t.* to feign.

erhitzen *v.t.* to heat; (sich) ~ *v.refl.* to grow hot; (*fig.*) to get angry.

erhoffen *v.t.* to hope for.

erhöhen *v.t.* to heighten; to enhance; to raise, to increase.

Erhöhung *f.* (-, -en) rise, increase.

erholen (sich) *v.refl.* to recover.

Erholung *f.* (-, -en) recovery; recreation.

Erholungs... recreational.

Erholungsstätte *f.* rest centre.

erhören *v.t.* to hear; to grant.

erinnerlich *a. soviel mir ~ ist*, so far as I can recollect.

erinnern *v.t.* to remind; (sich) ~ *v.refl.* to remember; to recollect.

Erinnerung *f.* (-, -en) remembrance; reminiscence.

erjagen *v.t.* to get (by hunting).

erkalten *v.i.* (*s*) to cool down.

erkälten (sich) *v.refl.* to catch (a) cold.

Erkältung *f.* (-, -en) cold.

erkämpfen *v.t.* to gain by fighting.

erkennen *v.t.st.* to perceive; to discern; to realize, to see; to know; to recognize; to decide.

erkenntlich *a.* grateful.

Erkenntnis *f.* (-nisses, -nisse) knowledge; cognition; perception.

Erker *m.* (-s, -) bay, projection.
erklären *v.t.* to explain, to interpret; to declare; to account for; (sich) ~ *v.refl.* to declare oneself.
erklärlich *a.* explicable; *leicht* ~, easily accounted for, easily explained.
erklärt *a.* professed; sworn.
erklärtermassen *adv.* professedly.
Erklärung *f.* (-, -en) explanation; declaration.
erklingen *v.i.st.* (*s*) to resound, to ring.
erkranken *v.i.* (*s*) to fall ill.
Erkrankung *f.* (-, -en) attack of illness.
erkühnen (sich) *v.refl.* to make bold.
erkunden *v.t.* to ascertain; (*mil.*) to reconnoitre.
erkundigen (sich) *v.refl.* to make inquiries.
Erkundigung *f.* (-, -en) inquiry.
erlahmen *v.i.* (*s*) to get tired *or* weak.
erlangen *v.t.* to attain; to obtain.
Erlass *m.* (-lasses, -lasse) remission, pardon; decree.
erlassen *v.t.st.* to issue; (*Gesetz*) to enact; (*nachlassen*) to remit.
erlauben *v.t.* to permit, to allow; *ich erlaube mir zu* ..., I beg to.
Erlaubnis *f.* (-, 0) permission, leave; *mit* ~ *von*, by permission of; *mit gütiger* ~ *von*, courtesy of ...
erläutern *v.t.* to illustrate, to elucidate.
Erläuterung *f.* (-, -en) illustration.
Erle *f.* (-, -n) alder.
erleben *v.t.* to live to see; to experience.
Erlebnis *n.* (-nisses, -nisse) experience.
erledigen *v.t.* to discharge; to dispatch; to settle; (sich) ~ *v.refl.* to be settled.
Erledigung *f.* (-, -en) dispatch, execution (of work); vacancy.
erlegen *v.t.* to kill; to pay down.
erleichtern *v.t.* to facilitate; to lighten, to ease; to alleviate.
Erleichterung *f.* (-, -en) relief; facilitation; (*von Bestimmungen*) relaxation.
erleiden *v.t.st.* to suffer, to bear.
erlernen *v.t.* to learn.
erlesen *a.* select, choice.
erleuchten *v.t.* to illuminate; to enlighten.
Erleuchtung *f.* (-, -en) illumination.
erliegen *v.i.st.* (*s*) to succumb.
erlogen *a.* false, untrue, forged.
Erlös *m.* (-ses, -se) proceeds *pl.*
erlöschen *v.t.* to extinguish; ~ *v.i.st.* (*s*) to go out; to become void.
erlösen *v.t.* to redeem, to deliver.
Erlöser *m.* (-s, -) Redeemer, Saviour.
Erlösung *f.* (-, -en) redemption.
ermächtigen *v.t.* to empower, to authorize.
Ermächtigung *f.* (-, -en) authorization; ~sgesetz *n.* enabling act.
ermahnen *v.t.* to admonish.
Ermahnung *f.* (-, -en) admonition, exhortation.

ermangeln *v.i.* to be wanting; to fail.
Ermangelung *f.* (-, 0) *in* ~ *von*, in default of.
ermässigen *v.t.* to abate, to reduce; *zu ermässigten Preisen*, at reduced rates.
Ermässigung *f.* (-, -en) abatement.
ermatten *v.i.* (*s*) to grow tired, to slacken.
ermessen *v.t.st.* to measure; to judge.
Ermessen *n.* (-s, 0) judgment; *nach meinem* ~, in my opinion.
ermitteln *v.t.* to find out, to ascertain.
Ermittlung *f.* (-, -en) inquiry.
ermöglichen *v.t.* to render possible.
ermorden *v.t.* to murder.
Ermordung *f.* (-, -en) assassination.
ermüden *v.t.* to tire, to fatigue; ~ *v.i.* (*s*) to get tired.
Ermüdung *f.* (-, -en) exhaustion.
ermuntern *v.t.* to animate, to cheer.
ermutigen *v.t.* to encourage.
Ermutigung *f.* (-, -en) encouragement.
ernähren *v.t.* to nourish; to support.
Ernährung *f.* (-, -en) nutrition.
ernennen *v.t.st.* to nominate, to appoint.
Ernennung *f.* (-, -en) appointment.
erneuen, erneuern *v.t.* to renew, to renovate.
Erneuerung *f.* (-, -en) renewal; revival.
erniedrigen *v.t.* to lower; to humble; (sich) ~ *v.refl.* to degrade oneself.
Ernst *m.* (-es, 0) seriousness.
ernst *a.* earnest, serious, grave, stern; *etwas* ~ *nehmen*, to take a thing seriously.
Ernstfall *m.* (*mil.*) case of war.
ernsthaft *a.* serious, grave.
ernstlich *a.* earnest, serious.
Ernte *f.* (-, -n) harvest; (*Ertrag*) crop.
Erntemaschine *f.* harvester.
ernten *v.t.* to reap, to harvest.
ernüchtern *v.t.* to sober, to disillusion.
Eroberer *m.* (-s, -) conqueror.
erobern *v.t.* to conquer.
Eroberung *f.* (-, -en) conquest.
eröffnen *v.t.* to open, to begin; to inaugurate; (*fig.*) to disclose, to make known.
Eröffnung *f.* (-, -en) opening, beginning; communication.
erörtern *v.t.* to discuss.
Erörterung *f.* (-, -en) discussion.
erotisch *a.* erotic.
erpicht *a.* bent (upon).
erpressen *v.t.* to extort.
Erpressung *f.* (-, -en) extortion; blackmail.
erproben *v.t.* to try, test.
erquicken *v.t.* to refresh.
erraten *v.t.* to guess, to divine.
errechnen *v.t.* to compute.
erregbar *a.* excitable; irritable.
erregen *v.t.* to stir up, to excite; to provoke; to produce.
erregt *a.* angry.

Erregung *f.* (-, -en) excitement.
erreichbar *a.* attainable; within reach.
erreichen *v.t.* to attain, to reach.
erretten *v.t.* to save, to rescue (from).
Errettung *f.* (-, -en) deliverance.
errichten *v.t.* to erect; to establish.
Errichtung *f.* (-, -en) erection; establishment.
erringen *v.t.st.* to obtain by exertion.
erröten *v.i.* (*s*) to blush.
Errungenschaft *f.* (-, -en) acquisition.
Ersatz *m.* (-es, 0) substitute; compensation, reparation; amends *pl.*
Ersatz: ~anspruch *m.* right of redress; ~batterie *f.* refill battery; ~rad *n.* (*mot.*) spare wheel; ~reifen *m.* spare tyre; ~stoff *m.* substitute; ~teil *m.* spare (part).
erschaffen *v.t.st.* to create.
Erschaffung *f.* (-, 0) creation.
erscheinen *v.i.st.* (*s*) to appear; (*Buch*) to come out.
Erscheinung *f.* (-, -en) appearance; apparition; phenomenon; symptom.
erschiessen *v.t.st.* to shoot (dead).
erschlaffen *v.i.* (*s*) to slacken.
erschlagen *v.t.st.* to slay.
erschlichen *a.* surreptitious.
erschliessen *v.t.st.* to make accessible.
erschöpfen *v.t.* to exhaust.
Erschöpfung *f.* (-, 0) exhaustion.
erschrecken *v.t.* to frighten, to startle; ~ *v.i.st.* (*s*) to be frightened.
erschrocken *a.* frightened, terrified.
erschüttern *v.t.* to shake, to shock.
Erschütterung *f.* (-, -en) shock; (*fig.*) emotion.
erschweren *v.t.* to aggravate.
erschwindeln *v.t.* to swindle.
erschwingen *v.t.st.* to afford.
ersehen *v.t.st.* to see, to find; to choose.
ersehnen *v.t.* to long for.
ersessenes Recht *n.* prescriptive right.
ersetzen *v.t.* to replace, to repair, to compensate; to refund.
ersichtlich *a.* evident, manifest.
ersinnen *v.t.st.* to contrive, to devise.
ersparen *v.t.* to spare, to save.
Ersparnis *f.* (-nisses, -nisse) savings *pl.*
erspriesslich *a.* useful, beneficial.
erst *adv.* first, at first; not until, only.
erstarken *v.i.* (*s*) to grow strong.
erstarren *v.i.* (*s*) to grow stiff *or* numb.
erstatten *v.t. Bericht* ~, to report (on).
Erstattung *f.* (-, -en) delivery.
Erstaufführung *f.* (-, -en) first night.
erstaunen *v.i.* (*s*) to be astonished.
Erstaunen *n.* (-s, 0) astonishment.
erstaunlich *a.* astonishing, amazing.
erstechen *v.t.st.* to stab.
erstehen *v.i.st.* (*s*) to arise; ~ *v.t.st.* to buy.
ersteigen *v.t.st.* to ascend, to climb.
erstens *adv.* firstly, in the first place.

Erstgeburt *f.* (-, -en) primogeniture.
ersticken *v.t.* to suffocate, to choke; ~ *v.i.* (*s*) to be suffocated.
erstklassig *a.* first-rate.
erstlich *adv.* firstly, at first.
erstreben *v.t.* to strive after.
erstrecken (sich) *v.refl.* to extend.
erstürmen *v.t.* to take by storm.
ersuchen *v.t.* to request, to beg.
ertappen *v.t.* to surprise, to catch; *auf der Tat* ~, to take in the act.
erteilen *v.t.* to impart, to confer; (*Verweis*) to administer.
ertönen *v.i.* (*s*) to resound.
Ertrag *m.* (-[e]s, -träge) produce, yield; proceeds *pl.*; returns *pl.*
Ertragfähigkeit *f.* productiveness.
ertragen *v.t.st.* (*fig.*) to bear, to endure.
erträglich *a.* tolerable, endurable.
ertränken *v.t.* to drown.
ertrinken *v.i.st* (*s*) to get drowned.
ertüchtigen *v.t.* to train.
erübrigen *v.t.* to save, to spare; to remain; *sich* ~, to be unnecessary.
erwachen *v.i.* (*s*) to awake.
erwachsen *v.i.st.* (*s*) to accrue; ~ *a.* grown-up.
Erwachsene[r] *m.* (-n, -n) adult, grown-up person.
erwägen *v.t.st.* (*fig.*) to weigh, to consider.
Erwägung *f.* (-, -en) consideration; *in* ~ *ziehen*, to take into consideration; *in* ~ *dass*, considering, seeing that...
erwählen *v.t.* to choose, to elect.
erwähnen *v.t.* to mention.
Erwähnung *f.* (-, -en) mention.
erwärmen *v.t.* to warm, to heat.
erwarten *v.t.* to expect; to wait for, to await.
Erwartung *f.* (-, -en) expectation.
erwecken *v.t.* to awaken.
Erweckung *f.* (-, -en) awakening.
erwehren (sich) *v.refl.* to keep off.
erweichen *v.t.* to soften, to mollify.
Erweis *m.* (-weises, -weise) proof.
erweisen *v.t.st.* to prove, to render; (*eine Gunst*) to bestow upon; *sich* ~ *als*, to turn out to be.
erweislich *a.* demonstrable.
erweitern *v.t.* to widen, to enlarge; to extend, to amplify.
Erweiterung *f.* (-, -en) enlargement; amplification, extension.
Erwerb *m.* (-[e]s, 0) acquisition; gain, earnings *pl.*; living.
erwerben *v.t.st.* to acquire, to gain.
erwerbsfähig *a.* able-bodied, capable of gaining one's living.
erwerbslos *a.* unemployed.
Erwerbslosenunterstützung *f.* (-, 0) unemployment benefit, dole.
Erwerbslosigkeit *f.* (-, 0) unemployment.
Erwerbung *f.* (-, -en) acquisition.

erwidern v.t. to return; to reply.
Erwiderung f. (-, -en) return; reply.
erwirken v.t. to procure.
erwischen v.t. to catch.
erwünscht a. desired, welcome.
erwürgen v.t. to strangle, to throttle.
Erz n. (-es, -e) ore; brass, bronze.
erzählen v.t. to tell, to narrate, to relate.
erzählend a. narrative.
Erzählung f. (-, -en) narrative, tale, story.
Erzbischof m. archbishop.
erzbischöflich n. archiepiscopal.
Erzbistum n. archbishopric.
Erzengel m. archangel.
erzeugen v.t. to beget, to engender, to produce; (Dampf) to generate.
Erzeugnis n. (-nisses, -nisse) (der Natur) produce; (des Geistes) product.
Erzeugung f. (-, -en) generation; production.
Erz: ~giesser m. brass-founder; ~herzog m. archduke.
erziehen v.t.st. to bring up, to educate.
Erzieher m. teacher, tutor.
Erzieherin f. (-, -nen) governess.
Erziehung f. (-, 0) education.
erzielen v.t. to obtain; to produce.
erzürnen v.t. to make angry; v.i. (s) (sich) ~ v.refl. to grow angry.
erzwingen v.t.st. to force, to enforce.
es pn. it; so.
Es n. (-, 0) E flat.
Esche f. (-, -n) ash (tree).
Esel m. (-s, -) ass; donkey.
Eselsohr n. (fig.) (im Buche) dog's ear.
Espe f. (-, -n) aspen, quaking-asp.
Espenlaub n. aspen leaves pl.
Essapfel m. eating apple.
essbar a. eatable, edible.
Esse f. (-, -n) smithy; chimney.
essen v.t. & i.st. to eat; to dine; to feed.
Essen n. (-s, -) food; dinner, meal; ohne ~ sein, to go without food.
Essenszeit f. dinner-time.
Essenz f. (-, -en) essence.
Essig m. (-[e]s, -e) vinegar.
Essig: ~gurke f. gherkin; ~sauer a. acetic; acetate of; ~saure Tonerde f. aluminium acetate; ~säure f. acetic acid.
Ess: ~löffel m. tablespoon; ein ~löffel voll, one tablespoonful of; ~tisch m. dining-table, dinner-table; ~waren pl. eatables, victuals pl.; ~zimmer n. dining-room.
Ess-Service n. dinner-set.
Estrich n. (-[e]s, -e) floor.
etablieren v.t. to establish; (sich) ~ v.refl. to settle; to set up in business.
Etablissement n. (-s, -s) establishment.
Etage f. (-, -n) storey, floor, flat.
Etagenwohnung f. flat; ~bau m. block of flats.
Etappe f. (-, -n) stage; (mil.) rear.

Etat (frz.) m. (-s, -s) budget, estimate.
Ethik f. (-, 0) ethics pl.
Etikett n. (-s, -s) label.
Etikette f. (-, -n) etiquette.
etliche a. pl. quite a number of, several.
Etui n. (-s, -s) case, box.
etwa adv. perhaps; nearly, about; say.
etwaig a. eventual.
etwas pn. something; some, any; ~ adv. somewhat.
Etymologie f. (-, -n) etymology.
etymologisch a. etymological.
euch pn. you.
euer pn. your; yours; euresgleichen, your equals.
Eugenik f. (-, -en) eugenics pl.
Eule f. (-, -n) owl, owlet.
Euphemismus m. (-, -men) euphemism.
eurethalben, euretwegen, um euretwillen, adv. for your sake.
eurige (der, die, das) pn. yours.
Euter n. (-s, -) udder, dug.
Euthanasie f. euthanasia.
evangelisch a. evangelical; Protestant.
Evangelist m. (-en, -en) evangelist.
Evangelium n. (-s, Evangelien) gospel.
eventuell a. & adv. possible, possibly, in a certain contingency.
ewig a. eternal, everlasting, perpetual; auf ~, in perpetuity.
Ewigkeit f. (-, -en) eternity.
exakt a. exact, accurate; ~e Wissenschaften, exact sciences.
Examen n. (-s, Examina) examination; ein ~ bestehen, to pass an examination.
Examinator m. (-s, -en) examiner.
examinieren v.t. to examine.
Exempel n. (-s, -) example.
Exemplar n. (-[e]s, -e) (eines Buches) copy; sample, specimen.
exemplarisch a. exemplary.
exerzieren v.t. & i. to exercise, to drill.
Exerzierplatz m. drill-ground.
Exil n. exile.
Existenz f. (-, -en) existence, livelihood.
Existenzminimum n. (minimum) living wage.
existieren v.i. to exist, to subsist.
expedieren v.t. to dispatch, to forward.
Expedition (-, -en) expedition.
Experiment n. (-[e]s, -e) experiment.
experimentieren v.i. to experiment.
explodieren v.i. (s) to explode.
Explosion f. (-, -en) explosion.
Explosionsmotor m. internal combustion engine.
Export m. (-[e]s, -e) export, exportation.
exportieren v.t. to export.
express a. & adv. express(ly).
Exterritorialität f. extraterritoriality.
extra adv. extra, besides, over and above; (fam.) especially, separately.
Extrablatt n. special edition.

Extrakt *m.* (-s, -e) extract.
Extrem *n.* (-[e]s, -e) extreme.
Extremitäten *f.pl.* extremities *pl.*
Exzellenz *f.* (-, -en) Excellency.

F

Fabel *f.* (-, -n) fable; fiction; plot.
fabelhaft *a.* fabulous, amazing.
fabeln *v.i.* to fable, to tell stories.
Fabrik *f.* (-, -en) factory, mill, works *pl.*
Fabrikant *m.* (-en, -en) manufacturer.
Fabrikat *n.* (-[e]s, -e) manufacture.
Fabrikation *f.* (-, -sarten) manufacture.
fabrikmässig *a. & adv.* by machinery.
Fabrikware *f.* manufactured goods *pl.*
fabrizieren *v.t.* to manufacture, to make.
Facette *f.* (-, -en) facet.
facettieren *v.t.* to cut in facets.
Fach *n.* (-[e]s, Fächer) compartment, partition; drawer, box, shelf; panel; (*im Schreibtisch*) pigeon-hole; (*fig.*) province, department; branch, line; (*Lehrfach*) subject.
Fach: ~arbeiter *m.* skilled worker; ~ausdruck *m.* technical term; ~berater *m.* technical adviser *or* consultant; ~bildung *f.* professional education.
fächeln *v.t.* to fan.
Fächer *m.* (-s, -) fan.
Fach: ~gelehrte[r], *m.* specialist; ~mann *m.* expert.
fachlich *a.* specialist.
fachmässig *a. & adv.* professional(ly).
Fach: ~schule *f.* professional *or* special school; ~studium *n.* professional study; ~werk *n.* timbered work; ~wissenschaft *f.* special branch of science.
Fackel *f.* (-, -n) torch.
Fackelzug *m.* torch-light procession.
fade *a.* flat, tasteless; insipid, dull.
Faden *m.* (-s, Fäden) thread; fathom.
Fadennudeln *f.pl.* vermicelli.
fadenscheinig *a.* threadbare.
Fagott *n.* (-[e]s, -e) bassoon.
fähig *a.* capable, able; fit, qualified.
Fähigkeit *f.* (-, -en) capacity; ability, faculty, talent.
fahl *a.* fallow, drab; livid.
fahnden *v.i. nach einem* ~, to search for.
Fahne *f.* (-, -n) standard, colours *pl.*, flag, banner.
Fahnenabzug *m.* (*typ.*) galley(-proof).
Fahnen: ~eid *m.* military oath; ~flucht *f.* desertion.
Fähnrich *m.* (-[e]s, -e) ensign; ~ *zur See*, midshipman.
Fahrausweis *m.* (*mil.*) travel order, travel permit.
fahrbar *a.* practicable (*Strasse*); mobile (*Kantine, etc.*).

Fähre *f.* (-, -n) ferry(boat).
fahren *v.i.st.* to drive; to cart, to wheel; to convey; ~ *v.i.st.* (*s*) to ride (in a carriage); to sail; to travel; to go; *aus der Haut* ~, to jump out of one's skin.
Fahrer *m.* (-s, -) driver.
Fahrgestell *n.* (*avi.*) undercarriage.
fahrig *a.* rash, fidgety.
Fahrkarte *f.* (-, -n) (*rail.*) ticket.
Fahrkartenausgabe *f.* booking-office.
fahrlässig *a.* negligent, careless.
Fahrlässigkeit *f.* (-, -en) negligence.
Fährmann *m.* ferryn.an.
Fahrordnung *f.* (-, -en) rule of the road.
Fahrplan *m.* time-table, (*Am.*) schedule.
fahrplanmässig *a.* regular; *adv.* to time; (*Am.*) scheduled, on schedule.
Fahr: ~preis *m.* fare; ~rad *n.* cycle, bicycle, (*fam.*) bike; ~schein *m.* ticket; ~stuhl *m.* (*im Hotel*) lift; bath-chair; ~weg *m.* carriage road.
Fahrt *f.* (-, -en) ride (in a carriage), drive; journey; (sea) voyage; row; course; *in voller* ~, at full speed.
Fahrtbefehl *m.* (*mil.*) travel order.
Fährte *f.* (-, -n) track, scent; *auf falscher* ~, on the wrong track.
Fahrtunterbrechung *f.* (*Am.*) stopover.
Fahrunterricht *m.*, Fahrschule *f.* (*mot.*) driving tuition.
Fahr: ~wasser *n.* channel; ~zeug *n.* vehicle.
faktisch *a. & adv.* actual(ly).
Faktor *m.* (-s, Faktoren) factor.
Faktur, Faktura *f.* (-, -ren) invoice.
Fakultät *f.* (-, -en) faculty.
falb *a.* fallow, sorrel, dun.
Falke *m.* (-n, -n) falcon, hawk.
Fall *m.* (-[e]s, Fälle) *m.* fall, accident; case; *im* ~*e dass*, in case; *den* ~ *setzen*, to suppose; *auf jeden* ~, at all events; *auf keinen* ~, on no account; *zu Fall bringen*, to ruin, to seduce.
Fallbeil *n.* guillotine.
Falle *f.* (-, -n) trap, snare; (*fig.*) pitfall.
fallen *v.i.st.* (*s*) to fall, to drop; (*Preise*) to decline (*com.*) to fail, to break; (*Schuss*) to be heard; *in die Augen* ~, to catch *or* strike the eye; *ins Gewicht* ~, to be of great weight; *in Ohnmacht* ~, to swoon, to faint; *es fällt mir schwer*, I find it hard.
fällen *v.t.* to fell; to cut down; *ein Urteil* ~, to pass a sentence.
Fallhammer *m.* drophammer.
fallieren *v.i.* to become bankrupt, to fail.
fällig *a.* due, payable; ~ *werden*, to become due; *sofort* ~*e Schulden*, liquid debts.
Fälligkeit *f.* (-, -en) maturity (*com.*).
falls *adv.* in case (that).
Fallschirm *m.* (-s, -e) parachute; *mit* ~ *abspringen*, to bail *or* bale out;

~springer *m.* parachutist; ~leucht-
bombe *f.* parachute flare; ~truppen *pl.*
paratroops.
Falltür *f.* trap-door.
falsch *a.* false, wrong; forged, counterfeit;
(*fig.*) faithless, deceitful; ~ *singen*, to
sing out of tune; ~ *spielen*, to cheat at
play.
fälschen *v.t.* to falsify; to adulterate;
(*Wechsel, Scheck*) to forge; (*Geld*) to
counterfeit; *gefälschte Stelle*, surreptitious passage.
Falschheit *f.* (-, -en) falsehood, false-
ness.
fälschlich *a.* false; ~ *adv.* falsely.
Falschmünzer *m.* (-s, -) coiner.
Falschspieler *m.* (-s, -) cardsharper.
Fälschung *f.* (-, -en) forgery.
Faltboot *n.* collapsible boat.
Falte *f.* (-, -n) fold, pleat, crease.
fälteln *v.t.* to pleat.
falten *v.t.* to fold, to pleat; *die Stirn* ~, to
knit one's brow; (*Hände*) to join.
Faltenwurf *n.* drapery.
Falter *m.* (-s, -) butterfly.
Falzbein *n.* (paper) folder.
falzen *v.t.* to fold; to flute; to groove.
familiär *a.* familiar, intimate.
Familie *f.* (-, -n) family.
Familien: ~name *m.* family name; ~un-
terstützung *f.* (*mil.*) separation allowance; ~urlaub *m.* compassionate leave;
~zulage *f.* family allowance.
famos *a.* (*fam.*) capital, first-rate, prime.
Fanatiker *m.* (-s, -) fanatic.
fanatisch *a.* fanatic(al).
Fanatismus *m.* (-, 0) fanaticism.
Fanfare *f.* (-, -n) flourish of trumpets.
Fang *m.* (-[e]s, Fänge) catch, capture;
fang, tusk; claw, talon; thrust, stab.
fangen *v.t.st.* to catch; to seize, to take;
(sich) ~ *v.refl.st.* to get caught.
Farbband *n.* (-[e]s, -bänder) typewriter
ribbon.
Farbe *f.* (-, -n) colour; dye, paint; hue,
complexion.
färben *v.t.* to colour, to tinge; to dye.
farbenblind *a.* colour-blind.
Farbendruck *m.* colour-printing.
Färber *m.* (-s, -) dyer, stainer.
farbig *a.* coloured.
Farbkasten *m.* (-s, -kästen) colour-box.
Farbstift *m.* (-[e]s, -e) crayon.
Farbstoff *m.* dyestuff; colouring matter.
Färbung *f.* (-, -en) coloration, colouring;
tinge, shade.
Farce *f.* (-, -n) farce.
Farnkraut *n.* fern.
Fasan *m.* (-[e]s, -e[n]) pheasant.
Faschine *f.* (-, -n) fagot, fascine, bavin.
Fasching *m.* (-s, -e) carnival.
Faschist *m.* (-en, -en) fascist.
faseln *v.i.* to drivel, to twaddle.

Faser *f.* (-, -n), Faserstoff *m.* fibre; Faserbrett *n.* fibreboard.
faserig *a.* fibrous.
fasern (sich) *v.refl.* to get frayed.
Fassade *f.* (-, -n) façade.
Fass *n.* (Fasses, Fässer) barrel, cask;
(*offenes*) tub, vat; *Bier vom* ~, beer on
draught.
fassbar *a.* seizable, comprehensible.
fassen *v.t.* to lay hold of, to seize; to contain; to conceive, to comprehend; (sich)
~ *v.refl.* to compose oneself; *sich kurz*
~, to be brief; *Edelsteine* ~, to set, to
mount; *in Worte* ~, to put into words;
einen Entschluss ~, to come to a decision.
fasslich *a.* intelligible, easy to understand.
Fasson *f.* (-, -en) shape.
Fassung *f.* (-, -en) setting (of stones);
wording, draft; composure.
fassungslos *a.* beside oneself.
fast *adv.* almost, nearly.
fasten *v.i.* to fast.
Fastenzeit *f.* Lent.
Fastnacht *f.* Shrove-Tuesday; Shrovetide.
Fasttag *m.* fast-day.
Faszikel *m.* (-s, -) bundle, file.
faszinieren *v.t.* to fascinate.
fatal *a.* unlucky, disagreeable; odious.
fauchen *v.i.* to spit.
faul *a.* putrefied, rotten; lazy, idle, sloth-
ful.
faulen *v.i.* (s) to rot, to putrefy.
faulenzen *v.i.* to idle, to lounge.
Faulenzer *m.* (-s, -) sluggard, idler.
Fäulnis *f.* (-, 0) rottenness, putrefaction.
Faust *f.* (-, Fäuste) fist.
Fäustchen *n.* (-s, -) *sich ins* ~ *lachen*, to
laugh in one's sleeve.
Fausthandschuh *m.* mitten.
Faustschlag *m.* cuff.
Fauteuil *n.* (-s, -s) armchair.
Fazit *n.* (-s, -s *or* -e) result, sum total.
Februar *m.* (-s, -e) February.
fechten *v.i.st.* to fight; (*kunstgerecht*) to
fence; (*fig.*) to beg one's way.
Fechter *m.* (-s, -) swordsman, fencer.
Feder *f.* (-, -n) feather; pen; spring.
Feder: ~ball *m.* shuttle-cock; ~bett *n.*
feather-bed; ~busch *m.* plume; crest;
~halter *m.* penholder.
federleicht *a.* light as a feather.
Federlesen *n. nicht viel* ~*s machen*, to
make short work of one.
Federmesser *n.* (-s, -) penknife.
federn *v.i.* to rebound; to be elastic.
Federstrich *m.* stroke of the pen.
Fee *f.* (-, -n) fairy.
feenhaft *a.* fairy-like.
Fegefeuer *n.* (-s, 0) purgatory.
fegen *v.t.* to sweep.
Fehde *f.* (-, -n) quarrel, feud; challenge.
Fehdehandschuh *m.* gauntlet.

Fehl *m.* (-s, 0) blemish.
fehl *adv.* amiss, wrong.
fehlbar *a.* fallible.
Fehl: -betrag *m.* deficit; ~bitte *f.* vain request.
fehlen *v.i.* to be missing; ~ *v.t.* to miss; *was fehlt dir?*, what is the matter with you?
Fehler *m.* (-s, -) fault, defect; error, mistake, blunder.
fehlerhaft *a.* faulty, incorrect.
Fehlgeburt *f.* miscarriage.
fehlgehen *v.i.st.* (*s*) to go wrong.
fehlgreifen *v.i.st.* to make a mistake.
Fehlgriff *m.* mistake; blunder.
Fehlschlag *m.* miss; failure.
fehlschlagen *v.i.st.* to miscarry, to fail.
Fehltritt *m.* false step; (*fig.*) error, mistake.
Fehlurteil *n.* (-s, -e) miscarriage of justice.
Feier *f.* (-, 0) celebration; festival; rest.
Feierabend *m.* cessation from work, time of rest.
feierlich *a.* festive, solemn; ceremonious.
Feierlichkeit *f.* (-, -en) ceremony.
feiern *v.i.* to rest from labour; ~ *v.t.* to solemnize; to celebrate.
Feiertag *m.* holiday; *gebotener* ~, holiday of obligation; *gesetzlicher* ~, public holiday.
feig(e) *a.* cowardly.
Feige *f.* (-, -n) fig.
Feigheit *f.* (-, -en) cowardice.
Feigling *m.* (-[e]s, -e) coward.
feil *a.* for sale, venal; mercenary.
feilbieten *v.t.st.* to offer for sale.
Feile *f.* (-, -n) file.
feilen *v.t.* to file; to refine, to polish.
feilschen *v.t.* to bargain, to haggle.
fein *a.* fine; delicate, elegant, refined, polite, genteel; subtle; *extra* ~, superfine.
Feind *m.* (-[e]s, -e) enemy; adversary, foe.
feind *a.* hostile, inimical.
feindlich *a.* inimical, hostile, adverse.
Feindschaft *f.* (-, -en) enmity, hostility.
feindselig *a.* hostile, malevolent.
Feindseligkeit *f.* (-, -en) hostility.
feinfühlig *a.* sensitive.
Feingehalt *m.* (-[e]s, -e) standard (of coins, gold, etc.).
Feinkost *f.* (-, 0) = Delikatessen.
Feinschmecker *m.* (-s, -) epicure.
feinsinnig *a.* delicate, sensitive.
feist *a.* fat, obese, adipose.
Feld *n.* (-[e]s, -er) field; plain; panel; (*Schach*) square.
Feld: -bahn *f.* field railway; ~bett *n.* camp-bed; ~geistlicher *m.* army chaplain, padre; ~geschrei *n.* war-cry; ~herr *m.* general; ~küche *f.* field-kitchen; ~lazarett *n.* field-hospital; ~marschall *m.* field-marshal; ~messer *m.* surveyor;

Chef der ~polizei *m.* provost-marshal, ~post *f.* army post, field post; ~postamt *n.* Army Post Office (APO); ~spat *m.* feldspar; ~stuhl *m.* camp-stool; ~webel *m.* sergeant-major; ~zug *m.* campaign.
Felge *f.* (-, -n) felloe, felly.
Fell *n.* (-[e]s, -e) hide; skin; coat; *ein dickes* ~ *haben*, to be thick-skinned.
Felleisen *n.* valise, portmanteau.
Fels *m.* (Felsen, Felsen), **Felsen** *m.* (-s, -) rock, crag.
felsenfest *a.* firm as a rock.
felsig *a.* rocky.
Fenster *n.* (-s, -) window.
Fenster: ~bank *f.* ~brett *n.* window-sill; ~kitt *m.* putty; ~laden *m.* shutter; ~putzer *m.* window-cleaner; ~rahmen *m.* window-frame; ~scheibe *f.* window-pane.
Ferien *pl.* vacation, holidays *pl.*; *in den* ~, on holiday.
Ferkel *n.* (-s, -) young pig.
ferkeln *v.t.* to farrow.
fern *a. & adv.* far, remote, distant.
Fernamt *n.* trunk exchange.
Fernaufklärung *f.* (*mil.*) long-range reconnaissance.
Ferne *f.* (-, -n) distance.
ferner *a.* farther, further; ~ *adv.* further, moreover.
fernerhin *adv.* henceforward, henceforth.
Ferngespräch *n.* trunk (*or* long-distance) call.
ferngesteuert *a.* remote-controlled.
Fernglas *n.* telescope.
fernhalten *v.t.st.* to keep off.
fernhin *adv.* to a distance, far away.
Fern: ~heizung *f.* long-distance heating; ~kampfartillerie, *f.* long-range artillery; ~rohr *n.* telescope; ~schreiben *n.* ~schreiber *m.* teletype; ~sehen *n.* television; ~sehapparat *n.* television set; ~sicht *f.* prospect, panorama.
Fernsprech: ~amt *n.* telephone exchange; ~zelle *f.* call box.
Fernsprecher *m.* (-s, -) telephone.
Fernsteuerung *f.* remote control.
Fernsteuerwaffe *f.* guided missile.
Ferse *f.* (-, -n) heel.
fertig *a.* ready; ready-made; finished; *ich bin* ~, I have (am) done; *mit einem* ~ *werden*, to manage one.
fertigen *v.t.* to manufacture, to make.
Fertigkeit *f.* (-, -en) skill, dexterity; fluency.
Fertigwaren *f.pl.* finished (*or* manufactured) goods.
fesch *a.* smart; dashing; stylish.
Fessel *f.* (-, -n) fetter, shackle; (*des Pferdes*) fetlock, pastern; ~ballon *m.* captive balloon.
fesseln *v.t.* to fetter; (*fig.*) to captivate; (*Blick*) to arrest.

fest a. fast; firm; solid; settled, fixed; forti-fied; ~er Schlaf, sound sleep; ~er Körper, solid; sich ~halten, to hold on; sich ~legen, to commit oneself; ~legen, to fix, lay down; ~machen, to fasten; ~nehmen, to arrest; ~setzen, ~stellen, to establish; ... fest a. resisting; **stossfest** a. shock resisting.

Fest n. (-es, -e) feast, festival.

Festbeleuchtung f. illumination.

Feste f. (-, -n) fastness, stronghold.

Festessen n. public dinner, banquet.

Festigkeit f. (-, 0) firmness; solidity; constancy; (Metall) strength.

Festland n. continent.

festlich a. festive, festival; solemn.

Festlichkeit f. (-, -en) festivity, solemnity.

Festnahme f. arrest.

festsetzen v.t. to fix, to settle, to appoint.

feststellen v.t. to ascertain; to establish.

Festtag m. feast, holiday.

Festung f. (-, -en) fortress.

Festzug m. procession, pageant.

Fetisch m. (-es, -e) fetish.

fett a. fat; greasy; (von Speisen) rich.

Fett n. (-[e]s, -e) fat; grease.

Fett: ~druck m. heavy type, bold face; ~gedruckt a. in thick or heavy type; ~flecken m. grease-spot.

fettig a. greasy, fatty.

Fettsäure f. fatty acid.

Fetzen m. (-s, -) shred, tatter, rag.

feucht a. moist, wet; damp.

Feuchtigkeit f. (-, -en) moisture, humidity.

Feuchtigkeitsmesser m. hygrometer.

feuchtigkeitssicher a. damp-proof.

feudal a. feudal.

Feuer n. (-s, -) fire; (fig.) ardour; (für Zigarren) light.

Feuer: ~bestattung f. cremation; ~bekämpfung f. fire-fighting.

feuerfest a. fire-proof.

feuergefährlich a. inflammable, combustible.

Feuer: ~gitter n. (am Kamin) fireguard; ~kraft f. (mil.) fire-power; ~leitung f. (mil.) fire direction; ~löschapparat m. fire extinguisher; ~melder m. fire-alarm.

feuern v.i. to fire.

feuerrot a. fiery red, red-hot.

Feuersbrunst f. (-, -brünste) fire, conflagration.

Feuersgefahr f. danger of fire.

feuersicher a. fireproof.

Feuer: ~spritze f. fire-engine; ~stein m. flint.

Feuerung f. (-, -en) fuel; firing.

Feuer: ~versicherung f. fire insurance; ~wache f. fire-station; ~wehr f. fire-brigade; ~wehrmann m. fireman; ~werk n. fireworks pl.; ~zange f. tongs pl.; ~zeug n. lighter.

feurig a. fiery; ardent.

FF! etwas aus dem ~ verstehen, to have a thing at one's finger ends.

Fiasko n. (-[s], -s) failure; ~ machen, to fail.

Fibel f. (-, -n) primer, spelling-book.

Fiber f. (-, -n) fibre, filament.

Fichte f. (-, -n) pine(-tree).

Fideikommiss, n. (-misses, -misse) entail.

fidel a. (fam.) merry, jolly.

Fieber n. (-s, -) fever; ~ haben, to have a temperature.

fieberhaft a. feverish.

fieberkrank a. feverish.

fiebern v.i. to be in a fever.

Fiedel f. (-, -n) fiddle.

Fiedelbogen m. fiddle-stick, bow.

fiedeln v.t. & n. to fiddle; to scrape.

Figur f. (-, -en) figure; diagram; (Schach) chessman.

Filet n. (-s, -s) netting; fillet of beef.

Filiale f. (-, -n) branch (establishment).

Filigranarbeit f. filigree.

Film m. (-s, -) film; (Am.) motion-picture.

Filmatelier n. studio.

filmen v.t. to film.

Filter m. or n. (-s, -) filter.

filtrieren v.t. to filter, to strain.

Filz m. (-es, -e) felt; (fig.) niggard.

Filzhut m. felt-hat.

filzig a. felt-like; (fig.) stingy, niggardly.

Finanzamt n. inland revenue office.

Finanzen f.pl. finances pl.; revenue.

finanziell a. financial.

finanzieren v.t. to finance.

Finanz: ~jahr n. fiscal year; ~mann m. financier; ~minister m. minister of finance; (in England) Chancellor of the Exchequer.

Findelhaus n. foundling-hospital.

finden v.t.st. to find, to discover; to meet with; to think, to deem; (sich) ~ v.refl.st. to be found; Vergnügen ~ an, to take pleasure in; Geschmack ~ an, to like, to relish; es wird sich ~, we shall see; sich ~ in, to put up with.

Finderlohn m. reward to the finder.

findig a. shrewd, ingenious.

Findling m. (-[e]s, -e) foundling.

Finger m. (-s, -) finger; einem auf die ~ sehen, to watch one closely; durch die ~ sehen, to wink at.

Fingerabdruck m. finger print.

Fingerhut m. thimble; (bot.) fox-glove.

fingern v.t. to finger.

Finger: ~satz m. (mus.) fingering; ~zeig m. hint.

fingieren v.t. to feign.

Fink[e] m. (-en -en) finch.

finster a. dark, obscure; gloomy, dim.

Finsternis f. (-, -nisse) darkness, obscurity; eclipse.

Finte f. (-, -n) feint; pretence; fib.

Firma f. (-, Firmen) firm; (*Name*) style.

Firmament n. (-[e]s, -e) firmament, sky.

Firmenname m. trade name.

Firm[el]ung f. (-, -en) confirmation.

Firnis m. (-nisses, -nisse) varnish.

firnissen v.t. to varnish.

First m. (-es, -e) & f. (-, -en) top; ridge of a roof.

Fis n. (-, 0) (*mus.*) F sharp.

Fisch m. (-es, -e) fish.

Fisch: ∼angel f. fishing-hook; ∼bein n. whalebone.

fischen v.t. to fish, to angle; *im Trüben* ∼, to fish in troubled waters.

Fischer m. (-s, -) fisherman, angler.

Fischerboot n. fishing-boat.

Fischhändler m. fishmonger.

fiskalisch a. fiscal.

Fiskus m. (-, 0) exchequer, treasury.

Fistel f. (-, -n) fistula; (*als Stimme*) falsetto.

Fittich m. (-[e]s, -e) wing, pinion.

fix a. fixed, firm; (*fig.*) quick, sharp; ∼ *und fertig*, quite ready.

fixieren v.t. to fix, to settle; (*phot.*) to fix; (*einen*) to stare at; *Fixierbad, Fixierlösung* (*phot.*) fixing solution.

Fixstern m. (-[e]s, -e) fixed star.

flach a. flat; plain, level; shallow.

Fläche f. (-, -n) plain, surface; plane.

Flächen: ∼inhalt m. area; ∼mass n. square measure; ∼raum m. area.

Flachrelief n. low relief.

Flachs m. (-es, -e) flax.

flackern v.i. to flare, to flicker.

Flagge f. (-, -n) flag, colours pl.

flaggen v.i. to hoist the flag(s).

Flamme f. (-, -n) flame, blaze; (*Liebchen*) love, sweetheart.

flammen v.i. to flame, to blaze.

Flammenwerfer m. flame-thrower.

Flanell m. (-[e]s, -e) flannel.

Flanke f. (-, -n) flank.

Flankenspiel n. (*mech.*) backlash.

flankieren v.t. to flank.

Flasche f. (-, -n) bottle flask; *auf* ∼n *ziehen*, to bottle.

Flaschen: ∼bier n. bottled beer; ∼gestell n. bottle-rack.

Flaschenzug m. pulley, tackle.

flatterhaft a. unsteady, fickle.

flattern v.i. to flit, to flutter; (*Fahne*) to wave, to stream.

flau a. flat, insipid; faint; (*com.*) dull.

Flaum m. (-[e]s, 0) down.

Flechte f. (-, -n) twist, plait, braid; (*med.*) herpes; (*Pflanze*) lichen.

flechten v.t.st. to twist, to plait; (*Kranz*) to wreathe.

Fleck m. (-[e]s, -e) spot; place; patch; blot, stain; tripe.

Flecken m. (-s, -) spot, stain; blemish; (*Ort*) market-town, hamlet.

flecken v.t. to stain.

Fleckfieber n. typhus.

fleckig a. spotted, speckled, stained.

Fledermaus f. bat.

Flegel m. (-s, -) flail; (*fig.*) churl.

Flegelei f. (-, -en) piece of insolence.

flehen v.i. to implore, to beseech.

flehend a. suppliant.

flehentlich a. & adv. imploring(ly), urgent(ly).

Fleisch n. (-es, 0) flesh; (butcher's) meat; (*des Obstes*) pulp.

Fleisch: ∼beschauer m. inspector of butcher's meat; ∼brühe f. broth, beeftea; gravy.

Fleischer m. (-s, -) butcher.

Fleischeslust f. carnal appetite.

Fleisch: ∼extrakt m. extract of meat; ∼farbe f. carnation (colour).

fleischfressend a. carnivorous.

fleischlich a. carnal.

Fleischpastete f. meat-pie.

Fleiss m. (-es, 0) diligence, application, industry.

fleissig a. diligent; industrious.

flektieren v.t. to inflect.

fletschen v.t. to grind (one's teeth).

flicken v.t. to mend, to patch, to botch.

Flickschuster m. cobbler.

Flieder m. (-s, -) (*spanischer*) lilac.

Fliege f. (-, -n) fly.

fliegen v.i.st. (s) to fly; to rush, to dash; ∼ lassen, to fly (a kite), to wave (a flag).

Fliegenpapier n. fly paper.

Flieger m. (-s, -) airman, flyer, aviator; pilot.

Fliegerabwehr... anti-aircraft-.

Fliegeralarm m. air-raid warning.

fliehen v.i.st. (s) to flee; ∼ v.t.st. to avoid, to shun.

Fliehkraft f. centrifugal power.

Fliese f. (-, -n) flag, slab; tile.

Fliess n. (-es, -e) fleece.

fliessen v.i.st. (s) to flow; (*vom Papier*) to blank.

fliessend a. & adv. fluent(ly); ∼es warmes *Wasser*, constant hot water.

Fliesspapier n. blotting-paper.

flimmern v.i. to twinkle, to flicker.

flink a. brisk, quick, nimble.

Flinte f. (-, -n) gun, musket; *die* ∼ *ins Korn werfen*, to give in, to throw up the sponge.

Flitterwochen f.pl. honeymoon.

Flocke f. (-, -n) flock; flake (of snow).

Floh m. (-[e]s, Flöhe) flea.

Flor m. (-[e]s, -e) (*Trauer*) crape, gauze.

Florett n. (-[e]s, -s u. -e) (fencing) foil.

florieren v.i. to flourish, to thrive.

Floskel f. (-, -n) flourish (of rhetoric), tirade, phrase.

Floss n. (-es, Flösse) float; raft.

Flosse, Flossfeder f. (-, -n) fin.

flössen *v.t.* to float.
Flöte *f.* (-, -n) flute.
Flötenbläser *m.* flute-player.
flott *a.* afloat, floating; slick; gay, fast; *wieder ~ machen,* to refloat; *~ leben,* to live fast.
Flotte *f.* (-, -n) fleet, navy.
Flottille *f.* (-, -n) squadron, flotilla.
Flöz *n.* (-es, -e) layer, stratum; seam.
Fluch *m.* (-[e]s, Flüche) curse, malediction; *(aus Gewohnheit)* oath.
fluchen *v.t.* to curse; to swear.
Flucht *f.* (-, 0) flight, escape; *(wilde)* rout; *(Reihe)* range, row.
flüchten *v.i.* (s) & *refl.* (sich) ~, to flee, to take to flight; ~ *v.t.* to secure, to carry to a place of safety.
flüchtig *a.* fugitive; *(oberflächlich)* careless, slight, fleeting.
Flüchtling *m.* (-[e]s, -e) refugee.
Flug *m.* (-[e]s, Flüge) flight.
Flug: ~anzug *m.* flying suit; ~bombe *f.* flying bomb.
Flügel *m.* (-s, -) wing; grand piano; leaf (of a door); blade (of a propeller).
Flügeltür *f.* folding-door.
Fluggast *m.* air-passenger.
flügge *a.* fledged.
Flug: ~hafen *m.* airport; ~platz *n.* aerodrome.
flugs *adv.* quickly, instantly.
Flug: ~sand *m.* quicksand; ~schrift *f.* pamphlet; ~zeug *n.* aircraft, aeroplane, airplane; ~zeughalle *f.* hangar; ~zeugträger *m.* (*nav.*) aircraft carrier.
Fluidum *n.* aura.
fluktuieren *v.i.* to fluctuate.
Flunder *m.* (-s, -n) & *f.* (-, -n) flounder.
Flunkerer *m.* (-s, -) story-teller.
flunkern *v.i.* to brag, to tell fibs.
Fluoreszenz...fluorescent.
Flur *f.* (-, -en) field, tilled plain; ~ *m.* (-[e]s, -e) *(Haus~)* entrance-hall; corridor.
Fluss *m.* (Flusses, Flüsse) flow; river, stream; flux.
Fluss: ~abschnitt *m.* reach; ~bett *n.* channel, river-bed; ~gebiet, ~becken *n.* river basin; ~pferd *n.* hippopotamus; ~übergang *m.* river crossing.
flüssig *a.* fluid, liquid.
Flüssigkeit *f.* (-, -en) fluidity; fluid, liquid.
flüstern *v.t.* to whisper.
Flut *f.* (-, -en) flood; high tide; (*fig.*) torrent, spate.
fluten *v.i.* to flow.
Fock: ~mast *m.* (-es, -e) foremast; ~segel *n.* foresail.
Föderalismus *m.* federalism.
fohlen *v.i.* to foal.
Fohlen *n.* (-s, -) foal, colt.
Föhn *m.* (-[e]s, -e) scorching south-wind.
Föhre *f.* (-, -n) (Scotch) fir

Folge *f.* (-, -n) succession, series; consequence; (*Zeit*) future, sequel; ~ leisten, to comply with; infolge, in consequence of, pursuant to; zufolge, according to.
folgen *v.i.* (s) to follow, to succeed; to result, to ensue; to obey; *im Folgenden,* hereinafter.
folgendermassen *adv.* in the following manner.
folgenreich *a.* big with consequences.
folgenschwer *a.* portentous, big with consequences.
folgerecht, folgerichtig *a.* consistent, logical.
folgern *v.t.* to conclude, to infer.
Folgerung *f.* (-, -en) deduction, conclusion, inference.
folgewidrig *a.* inconsistent.
Folgezeit *f.* time to come, after-ages *pl.*
folglich *adv.* consequently, therefore.
folgsam *a.* obedient; obsequious.
Foliant *m.* (-en, -en) folio (volume).
Folie *f.* (-, -n) foil.
Folio *n.* (-[s], -s *u.* Folien) folio.
Folter *f.* (-, -n) rack, torture.
foltern *v.t.* to put to the rack, to torture; (*fig.*) to torment.
Fonds *m.* (-, -) fund, capital, stock.
foppen *v.t.* to hoax, to mystify.
förderlich *a.* useful, beneficial.
fordern *v.t.* to demand, to claim, to call for; to require; (*zum Duell*) to challenge.
fördern *v.t.* to further, to forward; to promote; (*Bergwerk*) to haul; *zu Tage ~,* to bring to light, to unearth.
förderndes Mitglied *n.* sponsoring member.
Förderschacht *f.* engine-shaft.
Forderung *f.* (-, -en) demand, claim; challenge.
Förderung *f.* (-, -en) furtherance; promotion; hauling, output.
Forelle *f.* (-, -n) trout.
Form *f.* (-, -en) shape, form, figure; fashion; model, pattern; mould.
Formalität *f.* (-, -en) formality, form.
Format *n.* (-[e]s, -e) (*Buch*) size; form, shape.
Formel *f.* (-, -n) formula, form.
formell *a.* & *adv.* formal(ly), in due form.
formen *v.t.* to form, to shape, to mould.
Formenlehre *f.* (*gram.*) accidence.
formieren *v.t.* to form.
förmlich *a.* formal, in due form; ceremonious, stiff; explicit; regular, downright; ~ *adv.* actually; formally.
Förmlichkeit *f.* (-, -en) formality.
formlos *a.* shapeless; informal; rude.
Formular *n.* (-[e]s, -e) (printed) form, schedule.
formulieren *v.t.* to formulate; *neu ~,* to restate.

forsch a. (fam.) vigorous, lusty, strapping.

forschen v.i. to search, to inquire.

Forscher m. (-s, -) investigator, scholar.

Forschung f. (-, -en) research, investigation; **~sreisender** m. explorer.

Forst m. (-es, -e) forest.

Förster m. (-s, -) forester, ranger.

Forst: ~akademie f. school of forestry; **~amt** n. Forestry Commission.

fort adv. on; off, gone, away; in einem ~, without interruption; und so ~, and so on.

fortan adv. henceforth.

fortarbeiten v.i. to keep on working.

fortbegeben (sich) v.refl.st. to withdraw.

fortbestehen v.i.st. to continue to exist.

fortbewegen (sich) v.t. & refl. to move on.

fortbilden (sich) v.refl. to continue studying.

Fortbildungsschule f. continuation-school.

fortbleiben v.i.st. (s) to stay away.

fortbringen v.t.ir. to carry away; to help forward.

Fortdauer f. (-, 0) continuance.

fortdauern v.i. to continue, to last.

fortdürfen v.i.ir. to be permitted to go.

fortfahren v.i.st. (h) to continue, to go on.

fortführen v.t. to carry on.

Fortgang m. (-[e]s, 0) progress, success.

fortgehen v.i.st. (s) to go away.

Fortgeschrittener m. advanced student.

forthelfen v.t.st. to help on; (sich) ~ v.refl.st. to support oneself.

fortjagen v.t. to expel.

fortkommen v.i.st. (s) to prosper; gut, schlecht ~, to do well, ill.

Fortkommen n. (-s, 0) progress, success.

fortlassen v.t. to suffer to go.

fortlaufen v.i.st. (s) to run away.

fortlaufend a. continuous, continual.

fortleben v.i. to live on.

fortmachen v.i. (sich) ~ v.refl. to make off.

fortmarschieren v.i. (s) to march off or on.

fortmüssen v.i.ir. to be obliged to go.

fortpflanzen (sich) v.t. & refl. to propagate, to transmit; (Krankheit) to spread.

Fortpflanzung f. (-, 0) propagation, reproduction.

Fortpflanzungs... reproductive.

fortreisen v.i. (s) to depart.

fortrennen v.i.st. (s) to run off.

fortrücken v.t. (h) & i. (s) to move on, to remove; to advance, to make progress.

fortschaffen v.t. to carry off, to remove.

fortschicken v.t. to send away.

fortschleppen (sich) v.refl. to drag oneself on.

fortschreiten v.i.st. (s) to proceed, to make progress; to improve.

fortschreitend a. progressive.

Fortschritt m. (-[e]s, -e) progress.

fortsetzen v.t. to continue, to pursue.

Fortsetzer m. (-s, -) continuer.

Fortsetzung f. (-, -en) continuation.

forttragen v.t.st. to carry away.

fortwährend a. & adv. continual(ly).

fortwirken v.i. to continue to operate.

fortwollen v.i.ir. to want to go.

fortziehen v.t.st. to draw away; ~ v.i.st. (s) to move off; to leave (a house).

Fossil n. (-[e]s, -ien) fossil.

Fracht f. (-, -en) freight; load; cargo; (~geld) carriage; ~ bezahlt, carriage free.

Fracht: ~brief m. bill of lading; **~dampfer** m. cargo steamer.

frachtfrei a. carriage-paid.

Frack m. (-[e]s, -s, Fräcke) evening dress, tail-suit; **~hemd** n. dress shirt.

Frage f. (-, -n) question; issue; eine ~ stellen, to ask a question; in ~ stellen, to question; ohne ~, unquestionably.

fragen v.t. to ask, to demand; es fragt sich, it is doubtful, the question is whether...

Fragebogen m. questionnaire.

Frage: ~wort n. interrogative; **~zeichen** n. question-mark.

fraglich a. questionable; doubtful.

fragwürdig a. exciting suspicion, questionable.

Fraktion f. (-, -en) parliamentary group.

Frakturschrift f. German type; blackletter.

frank a. free, frank, ingenuous.

frankieren v.t. to stamp.

frankiert, franko a. post free.

Franse f. (-, -n) fringe.

fransig a. fringed.

Franziskaner m. (-s, -) Franciscan.

frappant a. striking.

Fräsmaschine f. milling machine.

fraternisieren v.i. to fraternize.

Fratz m. (-es u. -en, -en) brat, naughty child; guy.

Fratze f. (-, -n) grimace; caricature.

Frau f. (-, -en) woman; wife; lady; (auf Briefen) Mrs. (=Mistress).

Frauen: ~arzt m. specialist for women's diseases; **~hemd** n. chemise; **~kloster**, n. nunnery; **~zimmer** n. woman, female.

Fräulein n. (-s, -) Miss (title); young lady, single lady.

frech a. insolent, saucy, shameless.

Frechheit f. (-, -en) impudence.

Fregatte f. (-, -n) frigate.

Fregattenkapitän m. commander.

frei a. free; disengaged; exempt; vacant; im Freien, out of doors, in the open air; es steht dir ~, you are at liberty (to); es einem ~ stellen, to leave one at liberty (to); ~ Eisenbahn, free on rail; ~ Schiff, free on board; ~ Berufe or die professions; Angehöriger eines ~en Berufes, professional man; ~e Fahrt (mot.) open drive; ~e Wirtschaft, private enterprise;

aus ~er Hand, off-hand; *aus ~em Willen,* of one's own free will.
Frei: ~brief *m.* charter; ~denker *m.* free-thinker.
freien *v.t. & i.* to court, to woo.
Freier *m.* (-s, -) wooer, suitor.
Freiexemplar *n.* free copy, presentation copy.
Freifrau *f.* baroness.
Freigabe *f.* release.
freigeben *v.t.* to set free, to release.
freigebig *a.* liberal, generous.
Frei: ~geist *m.* freethinker; ~hafen *m.* freeport; ~handel *m.* free-trade.
Freihandzeichnen *n.* freehand drawing.
Freiheit *f.* (-, -en) freedom, liberty; *in ~,* at large.
freiheitlich *a.* liberal.
Freiheitsstrafe *f.* imprisonment.
Freiherr *m.* baron.
freiherrlich *a.* baronial.
Freiin *f.* (-, -nen) baron's daughter.
Freilauf *m.* freewheel.
freilich *adv.* indeed, certainly, to be sure, it is true, I admit.
Frei: ~luft...open air; ~machen *v.t.* to stamp; ~maurer *m.* freemason; ~maurerei *f.* freemasonry; ~mut *m.* frankness, candour.
freimütig *a.* candid, frank.
Freischärler *m.* (-s, -) guerilla.
freisinnig *a.* liberal.
freisprechen *v.t.st.* to acquit.
Frei: ~sprechung *f.* acquittal; ~staat *m.* republic; Free State; ~stätte *f.* refuge, asylum; ~stelle *f.* exhibition, scholarship (in a school); ~tag *m.* Friday; ~treppe *f.* outside stairs.
Freiübungen *f.pl.* callisthenics, light gymnastics *pl.*
freiwillig *a.* voluntary, spontaneous.
Freiwillige[r] *m.* (-n, -n) volunteer.
Freiwilligkeit *f.* (-, 0) spontaneity.
Freizügigkeit *f.* (-, 0) right of settlement.
fremd *a.* strange, foreign, outlandish.
fremdartig *a.* strange, odd.
Fremden: ~amt *n.* visitors' bureau; ~buch *n.* visitors' book; hotel register; ~führer *m.* guide; ~legion *f.* Foreign Legion; ~verkehr *m.* tourist traffic.
Fremde[r], *m.* (-n, -n) stranger; foreigner.
Fremdherrschaft *f.* (-, -en) foreign domination.
Fremdkörper *m.* foreign body.
Fremdling *m.* (-[e]s, -e) stranger.
Fremdsprache *f.* foreign language.
Fremdwort *n.* (-[e]s, -wörter) foreign word.
Frequenz *f.* (*elek.*) frequency.
Fresko *n.* (-s, Fresken) fresco(-painting).
fressen *v.t.st.* to eat; to devour.
Fressen *n.* (-s, -) food, meal.
Frettchen *n.* (-s, -) ferret.

Freude *f.* (-, -n) joy; enjoyment, pleasure, delight.
freudetrunken *a.* overjoyed, enraptured.
freudig *a.* joyful, joyous, cheerful.
freudlos *a.* joyless, cheerless.
freuen *v.t.* to gladden, to give pleasure; *das freut mich,* I am glad of that; (sich) ~ *v.refl.* (*über*) to be glad of; (*auf*) to look forward to.
Freund *m.* (-[e]s, -e) friend.
Freundin *f.* (-, -nen) (female) friend.
freundlich *a.* kind, friendly; (*Ort*) cheerful.
Freundlichkeit *f.* (-, -en) kindness.
Freundschaft *f.* (-, -en) friendship.
freundschaftlich *a.* amicable, friendly.
Frevel *m.* (-s, -) crime; outrage.
frevelhaft *a.* mischievous, criminal.
freveln *v.i.* to commit an outrage.
Frevler *m.* (-s, -) transgressor; offender.
Friede[n] *m.* (-dens, 0) peace; *im ~n,* at peace.
Friedens: ~bruch *m.* breach of the peace; ~richter *m.* Justice of the Peace, J.P.; ~schluss *m.* (conclusion of) peace; ~stifter *m.* peacemaker; ~vertrag *m.* peace treaty.
Friedhof *m.* church-yard, cemetery.
friedlich *a.* peaceable, peaceful.
friedliebend *a.* peaceable.
frieren *v.i.st.* to freeze; to feel cold.
Fries *m.* (-es, -e) (*arch.*) frieze; (*Zeug*) baize.
frisch *a.* fresh; new; (*fig.*) brisk, gay; vigorous; hale.
Frische *f.* (-, 0) freshness; vigour.
Friseur *m.* (-[e]s, -e) hair-dresser.
frisieren *v.t.* to dress the hair.
Frist *f.* (-, -en) time-limit; respite; (*Am.*) deadline.
fristen *v.t.* (*das Leben*) to gain one's living.
fristlos *a. & adv.* at a moment's notice.
Frisur *f.* (-, -en) hair-style, hair-do.
frivol *a. & adv.* frivolous(ly).
froh *a.* joyous, glad, joyful.
fröhlich *a.* joyous; merry; cheerful.
frohlocken *v.i.* to rejoice; to exult.
fromm *a.* pious, religious.
Frömmelei *f.* (-, -en) sanctimoniousness.
Frömmigkeit *f.* (-, 0) piety.
Frondienst *m.*, Fron(e) *f.* (-, -n) enforced labour.
frönen *v.i.* to indulge in.
Fronleichnamsfest *n.* Corpus Christi-day.
Front *f.* (-, -en) front, face.
Frosch *m.* (-es, Frösche) frog.
Frost *m.* (-es, Fröste) frost; chill; cold.
Frostbeule *f.* chilblain; frostbite.
frösteln *v.i.* to shiver, to feel chilly.
frostig *a.* frosty; chilly; frigid.
frottieren *v.t.* (*med.*) to rub; to brush.
Frucht *f.* (-, Früchte) fruit; (*fig.*) result, effect.

fruchtbar *a.* fruitful, productive, fertile.
Fruchtbarkeit *f.* (-, 0) fruitfulness, fertility; fecundity.
Fruchteis *n.* sundae.
fruchten *v.i.* (*fig.*) to be effectual.
fruchtlos *a.* fruitless; ineffectual.
Frucht: ~saft *m.* fruit-juice, squash; ~salat *m.* fruit-salad; ~wechsel *m.* rotation of crops.
früh *a.* & *adv.* early; in the morning.
Frühe *f.* (-, 0) early morning; *in aller* ~, early in the morning.
frühestens *adv.* at the earliest.
Früh: ~geburt *f.* premature birth; ~jahr *n.* spring.
Frühling *m.* (-s, -e) spring.
frühreif *a.* precocious, early-ripe.
Frühstück *n.* breakfast; (*zweites*) elevenses; ~ *anrichten*, to lay breakfast.
frühstücken *v.i.* to breakfast; to lunch.
frühzeitig *a.* early, premature; untimely.
Fuchs *m.* (Fuchses, Füchse) fox; sorrel horse; (*Student*) freshman.
Fuchsjagd *f.* fox-hunt.
Fuchtel *f.* (-, -n) ferule, rod.
fuchteln *v.i.* to fidget.
Fuder *n.* (-s, -) cart-load.
Fug *m.* (-[e]s, 0) *mit* ~ *und Recht*, with good cause.
Fuge *f.* (-, -n) juncture, joint; groove; (*mus.*) fugue; *aus den* ~*n sein*, to be out of joint.
fügen *v.t.* to join, to unite; (sich) ~ *v.refl.* to be suitable, to be convenient; to submit (to); to conform (to); to chance, to happen.
fügsam *a.* accommodating, docile.
Fügung *f.* (-, -en) contingency; dispensation of Providence.
fühlbar *a.* sensible, perceptible.
fühlen *v.t.* to feel; to be sensible *or* aware of.
Fühler *m.* (-s, -) antenna, feeler, tentacle.
Fühlung *f.* (-, -en) (*mil.*) touch; ~ *haben mit einem*, to be in touch with a person.
Fuhre *f.* (-, -n) conveyance; cartload.
führen *v.t.* to convey, to conduct; to lead, to guide; to manage; (*Bücher*) to keep; (*Waren*) to keep, to deal in; (*betreiben*) to carry on; *die Aufsicht* ~ *über*, to superintend; *den Beweis* ~, to show proof; *das Wort* ~, to be spokesman; *wohin soll das* ~? what are we coming to?
Führer *m.* (-s, -) leader; conductor; guide; pilot; guide-book.
Führer: ~prinzip *n.* leadership principle; ~prüfung *f.* (*mot.*) driving test.
Führerschaft *f.* (-, 0) leadership.
Führerschein *m.* (*mot.*) driving licence.
Fuhrmann *m.* waggoner, carrier.
Führung *f.* (-, -en) guidance, conduct; direction, management; (*mil.*) generalship.

Führungszeugnis *n.* certificate of good conduct.
Fuhrwerk *n.* carriage, vehicle.
Fülle *f.* (-, 0) plenty; abundance; *in Hülle und* ~, enough and to spare.
füllen *v.t.* to fill (up); to stuff; (*Zahn*) to stop.
Füllen *n.* (-s, -) foal, colt, filly.
Füllfeder *f.* fountain pen.
Füllung *f.* (-, -en) stuffing, dressing.
Fund *m.* (-[e]s, -e) find.
Fundament *n.* (-[e]s, -e) foundation.
Fund: ~büro *n.* lost property office; ~grube *f.* (*fig.*) store-house.
fünf *a.* **Fünf** *f.* (-, -en) five.
Fünfeck *n.* (-[e]s, -e) pentagon.
fünfeckig *a.* pentagonal.
fünferlei *a.* of five kinds.
fünffach, fünffältig *a.* fivefold, quintuple.
fünfhundert, five hundred.
Fünflinge *pl.* quintuplets *pl.*
fünfte Kolonne *f.* fifth column.
fünftens *adv.* fifthly; in the fifth place.
fünfzehn *a.* fifteen.
fünfzig *a.* fifty.
Fünfziger *m.* (-s, -) quinquagenarian.
fungieren *v.i.* to act as.
Funk *m.* (-s, 0) wireless, radio.
Funkaufklärung *f.* (-, -en) radio intelligence.
Funke[n] *m.* (-ken[s], -ken) spark, sparkle.
funkeln *v.i.* to sparkle.
funkelnagelneu *a.* brand-new.
funken *v.i.* & *t.* to wireless.
Funker *m.* (-s, -) wireless operator.
Funk: ~messgerät *n.* radar; ~peilung *f.* radio direction finding; ~spruch *m.* wireless message; ~telegramm *n.* radio-telegram; ~turm *m.* radio tower.
funktionieren *v.i.* to function, to work.
für *pr.* for; instead of; (*im Interesse von*) in behalf of; *an und* ~ *sich*, in itself; *Tag* ~ *Tag*, day by day; ~ *sich leben*, to live by oneself; *er* ~ *seine Person*, he, for one; ~ *und wider*, pro and con.
Furage *f.* forage.
Fürbitte *f.* (-, -n) intercession.
Furche *f.* (-, -n) furrow.
furchen *v.t.* to furrow; (*fig.*) to wrinkle.
Furcht *f.* (-, 0) fear, fright, dread.
furchtbar *a.* terrible, dreadful; awful.
fürchten *v.t.* to fear, to apprehend, to dread; (sich) ~ *v.refl.* to be afraid.
fürchterlich *a.* terrible, frightful.
furchtlos *a.* fearless, intrepid.
furchtsam *a.* timid, nervous, shy.
Furie *f.* (-, -n) fury.
Fürsprache *f.* (-, -n) intercession, good offices *pl.*
Fürsprecher *m.* (-s, -) intercessor, mediator.
Furnier *n.* (-s, -e) veneer.

furnieren *v.t.* to veneer, to inlay.
Fürsorge *f.* (-, 0) care, welfare work.
Fürsorgebeamter *m.* social worker, welfare officer.
Fürst *m.* (-en, -en) prince, sovereign.
Fürstin *f.* (-, -nen) princess.
fürstlich *a.* princely.
Furt *f.* (-, -en) ford.
Furunkel *m.* furuncle.
Fürwort *n.* (-[e]s, -wörter) (*gram.*) pronoun.
Fusion *f.* (-, -en) merger.
fusionieren *v.t.* to amalgamate.
Fuss *m.* (-es, Füsse) foot; base; footing, style; (*Münz~*) standard; *zu ~e*, on foot, afoot; *auf gutem, gespanntem ~e mit einem stehen*, to be on good, strained terms with one.
Fuss: ~ball *m.* football; ~balltoto *m.* football pool; ~boden *m.* floor.
fussen *v.i.* to rely upon a thing.
Fuss: ~gänger *m.* pedestrian; ~stapfe *f.* foot-step, trace, track; ~tritt *m.* kick; ~weg *m.* foot-path.
Futter *n.* (-s, -) lining; food, fodder, provender.
Futteral *n.* (-[e]s, -e) case.
Futtermittel *n.pl.* feeding stuffs.
futtern *v.t.* to line; to feed.
Fütterung *f.* (-, -en) feeding; lining.
Futur (*um*) *n.* (-s, -a) future tense.

G

G *n.* g; (*mus.*) sol.
Gabe *f.* (-, -n) gift, present; donation; alms; talent; (*med.*) dose.
Gabel *f.* (-, -n) fork; (*bot.*) tendril; (*eines Wagens*) thill, shafts *pl.*
gabeln (sich) *v.refl.* to fork, to bifurcate.
gackern *v.i.* to cackle.
gaffen *v.i.* to gape, to stare, to gaze at.
Gage *f.* (-, -n) salary, pay.
gähnen *v.i.* to yawn.
Gala *f.* (-, 0) gala, pomp.
Galakleid *n.* full dress, court-dress.
galant *a.* polite, courteous; gallant.
Galanterie *f.* (-, -[e]n) gallantry, courtesy.
Galanteriewaren *f.pl.* trinkets, fancy-articles *pl.*
Galeere *f.* (-, -n) galley.
Galerie *f.* (-, -[e]n) gallery.
Galgen *m.* (-s, -) gallows, gibbet.
Galgenfrist *f.* (*fam.*) respite, short delay.
Gallapfel *m.* (-s, -äpfel) gall-nut.
Galle *f.* (-, 0) gall; (*fig.*) bile.
Gallen: ~blase *f.* gall-bladder; ~stein *m.* gall-stone.
gallertartig *a.* gelatinous.
Gallert(e) *f.* (-, -n) jelly; gelatine.

gallig *a.* bilious; waspish.
Galopp *m.* (-[e]s, -e) gallop.
galoppieren *v.i.* to gallop.
galvanisch *a.* galvanic.
galvanisieren *v.t.* to galvanize.
Galvanismus *m.* (-, 0) galvanism.
Galvanostegie *f.* electroplating.
Gamaschen *f.* (-, -n) gaiters; spats.
Gang *m.* (-[e]s, -Gänge) walk, turn; gait; (*Maschine*) movement; alley, passage, corridor; (*Speisen*) course; (*Verlauf*) progress, course; (*Pferd*) pace; *im ~ sein*, to be in progress; *in vollem ~*, in full swing; *in ~ bringen*, to set going, to start.
gang und gäbe *a.* usual, common.
gangbar *a.* current, marketable.
Gängelband *n.* (-[e]s, -bänder) leading-strings *pl.*
gängeln *v.t.* to lead by the nose.
gängig *a.* usual.
Gangräne *f.* (-, 0) gangrene.
Gangwerk *n.* (-[e]s, -e) mechanism, movement.
Gans *f.* (-, Gänse) goose.
Gänse: ~blume *f.* daisy; ~braten *m.* roast goose; ~füsschen *n.pl.* inverted commas *pl.*; *es überläuft mich eine ~ haut*, my flesh creeps; ~klein *n.* (goose) giblets *pl.*; ~marsch *m.* single file.
Gänserich, Ganser[t] *m.* (-s, -e) gander.
ganz *a.* whole, entire, all; complete; ~ *adv.* quite, entirely, wholly; *eine ~e Note*, a semibreve; ~e *Zahl*, integer; *im ~en*, on the whole.
Ganze *n.* (-n, 0) whole; totality.
gänzlich *a.* whole, total; ~ *adv.* totally, wholly.
ganz: ~metall *a.* all-metal; ~wolle *a.* all-wool; ~zeitlich *a.* full-time.
gar *a.* (*gekocht*) done, sufficiently cooked; ~ *adv.* quite, very, fully; even; ~ *nicht*, not at all, by no means.
Garage *f.* (-, -n) garage.
Garantie *f.* (-, -[e]n) guarantee, security.
garantieren *v.t.* to warrant.
Garaus *m.* (-, 0) knockout blow; *den ~ machen*, to ruin, to do for someone.
Garbe *f.* (-, -n) sheaf.
Garde *f.* (-, -n) guard.
Garderobe *f.* (-, -n) wardrobe; cloakroom; clothes *pl.*
Gardine *f.* (-, -n) curtain.
gären *v.i.st.* to ferment.
Garn *n.* (-[e]s, -e) yarn, thread; *ins ~ gehen*, to fall into the net; *ins ~ locken*, to decoy.
Garneele *f.* (-, -n) shrimp.
garnieren *v.t.* to garnish, to trim.
Garnison *f.* (-, -en) garrison.
Garnitur *f.* (-, -en) set; (*Besatz*) trimming.
garstig *a.* dirty, nasty; ugly, naughty.
Garten *m.* (-s, Gärten) garden.

Garten: ~**haus** *n.* summer-house; ~**messer** *n.* pruning-knife.

Gärtner *m.* (-s, -) gardener.

Gärtnerei *f.* (-, -en) gardening.

Gärung *f.* (-, 0) fermentation.

Gas *n.* (-es, -e) gas.

Gasanstalt *f.* gas-works *pl.*

gasartig *a.* gaseous.

Gas: ~**beleuchtung** *f.* gas-lighting; ~**brenner** *m.* burner; ~**fusshebel** *m.* (*mot.*) accelerator.

gasförmig *a.* gaseous.

Gas: ~**glühlicht** *n.* incandescent light; ~**maske** *f.* gas mask; ~**messer** *m.* gas-meter.

Gaskrieg *m.* chemical warfare.

Gasometer *m.* (-s, -) gasometer.

Gaspedal *n.* (*mot.*) accelerator.

Gasrohr *n. u.* **Gasröhre** *f.* gas-pipe.

Gasse *f.* (-, -n) street; lane.

Gassenbube *m.* street-boy.

Gast *m.* (-[e]s, **Gäste**) guest; visitor: stranger; customer; *Gäste haben,* to have company; *zu ~ bitten,* to invite (to dinner or supper).

gastfrei, gastfreundlich *a.* hospitable.

Gastfreundschaft *f.* hospitality.

Gast: ~**geber** *m.* host; ~**geberin** *f.* hostess; ~**haus** *n.* restaurant, inn; ~**hof** *m.* hotel.

gastlich *a.* hospitable.

Gastmahl *n.* banquet, dinner-party.

gastrisch *a.* gastric.

Gast: ~**rolle** *f.* starring-part; ~**wirt** *m.* host, landlord; ~**wirtschaft** *f.* inn.

Gatte *m.* (-n, -n) husband, consort.

Gatter *n.* (-s, -) grate, lattice; railing.

Gattin *f.* (-. -nen) wife, spouse.

Gattung *f.* (-, -en) kind, sort; (*Naturgeschichte*) species, family genus.

Gattungsname *m.* appellative, generic name.

Gau *m.* (-[e]s, -e) district; county.

Gaukelei *f.* (-, -en) juggling; (*fig.*) trick, imposture.

gaukeln *v.i.* to juggle; to sway to and fro, to dangle.

Gaukelspiel *n.* (-[e]s, -e) delusion.

Gaukler *m.* (-s, -) conjurer, juggler.

Gaul *m.* (-[e]s, **Gäule**) horse, nag.

Gaumen *m.* (-s, -) palate.

Gauner *m.* (-s, -) cheat, sharper, swindler.

Gaze *f.* (-, -n) gauze.

Gazelle *f.* (-, -n) gazelle.

Geächtete[r] *m.* (-n, -n) outlaw.

Geächze *n.* (-s, 0) groaning.

geädert *a.* veined, veiny.

geartet *a.* disposed; *gut ~,* good-natured.

Gebäck *n.* (-[e]s, -e) pastry.

Gebälk *n.* (-[e]s, -e) timber-work, frame.

Gebärde *f.* (-, -n) gesture.

gebärden (sich) *v.refl.* to behave.

gebaren (sich) *v.refl.* to behave.

gebären *v.t.st.* to bear (a child), to give birth to.

Gebärmutter *f.* womb, uterus.

Gebäude *n.* (-s, -) building, edifice.

Gebein *n.* (-[e]s, -e) bones *pl.*; skeleton.

Gebell *n.* (-[e]s, 0) barking.

geben *v.t.st.* to give; to produce; to act, to perform; (*Karten*) to deal; *es gibt,* there is, there are; (sich) ~ *v.refl.st.* to abate; *Achtung ~,* to pay attention; *Nachricht ~,* to send word; *sich Mühe ~,* to take pains; *nichts auf einen ~,* to make no account of a person; *sich zufrieden ~,* to rest content (with).

Gebet *n.* (-[e]s, -e) prayer.

Gebetbuch *n.* prayer-book.

Gebiet *n.* (-[e]s, -e) district, territory; department; (*fig.*) province, sphere.

gebieten *v.t.st.* to command, to order; ~ *v.i.st.* (*über*) to rule; to control; to possess, to dispose of.

gebieterisch *a.* imperious, peremptory.

Gebilde *n.* (-s, -) structure, organization; form; image

gebildet *a.* cultured; educated.

Gebirge *n.* (-s, -) (range of) mountains.

gebirgig *a.* mountainous.

Gebirgskamm *m.* mountain-ridge.

Gebiss *n.* (-bisses, -bisse) set of teeth; (*künstliches*) denture.

geblümt *a.* flowered.

geboren *p.* & *a.* born; *ein ~er Leipziger,* a native of Leipzig; *sie ist eine ~e N.,* her maiden name is N., née N.

geborgen *a.* saved, out of harm's way.

Gebot *n.* (-[e]s, -e) command(ment), order; (*com.*) offer, bid; *zu ~ stehen,* to be at (someone's) disposal.

Gebräu *n.* (-s, -e) mixture, concoction.

Gebrauch *m.* (-[e]s, -bräuche) use, usage; custom; rite; *ausser ~ sein,* to be obsolete; *ausser ~ kommen,* to fall into disuse.

gebrauchen *v.t.* to use, to employ.

gebräuchlich *a.* usual, customary; ~**er,** more widely used.

Gebrauchsanweisung *f.* directions for use.

gebrauchsfertig *a.* ready-made.

Gebrechen *n.* (-s, -) infirmity, defect.

gebrechlich *a.* fragile; infirm, weak.

gebrochen *p.* & *a.* broken, fractured; *mit ~em Herzen,* broken-hearted.

Gebrüder *m.pl.* brothers *pl.*

Gebrüll *n.* (-[e]s, 0) roar; lowing.

Gebühr *f.* (-, -en) duty, due; fee; tax; *eine ~ erheben,* to charge a fee for; *nach ~,* deservedly; *über ~,* unduly.

gebühren *v.i. & refl.* (*sich*) to be due; to be proper, to be meet.

gebührlich *a.* due, suitable, proper.

Geburt *f.* (-, -en) delivery, childbirth; birth; extraction.

Geburten: ~kontrolle *f.* birth-control; ~ziffer *f.* birthrate.

gebürtig *a.* born, a native of.

Geburts: ~helfer *m.* accoucheur; ~hilfe *f.* midwifery, obstetrics *pl.*; ~land *n.* native country; ~ort *m.* native place, birthplace; ~schein *m.* certificate of birth; ~tag *m.* birthday.

Gebüsch *n.* (-[e]s, -e) underwood, copse.

Geck *m.* (-en, -en) fop, coxcomb.

geckenhaft *a.* foppish, dandyish.

Gedächtnis *n.* (-nisses, 0) memory.

Gedanke *m.* (-ns, -n) thought, idea.

Gedankengang *m.* train of thought.

gedankenlos *a.* thoughtless.

Gedankenstrich *m.* dash.

gedankenvoll *a.* thoughtful, pensive.

Gedärm *n.* (-[e]s, -e) bowels *pl.*

Gedeck *n.* (-[e]s, -e) table-cloth; plate; cover (at table), knife and fork.

gedeihen *v.i.st.* (*s*) to thrive; to prosper.

Gedeihen *n.* (-s, 0) prosperity.

gedeihlich *a.* prosperous; wholesome.

gedenken *v.i. & t.ir.* to think of; to remember; to intend.

Gedenkfeier *f.* commemoration.

Gedicht *n.* (-[e]s, -e) poem.

gediegen *a.* solid; pure; sterling.

Gedränge *n.* (-s, 0) crowd, throng.

gedrängt *a.* crowded; concise.

gedrungen *a.* compact; square-built.

Geduld *f.* (-, 0) patience; forbearance.

gedulden (sich) *v.refl.* to have patience.

geduldig *a.* patient, forbearing.

gedunsen *a.* bloated, sodden.

Geehrte(s) *n.* (-...ten, 0) (*Schreiben*) favour.

geeignet *a.* fit, adapted, suitable.

Gefahr *f.* (-, -en) danger, peril, risk; ~ laufen, to run the risk; *auf eigene* ~, at owner's risk; *auf Ihre* ~, at your peril.

gefährden *v.t.* to endanger, to imperil.

gefährlich *a.* dangerous.

gefahrlos *a.* free from danger; safe.

Gefährte *m.* (-n, -n) companion, comrade, associate, mate.

gefahrvoll *a.* perilous.

Gefälle *n.* (-s, -) fall, descent; *starkes* ~, (*mot.*) steep hill down.

gefallen *v.i.st.* to please, to like; *sich* ~ *lassen*, to submit to.

Gefallen *m.* (-s, 0) pleasure; liking; *einen* ~ *erweisen*, to do a favour.

gefällig *a.* pleasing; agreeable, obliging.

Gefälligkeit *f.* (-, -en) favour.

gefälligst *adv.* please.

gefallsüchtig *a.* coquettish.

gefangen *a.* imprisoned; captured, captive; ~*nehmen*, to take prisoner; ~*setzen*, to imprison; *sich* ~ *geben*, to surrender, to give oneself up.

Gefangene[r] *m.* (-n, -n) prisoner, captive.

Gefangennahme *f.* (-, 0) imprisonment; *ungesetzliche* ~, false imprisonment.

Gefangenschaft *f.* (-, 0) captivity.

Gefängnis *n.* (-nisses, -nisse) prison, jail; *ein Jahr* ~, one year's imprisonment; ~strafe *f.* sentence of imprisonment; ~wärter *m.* warder; ~wärterin *f.* wardress.

Gefasel *n.* (-s, 0) drivel.

Gefäss *n.* (-es, -e) vessel.

gefasst *a.* composed, collected, calm; ~ *auf*, prepared, ready for; *sich* ~ *machen*, to prepare oneself.

Gefecht *n.* (-[e]s, -e) fight, combat, engagement.

gefedert *a.* (*mech.*) sprung.

gefeit (gegen) *a.* immune (from).

Gefieder *n.* (-s, -) plumage.

gefiedert *a.* feathered.

Gefilde *n.* (-s, -) plain, fields *pl.*

Geflecht *n.* (-[e]s, -e) texture; wickerwork.

gefleckt *a.* speckled, spotted.

geflissentlich *a.* intentional, wilful.

geflochten *a.* plaited.

Geflügel *n.* (-s, 0) poultry, fowls *pl.*

Geflügelhändler *m.* poulterer.

geflügelt *a.* winged; ~es Wort *n.* familiar quotation.

Geflüster *n.* (-s, 0) whisper(ing).

Gefolge *n.* (-s, -) train, retinue, suite, attendants *pl.*

Gefolgschaft *f.* (-, -en) followers *pl.*

gefragt *a.* in request.

gefrässig *a.* voracious, gluttonous, greedy.

Gefreite[r] *m.* (-n, -n) lance-corporal.

gefrieren *v.i.st.* (*s*) to freeze; to congeal.

Gefrierfleisch *n.* frozen meat.

Gefrierpunkt *m.* (-[e]s, 0) freezing-point, zero.

Gefrorene[s] *n.* (-nen, 0) ice-cream.

Gefüge *n.* (-s, 0) texture, tissue.

gefügig *a.* pliant; (*fig.*) docile.

Gefühl *n.* (-[e]s, -e) feeling.

gefühllos *a.* unfeeling, insensible.

gefühlvoll *a.* feeling, tender.

gegen *pr.* towards; against; versus; to; in exchange for; contrary to; about, nearly; ~ *bar*, for cash.

Gegen: ~angriff *m.* counter-attack; ~antrag *m.* counter-motion, counterproposal; ~besuch *m.* return-visit.

Gegend *f.* (-, -en) region; country.

Gegen: ~forderung *f.* counter-claim; ~gewicht *n.* counterpoise, counterweight; ~gift *n.* antidote; ~kandidat *m.* rival candidate; ~leistung *f.* return, equivalent; ~massregel *f.* preventive measure; ~mittel *n.* antidote, remedy; ~papst *m.* antipope; ~partei *f.* opposite party; ~probe *f.* counter-test; ~satz *m.* contrast, opposition, antithesis; ~sätzlich *a.* contrary, opposite; ~schlag _m._ counter-stroke; ~seite _f._ opposite side; opponent.

gegenseitig _a._ mutual, reciprocal.

Gegen: ~seitigkeit _f._ reciprocity; ~stand _m._ object; subject.

gegenstandslos _a._ useless.

Gegen: ~stoss _m._ counter-thrust; ~stück _n._ counterpart; ~teil _n._ contrary, reverse; _im_ ~, on the contrary.

gegenteilig _a._ opposite.

gegenüber _adv. & p._ opposite (to).

Gegenüberstellung _f._ confrontation.

Gegenwart _f._ (-, 0) presence; (_Zeit_) the present.

gegenwärtig _a._ present; ~ _adv._ at present.

Gegen: ~wehr _f._ defence, resistance; ~wert _m._ equivalent; ~wind _m._ headwind; ~wirkung _f._ reaction.

gegenzeichnen _v.t._ to countersign.

Gegenzug _m._ counter-move.

Gegner _m._ (-s, -) opponent, adversary; _sich zum_ ~ _machen,_ to antagonize.

gegnerisch _a._ antagonistic, adverse.

Gegnerschaft _f._ (-, -en) antagonism; opponents _pl._

Gehalt _m._ (-[e]s, 0) contents _pl._; value, merit; (_chem._) proportion of; ~ _n._ (-[e]s, _u._ -hälter) salary, wages _pl._

Gehaltsskala _f._ (-, -skalen) salary-scale.

Gehaltszulage _f._ (-, -n) increase of salary.

gehaltvoll _a._ substantial.

Gehänge _n._ (-s, -) festoon, garland.

geharnischt _a._ clad-in-armour; (_fig._) angry, aggressive.

gehässig _a._ malicious, spiteful.

Gehässigkeit _f._ (-, -en) animosity, ill-will.

Gehäuse _n._ (-s, -) case; capsule (_Obst_) core; shell.

geheim _a._ secret; clandestine; ganz ~, ~e _Kommandosache,_ top secret.

Geheimbund _m._ (-[e]s, -bünde) secret alliance, society.

Geheimdienst _m._ secret service.

Geheimmittel _n._ (-s, -) nostrum, patent medicine.

Geheimnis _n._ (-nisses, -nisse) secret, mystery, arcanum

Geheimniskrämer _m._ secret-monger.

geheimnisvoll _a._ mysterious.

Geheimpolizei _f._ secret police.

Geheimschrift _f._ (-, -en) cipher; code.

Geheimsprache _f._ (-, -n) secret language.

Geheimtuerei _f._ (-, -en) secretiveness.

Geheiss _n._ (-es, 0) order, bidding.

gehen _v.i.st._ (_s_) to go, to walk; to sell (_v.i._); (_Maschinen_) to work; _zum Fischen_ ~, to go fishing; _wie geht es Ihnen?,_ how are you?; _es geht nicht,_ it won't do!; _vor sich_ ~, to take place; _sich_ ~ _lassen,_ to indulge one's humour.

geheuer _a._ safe; _nicht_ ~, haunted; unsafe.

Geheul _n._ (-[e]s, 0) howl(ing).

Gehilfe _m._ (-n, -n) assistant, mate.

Gehirn _n._ (-[e]s, -e) brain, brains _pl._

Gehirn: ~erschütterung _f._ concussion of the brain; ~erweichung _f._ softening of the brain; ~hautentzündung _f._ meningitis; ~schlag _m._ apoplexy.

Gehöft _n._ (-[e]s, -e) homestead.

Gehölz _n._ (-es, -e) wood, copse.

Gehör _n._ (-[e]s, 0) hearing; audience; _sich_ ~ _verschaffen,_ to make oneself heard; ~ _finden,_ to be heard; _ein gutes_ ~, a good ear.

gehorchen _v.i._ to obey.

gehören _v.i._ to belong; to appertain; (_sich_) ~ _v.refl._ to be proper.

Gehörgang _m._ acoustic duct.

gehörig _a._ belonging, appertaining; proper, due; ~ _adv._ duly, soundly.

Gehörnerv _m._ auditory nerve.

gehörnt _a._ horned; antlered.

Gehörorgan _n._ organ of hearing.

Gehörrohr _n._ (-s, -e) ear-trumpet.

gehorsam _a._ dutiful, obedient.

Gehorsam _m._ (-[e]s, 0) obedience.

Gehörsinn _m._ sense of hearing.

Gehverwundeter _m._ walking wounded.

Geier _m._ (-s, -) vulture.

Geifer _m._ (-s, 0) slaver; (_fig._) venom.

geifern _v.i._ to slaver; to foam.

Geige _f._ (-, -n) violin, fiddle.

geigen _v.i._ to play the violin, to fiddle.

Geigen: ~bogen _m._ fiddle-stick; bow; ~kasten _m._ violin case.

Geiger _m._ (-s, -) violinist, fiddler.

geil _a._ rank; lascivious, lewd.

Geisel _m._ (-s, -n) hostage.

Geiss _f._ (-, -en) goat; roe.

Geiss: ~blatt _n._ honeysuckle; ~bock _m._ he-goat.

Geissel _f._ (-, -n) whip, lash, scourge.

geisseln _v.t._ to scourge, to whip.

Geist _m._ (-es, -er) spirit; wit; mind, intellect; spectre, ghost.

geisterhaft _a._ spectral, ghostly.

geistesabwesend _a._ absent-minded.

Geistes: ~abwesenheit _f._ absent-mindedness; ~blitz _m._ brainwave; ~gegenwart _f._ presence of mind.

geisteskrank _a._ insane, of unsound mind.

Geisteskranker _m._ mental patient, mental case.

geistesschwach _a._ feeble-minded, imbecile.

Geistesstorung _f._ mental disorder.

geistig _a._ (_Getränke_) alcoholic; intellectual, mental; spiritual.

geistlich _a._ spiritual; ecclesiastical, clerical.

Geistliche[r] _m._ (-n, -n) clergyman, minister, divine.

Geistlichkeit _f._ (-, 0) clergy; priesthood.

geist: ~los _a._ spiritless, flat, dull; ~reich _a._ witty, gifted, racy, spirited; ~voll _a._ ingenious, witty, bright.

Geiz m. (-es, 0) avarice.
geizen v.i. to covet; to pinch, to stint.
Geizhals m. miser, niggard, curmudgeon.
geizig a. avaricious, covetous, stingy.
Gejammer n. (-s, 0) lamentation.
Geklapper n. (-s, 0) clatter, rattling.
Geklingel n. (-s, 0) tinkling, jingling.
Gekreisch n. (-s, 0) shrieking, screaming.
gekünstelt a. artificial, affected.
Gelächter n. (-s, 0) laughter.
Gelage n. (-[e]s, -e) banquet, carouse.
Gelände n. (-s, -) terrain; ~abschnitt m. (mil.) sector.
Geländer n. (-s, -) railing, balustrade, bannisters pl.
gelangen v.i. (s) to arrive at; to attain (to).
gelassen a. composed, resigned, quiet, calm.
Gelatine f. gelatine.
geläufig a. fluent, voluble; familiar.
gelaunt a. disposed, humoured.
Geläute n. (-s, -) ringing, peal (of bells).
gelb a. yellow; (Ei) ~ n. yolk; ~es Fieber, yellow fever.
Gelb:~sucht f. jaundice.
Geld n. (-[e]s, -er) money; bares ~, cash.
Geld: ~beutel m. purse; ~schrank m. safe; ~strafe f. fine; ~stück n. coin, piece of money; ~ wechsler m. money-changer.
gelegen a. situated; opportune.
Gelegenheit f. (-, en) occasion, opportunity; ~ ergreifen, to take an opportunity.
Gelegenheits: ~arbeiter m. casual worker; ~arbeiten pl. odd jobs.
gelegentlich a. occasional.
gelehrig a. docile, tractable.
Gelehrsamkeit f. (-, 0) learning, erudition.
gelehrt a. learned, erudite; die ~en Berufe pl. the professions.
Gelehrte[r] m. (-n, -n) scholar.
Geleise n. (-s, -) track; (rail.) rails pl.
Geleit n. (-[e]s, -e) escort, safe-conduct.
geleiten v.t. to conduct, to escort; to convoy.
Geleitzug m. (nav.) convoy.
Gelenk n. (-[e]s, -e) joint, articulation, link.
gelenkig a. flexible, pliable, supple.
Gelenkrheumatismus m. articular rheumatism.
gelernter Arbeiter m. skilled worker.
Geliebte m. & f. (-n, -n) lover; sweetheart; mistress.
gelind[e] a. soft, smooth; gentle; lenient.
gelingen v.i.st. (s) to succeed, to prosper; es gelang ihm, he succeeded (in).
Gelingen n. (-s, 0) success.
gellen v.t. to yell, to shrill.
geloben v.t. to vow, to promise solemnly.
Gelöbnis n. (-nisses, -nisse) vow.
gelt a. barren; i. is it not so? to be sure!

gelten v.i.st. to be worth, to be valid; to have influence; ~ für, to pass for; ~ lassen, to let pass, to admit; das gilt nicht!, it is not fair!
geltend p. & a. in force; ~ machen, to assert.
Geltung f. (-, 0) value; recognition; zur ~ bringen, to enforce, to assert; zur ~ kommen, to get into favour.
Gelübde n. (-s, -) vow, solemn promise.
gelungen a. (fam.) odd; amusing.
gelüsten v.i. to long for, to hanker after.
gemach i. peace!
Gemach n. (-[e]s, -mächer) apartment, chamber.
gemächlich a. easy, comfortable.
Gemahl m. (-[e]s, -e) husband.
Gemahlin f. (-, -nen) consort, wife.
Gemälde n. (-s, -) picture, painting.
Gemäldegalerie f. picture-gallery.
gemäss a. & p. according to.
gemässigt a. (Klima) temperate; moderate.
Gemäuer n. (-s, -) walls pl.
gemein a. common; low, vulgar; der ~e Mann, the common people; der ~e Soldat, the private.
Gemeinde f. (-, -n) community; (Stadt) municipality; parish; congregation.
Gemeinde... communal.
Gemeinde: ~rat m. town-council; ~steuer f. rate.
gemeingefährlich a. dangerous to the public.
Gemeingut n. common property.
Gemeinheit f. (-, -en) vulgarity; baseness; dirty trick.
gemeinhin adv. commonly.
gemeinnützig a. of public utility; ~e Organisation, non-profitmaking organization.
Gemeinplatz m. common-place, truism.
gemeinsam a. common; mutual, joint.
Gemeinschaft f. (-, -en) communion; intercourse, communication; society, association; partnership.
gemeinschaftlich a. common, joint.
Gemeinsinn m. public spirit.
gemeint a. intended.
gemeinverständlich a. generally intelligible, popular.
Gemein: ~wesen n. commonwealth; ~wohl n. public weal.
Gemenge n. (-s, -) mixture, medley.
gemessen a. measured; formal.
Gemetzel n. (-s, 0) slaughter, butchery.
Gemisch n. (-es, -e) mixture.
gemischtes Doppel n. (Tennis) mixed double.
Gemme f. (-, -n) gem.
Gemse f. (-, -n) chamois.
Gemunkel n. (-s, 0) secret talk.
Gemurmel n. (-s, 0) murmur(ing).

Gemüse n. (-s, -) greens, vegetables pl.

Gemüsehändler m. greengrocer.

Gemüt n. (-[e]s, -er) mind, soul, heart.

gemütlich a. good-natured; cosy, snug.

Gemütlichkeit f. (-, 0) good-nature; cosiness; comfort.

genagelt a. (Schuhe) hobnailed.

genau a. close; strict, precise; exact, accurate; es ~ nehmen, to be particular.

Genauigkeit f. (-, 0) accuracy, precision, exactness.

Gendarm m. (-en, -en) gendarme.

Gendarmerie f. rural police.

Genealogie f. (-, -n) genealogy.

genehm a. agreeable; acceptable.

genehmigen v.t. to approve of.

Genehmigung f. (-, -en) approval; assent, sanction; ratification.

geneigt a. inclined; prone; favourable.

General m. (-[e]s, -e) general; ~ der Flieger, air marshal.

General: ~agent m. agent-general; ~direktor m. general manager.

General: ~konsul m. consul-general; ~stab m. general staff; ~stabskarte f. ordnance survey map; ~versammlung f. general meeting.

Generation f. (-, -en) generation.

Generator m. generator; ~gas n. producer gas.

genesen v.i.st. (s) to recover, to be restored to health.

Genesung f. (-, -en) convalescence, recovery; ~sheim n. convalescent home.

genial a. inspired, gifted, full of genius.

Genick n. (-[e]s, -e) nape, back of the neck.

Genie n. (-s, -s) genius; man of genius.

genieren v.t. to molest, to bother; (sich) ~ v.refl. to feel embarrassed.

geniessbar a. eatable; palatable.

geniessen v.t.st. to enjoy; to eat or drink.

Genitalien pl. genitals.

Genitiv m. (-s, -e) genitive case.

Genoss, Genosse m. (-nossen, -nossen) companion, comrade, partner, mate.

Genossenschaft f. (-, -en) company, partnership; association.

genug a. & adv. enough, sufficient.

Genüge f. (-, 0) zur ~, sufficiently; ~ tun, to satisfy.

genügen v.i. to suffice; to satisfy; sich ~ lassen, to be satisfied (with).

genügend a. sufficient, enough.

genügsam a. easily satisfied; frugal.

Genugtuung f. (-, -en) satisfaction.

Genuss m. (-nusses, -nüsse) enjoyment; pleasure, delight; use, profit; eating, drinking.

genusssüchtig, a. pleasure-seeking.

Geograph m. (-en, -en) geographer.

Geographie f. (-, 0) geography.

geographisch a. geographical.

Geolog m. (-en, -en) geologist.

Geometer m. (-s, -) geometrician; surveyor.

Geometrie f. (-, -n) geometry.

geometrisch a. geometrical.

Gepäck n. (-[e]s, -e) luggage, baggage.

Gepäck: ~abfertigung f. parcels office; ~aufbewahrungsstelle f. cloakroom, left-luggage office; ~aufgabeschein m. registration-slip; ~netz n. luggage-rack; ~träger m. railway-porter; ~wagen m. luggage-van.

Gepflogenheit f. (-, -en) custom, habit.

Geplänkel n. (-s, 0) skirmishing.

Geplapper n. (-s, 0) babbling, chatter.

Geplätscher n. (-s, 0) splashing, plashing.

Geplauder n. (-s, 0) small-talk.

Gepräge n. (-s, -) impression, stamp, coin-age.

Gepränge n. (-s, 0) pomp, ceremony, pageantry.

gerade a. straight; direct, right; upright, honest; (Zahl) even; ~aus, straight on; ~ heraus, frankly.

gerade adv. just, exactly.

geradezu adv. bluntly; actually, no less than.

gerad: ~linig a. rectilineal, rectilinear; ~sinnig a. upright, straightforward.

Gerassel n. (-s, 0) rattling, din.

Gerät n. (-[e]s, -e) tool, implement, appliance, utensil.

geraten v.i.st. (s) to come, to get (into); to succeed, to turn out well, to prosper; in Brand ~, to catch fire; ins Stocken ~, to come to a standstill.

geraten a. advisable.

Geratewohl n. aufs ~, haphazard.

Gerätschaften f.pl. tools, implements pl.

geraum a. long; ~e Zeit, (for) a long time.

geräumig a. spacious, roomy, ample.

Geräusch n. (-[e]s, -e) noise, bustle.

geräusch: ~los a. noiseless; ~voll, noisy.

gerben v.t. (rot) to tan.

Gerber m. (-s, -) tanner.

Gerbsäure f. (-, 0) Gerbstoff m. (-[e]s, -e) tannic acid, tannin.

gerecht a. just; righteous.

Gerechtigkeit f. (-, 0) justice.

Gerechtsame f. (-, -n) privilege.

Gerede n. (-s, 0) talk, rumour.

gereichen v.i. to tend, to turn to.

gereizt a. & p. irritated, angry.

Gereiztheit f. (-, 0) irritation, anger.

gereuen v.imp. es gereut mich, I repent (of it), I regret (it).

Gericht n. (-[e]s, -e) court of justice, tribunal; judgment; dish, food; das jüngste ~, Doomsday, the Last Judgment; vor ~ stellen, to bring to trial, to try.

gerichtlich a. judicial, legal; forensic; ~ vorgehen gegen, to take proceedings against.

Gerichts: ~barkeit f. jurisdiction; *streitige*
~barkeit, contentious jurisdiction; ~ent-
scheidung f. ruling; ~ferien *pl.* recess,
vacation; ~gebäude *n.* courthouse;
~hof *m.* court of justice; ~kosten *pl.*
costs; ~saal *m.* courtroom; ~schreiber
m. clerk of the court; ~stand *m.* venue;
~vollzieher *m.* bailiff; ~wesen *n.*
judiciary, judicature.
gerieben *a.* cunning, wide-awake.
gering *a.* small, little, mean; scanty, slight,
unimportant; inferior, poor; *nicht im
~sten*, not in the least.
geringfügig *a.* unimportant, slight; trifling.
geringschätzen *v.t.* to think little of...
geringschätzig *a.* disdainful.
Geringschätzung f. (-, 0) contempt, scorn.
gerinnen *v.i.st.* (s) to coagulate, to curdle.
Gerippe *n.* (-s, -) skeleton; framework.
gerissen *a.* cunning, wide-awake.
germanisieren *v.t.* to germanize.
gern *adv.* with pleasure, willingly, readily,
easily; *~ haben*, to be fond of; *~ sehen*,
to like; *nicht ~ gesehen*, unwelcome.
Geröll *n.* (-[e]s, -e) rubble, boulders *pl.*
Gerste f. (-, -n) barley.
Gerstengra¹pen *pl.* pearl barley.
Gerte f. (-, -n) switch, rod.
Geruch *m.* (-[e]s, -rüche) smell; scent,
odour.
geruchlos, *a.* without smell.
Geruchs: ~sinn *m.* sense of smell; ~til-
gendes Mittel *n.* deodorant.
Gerücht *n.* (-[e]s, -e) rumour, report,
news *pl.*; *es geht das ~*, it is rumoured.
geruhen *v.i.* to be pleased, to deign.
Gerümpel *n.* (-s, 0) trash, lumber.
Gerundium *n.* (-s, -dien) gerund.
Gerüst *n.* (-[e]s, -e) scaffold, stage, scaf-
folding, frame(work).
Ges *n.* (-, 0) (*mus.*) G flat.
gesamt *a.* whole, total, aggregate.
Gesamtbetrag *m.* sum total.
Gesamtheit f. (-, 0) totality.
Gesandte[r] *m.* (-n, -n) minister, envoy.
Gesandtschaft f. (-, -en) legation. ,
Gesandtschaftsrat *m.* counsellor of lega-
tion.
Gesang *m.* (-[e]s, -sänge) singing; song,
air; canto (of a long poem).
Gesangbuch *n.* hymn-book.
Gesäss *n.* (-es, -e) bottom, backside.
Geschädigte *m.* (*law*) the injured person.
Geschäft *n.* (-[e]s, -e) business; employ-
ment, occupation; shop, establish-
ment; transaction.
geschäftig *a.* busy, bustling, active.
geschäftlich *a.* business-, commercial; *~e
Verbindung haben mit*, to do (transact)
business with.
Geschäfts: ~aufsicht f. legal control;
~brief *m.* business-letter; ~bücher *n.pl.*
the books (of a firm); ~fähigkeit f.

(*law*) legal capacity; ~führer *m.* manager; ~mann *m.* business man; ~num-
mer f., ~zeichen *n.* reference (number);
~ordnung f. agenda *pl.*; ~papiere *n.*
(*Post*) commercial papers; ~reisender
m. commercial traveller; ~stunden
f.pl. office hours; ~träger *m.* chargé
d'affaires; ~verkehr *m.* business deal-
ings *pl.*; ~zeit f. office-hours *pl.*;
~zweig *m.* line of business.
geschehen *v.i.st.* (s) to come to pass, to
occur, to happen; *~ lassen*, to permit;
es geschieht ihm recht, it serves him
right.
gescheit *a.* clever, intelligent.
Geschenk *n.* (-[e]s, -e) gift, present.
Geschichte f. (-, -n) history; story; (*fam.*)
affair.
geschichtlich *a.* historic(al).
Geschichtschreiber *m.* historian.
Geschick *n.* (-[e]s, -e) dexterity, skill; destiny, fate.
Geschicklichkeit f. (-, -en) dexterity,
adroitness, skill.
geschickt *a.* fit, apt, clever; skilled.
geschieden *a.* divorced.
Geschirr *n.* (-[e]s, -e) vessel; (*Silber*) plate;
(*irdenes*) crockery, earthenware; tools
pl.; (*Pferde~*) harness.
Geschlecht *n.* (-[e]s, -er) sex; kind, race;
lineage; generation; (*gram.*) gender.
geschlechtlich *a.* sexual.
Geschlechts: ~krankheit f. venereal disease; ~reife f. puberty; ~teile *m.pl.*
genitals *pl.*; ~trieb *m.* sexual instinct;
~wort *n.* article.
geschliffen *a.* polished; (*Glas*) cut.
geschlossen *a.* close, compact; concen-
trated; solid, in a body.
Geschmack *m.* (-[e]s, -schmäcke) taste;
savour, flavour, relish.
geschmacklos *a.* tasteless; in bad taste.
Geschmacklosigkeit f. (-, -en) bad taste.
Geschmackssache f. matter of taste.
geschmackvoll *a.* tasteful, elegant.
Geschmeide *n.* (-s, -) trinkets, jewels *pl.*
geschmeidig *a.* flexible, pliant, supple.
Geschmeiss *n.* (-es, 0) low rabble; vermin.
geschniegelt *a.* spruce, trim.
Geschöpf, *n.* (-[e]s, -e) creature.
Geschoss *n.* (-schosses, -schosse) projectile, missile; storey, floor.
geschraubt *a.* stilted.
Geschrei *n.* (-es, -e) cry, clamour, shout-
ing.
Geschütz *n.* (-es, -e) cannon, gun.
Geschütz: ~feuer *n.* gunfire; ~stand *m.*
emplacement; ~turm *m.* turret.
Geschwader *n.* (-s, -) squadron; (*avi.*)
wing; ~kommandeur *m.* wing commander.
Geschwätz *n.* (-es, 0) gossip.
geschwätzig *a.* talkative, garrulous.

geschweige denn, not to mention, let alone.
geschwind *a.* quick, fast, swift.
Geschwindigkeit *f.* (-, -en) quickness, speed; velocity.
Geschwindigkeitsmesser *m.* speedometer.
Geschwirr *n.* (-[e]s, 0) whirr, buzz.
Geschwister *pl.* brothers and sisters *pl.*
Geschworne[r] *m.* (-n, -n) juryman, juror.
Geschwornengericht *n.* jury.
Geschwulst *f.* (-, -schwülste) tumour; swelling.
Geschwür *n.* (-[e]s, -e) ulcer, abscess.
Gesell, Geselle *n.* (-[e]n, -[e]n) journeyman; companion, comrade.
gesellen (sich) *v.refl.* to associate (with).
gesellig *a.* social, sociable, convivial; **~e Zusammenkunft** *f.* social.
Geselligkeit *f.* (-, 0) social intercourse.
Gesellschaft *f.* (-, -en) society; company; party; *eine ~ gründen,* to form a company.
Gesellschafter *m.* (-s, -) companion; associate; (*com.*) partner.
Gesellschafterin *f.* (-, -nen) (lady) companion.
gesellschaftlich *a.* social.
Gesellschafts: **~anzug** *m.* evening dress; **~reise** *f.* conducted tour; **~spiel** *n.* society game, parlour game; **~tanz** *m.* ballroom dancing; **~vertrag** *m.* deed of partnership.
Gesetz *n.* (-es, -e) law, statute; rule.
Gesetzblatt *n.* law gazette.
Gesetz: **~buch** *n.* code; **~entwurf** *m.* bill.
Gesetzeskraft *f.* force of law, legal force.
gesetzgebend *a.* legislative; **~e Körperschaft** *f.* legislative body.
Gesetz: **~geber** *m.* legislator; **~gebung** *f.* legislation; legislature.
gesetzlich *a.* lawful, legal, statutory; **~ geschützt** *a.* legally registered, proprietary.
gesetzlos *a.* lawless, illegal.
Gesetzlosigkeit *f.* (-, -en) anarchy.
gesetzmässig *a.* lawful, legitimate; legal.
gesetzt *a.* steady; sedate; **~ dass,** suppose, supposing that.
gesetzwidrig *a.* unlawful, contrary to law.
gesichert *a.* safe, secured.
Gesicht *n.* (-[e]s, -er *u.* -e) face; countenance, mien; apparition; vision.
Gesichts: **~farbe** *f.* complexion; **~kreis** *m.* horizon; (*fig.*) intellectual horizon; **~punkt** *m.* point of view; **~zug** *m.* feature.
Gesims *n.* (-simses, -simse) shelf; cornice; mantelpiece.
Gesinde *n.* (-s, 0) servants, domestics *pl.*
Gesindel *n.* (-s, 0) mob, rabble.
gesinnt *a.* minded, disposed.
Gesinnung *f.* (-, -en) intention; disposition, opinion; mind; conviction.
Gesittung *f.* (-, 0) civilization.

gesoanen *a.* disposed, resolved.
Gespann *n.* (-[e]s, -e) team; yoke (of oxen).
gespannt *a. & p.* strained; intent, wrought up; anxious to know; *auf ~em Fuss,* on bad terms.
Gespenst *n.* (-es, -er) spectre, ghost.
gespenstisch *a.* spectral.
gesperrt *a.* closed; (*Druck*) spaced; **~ für Zutritt,** out of bounds, (*Am.*) off limits.
Gespött *n.* (-[e]s, 0) mockery, raillery.
Gespräch *n.* (-[e]s, -e) conversation, talk.
gesprächig *a.* talkative, communicative.
gespreizt *a.* pompous.
gesprenkelt *a.* speckled.
Gestade *n.* (-s, -) shore, beach, bank.
Gestalt *f.* (-, -en) form, figure, shape; frame; size, stature; fashion, manner.
gestalten *v.t.* to form, to shape; (sich) **~** *v.refl.* to turn out.
Gestaltung *f.* (-, -en) formation; configuration; condition.
geständig *a.* confessing; **~ sein,** to confess.
Geständnis *n.* (-nisses, -nisse) confession.
Gestank *m.* (-[e]s, -stänke) stink, stench.
gestatten *v.t.* to permit, to allow.
Geste *f.* (-, -n) gesture.
gestehen *v.t.st.* to confess, to avow, to admit.
Gestehungskosten *pl.* prime cost, cost price.
Gestein *n.* (-[e]s, -e) rock.
Gestell *n.* (-[e]s, -e) frame; rack, stand; trestle.
gestern *adv.* yesterday.
gestiefelt *a.* booted.
Gestirn *n.* (-[e]s, -e) star; constellation.
gestirnt *a.* starred, starry.
Gestotter *n.* (-s, 0) stammering.
Gesträuch *n* (-[e]s, -e) thicket, shrubs *pl.*
gestreng *a.* strict, severe, rigorous.
gestrig *a.* yesterday's.
Gestrüpp *n.* (-[e]s, -e) underwood.
Gestüt *n.* (-[e]s, -e) stud-farm.
Gesuch *n.* (-[e]s, -e) application, request; **~ einreichen,** to make an application; **ein ~ bewilligen,** to grant (approve) an application.
gesucht *a.* in demand; affected.
gesund *a.* sound, healthy; well, in good health; (*Ansicht*) sane; (*Speisen etc.*) wholesome; (*Klima*) salubrious.
gesunden *v.i.* (*s*) to recover (health), convalesce.
Gesundheit *f.* (-, 0) health; sanity; *eine ~ ausbringen,* to drink a person's health.
gesundheitlich *a.* sanitary.
Gesundheits: **~pflege** *f.* hygiene; **~polizei** *f.* sanitary service.
gesundheitsschädlich *a.* insanitary.
getäfelt *a.* wainscoted.
Getöse *n.* (-s, 0) noise, din.

Getrampel n. (-s, 0) trampling.
Getränk n. (-[e]s, -e) beverage, drink.
getrauen (sich) v.refl. to dare, to venture; ich getraue mich nicht hinein, I dare not go in.
Getreide n. (-s, -) corn, grain.
Getreidespeicher m. grain elevator.
getreu a. faithful, true, trusty; loyal.
Getriebe n. (-s, -) gear; (Uhr, Klavier) works; bustle; ~kasten m. gear box.
getrost a. confident; ~! i. courage!
Getümmel n. (-s, 0) bustle.
geübt a. practised, expert.
Gewächs n. (-es, -e) plant, vegetable; (Wein) vintage; (med.) growth.
gewagt a. risky.
gewählt a. select, choice.
gewachsen a. equal to, a match for.
Gewächshaus n. greenhouse, hot-house, conservatory.
gewahr a. aware (of).
Gewähr f. (-, 0) guarantee; ohne ~, subject to correction.
gewahren v.t. to perceive.
gewähren v.t. to give, to allow, to grant; einen ~ lassen, to let a person alone.
gewährleisten v.t. to guarantee.
Gewahrsam m. (-s, 0) safe-keeping, safe-custody; in ~, under restraint.
Gewährsmann m. informant; authority.
Gewalt f. (-, -en) power, authority; force, violence; höhere ~, act of God.
gewaltig a. mighty, enormous.
Gewaltmarsch m. forced march.
gewaltsam a. forcible, violent; eines ~en Todes sterben, to die a violent death.
gewalttätig, a. violent, outrageous.
Gewalttätigkeit f. (-, -en) rowdyism; outrage.
Gewand n. (-[e]s, -e (poet.) u. -wänder) dress, garment; drapery.
gewandt a. dexterous, smart, adroit.
gewärtigen v.t. to expect.
Gewäsch n. (-es, 0) twaddle, bosh.
Gewässer n. (-s, -) waters pl., flood.
Gewebe n. (-s, -) texture, tissue, fabric.
geweckt a. bright, clever, lively.
Gewehr n. (-[e]s, -e) weapon; gun, rifle.
Gewehrkolben m. butt.
Geweih n. (-[e]s, -e) antlers pl.
geweiht a. consecrated.
Gewerbe n. (-s, -) trade; calling; industry.
Gewerbe: ~freiheit f. liberty of trade; ~ordnung f. trade regulations pl.; ~schein m. licence; ~schule f. technical school; ~steuer f. trade-tax.
gewerblich a. industrial.
gewerbetreibend a. manufacturing.
gewerbsmässig a. professional.
Gewerkschaft f. (-, -en) trade(s)-union.
Gewicht n. (-[e]s, -e) weight.
gewichtig a. weighty.
gewillt a. willing, disposed.

Gewimmel n. (-s, 0) swarm, crowd.
Gewinde n. (-s, -) worm, thread.
Gewindebohrer m. (mech.) tap.
Gewinn m. (-[e]s, -e) gain, profit, advantage; mit ~, at a profit; ~ und Verlustkonto, profit and loss account; ~beteiligung f. profit sharing.
Gewinnanteil m. dividend.
gewinnbringend a. profitable.
gewinnen v.i. & t.st. to win; to gain, to get, to earn; über sich ~, to get oneself to do.
gewinnsüchtig a. greedy (of gain).
Gewinsel n. (-s, 0) whimper, whine.
Gewirr n. (-[e]s, 0) confusion; criss-cross.
gewiss a. certain; sure; constant, fixed; ~ adv. certainly, no doubt.
Gewissen n. (-s, -) conscience.
gewissenhaft a. conscientious.
gewissenlos a. unscrupulous.
Gewissens: ~biss, m. remorse; ~freiheit, f. liberty of conscience.
gewissermassen adv. so to speak.
Gewissheit f. (-, -en) certainty, surety.
Gewitter n. (-s, -) (thunder)storm.
gewitzigt a. taught wisdom by experience.
gewogen a. favourable, kindly disposed.
gewöhnen v.t. to accustom.
gewohnt a. wonted, habitual; in the habit of...
Gewohnheit f. (-, -en) custom; habit.
Gewohnheitsverbrecher m. habitual criminal.
gewöhnlich a. usual; common, vulgar; ~ adv. usually, as a rule.
Gewölbe n. (-s, -) vault, arch; store.
gewölbt a. vaulted, arched.
Gewühl n. (-[e]s, 0) throng, crowd.
gewunden a. & p. tortuous.
Gewürz n. (-es, -e) spice; seasoning.
Gewürzhändler m. grocer.
Gewürznelke f. clove.
Gezänk n. (-[e]s, -e) quarrel, squabble.
gezeichnet a. (gez.) signed.
geziemen (sich) v.i. & refl. to become, to befit; to be fitting.
geziemend a. proper, befitting, becoming.
geziert a. affected, finicking, finicky.
Gezwitscher n. (-s, 0) chirping, twitter.
gezwungen a. constrained, forced.
Gicht f. (-, 0) gout.
Giebel m. (-s, -) gable, gable-end.
Gier f. (-, 0) raging desire, greed(iness).
gierig a. eager, greedy.
Giessbach m. torrent.
giessen v.t.st. to pour; (Blumen) to water; (Metall) to cast, to found; Öl ins Feuer ~, to add fuel to the flames.
Giesserei f. (-, -en) foundry.
Giesskanne f. watering-can.
Gift n. (-[e]s, -e) poison; (fig.) spite.
giftig a. poisonous; (fig.) angry.
Giftpflanze f. poisonous plant.

Gigant *m.* (-en, -en) giant.
Gilde *f.* (-, -n) guild; corporation.
Ginster *m.* (-s, -) broom, furze; gorse.
Gipfel *m.* (-s, -) summit, peak; top; (*fig.*) height, acme.
gipfeln *v.i.* to culminate.
Gips *m.* (-es, -e) gypsum, plaster of Paris.
Gipsabdruckabguss *m.* plaster-cast.
Gipsverband *m.* plaster-dressing.
Giraffe *f.* (-, -n) giraffe.
girieren *v.t.* to endorse (a bill of exchange); to circulate.
Giro *n.* (-[s], -s) endorsement.
Giro: ~**konto** *n.* banking account; ~**verkehr** *m.* clearance-house business.
girren *v.i.* to coo.
Gis *n.* (-, 0) (*mus.*) G sharp.
Gischt *m.* (-[e]s, -e) froth, spray.
Gitarre *f.* (-, -n) guitar.
Gitter *n.* (-s, -) trellis, grating, grille, lattice.
Glacéhandschuh *m.* kid-glove.
Glanz *m.* (-es, 0) lustre, gloss; polish, sheen; brightness, splendour.
glänzen *v.i.* to glitter; to shine.
glänzend *a.* bright, brilliant.
Glanz: ~**leder** *n.* patent-leather; ~**leistung** *f.* brilliant feat.
Glas *n.* (-es, Gläser) glass; *buntes ~*, stained glass.
Glasbläser *m.* glass-blower.
Glaser *m.* (-s, -) glazier.
gläsern *a.* glassy; of glass.
Glas: ~**glocke** *f.* glass-shade; bell-glass; ~**hütte** *f.* glass-works *pl.*
glasieren *v.t.* to glaze; to varnish.
Glasur *f.* (-, -en) glazing.
Glasware *f.* glass-ware.
glatt *a.* smooth, sleek; ~**rasiert** *a.* clean-shaven.
Glatteis *n.* (-es, 0) glazed frost.
glätten *v.t.* to smooth; (*mech.*) to face.
Glatze *f.* (-, -n) bald-head, pate.
Glaube *m.* (~**ns**, 0) faith, belief, credit; religion; creed; *auf Treu und ~*, in good faith, on trust; *in gutem Glauben*, (*law*) bona fide, in good faith.
glauben *v.t.* to believe, to trust; to think, to suppose.
Glaubens: ~**artikel** *m.* article of faith; ~**bekenntnis** *n.* confession of faith, creed; ~**genosse** *m.* co-religionist; ~**satz** *m.* dogma.
glaubhaft *a.* credible, believable.
gläubig *a.* believing; faithful; devout.
Gläubige[r] *m.* (-n, -n) (true) believer.
Gläubiger *m.* (-s, -) creditor.
glaublich *a.* credible; probable.
glaubwürdig *a.* credible; authentic.
gleich *a.* equal, like; ~ *adv.* equally, just, alike; presently, directly; *meinesgleichen*, my equals *pl.* people like me.
gleichartig *a.* homogeneous.

gleichbedeutend *a.* synonymous, equivalent.
Gleichberechtigung *f.* (-, 0) equality of status.
gleichen *v.i.st.* to be alike, to resemble; to equal.
gleicherweise *adv.* likewise.
gleichfalls *adv.* likewise, also, equally.
gleichförmig *a.* uniform; conform.
gleichgesinnt *a.* like-minded, congenial.
Gleichgewicht *n.* (-[e]s, 0) balance, equilibrium; *das ~ halten*, to counter-balance.
gleichgültig *a.* indifferent; irrelevant; ~ *wie*, no matter how.
Gleichgültigkeit *f.* (-, 0) indifference.
Gleichheit *f.* (-, 0) equality; likeness.
Gleichheitszeichen *n.* (*ar.*) sign of equality.
gleichlaufend *a.* parallel.
gleich: ~**lautend** *a.* identical; ~**machen** *v.t.*; *dem Boden ~machen*, to level; ~**mässig** *a.* uniform, regular.
Gleichmass *n.* (-es, 0) symmetry, proportion.
Gleichmut *m.* (-[e]s, 0) equanimity.
gleichmütig *a.* calm, even-tempered.
gleichnamig *a.* bearing the same name.
Gleichnis *n.* (-nisses, -nisse) parable.
gleichordnen *v.t.* to co-ordinate.
Gleichrichter *m.* (-s, -) (*elek.*) rectifier.
gleichsam *adv.* as it were, as if.
Gleichschaltung *f.* (*political*) co-ordination.
gleichschenk(e)lig *a.* (*geom.*) isosceles.
gleichseitig *a.* equilateral.
Gleichstellung *f.* (-, -en) equalization.
Gleichstrom *m.* (*elek.*) direct current (D.C.).
Gleichung *f.* (-, -en) equation.
gleichviel *adv.* no matter, all the same.
gleichwertig *a.* equivalent.
gleichwie *c.* as, even as.
gleichwohl *c.* yet, however.
gleichzeitig *a.* contemporary; simultaneous.
Gleis *n.* = Geleise.
gleiten *v.i.st.* (*s*) to glide; to slide.
Gletscher *m.* (-s, -) glacier.
Glied *n.* (-[e]s, -er) limb; member; link; rank, file (of soldiers); *männliches ~*, penis.
gliedern *v.t.* to articulate; to organize.
Gliederpuppe *f.* lay-figure.
Gliederung *f.* (-, -en) (*auch mil.*) organization.
Gliedmassen *pl.* limbs *pl.*
glimmen *v.i.* to glimmer, to glow.
Glimmer *m.* (-s, 0) glimmer; mica.
glimpflich *a.* gentle, mild, lenient.
glitschen *v.i.* (*s*) to slide, to glide.
glitscherig *a.* slippery.
glitzern *v.i.* to glitter, to sparkle.
Globus *m.* (-, -se) globe.

G.D.

Glocke f. (-, -n) bell.
Glockenspiel n. chimes pl.
Glorie f. (-, 0) glory; halo.
glorreich a. glorious.
Glossar n. (-s, -e u. -ien) glossary.
Glosse f. (-, -n) gloss, comment.
glotzen v.i. to stare.
Glück n. (-[e]s, 0) luck, good luck; happiness, prosperity; fortune; ~ haben, to be in luck; kein ~ haben, to be unlucky; viel ~! good luck!; es war ein ~, it was fortunate; ~ wünschen, to congratulate.
glucksen v.i. to squelch.
glücken v.i. (s) to succeed, to prosper.
glücklich a. happy, fortunate; lucky.
Glückseligkeit f. (-, -en) bliss, happiness.
Glücksspiel n. game of chance.
Glückwunsch m. congratulation.
Glühbirne f. electric bulb, incandescent lamp.
glühen v.i. to glow.
Glut f. (-, -en) fire, heat; embers; (fig.) fervour, ardour.
Gnade f. (-, -n) grace, favour; pardon, mercy; quarter.
Gnadengesuch n. clemency plea, petition for clemency or mercy.
gnädig a. gracious; ~e Frau, madam.
Gobelin m. (-s, -s) tapestry.
Gold n. (-[e]s, 0) gold.
golden a. gold; (fig.) golden.
goldhaltig a. auriferous.
Gold: ~regen m. (bot.) laburnum; ~schmied m. goldsmith; ~schnitt m. gilt edges; ~standard m., ~währung f. gold standard.
Golf m. (-[e]s, -e) gulf; (Spiel) golf.
Golf: ~platz m. golf course, golf links; ~spieler m. golfer; ~schläger m. golf club.
Golfstrom m. Gulf-stream.
Gondel f. (-, -n) gondola.
gönnen v.t. not to envy, not to grudge; to allow, to grant.
Gönner m. (-s, -) patron, well-wisher.
gönnerhaft a. patronizing.
Gorilla m. (-s, -s) gorilla.
Gosse f. (-, -n) gutter, drain, sink sewer.
Gotik f. (-, 0) gothic style.
gotisch a. Gothic.
Gott m. (-s, Götter) God; um ~es willen, for God's sake; ~ sei Dank! thank God, thank goodness!; leider Gottes! alas!
göttergleich a. god-like.
Gottesdienst m. public worship, divine service.
gottesfürchtig a. pious, God-fearing.
Gotteslästerung f. blasphemy.'
Gottheit f. (-, -en) deity; divinity; godhead.
Göttin f. (-, -nen) goddess.
göttlich a. divine; godlike.
Göttlichkeit f. (-, 0) divinity; divine origin.

gottlos a. godless, impious, wicked.
Gottvertrauen n. trust in God.
gottvoll a. divine; (fam.) capital, grand.
Götze m. (-n, -n) false deity, idol.
Götzendienst m. idolatry.
Gouvernante f. (-, -n) governess.
Gouverneur m. (-s, -e) governor.
Grab n. (-[e]s, Gräber) grave, tomb, sepulchre.
Graben m. (-s, Gräben) ditch, trench; moat.
graben v.t.st. to dig; to engrave, to cut.
Grab: ~mal n. tomb, sepulchre; ~rede f. funeral sermon; ~schrift f. epitaph; ~stätte f., ~stelle f. grave, tomb; ~stein m. tombstone, gravestone.
Grad m. (-[e]s, -e) degree; grade; rate; in hohem ~, highly; im höchsten ~, exceedingly, to the last degree.
Gradeinteilung f. (-, -en) scale.
graduieren v.i. to graduate.
Graf f. (-en, -en) count; (englischer) earl.
Gräfin f. (-, -nen) countess.
Grafschaft f. (-, -en) earldom; county.
Gramm m. (-[e]s, -e) gramme, gram.
grämen (sich) v.refl. to grieve, to be grieved, to fret, to pine.
grämlich a. sullen, peevish, ill-humoured.
Gramm n. (-[e]s, -e) gramme, gram.
Grammatik f. (-, -en) grammar.
Grammatiker m. (-s, -) grammarian.
grammatisch a. & adv. grammatical(ly).
Grammophon n. (-s, -e) gramophone, (Am.) phonograph; ~platte f. record.
Granatapfel m. pomegranate.
Granate f. (-, -n) grenade, shell.
Granattrichter m. (shell) crater.
Granatwerfer m. mortar.
grandios a. grand.
Granit m. (-[e]s, -e) granite.
Graphik f. (-, -en) graphic art; engraving.
graphisch a. graphic; ~e Darstellung f. graphic representation, graph; ~es Zeichen n. symbol.
Graphit m. (-[e]s, -e) graphite, plumbago.
Grapholog m. (-en, -en) graphologist.
Gras n. (-es, Gräser) grass, herbage; ins ~ beissen, to bite the dust.
grasen v.i. to graze.
Grashalm m. blade of grass.
grass a. hideous, horrible.
grassieren v.i. to spread, to rage.
grässlich a. ghastly, dreadful, horrible.
Grat a. (-[e]s, -e) edge, ridge; (mech.) burr.
Gräte f. (-, -n) fish-bone.
grätig a. full of (fish-)bones.
gratis adv. free of charge.
Gratulation f. (-, -en) congratulation.
gratulieren v.i. to congratulate (on).
grau a. gray, grey; grizzled; ~er Star, cataract.
grauen v.imp. to shudder (at); to dawn.

Grauen n. (-s, 0) dread, horror; dawn.

grauenhaft, grauenvoll a. ghastly.

Graupe f. (-, -n) groats pl.; pearl barley.

graupeln v.i.imp. to sleet.

Graus m. (-[e]s, 0) horror, dread.

grausam a. cruel.

Grausamkeit f. (-, -en) cruelty.

grausen v.i.imp. to shudder (at).

grausig a. dreadful, gruesome, awful.

Graveur m. (-[e]s, -e) engraver.

gravieren v.t. to engrave.

gravierend a. aggravating; suspicious.

gravitätisch a. grave, solemn.

Grazie f. (-, -n) grace, charm.

graziös a. graceful, pretty.

Greif m. (-[e]s, -e) griffin.

greifbar a. tangible, palpable; on hand.

greifen v.t.st. to seize, to lay hold on; to grasp, to catch.

greis a. grey, hoary; very old.

Greis m. (-es, -e) old man.

Greisenalter n. old age.

greisenhaft a. senile.

grell a. (Licht, Farbe) glaring, dazzling.

Grenadier m. (-s, -e) grenadier.

Grenzberichtigung f. (-, -en) frontier readjustment.

Grenze f. (-, -n) frontier, boundary; limit.

grenzen v.i. to border on, to adjoin.

grenzenlos a. boundless; immense.

Grenzfall m. borderline case.

Grenzlinie f. boundary-line.

Greuel m. (-s, -) abomination, outrage.

Greueltat f. atrocity.

greulich a. horrible, heinous.

Griesgram m. (-[e]s, -e) grumbler.

griesgrämig a. morose, sullen, grumbling.

Griess m. (-sses, -sse) semolina pl.

Griesszucker m. granulated sugar.

Griff m. (-[e]s, -e) grip, grasp, hold.

Griffbrett n. (Geige) fret-board, neck.

Griffel m. (-s, -) style, slate-pencil.

Grille f. (-, -n) cricket (insect); (fig.) whim, caprice, fad.

Grimasse f. (-, -n) grimace, wry face.

Grimm m. (-[e]s, 0) fury, rage, wrath.

grimm a. grim, furious.

grimmig a. grim, furious.

Grind m. (-[e]s, -e) scab, scurf.

grinsen v.i. to grin, to smirk.

Grippe f. (-, 0) (med.) influenza (fam.) flu.

grob a. coarse, gross, thick; clumsy; rude, insolent; rough; ~e Berechnung f. rough calculation.

Grobian m. (-s, -e) churl, lout, boor.

gröhlen, grölen v.i. to scream, to squall.

Groll m. (-[e]s, 0) rancour, grudge, resentment.

grollen v.i. to bear a grudge or ill-will; (Donner) to rumble.

Gros n. (Grosses, Grosse) gross (12 dozen).

gross a. large; (dick) big; (Wuchs) tall; (fig.) great; high, eminent; ~er Buchstabe m. capital (letter); ~tun, to brag, to give oneself airs.

grossartig a. grand, sublime.

Grossbetrieb m. large undertaking.

Grösse f. (-, -n) size; (fig.) greatness, magnitude; quantity; ~ über alles, overall size.

Gross: ~einkauf m. bulk purchase; ~eltern pl. grandparents pl.; ~enkel m. great-grandson.

grossenteils adv. in a large measure.

Grössenwahn m. megalomania.

Gross: ~grundbesitzer m. large estate owner; ~handel m. wholesale business; ~händler m. wholesale merchant.

grossherzig a. magnanimous.

Grossherzog m. grand-duke.

Grossindustrie f. big industry pl.

grossjährig a. of age.

Gross: ~kampfschiff n. capital ship; ~macht f. great power.

Grossmut f. magnanimity, generosity.

grossmütig a. magnanimous, generous.

Gross: ~mutter f. grandmother; ~neffe m. grand-nephew; ~nichte f. grandniece; ~sprecher m. swaggerer, braggart; ~sprecherei f. big talk.

gross: ~ sprecherisch a. swaggering, vainglorious.

Gross: ~ stadt f. large city.

Gross: ~ städter m. inhabitant of a large city.

gross: ~ städtisch a. after the manner of a large city.

grösstenteils adv. for the most part.

Gross: ~tat f. achievement, exploit; ~vater m. grandfather; ~zügig a. on a large scale, generous.

grotesk a. grotesque.

Grotte f. (-, -n) grotto.

Grube f. (-, -n) pit; mine; (fig.) grave.

Grübelei f. (-, -en) musing, brooding.

grübeln v.i. to brood, to ponder.

Gruben: ~klotz m. prop; ~licht n. miner's lamp.

Gruft f. (-, Grüfte) tomb, vault.

grün a. green; fresh; (fig.) unripe; ~er Tisch, red tape.

Grün n. (-s, 0) green colour; verdure.

Grund m. (-[e]s, Gründe) ground; bottom; foundation; reason, motive; argument; auf ~ von, on the strength of; von ~ aus, thoroughly; im ~e, after all, at bottom; auf ~ laufen, to run aground; zu ~e richten, to ruin; zu ~e gehen, to perish.

Grund: ~bedingung f. main condition; ~begriff m. fundamental notion; ~besitz m. landed property, real estate; ~besitzer m. landowner; ~bestandteil m. main element, essential ingredient; ~buch n. land register, (Am.) real estate register; ~**buchamt** n. land registry; ~**dienstbarkeit**, (law) encumbrance.

Grund: ~**eigentum** n. landed property; ~**eigentümer** m. ground landlord.

gründen v.t. to establish, to found, to promote, to float; (sich) ~ v.refl. to rest (upon).

Gründer m. (-s, -) founder.

grundfalsch a. radically wrong or false.

Grund: ~**farbe** f. ground colour, priming; ~**fläche** f. base, basis; ~**gedanke** m. fundamental idea; ~**gehalt** m. basic salary.

Grundgesetz n. fundamental law.

grundieren v.t. to prime.

Grund: ~**irrtum**, fundamental error; ~**kapital** n. original stock; ~**lage** f. foundation, ground-work, substructure, base; ~**legung** f. foundation.

gründlich a. profound, thorough; solid.

Grund: ~**linie** f. basis; base line; ~**lohn** m. basic wage.

grundlos a. bottomless; groundless.

Gründonnerstag m. Maundy-Thursday.

Grund: ~**rechte** n.pl. rights of man pl.; ~**regel** f. basic rule; ~**rente** f. ground-rent; ~**riss** m. ground-plan; (Buch) outline; ~**satz** m. principle, maxim.

grundsätzlich a. fundamental; ~ adv. on principle.

Grund: ~**stein** m. foundation-stone; ~**steuer** f. land-tax; ~**stock** m. basis, foundation, nucleus; ~**stück** n. real estate; ~**ton** m. key-note.

Gründung f. (-, -en) foundation, establishment.

Grundursache f. original cause.

grundverschieden a. radically different.

Grund: ~**wasser** n. subterranean water; ~**zahl** f. cardinal number; ~**zins** m. ground-rent; ~**zug** m. main feature.

grünen v.i. to grow green.

grünlich a. greenish.

Grünschnabel m. greenhorn, (Am.) sucker.

Grünspan m. verdigris.

grunzen v.i. to grunt.

Grünzeug n. (-es, 0) greens pl.

Gruppe f. (-, -n) group; (avi.) group.

Gruppenkommandeur m. (avi.) group commander.

gruppieren v.t. to group.

Gruppierung f. (-, -en) grouping.

Grus m. (-es, 0) (coal) slack.

gruselig a. uncanny, creepy.

gruseln v.t.imp. mich gruselt, my flesh creeps, I shudder.

Gruss m. (-es, Grüsse) salutation, greeting; salute; compliment.

grüssen v.t. to greet; to salute; ~ lassen, to send one's kind regards.

Grütze f. (-, 0) groats pl.; (fig.) brains.

gucken v.i. to peep, to look.

Gulden m. (-s, -) florin; (holländischer) guilder.

gültig a. valid, available; good, current; ~ machen, to validate.

Gültigkeit f. (-, 0) validity, legality.

Gummi n. (-s, 0) rubber, India-rubber.

Gummiband n. elastic.

gummieren v.t. to gum.

Gummi: ~**knüppel** m. truncheon; ~**schuhe** m.pl. goloshes pl.

Gunst f. (-, 0) favour, kindness; zu ~en, in favour of.

günstig a. favourable.

Günstling m. (-[e]s, -e) favourite.

Gurgel f. (-, -n) throat, gullet.

gurgeln v.i. to gargle.

Gurke f. (-, -n) cucumber; saure ~, pickled cucumber, gherkin.

Gurt m. (-[e]s, -e) girth; girdle; strap.

Gürtel m. (-s, -) girdle; belt; (geog.) zone.

Gürtelrose f. (med.) shingles pl.

gürten v.t. to gird, to girdle.

Guss m. (Gusses, Güsse) (Schrift) fount; gush, shower.

Guss: ~**eisen** n. cast-iron; ~**stahl** m. cast-steel.

gut a. good; well; ~ heissen, to approve of; es ~ haben, to have a good time; ~ schreiben, to credit, to place to one's credit; einem etwas zu ~e halten, to make allowance for a thing; sich etwas zu ~ tun, to pique oneself upon; kurz und ~, in short; mit einem ~ stehen, to be on good terms with a person.

Gut n. (-[e]s, Güter) good; estate; (com.) commodity, article, goods pl.

Gutachten n. (-s, -) expert opinion, expert evidence.

gutartig a. good-natured; (med.) benign.

Gutdünken n. judgment, discretion.

Güte f. (-, 0) goodness; (com.) (good) quality.

Güter: ~**bahnhof** m. goods-station, goods-yard, (Am.) freight yard; ~**gemeinschaft** f. community of goods; ~**recht** n. regime; ~**trennung** f. separation of property; ~**verkehr** m. goods traffic; ~**wagen** m. (rail.) truck, (Am.) freight-car; ~**zug** m. goods train, (Am.) freight train.

gut: ~**gelaunt** a. good-humoured; ~**gesinnt**, well disposed; ~**gläubig**, bona fide, in good faith.

Guthaben n. (-s, -) (credit) balance.

gutherzig a. kind-hearted.

gütig a. kind, benignant.

gütlich a. amicable.

gutmütig a. good-natured.

Gutmütigkeit f. (-, 0) good-nature.

Gutsbesitzer m. (-s, -) land-owner.

Gutschein m. (-s, -e) voucher.

gutschreiben v.t. to enter to one's credit.

Gutschrift f. credit.

Gutshof m. farmyard.
gutwillig a. voluntary; friendly.
Gymnasial: ~bildung f. classical education; ~direktor m. headmaster of a grammar school; ~lehrer m. grammar-school master.
Gymnasiast m. (-en, -en) grammar-school boy.
Gymnasium n. (-s, -ien) grammar school.
Gymnastik f. (-, 0) gymnastics pl.
gymnastisch a. gymnastic.

H

Haar n. (-[e]s, -e) hair; die ~e standen ihm zu Berge, his hair stood on end; einander in die ~e geraten, to come to blows; sich die ~e machen, to do one's hair.
Haar: ~ausfall m. loss of hair; ~bürste f. hair-brush.
haaren v.i. sich ~, to lose one's hair.
haarig a. hairy; kurz~, ~ort-haired; lang~, long-haired.
haarklein adv. minutely.
Haarnadel f. hair-pin, bodkin.
haarscharf a. very subtle, very keen.
Haarspalterei f. (fig.) hair-splitting.
haarsträubend a. revolting, shocking.
Haar: ~wasser n. hair-lotion; ~wuchsmittel n. hair tonic.
Habe f. (-, 0) property, effects pl.; Hab' und Gut, goods and chattels pl.
haben v.t.ir. to have; da haben wir's! there we are!
Haben n. (-s, -) (com.) credit.
Habgier f. (-, 0) covetousness, greediness.
habgierig a. covetous, greedy.
habhaft a. ~ werden, to get hold of.
Habicht m. (-[e]s, -e) hawk.
habilitieren (sich) v.refl. to be admitted as lecturer at a German university.
Habseligkeiten pl. belongings pl.
Habsucht f. (-, 0) avarice, covetousness.
habsüchtig a. avaricious, covetous.
Hack: ~beil n. chopper, hatchet; ~block m. chopping-block; ~brett n. chopping-board; (mus.) dulcimer.
Hacke f. (-, -n) hoe, mattock· heel.
hacken v.t. to chop, to hack, to cleave; to mince; to hoe.
Hackfleisch n. minced meat.
Hackfrüchte f.pl. root crops.
Häcksel m. or n. (-s, 0) chopped straw.
Hader m. (-s, -n) quarrel, brawl.
hadern v.i. to quarrel, to wrangle.
Hafen m. (-s, Häfen) harbour, port, haven; (Topf) pot, jar.
Hafen: ~arbeiter m. longshoreman; ~gebühren f.pl. harbour dues, port dues; ~stadt f. sea-port.

Hafer m. (-s, 0) oats pl.
Hafer: ~brei m. porridge; ~mehl n. oatmeal; ~schleim m. gruel.
Haft f. (-, 0) custody, arrest.
haftbar a. liable, responsible.
Haftbefehl m. warrant (of arrest).
haften v.i. to stick, to adhere; ~ für, to be liable for.
Häftling m. (-s, -e) detainee.
Haftpflicht f. liability; mit beschränkter ~, Limited.
haftpflichtig a. liable.
Hagebutte f. (-, -n) hip, haw.
Hagedorn m. hawthorn.
Hagel m. (-s, 0) hail.
Hagelkorn n. hail-stone.
hageln v.i.imp. to hail.
Hagel: ~schaden m. damage caused by hail; ~schaden-Versicherung f. hail-insurance; ~wetter n. hail-storm.
hager a. lean, gaunt, meagre.
Häher m. (-s, -) jay.
Hahn m. (-[e]s, Hähne) cock; stop-cock.
Hahnenkamm m. cock's-comb.
Hahnrei m. (-[e]s, -e) cuckold.
Hai(fisch) m. (-[e]s, -e) shark.
Hain m. (-[e]s, -e) grove, wood.
Häkchen n. (-s, -) small hook.
Häkelarbeit f. crochet-work.
Häkelmuster n. crochet-pattern.
häkeln v.t. to crochet.
Häkelnadel f. crochet-needle.
Haken m. (-s, -) hook, clasp; das hat einen ~, there's a snag somewhere.
Hakenkreuz n. swastika.
halb a. & adv. half; ~e Note f. (mus.) minim; ~er Ton m. semitone; auf ~em Wege, halfway.
halbamtlich a. semi-official.
Halbbruder m. (-s, -brüder) half-brother.
Halbdunkel n. dusk, twilight.
Halbedelstein m. half- (or semi-) precious stone.
halbfertig a. semi-finished.
halbfranz a. half-bound.
halbgar a. underdone, (Am.) rare.
Halbgott m. demi-god.
Halbheit f. (-, -en) half-measure.
halbieren v.t. to halve; to bisect.
Halbinsel f. peninsula.
halb: ~jährig a. lasting six months; ~jährlich a. half-yearly; ~ adv. every six months.
Halb: ~kreis m. semicircle; ~kugel f. hemisphere.
halblaut a. & adv. in an undertone.
Halb: ~leinen n. half-linen; ~mast m. half-mast; ~messer m. radius; ~mond m. half-moon, crescent.
halboffen a. ajar.
Halb: ~schlaf m. somnolence; ~schuh m. (low) shoe; ~seiden a. half-silk; ~steif a. semi-stiff; ~stiefel m. (Damen) bootee.

halb: ~stündlich *a.* half-hourly; ~wegs *adv.* half-way, midway.
Halb: ~welt *f.* demimonde; ~wolle *f.* linsey-woolsey; ~zeit *f.* half-time.
Halde *f.* (-, -n) declivity, slope; dump.
Hälfte *f.* (-, -n) half; middle.
Halfter *f.* (-, -n) *m. & n.* (-s, -) halter.
halftern *v.t.* to halter, to put a halter on.
Halle *f.* (-, -n) hall; porch.
hallen *v.i.* to sound, to resound, to clang.
hallo! *i.* hullo!; *Hallo n.* fuss.
Halluzination *f.* hallucination.
Halm *m.* (-[e]s, -e) stalk, blade; straw.
Hals *m.* (Halses, Hälse) neck; throat; *vom Halse,* off one's hands; *bis zum Halse,* neck-deep; ~ *über Kopf,* head-long, helter-skelter; *einen auf den ~e haben,* to be encumbered with one; *sich vom ~e schaffen,* to get rid of; *um den ~ fallen,* to embrace.
Hals: ~abschneider *m.* cut-throat; ~ader *f.* jugular vein; ~band *n.* necklace.
halsbrecherisch *a.* break-neck.
Halsentzündung *f.* angina.
halsstarrig *a.* stubborn, obstinate.
Hals: ~tuch *n.* neckerchief; *(von Wolle)* comforter; ~weh *n.* sore throat.
Halt *m.* (-[e]s, -e) hold, footing; halt, stop; support, stay; ~ *machen,* to halt, to stop.
halt! *i.* hold! stop!
haltbar *a.* tenable; durable.
halten *v.t. & i.st.* to hold; to keep; to con-tain; to deem, to estimate; *(mil.)* to hold on to; (sich) ~ *v.refl.* to keep (good); to hold one's own; *länger ~ (von Sachen),* to have longer wear; *reinen Mund ~,* to think highly of one; *reinen Mund ~,* not to breathe a syllable about it; *den ~ halten,* to hold one's tongue; *eine Predigt ~,* to preach a ser-mon; *eine Rede ~,* to make a speech; *im Zaume ~,* to keep a tight hand on; *Wort ~,* to keep one's word; *sich ~ an,* to have recourse to.
Haltestelle *f.* station, stop.
haltlos *a.* unsteady, fickle.
Haltung *f.* (-, -en) attitude; bearing, car-riage; *(Körper~)* posture.
Halunke *m.* (-n, -n) scoundrel, rascal.
hämisch *a.* malicious, sneering.
Hammel *m.* (-s, -) wether.
Hammel: ~braten *m.* roast mutton; ~fleisch *n.* mutton; ~keule *f.* leg of mutton.
Hammer *m.* (-s, Hämmer) hammer.
hämmerbar *a.* malleable.
hämmern *v.t.* to hammer.
Hämorrhoiden *f.pl.* piles *pl.*, hæmorrhoids *pl.*
Hamster *m.* (-s, -) hamster, marmot.
Hamsterer *m.* (-s, -) food-hoarder.
hamstern *v.t.* to hoard.

Hand *f.* (-, Hände) hand; *mit der ~,* by hand; *vor der ~,* for the present; *zu Händen,* attention; *sich die Hände reiben,* to rub one's hands (together); *tote ~,* mortmain; *die ~ drücken,* to shake hands; *aus der ~ in den Mund leben,* to live from hand to mouth; *die Hände in den Schoss legen,* to remain idle; *unter der ~,* underhand, secretly; *die Hände im Spiel haben,* to have a finger in the pie; *bei der ~, zur Hand,* at hand, forthcoming.
Hand: ~akten *pl.* personal files; ~arbeit *f.* manual labour; *(weibliche)* needlework; ~bibliothek *f.* reference library.
handbreit *a.* of a hand's breadth.
Handbuch *n.* manual, handbook.
Hände: ~druck *m.* handshake; ~klat-schen *n.* applause.
Handel *m.* (-s, 0) trade, traffic, commerce; bargain; affair; *einen ~ abschliessen,* to strike a bargain; ~ *treiben,* to trade; *pl. Händel,* quarrel(s).
handeln *v.i.* to act; to deal; to trade, to do business; to bargain, to chaffer; *es handelt sich um...,* the point in ques-tion is...
Handels: ~adressbuch *n.* commercial directory; ~bilanz *f.* balance of trade; ~einig werden, to come to terms; ~flotte *f.* mercantile marine, merchant navy; ~gärtner *m.* market-gardener; ~gericht *n.* commercial court; ~gesell-schaft *f.* trading company; *offene ~gesellschaft,* (general) partnership; ~gesetzbuch *n.* commercial code; ~hochschule *f.* commercial college of university standing; ~kammer *f.* cham-ber of commerce; ~recht *n.* commercial law; ~schiff *n.* merchant ship; ~schif-fahrt *f.* merchant marine; ~schule *f.* commercial school; ~teil *(einer Zeit-ung) m.* city page; ~vertrag *m.* com-mercial treaty.
Handfertigkeit *f.* manual skill.
handfest *a.* strong, stout, strapping.
Hand: ~feuerwaffen *pl.* small arms; ~fläche *f.* palm of the hand; ~geld *n.* earnest-money; *(mil.)* bounty; ~gelenk *n.* wrist; *etwas aus dem ~ machen,* to do a thing with one's little finger.
handgemein *a.* at close quarters.
Hand: ~gemenge *n.* hand-to-hand fight-ing; ~gepäck *n.* hand-luggage.
hand: ~geschneidert *a.* hand-tailored; ~greiflich *a.* palpable.
Hand: ~granate *f.* hand grenade; ~griff *m.* grasp; handle; *(fig.)* knack; ~habe *f.* handle.
handhaben *v.t.* to handle; to manage.
Handkoffer *m.* suitcase.
Handlanger *m.* hodman.
Händler *m.* (-s, -) dealer, tradesman.

handlich *a.* handy; manageable.
Handlung *f.* (-, -en) act, action, deed; trade, business; shop.
Handlungs: ~**reisende(r)** *m.* commercial traveller; ~**weise** *f.* way of acting, mode of dealing.
Handschrift *f.* handwriting; manuscript.
handschriftlich *a.* in manuscript, written.
Hand: ~**schuh** *m.* glove; ~**streich** *m.* coup de main; ~**tasche** *f.* attaché case, handbag; ~**tuch** *n.* towel; ~**umdrehen** *n.*, *im* ~, in no time, in a trice; ~**voll** *f.* handful; ~**werk** *n.* handicraft, trade, small business; *einem das* ~ *legen*, to render a person innocuous.
Handwerker *m.* (-s, -) artisan, mechanic.
Handwerkszeug *n.* implements, tools *pl.*
Handwörterbuch *n.* dictionary.
Hanf *m.* (-[e]s, 0) hemp.
hänfen *a.* hempen.
Hänfling *m.* (-[e]s, -e) linnet.
Hanfzwirn *m.* hemp-yarn.
Hang *m.* (-[e]s, 0) slope, declivity; propensity, bias, bent.
Hänge: ~**brücke** *f.* suspension-bridge; ~**lampe** *f.* swinging lamp; ~**matte** *f.* hammock.
hängen *v.t.* to hang; to suspend.
hänseln *v.t.* to quiz, to hoax, to chaff.
Hansestadt *f.* Hanseatic town.
Hanswurst *m.* Jack-pudding, harlequin.
Hanteln *f.pl.* dumb-bells *pl.*
hantieren *v.t.* to handle, to manage.
hapern *v.i.impers.* to stick, to be amiss.
Happen *m.* (-s, -) morsel.
happig *a.* (*vulg.*) greedy, eager.
Harfe *f.* (-, -n) harp.
Harfenist *m.* (-en, -en) harper.
Harke *f.* (-, -n) rake.
harken *v.t.* to rake.
Harlekin *m.* (-s, -s) harlequin.
Harm *m.* (-[e]s, 0) grief, sorrow; injury.
härmen (sich) *v.refl.* to grieve, to pine for.
harmlos *a.* harmless.
Harmonie *f.* (-, -n) harmony; concord.
harmonieren *v.i.* to agree, to harmonize.
Harmonika *f.* (-, -s) accordion.
harmonisch *a.* harmonious.
Harn *m.* (-[e]s, 0) urine.
Harnblase *f.* bladder.
harnen *v.i.* to make water, to urinate.
Harnisch *m.* (-[e]s, -e) armour.
Harnröhre *f.* urethra.
Harnsäure *f.* uric acid.
harntreibend *a.* diuretical.
Harpune *f.* (-, -n) harpoon.
harsch *a.* harsh, rough, stiff.
hart *a.* hard; stiff; severe, austere; cruel.
Härte *f.* (-, -n) hardness; severity; cruelty.
härten *v.t.* to harden; (*Stahl*) to temper, to chill.
Hartgummi *m.* ebonite, hard rubber.

hart: ~**herzig** *a.* hard-hearted; ~**hörig** *a.* hard of hearing; ~**näckig** *a.* stubborn; headstrong, obstinate.
Harz *n.* (-es, -e) resin, rosin.
harzig *a.* resinous.
Hasardspiel *n.* game of chance, gambling.
haschen *v.t.* to snatch, to seize, to snap up; ~ *v.i.* (*nach*) to aspire to.
Hase *m.* (-n, -n) hare.
Haselnuss *f.* hazel-nut.
Hasenfuss *m.* coward.
Hasenscharte *f.* hare-lip.
Haspel *m.* (-s, -) reel, windlass, winch.
haspeln *v.t. & i.* to reel, to wind on a reel.
Hass *m.* (Hasses, 0) hate, hatred; grudge.
hassen *v.t.* to hate.
hassenswert *a.* hateful.
hässlich *a.* ugly, deformed.
Hast *f.* (-, 0) haste, hurry, precipitation.
hasten *v.i.* to hasten, to hurry.
hastig *a.* hasty, hurried.
hätscheln *v.t.* to coddle, to caress.
Haube *f.* (-, -n) cap; coif, hood.
Haubitze *f.* (-, -n) howitzer.
Hauch *m.* (-[e]s, -e) breath, whiff.
hauchen *v.i.* to breathe; to aspirate.
Hauchlaut *m.* spirant.
Haudegen *m.* swordsman.
Haue *f.* (-, -n) hoe, mattock; ~ *pl.* blows.
hauen *v.t.st.* to hew, to cut; to strike; *einen übers Ohr* ~, to make one pay through the nose.
Hauer *m.* (-s, -) hewer, cutter; fang, tusk.
Haufe[n] *m.* (-ns, -n) heap; pile; crowd, rabble; *über den* ~*n werfen*, to overthrow.
häufen (sich) *v.refl.* to accumulate.
haufenweise *adv.* in heaps.
Haufenwolke, *f.* cumulus cloud.
häufig *a.* frequent; copious, abundant.
Häufigkeit *f.* (-, 0) frequency.
Häufung *f.* (-, 0) accumulation.
Haupt *n.* (-[e]s, Häupter) head; (*fig.*) chief, chieftain.
Haupt...chief, main, principal.
Haupt: ~**buch** *n.* ledger; ~**fach** *n.* main subject; ~**geschäftsstelle** *f.* headquarters, head office, main office; ~**geschäftszeit** *f.* rush hours; ~**inhalt** *m.* summary, substance.
Häuptling *m.* (-[e]s, -e) chieftain.
Haupt: ~**linie** *f.* main line, trunk line; ~**mann** *m.* captain; ~**mast** *m.* mainmast; ~**nenner** *m.* (*ar.*) common denominator; ~**probe** *f.* dress-rehearsal; ~**quartier** *n.* head-quarters *pl.*; ~**rolle** *f.* principal *or* leading part; ~**sache** *f.* main point.
hauptsächlich *a.* chief, principal; ~ *adv.* chiefly, principally.
Haupt: ~**satz** *m.* (*gram.*) principal clause; ~**stadt** *f.* capital; metropolis; ~**strasse** *f.* main street; ~**schriftleiter** *m.* editor-

in-chief; ~täter *m.* (*law*) principal; ~wort *n.* noun, substantive.

Haus *n.* (-es, Häuser) house; *zu Hause*, at home; *ich bin für niemanden zu ~e*, I am not in for anybody; *nach ~e*, home; *von ~ aus*, originally.

Haus: ~angestellte[r] *m.f.* domestic servant; ~arbeiten *pl.* home work; ~arzt *m.* family doctor.

hausbacken *a.* home-bred.

Haus: ~besitzer *m.* landlord; ~brand *m.* domestic fuel.

Häuschen *n.* (-s, -) *aus dem ~ sein*, to be quite upset.

hausen *v.i.* to dwell; to keep house.

Hausenblase *f.* isinglass.

Häusermakler *m.* house agent.

Haus: ~flur *f.* vestibule, hall; ~frau *f.* housewife; ~halt *m.* household; *den ~halt führen*, to keep house; ~halten *v.i.* to economize; ~hälterin *f.* housekeeper.

haushälterisch *a.* economical, thrifty.

Haushalts...housekeeping...

Haushalts: ~ausschuss *m.* Committee of Supply; ~jahr *n.* fiscal year, financial year; ~kunde *f.* domestic subjects *pl.*; ~plan *m.* budget; ~voranschlag *m.* budget estimates; ~vorstand *m.* householder.

haushoch *a.* as high as a house.

hausieren *v.i.* to go peddling, to hawk.

Hausierer *m.* (-s, -) pedlar, hawker.

Haus: ~kleid *n.* house dress; ~knecht *m.* boots.

häuslich *a.* domestic; economical, frugal.

Häuslichkeit *f.* (-, 0) home.

Haus: ~mädchen *n.* housemaid; ~meister *m.* caretaker; ~schlüssel *m.* frontdoor key; ~schuh *m.* slipper; ~suchung *f.* house search; ~suchungsbefehl *m.* search warrant; ~tier *n.* domestic animal; ~tür *f.* frontdoor; ~vater *m.* father of the family; ~verwalter *m.* house-manager; ~wesen *n.* household; ~zins *m.* house-rent; ~zinssteuer *f.* rent-tax.

Hausse *f.* (-, -n) rise (of prices), boom.

Haussier (*frz.*) (-s, -s) bull.

Haut *f.* (-, Häute) skin, hide; (*auf Flüssigkeit*) (*anat.*) membrane; (*fam.*) *gute, ehrliche ~*, good fellow; *aus der ~ fahren*, to lose all patience; *sich seiner ~ wehren*, to defend one's own life.

Hautausschlag *m.* rash, cutaneous eruption.

Häutchen *n.* (-s, -) cuticle, pellicle; film.

häuten *v.refl.* to cast or change one's skin.

Hautfarbe *f.* complexion.

Hautwasser *n.* lotion.

Havarie *f.* (-, -en) damage by sea; average.

Hebamme *f.* midwife.

Hebebock *m.* (*mech.*) jack.

Hebel *m.* (-s, -) lever.

heben *v.t.st.* to raise, to lift; to elevate; (sich) ~ *v.refl.* to lift; (*von Zahlen*) to cancel.

Hebung *f.* (-, -en) lifting, raising; (*fig.*) improvement.

hecheln *v.t.* to hackle.

Hecht *m.* (-[e]s, -e) pike.

Heck *n.* (-[e]s, -e) (*nav.*) stern; (field-) gate.

Hecke *f.* (-, -n) hedge.

hecken *v.i. & t.* to breed, to hatch.

Heckenrose *f.* dog-rose.

Heckenschütze *m.* (*mil.*) sniper.

heda! *i.* hullo!

Heer *n.* (-[e]s, -e) army; host; great number; *stehende[s] ~*, standing army.

Heer(es)dienst *m.* military service.

Heerführer *m.* general.

Heerschau *f.* military review, parade.

Hefe *f.* (-, -n) barm, yeast; (*fig.*) dregs *pl.*

Heft *n.* (-[e]s, -e) hilt; (*Schule*) writing-book; (*Lieferung*) part, number.

heften *v.t.* to fasten; to pin; to stitch; *geheftet a.* in sheets.

heftig *a.* violent, vehement.

Heft: ~klammer *f.* staple; ~maschine *f.* stapling machine; ~pflaster *n.* adhesive plaster; ~verband *m.* adhesive dressing.

hegen *v.t.* to foster, to cherish; (*Zweifel*) to entertain.

Hegemonie *f.* (-, -n) hegemony.

Hehl *n.* (-[e]s, 0) concealment; *kein ~ daraus machen*, to make no secret of.

Hehler *m.* (-s, -) receiver (of stolen goods).

hehr *a.* sublime, august.

Heide *f.* (-, -n) heath; (*Kraut*) heather.

Heide *m.* (-n, -n) pagan, heathen, gentile.

Heidekraut *n.* heather, heath.

Heidelbeere *f.* bilberry; whortleberry.

Heidelerche *f.* woodlark.

Heiden: ~angst *f.* (*fam.*) blue funk; ~geld *n.* no end of money.

Heidentum *n.* (-[e]s, 0) paganism.

heidnisch *a.* heathenish.

heikel, heiklig *a.* dainty, fastidious; delicate, ticklish, thorny.

heil *a.* unhurt; *mit ~er Haut davonkommen*, to come off scot-free.

Heil *n.* (-[e]s, 0) salvation; ~! *i.* hail!; *sein ~ versuchen*, to try one's luck.

Heiland *m.* (-[e]s, -e) Saviour, Redeemer.

Heil: ~anstalt *f.* medical establishment, sanatorium; ~bad *n.* watering place, spa.

heilbar *a.* curable.

heilbringend *a.* salutary.

heilen *v.t.* to cure, to heal; ~ *v.i.* to heal.

heilig *a.* holy; (*geweiht*) sacred; *Heiliger Abend*, Christmas Eve; ~halten, to keep holy, to observe religiously.

Heilige[r] *m.* (-n, -n) saint.

heiligen *v.t.* to sanctify, to hallow.

Heiligenschein *m.* halo.
Heiligkeit *f.* (-, 0) holiness; sanctity; sacredness.
heiligsprechen *v.t.* to canonize.
Heiligtum *n.* (-[e]s, -tümer) sanctuary.
Heiligung *f.* (-, 0) sanctification.
Heilkraft *f.* healing power *or* virtue.
heilkräfti g *a.* sanative, healing, curative.
Heilkunde *f.* medicine.
heillos *a.* dreadful.
Heil: ~**mittel** *n.* remedy, medicine; ~**quelle** *f.* medicinal spring.
heilsam *a.* wholesome, salutary.
Heilsarmee *f.* Salvation Army.
Heilserum *n.* (-s, 0) anti-toxic serum.
Heilung *f.* (-, -en) cure.
Heilverfahren *n.* (-s, -) medical treatment.
heim *adv.* home.
Heim *n.* (-[e]s, -e) home, homestead.
Heimarbeit *f.* homework.
Heimat *f.* (-, -en) home, native place *or* country; (*mil.*) zone of the interior (ZI).
Heimat: ~**adresse** *f.* home address; ~**hafen** *m.* port of registry.
heimatlich *a.* native; home-like.
heimatlos *a.* homeless.
Heimchen *n.* (-s, -) cricket.
Heimfahrt *f.* return, homeward journey.
Heimfall *m.* (*law*) reversion.
heimfallen *v.i.st.* (s) to revert (to).
heimführen *v.t.* to lead home; to marry.
Heimgang *m.* decease.
heimgehen *v.i.st.* (s) to go home.
heimisch *a.* domestic, homelike, homely; native, indigenous.
Heimkehr *f.* return.
heimkehren *v.i.* (s) to return home.
Heimkunft *f.* return home.
heimlich *a.* secret, clandestine, furtive; private.
Heimlichkeit *f.* (-, -en) secrecy.
Heimreise *f.* return.
heimsuchen *v.t.* to visit; to afflict; to punish.
Heimsuchung *f.* (-, -en) affliction.
Heimtücke *f.* (-, 0) treachery.
heimtückisch *a.* treacherous.
heimwärts *adv.* homeward(s).
Heim: ~**weg** *m.* way home, return; ~**weh** *n.* home-sickness, nostalgia; *Heimweh haben*, to be homesick.
heimzahlen *v.t. einem etwas* ~, to pay someone out for a thing.
Heinzelmännchen *n.* brownie, Robin Goodfellow.
Heirat *f.* (-, -en) marriage; match.
heiraten *v.t.* to marry; ~ *v.i.* to get married.
Heiratsantrag *m.* offer *or* proposal of marriage.
heiratsfähig *a.* marriageable.
Heiratsgut *n.* dowry.
heisa! *i.* hurrah!

heischen *v.t.* to demand, to require.
heiser *a.* hoarse, husky.
Heiserkeit *f.* (-, 0) hoarseness, raucity.
heiss *a.* hot; (*Zone*) torrid; fervent, ardent.
heissblütig *a.* hot-blooded.
heissen *v.t.st.* to call; to bid, to command; ~ *v.i.st.* to be called; to signify, to mean; *etwas gut* ~, to approve of a thing; *wie heisst das auf französisch?* what do you call this in French?; *das heisst*, that is to say.
Heisshunger *m.* ravenous hunger.
heisshung(e)rig *a.* ravenous, voracious.
Heiss: ~**sporn** *m.* hotspur, firebrand.
heiter *a.* serene, clear, bright; fair; cheerful.
Heiterkeit *f.* (-, 0) serenity; hilarity.
heizbar *a.* containing a fireplace *or* stove.
heizen *v.t.* to heat, to make a fire (in) to stoke.
Heizer *m.* (-s, -) (*rail.*) fireman, stoker.
Heiz: ~**körper** *m.* radiator; ~**material** *n.* fuel; ~**öl** *n.* fuel oil; ~**platte** *f.* hot plate; elektrische ~**vorrichtung** *f.* electric heater.
Heizung *f.* (-, -en) heating, firing.
Hektar *m.n.* (-e, -e) hectare.
Hekto . . . = hecto . . .
Hektograph *m.* mimeograph.
Held *m.* (-en, -en) hero.
helden: ~**haft**, ~**mütig** *a.* heroic.
Helden: ~**tod** *m.* heroic death, hero's death; ~**tum** *n.* heroism.
Heldin *f.* (-, -nen) heroine.
helfen *v.i.st.* to help; to aid, to assist; to avail, to do good, to remedy.
Helfer *m.* (-s, -) helper, assistant.
Helfershelfer *m.* accomplice, abettor.
hell *a.* clear, bright; *am* ~*en Tage*, in broad daylight; ~*er Wahnsinn*, sheer madness.
hellblau *a.* light blue.
Helldunkel *n.* clair-obscure.
Helle *f.* = Helligkeit.
Hellebarde *f.* (-, -n) halberd.
Heller *m.* (-s, -) farthing, doit; *bei* ~ *und Pfennig*, to the last farthing.
Helligkeit *f.* (-, 0) clearness, brightness.
Hellseher *m.* clairvoyant.
hellsichtig *a.* clear-sighted.
Helm *m.* (-[e]s, -e) helmet; (*nav.*) helm.
Helmbusch *m.* crest, plume.
Hemd *n.* (-[e]s, -en) shirt; (*Frauen*~) chemise, shift.
Hemd: ~**ärmel** *m.* shirt-sleeve; ~**hose** *f.* combinations, cami-knickers.
Hemdenstoff *m.* shirting.
hemmen *v.t.* to stop, to hinder, to check.
Hemm: ~**nis** *n.* check, obstruction; ~**schuh** *m.* drag.
Hemmung *f.* (-, -en) check, restraint.
Hengst *m.* (-[e]s, -e) horse, stallion.

Henkel m. (-s, -) handle; ear.
henken v.t. to hang.
Henker m. (-s, -) hangman; executioner.
Henne f. (-, -n) hen.
her adv. hither, here; *her damit!* out with it!; *hin und ~,* to and fro; *nicht weit ~ (sein),* not much to boast of.
herab adv. down; downwards.
herablassen (sich) v.refl. to condescend.
Herablassung f. (-, 0) condescension.
herabsetzen v.t. to disparage; to reduce.
Herabsetzung f. (-, 0) disparagement; reduction, lowering.
herabsteigen v.i.st. (s) to descend; (*vom Pferde*) to dismount.
herabwürdigen v.t. to abase; to disparage; (sich) ~ v.refl. to demean oneself.
Heraldik f. (-, 0) heraldry.
heran adv. on, up, near.
heranbilden v.t. to train, to educate.
heranführen v.t. (*mil.*) to bring up, to move up.
herankommen v.i.st. (s) to come on.
heranmachen (sich) (an) v.refl. to sidle up to.
herannahen v.i. (s) to approach.
heranreifen v.i. (s) to come to maturity.
heranrücken v.i. (s) to advance.
heranwachsen v.i.st. (s) to grow up.
herauf adv. up, upwards.
heraufbeschwören v.t. to conjure up, to precipitate.
heraufsetzen v.t. (*Preis*) to put up.
heraufziehen v.t.st. to draw up; ~ v.i.st. (s) to draw near.
heraus adv. out; ~ ! come out i; *er hat's ~,* he has got the knack of it.
herausbekommen v.t.st. to get back (change); to find out.
herausbringen v.t.ir. to bring out; to find *or* make out.
herausfinden v.t. to find out.
herausfordern v.t. to challenge; to provoke.
Herausforderung f. (-, -en) challenge; provocation.
Herausgabe f. (-, 0) delivery; publication.
herausgeben v.t. to give up, to deliver up; to give change; to publish; to edit.
Herausgeber m. (-s, -) (*Leiter*) editor; publisher.
herauskommen v.i.st. (s) to come out; to transpire; *au eins ~,* to come to the same thing; *dabei kommt nichts heraus,* it's no use, it doesn't pay.
herausnehmen (sich) v.refl.st. (*etwas*) to presume, to make bold.
herausplatzen v.i. (s) (*mit*) to blurt out.
herausputzen v.t. to dress up, to rig out.
herausreden (sich) v.refl. to get off by prevarication, to extricate oneself.
herausrücken v.i. (s) (*mit dem Gelde*) to fork out, to come down; (*mit der Sprache*) to speak frankly.

herausschlagen v.t.st. to make (money).
herausstellen (sich) v.refl.imp. to turn out, to become apparent.
herausstreichen v.t.st. to extol, to praise; to puff.
heraustreten v.i.st. (s) to step out; to protrude.
herauszahlen v.t. to pay back, to give back (as change).
herb, herbe a. tart, acrid; (*fig.*) harsh, austere.
herbei adv. hither, near; on.
herbeiführen v.t. to bring about, to entail.
herbeischaffen v.t. to produce, to procure.
herbemühen v.t. to give one the trouble of coming here; (sich) ~ v.refl. to take the trouble of coming.
Herberge f. (-, -n) hostel.
herbestellen v.t. to appoint, to send for.
herbitten v.t.st. to invite.
herbringen v.t.ir. to bring (hither).
Herbst m. (-es, -e) autumn, (*Am.*) fall.
herbstlich a. autumnal.
Herbstzeitlose f. (-, -n) (*bot.*) meadowsaffron.
Herd m. (-[e]s, -e) fireplace; kitchen-range; (*einer Epidemie*) centre.
Herde f. (-, -n) (*Schafe*) flock; herd.
herein adv. in; ~! i. come in!
hereindürfen v.i.ir. to be allowed in.
Hereinfall m. (*fam.*) sell, take in.
hereinfallen v.i. to be taken in, to be sold.
hereinlassen v.t. to let in.
herfallen (über) v.i.st. to fall upon.
Hergang m. (-[e]s, -gänge) proceedings pl., course of events, circumstances pl.
hergeben v.t.st. to surrender, to give up; (sich) ~ v.refl. to lend oneself.
hergebracht a. traditional, established.
hergehen v.i.st. to happen; (*lustig, etc.*) to be going on.
hergehören v.i. to belong to the matter.
hergelaufen a. *ein ~er Mensch,* undesirable newcomer.
herholen v.t. to fetch.
Hering m. (-[e]s, -e) herring.
herkommen v.i.st. (s) to come on; to come from; to originate in.
Herkommen n. (-s, 0) usage, custom.
herkömmlich a. customary, usual, traditional.
Herkunft f. (-, 0) descent, origin.
herlegen v.t. to put down (here).
herleiern v.t. to reel off.
herleiten v.t. to conduct; to derive.
hermachen (sich) v.refl. (*über*) to set about.
Hermelin n. (-[e]s, -e) ermine.
hermetisch a. & adv. hermetic(ally).
hernach adv. afterwards.
hernehmen v.t.st. to take from.
heroisch a. & adv. heroic(ally).
Herold m. (-[e]s, -e) herald.
herplappern v.t. to rattle off.

Herr m. (-n, -en) master; lord; gentleman; Sir; *Herr Braun*, Mr. (Mister) B.; ~ *werden*, to master, to overcome.

Herreise f. (-, 0) journey hither.

herreisen v.i. (s) to travel thither.

Herrenhaus n. manor-house, hall.

herrenlos a. stray.

Herrenreiter m. gentleman rider.

Herrgott m. (fam.) the Lord, God.

herrichten v.t. to fit up, to arrange.

Herrin f. (-, -nen) mistress, lady.

herrisch a. imperious, masterful.

herrlich a. magnificent, splendid.

Herrlichkeit f. (-, -en) magnificence, splendour, glory; excellence.

Herrschaft f. (-, -en) dominion, mastery; master and mistress; *meine ~en*, ladies and gentlemen.

herrschaftlich a. high class.

herrschen v.i. to rule, to govern; to prevail.

Herrscher m. (-s, -) ruler, sovereign.

Herrscherfamilie f. dynasty.

Herrschsucht f. thirst of power.

herrschsüchtig a. imperious, ambitious.

herrücken v.i. to move near.

herrühren v.i. to originate in.

hersagen v.t. to recite, to repeat.

herschaffen v.t. to procure, to produce.

herschreiben (sich) v.refl.st. to date from.

herstellen v.t. to manufacture, to produce, to turn out; to restore (to health).

herüber adv. over, across, on this side.

herum adv. round; about; *hier ~*, hereabout(s); *die Reihe ~*, each one in his turn.

herumführen v.t. to show over a place; *an der Nase ~*, to lead by the nose.

herumkommen v.i.st. (s) *weit ~*, to see the world.

herumlaufen v.i. to run about.

herumliegen v.i. to lie about.

herumlungern, herumstehen, v.i. to loiter.

herumpfuschen (an) v.i. to tamper with.

herumreichen v.t. to hand round.

herumschlagen v.t.st. to wrap about; *sich ~ mit*, to scuffle with.

herumtreiben (sich) v.refl.st. to rove or stroll about.

herumziehend a. ambulatory.

herunter adv. down, off; (fam.) low, weak.

herunterbringen v.t.ir. to bring down; to reduce; to take it out of a person.

herunterkommen v.i.st. (s) to come down; to decay, to go to the bad.

herunterlassen v.t. to lower.

heruntermachen v.t. to run down.

herunterreissen v.t. to tear down.

herunterschlucken v.t. to swallow.

heruntersteigen v.i.st. (s) to descend.

hervor adv. forth, out.

hervorbringen v.t.ir. to bring forth, to produce; to effect.

hervorgehen v.i.st. (s) to proceed; to result; to come off.

hervorheben v.t.st. to emphasize; to set off.

hervorragen v.i. to stand out; to project.

hervorrufen v.t.st. to call forth, to cause.

hervorstechen v.i.st. to be prominent.

hervortreten v.i.st. (s) (fig.) to excel, to stand pre-eminent.

hervortun (sich) v.refl.st. to distinguish oneself.

Herweg m. (-[e]s, -e) way hither.

Herz, n. (-ens, -en) heart; breast; (*Kern*) core; (fig.) courage; *ans ~ legen*, to urge, to enjoin; *es liegt mir am ~en*, I have it at heart; *ich kann es nicht übers ~ bringen*, I cannot find it in my heart; *von ~en*, with all my heart; (*sich*) *etwas zu ~en nehmen*, to take a thing to heart.

Herz... cardiac.

Herzbeutel m. pericardium.

herzbrechend a. heart-rending.

Herzeleid n. heart-ache, grief, anguish.

herzen v.t. to hug, to caress.

Herzerweiterung f. dilatation of the heart.

herzhaft a. courageous, bold; hearty.

herzig a. lovely, sweet.

Herz: ~kammer f. ventricle (of the heart); **~klopfen** n. palpitation.

herzlich a. hearty.

herzlos a. heartless.

Herzog m. (-[e]s, Herzöge) duke.

Herzogin f. (-, -nen) duchess.

herzoglich a. ducal.

Herzogtum n. (-[e]s, -tümer) dukedom, duchy.

Herzschlag m. heart-throb; heart-failure.

herzzerreissend a. heart-rending.

Hetze f. (-, -n) hunt, chase; (fig.) hurry, rush; agitation; persecution, baiting.

hetzen v.t. to hunt; to set on; to agitate; to incite; to bait.

Hetzer m. (-s, -) agitator.

Heu n. (-[e]s, 0) hay.

Heuboden m. hay-loft.

Heuchelei f. (-, -en) hypocrisy.

heucheln v.t. to feign, to put on, simulate; *~ v.i.* to dissemble.

Heuchler m. (-s, -) **Heuchlerin** f. (-, -nen) hypocrite.

heuchlerisch a. hypocritical.

heuer adv. this year's.

heurig a. this year's.

Heu: ~ernte f. hay-time, hay-making; **~gabel** f. pitchfork; **~haufen** m. haystack.

heulen v.i. to howl; to cry, to whine.

Heuschnupfen m. (-s, 0) hay fever.

Heuschrecke f. (-, -n) grasshopper.

heute adv. to-day.

heutig a. this day's, present day.

heutzutage adv. nowadays.

Hexe (*hekse*) *f.* (-, -n) witch.
hexen (*heksen*) *v.i.* to practise witchcraft.
Hexenschuss *m.* lumbago.
Hexerei *f.* (-, -en) sorcery, witchcraft.
Hieb *m.* (-[e]s, -e) cut, stroke; (*fig.*) hit.
hiemit = hiermit.
hienieden *adv.* here below.
hier *adv.* here; present; ~ *zu Lande*, in this country.
Hierarchie *f.* (-, -[e]n) hierarchy.
hierauf *adv.* hereupon; after this.
hieraus *adv.* from this; hence.
hierbei *adv.* at, by, with this.
hierbleiben *v.i.* to stay here.
hierdurch *adv.* by this, hereby.
hierfür *adv.* for this.
hiergegen *adv.* against this.
hierher *adv.* hither, this way; *bis* ~, so far, hitherto.
hierherum *adv.* about here, hereabouts.
hierhin *adv.* this way.
hierin *adv.* in this.
hiermit *adv.* with this, herewith.
hiernach *adv.* after this, according to this.
Hieroglyphe (-*glife*) *f.* (-, -n) hieroglyph.
hierorts *adv.* in this place.
Hiersein *n.* (-s, 0) presence, stay here.
hierüber *adv.* over here; about this.
hierum *adv.* about this.
hierunter *adv.* under this, among these.
hiervon *adv.* of, from this; about this.
hierwider *adv.* against this.
hierzu *adv.* to this; ~ *kommt noch*, add to this.
hiesig *a.* of this place.
Hilfe *f.* (-, -n) help, aid, assistance, relief; *erste* ~, first aid; *einem zu Hilfe* ~ *kommen*, to come to the rescue of; ~ *leisten*, to aid, to assist.
Hilfeleistung *f.* assistance.
Hilferuf *m.* cry for help.
hilflos *a.* helpless.
hilfreich *a.* helpful; benevolent.
Hilfsarbeiter *m.* assistant.
Hilfsbedürftig *a.* requiring help.
Hilfs: ~**fonds** *m.* relief fund; ~**mittel** *n.* resource, expedient; ~**quelle** *f.* resource; ~**truppen** *pl.* auxiliary troops *pl.*; ~**unterstützung** *f.* grant-in-aid; ~**zeitwort** *n.* auxiliary (verb).
Himbeere *f.* (-, -n) raspberry.
Himmel *m.* (-s, -) heaven; heavens *pl.*; (*sichtbarer*) sky; (*eines Bettes*) canopy.
Himmelbett *n.* four-poster.
himmelblau *a.* azure, sky-blue.
Himmelfahrt *f.* Ascension; (*Mariä*) Assumption.
Himmelfahrtstag *m.* Ascension-day.
himmelhoch *a.* sky-high.
Himmelreich *n.* kingdom of heaven.
himmelschreiend *a.* crying to heaven.
Himmels: ~**gewölbe** *n.* firmament; ~**körper** *m.* celestial body; ~**richtung** *f.*

point of the compass; ~**schrift** *f.* sky-writing.
himmelwärts *adv.* heavenward(s).
himmelweit *a.* & *adv.* widely.
himmlisch *a.* celestial, heavenly.
hin *adv.* thither, there, along; gone, lost; ~ *und her*, to and fro, backwards and forwards; ~ *und wieder*, now and then; ~ *und zurück*, there, and back.
hinab *adv.* down.
hinarbeiten *v.i.* to aim at.
hinauf *adv.* up, up to; upstairs.
hinaufarbeiten (sich) *v.refl.* to work one's way up.
hinaufsteigen *v.i.st.* (s) to ascend, to step up.
hinaus *adv.* out; *darüber* ~, beyond that.
hinausgehen *v.i.st.* (s) to go out; to surpass, to exceed; to face.
hinaus: ~**laufen**, ~**kommen** *v.i.st.* (s) *auf dasselbe* ~, to come to the same thing.
hinausschieben *v.t.st.* (*fig.*) to defer, to put off, to postpone.
hinauswerfen *v.t.st.* to throw out.
hinauswollen *v.i.ir.* to want to get out; to be driving at.
hinbegeben (sich) *v.refl.st.* to repair to.
Hinblick *m.* (-[e]s, 0) consideration; *im* ~ *auf*, with a view to, in consideration of.
hinbringen *v.t.ir.* to carry to; (*Zeit*) to pass away.
hinderlich *a.* hindering, in the way.
hindern *v.t.* to hinder, to prevent, to impede.
Hindernis *n.* (-nisses, -nisse) hindrance, impediment, obstacle.
Hindernisrennen *n.* steeplechase.
hindeuten *v.i.* to point to *or* at.
Hindin *f.* (-, -nen) hind.
hindurch *adv.* through, throughout; across.
hinein *adv.* in; *in den Tag* ~, at random, at a venture.
hineinarbeiten (sich) *v.refl.* to familiarize oneself with.
hineinbegeben (sich) *v.refl.st.* to enter, to go in.
hineindenken (sich) *v.refl.ir.* to transfer oneself mentally into.
hineinfahren *v.i.* to run into.
hineinfinden (sich) *v.refl.* to make the best of a thing.
hineingeh(e)n *v.i.st.* to enter; *es wird nicht mehr* ~, it will hold no more.
hineinstecken, hineintun *v.t.* to put into.
hineinwagen (sich) *v.refl.* to venture in.
Hinfahrt *f.* (-, -en) journey to, drive, passage to; outward journey.
hinfallen *v.i.st.* (s) to fall down.
hinfällig *a.* frail, weak.
hinfliehen *v.i.st.* (s) to fly to; to fly away.
hinführen *v.t.* to conduct to, to lead to.
Hingabe *f.* (-, 0) devotion, surrender.

Hingang m. (-[e]s, 0) decease.
hingeben v.t.st. to give up; (sich) ~, to devote oneself (to), to indulge (in).
hingebend a. devoted, fond.
Hingebung f. (-, 0) resignation; devotion.
hingegen adv. on the other hand.
hingehen v.i.st. (s) to go; to pass; ~ lassen, to wink at, to let pass.
hinhalten v.t.st. to hold out; to put off, to delude with hopes.
hinken v.i. to limp, to halt.
hinkommen v.i.st. (s) to come to, to get to.
hinlänglich a. sufficient, adequate.
hinnehmen v.t.st. to put up with.
hinraffen v.t. (fig.) to carry off, to cut off (in the prime of life).
hinreichen v.t. to hand, to offer; ~ v.i. to suffice.
hinreichend a. sufficient.
Hinreise f. (-, -n) journey to, voyage out.
hinreisen v.i. (s) to travel to.
hinreissen v.t.st. to ravish, to transport.
hinreissend a. charming, ravishing.
hinrichten v.t. to execute.
Hinrichtung f. (-, -en) execution.
hinschaffen v.t. to convey to.
hinscheiden v.i.st. to depart (life).
hinschlagen v.i.st. to fall down.
hinschlachten v.t. to massacre.
hinschlendern v.i. (s) to saunter.
hinschwinden v.i.st. (s) to dwindle.
hinsehen v.i. to look.
hinsein v.i.st. (s) to be lost, to be gone.
hinsetzen v.t. to set down; (sich) ~ v.refl. to sit down.
Hinsicht f. (-, -en) respect, regard; in ~ auf..., with regard to.
hinsichtlich a. with regard to.
hinsiechen v.i. (h, s) to pine away.
hinsterben v.i.st. (s) to die away.
hinstrecken v.t. (fig.) to knock down; sich ~, to lie down.
hintansetzen v.t. (fig.) to slight.
Hintansetzung f. (-, -en) neglect; mit ~, regardless of.
hinten adv. behind; (nav.) aft; ~nach, afterwards.
hinter pr. behind, after; ~einander, one after another; ~s Licht führen, to dupe; etwas ~ sich haben, to have got over a thing; ~hersein, to pursue diligently.
Hinterbein n. hind-leg.
Hinterbliebene[r] m. (-s, -) survivor.
hinterbringen v.t. to inform.
Hinterdeck n. poop.
hinterdrein adv. afterwards, after; too late.
Hintere[r] m. (-n, -n) backside.
hintere[r] a. hind, hinder, back.
Hinterfuss m. hind-foot.
Hintergedanke m. mental reservation.
hintergehen v.t. to deceive.
Hinter: ~grund m. background; ~halt m. (-[e]s, -e) ambush.

hinterhältig a. reserved, crafty.
Hinterhaus n. backbuilding, outhouse.
hinterher adv. afterwards.
Hinter: ~kopf m. back of the head; occiput; ~land n. hinterland.
hinterlassen v.t.st. to leave (behind); to leave word.
Hinterlassene[r] m. (-n, -n) survivor.
Hinterlassenschaft f. (-, -en) inheritance.
hinterlegen v.t. to deposit.
Hinterlist f. fraud, deceit, cunning.
hinterlistig a. cunning, deceitful.
Hintern m. (-, -) behind, backside.
Hinter: ~mann m. backer; ~rad n. rear wheel.
hinterrücks adv. from behind, insidiously.
Hintersitz m. back-seat.
hinterste[r] a. hindmost.
Hinter: ~teil n. back-part; backside; (nav.) stern; ~treppe f. back-stairs pl.
hintertreiben v.t.st. to frustrate.
Hinter: ~tür f. back-door; loop-hole; ~wäldler m. (-s, -) backwoodsman.
hinterziehen v.t.st. to evade (taxes).
hintun, v.t. to put.
hinüber adv. over, across.
hinunter adv. down; downstairs.
hinunter: ~schlucken v.t. to swallow; ~würgen v.t. to gulp down.
hinwagen (sich) v.refl. to venture to go somewhere.
Hinweg m. (-[e]s, -e) way thither.
hinweg adv. away, off; ~! begone!; über etwas ~gehen, to pass lightly over a thing; ~raffen, to cut off, to sweep away; ~sehen über etwas, to overlook a thing; sich über etwas ~setzen, not to mind a thing, to make light of it.
Hinweis m. (-weises, -weise) hint; reference.
hinweisen (auf) v.i.st. to point out.
hinweisend a. (gram.) demonstrative.
hinwerfen v.t.st. to throw down; to fling to; to dash off, to utter carelessly.
hinwieder adv. again; on the other hand.
hinwirken (auf) v.i. to work in the direction of.
hinziehen v.t.st. to draw to, to protract sich ~, to drag on.
hinzielen v.i. to aim at; (fig.) to have in view.
hinzu adv. to it; in addition; near.
hinzudenken v.t.ir. to supply mentally.
hinzufügen v.t. to add; to subjoin.
hinzukommen v.i.st. (s) to come to; to be added.
hinzurechnen v.t. to add to.
hinzusetzen v.t. to add, to subjoin.
hinzuziehen v.t.st. to include, to add; (einen Arzt) to consult.
Hiobspost f. (-, -en) bad news.
Hirn n. (-[e]s, -e) brain, brains pl.
Hirngespinst n. (-[e]s, -e) fancy, chimera.

hirnlos *a.* brainless, hare-brained.

Hirnschale *f.* skull, cranium.

hirnverbrannt *a.* mad.

Hirsch *m.* (-[e]s, -e) stag, hart.

Hirsch: ~**fänger** *m.* hanger, cutlass; ~**geweih** *n.* antlers *pl.*, hartshorn; ~**käfer** *m.* stag-beetle; ~**kuh** *f.* hind, doe; ~**leder** *n.* buckskin.

Hirse *f.* (-, 0) millet.

Hirt *m* (-en, -en) shepherd.

Hirtenbrief *m.* pastoral letter.

His (*mus.*) B sharp.

hissen *v.t.* to hoist (up).

Historiker *m.* (-s, -) historian.

historisch *a.* historical.

Hitze *f.* (-, 0) heat; hot weather; (*fig.*) ardour, passion.

Hitzewelle *f.* heat wave.

hitzig *a.* hot; ardent, fervid; passionate.

Hitzkopf *m.* spit-fire, hotspur.

hitzköpfig *a.* hot-headed.

Hitzschlag *m.* sunstroke.

Hobel *m.* (-s, -) plane.

Hobelbank *f.* joiner's bench.

Hobelmaschine *f.* (-, -n) planer.

hobeln *v.t.* to plane.

Hobelspäne *f.pl.* shavings *pl.*

Hoboe *f.* (-, -n) oboe, haut-boy.

Hoboist *m.* (-en, -en) oboist.

hoch *a.* high; lofty, sublime; eminent; *dre Mann* ~, three men strong; *hohe See,* high seas; *hohe Strafe,* heavy penalty; *wenn es* ~ *kommt,* at most; *hoch lebe!* long live!; **ein Hoch** *n.* (*Wetterkunde*) a high.

hochachten *v.t.* to esteem, to respect, to value.

Hochachtung *f.* (-, 0) esteem, respect.

hochachtungsvoll *adv.* yours faithfully.

Hoch: ~**amt** *n.* high mass; ~**bahn** *f.* overhead railway; ~**bau** *m.* overground building; ~**burg** *f.* stronghold.

hochdeutsch *a.* High-German.

Hochdruck *m.* high pressure.

Hochebene *f.* table-land.

hoch: ~**fahrend** *a.* haughty; ~**fein** *a.* superfine; ~**fliegend** *a.* (*fig.*) lofty.

Hoch: ~**format** *n.* upright size; ~**frequenz** *f.* high frequency.

Hochgenuss *m.* treat, delight.

hochgradig *a.* to a high degree.

hoch: ~**herzig** *a.* high-minded, magnanimous; ~**kirchlich** *a.* High Church.

Hochland *n.* (-[e]s, -e *u.* -länder) highland.

höchlich *adv.* highly.

Hochmut *m.* arrogance, haughtiness.

hochmütig *a.* haughty, proud.

Hochofen *m.* blast-furnace.

hochrot *a.* light-red, crimson.

hochschätzen *v.t.* to esteem highly.

Hoch: ~**schätzung** *f.* high esteem; ~**schule** *f.* university, college (of university rank); ~**seeschlepper** *m.* sea-going tug; ~**spannung** *f.* high tension *or* voltage; ~**spannungsleitung** *f.* high tension cable, power line; ~**sprung** *m.* high jump.

hochschwanger *a.* far advanced in pregnancy.

höchst *a.* & *adv.* highest; extremely; ~*e Zeit,* high time.

Hochstapler *m.* (-s,) swindler, confidence trickster.

Höchst: ~**belastung** *f.* maximum load; ~**geschwindigkeit** *f.* speed limit, top speed; ~**grenze** *f.* ceiling; ~**leistung** *f.* record; ~**preis** *m.* maximum price.

höchstens *adv.* at most, at best.

hoch: ~**trabend** *a.* high-sounding, bombastic; ~**verdient** *a.* of great merit.

Hoch: ~**verrat** *m.* high treason; ~**wasser** *n.* flood; ~**wertig** *a.* high grade.

Hochwürden, Ew. ~ Your Reverence.

hochwürdig *a.* reverend.

Hochzeit *f.* wedding.

hochzeitlich *a.* nuptial.

Hochzeitsreise *f.* honeymoon.

hocken *v.i.* to squat.

Höcker *m.* (-s, -) bump; knoll; hunch, hump-back.

höckerig *a.* uneven; hunch-backed.

Hode *f.* (-, -n) testicle.

Hodensack *m.* scrotum.

Hof *m.* (-[e]s, Höfe) yard; court; farm; (*um den Mond*) halo; (*opt.*) cornea; *den* ~ *machen,* to court.

Hofdame *f.* lady-in-waiting.

Hoffart *f.* (-, 0) pride, haughtiness.

hoffen *v.i.* to hope; to expect; to trust.

hoffentlich *adv.* as I hope, I trust that...

Hoffnung *f.* (-, -en) hope; expectation; *sich* ~ *machen,* to indulge in the hope of; *guter* ~ *sein (von Frauen)* to be expecting a baby.

hoffnungs: ~**los** *a.* hopeless, past hope; ~**voll** *a.* hopeful; promising.

hofieren *v.i.* to court, to flatter.

höfisch *a.* courtly, courtier-like.

höflich *a.* courteous, polite.

Höflichkeit *f.* (-, -en) courteousness, courtesy, politeness.

Hof: ~**mann** *m.* courtier; ~**staat** *m.* royal *or* princely household.

Höhe *f.* (-, -n) height; hill; (*Luft, Geogr.*) altitude; (*der Preise*) level; *auf der* ~, up to date; *nicht ganz auf der* ~, not quite up to the mark; *auf der* ~ *von,* (*nav.*) off.

Hoheit *f.* (-, -en) grandeur; (*Titel*) Highness.

Hoheits: ~**abzeichen** *n.* (*mil.*) marking; ~**gewässer** *n.* territorial waters; ~**grenze** *f.* limit of territorial waters.

Hoheitsrecht *n.* royal prerogative.

Hohelied *n.* Song of Solomon.

Höhen: ~kurort *m.* high-altitude health resort; ~messer *m.* (*avi.*) altimeter; ~sonne *f.* ultra-violet rays *or* lamp; ~steuer *n.* (*avi.*) elevator.

Höhepunkt *m.* climax, acme, peak.

hohl *a.* hollow; concave.

Hohl: ~mass *n.* capacity measure; ~raum *m.* cavity; ~saum *m.* hemstitch; ~spiegel *m.* concave mirror; ~weg *m.* sunken road.

Höhle *f.* (-, -n) cave, den, cavern.

Höhlung *f.* (-, -en) excavation, cavity.

Hohn *m.* (-[e]s, 0) sneer, mockery.

höhnen *v.t.* to scoff, to sneer (at).

höhnisch *a.* scornful, sneering.

hohnlachen *v.i.* to jeer, to deride.

hohnsprechen *v.i.* to scorn.

Höker *m.* (-s, -) hawker, huckster.

hökern *v.i.* to huckster.

Hokuspokus *m.* (-, 0) hocus-pocus.

hold *a.* lovely, propitious.

holdselig *a.* charming, lovely.

holen *v.t.* to fetch; *sich etwas* ~, to catch; *Atem* ~, to breathe; ~*lassen*, to send for.

holla! *i.* hullo! hulloa!

Hölle *f.* (-, 0) hell.

Höllenangst *f.* mortal fright.

höllisch *a.* hellish, infernal.

holpern *v.i.* to jolt, to be uneven.

holp(e)rig *a.* rough, rugged; rude.

Holunder *m.* (-s, -) elder.

Holz *n.* (-[e]s, Hölzer) wood, timber; bush, forest.

Holz: ~arbeit *f.* woodwork; ~arbeiter *m.* woodworker.

Holzbock *m.* sawing-block, jack.

hölzern *a.* wooden; (*fig.*) clumsy, awkward.

Holzgas *n.* producer gas.

Holz: ~hacker *m.* wood-chopper; ~handel *m.* timber-trade; ~händler *m.* timber-merchant.

holzig *a.* woody, wooded.

Holz: ~klotz *m.* log; ~kohle *f.* charcoal; ~pflock *m.* peg; ~scheit *m.* stick of wood; ~schnitt *m.* woodcut; ~schnitzer *m.* wood-carver; ~schnitzerei *f.* wood-carving; ~schuh *m.* clog; ~stoss *m.* pile of wood; ~span *m.* wood shaving; ~weg *m., auf dem ~wege sein*, to be on the wrong track; ~wolle *f.* wood-wool; ~zellstoff *m.* wood-pulp.

Holzung *f.* (-, -en) forest, wood.

homogen *a.* homogeneous.

Homöopathie *f.* (-, 0) homœopathy.

Honig *m.* (-s, 0) honey.

Honigwabe *f.* honeycomb.

Honorar *n.* (-s, -e) fee; *ein* ~ *berechnen*, to charge a fee.

Hopfen *m.* (-s, 0) hop; *an ihm ist* ~ *und Malz verloren*, he is past hope of amendment.

Hopfenstange *f.* hop-pole; (*fam. von Menschen*) maypole, Long Meg.

hopp! *i.* hop! jump!

hopsen *v.i.* (*s*) to jump.

hörbar *a.* audible.

horch! *i.* hark!

horchen *v.i.* to listen, to hearken.

Horde *f.* (-, -n) horde.

hören *v.t.* to hear; to listen; *schwer* ~, to be hard of hearing; *hören Sie mal*, I say; *das lässt sich* ~, that sounds fair enough; *bei einem Professor* ~, to attend a professor's lectures.

Hörensagen *n.* hearsay; *von* ~, by hearsay.

Hörer *m.* (-s, -) (*Radio*) listener.

Hörerschaft *f.* (-, -en) audience.

hörig *a.* enslaved; bond.

Hörigkeit *f.* (-, 0) bondage.

Horizont *m.* (-[e]s, -e) horizon.

Hormon *n.* (-, -e) hormone; ~drüsen *f.pl.* ductless glands.

Horn *n.* (-[e]s, Hörner) horn; French horn, bugle.

Hörnchen *n.* (*Gebäck*) crescent.

hörnern *a.* of horn.

Hornhaut *f.* cornea (*Auge*); horny skin.

Hornisse *f.* (-, -n) hornet.

Hornist *m.* (-en, -en) cornet-player.

Horoskop *n.* (-es, -e) horoscope; *das* ~ *stellen*, to cast a horoscope.

Hör: ~rohr *n.* ear-trumpet; ~saal *m.* lecture-room.

Horst *m.* (-es, -e) eyrie, nest (of a bird of prey).

Hort *m.* (-[e]s, -e) hoard; (*fig.*) stronghold, retreat; protector; (*Kinder-*) ~, day nursery.

Hortensie *f.* (-, -n) hydrangea.

Hörweite *f.* hearing, earshot.

Hose *f.* (-, -n) trousers *pl.*, (*Am.*) pants; (*Knie~*) breeches *pl.*, knickerbockers, plus-fours *pl.*

Hosen: ~aufschläge *pl.* turn-ups; ~bandorden *m.* Order of the Garter; ~boden *m.* seat of the trousers; ~träger *pl.* braces, (*Am.*) suspenders.

Hospital *n.* (-[e]s, Hospitäler) hospital.

Hostie *f.* (-, -n) host, holy wafer.

Hotel *n.* (-s, -s) hotel; ~apartement *n.* suite.

Hub *m.* (-es, Hübe) lift; (*Kolben*) stroke.

hüben *adv.* on this side; ~ *und drüben*, on each (either) side.

hübsch *a.* pretty, fair; proper; *das ist nicht* ~ *von ihm*, that's hardly fair of him.

huckepack *adv.* pick-a-pack.

hudeln *v.t.* to bungle.

Huf *m.* (-[e]s, -e) hoof.

Hufbeschlag *m.* (horse)-shoeing.

Hufe *f.* (-, -n) hide of land

Hufeisen *n.* horse-shoe.

Hufschmied *m.* farrier; ~e *f.* shoeing-forge.

Hüftbein *n.* hip-bone.
Hüfte *f.* (-, -n) hip, haunch.
Hüftgelenk *n.* hip-joint.
Hügel *m.* (-s, -) hill, hillock, knoll.
hüg[e]lig *a.* hilly.
Huhn *n.* (-[e]s, Hühner) fowl; hen.
Hühnchen *n.* (-s, -) chicken, pullet.
Hühner: ~auge *n.* corn (on the foot);
  ~braten *m.* roast chicken; ~korb *m.*
  hencoop; ~stall *m.* chicken-house;
  ~stange, ~steige, *f.* hen-roost.
Huld *f.* (-, 0) grace, favour.
huldigen *v.i.* to pay, render, *or* do homage;
  to hold (an opinion); to indulge in.
Huldigung *f.* (-, -en) homage.
huldvoll *a.* benevolent.
Hülfe = Hilfe.
Hülle *f.* (-, -n) cover, veil, wrapper; ~ *und*
  Fülle, abundance, enough and to spare.
hüllen *v.t.* to cover, to wrap.
Hülse *f.* (-, -n) husk; (*Patronen*) case.
Hülsenfrucht *f.* legume.
human *a.* humane.
Humanismus *m.* (-, 0) humanism.
Humanität *f.* (-, 0) humanity.
Humbug *m.* (-s, 0) humbug, eyewash.
Hummel *f.* (-, -n) humble-bee.
Hummer *m.* (-s, -n) lobster.
Humor *m.* (-s, -e) humour.
Humoreske *f.* (-, -n) humorous sketch.
humpeln *v.i.* (*h, s*) to hobble, to limp.
Humpen *m.* (-s, -) tankard.
Hund *m.* (-[e]s, -e) dog, hound; *auf den* ~
  kommen, to go to the dogs.
Hunde: ~halsband *n.* dog-collar; ~hütte *f.*
  kennel; ~kälte *f.* bitter, sharp cold;
  ~kuchen *m.* dog-biscuit; ~leben *n.*
  dog's life.
hundert *a.* hundred.
hunderterlei *a.* of a hundred sorts.
hundertfach *a.* hundredfold.
Hundertjahrfeier *f.* centenary.
Hundertjährige[r] *m.* centenarian.
hundertste *a.* hundredth.
Hündin *f.* (-, -nen) bitch.
hündisch *a.* cringing.
Hundstage *m.pl.* dog-days *pl.*
Hüne *m.* (-n, -n) giant.
Hünengrab *n.* barrow, cairn.
Hunger *m.* (-s, 0) hunger; ~ *haben,* to be
  hungry; ~ *leiden,* to starve; ~*s sterben,*
  to die of hunger, to starve to death.
hung(e)rig *a.* hungry.
Hungerleider *m.* (-s, -) starveling.
Hungerlohn *m.* starvation wages, pittance.
hungern *v.i.imp.* to hunger, to be hungry.
Hungersnot *f.* famine.
Hunger: ~streik *m.* hunger strike; ~tod
  m. starvation.
Hupe *f.* (-, -n) horn.
hupen *v.i.* to hoot.
hüpfen *v.i.* (*s*) to hop, to skip.
Hupzeichen *n.* horn-signal.

Hürde *f.* (-, -n) hurdle; pen, fold.
Hure *f.* (-, -n) prostitute, whore.
huren *v.i.* to whore, to fornicate.
Hurerei *f.* (-, 0) whoring, whoredom.
hurra *i.* hurrah!
hurtig *a.* quick, swift, nimble, agile.
Husar *m.* (-en, -en) hussar.
husch *i.* hush! quick!
huschen *v.i.* (*s*) to scurry, to whisk.
Husten *m.* (-s, 0) cough.
husten *v.i.* to cough.
Hut *m.* (-[e]s, Hüte) hat, bonnet; (*Zucker*)
  loaf; ~ *f.* keeping, charge, guard; *auf*
  der ~ *sein,* to be on one's guard.
hüten *v.t.* to guard, to watch, to tend, to
  keep;(sich)~ *v.refl.* to be on one's guard,
  to beware (of); *das Bett, das Zimmer* ~,
  to be confined to one's bed, room.
Hüter *m.* (-s, -) keeper, guardian.
Hut: ~krempe *f.* brim (of a hat); ~macher
  m. hatter; ~schachtel *f.* hat-box.
Hütte *f.* (-, -n) hut, cottage; (*Werkhaus*)
  foundry, smelting works, forge.
Hüttenwesen *n.* metallurgy.
Hyäne *f.* (-, -n) hyena.
Hyazinthe *f.* (-, -n) hyacinth.
hydraulisch *a.* hydraulic.
Hygiene *f.* (-, 0) hygiene.
hygienisch *a.* hygienic.
Hymne *f.* (-, -n) hymn.
Hyperbel (-, -n) hyperbole; (*geom.*) hyper-
  bola.
hyperbolisch *a.* hyperbolical.
Hypnose *f.* (-, -n) hypnosis.
hypnotisieren *v.t.* to hypnotize.
Hypochonder *m.* (-s, -) hypochondriac.
Hypochondrie *f.* (-, 0) hypochondria.
hypochondrisch *a.* hypochondriacal.
Hypothek *f.* (-, -en) mortgage; *eine* ~ *für*
  verfallen erklären, to foreclose a mortgage; ~enschuld *f.* debt on mortgage.
hypothekarisch *a.* hypothecary.
Hypothese *f.* (-, -n) hypothesis.
Hysterie *f.* (-, 0) hysteria, hysterics.
hysterisch *a.* hysterical.

I

iambisch *a.* iambic.
ich *pn.* I, I myself.
Ideal *n.* (-[e]s, -e) ideal; ~ *a.* ideal.
idealisieren *v.t.* to idealize.
Idee *f.* (-, -n) idea, notion; *um eine* ~ *zu*
  lang, just a thought too long.
identifizieren *v.t.* to identify.
identisch *a.* identical.
Identität *f.* (-, -en) identity.
Ideologie *f.* (-, -n) ideology.
ideologisch *a.* ideological.
Idyll *n.* (-s, -en) idyll.
Igel *m.* (-s, -) hedgehog.

Ignorant *m.* (-en, -en) *(fam.)* ignoramus.
ignorieren *v.t.* to take no notice of; *(einen)* to cut.
ihm *pn.* (to) him; (to) it.
ihn *pn.* him, it.
ihnen *pn.* (to) them.
ihr *pn.* (to) her, their.
ihrerseits *adv.* on their (her) part.
ihrethalben, ihretwegen, um ihretwillen *adv.* for her, their sake; *Ihrethalben, etc.* for your sake.
ihrige *pn.* hers, theirs; *Ihrige,* yours.
illuminieren *v.t.* to illuminate; to colour.
illustrieren *v.t.* to illustrate.
Iltis *m.* (-tisses, -tisse) polecat.
im = in dem.
Imbiss *m.* (-bisses, -bisse) light meal.
Imbissraum *m.* teashop, snackbar.
Imker *m.* (-s, -) beekeeper.
immatrikulieren *v.t.* to matriculate.
immer *adv.* always, ever; *noch ~,* still; *~ besser,* better and better; *~ wieder,* again and again, over and over again; *~zu,* continually.
immerdar *adv.* for ever.
immerfort *adv.* for ever and ever, continually.
Immergrün *n.* (-s, 0) evergreen.
immerhin *adv.* for aught I care, so far as I am concerned; still, yet.
immer mehr *adv.* more and more.
immerwährend *a.* perpetual.
Immobilien *pl.* immovables *pl.* real, estate.
Immunität *f.* (-, -en) immunity.
Imperativ *m.* (-s, -e) imperative.
Imperfektum *n.* imperfect tense.
impfen *v.t.* to vaccinate, to inoculate.
immun *a.* immune (from).
Immunität *f.* (-, 0) immunity.
Impfschein *m.* certificate of vaccination.
Impfstoff *m.* vaccine, lymph.
Impfung *f.* (-, -en) vaccination.
implizieren *v.t.* to implicate; *(stillschweigend)* to imply.
Imponderabilien *pl.* imponderables *pl.*
imponieren *v.i.* to impress forcibly, to overawe; *~d a.* imposing.
Import *m.* (-s, -en) importation; imports.
imposant *a.* imposing.
Impotenz *f.* (-, 0) impotence.
imprägniert *a.* proofed.
imstande *adv.* able.
in *pr.* in, into; at; within.
Inangriffnahme *f.* taking in hand.
Inanspruchnahme *f.* (-, -n) strain.
Inbegriff *m.* essence, substance.
inbegriffen *a.* included, inclusive of.
Inbetriebstellung *f.* (-, -en) opening.
Inbrunst *f.* (-, 0) fervour.
inbrünstig *a.* ardent, fervent.
indem *c.* while, when; as, because.
indes, indessen *c.* however.

Indienststellung *f.* (-, -en) *(Kriegsschiff)* commissioning.
Indigo *m.* (-s, 0) indigo.
Indikativ *m.* (-s, -e) indicative.
indirekt *a.* indirect.
indiskret *a.* indiscreet, ill-advised.
Indiskretion *f.* (-, -en) indiscretion.
Individualität *f.* (-, -en) individuality.
individuell *a.* individual.
Individuum *n.* (-s, -duen) individual.
Indizienbeweis *m.* circumstantial evidence.
Indossant *m.* (-en, -en) endorser.
Indossat *m.* (-en, -en) endorsee.
indossieren *v.t.* to endorse.
Induktion *f.* (-, -en) induction; **induzieren** *v.t.* *(elek.)* to induce.
Industrie *f.* (-, -[e]n) industry.
industriell *a.* industrial.
ineinandergreifen *v.i.* *(mech.)* to mesh.
Ineinanderspiel *n.* (-[e]s, 0) interplay.
infam *a.* infamous, scandalous.
Infamie *f.* (-, 0) infamy, enormity.
Infanterie *f.* (-, 0) infantry.
Infanterist *m.* (-en, -en) foot-soldier.
Infektionskrankheit *f.* (-, -en) contagious disease.
Infinitiv *m.* (-s, -e) infinitive.
infizieren *v.t.* to infect.
Inflation *f.* inflation.
infolge *pr.* owing to, in consequence of; *~dessen adv.* consequently.
informieren *v.t.* to inform.
Infusorien *pl.* infusoria.
Ingenieur *m.* (-s, -e) engineer.
Ingrimm *m.* (-[e]s, 0) anger, spite, wrath.
ingrimmig *a.* angry, wrathful.
Ingwer *m.* (-s, 0) ginger.
Inhaber *m.* (-s, -) possessor, holder; occupant; *(eines Wechsels)* payee, bearer.
Inhaberaktie *f.* bearer share.
inhaftieren *v.t.* to imprison.
inhalieren *v.t.* to inhale.
Inhalt *m.* (-[e]s, -e) contents, tenor, substance; volume; *des ~s,* to the effect.
inhaltlich *a.& adv.* material; in substance.
Inhaltsangabe *f.* summary, synopsis.
inhalt[s]leer, inhalt[s]los *a.* empty, meaningless.
Inhaltsverzeichnis *n.* table of contents, index.
Initiative *f.* (-, 0) initiative; *die ~ ergreifen,* to take the initiative.
Injurie *f.* (-, -n) insult.
Inkasso *n.* (-, -s) cashing, collection.
Inkonsequenz *f.* (-s, -en) inconsistency.
Inkrafttreten *n.* (-s, 0) coming into force.
Inkunabel *f.* (-, -n) incunabula.
Inland *n.* (-[e]s, 0) inland, interior; *im In~ und Ausland,* at home and abroad.
Inländer *m.* (-s, -) native.
inländisch *a.* native, inland; indigenous.
Inlaut *m.* (-s, -e) medial sound.
Inlett *n.* (-s, -e) tick, ticking.

inliegend a. enclosed.

inmitten pr. in the midst of.

inne: ~haben v.t.ir. to possess; ~halten v.i.st. to stop, to pause; ~werden v.t.ir. to become aware of.

innen adv. within, inside, indoors; nach ~, inwards, inwardly; von ~, (from) within, on the inside; von ~ und aussen kennen, to know the ins and outs of. ↵

Innen: ~dekoration f. interior decoration; ~leben n. inner life; ~politik f. domestic politics; ~raum m. interior.

Innenseite f. inside, inner side.

inner a. interior, internal, inner.

Innere n. (-[e]n, 0) inside, interior; Home Office (England), Ministry of the Interior.

innerhalb pr. within.

innerlich a. inward; internal, intrinsic.

innerst a. inmost, innermost.

Innerzonen...intrazonal.

innig a. hearty, heartfelt; intimate.

Innigkeit f. (-, 0) cordiality, fervour.

Innung f. (-, -en) corporation, guild.

inoffiziell a. unofficial.

ins = in das.

Insasse m. (-n, -n) inmate (Haus); (Schiff, Abteil) occupant.

insbesondere adv. especially.

Inschrift f. (-, -en) inscription.

Insekt n. (-[e]s, -en) insect.

Insektenlehre f. entomology.

Insektenpulver n. insecticide, insect powder.

Insel f. (-, -n) island, isle.

Inserat n. (-[e]s, -e) advertisement.

inserieren v.t. & i. to advertise.

insgeheim adv. privately, secretly.

insgemein adv. generally, commonly.

insgesamt adv. altogether, collectively.

Insignien pl. insignia pl., badge of office.

insofern adv. so far as.

insolvent a. insolvent.

Insolvenz f. (-, -en) insolvency.

insoweit adv. (in) so far.

inspizieren v.t. to inspect, to superintend.

inspirieren v.t. to inspire.

Installateur m. (-s, -e) plumber; electric or gas fitter.

installieren v.t. to install.

Instandhaltung f. (-, -en) maintenance.

inständig a. instant, urgent.

instandsetzen v.t. to enable; to repair.

Instanz f. (-, -en) instance; höhere ~, superior court; höchste ~, highest court of appeal; in der letzten ~, in the last resort; im ~enweg, through (official) channels.

Instinkt m. (-[e]s, -e) instinct.

instinktmässig a. & adv. instinctive(ly).

Institut n. (-[e]s, -e) institution.

instruieren v.t. to instruct.

Instrument n. (-[e]s, -e) instrument.

instrumentieren v.t. (mus.) to score.

inszenieren v.t. to stage, to produce (a play).

Integralrechnung f. integral calculus.

Intelligenz f. (-, 0) intelligence.

Intendant m. (-en, -en) superintendent; (theat.) stage manager.

Intendantur, Intendanz f. (-, -en) superintendent's office; (mil.) commissariat.

interessant a. interesting.

Interesse n. (-s, -n) interest.

Interessent m. (-en, -en) prospective customer.

interessieren v.t. to interest, to concern; (sich) ~ v.refl. to take an interest (in).

interessiert a. interested; grasping.

interimistisch a. temporary.

Intermezzo n. (-[e]s, -s) interlude.

Internat n. (-[e]s, -e) boarding school.

internieren v.t. to intern.

Internierter m. (-ten, -ten) internee.

Internierung f. (-, -en) internment.

interpretieren v.t. to interpret.

Interpunktion f. (-, -en) punctuation.

intervenieren v.i. to intervene.

intim, a. intimate.

intravenös a. intravenous.

intrigieren v.i. to plot, to intrigue.

Invalide m. (-n, -n) invalid, disabled person.

Invalidenversicherung f. disablement insurance.

Inventar n. (-s, -e) inventory; das ~ aufnehmen, to take stock, to inventory.

inventarisieren v.t. to inventory.

Inventur f. (-, -en) stock-taking.

investieren v.t. to invest.

Investierung f. (-, -en) investment.

inwendig a. interior, inner; ~ adv. inside, within.

inwiefern, inwieweit adv. (in) how far.

Inzucht f. (-, 0) in-breeding.

inzwischen adv. meanwhile.

ionisiert a. (elek.) ionized.

irden a. earthen.

irdisch a. earthy; temporal; worldly.

irgend adv. at all, possibly; any(where); wenn ~ möglich, if at all possible; ~ etwas, anything, something; ~ jemand, anybody, somebody.

irgendein pn. any(one), anybody.

irgendwie adv. anyhow.

irgendwo adv. anywhere, somewhere.

irgendwoher adv. from some place (or other).

Ironie f. (-, 0) irony.

ironisch a. & adv. ironical(ly).

irre a. & adv. astray, wrong; insane; ~ werden (an), to lose confidence (in); ~gehen, to lose one's way; ~führen, to lead astray; sich nicht ~machen lassen, not to be easily put out or perplexed.

Irre[r] m. (-n, -n) madman, lunatic.

irren *v.i.* to err; to go astray; (sich) ~ *v.refl.* to be mistaken.
Irren: ~anstalt *f.*, ~haus *n.* lunatic asylum, mental institution; ~arzt *m.* alienist.
Irr: ~fahrt *f.* wandering, vagary; ~garten *m.* maze.
irrgläubig *a.* heterodox, heretical.
irrig *a.* erroneous, wrong, false.
Irr: ~lehre *f.* heterodoxy; false doctrine; ~lehrer *m.* heretic; ~licht *n.* will-o'-the-wisp.
Irrsinn *m.* madness, insanity.
irrsinnig *a.* insane, deranged.
Irrtum *m.* (-[e]s, -tümer) error, mistake.
irrtümlich *a.* mistaken, erroneous.
Irrung *f.* (-, -en) error; misunderstanding, mistake.
Irrwahn *m.* delusion.
Ischias *f.* (-, 0) sciatica.
isländisch *a.* Icelandic.
Isolator *m.* (-s, -en) insulator.
Isolierband *n.* (*elek.*) insulating tape.
isolieren *v.t.* to isolate; to insulate (electric wire).
Istbestand *m.* (-[e]s, -bestände) actual stock.
Iststärke *f.* (-, -n) actual strength.
I-tüpfelchen *n.* dot over the i.

J

ja *adv.* yes; aye; even; *er ist ~ mein Bruder,* he is my brother, you know.
Jacht *f.* (-, -en) yacht.
Jacke *f.* (-, -n) jacket; jerkin.
Jackett *n.* (-s, -e) jacket.
Jagd *f.* (-, -en) chase; hunting; shooting; shoot; *auf die ~ gehen,* to go hunting, shooting.
Jagd: ~flinte *f.* shotgun; ~flugzeug *n.* fighter; ~gesetz *n.* game law; ~hütte *f.* shooting box; ~saison *f.* open season; ~schein *m.* hunting or shooting licence.
jagen *v.t.* to chase, to hunt; *ins Bockshorn ~,* to bully, to intimidate; ~ *v.i.* (s) to rush.
Jäger *m.* (-s, -) hunter; sportsman.
Jägerlatein *n.* tall stories *pl.*
jäh *a.* steep, precipitous; rash, sudden.
jählings *adv.* suddenly, abruptly.
Jahr *n.* (-[e]s, -e) year; *übers ~,* a year hence; *von ~ zu ~,* one year after another; ~ *ein, ~ aus,* from year's end to year's end.
Jahrbuch *n.* year-book.
jahrelang *a. & adv.* for years.
jähren (sich) *v.refl.* to be a year ago.
Jahres: ~bericht *a.* annual report; ~frist *f.* a year's time; ~tag *m.* anniversary; ~urlaub *m.* (*mil.*) annual leave;

~wende *f.*, ~wechsel *m.* New Year; ~zahl *f.* (date of the) year; ~zeit *f.* season.
Jahrgang *m.* annual set; ~ 1902, persons born in 1902 (*esp. mil.*); (*Wein*) vintage.
Jahrhundert *n.* (-s, -e) century.
Jahrhundertfeier *f.* centenary.
jährlich *a.* yearly, annual; ~ *adv.* annually.
Jahrmarkt *m.* fair.
Jahrtausend *n.* (-s, -e) millennium.
Jahrzehnt *n.* (-[e]s, -e) decade.
Jähzorn *m.* sudden passion.
jähzornig *a.* irritable, passionate.
Jakob *m.* Jacob, James.
Jakobiner *m.* (-s, -) Jacobin.
Jalousie *f.* (-, -n) Venetian blind.
Jammer *m.* (-s, 0) lamentation; misery.
jämmerlich *a.* miserable, wretched.
jammern *v.i.* to lament, to wail; ~ *v.t.pers. & imp.* to feel pity, to pity.
jammerschade *a.* a thousand pities.
Jammertal *n.* vale of tears.
jammervoll *a.* deplorable, piteous.
Jänner *m.* (-s, -), Januar *m.* (-s, -e) January.
Jasmin *m.* (-s, -e) jasmine, jessamine.
Jaspis *m.* (-pisses, -pisse) jasper.
jäten *v.i.* to weed.
Jauche *f.* (-, -n) liquid manure.
jauchzen *v.i.* to shout, to exult.
jawohl *adv.* yes (indeed).
Jawort *n.* consent.
Jazz *m.* (-es, -e) jazz; ~bande *f.* jazzband.
je *adv.* ever; *von ~her,* from the remotest times; ~ *nachdem,* according as; ~ *nach,* in proportion to; ~ *zwei,* two at a time; every two; ~ *zwei Mark,* two shillings each; ~ *mehr desto besser,* the more the better.
jedenfalls *adv.* at all events, at any rate.
jeder, jede, jedes *pn.* every, every one, each.
jedermann *pn.* (-[e]s) every one, everybody.
jederzeit *adv.* always, at any time.
jedesmal *adv.* every or each time; ~ *wenn,* whenever.
jedesmalig *a.* actual, existing; respective.
jedoch *c.* yet, however, nevertheless.
jedweder *pn.* each, every one.
jeglicher, jegliche, jegliches *pn.* every, each.
jemals *adv.* ever, at any time.
jemand *pn.* (-es) somebody, anyone.
jener, jene, jenes *pn.* that, that one, the former; yon, yonder.
jenseit(s) *pr.* beyond, over, on the other side (of).
jenseitig *a.* being on the other side, opposite.
Jenseits *n.* (-, 0) the other world.
Jesuit *m.* (-en, -en) Jesuit.

jesuitisch *a.* Jesuitical.
jetzig *a.* present, now existing; current.
jetzt *adv.* now, at present; *für ~,* for the present; *von ~ an,* henceforth, from this time forward.
Joch *n.* (-[e]s, -e) yoke; *(Brücken~)* arch; mountain-ridge.
Jochbein *n.* cheek-bone.
Jod *n.* (-[e]s, 0) iodine.
jodeln *v.t. & i.* to yodel.
Jodler *m.* (-s, -) yodeller; yodelling song.
Johannis: ~beere *f.* red-currant; ~würmchen *n.* glow-worm.
johlen *v.i.* to howl.
Jolle *f.* (-, -n) jolly-boat, yawl.
Jongleur *m.* (-s, -e) juggler, conjurer.
jonglieren *v.i.* to juggle.
Joppe *f.* (-, -n) (shooting) jacket.
Journal *(Schur...)* *n.* (-es, -e) journal, magazine, periodical; *(com.)* day-book.
Journalist *m.* (-en, -en) journalist.
Jubel *m.* (-s, 0) jubilation.
Jubelfeier *f.* jubilee.
jubeln *v.i.* to jubilate, to exult.
Jubilar *m.* (-s, -e) aged person or official of long service celebrating his jubilee.
Jubiläum *n.* (-s, Jubiläen) jubilee.
jubilieren *v.i.* to jubilate.
Juchtenleder *n.* Russian leather.
jucken *v.i.* to itch.
Jude *m.* (-n, -n) Jew; *der Ewige ~,* the Wandering Jew.
jüdeln *v.i.* to speak like a Jew.
Judenhetze *f.* Jew-baiting.
Judenschaft *f.* (-, 0) Jews *pl.* Jewry.
Judentum *n.* (-s, 0) Judaism.
Judenviertel *n.* Jewish quarter.
Jüdin *f.* (-, -nen) Jewess.
jüdisch *a.* Jewish.
Jugend *f.* (-, 0) youth; young people.
Jugend: ~gericht *n.* juvenile court; ~herberge *f.* youth hostel; ~richter *m.* juvenile court judge.
jugendlich *a.* youthful, young, juvenile.
Jugendlicher *m.* juvenile.
Juli *m.* (-s, -[s]) July.
jung *a.* young; new, recent; *(fig.)* green.
Jungbrunnen *m.* fountain of youth.
Junge *m.* (-n, -n) boy, lad.
Junge *n.* (-n, -n) young one (of animals), cub.
jungenhaft *a.* boyish.
Jungenstreich *m.* boyish prank.
Jünger *m.* (-s, -) disciple.
Jungfer *f.* (-, -n) maid, spinster.
Jungfern: virgin...; ~kranz *m.* bridal wreath; ~rede *f.* maiden speech.
Jungfernschaft *f.* (-, 0) virginity.
Jungfrau *f.* (-, -en) maid, virgin.
jungfräulich *a.* virgin, maidenly, maiden.
Junggesell[e] *m.* bachelor.
Jüngling *m.* (-[e]s, -e) young man, youth.
Jünglingsalter *n.* adolescence.

jüngst *adv.* lately, newly, of late.
jüngst *a.* youngest, last; *der Jüngste Tag,* Doomsday.
Juni *m.* (-[s], -[s]) June.
Junker *m.* (-s, -) squire.
Junker: ~ei *f.,* ~tum *n.* squirearchy.
Jura *pl.* the law; *~ studieren,* to read for the bar, to study the law.
Jurist *m.* (-en, -en) jurist, legal practitioner, barrister, lawyer; law-student.
juristisch *a.* legal, juridical; ~e Person *f.* body corporate.
just *adv.* just, exactly; just now, but just.
Justiz *f.* (-, 0) justice.
Justiz: ~beamte[r] *m.* officer of justice; ~gebäude *n.* law-courts *pl.;* ~minister *m.* Minister of Justice; *(in England)* Lord Chancellor; ~mord *m.* judicial murder.
Jute *f.* (-, 0) jute.
Juwel *n.* (-[e]s, -en) jewel, gem.
Juwelier *m.* (-s, -e) jeweller.
Jux *m.* (-es, -e) joke, lark, hoax.

K

Kabale *f.* (-, -n) cabal, intrigue.
Kabarett *n.* (-[e]s, -e) cabaret, night-club.
Kabel *n.* (-s, -), Kabeltau *n.* cable.
kabeln *v.t.* to cable.
Kabeldepesche *f.* cable(gram).
Kabeljau *m.* (-s, -e) cod(fish).
Kabinett *n.* (-[e]s, -e) cabinet; closet.
Kabine *f.* (-, -n) cabin.
Kachel *f.* (-, -n) Dutch tile.
Kachelofen *m.* porcelain stove.
Kader *n.* (-s, -) cadre, skeleton staff.
Kadett *m.* (-en, -en) cadet.
Kadetten: ~anstalt *f.,* ~haus *n.* military college; ~schiff *n.* training ship.
Kadaver *m.* (-s, -) carcass; *(med.)* corpse.
Käfer *m.* (-s, -) beetle; chafer.
Kaffee *m.* (-s, -s) coffee.
Kaffee: ~bohne *f.* coffee-bean; ~geschirr *n.* coffee-things; ~haus *n.* café; ~kanne *f.* coffee-pot; ~mühle *f.* coffee-mill; ~satz *m.* coffee-grounds.
Kaffer *m.* (-s u. -n, -n) Kaffer, Caffir; *(fam.)* boor.
Käfig *m.* (-s, -e) (bird-)cage.
kahl *a.* bald; *(fig.)* bare, naked.
Kahlkopf *m.* bald-head.
kahlköpfig *a.* bald headed.
Kahn *m.* (-[e]s, Kähne) boat, skiff, lighter, punt.
Kai *m.* (-s, -s) quay.
Kaiser *m.* (-s, -) emperor.
Kaiserin *f.* (-, -nen) empress.
kaiserlich *a.* imperial.
Kaiser: ~reich *n.* empire; ~schnitt *m.* Cæsarean operation.

Kaisertum n. (-s, 0) imperial dignity.
Kajüte f. (-, -n) cabin; erste ~, first class saloon; ~nbett n. berth.
Kakadu m. (-[e]s, -s) cockatoo.
Kakao m. (-[s], -s) cocoa.
Kaktus m. (-, -se) cactus.
Kalauer m. (-s, -) (fam.) joke, pun.
Kalb n. (-[e]s, Kälber) calf.
kalben v.i. to calve.
Kalb: ~fell n. calf's skin; (fig.) drum; ~fleisch n. veal; ~leder n. calf-leather, calf.
Kalbs: ~braten m. roast-veal; ~haxe f. knuckle of veal; ~keule f. leg of veal.
Kaldaunen pl. tripe; guts pl.
Kalender m. (-s, -) calendar, almanac.
Kalesche f. (-, -n) light carriage.
kalfatern v.t. (nav.) to caulk.
Kali n. (-s, 0) potash.
Kaliber n. (-s, -) calibre; sort.
Kalif m. (-en, -en) caliph.
Kalium n. (-s, 0) potassium.
Kalk m. (-[e]s, -e) lime; (gebrannter) quicklime; (gelöschter) slaked lime; (schwefelsaurer) carbonate of lime.
kalkhaltig a. calcareous.
Kalk: ~ofen m. lime-kiln; ~stein m. limestone.
Kalkstickstoff m. calcium cyanamide.
kalkulieren v.i. & t. to calculate, to compute.
Kalorie f. (-, -n) calorie.
kalt a. cold; frigid, indifferent; ~es Fieber, ague; ~er Brand, mortification; das lässt mich ~, that leaves me unmoved; ~ stellen, to shelve.
kaltblütig a. cool, cool-headed; ~ adv. in cold blood.
Kaltblütigkeit f. (-, 0) sang-froid.
Kälte f. (-, 0) cold; coldness, frigidity.
Kaltschale f. (-, -n) a cold soup.
kaltsinnig a. indifferent, cold.
Kaltwasserheilanstalt f. hydropathic establishment.
Kaltwasserkur f. cold-water cure.
Kamee f. (-, -n) cameo.
Kamel n. (-[e]s, -e) camel; (fam.) blockhead.
Kamelie f. (-, -n) camellia.
Kamera f. (-, -s) (phot.) camera.
Kamerad m. (-en, -en) comrade, mate.
Kameradschaft f. (-, -en) fellowship.
kameradschaftlich a. like comrades.
Kamille f. (-, -n) camomile.
Kamin m. (-[es], -e) chimney; fire-place.
Kamin: ~feger, ~kehrer m. chimneysweep(er); ~sims m. mantelpiece; ~vorleger m. hearthrug; ~vorsetzer m. fender.
Kamm m. (-[e]s, Kämme) comb; (Hahn) crest; (eines Berges) ridge.
kämmen v.t. to comb; (Wolle) to card.

Kammer f. (-, -n) room, chamber; (Parlament) chamber.
Kammerdiener m. valet.
Kammer: ~herr m. gentleman in waiting; ~jäger m. destroyer of vermin; ~konzert n. chamber concert; ~musik f. chamber music; ~zofe f. lady's maid.
Kammgarn n. worsted.
Kämpe m. (-n, -n) champion.
Kampf m. (-[e]s, Kämpfe) combat, fight, conflict; struggle; ~ ums Dasein, struggle for existence.
Kampfer m. (-s, 0) camphor.
kämpfen v.t. to combat, to fight; to struggle.
Kämpfer m. (-s, -) combatant; champion.
Kampf: ~fluzeug n. bomber (plane); ~platz m. arena, lists; ~preis m. prize; ~richter m. umpire, referee; ~stoff m. (mil.) chemical warfare agent.
kampfunfähig a. disabled.
kampieren v.i. to encamp, to camp out.
Kanal m. (-s, Kanäle) canal; channel; sewer, drain; the Channel.
Kanalisation f. (-, -en) (der Stadt) sewerage; (Fluss) canalization.
Kanapee n. (-s, -s) sofa.
Kanarienvogel m. canary(-bird).
Kandare f. (-, -n) curb-bit.
Kandelaber m. (-s, -) chandelier.
Kandidat m. (-en, -en) candidate.
kandidieren v.i. to be a candidate for; in einem Wahlkreis ~, to contest a seat.
Känguruh n. (-s, -s) kangaroo.
Kaninchen n. (-s, -) rabbit, cony.
Kanne f. (-, -n) can; quart; tankard; (Kaffee~) pot.
Kannegiesser m. pot-house politician.
kannelieren v.t. to channel, to flute.
Kannibale m. (-n, -n) cannibal.
Kanonade f. (-, -n) bombardment.
Kanone f. (-, -n) cannon, gun.
Kanonen: ~boot n. gun-boat; ~futter n. cannon fodder; ~kugel f. cannonball; ~rohr n. barrel of a cannon; ~stiefel m.pl. jack-boots pl.
Kanonier m. (-s, -e) gunner.
kanonieren v.t. to cannonade.
kanonisch a. canonical.
Kantate f. (-, -n) cantata.
Kante f. (-, -n) corner, edge; brim; list, border.
kantig a. angular, edged.
Kantine f. (-, -n) canteen.
Kanton m. (-s, -e) canton, district.
kantonieren v.t. to canton, to billet.
Kantor m. (-s, -en) precentor.
Kanu n. (-s, -s) canoe.
Kanüle f. (-, -n) tubule.
Kanzel f. (-, -n) pulpit.
Kanzlei f. (-, -en) chancery, secretariat.
Kanzlei: ~beamter m. clerk; ~diener m. office attendant; ~papier n. foolscap paper.

Kanzler m. (-s, -) chancellor.
Kap n. (-s, -s) cape, promontory.
Kapaun m. (-[e]s, -e) capon.
Kapelle f. (-, -n) chapel; (Musik~) band.
Kapellmeister m. conductor; bandmaster.
Kaper m. (-s, -) privateer.
Kaper f. (-, -n) (Beere) caper.
Kaperbrief m. letter of marque and reprisal.
Kaperei f. (-, -en) privateering.
kapern v.t. to capture, to seize.
Kaperschiff n. privateer.
Kapital n. (-es, Kapitalien) capital; principal.
Kapital: ~abgabe f. capital levy; ~anlage f. investment; ~verbrechen n. capital crime.
Kapitäl n. (-[e]s, -e u. -er), Kapitell n. (-[e]s, -e), (arch.) capital.
Kapitalist m. (-en, -en) capitalist.
Kapitän m. (-s, -e) captain.
Kapitel n. (-s, -) chapter.
kapitulieren v.i. to capitulate.
Kaplan m. (-es, Kapläne) chaplain.
Kappe f. (-, -n) cap, hood.
Kapriole f. (-, -n) caper, leap.
Kapsel f. (-, -n) capsule, case; box.
kaputt a. broken; out of order; busted.
Kapuze f. (-, -n) cowl, hood.
Kapuzinade f. (-, -n) Capuchin's sermon.
Kapuziner m. (-s, -) Capuchin (friar).
Karabiner m. (-s, -) carbine.
Karaffe f. (-, -n) carafe, decanter.
Karat n. (-[e]s, -e) carat.
karätig a. (in Zus.) 22 ~es Gold, 22 carat gold.
Karawane f. (-, -n) caravan.
Karawanserai f. (-, -en) caravansary.
Karbolsäure f. carbolic acid.
Karbunkel m. (-s, -) carbuncle.
Kardinal m. (-s, -näle) cardinal.
Karfreitag m. Good Friday.
Karfunkel m. (-s, -) carbuncle.
karg a. stingy, parsimonious; sterile.
kargen v.i. to be niggardly, to stint.
kärglich a. sparing, penurious.
kariert a. chequered; check.
Karikatur f. (-, -en) cartoon, caricature; ~streifen m. comic strip; (politischer) Karikaturist m. cartoonist.
karikieren v.t. to caricature.
Karmeliter m. (-s, -) Carmelite.
Karmesin n. (-[e]s, 0) crimson.
Karneval m. (-s, -s u. -e) carnival.
Karnickel n. (-s, -) (vulg.) rabbit, bunny.
Karo n. (-[s], -s) square; (in der Karte) diamonds pl.
Karosserie f. (mot.) body.
Karotte f. (-, -n) carrot.
Karpfen m. (-s, -) carp.
Karpfenteich m. carp-pond; er ist Hecht im ~, he is the wolf in the sheepfold.
Karre f. (-, -n), Karren m. (-s, -) cart.

Karree n. (-s, -s) square.
karren v.t. to cart.
Kärrner m. (-s, -) carter, drayman.
Karriere f. (-, -n) gallop; career.
Karsamstag m. Holy Saturday.
Karst m. (-[e]s, -e) mattock, hoe.
Kartätsche f. (-, -n) canister-shot, grape-shot.
Kartause f. (-, -n) Carthusian monastery.
Kartäuser m. (-s, -) Carthusian friar.
Karte f. (-, -n) card; map; chart; ticket; (Speise~) bill of fare; ein Spiel ~n, a pack of cards; alles auf eine ~ setzen, to stake everything on one throw.
Kartei f. (-, -en) card index.
Kartell n. (-s, -e) cartel.
Kartellträger m. second.
Karten: ~haus n. house of cards; ~legerin, ~schlägerin f. fortune-teller; ~masstab m. map scale; ~netz n. grid; ~spiel n. game at cards; pack of cards.
Kartoffel f. potato; ~n in der Schale, Pell ~n, potatoes in jackets; ~käfer m. Colorado beetle; ~püree n. mashed potatoes; Brat ~n, fried potatoes; Salz ~n, boiled potatoes; geröstete Kartoffelstreifen (pommes frites), chipped potatoes, chips.
Karton m. (-s, -s) cardboard; cardboard-box.
kartonieren v.t. to bind in boards.
Kartothek f. (-, -en) card index; filing cabinet.
Karussell n. (-[e]s, -s u. -e) merry-go-round.
Karwoche f. (-, 0) Holy Week.
Karzer m. (-s, -) students' lock-up.
Kaschmir m. (-s, 0) cashmere.
Käse m. (-s, -) cheese.
Käsebrot n. bread and cheese.
Kasematte f. (-, -n) casemate.
Kaserne f. (-, -n) barracks pl; unter ~narrest, confined to barracks.
käsig a. cheesy.
Kasino n. (mil.) officers' mess.
Kasperletheater n. Punch and Judy show.
Kasse f. (-, -n) booking-office; cash, ready money; gut, schlecht bei ~ sein, to be flush of money, to be short of cash.
Kassen: ~arzt m. panel doctor; ~bestand m. cash in hand; ~patient m. panel patient.
Kassette f. (-, -n) casket; (phot.) plate holder.
Kassier[er] m. (-s, -) cashier.
kassieren v.t. to get in (money); to cashier; to annul; (Urteil) to quash.
Kastanie f. (-, -n) chestnut.
Kästchen n. (-s, -) casket, little box.
Kaste f. (-, -n) caste; close corporation.
kasteien v.t. to mortify (the flesh).
Kastell n. (-s, -e) fort.

Kastellan m. (-s, -e) steward.
Kasten m. (-s, Kästen) chest, case, box.
Kastengeist m. caste-feeling.
Kastrat m. (-en, -en) eunuch.
kastrieren v.t. to castrate; (Tier) to doctor.
Kasuistik f. (-, 0) casuistry.
Katakomben f.pl. catacombs.
Katalog m. (-[e]s, -e) catalogue.
Katalysator m. (-s, -en) (chem.) catalyst.
Katarrh m. (-s, -e) catarrh, cold.
Kataster n. (-s, -) land regis.
katastrophal a. catastrophic.
Katastrophe f. (-, -n) catastrophe.
Katechismus m. (-, Katechismen) catechism.
Kategorie f. (-, -[e]n) category.
kategorisch a. categorical.
Kater m. (-s, -) tomcat; = Katzenjammer.
Katheder n. (-s, -) lecturing-desk.
Kathedrale f. (-, -n) cathedral, minster.
Katheter m. (-s, -) (surg.) catheter.
Kathode f. (-, -n) (elek.) cathode; ~strahlen, cathode-rays.
Katholik m. (-en, -en) Roman-Catholic.
katholisch a. Roman-Catholic.
Kattun m. (-[e]s, -e) calico, print.
katzbalgen (sich) v.refl. to scuffle.
katzbuckeln v.i. to cringe.
Katze f. (-, -n) cat; die ~ im Sack kaufen, to buy a pig in a poke.
Katzen: ~jammer m. hangover; ~sprung m. nur einen ~sprung entfernt, just round the corner.
Kauderwelsch n. (-es u. -en, 0) gibberish.
kauen v.t. to chew.
kauern v.i. to cower, to squat.
Kauf m. (-[e]s, Käufe) purchase, bargain; in den ~, into the bargain.
Kaufbrief m. purchase deed.
kaufen v.t. to buy, to purchase.
Käufer m. (-s, -), **Käuferin** f. (-, -nen) purchaser, buyer.
Kauf: ~fahrteischiff n. merchantman, trading-vessel; ~haus n. stores; ~kraft f. purchasing power; ~leute pl. merchants; shopkeepers.
käuflich a. venal.
Kaufmann m. merchant; shopkeeper.
kaufmännisch a. mercantile, commercial.
Kaufvertrag m. contract for sale.
Kaulbarsch m. (-es, -e) river-perch, ruff.
Kaulquappe f. (-, -n) tadpole.
kaum, adv. scarcely, hardly.
kaustisch a. caustic, sarcastic.
Kautabak m. chewing-tobacco.
Kaution f. (-, -en) security, bail.
Kautschuk m. (-s, -e) India rubber.
Kauz m. (-es, Käuze) screech-owl; (fig.) odd fellow, queer chap.
Kavalier m. (-es, -e) cavalier, gentleman.
Kavallerie f. (-, -[e]n) cavalry.
Kavallerist m. (-en, -en) horseman.
Kaviar m. (-s, 0) caviar(e).

Kebse (-, -n) f. **Kebsweib** n. concubine.
keck a. bold, daring; saucy, pert.
Kegel m. (-s, -) cone; ~ pl. ninepins, skittles pl.; kegelschieben, to play at ninepins or skittles; Kind und ~, bag and baggage.
Kegelbahn f. skittle-alley.
kegelförmig a. conical, cone-shaped.
kegeln v.i. to bowl, to play at ninepins.
Kegelrad n. (mech.) bevel gear.
Kegelschnitt m. conic section.
Kehle f. (-, -n) throat, gorge; aus voller ~, at the top of one's voice.
Kehl: ~kopf m. larynx; ~kopfspiegel m. laryngoscope; ~leiste f. (arch.) channel; cornice.
Kehraus m. (-, 0) last dance; (fig.) end.
Kehre f. (-, -n) turn, bend.
kehren v.t. to sweep, to brush; to turn; (sich) ~ v.refl. (an etwas) to mind a thing; vor seiner eignen Tür ~, to mind one's own business; kehrt! (mil.) right about face!
Kehricht m. & n. (-s, 0) sweepings pl.
Kehrreim m. burden, refrain.
Kehrseite f. reverse, back; seamy side.
kehrtmachen (mil.) to wheel right about.
keifen v.i. to scold.
Keil m. (-[e]s, -e) wedge; (mech.) key.
Keilerei f. (-, -en) (vulg.) free fight, row.
keilförmig a. wedge-shaped; cuneiform.
Keil: ~kissen n. wedge-shaped mattress; ~riemen m. (mech.) vee-belt; ~schrift f. cuneiform characters.
Keim m. (-[e]s, -e) germ; bud, sprout; m ~ ersticken, to nip in the bud.
keimen v.i. to germinate, to bud.
keimfrei a. sterile, aseptic.
Keimzelle f. germ cell.
kein (keiner, keine, kein[e]s) a. no, no one, not any, none.
keinerlei a. of no sort.
keinesfalls adv. on no account.
keineswegs adv. by no means.
keinmal adv. not once, never.
Keks n. (-es, -e) biscuit.
Kelch m. (-[e]s, -e) cup; chalice; (bot.) calyx.
Kelle f. (-, -n) trowel.
Keller m. (-s, -) cellar.
Kellergeschoss n. basement.
Kellner m. (-s, -) waiter.
Kellnerin f. (-, -nen) waitress.
Kelter f. (-, -n) wine-press.
keltern v.t. to tread (grapes), to press.
keltisch a. celtic.
kennbar a. recognizable, distinct.
kennen v.i.ir. to know; to be acquainted with; ~lernen, to become acquainted with, to get introduced to.
Kenner m. (-s, -) connoisseur, expert.
Kennkarte f. identity card.
kenntlich a. recognizable.

Kenntlichmachung f. labelling.

Kenntnis f. -, (-nisse) knowledge; ~ von etwas nehmen, to take note or cognizance of a thing; in ~ setzen, to inform of; ohne ~ von, unaware of; zur Kenntnisnahme, for information.

kenntnisreich a. well-informed, learned.

Kennwort n. motto; password.

Kennzeichen n. mark, badge; characteristic, criterion.

kennzeichnen v.t. to mark; to characterize.

kentern v.t. to cant, to capsize.

Keramik f. ceramics pl.

Kerbe f. (-, -n) notch.

kerben v.t. to notch, to indent.

Kerker m. (-s, -) prison, jail, dungeon.

Kerl m. (-[e]s, -e) fellow; chap.

Kern m. (-[e]s, -e) kernel; stone; nucleus; (fig.) core.

Kern... (phys.) nuclear.

kerngesund a. thoroughly healthy.

kernig a. pithy, solid.

Kern: ~obst n. stone fruit; ~physik f. nuclear physics; ~teilung f. (phys.) nuclear fission; ~truppen pl. crack troops.

Kerosin-n. (-s, 0) kerosene.

Kerze f. (-, -n) candle; taper.

kerzeng[e]rade a. bolt-upright.

Kerzenstärke f. candle power.

Kessel m. (-s, -) kettle, cauldron; (Dampf) boiler; (mil.) pocket.

Kessel: ~flicker m. tinker; ~schmied m. boilermaker, coppersmith; ~stein m. scale, fur; ~wagen m. (rail.) fuel tanker, tank car.

Kette f. (-, -n) chain; necklace; (Berg~) range; (Weberei) warp; (avi.) flight; (mil., Panzer) track.

Kettenbrücke f. suspension-bridge.

Ketzer m. (-s, -) heretic.

Ketzerei f. (-, -en) heresy.

ketzerisch a. heretical.

keuchen v.i. to pant, to puff.

Keuchhusten m. whooping-cough.

Keule f. (-, -n) club; leg (of mutton, etc.).

keusch a. chaste, pure.

Keuschheit f. (- 0) chastity.

kichern v.t. to titter, to giggle.

Kiebitz m. (-[e]s, -e) lapwing, peewit.

Kiefer f. (-, -n) Scotch fir; ~ m. (-s, -) jawbone.

Kiel m. (-[e]s, -e) quill; (nav.) keel.

Kielwasser n. wake.

Kieme f. (-, -n) gill.

Kies m. (Kieses, Kiese) gravel.

Kiesel m. (-s, -) flint, pebble.

Kilo... (in Zus.) kilo...

Kilometerzähler m. (mot.) mileage indicator.

Kind n. (-[e]s, -er) child; kleines ~, infant, baby.

Kindbett n. child-bed; lying-in.

Kinderei f. (-, -en) tomfoolery.

Kinder: ~fräulein n. mother's help; ~fürsorge f. child welfare; ~garten m. kindergarten; ~gärtnerin f. assistant in a kindergarten; ~hort m. children's centre; ~krippe f. crèche; spinale ~lähmung f. infantile paralysis.

kinderleicht a. very easy.

Kinder: ~mädchen n. nursemaid; ~spiel n. child's play; ~sterblichkeit f. infant mortality; ~stube f. nursery; ~wagen m. perambulator, baby-carriage.

Kindes: ~alter n. infancy; ~statt f. an ~ annehmen, to adopt.

Kindheit f. (-, 0) childhood.

kindisch a. childish.

kindlich a. infantile; childlike.

Kinn n. (-[e]s, -e) chin.

Kinn: ~backen m. jaw(bone); ~haken m. uppercut; ~lade f. jaw.

Kino n. (-s, -s) cinema, pictures.

Kippe f. (-, 0) tilt.

kippen v.t. to tilt, to set atilt.

Kirche f. (-, -n) church; divine service.

Kirchen: ~buch n. parish-register; ~geschichte f. ecclesiastical history; ~lied n. hymn; ~raub m. sacrilege; ~recht n. canon-law; ~schiff n. nave; ~staat m. Papal States pl.; ~steuer f. church rate; ~stuhl m. pew; ~vater m. Father (of the church).

kirchlich a. ecclesiastical.

Kirch: ~turm m. steeple; ~turmspitze f. spire; ~weih f. wake, fair.

Kirmes f. (-, -messen) village-fair.

kirre a. tame; tractable.

kirren v.t. to tame; to allure; to decoy.

Kirsch: ~baum m. cherry-tree; ~blüte f. cherry-blossom; ~branntwein m. cherry-brandy.

Kirsche f. (-, -n) cherry; (saure) morello, egriot.

Kirschkern m. cherry-stone.

Kissen n. (-s, -) cushion, pillow.

Kiste f. (-, -n) box, chest, case.

Kitsch m. (-es, 0) trash.

Kitt m. (-[e]s, -e) putty; glue.

Kittel m. (-s, -) smock, frock.

kitten v.t. to cement.

Kitzel m. (-s, 0) tickling; pruriency.

kitzeln v.t. to tickle.

kitzlig a. ticklish; (fig.) difficult.

Kladde f. (-, -n) rough copy; scribbling-book; (com.) day book.

Kladderadatsch m. (-es, 0) crash.

klaffen v.i. to gape, to yawn.

kläffen v.i. to yelp.

Kläffer m. (-s, -) yelping dog; (fig.) brawler, wrangler.

Klafter f. (-, -n) fathom; (Holz) cord of wood.

klagbar a. actionable.

Klage *f.* (-, -n) complaint; lament; (*gerichtliche*) suit, action.

klagen *v.i.* to complain, to lament; (*law*) to take action, to go to law.

Kläger *m.* (-s, -), **Klägerin** *f.* (-, -nen) plaintiff, complainant.

Klageschrift *f.* writ, plaint.

kläglich *a.* lamentable, woeful.

klamm *a.* tight, narrow; numb, clammy.

Klammer *f.* (-, -n) cramp, clasp, peg; bracket, parenthesis; paper-clip, clamp.

klammern *v.t.* to fasten, to clasp; (sich) ~ *v.refl.* to cling (to).

Klang *m.* (-[e]s, **Klänge**) sound; ring.

Klangfarbe *f.* timbre.

klangvoll *a.* sonorous, rich.

Klappe *f.* (-, -n) flap; valve; (*mus.*) key, stop.

klappen *v.i.* to clap, to clatter; (*fig.*) to go well, to tally.

Klapper *f.* (-, -n) rattle.

klapp[e]rig *a.* rattling; shaky.

klappern *v.i.* to clatter, to rattle; (*Zähne*) to chatter.

Klapperschlange *f.* rattle-snake.

Klapp: ~**kamera** *f.* folding camera; ~**pult** *n.* folding-desk.

Klaps *m.* (**Klapses, Klapse** *u.* **Kläpse**) flap, smack.

Klapp: ~**sitz** *m.* tip-up seat; ~**stuhl** *m.* camp-stool; ~**tisch** *m.* folding table.

klar *a.* clear; (*Wasser*) limpid; evident.

klarblickend clear-sighted.

klären *v.t.* to clear; to clarify.

Klarheit *f.* (-, -en) clearness; evidence.

Klarinette *f.* (-, -n) clarinet.

Klar: ~**legung,** ~**stellung** *f.* clearing up.

klarstellen *v.t.* to clear up.

im Klartext in clear.

Klasse *f.* (-, -n) class, form; order, rank.

Klassenkampf *m.* class-war.

Klassenlehrer *m.* form-master.

klassifizieren *v.t.* to classify, to break down.

Klassifizierung *f.* (-, -en) breakdown.

Klassiker *m.* (-s, -) classic (author).

klassisch *a.* classical.

klatsch *i.* crack! smack!

Klatsch *m.* (-[e]s, -e) clash; gossip, tittle-tattle.

Klatschbase *f.* gossip, tale-bearer.

klatschen; Beifall ~, to applaud; ~ *v.i.* to clack; to gossip.

Klatscher *m.* (-s, -) clapper; gossip.

Klatscherei *f.* (-, -en) chit-chat, gossip.

klatschhaft *a.* talkative, gossiping.

klauben *v.t.* to pick, to gnaw; to carp at.

Klaue *f.* (-, -n) claw, talon, paw; clutch.

klauen *v.t.* to pilfer, to collar.

Klause *f.* (-, -n) cell, hermitage.

Klausel *f.* (-, -n) clause, proviso.

Klausner *m.* (-s, -) hermit, recluse.

Klausurarbeit *f.* class exercise; test paper.

Klaviatur *f.* (-, -en) keyboard.

Klavier *n.* (-[e]s, -e) piano.

Klavier: ~**auszug** *m.* pianoforte arrangement; ~**stimmer** *m.* piano-tuner.

kleben *v.t.* to paste, to glue, to stick; ~ *v.i.* to adhere, to stick.

kleb[e]rig *a.* sticky, viscous; glutinous.

Klebe: ~**stoff** *m.* gum, (*Am.*) mucilage; ~**streifen** *m.* Scotch tape.

Klecks *m.* (-ses, -se) blot, ink-spot.

klecksen *v.t.* to blot, to blotch; to daub.

Klee *m.* (-[e]s, 0) clover, trefoil.

Kleeblatt *n.* leaf of trefoil; (*fig.*) trio.

Kleid *n.* (-[e]s, -er) garment; gown, dress; coat; ~**er** *pl.* clothes *pl.*

kleiden *v.t.* to dress, to clothe; (*passen*) to fit, to become; (sich) ~ *v.refl.* to dress.

Kleider: ~**bügel** *m.* coathanger; ~**bürste** *f.* clothes-brush; ~**schrank** *m.* wardrobe; ~**ständer** *m.* clothes-stand.

kleidsam *a.* becoming.

Kleidung *f.* (-, -en) clothing, dress, clothes *pl.*

Kleidungsstück *n.* garment; ~**e** *pl.* wearing apparel.

Kleie *f.* (-, -n) bran.

klein *a.* little; small; petty, mean; ~*es Geld,* small change; *kurz und* ~, in shivers; (*Gas*) ~ *drehen,* to turn down.

Klein: ~**bahn** *f.* local railway, narrow-gauge railway; ~**bürger,** petty bourgeois; ~**geld** *n.* small change; ~**handel** *m.* retail trade; ~**kaliber...,** subcaliber...

Kleinigkeit *f.* (-, -en) small matter, trifle, detail.

Kleinkinderbewahranstalt, Kleinkinderschule *f.* infant-school, crèche.

kleinlaut *a.* dejected, disheartened.

kleinlich *a.* mean, petty, paltry, fussy.

kleinmütig *a.* pusillanimous.

Kleinod *n.* (-[e]s, -e *u.* -ien) jewel, treasure, trinkets *pl.*; **Kleinodien** *pl.* insignia of royalty, regalia.

Kleinstaat *m.* minor state.

Kleinstädter *m.* provincial.

kleinstädtisch *a.* provincial.

Kleister *m.* (-s, 0) paste.

kleistern *v.t.* to paste.

Klemme *f.* (-, -n) clamp; straits *pl.*, fix, difficulty.

klemmen *v.t.* to pinch; to squeeze; (sich) ~ *v.refl.* to jam one's finger.

Klempner *m.* (-s, -) plumber, tinner.

Klepper *m.* (-s, -) nag, hack.

klerikal *a.* clerical.

Kleriker *m.* (-s, -) clergyman, priest.

Klette *f.* (-, -n) bur.

klettern *v.i.* to climb, to clamber.

Kletterpflanze *f.* climber, creeper.

Klient *m.* (-en, -en) client.

Klima *n.* (-s, -ta *u.* -te) climate, clime.

klimatisch *a.* climatic.

klimmen *v.i.st.* (*s*) to climb.
klimpern *v.i.* to jingle; to strum.
Klinge *f.* (-, -n) blade; sword.
Klingel *f.* (-, -n) small bell, hand-bell.
Klingelbeutel *m.* collection-bag.
Klingelleitung *f.* bell-circuit.
klingeln *v.i.* to ring the bell, to tinkle.
Klingelschnur *f.* bell-rope.
klingen *v.i.st.* to ring, to clink, to sound.
Klinik *f.* (-, -en) nursing home.
klinisch *a.* clinical.
Klinke *f.* (-, -n) latch, door-handle.
Klinker *m.* (-s, -) clinker.
Klippe *f.* (-, -n) cliff, crag.
klirren *v.i.* to clink, to clatter, to crash.
Klischee *n.* (-s, -s) (stereotype) block.
Klistier, *n.* (-s, -e) enema; **~spritze** *f.* squirt, syringe.
Kloake *f.* (-, -n) sink, sewer.
klobig *a.* coarse, rude, blockish.
klopfen *v.t.* to knock, to beat, to rap, to tap.
Klopfer *m.* (-s, -) knocker, rapper.
Klöppel *m.* (-s, -) clapper; drum-stick; bobbin, lace-bone.
klöppeln *v.t.* to make bone-lace.
Klöppelspitze *f.* bone-lace.
Klöppler *m.* (-s, -), **Klöpplerin** *f.* (-, -nen) lace-maker.
Klops *m.* (-ses, -se) dumpling.
Klosett *n.* (-[e]s, -e *u.* -s) water-closet.
Kloss *m.* (-es, Klösse) clod; dumpling.
Kloster *n.* (-s, Klöster) cloister; monastery; convent, nunnery.
Klosterfrau *f.* nun.
klösterlich *a.* monastic.
Klosterschule *f.* convent-school.
Klotz *m.* (-es, Klötze) block, log, trunk.
klotzig *a.* log-like; rude; enormous.
Klub *m.* (-s, -s) club.
Kluft *f.* (-, Klüfte) chasm, ravine, gulf.
klug *a.* prudent; intelligent; clever, sharp; *aus etwas nicht ~ werden,* to be puzzled by a thing.
Klügelei *f.* (-, -en) sophistry, subtilizing.
klügeln *v.i.* to subtilize.
Klugheit *f.* (-, 0) prudence, shrewdness.
Klumpen *m.* (-s, -) lump, clod.
Klumpfuss *m.* club-foot.
Klüngel *m.* (-s, 0) coterie.
Klüver *m.* (-s, -) (*nav.*) jib.
knabbern *v.t. & i.* to nibble, to gnaw.
Knabe *m.* (-n, -n) boy, lad.
Knabenalter *n.* boyhood.
knabenhaft *a.* boyish.
Knack(s) *m.* (-[e]s, -e *u.* Knackses, -se) crack(ing).
knacken *v.t.* to crack; **~** *v.i.* to break.
Knall *m.* (-[e]s, -e *u.* Knälle) clap, crack; report, detonation; *~ und Fall,* on a sudden.
Knall: ~bonbon *n.* cracker; **~effekt** *m.* stage effect.

knallen *v.t.* to crack (a whip); **~** *v.i.* to detonate, to pop.
knallrot *a.* glaring red.
knapp *a.* close, tight, narrow; scarce, scanty; (*Stil*) concise; **~** *halten,* to keep (one) short.
Knappe *m.* (-n, -n) esquire; miner.
Knappheit *f.* (-, -en) shortage.
Knappschaft *f.* (-, -en) miners' union.
knarren *v.i.* to creak, to jar.
knattern *v.i.* to rattle, to clatter.
Knäuel *m.* (-s, -) clue, ball of thread; throng.
Knauf *m.* (-[e]s, Knäufe) head, knob.
Knauser *m.* (-s, -) niggard, curmudgeon.
Knauserei *f.* (-, -en) stinginess.
knauserig *a.* stingy, close.
knausern *v.i.* to be stingy.
Knebel *m.* (-s, -) gag.
Knebelbart *m.* moustache.
knebeln *v.t.* to tie, to bind; to gag.
Knecht *m.* (-[e]s, -e) man-servant, man.
knechten *v.t.* to enslave.
knechtisch *a.* slavish, servile, menial.
Knechtschaft *f.* (-, 0) servitude, slavery.
kneifen *v.t.st.* to pinch, to nip.
Kneifer *m.* (-s, -) folders, glasses *pl.*
Kneifzange *f.* pincers *pl.*
Kneipe *f.* (-, -n) tavern, public house.
Kneiperei *f.* (-, -en) drinking-bout.
kneten *v.t.* to knead.
Knick *m.* (-[e]s, -e) crack, break.
knicken *v.t.* to crack, to break; (*fig.*) ge-*knickt,* broken-down.
Knickerei *f.* (-, -en) niggardliness.
knickerig *a.* niggardly.
knickern *v.i.* to be stingy.
Knicks *m.* (Knickses, Knickse) curtsy.
knicksen *v.i.* to drop a curtsy.
Knie *n.* (-[e]s, -[e]) knee.
Kniebeugung *f.* genuflection.
knie[e]n *v.i.* to kneel.
kniefällig *a.* upon one's knees.
Kniehose *f.* breeches, knickerbockers, plus-fours *pl.;* **~scheibe** *f.* knee-cap.
Kniff *m.* (-[e]s, -e) pinch; trick, dodge.
knifflich *a.* (*fam.*) queer, intricate.
knipsen *v.i.* to snap one's fingers; (*Fahrkarte*) to punch; (*phot.*) to snap.
Knirps *m.* (-es, -e) urchin.
knirschen *v.t.* to gnash (one's teeth); **~** *v.i.* to grate.
knistern *v.i.* to crackle.
knittern *v.i.* to crease; *nicht knitternd,* crease-resisting.
Knoblauch *m.* (-[e]s, 0) *m.* garlic.
Knöchel *m.* (-s, -) knuckle; joint; ankle; dice *pl.*
Knochen *m.* (-s, -) bone.
Knochen: ~bruch *m.* fracture (of a bone); **~frass** *m.* caries; **~gerüst** *n.* skeleton; **~mehl** *n.* bone-dust.
knochig *a.* bony.

Knödel *m.* (-s, -) dumpling.
Knolle *f.* (-, -n) tuber; bulb.
Knollen *m.* (-s, -) clod, lump.
knollig *a.* bulbous; knobby.
Knopf *m.* (-es, Knöpfe) button; pommel; (*Hemd*) stud, head.
Knopfloch *n.* button-hole.
knöpfen *v.t.* to button.
Knorpel *m.* (-s, -) cartilage, gristle.
Knorren *m.* (-s, -) knot, gnarl.
Knospe *f.* (-, -n) bud, eye.
knospen *v.i.* to bud.
knoten *v.t.* to knot.
Knoten *m.* (-s, -) knot; node.
Knotenpunkt *m.* (*rail.*) junction.
knüllen *v.t.* to rumple, to crumple.
knüpfen *v.t.* to tie; to knit, to unite, to connect.
Knüppel *m.* (-s, -) cudgel, stick.
knurren *v.i.* to growl, to snarl; to grumble.
knusp[e]rig *a.* (*Gebäck*) crisp, short.
knuspern *v.t.* to nibble, to munch.
Knute *f.* (-, -n) knout.
Knüttel *m.* (-s, -) cudgel.
Knüttelvers *m.* doggerel (line).
Koalition *f.* (-, -en) coalition.
Kobalt *m.* (-s, -e) cobalt.
Kobold *m.* (-[e]s, -e) hobgoblin; gnome.
Koch *m.* (-[e]s, Köche) (male) cook.
Kochbuch *n.* cookery-book, (*Am.*) cookbook.
kochen *v.t.* to boil, to cook; ~ *v.i.* to boil; to be cooking.
Kocher *m.* (-s, -) cooker.
Köcher *m.* (-s, -) quiver.
Köchin *f.* (-, -nen) (female) cook.
Koch: ~**löffel** *m.* ladle; ~**topf** *m.* saucepan, cooking-pot.
Köder *m.* (-s, -) bait, lure.
ködern *v.t.* to bait, to allure, to decoy.
Kodex *m.* (-, Kodizes) code.
Koffer *m.* (-s, -) trunk, box.
Kognak *m.* (-s, -s) brandy, cognac.
Kohl *m.* (-[e]s, 0) cabbage; kale; (*fam.*) twaddle, humbug.
Kohle *f.* (-, -n) charcoal; coal; carbon.
Kohle: ~**hydrat** *n.* carbohydrate; ~**hydrierung** *f.* hydrogenation; ~**papier** *n.* carbon paper.
kohlen *v.t.* to char, to carbonize; (*nav.*) to coal.
Kohlen: ~**bergwerk** *n.* coal mine, colliery; ~**feld**, ~**lager** *n.* coalfield; ~**grube** *f.* coalpit, colliery; ~**säure** *f.* carbonic acid; ~**schiff** *n.* collier; ~**schuppen** *m.* coal shed; ~**station** *f.* coaling station; ~**stoff** *m.* carbon; ~**stoffhaltig** *a.* carbonaceous; ~**wasserstoff** *m.* hydrocarbon.
Köhler *m.* (-s, -) charcoal-burner.
Kohlrabi *m.* (-[s], -[s]) kohl rabi.
Kohlrübe *f.* turnip-rooted cabbage.

Koje *f.* (-, -n) berth, cabin.
Kokarde *f.* (-, -n) cockade.
kokett *a.* coquettish.
Kokette *f.* (-, -n) coquette, flirt.
Koketterie *f.* (-, -n) coquetry, flirtation.
kokettieren *v.i.* to flirt.
Kokos: ~**nuss** *f.* cocoa-nut, coker-nut; ~**palme** *f.* cocoa-nut tree.
Koks *m.* (-es, 0) coke.
Kolben *m.* (-s, -) club; butt end; piston; alembic, retort.
Kolbenstange *f.* piston-rod.
Kolik *f.* (-, 0) colic, gripes *pl.*
Kolleg *n.* (-s, -ien) course of lectures.
Kollege *m.* (-s, -n) colleague.
Kollegium *n.* (-s, Kollegien) board, committee; staff (of teachers).
Kollekte *f.* (-, -n) (church-)collection; (*Gebet*) collect.
kollektiv *a.* collective; ~**e** Sicherheit *f.* collective security.
Koller *m.* (-s, 0) rage, madness.
kollern *v.t. & i.* to roll.
Kölnisch-Wasser, Kölnisches Wasser *n.* eau de Cologne.
Kolonialwaren *pl.* groceries; ~**händler** *m.* grocer.
Kolonie *f.* (-, -[e]n) colony.
Kolonist *m.* (-en, -en) colonist, settler.
kolonisieren *v.t.* to colonize.
Kolonne *f.* (-, -n) column.
Kolophonium *n.* (-s, 0) colophony.
Koloratur *f.* (-, -en) coloratura.
Kolorit *n.* (-s, 0) colouring.
Koloss *m.* (Kolosses, Kolosse) colossus.
kolossal *a.* colossal, huge.
kolportieren *v.t.* to hawk; to spread.
kombinieren *v.t.* to combine.
Komet *m.* (-en, -en) comet.
Komfort *m.* (-s, 0) comfort; *mit allem* ~, with all modern conveniences.
Komiker *m.* (-s, -) comic actor.
komisch *a.* comical; strange, odd, funny.
Komitee *n.* (-s, -s) committee.
Komma *n.* (-[s], -ta *u.* -s) comma.
Kommandant *m.* (-en, -en) commander.
kommandieren *v.t.* to command.
Kommanditgesellschaft *f.* limited company (with shares).
Kommando *n.* (-[s], -s) command; detachment (of soldiers); ~**brücke** *f.* (conning-)bridge.
Kommandogerät *n.* (*avi.*) predictor.
kommen *v.i.st.* (*s*) to come; to happen; to arrive at, to get to; *woher kommt das?* what is the cause of this? how is it that...?; ~ *lassen*, to send for, to write for; ~ *sehen*, to foresee; *abhanden* ~, to get lost, to be mislaid; *einem gleich* ~, to equal one; *zu kurz* ~, to be a loser; *teuer, hoch zu stehen* ~, to cost dear; *wenn es hoch kommt*, at most, in extreme cases; *auf etwas* ~, to think of;

ich konnte gestern nicht dazu ~, I could not find time for it yesterday; *nicht zu Worte* ~, to be unable to put in a word; *um etwas* ~, to lose a thing; *sich etwas zu Schulden* ~ *lassen*, to be guilty of a thing.

kommentieren *v.t.* & *i.* to comment (upon).

Kommers *m.* (-merses, -merse) (German students') drinking-bout.

Kommilitone *m.* (-n, -n) fellow-student.

Kommis *m.* (-, -) clerk; salesman.

Kommissar *m.* (-s, -e) commissioner, commissary.

Kommode *f.* (-, -n) chest of drawers.

kommunal *a.* communal, municipal.

Kommunal: ~**behörden** *pl.* local authorities; ~**verwaltung** *f.* local government.

Kommunismus *m.* (-, 0) communism.

kommunizieren *v.i.* to communicate.

Komödiant *m.* (-en, -en) actor, comedian.

Komödie *f.* (-, -n) comedy; play.

Kompa(g)nie *f.* (-, -n) company.

Kompagnon *m.* (-s, -s) partner.

Komparativ *m.* (-s, -e) comparative.

Kompass *m.* (-es, -e) compass.

kompensieren *v.t.* to compensate.

Kompetenz *f.* (-, -en) competence, jurisdiction.

komplett *a.* complete.

Komplize *m.* (-, -n) accomplice.

kompliziert *a.* complicated.

Komplott *n.* (-s, -e) plot.

komponieren *v.t.* to compose, to set (to music).

Komponist *m.* (-en, -en) composer.

Komposition *f.* (-, -en) *(mus.)* composition, setting.

Kompott *n.* (-[e]s, -e *u.* -s) stewed fruit.

Kompressor *m.* (-s, -en) *(mot.)* compressor, supercharger.

Kompromiss *n.* (-[e]s, -e) compromise.

kompromittieren *v.t.* to compromise; *sich* ~, to expose oneself.

kondensierte Milch *f.* condensed milk.

Konditor *m.* (-s, -en) confectioner.

Konditorei *f.* (-, -en) confectioner's (shop).

Konfekt *n.* (-[e]s, -e) confectionery.

Konfektion *f.* (-, 0) ready-made articles of dress.

Konferenz *f.* (-, -en) meeting, conference.

konferieren *v.i.* to confer.

Konfession *f.* (-, -en) denomination.

konfessionell *a.* denominational.

Konfirmand *m.* (-en, -en) candidate for confirmation.

konfiszieren *v.t.* to confiscate.

konfus *a.* confused, scatter-brained.

König *m.* (-s, -e) king.

Königin *f.* (-, -nen) queen.

königlich *a.* royal, regal.

Königreich *n.* kingdom.

Königtum *n.* (-[e]s, -tümer) royalty, kingship.

konjugieren *v.t.* to conjugate.

Konjunktion *f.* (-, -en) conjunction.

Konjunktiv *m.* (-s, -e) subjunctive.

Konjunktur *f.* (-, -en) boom; ~**forschung** *f.* market research.

konkav *a.* concave.

Konkordat *n.* (-[e]s, -e) concordat.

konkret *a.* concrete.

Konkubinat *n.* (-[e]s, -e) concubinage.

Konkurrent *m.* (-en, -en) competitor.

Konkurrenz *f.* (-, -en) competition.

konkurrenzfähig *a.* competitive.

konkurrieren *v.i.* to compete.

Konkurs *m.* (-kurses, -kurse) bankruptcy, insolvency; ~ *machen*, to become or go bankrupt.

Konkurs: ~**masse** *f.* bankrupt's estate; ~**ordnung** *f.* bankruptcy law; ~**verfahren** *n.* proceedings in bankruptcy.

können *v.i.i.ir.* to be able to know, to understand; *ich kann,* I can, I may; *ich kann nichts dafür,* it's no fault of mine, I can't help it.

Konnossement *n.* (-s, -s) bill of lading.

konsequent *a.* consistent.

Konsequenz *f.* (-, -en) consistency.

konservativ *a.* conservative.

Konservatorium *n.* (-s, -nen) academy of music.

Konservenbüchse *f.* (-, -n) tin, (*Am.*) can; *Konserven...*tinned, canned.

konservieren *v.t.* to preserve, to keep.

Konsolidieren *v.t.* to consolidate.

Konsonant *m.* (-en, -en) consonant.

Konsorte *m.* (-n, -n) associate.

Konsortialkredit *m.* syndicate credit.

Konsortium *n.* (-s, Konsortien) group, syndicate.

konstatieren *v.t.* to state, to notice.

konstitutionell *a.* constitutional.

konstruieren *v.t.* to construct.

Konstruktionsbüro *n.* drawing office.

Konsul *m.* (-s, -n) consul.

Konsulat *n.* (-s, -e) consulate.

konsultieren *v.t.* to consult.

Konsumverein *m.* (-s, -e) co-operative society.

Konter: ~**admiral** *m.* rear-admiral; ~**bande** *f.* contraband.

Kontinent *m.* (-s, -e) continent.

Kontingent *n.* (-[e]s, -e) quota, contingent.

Konto *n.* (-s, -n *u.* Konti) account; *Depositen* ~, deposit account; *fiktives* ~, fictitious account; *laufendes* ~, current account; *ein* ~ *eröffnen,* to open an account; ~**auszug** *m.* statement (of account); ~ **inhaber** *m.* account-holder.

Kontor *n.* (-s, -e) office, counting-house.

Kontra: ~**bass** *m.* bass-viol; ~**punkt** *m.* counterpoint.

Kontrahent *m.* (-en, -en) contracting party.

Kontrakt *m.* (-es, -e) contract.
kontraktlich *a. & adv.* by contract, contractual; ~ *verpflichtet*, under contract to...
Kontrollabschnitt *m.* counterfoil, (*Am.*) stub.
Kontrolle *f.* (-, 0) control.
kontrollieren *v.t.* to control, to check.
Kontroll: ~kasse *f.* cash register; ~marke *f.* check.
Kontur *f.* (-, -en) outline.
konventionell *a.* conventional.
Konversationslexikon *n.* encyclopædia.
konvertierbar *a.* convertible.
konvertieren *v.t.* to convert.
Konvertit *n.* (-en, -en) convert.
Konzentrationslager *n.* concentration camp.
konzentrieren *v.t.* to concentrate.
Konzept *n.* (-[e]s, -e) (rough) draft, sketch.
Konzern *m.* (-[e]s, -e) combine.
Konzert *n.* (-s, -e) concert; ~saal *m.* concert hall; ~zeichner *m.* (*Börse*) stag.
Konzession *f.* (-, -en) concession; licence; *sich eine* ~ *beschaffen,* to take out a licence; *mit Regierungs*~, under licence from the government; ~sinhaber *m.* licensee.
Konzil *n.* (-[e]s, -e *u.* -ien) council.
ko-optieren *v.t.* to co-opt.
koordinieren *v.t.* to co-ordinate.
Köper *m.* (-s, 0) twill.
Kopf *m.* (-es, Köpfe) head; (*fig.*) mind; (*Pfeifen*~) bowl; *aus dem* ~, from memory; *Hals über* ~, head over heels; *einen vor den* ~ *stossen,* to offend one; *sich auf den* ~ *stellen,* to strain every nerve; *sich den* ~ *über etwas zerbrechen,* to rack one's brains about a thing; *den* ~ *hängen lassen,* to hang one's head, to be dispirited.
Kopfarbeit *f.* brain-work.
köpfen *v.t.* to behead.
Kopf: ~hörer *m.* earphone, headphone; ~kissen *n.* pillow.
kopflos *a.* brainless, silly.
Kopf: ~nicken *n.* nod; ~rechnen *n.* mental arithmetic; ~salat *m.* cabbage-lettuce.
kopfscheu *a.* skittish, shy.
Kopf: ~schmerz *m.* headache; ~schuppen *pl.* dandruff; ~schütteln *n.* headshake; ~sprung *m.* header; ~stand *m.* (*avi.*) nose-landing, nose-over; ~steuer *f.* poll-tax; ~tuch *n.* kerchief, coif.
kopfüber *adv.* head foremost.
Kopf: ~weh *n.* head-ache; ~zerbrechen *n.* puzzling of one's head.
Kopie *f.* (-, -[e]n) copy; duplicate.
kopieren *v.t.* to copy; (*phot.*) to print.
Koppel *f.* (-, -n) sword-belt; (*Hunde*~) leash.
koppeln *v.t.* to couple.

Koralle *f.* (-, -n) coral.
Korb *m.* (-[e]s, Körbe) basket, hamper, crate; *einen* ~ *bekommen,* to meet with a refusal.
Korb: ~flechter, ~macher *m.* basket-maker; ~flechtwaren *pl.* wickerwork; ~möbel *n.* wicker furniture.
Kork *m.* (-[e]s, -e) cork; stopper; float (fishing).
korken *v.t.* to cork.
Korkzieher *m.* cork-screw.
Korn *n.* (-[e]s, Körner) corn; grain.
Kornblume *f.* corn-flower.
körnen *v.t. & i.* to granulate.
Körner *m.* (-s, -) (*mech.*) centre-punch.
Kornfeld *n.* corn-field.
körnig *a.* granulous, granular.
Kornkammer *f.* granary.
Körper *m.* (-s, -) body; (*toter*) corpse; (*phys.*) solid.
Körper: ~bau *m.* physique; ~beschädigung *f.* bodily harm *or* injury; ~haltung *f.* posture; ~kultur *f.* physical culture.
Körperchen *n.* (-s, -) corpuscle.
körperlich *a.* corporeal, bodily; physical.
Körperschaft *f.* corporation; ~ssteuer *f.* corporation profits tax.
Korps (*frz.*) *n.* (-, -) corps; body.
korrekt *a.* correct.
Korrektor *m.* (-s, -en) proof-reader.
Korrektur *f.* (-, -en) correction; proof-sheet, revise; ~bogen *m.* proof-sheet.
Korrelat *n.* (-[e]s, 0) correlate.
Korrespondent *m.* (-en, -en) (*com.*) correspondence clerk.
Korrespondenz *f.* (-, -en) correspondence.
korrespondieren *v.i.* to correspond.
Korridor *m.* (-s, -e) passage, corridor.
korrigieren *v.t.* to correct.
Korsar *m.* (-en, -en) corsair, pirate.
Korsett *n.* (-[e]s, -e *u.* -s) corset, stays *pl.*
Koryphäe *m.* (-n, -n) leader, head.
koscher *a.* kosher.
kosen *v.i.* to caress.
Kosename *m.* pet name.
Kosinus *m.* (*math.*) cosine.
Kost *f.* (-, 0) fare, food; board; *in* ~ *sein bei,* to board with.
kostbar *a.* costly, precious; (*fam.*) capital.
Kostbarkeit *f.* (-, -en) preciousness; valuables *pl.*
kosten *v.t.* to taste; to cost; to require.
Kosten *pl.* cost, costs, charges, expenses *pl.; die* ~ *tragen,* to bear the expenses; ~anschlag *m.* estimate; ~los *a.* free of charge; ~pflichtig abweisen (*law*), to dismiss with costs.
Kostenpunkt *m.* the question of expense.
Kost: ~gänger *m.* boarder; ~geld *n.* board; allowance; board-wages (*für Dienstboten*)
köstlich *a.* precious; delicious, dainty.
kostspielig *a.* expensive, costly.

Kostüm n. (-s, -e) costume, dress; ~**fest** n. fancy-dress ball.

Kot m. (-[e]s, 0) mud, dirt; excrement.

Kotelett f. (-, -s) cutlet, chop.

Köter m. (-s, -) cur.

Kotflügel m. mudguard.

Kothurn m. (-[e]s, -e) buskin.

kotzen v.i. (vulg.) to vomit.

Krabbe f. (-, -n) crab.

krabbeln v.i. to crawl.

Krach m. (-[e]s, -e) crack, crash; quarrel.

krachen v.i. to crack, to crash.

krächzen v.i. to croak, to caw.

kraft pr. by virtue of.

Kraft f. (-, Kräfte) strength; (Natur) force; (Macht) power; vigour; in ~, in force; in ~ setzen, to put into operation; ausser ~ setzen, to abrogate; in ~ treten, to come into force; aus Leibeskräften, with might and main.

Kraft: ~**brühe** f. bouillon, clear soup; ~**fahrer** m. motorist; ~**fahrkorps** n. motor corps; ~**fahrwesen** n. motor transport (service); ~**fahrpark** m. motor pool.

kräftig a. strong; powerful; vigorous; nourishing.

kräftigen v.t. to strengthen.

kraftlos a. weak, feeble; impotent.

Kraft: ~**probe** f. trial of strength; ~**wagen** m. motor-car; ~**werk** n. power station.

kraftvoll a. vigorous.

Kragen m. (-s, -) collar; cape.

Krähe f. (-, -n) crow.

krähen v.i. to crow.

krakeelen v.i. to kick up a row.

Krakeeler m. (-s, -) quarreller, brawler.

Kralle f. (-, -n) claw; clutch, talon.

Kram m. (-[e]s, Kräme) lumber.

kramen v.i. to rummage.

Krämer m. (-s, -) shopkeeper, grocer.

Krampf m. (-[e]s, Krämpfe) cramp; spasm, convulsion.

Krampfader f. varicose vein.

krampfhaft a. spasmodic, convulsive.

Kran m. (-[e]s, Kräne) crane; cock (of a barrel).

Kranich m. (-s, -e) crane.

krank a. ill, sick; ~werden, to fall ill; sich ~stellen, to feign illness, to malinger; ~ im Bett liegen, to be laid up; sich ~ melden (mil.), to go on sick-call.

Kranke[r] m. & f. (-n, -n) patient.

kränkeln v.i. to be ailing, to be sickly.

kranken v.i. to suffer from.

kränken (sich) v.t. & refl. to vex, to mortify; to injure.

Kranken: ~**appell** m. (mil.) sick-call; ~**bett** n. sick-bed; ~**haus** n. hospital; ins ~haus überführen, to hospitalize; ~**kasse** f. health insurance; ~**kraftwagen** m. motor ambulance; ~**pflege** f. nursing; ~**pfleger** m., ~**wärter** m. male

nurse; ~**schwester** f. hospital-nurse; ~**träger** m. stretcher-bearer; ~**urlaub** m. sick leave; ~**versicherung** f. health insurance; ~**wagen** m. ambulance.

krankhaft a. morbid.

Krankheit f. (-, -en) disease, sickness; die englische ~, the rickets.

kränklich a. sickly, ailing, poorly.

Kränkung f. (-, -en) insult, mortification.

Kranz m. (-es, Kränze) wreath, garland.

kränzen v.t. to wreathe, to crown.

Krapfen m. (-s, -) doughnut.

Krapp m. (-[e]s, 0) madder.

krass a. coarse, gross.

Krater m. (-s, -) crater.

Kratzbürste f. scraper.

kratzbürstig a, cross-grained, rasping.

Krätze f. (-, 0) itch, mange, scabies.

kratzen v.t. to scratch, to scrape; (Wolle) to card; ~ v.i. (von Federn) to spurt.

kraus a. crisp, curled, frizzled.

Krause f. (-, -n) ruff; frill.

kräuseln v.t. to curl, to frizzle.

Krauskopf m. curly-head.

Kraut n. (-[e]s, Kräuter) herb; plant; cabbage; (offizinell) simple.

Krawall m. (-[e]s, -e) row, riot.

Krawatte f. (-, -n) (neck)-tie, scarf.

Kreatur f. (-, -en) creature.

Krebs m. (Krebses, Krebse) crayfish; crab; (med.) cancer.

krebsartig a. cancerous.

kredenzen v.t. to hand (a cup of wine, after first tasting it).

Kredit m. (-[e]s, -e) credit; trust; reputation.

Kredit: ~**brief** m. letter of credit; ~**kassenschein** m. credit voucher.

kreditfähig a. credit-worthy, sound.

kreditieren v.t. to credit.

Kreide f. (-, -n) chalk; crayon.

Kreis m. (Kreises, Kreise) circle, quarter; orbit; sphere; district.

Kreis: ~**abschnitt** m. segment; ~**ausschnitt** m. sector.

kreischen v.i. to scream.

Kreisel m. (-s, -) top; ~**kompass** m. gyroscope.

kreiseln v.i. to turn like a top.

kreisen v.i. to revolve.

Kreisfläche f. circular surface.

kreisförmig a. circular.

Kreis: ~**lauf** m. circulation; periodical return; ~**linie** f. circumference of a circle; ~**säge** f. circular saw.

Kreislauf...circulatory, a.

kreissen v.i. to be in labour.

Krematorium n. (-s, -rien) crematorium.

Krempe f. (-, -n) brim (of a hat).

Krempel m. (-s, 0) rubbish.

krempen v.t. to turn up.

Kreosot n. (-s, 0) creosote.

krepieren v.i. (s) to die a miserable death; (Geschoss) to burst.

Krepp m. (-s, 0) crape.

Kresse f. (-, -n) (water-)cress.

Kreuz n. (-es, -e) cross; (in der Karte) club; (fig.) cross, tribulation; kreuz und quer, right and left, in all directions.

Kreuzband n. wrapper; unter ~ versenden, to send by book-post.

kreuzen v.t. to cross; to interbreed; ~ v.i. (nav.) to cruise; sich ~ v.refl. to intersect; die beiden Briefe kreuzten sich, the two letters crossed.

Kreuzer m. (-s, -) (nav.) cruiser.

Kreuz: ~fahrer m. crusader; ~fahrt f. crusade.

Kreuzgang m. cloisters pl.

kreuzigen v.t. to crucify.

Kreuzigung f. crucifixion.

Kreuz: ~otter f. viper; ~stich m. cross-stitch.

Kreuzung f. (-, -en) cross-breeding.

Kreuz: ~verhör n. cross-examination; ~wegstationen pl. stations of the Cross.

kreuzweise adv. across, cross-wise.

Kreuzworträtsel n. crossword puzzle.

Kreuzzug m. crusade.

kribbeln v.i. to tickle, to itch.

kriechen v.i.st. (h. u. s.) to creep, to crawl; (fig.) to cringe, to fawn, to toady.

Kriecher m. (-s, -) (fig.) crawler, toady; tuft-hunter.

Kriecherei f. (-, -en) toadyism, servility.

Krieg m. (-[e]s, -e) war; contest, quarrel; ~ führen, to make war (upon).

kriegen v.t. (fam.) to get, to obtain.

Krieger m. (-s, -) warrior.

Kriegerdenkmal n. war-memorial.

kriegerisch a. warlike, martial.

Kriegs: ~artikel pl. articles of war; ~beschädigte[r] m. disabled ex-service man; ~blind a. war-blinded; ~brücke f. military bridge; ~dienst m. military service; ~dienstverweigerer m. conscientious objector; ~einsatz m. war effort; ~erklärung f. declaration of war; ~flotte f. navy; ~fuss m. war-establishment; ~gebiet n. theatre of operations; ~gefangene[r] m. prisoner of war; ~gefangenschaft f. captivity; ~gericht n. court-martial; ~gewinnler m. war-profiteer; ~gliederung f. order of battle; ~hafen m. naval base; ~hetzer m. war-monger; ~klausel f. war clause; ~list f. stratagem; ~material n. (Am.) matériel; ~ministerium n. War Office; ~potential n. war potential; ~recht n. military law; ~risiko n. war risk; ~schauplatz m. theatre of war; ~schiff n. man-of-war, warship; ~spiel n. (mil.) map manœuvre; ~wichtiges Ziel n. military target or objective;

~wissenschaft f. military science; ~zulage f. war bonus.

Kriminalität f. (-, 0) delinquency.

Kriminalpolizei f. criminal investigation department; detective police.

Kriminologe m. (-n, -n) criminologist.

Krippe f. (-, -n) crib, manger; crèche.

Krise, Krisis f. (-, Krisen) crisis.

Kristall m. (-[e]s, -e) crystal.

kristallen a. crystalline.

Kristallglas n. flint-glass.

kristallisieren v.i. to crystallize.

Kritik f. (-, -en) criticism; critique, review; unter aller ~, below contempt.

Kritiker m. (-s, -) critic.

kritisch a. critical.

kritisieren v.t. to criticize; to review.

kritzeln v.i. to scrawl, to scribble.

Krokodil n. (-[e]s, -e) crocodile.

Krone f. (-, -n) crown; coronet.

krönen v.t. (also fig.) to crown.

Kron: ~leuchter m. chandelier, lustre; ~prinz m. crown-prince.

Kronzeuge werden, to turn king's evidence.

Krönung f. (-, -en) coronation.

Kropf m. (-[e]s, Kröpfe) goitre, struma.

Kröte f. (-, -n) toad.

Krücke f. (-, -n) crutch.

Krug m. (-[e]s, Krüge) pitcher; jug; (Henkel~) mug; inn.

Krume f. (-, -n) crumb; (Acker) mould.

krümelig a. crumbling, crummy.

krümeln (sich) v.i. & refl. to crumble.

krumm a. crooked; curved; etwas ~ nehmen, to take a thing (in) ill (part).

krümmen v.t. to bend, to crook; (sich) ~ v.refl. to cringe, to stoop; (vor Schmerz) to writhe; (Fluss) to bend, to wind; einem kein Haar ~, not to hurt a hair of a person's head.

Krummstab m. crosier.

Krümmung f. (-, -en) bend, winding.

Krüppel m. (-s, -) cripple.

krüppelhaft, krüppelig a. crippled, lame.

Kruste f. (-, -n) crust.

Krustentier n. crustacean.

Kruzifix n. (-es, -e) crucifix.

Krypta f. (-, Krypten) crypt.

Kübel m. (-s, -) tub.

Kubik- (in Zus.) cubic.

Kubik: ~wurzel f. cube root; ~zahl f. cube (number).

Küche f. (-, -n) kitchen; cooking, cookery, cuisine; kalte ~, cold meat.

Kuchen m. (-s, -) cake, pastry.

Küchenartikel m.pl. kitchen appliances.

Kuchenbäcker m. pastry-cook.

Küchenchef m. chef.

Küchlein n. (-s, -) chicken.

Kuckuck m. (-s, -e) cuckoo.

Kufe f. (-, -n) skid, runner.

Küfer m. (-s, -) cooper.

Kugel f. (-, -n) ball; (Flinte) bullet; (math.) sphere, globe.
kugelfest a. bullet-proof.
kugelförmig a. spherical.
Kugel: ~gelenk n. socket joint; (mech.) ball and socket; ~lager n. ball bearing.
kugeln v.t. & i. to roll, to bowl.
Kuh f. (- Kühe) cow; junge ~, heifer.
kühl a. cool, fresh.
Kühlapparat, m. refrigerator.
Kühle f. (-, 0) coolness.
kühlen v.t. to cool; ~ v.i. to grow cool.
Kühler m. (-s, -) (mot.) radiator.
Kühlflüssigkeit f. (-, -en) (mech.) coolant.
Kühlraum n. cold storage.
Kühlung f. (-, -en) cooling.
kühn a. bold, daring, audacious.
Kuhstall m. cow-shed.
Küken n. (-s, -) chicken; (fam.) chick.
kulant a. (com.) fair.
Kuli m. (-s, -s) coolie.
Kulisse f. (-, -n) wing, side-scene; hinter den ~n, behind the scenes.
kultivieren v.t. to cultivate; to culture.
Kultur f. (-, -en) culture; civilization; cultivation.
Kulturfilm m. documentary film.
Kultus m. (-, Kulte) (public) worship.
Kultusminister m. minister of education.
Kümmel m. (-s, -) caraway.
Kummer m. (-s, 0) grief, sorrow, distress.
kümmerlich a. miserable; scanty.
kümmern (sich) v.refl. to care for, to mind.
kummervoll a. grievous, afflicted.
Kumpan m. (-[e]s, -e) companion, pal.
kund a. ~ tun, to notify, to give notice; sich ~geben, to manifest oneself.
kündbar a. recallable (of a loan).
Kunde f. (-, -n) knowledge; information; tidings pl., intelligence; ~ m. (-n, -n) customer, client.
künden v.t. to make known.
Kundgebung f. (-, -en) demonstration.
kundig a. skilled, versed (in).
kündigen v.t. to give warning or notice.
Kündigung f. (-, -en) notice, warning; Geld auf tägliche ~, call-money; auf monatliche ~, at a month's notice; ~sfrist f. period of notice.
Kundschaft f. (-, -en) customers; patronage.
kundschaften v.i. to reconnoitre.
Kundschafter m. (-s, -) scout; spy.
künftig a. future, to be, next; ~ adv. in future.
Kunst f. (-, Künste) art; skill.
Kunst...synthetic.
Kunst: ~akademie f. academy of arts; ~ausdruck m. technical term; ~ausstellung f. art-exhibition; ~dünger m. artificial manure.
Künstelei f. (-, -en) affectation.

Kunst: ~fertigkeit f. skill; ~gegenstand m. object of art.
kunstgerecht a. (technically) correct, workmanlike.
Kunst: ~gewerbe n. arts and crafts; ~griff m. trick, artifice; ~händler m. art-dealer; ~handlung f. fine-art shop; ~handwerk n. industrial art; ~kenner m. connoisseur; ~leder n. imitation leather.
Künstler m. (-s, -) artist.
künstlerisch a. artistic.
künstlich a. artificial; artful.
kunstlos a. artless, plain.
kunstsinnig a. art-loving.
Kunst: ~sammlung f. art collection; ~seide f. artificial silk, rayon; ~schule f. school of art; ~stopferei f. invisible mending; ~stück n. feat, trick, stunt; ~tischler m. cabinet-maker.
kunst: ~verständig a. expert; ~voll a. artistic, elaborate.
Kunstwerk n. work of art.
kunterbunt a. & adv. higgledy-piggledy.
Kupfer n. (-s, -) copper.
Kupfer: ~bergwerk n. copper-mine; ~blech n. sheet-copper; ~druck m. copper-plate.
Kupfermünze f. copper (coin).
kupfern a. copper.
Kupferplatte f. copper-plate.
kupferrot a. copper-coloured.
Kupfer: ~schmied m. coppersmith, brazier; ~stecher m. engraver (in copper); ~stich m. engraving, copperplate, print.
Kuppe f. (-, -n) curved top, summit.
Kuppel f. (-, -n) cupola, dome.
Kuppelei f. (-, -en) pimping.
kuppeln v.t. to couple, to link, to join; ~ v.i. to procure.
Kupplung f. (-, -en) coupling; clutch.
Kuppler m. (-s, -) pander, pimp.
Kupplerin f. (-, -nen) procuress, bawd.
Kur f. (-, -en) cure, medical treatment.
Kürassier m. (-[e]s, -e) cuirassier.
Kuratel f. (-, -en) guardianship, trusteeship.
Kurator m. (-s, -en) guardian, trustee.
Kurbel f. (-, -n) winch, crank.
kurbeln v.t. to crank; (film) to reel off.
Kurbelwelle f. (mech.) crankshaft.
Kürbis m. (-bisses, -bisse) gourd, pumpkin.
Kur: ~fürst m. elector; ~fürstentum n. electorate; ~fürstin f. electress.
kurfürstlich a. electoral.
Kur: ~gast m. visitor at a watering-place; ~haus m. pump room; casino (of a watering-place).
Kurier m. (-[e]s, -e) courier.
kurieren v.t. to cure.
kurios a. curious, odd.

Kurliste f. visitors' list at a watering-place.

Kurort m. health-resort, spa, watering-place.

Kurpfuscher m. quack.

Kurrentschrift f. running-hand.

Kurs m. (-ses, -se) (rate of) exchange; price; (nav.) course; ausser ~ (Geld, Briefmarke), out of course.

Kurs: ~buch n. railway-guide, time-tables pl.; ~wagen m. (rail.) through carriage; ~zettel m. exchange list.

Kürschner m. (-s, -) furrier, skinner.

kursieren v.i. to be current, to circulate.

kursiv: ~ gedruckt, printed in italics.

Kursivschrift f. italics pl.

Kursus m. (-, Kurse) course (of lessons).

Kurve f. (-, -n) curve, bent.

Kurvenbild n. graph.

kurz a. short; brief, abrupt; ~ adv. in short, briefly; ~ und gut, in a word; ~um, in short; ~weg, briefly, in brief; ~ und bündig, concise(ly), terse(ly); in ~em, shortly, soon; vor ~em, recently, the other day; über ~ oder lang, sooner or later; zu ~ kommen, to get short measure; den kürzeren ziehen, to get the worst of it.

kurzatmig a. short-winded.

Kürze f. (-, -) shortness; brevity.

kürzen v.t. to shorten, to curtail; (Schriftliches) to abridge.

Kurz: ~fristig a. short term; ~geschichte f. short story; ~welle f. (Radio) short wave.

kürzlich adv. lately, recently.

Kurz: ~schluss m. short circuit; ~schrift f. shorthand (writing).

kurzsichtig a. near-sighted, short-sighted, narrow-minded.

Kürzung f. (-, -en) abbreviation; curtailment, cut.

Kurzwaren pl. haberdashery; hardware.

Kurzweil f. (-, 0) pastime.

kurzweilig a. merry, diverting, amusing.

kuschen v.i. (von Hunden) to crouch, to lie down; kusch (dich)! lie down!

Kuss m. (Kusses, Küsse) kiss.

küssen v.t. to kiss.

Kusshand f. blown kiss.

Küste f. (-, -n) coast, shore.

Küsten… coastal.

Küstenfahrer m. coasting-vessel, coaster.

Küster m. (-s, -) sexton, verger.

Kustos m. (-, Kustoden) curator, custodian.

Kutschbock m. coach-box.

Kutsche f. (-, -n) carriage, coach.

Kutscher m. (-s, -) coachman, driver.

kutschieren v.i. to drive a coach.

Kutte f. (-, -n) cowl.

Kutter m. (-s, -) (nav.) cutter.

Kuvert n. (-s, -s) envelope; (Gedeck) cover.

Kux m. (-es, -e) mining-share.

G.D.

L

laben v.t. to refresh, to comfort; (sich) ~ v.refl. to refresh oneself.

labil a. unstable.

Laboratorium n. (-s, -torien) laboratory.

laborieren v.i. ~ an, to labour under.

Labsal n. (-[e]s, -e) restorative, cordial.

Lache f. (-, -n) pool, puddle.

lächeln v.i. to smile.

lachen v.i. to laugh.

Lachen n. (-s, 0) laughter, laugh.

Lacher m. (-s, -) laughter.

lächerlich a. laughable, ridiculous.

Lachkrampf m. convulsive laughter.

Lachs m. (-ses, -se) salmon.

Lachsschinken m. (-s, -) fillet of smoked ham.

Lack m. (-[e]s, -e) gum-lac; varnish, lacquer.

lackieren v.t. to varnish, to lacquer, to japan.

Lackmus n. (-, 0) litmus.

Lackstiefel m. patent-leather boots.

Lade f. (-, -n) box, chest, trunk.

laden v.t.st. to load, to charge; to summon, to cite; to invite.

Laden m. (-s, -Läden) shop; (Am.) store.

Laden: ~dieb m. shoplifter; ~diebstahl f. shoplifting; ~fenster n. shop-window; ~hüter m. unsaleable article, drug; ~mädchen n. shop-girl, saleslady, (Am.) salesgirl; ~preis m. retail price; (Bücher) publication price; ~tisch m. counter.

Lader m. (avi.) supercharger.

Laderampe f. loading ramp.

Ladung f. (-, -en) freight, cargo, shipment; (Gewehr~) (elek.) charge.

Ladungsaufseher m. supercargo.

Lafette f. (-, -n) gun-carriage, mount.

Laffe m. (-n, -n) fop, puppy.

Lage f. (-, -n) situation, position; condition; layer, stratum; (mech.) thickness; ~ ziegel, course of bricks; ~karte f. (mil.) situation map; ~meldung f. (mil.) situation report.

Lager n. (-s, -) couch, bed; warehouse; (von Tieren) lair; (Vorrat) stock; (Erz) deposit; (mil.) camp.

Lager: ~bier n. lager; ~geld n., ~gebühr f. storage (charge); ~haus n. warehouse.

Lagerist m. warehouse clerk.

lagern v.t. to lay, to store, to warehouse; ~ v.i. to (en)camp; to be stored; (sich) ~ v.refl. to lie down.

Lagerstätte f. resting-place; depot.

Lagune f. (-, -n) lagoon.

lahm a. lame, halt.

lahmen v.i. to be lame, to halt.

lähmen v.t. to lame, to paralyse.

lahmlegen v.t. to paralyse.

Lähmung f. (-, -en) paralysis.

Laib *m.* (-[e], -e) loaf.
Laich *m.* (-[e]s, Ø) spawn.
laichen *v.i.* to spawn.
Laie *m.* (-n, -n) layman.
Laienbruder *m.* lay-brother.
Lakai *m.* (en, -en) footman, lackey.
Lake *f.* (-, -n) brine, pickle.
Laken *n.* (-s, -) sheet; (*Toten.*) pall.
lakonisch *a. & adv.* laconic(ally).
Lakritze *f.* (-, -n) liquorice.
Lakritzenholz *n.* stick-liquorice.
lallen *v.t. & i.* to stammer.
Lamelle *f.* (-, -n) (*elek.*) lamina.
Lamm *n.* (-[e]s, Lämmer) lamb.
Lammbraten *m.* roast-lamb.
Lammfleisch *n.* lamb.
Lampe *f.* (-, -n) lamp.
Lampen: ~fieber *n.* stage-fright; ~schirm
  m. lamp-shade.
Land *n.* (-[e]s, Länder *or*, poet. Lande)
  land; country; territory; *zu ~*, by land;
  auf dem ~, in the country.
Landauer *m.* (-s, -) landau.
landen *v.t.* (*h*) *& i.* (*s*) to land; to get
  ashore, to disembark.
Landenge *f.* isthmus.
Länderei *f.* (-, -en) landed property.
Länderkunde *f.* geographical knowledge.
Landes...regional *a.*
Landes: ~farben *pl.* national colours;
  ~herr *m.* sovereign; ~kirche *f.* national
  or established church; ~tracht *f.*
  national costume.
landesüblich *a.* customary, usual.
Landes: ~verrat *m.* treason; ~verteidi-
  gung *f.* defence.
Land: ~friede[n] *m.* the king's peace;
  ~gericht *n.* county court; ~gut *n.*
  estate, manor; ~haus *n.* county-seat;
  ~karte *f.* map; ~kriegsordnung *f.* rules
  of land warfare.
landläufig *a.* in current use.
ländlich *a.* rural.
Landmesser *m.* surveyor.
Landschaft *f.* (-, -en) landscape; scenery;
  countryside.
landschaftlich *a.* provincial; scenic.
Landsitz *m.* country-seat.
Lands: ~knecht *m.* hired foot-soldier;
  ~mann *m.* countryman, compatriot.
Land: ~strasse *f.* highroad, highway
  ~streicher *m.* vagrant, tramp, (*Am.*)
  hobo; ~strich *m.* tract, district; ~tag
  m. Diet; ~truppen *pl.* ground forces.
Landung *f.* (-, -en) landing, descent.
Landungs: ~brücke *f.* landing-stage;
  ~platz *m.* landing-place.
Land: ~wirt *m.* farmer; agriculturist;
  ~wirtschaft *f.* agriculture, farming.
landwirtschaftlich *a.* agricultural; ~er
  Betriebsleiter *m.* farm manager.
lang *a.* long; tall; *Tage ~ for* days together.

langatmig *a.* long-winded, lengthy.
lange *adv.* long; ~ *her*, long ago.
Länge *f.* (-, -en) length; tallness; longitude; *auf die ~*, in the long run; *der ~
  nach*, lengthwise.
langen *v.t.* to hand, to give, to reach;
  ~ *v.i.* to suffice, to be enough.
Längen: ~grad *m.* degree of longitude;
  ~kreis *m.* longitude; ~mass *n.* long *or*
  linear measure.
Langeweile *f.* (-, Ø) boredom.
lang: ~fristig *a.* longterm; ~jährig *a.* of
  long standing; ~lebig *a.* long-lived.
länglich *a.* oblong.
Langmut *f.* (-, Ø) long-suffering.
langmütig *a.* forbearing, long-suffering.
längs *pr.* along
langsam *a.* slow; tardy.
längst *adv.* long ago.
längstens *adv.* at the longest, at latest.
langweilen *v.t.* to tire, to bore; (sich) ~
  v.refl. to feel dull, to be bored.
langweilig *a.* dull; ~e *Person*, bore.
Langwelle *f.* (*Radio*) long wave.
langwierig *a.* lengthy, protracted.
Lanze *f.* (-, -n) lance, spear.
Lanzette *f.* (-, -n) lancet.
lanzieren *v.t.* to start, to launch.
Lappalie *f.* (-, -n) trifle.
Lappen *m.* (-s, -) rag; patch.
läppisch *a.* silly, foolish.
Lärche *f.* (-, -n) larch.
Lärm *m.* (-[e]s, Ø) noise, din; alarm;
  blinder ~, false alarm; ~ *schlagen*, to
  sound the alarm.
lärmen *v.i.* to make a noise *or* row.
Larve *f.* (-, -n) mask; larva.
Lasche *f.* (-, -n) (*Kleid*) stripe, flap.
lassen *v.t.st.* to let; to allow, to suffer;
  to order, to cause; to leave; *sein Leben
  ~*, to sacrifice one's life: *einen in Ruhe
  oder zufrieden ~*, to leave (let) one
  alone; *kommen ~*, to send for, to order;
  machen ~, to have done; *sehen ~*, to
  show; *sagen ~*, to send word; *übrig ~*,
  to leave; *sein Tun und Lassen*, all his
  doing; *lass das!* don't!; *das lässt sich
  hören*, it is pleasant to hear; there is
  something in that.
lässig *a.* lazy, sluggish, indolent; weary.
lässlich *a.* venial, pardonable.
Last *f.* (-, -en) load, charge, burden;
  tonnage; *zu Ihren ~en*, at your debit;
  zur ~ fallen, to be a burden on.
lasten *v.i.* to weigh upon, to press.
Laster *n.* (-s, -) vice; crime.
lasterhaft *a.* vicious, profligate.
Lästermaul *n.* slanderer, scandalmonger.
lästern *v.t.* to slander; to blaspheme.
Lästerung *f.* (-, -en) calumny; blasphemy.
lästig *a.* burdensome, troublesome.
Last: ~kraftwagen *m.* motor lorry *or*
  truck; ~tier *n.* beast of burden; ~

träger *m.* porter; ~wagen *m.* cart, truck, waggon.

Latein *n.* (-s, 0) Latin.

lateinisch *a.* Latin.

Laterne *f.* (-, -n) lantern; (street-)lamp.

Laternenpfahl *m.* lamp-post.

Latsche *f.* (-, -n) dwarf pine.

latschen *v.i.* to shuffle along.

Latte *f.* (-, -n) lath.

Lattich *m.* (-[e]s, -e) lettuce.

Latwerge *f.* (-, -n) electuary.

Latz *m.* (-es, Lätze) flap; bib; tucker.

lau(warm) *a.* tepid; (*fig.*) lukewarm.

Laub *n.* (-[e]s, 0) leaves *pl.*; foliage.

Laubbaum *m.* deciduous tree.

Laube *f.* (-, -n) arbour, bower.

Laubengang *m.* arcade.

Laubfrosch *m.* tree-frog.

laubig *a.* leafy, leaved.

Laubsäge *f.* fret-saw.

Lauch *m.* (-[e]s, -e) leek.

Lauer *f.* (-, 0) lurking-place, ambush; *au der ~ sein,* to lie in wait.

lauern *v.i.* to lurk, to lie in wait.

Lauf *m.* (-[e]s, Läufe) course; run; race; (*Gewehr~*) barrel; leg (of game); (*mus.*) roulade.

Lauf: ~bahn *f.* course, career; ~bursche *m.* errand-boy.

laufen *v.i.st.* (*s*) to run, to flow, to leak.

laufend *a.* running; current; *auf dem ~en sein,* to be well informed; *auf dem ~en halten,* to keep informed; ~e Arbeiten *pl.* routine work; ~es Band *n.* conveyor belt; ~e Nummer *f.* serial number; ~es Wasser *n.* running *or* constant water.

Läufer *m.* (-s, -) runner; stair-carpet; (*Schach*) bishop.

Lauferei *f.* (-, -en) wearisome trotting about.

Lauffeuer *n.*, *wie ein ~,* like wildfire.

Laufffläche *f.* (*eines Reifens*) tread.

Lauf: ~kran *m.* travelling crane; ~ masche *f.* ladder; ~schritt *m.* double time; ~ställchen *n.* play-pen; ~weg *m.* (*nav.*) slipway.

Lauge *f.* (-, -n) lye, buck.

Laune *f.* (-, -n) whim, caprice; humour, temper, mood.

launig *a.* humorous.

launisch *a.* capricious, wayward.

Laus *f.* (-, Läuse) louse (*pl.* lice).

Lausbub *m.* (-en, -en) scamp.

Lauscher *m.* (-s, -) listener.

lauschig *a.* snug, cosy, quiet.

lausig *a.* lousy, wretched.

Lausjunge, Lausekerl *m.* blackguard.

Laut *m.* (-[e]s, -e) sound.

laut *a.* loud; ~ *adv.* aloud, loud(ly); ~ *pr.* as per, according to.

Laute *f.* (-, -n) lute.

lauten *v.i.* to sound; to run, to read.

läuten *v.i. & t.* to ring.

lauter *a.* clear; pure; mere, none but, nothing but; sincere, ingenuous.

Lauterkeit *f.* (-, 0) purity; integrity.

läutern *v.t.* to purify, to refine.

Läuterung *f.* (-, -en) purification.

Lautgesetz *n.* phonetic law.

lautlos *a.* silent, mute; hushed.

Laut: ~sprecher *m.* loudspeaker, speaker; ~sprecherwagen *m.* loudspeaker van; ~stärke *f.* (*Radio*) volume; ~stärkeneinstellung *f.* volume control; ~zeichen *n.* phonetic symbol.

Lava *f.* (-, Laven) lava.

Lavendel *m.* (-s, 0) lavender.

lavieren *v.i.* to veer, to tack.

Lawine *f.* (-, -n) avalanche.

lax *a.* lax, loose.

Lazarett *n.* (-[e]s, -e) military hospital.

Lazarettschiff *n.* hospital ship; Lazarettzug *m.* hospital train.

Lebenlang *n.*, *mein ~,* all my life.

Lebemann *m.* man about town; epicure.

leben *v.i.* to live, to be alive; *lebe wohl!* farewell; *hoch ~ lassen,* to cheer.

Leben *n.* (-s, -) life; (*fig.*) animation; *am ~ bleiben,* to live; *ums ~ bringen,* to kill; *ums ~ kommen,* to perish; *sich sein ~ verdienen,* to earn *or* make a living.

lebend *a.* living; alive; ~e Sprachen, modern languages; ~e Bilder, tableaux vivants.

lebendig *a.* living, alive; quick, lively.

Lebens: ~alter *n.* age; ~beschreibung *f.* biography, life; ~dauer *f.* (*auch von Dingen*) life; *von langer ~dauer,* long-lived; *mutmassliche ~dauer,* expectation of life.

lebensfähig *a.* capable of living, viable.

Lebensfrage *f.* vital question.

lebensgefährlich *a.* perilous; *~ verwundet od. krank,* in critical condition.

Lebens: ~grösse *f.* full length, lifesize; ~haltung *f.* standard of life *or* living; ~haltungskosten *pl.* cost of living.

lebenslänglich *a.* for life, life-long; ~er Niessbrauch, (*law*) life-interest.

Lebenslauf *m.* career; curriculum vitae.

lebenslustig *a.* cheery, enjoying life.

Lebensmittel *pl.* provisions, victuals; ~karten *pl.* ration book.

lebensmüde *a.* weary of life.

Lebens: ~unterhalt *m.* (means of) livelihood; ~versicherung *f.* life-insurance; abgekürzte ~versicherung *f.* endowment insurance; ~wandel *m.* conduct; ~weise *f.* mode of life; ~weisheit *f.* practical wisdom; ~wichtig *a.* vital; ~zeichen *n.* sign of life; *auf ~zeit,* for life.

Leber *f.* (-, -n) liver.

Leber: ~fleck *u.* ~flecken *m.* freckle, mole; ~tran *m.* cod-liver oil.

Lebewesen *n.* living object.

Lebewohl n. (-[e]s, -e u. -s) farewell.
lebhaft a. vivid, lively, brisk, animated.
Lebhaftigkeit f. (-, 0) vivacity, animation.
Lebkuchen m. spiced honey cake.
leblos a. lifeless, inanimate; heavy, dull.
Lebzeiten f.pl. lifetime.
lechzen v.i. to pant, to languish.
leck a. leaky; ~ werden, to spring a leak.
Leck n. (-[e]s, -e) leak.
lecken v.t. to lick, to lap; ~ v.i. (nav.) to leak.
lecker a. dainty, nice; fastidious.
Leckerbissen m. tit-bit, choice morsel.
Leder n. (-s, -) leather.
Lederband m. (Buch) calf-binding.
ledern a. leather, leathern; (fig.) dull.
Lederzeug n. leather straps and belts pl.
ledig a. unmarried, single; ~e Frau f. spinster.
lediglich adv. solely, only.
Lee n. (-, 0) (nav.) lee-side.
leer a. empty, void; vacant.
Leere f. (-, 0) void, vacuum.
leeren v.t. to empty, to clear.
Leerlauf m. (-[e]s, 0) idle motion, idle gear.
leerstehend a. unoccupied.
Legat n. (-[e]s, -e) legacy; ~ m. (-en, -en) legate.
egen v.t. to lay, to put, to place; (sich) ~ v.refl. to lie down; (wind) to abate; Karten ~, to tell fortunes from cards; einem das Handwerk ~, to stop one's little game; nahe~, to suggest, to impress upon; an den Tag ~, to manifest, to evince; sich auf etwas ~, to apply oneself to ; sich ins Mittel ~, to step in, to interpose.
Legende f. (-, -n) legend.
legieren v.t. to alloy; (law) to bequeath.
Legierung f. (-, -en) alloy(ing).
legitim a. legitimate, lawful.
Legitimationspapier n. certificate of identity; ~e pl. identity papers.
legitimieren v.t. to legitimate; sich ~ v. refl. to prove one's identify.
Legitimität f. (-, 0) legitimacy.
Leh(e)n n. (-s, -) fief.
Leh(e)nsrecht n. feudal law.
Lehm m. (-[e]s, -e) loam, clay.
Lehne f. (-, -n) back (of a chair).
lehnen v.t. & i. & refl. (sich) to lean (against).
Lehnsessel, -stuhl m. arm-chair.
Lehr: ~amt n. professorship; ~anstalt f. academy, school.
lehrbar a. teachable.
Lehrbuch n. text-book.
Lehre f. (-, -n) doctrine; instruction, precept; moral, warning; lesson; apprenticeship; in der ~ sein, to serve one's apprenticeship; ~ f. gauge (mech.).
lehren, v.t. to teach, to instruct.

Lehrer m. (-s, -) teacher; tutor.
Lehrerin f. (-, -nen) (female) teacher.
Lehr: ~fach n. subject; ~gang m. course of instruction; ~film m. instructional film; ~jahre n.pl. apprenticeship.
Lehrkörper m. (-s, -) teaching staff.
Lehrling m. (-[e]s, -e) apprentice.
Lehr: ~meister m. instructor; ~mittel n. means of instruction; ~plan m. curriculum.
lehrreich a. instructive.
Lehr: ~satz m. theorem, maxim; ~stuhl m. (professor's) chair; ~zeit f. apprenticeship.
Leib m. (-[e]s, -er) body; (Bauch) belly; sich vom ~ halten, to keep at a distance.
Leib: ~ arzt m. physician in ordinary; ~binde f. (flannel) belt.
Leibchen n. (-s, -) bodice, corsage.
Leibeigene[r] m. (-n, -n) serf.
Leibes: ~erben m.pl. issue; ~frucht f. fœtus.
Leibesübung f. physical exercise.
leiblich a. physical, bodily.
Leibgarde f. body-guard, life-guards pl.
leibhaftig a. real.
leiblich a. physical, bodily.
Leib: ~lied n. favourite ditty; ~rente f. life-annuity; ~schmerzen m.pl. stomach-ache; ~wache f. body-guard.
Leiche f. (-, -n) corpse.
Leichen: ~begängnis, n. funeral, burial; ~beschauer m. coroner.
leichenblass, a deadly pale.
Leichen: -feier f. obsequies, pl.; ~schau f. inquest; ~verbrennung f. cremation.
Leichnam m. (-[e]s, -e) corpse; carcass.
leicht a. light; easy, slight; (Tabak) mild; ~ adv. easily.
Leichtathletik f. athletics pl.
leicht: ~blütig a. sanguine; ~fertig a. light, wanton, frivolous.
Leichter m. (-s, -s) (nav.) lighter.
Leichtgewicht n. (sport) light-weight.
leicht: ~gläubig a. credulous; ~herzig a. light-hearted.
leichthin adv. lightly.
Leichtigkeit f. (-, -en) ease, facility.
leichtlebig a. easy-going.
Leichtmetall n. light metal.
Leichtsinn m. levity, frivolity.
leichtsinnig a. frivolous, light-hearted, heedless.
Leid n. (-[e]s, 0) grief, sorrow; pain, harm; einem etwas zu ~e tun, to harm, to wrong, to hurt one; es tut mir leid, I am sorry (for it).
leiden v.t. & i.st. to suffer, to endure; to tolerate; nicht ~ können, not to be able to stand.
Leiden n. (-s, -) suffering; disease.
Leidenschaft f. (-, -en) passion.
leidenschaftlich a. passionate, vehement.

Leidensgefährte m. fellow-sufferer.
leider adv. unfortunately; ~ i. alas!
leidig a. tiresome, unpleasant.
leidlich a. tolerable.
Leidtragende[r] m. mourner.
leidvoll a. sorrowful.
Leidwesen n. regret.
Leier f. (-, -n) lyre; die alte ~, the old story.
Leierkasten m. barrel-organ.
leiern v.i. to grind a barrel-organ.
Leihbibliothek f. circulating-library.
leihen v.t.st. to lend; to borrow.
Leihhaus n. pawnbroker's shop.
leihweise adv. as a loan, by way of loan.
Leim m. (-[e]s, -e) glue; size; aus dem ~ gehen, to get out of joint; auf den gehen, to fall into the trap.
leimen v.t. to glue; (Papier) to paste.
Leine f. (-, -n) line, cord.
leinen a. linen.
Leinen n. (-s, -) linen (goods) pl.
Leinenband m. (Buch) cloth binding.
Lein: ~öl n. linseed oil; ~samen m. linseed.
Leinwand f. (-, 0) linen; (Maler~) canvas.
Leinwandhändler m. linen-draper.
leise a. low, soft, gentle; ~ adv. softly, in a low voice; ~r reden, to lower one's voice.
Leiste f. (-, -n) ridge, ledge.
Leisten m. (-s, -) last, form; boot tree.
leisten v.t. to do, to perform; (Dienst) to render; (Eid) to take; (Grosses) to achieve (great things); Gesellschaft ~, to keep (someone) company; ich kann mir das ~, I can afford it.
Leisten: ~bruch m. (med.) hernia; ~gegend f. (med.) groin.
Leistung f. (-, -en) performance; accomplishment.
leistungsfähig a. efficient; productive.
Leistungsfähigkeit f. (-, 0) efficiency; productivity; (Maschine) power, (working) capacity.
Leitartikel m. leading-article, leader.
Leitartikler m. (-s, -) leader writer.
leiten v.t. to lead, to guide, to conduct; to manage, to direct.
Leiter m. (-s, -) manager; leader, conductor; (elek.) conductor.
Leiter f. (-, -n) ladder; steps.
Leit: ~fähigkeit f. (elek.) conductivity; ~faden m. (Buch) manual; ~hammel m. bell-wether.
Leitung f. (-, -en) guidance; management; direction; (Röhre) conduit; (elek.) line; die ~ von etwas haben, to be in charge of.
Lektion f. (-, -en) lesson; (fig.) lecture.
Lektüre f. (-, 0) reading; books pl.
Lende f. (-, -n) loin; haunch, thigh.
Lendenbraten m. sirloin; rump of beef.
lenken v.t. to direct, to rule; to steer.
Leuksäule f. (mot.) steering column.

Lenkstange f. (-, -n) handlebar.
Lenz m. (-es, -e) spring.
Leopard m. (-en, -en) leopard.
Lerche f. (-, -n) lark, skylark.
lernbar a. learnable, acquirable by study.
lernen v.t. to learn.
Lesart f. reading, variant.
lesbar a. legible; (fig.) readable.
Lese f. (-, -n) vintage.
Lesebuch n. reader.
lesen v.t. & i.st. to gather, to glean; to read; to lecture; (Messe) to say.
Leser m. (-s, -) reader; gleaner.
leserlich a. legible.
Lesesaal m. reading-room.
Lesung f. (-, -en) reading.
Letter f. (-, -n) letter, type.
letzen sich ~ an, to enjoy, to relish.
letzt a. last, final; ~e Ölung, extreme unction; zu guter Letzt, finally.
letztere[r] a. latter.
letzthin adv. lately, the other day.
letztlich adv. lastly.
letztwillig a. testamentary.
Leuchte f. (-, -n) lamp, lantern; (fig.) shining light.
leuchten v.i. to shine; to beam.
Leuchter m. (-s, -) candlestick; lustre.
Leucht: ~feuer n. beacon; ~käfer m. glow-worm; ~kugel f. fire-ball; ~pfad m. (avi.) flare-path; ~pistole f. Very pistol; ~spurteschoss n. tracer bullet; ~turm m. lighthouse; ~uhr f. luminous watch.
leugnen v.t. to deny, to disown.
Leumundszeugnis n. character, testimony of good conduct.
Leute pl. people, persons pl.; servants, pl.
Leuteschinder m. slave-driver.
Leutnant m. (-[e]s, -s) lieutenant.
leutselig a. affable, condescending.
Levkoje f. (-, -n) stock, gilly flower.
Lexikon n. (-s, Lexika) dictionary.
Libelle f. (-, -n) dragon-fly.
liberal a. liberal; generous, open-handed.
Licht n. (-[e]s, -er u. -e) light; candle; bei ~e, (fig.) closely; ungeschütztes ~, naked light; einem ein ~ aufstecken, to open one's eyes; hinters ~ führen, to dupe, to impose upon; ans ~ bringen, to bring to light; ins rechte ~ setzen, to show in its true colours.
licht a. light, bright; lucid; clear; ~e Höhe f. overhead clearance.
Licht: ~bild n. photograph; lantern slide; ~ervortrag m. lantern lecture; ~blick m. ray of hope; ~bogen m. electric arc; ~bogenschweissung f. arc welding; ~druck m. collotype; ~empfindlich a. (phot.) sensitive.
lichten v.t. (Wald) to clear, to thin; den Anker ~, to weigh anchor.
lichterloh a. blazing.

lichtscheu *a.* (*fig.*) shunning publicity.

Licht: ~**spiele** *n.pl. or* ~**spieltheater** *m.* cinema, pictures, movies; ~**seite** *f.* bright side (of things); ~**strahl** *m.* ray of light, beam.

Lichtung *f.* (-, -en) clearing, glade.

lichtvoll *a.* luminous, lucid.

Lid *n.* (-[e]s, -er) eyelid.

lieb *a.* dear, beloved; agreeable.

liebäugeln *v.i.* to ogle, to make eyes at.

Liebe *f.* (-, 0) love; (*christliche*) charity.

Liebedienerei *f.* (-, -en) time-serving.

liebedienerisch *a.* time-serving.

Liebelei *f.* (-, -en) love-intrigue.

lieben *v.t.* to love; to like; ~ *v.i.* to be in love.

liebenswürdig *a.* amiable, sweet; kind.

Liebenswürdigkeit *f.* (-, -en) kindness; winning ways *pl.*

lieber *adv.* rather, sooner.

Liebes: ~**dienst** *m.* good turn, (act of) kindness; ~**gabe** *f.* present to soldiers in the field; ~**paar** *n.* couple of lovers.

liebevoll *a.* loving.

Liebhaber *m.* (-s, -) lover; amateur.

Liebhaberei *f.* (-, -en) hobby.

Liebhabertheater *n.* private theatricals *pl.*

liebkosen *v.t.* to caress, to fondle.

lieblich *a.* lovely; charming, sweet.

Liebling *m.* (-[e]s, -e) favourite, pet, darling.

Lieblingsbuch *n.* favourite book.

lieblos *a.* unkind, uncharitable.

liebreich *a.* kind, loving.

Liebreiz *m.* charm, attraction.

liebreizend *a.* charming, lovely.

Liebste[r] *m.* (-, -n), **Liebste** *f.* (-n -n) love, lady-love, sweetheart.

Lied *n.* (-[e]s, -er) song, air; (*Kirchen*~) hymn.

liederlich *a.* loose, dissolute, immoral.

Lieferant *m.* (-n, -en) purveyor.

Lieferanteneingang *m.* tradesman's entrance.

liefern *v.t.* to deliver; to furnish; to supply; *eine Schlacht* ~, to give battle.

Lieferschein *m.* delivery note.

Lieferung *f.* (-, -en) delivery, supply; number, part (of a book).

Lieferwagen *m.* delivery van.

Lieferzeit *f.* term of delivery.

Liege: ~**geld** *n.* (*nav.*) demurrage; ~ **kur** rest cure.

liegen *v.i.st.* to lie; to be situated; *vor Anker* ~, to ride at anchor; ~*lassen,* to leave (behind); to leave alone, to give up; *~bleiben,* to be left (unfinished, unsettled); *es liegt an mir,* it is my fault; *es liegt nichts daran,* it's of no consequence; *die Sache liegt ganz anders,* the case is different altogether.

Liegenschaften *pl.* real estate, immovables *pl.*

Liegestuhl *f.* deck-chair.

Liga *f.* (-, 0) league.

Likör *m.* (-[e]s, -e) cordial, liqueur.

lila (*farben*) *a.* lilac.

Lilie *f.* (-, -n) lily; (*Wappen*) fleur-de-lis.

Limonade *f.* (-, -n) lemonade.

Limousine *f.* (-, -n) sedan.

lind *a. & adv.* soft(ly), mild(ly).

Linde *f.* (-, -n) lime-tree, linden.

lindern *v.t.* to soften, to mitigate.

Lineal *n.* (-[e]s, -e) ruler, rule.

Linie *f.* (-, -n) line; lineage, descent; *in absteigender* ~, in the descending line; *in aufsteigender* ~, in the ascending line; *in gerader* ~, in the direct line.

Linien: ~**blatt** *n.* (sheet with) ink lines; ~**papier** *n.* ruled paper.

linieren *v.t.* to rule.

link *a.* left; left hand.

Linke *f.* (-n, 0) left hand or side; (*im Reichstage*) the left.

linkisch *a.* awkward.

links *adv.* to the left; on the left-hand side; ~**händig** *a.* left-handed; ~ *schwenkt marsch!,* left wheel!; ~ *um, kehrt!,* (left) about turn!, (*Am.*) left, face!

Linse *f.* (-, -n) lentil; (*opt.*) lens.

Lippe *f.* (-, -n) lip.

Lippenstift *m.* lipstick.

Liquidationstag *m.* (*Börse*) settling day.

liquidieren *v.t.* to liquidate, to wind up.

lispeln *v.i.* to lisp; to whisper.

List *f.* (-, -en) cunning, craft; trick, stratagem.

Liste *f.* (-, -n) list, roll, catalogue; *von der* ~ *streichen,* to strike off the list.

listig *a.* cunning, crafty, sly, artful.

Litanei *f.* (-, -en) litany.

Liter *n.* (-s, -) litre (= ⅞ quart).

Literarhistoriker *m.* literary historian.

literarisch *a.* literary.

Literat *m.* (-en, -en) man of letters.

Literatur *f.* (-, -en) literature, letters *pl.*

Lithograph *m.* (-en, -en) lithographer.

Liturgie *f.* (-, -n) liturgy.

Litze *f.* (-, -n) lace, tape, braid; (*elek.*) flex(ible).

Litzenbesatz *m.* piping.

Livree *f.* (-, -[e]n) livery.

Lizenz *f.* (-, -en) licence; ~**gebühr** *f.* royalty.

Lizenz: ~**inhaber;** ~**träger** *m.* licensee.

Lob *n.* (-[e]s, 0) praise; commendation.

loben *v.t.* to praise, to commend.

lobenswert *a.* praiseworthy.

Lobgesang *m.* song of praise.

lobhudeln *v.t.* to cry up, to magnify.

löblich *a.* laudable, commendable.

Lobrede *f.* panegyric, eulogy.

Lobredner *m.* panegyrist.

Loch *n.* (-[e]s, Löcher) hole; dungeon.

lochen *v.t.* to perforate, to punch.

Locher *m.* (-s, -) perforator.

löcherig *a.* full of holes, in holes.
Locke *f.* (-, -n) lock, curl, ringlet.
locken *v.t.* to allure, to entice; to curl.
locker *a.* loose; licentious, dissolute.
lockern *v.t.* to loosen.
lockig *a.* curled, curly.
Lockmittel *n.* lure, bait.
Loden *m.* (-s, -) coarse woollen stuff.
lodern *v.i.* to blaze; (*fig.*) to glow (with).
Löffel *m.* (-s, -) spoon; (*Schopf*) ladle.
löffeln *v.t.* to ladle.
Log *n.* (-s, -s) (*nav.*) log.
Logarithmus *m.* (-, -men) logarithm.
Loge *f.* (-, -n) box; (*der Freimaurer*) lodge.
Logenschliesser *m.* box-keeper.
logieren *v.i.* to lodge.
Logik *f.* (-, 0) logic.
Logiker *m.* (-s, -) logician.
logisch *a.* logical.
Lohe *f.* (-, -n) tan; (*Flamme*) flame.
lohen *v.t.* to tan; ~, *v.i.* to blaze.
Lohgerber *m.* tanner.
Lohn *m.* (-[e]s, Löhne), reward; wages *pl.*,
    pay; salary, fee.
Lohn: ~buchhalter *m.* timekeeper; ~em-
    pfänger *m.* wage-earner; ~erhöhung *f.*
    rise; ~schreiber *m.* hack-writer; ~tarif
    m. wage tariff; ~tüte *f.* pay envelope.
lohnen *v.t. & i.* to reward, to recompense,
    to pay; *es lohnt (sich) nicht (der Mühe)*,
    it is not worth while.
lohnend *a.* remunerative.
Löhnung *f.* (-, -en) payment, pay.
Lokal *n.* (-[e]s, -e) locality, place, shop,
    premises *pl.*; (*Gastwirtschaft*) tavern,
    café.
lokalisieren *v.t.* to locate; to prevent from
    spreading.
Lokomotive *f.* (-, -n) (locomotive) engine.
Lokomotivführer *m.* engine-driver.
Lorbeer *m.* (-s, -en) laurel, bay.
Lore *f.* (-, -n) lorry, load.
Lorgnette *f.* (-, -n) eye-glass, lorgnette.
Los *n.* (Loses, Lose) lot, destiny, fate;
    lottery-ticket; *das grosse* ~, the first
    prize.
los *a.* loose, untied; *was ist los?* what is the
    matter? *ich bin es los*, I am rid of it;
    etwas ~ haben, to have the knack; *etwas
    ~kriegen*, to get the hang of a thing.
lösbar *a.* soluble.
losbinden *v.t.st.* to untie.
losbrechen *v.t.st.* to break loose *or* off;
    ~ *v.i.st.* (*s*) to burst out.
Lösch: ~blatt *n.* blotting paper; ~eimer,
    fire-bucket.
löschen *v.t.* to extinguish; (*Durst*) to
    quench; (*Kalk*) to slake; (*Schiff*) to un-
    load; (*Ladung*) to unload.
Löschpapier *n.* blotting-paper.
lose *a.* loose; dissolute, wanton.
Lösegeld *n.* ransom.
losen *v.i.* to cast *or* draw lots.

lösen *v.t.* to loosen, to untie; to free, **to**
    deliver; (*Aufgabe*) to solve; (*Fahrkarte*)
    to take, to get.
losfahren *v.i.st.* (*s*) to fly (at one).
losgehen *v.i.st.* (*s*) to come off; to get
    loose; to go off; to rush upon, to fight;
    to begin, to commence.
loskaufen *v.t.* to redeem, to ransom.
loskommen *v.i.st.* (*s*) to get away.
loslassen *v.t.st.* to let go.
löslich *a.* soluble.
losmachen *v.t.* to disengage, to free.
losplatzen *v.i.* (*s*) to blurt out.
losreissen *v.t.st.* to tear off; to separate;
    (sich) ~ *v.refl.* to tear oneself away.
lossagen (sich) *v.refl.* to renounce.
losschlagen *v.t.st.* to knock off; (*verkaufen*)
    to dispose of, to sell off; ~ *v.i.* to begin
    to fight.
lossprechen *v.t.st.* to absolve.
Lossprechung *f.* (-, -en) absolution.
lossteuern (auf) *v.i.* to make for.
Lösung *f.* (-, -en) solving, loosening; solu-
    tion.
Losung *f.* (-, -en) (*mil.*) password; watch-
    word.
loswickeln *v.t.* to reel off.
losziehen *v.i.st.* (*s*) (*fig.*) to inveigh against
    one.
Lot *n.* (-[e]s, -e) half an ounce; plummet,
    lead; solder.
loten *v.i.* to take soundings.
löten *v.t.* to solder.
lotrecht *a.* perpendicular.
Lötrohr *n.* blowpipe.
Lotse *m.* (-n, -n) pilot.
lotsen *v.t.* to pilot; (*fig.*) to take in
    tow.
Lotsengebühr *f.* pilotage.
Lotterie *f.* (-, -[e]n) lottery.
Lotterielos *n.* lottery ticket.
Löwe *m.* (-n, -n) lion.
Löwen: ~anteil *m.* the lion's share;
    ~maul *n.* (*bot.*) snap-dragon; ~zahn *m.*
    (*bot.*) dandelion.
Löwin *f.* (-, -nen) lioness.
Luchs *m.* (Luchses, Luchse) lynx.
Lücke *f.* (-, -n) gap; (*fig.*) void, blank;
    omission, deficiency, hiatus.
Lückenbüsser *m.* (-s, -) stop-gap.
lückenhaft *a.* defective, fragmentary.
lückenlos *a.* without a gap.
Luder *n.* (-s, -) wretch, hussy.
Luft *f.* (-, Lüfte) air; breath; breeze;
    frische ~ *schöpfen*, to take the air; *in
    die* ~ *sprengen*, to blow up.
Luft: ~angriff *m.* air raid; ~aufklärung *f.*
    (*mil.*) air reconnaissance; ~aufnahme
    f., ~bild *n.* air photograph.
Lüftchen *n.* (-s, -) breeze.
luftdicht *a.* air-tight, hermetic.
Luft: ~druck *m.* atmospheric pressure;
    ~druckbremse *f.* pneumatic brake.

lüften *v.t.* to air, to ventilate; to raise, to lift up.

Luft: ~**fahrtgesellschaft** *f.* airline; ~**geschwindigkeitsmesser** *m.* airspeed indicator.

luftig *a.* airy; (*dress*) thin.

luftleer *a.* void of air; ~*er Raum*, vacuum.

Luft: ~**kurort** *m.* climatic health resort; ~**linie(nentfernung)** *f.* as the crow flies; ~**loch** *n.* air pocket; ~**post** *f.* airmail; ~**röhre** *f.* windpipe; ~**schiff** *n.* airship; ~**schiffahrt** *f.* aeronautics; ~**schloss** *n.* (*fig.*) castle in the air; ~**schraube** *f.* propeller; ~**schraubenblatt** *n.* propeller blade; ~**schutz** *m.* air raid protection (ARP); ~**schutzanzug** *m.* siren suit; ~**schutzwart** *m.* air-raid warden; ~**störungen** *pl.* (*Radio*), atmospherics.

Lüftung *f.* (-, -en) airing, ventilation.

Luftveränderung *f.* change of air.

Lug *m.* (-[e]s, 0) lying, lie.

Lüge *f.* (-, -n) lie, falsehood.

lugen *v.i.* to look out, to peep.

lügen *v.i.st.* to lie, to tell a lie.

lügenhaft *a.* lying, false, mendacious.

Lügner *m.* (-s, -) liar.

lügnerisch *a.* lying, false.

Luke *f.* (-, -n) (*nav.*) hatch(way).

lullen *v.t. & i.* to lull (to sleep).

Lümmel *m.* (-s, -) ruffian, lubber, lout.

lümmelhaft *a.* lubberly, loutish.

Lump *m.* (-[e]s, -e) rascal, blackguard.

Lumpen *m.* (-s, -) rag, tatter.

Lumpensammler *m.* rag-picker.

Lumperei *f.* (-, -en) trash.

lumpig *a.* (*fig.*) shabby, paltry.

Lunge *f.* (-, -n) lung[s]; lights (of animals) *pl.*

Lungen: ~**entzündung** *f.* pneumonia; ~**flügel** *m.* lobe of the lung; ~**schwindsucht** *f.* consumption.

lungern *v.i.* to idle, to lounge, to skulk.

Lunte *f.* (-, -n) match; ~ *riechen* (*fam.*) to smell a rat.

Lupe *f.* (-, -n) magnifying-glass.

Lupine *f.* (-, -n) (*bot.*) lupin.

Lust *f.* (-, Lüste) joy, delight; inclination; desire, lust; *keine* ~ *zu etwas haben*, to have no mind (for, to...).

Lustbarkeit *f.* (-, -en) amusement, sport.

lüstern *a.* desirous, longing (for); (*sinnlich*) lascivious, lustful.

lustig *a.* gay, merry, cheerful; funny, droll; *sich über einen* ~ *machen*, to make fun of one, to laugh at one.

Lust: ~**mord** *m.* murder and rape; ~**schloss** *n.* country-seat; ~**seuche** *f.* venereal disease, syphilis; ~**spiel** *n.* comedy.

lustwandeln *v.i.* (*h u. s*) to take a walk.

lutherisch *a.* Lutheran.

Luthertum *n.* (-s, 0) Lutheranism.

lutschen *v.i.* to suck.

Luvseite *f.* (*nav.*) weather-side.

luxuriös *a.* luxurious.

Luxus *m.* (-, 0) luxury.

Luxus... de luxe, *a.*

Luxuszug, *m.* saloon-train.

Luzerne *f.* (-, -n) (*bot.*) lucern.

Lymphe *f.* (-, -n) lymph.

lynchen *v.t.* to lynch.

Lyrik *f.* (-, 0) lyric poetry.

Lyriker *m.* (-s, -) lyric poet.

lyrisch *a.* lyric.

Lysol *n.* (-s, 0) lysol(e).

Lyzeum *n.* (-s, -zeen) high schoo for girls.

M

Maat *m.* (-[e]s, -e) (*nav.*) (ship-)mate, petty officer.

Machart *f.* (-, -en) style.

Mache *f.* (-, 0) making, workmanship.

machen *v.t.* to make; to do; *was macht das?* how much is it?; *das macht nichts*, that does not matter; *die Rechnung macht so und so viel*, it comes to so much in all; *Licht* ~, to strike a light; *Ernst* ~ *mit etwas*, to be in earnest about a thing; *zu Gelde* ~, to sell, to turn into money; *sich auf den Weg* ~, to set out; *sich daraus nichts* ~, not to care about it.

Machenschaften *pl.* machinations *pl.*

Macht *f.* (-, Mächte) power; might; forces.

Macht: ~**befugnis** *f.* competence; ~**bereich** *m.* sphere of power.

Machthaber *m.* (-s, -) potentate, ruler.

mächtig *a.* powerful; mighty.

machtlos *a.* powerless.

Macht: ~**vollkommenheit** *f.* absolute power, authority; ~**wort** *n.* word of command.

Machwerk *n.* bungling work.

Mädchen *n.* (-s, -) girl; maid, lass; servant; ~ *für alles*, maid-of-all-work.

Mädchenname *m.* (*der Frau*) maiden name.

Made *f.* (-, -n) maggot, mite.

Mädel = **Mädchen.**

Magazin *n.* (-[e]s, -e) store; (*Zeitschrift*) magazine.

Magd *f.* (-, Mägde) maid-servant.

Magen *m.* (-s, -) stomach.

Magenbeschwerden *pl.* indigestion, dyspepsia.

magenleidend *a.* suffering from a disorder of the stomach.

Magen: ~**pumpe** *f.* stomach pump; ~**säure** *f.* (gastric) acid.

mager *a.* lean, thin; meagre.

Magermilch *f.* skimmed milk.

Magie *f.* (-, 0) magic.

Magier *m.* (-s, -) magician.

magisch *a.* magical.
Magistrat *m.* (-[e]s, -e) mayor and alder-men, corporation.
Magnet *m.* (-[e]s, -e) magnet.
magnetisch *a.* magnetic.
magnetisieren *v.t.* to magnetize.
Magnetismus *m.* (-, 0) magnetism.
Magnetnadel, *f.* magnetic needle.
Magnetzünder *m.* (*mot.*) magneto.
Mahagoni *n.* (-s, 0) mahogany.
mähen *v.t.* to mow.
Mahl *n.* (-[e]s, -e *u.* Mähler) meal, repast.
mahlen *v.t.st.* to grind.
Mahlzeit *f.* meal, repast.
Mähmaschine *f.* mower, reaping machine.
Mähne *f.* (-, -n) mane.
mahnen *v.t.* to remind, to admonish.
Mahnung *f.* (-, -en) admonition.
Mähre *f.* (-, -n) mare; (*Schind.*) jade.
Mai *m.* (- *u.* -[e]s, -e) May.
Maibaum *m.* May-pole; birch.
Maid *f.* (-, 0) (*poet.*) maid.
Mai: ~glöckchen *n.* lily of the valley; ~käfer *m.* cockchafer.
Mais *m.* (- *u.* -ses, 0) maize, Indian corn.
Majestät *f.* (-, -en) majesty.
majestätisch *a.* majestic.
Major *m.* (-[e]s, -e) major.
Majorat *n.* (-[e]s, -e) entail(ed estate); primogeniture.
majorenn *a.* of age.
Majorität *f.* (-, 0) majority.
Makel *m.* (-s, -) spot; blemish.
makellos *a.* unblemished.
mäkeln *v.i.* to find fault (with).
Makler *m.* (-s, -) broker; middle-man.
Maklergebühr *f.* brokerage.
Makrele *f.* (-, -n) mackerel.
Makrone *f.* (-, -n) macaroon.
Makulatur *f.* (-, -en) waste-paper.
Mal *n.* (-[e]s, -e) time; mark, sign, monu-ment; (*am Körper*) mole; *einmal*, once; *noch einmal*, once more; *auf einmal*, at once; *ein für allemal*, once for all.
mal *adv.* once, just.
malen *v.t.* to paint; to portray; *sich ~ lassen*, to sit for one's portrait.
Maler *m.* (-s, -) painter, artist.
Malerei *f.* (-, -en) painting; picture.
malerisch *a.* picturesque.
Malkasten *m.* paint-box.
Malter *m. & n.* (-s, -) (*Getreidemass*) twelve bushels.
malträtieren *v.t.* to maltreat, (*Am.*) to mistreat.
Malz *n.* (-es, 0) malt.
malzen *v.i.* to malt.
Mälzer *m.* (-s, -) maltster.
Mama *f.* (-, -s) mamma; (*fam.*) ma.
Mammut *n.* (-s, -s) mammoth.
man *pn.* they, people, one.
mancher, manche, manches *pn.* many a, many a man; *manche pl.* some.

mancherlei *a.* various, divers.
manchmal *adv.* sometimes.
Mandant *m.* (-en, -en) client.
Mandarine *f.* tangerine.
Mandat *n.* (-[e]s, -e) mandate, commis-sion, writ.
Mandel *f.* (-, -n) almond; (*anat.*) tonsil.
Mandelentzündung *f.* tonsillitis.
Mandoline *f.* (-, -n) mandolin.
Mangan *n.* (-[e]s, 0) manganese.
Mangel *f.* (-, -n) mangle.
Mangel *m.* (-s, Mängel) want; deficiency; defect; shortage.
mangelhaft *a.* incomplete; defective.
mangeln *v.t.* to mangle; ~ *v.i.* to want.
mangels *p.* in default of.
Mangelware *f.* goods in short supply *pl.*
Manie *f.* (-, -[e]n) mania.
Manier *f.* (-, -en) manner.
manieriert *a.* affected, mannered.
manierlich *a.* mannerly, polite, civil.
Manifest *n.* (-[e]s, -e) manifesto.
Maniküre *f.* manicure; ~n *v.t.* to mani-cure.
Mann *m.* (-[e]s, Männer) man; husband.
mannbar *a.* marriageable.
Männchen *n.* (-s, -) (*von Tieren*) male; (*von Vögeln*) cock.
mannhaft *a.* manly, manful, stout.
mannigfach, mannigfaltig *a.* manifold.
Mannigfaltigkeit *f.* (-, 0) variety.
männlich *a.* male; (*gram.*) masculine; (*fig.*) manly.
Mannschaft *f.* (-, -en) (*Schiffs~*) crew (*Sport*) team.
Mannschaftstransportwagen *m.* (*mil.*) per-sonnel carrier.
mannstoll *a.* nymphomaniac.
Mannweib *n.* virago, amazon.
Manöver *n.* (-s, -) manœuvre.
manövrieren *v.i.* to manœuvre.
Mansarde *f.* (-, -n) attic, garret; mansard-roof.
manschen *v.i.* to dabble, to paddle; to mix.
Manschette *f.* (-, -n) cuff.
Manschettenknopf *m.* sleeve link.
Mantel *m.* (-s, Mäntel) overcoat, mantle; cloak; outer cover of a tyre.
Manufaktur *f.* (-, -en) manufactory.
Manuskript *n.* (-[e]s, -e) manuscript.
Mappe *f.* (-, -n) brief-case, portfolio; satchel.
Märchen *n.* (-s, -) (fairy-)tale; fable, fiction; (*Lüge*) fib.
märchenhaft *a.* fabulous, legendary.
Marder *m.* (-s, -) marten.
Margarine *f.* (-, -n) margarine.
Marienkäfer *m.* ladybird.
Marine *f.* (-, -n) marine, navy.
Marine: ~minister *m.* Navy Minister; First Lord of the Admiralty; ~offizier *m.* naval officer; ~werft *f.* navy-yard.
marinieren *v.t.* to pickle.

Marionette *f.* (-, -n) (wire-)puppet.

Marionettentheater *n.* puppet show.

Mark *n.* (-[e]s, 0) marrow, pith; ~ *j.* (-, -en) border, marches *pl.*; district; (*Münze*) Mark.

Marke *f.* (-, -n) brand; (*Brief~*) (postage-) stamp; (*Spiel~*) counter.

Markenartikel *m.* proprietary article.

Marketenderin *f.* (-, -nen) canteen woman.

markieren *v.t.* to mark.

markig *a.* pithy, marrowy.

Markise *f.* (-, -n) awning.

Markstein *m.* boundary stone.

Markt *m.* (-e[s], Märkte) market; market-place; mart; *auf den ~ bringen,* to place on the market; *auf den ~ kommen,* to come into the market.

Marktbericht *m.* market report.

Marktflecken *m.* market town.

marktgängig *a.* current.

marktschreierisch *a.* puffing.

Marmelade *f.* (-, -n) jam; (*Apfelsinen~* marmalade.

Marmor *m.* (-s, 0) marble.

marmorn *a.* marble.

marode *a.* knocked-up, dog-weary.

Marodeur *m.* (-s, -e) marauder.

Marone *f.* (-, -n) edible chestnut.

Maroquin *m.* (-s, 0) morocco (-leather).

Marotte *f.* (-, -n) fad.

Marquise *f.* (-, -n) marchioness.

marsch! *i.* march!; be off! get out!

Marsch *m.* (-es, Märsche) march.

Marsch *f.* (-, -en) (salt-)marsh, fen.

Marschall *m.* (-[e]s, -schälle) marshal.

Marschallsstab *m.* marshal's baton.

Marschbefehl *m.* marching-order.

marschieren *v.i.* (*h u. s*) to march.

Marssegel *n.* topsail.

Marstall *m.* (-[e]s, ~ställe) royal stables *pl.*

Marter *f.* (-, -n) torture.

Marterkammer *f.* torture-chamber.

martern *v.t.* to rack, to torture.

martialisch *a.* martial.

Märtyrer *m.* (s, -) martyr.

Martyrium *n.* (-s, 0) martyrdom.

März *m.* (- *u.* -en, -e) March.

Marzipan *m.* (-s, -e) marzipan.

Masche *f.* (-, -n) mesh; stitch (in knitting).

Maschine *f.* (-, -n) machine, engine.

Maschinen: ~bauer *m.* mechanical engineer; ~gewehr *n.* machine-gun; ~gewehrnest *n.* pillbox; ~pistole *f.* sub-machine-gun, tommy-gun; ~schrift *f.* typewriting, typescript.

Maschinerie *f.* (-, -[e]n) machinery.

Maschinist *m.* (-en, -en) machinist.

Maser *f.* (-, -n) spot, speckle; (*Holz*) vein, grain; ~n *pl.* measles *pl.*

masern *v.t.* to vein, to grain.

Maske *f.* (-, -n) mask.

Masken: ~anzug *m.* fancy-dress; ~ball *m.* fancy-dress ball.

Maskerade *f.* (-, -n) masquerade.

maskieren (sich) *v.t.* & *refl.* to mask; to disguise oneself.

Mass *n.* (-es, -e) measure; (*fig.*) moderation; ~ *halten,* to observe moderation; *nach ~,* to measure; ~ *nehmen,* to take a person's measurement(s).

Mass *f.* (-, -e) quart, pot.

Massage *f.* massage.

Masse *f.* (-, -n) mass, bulk; large quantity, multitude.

Masseinheit *f.* unit of measurement.

Massen: ~artikel *pl.* staple goods; ~erzeugung *f.* mass production.

massenhaft *a.* wholesale.

Massenproduktion *f.* mass production.

massenweise *adv.* in large quantities.

Massgabe *f. nach ~,* according to.

massgearbeitet *a.* made-to-measure.

massgebend *a.* authoritative; standard.

mässig *a.* moderate; frugal; ~e Preise *pl.* reasonable prices.

massieren *v.t.* to massage.

mässigen *v.t.* to moderate; to temper.

Mässigkeit *f.* (-, 0) temperance, frugality.

Mässigung *f.* (-, 0) moderation; self-control.

massiv *a.* massive, solid.

Masskrug *m.* quart, tankard.

masslos *a.* immoderate, boundless.

Mass: ~nahme, ~regel *f.* measure; ~n *treffen,* to take measures; ~stab *m.* measure; scale; standard.

massregeln *v.t.* to take measures against somebody.

Masschneider *m.* bespoke tailor.

massvoll *a.* moderate, measured.

Mast *m.* (-es, -en) mast; (*elek.*) pylon.

Mast *f.* (-, -en) fattening; food, mast.

Mast: ~baum *m.* mast; ~darm *m.* rectum.

mästen *v.t.* to feed, to fatten.

Mast: ~korb *m.* top, masthead, crow's nest; ~vieh *n.* beef cattle.

Material *n.* (-[e]s, -ien) material.

Materialismus *m.* (-, 0) materialism.

Materialist *m.* (-en, -en) materialist.

Materie *f.* (-, -n) matter; subject.

materiell *a.* material; worldly.

Mathematik *f.* (-, 0) mathematics *pl.*

Mathematiker *m.* (-s, -) mathematician.

mathematisch *f.* mathematical.

Matinée *f.* matinée.

Matratze *f.* (-, -n) mattress.

Matratzenbezug *m.* ticking.

Mätresse *f.* (-, -n) mistress.

Matrikel *f.* (-, -n) register, roll.

Matrize *f.* (-, -n) matrix; (*Stempel*) die.

Matrose *m.* (-n, -n) sailor, mariner.

Matsch *m.* (-[e]s, 0) mud.

matt *a.* tired, feeble, languid, faint; (*Gold*) dull; (*Schach*) (check-)mate ;~ *setzen,* to mate.

Matte *f.* (-, -n) mat; alpine meadow.

Mattglas n. frosted glass.

mattherzig a. faint-hearted.

Mattscheibe f. (*phot.*) ground glass or disc.

Mauer f. (-, -n) wall.

Mauerblümchen n. wallflower.

mauern v.t. to make a wall, to build.

Maul n. (-[e]s, Mäuler) mouth; *das ~ halten,* to hold one's tongue, to shut up.

Maulbeere f. mulberry.

Maulesel m. mule; hinney.

Maul: **~korb** m. muzzle; **~tier** n. mule; **~und Klauenseuche** f. foot-and-mouth disease; **~wurf** m. mole; **~wurfshaufen,** **~wurfshügel** m. mole-hill.

Maurer m. (-s, -) mason, bricklayer.

Maus f. (-, Mäuse) mouse.

mauscheln v.i. to talk like a Jew.

mäuschenstill a. stock still.

Mausefalle f. mouse-trap.

mausen v.t. to pilfer; *~ v.i.* to catch mice, to mouse.

mausern (sich) v.refl. to moult.

Maximal… maximum, a.

Mäzen m. (-[e]s, -e) patron of arts.

Mechanik f. (-, -en) mechanics pl.; mechanism.

Mechaniker m. (-s, -) mechanician.

mechanisch a. & adv. mechanical(ly); by rote.

meckern v.i. to bleat; (*fig.*) to grumble.

Medaille f. (-, -n) medal; locket.

Medikament n. (-[e]s, -e) medicine.

Medizin f. (-, -en) medicine; physic.

Mediziner m. (-s, -) medical man or student.

medizinisch a. medical; medicinal; **~es Gutachten** n. medical opinion.

Meer n. (-[e]s, -e) sea, ocean; *offenes ~,* main, high sea.

Meer: **~busen** m. bay, gulf; **~enge** f. straits pl.

Meeres: **~boden** m. sea-bed; **~spiegel** m. sea-level.

Meer: **~rettich** m. horse-radish; **~schaum** m. meerschaum; **~schweinchen** n. guinea-pig.

Megahertz n. (*elek.*) megacycle.

Megaphon n. (-s, -e) megaphone.

Mehl n. (-[e]s, 0) meal; (*feines*) flour.

Mehlbrei m. porridge, pap.

Mehlspeise f. pudding.

mehlig a. mealy, farinaceous; (*Früchte*) sleepy.

mehr a. & adv. more; *um so ~,* so much the more; *nicht ~,* no more, no longer; *immer ~,* more and more; *nicht ~ als,* not exceeding.

Mehr: **~bedarf** m. extra requirement; **~betrag** m. surplus.

mehrdeutig a. ambiguous.

Mehreinnahme f. increased receipts pl.

mehren v.t. to increase, to augment; (sich) *~ v.refl.* to multiply.

mehrere a.pl. several.

mehrfach a. & adv. repeated(ly).

Mehrheit f. (-, -en) majority, plurality.

Mehrkosten pl. extra expense.

mehrmalig a. repeated.

mehrmals adv. several times.

mehrseitig a. multilateral.

mehrstimmig a. (*mus.*) arranged for several voices.

Mehrzahl f. plural (number); majority.

meiden v.t.st. to avoid, to shun.

Meile f. (-, -n) mile.

meilenweit adv. for miles; miles off.

Meiler m. (-s, -) charcoal-pile.

mein, meine, mein pn. my; mine; *Streit um das ~ und dein,* contention for the *meum* and *tuum*; *~esgleichen,* people like me.

Meineid m. perjury.

meineidig a. perjured.

meinen v.t.st. to mean, to think.

meinethalben, meinetwegen adv. for aught I care.

meinige (*der, die, das*) a. mine.

Meinung f. (-, -en) opinion; meaning; intention; *nach meiner ~,* in my opinion.

Meinungsverschiedenheit f. divergence of opinion.

Meise f. (-, -n) titmouse, tomtit.

Meissel m. (-s, -) chisel.

meisseln v.t. to chisel, to carve.

meist adv. most, mostly.

Meistbegünstigungsklausel f. most-favoured-nation clause.

Meistbietende[r] (-n, -n) highest bidder.

meistens adv. mostly, generally.

meistenteils adv. for the most part.

Meister m. (-s, -) master; (sport) champion.

meisterhaft a. masterly.

meistern v.t. to master; to surpass.

Meisterschaft f. (-, 0) mastery, perfection; (sport) championship.

Meister: **~stück** n. master-piece; **~werk** n. masterly work.

Meistgebot n. (-es, -e) highest bid.

Melancholie f. (-, 0) melancholy.

melancholisch a. melancholy.

Melasse f. (-, 0) molasses pl.

Melde: **~amt** n. police registration office; **~formular** n. report form; **~gänger** m. (*mil.*) dispatch rider; **~hund** m. messenger dog.

melden v.t. to notify, to announce; (sich) *~ v.refl.* to register; *sich ~ lassen,* to send in one's name; *sich zu etwas ~,* to enter for.

Meldesammelstelle f. (*mil.*) message centre.

Meldung f. (-, -en) report; mention, announcement, notification; entry.

melken *v.t.st.* to milk.
Melodie *f.* (-, -[e]n) melody; tune; air.
melodisch *a.* melodious, tuneful.
Melone *f.* (-, -n) melon.
Meltau *m.* (-[e]s, 0) mildew.
Membran *f.* (-, -e) membrane.
Menagerie *f.* (-, -[e]n) menagerie.
Menge *f.* (-, -n) multitude; quantity; great deal, lots *pl.*; a great many.
mengen *v.t.* to mix, to mingle.
Mennig *m.* (-s, 0) red-lead, minium.
Mensch *m.* (-en, -en) man, human being; ~ *n.* (-es, -er) hussy, wench.
Menschen: ~fresser *m.* cannibal; maneater; ~freund *m.* philanthropist.
menschenfreundlich *a.* humane, philanthropic.
Menschen: ~gedenken *n.* memory of man; *seit* ~, time out of mind; ~hass *m.* misanthropy; ~kenner *m.* judge of human nature.
menschenleer *a.* deserted.
Menschenliebe *f.* philanthropy, charity.
menschenmöglich *a.* in the power of man.
Menschen: ~opfer *n.* human sacrifice; ~recht *n.* right of man.
menschenscheu *a.* shy, unsociable.
Menschheit *f.* (-, 0) human race, mankind; humanity.
menschlich *a.* human; *(mild)* humane.
Menschlichkeit *f.* (-, 0) humanity.
Mensur *f.* (-, -en) students' fencing match.
Menuett *n.* (-[e]s, -e) minuet.
Mergel *m.* (-s, -) marl.
Meridian *m.* (-s, -e) meridian.
merkbar *a.* perceptible.
Merkblatt *n.* instructional pamphlet, booklet.
merken *v.t.* to note, to perceive; to remember; ~ *lassen*, to betray; to show.
merklich *a.* noticeable.
Merkmal *n.* (-[e]s, -e) mark, sign.
merkwürdig *a.* remarkable; curious.
Merkwürdigkeit *f.* (-, -en) curiosity.
Mesner *m.* (-s, -) sacristan.
Messband *n.* tape measure.
messbar *a.* measurable.
Messbuch *n.* missal.
Messe *f.* (-, -n) mass; fair; *(nav. & mil.)* mess; *stille* ~, low mass; ~ *lesen*, to say mass.
messen *v.t.st.* to measure.
Messer *n.* (-s, -) knife; ~ *m.* meter.
Messer: ~schmied *m.* cutler; ~stiel *m.* knife-handle.
Messing *n.* (-s, 0) brass.
Messung *f.* (-, -en) mensuration.
Met *m.* (-[e]s, 0) mead.
Metall *n.* (-[e]s, -e) metal.
metallen *a.* (of) metal.
Metallfutter *n.* *(mech.)* bush.
metallisch *a.* metallic.

Metallsäge *f.* *(mech.)* hacksaw.
Metallwaren *f.pl.* hardware.
Metapher *f.* (-, -n) metaphor.
Metaphysik *f.* (-, 0) metaphysics *pl.*
Meteor *m.* (-s, -e) meteor.
Meteorolog *m.* (-en, -en) meteorologist.
Meter *n. & m.* (-s, -) metre.
Methode *f.* (-, -n) method.
methodisch *a.* methodical.
Metrik *f.* (-, 0) prosody.
metrisch *a.* metrical; ~es System *n.* metric system.
Metrum *n.* (-s, Metra *u.* Metren) metre.
Mette *f.* (-, -n) matins *pl.*
Mettwurst *f.* (kind of) smoked mince sausage.
Metzelei *f.* (-, -en) massacre, butchery.
metzeln *v.t.* to massacre, to butcher.
Metzger *m.* (-s, -) butcher.
Meuchel: ~mord *m.* assassination; ~mörder *m.* assassin.
meuchlings *adv.* treacherously.
Meute *f.* (-, -n) pack of hounds.
Meuterei *f.* (-, -en) mutiny.
Meuterer *m.* (-s, -) mutineer.
meuterisch *a.* mutinous.
meutern *v.i.* to mutiny, to revolt.
mich, *pn.acc.* me.
Mieder *n.* (-s, -) bodice, corsage.
Miene *f.* (-, -en) mien, air, countenance; ~ *machen*, to threaten (to do).
mies *a.* *(sl.)* bad, rotten.
Miesmacher *m.* (-s, -) defeatist.
Miete *f.* (-, -n) rent; hire; stack, rick.
Mieteinigungsamt *n.* rent tribunal.
mieten *v.t.* to hire, to rent; to take; *(Schiff)* to charter.
Mieter *m.* (-s, -) tenant, lodger.
mietfrei *a.* rent-free.
Miets: ~flugzeug *n.* taxi plane; ~truppen *pl.* hired troops, mercenaries.
Mietsumme *f.* rental.
mietweise *adv.* on hire.
Miet: ~(s)wohnung *f.* hired house *or* lodgings; ~zins *m.* house-rent.
Migräne *f.* (-, 0) sick headache.
Mikrometer *m.* (-s, -) micrometer.
Mikrophon *n.* (-s, -e) microphone.
Mikroskop *n.* (-[e]s, -e) microscope.
mikroskopisch *a.* microscopic(al).
Milbe *f.* (-, -n) mite.
Milch *f.* (-, 0) milk; *(der Fische)* milt.
Milch: ~halle *f.* milk bar; ~strasse *f.* milky way, galaxy; ~zahn *m.* milktooth.
mild *a.* mild, soft, gentle; liberal, charitable.
Milde *f.* (-, 0) softness, mildness.
mildern *v.t.* to mitigate, to soften.
mildernd *a.* extenuating; ~e Umstände *pl.* extenuating circumstances.
Milderung *f.* (-, -en) mitigation.
mildtätig *a.* charitable.

Militär n. (-[e]s, 0) military, soldiery.

Militär m. (-[e]s, -s) military man.

Militär: -regierung f. military government; ~strafgesetzbuch n. military code.

militärisch a. military.

Miliz f. (-, -en) militia.

Milliarde f. (-, -n) milliard (a thousand millions), (Am.) billion.

Million f. (-, -en) million.

Millionär m. (-s, -e) millionaire.

Milz f. (-, -en) milt, spleen.

Milzbrand m. anthrax.

Milzsucht f. (-, 0) spleen.

minder a. less; minor, inferior.

Minderheit f. (-, -en) minority.

minderjährig a. under age, minor.

mindern v.t. to diminish, to lessen, to abate; (sich) ~ v.refl. to decrease.

Minderung f. (-, -en) diminution, decrease.

minderwertig a. (of) inferior (quality).

Minderzahl f. minority.

mindest a. least, lowest; zum ~en, at (the) least, to say the least.

mindestens adv. at least.

Mindestmass, n. minimum (size).

Mine f. (-, -n) mine.

Minen: -feld n. minefield; ~sucher m. minesweeper.

Mineral n. (-[e]s, -e u. -ien) mineral.

mineralisch a. mineral.

Mineralogie f. (-, 0) mineralogy.

Mineralreich n. mineral kingdom.

Miniaturgemälde n. miniature.

minieren v.t. to (under)mine, to sap.

minimal a., Minimal…minimum a.

Minister m. (-s, -) minister (of State).

Minister: -präsident m. Prime Minister; ~rat m. Cabinet Council.

Ministerium n. (-s, Ministerien) ministry.

Minne f. (-, 0) love.

minorenn a. under age.

Minute f. (-, -n) minute.

Minutenzeiger m. minute-hand.

Minze f. (-, 0) mint.

mir pn. me, to me.

Mischehe f. mixed marriage (between persons of different creeds).

mischen v.t. to mix, to blend; (Karten) to shuffle.

Mischling m. (-s, -e) hybrid, mongrel, half-caste.

Mischmasch m. (-es, -e) medley.

Mischung f. (-, -en) mixture, blend.

miserabel a. wretched, miserable.

missachten v.t. to disregard, to slight.

Missachtung f. (-, 0) disregard; ~ des Gerichtes, contempt of court.

Missbehagen n. (-s, 0) uneasiness.

missgebildet a. malformed.

Missbildung f. (-, -en) deformity, malformation.

missbilligen v.t. to disapprove (of).

Missbilligung f. (-, 0) disapproval.

Missbrauch m. (-[e]s, -bräuche) abuse; misuse.

missbrauchen v.t. to misuse, to abuse.

missdeuten v.t. to misinterpret.

Missdeutung f. (-, -en) misconstruction.

missen v.i. to miss, to want.

Misserfolg m. (-[e]s, -e) failure.

Missernte f. (-, -n) bad harvest.

Missetat f. (-, -en) misdeed, crime.

Missetäter m. (-s, -) malefactor, criminal.

missfallen v.i.st. to displease.

Missfallen n. (-s, 0) displeasure.

missfällig a. displeasing.

Missgeburt f. (-, -en) monster, abortion.

Missgeschick n. (-[e]s, -e) mishap, misfortune.

missglücken v.i. (s) to fail, to miscarry.

missgönnen v.t. to grudge, to envy.

Missgriff m. (-[e]s, -e) mistake, blunder.

Missgunst f. (-, 0) ill-will, grudge, envy.

missgünstig a. envious, jealous.

misshandeln v.t. to ill-treat, to maltreat, (Am.) to mistreat.

Misshandlung f. ill usage, illtreatment, maltreatment.

Missheirat f. (-, -en) misalliance.

Missheiligkeit f. (-, -en) difference, misunderstanding, dissension.

Mission f. (-, -en) mission.

Missionar m. (-s, -e) missionary.

Missklang m. (-[e]s, -klänge) dissonance.

Misskredit m. (-[e]s, 0) disrepute.

misslich a. awkward.

missliebig a. unpopular, objectionable.

misslingen v.i.st. (s) to fail, to miscarry.

Missmut m. (-[e]s, low spirits pl.

missmutig a. discouraged, dejected.

missraten v.i.st. (s) to miscarry.

Miss: ~ stand m. (-[e]s, -stände) nuisance.

Miss: ~ stimmung f. (-, -en) bad temper.

Misston m. (-[e]s, -töne) false note.

misstrauen v.i. to distrust.

Misstrauen n. (-s, 0) distrust.

Misstrauensvotum n. vote of censure.

misstrauisch a. suspicious; diffident.

missvergnügt a. discontented.

Missverhältnis n. (-nisses, -nisse) disproportion; incongruity.

Missverständnis n. (-nisses, -nisse) misunderstanding.

missverstehen v.t.st. to misunderstand.

Mist m. (-es, 0) dung, manure.

Mistel f. (-, -n) mistletoe.

misten v.t. to manure; ~ v.i. to dung.

Mist: ~gabel f. dung-fork; ~haufen m. dung-hill; ~käfer m. dung beetle.

Miszellen f.pl. miscellanies, scraps pl.

mit pr. with; by, at; ~ der Post, by post; ~ der Zeit, in time; ~einander, together, jointly; ~ dabei sein, to make one (of a party).

mitarbeiten *v.i.* to collaborate, to co-operate.

Mitarbeiter *m.* fellow-worker, collaborator, colleague, associate.

Mitbesitzer *m.* joint-proprietor.

Mitbewerber *m.* competitor.

mitbringen *v.t.ir.* to bring (along with one).

Mitbruder *m.* (-s, -brüder) fellow.

Mitbürger *m.* fellow-citizen.

Miteigentümer *m.* (-s, -) joint owner.

miteinander *adv.* together.

mitempfinden *v.t.st.* to sympathize in.

Miterbe *m.* co-heir, joint-heir.

Mitesser *m.* pimple, blackhead.

mitfühlen *v.i.* to sympathize (with).

Mitgefühl *n.* sympathy.

mitgehen *v.i.st.* (s) to go along (with), to come (with one).

Mitgift *f.* dowry, portion.

Mitglied *n.* member; fellow.

Mitgliedschaft *f.* membership.

Mitglieds: ~beitrag *m.* membership subscription; ~karte *f.* membership card.

mithelfen *v.i.st.* to lend a hand.

Mithilfe *f.* assistance, co-operation.

mithin *c.* consequently.

Mitkämpfer *m.* fellow-combatant.

mitklingen *v.i.st.* to resonate.

Mitläufer *m.* (-s, -) 'fellow-traveller' (*einer Partei*).

Mitlaut[er] *m.* (-s, -) consonant.

Mitleid *n.* compassion, pity.

Mitleidenschaft *f.* implication in another's loss *or* damage; *einen in ~ ziehen*, to implicate another in one's misfortune *or* loss.

mitleidig *a.* compassionate.

mitleidlos *a.* pitiless, ruthless.

mitmachen *v.i.* to take part in.

Mitmensch *m.* fellow-man *or* -creature.

mitnehmen *v.t.st.* to take along with one; (*fig.*) to weaken, to exhaust.

mitrechnen *v.t.* to include in the number.

mitreden *v.i.* to join in the conversation; to have one's say in a matter.

mitsamt *pr.* together with.

mitschreiben *v.i. & t.st.* to take down (a speech, etc.).

Mitschuld *f.* complicity.

Mitschuldig[r] *m.* accomplice, accessory.

Mitschüler *m.* schoolfellow.

mitspielen *v.i.* to join in a game; *einem übel ~*, to do one an ill turn.

Mittag *m.* (-s, -e) mid-day, noon; *zu ~ essen, speisen*, to dine.

mittags *adv.* at noon.

Mittag(s)essen *n.* (-s, -) dinner, lunch.

Mitte *f.* (-, 0) middle, midst.

mitteilbar *a.* fit to be told *or* printed.

mitteilen *v.t.* to communicate.

mitteilsam *a.* communicative.

Mitteilung *f.* communication, notice.

Mittel *n.* (-s, -) medium, average, mean; means, expedient, way; remedy; (*Geld*) means; *sich ins ~ legen*, to step in.

Mittelalter *n.* the Middle Ages *pl.*

mittelalterlich *a.* mediæval.

mittelbar *a.* indirect.

Mittelding *n.* intermediate thing.

mitteleuropäisch *a.* Central European.

Mittel: ~finger *m.* middle finger; ~gross *a.* medium sized; ~grösse, *f.* medium size; ~gut *a.* of second quality.

mittelhochdeutsch *a.* Middle High German.

mittelländisch *a.* Mediterranean; inland.

mittellos *a.* penniless, destitute.

mittelmässig *a.* middling; mediocre.

Mittel: ~meer *n.* Mediterranean; ~punkt *m.* centre.

mittels, mittelst *pr.* by means of.

Mittelschule *f.* secondary school.

Mittelsmann *m.*, Mittelsperson *f.* intermediary.

Mittel: ~stand *m.* middle class(es); ~stürmer *m.* (sport) centre forward; ~weg *m.* middle course.

Mittelwelle *f.* (*Radio*) medium wave.

mitten *adv.* midst; ~ im Winter, in the depth of winter; ~ durch, through the midst; ~ entzwei, in twain, broken right in two; ~ in, in the middle of.

Mitternacht *f.* (-, -nächte) midnight.

Mittler *m.* (-s, -) mediator.

Mittleramt *n.* mediatorship, umpireship.

mittlere[r] *a.* middle, mean.

mittlerweile *adv.* meanwhile.

mittun *v.t.st.* to join in doing.

Mitwisser *m.* person in the secret.

Mittwoch *m.* (-s, -e) Wednesday.

mitunter *adv.* now and then.

Mitwelt *f.* (-, 0) contemporaries.

mitwirken *v.i.* to co-operate, to concur.

Mitwirkung *f.* (-, 0) co-operation.

Mitwissen *n.* (-s, 0) knowledge.

Möbel *n.* (-s, -) piece of furniture.

Möbel: ~händler *m.* upholsterer, dealer in furniture; ~magazin *n.* furniture warehouse; ~schreiner, ~tischler *m.* cabinet-maker; ~wagen *m.* furniture-van.

mobil *a.* active, quick; ~ machen, to mobilize.

Mobilmachung *f.* (-, 0) mobilization.

mobilisieren *v.t.* to mobilize.

möblieren *v.t.* to furnish.

Mode *f.* (-, -n) mode, fashion.

Modell *n.* (-s, -e) model, sitter; pattern; mould.

modellieren *v.t.* to model, to mould.

modeln *v.t.* to fashion, to form.

Moder *m.* (-s, 0) mould; mud; decay.

moderig *a.* musty, mouldy.

modern *v.i.* (s) to moulder, to decay.

modern *a.* fashionable; modern.

modernisieren *v.t.* to modernize.

Modewaren n. f.pl. fancy-goods pl.
modifizieren v.t. to modify.
modisch a. fashionable, stylish.
Modistin f. (-, -nen) milliner, dressmaker.
mogeln v.i. (vulg.) to cheat (at cards).
mögen v.i. & t.ir. to like, to wish; ich mag, I may, I can; I like; ich möchte, I should like; ich möchte lieber, I would rather.
möglich a. possible.
Möglichkeit f. (-, -en) possibility.
Möglichkeiten pl. potentialities; Feind-möglichkeiten (mil.), enemy capabilities.
möglichst adv. as much as possible.
Mohn m. (-[e]s, -e) poppy, poppy-seed.
Mohnsaft m. opium.
Mohr m. (-en, -en) Moor; blackamoor.
Mohrrübe f. carrot.
Molch m. (-es, -e) salamander.
Molekül n. (-s, -e) molecule.
Molke f. (-, -n) Molken pl. whey.
Molkerei f. (-s, -en) dairy.
moll a. (mus.) minor, flat.
mollig a. comfortable, snug.
Molltonart f. (-, -en) minor key.
Moment m. (-[e]s, -e) moment.
momentan a. momentary.
Momentaufnahme f. (phot.) snapshot.
Monarch m. (-en, -en) monarch.
Monarchie f. (-, -[e]n) monarchy.
monarchisch a. monarchical.
Monat m. (-[e]s, -e) month.
monatlich a. & adv. monthly.
Monatsschrift f. monthly (magazine).
Mönch m. (-[e]s, -e) monk, friar.
mönchisch a. monkish; monastic.
Mönchskloster n. monastery.
Mond m. (-[e]s, -e) moon.
Mondfinsternis f. eclipse of the moon.
mondhell a. moonlight.
Mond: ~schein m. moonlight; ~sichel f. crescent.
mondsüchtig a. moonstruck.
Monographie f. (-, -n) monograph.
monolithisch a. monolithic.
Monolog m. (-s, -e) monologue.
Monopol n. (-[e]s, -e) monopoly.
monopolisieren v.t. to monopolize.
monoton a. monotonous.
Monotonie f. (-, 0) monotony.
Monstranz f. (-, -en) pyx, monstrance.
Montag m. (-[e]s, -e) Monday.
montags adv. on Monday(s).
Montanaktien f.pl. mining shares.
Montanindustrie f. mining industry.
Monteur m. (-s, -e) engine fitter.
montieren v.t. (mech.) to mount, to fit, to assemble.
Montierung f. (-, -en) (mil.) equipment.
Moor n. (-[e]s, -e) moor, fen, bog.
Moos n. (-es, -e) moss.
moosig a. mossy.
Mops m. (Mopses, Möpse) pug(dog).

Moral f. (-, 0) moral philosophy; (einer Fabel) moral; morals pl.
moralisch a. moral.
moralisieren v.i. to moralize.
Morast m. (-es, -e u. Moräste) morass.
Moratorium n. (-s, -rien) moratorium.
Morchel f. (-, -n) morel (mushroom).
Mord m. (-[e]s, -e) murder, homicide.
morden v.t. & i. to murder.
Mörder m. (-s, -) murderer.
Mörderin f. (-, -nen) murderess.
mörderisch a. murderous.
Mord(s)kerl m. devil of a fellow.
mordsmässig a. (fam.) tremendous.
Mordtat f. murder.
morganatisch a. morganatic.
Morgen m. (-s, -) morning; east; ⅝ acre (of land).
Morgen adv. to-morrow; heute ~, this morning; ~ früh, to-morrow morning.
Morgenland n. Orient, East.
Morgen: ~rot n. u. ~röte f. dawn, aurora, blush of dawn; ~stern m. morning-star.
morgens adv. in the morning.
morgig a. of to-morrow, to-morrow's.
Morphium n. (-s, 0) morphine.
morsch a. rotten, decayed.
Mörser m. (-s, -) mortar; (mil.) howitzer.
Mörserkeule f. pestle.
Mörtel m. (-s, -) mortar, cement.
Mosaik n. (-[s], -en) mosaic.
Moschee f. (-, -[e]n) mosque.
Moschus m. (-, 0) musk.
Moskito m. (-s, -s) mosquito.
Most m. (-es, -e) mus; (Apfel~) cider.
Mostrich m. (-s, -) mustard.
Motiv n. (-s, -e) motive; (mus.) motif.
motivieren v.t. to motivate.
Motor m. (-s, -e) motor, engine.
Motor: ~barkasse f. motor-launch; ~boot n. motor boat; ~fahrzeug n. motor vehicle; ~haube f. engine cowling; ~rad n. motor-bicycle; ~unterbau m. engine-bed.
motorisieren v.t. to motorize.
Motte f. (-, -n) moth; von ~n zerfressen, moth-eaten.
Motten: ~frass m. damage caused by moths; ~pulver n. moth powder; ~sicher a. moth-proof.
Motto n. (-s, -s) motto.
moussieren v.i. to effervesce, to sparkle.
Möwe f. (-, -n) sea-gull, sea-mew.
Mucke f. (-, -n) caprice, whim.
Mücke f. (-, -n) gnat, midge.
mucken v.i. to grumble.
Mucker m. (-s, -) hypocrite, precisian.
müde a. weary, tired.
Müdigkeit f. (-, 0) weariness, fatigue.
Muff m. (-[e]s, -e) muff.
Muffel f. (-, -en) muffle (chem. and tech.).
muffig a. musty; sulky.

Mühe f. (-, -n) trouble, effort; pains pl.; sich ~ geben, to take pains; der ~ wert sein, to be worth while.

mühelos a. without trouble, easy.

mühen (sich) v.refl. to trouble oneself.

mühevoll a. laborious, irksome.

Mühle f. (-, -n) mill, windmill.

Mühlstein m. millstone.

Mühsal n. (-[e]s, -e) f. (-, -e) misery.

mühsam a. troublesome, toilsome.

mühselig a. toilsome; miserable.

Mulatte m. (-n, -n) mulatto.

Mulde f. (-, -n) tray, trough.

Mull m. (-[e]s, 0) book-muslin, mull.

Müll m. (-[e]s, 0) dust, rubbish.

Müll ~abfuhr f. refuse clearance; ~eimer m. dustbin, (Am.) ashcan.

Müller m. (-s, -) miller.

multiplizieren v.t. to multiply.

Mumie f. (-, -n) mummy.

Mund m. (-[e]s, -e u. Münder) mouth; (fig.) orifice; den ~ halten, to hold one's tongue; von der Hand in den ~ leben, to live from hand to mouth.

Mundart f. dialect.

mundartlich a. dialectic(al).

Mündel n. (-s, -) ward; pupil.

Mündelgelder n.pl. trust money.

mündelsicher a. trustee (securities).

munden v.i.imp. to taste nice.

münden v.i. to fall into.

Mundharmonika f. mouth-organ.

mundgerecht a. palatable.

mündig a. of age; ~ werden, to come of age.

Mündigkeit f. (-, 0) majority, full age.

Mündigkeitsalter n. age of consent.

mündlich a. verbal, oral.

Mundstück n. mouth-piece.

Mündung f. (-, -en) mouth; estuary; (einer Flinte) muzzle; orifice.

Munition f. (-, -en) ammunition.

munkeln v.i. to whisper, to mutter.

Münster n. or m. (-s, -) minster, cathedral.

munter a. awake; lively, gay, brisk.

Münze f. (-, -n) coin; medal; mint; (bot.) mint; klingende ~, hard cash.

Münzeinheit f. monetary unit.

münzen v.t. to mint, to coin.

Münz: ~fuss m. standard (of coinage); ~kunde f. numismatics pl.

mürbe a. mellow; tender, soft.

Murmel f. (-, -n) marble.

murmeln v.t. & i. to murmur; to mutter.

Murmeltier n. marmot.

murren v.i. to grumble, to growl.

mürrisch a. morose, surly, peevish.

Mus n. (-es, -e) pulp, pap; (Früchte) jam, fool.

Muschel f. (-, -n) shell, mussel.

Muse f. (-, -n) muse.

Muselman m. (-s, -en) Moslem.

Museum n. (-s, Museen) museum.

Musik f. (-, 0) music.

Musikalien pl. music.

Musikalienhandlung f. music(-seller's) shop.

musikalisch a. musical.

Musikant m. (-en, -en) (inferior) musician.

Musiker m. (-s, -) musician.

Musiklehrer m. music-master.

musizieren v.i. to make music.

Muskat m. (-[e]s, -e) nutmeg.

Muskateller m. (-s, 0) (Wein) muscatel.

Muskel m. (-s, -n) muscle.

Muskete f. (-, -n) musket.

Musketier m. (-[e]s, -e) musketeer.

Muskulatur f. (-, -en) muscular system.

muskulös a. muscular.

Musse f. (-, 0) leisure; mit ~, at leisure.

Musselin m. (-[e]s, -e) muslin.

müssen v.i.ir. to be obliged, to be forced, to be constrained, to have to.

müssig a. unemployed, idle.

Müssiggang m. (-[e]s, 0) idleness, idling.

Müssiggänger m. (-s, -) idler, loafer.

Muster n. (-s, -) pattern; sample; design; nach ~, according to sample.

mustergültig a. standard; classical.

musterhaft a. exemplary, model.

mustern v.t. to review, to muster; (Stoffe) to figure.

Musterrolle f. muster-roll.

Musterschutz m. copyright in designs.

Musterung f. (-, -en) review, inspection; (eines Fells) marking.

Musterzeichner m. designer (of patterns).

Mut m. (-[e]s, 0) courage; spirit, mettle.

mutig a. courageous, spirited, plucky.

mutlos a. discouraged.

mutmassen v.t. to conjecture.

mutmasslich a. presumptive.

Mutter f. (-, Mütter) mother; (Schrauben~) nut; werdende ~, expectant mother.

Mutter: ~gesellschaft f. parent company; ~kompass m. master-compass; ~mal n. birthmark; ~leib m. womb.

mütterlich a. motherly; maternal.

Mutterschaft f. (-, 0) motherhood; maternity.

Mutter: ~schoss m. womb; ~schwein n. sow.

mutterseelenallein adv. quite alone.

Mutter: ~söhnchen n. milksop, spoiled child; ~sprache f. mother-tongue; ~witz m. mother-wit, common-sense.

Mutung f. (-, -en) (min.) claim.

Mutwille (-ns, 0) wantonness.

mutwillig a. wanton.

Mütze f. (-, -n) cap.

Myrrhe f. (-, -n) myrrh.

Myrte f. (-, -n) myrtle.

mysteriös a. mysterious.

Mysterium n. (-s, -rien) mystery.

mystifizieren v.t. to mystify.

Mystik f. (-, -e-) mysticism.
Mystiker m. (-s, -) mystic.
Mythe, f. (-, -n) fable, myth.
Mythologie f. (-, -[e]n) mythology.
Mythus m. (-, -then) myth.

N

na! i. well! now!
Nabe f. (-, -n) nave, hub; boss.
Nabel m. (-s, -) navel.
Nabelschnur f. umbilical cord.
nach pr. & adv. after, behind; according to; past; to; ~ und ~, little by little; ~ Gewicht, by weight; ~ der Reihe, in turn; ~ wie vor, now as before.
nachäffen v.t. & i. to ape, to mimic.
nachahmen v.t. to imitate; to copy.
Nachahmer m. (-s, -) imitator.
Nachahmung f. (-, -en) imitation.
Nachbar m. (-s u. -n, -n), Nachbarin f. (-, -nen) neighbour.
nachbarlich a. neighbourly.
Nachbarschaft f. (-, 0) neighbourhood.
nachbestellen v.t. to order again.
Nachbestellung f. (-, -en) repeat order.
nachbeten v.t. (fig.) to echo.
nachbilden v.t. to copy, to imitate.
nachblicken v.t. to look after.
nachdatieren v t. to postdate.
nachdem adv. afterwards, after that; ~ c. after; je ~, according as.
nachdenken v.i.ir. to meditate, to muse.
Nachdenken n. (-s, 0) reflection.
nachdenklich a. thoughtful, wistful.
nachdrängen (h) v.i., nachdringen (s) v.i.st. to crowd after, to press in after.
Nachdruck m. (-[e]s, -e) energy, emphasis, stress; pirated edition.
nachdrucken v.t. to reprint; to pirate.
nachdrücklich a. energetic, emphatic.
nacheifern v.i. to emulate.
Nacheiferung f. (-, 0) emulation.
nacheilen v.i. (s) to hasten after.
nacheinander adv. one after another.
nachempfinden v.t.st. to feel with.
Nachen m. (-s, -) boat, skiff.
nacherzählen v.t. to repeat a story.
nachfahren v.i.st. (s) to follow (in a carriage).
Nachfolge f. succession; imitation.
nachfolgen v.i. (s) to succeed; to imitate.
Nachfolger m. (-s, -) follower; successor; imitator.
Nachforderung f. (-, -en) additional claim or charge.
nachforschen v.i. to search after; to inquire into, to investigate.
Nachforschung f. (-, -en) search, inquiry, investigation.
Nachfrage f. demand, request; inquiry.

nachfragen v.i. to inquire after.
nachfühlen v.t. to feel with someone.
nachfüllen v.t. to refill.
nachgeben v.t. & i.st. to yield, to comply.
nachgeboren a. posthumous; born later.
Nachgeburt f. afterbirth.
nachgehen v.i.st. (s) to follow; (einer Sache) to investigate; (Uhr) to be slow.
nachgelassen a. posthumous.
nachgemacht a. counterfeit.
nachgerade adv. by this time.
nachgeraten (einem) v.i.st. to take after a person.
Nachgeschmack m. aftertaste, tang.
nachgiebig a. yielding, complying.
nahhaltig a. lasting, enduring.
nachhängen v.i. to indulge in.
nachhelfen v.i.st. to lend a helping hand.
nachher adv. afterwards.
nachherig a. subsequent.
Nachhilfe f. help, aid; coaching.
nachholen v.t. to make up for.
Nachhut f. (-, 0) rear-guard.
nachjagen (s. fig. h) v.i. to pursue.
Nachklang m. resonance; after-effect.
Nachkomme m. (-n, -n) descendant.
nachkommen v.i.st. (s) to come after; (fig.) to conform to, to obey.
Nachkommenschaft f. (-, -en) issue, descendants pl., posterity.
Nachlass m. (-lasses, -lasse u. -lässe) remission; estate, inheritance; ~steuer f. estate duty.
nachlassen v.t.st. to slacken, to relax; (vom Preise) to reduce; ~ v.i.st. to abate, to subside.
Nachlassen n. let-up.
nachlässig a. negligent, careless.
Nachlässigkeit f. (-, -en) negligence.
nachlaufen v.i.st. (s) to run after.
Nachlese f. (-, -n) gleaning.
nachlesen v.t.st. to glean; to look up (a passage).
Nachlieferung f. (-, -en) subsequent delivery.
nachmachen v.t. to counterfeit.
nachmalig a. subsequent.
nachmals adv. afterwards, subsequently.
nachmessen v.t.st. to measure again.
Nachmittag m. afternoon.
nachmittags adv. in the afternoon.
Nachnahme f. (-, -n) (com.) cash on delivery.
nachplappern v.t. & i. to repeat (another's words) mechanically.
nachprüfen v.t. to verify, to re-examine.
nachrechnen v.t. to check (an account).
Nachrede f. (-, -n) üble ~, slander.
nachreden v.t. to repeat (another's words).
Nachricht f. (-, -en) advice, information, news.
Nachrichten: ~abteilung f. intelligence department; ~büro n. news agency;

~dienst *m*. intelligence service; ~stelle, zentrale *f*. (*mil*.) message centre, signal centre; ~wesen *n*. (*mil*.) signal communications; ~truppen *pl*. signal troops.

nachrücken *v.i.* (*mil*.) to move up.

Nachruf *m*. obituary (notice).

Nachruhm *m*. posthumous fame.

nachrühmen *v.t*. to say to someone's credit.

nachsagen *v.t*. to relate of, to repeat of (a person).

Nachsatz *m*. (*gram*.) final clause.

nachschicken *v.t*. to forward.

Nachschlage: ~bibliothek *f*. reference library; ~buch *n*. reference book.

nachschlagen *v.t.st*. to look up; to refer to, to consult (a book); ~ *v.i.st.* to take after.

nachschleichen *v.i.st.* (*s*) to steal after.

Nachschlüssel *m*. false key, picklock.

Nachschub *m*. (-[e]s, -schübe) (*mil*.) supply.

nachsehen *v.t*. & *i.st*. to look after; to pardon, to excuse; to look up (in a book).

nachsenden *v.t.ir.* (*Briefe*) to forward; *bitte ~!* please forward!

nachsetzen *v.i.* (*s*) to pursue.

Nachsicht *f*. (-, 0) indulgence.

nachsichtig *a*. indulgent, considerate.

Nachsilbe *f*. suffix.

nachsinnen *v.i.st.* to muse.

Nachsommer *m*. Indian summer.

Nachspiel *n*. sequel.

nachsprechen *v.t.st*. to repeat.

nachspüren *v.i.* to trace; to investigate.

nächst *pr.* next to; ~beste[r] *a*. second-best.

Nächste[r] *m*. (-n, -n) neighbour.

nachstehen *v.i.st.* to be inferior to.

nachstellen *v.i.* to waylay; ~ *v.t.* (*Uhr*) to put back.

Nachstellung *f*. (-, -en) pursuit.

Nächstenliebe *f*. charity.

nächstens *adv*. soon, shortly.

nachstreben *v.i.* to strive for; to emulate.

nachsuchen *v.i.* to petition for.

Nacht *f*. (-, Nächte) night; *bei ~*, at night; *über ~*, during the night.

nachtanken *v.t*. to refuel.

Nacht: ~anzug *m*. nightdress; ~blindheit *f*. nightblindness.

Nachtdienst *m*. night-duty.

Nachteil *m*. (-[e]s, -e) disadvantage.

nachteilig *a*. disadvantageous.

Nachthemd *n*. nightshirt; (*Frauen~*) nightdress.

Nachtigall *f*. (-, -en) nightingale.

nächtigen *v.i.* to pass the night.

Nachtisch *m*. dessert.

Nacht: ~jacke *f*. bed-jacket; ~jäger *m*. (*avi*.) night-fighter.

nächtlich *a*. nightly, nocturnal.

Nachtrab *m*. (-[e]s, -e) rear(-guard).

Nachtrag *m*. (-[e]s, -träge) supplement.

nachtragen *v.t.st*. to add, to append; *einem etwas ~*, to bear someone a grudge.

nachträglich *a*. subsequent, supplementary.

Nachtruhe *f*. night-rest.

nachts *adv*. in the night(-time), at night.

Nacht: ~schatten *m*. (*bot*.) (deadly) nightshade; ~tisch *m*. bed(side)-table; ~wache *f*. night-watch; ~wächter *m*. watchman; ~wandler *m*. sleep-walker.

nachwachsen *v.i.st.* (*s*) to grow again.

Nach: ~wahl *f*. by-election; ~wehen, painful consequences *pl*.

Nachweis *m*. (-weises, -weise) proof.

nachweisen *v.t*. to prove.

Nachweisung *f*. (-, -en) information.

Nachwelt *f*. posterity.

nachwirken *v.i.* to have an after-effect.

Nach: ~wirkung *f*. after-effect; ~wort *n*. concluding remarks *pl*., postscript.

Nachwuchs *m*. (-es, 0) rising generation.

nachzahlen *v.t*. to pay in addition.

nachzählen *v.t*. to count over again.

Nachzahlung *f*. after-payment.

nachzeichnen *v.t*. to copy, to draw from.

nachziehen *v.i.st.* (*s*) to march after.

Nachzügler *m*. (-s, -) straggler.

Nacken *m*. (-s, -) nape.

nackend, nackt *a*. & *adv*. naked, nude.

Nadel *f*. (-, -n) needle; pin.

Nadelbaum *m*. coniferous tree.

Nadel: ~öhr *n*. eye of a needle; ~spitze *f*. point of a needle *or* pin; ~stich *m*. pin-prick.

Nagel *m*. (-s, Nägel) nail.

Nagelbürste *f*. nail-brush.

nageln, *v.t*. to nail.

nagelneu *a*. brand-new.

Nagel: ~schere *f*. nail-scissors; ~schmied *m*. nail-smith.

nagen *v.t*. & *i.* to gnaw; (*fig*.) to rankle.

Nager *m*. (-s, -), Nagetier *n*. rodent.

nah[e] *a*. near, close, nigh; imminent; *das geht mir ~*, that grieves me; *einem zu ~ treten*, to hurt someone's feelings.

Nahaufklärung *f*. (*mil*.) close reconnaissance.

Nahaufnahme *f*. (*Film*) close-up.

Nähe *f*. (-, -n) nearness, proximity; *in der ~*, at hand.

nahen *v.i.* (*s*) to approach.

nähen *v.t*. to sew, to stitch.

Nähere(s) *n*. details, particulars *pl*.

Näherei *f*. (-, -en) needlework.

Näherin *f*. (-, -nen) seamstress, needle-woman.

nähern (sich) ~ *v.refl.* to draw near.

nahestehen (einem) *v.i.st.* to be intimate with.

Näh: ~beutel *m*. workbag; ~kästchen *n*. workbox; ~korb *m*. work basket; ~maschine *f*. sewing machine; ~nadel *f*.

sewing needle; ~**seide** f. sewing silk; ~**zeug** n. sewing kit.

Nähr... nutritive, a.; ~**wert** m. nutritive value.

Nährboden m. breeding ground, hotbed (also fig.).

nähren v.t. to feed, to nourish; to nurse; (fig.) to foster.

nahrhaft a. nutritious, nourishing; (fig.) profitable, lucrative.

Nahrung f. (-, 0) nourishment, food; livelihood, means of subsistence.

Nahrungs- ~**mittel** n. (article of) food; pl. victuals, provisions pl.; ~**sorgen** pl. cares for daily bread.

Nährwert, m. nutritive quality.

Naht f. (-, Nähte) seam; suture.

Nahverkehr m. local traffic.

naiv a. naïve, unsophisticated.

Naivität f. (-, -en) naïveté, artlessness.

Name[n], m. (-ns, -n) name; title; (fig.) reputation, fame; dem ~ nach, by name only; nominal.

namenlos, a. nameless; unspeakable.

namens adv. in the name of, on behalf; ~ N, of the name of N.

Namens- ~**aktie** f. registered share; ~**liste** f. (mil.) roster; ~**schild** n. plate; ~**tag** m. name-day; ~**vetter** m. name-sake.

namentlich adv. by name; particularly.

namhaft a. considerable, well-known; ~ **machen,** to name, to specify.

nämlich a. the same; ~ adv. namely, viz.

Napf m. (-[e]s, Näpfe) basin, bowl.

Narbe f. (-, -n) scar; cicatrice.

narbig a. scarred, scarry; grained.

Narkose f. (-, -n) narcosis.

narkotisch a. narcotic.

Narr m. (-en, -en) fool; buffoon, jester; einen zum ~en haben, to fool someone.

narren v.t. to make a fool of, to chaff.

Narretei f. (-, 0) tomfoolery, buffoonery.

närrisch a. foolish; mad; odd, queer.

Narzisse f. (-, -n) narcissus.

naschen v.t. & i. to eat (sweets) on the sly.

Näscherei f. (-, -en) ~**en** f.pl. dainties pl.

naschhaft a. fond of dainties.

Nase f. (-, -n) nose; (Tier~) snout; (fig.) reprimand; die ~ rümpfen, to turn up one's nose (at); an der ~ herumführen, to lead by the nose.

näseln v.i. to speak through the nose.

Nasenbluten n. (-s, 0) nose-bleeding.

Nasen- ~**loch** n. nostril; ~**spitze** f. tip of the nose.

naseweis a. pert, saucy, impertinent.

Nashorn n. rhinoceros.

nass a. wet, moist.

Nässe f. (-, 0) wetness, moisture.

nässen v.t. to wet, to moisten.

nasskalt a. raw, damp and cold.

Nation f. (-, -en) nation.

national a. national.

nationalisieren v.t. to nationalize.

Nationalität f. nationality.

Natrium n. (-s, -0) sodium.

Natron n. (-s, 0) soda; doppeltkohlensaures ~, (bi)carbonate of soda.

Natter f. (-, -n) adder, viper.

Natur f. (-, -en) nature; disposition; von ~, by nature, naturally.

naturalisieren v.t. to naturalize; sich ~ lassen, to become naturalized.

Naturalleistung f. payment in kind.

Naturell n. (-[e]s, -e) natural disposition.

Natur- ~**forscher** m. man of science, scientist, (natural) philosopher.

Naturgas n. natural gas.

naturgemäss a. & adv. natural, normal; in accordance with nature.

Naturgeschichte f. natural history.

naturgetreu a. true to nature or life.

Naturkunde f. science, physics pl.

natürlich a. natural; innate; unaffected; ~ adv. of course.

Naturrecht n. natural right; law of nature.

Naturvolk n. primitive race.

naturwidrig a. unnatural.

Naturwissenschaft f. (natural) science.

Nautik f. (-, 0) art of navigation.

Nebel m. (-s, -) mist, fog; (mil.) smoke; ~**wand** f. smoke-screen.

nebelhaft a. nebulous; misty, obscure.

neb(e)lig a. misty, foggy.

neben pr. near, by, beside; at, next to.

Nebenabsicht f. secondary intention.

nebenan adv. next door; close by.

Neben- ~**anschluss** m. (tel.) extension; ~**ausgaben** pl. incidentals, sundries.

nebenbei adv. by the way; besides; ~ bemerkt, incidentally.

Neben- ~**beschäftigung** f. side-line; ~**beruf** m. side-line; ~**branche** f. side-line ~**buhler(in)** m. (& f.) rival.

nebeneinander adv. side by side, abreast.

Nebeneinanderschaltung f. (elek.) parallel connection.

Neben- ~**einkünfte** pl. extras, perquisites pl.; ~**fach** n. subsidiary subject; ~**fluss** m. tributary (river); ~**gebäude** n. outbuilding; ~**gelass** n. domestic offices; ~**gleis** n. siding.

nebenher adv. besides; by the way.

Neben- ~**kosten** pl. extras; ~**linie** f. collateral line; (rail.) branch-line; ~**mann** m. next man; ~**mensch** m. fellow-creature; ~**person** f. inferior or secondary character; ~**produkt** n. by-product; ~**rolle** f. subordinate part; ~**sache** f. matter of secondary importance; ~**satz** m. subordinate clause; ~**umstand** m. accessory or accidental circumstance; ~**verdienst** m. extra earnings pl.; perquisites, emoluments pl.; ~**zimmer** n. adjoining room.

nebensächlich *a.* of secondary importance.

nebst *pr.* together with, besides.

necken *v.t.* to tease; to banter.

Neckerei *f.* (-, -en) banter.

Neffe *m.* (-n, -n) nephew.

negativ *a.* negative.

Neger *m.* (-s, -) negro; nigger.

Negerin *f.* (-, -nen) negress.

nehmen *v.t.st.* to take; *es genau ~,* to be very particular; *es leicht ~,* to take things easy, to make light of.

Neid *m.* (-es, 0) envy, grudge.

neiden *v.t.* to envy.

Neider *m.* (-s, -) Neidhammel (-s, -) Neidhart *m.* (-[e]s, -e) envious person.

neidisch *a.* envious.

Neige *f.* (-, -n) dregs, *pl. auf die ~ gehen,* to be on the decline; to run short.

neigen *v.t. & i.* to incline; (sich) *~ v. refl.* to bow, to decline; to feel inclined.

Neigung *f.* (-, -en) inclination; bias, affection; dip, slope, gradient.

nein *adv.* no; nay.

Nektar *m.* (-s, 0) nectar.

Nelke *f.* (-, -n) pink; (*gefüllte*) carnation.

nennen *v.t. ir.* to name, to call, to mention.

nennenswert *a.* worth mentioning.

Nenner *m.* (-s, -) (*ar.*) denominator.

Nenn: ~wert *m.* nominal value; (*Banknote, Scheck*) denomination; ~wort *n.* noun.

Neon *n.* neon; ~röhre, *f.* neon-tube.

neppen *v.t.* (*sl.*) to overcharge.

Nerv *m.* (-es, -en) nerve; *seine ~n verlieren* to lose one's nerve.

Nerven: ~fieber *n.* typhoid fever; ~heilanstalt, sanatorium (for nervous diseases); ~knoten *m.* ganglion.

nervenkrank, nervenschwach *a.* neurasthenic.

Nerven: ~krankheit *f.* nervous disease; ~leiden *n.* nervous complaint.

nervenstärkend *a.* tonic.

Nervensystem *n.* nervous system.

nervig *a.* nervous; sinewy.

nervös *a.* nervous; highly strung.

Nerz *m.* (-es, -e) mink, small otter.

Nessel *f.* (-, -n) nettle.

Nesselausschlag *m.* nettle-rash.

Nest *n.* (-es, -er) nest; (*Stadt*) hole.

Nesthäkchen *n.* youngest child, pet.

nett *a.* neat, fair, nice, pretty.

netto *adv.* (*vom Preise, Gewichte*) net.

Netto: ~betrag *m.* net amount; ~einnahme *f.* net receipts *pl.*; ~ertrag *m.* net proceeds *pl.*

Netz *n.* (-es, -e) net; network.

netzen *v.t.* to wet, to moisten.

netzförmig *a.* reticular.

Netzhaut *f.* retina.

neu *a.* new, recent; *aufs ~e, von ~em,* anew, again; ~e[re] *Zeit,* modern times; ~ere *Sprache,* modern language.

neuartig *a.* novel.

Neubau *m.* (-[e]s, ~bauten) new building.

Neubearbeitung *f.* (-, -en) revised edition.

neubenennen *v.t. ir.* to redesignate.

Neudruck *m.* reprint.

neuerdings *adv.* lately, recently.

Neuerer *m.* (-s, -) innovator.

Neuerscheinung *f.* (-, -en) new publication.

Neuerung *f.* (-, -en) innovation.

neuformen *v.t.* to reshape.

neugeboren *a.* new-born.

neugestalten *v.t.* to reorganize.

Neugierde *f.* (-, 0) curiosity.

neugierig *a.* inquisitive, curious.

neugültig machen *v.t.* to revalidate.

Neuheit *f.* (-, -en) newness; novelty.

Neuigkeit *f.* (-, -en) news.

Neujahr *n.* (-[e]s, -e) New-Year's day.

neulich *adv.* recently, the other day.

Neuling *m.* (-[e]s, -e) novice, beginner.

neumodisch *a.* newfangled.

Neumond *m.* new moon.

neun *a.* nine.

Neunauge *n.* lamprey.

neunfach *a.* ninefold.

neunmal *adv.* nine times

neunmalig *a.* nine times repeated.

neunzehn *a.* nineteen.

neunzig *a.* ninety.

Neuphilolog[e] *m.* student *or* teacher of modern languages.

neutral *a.* neutral.

Neutralität *f.* (-, 0) neutrality.

Neutrum *n.* (-s, Neutra) (*gram.*) neuter.

neuvermählt *a.* newly married.

Neuzeit *f.* modern times, our days *pl.*

nicht *adv.* not; *auch ~,* not; *~ einmal,* not even; *durchaus ~,* not at all; *gar ~,* not at all, by no means; *noch ~,* not yet; *~ mehr,* no more, no longer.

nichtalkoholische Getränke *pl.* soft drinks.

Nichtangriff *m.* non-aggression.

nichtansässig *a.* non-resident.

Nichtbeachtung, Nichtbefolgung *f.* (-, 0) inattention, noncompliance, nonobservance.

Nichte *f.* (-, -n) niece.

Nichteinmischung *f.* (-, 0) non-intervention.

Nichteisenmetall *n.* non-ferrous metal.

Nichterfüllung *f.* non-fulfilment.

Nichterscheinen *n.* non-attendance.

nichtig *a.* null, void; vain, empty.

Nichtigkeit *f.* (-, -en) invalidity, nullity, futility; vanity, emptiness.

Nichtigkeitsklage *f.* writ of error, plea of nullity.

Nichtkriegführender *m.* non-belligerent.

Nichtmitglied *n.* non-member.

Nichtraucher *m.* non-smoker.

nichts *adv.* nothing; nought; *~ als,* nothing but; *~ weniger als,* anything but this; *mir ~ dir ~,* unexpectedly.

Nichts *n.* (-, 0) nothing(ness), nonentity.
nichtsdestoweniger *adv.* nevertheless.
Nichtsnutz *m.* (-es, -e) ne'er-do-well.
nichtssagend *a.* meaningless, unmeaning.
nichtswürdig *a.* vile, worthless.
Nickel *m.* (-s, -) nickel.
nicken *v.i.* to nod; to nap.
nie *adv.* never.
nieder *a. & adv.* low, lower, nether; down; *auf und ~,* up and down.
niederbeugen *v.t.* to bend down.
niederbrennen *v.t. & i.ir.* to burn down.
niederdeutsch *a.* Low-German.
Niederdruck *m.* (-s, 0) low pressure.
niederdrücken *v.t.* to press down; (*fig.*) to depress, to oppress.
niederfallen *v.i.st.* (*s*) to fall down.
Niedergang *m.* decline.
niedergehen *v.i.st.* (*s*) to go down.
niedergeschlagen *a.* dejected, downcast.
niederhalten *v.t.st.* to keep down.
niederknie[e]n *v.i.* (*s*) to kneel down.
niederkommen *v.i.st.* (*s*) to be confined.
Niederkunft *f.* (-, 0) confinement.
Niederlage *f.* (-, -n) defeat; warehouse, depository.
niederlassen (sich) *v.refl.st.* to establish oneself, to settle down; to set up (in business).
Niederlassung *f.* (-, -en) establishment; settlement.
niederlegen *v.t.* to lay down; to retire from; (*Arbeit*) to strike, to knock off.
niedermachen *v.t.* to kill, to slay.
niedermetzeln *v.t.* to massacre.
niederreissen *v.t.st.* to pull down.
Niederschlag *m.* rain; (*chem.*) precipitate.
Niederschlagsmenge *f.* (-, -n) rainfall.
niederschlagen *v.t.st.* to knock down; (*die Augen*) to cast down; (*law*) to quash (a charge); (*chemisch*) to precipitate.
niederschmettern *v.t.* to crush.
niederschreiben *v.t.st.* to write down.
niederschreien *v.t.st.* to shout down.
Niederschrift *f.* (-, -en) writing down, copy.
niedersetzen *v.t.* to set *or* put down; (sich) ~ *v.refl.* to sit down.
niederträchtig *a.* base, abject, vile.
Niederträchtigkeit *f.* (-, -en) baseness.
niedertreten *v.t.st.* to trample down.
Niederung *f.* (-, -en) low ground.
niederwerfen *v.t.st.* to throw down; (sich) ~ *v.refl.* to prostrate oneself.
niedlich *a.* neat, nice; dainty, elegant.
niedrig *a.* low; mean, vile, base.
Niedrigkeit *f.* (-, -en) lowness; baseness.
niemals *adv.* never.
niemand *pn.* nobody.
Niere *f.* (-, -n) kidney; reins *pl.*
Nieren: ~braten *m.* roast-loin; ~entzündung *f.* nephritis.
niesen *v.i.* to sneeze

Nieswurz *f.* (-, 0) hellebore.
Niete *f.* (-, -n) rivet.
nieten *v.t.* to rivet.
Nilpferd *n.* hippopotamus.
Nimbus *m.* (-, 0) nimbus, halo; prestige.
nimmer, nimmermehr, *adv.* never, nevermore, no more; by no means, nowise.
nippen *v.t.* to sip.
Nippsachen *pl.* (k)nic(k)nacks *pl.*
nirgend[s] *adv.* nowhere.
Nische *f.* (-, -n) niche.
nisten *v.i.* to nest; to build; to nestle.
Nitrat *n.* (-s, -e) nitrate.
Nitroglyzerin *n.* nitro-glycerine.
Niveau *n.* (-s, -s) level.
nivellieren *v.t.* to level.
Nixe *f.* (-, -n), water-fairy, nixie.
nobel *a.* noble; generous; magnificent.
noch *adv.* still, yet; ~ *einmal,* once more; ~ *etwas,* something more; ~ *immer,* still; ~ *nicht,* not yet.
nochmalig *a.* repeated.
nochmals *adv.* once again.
Nockenwelle *f.* (*mech.*) camshaft.
Nomade *m.* (-n, -n) nomad.
Nonius *m.* (*mech.*) vernier.
Nonne *f.* (-, -n) nun.
Nonnenkloster *n.* nunnery, convent.
Nord(en) *m.* (-s, 0) North.
nordisch *a.* Northern; Nordic.
Nordländer *m.* (-s, -) northerner.
nördlich *a.* northerly, northern; arctic; ~*e Breite,* Northern latitude.
Nordlicht *n.* aurora borealis.
Nordost *m.* (-ens, 0) north-east.
Nord: ~pol *m.* North Pole; ~polarkreis *m.* arctic circle.
Nordsüd... north-and-south, *a.*
nordwärts *adv.* northward.
Nordwest *m.* (-ens, 0) north-west.
Nordwind *m.* north wind.
nörgeln *v.i.* to grumble, to nag.
Norm *f.* (-, -en) standard, rule.
normal *a.* normal, standard.
Normalzeit *f.* mean time.
normen, normieren *v.t.* to standardize.
Not *f.* (-, Nöte) need, misery; necessity, distress, trouble; *zur ~,* if need be; *mit knapper ~,* barely, with great difficulty.
Not... emergency...
Nota... *f.* (-, 0) memorandum.
Notar *m.* (-s, -e) notary public.
Notariat *n.* (-[e]s, -e) notary's office.
notariell *a.* attested by a notary.
Not: ~ausgang *m.* emergency exit; ~behalf *m.* shift, makeshift; ~bremse *f.* communication cord.
Notdurft *f.* (-, 0) *seine ~ verrichten,* to ease oneself.
notdürftig *a.* indigent; scant.
Note *f.* (-, -n) note; bill; mark; ~n *pl.* music; *ganze ~,* semibreve; *halbe ~,* minim.

Noten: ungedeckte ~ausgabe f. fiduciary issue; ~bank f. issuing bank; ~blatt n. sheet of music; ~linien pl. staff; ~papier n. music-paper; ~pult n. music stand.

Notfall m. case of need, emergency.

notgedrungen adv. needs.

Notgeld n. emergency money.

notieren v.t. to note (down); (com.) to quote; to be quoted.

nötig a. necessary; etwas ~ haben, to stand in need of, to need.

nötigen v.t. to compel, to force, to urge.

nötigenfalls adv. in case of need.

Nötigung f. (-, -en) compulsion; durch ~, (law) under duress.

Notiz f. (-, -en) notice; memorandum; ~en pl. notes, jottings.

Notizbuch n. notebook.

Notlandung f. forced landing.

Notlage f. distressed condition.

notleidend a. indigent, needy.

notorisch a. notorious.

Not: ~pfennig m. savings pl., nest-egg; ~signal n. distress signal; ~stand m. state of distress or need; ~standsgebiet n. distressed area; ~standsarbeiten pl. relief work; ~verband m. provisional dressing; ~verbandskasten m. first-aid outfit; ~verordnung f. emergency decree; ~wehr f. (-, 0) self-defence.

notwendig a. necessary.

Notwendigkeit f. (-, 0) necessity.

Notzucht f. rape, violation.

notzüchtigen v.t. to ravish, to violate.

Novelle f. (-, -n) short story, novelette.

November m. (-s, -) November.

Novize m. (-n, -n) f. (-, -n) novice.

Nu n. (-, 0) moment; in einem ~, in a twinkling, in a trice.

Nüance f. (-, -n) shade (fig.).

nüancieren v.t. to shade.

nüchtern a. fasting, sober; (fig.) bald, matter-of-fact; dreary, prosaic; noch ~ sein, not to have eaten anything yet.

Nudeln f.pl. noodles.

null a. null; ~ und nichtig, null and void.

Null f. (-, -en) zero; nought.

Nullpunkt m. zero, freezing-point.

numerieren v.t. to number.

numerisch a. numerical.

Nummer f. (-, -n) number.

Nummernschild n. number-plate.

nun adv. & c. now, at present; therefore; ~? well?

nunmehr adv. now, by this time.

Nuntius, Nunzius m. (-, -zien) nuncio.

nur adv. only, but solely.

Nuss f. (-, Nüsse) nut; eine harte ~ a hard nut to crack.

Nuss: ~baum m. walnut-tree; ~holz n. walnut(-wood); ~knacker m. nutcracker; ~schale f. nutshell.

Nüster f. (-, -n) nostril.

Nute f. (-, -n) (mech.) keyway.

Nutz m. = Nutzen: sich zu ~e machen, to turn to account.

nutz a. = nütze.

Nutzanwendung f. moral (application).

nutzbar a. useful; profitable.

Nutzeffekt m. efficiency.

nutzen, nützen v.t. to make use of, to use, to turn to account; ~ v.i. to be c f use, to serve.

Nutzen m. (-s, 0) use; profit, benefit.

Nutzholz n. timber.

Nutzlast f. useful load.

nützlich a. useful, profitable; conducive (to).

Nützlichkeit f. (-, 0) usefulness, utility.

nutzlos a. useless, of no use.

Nutzniesser m. (-s, -) usufructuary.

Nutzniessung f. (-, 0) usufruct.

Nutzung f. (-, -en) use; usufruct.

Nutzwert m. practical value.

Nylon n. nylon.

Nymphe f. (-, -n) nymph.

O

o! i. o! oh!; ~ weh! alas! oh dear!

Oase f. (-, -n) oasis.

ob c. whether; if; als ~, as if; na ~! (fam.) rather!

Obacht f. (-, 0) heed, care; ~ geben, to pay attention.

Obdach n. (-[e]s, 0) shelter, lodging.

obdachlos a. houseless, homeless.

Obdachlosenasyl n. casual ward.

Obduktion f. (-, -en) post-mortem examination.

O-Beine n.pl. bandy legs.

o-beinig a. bandy-legged.

oben adv. above; on the surface; upstairs; von ~ herab, in a superior way; von ~ bis unten, from top to bottom; diese Seite nach ~, this side up; das zweite von ~, the second down; ~erwähnt a. above-mentioned.

obendrein adv. besides, into the bargain.

obenhin adv. superficially.

ober a. upper, higher; (fig.) chief; ~e rechte Ecke, top righthand corner.

Ober m. (-s, -) (fam.) (head-)waiter.

Ober: ~arm m. upper arm; ~arzt m. head physician; ~befehl m. chief command; ~befehlshaber m. commander-in-chief; ~deck n. upper-deck.

oberdeutsch a. Upper German.

Obere[r] m. (-n, -n) superior.

Oberfläche f. surface; superficies.

oberflächlich a. & adv. superficial(ly).

oberhalb pr. above.

Ober: ~hand *f.* upper hand; ~haupt *n.* head, chief; ~haus *n.* House of Lords; ~hemd *n.* shirt; ~hoheit *f.* supremacy, suzerainty.

Oberin *f.* (-, -nen) mother superior; matron.

oberirdisch *a.* overground.

Ober: ~kellner *m.* head waiter; ~kiefer *n.* upper jaw; ~körper *m.* upper part of the body; ~kommando *n.* high command; ~leder *n.* upper leather, uppers *pl.*; ~leitung *f.* (*elek.*) overhead wire, overhead cable; ~licht *n.* sky-light; ~lippe *f.* upper lip; ~satz *m.* (*Logik*) major term; ~schenkel *m.* thigh; ~schwester *f.* sister.

oberst *a.* uppermost; supreme; top.

Oberst *m.* (-en, -en) colonel.

Oberstleutnant *m.* lieutenant-colonel.

Ober: ~studiendirektor *m.* head master; ~wasser *n.* (*fig.*) ~ bekommen, to get the upper hand.

obgleich *c.* though, although.

Obhut *f.* (-, 0) protection, care.

obig *a.* above; foregoing, former.

objektiv *a.* objective; impartial.

Oblate *f.* (-, -n) wafer.

obliegen *v.i.st.* to be incumbent on; to apply oneself to; *es liegt mir ob*, it is my duty.

Obliegenheit *f.* (-, -en) duty, obligation.

Obligation *f.* (-, -en) (*com.*) debenture.

Obmann *m.* chairman.

Oboe *f.* (-, -n) hautboy, oboe.

Obrigkeit *f.* (-, -en) authorities *pl.*, government.

obrigkeitlich *a.* government.

obschon *c.* (al)though, albeit.

Observatorium *n.* (-[s], -rien) observatory.

obskur *a.* obscure.

Obst *n.* (-es, 0) fruit.

Obst: ~baum *m.* fruit-tree; ~garten *m.* orchard; ~händler *m.* fruiterer; ~kern *m.* stone, pip.

obszön *a.* obscene.

obwalten *v.i.* to prevail.

obwohl *c.* though, although.

Ochs *m.* (Ochsen, Ochsen) bull, bullock; (*fig.*) blockhead.

Ochsenfleisch *n.* beef.

Ocker *m.* (-s, 0) ochre.

Ode *f.* (-, -n) ode.

öde *a.* desert, desolate, waste; dull.

Öde *f.* (-, -n) *f.* desert, wilderness.

Odem *m.* (-s, 0) breath.

oder *c.* or; or else.

Ödland *n.* (-[e]s, -länderelen) wasteland.

Ofen *m.* (-s, -Öfen) stove, oven; furnace, kiln.

Ofen: ~kachel *f.* Dutch tile; ~loch *n.* mouth of an oven; ~röhre *f.* stove-pipe; ~schirm *m.* fire-screen ; ~setzer *m.* stove-fitter.

offen *a.* open; (*Stelle*) vacant; (*fig.*) frank; (*Wechsel*) blank cheque.

offenbar *a.* evident, manifest.

offenbaren *v.t.* to make known; to disclose, to reveal.

Offenbarung *f.* (-, -en) revelation.

Offenbarungseid *m.* oath of manifestation.

offenhalten *v.t.st.* to reserve.

offenherzig *a.* open-hearted, frank.

offenkundig *a.* notorious, public.

offensichtlich *a.* manifest.

offensiv *a.* offensive.

öffentlich *a.* public; ~e Einrichtung *f.* public utility.

Öffentlichkeit *f.* (-, 0) public, publicity; *unter Ausschluss der* ~, (*law*) in camera.

offerieren *v.t.* to offer.

Offerte *f.* (-, -en) offer, tender.

offiziell *a.* official.

Offizier *m.* (-[e]s, -e) officer.

Offizierkorps *n.* body of officers.

Offiziersanwärter *m.* officer candidate.

Offizin *f.* (-, -en) dispensary, chemist's shop; printing-office.

offiziös *a.* semi-official.

öffnen (sich) *v.t. & refl.* to open.

Öffner *m.* (-s, -) opener.

Öffnung *f.* (-, -en) opening; aperture.

Öffnungszeiten *pl.* opening hours *pl.*

oft(mals) *adv.* often, frequently.

öfter *a.* frequent, repeated; ~ *adv.* oftener.

öfters *adv.* repeatedly.

oh! *i.* oh! **oha!** *i.* oho!

Oheim, Ohm *m.* (-s, -e) uncle.

Ohm *n.* (*elek.*) ohm.

ohne *pr.* without; but for, except; ~ *weiteres*, without ceremony, without more ado; *es ist nicht* ~, (*fam.*) it is not to be despised.

ohnedies, ohnehin *adv.* anyhow.

Ohnmacht *f.* (-, -en) swoon, fainting fit; weakness.

ohnmächtig *a.* weak, powerless; fainting, in a swoon.

Ohr *n.* (-[e]s, -en) ear; *die* ~*en spitzen*, to prick up one's ears; *einen übers* ~ *hauen*, to make someone pay through the nose; *bis an, bis über die* ~*en*, over head and ears.

Öhr *n.* (-[e]s, Öhre) eye (of a needle).

Ohren: ~arzt *m.* ear specialist; ~beichte *f.* auricular confession; ~brausen *n.* buzzing in the ear; ~sausen *n.* = ~brausen; ~schmalz *n.* ear-wax; ~zeuge *m.* ear-witness.

Ohrfeige *f.* box on the ear.

ohrfeigen *v.t.* to box a person's ears.

Ohr: ~läppchen *n.* lobe of the ear; ~**ring** *m.* ear-ring; ~wurm *m.* earwig.

Oker = Ocker.

Okkultismus *m.* (-, 0) occultism.

Ökonom *m.* (-en, -en) farmer.

Ökonomie f. (-, -[e]n) farmyard; economy.
ökonomisch a. economical.
Oktan n. (-s, 0) (mot.) octane; ~zahl f. octane rating.
Oktavband m. octavo (volume).
Oktave f. (-, -n) (mus.) octave.
Oktober m. (-s, -) October.
oktroyieren v.t. to dictate to, to impose upon.
okulieren v.t. to inoculate, to ingraft.
Okzident m. (-s, 0) occident.
Öl n. (-[e]s, -e) oil; ~ ins Feuer giessen, (fig.) to add fuel to the fire.
Öl: ~baum m. olive-tree; ~berg m. Mount of Olives; ~bild n. oil-painting; ~druck m. chromo(lithograph), oleograph.
Oleander m. (-s, -) oleander.
ölen v.t. to oil; to anoint.
Öl: ~farbe f. oil-paint; ~gemälde n. oil-painting.
ölig a. oily, oleaginous.
Olive f. (-, -n) olive.
Olivenöl n. olive-oil.
Öl: ~kanne f. oil can; ~kuchen m. oil-cake; ~malerei f. painting in oil; ~raffinerie f. oil refinery; ~stand m. oil level; ~standzeiger m. oil gauge; ~tankschiff n. oil tanker.
Ölung f. (-, -en) oiling; lubrication; letzte ~, extreme unction.
Ölzweig m. olive-branch.
Omelett n. omelet.
Omnibus m. (-sses, -sse) (omni)bus.
Omnibushaltestelle f. bus stop.
ondulieren v.t. to wave.
Onkel m. (-s, -) uncle.
Opal m. (-s, -e) opal.
Oper f. (-, -n) opera.
Operateur m. (-s, -e) operator.
Operation f. (-, -en) operation.
Operationsgebiet n. (mil.) zone of operations.
operativ a. (mil.) operational.
Operette f. (-, -n) operetta, musical comedy.
operieren v.t. & i. to operate; sich ~ lassen (med.), to be operated on.
Opern: ~gucker m. opera-glass; ~haus, n. opera-house; ~sänger(in) m. (& f.) opera-singer; ~text m. libretto, book.
Opfer n. (-s, -) offering; sacrifice; victim; ein ~ bringen, (fig.) to make a sacrifice.
Opfergabe f. offering.
opfern v.t. to immolate; to sacrifice.
Opferung f. (-, -en) immolation; sacrifice.
Opium n. (-s, 0) opium.
opponieren v.t. to oppose.
Opportunist m. opportunist.
optieren v.i. to opt.
Optik f. (-, 0) optics pl.
Optiker m. (-s, -) optician.
Optimismus m. (-, 0) optimism.

optisch a. optical.
Orakel n. (-s, -), Orakelspruch m. oracle.
orakelhaft, orakelmässig a. oracular.
orakeln v.i. to speak oracularly.
Orange f. (-, -n) bitter orange.
orangefarben a. orange(-coloured).
Orangenbaum m. orange-tree.
Orangerie f. (-, -[e]n) orangery; greenhouse.
Orang-Utan m. (-s, -s) Orang-Utang.
Oratorium n. (-s, -rien) (mus.) oratorio.
Orchester n. (-s, -) orchestra.
Orchestermusik f. orchestral music.
Orchidee f. (-, -n) orchid.
Orden m. (-s, -) order; decoration, medal.
Ordens: ~band n. ribbon (of an order); ~regel f. monastic rule; ~schwester f. sister, nun.
ordentlich a. orderly, tidy; ordinary, usual, regular; ~er Professor, (senior) professor.
ordinär a. vulgar, mean, low.
ordinieren v.t. to ordain; sich ~ lassen, to take (holy) orders.
ordnen v.t. to put in order; to arrange, to regulate; to classify.
Ordnung f. (-, -en) order, arrangement; class; zur ~ rufen, to call to order; etwas in ~ bringen, to straighten out; ~ schaffen, to establish order.
ordnungsmässig a. orderly, regular.
ordnungswidrig a. irregular, illegal; ~es Benehmen n. disorderly conduct.
Ordnungszahl f. ordinal number.
Ordonnanz f. (-, -en) (royal) order; (Person) orderly.
Organ n. (-[e]s, -e) organ; voice.
organisch a. organic.
organisatorisch a. organizational.
organisieren v.t. to organize.
Organismus m. (-e, -men) organism.
Organist m. (-en, -en) organist.
Orgel f. (-, -n) organ.
Orgelbauer m. organ-builder.
Orgel: -pfeife f. organ-pipe; ~register n. organ stop; ~spieler m. organist.
Orgie f. (-, -n) orgy.
Orient m. (-[e]s, 0) Orient, East(ern countries).
orientalisch a. Oriental.
orientieren v.t. to orientate, to inform; ~ v.refl. (fig.) to see one's way.
Orientierung f. zu Ihrer ~, for your guidance.
Original n. (-[e]s, -e) original.
original a. original.
originell a. original, eccentric.
Orkan m. (-[e]s, -e) hurricane, tornado.
Ornat n. (-[e]s, -e) vestments, robes.
Ort n. (-es, -e) place; spot, locality; an ~ und Stelle, on the spot.
orthopädisch a. orthopædic.
örtlich a. local.

Örtlichkeit f. (-, -en) locality.
Ortsangabe f. statement of place.
Ortschaft f. (-, -en) village.
ortsfest a. (mil.) fixed, static.
Ortsgespräch n. (tel.) local call.
ortskundig a. acquainted with the locality.
Öse f. (-, -n) eye (for a hook).
Ost, Osten m. (Ostens, 0) east.
Osterei n. (-s, -er) Easter-egg.
Oster: ~fest n. Easter; ~lamm n. paschal lamb.
österlich a. paschal, Easter...
Ostern n. or pl. Easter.
Ostertag m. Easter day.
östlich a. eastern, easterly; oriental.
ostwärts adv. eastward.
Ostwind m. east wind.
Otter f. (-, -n) otter; adder, viper.
Ottomane f. (-, -n) ottoman.
Ouvertüre f. (-, -n) (mus.) overture.
oval a. oval.
Oxhoft n. (-[e]s, -e) hogshead.
Oxyd n. (-[e]s, -e) oxide.
oxydieren v.t.i. to (become) oxidize(d).
Ozean m. (-s, -e) ocean.
Ozon n. (-s, 0) ozone.

P

Paar n. (-[e]s, -e) pair, couple; (Wildge-flügel) brace; ein paar, a few.
paaren (sich) v.t. & refl. to pair; to couple; to copulate.
Paarung f. (-, -en) copulation; pairing.
paarweise adv. by pairs, in twos.
Pacht m. (-[e]s, -e) & f. (-, -en) tenure, lease; rent.
pachten v.t. to farm, to rent, to take on lease.
Pächter m. (-s, -) tenant, leaseholder; farmer.
Pacht: ~geld n. rental, rent; ~gut n. farm, leasehold estate; ~vertrag m. lease.
Pachtung f. (-, -en) leaseholding.
pachtweise adv. on lease.
Pack m. (-[e]s, -e u. Päcke) pack, bundle, parcel; (fig.) ~ n. rabble.
Päckchen n. (-s, -) small parcel.
Packeis n. (-es, 0) pack(-ice).
packen v.t. to pack up; to lay hold of, to seize; (ergreifen) to affect; (sich) ~ v.refl. to be gone.
Packen m. (-s, -) pack; bale.
packend a. thrilling.
Pack: ~papier n. brown paper; ~pferd n. pack-horse; ~sattel, m. packsaddle; ~träger m. porter; ~wagen m. luggage van.
Packung f. (-, -en) pack, package.
Pädagog[e] m. (-en, -en) pedagogue.
Pädagogik f. (-, 0) science of education.

Pädagogisch a. educational.
Paddelboot n. (-es, -e) canoe.
paffen v.i. to puff away.
Page m. (-n, -n) page (boy).
Pagen: ~kopf m. bobbed hair; ~streich m. page's trick, escapade.
paginieren v.t. to page (a book).
pah! i. pshaw! pooh!
Pair m. (-s, -s) peer.
Paket n. (-[e]s, -e) packet, parcel.
Paketpost f. parcel-post.
Paketfahrtgesellschaft f. parcel-company; (Am.) express company.
Pakt m. (-[e]s, -e) agreement, (com)pact.
paktieren v.i. to come to terms, to agree (on).
Palast m. (-[e]s, Paläste) palace.
Paletot m. (-[s], -s) over-coat.
Palette f. (-, -n) palette.
Palissade f. (-, -n) palisade.
Palme f. (-, -n) palm-tree.
Palmsonntag m. Palm Sunday.
Panier n. (-[e]s, -e) banner, standard.
panieren v.t. to roll in crumbs.
Panik f. (-, -en) panic.
panisch a. panic; ~er Schrecken, panic.
Panne f. (-, -n) breakdown; (Reifen) puncture, flat tire; eine ~ haben, to break down.
panschen v.t. (Milch) to water.
Panther m. (-s, -) panther.
Pantoffel m. (-s, -) slipper; (fig.) unter dem ~ stehen, to be hen-pecked.
Pantoffelheld m. hen-pecked husband.
Pantomime f. (-, -n) pantomime.
Panzer m. (-s, -) armour; cuirass; (Schiffs~) armour(-plating).
Panzer: ~abwehrkanone f. anti-tank gun; ~fahrer m. tank driver; ~glas n. bullet-proof glass; ~jäger pl. anti-tank troops; ~kreuzer m. armoured cruiser, pocket battleship.
panzern v.t. (Schiffe) to plate.
Panzer: ~platte f. armour-plate; ~truppen pl. armoured troops; ~wagen m. armoured car; ~zug m. armoured train.
Päonie f. (-, -n) peony.
Papa m. (-s, -s) papa, dad.
Papagei m. (-en u. -[e]s, -en) parrot.
Papier n. (-[e]s, -e) paper; ein Buch ~, a quire of paper; zu ~ bringen, to commit to paper; ~e pl. stocks, securities pl.
papieren a. (of) paper.
Papier: ~fabrik f. paper-mill; ~geld n. paper-money; ~handlung f. stationer's shop; ~korb m. waste-paper basket; ~serviette f. paper napkin.
papistisch a. popish, papistical.
Papp: ~arbeit f. pasteboard-work; ~band m. (binding in) boards; ~deckel = Pappendeckel.
Pappe f. (-, -en) cardboard, pasteboard.
Pappel f. (-, -n) poplar.

pappen *v.t.* to paste.
Pappen: ~deckel *m.* pasteboard; ~stiel *m.* (*fig.*) trifle.
Pappschachtel *f.* cardboard-box.
Papst *m.* (-es, Päpste) pope.
päpstlich *a.* papal.
Papsttum *n.* (-, 0) papacy; pontificate.
Parabel *f.* (-, -n) parable; (*geom.*) parabola.
Parade *f.* (-, -n) parade; (*fig.*) display; (*mil.*) review; (*Fechten*) parry.
Parade: ~anzug *m.* full dress; ~marsch *m.* march-past; ~platz *m.* parade-ground.
paradieren *v.t.* & *i.* to parade.
Paradies *n.* (-es, -se) paradise.
paradiesisch *a.* paradisiacal.
paradox *a.* paradoxical.
Paragraph *m.* (-en, -en) paragraph.
parallel *a.* parallel.
Parallele *f.* (-, -n) parallel, parallel line.
Parallelversammlung *f.* overflow meeting.
paraphieren *v.t.* to initial.
Parasit *m.* (-en, -en) parasite.
Paratyphus *m.* (-, 0) paratyphoid (fever).
Pardon *m.* (-s, 0) pardon.
Parfüm *n.* (-s, -e) perfume, scent.
Pari *n.* (-[s], 0) par (of exchange).
pari *adv.* at par.
parieren *v.t.* to parry; ~ *v.i.* to obey.
Parität *f.* (-, -en) parity.
Park *m.* (-[e]s, -e) park.
parken *v.t.* & *i.* to park; ~ verboten, no parking!
Parkett *n.* (-[e]s, -e) parquet (floor).
Parkplatz *m.* parking lot.
Parlament *n.* (-[e]s, -e) Parliament.
Parlamentarier *m.* (-, -) parliamentarian.
parlamentarisch *a.* parliamentary.
Parodie *f.* (-, -[e]n) parody.
Parole *f.* (-, -n) watchword, parole.
Partei *f.* (-, -en) party, side; ~ ergreifen, to take sides, to side (with).
Partei: ~funktionär *m.* party official; ~gänger *m.* partisan.
parteiisch, parteilich *a.* partial.
parteilos *a.* impartial, neutral.
Parteitag *m.* party conference.
Parteiung *f.* (-, -en) division into parties.
Parterre *n.* (-[s], -s) ground-floor; flower-bed; (*im Theater*) pit.
Partie *f.* (-, -[e]n) parcel, lot; (*Heirat*) match; (*Spiel*) game; (*Ausflug*) excursion.
Partitur *f.* (-, -en) score.
Partikel *f.* (-, -n) particle.
Partisane *m.* (-n, -n) (*mil.*) partisan.
Partizip *n.* (-s, -zipien) participle.
Partner *m.* (-s, -) partner.
Parze *f.* (-, -n) Fate, weird sister.
Parzelle *f.* (-, -n) plot (of land).
parzellieren *v.t.* to parcel out.
Pascha *m.* (-s, -s) pasha.

Pasquill *n.* (-[e]s, -e) lampoon.
Pass *m.* (Passes, Pässe) pass, defile; passport; (*Ritt*) amble.
Passagier *m.* (-[e]s, -e) passenger; blinder ~, stowaway.
Passagierflugzeug *n.* airliner.
Passah *n.* (-s, -s) Passover.
Passant *m.* (-en, -en) passer-by.
Passanten: ~hotel *n.* Am. transient hotel; ~quartier *n.* transient billets.
Passatwind *m.* tradewind.
passen *v.i.* to fit, to suit, to wait, to watch; (*im Spiel*) to pass; (sich) ~ *v.refl.* to be fit or convenient.
passend *a.* fitting, suitable; convenient.
passieren *v.t.* to pass, to cross; ~ *v.i.* to happen.
Passierschein *m.* pass, permit.
passiv *a.* passive; indolent, inactive.
Passiva, Passiven (*pl.*) liabilities.
Passivhandel *m.* adverse trade.
Passiv[um] *n.* (-s, -en u. -va) passive voice.
Pastell(stift) *m.* (-[e]s, -e) pastel, crayon.
Pastete *f.* (-, -n) pie, pastry.
Pastetenbäcker *m.* pastry-cook.
pasteurisieren *v.t.* to pasteurize.
Pastille *f.* (-, -n) lozenge, pastil.
Pastor *m.* (-s, u. -en, -en) pastor, minister.
Pate *m.* (-n, -n) & *f.* (-, -n) godfather, godmother.
Patenkind *n.* god-child.
Patent *n.* (-[e]s, -e) patent; (*mil.*) commission; angemeldetes ~, pending patent.
Patent: ~amt *n.* patent office; ~anmeldung *f.* application for a patent; ~anwalt *m.* patent agent or lawyer; ~beschreibung *f.* specification; ~erteilung *f.* patent-grant.
patentieren *v.* to patent; sich etwas ~ lassen, to take out a patent for a thing.
Patent: ~inhaber *m.* patentee; ~inhabergesellschaft *f.* patent holding company; ~verlängerung *f.* renewal of a patent.
pathetisch *a.* & *adv.* pathetic(ally).
Patholog *m.* pathologist.
Pathologie *f.* pathology.
pathologisch *a.* pathological.
Patient *m.* (-en, -en) patient.
patriarchalisch *a.* patriarchal; paternal.
Patriot *m.* (-en, -en) patriot.
Patrizier *m.* (-s, -) patrician.
Patron *m.* (-[e]s, -e) patron, protector, supporter.
Patronat *n.* (-[e]s, -e) patronage; (*einer Pfründe*) advowson.
Patrone *f.* (-, -n) pattern; cartridge.
Patronentasche *f.* cartridge-box, pouch.
Patrouille *f.* (-, -) patrol.
Patsche *f.* (-, -n) (*fig.*) pickle, mess, fix
patschen *v.i.* to splash; to slap.
Pauke *f.* (-, -n) kettle-drum.
pauken *v.i.* to beat the kettle-drums.
pausbackig *a.* chubby(-faced).

Pauschalsumme f. lump sum.
Pause f. (-, -n) pause, stop; (mus.) rest; interval, break; traced design.
pausen v.t. to trace, to counterdraw.
pausieren v.i. to pause.
Pauspapier n. tracing paper.
Pavian m. (-s, -e) baboon.
Pavillon m. (-s, -s) pavilion.
Pazifist m. (-en, -en) pacifist.
Pech n. (-[e]s, -e) pitch; (fig.) bad luck.
pechfinster a. pitch-dark.
pechschwarz a. jet-black, pitch-dark.
Pechvogel m. (fig.) unlucky beggar.
Pedal n. (-[e]s, -e) pedal.
Pedant m. (-en, -en) pedant, prig.
Pedanterie f. (-, 0) pedantry.
pedantisch a. pedantic; over-punctilious.
Pedell m. (-es u. -en, -e[n]) beadle.
Pegel m. (-s, -) water-gauge.
peilen v.t. (nav.) to sound, to take soundings, to take the bearings of.
Peilung f. (-, -en) direction finding.
Pein f. (-, 0) pain, torment.
peinigen v.t. to torment, to torture.
peinlich a. painful, embarrassing.
Peitsche f. (-, -n) whip, scourge.
peitschen v.t. to whip.
pekuniär a. pecuniary.
Pelikan m. (-[e]s, -e) pelican.
pellen v.t. to peel, to skin.
Pellkartoffeln pl. potatoes in jackets.
Pelz m. (-es, -e) fur, pelt; fur-coat.
Pelzhändler m. furrier.
Pelz: ~kragen m. fur collar; ~mantel m. fur coat; ~mütze f. fur cap.
Pendel m. (-s, -) pendulum.
pendeln v.i. to oscillate.
Pendelverkehr m. shuttle service.
Penizillin n. (-s, 0) penicillin.
Pension f. (-, -en) pension; half-pay; board; boarding-house.
Pensionär m. (-[e]s, -e) pensioner.
Pensionat n. (-[e]s, -e) boarding-school.
pensionieren v.t. to pension (off); sich ~ lassen, to retire on half-pay.
Pensionierung f. (-, -en) retirement.
pensions: ~berechtigt a. pensionable, superannuable; ~fähig a. pensionable.
Pensum n. (-s, -sa u. -sen) task, lesson.
Perfekt(um) n. (-s, -ta, -te) perfect (tense).
perfid a. perfidious.
Pergament n. (-[e]s, -e) parchment.
Periode f. (-, -n) period.
periodisch a. & adv. periodical(ly).
Peripherie f. (-, -[e]n) circumference, periphery.
Perle f. (-, -n) pearl; (Glas) bead.
perlen v.i. to sparkle, to rise in pearls.
Perl: ~graupen f.pl. pearl-barley; ~huhn n. guinea-fowl; ~mutter f. mother-of-pearl.
perniziöse Anämie f. pernicious anæmia.
per procura (p.p.), for and on behalf of.

Person f. (-, -en) person.
Personal n. (-s, -e) staff, personnel.
Personal... personnel-; ~abbau m. reduction of staff; ~abteilung f. personnel section; ~akten pl. personnel file.
Personalien pl. particulars.
Personen: ~zug m. (rail.) passenger train; ~verkehr m. passenger traffic.
personifizieren v.t. to personify.
persönlich a. personal; ~er Wert m. sentimental value; ~ adv. in person.
Persönlichkeit f. (-, -en) personality.
Perspektive f. (-, -n) perspective.
Perücke f. (-, -n) wig, periwig.
pervers a. perverse.
Pessimismus m. (-, 0) pessimism.
Pest f. (-, -en) plague, pest(ilence).
Petersilie f. (-, 0) parsley.
Petition f. (-, -en) petition.
Petroleum n. (-s, 0) petroleum.
Petschaft n. (-[e]s, -e) seal, signet.
in petto haben, to have up one's sleeve.
Pfad m. (-es, -e) path.
Pfadfinder m. (-s, -) boy scout; ~in f. girl guide.
Pfaffe m. (-n, -n) (verächtlich) parson.
Pfahl m. (-[e]s, Pfähle) pale, post, pole.
Pfahlbau m. pile dwelling.
Pfand n. (-[e]s, Pfänder) pledge, pawn; security; (Spiel) forfeit.
pfändbar a. distrainable.
Pfandbrief m. mortgage bond.
pfänden v.t. to distrain, to seize.
Pfänderspiel n. game of forfeits.
Pfand: ~haus n. pawn-shop; ~leiher m. pawnbroker; ~schuldner m. pledger.
Pfändung f. (-, -en) distraint, distress; ~sbefehl m. distress warrant.
Pfanne f. (-, -n) pan.
Pfannkuchen m. pancake.
Pfarre f. (-, -n) living; rectory, parsonage, vicarage; parish.
Pfarrer m. (-s, -) vicar, rector.
Pfarr: ~haus n. parsonage, vicarage; ~kirche f. parish church.
Pfau m. (-[e]s u. -en, -en) peacock.
Pfeffer m. (-s, 0) pepper.
Pfefferminze f. peppermint.
pfeffern v.t. to pepper.
Pfeife f. (-, -n) (tobacco-)pipe; whistle; eine ~ stopfen, to fill a pipe.
pfeifen v.i. & i.st. to pipe; to whistle.
Pfeifenreiniger m. pipe cleaner.
Pfeifer m. (-s, -) piper; whistler.
Pfeil m. (-[e]s, -e) arrow; bolt, dart.
Pfeiler m. (-s, -) pillar; pier.
Pfeilspitze f. arrow-head.
Pfennig m. (-s, -e) small coin (⅛ penny).
Pferch m. (-[e]s, -e) fold, pen.
pferchen v.t. to pen, to fold; to coop up.
Pferd n. (-[e]s, -e) horse; (Turnen) vaulting-horse; zu ~e, on horseback.

Pferde...horsedrawn, *a.*; ~kraft *f.* horsepower.

Pferde: ~rennen *n.* (horse-)race; ~zucht *f.* breeding of horses.

Pfiff *m.* (-[e]s, -e) whistle; trick.

pfiffig *a.* sly, sharp, smart.

Pfingsten *n. or f. or pl. u.* Pfingstfest *n.* Whitsuntide; Pentecost.

Pfingstmontag *m.* Whit-Monday.

Pfirsich *m.* (-, -e) peach.

Pflanze *f.* (-, -n) plant.

pflanzen *v.t.* to plant, to set.

Pflanzen: ~faser *f.* vegetable fibre; ~fett *n.* vegetable fat; ~kost, ~nahrung *f.* vegetable diet or food; ~öl *n.* vegetable oil; ~reich *n.* vegetable kingdom; ~schädling *m.* pest.

Pflanzer *m.* (-s, -) planter.

Pflanzung *f.* (-, -en) plantation.

Pflaster *n.* (-s, -) plaster; pavement; *englisches* ~, court-plaster.

pflastern *v.t.* to pave.

Pflasterstein *m.* paving-stone.

Pflaume *f.* (-, -n) plum; *getrocknete* ~, prune.

Pflege *f.* (-, 0) care, cultivation.

Pflege: ~eltern *pl.* foster-parents *pl.*; ~kind *n.* foster-child; ~mutter *f.* foster-mother.

pflegen *v.t.* to foster, to nurse, to take care of, to attend to; ~ *v.i.* to be accustomed, to use; (sich) ~ *v.refl.* to take great care of oneself; *Umgang* ~, to see a good deal (of).

Pflege: ~sohn *m.* foster-son; ~tochter *f.* foster-daughter; ~vater *m.* foster-father.

Pflegling *m.* (-[e]s, -e) foster-child.

Pflicht *f.* (-, -en) duty; obligation.

Pflicht: ~eifer *m.* zeal, dutifulness; ~gefühl *n.* sense of duty.

pflicht: ~gemäss *a.* in fulfilment of a duty; ~ *adv.* as in duty bound; ~getreu *a.* dutiful, conscientious; ~mässig *a.* prescribed by duty; ~teil *m.* compulsory portion; ~vergessen *a.* undutiful; ~verletzung *f.* breach of duty; ~versäumnis *f.* neglect of duty.

Pflock *m.* (-[e]s, Pflöcke) plug, peg.

pflöcken *v.t.* to peg.

pflücken *v.t.* to pluck; to pick.

Pflug *m.* (-[e]s, Pflüge) plough.

Pflugbagger *m.* bulldozer.

pflügen *v.t.* to plough.

Pflugschar *f.* plough-share.

Pforte *f.* (-, -n) gate; (*nav.*) port-hole.

Pförtner *m.* (-s, -) door-keeper, porter.

Pfosten *m.* (-s, -) post; pale, stake.

Pfote *f.* (-, -n) paw, claw.

Pfriem *m.* (-[e]s, -e), Pfriemen *m.* (s, -), Pfrieme *f.* (-, -n) awl, punch.

Pfropf *m.* (-[e]s, -e *u.* Pfröpfe), Pfropfen *m.* (-s, -) cork, stopper; (*Holz*) plug.

pfropfen *v.t.* to cram; (*Pflanzen*) to graft; to cork.

Pfründe *f.* (-, -n) benefice, living.

Pfuhl *m.* (-[e]s, -e) pool, puddle, slough.

pfui! *i.* fie! shame!; ~ *schäme dich!* fie upon you!

Pfund *n.* (-[e]s, -e) pound.

pfündig *a.* (*in Zus.*) of (so many) pounds.

pfundweise *adv.* by the pound.

pfuschen *v.i.* to bungle, to botch; *einem ins Handwerk* ~, (*fig.*) to trespass on another's field.

Pfütze *f.* (-, -n) puddle.

Phänomen *n.* (-s, -e) phenomenon.

Phantasie *f.* (-, -[e]n) fancy; imagination.

phantasiereich *a.* fanciful, imaginative.

phantasieren *v.i.* to indulge one's imagination; (*med.*) to wander, to rave; (*mus.*) to improvise.

Phantast *m.* (-en, -en) visionary.

phantastisch *a.* fantastic, whimsical, wild.

Pharisäer *m.* (-s, -) Pharisee.

pharisäerhaft, pharisäisch *a.* pharisaical.

Pharmazeut *m.* (-en, -en) student of pharmacy.

Phase *f.* (-, -n) (*astr.*) phase; stage.

Philanthrop *m.* (-en, -en) philanthropist.

Philister *m.* (-s, -) Philistine.

philisterhaft, philiströs *a.* narrow-minded.

Philolog(e) *m.* (-en, -en) philologist.

Philologie *f.* (-, 0) philology.

philologisch *a.* philological.

Philosoph *m.* (-en, -en) philosopher.

Philosophie *f.* (-, -[e]n) philosophy.

philosophieren *v.i.* to philosophize.

philosophisch *a.* philosophical.

Phlegma *n.* (-[s], 0) phlegm.

phlegmatisch *a.* phlegmatic.

Phlegmone *f.* (-, -n) (*med.*) phlegmon.

Phonetik *f.* (-, -en) phonetics.

phonetisch *a.* phonetic.

Phosphor *m.* (-s, -e) phosphorus.

phosphoreszieren *v.i.* to phosphoresce.

Phosphorsäure *f.* phosphoric acid.

Photograph *m.* (-en, -en) photographer.

Photographie *f.* (-, -[e]n) photograph. (*fam.*) photo; (*Kunst*) photography.

photographieren *v.t.* to photograph.

Photogravüre *f.* photogravure, photo-engraving.

Photokopie *f.* (-, -n) photostatic copy, photo-copy.

Photozelle *f.* photo-electric cell.

Phrase *f.* (-, -n) phrase, idiom; tall talk.

phrasenhaft *a.* empty, grandiloquent.

Physik (*Phü-*) *f.* (-, 0) physics *pl.*

physikalisch *a.* physical.

Physiker *m.* (-s, -) physicist.

Physiolog *m.* physiologist.

physisch *a.* physical.

Pianino *n.* (-[s], -s) (cottage) piano.

Piano(forte) *n.* (-s, -s) piano.

Picke *f.* (-, -n) pick-axe.

Pickel *m.* (-s, -) stonemason's hammer; pimple.

picken *v.i.* to peck, to pick.

piepen, piepsen *v.i.* to chirp, to peep.

Pietät *f.* (-, 0) reverence.

pietätvoll *a.* reverent, reverential.

Pietist *m.* (-en, -en) pietist.

Pik *n.* (-[s], -[s]) (*in der Karte*) spade.

pikant *a.* piquant, spicy, pungent; racy.

Pikee *m.* & *n.* (-s, -s) (*Stoff*) quilting.

pikfein *a.* spick and span.

Pilger *m.* (-s, -) pilgrim.

Pilgerfahrt *f.* pilgrimage.

pilgern *v.i.* (*s, h*) to go on a pilgrimage.

Pille *f.* (-, -n) pill.

Pilot *m.* (-en, -en) pilot.

Pilz *m.* (-es, -e) mushroom; (*giftiger*) toadstool.

Pinie *f.* (-, -n) stone-pine.

Pinscher *m.* (-s, -) terrier.

Pinsel *m.* (-s, -) (painter's) brush; (*fig.*) simpleton.

Pinzette *f.* (-, -n) pair of tweezers.

Pionier *m.* (*mil.*) engineer; (*fig.*) pioneer.

Pirat *m.* (-en, -en) pirate.

pirschen *v.t.* to go deer-stalking.

pissen *v.i.* to piss.

Pistazie *f.* (-, -n) pistachio.

Pistole *f.* (-, -n) pistol, (*Am.*) gun.

placken *v.t.* to harass, to pester; (sich) ~ *v.refl.* to toil, to drudge.

Plackerei *f.* (-, -en) toil, drudgery; vexation.

plädieren *v.i.* to plead.

Plage *f.* (-, -n) plague, torment, bother.

Plagegeist *m.* bore.

plagen *v.t.* to plague, to trouble to vex; (sich) ~ *v.refl.* to drudge, to slave.

Plagiat *n.* (-[e]s, -[e]) plagiarism, plagiary.

Plakat *n.* (-[e]s, -e) poster, placard, bill.

Plan *m.* (-[e]s, -e *u.* Pläne) plan; design, scheme.

plan *a.* plain, level.

planen *v.t.* to plan, project.

Planet *m.* (-en, -en) planet.

planieren *v.t.* to level; to plane.

Planimetrie *f.* (-, 0) plane geometry.

Planke *f.* (-, -n) plank, board.

Plänkelei *f.* (-, -en) skirmishing.

plänkeln *v.i.* (*mil.*) to skirmish.

planlos *a.* aimless, without a plan; ~ *adv.* at random.

planmässig *a.* established, scheduled, (*Beamter*) permanent; ~ *adv.* according to plan.

planschen, plantschen *v.i.* to splash.

Planspiel *n.* (*mil.*) map exercise.

Plantage *f.* (-, -n) plantation.

Planwirtschaft *f.* planned economy.

plappern *v.i.* to prattle, to chatter.

plärren *v.t.* to blubber; (*singend*) to drawl.

Plastik *f.* (-, 0) plastic art.

plastisch *a.* plastic; ~e Chirurgie *f.* plastic surgery.

Platane *f.* (-, -n) plane-tree.

Platin *n.* (-s, 0), platinum.

plätschern *v.i.* to splash, to dabble.

platt *a.* flat, level; (*fam.*) amazed.

Plättbrett *n.* ironing-board.

plattdeutsch *a.* Low German.

Platte *f.* (-, -n) plate; bald head, pate; (*Stein*) flag, slab; (*Teller*) tray, silver; (*Tisch*) leaf; (*Grammophon*) record.

Plätteisen *n.* (flat)-iron.

plätten *v.t.* to iron.

Plattenspieler *m.* (*Grammophon*), elektrischer ~, electric record player.

Platt: ~form *f.* platform; ~fuss *m.* flat foot; ~fusseinlage *f.* arch support, foot support.

plattfüssig *a.* flat-footed.

Plattheit *f.* (-, -en) flatness, platitude.

Plätt: ~wäsche *f.*, ~zeug *n.* washing, linen to be ironed.

Platz *m.* (-es, Plätze) place; room space; public place, square; seat; ~ machen, to make room; ~ nehmen, to take a seat.

Plätzchen *n.* (-s, -) (chocolate) drop; small cake.

platzen *v.i.* to burst; to explode.

Platz: ~patrone *f.* blank cartridge; ~regen *m.* downpour.

Plauderei *f.* (-, -en) chat.

plaudern *v.i.* to chatter, to gossip, to chat.

Pleite *f.* (-, -n) (*vulg.*) bankruptcy; ~ sein, ~ gehen, to fail, to go smash.

Plenarsitzung *f.* (-, -en) plenary session.

Plenum *n.* (-s, 0) plenary meeting.

Pleuelstange *f.* (-, -n) connecting rod.

Plexiglas *f.* safety glass.

Plissee *n.* (-s, -s) pleating.

Plombe *f.* (-, -n) lead seal; stopping (of teeth).

plombieren *v.t.* to seal with lead; to plug, to stop (a tooth).

plötzlich *a.* sudden; ~ *adv.* suddenly, all of a sudden.

plump *a.* unwieldy, clumsy; coarse.

plumpsen *v.i.* (*s*) (*fam.*) to plump.

Plunder *m.* (-s, 0) trumpery, lumber, trash.

plündern *v.t.* to pillage, to plunder.

Plünderung *f.* (-, -en) plundering, sack.

Plural *m.* (-s, -e) plural (number).

Plüsch *m.* (-es, -e) plush.

Plusquamperfekt(um) *n.* (-s, -fekte) pluperfect.

Pöbel *m.* (-s, 0) mob, rabble, populace.

pöbelhaft *a.* vulgar, low.

pochen *v.t.* to knock; (*vom Herzen*) to beat, to throb; (*fig.*) to boast (of).

Pocken *f.pl.* small-pox.

Pockennarbe *f.* pock mark.

Poesie *f.* (-, -[e]n) poetry, poesy.

Poetik *f.* (-, -en) poetics.

poetisch *a.* & *adv.* poetical(ly); poetic.
Pokal *m.* (-[e]s, -e) goblet; (*Sport*) cup.
Pökelfleisch *n.* salt meat.
pökeln *v.t.* to pickle, to salt.
Pol *m.* (-[e]s, -e) Pole.
Polar..., polar.
Polarstern *m.* Pole-star.
Polemik *f.* (-, 0) controversy.
Police *f.* (-, -n) policy; ~inhaber *m.* policy-holder.
Polier *m.* (-[e]s, -e) foreman (of masons).
polieren *v.t.* to polish, to burnish.
Politik *f.* (-, 0) politics *pl.*; policy.
Politiker *m.* (-s, -) politician.
politisch *a.* political; ~ massgebende Person *f.* policy-maker; ~ prüfen *v.t.* to screen.
politisieren *v.i.* to talk politics.
Politur *f.* (-, -en) polish.
Polizei *f.* (-, -en) police; police-office; *sich der ~ stellen*, to give oneself up to the police; ~aufsicht *f.* police supervision; ~präsidium *n.* police headquarters.
polizeilich *a.* of the police.
Polizeiwache *f.* police-station.
polizeiwidrig *a.* contrary to the police regulations.
Polizist *m.* (-en, -en) policeman.
Polster *n.* (-s, -) cushion; bolster.
polstern *v.t.* to stuff, to pad.
Polterabend *m.* wedding eve.
poltern *v.i.* to racket, to rattle; to bluster.
Polyp *m.* (-en, -en) polyp(us).
Polytechnikum *n.* (-[s], -techniken) polytechnic school, engineering college.
Pomade *f.* (-, -n) pomade.
pomadig *a.* (*vulg.*) cool, indifferent.
Pomeranze *f.* (-, -n) orange, lime.
Pomp *m.* (-[e]s, 0) pomp, splendour.
pomphaft *a.* stately, pompous.
pompös *a.* stately, magnificent.
Ponton *m.* pontoon, (*Am.*) ponton.
Pony *n. or m.* (-s, -s) pony.
Popanz *m.* (-es, -e) bugbear.
Popo *m.* (-s, -s) (*fam.*) backside.
populär *a.* popular.
Popularität *f.* (-, 0) popularity.
Pore *f.* (-, -n) pore.
pornographisch *a.* pornographic.
porös *a.* porous.
Porphyr *m.* (-s, -e) porphyry.
Portal *n.* (-[e]s, -e) porch.
Portefeuille *n.* (-[s], -s) portfolio.
Portemonnaie *n.* (-s, -s) purse.
Portier *m.* (-s, -s) porter, (*Am.*) janitor; (*Hotel*) hall-porter, desk-clerk.
Portion *f.* (-, -en) portion, ration; *zweite ~*, second helping; *eine ~ Kaffee*, coffee for one.
Porto *n.* (-s, -s *u.* Porti) postage.
portofrei *a.* post free, (pre)paid.
Portospesen *pl.* postal expenses.

Porträt *n.* (-s, -s) portrait.
portraitieren *v.t.* to portray.
Porzellan *n.* (-[e]s, -e) china, porcelain.
Posaune *f.* (-, -n) trombone.
posaunen *v.t.* (*fig.*) to trumpet.
Pose *f.* (-, -n) attitude.
positiv *a.* positive.
Positur *f.* (-, -en) posture.
Posse *f.* (-, -n) jest; farce, burlesque.
possierlich *a.* droll, funny.
Post *f.* (-, -en) post, mail; post-office; *mit der ~*, by post; *gewöhnliche ~* (*nicht Luftpost*), surface mail; *mit umgehender ~ postwendend*, by return of post.
Postament *n.* (-[e]s, -e) pedestal, base.
Post: ~amt *n.* post-office; ~anweisung *f.* money-order; ~bote *m.* postman; ~dampfer *m.* mail-steamer.
Posten *m.* (-s, -) post, station, place; (*mil.*) outpost, sentry; (*com.*) item, sum; parcel, lot; entry.
Postenkette *f.* line of sentries.
Postfach *n.* post-office box.
Postkarte *f.* postcard; *farbige ~*, colour postcard.
Postkutsche *f.* stage-coach, mail-coach.
postlagernd *a.* & *adv.* (*auf Briefen*) to be (kept till) called for, post restante.
Post: ~ministerium *n.* Ministry of Post; (*in Eng.*) Offices of the Postmaster General; ~paket *n.* parcel sent by post; ~scheck *m.* postal cheque; ~scheckkonto *n.* postal check(ing) account; ~sparkasse *f.* post-office savings bank; ~stempel *m.* post-mark.
postnumerando *adv.* pay after receipt.
Potentat *m.* (-en, -en) potentate.
Potenz *f.* (-, -en) (*math.*) power.
potenzieren *v.t.* to raise to a higher power.
poussieren *v.t.* to promote; ~ *v.i.* to flirt.
Pracht *f.* (-, 0) splendour, pomp, state.
prächtig *a.* magnificent, splendid.
prachtvoll *a.* splendid.
Prädikat *n.* (-[e]s, -e) predicate; title.
prägen *v.t.* to coin, to stamp.
Prägestock *m.* die, matrice.
prägnant *a.* pregnant, pithy.
prahlen *v.i.* to boast, to brag.
Prahler *m.* (-s, -) braggart, boaster.
Prahlerei *f.* (-, -en) boasting.
prahlerisch *a.* boastful, ostentatious.
Praktik *f.* (-, -en) trick, machination.
Praktikant *m.* (-en, -en) probationer.
Praktiker *m.* (-s, -) practical man.
praktisch *a.* practical; ~e Arzt *m.* general practitioner.
praktizieren *v.t.* to practise.
Prälat *m.* (-en, -en) prelate.
Praliné *n.* (-s, -s), Praline *f.* (-, -n) (filled) chocolate; ~schachtel *f.* box of chocolates.
prall *a.* stuffed out; tight.
prallen *v.i.* to rebound.

Prämie f. (-, -n) premium; prize.
prämiieren v.t. to award a prize.
Prämisse f. (-, -n) premise.
prangen v.i. to glitter.
Pranger m. (-s, -) pillory.
pränumerando adv. pay in advance.
Präparat n. (-[e]s, -e) preparation, mixture.
präparieren v.t. to prepare.
Präsens n. (-, e) present (tense).
präsentieren v.t. to present.
Präsenz f. (-, -en) presence; ~liste f. list of those present; ~stärke f. actual strength.
Präsident m. -en, -en) president, chairman.
präsidieren v.t. & i. to preside over, to be in the chair.
Präsidium n. (-s,-dien) chair(man's office), presidency; directorate.
prasseln v.i. to crackle.
prassen v.i. to gormandize, to revel.
Prätendent m. (-en, -en) pretender.
Präteritum n. (-s, -ta) preterite, past tense.
Praxis f. (-, 0) practice; exercise; (Arzt, Rechtsanwalt) connection.
Präzedenzfall m. precedent.
präzis a. punctual, exact.
Präzision f. (-, 0) precision; ~sarbeiter m. precision worker; ~swerkzeug n. precision tool.
predigen v.t. to preach.
Prediger m. (-s, -) preacher.
Predigt f. (-, -en) sermon; lecture.
Preis m. (Preises, Preise) (Belohnung) prize; (Wert) price, rate, cost, figure; (Lob) praise, glory; um keinen ~, not for the world.
Preis: ~angabe f. quotation (of price); ~ausschreiben n. competition.
preisen v.t.st. to extol.
preisgeben v.t. to expose; to abandon.
preisgekrönt a. prize-medalled.
Preis: ~lage f. range of prices; in niedriger ~lage, low-priced; ~richter m. adjudicator; ~träger m. winner (of a competition); ~sturz m. sudden fall of prices; ~überwachung f. price-control.
preiswert a. cheap.
Preisselbeere u. **Preiselbeere** f. cranberry.
prekär a. precarious.
Prellbock m. buffers pl.
prellen v.t. to toss; to defraud, to cheat.
Prellung f. (-, -en) (med.) concussion.
Presse f. (-, -n) press.
Presse: ~besprechung f. press conference; ~korrespondenz f. press service; ~tribüne f. press gallery.
pressen v.t. to press, to squeeze.
Press: ~freiheit f. liberty of the press; ~gesetz n. press-law; ~kohle f. briquette.

pressieren v.i. to be urgent.
preussischblau a. Prussian blue.
prickeln v.t. to prickle, to itch.
prickelnd a. pointed, sharp, pungent.
Priester m. (-s, -) priest.
Priesterin f. (-, -nen) priest(ess).
Priesterschaft f. clergy; priesthood.
Priestertum n. priesthood.
Priesterweihe f. ordination of a priest.
Prima f. (-, -men) top-class; 8th and 9th form in secondary school.
Primaner m. (-s, -) sixth-form boy.
Primas m. (-, -) primate.
Primawechsel m. first of exchange.
Primel f. (-, -n) primrose, cowslip.
primitiv a. primitive.
Primzahl f. (ar.) prime number.
Prinz m. (-en, -en) prince.
Prinzessin f. (-, -nen) princess.
Prinzip n. (-[e]s, -e u. -ien) principle.
Prinzipal m. (-[e]s, -e) principal, chief.
Prise f. (-, -n) prize; (Schnupftabak) pinch.
Prisengericht n. prize-court.
Prisma n. (-s, -men) prism.
prismenförmig a. (mech.) vee-.
Pritsche f. (-, -n) wooden couch, bunk.
privat a. private.
Privatdozent m. unsalaried lecturer (at German Universities).
privatim adv. privately.
privatisieren v.i. to live as a private gentleman.
Privat: ~mann m. private person; ~recht n. civil law.
privilegieren v.t. to privilege.
Privilegium n. (-s, -gien) privilege.
pro, pr. per; ~ Jahr, per annum.
Probe f. (-, -n) experiment, trial; test; (Waren~) sample; (Theater) rehearsal; auf ~, on probation; auf die ~ stellen, to put to the test.
Probe... probationary, a.
Probe: ~dienst m. probationary service; ~exemplar n. specimen copy; ~fahrt f. trial run; ~flug m. test flight; ~zeit f. term of probation, qualifying period.
proben v.i. & t. to rehearse.
probieren v.t. to try, to test; to taste.
Problem n. (-s, -e) problem, question.
Produkte f. produce; ~nbörse f. produce exchange.
Produktion f. (-, -en) production.
Produzent m. (en, -en) producer.
produzieren v.t. to produce.
profan a. profane.
profanieren v.t. to profane, to desecrate.
Profession f. (-, -en) profession; trade.
Professor m. (-s, -en) professor.
Professur f. (-, -en) professorship.
Profil n. (-s, -e) profile.
profitieren v.i. to profit (by).
Prognose f. (-, -n) prognosis.
Programm n. (-[e]s, -e) programme.

Projekt n. (-[e]s, -e) project, scheme.
Projektionsapparat m. projector.
Projektionsschirm m. screen.
projizieren v.t. to project.
proklamieren v.t. to proclaim.
Prokura f. (-, 0) proxy.
Prokurist m. (-en, -en) confidential clerk.
Proletariat n. (-[e]s, 0) proletariat(e).
Proletarier m. (-s, -) proletarian.
Prolog m. (-[e]s, -e) prologue.
prolongieren v.t. to renew, to prolong.
Promenade f. (-, -n) promenade, walk.
Promotion f. (-, -en) graduation, taking of a degree.
promovieren v.i. to graduate.
prompt a. prompt, quick.
Pronomen n. (-s, -mina) pronoun.
Propeller m. (-s, -) propeller.
Prophet m. (-en, -en) prophet.
prophetisch a. prophetic.
prophezeien v.t. to prophesy.
Prophezeiung f. (-, -en) prophecy.
proportional a. proportional; umgekehrt ~, inversely proportioned.
Propst m. (-es, Pröpste) provost.
Prosa f. (-, 0) prose.
Prosaiker m. (-s, -) prose-writer.
prosaisch a. prosaic; (fig.) prosy.
prosit! (vulg.) prost! i. much good may it do you!
Prospekt m. (-[e]s, -e) prospectus.
Prostituierte f. (-n, -n) prostitute.
Proszeniumsloge f. stage-box.
Protektorat n. (-es, -e) protectorate.
Protest m. (-es, -e) protest; ~ erheben, to enter a protest.
Protestant m. (-en, -en) Protestant.
protestantisch a. Protestant.
protestieren v.t. to protest.
Protokoll n. (-[s], -e) minutes pl.; ~ führen, to keep the minutes; zu ~ geben, to place on record; zu ~ nehmen, to take down.
protokollieren v.t. to write a minute of.
Protz m. (-n, -n) swell; snob.
Protze f. (-, -n) limber (of a gun).
protzig a. purse-proud, insolent.
Proviant m. (-[e]s, 0) provisions, stores.
Provinz f. (-, -en) province.
Provision f. (-, -en) commission.
Provisor m. (-s, -en) chemist's assistant.
provisorisch a. provisional, temporary.
provozieren v.t. to provoke.
Prozent n. (-[e]s, -e) per cent.
Prozess m. (-zesses, -zesse) process; law-suit (action); proceedings pl.; kurzen ~ machen mit, to make short work of.
Prozessakten f.pl. minutes (pl.) of a law case.
prozessieren v.i. to go to law.
Prozession f. (-, -en) procession.
Prozesskosten f.pl. law-costs pl.
Prozessverfahren n. legal procedure.

prüde a. prudish, squeamish.
Prüderie f. (-, 0) prudery.
prüfen v.t. to try, to test; to examine; to censor; von der Zensur geprüft, censored.
Prüfung f. (-, -en) trial; examination; eine ~ machen, to take an examination or test; sich einer ~ unterziehen, to sit for an examination or test.
Prüfungs: ~aufgaben pl. examination papers; ~kommission f. examination board.
Prügel m. (-s, -) stick, cudgel.
Prügelei f. (-, -en) f. fight, row, scuffle.
prügeln v.t. to cudgel, to thrash.
Prügelstrafe f. corporal punishment.
Prunk m. (-es, 0) ostentation, show.
prunken v.i. to make a show.
prunkvoll a. gorgeous, splendid.
Psalm m. (-s, -en) psalm.
pst! i. hush!
psychiatrisch, psychiatric; ~e Klinik f. mental hospital.
Psychiater m. (-s, -) psychiatrist.
psychisch a. psychic(al).
Psychoanalyse f. psycho-analysis.
Psycholog m. (-en, -en) psychologist.
Psychologie f. psychology.
Pubertät f. (-, 0) puberty.
Publikum n. (-[s], 0) public.
publizieren v.t. to publish.
Pudding m. (-s, -s) pudding.
Pudel m. (-s, -) poodle.
Puder m. (-s, 0) (toilet) powder.
pudern v.t. to powder.
Puderquaste f. (powder-)puff.
Puff m. (-[e]s, -e) cuff, thump; puff; (Knall) pop, report.
puffen v.t. & i. to cuff, to thump.
Puffer m. (-s, -) buffer.
Puls m. (-es, Pulse) pulse.
Pulsader f. artery.
pulsen, pulsieren v.i. to pulsate, to throb; (fig.) to pulse.
Pult n.(-es, -e) desk.
Pulver n. (-s, -) powder; gun-powder.
pulverisieren, pulvern v.t. to pulverize.
Pump m. (-[e]s, -e) (vulg.) credit; auf ~, on tick.
Pumpe f.(-, -n) pump.
pumpen v.t. to pump; to lend; to borrow.
Pumpenschwengel m. pump-handle.
Punkt m. (-[e]s, -e) point, dot; (gram.) full stop; article, item; Punkt 7 Uhr, seven o'clock sharp; der wunde ~, the sore point or spot.
punktieren v.t. to point, to dot; to punctuate; (med.) to tap.
Punktion f. (med.) puncture.
pünktlich a. punctual; ~ adv. punctually.
Punktsieg m. (Boxen) winning on points.
Punsch m. (-es, -e u. Pünsche) punch.
Punze f. (-, -n), Punzen m. (-, -) punch.

punzen *v.t.* to punch, to stamp.
Pupille *f.* (-, -n) (*des Auges*) pupil.
Puppe *f.* (-, -n) doll; puppet; chrysalis.
Puppenspiel *n.* puppet-show.
pur, *a.* pure, mere.
purgieren *v.t. & i.* to purge.
Purpur *m.* (-s, 0) purple; purple robe.
purpurn *a.* purple, crimson.
purpurrot *a.* purple.
Purzelbaum *m.* somersault.
purzeln *v.i.* (*s*) to tumble.
Pustel *f.* (-, -n) pustule.
pusten *v.i.* to breathe hard, to puff.
Pute, Puthenne *f.* (-, -n) turkey-hen.
Putsch *m.* (-es, -e) putsch.
Putz *m.* (-es, 0) dress, finery, attire; (*Mauer*) rough-cast.
putzen *v.t.* to clean, to polish; (*die Nase*) to blow, to wipe.
putzig *a.* droll, queer.
Putzlappen *m.* (-s, -) cleaning rag.
Putzmacherin *f.* (-, nen) milliner.
Putzpulver *n.* polishing powder.
Putzzeug *n.* cleaning utensils *pl.*
Pyramide *f.* (-, -n) pyramid.
pyramidenförmig *a.* pyramidal.
pythagoreisch *a.* Pythagorean; ∼er *Lehrsatz*, Pythagorean theorem.

Q

Quacksalber *m.* (-s, -) quack.
Quaderstein *m.* square *or* hewn stone.
Quadrat *n.* (-[e]s, -e) square; *im*∼, square.
quadratisch *a.* quadratic, square.
Quadratwurzel *f.* square root.
quaken *v.i.* to croak; to quack.
quäken *v.i.* to scream, to squeak.
Quäker *m.* (-s, -) Quaker, Friend.
Qual *f.* (-, -en) pain, torment, agony.
quälen *v.t.* to torment, to vex; (sich) ∼ *v.refl.* to toil, to drudge.
Quälerei *f.* (-, -en) vexation, annoyance.
Quälgeist *m.* tormentor.
qualifizieren (sich) *v.t. & refl.* to qualify.
Qualität *f.* (-, -en) quality.
Qualitäts. . . quality-.
Qualm *m.* (-[e]s, 0) thick smoke.
qualmen *v.i.* to smoke.
qualvoll *a.* very painful.
Quantität *f.* (-, -en) quantity.
Quantum *n.* (-[s], -ta) quantum.
Quarantäne *f.* (-, -n) quarantine.
Quark *m.* (-[e]s, 0) curds *pl.*; (*vulg.*) trifle; trash, rubbish.
Quarkkäse *m.* white cheese.
Quart *n.* (-[e]s, -e) quart; *in* ∼, in quarto.
Quarta *f.* (-, -ten) (lower) fourth form.
Quartel *n.* (-[e]s, -e) quarter (of the year); quarter-day.
Quartaner *m.* (-s, -) fourth-form boy.

Quart: **-band** *m.* quarto volume; ∼**blatt** *n.* quarter of a sheet.
Quart[e] *f.* (-, -n) (*mus.*) fourth.
Quartett *n.* (-[e]s, -e) quartet(te).
Quartier *n.* (-[e]s, -e) quarters *pl.*
quartieren *v.t.* to quarter, to billet.
Quartiermeister *m.* (*mil.*) quartermaster.
Quarz *m.* (-es, -e) quartz.
quasseln *v.i.* to prate, to twaddle.
Quast *m.* (-es, -en), **Quaste** *f.* (-, -n) tassel, tuft; puff; mop, brush.
Quatember *m.* (-s, -) Ember-day.
Quatsch *m.* (-es, 0) foolish talk, twaddle.
quatschen *v.i.* to talk nonsense.
Quatschkopf *m.* twaddler.
Quecksilber *n.* quicksilver, mercury.
Quell *m.* (-s, 0) **Quelle** *f.* (-, -n) well, spring, source.
quellen *v.t.* to soak, to swell; ∼ *v.i.st.* (*s*) to spring, to gush, to flow; to swell.
quengeln *v.i.* to grumble, to jangle.
quer *a.* cross; oblique, transverse; ∼ *adv.* across, athwart.
Querbalken *m.* cross-beam.
querdurch *adv.* straight across.
Quere *f.* (-, 0) oblique direction; *der* ∼ *nach*, athwart, crosswise; *in die* ∼ *kommen*, to thwart.
querfeldein *adv.* across country.
Quer: ∼**linie** *f.* cross-line; ∼**schiff**, *n.* transept; ∼**schnitt** *m.* cross-section; ∼**strasse** *f.* branch-road, turning; ∼**stück** *n.* (*mech.*) traverse.
querüber *adv.* over against, athwart.
Querulant *m.* (-en, -en) litigious person; grumbler.
quetschen *v.t.* to squeeze, to squash, to bruise.
Quetschung *f.* (-, -en) contusion, bruise.
Queue *n.* (-s, -s) cue, billiard-stick.
quick *a.* quick, lively, brisk.
quieken, quietschen *v.i.* to squeak.
Quinta *f.* (-, -ten) fifth form.
Quintaner *m.* (-s, -) fifth-class boy.
Quinte *f.* (-, -n) (*mus.*) fifth.
Quintessenz *f.* (-, -en) quintessence, gist.
Quintett *n.* (-[e]s, -e) quintet(te).
quitt *adv.* quits, even; rid, free.
quittieren *v.t.* to receipt (a bill); to quit.
Quittung *f.* (-, -en) receipt.
Quittungsmarke *f.* **Quittungsstempel** *m.* receipt-stamp.
Quote *f.* (-, -n) quota, share.
Quotient *m.* (-en, -en) (*ar.*) quotient.

R

Rabatt *m.* (-[e]s, 0) abatement, discount.
Rabbiner *m.* (-s, -) rabbi.
Rabe *m.* (-n, -n) raven.
Rabulist *m.* (-en, -en) pettifogger.

Rache f. (-, 0) revenge, vengeance.
Rachen m. (-s, -) mouth (of an animal), jaws pl.; back part of the mouth; (fig.) abyss.
rächen v.t. to avenge, to revenge; (sich) ~ v.refl. to take vengeance.
Rächer m. (-s, -) avenger.
Rachitis f. (-, 0) rickets pl.
Rachsucht f. vindictiveness.
rachsüchtig a. vindictive.
Rad n. (-[e]s, Räder) wheel; bicycle; fünftes ~ am Wagen sein, to be superfluous.
Radachse f. axle-tree.
Radau m. (-s, 0) (vulg.) noise, row.
Raddampfer m. paddle-steamer.
radebrechen v.t. to mangle (a language).
radeln v.i. to cycle, to bike.
Rädelsführer m. ringleader.
rädern v.t. to break on the wheel.
Räderwerk n. gearing.
radfahren v.i. to cycle, to wheel.
Radfahrer m. (-s, -) cyclist.
Radfahrweg m. cyclists' path.
Radialbohrmaschine f. radial drill.
radieren v.t. to erase; (Kunst) to etch.
Radiergummi n. (India) rubber.
Radierung f. (-, -en) erasure; etching.
Radieschen n. (-s, -) radish.
Radio n. (-s, 0) radio, wireless; ~apparat m. wireless set.
radioaktive a. radio-active.
Radiotherapie f. radiotherapeutics.
radikal a. radical.
Radium n. radium.
Radius m. (-, -dien) radius.
raffen v.t. to snatch up; to gather.
raffinieren v.t. to refine.
raffiniert p. & a. refined; (fig.) crafty, wily; exquisite.
ragen v.i. to project, to be prominent.
Ragout m. (-s, -s) stew, ragout.
Rahm m. (-[e]s, 0) cream.
Rahmen m. (-s, -) frame; im ~ von, within the framework of.
rahmen v.t. to frame.
Rahmkäse m. cream-cheese.
Rakete f. (-, -n) rocket.
Raketenwurfmaschine f. (mil.) rocket launcher or projector.
Rakett n. (-s, -s) racket.
rammen v.t. to ram, to drive in.
Rampe f. (-, -n) ramp, sloping drive.
Rampenlicht n.pl. footlights pl.
ramponieren v.t. to knock about.
Ramsch m. (-es, -e) refuse, rubbish.
Ramschverkauf m. rummage sale.
Rand m. (-es, Ränder) edge; (Hut) brim; (Buch) margin; (Teller) rim; (Wunde) lip; (fig.) brink, verge; border.
Randbemerkung f. marginal note.
rändeln v.t. (mech.) to knurl.
Ranft m. (-es, Ränfte), Ränftchen n. (-s, -) crust.

Rang m. (-[e]s, Ränge) rank, order; quality, rate; (Theater) circle, row, tier; erster ~, dress circle; zweiter ~, upper circle.
rangältest a. senior.
Range m. (-n, -n) ~ f. (-, -n) naughty boy; romp; hoyden.
Rangierbahnhof m. marshalling yard.
rangieren v.t. (rail.) to shunt; ~ v.i. to rank.
Rangiergleis n. siding.
Rang: ~liste f. army list; ~ordnung (order of) precedence; ~stufe f. degree, order.
Ranke f. (-, -n) tendril, creeper.
Ränke m.pl. intrigues.
ranken (sich) v.refl. to climb, to creep.
Ränkeschmied m. intriguer, trickster.
ränkesüchtig, ränkevoll a. intriguing.
Ränzel n. (-s, -), Ranzen m. (-s, -) knapsack.
ranzig a. rancid, rank.
Rapier n. (-[e]s, -e) foil, rapier.
Rappe m. (-n, -n) black horse.
rappelköpfig a. crazy, flighty, cracked.
Rapport m. (-[e]s, -e) report.
Raps m. (-ses, 0) rape-seed, colza.
rar a. rare; exquisite; scarce.
Rarität f. (-, -en) curio; rarity.
rasch a. speedy, swift; brisk, prompt.
rascheln v.i. to rustle.
Rasen m. (-s, -) turf, lawn.
rasen v.i. to rave, to rage; to rush.
Rasen: ~mähmaschine f. lawn-mower; ~platz m. grass-plot, lawn, green; ~stück n. sod.
rasend a. furious, frantic.
Raserei f. (-, -en) delirium, frenzy.
Rasierapparat m. (-es, -e) safety razor.
rasieren v.t. to shave.
Rasier: ~krem n. shaving cream; ~krem ohne Pinsel, brushless shaving cream; ~messer n. razor; ~seife f. shaving-soap, shaving-stick; ~zeug n. shaving things or tackle.
Raspel f. (-, -n) rasp, coarse file, grater.
raspeln v.t. to rasp.
Rasse f. (-, -n) breed, race; von reiner ~, thoroughbred.
Rassehund m. breed-dog, pedigree-dog.
rasseln v.i. to rattle.
Rassen...racial, a.; ~mischung f. miscegenation.
rassig a. racy.
Rast f. (-, 0) rest, repose; halt.
rasten v.i. to rest, to repose; to halt.
rastlos a. & adv. restless(ly).
Rasttag m. day of rest.
Rat m. (-[e]s, Räte) counsel, advice; consultation; council, board; (Person) councillor; zu ~e ziehen, to consult; mit sich zu ~e gehen, to take counsel with oneself; um ~ fragen, to ask advice

(of); *mit ~ und Tat*, with advice and assistance.

Rate f. (-, -n) (*com.*) instalment; (*Statistik*) rate; *in ~n, ratenweise*, by instalments; **~nzahlung** f. payment by instalments.

raten v.t.st. to guess, to divine; to counsel, to advise.

Rat: **~geber** m. adviser; **~haus** n. town-hall, council house.

ratifizieren v.t. to ratify.

Ration f. (-, -en) ration, allowance.

rationell a. rational.

rationieren v.t. to ration; *nicht mehr rationiert sein*, to come off the ration; *rationiert werden*, to go on rations.

Rationierung f. (-, -en) rationing; *von der ~ befreien*, to de-ration.

rätlich a. advisable.

ratlos a. perplexed, helpless, at a loss.

ratsam a. advisable, expedient.

Ratschlag m. advice, counsel.

ratschlagen v.i. to consult, to deliberate.

Ratschluss m. decree, resolution.

Rätsel n. (-s, -) riddle, enigma; mystery; problem.

rätselhaft a. enigmatical, mysterious.

Ratte f. (-, -n) rat.

Ratten: **~fänger** m. rat-catcher; **~gift** n. ratsbane.

Raub m. (-[e]s, 0) robbery, piracy; prey.

rauben v.t. to rob; (*Kinder*) to kidnap.

Räuber m. (-s, -) robber, highwayman.

Räuberbande f. gang of robbers.

Räuberei f. (-, -en) robbery.

räuberisch a. rapacious, predatory.

Raub: **~gier** f. rapacity; **~mord** m. murder with robbery; **~tier** n. beast of prey; **~vogel** m. bird of prey; **~zug** m. raid.

Raubritter m. (-s, -) robber-baron.

Rauch m. (-[e]s, 0) smoke, fume.

rauchen v.t. & i. to smoke; *Rauchen verboten*, no smoking!

Raucher m. (-s, -) smoker; *starker ~*, heavy smoker.

Raucherabteil n. smoking compartment.

Räucherhering m. kipper.

räuchern v.t. to perfume; to cure, to smoke(dry); to fumigate.

Rauchfang m. chimney; flue.

Rauch: **~tabak** m. smoking tobacco; **~waren** f.pl. furs pl.; **~zimmer** n. smoking-room.

Räude f. (-, 0) mange, scab.

räudig a. scabbed, mangy.

Raufbold m. bully, hector.

Raufe f. (-, -n) flax-comb; rack (for hay).

raufen v.t. to pluck; (sich) *~* v.refl. to scuffle, to fight.

Rauferei f. (-, -en) row, brawl, scuffle.

rauh a. rough, rugged; boisterous; (*Wetter*) raw; (*im Halse*) hoarse; (*fig.*) harsh, rude.

Rauhreif m. (-[e]s, 0) hoar-frost.

Raum m. (-[e]s, Räume) room, space, place; (*Schiff*) hold; *leerer ~*, vacuum; *~ geben*, (*der Hoffnung*) to indulge in; (*dem Gedanken*) to give way to; (*der Bitte*) to grant.

räumen v.t. to clear away, to remove; (*Platz*) to evacuate; *aus dem Wege ~*, to put out of the way.

Raum: **~gehalt** m. tonnage; **~inhalt** m. volume, capacity; **~kunst** f. interior decoration.

räumlich a. relating to space.

Räumung f. (-, -en) removal; evacuation.

Räumungsausverkauf m. clearance sale.

raunen v.t. & i. to whisper.

Raupe f. (-, -n) caterpillar.

Raupenfahrzeuge pl. tracked vehicles.

Rausch m. (-es, Räusche) intoxication; (*fig.*) frenzy (of love, etc.).

rauschen v.i. to rustle, to rush.

Rauschgift n. (-[e]s, -e) drug, narcotic; **~süchtiger** m. drug addict.

räuspern (sich) v.refl. to clear one's throat, to hem and haw.

Raute f. (-, -n) rhomb diamond.

rautenförmig a. rhombic.

Rayonchef m. (-s, -s) shopwalker, (*Am.*) floorwalker.

Razzia f. (-, Razzien) round-up, swoop; *eine ~ veranstalten*, to round-up.

Reagensglas n. test-tube.

reagieren v.i. to react (upon).

Reaktion f. (-, -en) reaction.

Reaktionär m. (-[e]s, -e) reactionary.

real a. real.

realisieren v.t. to realize; to turn into money.

Realschule f. non-classical secondary school.

Rebe f. (-, -n) vine, vine-branch.

Rebell m. (-en, -en) rebel, mutineer.

rebellieren v.i. to rebel, to mutiny.

Rebellion f. (-, -en) rebellion.

rebellisch a. rebellious.

Reb: **~huhn** n. partridge; **~laus** f. phylloxera; **~stock** m. vine.

Rechen m. (-s, -) rake.

rechen v.t. to rake.

Rechen: **~aufgabe** f. sum, mathematical problem; **~buch** n. arithmetic-book; **~exempel** n. sum, arithmetical problem; **~fehler** m. miscalculation; **~kunst** f. arithmetic; **~maschine** f. calculating machine.

Rechenschaft f. (-, 0) account; *~ ablegen*, to give an account; *zur ~ ziehen*, to call to account.

Rechenschieber m. slide rule.

rechnen v.t. & i. to count, to reckon, to compute, to calculate; *auf einen ~*, to depend, to rely, to count on one; *~ zu*, to class with.

Rechnung f. (-, -en) reckoning, calculation, computation; (*Nota*) bill, account; *die ~ stimmt, trifft zu,* the account squares, is correct; *auf die ~ setzen,* to charge in the bill; *in ~ stellen,* to carry to account; *auf ~ bestellen,* to order for account; *auf eigene, fremde ~,* on one's own account, for account of another; *einen Strich durch die ~ machen,* to thwart one's plans; *den Umständen ~ tragen,* to accommodate oneself to circumstances.

Rechnungs: ~ablage, ~ablegung *f.* rendering of account; ~abschluss *m.* balance of account; ~jahr *n.* business year; ~prüfer *m.* auditor; ~wesen *n.* bookkeeping, accounts *pl.*

recht *a.* right, just; convenient, fitting; correct, proper; ~ *adv.* right, fairly; well; *ein ~er Winkel,* a right angle; *~e Seite,* right-hand side; *zur ~en Zeit,* in time; ~ *haben,* to be right; **rechts** *adv.* on the right hand.

Recht *n.* (-[e]s, -e) right; justice; title, claim; law, jurisprudence; *mit Fug und ~,* with good reason, in all conscience; *~ sprechen,* to administer justice; *die ~e studieren,* to study law, to read for the bar; *von ~s wegen,* by right, according to law.

Rechte *f.* (-n, -n) right hand.

Rechteck *n.* (-s, -e) rectangle.

rechteckig *a.* rectangular.

rechten *v.i.* to contest, to dispute.

rechtfertigen *v.t.* to justify, to vindicate.

Rechtfertigung *f.* (-, -en) justification.

rechtgläubig *a.* orthodox.

Rechtgläubigkeit *f.* (-, 0) orthodoxy.

Rechthaberei *f.* (-, -en) positiveness.

rechthaberisch *a.* dogmatic, obstinate.

rechtlich *a.* legal, lawful.

rechtlos *a.* illegal, outlawed.

Rechtlosigkeit *f.* (-, 0) outlawry.

rechtmässig *a.* lawful, legitimate.

Rechtmässigkeit *f.* (-, 0) legitimacy, legality.

Rechts: ~anwalt *m.* counsel, lawyer, solicitor; *(vor Gericht auftretender)* barrister; *als ~anwalt praktizieren,* to practice at the bar; ~beistand *m.* counsel, legal adviser; ~beugung *f.* miscarriage of justice.

rechtschaffen *a.* righteous, honest.

Rechtschreibung *f.* spelling, orthography.

Rechts: ~einwand *m.* demurrer; ~fähigkeit *f.* legal competence; ~fall *m.* case (at law); ~gelehrter *m.* jurist; ~grund *m.* legal argument.

rechtsgültig *a.* legal, valid.

Rechts: ~hülfe *f.* legal aid; ~kraft *f.* force of law.

rechtskräftig *a.* legal, valid.

Rechts: ~lehrer *m.* professor of jurisprudence; ~mittel *n.* legal remedy,

appeal; ~pflege *f.* administration of justice; ~sache *f.* lawsuit, case.

Rechtsprechung *f.* administration of justice.

Rechts: ~stellung *f.* legal status; ~titel *m.* (legal) title.

rechts schwenkt, marsch! right wheel!; *rechts um, kehrt!,* right about turn! *(Am.)* right face!

rechtswidrig *a.* contrary to law, illegal.

Rechtswissenschaft *f.* jurisprudence.

recht: ~wink[e]lig *a.* rectangular; ~zeitig *a.* well-timed; ~ *adv.* in due time.

Reck *n.* (-[e]s, -e) horizontal bar.

Recke *m.* (-n, -n) hero, warrior.

recken *v.t.* to extend, to stretch, to rack; *(Hals)* to crane.

Redakteur *m.* (-[e]s, -e) editor.

Redaktion *f.* (-, -en) editorship; editor's office; editorial staff; wording.

Rede *f.* (-, -n) speech; oration, address; *eine ~ halten,* to make a speech; *in die ~ fallen,* to interrupt; *zur ~ stellen,* to call to account; *~ stehen,* to give an account; *nicht der ~ wert,* not worth mentioning.

Rede: ~freiheit *f.* freedom of speech; ~kunst *f.* rhetoric; oratory.

reden *v.t. & i.* to speak, to talk.

Redensart *f.* phrase; idiom; **Redensarten** *pl.* empty phrases.

Redewendung *f.* figure of speech.

redigieren *v.t.* to edit.

redlich *a.* honest, just, candid.

Redner *m.* (-s, -) orator, speaker; lecturer.

Rednerbühne *f.* platform.

rednerisch *a.* oratorical, rhetorical.

Redoute *f.* (-, -n) masquerade.

redselig *a.* talkative.

reduzieren *v.t.* to reduce, to diminish.

Reede *f.* (-, -n) road, roadstead.

Reeder *m.* (-s, -) ship-owner.

Reederei *f.* (-, -en) shipping company.

reell *a.* honest, respectable, solid.

Reep *n.* (-[e]s, -e) *(nav.)* rope.

Referendar *m.* (-s, -e) young member of the legal profession qualifying, by practical work, for the 'Assessor'-examination.

Referenz *f.* (-, -en) reference.

referieren *v.t.* to report.

reffen *v.t.* to reef (the sails).

reflektieren *v.t. & i.* to reflect; *~ auf,* to be inclined to (buy, etc.).

Reflex *m.* (-es, -e) reflex.

Reflexion *f.* (-, -en) reflexion.

reformieren *v.t.* to reform.

reformiert *a.* Reformed, Calvinistic.

Refrain *m.* (-s, -s) burden, refrain.

Regal *n.* (-[e]s, -e) shelf, shelves *pl.*

Regatta *f.* (-, -ten) boat race, regatta.

rege *a.* stirring, brisk; active.

Regel *f.* (-, -n) rule, regulation; *(med.)*

menses; ~detri f. rule of three; *in der* ~, as a rule, generally.

regel: ~los *a.* irregular; ~mässig *a.* regular.

Regelmässigkeit f. (-, -en) regularity.

regeln *v.t.* to regulate; to settle.

regelrecht *a.* regular, correct.

Regelung f. (-, -en) ordering, settlement.

regelwidrig *a.* contrary to rule.

regen (sich) *v.refl.* to stir.

Regen *m.* (-s, 0) rain; (*fig.*) shower.

Regen: ~bogen *m.* rainbow; ~bogenfarben *f.pl.* prismatic colours *pl.*; ~bogenhaut f. iris; ~dach *n.* eaves *pl.*

Regen: ~guss *m.* downpour; ~mantel *m.* raincoat; ~messer *m.* rain-gauge; ~schauer *m.* shower; ~schirm *m.* umbrella; ~schirmständer *m.* umbrella stand.

Regent *m.* (-en, -en) regent.

Regentschaft f. (-, -en) regency.

Regen: ~wurm *m.* earthworm; ~zeit f. rainy season.

Regie f. (-, -[e]n) administration.

regieren *v.i.* to rule, to reign; ~ *v.t.* to govern, to rule.

Regierung f. (-, -en) government; reign.

Regierungs: ~antritt *m.* accession; ~bezirk *m.* administrative district; ~umbildung f. government reshuffle; ~zeit f. reign.

Regiment *n.* (-[e]s, -er) regiment.

Regisseur *m.* (-s, -e) producer.

Register *n.* (-s, -) register; index; (*Orgel*) stop.

Registrator *m.* (-s, -en) registrar.

Registratur f. (-, -en) registry.

registrieren *v.t.* to record, to register.

Regler *m.* (-s, -) (*elek.*) regulator.

regnen *v.i.* to rain; *fein* ~, to drizzle.

regnerisch *a.* rainy.

Regress *m.* (-es, -e) recourse; ~ *nehmen,* to have recourse, to seek recovery; ~pflichtiger *m.* person liable to recourse.

regsam *a.* quick, agile, active.

regulär *a.* regular.

regulieren *v.t.* to regulate, to adjust; *die Uhr* ~, to set a watch.

Regung f. (-, -en) impulse.

regungslos *a.* motionless.

Reh *n.* (-[e]s, -e) roe; (*weibliches*) doe.

Reh: ~bock *m.* roebuck; ~braten *m.* venison; ~keule f. haunch of venison.

rehabilitieren *v.t.* to rehabilitate.

Reibeisen *n.* grater.

reiben *v.t.st.* to rub; to grate; to grind; *wund* ~, to gall, to chafe.

Reiberei f. (-, -en) provocation; friction.

Reibung f. (-, -en) friction.

Reibungsfläche f. friction surface.

reich *a.* rich, opulent, wealthy; copious.

Reich *n.* (-[e]s, -e) empire, kingdom.

reichen *v.t.* to reach; to pass, to hand; ~ *v.i.* to reach, to extend (to); to suffice.

reichhaltig *a.* copious, comprehensive.

reichlich *a.* copious, plentiful.

Reichs: ~bahn f. Reich railway; ~gericht *n.* Supreme Court of the Reich; ~post f. Reich post (office); ~stadt f. free (Imperial) city; ~tag *m.* Reichstag; ~tagsabgeordnete(r) *m.* Member of the Reichstag.

Reichswehr f. German army.

Reichtum *m.* (-s, -tümer) riches, wealth; abundance.

reif *a.* ripe; mature; *in reiferen Jahren,* advanced in years; ~ *zu, für,* ripe for.

Reif *m.* (-[e]s, 0) rime, hoar-frost; (*pl.*) (-e) hoop, ring.

Reife f. (-, 0) maturity, ripeness; matriculation standard.

reifen *v.t.* to mature; ~ *v.i.* to ripen, to grow ripe.

Reifen *m.* (-s, -) tyre, (*Am.*) tire; ~panne f. puncture, (*Am.*) flat tire.

Reife: ~prüfung f. leaving examination; ~zeugnis *n.* leaving certificate.

reiflich *a.* mature; ~ *adv.* maturely, thoroughly.

Reifrock *m.* crinoline.

Reigen *m.* (-s, -) round dance.

Reihe f. (-, -n) row, line; rank; range; series; turn; *in Reih und Glied,* with closed ranks; *er ist an der* ~, *er kommt an die* ~, *die* ~ *ist an ihm,* it is his turn; *nach der* ~, by turns.

reihen *v.t.* to range, to rank; to string.

Reihen *m.* (-s, -) round dance.

Reihenfolge f. succession, sequence, order.

Reihengeschäft *n.* chain-store.

Reihenschaltung f. (*elek.*) series connection.

reihenweise *adv.* in rows; by files.

Reiher *m.* (-s, -) heron.

reihum *adv.* by turns.

Reim *m.* (-[e]s, -e) rhyme.

reimen *v.t.* to rhyme; (sich) ~ *v.refl.* (*fig.*) to rhyme.

reimlos *a.* blank, unrhymed.

rein *a.* clean, pure; clear; *der* ~*e Zufall,* the merest accident; *ins* ~*e schreiben,* to make a fair copy; *ins* ~*e bringen,* to settle, to arrange.

Rein: ~ertrag *m.* net proceeds *pl.*; ~fall (*vulg.*) 'sell'; coming to grief; ~gewinn *m.* net profit.

Reinheit f. (-, 0) cleanness, purity.

reinigen *v.t.* to clean, to purify.

reinlich *a.* cleanly, neat; ~ *adv.* cleanly.

Reinlichkeit f. (-, 0) cleanliness.

Reinschrift f. fair copy.

reinweg *adv.* clean, flatly.

Reis *n.* (Reises, Reiser) scion; sprig.

Reis *m.* (Reises, 0) rice.

Reise f. (-, -n) journey, tour; (See) voyage; travels pl.; eine ~ antreten, to go upon a journey; auf ~n sein, to be travelling.

Reise: ~agent m. tourist agent; ~agentur f. travel agency; ~artikel pl. travel goods; ~büro n. tourist office; ~decke f. travel rug.

Reise: ~führer m. guide(-book); ~handbuch n. guide(-book).

reisen v.i. (h) to travel, to journey; (s) to go (to).

Reisende[r] m. (-n, -n) traveller.

Reise: ~omnibus m. motor-coach; ~pass m. passport; ~route f. itinerary; ~scheck m. traveller's cheque; ~tasche f. travelling bag.

Reisig n. (-s, 0) brushwood.

Reissaus nehmen v.i. to take to one's heels.

Reissbrett n. drawing-board.

reissen v.t.st. to tear, to rend, to pull; ~ v.st. to burst; to split; entzwei, to tear to pieces; Witze ~, to crack jokes; an sich ~, to take hold of; sich um einen oder etwas ~, to scramble for, to fight for; das reisst in den Geldbeutel, that runs into money; mir reisst die Geduld, I am losing patience; wenn alle Stränge ~, if the worst comes to the worst.

Reissen n. (-s, 0) rheumatism, ache.

reissend a. rapid.

Reisser m. (-s, -) (Buch) best-seller.

Reiss: ~feder f. drawing pen; ~nadel f. (mech.) scriber; ~nagel m. drawing pin, (Am.) thumb-tack; ~verschluss m. zip fastener, (Am.) slide fastener; ~zeug n. case of mathematical instruments.

Reitbahn f. riding-school, manège.

reiten v.t. & i.st. to ride, to go on horseback; auf etwas immer herum~, to be always harping on the same string.

Reiter m. (-s, -) rider, horseman.

Reiterei f. (-, -en) cavalry.

Reiterin f. (-, -nen) horse-woman.

Reit: ~gerte, ~peitsche f. riding-whip; ~hose f. riding breeches; ~kleid n. riding habit; ~knecht m. groom; ~kunst f. horsemanship; ~pferd n. saddle-horse; ~schule f. riding-school; ~stiefel m.pl. boots, top-boots; ~stock m. (mech.) tailstock; ~weg m. bridle-path; ~zeug n. riding equipment.

Reiz m. (-es, -e) charm, attraction; incentive, stimulus; irritation.

reizbar a. sensitive; irritable.

reizen v.t. to stimulate; to charm; to irritate.

reizend a. charming.

reizlos a. unattractive.

Reizmittel n. incentive; (med.) stimulant.

reizvoll a. attractive.

rekapitulieren v.t. to recapitulate.

Reklame f. (-, -n) advertisement; pub-

licity; ~ machen, to advertise; ~wirkung f. appeal.

reklamieren v.t. to claim; ~ v.i. to protest.

rekognoszieren v.t. to reconnoitre.

Rekonvaleszent m. (-en, -en) convalescent.

Rekord m. (-[e]s, -e) record.

Rekrut m. (-en, -en) recruit.

rekrutieren v.t. to recruit.

Rektor m. (-s, -toren) rector; headmaster; principal (of a college).

Rektorat n. (-[e]s, -e) rectorship.

Relais n. relay.

relativ a. relative.

Relativität f. (-, -en) relativity.

relegieren v.t. to expel; to rusticate.

Relief n. (-s, -s) relief.

Religion f. (-, -en) religion.

religiös a. religious.

Reliquie f. (-, -n) relic.

Renegat m. (-en, -en) renegade.

Rennbahn f. race-course; track.

rennen v.i.ir. to run hard; to race.

Rennen n. (-s, -) race; run; heat.

Rennpferd n. racehorse.

Renn: ~platz m. race-course; ~sport m. racing, the turf; ~stall m. racing stud; ~tier n. reindeer.

renommieren v.i. to brag, to show off.

renommiert a. well-known, renowned.

rentabel a. profitable, economic.

Rentabilität f. (-, 0) profitableness.

Rentamt n. revenue office.

Rente f. (-, -n) revenue; pension.

Rentier m. (-s, -s) gentleman of private means.

rentieren (sich) v.refl. to pay.

Rentner m. (-s, -) pensioner.

Reparatur f. (-, -en) repair; ~werkstatt f. repair shop.

reparieren v.t. to repair.

Repertoire (...toar), n. (-s, -s) (theat.) stock, repertoire, repertory.

repetieren v.t. to repeat.

Replik f. (-, -en) replica; reply.

Report m. (-s, -e) contango.

Repräsentant m. (-en, -en) representative.

Repräsentantenhaus f. (Am.) House of Representatives.

repräsentieren v.t. to represent.

Repressalien pl. reprisals pl.

reproduzieren v.t. to reproduce.

Reptil n. (-s, -ien) reptile.

Republik f. (-, -en) republic.

Republikaner m. (-s, -) republican.

republikanisch a. republican.

requirieren v.t. (mil.) to requisition.

Reserve f. (-, -n) reserve.

reservieren v.t. to reserve.

Reservist m. (-en, -en) reservist.

Residenz f. (-, -en) (monarch's) residence.

residieren v.i. to reside.

Resonanzboden m. sounding-board.

Respekt m. (-[e]s, 0) respect, regard.

respektieren v.t. to respect, to honour.
respektlos a. without respect.
respektvoll a. respectful.
Ressort (frz.), n. (-s, -s) department.
Rest m. (-[e]s, -e) rest, residue, remainder; remnant; arrears pl.
Restaurant n. restaurant; ~ mit Selbstbedienung f. cafeteria.
Restaurateur m. (-[e]s, -e) inn-keeper.
Restauration f. (-, -en) restoration; refreshment-room, restaurant.
restaurieren v.t. to restore, to renovate (a building, etc.).
Restbestand m. remainder; residue.
restlos a. & adv. completely.
Restsumme f. balance.
Resultat n. (-[e]s, -e) result; (Rechnung) answer.
resümieren v.t. to summarize.
Retorte f. (-, -n) retort, alembic.
retour adv. back.
retten v.t. & refl. (sich) to save, to rescue, to preserve; to save oneself.
Rettich m. (-[e]s, -e) black radish.
Rettung f. (-, -en) rescue.
Rettungs: ~boot n. life-boat; ~gürtel m. life-belt.
rettungslos adv. irretrievably.
retuschieren v.t. to retouch.
Reue f. (-, 0) repentance.
reuelos a. impenitent; unrepentant.
reuen v.t.imp. es reut mich, I repent (of it).
reuig, reumütig a. repentant.
reuvoll a. repentant.
revanchieren (sich) v.refl. to return (a service, etc.).
Reverenz (-, -en) curtsy, bow.
Revers m. (Reverses, Reverse) bond, written promise; (von Münzen) reverse.
revidieren v.t. to revise; to check.
Revier n. (-[e]s, -e) (hunting-)district; quarter, district; beat; (mil.) sick-bay, sickward, infirmary.
Revision f. (-, -en) revision; inspection; (Druck~) revise; (law) review.
Revolution f. (-, -en) revolution.
revolutionär a. revolutionary.
Revolutionär m. (-[e]s, -e) revolutionist.
Revolver m. (-s, -) revolver.
Revue f. (-, -n) review.
Rezensent m. (-en, -en) reviewer, critic.
rezensieren v.t. to review.
Rezension f. (-, -en) review.
Rezept n. (-es, -e) prescription; recipe.
rezitieren v.t. to recite.
Rhabarber m. (-s, 0) rhubarb.
Rheinwein m. hock, Rhenish (wine).
Rhetorik f. (-, 0) rhetoric.
rhetorisch a. rhetorical.
rheumatisch a. rheumatic.
Rheumatismus m. (-, 0) rheumatism.
Rhinozeros n. (-ses, -se) rhinoceros.
rhythmisch a. rhythmical.

Rhythmus m. (-, -men) rhythm.
richten v.t. to direct; to judge; sich ~ nach, to be determined by; eine Bitte an einen ~, to make a request of one; zu Grunde ~, to ruin, to destroy.
Richter m. (-s, -) judge, justice.
richterlich a. judicial.
Richterspruch m. sentence.
richt Euch! dress right or left!
richtig a. & adv. right(ly), exact(ly); correct(ly); die Uhr geht nicht ~, the watch does not go right.
Richtigkeit f. (-, 0) accuracy; correctness.
richtigstellen v.t. to rectify.
Richtlinie f. directive.
Richtschnur f. rule of conduct.
Richtstrahler m. (Radio) directional aerial.
Richtung f. (-, -en) direction.
riechen v.t. & i.st. to smell; to scent; ~ nach, to smell of.
Riegel m. (-s, -) bar, bolt.
Riemen m. (-s, -) strap, thong; (nav.) oar.
Ries n. (Rieses, Riese) ream (of paper).
Riese m. (-n, -n) giant.
Rieselfeld n. field irrigated with sewage.
rieseln v.i. to murmur, to babble.
riesengross, riesenhaft, riesig a. gigantic.
Riesen: ~schlange f. boa constrictor; ~schritt m. giant-stride.
Riff n. (-[e]s, -e) reef, ridge.
Rille f. (-, -n) small groove.
Rimesse f. (-, -n) (com.) remittance.
Rind n. (-[e]s, -er) neat; ox, cow, cattle.
Rinde f. (-, -n) bark, rind; (des Brotes) crust.
Rinder: ~braten m. roast-beef; ~pest, ~seuche f. cattle-plague.
Rindfleisch n. beef.
Rindvieh n. horned cattle; (vulg.) blockhead.
Ring m. (-[e]s, -e) ring; circle; link.
Ringellocke f. ringlet.
ringeln v.t. & refl. (sich) to curl.
ringen v.t.st. to wring, to wrest; to struggle, to wrestle; to strive (after).
Ringer m. (-s, -) wrestler.
ringförmig a. annular.
Ringkampf m. wrestling-match.
rings adv. around.
ringsum(her) adv. round about.
ringsum(her) adv. round about.
Rinne f. (-, -n) groove, channel; gutter.
rinnen v.i. (s, h) to run; to leak.
Rinnsal n. (-[e]s, -e), **Rinnsel** n. (-s, -) water-course, channel.
Rinnstein m. gutter(-stone), sink.
Rippe f. (-, -n) rib; (arch.) groin.
rippen v.t. to rib; gerippt, ribbed.
Rippen: ~fell n. pleura; ~fellentzündung f. pleurisy.
Risiko n. (-s, -s) risk.
riskant a. hazardous, risky.
riskieren v.t. to risk.

Riss *m.* (Risses, Risse) crevice, chink, cleft; rent, tear; breach, schism.

Rist *m.* (-es, -e) instep; (*Hand*) wrist; (*eines Pferdes*) withers *pl.*

Ritt *m.* (-[e]s, -e) ride.

Ritter *m.* (-s, -) knight, cavalier.

ritterbürtig *a.* of noble descent.

Ritter: ~gut *n.* estate, manor; ~gutsbesitzer *m.* landed gentleman.

ritterlich *a.* chivalrous, knightly.

rittlings *adv.* astride, astraddle.

Rittmeister *m.* cavalry captain.

rituell *a.* ceremonial.

Ritus *m.* (-, - *u.* Riten) rite.

Ritz *m.* (-es, -e), Ritze *f.* (-, -n) chink.

ritzen *v.t.* to scratch.

rivalisieren *v.i.* to rival.

Rizinusöl *n.* castor oil.

Robbe *f.* (-, -n) seal.

Robe *f.* (-, -n) gown.

röcheln *v.i.* to rattle in the throat.

Rock *m.* (-[e]s, Röcke), coat; petticoat; skirt.

rodeln *v.i.* to toboggan.

Rodel: ~bahn *f.* tobogganning course; ~schlitten *m.* toboggan; (*mit Steuerung*) bobsleigh; skeleton.

roden *v.t.* to root out; to clear (for cultivation).

Rodung *f.* (-, -en) clearing, cleared land.

Rogen *m.* (-s, -) roe, spawn.

Roggen *m.* (-s, 0) rye.

roh *a.* raw, crude, rude.

Roheisen *n.* pig-iron.

Roh: ~gummi *m.* crude rubber; ~material *n.* raw material; ~öl *n.* crude oil.

Rohr *n.* (-[e]s, -e) reed, cane; pipe; tube; barrel.

Röhre *f.* (-, -n) tube, pipe; funnel; conduit; (*radio*) valve, (*Am.*) tube.

Röhrenapparat *m.* (*radio*) valve set.

röhrenförmig *a.* tubular.

Röhrenleitung *f.* conduit-pipes *pl.*

Röhricht *n.* (-[e]s, -e) reed-bank.

Rohr: ~leitung *f.* pipeline; ~post *f.* pneumatic post; ~stuhl *m.* cane-bottomed chair; ~zucker *m.* cane-sugar.

Roh: ~seide *f.* raw silk; ~stoff *m.* raw material.

Rolladen *m.* (-s, -) window-blind.

Rolle *f.* (-, -n) roll, roller; register; (*theat. und fig.*) part; pulley; *Geld spielt keine ~*, money is no object.

rollen *v.t. & i.* to roll, to rumble.

Rollenbesetzung *f.* cast.

Rollenlager *n.* (*mech.*) roller-bearing.

Roll: ~film *m.* roll film; ~holz *n.* rolling-pin; ~schuh *m.* roller-skate; ~sitz *m.* sliding seat; ~stuhl *m.* bath-chair; ~treppe *f.* escalator.

Roman *m.* (-[e]s, -e) novel; romance.

romanisch *a.* Romanic, Romance, (*arch.*) Romanesque.

Romanschreiber *m.* novelist.

Romantik *f.* romanticism; romance.

romantisch *a.* romantic.

römische Zahl *f.* Roman numeral.

Röntgen: ~bild *n.* radiograph; ~röhre *f.* X-ray tube; ~strahlen *pl.* X-rays *pl.*

rosa *a.* pink.

Rose *f.* (-, -n) rose.

rosenfarben *a.* rose-coloured, rosy.

Rosen: ~kohl *m.* Brussels sprouts *pl.*; ~kranz *m.* rosary.

rosenrot *a.* rose-coloured.

Rosenstock *m.* rose-tree.

rosig *a.* rosy, roseate.

Rosine *f.* (-, -n) raisin; (*kleine*) currant.

Ross *n.* (Rosses, Rosse) horse.

Ross: ~haar *n.* horsehair; ~kastanie *f.* horse-chestnut.

Rost *m.* (-[e]s, -e) rust; gridiron, grate.

Rostbraten *m.* roast-meat, roast-beef.

rosten *v.i.* to rust, to grow rusty.

rösten *v.t.* to roast, to grill; (*Brot*) to toast.

Rostfleck *m.* iron-mould.

rostfrei *a.* (*Stahl*) stainless.

rostig *a.* rusty.

rot *a.* red.

Rot *n.* (-es, 0) red colour.

Rotationsmaschine *f.* rotary machine.

rotbäckig *a.* red-cheeked.

rotbraun *a.* reddish-brown, ruddy; bay.

Rot: ~buche *f.* copper-beech; ~dorn *m.* pink hawthorn.

Röte *f.* (-, 0) redness; blush.

Röteln *pl.* German measles *pl.*

röten *v.t.* to redden.

rote Rübe *f.* red beet, beetroot.

Rotes Kreuz *n.* Red Cross.

Rotfuchs *m.* sorrel *or* bay horse.

rotgelb *a.* orange-coloured, flame-coloured.

rotglühend *a.* red-hot.

Rotglut *f.* red-heat.

rothaarig *a.* red-haired, carroty.

Rot: ~haut *f.* redskin; ~käppchen *n.* Little Red Ridinghood; ~kehlchen *n.* robin red-breast; ~lauf *m.* erysipelas; (*des Schweins*) red murrain.

rotieren *v.i.* to rotate.

rötlich *a.* reddish.

Rot: ~wein *m.* red wine; ~stift *m.* red pencil.

Rotte *f.* (-, -n) band, gang; (*mil.*) troop.

Rotwild *n.* red deer.

Rotz *m.* (-es, 0) mucus; (*vulg.*) snot; (*der Pferde*) glanders *pl.*

Rouleau *n.* (-[s], -s *u.* -x) (roller-)blind.

routiniert *a.* experienced; smart.

Rübe *f.* (-, -n) rape; (*weisse*) turnip; (*gelbe*) carrot; (*rote*) beet-root.

Rubel *m.* (-s, -) rouble.

Rübenzucker *m.* beet sugar.

Rubin *m.* (-[e]s, -e) ruby.

Rüböl *n.* rape-seed oil.
Rubrik *f.* (-, -en) rubric; column.
rubrizieren *v.t.* to distribute in columns.
Rübsamen *m.* rape-seed.
ruchbar *a.* notorious, rumoured.
ruchlos *a.* profligate, reprobate.
Ruck *m.* (-[e]s, -e) jolt, jerk, start.
Rück: ~anschrift *f.* return address; ~antwort *f.* reply; ~blick *m.* retrospect.
rücken *v.t.* to move, to push; ~ *v.i.* (*s*) to move, to budge; *näher* ~, to draw near; *ins Feld* ~, to take the field.
Rücken *m.* (-s, -) back; ridge; (*mil.*) rear; *einem den* ~ *kehren*, to turn one's back on one.
Rücken: ~deckung *f.* (*mil.*) rear cover; ~lehne *f.* back (of a chair); ~mark *n.* spinal cord; ~schmerz *m.* backache; ~schwimmen *n.* back stroke; ~stück *n.* sirloin; ~wirbel *m.* vertebra.
Rück:~erstattung *f.* refund; ~fahrkarte *f.* return ticket; ~fahrt *f.* return; ~fall *m.* relapse.
rückfällig *a.* relapsing; revertible.
Rückfracht *f.* freight back; return cargo.
Rückfrage *f.* further inquiry.
Rückführung *f.* repatriation.
Rückgabe *f.* restitution, return.
Rückgang *m.* retrogression; decline.
rückgängig *a.* retrograde; ~ *machen*, to annul, to cancel.
Rückgrat *n.* backbone, spine; ~los *a.* spineless.
Rückhalt *m.* reserve; support.
rückhaltlos *a.* & *adv.* unreserved(ly).
Rückkauf *m.* redemption, buying back.
Rückkehr, Rückkunft *f.* (-, 0) return.
Rückkoppelung *f.* (*radio*) reaction.
rückläufig *a.* recurrent; retrograde.
rücklings *adv.* backward; from behind.
Rückmarsch *m.* march back; return, retreat.
Rückporto *n.* return postage.
Rückreise *f.* return journey; *auf der* ~, homeward bound.
Rückruf *m.* recall.
Rucksack *m.* loose knapsack, rucksack.
Rückschlag *m.* set-back.
Rückschluss *m.* inference, conclusion.
Rückschreiben *n.* rescript; reply
Rückschritt *m.* retrocession; falling-off.
rückschrittlich *a.* reactionary.
Rückseite *f.* back, reverse.
Rücksicht *f.* (-, -en) regard, consideration, respect; *in* ~ *auf*, in consideration of, with regard to; ~ *nehmen auf*, to take notice of; to make allowance for.
rücksichtlich *adv.* with regard to.
rücksichtslos *a.* inconsiderate, reckless.
rücksichtsvoll *a.* considerate.
Rücksitz *m.* back-seat.
Rücksprache *f.* consultation; ~ *nehmen mit*, to confer with.

Rückstand *m.* arrears *pl.*; residue; (*Am.*, *bei der Arbeit*) backlog.
rückständig *a.* outstanding, overdue; in arrears; backward.
Rückstoss *m.* recoil; repulsion.
Rücktritt *m.* withdrawal, resignation; ~bremse *f.* back pedalling brake.
Rückübersetzung *f.* retranslation.
Rückvergütung *f.* repayment.
Rückversicherung *f.* reinsurance.
rückwärtig *a.* rear; ~es Gebiet *n.* rear area.
rückwärts *adv.* backwards; reverse; ~gang *m.* reverse gear.
Rückweg *m.* way back, return.
ruckweise *adv.* by fits and starts.
rückwirkend *a.* retroactive; *mit* ~*er Kraft*, with retroactive effect.
Rückwirkung *f.* reaction.
Rückzahlung *f.* repayment.
Rückzug *m.* retreat.
rüde *a.* rude, coarse.
Rudel *n.* (-s, -) pack troop.
Ruder *n.* (-s, -) oar; rudder; (*fig.*) helm.
Ruderboot *n.* sculling-boat.
Ruderer *m.* (-s, -) rower, oarsman.
rudern *v.t.* & *i.* to row.
Ruf *m.* (-[e]s, -e) call; vocation; report; reputation; (*com.*) credit, standing; *in gutem* ~*e stehen*, to be well reputed.
rufen *v.i.* & *t.st.* to call; to cry, to shout; *um Hilfe rufen*, to cry for help; *etwas ins Leben* ~, to start a thing; ~ *lassen*, to send for, to summon.
Rüffel *m.* (-s, -) (*fam.*) wigging.
rüffeln *v.t.* (*fam.*) to blow up.
Rufweite *f. in* ~, within call.
Rufzeichen *n.* exclamation mark.
Rüge *f.* (-, -n) censure, blame, rebuke.
rügen *v.t.* to censure, to reprehend.
Ruhe *f.* (-, 0) rest, repose; quiet, tranquility; *sich zur* ~ *setzen*, to retire from business (office, active life); ~ *stiften*, to make peace; ~! hush! be quiet!; *in* ~ *lassen*, to let alone.
ruhelos *a.* restless.
ruhen *v.i.* to rest, to repose; *ein Verdacht ruht auf ihm*, he is under suspicion (of).
Ruhe: ~stand *m.* retirement; *im* ~*stand*, retired; *in den* ~*stand versetzen*, to retire, to put on the retired list; ~störung *f.* disturbance.
ruhig *a.* quiet; calm; silent.
Ruhm *m.* (-[e]s, 0) fame, glory, renown.
rühmen *v.t.* to praise, to extol; (*sich*) ~ *v.refl.* to boast of, to glory (in).
rühmlich *a.* glorious; praiseworthy.
ruhmlos *a.* inglorious.
ruhmredig *a.* vainglorious.
Ruhr *f.* (-, 0) dysentery.
Rührei *n.* scrambled *or* buttered eggs *pl.*
rühren *v.t.* & *i.* to stir; to beat (the drum, eggs); (*sich*) ~ *v.refl.* to stir, to bestir

oneself; *sich nicht vom Flecke* ~, not to budge; *rührt euch!* (*mil.*) stand at ease; *rührende Worte*, touching words; *ich bin ganz gerührt*, I am deeply affected.

rührig *a.* active, stirring, bustling.

rührselig *a.* sentimental.

Rührung *f.* (-, -en) emotion.

Ruin *m.* (-[e]s, 0) ruin, overthrow.

Ruine *f.* (-, -n) ruins *pl.*

ruinieren *v.t.* to ruin, to spoil; (*einen*) to undo (one).

rülpsen *v.i.* to belch, to eructate.

Rum *m.* (-s, -s) rum.

Rummel *m.* (-s, 0) noise, row.

Rumor *m.* (-s, 0) bustle, hubbub.

rumoren *v.i.* to make a noise or row.

Rumpelkammer *f.* lumber room.

Rumpf *m.* (-[e]s, Rümpfe) trunk; torso; (*Schiffs~*) hull; (*Flugzeug*) fuselage.

rümpfen *v.t. die Nase* ~, to turn up one's nose.

rund *a.* round; plain; ~e Summe *f.* round sum.

Rundbogen *m.* Roman arch.

Runde *f.* (-, -n) round.

Rund: ~erlass *m.* circular (decree); ~funk *m.* broadcasting; ~funksender *m.* broadcasting station, radio station; ~gang *m.* round; ~frage *f.* inquiry.

rundfunken *v.t.* to broadcast.

rundlich *a.* roundish.

Rund: ~reise *f.* (circular) tour; ~reisekarte *n.* tourist-ticket; ~schreiben *n.* circular.

rundweg *adv.* flatly, plainly.

Rune *f.* (-, -n) Rune, Runic character.

Runkelrübe *f.* beet-root.

Runzel *f.* (-, -n) wrinkle; (*um die Augen*) crow's feet *pl.*

runz(e)lig *a.* wrinkled.

runzeln *v.t.* to wrinkle; *die Stirn* ~, to knit one's brows.

Rüpel *m.* (-s, -) lout, boor.

Rüpelei *f.* (-, -en) insolence.

rüpelhaft *a.* unmannerly, clownish.

rupfen *v.t.* to pluck; (*fig.*) to fleece.

Rupie *f.* (-, -n) rupee.

ruppig *a.* shabby; rude.

Russ *m.* (-es, 0) soot.

Rüssel *m.* (-s, -) snout, trunk, proboscis.

russen *v.i.* to soot, to smoke.

russig *a.* sooty.

rüsten *v.t.* to arm; to prepare; ~ *v.i.* to prepare for war.

rüstig *a.* stout, vigorous, robust, strong.

Rüstung *f.* (-, -en) armament; armour.

Rüstzeug *n.* tool, instrument.

Rute *f.* (-, -n) rod, wand, twig, switch; (*Mass*) perch (=12 feet).

Rutsch *m.* (-es, -e) slide, landslip.

Rutschbahn *f.* slide.

rutschen *v.i.* (*s*) to slide; to skid.

rütteln *v.t.* to shake, to jolt.

S

Saal *m.* (-[e]s, Säle) hall, (large) room.

Saat *f.* (-, -en) seed; standing corn; sowing.

Saatkorn *n.* seed-corn.

Sabbat *m.* (-[e]s, -e) sabbath.

Säbel *m.* (-s, -) sabre, sword.

sabotieren *v.t.* to sabotage.

Sacharin *n.* (-s, 0) saccharine.

Sachbeschädigung *f.* damage to property.

Sache *f.* (-, -n) thing, matter; affair, business; cause; (*Prozess*) case; *es ist seine* ~, it is up to him; *das gehört nicht zur* ~, that is beside the question; *bei der* ~ *bleiben*, to stick to the point; *nicht bei der* ~, inattentive, absent-minded; *gemeinschaftliche* ~ *mit einem machen*, to make common cause with; ~**nrecht** *n.* law of property.

sachgemäss *a.* appropriate; relevant.

Sach: ~kenner *m.* expert; affair; ~kenntnis *f.* knowledge of a subject, experience.

sachkundig *a.* expert.

Sachleistung *f.* delivery in kind.

Sachlage *f.* (-, 0) state of affairs.

sachlich *a.* real, to the point; material (not formal); impartial, objective.

sächlich *a.* (*gram.*) neuter.

Sachregister *n.* subject-index.

sacht *a.* & *adv.* soft(ly), gentle(tly).

Sachverhalt *m.* (-[e]s, 0) facts *or* bearings (of a case) *pl.*

sachverständig *a.* expert.

Sachverständige[r] *m.* (-n, -n) expert.

Sachwalter *m.* (-s, -) advocate.

Sachwert *m.* real value.

Sack *m.* (-[e]s, Säcke) bag, sack; *mit* ~ *und Pack*, bag and baggage.

Säckel *m.* (-s, -) purse.

sacken *v.i.* to sink.

Sackgasse *f.* blind alley.

Sä[e]: ~mann *m.* sower; ~maschine *f.* sowing-machine.

säen *v.t.* to sow.

Saffian *m.* (-[s], -e) Morocco-leather.

Safran *m.* (-s, 0) saffron.

safrangelb *a.* saffrony.

Saft *m.* (-[e]s, Säfte) juice; (*der Bäume*) sap.

saftig *a.* juicy, sappy, succulent.

saftlos *a.* sapless; (*fig.*) insipid, stale, dry.

Sage *f.* (-, -n) myth; saga; tale, legend; *die* ~ *geht*, it is rumoured.

Säge *f.* (-, -n) saw.

Säge: ~bock *m.* sawing horse; ~mehl *n.* saw-dust; ~mühle *f.* saw-mill; ~späne *pl.* shavings.

sägen *v.t.* to saw.

sagen *v.t.* to say, to tell; ~ *lassen*, to send word; *er lässt sich nichts* ~, he will not listen to reason; *das hat nichts zu* ~, that does not matter; *das will nicht viel sagen*, there is not much in that; *so zu ~*, as it were; *Dank ~*, to return thanks.

sagenhaft *a.* fabulous, legendary.

Sägespäne *m.pl.* saw-dust.

Sago *m.* (-s, 0) sago.

Sahne *f.* (-, 0) cream.

Saison (*frz.*) *f.* (-, -s) season.

Saite *f.* (-, -n) string, chord.

Saitenspiel *n.* string-music; lyre.

Sakko *m.* (-s, -s) lounge suit.

Sakrament *n.* (-[e]s, -e) sacrament.

Sakristan *m.* (-[e]s, -e) sacristan, sexton.

Sakristei *f.* (-, -en) vestry, sacristy.

säkularisieren *v.t.* to secularize.

Salamander *m.* (-s, -) salamander.

Salat *m.* (-[e]s, -e) salad; lettuce.

Salatsauce *f.* salad dressing.

salbadern *v.i.* to twaddle.

Salbe *f.* (-, -n) salve, ointment.

Salbei *m.* (-s, -e) *f.* (-, -en) sage.

salben *v.t.* to anoint.

Salböl *n.* consecrated oil.

Salbung *f.* (-, -en) unction.

salbungsvoll *a.* unctuous.

Saldo *m.* (-[s], -s *u.* -di) balance; *den ~ ziehen*, to strike a balance; *per ~ quittieren*, to receipt in full.

Saldobetrag *m.* (amount of) balance.

Saline *f.* (-, -n) salt-works *pl.*

Salizylsäure *f.* salicylic acid.

Salm *m.* (-[e]s, -e) salmon.

Salmiak *m.* (-s, 0) sal-ammoniac.

Salmiakgeist *m.* ammonia.

Salon *m.* (-s, -s) drawing-room; saloon.

salopp *a.* lackadaisical.

Salpeter *m.* (-s, 0) nitre, saltpetre.

salpetersauer *a.*, **salpetersaures Salz**, nitrate.

salpetrig *a.* nitrous; *~e Säure*, nitric acid.

Salut *m.* (-[e]s, -e) salute.

Salve *f.* (-, -n) volley; salute.

Salz *n.* (-es, -e) (*also fig.*) salt.

Salzbrühe *f.* pickle, brine.

salzen *v.t.* to salt, to corn; **gesalzen** *a.* (*fig.*) biting, smart.

Salz: *~fass n.* salt-cellar, (*Am.*) salt-shaker; *~kartoffeln pl.* boiled potatoes.

salzig *a.* salt(y), briny.

Salzsäure *f.* hydrochloric (*or* muriatic) acid.

Sämaschine *f.* sowing machine.

Same(n) *m.* (-ns, -n) seed; sperm.

Sämerei *f.* (-, -en) seeds (of plants) *pl.*

Sammelbüchse *f.* collecting-box.

sammeln *v.t.* to gather, to collect; (sich) *~ v.refl.* to assemble; (*fig.*) to collect oneself.

Sammel: *~platz m.* meeting-place; *~punkt m.* rallying-point.

Sammelsurium *n.* (-[s], -surien) omnium-gatherum.

Sammet, Samt *m.* (-[e]s, -e) velvet.

Sammler *m.* (-s, -) collector, gatherer.

Sammlung *f.* (-, -en) collection; composure.

Samstag *m.* Saturday.

samt *pr. & adv.* together with; *~ und sonders*, each and all.

sämtlich *a.* all, entire, complete.

Sand *m.* (-[e]s, 0) sand; *einem ~ in die Augen streuen*, to throw dust in a person's eyes.

Sandale *f.* (-, -n) sandal.

Sand: *~bank f.* sand-bank, sands *pl.*; *~papier n.* sand paper; *~sack m.* sand-bag; *~stein m.* freestone; *~uhr f.* hour-glass.

sanft *a.* soft, gentle, mild; meek.

Sänfte *f.* (-, -n) sedan-chair, litter.

Sanftmut *f.* (-, 0) meekness.

sanftmütig *a.* gentle, mild.

Sang *m.* (-[e]s, Sänge) song; *ohne ~ und Klang*, quietly.

Sänger *m.* (-s, -) singer.

Sängerin *f.* (-, -nen) (female) singer.

Sanguiniker *m.* (-s, -) sanguine person.

sanguinisch *a.* sanguine.

sanieren *v.t.* to reorganize.

Sanitäts: *~behörde f.* Public Health Department; *~dienst m.* medical service; *~kolonne f.* ambulance column; *~wache f.* ambulance station

sanktionieren *v.t.* to sanction.

Saphir *m.* (-s, -e) sapphire.

Sardine *f.* (-, -n) sardine.

Sarg *m.* (-[e]s, Särge) coffin.

Sarkophag *m.* (-s, -e) sarcophagus.

Satan *m.* (-s, -e) Satan.

satanisch *a.* satanic.

Satire *f.* (-, -n) satire.

Satiriker *m.* (-s, -) satirist.

satt *a.* satisfied; *etwas ~ haben*, to be sick of a thing; *es ~ bekommen*, to get sick of a thing.

Sattel *m.* (-s, Sättel) saddle.

Satteldecke *f.* saddle-cloth.

satteln *v.t.* to saddle.

sättigen *v.t.* to satiate; (*chem.*) to saturate.

Sättigung *f.* (-, -en) (*chem.*) saturation.

Sattler *m.* (-s, -) saddler.

sattsam *adv.* sufficiently, enough.

Satz *m.* (-es, Sätze) leap, jump; (*Boden~*) sediment, dregs *pl.*; (*gram.*) sentence, clause; (*mus.*) movement; (*log.*) proposition; (*Druck*) composition; (*gleichartige Dinge*) set; (*Verhältnis*) rate.

Satzlehre *f.* syntax.

Satzung *f.* (-, -en) statute, regulation.

satzungsgemäss *a.* statutory.

Sau *f.* (-, -en) sow, hog; (*fig. vulg.*) slut.

sauber *a.* clean, neat; fine, pretty.

Sauberkeit *f.* (-, 0) cleanliness; neatness.

säuberlich *adv.* gently; properly.

säubern *v.t.* to clean, to cleanse, to purge; (*mil.*) to mop up.

Säuberung f. (-, -en) (pol.) purge.
Saubohne f. broad bean.
Sauce f. (-, -n) gravy; sauce.
sauer a. sour; acid; morose; ~ werden, to go sour.
Sauerampfer m. sorrel.
Sauerkraut n. pickled cabbage, sauerkraut.
säuerlich a. acidulous.
Sauermilch f. curdled milk.
Sauer: ~stoff m. oxygen; ~teig m. leaven.
Sauerstoffgerät n. oxygen apparatus.
saufen v.t. & i.st. to drink to excess.
Säufer m. (-s, -) drunkard.
Sauferei f. (-, -en) drinking-bout, booze.
Säuferwahnsinn m. delirium tremens.
Saufgelage n. drinking-bout.
saugen v.t. & i.st. to suck.
säugen v.t. to suckle, to nurse.
Sauger m. (-s, -) sucker; (der Flasche) nipple.
Säugetier n. mammal.
Saugflasche f. feeding-bottle.
Säugling m. (-s, -e) baby, suckling.
Säuglingssterblichkeit f. infant mortality.
Säule f. (-, -n) pillar, column; (galvanic) pile.
Säulen: ~bohrmaschine f. pillar drill; ~gang m. colonnade; ~halle f. portico; ~schaft m. shaft of a column.
Saum m. (-[e]s, Säume) border, edge; seam, hem.
säumen v.t. to hem; ~ v.i. to delay, to tarry.
säumig a. tardy, dilatory.
saumselig a. tardy, dilatory; negligent.
Säure f. (-, -n) (chem.) acid.
säurebeständig a. acid-proof.
Sauregurkenzeit f. silly season.
Saus m. (-ses, 0) ~ und Braus, riot and revelry.
säuseln v.i. to rustle.
sausen v.i. to whistle, to whiz.
Saustall m. pig-sty; (fig.) mess.
Schabe f. (-, -n) cockroach.
Schabefleisch n. scraped meat.
schaben v.t. to scrape; to rub.
Schabernack m. (-[e]s, -e) hoax; practical joke.
schäbig a. shabby; mean.
Schablone f. (-, -n) pattern; stencil.
Schabracke f. (-, -n) caparison.
Schach n. (-s, 0) chess; check!; ~ bieten, to check; einen im ~ halten, to keep one in check.
Schachbrett n. chess-board.
Schacher m. (-s, 0) mean or unfair traffic, petty trade.
schachern v.t. to bargain; to haggle.
Schach: ~feld n. square; ~figur f. chessman.
schachmatt a. checkmate.
Schacht m. (-[e]s, Schächte) pit, shaft.

Schachtel f. (-, -n) box; bandbox; (fig.) alte ~, old frump.
schächten v.t. to slaughter in the Jewish fashion.
Schachzug m. move.
schade es ist ~, it is a pity.
Schade[n] m. (-ns, Schäden) damage, prejudice, hurt; ~n leiden, nehmen, zu ~n kommen, to come to grief, to be hurt.
Schädel m. (-s, -) skull.
Schädelbruch m. fracture of the skull.
schaden v.i. to hurt, to injure, to damage; es schadet nichts, it does not matter.
Schaden: ~ersatz m. indemnification; damages pl., compensation; ~freude f. malicious joy.
schadhaft a. damaged, defective, faulty.
schädigen v.t. to damage, to injure.
schädlich a. hurtful, detrimental.
schadlos a. sich ~ halten, to recover one's losses.
Schädling m. (-s, -e) (insect) pest; noxious creature.
Schaf n. (-[e]s, -e) sheep; (fig.) simpleton.
Schaf: ~blattern f. pl. chicken-pox; ~bock m. ram.
Schäfchen n. (-s, -) lamb, lambkin.
Schäfer m. (-s, -) shepherd.
Schäferhund m. shepherd's dog; Alsatian.
Schaffell n. sheepskin.
schaffen v.t.st. to create; ~ v.t. to afford, to procure; to convey; ~ v.i. to be active, to work, to do; aus dem Wege ~, to remove; sich vom Halse ~, to rid oneself of; zu ~ machen, to give trouble; sich zu ~ machen, to busy oneself.
Schaffner n. (-s, -) steward; (rail.) guard; (Am. Strassenbahn) conductor.
Schaf: ~fleisch n. mutton; ~hürde f. sheep-fold.
Schafott n. (-[e]s, -e) scaffold.
Schafschur f. sheep-shearing.
Schaf(s)kopf m. blockhead.
Schaft m. (-[e]s, Schäfte) shaft; leg (of a boot); (Baum) trunk; (Blumen) stalk; (tech.) shank.
Schaftstiefel m. Wellington boot.
Schaf: ~weide f. sheep-walk; ~zucht f. sheep-farming.
Schakal m. (-s, -e) jackal.
Schäker m. (-s, -) joker, wag; rogue.
schal a. stale, flat, insipid.
Schal m. (-s, -s) shawl.
Schale f. (-, -n) shell; peel; husk, pod; dish; bowl, saucer; (Wage) scale; (fig. outside.
schälen v.t. to shell; to peel, to pare; to husk; to bark; (sich) ~ v.refl. to peel off, to come off.
Schalk m. (-[e]s, -e) rogue; wag.
schalkhaft a. waggish, roguish, arch.

Schall *m.* (-[e]s, -e) sound.
Schalldämpfung *f.* sound insulation.
schallen *v.i.* to sound, to ring.
Schallplatte *f.* gramophone record.
Schallwelle *f.* sound-wave.
Schaltbrett *n.* switch-board.
schalten *v.i.* to act, to command; to switch; ~ *und walten,* to manage.
Schalthebel *m.* control *or* gear lever.
Schalter *m.* (-s, -) booking-office; counter; (*elek.*) switch.
Schaltgerät *n.* (*elek.*) switch-gear.
Schaltjahr *n.* leap-year.
Schaltung *f.* (-, -en) (*elek.*) connection.
Schaluppe *f.* (-, -n) sloop; yawl.
Scham *f.* (-, 0) shame; privy parts *pl.*
schämen (sich) *v.refl.* to be ashamed.
schamhaft *a.* bashful, shamefaced.
Schamleiste *f.* groin.
schamlos *a.* shameless; indecent.
Schamotte *f.* (-, -) chamotte, fire-clay.
schamponieren *v.t.* to shampoo.
schamrot *a.* blushing.
Schande *f.* (-, 0) shame, disgrace; *zu* ~*n machen,* to destroy, to ruin.
schänden *v.t.* to violate, to deflower.
Schandfleck, *m.* stain, blemish.
schändlich *a.* disgraceful, shameful.
Schandtat *f.* crime.
Schankwirtschaft *f.* public-house.
Schankgerechtigkeit *f.* licence; *mit* ~, licensed.
Schanze *f.* (-, -n) earth-work, entrenchment.
Schar *f.* (-, -en) troop, band.
Scharade *f.* (-, -n) charade.
scharen (sich) *v.refl.* to assemble, to collect, to flock together, to rally.
scharf *a.* sharp, keen; (*spitz*) acute; (*Geschmack*) acrid, pungent.
Scharfblick *m.* (-[e]s, 0) penetration.
Schärfe *f.* (-, -en) sharpness; acuteness; pungency; acrimony; severity; edge.
schärfen *v.t.* to sharpen, to whet; *Minen*~, to fuse mines.
Scharf: ~**macher** *m.* firebrand; ~**richter** *m.* executioner; ~**schütze** *m.* marksman.
scharfsichtig *a.* sharp-sighted.
Scharfsinn *m.* (-[e]s, 0) acumen, sagacity.
scharfsinnig *a.* sagacious, shrewd.
Scharlach *m.* (-[e]s, 0) scarlet.
Scharlachfieber, *n.* scarlet-fever.
Scharlatan *m.* (-s, -e) charlatan, quack.
Scharmützel *n.* (-s, -) skirmish.
Scharnier *n.* (-[e]s, -e) hinge, joint.
Schärpe *f.* (-, -n) sash, sling.
Scharpie *f.* (-, 0) lint.
scharren *v.t. & i.* to scrape, to take.
Scharte *f.* (-, -n) notch, jag.
schartig *a.* notched, jagged.

Schatten *m.* (-s, -) shade, shadow; *in* ~ *stellen,* (*fig.*) to throw into the shade.
Schatten: ~**bild** *n.* shade, phantom; ~**riss** *m.* silhouette; ~**seite** *f.* drawback.
schattieren *v.t.* to shade.
Schattierung *f.* (-, -en) shade, nuance.
schattig *a.* shady, shadowy.
Schatulle *f.* (-, -n) cash-box.
Schatz *m.* (-es, Schätze) treasure; store; (*fig.*) darling, love.
Schatzamt *n.* treasury, exchequer.
Schatzanweisung *f.* (-, -en) treasury bond, (*Am.*) treasury certificate.
schätzbar *a.* valuable, estimable.
schätzen *v.t.* to value, to esteem; to estimate; *geschätzt auf,* put at.
schätzenswert *a.* estimable.
Schätzer *m.* (-s, -) appraiser, valuer.
Schatz: ~**gräber,** *m.* treasure-hunter; ~**schein** *m.* treasury bond.
Schätzung *f.* (-, -en) valuation; estimate.
Schatzwechsel *m.* treasury bill.
Schau *f.* (-, 0) view; show; *zur* ~ *stellen,* to exhibit, to display; *zur* ~ *tragen,* to parade, to sport; to boast of.
Schau: ~**bude** *f.* show-booth; ~**budenbesitzer** *m.* showman.
Schauder *m.* (-s, -) shudder; horror.
schauderhaft, schaudervoll *a.* horrible, dreadful, shocking.
schaudern *v.i.* to shudder, to shiver.
schauen *v.t. & i.* to view, to gaze.
Schauer *m.* (-s, -) beholder; shivering fit; horror, awe; (*Regen*~) shower.
schauerlich *a.* awful, thrilling.
Schaufel *f.* (-, -n) shovel; ladle; paddle.
schaufeln *v.t.* to shovel.
Schaufelrad *n.* paddle-wheel.
Schaufenster *n.* show-window; ~**dekorateur** *m.* window-dresser.
Schaukasten *m.* showcase.
Schaukel *f.* (-, -n) swing.
schaukeln *v.t. & i.* to swing, to rock.
Schaukelpferd *n.* rocking-horse.
schaulustig *a.* curious.
Schaum *m.* (-[e]s, Schäume) foam, froth.
schäumen *v.i.* to foam, to froth.
schaumig *a.* foamy, foaming.
Schaumwein *m.* sparkling wine.
schaurig *a.* awful, horrid.
Schau: ~**platz** *m.* scene; (*fig.*) theatre; ~**spiel** *n.* spectacle, sight; play, drama; ~**spieldirektor** *m.* manager of a theatre; ~**spieler** *m.* actor, player; ~**spielerei** *f.* hypocrisy; ~**spielerin** *f.* actress.
schauspielerisch *a.* stagey, theatrical.
Schau: ~**spielhaus** *n.* theatre; ~**spielkunst** *f.* dramatic art.
Scheck *m.* cheque, (*Am.*) check; *einen* ~ *sperren,* to stop payment on a cheque.
scheckig *a.* piebald, dapple.
scheel *a.* squint-eyed; envious; ~ *adv.* askance.

Scheffel, *m.* (-s, -) bushel.
scheffelweise *a. & adv.* by the bushel.
Scheibe *f.* (-, -n) disk, orb; target; (*Glas* ~) pane; (Schnitte) cut, slice.
Scheibenschiessen *n.* target-practice.
Scheibenwischer *m.* (*mot.*) windscreen wiper.
Scheide *f.* (-, -n) sheath; (*anat.*) vagina.
Scheidemünze *f.* small coin.
scheiden *v.t.st.* to divide, to separate; to divorce; ~ *v.i.* to depart, to part, to leave.
Scheidewand *f.* partition; (*fig.*) barrier.
Scheidung *f.* (-, en) separation; divorce.
Scheidungsklage *f.* divorce-suit.
Schein *m.* (-[e]s, -e) shine; lustre, splendour; appearance; pretext; certificate, bill; *zum* ~, seemingly.
Scheinangriff *m.* (*mil.*) feint attack.
scheinbar *a.* apparent, ostensible.
Scheinbeweis *m.* sophism.
scheinen *v.i.st.* to shine; to seem, to appear.
Scheingeschäft *n.* fictitious transaction.
scheinheilig *a.* sanctimonious.
Schein: -heiligkeit *f.* hypocrisy; ~tod, *m.* apparent death, catalepsy; ~werfer *m.* searchlight; *mit* ~*werfer beleuchten,* to floodlight; ~werferlicht *n.* spotlight; (*mot.*) headlights.
scheissen *v.i.* (*vulg.*) to shit.
Scheit *n.* (-[e]s, -e) piece of wood, billet.
Scheitel *m.* (-s, -) (*Haar* ~) parting.
Scheiterhaufen *m.* funeral pile, stake.
scheitern *v.i.* to be wrecked; (*fig.*) to miscarry, to fail.
Schellack *m.* (-[e]s, -e) shellac.
Schelle *f.* (-, -n) (small) bell; manacle; box on the ear.
schellen *v.i.* to ring the bell.
Schellfisch *m.* haddock.
Schelm *m.* (-[e]s, -e) rogue, knave.
schelmisch *a.* roguish, knavish.
Schelte *f.* (-, -n) scolding.
schelten *v.t. & i.st.* to scold, to chide; to rebuke; to abuse.
Scheltwort *n.* invective, abusive term.
Schema *n.* (-s, -s *u.* -mata) sketch, model, plan.
schematisch *a.* mechanical.
Schemel *m.* (-s, -) foot-stool.
Schenke *f.* (-, -n) inn, public-house.
Schenkel *m.* (-s, -) thigh, shank; leg; (*des Winkels*) side.
schenken *v.t.* to retail (liquor); to pour out; to make a present of, to give, to grant; *die Strafe* ~, to remit a punishment.
Schenker *m.* (-s, -) donor.
Schenktisch *m.* bar.
Schenk:ung *f.* (-, -en) donation.
Schenkungsurkunde *f.* deed of gift.
Scherbe *f.* (-, -n), Scherben *m.* (-s, -) potsherd; fragment; (*nav.*) scarf.

Schere *f.* (-, -n) scissors; (*grosse*) pair of shears *pl.*; (*Hummer* ~) claw.
scheren *v.t.st.* to shear, to clip; to fleece, to cheat; *sich um etwas* ~, to trouble oneself about a thing; *sich zum Teufel* ~, to go to the devil; *das schert mich nichts*, I don't care a straw for it.
Scherenschleifer *m.* knife-grinder.
Schererei *f.* (-, -en) vexation, bother.
Scherflein *n.* (-s, -) mite.
Scherz *m.* (-es, -e) joke, pleasantry; ~ *beiseite,* joking apart.
scherzen *v.i.* to jest, to joke; ~ *über,* to make fun of.
scherzhaft *a.* jocose, playful, funny.
scherzweise *adv.* jestingly, in fun.
scheu *a.* shy; timid, bashful.
Scheu *f.* (-, 0) shyness; aversion; awe.
scheuchen *v.t.* to frighten away; to scare.
scheuen *v.t.* to shun, to avoid; ~ *v.i.* to shy (at); (sich) ~ *v.refl.* to be shy; to fight shy (of).
Scheuer *f.* (-, -n) shed, barn.
Scheuer: ~frau *f.* charwoman; ~lappen *m.* dish-cloth.
scheuern *v.t.* to scour; to scrub.
Scheuklappe *f.*, Scheuleder *n.* blinker.
Scheune *f.* (-, -n) barn, shed.
Scheusal *n.* (-[e]s, -e) monster.
scheusslich *a.* frightful, hideous.
Schicht *f.* (-, -en) layer, bed, stratum; (*Gesellschafts* ~) class, rank; shift, task.
schichten *v.t.* to dispose in layers, to pile up; to arrange.
schichtweise *a. & adv.* in layers.
Schick *m.* (-[e]s, 0) skill, tact.
schick *a.* stylish, smart.
schicken *v.t.* to send, to dispatch; (sich) ~ *v.refl.* to be suitable, to be proper.
schicklich *a.* suitable, decent, proper.
Schicklichkeit *f.* (-, 0) propriety, decorum.
Schicksal *n.* (-[e]s, -e) fate; destiny.
Schickung *f.* (-, -en) dispensation.
Schiebefenster *n.* sash window.
schieben *v.t.st.* to shove, to push; (*fig.*) to act corruptly; *Kegel* ~, to play at ninepins; *einem etwas in die Schuhe* ~, to lay a fault at someone's door.
Schieber *m.* (-s, -) bolt, slide; slide-valve; (*am Ofen*) damper, register; profiteer.
Schiebe: ~tür *f.* sliding door; ~ventil *n.* slide-valve.
Schiebung *f.* (-, -en) graft, jobbery, racket.
Schieds: ~gericht *n.* court of arbitration; ~richter *m.* arbitrator, umpire; referee; ~spruch *m.* award.
schief *a.* oblique, wry, crooked; ~ *adv.* askew, awry; ~*gehen* (*fig.*), to go wrong; ~*e Ebene*, inclined plane.
Schiefer *m.* (-s, -) slate; splinter.
Schiefer: ~dach *n.* slated roof; ~decker *m.* slater; ~platte *f.* slab of slate; ~tafel *f.* (school-)slate.

schielen v.i. to squint; to leer (at).
schielend a. squint-eyed, squinting.
Schienbein n. shin(-bone).
Schiene f. (-, -n) splint; (rail.) rail.
schienen v.t. to splint; (Rad) to shoe.
schier adv. sheer, pure; (adv.) almost.
Schierling m. (-[e]s, -e) hemlock.
Schiessbaumwolle f. gun-cotton.
schiessen v.t. & i.st. to shoot, to discharge, to fire; (football, Tor ~) to score; to rush; die Zügel ~ lassen, to let go the reins; einen Bock ~, (fam.) to make a blunder.
Schiessfertigkeit f. marksmanship.
Schiess: ~gewehr n. fire-arm; ~pulver n. gunpowder; ~scharte f. embrasure, loop-hole; ~scheibe f. target.
Schiff n. (-[e]s, -e) ship, vessel, boat; (Kirchen~) nave; (Weber) shuttle.
Schiffahrt f. (-, 0) navigation.
schiffbar a. navigable.
Schiff: ~bruch m. shipwreck; ~bruch leiden, to be shipwrecked.
schiffbrüchig a. shipwrecked.
Schiffbrücke f. pontoon-bridge.
schiffen v.i. to navigate, to sail.
Schiffer m. (-s, -) ship's-master, skipper.
Schiffs: ~junge m. cabin-boy; ~raum m. shipping space; ~spediteur m. shipping-agent.
Schikane f. chicanery, trickery.
schikanieren v.t. to vex.
schikanös a. vexatious.
schilaufen v.i. to ski.
Schild m. (-es, -e) shield, buckler.
Schild n. (-es, -er) sign-board; door-plate; label.
Schilddrüse f. thyroid gland.
schildern v.t. to describe, to picture.
Schilderung f. (-, -en) description.
Schild: ~kröte f. turtle, tortoise; ~laus f. cochineal kermes; ~wache f. sentinel, sentry.
Schilf n. (-[e]s, -e) reed, rush; sedge.
Schilfgras n. reed-grass, sedge.
Schilfrohr n. reed.
schillern v.i. to be iridescent, to glitter.
schillernd a. glistening, iridescent.
Schilling m. (-s, -e) (Münze) shilling.
Schimäre f. (-, -n) chimera, bogy.
Schimmel m. (-s, -) mould, mustiness; white horse.
schimm[e]lig a. mouldy, musty.
schimmeln v.i. to get mouldy, to mould.
Schimmer m. (-s, -) glitter, gleam, glimmer; (fig.) idea; keinen ~, not the faintest notion.
schimmern v.i. to glitter, to glisten.
Schimpanse m. (-n, -n) chimpanzee.
Schimpf m. (-[e]s, -e) affront, insult; disgrace.
schimpfen v.t. to abuse, to revile.
schimpflich a. disgraceful.

Schimpfwort n. invective, term of abuse.
Schindeldach n. shingle-roof.
schinden v.t.st. to flay; (fig.) to oppress, to grind; sich ~, to slave.
Schinderei f. (-, -en) drudgery.
Schinken m. (-s, -) ham.
Schirm m. (-[e]s, -e) screen; shade; (Regen~) umbrella; (Sonnen~) parasol; (Mützen~) peak; (fig.) shelter, protection.
schirmen v.t. to shelter, to protect.
Schirm: ~rippe, ~stange f. rib; ~ständer m. umbrella stand.
Schisma n. (-s, -s u. -mata) schism.
schismatisch a. schismatic.
Schlacht f. (-, -en) battle; eine ~ liefern, to fight a battle.
Schlachtbank f. shambles pl.
schlachten v.t. to slaughter, to kill.
Schlächter m. (-s, -) butcher.
Schlacht: ~kreuzer m. battle-cruiser; ~feld n. battle-field; ~ruf m. war-cry; ~schiff n. battleship.
Schlacke f. (-, -n) dross, slag, scoria.
Schlackwurst f. German salami.
Schlaf m. (-[e]s, 0) sleep; im ~e, asleep.
Schlafanzug m. pyjamas pl., (Am.) pajamas.
Schläfe f. (-, -n) temple.
schlafen v.i.st. to sleep.
Schläfer m. (-s, -) sleeper.
schlaff a. limp, slack, flabby; indolent.
Schlaffheit f. (-, 0) slackness, indolence.
Schlafkrankheit f. sleeping sickness.
schlaflos a. sleepless.
Schlaf: ~mittel n. soporific; ~mütze f. nightcap; (fig.) dullard, slowcoach.
schläfrig a. sleepy, drowsy; sluggish.
Schlaf: ~rock m. dressing-gown; ~sack m. sleeping-bag.
schlaftrunken a. drowsy.
Schlaf: ~wagen m. sleeping-car, sleeper; ~wagenschaffner m. sleeping-car attendant; ~wandler m. sleep-walker; ~zimmer n. bedroom.
Schlag m. (-[e]s, Schläge) stroke, blow; (elek.) shock; apoplexy, fit; (fig.) kind, sort; (Donner~) clap; (Puls~) beat; ~ auf ~, in rapid succession, as thick as hail; ~ zwölf Uhr, at twelve o'clock sharp.
Schlag: ~ader f. artery; ~anfall m. apoplectic fit; ~baum m. bar, turnpike.
Schlägel = **Schlegel**.
schlagen v.t.st. to beat, to strike; (den Feind) to defeat; (Eier) to beat; ~ v.i. (Uhr) to strike; es schlägt 12 Uhr, it strikes 12; ~ v.refl. sich schlagen, to fight; Holz ~, to fell wood; eine Brücke ~, to throw a bridge; Geld ~, to coin money; ein Kreuz ~, to make the sign of the Cross; Alarm ~, to sound the

alarm; *ans Kreuz* ~, to crucify; *zum Ritter* ~, to knight.
schlagend *a.* striking.
Schlager *m.* (-s, -) (*theat.*) hit.
Schläger *m.* (-s, -) (*Tennis*) racket, (*Kricket*) bat.
Schlägerei *f.* (-, -en) scuffle, row.
schlagfertig *a.* quick at repartee.
Schlag: ~kraft *f.* striking power; ~sahne *f.* whipped cream; ~weite *f.* striking distance; ~wetter *n.* firedamp; ~wort *n.* catchword; slogan.
Schlamassel *n.* (-s, -) scrape, predicament.
Schlamm *m.* (-[e]s, 0) mud; mire, slime.
Schlampe *f.* (-, -n) slut, slattern, hussy.
schlampig *a.* slovenly.
Schlange *f.* (-, -n) snake, serpent; coil; (*Reihe*) queue.
schlängeln (sich) *v.refl.* to meander.
schlangenförmig *a.* serpentine.
schlank *a.* slender, slim.
schlankweg *adv.* right away.
schlapp = schlaff.
Schlappe *f.* (-, -n) check, reverse.
Schlapphut *m.* slouched hat.
Schlaraffenland *n.* Land of Cockayne.
schlau *a. & adv.* sly (slily); cunning(ly), crafty(ily).
Schlauberger, Schlaukopf, Schlaumeier *m.* (*fam.*) slyboots, artful dodger.
Schlauch *m.* (-[e]s, Schläuche) hose; (*Fahrrad*) tube.
Schlauch: ~boot *n.* rubber dinghy; ~mantel *m.* cover of a tyre.
Schlauheit *f.* (-, -en) cunning, slyness.
schlecht *a.* mean, base, bad, wicked; (*Geld*) base; vile; ill; *mir ist* or *wird* ~, I feel ill; *es ~ haben*, to have a bad time; *es geht ihm* ~, he is unwell or badly off.
schlechtgesinnt *a.* evil-minded.
schlechterdings *adv.* absolutely.
schlechthin *adv.* plainly; positively.
Schlechtigkeit *f.* (-, -en) meanness, baseness, badness.
schlechtweg *adv.* plainly, simply.
schlecken *v.t. & i.* to lick.
Schleckerei *f.* (-, -en) sweets, dainties *pl.*
Schlegel *m.* (-s, -) mallet; leg (of mutton, etc.); drumstick.
Schlehdorn *m.* blackthorn.
Schlehe *f.* (-, -n) sloe.
schleichen *v.i.st.* (*s*) to sneak, to steal, to glide, to slink; (*sich fort*~, to steal away, to sneak off.
schleichend *a.* sneaking; (*fig.*) lingering.
Schleich: ~handel *m.* black market; ~händler *m.* black marketeer; ~weg *m.* (*fig.*) crooked way.
Schleie *f.* (-, -n) (*Fisch*) tench.
Schleier *m.* (-s, -) veil.
schleierhaft *a.* (*fig.*) unaccountable; *das ist mir* ~, I don't know what to make of it.

Schleife *f.* (-, -n) loop; knot, bow; sledge drag.
schleifen *v.t. & i.* to drag, to trail; to raze; to glide, to slide; ~*v.t.st.* to grind, to polish; to cut (glass).
Schleifer *m.* (-s, -) grinder, polisher; (*Edelstein*~) cutter.
Schleifmittel *n.* abrasive.
Schleifstein *m.* whetstone, grindstone.
Schleim *m.* (-[e]s, -e) slime; phlegm; mucus.
Schleimhaut *f.* mucous membrane.
schlemmen *v.i.* to gormandize, to revel.
Schlemmer *m.* (-s, -) glutton.
schlendern *v.i.* (*s*) to saunter, jog along.
Schlendrian *m.* (-s, 0) jog-trot, routine.
schlenkern *v.t. & i.* to swing; to dangle.
Schleppdampfer *m.* steam-tug.
Schleppe *f.* (-, -n) train (of a dress).
schleppen *v.t. & i.* to drag; to trail; (*nav.*) to tow, to tug.
schleppend *a.* flagging, lengthy, heavy.
Schlepper *m.* (-s, -) tug.
Schlepp: ~kleid *n.* dress with a train; ~tau *n.* tow-rope; *ins* ~ *nehmen*, to take in tow.
Schleuder *f.* (-, -n) sling.
Schleuderausfuhr *f.* dumpling.
schleudern *v.t.* to sling, to throw; ~ *v.i.* to swing.
Schleuderpreis *m. zu Schleuderpreisen*, dirt cheap.
schleunig *a.* quick, speedy.
Schleuse *f.* (-, -n) sluice, lock, flood-gate.
Schlich *m.* (-[e]s, -e) trick, dodge; *hinter die* ~*e kommen*, to be up to one's dodges or tricks.
schlicht *a.* plain; sleek, smooth.
schlichten *v.t.* to smooth; (*fig.*) to settle, to arrange, to adjust.
Schlichter *m.* (-s, -) arbitrator.
Schlichtung *f.* (-, 0) settling (of differences); ~samt *n.* conciliation board; ~ausschuss *m.* court of arbitration.
schliessen *v.t. & i.st.* to shut, to close, to bolt; to conclude; (*Ehe*) to contract; *in sich* ~, to include.
Schliesser *m.* (-s, -) jailer; doorkeeper.
Schliessfach *n.* post-office box.
schliesslich *adv.* lastly, finally.
Schliessung *f.* (-, -en) closure.
Schliff *m.* (-[e]s, -e) (*fig.*) polish.
schlimm *a.* bad, evil, serious.
Schlinge *f.* (-, -n) noose, knot; loop, snare; (*med.*) sling.
Schlingel *m.* (-s, -) rascal; naughty boy.
schlingen *v.t. & i.st.* to swallow, to gulp (down); to twist, to entwine; (sich) ~ *v.refl.st.* to wind, to twine (round).
schlingern *v.i.* (*nav.*) to roll.
Schlingpflanze *f.* creeper.
Schlips *m.* (-es, -e) (neck-)tie.
Schlipsnadel *f.* tie-pin.

Schlitten m. (-s, -) sledge, sleigh; (kleiner) toboggan; (mech.) slide, carriage.

Schlittschuh m. skate; ~ laufen, to skate.

Schlittschuhläufer m. skater.

Schlitz m. (-es, -e) slit, slash; fissure; slot.

schlitzen v.t. to slit, to slash.

Schloss n. (Schlosses, Schlösser) lock; castle; palace; unter ~ und Riegel, under lock and key.

Schlosser m. (-s, -) locksmith.

Schlot m. (-[e]s, -e u. Schlöte) chimney.

schlotterig a. wabbling.

schlottern v.i. to wobble, to hang loose.

Schlucht f. (-, -en) cleft, ravine.

schluchzen v.i. to sob.

Schluck m. (-[e]s, Schlucke) gulp, drink.

schlucken v.i. & t. to gulp (down), to swallow; (fig.) to stomach.

Schlucker m. (-s, -) hiccup; armer ~, poor wretch.

Schlummer m. (-s, 0) slumber; doze.

schlummern v.i. to slumber, to doze.

Schlund m. (-[e]s, Schlünde) throat, gullet; gulf, abyss.

schlüpfen v.i. (s) to slip, to slide.

Schlüpfer m. (-s, -) (pair of) knickers.

Schlupf: ~loch n. loop-hole; ~winkel m. hiding place, den.

schlüpfrig a. slippery; prurient, obscene.

schlürfen v.t. to sip, to lap; v.i. to shuffle (along).

Schluss m. (Schlusses, Schlüsse) conclusion, end; (log.) inference; closure.

Schlüssel m. (-s, -) key; (mus.) key.

Schlüssel: ~bein n. collar-bone; ~blume f. cowslip, primrose; ~bund m. bunch of keys; ~loch n. keyhole; ~ring m. split ring; ~stellung f. key position.

Schluss: ~examen n. final examination; ~feier f. (Schule) speech day; ~folgerung f. inference, conclusion.

schlüssig a. conclusive; sich ~ werden, to make up one's mind.

Schluss: ~licht n. rear lamp or light; ~notierung f. closing price; ~satz m. concluding sentence; (mus.) finale; ~stein m. keystone.

Schmach f. (-, 0) ignominy; insult.

schmachten v.i. to languish, to long for, to pine.

schmächtig a. slender, slim.

schmachvoll a. ignominious; disgraceful.

schmackhaft a. savoury, tasty.

schmähen v.t. to revile.

schmählich a. ignominious, injurious.

Schmähschrift f. libel, lampoon.

Schmähung f. (-, -en) abuse, invective.

schmal a. narrow; small; scanty; slim.

schmälern v.t. to lessen; to belittle.

Schmalspur f. narrow gauge.

Schmalz n. (-es, 0) lard.

schmalzig a. greasy; (fig.) sentimental.

schmarotzen v.i. to sponge (on others).

Schmarotzer m. (-s, -) parasite.

schmatzen v.t. & i. to smack one's lips

Schmaus m. (-ses, Schmäuse) feast, treat.

schmausen v.i. to feast, to banquet.

schmecken v.t. & i. to taste (nach, of); to savour; to taste well; wie schmeckt dir ...? how do you like?

Schmeichelei f. (-, -en) flattery.

schmeichelhaft a. flattering.

schmeicheln v.i. to flatter.

schmeichlerisch a. flattering, fawning.

schmeissen v.t.st. to chuck, to fling.

Schmelz m. (-es, -e) enamel.

schmelzen v.t.st. to melt; (Erze) to smelt; to fuse; ~ v.i.st. to melt (away).

schmelzend a. melodious; languishing.

Schmelz: ~punkt m. melting point; ~tiegel m. crucible.

Schmerz m. (-es, -en) pain, ache; grief.

schmerzen v.t. to hurt, to grieve.

schmerzhaft a. painful, grievous.

schmerzlich a. painful.

schmerzlos a. painless.

schmerzstillend a. anodyne; soothing.

Schmetterling m. (-[e]s, -e) butterfly.

schmettern v.i. (von Trompeten) to bray, to blare; (von Singvögeln) to warble.

Schmied m. (-[e]s, -e) (black-)smith.

Schmiede f. (-, -n) forge, smithy.

Schmiede: ~eisen n. wrought iron; ~hammer m. sledge(-hammer).

schmieden v.t. to forge; (fig.) to plan, to frame, to concoct.

schmiegen (sich) v.refl. to nestle, to cling.

schmiegsam a. (fig.) pliant, supple.

Schmiere f. (-, -n) grease; salve; (vulg.) low theatre.

schmieren v.t. & i. to grease, to lubricate: (Butter) to spread; (sudeln) to scrawl; (fig.) to bribe; es geht wie geschmiert, things go swimmingly.

Schmierfink m. (fam.) dirty fellow.

schmierig a. greasy; dirty; (fig.) sordid.

Schmierseife f. soft-soap.

Schminkdose f., **Schminktopf** m. rouge-pot.

Schminke f. (-, -n) paint, rouge, make-up.

schminken v.t. to paint; to lay on rouge.

Schmirgel m. (-s, 0) emery.

Schmiss m. (Schmisses, Schmisse) stroke, blow; cut, slash; (fig.) smartness.

schmissig a. snappy.

Schmöker m. (-s, -) (fam.) worthless old book.

schmollen v.i. to pout, to sulk.

Schmorbraten m. stewed joint of beef.

schmoren v.t. & i. to braise, to stew.

Schmu m. (-s, 0) (fam.) unfair gain.

Schmuck m. (-[e]s, 0) ornament, jewels pl.

schmuck a. neat, spruce, trim, dandy.

schmücken v.t. to adorn; to dress up; to trim; to decorate.

schmucklos a. plain, unadorned.

Schmucksachen *f.pl.* jewellery.
Schmuckstück *n.* ornament.
Schmuggel *m.* (-s, 0) smuggling.
schmuggeln *v.t.* to smuggle.
Schmuggelware *f.* contraband.
schmunzeln *v.i.* to smirk; to chuckle.
Schmus *m.* (-es, 0) (*fam.*) soft soap.
Schmutz *m.* (-es, 0) dirt, soil, filth.
Schmutz… (*fig.*) pornographic.
schmutzen *v.t. & i.* to soil; to get dirty.
Schmutz: ~**fink** *m.* dirty fellow; ~**fleck** *m.* stain.
schmutzig *a.* dirty, filthy; sordid; obscene.
Schnabel *m.* (-s, Schnäbel) bill, beak.
Schnake *f.* (-, -n) gnat, midge.
schnakisch *a.* droll, odd, funny.
Schnalle *f.* (-, -n) buckle.
schnallen *v.t.* to buckle.
schnalzen *v.i.* to smack; to crack (a whip).
schnappen *v.i.* to snap, to snatch; *nach Luft ~,* to gasp for breath.
Schnappschloss *n.* spring-lock.
Schnaps *m.* (Schnapses, Schnäpse) strong liquor; dram.
schnarchen *v.i.* to snore.
Schnarre *f.* (-, -n) rattle.
schnarren *v.i.* to rattle.
schnattern *v.i.* to cackle; chatter.
schnauben *v.i.* to snort.
schnaufen *v.i.* to snort.
Schnauze *f.* (-, -n) snout, muzzle.
Schnecke *f.* (-, -n) snail, slug; (*Gebäck*) sweet-roll.
schneckenförmig *a.* spiral, helical.
Schnecken: ~**haus** *n.* snail-shell; ~**rad** *n.* (*mech.*) wormgear; ~**windung** *f.* volution, spiral turning.
Schnee *m.* (-[e]s, 0) snow.
Schneeball *m.* snowball.
Schnee: ~**brille** *f.* dark goggles *pl.*; ~**flocke** *f.* snow-flake; ~**glöckchen** *n.* snowdrop.
Schneewetter *n.* snowy weather.
Schneid *m.* (-s, 0) pluck, dash.
Schneide *f.* (-, -n) (cutting) edge.
schneiden *v.t.st.* to cut; to carve; to saw; to reap; to pull (faces); (sich) ~ *v.refl.* (*math.*) to intersect.
schneidend *a.* cutting, caustic, trenchant.
Schneider *m.* (-s, -) tailor.
Schneiderin *f.* (-, -nen) dressmaker.
schneidern *v.i.* to make clothes, to tailor.
Schneidezahn *m.* incisor.
schneidig *a.* plucky, dashing.
schneien *v.i.imp.* to snow.
Schneise *f.* (-, -n) glade.
schnell *a.* quick, swift, speedy, fast; rapid; prompt.
Schnellboot *n.* speedboat.
schnellen *v.t.* to let fly, to jerk, to toss; ~ *v.i.* (*s*) to spring.
Schnell: ~**feuer** *n.* rapid fire; ~**feuerge-schütz** *n.* quick-firing gun; ~**gang** *m.*

(*mot.*) overdrive; ~**gericht** *n.* court of summary jurisdiction.
Schnelligkeit *f.* (-, 0) quickness, velocity, rapidity, speed.
Schnell: ~**kraft** *f.* elasticity; ~**verfahren** *n.* (*law*) summary procedure; ~**wirk-end**, *a.* quick-acting; ~**zug** *m.* fast train, express.
Schnepfe *f.* (-, -n) woodcock.
schneuzen (sich) *v.refl.* to blow one's nose.
schniegeln *v.t.* to make smooth.
Schnippchen *n.* (-s, -) *ein ~ schlagen,* to trick.
schnippisch *a.* snappish, pert.
Schnitt *m.* (-[e]s, -e) cut; incision; (*Buch~*) edge; fashion, pattern; section.
Schnitte *f.* (-, -n) slice, steak, cut.
Schnitter *m.* (-s, -) reaper.
Schnitt: ~**lauch** *m.* chives *pl.;* ~**muster** *n.* pattern; ~**punkt** *m.* intersection; ~**waren** *pl.* drapery, dry goods.
Schnitzel *n.* (-s, -) chip, shred; *Wiener ~,* veal-steak.
schnitzen *v.t.* to carve, to cut.
Schnitzer *m.* (-s, -) carver; blunder.
Schnitzerei *f.* (-, -en) carved work.
schnoddrig *a.* cheeky.
schnöde *a.* scornful; base, vile.
Schnörkel *m.* (-s, -) (*arch.*) scroll; flourish.
schnüffeln *v.i.* to sniff; to pry.
Schnüffler *m.* (-s, -) spy.
Schnuller *m.* teat.
schnupfen *v.t. & i.* to take snuff.
Schnupfen *m.* (-s, 0) cold (in the head); *sich den ~ holen,* to catch cold.
Schnupf: ~**tabak** *m.* snuff; ~**tabaksdose** *f.* snuff-box; ~**tuch** *n.* (pocket-)handker-chief.
schnuppern *v.i.* to sniff, to snuffle.
Schnur *f.* (-, Schnüre) string, cord.
Schnürchen *n.* (-s, -) *wie am ~,* like clock-work.
schnüren *v.t.* to lace; to cord, to tie up.
schnurgerade *a.* straight.
Schnurrbart *m.* moustache.
schnurren *v.i.* to hum, to whiz, to whir; (*von Katzen*) to purr.
schnurrig *a.* droll, funny.
Schnür: ~**senkel** *m.* boot-lace; ~**schuh**, ~**stiefel** *m.* lace-boot.
schnurstracks *adv.* directly.
Schober *m.* (-s, -) stack, rick.
schockweise *adv.* by threescores.
schofel *a.* mean, paltry.
Schöffe *m.* (-n, -n) juror, juryman, lay-judge.
Schöffengericht *n.* lowest court of law.
Schokolade *f.* (-, -n) chocolate.
Scholle *f.* (-, -n) clod, glebe; (*Fisch*) plaice.
schon *adv.* already; surely.
schön *a.* fine, fair, beautiful, handsome; ~**e Künste** *pl.* fine arts.

schonen *v.t.* to spare, to save; **(sich)** ~ *v.refl.* to take great care of oneself.
Schoner *m.* (-s, -) schooner.
Schönfärberei *f.* (-, -en) *(fig.)* embellishment, rose-coloured statements.
Schöngeist *m.* wit, *bel-esprit.*
schöngeistig *a.* æsthetical.
Schönheit *f.* (-, -en) beauty.
Schönheitssalon *m.* beauty parlour.
Schonung *f.* (-, -en) forbearance, indulgence; sparing; nursery for young trees.
schonungslos *a.* unsparing, relentless.
Schonzeit *f.* close time *or* season.
Schopf *m.* (-[e]s, Schöpfe) head of hair.
schöpfen *v.t.* to draw (water); to obtain, to get; *Luft* ~, to take the air; *Verdacht* ~, to conceive a suspicion; *Hoffnung* ~, to be reanimated by hope.
Schöpfer *m.* (-s, -) creator; author.
schöpferisch *a.* creative, productive.
Schöpflöffel *m.* ladle, scoop.
Schöpfung *f.* (-, -en) creation.
Schoppen *m.* (-s, -) pint.
Schöps *m.* (Schöpses, Schöpse) wether; *(fig.)* simpleton.
Schöpsenbraten *m.* roast-mutton.
Schorf *m.* (-[e]s, -e) scab, scurf.
schorfig *a.* scabby, scurfy.
Schornstein *m.* chimney; *(Am.)* smoke-stack.
Schornsteinfeger *m.* chimney-sweep.
Schoss *m.* (Schosses, Schosse *u.* Schossen) sprig, shoot.
Schoss *m.* (-es, Schösse) lap; *(fig.)* womb; *(Rock~)* flap, skirt, coat-tail; *die Hände in den ~ legen*, to sit with folded hands.
Schoss: ~**hund** *m.* lapdog; ~**kind** *n.* darling, pet child.
Schössling *m.* (-[e]s, -e) shoot, sprout.
Schoten *f.pl.* green peas.
Schott *n.* (-[e]s, -e) *(nav.)* bulkhead.
Schotter *m.* (-s, -) broken stones *pl.*
schottern *v.t.* to macadamize.
schraffieren *v.t.* to hatch.
schräg *a.* oblique, slanting; transverse; ~**er Anschnitt** *m.* *(mech.)* bevel.
Schräge *f.* (-, 0) obliquity.
Schramme *f.* (-, -n) scratch, slight wound.
schrammen *v.t.* to scratch, to graze.
Schrank *m.* (-[e]s, Schränke) cupboard; wardrobe; *(Am.)* closet.
Schranke *f.* (-, -n) bar, barrier; bound, limit; *(Eisenbahn)* gate.
schrankenlos *a.* boundless.
Schrankenwärter *m.* gateman.
Schraube *f.* (-, -n) screw; *(Dampfer~)* propeller.
schrauben *v.t.* to screw.
Schrauben: ~**dampfer** *m.* screw-steamer; ~**gewinde** *n.* worm *or* thread of a screw; ~**mutter** *f.* nut; ~**schlüssel** *m.* wrench, spanner; ~**zieher** *m.* screwdriver.
Schraubstock *m.* vice.

Schrebergarten *m.* allotment.
Schreck *m.* (-[e]s, -) fright, terror.
Schreckbild *n.* bugbear, fright.
schrecken *v.t.* to frighten, to affright.
Schrecken *m.* (-s, -) fright, terror; *ein blinder* ~, a false alarm.
schreckenerregend *a.* horrific.
Schreckensherrschaft *f.* reign of terror, terrorism.
schreckhaft *a.* easily frightened.
schrecklich *a.* awful, dreadful, terrible.
Schreckschuss *m.* shot in the air; *(fig.)* false alarm.
Schrei *m.* (-[e]s, -e) cry, shriek, scream.
Schreibblock *m.* writing-pad, writing-tablet.
schreiben *v.t.st.* to write; to type(write); *ins Reine* ~, to copy out; *einem auf die Rechnung* ~, to put down to one's account.
Schreiben *n.* (-s, -) letter, epistle; (art of) writing.
Schreiber *m.* (-s, -) clerk, copyist.
Schreib: ~**feder** *f.* nib; ~**fehler** *m.* slip of the pen, clerical error; ~**heft** *n.* exercise-book; ~**maschine** *f.* typewriter; ~**papier** *n.* writing-paper; ~**pult** *n.* writing desk; ~**stube** *f.* *(mil.)* orderly room; ~**tisch** *m.* writing-table; ~**waren** *f.pl.* stationery; ~**warenhändler** *m.* stationer.
schreien *v.t. & i.st.* to cry, to scream.
Schreier *m.* (-s, -), **Schreihals** *m.* crier; brawler; squalling child.
Schrein *m.* (-[e]s, -e) shrine.
Schreiner *m.* (-s, -) joiner, cabinet-maker.
schreiten *v.i.st.* (s) to stride, to step.
Schrift *f.* (-, -en) writing; handwriting; script; type; book; Scripture, Bible.
Schrift: ~**führer** *m.* secretary; ~**giesserei** *f.* typefoundry; ~**leiter** *m.* editor.
schriftlich *a.* written; ~ *adv.* in writing, by letter; ~**er Lehrkurs** *m.* correspondence course.
Schrift: ~**satz** *m.* *(law)* brief; ~**setzer** *m.* compositor, typesetter; ~**sprache** *f.* written language; ~**stelle** *f.* Scripture text; ~**steller** *m.* writer, author; ~**stellerei** *f.* authorship; ~**stellername** *m.* pen-name.
schriftstellerisch *a.* literary.
Schrift: ~**stück** *n.* document, letter; ~**wechsel** *m.* exchange of letters; ~**zeichen** *n.* character.
schrill *a.* shrill, piercing.
Schritt *m.* (-[e]s, -e) step, stride, pace; gait; demarche; ~ *vor (für)* ~, step by step; *für einen* ~*e tun*, to take steps in behalf of one; *im* ~ *gehen*, to walk, to pace; ~ *mit einem halten*, to keep pace with one; *aus dem* ~ *kommen*, to fall out of time; ~ *reiten, fahren*, to pace, to walk.

Schrittmacher m. pace-maker.
schrittweise adv. step by step.
schroff a. steep, rugged; (fig.) gruff.
schröpfen v.t. to cup; (fig.) to fleece.
Schrot n. (-[e]s, -e) due weight (of a coin); small shot.
Schrotflinte f. fowling-piece.
Schrott m. (-s, 0) scrap(iron).
schrubben v.t. to scrub.
Schrulle f. (-, -n) fad, whim.
schrullenhaft a. whimsical.
schrumpfen v.i. (s) to shrink, to shrivel.
Schub m. (-[e]s, Schübe) shove, push.
Schub: ~fach n. drawer; ~fenster n. sash-window; ~karren m. wheel-barrow; ~lade f. drawer.
schüchtern a. shy, coy, bashful.
Schuft m. (-[e]s, -e) blackguard, scoundrel.
schuften v.i. (vulg.) to work hard.
schuftig a. base, abject.
Schuh m. (-[e]s, -e) shoe; (fig.) einem etwas in die ~e schieben, to lay a fault at one's door.
Schuh: ~band n. shoe-lace; ~einlage f. insole, sock; ~flicker m. cobbler; ~leisten m. shoe-tree; ~litze f. shoe-lace (Am.) shoe-string; ~löffel m. shoe-horn; ~macher m. shoemaker; ~putzer m. boot-black; ~riemen m. boot-lace; ~wichse f. shoe polish.
Schulbank f. form.
Schuld f. (-, -en) guilt, fault; debt; einem ~ geben, to blame; sich etwas zu ~en kommen lassen, to be guilty of a thing; ich bin daran ~, it is my fault; eine ~ abtragen, to pay off a debt.
schuldbewusst a. conscious of guilt.
schulden v.t. to owe, to be indebted to.
Schulden f.pl. debts; ~ eingehen, machen, to contract or incur debts.
schuldenfrei a. unencumbered.
Schuldentilgung f. liquidation of debts.
Schuldforderung f. claim, demand.
Schuldirektor m. head-master.
schuldig a. guilty, culpable; due; indebted, owing; etwas ~ bleiben, to remain one's debtor for a thing; einen ~ sprechen, to find a person guilty.
Schuldigerklärung f. (law) conviction.
Schuldigkeit f. (-, 0) obligation, duty.
Schuldklage f. action for debt.
schuldlos a. guiltless; innocent.
Schuldner m. (-s, -) debtor.
Schuld: ~schein m., ~verschreibung f. promissory note, I.O.U. (I owe you).
Schule f. (-, -n) school; school-house; eine ~ besuchen, in die ~ gehen, auf der ~ sein, to go to school, to be at school.
schulen v.t. to school; to train.
Schulentlassungsalter n. school-leaving age.

Schüler m. (-s, -), **Schülerin** f. (-, -nen) schoolboy, schoolgirl; pupil, scholar.
schülerhaft a. blundering, bungling.
Schul: ~fall m. test case; ~feier f. speech day; ~geld n. school-fees pl., schooling; ~jahr n. session, scholastic year; ~kamerad m. schoolfellow; ~mappe f. satchel.
schulmeistern v.t. to censure.
Schulpflicht f. compulsory school-attendance.
schulpflichtig a. bound to attend school; ~es Alter, school age.
Schulschiff n. training ship.
Schulter f. (-, -n) shoulder; die kalte ~ zeigen, to coldshoulder.
Schulterblatt n. shoulder-blade.
schultern v.t. to shoulder.
Schultertasche f. (für Damen) shoulder-bag.
Schulung f. (-, -en) training, practice.
Schul: ~zeugnis n. report; ~zwang m. compulsory education.
Schund m. (-[e]s, 0) offal, trash, rubbish.
Schuppe f. (-, -n) scale; scurf.
schuppen, (sich) ~ v.refl. to scale off.
Schuppen m. (-s, -) coach-house; shed.
schuppig a. scaly, squamous.
Schur f. (-, -en) shearing; fleece.
schüren v.t. to stoke; (fig.) to stir up.
schürfen v.t. to scratch, to cut; to prospect (nach, for); to open a mine.
Schurke m. (-n, -n) rogue, rascal, villain.
Schurkenstreich m. villainy.
schurkisch a. knavish, rascally.
Schurz m. (-es, -e) apron.
Schürze f. (-, -n) apron.
schürzen v.t. to tuck up.
Schurzfell n. leather-apron.
Schuss m. (Schusses, Schüsse) shot.
Schussfeld n. range.
Schuss: ~waffe f. fire-arm; ~weite ,. range; ~wunde f. gunshot wound.
Schüssel f. (-, -n) dish, platter.
Schuster m. (-s, -) shoemaker.
schustern v.i. to cobble.
Schutt m. (-[e]s, 0) rubbish.
Schüttelfrost m. shivers pl., cold fit.
schütteln v.t. to shake, to toss; einem die Hand ~, to shake hands with a person; aus dem Ärmel ~, to produce offhand.
schütten v.t. & i. to shed, to pour; to heap.
Schutz m. (-es, 0) protection, shelter; in ~ nehmen, to take under one's protection.
Schutz: ~befohlene[r] m. protégé, client; ~blech n. mudguard; ~brille f. goggles.
Schütz m. (-es, -e) (elek.) contactor.
Schütze m. (-n, -n) shot, marksman; (mil.) rifleman.
schützen v.t. to protect, to guard, shelter.
Schützengraben m. trench, rifle-pit.
Schutzengel m. guardian angel.

Schützenregiment n. rifle regiment.
Schutz: ~frist f. term of copyright; ~haft f. protective custody; ~impfung f. immunization; ~herr m. patron, protector.
Schützling m. (-[e]s, -e) protégé.
schutzlos a. defenceless, unprotected.
Schutz: ~mann m. policeman, constable; ~marke f. trade-mark; ~raum m. (*Luftschutz*) shelter; ~rücken m. (*Buch*) cover; ~umschlag m. (publisher's) jacket, dust-cover; ~zoll m. protection; ~zöllner m. protectionist.
schwäbeln v.i. (*fam.*) to speak like a Swabian.
schwach a. weak, feeble, infirm; *mir wird* ~, I feel faint.
Schwäche f. (-, -) weakness, feebleness.
schwächen v.t. to weaken, to enfeeble.
Schwachheit f. (-, -en) weakness, frailty, infirmity.
Schwachkopf m. simpleton, idiot.
schwachköpfig a. weak-headed, soft.
schwächlich a. infirm, feeble, sickly.
Schwächling m. (-s, -e) weakling.
Schwachsinn m. mental deficiency.
schwachsinnig a. feeble-minded, mentally deficient or defective.
Schwachstrom m. weak current.
Schwaden m. (-s, 0) swath; vapour, steam.
Schwadron f. (-, -en) squadron, squad.
Schwager m. (-s, Schwäger) brother-in-law.
Schwägerin f. (-, -nen) sister-in-law.
Schwägerschaft f. (-, 0) relationship by marriage.
Schwalbe f. (-, -n) swallow.
Schwall m. (-[e]s, 0) swell, flood.
Schwamm m. (-[e]s, Schwämme) sponge; mushroom, fungus; *Haus*~, dry rot.
Schwammbeutel m. sponge-bag.
schwammig a. spongy.
Schwan m. (-[e]s, Schwäne) swan.
schwanen v.imp. to have a foreboding; *es schwant mir*, my heart misgives me.
Schwanengesang m. swan's song.
Schwang m. (-[e]s, 0) swing; (*fig.*) vogue.
schwanger a. pregnant; with child.
schwängern v.t. to get with child; (*fig.*) to impregnate; (*chem.*) to saturate.
Schwangerschaft f. (-, -en) pregnancy.
Schwangerschaftsunterbrechung f. interruption of pregnancy.
Schwank m. (-[e]s, Schwänke) merry tale; (*theatr.*) farce.
schwanken v.i. to totter, to stagger; (*fig.*) to waver; to fluctuate.
Schwankung f. (-, -en) fluctuation.
Schwanz m. (-es, Schwänze) tail.
schwänzen v.t. (*die Schule, etc.*) to shirk, to play the truant.
Schwäre f. abscess, ulcer.

schwären v.i. to fester, to suppurate.
Schwarm m. (-[e]s, Schwärme) swarm.
schwärmen v.i. to swarm; to riot, to revel; ~ *für*, to be mad about.
Schwärmer m. (-s, -) fanatic, enthusiast.
Schwärmerei f. (-, -en) enthusiasm.
schwärmerisch a. enthusiastic, fanatic.
schwarz a. black; *es wird einem* ~ *vor den Augen*, his head begins to swim; *ins Schwarze treffen*, to hit the mark; ~ *auf weiss*, in black and white; ~e Liste, black list; ~es Brett n. notice board, bulletin board.
Schwarz n. (es, 0) black colour.
Schwarz: ~brot f. rye bread; ~dorn m. blackthorn.
Schwärze f. (-, -n) blacking; (printer's) ink.
schwärzen v.t. to black(en); to smuggle.
Schwarzkünstler m. necromancer.
schwärzlich a. blackish.
Schwarz: ~markt m. black market; ~seher m. pessimist; ~wald m. the Black Forest.
schwarzweiss a. black-and-white.
schwatzen v.i. to chatter, to talk idly.
Schwätzer m. (-s, -) tattler, babbler.
schwatzhaft a. talkative, garrulous.
Schwebe f. (-, 0) suspense; *in der* ~, undecided, trembling in the balance.
Schwebebahn f. suspension railway.
schweben v.i. to hover, to float; to be pending; *in Gefahr* ~, to be in danger; *die Sache schwebt noch*, the matter is still pending; ~de Schuld, floating debt.
Schwefel m. (-s, -) sulphur, brimstone.
schwefelig s. sulphur(e)ous.
Schwefelsäure f. sulphuric acid.
Schweif m. (-[e]s, -e) tail; train.
schweifen v.i. to ramble, to stray.
Schweigegeld n. hush-money.
schweigen v.i.st. to be silent, to hold one's tongue.
Schweigen n. (-s, 0) silence.
schweigsam a. taciturn.
Schwein n. (-[e]s, -e) pig, hog, swine; (*fam.*) luck.
Schweine: ~braten m. roast pork; ~fett n. lard; ~fleisch n. pork; ~hirt m. swineherd.
Schweinerei f. (-, -en) filth, mess; (*fig.*) obscenity.
Schweinestall m. pig-sty.
Schweinhund m. filthy fellow.
schweinisch a. swinish, filthy.
Schweins: ~borste f. hog's bristle; ~keule f. leg of pork; ~leder n. pig-skin.
Schweiss m. (-es, 0) sweat; perspiration.
schweissen v.t. to weld.
Schweisser m. (-s, -) (*mech.*) welder.
schweisstreibend a. sudorific.
Schweizer m. (-s, -) Alpine dairyman.
schwelen v.i. to smoulder.

schwelgen *v.i.* to revel, to riot.
Schwelger *m.* (-s, -) reveller, glutton.
schwelgerisch *a.* luxurious.
Schwelle *f.* (-, -n) threshold, sill; (*rail.*) sleeper.
schwellen *v.i.* (*s*) to swell, to heave.
Schwellung *f.* (-, -en) swelling, tumour.
schwemmen *v.t.* to soak.
Schwengel *m.* (-s, -) (*Glocken~*) clapper; (*Pumpen~*) handle.
schwenken *v.t.* to swing; to flourish, brandish; ~ *v.i.* to wheel.
Schwenkung *f.* (-, -en) evolution, wheeling about; sudden change.
schwer *a.* heavy, weighty; difficult, hard; (*Wein*) strong; grave; grievous; ~e Artillerie *f.* medium artillery; *ein Pfund ~,* weighing one pound; *es fällt mir ~,* I find it hard.
Schwer: ~arbeiter *m.* heavy worker; ~beschädigter *m.* seriously disabled ex-service man.
Schwere *f.* (-, 0) gravity; heaviness.
schwerfällig, *a.* unwieldy; clumsy.
Schwergewicht *n.* weight; (*Boxer*) heavyweight.
schwerhalten *v.i.st.* to be difficult.
schwerhörig *a.* hard of hearing.
Schwer: ~kraft *f.* gravitation; ~industrie *f.* heavy industries.
schwerlich *adv.* hardly, scarcely.
Schwermut *f.* melancholy.
schwermütig *a.* melancholy.
Schwerpunkt *m.* centre of gravity.
schwerste Artillerie *f.* heavy artillery.
Schwert *n.* (-[e]s, -er) sword.
schwer: ~verständlich *a.* hard to understand, abstruse; ~verwundet *a.* severely wounded.
Schwester *f.* (-, -n) sister; nun; nurse.
schwesterlich *a.* sisterly.
Schwibbogen *m.* arch.
Schwieger: ~eltern *pl.* parents-in-law *pl.*; ~mutter *f.* mother-in-law; ~sohn *m.* son-in-law; ~tochter *f.* daughter-in-law; ~vater *m.* father-in-law.
Schwiele *f.* (-, -n) callus, callosity; wale.
schwielig *a.* callous, horny.
schwierig *a.* hard, difficult.
Schwierigkeit *f.* (-, -en) difficulty.
Schwimm: ~anstalt *f.* swimming-bath; ~anzug *m.* swimsuit; ~bad *n.* swimming pool; ~dock *n.* floating dock.
schwimmen *v.i.st.* to swim; to float.
Schwimm: ~flosse *f.* fin; ~gestell *n.* (*avi.*) float; ~gürtel *m.* life-belt; ~weste *f.* life jacket.
Schwindel *m.* (-s, 0) giddiness, dizziness; swindle, cheat, humbug, bubble.
Schwindelei *f.* swindle, humbug; (*Lüge*) fib.
schwindelfrei *a.* free from giddiness.
schwindelhaft *a.* fraudulent.

schwind(e)lig *a.* dizzy, giddy.
schwindeln *v.i.imp.* to be giddy; to humbug, to cheat.
Schwindelpreis *m.* extortionate price.
schwinden *v.t.st.* (*s*) to disappear, to vanish; (*Radio*) to fade.
Schwindler *m.* (-s, -) swindler, cheat, humbug.
schwindlerisch *a.* swindling.
Schwindsucht *f.* consumption.
schwindsüchtig *a.* consumptive.
Schwinge *f.* (-, -n) wing; fan, winnow.
schwingen *v.t. & i.st.* to brandish; to fan, to winnow; to swing; to vibrate, to oscillate.
Schwingung *f.* (-, -en) vibration, oscillation.
Schwips *m.* (Schwipses, Schwipse) *einen ~ haben,* to be slightly elevated.
schwirren *v.i.* to whir; to buzz.
Schwitzbad *n.* steam-bath, Turkish bath.
schwitzen *v.i.* to sweat, to perspire.
Schwitzkur *f.* sweating-cure.
schwören *v.t.st.* to swear; *einen Eid ~,* to take an oath; *auf etwas ~, bei etwas ~,* to swear by; *falsch ~,* to swear false.
schwül *a.* sultry.
Schwüle *f.* (-, 0) sultriness.
Schwulst *m.* (-es, 0) bombast.
schwülstig *a.* bombastic, inflated.
Schwund *m.* (-[e]s, 0) decay, wasting away.
Schwung *m.* (-[e]s, Schwünge) swing, vibration; flight, strain; rapture; *etwas ist im ~, kommt in ~,* a thing is in full swing, is getting into vogue.
schwunghaft *a.* flourishing, spirited.
Schwung: ~kraft *f.* tangential force; ~rad *n.* fly-wheel.
schwungvoll *a.* full of fire.
Schwur *m.* (-[e]s, Schwüre) oath.
Schwurgericht *n.* assizes *pl.*; ~sverhandlung, *f.* trial by jury.
sechs *a.* six.
Sechs *f.* (-, 0) number six.
Sechsachteltakt *m.* six-eight time.
Sechseck *n.* (-[e]s, -e) hexagon.
sechserlei *a.* of six kinds.
sechsfach *a.* sixfold.
sechsmal *adv.* six times.
sechsmonatlich *a.* half-yearly.
sechsseitig *a.* hexagonal.
sechstens *adv.* sixthly.
sechzehn *a.* sixteen.
Sechzehntel *n.* (-s, -) sixteenth part; note, *f.* (*mus.*) semiquaver.
sechzig *a.* sixty; *ein Mann in den ~ern, ein Sechziger,* a sexagenarian.
See *m.* (-[e]s, -[e]n) lake; ~ *f.* (-, 0) sea; *zur ~,* at sea; *hohe (offene) ~,* main or open sea; *in ~ gehen,* to put to sea.
See: ~bad *n.* seaside resort; ~fahrt *f.* voyage, cruise; navigation.

seefest *a.* seaworthy; ∼ *sein*, to be a good sailor.

See: ∼**gang** *m.* motion of the sea; ∼**gefecht** *n.* naval action; ∼**gras** *n.* seaweed; ∼**hafen** *m.* sea-port; ∼**handel** *m.* maritime trade; ∼**herrschaft** *f.* naval supremacy; ∼**hund** *m.* seal; ∼**kadett** *m.* naval cadet; ∼**karte** *f.* chart.

seekrank *a.* sea-sick.

See: ∼**krankheit** *f.* sea-sickness; ∼**krieg** *m.* naval war; ∼**kriegsleitung** *f.* naval operations staff; ∼**küste** *f.* sea-coast, sea-board.

Seele *f.* (-, -n) soul; *mit Leib und* ∼, body and soul.

Seelenamt *n.* office for the dead.

seelenfroh *a.* heartily glad.

Seelen: ∼**grösse** *f.* greatness of mind; ∼**heil** *n.* spiritual welfare; ∼**hirt** *m.* pastor; ∼**messe** *f.* requiem; ∼**ruhe** *f.* composure, calmness.

seelenlos *a.* soulless.

seelenvergnügt *a.* thoroughly happy.

Seelenwanderung *f.* transmigration of souls.

Seeleute *pl.* seamen, mariners *pl.*

seelisch *a.* mental.

Seel: ∼**sorge** *f.* cure of souls; ∼**sorger** *m.* pastor.

Seeluft *f.* sea-air.

See: ∼**macht** *f.* maritime power; ∼**mann** *m.* sailor, mariner; ∼**meile** *f.* nautical mile, knot; ∼**not** *f.* distress; ∼**offizier** *m.* naval officer; ∼**räuber** *m.* pirate, corsair; ∼**räuberei** *f.* piracy; ∼**recht** *n.* maritime law; ∼**reise** *f.* voyage, cruise; ∼**rose** *f.* water-lily; ∼**schiffahrt** *f.* ocean navigation; ∼**schlacht** *f.* naval battle; ∼**sieg** *m.* naval victory; ∼**soldat** *m.* marine.

seetüchtig *a.* seaworthy.

See: ∼**ufer** *n.* shore, strand; ∼**warte** *f.* naval observatory.

seewärts *adv.* seaward, outward.

See: ∼**weg** *m.* sea-route; *auf dem* ∼*e*, by sea; ∼**wesen** *n.* naval affairs *pl.*; ∼**zunge** *f.* (*Fisch*) sole.

Segel *n.* (-s, -) sail; ∼ *setzen*, to set sail; ∼ *streichen*, to strike sail.

Segelboot *n.* sailing-boat.

Segel: ∼**flug** *m.* gliding; ∼**flieger** *m.* glider.

segeln *v.i.* (*s, h*) to sail.

Segel: ∼**schiff** *n.* sailing-vessel; ∼**tuch** *n.* canvas, sail-cloth.

Segen *m.* (-s, -) blessing, benediction; abundance.

segensreich *a.* blessed.

segensvoll *a.* blessed, fruit-bearing.

Segenswunsch *m.* blessing, kind wishes *pl.*

Segler *m.* (-s, -) (*Schiff*) sailer.

segnen *v.t.* to bless.

Segnung *f.* (-, -en) blessing, benediction.

sehen *v.i.* & *t.st.* to see, to look, to behold;

einem auf die Finger ∼, to watch one closely; *durch die Finger* ∼, to connive at, to wink at; *ungern* ∼, to dislike; *ähnlich* ∼, to look like, to resemble; ∼ *nach*, to look for; (*sorgen*) to look after; *vom* ∼, by sight.

sehenswert *a.* worth seeing.

Sehenswürdigkeit *f.* (-, -en) sight, place of interest.

Seher *m.* (-s, -) seer, prophet.

Sehergabe *f.* gift of prophecy.

Seh: ∼**feld** *n.* range of vision; ∼**kraft** *f.* visual faculty, eyesight.

Sehne *f.* (-, -n) sinew, tendon; (*Bogen*∼) string; (*math.*) chord.

sehnen (sich) *v.refl.* to long (for).

Sehnerv *m.* optic nerve.

sehnig *a.* sinewy; wiry.

sehnlich *a.* longing, earnestly desirous; ∼ *adv.* eagerly, ardently.

Sehnsucht *f.* (-, 0) intense longing.

sehnsüchtig *a.* longing, yearning.

sehr *adv.* very, much, greatly.

seicht *a.* shallow, flat, superficial.

Seide *f.* (-, 0) silk.

Seidel *n.* (-s, -) ⅜ pint; tankard.

seiden *a.* silk(en).

Seiden: ∼**händler** *m.* silk-mercer; ∼**papier** *n.* tissue-paper; ∼**raupe** *f.* silk-worm; ∼**wurm** *m.* silk-worm.

Seife *f.* (-, -n) soap.

seifen *v.t.* to soap.

Seifen: ∼**blase** *f.* soap-bubble; ∼**schaum** *m.* lather; ∼**flocken** *pl.* soap-flakes; ∼**sieder** *m.* soapmaker.

seihen *v.t.* to strain, to filter.

Seiher *m.* (-s, -) strainer.

Seihtuch *n.* straining-cloth.

Seil *n.* (-[e]s, -e) rope, cord, line.

Seiler *m.* (-s, -) rope-maker, roper.

Seiltänzer *m.* rope-dancer.

sein *pn.* his, of him; its, of it; *das Seine*, his property; *die Seinen*, his people.

sein *v.i.i.r.* (*s*) to be, to exist.

Sein *n.* (-s, 0) being, existence.

seinerseits *adv.* on his part.

seinetwegen *adv.* on his account, for his sake.

Seinige *n.* (-n, 0) his; *die* ∼**n** *pl.* his family.

seit *pr.&c.* since; ∼ *alters*, time out of mind.

seitdem *adv.* since then.

Seite *f.* (-, -n) side, part, flank; page; party; *schwache* ∼, foible; *bei* ∼, aside; *sich auf eines* ∼ *stellen*, to side with one; *bei* ∼ *schaffen*, to put out of the way, to make away with; *auf eines* ∼ *stehen*, to take one's part.

Seiten: ∼**angriff** *m.* flank-attack; ∼**ansicht** *f.* profile, side-view; ∼**blick** *m.* sidelong glance; ∼**flügel** *m.* side-aisle, wing; ∼**gewehr** *n.* side-arms *pl.*; ∼**hieb** *m.* (*fig.*) innuendo.

seitenlang a. of many pages; ~ adv. for pages and pages.

Seiten: ~linie f. collateral line; ~loge f. side box; ~schiff n. aisle; ~schwimmen n. side-stroke; ~sprung f. escapade; ~stechen n. pain in the side, stitch; ~steuer n. (avi.) rudder; ~stück n. counterpart; ~tür f. side-door; ~verwandte[e]r m. collateral relation.

seitens pr. von Seiten, at the hands of.

seither adv. since (that time).

seitlich a. lateral, collateral.

seitwärts adv. sideways, aside.

Sekretär m. (-s, -e) secretary.

Sekretariat n. (-[e]s, -e) secretariat.

Sekt m. (-[e]s, -e) champagne.

Sekte f. (-, -n) sect.

Sektierer m. (-s, -) sectarian.

Sektion f. (-, -en) section; post-mortem (examination).

Sekunda f. (-, -den) second form (=fifth form in English schools).

Sekundaner m. (-s, -) second-form boy.

Sekundant m. (-en, -en) second.

sekundär a. secondary.

Sekunde f. (-, -n) second; Bruchteil einer ~, split-second.

Sekundenzeiger m. second-hand (of a watch).

selber pn. myself, himself, etc., personally (cp. derselbe).

selbst pn. self; myself, etc.; ~ adv. even.

Selbstachtung f. self-respect.

selbständig a. independent.

Selbständigkeit f. (-, 0) independence.

Selbst: ~anschlusstelephon n. automatic telephone; ~beherrschung f. self-control; ~bestimmung f. self-determination; ~betrug m. self-deception.

selbstbewusst a. self-confident.

Selbst: ~bewusstsein n. self-awareness; ~erhaltung f. self-preservation; ~erkenntnis f. self-knowledge.

Selbstfahr... (mil.) (on) self-propelled (mounts).

selbstgefällig a. smug, self-complacent.

Selbstgefühl n. self-confidence.

selbst: ~genügsam a. self-sufficient; ~gerecht a. self-righteous.

Selbst: ~gespräch n. monologue, soliloquy; ein ~ führen, to soliloquize; ~hilfe f. self-help.

selbstisch a. selfish.

Selbst: ~kostenpreis m. cost-price; ~laut-[er] m. vowel.

selbstlos a. unselfish, disinterested.

Selbstlosigkeit f. unselfishness, altruism.

Selbst: ~mord m. suicide; ~mord begehen, to commit suicide; ~mörder m. suicide.

selbstredend a. self-evident; (adv.) of course.

Selbstschuss m. spring-gun.

selbstsicher a. self-reliant.

Selbstsucht f. (-, 0) selfishness.

selbstsüchtig a. selfish, self-seeking.

selbsttätig a. spontaneous; automatic.

Selbsttäuschung f. self-delusion.

Selbst: ~überwindung f. self-conquest; ~verleugnung f. self-denial.

selbstverständlich a. self-evident; (adv.) of course; needless to say, obviously, it goes without saying.

Selbst: ~vertrauen m. self-confidence, self-reliance; ~verwaltung, f. self-government; ~zufriedenheit f. self-satisfaction; ~zweck m. end in itself.

Selen n. (-s, 0) selenium.

selig a. blessed, blissful; deceased, late; ~sprechen, to beatify; ~ werden, to be saved.

Seligkeit f. (-, -en) beatitude; salvation.

seligmachend a. beatific; saving.

Seligsprechung f. (-, -en) beatification.

Sellerie m. (-s, -s) celery.

selten a. rare, scarce; ~ adv. seldom, rarely.

Seltenheit f. (-, -en) rarity, scarcity; curiosity, curio.

seltsam a. singular, strange, odd.

Selterwasser n. artificial mineral water.

Semester n. (-s, -) academic term.

Seminar n. (-s, -e) training college; seminary.

Semit m. (-en, -en) semite.

Semmel f. (-, -n) roll; milk loaf.

Senat m. (-s, -e) senate.

Sendbote m. emissary.

senden v.t.ir. to send, to dispatch; nach einem ~, to send for one; Waren mit der Post ~, to send things through the post.

Sender m. (-s, -) transmitter.

Senderaum m. (Radio) studio.

Sendestation f. radio or broadcasting station.

Sendung f. (-, -en) mission; consignment, parcel.

Senf m. (-[e]s, -e) mustard.

Senfkorn n. mustard-seed.

sengen v.t. to singe, to scorch; to scald; ~ und brennen, to lay waste by fire.

Senkblei n. plummet.

senken v.t. to let down, to lower; (sich) ~ v.refl. to sink.

Senkgrube f. cesspool, sink.

senkrecht a. perpendicular; vertical.

Senkschraube f. countersunk screw.

Senkung f. (-, -en) sinking; depression; (Preise) reduction; unstressed syllable.

Senn (-[e]s, -e), **Senne** (-n, -n) **Senner** m. (-s, -) (Alpine) herdsman and dairyman.

Sennerei (-, -en), **Sennhütte** f. Alpine cheese-dairy.

Sennerin f. (-, -nen) (Alpine) dairymaid.

Sense f. (-, -n) scythe.

sentimental *a.* sentimental.

separat *a.* separate.

September *m.* (-s, -) September.

sequestrieren *v.t.* to sequestrate.

Serail *m. n.* (-s, -s) seraglio.

Sergeant *m.* (-en, -en) sergeant.

Serie *f.* (-, -n) series.

Serum *n.* (-s, -ra, -ren) serum.

Service, *f.* service, set.

servieren *v.t.* to serve.

servierfertig, *a.* ready-to-serve.

Serviette *f.* (-, -n) serviette, (table)-napkin.

Sessel *m.* (-s, -) easy chair, arm chair.

sesshaft *a.* sedentary resident.

Setzei *n.* fried egg.

setzen *v.t.* to set, to put, to place; to stake; to compose; ~ *v.i.* to leap; (sich) ~ *v.refl.* to sit down; to settle; *alles auf eine Karte* ~, to stake everything on one card; *aufs Spiel* ~, to stake, to risk; *instand* ~, to enable; to repair; *in Schrecken* ~, to frighten; *unter Wasser* ~, to inundate; *alles daran* ~, to risk everything; *sich zur Ruhe* ~, to retire into private life; *sich zur Wehr* ~, to offer resistance; *über den Fluss* ~, to cross the river; *gesetzt den Fall*, put the case, suppose.

Setzer *m.* (-s, -) compositor, typesetter.

Setzreis *n.* layer, shoot.

Seuche *f.* (-, -n) epidemic; pestilence.

seuchenartig *a.* epidemic, contagious.

seufzen *v.i.* to sigh, to groan.

Seufzer *m.* (-s, -) sigh, groan; ~ *ausstossen*, to heave sighs, to utter groans.

Sexta *f.* (-, -ten) sixth *or* lowest class of secondary school.

Sextaner *m.* (-s, -) sixth-class boy.

Sextett *n.* (-[e]s, -e) sextet(te).

sexuell *a.* sexual.

sezieren *v.t.* to dissect.

Seziermesser *n.* dissecting-knife.

Sibylle *f.* (-, -n) Sibyl, prophetess.

sich *pn.* oneself, himself, etc.; each other; *an und für* ~, in itself; *wieder zu* ~ *kommen*, to come to, to recover consciousness; *es hat nichts auf* ~, it is of no consequence.

Sichel *f.* (-, -n) sickle; (*Mond*~) crescent.

sicher *a.* sure, certain; secure, safe; ~ *adv.* for sure, for certain; ~ *wissen*, to be sure; ~*e Hand*, steady hand; ~*es Geleit*, safe-conduct; (*sich*) ~ *stellen*, to secure (oneself).

Sicherheit *f.* (-, -en) security; surety, safety; *in* ~ *bringen*, to secure; ~ *leisten*, to go bail, to give security; *in* ~, (in a place of) safety.

Sicherheits: ~*ausschuss m.* (*Am.*) vigilantes; ~*glas n.* shatterproof glass, safety-glass; ~*lampe f.* safety-lamp; ~*massregeln pl.* precautions; ~*nadel f.*

safety-pin; ~*schloss n.* safety-lock; ~*ventil n.* safety-valve; ~*zündholz n.* safety-match.

sicherlich *adv.* surely, certainly.

sichern *v.t.* to secure.

Sicherung *f.* (-, -en) (*am Gewehr*) safety bolt; (*elek.*) fuse.

Sicht *f.* (-, 0) sight; *auf* ~, at *or* on sight; *nach* ~, after sight; *auf kurze* ~, at short date; *auf 8 Tage* ~, seven days after sight; *auf 2 Monate* ~, at two months' sight; *ausser* ~ *sein*, to be out of sight.

sichtbar *a.* visible; (*fig.*) evident.

sichten *v.t.* to sift; (*nav.*) to sight.

sichtlich *a.* perceptible.

Sichtvermerk *m.* (-s, -e) visa.

Sichtwechsel *m.* bill payable at sight.

sickern *v.i.* to trickle, to ooze.

sie *pn.* she, her; they, them.

Sie *pn.* you.

Sieb *n.* (-[e]s, -e) sieve; strainer.

sieben *v.t.* to sift, to bolt.

sieben *a.* seven; *es ist halb* ~, it is half-past six.

siebenerlei *a.* of seven kinds.

siebenfach, siebenfältig *a.* sevenfold.

siebenmal *adv.* seven times.

Siebenmeilenstiefel *pl.* seven-league boots *pl.*

Siebensachen *pl.* one's belongings.

siebzehn *a.* seventeen.

siebzig *a.* seventy.

Siebziger *m.* (-s, -) septuagenarian.

siech *a.* sick, sickly, infirm.

Siechbett *n.* sick-bed.

siechen *v.i.* to be sickly; to pine away.

Siechtum (-s, 0) *n.* protracted sickness.

siede(nd)heiss *a.* scalding hot.

Siedehitze *f.* boiling heat.

siedeln *v.i. & t.* to colonize, to settle.

sieden *v.t. & i.st.* to seethe, to boil; to simmer.

Siedepunkt *m.* boiling-point.

Siedler *m.* (-s, -) settler.

Siedlung *f.* (-, -en) settlement.

Sieg *m.* (-[e]s, -e) victory; triumph.

Siegel *n.* (-s, -) seal; *sein* ~ *drauf drücken*, to set one's seal to it.

Siegel: ~*abdruck m.* impress (of a seal); ~*lack m.* sealing-wax.

siegeln *v.t.* to seal.

Siegelring *m.* signet-ring.

siegen *v.i.* to conquer, to win, to be victorious (over).

Sieger *m.* (-s, -) conqueror, victor; (*Sport*) winner.

siegreich *a.* victorious, triumphant.

sieh! *i.* see! lo!; ~ *einmal!* ~ *da!* look there!

Signal *n.* (-[e]s, -e) signal.

signalisieren *v.t.* to signal.

Signalwächter *m.* (*rail.*) signalman.

Signatarmächte *pl.* signatory powers.

Signatur f. (-, -en) mark, brand; (*fig.*) stamp.

Silbe f. (-, -n) syllable.

Silben: ~rätsel n. charade; ~schrift f. syllabic writing; ~teilung f. syllabication.

Silber n. (-s, 0) silver; *gediegenes* ~, solid silver.

Silber: ~barre f., ~barren m. ingot of silver; ~geschirr n. (silver-) plate.

silbern a. (of) silver; ~e *Hochzeit*, silver wedding.

Silber: ~pappel f. white poplar; ~streifen m. silver lining; ~währung f. silver standard; ~waren pl. silver ware, plate.

Silberzeug n. silver-plate.

Silentium! i. silence!

Silhouette f. (-, -n) silhouette.

Silvesterabend m. New Year's Eve.

Simili m. (-s, -s) paste(stone).

simpel a. simple, plain.

Simpel m. (-s, -) simpleton.

Sims m. & n. (-es, -e), cornice, moulding; shelf; pediment; mantelpiece.

Simulant m. (-en, -en) malingerer.

simulieren v.t. to malinger, to simulate (illness).

Simultanschule f. undenominational school.

Sinekure f. (-, -n) sinecure.

singen v.i. & t.st. to sing; *vom Blatt* ~, to sing at sight; *nach Noten* ~. to sing from notes.

Sing: ~sang m. sing-song; ~stimme f. vocal part; ~vogel m. singing-bird; ~weise f. melody, tune.

Singular m. (-s, -e) singular.

sinken v.i.st. (s) to sink, to decline; *den Mut* ~ *lassen*, to get discouraged.

Sinn m. (-[e]s, -e) sense; mind; liking, taste (for, *für*); meaning; *im* ~ *haben*, to intend; *nicht nach meinem* ~, not to my mind; *die fünf* ~*e*, the five senses; *bei* ~*en sein*, to have one's wits about one.

Sinnbild n. symbol, emblem; allegory.

sinnbildlich a. symbolic(al), emblematic.

sinnen v.i.st. to meditate, to reflect, to muse; *anders gesinnt sein*, to be otherwise inclined; *nicht gesonnen sein*, to feel disinclined; *all sein Sinnen und Trachten*, all his thoughts and aspirations.

Sinnen: ~genuss m. sensual pleasure; ~lust f. sensuality; ~welt f. external world.

Sinnes: ~änderung f. change of mind; ~art f. disposition, character; ~täuschung f. illusion; hallucination; delusion; ~werkzeug n. sense organ.

Sinngedicht n. epigram.

sinnig a. thoughtful; sensible.

sinnlich a. sensual; sensuous, material.

Sinnlichkeit f. (-, 0) sensuality.

sinnlos a. senseless; irrational; useless.

sinnreich a. ingenious; clever.

Sinnspruch m. maxim, motto, device.

sinnverwandt a. synonymous.

sintemal c. since, especially as.

Sintflut f. (great) flood.

Sinus m. (-, -) sine.

Sippe f. (-, -n), **Sippschaft** f. kindred; tribe, family.

Sippenhaftung f. liability of kin.

Sirene f. (-, -n) siren.

Sirup m. (-s, -e) treacle; syrup.

sistieren v.t. to stop; to arrest; (*Prozess*) to nonsuit.

Sistierung f. (-, -en) (*Klage*) nonsuit.

Sitte f. (-, -n) custom, usage, fashion.

Sitten n.pl. manners; morals pl.

Sitten: ~gesetz n. moral law; ~lehre f. moral philosophy, ethics pl.

sittenlos a. immoral.

Sittenlosigkeit f. (-, 0) immorality.

sittenrein a. (morally) pure.

Sittenstrenge f. austerity.

sittlich a. moral.

Sittlichkeit f. (-, 0) morality.

Sittlichkeitsvergehen n. indecent assault.

sittsam a. modest; demure.

situiert a. *gut* ~, well off.

Sitz m. (-es, -e) seat; residence; chair.

Sitzbad n. hip-bath.

sitzen v.i.st. to sit; to fit; to be imprisoned; *gut* ~, to fit well; *auf sich* ~ *lassen*, to pocket; *ein Mädchen* ~ *lassen*, to jilt a girl, to throw a girl over; ~*bleiben*, to remain a spinster; (*in der Schule*) not to get one's remove; *das Kleid sitzt gut*, the dress is an excellent fit; *sitzende Lebensweise*, sedentary life.

. . .**sitzer** m. (*in Zus.*) seater.

Sitz: ~fleisch n. (*fig.*) steadiness; ~gelegenheit f. seating accommodation; ~platz m. seat; ~streik m. sit-down strike.

Sitzung f. (-, -en) sitting, session.

Sitzungsbericht m. minutes, (report of) proceedings pl.

Skala f. (-, -len) scale.

skalpieren v.t. to scalp.

Skandal m. (-[e]s, -e) scandal; row.

skandalös a. scandalous.

skandieren v.t. to scan.

Skat m. (-[e]s, -e) a German national card-game.

Skelett n. (-[e]s, -e) skeleton.

Skeptiker m. (-s, -) sceptic.

skeptisch a. sceptical.

Skizze f. (-, -n) sketch.

Skizzenbuch n. sketch-book.

skizzieren v.t. to sketch.

Sklave m. (-n, -n) slave.

Sklaven: ~halter m. slave-owner; ~handel m. slave-trade; ~händler m. slave-trader.

Sklaverei *f.* (-, 0) slavery.
Sklavin *f.* (-, -nen) female slave.
sklavisch *a.* slavish, servile.
Skonto *m.* (-[s], 0) discount.
Skorbut *m.* (-[e]s, 0) scurvy.
Skorpion *m.* (-[e]s, -e) scorpion.
Skrofeln *f. pl.* scrofula.
skrofulös *a.* scrofulous.
Skrupel *pl.* scruples *pl.*; *sich keine ~ machen*, to have no scruple (of).
skrupulös *a.* scrupulous.
skrupellos *a.* unscrupulous.
Skulptur *f.* (-, -en) sculpture.
S-Kurve *f.* (-, -n) hairpin-bend.
Smaragd *m.* (-[e]s, -e) emerald.
Smoking *m.* (-s, -s) dinner-jacket.
so *adv. & c.* so, thus, in such a manner, like this; *sobald als*, as soon as; *sowohl ..., als auch*, as well as; *~ und ~ viel*, so and so much; *~ reich er auch ist*, rich as he may be; *~ sehr auch, wenn auch noch ~ sehr*, however much, if...ever so much; *~ ein Mann*, such a man; *~ etwas*, such a thing; *um ~ besser*, so much the better; *zweimal soviel*, twice as much? *wieso?* how so? how do you mean?
Socke *f.* (-, -n) sock.
Sockel *m.* (-s, -) plinth.
Sockenhalter *m.* suspender.
Soda *f.* (-, 0) soda.
sodann *adv.* then.
Sodawasser *n.* soda(-water).
Sodbrennen *n.* heart-burn.
soeben *adv.* just now, this minute.
Sofa *n.* (-s, -s) sofa.
sofern *c.* inasmuch as, so far as.
sofort *adv.* at once, immediately.
sofortig *a.* immediate, instantaneous.
sogar *adv.* even.
sogenannt *a.* so-called; pretended.
sogleich *adv.* immediately, directly.
Sohle *f.* (-, -n) sole.
sohlen *v.t.* to sole.
Sohn *m.* (-[e]s, Söhne) son; *der verlorene ~*, the Prodigal Son.
solange, als, as long as.
Solawechsel *m.* single-bill, sole-bill.
solcher, solche, solch[es] *pn.* such; the same.
solchergestalt *a.* thus, in such manner.
solcherlei *a.* of such a kind.
Sold *m.* (-[e]s, 0) (military) pay; *(fig.)* wages; *in ~ stehen*, to be the hireling of...
Soldat *m.* (-en, -en) soldier; *gemeiner ~* private (soldier); *~ werden*, to enlist, to go for a soldier.
Soldatenleben *n.* soldiering.
Soldateska *f.* (-, 0) (brutal) soldiery.
soldatisch *a.* soldier-like, military.
Söldner *m.* (-s, -) mercenary, hireling.
Soldliste *f.* (*mil.*) pay-roll.

Sole *f.* (-, -n) salt-water, brine.
solenn *a.* solemn; splendid.
solid(e) *a.* solid, strong; *(fig.)* respectable, steady, safe, solvent.
solidarisch *a.* jointly and separately liable.
Solidarität *f.* (-, 0) solidarity.
Solidität *f.* (-, 0) solidity; *(com.)* respectability, acknowledged standing.
Solist *m.* (-en, -en) soloist.
Soll *n.* (-[s], -[s]) debit; *~ und Haben*, debit and credit.
sollen *v.i.ir.* shall, to be to; to be said, be supposed to; *was soll das?* what does this mean?
Solo *n.* (-s, -s *u.* Soli) solo.
Solquelle *f.* saline-spring.
somit *adv.* therefore; consequently.
Sommer *m.* (-s, -) summer.
Sommer: *~aufenthalt m.* summer-resort; *~fahrplan m.* summer-service time-tables; *~läden m.pl.* gossamer; *~frische f.* summer-resort; *~gäste pl.* visitors.
sommerlich *a.* summerlike.
Sommersprosse *f.* freckle.
sommersprossig *a.* freckled.
Sommerzeit *f.* summer-time.
somnambul *a.* somnambulistic.
sonach *adv.* therefore, accordingly.
Sonate *f.* (-, -n) sonata.
Sonde *f.* (-, -n) (sounding-)lead; *(med.)* probe.
Sonderausgabe *f.* special edition.
sonderbar *a.* strange, singular, odd.
Sonderberichterstatter *m.* special correspondent.
sondergleichen *a. & adv.* without equals.
Sonderinteresse *n.* special interest.
sonderlich *a.* special, particular; important.
Sonderling *m.* (-[e]s, -e) odd character.
sondern *v.t.* to separate, to sever; *~ c.* but; *nicht nur..., ~ auch*, not only... but also.
Sonder: *~recht n.* privilege; *~zug m.* special train.
Sonderstellung *f.* unique *or* exceptional position.
Sonderung *f.* (-, -en) separation.
sondieren *v.t.* (*med.*) to probe; to sound; *(fig.)* to explore, to feel one's way.
Sonett *n.* (-[e]s, -e) sonnet.
Sonnabend *m.* (-s, -e) Saturday.
Sonne *f.* (-, -n) sun.
sonnen, (sich) *~ v.refl.* to bask in the sun.
Sonnen: *~aufgang m.* sunrise; *~bad n.* sun-bath; *~blume f.* sunflower; *~brand m.* sunburn; *~brille f.* sun-glasses, sun-spectacles; *~finsternis f.* solar eclipse; *~fleck m.* sun-spot.
Sonnenjahr *n.* solar year.
sonnenklar *a.* as clear as daylight.
Sonnen: *~licht n.* sunlight; *~schein m.* sunshine; *~schirm m.* parasol, sun-

shade; ~spektrum *n.* solar spectrum; ~stich *m.* sunstroke; ~strahl *m.* sunbeam; ~system *n.* solar system; ·~uhr *f.* sun-dial.

Sonnenuntergang *m.* sunset, (*Am.*) sundown.

sonnenverbrannt *a.* sunburnt.

Sonnenwende *f.* solstice.

sonnig *a.* sunny, sunshiny.

Sonntag *m.* (-s, -e) Sunday.

sonntäglich *a.* Sunday.

sonst *adv.* else, otherwise; besides; formerly; ~ *etwas*, anything else; ~ *jemand*, anybody else; ~ *nichts*, nothing else; ~ *nirgends*, nowhere else; ~ *wo*, elsewhere.

sonstig *a.* other, remaining; former.

Sophistik *f.* (-, 0) sophistry.

sophistisch *a.* sophistic(al).

Sopran *m.* (-[e]s, -e) soprano, treble.

Sorge *f.* (-, -n) care; worries *pl.*; *sich ~ machen über etwas, um sinen,* to be concerned about...

sorgen *v.i.* to be anxious, to worry; to care, provide; *sich um etwas ~,* to be concerned about a thing; *~ für,* to provide for, to see to it, to look after, to take care of.

sorgenfrei, sorgenlos *a.* free from care.

Sorgenkind *n.* delicate child.

sorgenschwer *a.* anxious, uneasy.

sorgenvoll *a.* anxious, uneasy.

Sorgfalt *f.* (-, 0) care(fulness).

sorgfältig *a.* careful, heedful.

sorglich *a.* anxious; careful.

sorglos *a.* careless, thoughtless.

sorgsam *a.* heedful, careful.

Sorte *f.* (-, -n) sort, kind.

sortieren *v.t.* to (as)sort.

Sortierer *m.* (-s, -) sorter.

Sortimenter *m.* (-s, -), Sortimentsbuchhändler *m.* retail bookseller.

Souffleur *m.* (-[e]s, -e) prompter.

Souffleurkasten *m.* prompter's box.

soufflieren *v.i.* to prompt.

Souterrain *n.* (-[s], -s) basement (story).

souverän *a.* sovereign.

Souverän *m.* (-[e]s, -e) sovereign.

Souveränität *f.* (-, 0) sovereignty.

Sowjet *m.* (-s, -s) Soviet.

soweit *c.* as far as.

sowieso *adv.* anyhow, (*Am.*) anyway.

sozial *a.* social.

Sozialdemokrat *m.* (-en, -en) Social Democrat.

sozialdemokratisch *a.* social-democratic.

sozialisieren *v.t.* to socialize.

Sozialismus *m.* (-, 0) socialism.

Sozialwissenschaft *f.* sociology.

Soziologie *f.* (-, 0) social science, sociology.

Sozius *m.* (-, Sozii) (*com.*) partner.

sozusagen *adv.* as it were, so to speak.

Soyabohne *f.* soya bean, (*Am.*) soy bean

Spagat *m.* (-[e]s, -e) string.

spähen *v.i. & t.* to spy, to explore.

Späher *m.* (-s, -) spy, scout.

Spähtrupp *m.* patrol; ~tätigkeit *f.* patrol activity.

Spalier *n.* (-[e]s, -e) espalier, trellis; (*fig.*) lane.

Spalierobst *n.* well-fruit.

Spalt *m.* (-[e]s, -e), Spalte *f.* (-, -n) crack, crevice, fissure; *Spalte* (newspaper) column.

spalten *v.t.* to split, to cleave, to slit; (sich) ~ *v.refl.* to divide; to bifurcate.

spaltig *a.* fissured, cracked.

Spaltung *f.* (-, -en) division, cleavage, schism; (*Atomkern, Zelle*) fission.

Span *m.* (-[e]s, Späne) chip, splinter; *Späne pl.* shavings, chips *pl.*

Spanferkel *n.* sucking-pig.

Spange *f.* (-, -n) buckle, clasp; bracelet.

spanisch *a.* Spanish; ~er *Pfeffer*, Guinea-pepper, red-pepper; ~e *Fliege*, cantharides *pl.*

Spann *m.* (-[e]s, -e) instep.

Spanne *f.* (-, -n) span; (*fig.*) short space; (*com.*) margin.

spannen *v.t.* to stretch, to strain; to extend; to span; (*den Bogen*) to bend; (*das Gewehr*) to cock; *seine Forderungen zu hoch ~,* to pitch one's claims too high; *einen auf die Folter ~,* to put one to the rack.

spannend *a.* deeply interesting, thrilling.

Spanner *m.* (-s, -) (*mech.*) spanner, (*Am.*) wrench.

Spann-: ~feder *f.* spring; ~futter *f.* (*mech.*) chuck; ~kraft *f.* elasticity.

Spannung *f.* (-, -en) tension; (*elek.*) voltage; strained relations *pl.*

spannungslos *a.* (*elek.*) dead.

Spannweite *f.* spread; span.

sparen *v.t.* to save, to spare; to lay by.

Spargel *m.* (-s, -) asparagus.

Sparkasse *f.* savings-bank.

spärlich *a.* scanty, meagre, frugal.

Sparmassnahmen *pl.* economy measures.

sparsam *a.* economical, thrifty.

Sparsamkeit *f.* (-, 0) thrift, economy.

Sparschein *m.* savings certificate.

spartanisch *a.* Spartan.

Sparte *f.* (-, -n) department, branch.

Spass *m.* (-es, Spässe) jest, joke, sport; *das macht mir ~,* it amuses me; *das ist kein ~,* this is no laughing matter; *zum ~,* for fun.

spassen *v.i.* to jest, to joke.

spasshaft *a.* waggish, funny, jocular.

spassig *a.* funny, jocular, facetious.

Spassmacher, Spassvogel *m.* wag; buffoon.

Spat *m.* (-[e]s, -e) (*Mineral*) spar.

spät *a. & adv.* late; *wie ~ ist es?* what is the time?; *früher oder später,* sooner or later; ~ am Tage, im Jahre, late in the day, in the year.

Spaten m. (-s, -) spade.

späterhin adv. later on.

spätestens adv. at the latest.

Spät: ~herbst m. late Autumn; ~obst n. late fruit; late summer.

Spatz m. (-en, -en) sparrow.

spazieren v.i. (s) to take a walk, to stroll; ~gehen to go for a walk.

Spazier: ~gang m. walk, stroll; promenade; ~stock m. walking-stick; ~weg m. walk, promenade.

Specht m. (-[e]s, -e) woodpecker.

Speck m. (-[e]s, 0) bacon.

speckig a. fat.

Speck: ~schwarte f. rind, skin of bacon; ~seite f. flitch of bacon.

spedieren v.t. to dispatch, to forward.

Spediteur m. (-s, -) forwarding agent, carrier; furniture remover.

Speditionskosten pl. transport or forwarding charges.

Speer m. (-[e]s, -e) spear; javelin.

Speiche f. (-, -n) spoke.

Speichel m. (-s, 0) spittle, saliva.

Speichellecker m. lick-spittle, toady.

Speicher m. (-s, -) granary; warehouse.

speichern v.t. to warehouse.

speien v.i. & t.st. to spit; to vomit.

Speise f. (-, -n) food, meat; dish.

Speise: ~kammer f. larder, pantry; ~karte f. bill of fare, menu.

speisen v.t. to feed; ~ v.i. to eat; to dine.

Speise: ~öl n. salad-oil; ~röhre f. gullet, œsophagus; ~saal m. dining-room; ~wagen m. dining-car, restaurant-car; ~wagenschaffner m. dining-car attendant; ~zimmer n. dining-room.

Spektakel m. & n. (-s, -) noise, row.

Spektralanalyse f. spectral-analysis.

Spekulant m. (-en, -en) speculator.

Spekulation f. (-, -en) speculation.

spekulieren v.i. to speculate (in, on).

Spelt m. (-[e]s, -e) (bot.) spelt.

Spelunke f. (-, -n) den; low gin-shop.

Spende f. (-, -n) dole; donation.

spenden v.t. to contribute (to).

Spender m. (-s, -) donor.

spendieren v.t. to give liberally.

Spengler m. (-s, -) tinner, plumber.

Sperber m. (-s, -) sparrow-hawk.

Sperling m. (-s, -e) sparrow.

Sperrdruck m. spaced-out type.

Sperre f. (-, -n) bar, barrier; (nav.) embargo, blockade; (Strassen~) block.

sperren v.t. to shut up, to bar, to stop; (Druck) to space; (Strasse) to block; (sich) ~ v.refl. to turn restive.

Sperr: ~feuer n. barrage; ~holz n. plywood; ~konto n. blocked account; ~rad n. ratchet(-wheel); ~sitz m. (theat.) stalls pl.

Sperrung f. (-, -en) embargo, blockade.

Spesen f.pl. charges, expenses pl.

Spezerei f. (-, -en) grocery; spices pl.

Spezialarzt m. specialist.

spezialisieren v.t. to specialize, to detail.

Spezialist m. (-en, -en) specialist.

Spezialität f. (-, -en) special line.

speziell a. specific, special.

spezifisch a. specific; ~es Gewicht, specific gravity.

Sphäre f. (-, -n) sphere; province, range.

sphärisch a. spherical.

spicken v.t. to lard.

Spiegel m. (-s, -) mirror, looking-glass.

Spiegelbild n. reflected image.

Spiegel: ~ei n. fried egg; ~fechterei f. delusion, jugglery; ~fläche f. smooth surface; ~glas n. plate-glass.

spiegelglatt a. smooth as a mirror.

spiegeln v.i. to glitter, to shine; ~ v.t. to reflect; (sich) ~ v.refl. to be reflected.

Spiegelung f. (-, -en) reflection; mirage.

Spiel n. (-[e]s, -e) play; game; auf dem ~e stehen, to be at stake; aufs ~ setzen, to risk, to stake; etwas anderes ist dabei im ~, there is something else in the case; die Hand dabei im ~ haben, to have a finger in the pie; einen aus dem ~ lassen, to let one alone.

Spiel: ~art f. variety; (Biol.) sport; ~ball m. (fig.) sport, plaything; ~bank f. gaming table.

spielen v.t. & i. to play; to gamble; to act, to perform; falsch ~, to cheat at play; vom Blatte ~, to play at sight; einem, einen Streich ~, to play one a trick.

spielend a. & adv. (fig.) easy; easily.

Spieler m. (-s, -) player; gambler.

Spielerei f. (-, -en) child's play, sport.

spielerisch a. playful, sportive.

Spiel: ~hölle f. gambling-hell; ~karte f. playing-card; ~leiter m. stage manager; ~plan m. (theat.) repertory; ~platz m. play-ground; ~raum m. elbow-room, play, scope; ~regel f. rule of a game; ~sache f. plaything, toy; ~verderber m. marplot, kill-joy; ~zeug n. plaything(s), toy(s pl.).

Spiess m. (-es, -e) spear, pike; (Brat~) spit; den ~ umkehren, (fig.) to turn the tables (upon).

Spiessbürger m. Philistine.

spiessbürgerlich a. humdrum, Philistine.

Spiesser m. (-s, -) = Spiessbürger.

spiessig a. = spiessbürgerlich.

Spiess: ~geselle m. accomplice; ~ruten f.pl. ~ laufen, to run the gauntlet (of).

Spill n. (-s, -e) capstan.

Spinat m. (-[e]s, 0) spinach.

Spind n. (-es, -e) press, wardrobe.

Spindel f. (-, -n) spindle; distaff; (mech.) mandrel.

spindeldürr a. thin as a lath.

Spindelstock *m.* (*mech.*) headstock.
Spinett *n.* (-[e]s, -e) spinet, harpsichord.
Spinne *f.* (-, -n) spider.
spinnen *v.i.* & *t.st.* to spin.
Spinnwebe *f.* cobweb.
Spinnerei *f.* (-, -en) spinning-mill.
Spinn: **~maschine** *f.* spinning-jenny; **~rad** *n.* spinning-wheel; **~rocken** *m.* distaff.
spintisieren *v.i.* to subtilize, to ponder.
Spion *m.* (-[e]s, -e) spy.
Spionage *f.* (-, 0) espionage.
Spionageabwehr *f.* counter-espionage.
spionieren *v.i.* to spy.
Spirale *f.* (-, -n) spiral (line).
Spiralfeder *f.* spiral spring.
spiralförmig *a.* spiral.
Spiritismus *m.* (-, 0) spiritualism.
Spiritist *m.* (-en, -en) spiritualist.
Spirituosen *pl.* spirits *pl.*
Spiritus *m.* (-, - *u.* -tusse) spirit, alcohol.
Spiritusbrennerei *f.* distillery.
Spital *n.* (-[e]s, -täler), **Spittel** *m.* & *n.* (-s, -) hospital, infirmary.
spitz *a.* pointed; (*math.*) acute; (*fig.*) sharp; ~ zulaufen, to taper.
Spitz *m.* (-es, -e) Pomeranian dog.
Spitz: **~bart** *m.* pointed beard; **~bogen** *m.* (*arch.*) pointed or Gothic arch; **~bube** *m.* rogue; thief.
spitzbübisch *a.* rascally; thievish.
Spitze *f.* (-, -n) point; (*Gewebe*) lace; (*Feder-*) nib; (*mil.*) spearhead; *auf die* ~ *treiben*, to carry to extremes; *an der* ~ *stehen*, to be at the head (of).
Spitzel *m.* (-s, -) police-spy, informer.
spitzen *v.t.* to point; to sharpen; *die Ohren* ~, to prick up one's ears.
Spitzenklöppel, *m.* lace-bobbin.
spitzfindig *a.* subtle; shrewd; cavilling.
Spitzfindigkeit *f.* (-,-en) subtlety, sophistry.
Spitzhacke *f.* pick-axe.
spitzig *a.* pointed, sharp; poignant.
Spitzname *m.* nickname.
spitzwinklig *a.* acute-angled.
spleissen *v.t.* & *i.st.* to split; to cleave.
splendid *a.* liberal.
Splitter *m.* (-s, -) splinter, chip.
splittern *v.i.* to splinter, to split; ~ *v.t.* to shiver.
splitternackt *a.* stark naked.
Splitterrichter *m.* fault-finder.
splittersicher *a.* splinter-proof.
spontan *a.* spontaneous.
sporadisch *a.* sporadic(al).
Spore *f.* (-, -n) (*bot.*) spore.
Sporn *m.* (-[e]s, Sporen) spur.
spornen *v.t.* to spur.
spornstreichs *adv.* post-haste.
Sport *m.* (-s, -s) sport; turf.
Sporteln *f.pl.* perquisites, fees *pl.*
Sportkleidung *f.* sports wear.
sportlich, sportsmässig *a.* sporting, sportsmanlike.

Spott *m.* (-[e]s, 0) derision, raillery, mockery, scorn; laughing-stock.
spottbillig *a.* dirt-cheap.
Spöttelei *f.* (-, -en) sneer, taunt, gibe.
spötteln *v.i.* to mock, to sneer at.
spotten *v.i.* to mock, to deride; *das spottet aller Beschreibung,* it beggars description.
Spötter *m.* (-s -) mocker, scoffer.
spöttisch *a.* satirical, ironical, scoffing.
Sprache *f.* (-, -n) language, tongue; speech, voice; *zur* ~ *bringen,* to broach (a subject); *zur* ~ *kommen,* to be mentioned.
Sprach[en]kunde *f.* linguistics *pl.*
Sprach: **~fehler** *m.* defect of speech; **~forscher** *m.* linguist, philologist; **~forschung** *f.* philology; **~führer** *m.* phrase-book; **~gebrauch** *m.* usage (in language); **~lehre** *f.* grammar.
sprachlich *a.* grammatical, lingual.
sprachlos *a.* speechless; (*fig.*) dumb.
Sprachreiniger *m.* purist.
Sprachrohr *n.* speaking tube; (*fig.*) mouth-piece.
sprachwidrig *a.* ungrammatical.
Sprachwissenschaft *f.* science of language.
sprechen *v.t.* & *i.st.* to speak; to talk; *er ist nicht zu* ~, you cannot see him now.
sprechend *a.* & *adv.* striking(ly); ~ *ähnlich a.* (of a) speaking likeness.
Sprech: **~film** *m.* talking film, talkie; **~stunden** *pl.* consulting hours, (*Stellen*) interviewing hours; **~zimmer** *n.* consulting room.
Spreize *f.* (-, -n) stay, prop.
spreizen *v.t.* to spread open, to stretch, to straddle.
Sprengel *m.* (-s, -) diocese; parish.
sprengen *v.t.* & *i.* to sprinkle, to water; to burst open; (*Bank*) to break; to blow up, to blast; to gallop.
Spreng: **~geschoss** *n.* explosive, shell; **~kapsel** *f.* detonator; **~stoff** *m.* high explosive.
sprenkeln *v.t.* to speckle.
Spreu *f.* (-, 0) chaff.
Sprichwort *n.* proverb, adage.
sprichwörtlich *a.* & *adv.* proverbial(ly).
spriessen *v.i.st.* (*s, h*) to sprout, to shoot.
Spring: **~brett** *n.* spring board; **~brunnen** *m.* fountain, jet.
springen *v.i.st.* (*s, h*) to spring; to leap, to jump; to crack, to burst; *entzwei* ~, to burst asunder; *in die Augen* ~, to be obvious.
Springer *m.* (-s, -) (*im Schachspiel*) knight.
Spring: **~feder** *f.* spring; **~federmatratze** *f.* spring mattress; **~flut** *f.* spring-tide; **~kraft** *f.* elasticity; **~quelle** *f.* spring, fountain.
Sprit *m.* (-s, 0) alcohol.

Spritze f. (-, -n) squirt, syringe; spray; fire-engine.
spritzen v.t. to spout, to squirt.
Spritzer m. (-s, -) squirt; spray, drop.
spröde a. brittle; (Haut) rough; (fig.) coy, reserved, prim.
Sprödigkeit f. (-, 0) brittleness; coyness.
Spross m. (Sprosses, Sprossen) shoot, sprout; scion, offspring.
Sprosse f. (-, -n) step, round, rung.
sprossen v.i. to sprout, to pullulate.
Sprössling m. (-[e]s, -e) sprout, shoot, (fig.) scion.
Sprotte f. (-, -n) sprat.
Spruch m. (-[e]s, Sprüche) maxim, saying; (Bibel⁓) text.
spruchreif a. ripe for decision.
Sprudel m. (-s, -) bubbling well, spring.
sprudeln v.i. to bubble; to spout.
sprühen v.t. to sprinkle, to emit; ⁓ v.i. to emit sparks, to scintillate.
Sprühregen m. drizzle.
Sprung m. (-[e]s, Sprünge) spring; leap jump; chink, crack, fissure; auf dem ⁓e sein, stehen, to be on the point of.
Sprung: ⁓brett n. spring-board; ⁓feder f. (elastic) spring.
sprungweise adv. by leaps.
Spucke f. (-, 0) spittle.
spucken v.i. to spit.
Spucknapf m. spittoon.
Spuk m. (-[e]s, -e) apparition, spectre.
spuken v.i. to haunt; to be haunted.
Spukgeschichte f. ghost-story.
Spule f. (-, -n) spool, bobbin; (Feder) quill; (elek.) coil.
spulen v.t. to spool, to reel.
spülen v.t. to rinse; to wash.
Spülicht n. (-[e]s, 0) dish-water; slops pl.
Spülwasser n. dish-water.
Spund m. (-[e]s, Spünde) bung, plug.
Spundloch n. bung-hole.
Spur f. (-, -en) track, trace; vestige; (Wagen⁓) rut; keine ⁓ von, not an idea or inkling of.
spüren v.t. to track, to trace; to perceive, to feel.
Spürhund m. pointer; (fig.) spy.
spurlos adv. without leaving a trace.
Spürsinn m. sagacity.
Spurweite f. (rail.) gauge.
sputen (sich) v.refl. to make haste.
Staat m. (-s, -en) state; pomp, show.
Staatenbund m. confederacy.
staatlich a. state-..., public; politic(al).
staatlich unterstützt, state-aided.
Staats: ⁓amt n. public office; ⁓angehörige[r] m. national, subject; ⁓angehörigkeit f. nationality; citizenship; ⁓anleihe f. government-loan; ⁓anwalt m. public prosecutor; (in England) Attorney-General; ⁓anwaltschaft f.

public prosecutor; ⁓anzeiger m. official gazette; ⁓beamte[r] m. civil servant.
Staats: im Staatsbesitz, state-owned; ⁓bürger m. subject, citizen; ⁓dienst m. public or civil service; ⁓einkünfte pl. revenue.
staatsgefährlich a. dangerous to the state.
Staats: ⁓gesetz n. law of the land, statute law; ⁓gewalt f. supreme or executive power; ⁓haushalt m. budget; ⁓kirche f. Established Church.
staatsklug a. politic, diplomatic.
Staats: ⁓kunst f. statesmanship; ⁓mann m. (-[e]s, -männer) statesman.
staatsmännisch a. statesmanlike.
Staats: ⁓minister m. minister of state; ⁓oberhaupt n. head of a state; ⁓papiere n.pl.. Stocks, public funds pl.; ⁓recht n. public law; ⁓schuld f. national debt; ⁓sekretär m. Secretary of State; ⁓streich m. coup d'état; ⁓verfassung f. constitution; ⁓verwaltung f. government, public administration; ⁓wesen n. state-affairs, pl. politics; ⁓wissenschaft f. political science, politics pl.
Stab m. (-[e]s, Stäbe) staff, stick; bar; (mil.) staff.
Stabreim m. alliteration.
stabil a. stable.
stabilisieren v.t. to stabilize.
Stabs: ⁓arzt m. medical officer (captain); ⁓offizier m. field officer.
Stachel m. (-s, -u) (Insekten⁓) sting; prickle, thorn; (fig.) sting, edge; stimulus.
Stachel: ⁓beere f. gooseberry; ⁓draht m. barbed wire.
stach(e)lig, a. prickly, thorny.
stacheln v.t. to goad; (fig.) to stimulate.
Stachelschwein n. porcupine.
Stadel m. (-s, -) barn, shed.
Stadion n. (-s, -dien) stadium.
Stadium n. (-[s], -dien u. -dia) stage.
Stadt f. (-, Städte) town; city.
Stadt: ⁓amt n. municipal office; ⁓bahn f. (in London) Metropolitan (railway).
Städtebau m. town-planning.
Städter m. (-s, -) townsman, citizen.
Stadtgespräch n. town-talk.
städtisch a. municipal; townlike.
Stadt: ⁓kämmerer m. city-treasurer; ⁓mauer f. city-wall; ⁓rat m. municipal council; town-councillor; ⁓verordnete[r] m. town-councillor; ⁓viertel n. quarter (of a town).
Stafette f. (-, -n) courier, express; (Sport) relay.
Staffel f. (-, -n) step, rung; degree; (Sport) relay; (mil.) echelon; (avi.) squadron.
Staffelei f. (-, -en) easel.
Staffel: ⁓kapitän m. squadron-leader,

~lauf *m.* relay race; ~tarif *m.* differential tariff.

staffeln *v.t.* to graduate; *gestaffelt*, *(mil.)* in echelon formation; gestaffelte Ferien *pl.* staggered holidays.

stagnieren *v.n.* to stagnate.

Stahl *m.* (-[e]s, Stäble) steel; *(mech.)* tool; *weicher* ~, mild steel.

stählen *v.t.* to temper, to harden; *(fig.)* to brace (up), to steel.

stählern *a.* (of) steel; steely.

Stahl: ~feder *f.* nib; ~halter *m.* *(mech.)* tool-holder; ~helm *m.* steel-helmet, *(sl.)* tin-hat; ~stich *m.* steel-engraving; ~werk *n.* steel-works *pl.*; ~wolle *f.* steel-wool.

staken *v.t.* to pole, to punt.

Stall *m.* (-[e]s, Ställe) stable.

Stallknecht *m.* groom.

Stallung *f.* (-, -en) stabling, stable-room.

Stamm *m.* (-[e]s, Stämme) stem, stalk; trunk, body; stock, race, family, tribe; *(gram.)* root.

Stamm: ~aktie *f.* ordinary share, *(Am.)* common stock; ~baum *m.* pedigree; ~buch *n.* album.

stammeln *v.t. & i.* to stammer, to stutter.

Stammeltern *pl.* first parents *pl.*

stammen *v.i.* (s) to originate, to proceed; to descend from; to be derived.

Stamm: ~gast *m.* regular customer; ~halter *m.* son and heir.

stämmig *a.* stout, strong.

Stammkapital *n.* nominal capital.

Stammler *m.* (-s, -) stammerer, stutterer.

Stamm: ~personal *n.* skeleton staff; ~rolle *f.* muster roll; ~tisch *m.* table reserved for regular customers; ~vater *m.* ancestor.

stammverwandt *a.* cognate, kindred.

stampfen *v.i. & t.* to stamp; to pound.

Stand *m.* (-[e]s, Stände) state, condition; *(Verkaufs-.)* stall; station, situation; rank, profession, order, class; *(im Stall)* stall; *(Barometer, etc.)* reading; *neu in* ~ *setzen*, to recondition.

Standarte *f.* (-, -n) standard.

Standbild *n.* statue.

Ständchen *n.* (-s, -) serenade.

Stände *m.pl.* estates *(pl.)* of the realm.

Ständer *m.* (-s, -) stand, upright; *(elek.)* stator.

Ständerlampe *f.* standard lamp.

Standesamt *n.* registrar's office.

standesamtlich *a.* before the registrar.

Standesbeamte[r] *m.* registrar.

standesgemäss *a.* in accordance with one's rank.

standhaft *a.* firm, steady, steadfast; constant.

Standhaftigkeit *f.* (-, 0) constancy.

ständig *a.* permanent, fixed.

standhalten *v.i.st.* to hold one's ground.

Stand: ~ort *m.* location; *(mil.)* (military) post; ~punkt *m.* point of view; standpoint; ~recht *n.* martial law.

standrechtlich *a.* according to martial law.

Stange *f.* (-, -n) pole, perch; bar; stick; ~bohne *f.* kidney bean, scarlet runner.

Stänkerei *f.* (-, -en) quarrel, row.

stänkern *v.i.* *(fig.)* to quarrel, to pick quarrels; to find fault.

Stanniol *n.* (-[e]s, 0) tinfoil.

Stanze *f.* (-, -n) stanza; *(Druckerei)* stamp, die.

stanzen *v.t.* to stamp, to punch.

Stapel *m.* (-s, -) heap, pile; staple, emporium; *vom* ~ *lassen*, to launch (a ship, an enterprise).

Stapellauf *m.* launching.

stapeln *v.t.* to pile up.

Stapelplatz *m.* staple, emporium.

Star *m.* (-[e]s, -e) starling; *(med.)* cataract; *grüner* ~, glaucoma; *schwarzer* ~, amaurosis; *den* ~ *stechen*, to operate for, to couch cataract.

stark *a.* strong, robust; stout, fat; intense; ~e *Seite*, strong point.

starkbesetzt *a.* well attended, crowded.

Stärke *f.* (-, 0) strength, force, vigour; starch; thickness.

stärkehaltig *a.* containing starch.

Stärkemehl *n.* starch-flour.

stärken *v.t.* to strengthen; to corroborate; to comfort; to starch.

Stärkenachweisung *f.* *(mil.)* table of organization, strength report.

stärkend *a.* strengthening, restorative, invigorating.

Starkstrom *m.* power current.

Stärkung *f.* (-, -en) strengthening; consolation; refreshment, food.

Stärkungsmittel *n.* restorative.

starr *a.* stiff, rigid; fixed; ~ *sein vor Erstaunen*, to be dumb with astonishment.

starren *v.i.* to stare; *von Schmutze* ~, to be stiff with dirt; *(von Fehlern, etc.)* to bristle with.

Starrheit *f.* stiffness, rigidity; obstinacy.

Starrkopf *m.* stubborn fellow.

starrköpfig *a.* stubborn, headstrong.

Starr: ~krampf *m.* tetanus; ~sinn *m.* stubbornness.

starrsinnig *a.* stubborn, headstrong.

Startbahn *f.* *(avi.)* runway.

Startplatz *m.* starting place.

Statik *f.* (-, 0) statics.

Station *f.* (-, -en) station; stopping-place, stage.

stationieren *v.t.* *(mil.)* to station.

Stationsvorsteher *m.* station-master.

Statist *m.* (-en, -en), Statistin *f.* (-, -nen) *(theat.)* super, mute person.

Statistik *f.* (-, -en) statistics.

statistisch *a.* statistic(al).

Stativ n. (-s, -e) stand; (*phot.*) tripod.

Statt f. (-, 0) place, stead; *an meiner* ~, in my place; *an Kindes* ~ *annehmen*, to adopt.

statt *pr.* instead of, in lieu of; ~ *dessen*, instead of this; ~ *dass*, instead of...

Stätte f. (-, -n) place, spot.

stattfinden v.i.st. to take place.

stattgeben v.i.st. to grant.

statthaben v.i.st. to take place.

statthaft a. admissible, allowable, lawful.

Statthalter m. Stadholder; governor.

stattlich a. stately; considerable.

Statue f. (-, -n) statue.

Statuette f. (-, -n) statuette.

Statur f. (-, -en) stature, size.

Statut n. (-[e]s, -e) statute, regulation.

statutenmässig a. statutory.

Staub m. (-[e]s, 0) dust; powder; *sich aus dem* ~*e machen*, to make off, to abscond.

Stäubchen n. (-s, -) mote.

stauben v.i. to give off dust, to be dusty.

stäuben v.i. to raise dust; ~ v.t. to dust.

Staubgefäss n. stamen, pl. stamina.

staubig a. dusty.

Staubtuch n. duster.

Staude f. (-, -n) shrub; bush.

stauen v.t. to dam up, to bank up; *das Wasser staut sich*, the water is dammed up.

staunen v.i. to be astonished, to be surprised, to be amazed.

staunenswert a. amazing, marvellous.

Staupe f. (-, 0) (*Hunde*~) distemper.

Stearin n. (-[e]s, 0) stearin.

stechen v.t.st. to sting, to prick; to stab; (*Torf*) to cut; ~ v.i.st. (*Sonne*) to burn; *in die Augen* ~, to strike the eye; *in See* ~, to put to sea, to set sail.

Stech: ~**heber** m. pipette; ~**palme** f. holly; ~**schritt** m. goose-step.

Steckbrief m. warrant of apprehension.

steckbrieflich a. & adv. *einen* ~ *verfolgen*, to issue a warrant against someone.

Steckdose f., **Stecker** m. (*elek.*) plug.

stecken v.t. to stick; ~ v.i.st. to stick, to be fixed; ~**bleiben**, to stick fast; *was steckt dahinter?* what can be at the bottom of it?; *Geld in ein Unternehmen* ~, to invest money in an undertaking; *sich hinter einen* ~, to induce a person to act in one's interest; *mit einem unter einer Decke* ~, to play into each other's hands.

Stecken m. (-s, -) stick, staff.

Steckenpferd n. hobby-horse; (*fig.*) hobby, fad.

Stecker m. (-s, -) plug.

Steckkontakt m. (*elek.*) socket.

Steck: ~**nadel** f. pin; ~**nadelkopf** m. pinhead; ~**rübe** f. Swedish turnip.

Steg m. (-[e]s, -e) path; small bridge; (*Geigen*~) bridge.

Stegreif m. *aus dem* ~*e*, extempore, offhand; *aus dem* ~ *sprechen*, to extemporize.

stehen v.i.st. to stand; to suit (well, ill); to be; *es steht fest*, it is beyond doubt that; *frei*~, to be permitted; *es steht Ihnen frei*, you are at liberty to; *es steht in der Zeitung*, it's in the paper; *Modell* ~, to serve as model (to); *wie steht's?* how are you?; *sich gut* ~, to be well off; *sich auf* 3000 M. (*Einkommen*) ~, to have an income of 3000 M. a year: *die Aktien* ~ *auf*..., the shares stand at...; *seinen Mann* ~, to hold one's own; ~**bleiben**, to stop, to pause; *Geld bei einem* ~ *haben*, to have deposited money with one; *sich den Bart* ~ *lassen*, to let one's beard grow; *es steht zu erwarten*, it is to be expected; *zum* ~ *bringen*, to bring to a stand.

stehend a. standing; ~*es Heer*, standing army; ~*e Redensart*, standing phrase; stock phrase.

Stehkragen m. stand-up collar.

Stehlampe f. standard lamp.

stehlen v.t.st. to steal; to pilfer; *sich aus dem Hause* ~, to steal out of the house.

Steh: ~**platz** m. standing-room; ~**pult** n. standing-desk.

steif a. stiff; rigid; awkward; formal; ~ *werden*, to stiffen; ~ *und fest behaupten*, to maintain obstinately; ~*er Grog*, strong grog.

steifen v.t. to stiffen.

Steifheit f. (-, -en) stiffness; (*fig.*) formality, pedantry.

Steig m. (-[e]s, -e) path.

steigen v.i.st. (*s*) to mount, to ascend, to rise; to increase; to climb; *die Haare* ~ *mir zu Berge*, my hair stands on end; *die Aktien* ~, the shares are going up.

Steiger m. (-s, -) overseer of miners.

steigern v.t. to raise (the price), to enhance, to increase.

Steigerung f. (-, -en) rise, increase, gradation; (*gram.*) comparison.

Steigerungsgrad m. (*gram.*) degree of comparison.

Steigung f. (-, -en) rising, ascent; (*rail.*) gradient; (*mot.*) (steep) hill (up).

steil a. steep, stiff.

Steilfeuer n. high-angle fire.

Stein m. (-[e]s, -e) stone; (*im Schachspiele*), piece; ~ *des Anstosses*, stumbling-block; ~ *der Weisen*, philosophers' stone; *es fällt mir ein* ~ *vom Herzen*, a great weight is taken off my mind; *wie ein Tropfen auf einen heissen* ~, altogether insufficient.

Stein: ~**bild** n. statue; ~**bock** m. ibex; (*Sternbild*) Capricorn; ~**bruch** m.

quarry; ~butt *m.*, ~butte *f.* turbot; ~druck *m.* lithography.

steinern *a.* (of) stone; (*fig.*) stony.

Steingut *n.* earthenware, crockery.

steinhart *a.* hard as stone, stony.

steinig *a.* stony, rocky.

Steinigung *f.* (-, -en) stoning.

Stein: ~kohle *f.* hard coal; ~metz *m.* stone-mason; ~obst *n.* stone-fruit; ~öl *n.* petroleum; ~pilz *m.* white (edible) mushroom; ~platte *f.* slab, flagstone.

steinreich *a.* enormously rich.

Stein: ~salz *n.* rock-salt; ~setzer *m.* pavier; ~wurf *m.* stone's throw; ~zeit *f.* stone-age.

Steiss *m.* (-[e]s, -e) backside, rump, buttocks *pl.*

Steissbein *n.* rump-bone, coccyx.

Stelldichein *n.* (-[s], -) rendezvous.

Stelle *f.* (-, -n) place, spot; situation, office; (*Buch.*) passage; *an höchster ~*, on top level; *auf der ~ treten*, to mark time; *nicht von der ~ kommen*, not to get on; *sich nicht von der ~ rühren*, not to stir an inch; *an Ort und ~ sein*, to be on the spot; *an ~ von*, in lieu of; *sich zu einer ~ melden*, to apply for a situation; *auf der ~*, at once, on the spot.

stellen *v.t.* to put, to place, to set; to regulate; (sich) ~ *v.refl.* to step, to stand; (*Preis*) to amount to; to dissemble, to make believe; *bereit.*, to place in readiness; *sich krank ~*, to feign sickness; *sich ~ als ob*, to pretend, to make believe; *eine Uhr richtig ~*, to set a watch; *einem ein Bein ~*, to trip someone up; *nach dem Leben ~*, to attempt one's life; *einen Antrag ~*, to move.

Stellen: ~besetzung *f.* placement; ~gesuch *n.* (*Zeitung*) situation wanted.

Stellenjäger *m.* place-hunter.

Stellenvermittlungsbüreau *n.* employment agency.

stellenweise *a.* sporadically, in parts.

Stellmacher *m.* (-s, -) cartwright.

Stellschraube *f.* adjusting screw.

Stellung *f.* (-, -en) position; situation; (*Körper.*) posture.

Stellungnahme *f.* comment(s).

Stellungskrieg *n.* position warfare.

Stellvertreter *m.* representative, substitute; proxy.

Stellwerk *n.* signal box.

Stelze *f.* (-, -n) stilt.

Stelzfuss *m.* wooden leg.

Stemmeisen *n.* chisel.

stemmen *v.t.* (*Flut, usw.*) to stem; (sich) ~ *v.refl.* to lean (against); to resist; *die Hände in die Seiten ~*, to set one's arms akimbo; *sich gegen etwas ~*, to set one's face against a thing.

Stempel *m.* (-s, -) stamp; pestle; (*bot.*) pistil; post-mark; (*mech.*) piston.

Stempel: ~gebühr *f.* stamp-duty; ~kissen *n.* stamp-pad; ~marke *f.* stamp.

stempeln *v.t.* to stamp, to mark; ~ gehn *v.i.* to be on the dole.

Stengel *m.* (-s, -) stalk, stem.

Stenograph *m.* (-en, -en) shorthand-writer.

Stenographie (-, -en) shorthand.

stenographieren *v.t. & i.* to write (in) shorthand.

Stenotypistin *f.* (-n, -nen) shorthand typist.

Steppdecke *f.* quilt, eiderdown.

Steppe *f.* (-, -n) steppe.

steppen *v.t.* to quilt, to stitch.

Sterbe: ~bett *n.* death-bed; ~kasse *f.* (fund of a) burial-club.

sterben *v.i.st.* (*s*) to die; *eines natürlichen Todes ~*, to die a natural death; *Hungers ~*, to die of hunger.

Sterben *n.* (-s, -) dying; mortality, epidemic; *im ~ liegen*, to be dying.

sterbenskrank *a.* dangerously ill.

Sterbenswörtchen *n.* a single word, a syllable.

Sterbesakramente *pl.* the last sacraments.

sterblich *a.* mortal; ~ *verliebt*, desperately in love.

Sterblichkeit *f.* (-, 0) mortality; ~ziffer *f.* death rate, mortality.

Stereometrie *f.* (-, 0) stereometry, solid geometry.

stereoskopisch *a.* stereoscopic.

stereotyp *a.* stereotyped.

stereotypieren *v.t.* to stereotype.

sterilisieren *v.t.* to sterilize.

Stern *m.* (-[e]s, -e) star; (*im Druck*) asterisk.

Sternbild *n.* constellation.

Sternchen *n.* (-s, -) asterisk.

Sterndeuter *m.* (-s, -) astrologer.

Sternen: ~banner *n.* stars and stripes; ~licht *n.* starlight.

Sternfahrt *f.* (*mot.*) motor rally.

sternförmig *a.* star-shaped stellar.

sternhell *a.* starlight, starry.

Stern: ~himmel *m.* firmament, starry sky; ~kunde *f.* astronomy; ~schnuppe *f.* shooting star; ~warte *f.* observatory.

Sterz *m.* (-es, -e) tail, plough-tail.

stet *a.* steady, constant, continued.

stetig *a.* continual, continuous.

Stetigkeit *f.* (-, 0) continuity, constancy, stability.

stets *adv.* continually, always, ever.

Steuer *n.* (-s, -) rudder, helm.

Steuer *f.* (-, -n) (*Staats.*) tax; (*Gemeinde.*) rate; (*Zoll*) duty.

steuerbar *a.* assessable, liable to duty.

Steuer: ~beamter *m.* tax-collector, revenue officer; ~behörde *f.* board of inland revenue; ~bord *n.* starboard; ~einnehmer *m.* tax-collector; ~er-

klärung f. income-tax return; **~erlass** m. tax remission.
steuerfrei a. exempt from taxes, duty-free.
Steuer: ~freiheit f. exemption from taxes; **~hinterziehung** f. evasion of taxes.
Steuer: ~mann m. mate; **~marke** f. revenue stamp.
steuern v.t. to steer; to pilot; **~** v.i. to steer; (einem Dinge) to check, to repress.
Steuern hinterziehen, to defraud the revenue.
Steuer: ~nachlass m. tax remission; **~pflichtig** a. dutiable, subject to taxation; **~politik** f. fiscal policy; **~rad** n. (mot.) steering wheel; **~rückvergütung** f. tax refund; **~ruder** n. helm, rudder; **~satz** m. rate of assessment; **~schuld** f. tax arrears.
Steuerung f. (-, -en) (mech.) control.
Steuer: ~veranschlagung f. assessment; **~zahler** m. rate-payer, tax-payer.
Steven m. (-s, -) (nav.) posts at bow or stern.
stibitzen v.t. (fam.) to pilfer, to filch.
Stich m. (-[e]s, -e) puncture; stab; (Nadel) prick; sting; (Näh.) stitch; engraving; **~** halten, to hold good; im **~** lassen, to leave in the lurch.
Stichel f. (-s, -) burin.
Stichelei f. (-, -en) taunt, raillery, sneer.
sticheln v.i. (auf einen) to taunt.
Stichflamme f. (-, -n) pilot jet.
stichhaltig a. valid, sound.
Stichprobe f. (-, -n) (Am.) spotcheck; **~machen**, to spotcheck.
Stichtag m. qualifying date, reference date.
Stichwort n. cue; catchword.
sticken v.t. to embroider.
Stickerei f. (-, -en) embroidery.
Stickerin f. (-, -nen) embroideress.
Stick: ~luft f. stuffy air; **~muster** n. pattern for embroidering, sampler; **~rahmen** m. embroidery-frame; **~stoff**, m. nitrogen.
stickstoffhaltig a. nitrogenous.
Stickstoffverbindung f. nitrous compound.
Stiefbruder m. step-brother, half-brother.
Stiefel m. (-s, -) boot.
Stiefelknecht m. bootjack.
Stiefelputzer m. bootblack.
Stiefeltern pl. step-parents pl.
Stief: ~geschwister pl. step-brother[s] and sister[s]; **~kind** n. step-child; **~mutter** f. step-mother; **~mütterchen** n. (bot.) pansy.
stiefmütterlich a. step-motherly.
Stief: ~schwester f. step-sister; **~sohn** m. step-son; **~tochter** f. step-daughter; **~vater** m. step-father.
Stiege f. (-, -n) staircase, (Am.) stairway.
Stieglitz m. (-es, -e) thistle-finch.

Stiel m. (-[e]s, -e) handle, helve; (bot.) stalk, pedicle; mit Stumpf und **~**, root and branch.
Stier m. (-[e]s, -e) bull.
stieren v.i. to stare.
Stier: ~fechter m. toreador; **~gefecht** n. bull-fight.
Stift m. (-[e]s, -e) tag, peg; pencil, crayon; (fam.) office boy, 'nipper.'
Stift n. (-[e]s, -e u. -er) (charitable) foundation; home for old people; chapter-house; college.
stiften v.t. to establish; to found; Gutes, Nutzen **~**, to do good, to be useful.
Stifter m. (-s, -) founder, author.
Stiftung f. (-, -en) establishment; institution; pious or charitable foundation.
Stiftungs, Stiftungsfest n. founder's day.
Stil m. (-[e]s, -e) style; manner.
Stilistik f. (-, -en) theory of style.
stilistisch a. relating to style.
still a. stii, silent; calm, quiet, tranquil; **~**! hush!; im **~en**, quietly; **~halten**, to keep still; **~schweigen**, to be silent, to keep silence; **~sein**, to be quiet; **~stehen**, to stand still; der **~e** Ozean, the Pacific; **~er Teilhaber** m. silent partner, sleeping partner.
Stille f. (-, 0) silence, tranquillity; in aller **~**, secretly.
stillegen v.t. to close down.
Stillegung f. (-, -en) shut down.
stillen v.t. to quiet, to appease, to quench; (Blut) to staunch; (Begierden) to gratify; (ein Kind) to feed, to nurse.
stillgestanden! (mil.) attention.
stilliegend a. **~e** Fabrik, idle factory.
stillos a. lacking in style.
Still: ~leben n. (Malerei) still life; **~schweigen** n. silence.
stillschweigend a. silent, tacit; **~** dulden, to connive at; **~e** Einwilligung f. connivance.
Stillstand m. standstill, stop, deadlock.
Stilmöbel n.pl. period furniture.
stilvoll a. in (correct) style.
Stimmband n. vocal chord.
stimmberechtigt a. entitled to vote.
Stimmbruch m. breaking of the voice.
Stimme f. (-, -n) voice; (Wahl**~**) vote; (mus.) part; seine **~** abgeben, to cast one's vote.
stimmen v.t. to tune; (fig.) to dispose; **~** v.t. to vote; das stimmt! that's true enough; die Rechnung stimmt, the account is square or correct; er ist heute schlecht gestimmt, he is in a bad humour to-day.
Stimm(en)abgabe f. voting.
Stimmen: ~gleichheit f. equality of votes, tie; **~mehrheit** f. majority of votes.
Stimmer m. (-s, -) tuner.
stimmfähig a. entitled to vote.

Stimmgabel *f.* tuning-fork.
stimmhaft *a.* voiced.
stimmlos *a.* voiceless.
Stimmrecht *n.* suffrage, right of voting.
Stimmung *f.* (-, -en) mood, humour, disposition; (*mil.*) morale, general feeling.
Stimmwechsel *m.* breaking of the voice.
Stimmzettel *m.* ballot-paper.
stinken *v.i.st.* to stink (of).
Stipendiat *m.* (-en, -en) exhibitioner.
Stipendium *n.* (-[s], -dien) scholarship, exhibition.
stippen *v.t.* to dip, to steep.
Stirn *f.* (-, -en) forehead; front; (*fig.*) insolence; *einem die ~ bieten,* to show a bold front.
Stirn: ~angriff *m.* frontal attack; ~runzeln *n.* frown(ing).
stöbern *v.i.* (*nach*) to rummage (for).
stochern *v.i.* to poke, to stir.
Stock *m.* (-[e]s, Stöcke) stick; staff; cane; log, block, trunk; (*Stockwerk*) storey, floor, flat; (*Stock-* (vor Nationennamen) *z. B. Stock-Russe*), to the backbone, genuine.
stockblind *a.* stone-blind.
stockdumm *a.* utterly stupid.
stockdunkel *a.* pitch-dark.
stocken *v.i.* to stop; (*gerinnen*) to curdle; (*fig.*) to hesitate; *die Geschäfte ~,* business is at a standstill.
Stocken *n.* (-s, 0) *ins ~ geraten,* to come to a standstill.
stockfinster *a.* pitch-dark.
Stockfisch *m.* stockfish, dried cod.
stocksteif *a.* stiff as a poker.
stocktaub *a.* stone-deaf, deaf as a post.
Stockung *f.* (-, -en) stagnation; interruption, block; (*med.*) congestion.
Stockwerk *n.* floor, storey.
Stoff *m.* (-[e]s, -e) stuff, material, fabric; matter, subject.
stofflich *a.* material.
Stoffwechsel *m.* (*med.*) metabolism.
stöhnen *v.i.* to groan.
Stoiker *m.* (-s, -) stoic.
stoisch *a.* stoic(al).
Stoizismus *m.* (-, 0) stoicism.
Stola *f.* (-, en) stole.
Stollen *m.* (-s, -) (mining) adit, gallery.
stolpern *v.i.* (*s*) to stumble, to trip.
stolz *a.* proud; stately.
Stolz *m.* (-es, 0) pride; *seinen ~ in etwas setzen,* to take a pride in a thing.
stolzieren *v.i.* (*s*) to flaunt, to strut.
stopfen *v.t.* to stop; to stuff, to cram; to fill (a pipe); to obstruct; (*mit Garn*) to darn; (*med.*) to constipate.
Stoppel *f.* (-, -n) stubble.
stoppen *v.t.* (*nav.*) to stop.
Stoppuhr *f.* stop-watch.
Stöpsel *m.* (-s, -) stopper, cork.
stöpseln *v.t.* to cork, to plug.

Stör *m.* (-[e]s, -e) sturgeon.
Storch *m.* (-[e]s, Störche) stork.
stören *v.t.* to disturb, to trouble; (*Radio*) to jam; ~ *v.i.* to be in the way.
Störenfried *m.* (-[e]s, -e) mischief-maker, marplot.
störrig, störrisch *a.* stubborn, refractory.
Störung *f.* (-, -en) disturbance, interruption; ~en, (*Radio*) atmospherics *pl.*
Störungsangriff *m.* (*avi.*) nuisance raid.
Stoss *m.* (-es, Stösse) thrust, push; shock; (*Fuss*) kick; jolt; (*phys.*) impact; (*Billiard*) stroke; (*Haufen*) pile, heap; (*Akten.*) file, bundle.
Stössel *m.* (-s, -) pestle.
stossen *v.t.st.* to thrust, to push; to kick, to knock; (*im Mörser*) to pound; ~ *v.i. st.* (*Wagen*) to jolt; to butt; (*an etwas*) to border (on); to strike against; (*auf etwas*) to come across; (sich) ~ *v.refl.* to knock against; to hurt oneself; *einen vor den Kopf ~,* to offend one; *über den Haufen ~,* to overturn; *sich an etwas ~,* to take offence at.
Stossdämpfer *m.* (*mot.*) shock absorber.
Stoss: ~maschine *f.* slotting machine, slotter; ~truppen *pl.* shock troops *pl.*
stossweise *adv.* by fits and starts.
stottern *v.i.* to stutter, to stammer.
stracks *adv.* straightway, immediately.
Straf... punitive *a.*
Straf: ~anstalt *f.* house of correction; ~antrag *m.* (*jur.*) demand for punishment; ~arbeit *f.* imposition (in schools).
strafbar *a.* punishable; ~ *sein,* to be liable to prosecution.
Straf: ~befugnis *f.* right to impose penalties; ~bestimmung *f.* clause in penal code; ~buch *n.* book of fines.
Strafe *f.* (-, -n) punishment; (*Geld*) fine, penalty; *seine ~ erleiden,* to undergo one's punishment; *es ist bei ~ verboten,* it is forbidden on pain of (the Law, a fine, etc.); *seine ~ absitzen,* to serve one's sentence.
strafen *v.t.* to punish, to chastise; (*an Geld*) to fine; *einen Lügen ~,* to give someone the lie.
Straferlass *m.* amnesty.
straff *a.* tight, tense; (*nav.*) taut.
straffällig *a.* punishable.
straffen (sich) *v.t. & refl.* to tauten.
Straf: ~gefangene[r] *m.* convict; ~gericht *n.* judgment; ~gesetz *n.* penal law; ~gesetzbuch *n.* penal code; ~kolonie *f.* penal settlement.
sträflich *a.* punishable.
Sträfling, *m.* (-[e]s, -e) convict.
straflos *adv.* with impunity.
Straf: -mass *n.* degree of punishment, ~porto *n.* surcharge; ~predigt *f.* lecture; reprimand; ~prozess *m.* criminal case;

criminal procedure; **~prozessordnung** f. code of criminal procedure; **~punkt** m. (*Sport*) penalty; **~recht** n. criminal law; **~rechtspflege** f. criminal justice; **~rechtsreform** f. penal reform; **~rechtlich** a. criminal, penal; **~register,** n. criminal register; **~richter** m. criminal judge; **~sache** f. criminal case; **~summe** f. penalty, fine; **~umwandlung** f. commutation of sentence; **~urteil** n. sentence; **~verfahren** n. criminal proceedings; **~versetzung** f. disciplinary transfer; **~vollstreckung** f., **~vollzug** m. penal administration; **~zeit** f. prison term.

strafwürdig a. punishable.

Strahl m. (-[e]s, -en) beam, ray flash; (*Wasser~*) jet.

strahlen v.t. & i. to radiate, to beam.

Strahlenbrechung f. refraction.

strahlend a. radiant, shining.

strahlenförmig a. radial.

Strähne f. (-, -n) strand, skein.

stramm a. tight; sturdy, strapping; erect; (*im Dienst*) strict.

strammstehen v.i. to stand to attention.

strampeln v.i. to kick, to struggle.

Strand m. (-[e]s, -e) strand, shore, beach; *auf den ~ laufen,* to run ashore.

stranden v.i. (s) to strand, to be stranded.

Strand: ~gut n. jetsam, flotsam, wreck; **~korb** m. wicker chair for the beach.

Strang m. (-[e]s, Stränge) rope; (*Galgen~*) halter; (*Schienen~*) track.

strangulieren v.t. to strangle.

Strapaze f. (-, -n) fatigue, over-exertion.

strapazieren v.t. (*Kleid*) to wear hard.

Strapazierfähigkeit f. resistance to wear.

Strasse f. (-, -n) road, highway; street; (*Meeresenge*) straits pl.

Strassen: ~anzug m. lounge suit; **~arbeiter** m. road-maker, navvy; **~bahn** f. tramway; **~bahnwagen** m. (*Am.*) street-car, trolley; **~bau** m. road-making; **~gabel** f. road-junction; **~kehrer** m. scavenger; **~kleid** n. walking-dress; **~kreuzung** f. intersection, crossing, cross-roads; **~pflaster** n. pavement; **~raub** m. highway-robbery; **~räuber** m. highwayman; **~sperre** f. (*mil.*) road-block; **~unterbau** m. road-bed; **~verkehrsordnung** f. rule of the road; **~verkäufer** m. street vendor.

Stratege m. (-en, -en) strategist.

Strategie f. (-, 0) strategy.

strategisch a. strategic(al).

sträuben (sich) ~ v.refl. to strive against, to struggle.

Strauch m. (-[e]s, Sträuche[r] bush, shrub.

straucheln v.i. (s) to stumble.

Strauss m. (-es, -e) ostrich; (*pl. Sträusse*) bunch, bouquet, nosegay; combat.

streben v.i. to strive, to aspire.

Streben n. (-s, 0) effort, endeavour.

Strebepfeiler m. buttress.

Streber m. (-, -) place-hunter.

strebsam a. active, industrious.

streckbar a. ductile.

Strecke f. (-, -n) extent, trace; distance; (*rail.*) section.

strecken v.t. to stretch; to extend; *die Waffen ~,* to lay down one's arms; *zu Boden ~,* to fell.

streckenweise adv. in sections.

Streich m. (-[e]s, -e) stroke, blow, lash; trick; *auf einen ~,* at one blow; *einem einen ~ spielen,* to play someone a trick; *ein dummer ~,* a foolish trick; *ein lustiger ~,* a 'lark.'

streicheln v.t. to stroke, to caress.

streichen v.t.st. to rub; (*Butter*) to spread; (*die Flagge*) to strike; (*Segel*) to lower; (*ausstreichen*) to strike out, to erase; ~ v.i. (s) to rove, to stroll.

Streich: ~holz, ~hölzchen n. match; **~instrument** n. stringed instrument; **~music** f. string-music; **~riemen** m. razor-strop.

Streichquartett n. string-quartet.

Streichung f. (-, -en) cut, deleted passage.

Streif m. (-[e]s, -e), **Streifen** m. (-s, -) stripe, streak; strip.

Streifband n. wrapper, cover.

Streife f. (-, -n) raid, razzia; patrol.

streifen v.t. to graze, to touch slightly, to brush; to stripe, to streak; ~ v.i. (s) to ramble, to rove; (h) (*an etwas*) to border, or verge (upon) *in die Höhe ~,* to tuck up (one's sleeves).

streifig a. striped; streaky (bacon).

Streif: ~licht n. side-light; **~schuss** m. grazing shot; **~zug** m. inroad, raid.

Streik m. (-s, -e) strike (of workmen).

Streikbrecher m. (-s, -) blackleg.

streiken v.i. to strike.

streikend a. on strike.

Streik: ~kasse f. strike-fund; **~posten** m. picket.

Streit m. (-[e]s, -e) fight; contest, dispute, quarrel; conflict; *in ~ geraten,* to fall out, to get into a quarrel.

Streitaxt f. battle-axe.

streitbar a. warlike, valiant.

streiten v.i.st. to fight; to dispute, to quarrel; to disagree; *darüber lässt sich ~,* that is a matter of opinion; *die streitenden Parteien,* the contending parties.

Streit: ~frage f. moot point, controversial question; **~gegenstand** m. (*law*) matter in controversy; **~handel** m. dispute.

streitig a. contested, controversial; *einem etwas ~ machen,* to contest one's right to a thing.

Streitigkeit f. (-, -en) contention; controversy; quarrel.

Streit: ~kräfte pl. (military) forces; ~lust f. quarrelsome disposition.

streitlustig a. contentious, litigious.

Streit: ~punkt m. point at issue; ~schrift f. polemic treatise; ~sucht f. contentiousness.

streitsüchtig a. litigious, quarrelsome.

streng[e] a. severe, stern; (Charakter) austere; strict, stringent; ~genommen, strictly speaking.

Strenge f. (-, 0) severity; austerity; rigour (of climate).

strenggläubig a. orthodox.

Streu f. (-, -en) litter.

Streubüchse f. sugar-box.

streuen v.t. to strew; to scatter, to spread; to litter.

Streuzucker m. castor sugar.

Strich m. (-[e]s, -e) stroke, line, dash; (Land~) tract; in einem ~, at a stretch; das macht einen ~ durch die Rechnung, that upsets the whole plan; gegen oder wider den ~, against the grain.

Strichpunkt m. semi-colon.

strichweise adv. here and there.

Strick m. (-[e]s, -e) cord, rope; halter.

Strickbeutel m. knitting-bag.

stricken v.t. to knit.

Strickerei f. (-, -en) knitting.

Strick: ~leiter f. rope-ladder; ~nadel f. knitting-needle; ~waren pl. knitwear.

Striegel m. (-s, -) curry-comb.

striegeln v.t. to curry; (vulg.) to cudgel.

Striemen m. (-s, -), Strieme f. (-, -n) stripe, weal.

strikt a. strict.

Strippe f. (-, -n) strap, band.

strittig a. = streitig.

Stroh n. (-[e]s, 0) straw.

Strohdach n. thatch.

strohern a. (of) straw.

Stroh: ~halm m. straw; ~hut m. strawhat; ~hütte f. thatched hut; ~sack m. straw-mattress, palliasse; ~witwe f. grass-widow; ~witwer m. grasswidower.

Strolch m. (-[e]s, -e) tramp, vagrant.

strolchen v.i. (s) to loaf or prowl about.

Strom m. (-[e]s, Ströme) large river; (elek. usw.) current; (fig.) torrent, flood; gegen den ~, mit dem ~e schwimmen, to swim against, with the stream or the tide.

stromabwärts adv. down stream.

stromaufwärts adv. up stream.

strömen v.i. (s) to stream, to flow; to pour.

Stromer m. (-s, -) vagabond, tramp.

Strom: ~gebiet n. basin; ~kreis m. circuit; ~linien...., streamlined, a.; ~messer m. (elek.) ammeter; ~schnelle f. rapid; ~stärke f. amperage.

Strömung f. (-, -en) current, drift.

Strophe f. (-, -n) stanza, verse.

strophisch a. strophic, in stanzas.

strotzen v.i. to swell, to bulge; teem (with).

Strudel m. (-s, -) whirlpool, eddy; vortex.

Struktur f. (-, -en) structure.

strukturell a. structural.

Strumpf m. (-[e]s, Strümpfe) stocking; (Glüh~), mantle.

Strumpf: ~band n. garter; ~halter m. suspender; ~händler m. hosier; ~ware f. hosiery; ~wirker m. hosiery worker.

struppig a. tousled, bristly, matted (hair).

Struwwelkopf m. tousle-head.

Strychnin (Strich~), n. (-[e]s, 0) strychnine.

Stube f. (-, -n) (living) room, chamber.

Stuben: ~arrest m. confinement in one's own room; ~hocker m. stay-at-home; ~mädchen n. chamber-maid.

Stuck m. (-[e]s, 0) stucco(-work).

Stück n. (-[e]s, -e) piece, bit, morsel; fragment; (Theater) piece, play; (Zucker) lump; ~ für ~, piece by piece; im ~, in the piece; grosse ~e auf einen halten, to think much of someone; aus freien ~en, of one's own accord; in allen ~en, in every respect.

Stückgüter pl. (com.) piece-goods, sundries pl.

stückweise adv. by the piece, piecemeal.

Stückzucker m. lump-sugar.

Student m. (-en, -en) student, undergraduate.

Studentenverbindung f. students' society.

Studentenschaft f. (-, 0) students.

studentisch a. student-like, student.

Studie f. (-, -n) (Maler~) (painter's) study; essay, sketch.

Studien: ~direktor m. head-master (of a secondary school); ~gang m. course of study; ~kopf m. study of a head; ~rat m. assistant master (of a secondary school).

studieren v.t. & i. to study; to read.

Studierende[r] m. (n, -n) = Student.

Studier: ~lampe f. reading-lamp; ~stube f. study.

Studiosus m. (-, -sen u. -si) student, undergraduate.

Studium n. (-s, Studien) study.

Stufe f. (-, -n) step; degree.

stufenartig a. gradual, graduated.

Stufen: ~leiter f. scale; (fig.) gradation; ~scheibe f. (mech.) cone-pulley.

stufenweise adv. gradually, by degrees.

Stuhl m. (-[e]s, Stühle) chair, seat; (ohne Lehne) stool; (Kirchen~) pew; (Stuhlgang) stool; der apostolische ~, the Holy See; sich zwischen zwei Stühle setzen, (fig.) to fall between two stools.

Stuhl: ~bein n. leg of a chair; ~drang m. need of relieving the bowels; ~gang m. (med.) stool; ~lehne f. back of a chair.

Stukkateur *m.* (-s, -e) stucco-worker.

Stukkatur *f.* (-, -en) stucco(-work).

Stulle *f.* (-, -n) slice of bread and butter.

stülpen *v.t.* to cock (a hat); to tilt, to turn up; to put over.

Stulp[en]stiefel *m.* top-boot.

stumm *a.* dumb, mute, silent; ~*er Film m.* silent film.

Stummel *m.* (-s, -) stump, cigar-end.

Stümper *m.* (-s, -) bungler.

Stümperei *f.* (-, -en) bungling.

stümperhaft *a.* bungling.

stümpern *v.t.* to bungle, to botch.

stumpf *a.* obtuse; blunt; dull; ~*er Winkel*, obtuse angle.

Stumpf *m.* (-[e]s, Stümpfe) stump, trunk.

Stumpf: ~**nase** *f.* snub-nose; ~**sinn** *m.* dullness.

stumpfsinnig *a.* stupid, dull.

Stunde *f.* (-, -n) hour; lesson.

stunden *v.t.* to respite.

Stunden: ~**geld** *n.* fee for a lesson; ~**glas** *n.* hour-glass.

stundenlang *a.* lasting for hours.

Stunden: ~**plan** *m.* time-table; ~**zeiger** *m.* hour-hand.

stündlich *a.* & *adv.* hourly; every hour.

Stundung *f.* (-, -en) delay (of payment), respite.

Stundungsfrist *f.* (*com.*) days of grace.

Sturm *m.* (-[e]s, Stürme) gale, storm; tempest; (*mil.*) assault.

Sturm: ~**angriff** *m.* assault; ~**warnung** *f.* gale warning.

stürmen *v.t.* & *i.* to storm; to rush; to assault.

Stürmer (-s, -) (*Fussball*) forward.

stürmisch *a.* stormy, tempestuous.

Sturmwind *m.* heavy gale.

Sturz *m.* (-es, Stürze) rush; fall, ruin; plunge; (*fig.*) overthrow.

Sturzbach *m.* torrent.

sturzbomben *v.t.* to dive-bomb.

stürzen *v.t.* to tilt, to shoot; (*fig.*) to overthrow, to ruin; ~ *v.i.* (*s*) to fall, to tumble down; to rush; *sich in Gefahren* ~, to rush into dangers; *sich in Schulden, Kosten* ~, to plunge into debt, to incur heavy expenses; *ins Elend* ~, to reduce to beggary; *ins Verderben* ~, to undo, to ruin; *ein Ministerium* ~, to overthrow a ministry.

Sturzflug *m.* (*avi.*) nose-dive.

Sturzkampfflieger *m.* dive-bomber.

Stute *f.* (-, -n) mare.

Stutenfüllen *n.* filly.

Stütze *f.* (-, -n) prop, stay; support.

stutzen *v.t.* to curtail; to prune; to crop (ears); to clip, to lop, to trim; ~ *v.i.* to be startled; to stop short.

stützen *v.t.* to prop, to support; to base on; (sich) ~ *v.refl.* to rely upon, to lean against; to refer to.

Stutzer *m.* (-s, -) dandy.

stutzerhaft *a.* dandified.

Stutzflügel *m.* baby grand (piano).

stutzig *a.* ~ *machen*, to startle.

Stützpunkt *m.* point of support; (*des Hebels*) fulcrum; (*mil.*) base.

Stutzschwanz *m.* bob-tail.

subaltern *a.* subaltern, inferior.

Subhastation *f.* (-, -en) forced sale.

Subjekt *n.* (-[e]s, -e) subject; (*fam.*) person, fellow.

subjektiv *a.* subjective.

Subkontrahent *m.* (-en, -en) subcontractor.

Sublimat *n.* (-s, -e) sublimate.

Submission *f.* (-, -en) tender(s).

subordinieren *v.t.* to subordinate.

Subsidiengelder *pl.* subsidies

subskribieren *v.t.* to subscribe (to).

Subskription *f.* (-, -en) subscription.

Substantiv *n.* (-s, -e) noun.

Substanz *f.* (-, -en) substance.

Substrat *n.* (-[e]s, -e) substratum.

subtil *a.* subtle.

Subtrahend *m.* (-en, -en) subtrahend.

subtrahieren *v.t.* to subtract.

subtropisch *a.* subtropic(al).

subventionieren *v.t.* to subsidize.

Subventionierung *f.* (-, -en) subvention, subsidy.

Suche *f.* (-, -n) search; *auf der* ~ *sein*, to be in search (of).

suchen *v.t.* to seek, to look for; (*versuchen*) to endeavour, to try; *er hat hier nichts zu* ~, he has no business here; *gesucht*, wanted; affected; far-fetched.

Sucher *m.* (-s, -) (*phot.*) viewfinder.

Sucht *f.* (-, 0) mania, passion; disease; *fallende* ~, *f.* falling-sickness, epilepsy.

Süden *m.* (-s, 0) south.

Sudelei *f.* (-, -en) bungling work.

sudeln *v.t.* to daub, to scrawl.

Südfrüchte *pl.* fruits grown in the south.

südlich *a.* south(ern).

Südost[en], *m.* south-east.

südöstlich *a.* south-east(ern).

Süd: ~**pol** *m.* South-Pole; ~**see** *f.* South-Sea; ~**seite** *f.* south side.

südwärts *adv.* southward.

Südwester *m.* (-s, -) (*Seemannshut*) southwester, sou'wester.

südwestlich *a.* south-west(ern).

Suff *m.* (-[e]s, 0) (*vulg.*) toping, tippling.

suggerieren *v.t.* to suggest.

Sühne *f.* (-, -n) expiation, atonement.

sühnen *v.t.* to expiate, to atone for.

Sühneverfahren *n.* (-s, -) conciliation proceedings.

Sühneversuch *m.* attempt at reconciliation.

Suite *f.* (-, -n) retinue; set of things.

sukzessiv *a.* successive.

Sultan *m.* (-[e]s, -e) sultan.
Sultanine *f.* (-, -n) sultana.
Sülze *f.* (-, -n) brawn.
Summa *f.* (-, Summen) sum (total).
summarisch *a.* summary.
Summe *f.* (-, -n) sum; sum-total.
summen *v.i.* to buzz, to hum; (*vom Ohr*) to tingle.
summieren (sich) *v.t. & refl.* to add up (to).
Sumpf *m.* (-[e]s, Sümpfe) bog, fen, marsh, swamp.
sumpfig *a.* boggy, marshy, swampy.
Sumpfhuhn *n.* moor-hen.
Sund *m.* (-[e]s, -e) straits *pl.*, sound.
Sünde *f.* (-, -n) sin.
Sünden: ~bock *m.* scapegoat; ~fall *m.* fall (of man); ~vergebung *f.* remission of sins.
Sünder *m.* (-s, -), Sünderin *f.* (-, -nen) sinner.
Sündflut(=Sintflut) *f.* deluge, the Flood.
sündhaft *a.* sinful.
sündig *a.* sinful.
sündigen *v.i.* to sin.
sündlos *a.* sinless.
superklug *a.* (*fam.*) overwise.
Superlativ *m.* (-s, -e) superlative.
Suppe *f.* (-, -n) soup; *einem eine ~ ein-brocken*, to serve one an ill turn.
Suppen: ~fleisch *n.* boiled beef; ~löffel *m.* table-spoon, soup-ladle; ~schüssel *f.* tureen.
surren *v.i.* to hum, to buzz.
Surrogat *n.* (-[e]s, -e) substitute.
suspendieren *v.t.* to suspend.
süss *a.* sweet.
Süsse *f.* (-, 0) sweetness.
Süssen *v.t.* to sweeten.
Süssigkeit *f.* (-, -en) sweetness; *Süssig-keiten f.pl.* sweets, lollipops *pl.*
süsslich *a.* sweetish.
Süsswasser *n.* fresh water.
Sylphe *f.* (-, -n) sylph.
Syllogismus *m.* (-, -gismen) syllogism.
Sylvester[abend] *m.* New Year's eve.
Symbol *n.* (-[e]s, -e) symbol.
Symbolik *f.* (-, 0) symbolism.
symbolisch *a.* symbolic.
Symmetrie *f.* (-, -[e]n) symmetry.
symmetrisch *a.* symmetrical.
Sympathie *f.* (-, -[e]n) sympathy.
sympathisch *a.* congenial.
sympathisieren *v.i.* to sympathize (with).
Symphonie *f.* (-, -[e]n) symphony.
Symptom *n.* (-[e]s, -e) symptom.
symptomatisch *a.* symptomatic (of).
Syndikat *n.* (-es, -e) syndicate.
Syndikus *m.* (-, -dizi *u.* -diken) syndic (legal adviser to town council, etc.).
synkopieren *v.t.* to syncopate.
Synode *f.* (-, -n) synod.
synonym *a.* synonymous.
Syntax *f.* (-, 0) syntax.

Synthese *f.* (-, -n) synthesis.
synthetisch *a.* synthetic.
Syphilis *f.* (-, 0) syphilis.
Syrup *m.* (-s, 0) syrup, (*Am.*) molasses.
System *n.* (-[e]s, -e) system.
systematisch *a.* systematic.
Szene *f.* (-, -n) scene.
Szenerie *f.* (-, -en) scenery.
Szepter *n.* = Zepter.

T

Tabak *m.* (-[e]s, -e) tobacco.
Tabaks: ~beutel *m.* tobacco-pouch; ~dose *f.* snuff-box; ~regie *f.* government monopoly of tobacco.
tabellarisch *a.* tabular, tabulated.
Tabelle *f.* (-, -n) table(s), schedule.
Tablett *n.* (-s, -e) tray.
Tablette *f.* (-, -n) tabloid.
Tachometer *n.* (-s, -) speedometer.
Tadel *m.* (-s, -) blame, censure; fault, blemish.
tadelhaft *a.* blameable.
tadellos *a.* blameless, faultless, perfect.
tadeln *v.t.* to blame, to censure.
tadelnswert *a.* blameworthy.
Tadler *m.* (-s, -) censurer, fault-finder.
Tafel *f.* (-, -n) (dining-)table; (*Wand~*) black-board; (*Stein~*) slab; plate; slate; cake (of chocolate); dinner.
tafelförmig *a.* tabular, table-shaped.
Tafelgeschirr *n.* plate, dinner-service.
tafeln *v.i.* to dine, to sup, to feast.
täfeln *v.t.* to wainscot.
Täfelung *f.* (-, -en) wainscot(ing).
Taffet, Taft *m.* (-[e]s, -e) taffeta.
Tag *m.* (-[e]s, -e) day; light; *es ist heller ~*, it is broad day; *an den ~ kommen*, to come to light; *bei Tage*, in the daytime; *heute über acht ~e*, this day week; *in den ~ hinein*, thoughtlessly.
Tagbau *m.* (*min.*) open cast *or* work.
Tage: ~buch *n.* diary, journal; (*com.*) day-book; ~geld *n.* per diem allowance.
tagelang *a. & adv.* for days together.
Tage: ~lohn *m.* daily wages *pl.*; ~löhner *m.* day-labourer.
Tagemarsch *m.* day's march.
tagen *v.imp.* to dawn; ~ *v.i.* (of assemblies) to meet, to sit.
Tagereise *f.* day's journey.
Tages: ~anbruch *m.* day-break; ~angriff *m.* (*avi.*) daylight attack; ~befehl *m.* (*mil.*) order of the day; ~licht *n.* day-light; *ans ~licht kommem*, to come to light; ~ordnung *f.* agenda, order of the day; ~zeit *f.* time of the day.
tageweise *adv.* by the day.
Tagewerk *n.* day's work, day's task.

taghell *a.* light as day.

täglich *a.* daily; ~*es Geld n.* call money.

tagtäglich *adv.* every (mortal) day.

Tag- und Nachtgleiche *f.* equinox.

Tagung *f.* (-, -en) conference, rally, session.

Taifun *m.* (-s, -e) typhoon.

Taille *f.* (-, -n) waist; figure; bodice.

Takel *n.* (-s, -) (*nav.*) tackle.

takeln *v.t.* to tackle, to rig.

Takelwerk *n.* rigging.

Takt *m.* (-es, -e) time, measure; bar; (*fig.*) tact; ~ *halten*, to keep time; ~ *schlagen* to beat time; *im* ~, in time.

Taktik *f.* (-, -en) tactics *pl.*

Taktiker *m.* (-s, -) tactician.

taktisch *a.* tactical.

taktlos *a.* tactless.

Takt: Takt[ier]stock *m.* baton; ~strich *m.* (*mus.*) bar.

taktvoll *a.* tactful; discreet.

Tal *n.* (-[e]s, Täler) valley, dale, glen.

Talar *m.* (-[e]s, -e) gown, robe.

Talent *n.* (-[e]s, -e) talent; gift, aptitude.

talentvoll *a.* talented, gifted.

Talg *m.* (-[e]s, 0) tallow, suet.

Talglicht *n.* tallow-candle.

Talje *f.* (-, -n) tackle.

Talsperre *f.* dam; reservoir.

Tambour *m.* (-s, -e *u.* -s) drummer.

Tambourin *n.* (-[e]s, -e *u.* -s) tambourine; tambour.

Tand *m.* (-[e]s, 0) knicknacks *pl.* toy(s).

Tändelei *f.* (-, -en) trifling, toying.

tändeln *v.t.* to trifle, to toy, to dandle.

Tang *m.* (-[e]s, -e) sea-weed, sea-wrack.

Tangente *f.* (-, -n) tangent.

Tank *m.* (-[e]s, -s) tank; ~dampfer *m.* tanker.

tanken *v.i.* to refuel.

Tankstelle *f.* (-, -n) service station, petrol station, (*Am.*) gasoline station.

Tanne *f.* (-, -n) fir(-tree), silver-fir.

Tannenzapfen *m.* pine-cone, fir-cone.

Tannin *n.* (-[e]s, 0) tannic acid, tannin.

Tante *f.* (-, -n) aunt.

Tantieme *f.* (-, -n) royalty.

Tanz *m.* (-es, Tänze) dance.

tanzen *v.i.* to dance.

Tänzer[in] *m.* (-s, -) & *f.* (-, -nen) dancer.

Tanz: -gesellschaft *f.* dancing party; ~lehrer, ~meister *m.* dancing-master; ~stunde *f.* dancing-lesson.

Tapet *n.* (-[e]s, -e) (*obs.*) *aufs* ~ *bringen*, to broach *or* to introduce (a subject).

Tapete *f.* (-, -n) wall-paper.

tapezieren *v.t.* to paper; to hang with tapestry.

Tapezier[er] *m.* (-s, -) paper-hanger, upholsterer.

tapfer *a.* brave, valiant.

Tapferkeit *f.* (-, 0) valour, bravery.

tappen *v.i.* to grope; to fumble.

täppisch *a.* awkward, clumsy.

tapsen *v.i.* to lurch along.

tapsig *a.* awkward, clumsy.

Tara *f* (-, 0) (*Gewicht*) (*com.*) tare.

Tarantel *f.* (-, -n) tarantula; *wie von der* ~ *gestochen*, like one possessed.

Tarif *m.* (-s, -e) tariff; scale of wages; railway rate.

Tarifvertrag *m.* collective agreement.

tarnen *v.i.* (*mil.*) to camouflage.

Tarnung *f.* (-, -en) camouflage.

Tarock *m. & n.* (-s, 0) taroc.

Tasche *f.* (-, -n) pocket; bag; (*Schul* ~) satchel.

Taschen: ~ausgabe *f.* pocket edition; ~buch *n.* pocket-book; ~dieb *m.* pick-pocket; ~format *n.* pocket-size; ~geld *n.* pocket-money; ~krebs *m.* crab; ~lampe *f.* electric torch; ~messer *n.* pocket-knife; ~spiel *n.* juggling, sleight-of-hand; ~spieler *m.* conjurer, juggler; ~tuch *n.* pocket-handkerchief; ~uhr *f.* watch.

Tasse *f.* (-, -n) cup (and saucer).

Tastatur *f.* (-, -en) (*mus.*) key-board, keys *pl.*

Taste *f.* (-, -n) (*mus.*) key.

tasten *v.t. & i.* to grope, to feel, to touch.

Taster *m.* (-s, -) feeler, antenna.

Tasterzirkel *m.pl.* (*mech.*) callipers.

Tastsinn *m.* (sense of) touch, feeling.

Tat *f.* (-, -en) action, deed, fact, act; *in der* ~, indeed, as a matter of fact; *auf frischer* ~, in the very act; *mit Rat und* ~, by word and deed.

Tatbestand *m.* facts of the case *pl.*

Tatendrang, Tatendurst *m.* desire of doing great things.

tatenlos *a.* inactive.

Täter *m.* (-s, -) perpetrator (of crime).

tätig *a.* active; busy, industrious.

tätigen *v.t.* to effect, to carry out.

Tätigkeit *f.* (-, -en) activity; *ausser* ~ *setzen*, to suspend.

Tatkraft *f.* energy.

tatkräftig *a.* energetic.

tätlich: *einen* ~ *misshandeln*, to offer violence to someone; ~*werden*, to come to blows; ~*e Beleidigung*, assault and battery.

tätowieren *v.t.* to tattoo.

Tatsache *f.* (-, -n) fact.

tatsächlich *a. & adv.* actual(ly), as a matter of fact, in point of fact.

Tatze *f.* (-, -n) paw, claw.

Tau *n* (-[e]s, -e) cable rope.

Tau *m.* (-[e]s, 0) dew.

taub *a.* deaf.

Taube *f.* (-, -n) pigeon, dove.

Taubheit *f.* (-, 0) deafness.

Taubnessel *f.* dead nettle.

taubstumm *a.* deaf-and-dumb.

tauchen v.t. to dip, to steep, to duck; ~ v.i. to dive, to plunge.

Taucher m. (-s, -) diver.

Taucherglocke f. diving-bell.

tauen v.i.imp. to thaw.

Tauf: ~becken n. (baptismal) font; ~buch n. parish-register.

Taufe f. (-, -n) baptism, christening.

taufen v.t. to christen, to baptize.

Täufer m. (-s, -) Johannes der ~, St. John the Baptist.

Täufling m. (-[e]s, -e) child (or person) to be baptized.

Tauf: ~name m. Christian name; ~pate m. godfather; ~patin f. godmother; ~schein m. certificate of baptism.

taugen v.i. to be good or fit for; nichts ~, to be good for nothing.

Taugenichts m. (-, -nichtse) good-for-nothing; (scherzhaft) scapegrace.

tauglich a. fit, able, qualified; (mil.) able-bodied.

Taumel m. (-s, 0) ecstasy, passion.

taumeln v.i. (s) to reel, to stagger.

Tausch m. (-es, -e) exchange, barter.

tauschen v.t. to exchange, to barter.

täuschen v.t. to deceive, to delude; (sich) ~ v.refl. to be deceived; sich durch etwas ~ lassen, to be deceived by a thing.

täuschend a. deceptive.

Tauschhandel m. barter; ~ treiben, to barter, to truck.

Täuschung f. (-, -en) delusion, illusion; optische ~, optical illusion.

tauschweise adv. by way of exchange.

tausend a. thousand; zu Tausenden, by thousands, in their thousands.

Tausender m. (-s, -) thousand, figure denoting the thousand.

tausenderlei a. of a thousand kinds.

tausendfach, tausendfältig a. thousandfold.

Tausendfuss m. centipede, millipede.

tausendjährig a. millennial; das Tausendjährige Reich, the Millennium.

Tausendkünstler m. Jack-of-all-trades.

tausendmal adv. a thousand times.

Tauziehen n. tug of war.

Taxameter m. (-s, -) taximeter.

Taxator m. (-s, -toren) valuer.

Taxe f. (-, -n) fee, fixed scale of charges; taxi.

taxieren v.t. to value.

Taxushecke f. yew hedge.

Taxwert m. estimated value.

Technik f. (-, 0) technology; (in der Kunst) technique, execution.

Techniker m. (-s, -) (mechanical) engineer.

Technikum n. (-s, -ken) technical school.

technisch a. technical.

technischer Berater m. consulting engineer.

Teckel m. (-s, -) dachshund.

Tedeum n. (-[s], -[s]) Te Deum.

Tee m. (-s, -e u. -s) tea.

Tee: ~brett n. tea-tray; ~büchse f. tea-caddy; ~gesellschaft f. tea-party; ~kanne f. tea-pot; ~kessel m. tea-kettle; ~löffel m. tea-spoon; ~mütze f. tea-cosy; ~satz m. tea-leaves; ~sieb n. strainer; ~service n. tea-set; ~tischdecke f. tea-cloth.

Teer m. (-[e]s, -e) tar.

teeren v.t. to tar.

Teich m. (-[e]s, -e) pond.

Teig m. (-[e]s, -e) dough, paste.

Teil m. (-[e]s, -e) part, portion; division; teilhaben an, to participate; ~nehmen an, to take part in; beide ~e, both parties; zu gleichen ~en, in equal shares; ich für meinen ~, I, for one; for my part; zum ~, partly.

teilbar a. divisible.

Teilchen n. (-s, -) particle.

teilen v.t. to divide; to share.

Teiler m. (-s, -) (ar.) divisor.

Teilhaber m. (-s, -) partner.

Teilhaberschaft f. partnership.

teilhaft(ig) a. participating in; ~ werden, to partake of, to share.

...teilig a. consisting of ... parts.

Teilnahme f. (-, 0) participation; interest, sympathy.

Teilnahmslosigkeit f. (-, 0) indifference.

teilnehmend a. sympathetic.

Teilnehmer m. (-s, -) sharer, partaker; (tel.) subscriber.

teils adv. partly.

Teilung f. (-, -en) division, partition.

teilweise adv. in part(s), partially.

Teilzahlung f. part-payment, instalment.

Teint m. (-s, -s) complexion.

Telegramm n. (-s, -e) telegram, wire.

Telegrammadresse f. telegraphic address.

Telegraph m. (-en, -en) telegraph.

Telegraphen: ~amt n. telegraph office; ~leitung f. telegraph wire or line; ~linie f. telegraph line; ~stange f. telegraph pole.

Telegraphie f. (-, 0) telegraphy; drahtlose ~, wireless (telegraphy).

telegraphieren v.t. to telegraph, to wire; to cable.

telegraphisch a. & adv. telegraphic; by wire, by telegram.

Telegraphist m. (-en, -en) telegraph clerk, operator.

Telephon n. (-[e]s, -e) telephone; bleiben Sie am ~, hold the line, please; ~fräulein n. operator; ~gespräch n. telephone call; ~leitung f. telephone line; ~zelle f. telephone-box.

telephonieren v.t. to telephone.

Teleskop n. (-s, -e) telescope.

Teller m. (-s, -) plate; (hölzerner) trencher.

Tempel m. (-s, -) temple.

Temperafarbe f. distemper; tempera.
Temperament n. (-[e]s, -e) temper.
temperamentvoll a. fiery, spirited.
Temperatur f. (-, -en) temperature; ~ *nehmen*, to take the temperature.
temperieren v.t. to temper.
tempern v.t. (*mech.*) to temper.
Tempo n. (-s, -s u. -pi) (*mus.*) time; movement; pace; speed.
temporär a. temporary.
Tempus n. (-, **Tempora**) (*gram.*) tense.
Tendenz f. (-, -en) tendency; bias, slant.
Tender. m. (-s, -) (engine-)tender.
tendenziös a. biased, tendentious.
Tenne f. (-, -n) threshing-floor.
Tennis n. (-, 0) (lawn) tennis; ~**platz** *m.* tennis court; ~**schläger** m. racket.
Tenor m. (-[e]s, -e u. -nöre) tenor (voice).
Tenorist m. (-en, -en) tenor-singer.
Teppich m. (-[e]s, -e) carpet.
Teppichkehrmaschine f. carpet-sweeper.
Termin m (-[e]s, -e) term, time-limit, (*Am.*) deadline; *einen ~ anberaumen*, (*law*) to fix a hearing.
Termingeschäft n. (dealing) in futures.
Terminologie f. (-, -[e]n) terminology.
Termite f. (-, -n) termite.
Terpentin m. or n. (-s, 0) turpentine.
Terrain n. (-s, -s) ground.
Terrasse f. (-, -n) terrace.
Terrine f. (-, -n) tureen.
Territorium n. (-[s], -rien) territory.
terrorisieren v.t. to terrorize.
Tertia f. (-, -tien) third (in England) fourth and fifth form of a secondary school.
Tertianer m. (-s, -) third-form boy.
Terz f. (-, -en) (*mus.*) third; *grosse ~*, major third; (fencing) tierce.
Terzett n. (-[e]s, -e) terzetto, trio.
Testament n. (-[e]s, -e) testament, will.
testamentarisch, testamentlich a. testamentary, by will.
Testamentsvollstrecker m. executor.
testieren v.i. to make a will; to bequeath; to testify.
teuer a. dear; expensive; *wie ~ ist das?* how much is this?
Teuerung f. (-, -en) dearness, scarcity, dearth.
Teufel m. (-s, -) devil.
teuflisch a. devilish, diabolical.
Text m. (-es, -e) text; context; (*Lied~*) words; (*Opern~*) book.
Textbuch n. libretto, words pl.
Textilien pl. textiles.
Textilindustrie f. textile industry.
Theater n. (-s, -) theatre; stage.
Theater: ~**dichter** m. dramatist, playwright; ~**direktor** m. theatrical manager; ~**kasse** f. box-office; ~**loge** f. box; ~**stück** n. play; ~**zettel** m. play-bill.
theatralisch a. theatrical, stagey.

Theismus m. (-, 0) theism.
Theist m. (-en, -en) theist.
Thema n. (-s, -ta u. -men u. -s) theme, subject, topic.
Theolog m. theologian; divinity student.
Theologie f. (-, -[e]n) theology, divinity.
theologisch a. theological.
Theoretiker m. (-s, -) theorist.
theoretisch a. theoretical.
Theosophie f. theosophy.
Theorie f. (-, -[e]n) theory.
Therapie f. (-, -en) therapy.
Thermometer n. (m.) (-s, -) thermometer.
Thermosflasche f. thermos or vacuum flask.
These f. (-, -n) thesis.
Thomasschlacke f. Thomas slag,basic slag.
Thomasmehl n. Thomas meal.
Thron m. (-[e]s, -e) throne.
thronen v.i. to sit enthroned; to reign.
Thron: ~**erbe** m. heir to the throne; ~**rede** f. King's speech.
Thunfisch m. tunny.
Thymian m. (-s, 0) thyme.
Tiara f. (-, Tiaren) tiara, triple crown.
Tick m. (-[e]s, -e) tap; hobby, fad.
ticken v.i. (*von Uhren*) to tick.
tief a. deep; profound; low; (*von Farben*) dark.
Tief n. (-[e]s, -e) (*Wetterkunde*) low.
Tief: ~**bau** m. deep mining; underground constructions pl.; road construction; ~**blick** m. keen insight.
Tiefdruck m. low pressure.
tiefblickend a. deep-sighted.
Tiefe f. (-, -n) depth; profundity.
Tiefgang m. draught (of a ship).
tiefliegend a. deep-set, sunken.
Tief: ~**punkt** m. nadir; ~**sinn** m. melancholy; profoundness.
tiefsinnig a. thoughtful, pensive; melancholy; profound.
Tiegel (-s, -) crucible; stew pan.
Tier n. (-[e]s, -e) animal; beast, brute.
Tier: ~**arzneikunde** f. veterinary science; ~**arzt** m. veterinary surgeon, 'vet.'; ~**garten** m. Zoological Gardens, Zoo.
tierisch a. animal; brutish, bestial.
Tier: ~**kreis** m. zodiac; ~**quälerei** f. cruelty to animals; ~**reich** n. animal kingdom; ~**schutzverein** m. society for the prevention of cruelty to animals.
Tiger m. (-s, -) tiger.
Tilde f. (-, -n) sign of repetition.
tilgbar a. redeemable.
tilgen v.t. to extinguish, to annul, to cancel; (*eine Schuld*) to discharge.
Tilgung f. (-, -en) cancelling, amortization, payment.
Tilgungsfond m. sinking-fund.
Tinktur f. (-, -en) tincture.
Tinte f. (-, -n) ink; *in der ~ sitzen*, to be in a nice pickle.

Tinten: ~fass *n.* inkstand; ~fisch *m.* cuttle-fish, sepia; ~fleck, ~klecks *m.* blot, ink-spot; ~stift *m.* ink pencil.
Tipp *m.* (-[e]s, -e) tip.
tippen *v.t.* to touch gently, to tap; to type.
Tirade *f.* (-, -n) flourish, tirade.
Tisch *m.* (-es, -e) table; board; (*fig.*) dinner; *bei ~e,* at table; *zu ~e,* to dinner; *den ~ decken,* to lay the cloth; *reinen ~ machen,* to clean the slate.
Tisch: ~decke *f.* table-cloth; table-cover; ~gebet *n.* grace; dinner-party.
Tischler *m.* (-s, -) joiner, cabinet-maker.
Tischlerei *f.* (-, -en) joinery.
tischlern *v.i.* to do joiner's work.
Tisch: ~rücken *n.* table-turning; ~tuch *n.* table-cloth; ~zeug *n.* table-linen.
titanenhaft, titanisch *a.* titanic.
Titel *m.* (-s, -) title; style.
Titel: ~bild *n.* frontispiece; ~blatt *n.* title-page.
Titular...(*in Zus.*), nominal, brevet-.
Titulatur *f.* (-, -en) titles *pl.*
titulieren *v.t.* to style, to title; (sich) ~ *v.refl.* to style oneself.
Toast *m.* (-es, -e) toast; *einen ~ ausbringen,* to drink someone's health.
toben *v.i.* to rage, to storm.
Tobsucht *f.* raving madness, delirium.
Tochter *f.* (-, Töchter) daughter.
Tochtergesellschaft *f.* subsidiary (company).
Tod *m.* (-[e]s, Todesfälle) death, decease.
todbringend *a.* death-dealing, fatal.
Todes: ~angst *f.* agony, mortal fear; ~anzeige *f.* obituary (notice); ~art *f.* manner of death; ~fall *m.* death, decease; (*mil.*) fatal casualty; ~kampf *m.* agony; ~stoss *m.* death-blow; ~strafe *f.* capital punishment; *bei ~,* on pain of death; ~urteil *n.* sentence of death.
Todfeind *m.* deadly enemy.
todkrank *a.* dangerously ill.
tödlich *a.* mortal, deadly.
todmüde *a.* dead-tired, knocked up.
Todsünde *f.* mortal sin.
Toilette *f.* (-, -n) toilet, dressing-table; dress; lavatory; ~ngarnitur *f.* toilet-set; ~nseife *f.* toilet soap.
Toleranz *f.* (-, 0) toleration; (*mech.*) allowance.
toll *a.* mad, frantic.
tollen *v.i.* (*fam.*) to romp, to fool about.
Toll: ~haus *n.* madhouse, bedlam; ~häusler *m.* bedlamite.
Tollheit *f.* (-, -en) madness.
Tollkirsche *f.* deadly nightshade.
tollkühn *a.* foolhardy.
Tollwut *f.* hydrophobia, rabies.
Tolpatsch *m.* (-es, -e) awkward fellow.
Tölpel *m.* (-s, -) awkward fellow.
tölpelhaft, tölpisch *a.* clumsy, awkward.

Tomate *f.* (-. -n) tomato.
Ton *m.* (-[e]s, Töne) sound; tone; note; key; stress, accent; shade, tint; *guter, feiner ~,* 'good form'; *einen andern ~ anschlagen,* (*fig.*) to change one's note; *den ~ angeben,* to set the fashion.
Ton *m.* (-[e]s, -e) clay, potter's earth.
Ton: ~art *f.* (*mus.*) key; ~dichter *m.* musical composer.
tonen *v.t.* to sound; to resound; to tint.
tönern *a.* (of) clay, earthen.
Ton: ~erde *f.* clay; ~fall *m.* cadence; ~film *m.* sound film, talkie; ~kunst *f.* music, musical art; ~leiter *f.* scale, gamut.
tonlos *a.* toneless, feeble; unaccented (syllable).
Tonne *f.* (-, -n) (*Schiffs~*) ton; barrel, tun.
Tonnen: ~gehalt *n.* tonnage; ~gewölbe *n.* barrel-vault.
Tonspur *f.* (*Film*) sound-track.
Tonsur *f.* (-, -en) tonsure.
Tönung *f.* (-, -en) tinge, shading.
Topas *m.* (Topases, Topase) topaz.
Topf *m.* (-[e]s, Töpfe) pot, saucepan; *alles in einen ~ werfen,* (*fig.*) to treat all alike.
Töpfer *m.* (-s, -) potter.
Töpferscheibe *f.* potter's wheel.
Tor *n.* (-[e]s, -e) gate; (*Fussball*) goal.
Tor *m.* (-n, -en) fool.
Torf *m.* (-[e]s, -e *u.* Törfe) peat.
Torheit *f.* folly, foolishness.
Torhüter *m.* goalkeeper.
töricht *a.* foolish, silly.
torkeln *v.i.* (*s*) to stagger, to reel.
Tornister *m.* (-s, -) knapsack; pack; ~funkgerät *n.* pack radio set; ~empfänger *m.* pack receiver.
Torpedo *m.* (-[s] -e) torpedo.
Torpedo: ~boot *n.* torpedo-boat; ~zerstörer *m.* (torpedo) destroyer.
Torso *m.* (-s, -s) torso, trunk.
Tort *m.* (-[e]s, 0) *einem einen ~ antun,* to hurt someone's feelings.
Torte *f.* (-, -n) kind of large rich cake.
Tortur *f.* (-, -en) torture, rack.
Tor: ~wächter *m.* (*Fussball*) goalkeeper; ~weg *m.* gateway.
tosen *v.i.* to roar, to rage.
tot *a.* dead, deceased; *~e Hand,* mortmain; *~es Kapital,* idle capital; *~schlagen,* to slay; to kill (time); *~schiessen,* to shoot dead; *~schweigen,* to hush up (an affair); *sich ~lachen,* to die with laughter; *~geboren,* still-born; ~Geburt *f.* still-birth.
total *a.* total; *~er Krieg,* total war.
Total: ~ausfall *m.* total loss; ~betrag *m.* aggregate amount.
Totalisator *m.* (-s, -en) totalisator.
Tote[r] *m.* (-n, -n) dead person, dead man; *die ~n,* the dead.
töten *v.t.* to kill; (*Nerv*) to deaden

Toten: ~amt *n.* mass for the dead; ~bahre *f.* bier.
totenblass, totenbleich *a.* deadly pale.
Toten: ~feier *f.* obsequies; ~gedenktag *m.* memorial day; ~gräber *m.* gravedigger; ~hemd *n.* shroud, winding-sheet; ~kopf *m.* death's head; ~messe *f.* requiem, mass for the dead; ~schein *m.* certificate of death.
totenstill *a.* silent as the grave.
Totenstille *f.* dead calm.
Totschlag *m.* manslaughter.
totsicher *a.* cocksure.
Tötung *f.* (-, -en) killing, slaying.
Tour *f.* (-, -en) tour, trip.
Tourist *m.* (-en, -en) tourist.
Tournee *f.* (-, -n) tour.
Tournier *n.* (-[e]s, -e) tournament; ~hof *m.* tiltyard.
Trab *m.* (-[e]s, 0) trot; ~ reiten, to trot.
Trabant *m.* (-en, -en) footman; satellite.
traben *v.i.* (s) to trot.
Tracht *f.* (-, -en) fashion, costume; *eine ~ Prügel*, a thrashing.
trachten *v.i.* to strive.
trächtig *a.* in calf, in pup, etc.; pregnant.
traditionell *a.* traditional.
Trag: ~bahre *f.* stretcher, litter; ~balken *m.* beam, transom.
tragbar *a.* portable.
Trage *f.* (-, -n) hand-barrow, litter.
träge *a.* lazy, inert, idle, indolent.
tragen *v.t.st.* to bear; to carry; (*Kleider*) to wear; (sich) ~ *v.refl.* to wear (well, etc.); *bei sich ~*, to carry on the person; *kein Bedenken ~*, not to hesitate or scruple; *die Kosten ~*, to bear the expense; *sich mit etwas ~*, to have one's mind occupied with.
Träger *m.* (-s, -) bearer; carrier, porter; wearer; (*arch.*) beam, girder.
Trägerwelle *f.* (*Radio*) carrier wave.
Tragfähigkeit *f.* capacity.
tragfertig *a.* ready-to-wear.
Tragfläche *f.* (*avi.*) wing.
Trägheit *f.* (-, 0) laziness; (*phys.*) inertia.
Tragiker *m.* (-s, -) tragic poet; tragedian.
tragikomisch *a.* tragicomic(al).
tragisch *a.* tragic; ~ *adv.* tragically.
Tragkraft *f.* bearing-power.
Tragöde *m.* (-n, -n) tragic actor.
Tragödie *f.* (-, -n) tragedy.
Trag: ~riemen *m.* sling, strap; ~weite *f.* range; (*fig.*) bearing, significance.
Train *m.* (-s, 0) (*mil.*) train.
Trainer *m.* (-s, -) coach.
trainieren *v.t.* to train.
Traktat *m. or n.* (-[e]s, -e) treatise.
trällern *v.t.* to hum.
Trambahn *f.* tramway.
trampeln *v.i.* to trample.
Tran (-[e]s, -e) train-oil; blubber.
tranchieren *v.t.* to carve meat.

Tranchiermesser *n.* carving-knife, carver.
Träne *f.* (-, -n) tear.
tränen *v.i.* to run with tears.
tränenlos *a.* tearless.
Trank *m.* (-[e]s, Tränke) drink, beverage; potion, decoction.
Tränke *f.* (-, -n) watering-place (for animals).
tränken *v.t.* to water (cattle), to give to drink; to soak; to impregnate.
transatlantisch *a.* transatlantic.
Transformator *m.* (-s, -en) (*elek.*) transformer; ~enhaus *n.* transformer station.
Transit: ~handel *m.* transit-trade; ~verkehr *m.* transit-traffic.
transitiv *a.* transitive.
Transmission *f.* (-, -en) transmission.
transparent *n.* (-[e]s, -s) transparent picture.
Transport *m.* (-[e]s, -e) transport, haulage; ~flugzeug *n.* transport (plane); ~arbeiter *m.* transport worker; *auf dem ~*, in transit.
transportfähig *a.* transportable.
transportieren *v.t.* to transport.
Transport(mittel), *n.* (*Am.*) transportation.
Transportschiff *n.* transport.
Transportunternehmer *m.* haulage contractor.
transzendental, transcendental.
Trapez *n.* (-es, -e) (*math.*) trapezium; (*Gymnastik*) trapeze.
Trassant *m.* (-en, -en) (*com.*) drawer.
Trassat *m.* (-en, -en) (*com.*) drawee.
trassieren *v.t.* to draw.
Tratte *f.* (-, -n) draft.
Traualtar *m.* (marriage-)altar.
Traube *f.* (-, -n) bunch of grapes; cluster.
traubenförmig *a.* racemose.
Traubenzucker *m.* dextrose.
trauen *v.t.* to marry, to join in wedlock; ~ *v.i.* to trust, to confide in; (sich) ~ *v.refl.* to venture, to dare; *sich ~ lassen*, to get married.
Trauer *f.* (-, 0) mourning; mourning-dress; affliction; ~ *haben um*, to be in mourning for.
Trauer: ~fall *m.* death, mournful event; ~flor *m.* crape; ~geleit *n.* funeral procession; ~kleid *n.* mourning (dress); ~marsch *m.* funeral march.
trauern *v.i.* to mourn; to be in mourning (for).
Trauer: ~spiel *n.* tragedy; ~weide *f.* weeping-willow; ~zug *m.* funeral procession.
Traufe *f.* (-, -n) eaves *pl.*; gutter; water dripping from the eaves; *aus dem Regen in die ~ kommen*, to drop from the frying pan into the fire.
träufeln *v.t. & i.* to drip, to trickle.
traulich *a.* cordial, intimate; cozy.

Traum m. (-[e]s, Träume) dream.
träumen v.t. & i. to dream.
Träumer m. (-s, -) dreamer; (fig.) visionary.
Träumerei f. (-, -en) reverie.
träumerisch a. dreamy.
traumhaft a. dreamlike.
traurig a. mournful, sad, dismal.
Trau: ~ring m. wedding-ring; ~schein m. certificate of marriage.
Trauung f. (-, -en) marriage-ceremony.
Traverse f. (-, -n) (mech.) traverse.
Treff n. (-s, 0) (Kartenspiel) club.
treffen v.t.st. to hit; to meet (with); to befall; ihn trifft die Schuld, it is his fault; sein Bild ist gut getroffen, his portrait is a good likeness; es trifft sich gut, it is lucky; Anstalten, Vorkehrungen ~, to take measures, precautions; sich ~, to happen; to meet.
Treffen n. (-s, -) battle; meeting; rally.
treffend a. appropriate to the purpose.
Treffer m. (-s, -) prize (in a lottery).
trefflich a. excellent, exquisite.
Treffpunkt m. meeting place, venue.
Treibeis n. floating ice.
treiben v.t.st. to drive, to propel; (fig.) to urge, to impel, to incite; (Gewerbe) to carry on, to do, to exercise; (Blätter) to put forth; ~ v.i.st. to float, to drift; auf die Spitze, aufs Äusserste ~, to carry to excess; in die Enge ~, to drive into a corner; die Preise in die Höhe ~, to send or force the prices up; Musik ~, to study or practise music; alte Sprachen ~, to work at Latin and Greek; Aufwand ~, to live in great style; sein Wesen ~, to be at it (again).
Treibhaus n. hothouse, greenhouse.
Treib: ~holz n. drift-wood; ~jagd f. battue; ~rad n. driving-wheel; ~riemen m. driving-belt; ~sand m., Triebsand m. quicksands pl.
tremulieren v.t. to quaver, to trill.
trennbar a. separable.
trennen v.t. to separate, to sever; to disunite; (sich) ~v. refl. to part.
Trennschärfe f. (Radio) selectivity.
Trennung f. (-, -en) separation; parting.
trepanieren v.t. to trepan.
Treppe f. (-, -n) staircase, (Am.) stairway; stairs; flight of stairs; treppauf, treppab, up and down the stairs; eine, zwei ~n hoch wohnen, to live on the first, second floor.
Treppen: ~absatz m. landing; ~geländer, n. bannisters pl.
Tresor m. (-s, -s) safe, vault.
Tresse f. (-, -n) galloon, lace; (mil.) stripe.
treten v.i. & i.st. to tread; to step; to trample (upon); einem zu nahe ~, to hurt someone's feelings; an die Spitze ~, to take the lead; an die Stelle eines ~, to

take another's place; aus den Ufern ~, to overflow its banks; in den Vordergrund ~, to come to the front.
Tretmühle f. tread-mill.
treu a. faithful, true; zu ~en Händen, in trust.
Treubruch m. breach of faith.
treubrüchig a. faithless, perfidious.
Treue f. (-, 0) faithfulness, fidelity; allegiance, loyalty; auf Treu und Glauben, on trust.
Treueid schwören, to swear allegiance.
Treuhand f. trust; ~gesellschaft f. trust company.
treuherzig a. frank, artless.
Treuhänder m. trustee.
treulos a. faithless, perfidious.
Triangel m. (-s, -) triangle.
Tribunal n. (-[e]s, -e) tribunal.
Tribüne f. (-, -n) platform; (grand-) stand (at races).
Tribut m. (-[e]s, -e) tribute; seinen ~ entrichten, zollen, to pay one's tribute.
tributpflichtig a. tributary.
Trichine f. (-, -n) trichina.
Trichter m. (-s, -) funnel; (Granat~) crater.
Trick m. (-s, -s) trick, dodge.
Trickfilm m. cartoon film.
Trieb m. (-[e]s, -e) sprout, shoot; impulse, bent, instinct.
Trieb: ~feder f. motive; ~rad n. driving-wheel; ~wagen m. (rail.) motor carriage; ~werk n. mechanism, action, gear.
triefäugig a. blear-eyed.
triefen v.i. & st. to drip, to trickle; seine Augen ~, his eyes run.
triefnass a. dripping wet.
Triennium n. (-[s], -nien) period of three years.
Trift f. (-, -en) pasturage, common.
triftig a. weighty, cogent, forcible.
Trikot m. (-s, -s) tights, fleshings pl.
Trikotagen pl. stockinet goods.
Triller m. (-s, -) trill; quaver; shake.
trillern v.i. to trill, to quaver; (Vögel) to warble.
Trilogie f. (-, -n) trilogy.
Trinität f. (-, 0) Trinity.
trinkbar a. drinkable, potable.
Trinkbecher m. mug.
trinken v.t. & i.st. to drink; to imbibe; er trinkt, he is a drunkard.
Trinker m. (-s, -) drunkard.
Trink: ~gelage n. drinking-bout; ~geld n gratuity, tip; ~halm m. drinking straw ~wasser n. drinking water.
Trio n. (-[s], -e) trio.
Tripper m. (-s, -) (med.) gonorrhœa.
Triptychon n. triptych.
Tritt m. (-[e]s, -e) tread, step, pace; kick; (Spur) footstep; steps; ~ halten, to keep pace; im ~, in step.

Tritt: ~brett, *n.* step; (*mot.*) running-board; ~leiter *f.* steps *pl.*

Triumph *m.* (-[e]s, -e) triumph.

Triumphbogen *m.* triumphal arch.

triumphieren *v.i.* to triumph.

Triumphzug *m.* triumphal procession.

Triumvirat *n.* (-[e]s, -e) triumvirate.

trivial *a.* & *adv.* trite, trivial(ly).

Trivialität *f.* (-, -en) triviality, triteness; (*konkret*) platitude.

Trochäus *m.* (-, -chäen) trochee.

trocken *a.* dry, arid; barren; (*fig.*) plain; prosy; *auf dem Trocknen sitzen*, to be stony-broke.

Trocken: ~dock *n.* dry dock; ~ei *n.* dried egg; ~milch *f.* evaporated milk.

Trockenlegung *f.* drainage, draining.

trocknen *v.t.* & *i.* to dry, to dry up.

Troddel *f.* (-, -n) tassel.

Trödel *m.* (-s, 0) lumber, junk.

Trödelei *f.* (-, -en) (*fig.*) dawdling.

Trödelhandel *m.* second-hand *or* curiosity shop.

trödelhaft *a.* dilatory, dawdling.

trödeln *v.i.* to tarry, to dawdle.

Trog *m.* (-[e]s, Tröge) trough.

trollen (sich) *v.refl* to be off, to skedaddle.

Trommel *f.* (-, -n) drum.

Trommel: ~fell *n.* (*Ohr*) tympanum; ~feuer *n.* drum fire.

trommeln *v.i.* to drum, to beat the drum.

Trommel: ~schlegel *m.* drumstick; ~wirbel *m.* roll of drums.

Trommler *m.* (-s, -) drummer.

Trompete *f.* (-, -n) trumpet.

trompeten *v.i.* to (sound the) trumpet.

Trompeter *m.* (-s, -) trumpeter.

Tropen *pl.* tropics *pl.*

Tropf *m.* (-[e]s, Tröpfe) simpleton, dunce.

tröpfeln, tropfen *v.t.* &. *i.* to drop; to trickle, to drip.

Tropfen *m.* (-s, -) drop; bead (of perspiration).

tropfenweise *adv.* by drops.

Tropfstein *m.* stalactite.

Trophäe *f.* (-, -n) trophy.

tropisch *a.* tropical.

Tross *m.* (Trosses, Trosse) baggage-(train).

Trosse *f.* (-, -n) cable, hawser.

Trost *m.* (-es, 0) consolation, comfort; *schwacher* ~, cold comfort; *nicht recht bei* ~e *sein*, to be not all there.

trost: ~bedürftig *a.* in need of consolation; ~bringend *a.* consolatory.

trösten *v.t.* to console; *sich über etwas* ~, to get reconciled to a thing.

tröstlich *a.* comforting, consoling.

trostlos *a.* inconsolable, disconsolate.

trostreich *a.* comforting, consoling.

Tröstung *f.* (-, -en) consolation.

Trott *m.* (-[e]s, 0) trot.

Trottel *m.* (-s, -) milksop, fool, idiot.

trotten *v.i.* (*s*) to trot, to trudge.

Trottoir *n.* (-[e]s, -e *u.* -s) (foot-) pavement, sidewalk.

Trotz *m.* (-es, 0) defiance.

trotz *pr.* in spite of; ~dem *adv.* nevertheless; ~ *alledem*, for all that; ~dem (*dass*), although.

trotzen *v.i.* to brave, to defy.

trotzig *a.* defiant; pig-headed; sulky.

trüb(e) *a.* troubled, muddy, thick; dim, dull; *im trüben fischen*, (*fig.*) to fish in troubled waters.

Trubel *m.* (-s, 0) hubbub, bustle.

trüben *v.t.* to trouble, to dim.

Trübsal *f.* (-, -e) affliction, calamity.

trübselig *a.* woeful, doleful.

Trübsinn *m.* melancholy; dejection.

Trüffel *f.* (-, -n) truffle.

Trug *m.* (-[e]s, 0) deceit, fraud; delusion.

Trugbild *n.* phantom.

trügen *v.t.* & *i.st.* to deceive, to delude.

trügerisch, trüglich *a.* deceitful, illusory.

Trugschluss *m.* logical fallacy, sophism.

Truhe *f.* (-, -n) chest, trunk.

Trümmer *pl.* fragments; ruins *pl.*

trümmerhaft *a.* ruinous.

Trumpf *m.* (-[e]s, Trümpfe) trump.

trumpfen *v.t.* to trump.

Trunk *m.* (-[e]s, Trünke) potion.

trunken *a.* drunken; tipsy.

Trunkenbold *m.* (-[e]s, -e) drunkard.

Trunksucht *f.* dipsomania.

Trupp *m.* (-[e]s, -s) troop, band; flock.

Truppe *f.* (-, -n) troop.

Truppen *f.pl.* troops, forces *pl.*

Truppen: ~gattung *f.* arm *or* branch of service; ~teil *m.* organization; ~transportschiff *n.* troopship; ~übungsplatz *m.* troop training ground.

truppweise *adv.* in troops, in flocks.

Truthahn *m.* turkey(-cock).

Trutz *m.* (-es, 0) defiance, attack.

Tschako *m.* (-s, -s) shako.

Turberkel *f.* (-, -n) tubercle.

tuberkulös *a.* tubercular, tuberculous.

Tuberkulose *f.* (-, 0) tuberculosis.

Tuch *n.* (-[e]s, Tuche) cloth; (*pl. Tücher*) shawl; neckerchief; *Tuche pl.* different sorts of cloth.

tuchen *a.* (made of) cloth.

Tuch: ~händler *m.* cloth-merchant, draper; ~muster *n.* swatch.

tüchtig *a.* able, apt, fit; excellent; ~ *adv.* thoroughly.

Tücke *f.* (-, -n) treachery.

tückisch *a.* treacherous.

Tuff *m.* (-[e]s, -e), Tuffstein *m.* tufa, tuff.

Tüftelei *f.* (-, -en) subtlety, hair-splitting.

Tugend *f.* (-, -en) virtue.

tugendhaft *a.* virtuous.

tugendsam *a.* virtuous.
Tüll *m.* (-[e]s, -e) tulle, bobbinet.
Tulpe *f.* (-, -n) tulip.
Tulpenzwiebel *f.* tulip-bulb.
tummeln *v.t.* to exercise (*Pferd*); (sich) ~ *v.refl.* to bestir oneself.
Tummelplatz *m.* (-es, -) play-ground.
Tümpel *m.* (-s, -) pool, puddle.
Tumult *m.* (-[e]s, -e) tumult, riot.
tumultuarisch *a.* tumultuous, riotous.
tun *v.t. & i.st.* to do, to make; to perform, to act; ~ *als ob,* to make as if, to pretend to...; *mit einem schön~,* to cajole; *er tut nur so,* it's all a sham, it's all make-believe; *es tut nichts,* it does not matter; *es tut mir leid,* I am sorry (for); *ich kann nichts dazu ~,* I cannot help it; *das hat damit nichts zu ~,* that has nothing to do with it; *es ist mir sehr darum zu ~,* I feel very anxious about it
Tun *n.* (-s, 0) doing.
Tünche *f.* (-, -n) whitewash.
tünchen *v.t.* to whitewash.
Tunichtgut *m.* (-s, -se) ne'er-do-well.
Tunke *f.* (-, -n) gravy; sauce.
tunken *v.t.* to dip, to steep.
tunlich *a.* feasible, practicable.
Tunnel *m.* (-s, -[s]) tunnel.
tupfen *v.t. & i.* to tip; to dab.
Tür *f.* (-, Türen) door.
Turban *m.* (-[e]s, -e) turban.
Turbine *f.* (-, -n) turbine.
Tür: ~angel *f.* (door)hinge; ~flügel *m.* leaf of a door; ~füllung *f.* door-panel; ~hüter *m.* doorkeeper; ~rahmen *m.* door-frame; ~pfosten *m.* doorpost.
Türkis *m.* (-kises, -kise) turquoise.
türkisch *a.* Turkish; ~er Weizen, maize, Indian corn.
Tür: ~klinke *f.* latch, door handle; ~klopfer *m.* knocker.
Turm *m.* (-[e]s, Türme) tower; turret; (*im Schach*) rook castle.
türmen *v.t.* to run away; (sich) ~ *v.refl.* to tower.
turmhoch *a.* towering, very high.
Turnanstalt *f.* gymnasium.
turnen *v.t. & i.* to practise gymnastics *or* athletics.
Turnen *n.* (-s, 0) gymnastics.
Turner *m.* (-s, -) gymnast.
Turn: ~halle *f.* (covered) gymnasium; ~hose *f.* shorts *pl.*
Turnier *n.* (-[e]s, -e) tournament, joust.
turnieren *v.i.* to joust, to tilt.
Turnierplatz *m.* the lists *pl.*
Turn: ~schuh *m.* gym-shoe; ~übung *f.* gymnastic exercise, gymnastics.
Tür: ~schild *n.* door-plate; ~schwelle *f.* threshold.
Turteltaube *f.* turtle-dove.
Tusch *m.* (-es, -e) flourish.
Tusche *f.* (-, -n) Indian ink.

tuscheln *v.i.* to whisper secretly.
Tüte *f.* (-, -n) paper-bag.
tuten *v.t. & i.* to toot; (*mot.*) to honk.
Tüttelchen *n.* (-s, -) dot, jot.
Typ *m.* (-s, -en), Type *f.* (-, -n) type.
Typhus *m.* (-, 0) typhoid.
typisch *a.* typical.
typographisch *a.* typographical.
Typus *m.* (-, Typen) type.
Tyrann *m.* (-en, -en) tyrant.
Tyrannei *f.* (-, -en) tyranny.
tyrannisch *a.* tyrannic(al).
tyrannisieren *v.t.* to tyrannize over, to oppress; to bully.

U

U *n.* (the letter) U; *einem ein X für ein ~ machen,* to bamboozle, to hoodwink someone.
übel *a.* evil, bad; sick; ~ *adv.* ill, badly; *wohl oder ~,* willy-nilly; *es bekommt ihm ~,* it disagrees with him; *~nehmen,* to take ill *or* amiss; *~daran sein,* to be in a sad plight; *mir wird ~,* I feel sick.
Übel *n.* (-s, -) evil; disease; injury.
Übelbefinden *n.* indisposition.
übel: ~gelaunt *a.* cross, out of humour; ~gesinnt *a.* evil-minded; hostile.
Übelkeit *f.* (-, -en) sickness, nausea.
übellaunig *a.* ill-humoured, cross.
übelriechend *a.* strong-smelling.
Übel: ~stand *m.* inconvenience, nuisance; drawback; ~tat *f.* misdeed, crime; ~täter *m.* evil-doer, criminal.
übelwollend *a.* malevolent.
üben *v.t.* to exercise; to practise; (*mil.*) to drill, to train; *geübt sein in,* to be versed in.
über *pr.* over, above; about; across, beyond; by, on, upon; more than; ~ *und ~,* all over; ~ *Berlin reisen,* to travel via Berlin; *Fehler ~ Fehler,* blunder upon blunder; *~dies,* besides, moreover; *heute ~ 8 Tage,* this day week; ~ *zwanzig,* more than twenty; 10 *Minuten ~ 4 Uhr,* ten minutes past four; ~ *kurz oder lang,* sooner or later; *~Nacht,* over night; *tags~,* during daytime; *einem ~ sein,* to surpass someone; (*mil.*) *Gewehr über!* slope arms!
überall *adv.* everywhere, throughout; *von ~her,* from everywhere; *~hin,* in all directions.
Überangebot *n.* excessive supply.
überanstrengen *v.t.* to strain; (sich) ~ *v.refl.* to over-exert oneself.
Überanstrengung *f.* over-exertion.
überantworten *v.t.* to deliver (up).

überarbeiten *v.t.* to touch up, to retouch; (sich) ~ *v.refl.* to over-work oneself.
überaus *adv.* exceedingly.
Überbau *m.* superstructure.
überbelichten *v.t.* (*phot.*) to over-expose.
überbieten *v.t.st.* to outbid; to outdo.
Überbleibsel *n.* (-s, -) remainder.
Überblick *m.* general view; survey.
überblicken *v.t.* to survey.
überbringen *v.t.st.* to deliver, to bring.
Überbringer *m.* bearer.
überbrücken *v.t.* to bridge.
Überbrückungskredit *m.* (*com.*) short term credit, temporary accommodation.
Überbürdung *f.* (-, -en) excessive labour.
überdachen *v.t.* to roof in.
überdauern *v.t.* to outlast.
überdies *adv.* besides, moreover.
überdosieren *v.t.* to overdose.
Überdruck *m.* over-pressure; (*auf Marken*) surcharge.
Überdruss *m.* (-drusses, 0) disgust.
überdrüssig *a.* disgusted with.
übereilen *v.t.* to precipitate; (sich) ~ *v.refl.* to be over-hasty.
übereilt *a.* precipitate, rash.
Übereilung *f.* (-, -en) precipitation, rush.
übereinander *adv.* one upon another.
übereinkommen *v.i.st.* (*s*) to agree.
Übereinkommen *n.* (-s, -) agreement; *ein ~ treffen*, to make an agreement.
Übereinkunft *f.* (-, -künfte) agreement.
übereinstimmen *v.t.* to agree.
übereinstimmend *a.* in conformity with.
Übereinstimmung *f.* (-, -en) agreement.
überessen (sich) *v.refl.* to overeat.
überfahren *v.t.* to run over.
Über: ~fahrt *f.* passage; ~fall *m.* sudden attack; raid.
Überfallkommando *n.* flying squad.
überfallen *v.t.st.* to surprise, to attack suddenly; (*Nacht*) to overtake.
überfällig, *a.* overdue.
überfein *a.* over-refined, fastidious.
überfliegen *v.t.* to fly over; to glance over (a book).
überfliessen *v.i.st.* (*s*) to overflow.
überflügeln *v.t.* to outstrip.
Überfluss *m.* abundance, profusion.
überflüssig *a.* superfluous, needless.
überfluten *v.t.* to overflow.
überfordern *v.t.* to overcharge.
überführen *v.t.* to convey across; to convict; to convince.
Überführung *f.* (-, -en) conviction.
Überfülle *f.* superabundance.
überfüllen *v.t.* to cram, to glut.
überfüllt *a.* overcrowded.
Überfüllung *f.* overcrowding, congestion; repletion.

überfüttern *v.t.* to overfeed.
Übergabe *f.* delivery; surrender.
Übergang *m.* passage; change, transition; crossing; ~ *für Fahrzeuge*, vehicle crossing; ~ *für Fussgänger*, pedestrian crossing.
Übergangs: ~bestimmungen *pl.* temporary regulations *pl*; ~zeit *f.* period of transition, transition stage.
übergeben *v.t.* to deliver (up), to hand over, to turn over; (*mil.*) to surrender; (sich) ~ *v.refl.* to vomit; to surrender.
übergehen *v.t.st.* to pass over; to omit; to skip, to revise; *mit Stillschweigen ~* to pass over in silence; ~ *v.i.* (*s*) (*mil.*) to go over.
übergenug *adv.* enough and to spare.
Übergewicht *n.* over-weight, excess weight; preponderance.
überglücklich *a.* overjoyed.
übergreifen *v.i.* to encroach (on).
Übergriff *m.* encroachment.
übergross *a.* huge, oversized.
Überguss *m.* icing.
überhand *adv.* ~ *nehmen*, to gain too much ground.
überhäufen *v.t.* to overload.
überhaupt *adv.* in general; at all.
überheben *v.t.st.* (sich) ~ *v.refl.st.* to be overbearing.
überheblich *a.* arrogant.
Überhebung *f.* (-, -en) presumption.
überheizen *v.t.* to overheat.
überhin *adv.* superficially.
überhitzen *v.t.* to overheat.
überhoben *a.* ~ *sein*, to be spared (the trouble).
überholen *v.t.* to overhaul; to overtake, to pass (*Verkehr*).
überhören *v.t.* to miss a word; to overhear.
überirdisch *a.* superhuman, supernatural.
überkippen *v.i.* (*s*) to tilt over.
überkleben *v.t.* to paste over.
Überkleid *n.* outer garment; overall.
überklug *a.* overwise, conceited.
überkochen *v.i.* (*s*) to boil over.
überkommen *v.t.st.* to be transmitted.
Überkultur *f.* over-refinement.
überladen *v.t.st.* to overload.
Überland: ~reise *f.* overland journey; ~zentrale *f.* (*elek.*) (super) power station.
überlassen *v.t.st.* to cede; (sich) ~ *v.refl.st.* to give oneself up to.
Überlassung *f.* (-, -en) cession, abandonment.
überlaufen *v.t.st.* to overrun; to importune; *es überläuft mich,* I shudder; ~ *v.i.st.* (*s*) to go over.
Überläufer *m.* deserter; turncoat.
überlaut *a.* too *or* very loud, noisy.

überleben *v.t.* to outlive, to survive; *diese Sache hat sich überlebt*, the thing is out of date altogether.

Überlebende[r] *m.* survivor.

überlebensgross *a.* more than lifesize.

überlegen *v.t. & refl.* (*sich ~*) to reflect upon, to consider, to think over; ~ *a.* superior.

Überlegenheit *f.* (-, 0) superiority.

überlegt *a.* well-weighed, deliberate.

Überlegung *f.* (-, -en) deliberation; consideration.

überleiten *v.t.* to transmit.

Überleitung *f.* (-, -en) cross-over.

überlesen *v.t.st.* to read over.

überliefern *v.t.* to surrender; to hand down (to posterity, etc.)

Überlieferung *f.* tradition.

überlisten *v.t.* to outwit, to dupe.

übermachen *v.t.* to make over.

Übermacht *f.* preponderance; superior force, odds.

übermächtig *a.* overwhelming.

übermalen *v.t.* to paint over.

übermannen *v.t.* to overpower.

Übermass *n.* excess.

übermässig *a.* exorbitant, excessive.

Übermensch *m.* superman.

übermitteln *v.t.* to convey, to transmit.

übermorgen *adv.* the day after to-morrow.

Übermüdung *f.* (-, 0) over-fatigue.

Übermut *m.* insolence; sportiveness.

übermütig *a.* frolicsome; overweening.

übernachten *v.i.* to pass the night.

Übernachtungsunterkunft *f.* overnight, accommodation.

Übernahme *f.* (-, 0) taking possession of, taking charge of.

übernatürlich *a.* supernatural.

übernehmen *v.t.st.* to take possession of, to take upon oneself; (sich) ~ *v.refl.* to overtask oneself.

überordnen *v.t.* to place *or* set over.

Überproduktion *f.* over-production.

überqueren *v.t.* to cross.

überragen *v.t.* to surpass.

überraschen *v.t.* to surprise.

Überraschung *f.* (-, -en) surprise.

überreden *v.t.* to persuade.

Überredung *f.* (-, -en) persuasion.

überreich *a.* abounding (in).

überreichen *v.t.* to hand over, to present.

überreichlich *adv.* exuberantly.

überreif *a.* over-ripe.

überreizen *v.t.* to over-excite; to strain.

überrennen *v.t.* to overrun.

Überrest *m.* remainder, residue, remnant.

Überrock *m.* top-coat.

überrumpeln *v.t.* to (take by) surprise.

übers = über das.

übersäen *v.t.* to strew; to stud.

übersättigen *v.t.* to surfeit, to cloy.

überschatten *v.t.* to overshadow.

überschätzen *v.t.* to overrate.

Überschau *f.* (-, 0) review, survey.

überschauen *v.t.* to survey, to overlook.

überschäumen *v.i.* (*h, s*) to overflow with foam *or* froth.

überschicken *v.i.* to transmit.

überschiessen *v.i.* to overshoot.

Überschlag *m.* estimate, rough calculation; (*am Rock*) facing.

überschlagen *v.t.st.* to estimate.

überschnappen *v.i.* (*s*) to squeak; (*fig.*) to turn crazy.

überschneiden (sich) *v.refl.* to overlap partially.

überschreiben *v.t.st.* to transfer.

Überschreibung *f.* transfer.

überschreien *v.t.st.* to cry down; (sich) ~ *v.refl.st.* to overstrain one's voice.

überschreiten *v.t.st.* to pass, to exceed; to go beyond; to cross.

Über: ~schrift *f.* heading; title; ~schuh *m.* goloshes *pl.*

Überschuh *m.* overshoe.

überschuldet *a.* overburdened with debt.

Überschuss *m.* surplus, excess.

überschüssig *a.* surplus (money, etc.).

überschütten, *v.t.* to cover (with).

Überschwang *m.* exuberance.

überschwemmen *v.t.* to flood, to inundate, to submerge.

Überschwemmung *f.* inundation, flood.

überschwenglich *a.* exuberant.

Übersee *n.* oversea(s).

überseeisch *a.* transatlantic, oversea.

übersehbar *a.* admitting of estimation.

übersehen *v.t.st.* to omit; to overlook; to disregard; to let pass; to survey.

übersein, *v.ir.*(*fam.*) *das ist mir über*, I am sick of it; *er ist dir über*, he has the better of you.

übersenden *v.t.st.* to transmit.

Übersendung *f.* transmission.

übersetzen *v.t.* to ferry across; to translate; ~ *v.i.* (*s*) to leap over; to pass over, to cross.

Übersetzung *f.* (-, -en) translation, version; (*Fahrrad*) gear; *grosse ~*, high gear; *kleine ~*, low gear.

Übersicht *f.* (-, -en) survey; summary.

übersichtlich *a.* well arranged.

Übersichtstafel *f.* chart.

übersiedeln *v.i.* (*s*) to remove (to).

übersinnlich *a* metaphysical.

überspannen *v.t.* to span; to overstrain; (*fig.*) to exaggerate.

überspannt *a.* (*fig.*) eccentric.

überspringen *v.t.st.* to leap over; (*fig.*) to skip.

übersprudeln *v.i.* to bubble over.

überstehen *v.t.st.* to get over; (*einen Sturm*) to weather, to outride.

übersteigen *v.t.st.* to surmount; to surpass, to exceed.

überstellen *v.t.* to hand over.

überstimmen *v.t.* to outvote.

überstrahlen *v.t.* to outshine; to shine upon.

überströmen *v.t.* to flood, to overwhelm; ~ *v.i.* (*s*) to overflow; to abound.

Überstunden *pl.* overtime; ~ *machen*, to work overtime.

überstürzen *v.t.* to hasten, to precipitate; (sich) ~ *v.refl.* to act rashly.

übertäuben *v.t.* to stun, to deafen.

übertölpeln *v.t.* to dupe, to take in.

übertönen *v.t.* to drown a sound.

Übertrag *m.* (-[e]s, -träge) sum carried over; carry over.

übertragbar *a.* transferable; negotiable; (*med.*) catching.

übertragen *v.t.st.* to translate; to transfer; to carry over; to confer (an office upon one); (*Befugnis*) to delegate; (*Schrift*) to transcribe; (*Blut*) to transfuse; ~ *a.* figurative, metaphorical.

Übertragung *f.* (-, -en) transfer, cession; translation; (*tech.*) transmission.

übertreffen *v.t.st.* to surpass, to excel.

übertreiben *v.t.st.* to exaggerate; to overdo, to overact.

Übertreibung *f.* (-, -en) exaggeration.

übertreten *v.t.st.* to transgress, to trespass (against), to infringe; ~ *v.i.st.* (*s*) to go over.

Übertretung *f.* (-, -en) violation, transgression.

übertrieben *a.* excessive, exaggerated.

Übertritt *m.* (*Kirche*) conversion.

übertrumpfen *v.t.* to outdo.

übertünchen *v.t.* to whitewash.

übervölkern *v.t.* to overpopulate.

Übervölkerung *f.* (-, 0) over population.

übervoll *a.* overfull.

übervorteilen *v.t.* to overreach.

überwachen *v.t.* to superintend, to control.

Überwachung *f.* supervision, control, surveillance; ~sstelle *f.* control office.

überwältigen *v.t.* to overpower.

überweisen *v.t.st.* to assign, to transfer.

Überweisung *f.* transfer, remittance.

überwerfen *v.t.st.* to huddle on; sich ~ *v.refl.st.* to fall out (with).

überwiegen *v.t.st.* to preponderate (over).

überwiegend *a.* preponderating.

überwinden *v.t.st.* to overcome, to vanquish; (sich) ~ *v.refl.st.* to prevail on oneself.

Überwindung *f.* (-, -en) conquest; effort; (*Selbst~*) self-command.

überwintern *v.i.* to pass the winter; to hibernate.

überwölken (sich) *v.refl.* to get overcast.

überwuchern *v.t.* to overgrow luxuriantly, to stifle.

Überwurf *m.* cloak, wrapper.

Überzahl *f.* (-, 0) numerical superiority.

überzählig *a.* supernumerary, surplus.

überzeichnen *v.t.* (*com.*) to oversubscribe.

Überzeichnung *f.* (-, -en) oversubscription.

überzeugen *v.t.* to convince (of).

überzeugend *a.* convincing, conclusive.

Überzeugung *f.* (-, -en) conviction.

überziehen *v.t.st.* to cover; (*Bett*) to put fresh sheets on; (account) to overdraw; (sich) ~ *v.refl.st.* to become overcast.

Überzieher *m.* (-s, -) over-coat, top-coat.

überzuckern *v.t.* to candy, to ice.

Überzug *m.* cover, coat(ing); bed-slip.

überzwerch *a.* athwart, across.

üblich *a.* usual, customary, in use.

U-boot *n.* submarine; **U-boot Bunker** *m.* submarine pen.

übrig *a.* remaining, left; ~bleiben, to be left; *im übrigen*, for the rest; ~sein, to be left; ~behalten, to keep, to spare; ~haben, to have...left *or* to spare; ~lassen, to leave; *das Übrige, die Übrigen*, the rest.

übrigens *adv.* by the way.

Übung *f.* (-, -en) exercise, practice; (*mil.*) drill(ing); *aus der* ~, out of practice.

Ufer *n.* (-s, -) (*Fluss~*) bank; (*See~*) shore, beach.

uferlos *a.* boundless.

Uhr *f.* (-, -en) clock; (*Taschen~*) watch; *wieviel* ~ *ist es?* what is the time?; *es ist halb drei* (~), it is half past two; *eine* ~ *aufziehen*, to wind up a watch; *eine* ~ *stellen*, to set a clock *or* watch; *die* ~ *ist abgelaufen*, the watch has run down.

Uhr: ~**band** (**Leder**) *n.* watch-strap; ~**blatt** *n.* face.

Uhrenarmband *n.* watchband, watch-bracelet.

Uhr: ~**feder** *f.* watch spring; ~**gehäuse** *n.* watch-case; ~**macher** *m.* watchmaker, clockmaker; ~**werk** *n.* clock-work.

Uhrzeiger *m.* hand; *in der Richtung des* ~s, clockwise; *gegen die Richtung des* ~s, anticlockwise, counterclockwise.

Uhu *m.* (-s, -e *u.* -s) eagle owl.

Ukas *m.* (- *u.* Ukases, - *u.* Ukase) ukase

Ulan *m.* (-en, -en) uhlan, lancer.

Ulk *m.* (-[e]s, -e) (*fam.*) spree, lark, hoax

Ulme *f.* (-, -n) elm.

Ultimatum *n.* (-[s], -s *u.* -ta) ultimatum.

Ultimo *m.* (-[s], -s *u.* -timi) last day of the month.

Ultrakurzwelle f. (*Radio*) ultra-short wave.

ultramontan *a.*, Ultramontane[r] *m.* (-en, -en), ultramontane.

ultraviolett *a.* ultra-violet.

um *pr.* about, round; at; by; for; concerning; past; ~ 3 *Uhr*, at three (o'clock); *es ist gerade* ~, it is just past; ~ *so besser*, all the better; ~ *etwas kommen*, to lose a thing; ~ *zu*, in order to.

umackern *v.t.* to plough up.

umadressieren *v.t.* to redirect.

umändern *v.t.* to change, to alter.

Umänderung *f.* change, alteration.

umarbeiten *v.t.* to re-cast, to re-model.

umarmen *v.t.* to embrace, to hug.

Umarmung *f.* (-, -en) embrace.

umbauen *v.t.* to rebuild.

umbehalten *v.t.st.* to keep on (a wrap).

umbiegen *v.t.st.* to bend, to double up.

umbilden *v.t.* to transform; to re-model.

Umbildung *f.* transformation; re-cast.

umbinden *v.t.st.* to tie round, to put on.

umblasen *v.t.st.* to blow down.

umblättern *v.t.* to turn over (a leaf).

umblicken (sich) ~ *v.refl.* to look round.

umbrechen *v.t.st.* to break up.

umbringen *v.t.ir.* to kill.

Umbruch *m.* (*typ.*) page-proof.

umdrehen *v.t.* to turn, to twist, to wring; (sich) ~ *v.refl.* to turn round; to rotate, to revolve.

Umdrehung *f.* turn; rotation; (*mech.*) revolution.

Umdrehungszähler *m.* (*mot.*) tachometer.

umfahren *v.t.st.* to run down; to circumnavigate.

umfallen *v.i.st.* to fall over.

Umfang *m.* (-[e]s, -fänge) circumference, size; compass, extent.

umfangen *v.t.st.* to encircle; to embrace; to encompass.

umfangreich *a.* bulky.

umfassen *v.t.* to clasp; to comprise, to include, to embrace; (*mil.*) to envelop.

umfassend *a.* comprehensive.

umfassonieren *v.t.* (*Hut, Mantel*) to re-model.

Umfassung *f.* enclosure; embrace, grasp; (*mil.*) envelopment.

umfliegen *v.t.* to circle round.

umfluten *v.t.* to flow about, to wash.

umformen *v.t.* to re-model, to re-cast.

Umformer *m.* (*elek.*) converter.

Umfrage *f.* inquiry (all round).

umfried[ig]en *v.t.* to fence, to hedge in.

umfüllen *v.t.* to transfuse; to decant.

Umgang *m.* intercourse; (*Chor.*~) ambulatory.

umgänglich *a.* sociable, conversable.

Umgangssprache *f.* colloquial speech.

umgarnen *v.t.* (*fig.*) to ensnare.

umgeben *v.t.st.* to surround.

Umgebung *f.* (-, -en) environs, surroundings *pl.*; environment; (*Personen*) entourage.

Umgegend *f.* (-, 0) neighbourhood.

umgehen *v.t.st.* to evade, to elude, to bypass; ~ *v.i.st.* (*s*) to associate (with); *es geht in dem Schlosse um*, the castle is haunted; *mit einem umzugehen wissen*, to know how to deal with someone; *umgehend antworten*, to answer by return of post.

Umgehung *f.* (*Gesetz*) evasion.

Umgehungsstrasse *f.* by-pass road.

umgekehrt *a.* opposite, contrary, reverse; the other way round.

umgestalten *v.t.* to transform, to re-cast.

umgraben *v.t.st.* to dig (up).

umgrenzen *v.t.* to circumscribe.

umgruppieren *v.t.* to re-group, to re-align.

Umgruppierung *f.* (*mil.*) regrouping.

umgucken (sich) ~ *v.refl.* to look round.

umgürten *v.t.* to buckle on (a sword); (*fig.*) to encircle.

umhaben *v.i.ir.* to have on *or* about one.

umhalsen *v.t.* to hug, to embrace.

Umhang *m.* (-[e]s, -hänge) wrap.

umhängen *v.t.* to put on.

umhauen *v.t.st.* to fell, to cut down.

umher *adv.* around, (round) about.

umherschweifen *v.t.* (*s*) to rove, to wander.

umherziehend *a.* ambulatory; vagrant.

umhin *adv. ich kann nicht* ~, I cannot help.

umhüllen *v.t.* to wrap (up), to enshroud.

Umhüllung *f.* (-, -en) cover, wrapper, veil.

Umkehr *f.* (-, 0) return; complete change, revulsion (of feeling).

umkehren *v.t.* to turn (round), to invert; (*mech.*) to reverse; ~ *v.i.* (*s*) to turn back; *in umgekehrtem Verhältnis stehen*, to be in inverse ratio (to).

Umkehrung *f.* (-, -en) reversal.

umkippen *v.i.* (*s*) to tilt over; ~ *v.t.* to upset, to overturn.

umklammern *v.t.* to clasp, to cling to.

umkleiden (sich) *v.refl.* to change one's clothes.

umkommen *v.i.st.* (*s*) to perish; to spoil.

Umkreis *m.* (-kreises, -kreise) compass, circle; circumference; *im* ~ *von*, within a radius of...

umkreisen *v.t.* to encircle, to enclose.

umkrempeln *v.t.* to tuck up; to turn inside out.

umladen *v.t.st.* to transload.

Umladung *f.* (-, -en) transhipment.

Umlage *f.* (-, -n) assessment, impost.

umlagern *v.t.* to besiege, to invest.

Umlauf *m.* (-[e]s, -läufe) circulation; currency (of coins, words); *in* ~ *bringen, setzen*, to circulate; to issue; *im* ~ *sein*, to circulate.

umlaufen *v.i.st.* (*s*) to circulate.

Umlaut *m.* umlaut, modification.

umlauten *v.i.* to be mutated or modified.

umlegen *v.t.* to put round *or* on; (*Steuern*) to assess.

umleiten *v.t.* (*Verkehr*) to detour, to divert.

umlenken *v.t.* to turn round *or* back.

umlernen *v.t.* to readjust one's views.

umliegend *a.* surrounding, circumjacent.

ummauern *v.t.* to wall in.

umnachten *v.t.* to wrap in darkness.

umnebeln *v.t.* to dim.

umnehmen *v.t.st.* to put on.

umpacken *v.t.* to repack.

umpflanzen *v.t.* to transplant.

umpflügen *v.t.* to plough up.

umprägen *v.t.* to re-coin.

umquartieren *v.t.* to remove to other quarters.

umrahmen *v.t.* to frame, to encircle.

umrändern *v.t.* to border, to edge.

umranken *v.t.* to twine around.

umräumen *v.t.* to place otherwise *or* elsewhere.

umrechnen *v.t.* to convert.

Umrechnungskurs *m.* rate of exchange, parity.

umreissen *v.t.st.* to pull down; to sketch the outlines of.

umreiten *v.t.st.* to ride round.

umrennen *v.t.ir.* to run down *or* over.

umringen *v.t.* to encircle, to surround.

Umriss *m.* (-risses, -risse) sketch, outline, contour.

umrühren *v.t.* to stir.

ums = **um das**

umsatteln *v.i.* (*fig.*) to change one's profession.

Umsatz *m.* (-es, 0) turnover; **~steuer** *f.* turnover tax.

umschalten *v.t.* to switch (on), to reverse (the current).

Umschalter *m.* switch, commutator.

umschatten *v.t.* to shade.

Umschau *f.* (-, 0) survey; **~ halten**, to look round.

umschauen (**sich**) *v.refl.* to look back *or* round.

umschiffen *v.t.* to circumnavigate.

Umschlag *m.* (-[e]s, -schläge) envelope, wrapper; poultice, compress; sudden change, turn; (*Ärmel*) cuff, tuck; (*Waren*) transhipment.

umschlagen *v.t.st.* (*Saum*) to turn up; (*Kragen*) to turn down; (*Blatt*) to turn over; (*Ärmel*) to tuck up; to wrap round; to buy and sell; **~** *v.i.st.* (*s*) to capsize; to change suddenly; to turn sour; (*Stimme*) to break.

umschleichen *v.t.st.* to prowl round.

umschliessen *v.t.st.* to enclose.

umschlingen *v.t.st.* to embrace.

umschmeissen *v.t.st.* to overturn.

umschnallen *v.t.* to buckle on.

umschnüren *v.t.* to cord.

umschreiben *v.t.st.* to transcribe; to trans-

fer; (*Wechsel*) to re-indorse; (*mit Worten*) to paraphrase; (*math.*) to circumscribe.

Umschreibung *f.* (-, -en) paraphrase; transcription.

Umschrift *f.* (-, -en) (*auf Münzen*) legend; *phonetische* **~**, phonetic transcription.

Umschuldung *f.* debt-conversion.

Umschütten *v.t.* to spill.

umschwärmen *v.t.* to adore.

Umschweif *m.* (-[e]s, -e) digression.

umschwenken *v.i.* (*h*, *s*) to wheel round.

Umschwung *m.* (-[e]s, -schwünge) revolution; revulsion, the turning of the tide.

umsehen (**sich**) *v.refl.st.* to look round *or* back; (*nach*) to look out for; (*in*) to become acquainted (with); *im* **~**, in a twinkling.

um sein *v.i.ir.* (*s*) to be over.

umseitig *adv.* overleaf; *Fortsetzung* **~**, continued over.

umsetzen *v.t.* (*Pflanzen*) to transplant; to turn over; *in Taten* **~**, to translate into deeds.

Umsichgreifen *n.* (-s, 0) spreading.

Umsicht *f.* (-, 0) circumspection.

umsichtig *a.* circumspect.

Umsiedlung *f.* (-, -en) resettlement.

umsinken *v.i.st.* (*s*) to drop, to faint.

umsonst *adv.* gratis, for nothing; in vain; *nicht* **~**, not without good reason.

umspannen *v.t.* to span, to encompass.

umspringen *v.i.st.* (*s*) to veer (round), to turn; **~** *mit*, to manage, to handle.

Umstand *m.* (-[e]s, -stände) circumstance; **Umstände** *pl.* ceremonies, fuss; particulars *pl.*; *in andern Umständen sein* (*von Frauen*), to be in the family way.

umständlich *a.* involved.

Umstandswort *n.* adverb.

umstehend *a.* next (page); **~** *adv.* overleaf.

Umstehende[n], *m.pl.* bystanders *pl.*

umsteigen *v.i.st.* (*s*) to change (carriages).

umstellen *v.t.* to transpose; to surround.

Umstellung *f.* (-, -en) inversion; changeover.

umstimmen *v.t.* to bring (one) round.

umstossen *v.t.st.* to knock down; to quash (a sentence).

Umstossung *f.* (-, -en) rescission.

umstricken *v.t.* (*fig.*) to ensnare.

umstülpen *v.t.* to turn up *or* upside down.

Umsturz *m.* (-es, -stürze) overthrow; revolution.

umstürzen *v.t.* to throw down, to overturn; **~** *v.i.* (*s*) to be upset.

Umstürzler *m.* (-s, -) revolutionist.

umtaufen *v.t.* to give another name.

Umtausch *m.* (-[e]s, 0) exchange, barter.

umtauschen *v.t.* to exchange.

Umtrieb *m.* (-[e]s, -e) intrigue.

umtun *v.t.st.* to put on; *sich nach etwas* **~**, to look *or* cast about for.

Umwallung f. (-, -en) circumvallation.
umwälzen v.t. to revolutionize.
Umwälzung (-, -en) f. revolution.
umwandeln v.t. to change, to convert (in-to); (Strafe) to commute.
Umwandlung f. (-, -en) change, transformation; conversion.
umwechseln v.t. to (ex)change.
Umweg m. (-[e]s, -e) detour.
umwehen v.t. to blow down.
Umwelt f. (-, 0) environment.
umwenden v.t.ir. to turn (over).
umwerben v.t.st. to court.
umwerfen v.t.st. to overthrow.
umwerten v.t. to revalue.
Umwertung f. (-, -en) revaluation.
umwickeln v.t. to wrap up.
umwohnend a. surrounding.
umwölken (sich) v.refl. to get cloudy; (fig.) to darken.
umworben a. sought in marriage, courted.
umwühlen v.t. to rout up: to rummage.
umzäunen v.t. to hedge, to fence.
Umzäunung f. (-, -en) enclosure, fence.
umziehen v.i.st. (s) to move, to change one's habitation; jemand ~, to change somebody's clothes; (sich) ~ v.refl.st. to change (one's clothes); to become overcast.
umzingeln v.t. to encircle, to surround.
Umzug m. (-[e]s, -züge) procession; (Wohnungswechsel) removal, move.
unabänderlich a. irrevocable.
unabgeschreckt a. undeterred.
unabhängig a. independent.
Unabhängigkeit f. (-, 0) independence.
unabkömmlich a. indispensable.
unablässig a. unceasing, unremitting.
unabsehbar a. immeasurable, unbounded.
unabsetzbar a. irremovable.
unabsichtlich a. unintentional.
unabweisbar, unabweislich, a. imperative.
unabwendbar a. inevitable.
unachtsam a. inadvertent; careless.
Unachtsamkeit f. (-, -en) inadvertency.
unähnlich a. unlike, dissimilar.
unanfechtbar a. incontestable.
unangebracht a. out of place.
unangefochten a. unchallenged; unmolested.
unangekündigt a. unheralded.
unangemeldet a. without (previous) notice; unregistered.
unangemessen a. inadequate, unsuitable.
unangenehm a. disagreeable, unpleasant.
unangetastet a. untouched.
unangreifbar a. unassailable.
unannehmbar a. unacceptable.
Unannehmlichkeit f. (-, -en) inconvenience.
unansehnlich a. inconspicuous, poor-looking; homely; plain.
unanständig a. indecent; improper.

unanstössig a. unobjectionable, correct.
unantastbar a. unassailable.
unappetitlich a. unsavoury, nasty.
Unart f. (-, -en) naughtiness, bad habit.
unartig a. naughty, rude.
unartikuliert a. inarticulate.
unästhetisch a. unsightly.
unauffindbar a. undiscoverable.
unaufgefordert a. uncalled for, unasked.
unaufhaltsam a. irresistible.
unaufhörlich a. incessant.
unauflöslich a. indissoluble.
unaufmerksam a. inattentive.
unaufrichtig a. insincere.
unaufschiebbar a. urgent, pressing.
unaufspürbar a. untraceable.
unausbleiblich a. inevitable.
unausführbar a. impracticable.
unausgesetzt a. uninterrupted.
unauslöschlich a. indelible.
unaussprechlich a. ineffable.
unausstehlich a. insufferable.
unausweichlich a. inevitable.
unbändig a. unmanageable.
unbarmherzig a. merciless.
unbeabsichtigt a. unintentional.
unbeachtet a. unnoticed.
unbeanstandet a. unexceptionable.
unbeaufsichtigt a. unattended.
unbedacht, unbedächtig, unbedachtsam, a. inconsiderate, rash.
unbedenklich a. unhesitating; unobjectionable; ~ adv. without hesitation.
unbedeutend a. insignificant, trifling.
unbedingt a. unconditional, absolute; implicit; ~ adv. by all means.
unbeeinflusst a. uninfluenced.
unbefangen a. unprejudiced; unembarrassed; candid, natural.
unbefleckt a. immaculate, pure.
unbefriedigend a. unsatisfactory.
unbefugt a. unauthorized; incompetent.
unbegreiflich a. incomprehensible, inconceivable.
unbegrenzt a. unbounded, unlimited.
unbegründet a. unfounded, groundless.
unbegütert a. not rich, without landed property.
Unbehagen a. uneasiness, discomfort.
unbehaglich a. uneasy, uncomfortable.
Unbehaglichkeit f. discomfort.
unbehelligt a. unmolested.
unbehilflich a. awkward.
unbehindert a. unrestrained, unhindered.
unbeholfen a. awkward, clumsy.
unbekannt a. unknown.
unbekehrbar a. inconvertible.
unbekümmert a. unconcerned (about).
unbelebt a. inanimate; lifeless, dull.
unbeleckt a. untouched, untainted.
unbeleuchtet a. unlit.
unbeliebt a. unpopular.
unbemerkt a. unnoticed, unperceived.

unbemittelt *a.* poor, without means.
unbenannt *a.* anonymous; ∼*e Zahlen,* indefinite *or* abstract numbers.
unbenommen *a. es bleibt dir* ∼, you are quite free to...
unbenutzt *a.* unused, unemployed.
unbequem *a.* uncomfortable.
unberechenbar *a.* incalculable.
unberechtigt *a.* unauthorized; unlawful.
unberichtigt *a.* uncorrected; (*Rechnung*) unpaid.
unberücksichtigt *a.* disregarded.
unberufen *a.* uncalled for; *unberufen!* (*fig.*) touch wood!
unberührt *a.* untouched.
unbeschadet *adv.* without prejudice to.
unbeschädigt *a.* unhurt, uninjured.
unbescheiden *a.* immodest; indiscreet.
unbescholten *a.* blameless.
Unbescholtenheit *f.* blameless reputation.
unbeschränkt *a.* unlimited.
unbeschreiblich *a.* indescribable.
unbeseelt *a.* inanimate.
unbesehen *a.* unseen, unexamined; ∼ *adv.* without hesitation.
unbesetzt *a.* unoccupied, vacant.
unbesiegbar *a.* invincible.
unbesiegt *a.* unbeaten.
unbesoldet *a.* unsalaried, unpaid.
unbesonnen *a.* thoughtless, rash.
unbesorgt *a.* unconcerned; easy.
unbeständig *a.* inconstant, fickle.
Unbeständigkeit *f.* instability, fickleness.
unbestätigt *a.* unconfirmed.
unbestechlich *a.* incorruptible.
unbestellbar *a.* not deliverable.
unbestimmt *a.* indeterminate.
unbestreitbar *a.* indisputable.
unbestritten *a.* uncontested.
unbeteiligt *a.* not concerned (in).
unbeträchtlich *a.* inconsiderable.
unbeugsam *a.* inflexible.
unbewacht *a.* unguarded; unwatched.
unbewaffnet *a.* unarmed; *mit unbewaffnetem Auge,* with the naked eye.
unbewandert *a.* unversed in.
unbeweglich *a.* immovable; real (property); (*fig.*) inflexible.
Unbeweglichkeit *f.* immobility.
unbewohnbar *a.* uninhabitable.
unbewohnt *a.* uninhabited.
unbewusst *a.* unconscious (of); unknown.
unbezahlbar *a.* priceless.
unbezähmbar *a.* indomitable.
unbezeugt *a.* unattested, not proved.
unbezweifelt *a.* undoubted.
unbezwinglich *a.* invincible, impregnable.
unbiegsam *a.* not pliant; inflexible.
Unbill *f.* (-, -bilden) injury, wrong; (*des Wetters*) inclemency.
unbillig *a.* unfair, unjust.
unblutig *a.* bloodless.
unbotmässig *a.* unruly, refractory.

unbrauchbar *a.* useless, unserviceable.
unbussfertig *a.* impenitent.
und *c.* and; ∼ *wenn,* even if; ∼ *so weiter,* and so on; etc.; *der* ∼ *der,* so and so.
Undank *m.* (-[e]s, 0) *m.* ingratitude.
undankbar *a.* ungrateful; thankless.
undatiert *a.* undated.
undefinierbar *a.* undefinable.
undenkbar *a.* inconceivable.
undenklich *a.* immemorial.
undeutlich *a.* indistinct; inarticulate.
undicht *a.* not tight, leaking.
Unding *n.* absurdity.
unduldsam *a.* intolerant.
undurchdringlich *a.* impenetrable.
undurchführbar *a.* impracticable.
undurchlässig *a.* impervious to.
undurchsichtig *a.* opaque.
Undurchsichtigkeit *f.* opacity.
uneben *a.* uneven, rugged.
unebenbürtig *a.* of unequal birth *or* rank.
unecht *a.* not genuine; spurious, counterfeit, sham.
unedel *a.* ignoble, mean, base.
unehelich *a.* illegitimate.
Unehre *f.* dishonour, disgrace.
unehrerbietig *a.* irreverent, disrespectful.
unehrlich *a.* dishonest.
uneigennützig *a.* disinterested.
uneigentlich *a.* figurative, not literal.
uneinbringlich *a.* irrecoverable.
uneingedenk *a.* unmindful, forgetful (of).
uneingeschränkt *a.* unrestricted.
uneingeweiht *a.* uninitiated.
uneinig *a.* discordant, at variance.
Uneinigkeit *f.* disagreement, discord.
uneinnehmbar *a.* impregnable.
uneins = uneinig.
uneinträglich *a.* unprofitable, barren.
unempfänglich *a.* unsusceptible.
unempfindlich *a.* insensible; indifferent.
unendlich *a.* endless, infinite.
Unendlichkeit *f.* infinity; infinite space.
unentbehrlich *a.* indispensable.
unentgeltlich *a.* gratuitous; ∼ *adv.* gratis.
unenthaltsam *a.* incontinent.
Unenthaltsamkeit *f.* incontinence.
unentrinnbar *a.* inevitable, unavoidable.
unentschieden *a.* undecided; irresolute.
Unentschieden *n.* (-, -) (*sport*) draw.
unentschlossen *a.* irresolute.
Unentschlossenheit *f.* irresolution.
unentschuldbar *a.* inexcusable.
unentwegt *a.* unswerving, steady.
Unentwegte[r] *m.* (-n, -n) die-hard.
unentwickelt *a.* undeveloped.
unentwirrbar *a.* inextricable.
unerbittlich *a.* inexorable.
unerfahren *a.* inexperienced.
Unerfahrenheit *f.* (-, 0) inexperience.
unerfindlich *a.* incomprehensible.
unerforschlich *a.* inscrutable.
unerfreulich *a.* unpleasant.

unerfüllbar *a.* not to be fulfilled *or* complied with, unrealizable.
unergiebig *a.* unproductive.
unergründlich *a.* unfathomable.
unerheblich *a.* inconsiderable; irrelevant.
unerhört *a.* unheard of, unprecedented.
unerkannt *a.* unrecognized.
unerkennbar *a.* unrecognizable.
unerkenntlich *a.* ungrateful.
unerklärlich *a.* inexplicable.
unerlässlich *a.* indispensable.
unerlaubt *a.* illicit, unlawful.
unerledigt *a.* unattended, not dispatched.
unermesslich, *a.* immeasurable; immense.
Unermesslichkeit *f.* (-, 0) immensity.
unermüdlich *a.* indefatigable.
unerörtert *a.* undiscussed; undecided.
unerquicklich *a.* unpleasant, unedifying.
unerreichbar *a.* unattainable.
unerreicht *a.* unequalled.
unersättlich *a.* insatiable.
unerschlossen *a.* undeveloped.
unerschöpflich *a.* inexhaustible.
unerschrocken *a.* intrepid, undaunted.
unerschütterlich *a.* unshakable, imperturbable, firm, unshaken.
unerschwinglich *a.* beyond one's means; ~er Preis, prohibitive price.
unersetzlich, *a.* irreparable; irreplaceable.
unerspriesslich *a.* unprofitable.
unerträglich *a.* intolerable.
unerwähnt *a.* unmentioned; ~ lassen, to pass over (in silence).
unerwartet *a.* unexpected.
unerwidert *a.* unanswered; unreturned.
unerwiesen *a.* not proved.
unerwünscht *a.* undesirable.
unerzogen *a.* uneducated.
unfähig *a.* incapable, inefficient.
Unfähigkeit *f.* incapacity, inability.
Unfall *m.* accident; mischance.
Unfall: ~station *f.* ambulance station; ~versicherung *f.* accident insurance.
unfassbar *a.* inconceivable.
unfehlbar *a.* infallible.
Unfehlbarkeit *f.* (-, 0) infallibility.
unfein *a.* ungenteel, indelicate, coarse.
unfern *adv.* not far off; ~ *pr.* near, not far from.
unfertig *a.* unfinished, not ready.
Unflat *m.* (-[e]s, 0) filth, dirt.
unflätig *a.* nasty, filthy; obscene.
unfolgsam *a.* disobedient.
Unfolgsamkeit *a.* disobedience.
unförmig, unförmlich *a.* shapeless.
unfrankiert *a.* unstamped.
unfrei *a.* not free.
unfreiwillig *a.* involuntary; compulsory.
unfreundlich *a.* unkind; harsh.
Unfreundlichkeit *f.* unkindness.
Unfriede *m.* discord, dissension.
unfruchtbar *a.* barren, sterile.
Unfruchtbarkeit *f.* sterility, barrenness.

Unfruchtbarmachung *f.* sterilization.
Unfug *m.* (-[e]s, 0) mischief, nuisance, *grober* ~, gross misdemeanour.
unfügsam *a.* uncomplying, intractable.
ungangbar *a.* (*Weg*) impassable.
ungastlich *a.* inhospitable.
ungeachtet *pr.* notwithstanding.
ungeahnt *a.* unexpected, unthought-of.
ungebändigt *a.* untamed, unsubdued.
ungebärdig *a.* unruly.
ungebeten *a.* unbidden, uninvited.
ungebildet *a.* uneducated, uncultured.
ungebleicht *a.* unbleached.
ungeboren *a.* unborn.
ungebrannt *a.* unburnt.
ungebräuchlich *a.* unusual; obsolete.
ungebraucht *a.* unused; new.
ungebrochen *a.* unbroken.
ungebührlich *a.* improper, unmannerly.
ungebunden *a.* unbound; (*Bücher*) in sheets; (*fig.*) loose, licentious; ~e Rede, prose; ~es Wesen, dissolute ways *pl.*
ungedeckt *a.* uncovered; (*com.*) unpaid; ~er Kredit, unsecured credit.
ungedruckt *a.* unprinted.
Ungeduld *f.* impatience.
ungeduldig *a.* impatient.
ungeeignet *a.* unfit (for).
ungefähr *a.* approximate; ~ *adv.* about, nearly; *von* ~, by chance.
ungefährdet *a.* unendangered; safe.
Ungefälligkeit *f.* unkindness.
ungefärbt *a.* undyed, uncoloured.
ungefüge, ungefügig *a.* unwieldy.
ungefüttert *a.* not lined.
ungegliedert *a.* inarticulate.
ungehalten *a.* angry, indignant.
ungeheissen *a.* spontaneous, unbidden.
ungehemmt *a.* unchecked, unimpeded.
ungeheuchelt *a.* unfeigned.
ungeheuer *a.* immense, prodigious, huge.
Ungeheuer *n.* (-s, -) monster.
ungeheuerlich *a.* monstrous.
Ungeheuerlichkeit *f.* (-, -en) monstrosity.
ungehindert *a.* unchecked.
ungehobelt *a.* unplaned; (*fig.*) coarse.
ungehörig *a.* improper; unsuitable.
ungehorsam *a.* disobedient.
Ungehorsam *m.* disobedience.
ungeimpft *a.* unvaccinated.
ungekämmt *a.* uncombed, unkempt.
ungekränkt *a.* uninjured.
ungekünstelt *a.* unaffected.
ungekürzt *a.* unabridged.
ungeladen *a.* uninvited; unloaded.
ungeläufig *a.* unfamiliar.
ungeleckt *a.* unlicked; unrefined.
ungelegen *a.* inconvenient, inopportune.
Ungelegenheit *f.* inconvenience, trouble.
ungelehrig *a.* indocile, not docile.
ungelehrt *a.* unlettered, unlearned.
ungelenk *a.* stiff; clumsy, awkward.
ungelöscht *a.* unslaked (lime).

ungelernt a. unskilled.
Ungemach n. (-[e]s, -e) discomfort, adversity; trouble, hardship.
ungemein a. uncommon; extraordinary.
ungemessen a. unmeasured.
ungemildert a. unmitigated.
ungemischt a. unmixed.
ungemünzt a. uncoined.
ungemütlich a. uncomfortable.
ungenannt a. unnamed.
ungenau a. inaccurate, inexact.
Ungenauigkeit f. inaccuracy.
ungeneigt a. disinclined, indisposed (to).
ungeniert a. unceremonious.
ungeniessbar a. unpalatable.
ungenügend a. insufficient.
ungenügsam a. insatiable.
ungenützt a. unused, unemployed.
ungeöffnet a. unopened.
ungeordnet a. unarranged; unsettled.
ungeprüft a. untried; unexamined.
ungerächt a. unavenged.
ungerade a. (Zahl) odd; uneven.
ungeraten a. (Kind) spoiled.
ungerechnet adv. not counting.
ungerecht a. unjust.
Ungerechtigkeit f. injustice.
ungereimt a. (Vers) unrhymed; blank; (fig.) absurd, preposterous.
Ungereimtheit f. (-, -en) (fig.) absurdity.
ungern adv. unwillingly, reluctantly.
ungerufen a. uncalled.
ungerügt a. uncensored, unpunished.
ungerupft a. unplucked.
ungesagt a. unsaid.
ungesalzen a. unsalted; fresh.
ungesäuert a. unleavened.
ungesäumt a. (sofortig) immediate.
ungeschehen, ~ **machen**, to undo.
ungescheut a. without fear, fearless.
ungeschichtlich a. unhistorical.
Ungeschick n. (-[e]s, 0), **Ungeschicklichkeit**, **Ungeschicktheit** f. awkwardness, ineptitude.
ungeschickt a. awkward, clumsy.
ungeschlacht a. uncouth, coarse.
ungeschliffen a. (von Edelsteinen) rough; (fig.) unpolished, rude, unmannerly.
ungeschmälert a. undiminished.
ungeschminkt a. unvarnished.
ungeschoren a. unmolested.
ungeschwächt a. unimpaired.
ungesellig a. unsociable.
ungesetzlich a. illegal.
Ungesetzlichkeit f. illegality.
ungesetzmässig a. illegal, unlawful.
ungesittet a. unmannerly.
ungestalt(et) a. ill-shaped, misshapen.
ungestillt a. unquenched, unslaked.
ungestört a. undisturbed.
ungestraft a. unpunished; ~ adv. with impunity.
ungestüm a. impetuous.

Ungestüm n. (-[e]s, 0) impetuosity.
ungesucht a. unsought for; (fig.) artless.
ungesund a. unwholesome; unhealthy.
ungeteilt a. undivided.
ungetreu a. faithless.
ungetrübt a. cloudless, untroubled.
Ungetüm m. (-[e]s, -e) monster.
ungeübt a. unpractised; unskilled.
ungewandt a. awkward, unskilful.
ungewiss a. uncertain.
Ungewissheit f. uncertainty.
Ungewitter n. (thunder)storm.
ungewöhnlich a. unusual, uncommon.
ungewohnt a. unaccustomed, unfamiliar.
ungezählt a. unnumbered, untold.
ungezähmt a. untamed; (fig.) uncurbed.
Ungeziefer n. vermin.
ungeziemend a. unbecoming; improper.
ungezogen a. ill-bred, rude; naughty.
ungezügelt a. unbridled.
ungezwungen a. unaffected, easy.
Unglaube m. disbelief; (kirchlich) unbelief.
unglaubhaft a. unbelievable.
ungläubig a. unbelieving, infidel.
Ungläubige[r] m. infidel, unbeliever.
unglaublich a. incredible.
unglaubwürdig a. unworthy of belief.
ungleich a. unequal; unlike, dissimilar, uneven; odd; ~ adv. (by) far, much.
ungleichartig a. heterogeneous.
ungleichförmig a. not uniform.
Ungleichheit f. inequality, dissimilarity.
ungleichmässig a. disproportionate, unequal.
Unglimpf m. (-[e]s, 0) insult.
unglimpflich a. ungentle, harsh.
Unglück n. misfortune; adversity; ill-luck.
unglücklich a. unlucky, unhappy, unfortunate.
unglücklicherweise adv. unfortunately.
unglückselig a. miserable; disastrous.
Unglücks(fall) m. misfortune; accident; ~**gefährte** m. fellow-sufferer; ~**vogel** m. poor devil.
Ungnade f. disgrace, disfavour.
ungnädig a. ungracious, unkind, angry.
ungrammatisch a. ungrammatical.
ungründlich a. superficial, shallow.
ungültig a. invalid, void; (Fahrkarte) not available; für ~ erklären, ~ machen, to annul, to invalidate, to void.
Ungunst f. disfavour; (Wetter) inclemency.
ungünstig a. unfavourable.
ungut, nichts für ~! no offence!
unhaltbar a. untenable.
Unheil n. (-[e]s, 0) mischief, harm; calamity.
unheilbar a. incurable.
unheilig a. unholy, profane, unhallowed.
Unheilstifter m. mischief-maker.
unheilvoll a. calamitous, disastrous.
unheimlich a. uncanny.

unhistorisch *a.* unhistoric.
unhöflich *a.* uncivil, rude.
Unhöflichkeit *f.* rudeness, incivility.
Unhold *m.* (-[e]s, -e) monster; fiend.
unhörbar *a.* inaudible.
Uniform *f.* (-, -en) uniform.
unhygienisch *a.* insanitary.
Unikum *n.* (-[s], -ka) a unique object.
uninteressant *a.* uninteresting.
uninteressiert *a.* disinterested.
Unitarier *m.* (-s, -) Unitarian.
Union *f.* (-, -en) union.
universal *a.* universal.
Universalerbe *m.* sole heir.
Universität *f.* (-, -en) university.
Universum *n.* (-[s], 0) universe.
unkenntlich *a.* unrecognizable.
Unkenntnis *f.* (-, 0) ignorance.
unkeusch *a.* unchaste.
Unkeuschheit *f.* unchastity.
unkindlich *a.* unfilial; precocious.
unkirchlich *a.* not churchy, anti-clerical.
unklagbar *a.* not actionable.
unklar *a.* confused, unintelligible; *im*
  unklaren sein, to be in the dark (about).
unklug *a.* imprudent, indiscreet.
Unklugheit *f.* imprudence.
unkörperlich *a.* incorporeal, bodiless.
Unkosten *pl.* charges, expenses *pl.; lau-*
  fende ~, overhead expenses.
Unkraut *n.* (-[e]s, 0) weed.
unkriegerisch *a.* unwarlike.
Unkultur *f.* (-, 0) lack of civilization.
unkündbar *a.* irredeemable.
unkundig *a.* ignorant (of).
unkünstlerisch *a.* inartistic.
unlängst *adv.* of late, the other day.
unlauter *a.* impure; (*fig.*) unfair; *~er Wett-*
  bewerb, unfair competition.
unleidlich *a.* intolerable.
unlenksam *a.* unmanageable, unruly.
unlesbar *a.* unreadable.
unleserlich *a.* illegible.
unleugbar *a.* undeniable.
unlieb *a.* disagreeable.
unliebsam *a.* unpleasant.
unlogisch *a.* illogical.
unlösbar *a.* unsolvable.
unlöslich *a.* insoluble.
Unlust *f.* (-, 0) disinclination.
unmanierlich *a.* unmannerly.
unmännlich *a.* unmanly, effeminate.
Unmasse *f.* (*fam.*) vast quantity.
unmassgeblich *a.* without authority.
unmässig *a.* immoderate; intemperate.
Unmässigkeit *f.* intemperance; excess.
Unmenge *f.* vast quantity *or* number.
Unmensch *m.* monster, brute.
unmenschlich *a.* inhuman, cruel.
Unmenschlichkeit *f.* inhumanity, cruelty.
unmerklich *a.* imperceptible.
unmethodisch *a.* unmethodical.
unmittelbar *a.* immediate, direct.

unmöbliert *a.* unfurnished.
unmodern *a.* old-fashioned.
unmöglich *a.* impossible.
Unmöglichkeit *f.* impossibility.
unmoralisch *a.* immoral.
unmotiviert *a.* without any motive.
unmündig *a.* under age.
Unmündigkeit *f.* minority.
unmusikalisch *a.* unmusical.
Unmut *m.* ill-humour, discontent.
unmutig *a.* ill-humoured.
unnachahmlich *a.* inimitable.
unnachgiebig *a.* relentless, unyielding.
unnachsichtlich *a.* relentless.
unnahbar *a.* unapproachable.
Unnatur *f.* unnaturalness, affectation.
unnatürlich *a.* unnatural; affected.
unnennbar *a.* ineffable, unutterable.
unnötig *a.* unnecessary, needless.
unnütz *a.* useless, unprofitable.
unordentlich *a.* disorderly, untidy.
Unordnung *f.* disorder, untidiness.
unorganisch *a.* inorganic.
unparteiisch, unparteilich *a.* impartial.
Unparteiische(r) *m.* umpire.
Unparteilichkeit *f.* impartiality.
unpässlich *a.* indisposed.
unpassend *a.* unbecoming; improper.
Unpässlichkeit *f.* (-, 0) indisposition.
unpatriotisch *a.* unpatriotic.
unpersönlich *a.* impersonal.
unpolitisch *a.* non-political.
unpopulär *a.* unpopular.
unpraktisch *a.* unpractical.
unproduktiv *a.* unproductive.
unprovoziert *a.* unprovoked.
unpünktlich *a.* unpunctual.
unqualifizierbar *a.* unqualifiable.
Unrast *f.* (-, 0) restlessness.
Unrat *m.* (-[e]s, 0) dirt, rubbish.
unratsam *a.* inadvisable.
unrecht *a.* wrong; unjust; *an den Un-*
  rechten kommen, to catch a Tartar.
Unrecht *n.* wrong, injustice, injury; *~*
  haben, to be wrong; *ins ~ setzen,* to put
  in the wrong.
unrechtmässig *a.* unlawful, illegal.
unredlich *a.* dishonest.
Unredlichkeit *f.* dishonesty.
unreell *a.* dishonest.
unregelmässig *a.* irregular.
unreif *a.* unripe; (*fig.*) immature.
Unreife *f.* (-, 0) immaturity; unripeness.
unrein *a.* unclean, impure.
unreinlich *a.* uncleanly.
unrentabel *a.* unremunerative.
unrettbar *a.* past help, past recovery; *~*
  verloren sein, to be irretrievably lost.
unrichtig *a.* wrong, incorrect.
unritterlich *a.* unchivalrous.
Unruhe *f.* disquietude, trouble; disturbance; alarm; noise; restlessness; balance
  (of a watch).

unruhig *a.* restless; uneasy; turbulent.
unrühmlich *a.* inglorious.
uns *pn.* us, to us; ourselves.
unsäglich *a.* unspeakable.
unsanft *a.* hard, harsh, rough.
unsauber *a.* unclean, slovenly.
Unsauberkeit *f.* uncleanliness.
unschädlich *a.* harmless, innocuous.
unschätzbar *a.* inestimable, invaluable.
unscheinbar *a.* inconspicuous.
unschicklich *a.* improper, unseemly.
Unschicklichkeit *f.* impropriety.
Unschlitt *n.* (-[e]s, -e) tallow.
unschlüssig *a.* irresolute; ~ *sein*, to hesitate.
unschmackhaft *a.* unpalatable.
unschön *a.* plain, homely, not nice.
Unschuld *f.* innocence.
unschuldig *a.* innocent.
unschwer *adv.* easily.
unselbständig *a.* dependent, unable to act *or* judge by oneself.
unselig *a.* luckless, unfortunate, fatal.
unser *pn.* our, ours; ~*einer*, ~*eins*, the like of us.
uns[e]rige (*der, die, das*) *pn.* ours.
unsertwegen *adv.* for our sake.
unsicher *a.* unsafe; uncertain, dubious.
Unsicherheit *f.* insecurity; uncertainty.
unsichtbar *a.* invisible.
unsigniert *a.* unsigned.
Unsinn *m.* (-[e]s, 0) nonsense.
unsinnig *a.* nonsensical, absurd.
Unsitte *f.* bad habit.
unsittlich *a.* immoral.
Unsittlichkeit *f.* (-, -en) immorality.
unsolide *a.* dissipated, loose; unreliable.
unstatthaft *a.* inadmissible; illicit.
unsterblich *a.* immortal.
Unsterblichkeit *f.* (-, 0) immortality.
Unstern *m.* (-[e]s, 0) evil star, ill-luck.
unstet *a.* unsteady, unsettled.
unstillbar *a.* unquenchable.
unsträflich *a.* irreproachable.
unstreitig *a.* unquestionable.
Unsumme *f.* (*fam.*) immense number.
unsymmetrisch *a.* unsymmetrical.
unsympatisch *a.* distasteful; *mir ist es* ~, do not like.
untadelhaft, untadelig *a.* blameless.
Untat *f.* crime, outrage.
untätig *a.* inactive; idle.
Untätigkeit *f.* (-, 0) inactivity.
untauglich *a.* unfit; *für* ~ *erklären*, to condemn.
unteilbar *a.* indivisible.
unten *adv.* below; downstairs; at the bottom; *nach* ~, down(wards); *von oben bis* ~, from top to bottom; *weiter* ~, lower down; *der zweite von* ~, the second up.
unter *pr.* under, below; among, between; beneath; during; ~ *uns*, among our-

selves; ~ *uns gesagt*, between you and me.
unter *a.* inferior, lower, nether.
Unter *m.* (-s, -) (*im Kartenspiel*), knave.
Unter: ~*abteilung f.* subdivision; ~*arm m.* forearm; ~*art f.* sub-species; ~*bau m.* foundation, groundwork; (*rail.*) substructure; ~*beamte[r] m.* subaltern; ~*beinkleider n.pl.* (*Frauen*~) knickers *pl.* (*Männer*) pants *pl.*
Unterbelichtung *f.* (*phot.*) underexposure.
unterbewusst *a.* subconscious.
unterbieten *v.t.st.* to undercut, to undersell; (*Rekord*) to lower.
Unterbilanz *f.* deficit.
unterbinden *v.t.st.* to ligature (an artery); to cut off (supplies, etc.).
unterbleiben *v.i.st.* (*s*) to be left undone; not to take place.
unterbrechen *v.t.st.* to interrupt.
Unterbrechung *f.* (-, -en) interruption.
unterbreiten *v.t.* to submit (to).
unterbringen *v.t.ir.* to put up, to accommodate; to provide for; (*Waren*) to dispose of; to place (a loan); (*Wechsel*) to negotiate.
unterdes, unterdessen *adv.* meanwhile, in the meantime.
unterdrücken *v.t.* to oppress; to suppress, to crush, to quell.
Unterdrücker *m.* (-s, -) oppressor.
Unterdrückung *f.* (-, -en) oppression; suppression.
unterernährt *a.* underfed.
Unterernährung *f.* malnutrition.
unterfangen (sich) *v.refl.st.* to dare, to be bold enough.
Unterführung *f.* subway; (*Am.*) underpass.
Untergang *m.* (-[e]s, 0) decline; fall, ruin destruction.
untergeben *a.* inferior (to).
Untergebene[r] *m.* (-n, -n) subaltern, subordinate.
untergehen *v.i.st.* (*s*) to go down, to set.
untergeordnet *a.* subordinate, inferior.
untergeschoben *a.* supposititious; spurious, forged.
Untergestell *n.* truck, frame.
untergraben *v.t.st.* to undermine, to sap.
Untergrund *m.* subsoil; ~*bahn f.* underground railway, tube, (*Am.*) subway.
unterhalb *pr.* below.
Unterhalt *m.* (-[e]s, 0) maintenance; livelihood.
unterhalten *v.t.st.* to maintain, to support, to keep (up); to amuse, to entertain; (sich) ~ *v.refl.st.* to converse, to talk; to enjoy oneself.
unterhaltend *a.* entertaining, amusing.
Unterhaltung *f.* (-en, -en) entertainment; maintenance; conversation.
Unterhaltungs... recreational, recreative.
unterhandeln *v.i.* to negotiate, to treat.

Unterhändler *m.* negotiator, agent.
Unterhandlung *f.* negotiation.
Unterhaus *n.* Lower-House, House of Commons.
Unterhemd *n.* under-shirt.
unterhöhlen *v.t.* to undermine, to sap.
Unter: ~holz *n.* under-wood; ~hose = *Unterbeinkleid*; ~jacke *f.* (under)vest.
unterirdisch *a.* subterraneous, underground; subterranean.
unterjochen *v.t.* to subjugate, to subdue.
Unterkiefer *m.* lower jaw.
Unterkleid *n.* slip.
unterkommen *v.i.st.* (s) to find lodgings, employment, etc.
Unterkommen *n.* (-s, 0) shelter, accommodation, lodging; place, employment.
Unterkontrakt *m.* subcontract.
unterkriegen *v.t.* (*fam.*) to get under one's thumb, to get the better of.
Unterkunft *f.* (-, 0) shelter, (*mil.*) quarters.
Unterkunftshaus *n.*, Unterkunftshütte *f.* (mountain-)shelter.
Unterlage *f.* writing-pad, blotter; (*Beweis*) evidence; ~n *pl.* documentation.
Unterlass *m.* (-lasses, 0) intermission.
unterlassen *v.t.* to omit (to do).
Unterlassung *f.* (-, -en) omission.
Unterlauf *m.* lower course (of a river).
unterlaufen *v.i.* (s) *mit* ~, to slip in, to occur (accidentally); ~ *a.* bloodshot.
unterlegen *v.t.* to lay *or* put under; (*fig.*) to put (a construction) upon; *einer Melodie einen Text, Worte* ~, to adapt words to a melody.
Unterleib *m.* abdomen.
Unterleibs..., abdominal.
Unterlieferant *m.* (-en, -en) subcontractor.
unterliegen *v.i.st.* (s) to succumb; to be open to, to admit of (doubt).
Unterlippe *f.* lower-lip.
Unterlizenz *f.* sublicence; *in* ~ *vergeben*, to sublicense.
untermauern *v.t.* to underpin.
untermengen *v.t.* to intermix, to mingle.
Untermieter *m.* sub-tenant.
unterminieren *v.t.* to undermine.
unternehmen *v.t.st.* to undertake, to take upon oneself.
Unternehmen *n.* (-s, -) enterprise; (*mil.*) operation.
unternehmend *a.* enterprising, bold.
Unternehmer *m.* (-s, -) contractor; employer; entrepreneur.
Unternehmung *f.* (-, -en) enterprise.
unternehmungslustig *a.* enterprising.
unternormal *a.* subnormal.
Unteroffizier *m.* non-commissioned officer, corporal.
unterordnen *v.t.* to subordinate.
Unter: ~ordnung *f.* subordination; ~pfand *n.* pledge; pawn, mortgage; ~prima *f.* lower first (class); (in

Austria and England) lower sixth (form).
Unterproduktion *f.* underproduction.
unterreden (sich) *v.refl.* to converse.
Unterredung *f.* conversation; conference.
Unterricht *m.* (-[e]s, 0) instruction, tuition, teaching, lessons *pl.*
unterrichten *v.t.* to instruct, to teach; to inform.
Unterrichts: ~fach *n.* subject; ~ministerium *n.* Ministry of Public Instruction (*in Eng.*) M. of Education.
Unterrock *m.* petticoat.
unters = unter das.
untersagen *v.t.* to forbid, to prohibit.
Untersatz *m.* stand, support.
unterschätzen *v.t.* to underrate, to underestimate.
Unterschätzung *f.* (-, 0) undervaluation.
unterscheiden *v.i. & i.st.* to distinguish, to discern; to discriminate; sich ~ *v.refl.* to differ.
unterscheidend *a.* distinctive.
Unterscheidung *f.* distinction.
Unterschenkel *m.* shank, leg.
unterschieben *v.t.st.* to substitute; to father upon; to forge.
Unterschiebung *f.* (-, -en) substitution; forging.
Unterschied *m.* (-[e]s, -e) difference.
unterschieden *a.* different; distinct.
unterschiedlich *a.* distinct, various.
unterschiedslos *a.* indiscriminate.
unterschlagen *v.t.st.* (*Geld*) to embezzle; to intercept.
Unterschlagung *f.* (-, -en) embezzlement; interception (of letters).
Unterschleif *m.* (-[e]s, -e) fraud, embezzlement, malversation.
unterschreiben *v.t.st.* to subscribe; to sign.
Unterschrift *f.* signature.
Unterseeboot *n.* submarine.
unterseeisch *a.* submarine.
Unterseekabel *n.* submarine cable.
Untersekunda *f.* lower second (class); (in Austria and England) lower fifth (form).
untersetzt *a.* thick-set, stocky.
Untersetzungsgetriebe *f.* reduction gear.
untersinken *v.i.st.* (s) to go down, to sink.
unterspülen *v.t.* to wash away.
Unterspülung *f.* washout.
unterst *a.* lowest, undermost.
Unterstaatssekretär *m.* Under-Secretary of State.
Unterstand *m.* (*mil.*) dug-out.
unterstehen (sich) *v.refl.st.* to dare, to venture; *einem* ~, to be under another's orders.
unterstellen *v.t.* to place *or* put under; to insinuate, to impute; (sich) ~ *v.refl.* to stand up (under shelter),

Unterstellung f. (-, -en) imputation.
unterstreichen v.t.st. to underline.
Unterströmung f. undercurrent.
unterstützen v.t. to support; to assist.
Unterstützung f. (-, -en) aid, support;
assistance, relief.
Unterstützungskasse f. benevolent fund.
untersuchen v.t. to search; to examine, to
investigate.
Untersuchung f. (-, -en) inquiry, examination, investigation; (chem.) analysis.
Untersuchungs: ~haft f. imprisonment on
remand; in ~ nehmen, to commit for
trial; ~ anrechnen, to make allowance
for the period of custody; ~richter m.
examining magistrate.
untertags adv. by day.
untertan a. subject, obedient.
Untertan m. (-s, u. -en, -en) subject.
untertänig a. subject; submissive.
Untertasse f. saucer.
untertauchen v.t. & i. (s) to dip, to immerse, to duck; to dive.
Unter: ~teil n. & m. lower part; ~tertia f.
lower third (class); (in Austria and
England) lower fourth (form); ~titel
m. subtitle, subheading.
unterteilen v.t. to subdivide.
Unterton m. undertone.
Unterwäsche f. underwear.
Unterwasserbombe f. depth charge.
unterwegs adv. on the way; in transit, en
route.
unterweisen v.t.st. to instruct, to teach.
Unterweisung f. (-, -en) instruction.
Unterwelt f. underworld.
unterwerfen v.t.st. to subject; to subjugate, to subdue; (sich) ~ v.refl.st. to
submit.
Unterwerfung f. (-, 0) subjection; submission; resignation (to).
unterwühlen v.t. to undermine.
unterwürfig a. submissive.
unterzeichnen v.t. to subscribe; to sign.
Unterzeichner m. (-s, -) signatory.
Unterzeichnete[r] m. (-n, -n) undersigned.
Unterzeichnung f. (-, -en) signature; ratification (of a treaty).
Unterzeug n., Unterkleider pl. under-
clothing.
unterziehen (sich) v.refl.st. to undergo.
Untiefe f. shallow place, shoal.
Untier n. monster.
untilgbar a. (Schuld) irredeemable.
untragbar a. inadmissible.
untrennbar a. inseparable.
untreu a. unfaithful, faithless.
Untreue f. unfaithfulness.
untröstlich a. disconsolate.
untrüglich a. infallible, unerring.
untüchtig a. unfit, incapable; impotent.
Untüchtigkeit f. (-, 0) inefficiency.
Untugend f. vice; bad habit.

untunlich a. impracticable, not feasible.
unüberlegt a. rash, inconsiderate.
unübersehbar a. vast, immense.
unübersichtlich a. badly arranged.
unübersteigbar a. insurmountable.
unübertrefflich a. unequalled, unrivalled.
unübertroffen a. unbeaten, unsurpassed.
unüberwindlich a. invincible.
unumgänglich a. indispensable; adv. absolutely.
unumschränkt a. unlimited, absolute.
unumstösslich a. irrefutable; irrevocable.
unumwunden a. frank, plain.
ununterbrochen a. uninterrupted; ~ adv.
without interruption.
ununterscheidbar a. indistinguishable.
unveränderlich a. immutable; invariable.
unverändert a. unaltered.
unverantwortlich a. irresponsible.
unveräusserlich a. inalienable.
unverbesserlich a. incorrigible.
unverbindlich a. not binding; adv. without
any commitment.
unverblümt a. plain, frank, open.
unverbrüchlich a. inviolable.
unverbürgt a. unconfirmed.
unverdächtig a. unsuspected.
unverdaulich a. indigestible.
unvereinbar a. incompatible.
unverdaut a. undigested; crude.
unverdient a. undeserved, unmerited.
unverdorben a. incorrupt, unimpaired.
unverdrossen a. indefatigable, unwearied.
unvereidigt a. unsworn.
unvereinbar a. incompatible (with).
unverfälscht a. unadulterated, genuine.
unverfänglich a. not insidious, harmless.
unverfroren a. (fam.) impudent, cheeky.
unvergänglich a. imperishable.
unvergessen a. unforgotten.
unvergesslich a. unforgettable.
unvergleichlich a. incomparable.
unverhältnismässig a. disproportionate.
unverheiratet a. unmarried.
unverhofft a. unhoped-for, unexpected.
unverhohlen a. unconcealed, open.
unverkäuflich a. unsal(e)able.
unverkauft a. unsold.
unverkennbar a. unmistakable.
unverkürzt a. unabridged; uncurtailed.
unverletzbar, unverletzlich a. inviolable.
unverletzt a. intact, uninjured, inviolate.
unverlierbar a. never to be lost.
unvermeidlich a. inevitable.
unvermerkt a. unperceived; ~ adv. insen-
sibly, unawares.
unvermindert a. undiminished, unabated.
unvermittelt a. sudden, abrupt.
Unvermögen n. inability; impotence.
unvermögend a. unable; penniless.
unvermutet a. unexpected, unlooked-for.
unvernehmlich a. inaudible, indistinct.
Unvernunft f. unreasonableness.

unvernünftig *a.* unreasonable; irrational.
unverrichtet *a.* unperformed; ~er *Sache,* unsuccessfully; with empty hands.
unverrückt *a.* unmoved, fixed.
unverschämt *a.* impudent.
Unverschämtheit *f.* impudence.
unverschuldet *a.* undeserved.
unversehens *adv.* unawares.
unversehrt *a.* safe, uninjured, intact.
unversiegbar *a.* inexhaustible, perennial.
unversiegelt *a.* unsealed.
unversöhnlich *a.* irreconcilable.
unversorgt *a.* unprovided for.
Unverstand *m.* folly.
unverständig *a.* unwise, foolish.
unverständlich *a.* unintelligible.
Unverständnis *f.* (-nisses, 0) incomprehension.
unversucht *a.* untried.
unverträglich *a.* incompatible.
unverwandt *a.* unmoved, steadfast, fixed.
unverwehrt *a. es ist dir ~ zu...,* you are quite free to...
unverweilt *adv.* without delay.
unverwelklich *a.* unfading.
unverwundbar *a.* invulnerable.
unverwüstlich *a.* indestructible.
unverzagt *a.* intrepid, undaunted.
unverzeihlich *a.* unpardonable.
unverzinslich *a. & adv.* without (bearing) interest, free.
unverzollt *a.* duty unpaid.
unverzüglich *a. & adv.* immediate; without delay, immediately.
unvollendet *a.* unfinished.
unvollkommen *a.* imperfect.
Unvollkommenheit *f.* imperfection.
unvollständig *a.* incomplete.
unvollzählig *a.* incomplete.
unvorbereitet *a.* unprepared.
unvordenklich *a.* immemorial.
unvorhergesehen *a.* unforeseen.
unvorhersehbar *a.* unforeseeable.
unvorsätzlich *a.* unintentional.
unvorsichtig *a.* careless, heedless.
Unvorsichtigkeit *f.* (-, -en) imprudence.
unvorteilhaft *a.* unprofitable.
unwahr *a.* untrue, false, feigned.
Unwahrhaftigkeit *f.* untruthfulness.
Unwahrheit *f.* (-, -en) untruth, falsehood.
unwahrscheinlich *a.* improbable.
Unwahrscheinlichkeit *f.* (-, -en) improbability.
unwandelbar *a.* immutable, invariable.
unwegsam *a.* impassable.
unweiblich *a.* unwomanly.
unweigerlich *adv.* inevitably.
unweit *pr.* not far from, near.
unwert *a.* unworthy.
Unwesen *n.* (-s, 0) nuisance; *sein ~ treiben,* to be up to one's tricks.
unwesentlich *a.* immaterial, irrelevant.
Unwetter *n.* bad weather, storm.

unwichtig *a.* unimportant.
unwiderlegbar, unwiderleglich *a.* irrefutable.
unwiderruflich *a.* irrevocable.
unwidersprechlich *a.* incontestable.
unwiderstehlich *a.* irresistible.
unwiderbringlich *a.* irrecoverable.
Unwille *m.* displeasure, indignation.
unwillig *a. & adv.* indignant(ly), reluctant(ly).
unwillkommen *a.* unwelcome.
unwillkürlich *a.* involuntary.
unwirklich *a.* unreal.
unwirksam *a.* ineffectual, inefficacious; inoperative.
unwirsch *a.* cross, testy, nettled.
unwirtlich *a.* inhospitable.
unwirtschaftlich *a.* uneconomical.
unwissend *a.* ignorant.
Unwissenheit *f.* (-, 0) ignorance.
unwissenschaftlich *a.* unscientific.
unwissentlich *adv.* unknowingly.
unwohl *a.* indisposed, unwell; *sich ~ fühlen,* to feel unwell.
Unwohlsein *n.* (-s, 0) indisposition.
unwohnlich *a.* uninhabitable.
unwürdig *a.* unworthy; undeserving.
Unzahl *f.* (-, 0) immense number.
unzählbar, unzählig *a.* innumerable.
unzart *a.* indelicate, rude.
Unze *f.* (-, -n) ounce.
Unzeit *f. zur ~,* inopportunely.
unzeitig *a.* untimely, unseasonable.
unzerbrechlich *a.* unbreakable.
unzerreissbar *a.* untearable; (*fig.*) indissoluble.
unzerstörbar *a.* indestructible.
unzertrennlich *a.* inseparable.
unziemlich *a.* unseemly, unbecoming.
unzivilisiert *a.* uncivilized, uncultured.
Unzucht *f.* (-, 0) fornication.
unzüchtig *a.* lewd, unchaste.
unzufrieden *a.* discontented, dissatisfied.
Unzufriedene[r] *m.* (-n, -n) malcontent.
Unzufriedenheit *f.* discontent, dissatisfaction.
unzugänglich *a.* inaccessible.
unzulänglich *a.* insufficient, inadequate.
Unzulänglichkeit *f.* (-, -en) insufficiency, inadequacy.
unzulässig *a.* inadmissible.
unzurechnungsfähig *a.* non compos mentis; imbecile.
unzureichend *a.* insufficient.
unzusammenhängend *a.* incoherent.
unzuständig *a.* not competent.
Unzuständigkeit *f.* (-, 0) (*law*) incompetence.
unzuträglich *a.* disadvantageous; unhealthy; bad for.
Unzuträglichkeit *f.* (-, -en) inconvenience.
unzutreffend *a.* wrong.
unzuverlässig *a.* unreliable; uncertain.

unzweckmässig a. inexpedient.
unzweideutig a. unequivocal.
unzweifelhaft a. indubitable; ~ adv. doubtless, without doubt, indubitably.
üppig a. luxurious, wanton; luxuriant, rank.
Üppigkeit f. (-, -en) luxury.
Ur m. (-[e]s, -e) aurochs.
Urahn m. great-grandfather; ancestor.
uralt a. very old, very ancient.
Uraufführung f. (-, -en) first night.
urbar a. arable; ~ **machen**, to bring under cultivation.
Urbeginn m. first beginning.
Urbewohner m.pl. aborigines pl.
Urbild n. prototype; original.
Urchristentum n. primitive Christianity.
ureigen a. original, primitive.
Ureinwohner m. original inhabitant.
Ureltern pl. ancestors, first parents pl.
Urenkel m. great-grandson.
Urform f. primitive form.
Urgeschichte f. primitive history.
Urgestalt f. archetype, prototype.
Urgrossmutter f. great-grandmother.
Urgrossvater m. great-grandfather.
Urheber m. (-s, -), author, originator.
Urheberrecht n. copyright.
Urheberschaft f. (-, 0) authorship.
Urin m. (-[e]s, 0) urine; ~**lassen**, to urinate, to pass water.
urinieren v.i. to urinate.
urkomisch a. irresistibly ludicrous.
Urkraft f. original power.
urkräftig a. very powerful.
Urkunde (-, -n) record, deed, document.
Urkundenbeweis m. documentary evidence.
urkundlich a. authentic; documentary.
Urlaub m. (-[e]s, -e) leave (of absence), furlough; *bezahlter* ~, holidays with pay.
Urlauber m. (-s, -) soldier on furlough.
Urlaubsüberschreitung f. overstaying of leave.
Urmensch m. primitive man.
Urne f. (-, -n) urn.
urplötzlich a. very sudden.
Urquell m. fountain-head; first source.
Ursache f. (-, -n) cause; reason; motive.
ursächlich a. casual; causative.
Urschrift f. original (text).
Ursprache f. original language.
Ursprung m. (-[e]s, -sprünge) source, origin; *seinen* ~ *haben* or *nehmen von*, to originate in.
ursprünglich a. original, primitive.
Urteil n. (-[e]s, -e) judgment; sentence, verdict; *einem das* ~ *sprechen*, to pass sentence upon someone.
urteilen v.t. & i. to judge.
Urteilsbegründung f. reasons for the verdict.

Urteilsspruch m. sentence.
Urtext m. original (text).
Ururgrossvater m. great-great grandfather.
Urwähler m. primary elector.
Urwald m. virgin forest.
Urwelt f. primitive world.
urweltlich a. primeval.
urwüchsig a. original, native; rough.
Urzeit f. remote antiquity.
Urzeugung f. spontaneous generation.
Urzustand m. primitive condition.
Usance f. (-, -n) usage.
Usurpator m. (-s, -atoren) usurper.
Usus m. (-, 0) usage, custom.
Utensilien pl. utensils, implements pl.
Utilitarier m. (-s, -) utilitarian.
Utopie f. (-, -n) utopia, utopian scheme.
utopisch a. utopian.
uzen v.t. to tease, to chaff, to mock.

V

vag a. vague, loose.
Vagabund m. (-en, -en) vagabond.
vagabundieren v.i. to tramp (about).
vakant a. vacant.
Vakanz f. (-, -en) vacation.
Valuta f. (-, -uten) currency.
Vampir m. (-[e]s, -e) vampire.
Vandalismus m. (-, 0) vandalism.
Vanille f. (-, -n) vanilla.
Variante f. (-, -n) variant.
Varieté n. (-s, -s) music hall.
variieren v.t. & i. to vary; to fluctuate.
Vasall m. (-en, -en) vassal.
Vasallenstaat m. satellite state.
Vase f. (-, -n) vase.
Vaselin n. (-s, -e) vaseline.
Vater m. (-s, Väter) father; (*Tiere*) sire.
Vater: ~**haus** n. parental house, home; ~**land** n. native country, fatherland.
vaterländisch a. patriotic.
Vaterlandsliebe f. patriotism.
vaterlandsliebend a. patriotic.
vaterlandslos a. unpatriotic.
väterlich a. fatherly; paternal.
Vater: ~**mord** m. parricide; ~**mörder** m. parricide.
Vaterschaft f. (-, 0) paternity; fatherhood.
Vaterstadt f. native town.
Vaterunser n. (-s, -) Lord's prayer.
Vegetabilien pl. vegetables, plants.
vegetabilisch a. vegetable.
Vegetarier m. (-s, -) vegetarian.
vegetarisch a. vegetarian.
Vegetation f. (-, -en) vegetation.
vegetieren v.i. to vegetate.
Veilchen n. (-s, -) violet.
veilchenblau a. violet(-coloured).
Veitstanz m. St. Vitus' dance.

Velleität f. (-, -en) faint desire.
Vene f. (-, -n) vein.
Venenentzündung f. (med.) phlebitis.
Ventil n. (-[e]s, -e) valve.
Ventilation f. (-, -en) ventilation.
Ventilator m. (-s, -en) ventilator, fan.
ventilieren v.t. to ventilate.
verabfolgen v.i.& t. to deliver.
verabreden v.t., (sich) ~ v.refl. to agree upon; to make an appointment.
Verabredung f. (-, -en) appointment; nach ~, by appointment; eine Verabredung treffen, to make an appointment.
verabreichen v.t. to deliver, to give.
verabsäumen v.t. to neglect, to omit.
verabscheuen v.t. to detest.
verabscheuungswürdig a. abominable.
verabschieden v.t. to discuss, to discharge, to disband; (sich) ~ v.refl. to take leave.
Verabschiedung f. (-en) dismissal.
verachten v.t. to despise, to scorn, to contemn.
Verächter m. (-s, -) despiser.
verächtlich a. contemptible, despicable; (verachtend) contemptuous.
Verachtung f. (-, 0) contempt, scorn.
verallgemeinern v.t. to generalize.
veralten v.i. (s) to become obsolete.
veraltet a. obsolete, antiquated.
Veranda f. (-, -den) veranda(h).
veränderlich a. variable; changeable.
verändern v.t. to alter; to change.
Veränderung f. (-, -en) change, alteration.
verankern v.t. (nav.) to moor; (fig.) to establish firmly; (mech.) to stay.
veranlagen v.t. to assess (taxes); gut veranlagt, gifted, clever.
Veranlagung f. (-, -en) assessment; talent, aptitude (for).
veranlassen v.t. to occasion; to cause; to induce (one to do something).
Veranlassung f. (-, -en) occasion.
veranschaulichen v.t. to illustrate.
veranschlagen v.t. to estimate (at).
veranstalten v.t. to arrange, to organize.
Veranstaltung f. (-, -en) function; (Sport) event.
verantworten v.t. to answer for; (sich) ~ v.refl. to justify or defend oneself.
verantwortlich a. responsible, accountable.
Verantwortung f. (-, 0) responsibility; zur ~ ziehen, to call to account.
verantwortungsvoll a. involving great responsibility, responsible.
verarbeiten v.t. to make up.
verargen v.t. to blame (one) for.
verärgert a. annoyed.
verarmen v.i. (s) to become poor.
verarmt a. impoverished.
verästeln; (sich) ~ v.refl. to ramify.
Verästelung f. (-, -en) ramification.
verauktionieren v.t. to sell by auction.

verausgaben v.t. to pay away, to spend (in, on); (sich) ~ v.refl. to run out of money; to exhaust oneself.
veräusserlich a. alienable.
veräussern v.t. to alienate, to dispose of.
Verb n. (-s, -en) verb.
verballhornen v.t. to spoil text of book.
Verband m. (-[e]s, -bände) association, federation, union; (einer Wunde) dressing, bandage.
Verbandplatz m. dressing station.
Verbandskasse f. funds of a federation.
Verbandzeug n. dressings and bandages pl.
verbannen v.t. to banish.
Verbannte[r] m. (-n, -n) exile.
Verbannung f. (-, 0) banishment, exile.
verbarrikadieren v.t. to barricade.
verbauen v.t. (fig.) to obstruct.
verbeissen v.t.st. (fig.) to suppress by an effort.
verbergen v.t.st. to conceal, to hide.
verbessern v.t. to correct; to improve.
verbesserungsfähig a. capable of improvement.
verbeugen (sich) v.refl. to bow (to).
Verbeugung f. (-, -en) bow; curtsey.
verbiegen v.t.st. to bend out of shape.
verbieten v.t.st. to forbid, to prohibit, to ban.
verbilden v.t. to spoil, to vitiate.
verbilligen v.t. to lower the prices.
verbinden v.t.st. to dress (a wound); to join; to connect; (Telephon) to put through; (sich) ~ v.refl. to unite oneself (with), to join.
verbindlich a. obliging; obligatory, binding.
Verbindlichkeit f. (-, -en) obligation, liability, engagement; civility, obligingness.
Verbindung f. (-, -en) connection; union, alliance; junction; society, club; communication; (chem.) compound; mit einem in ~ stehen, to be in touch with one; in ~ bleiben, to keep in touch; sich in ~ setzen, to get in touch.
Verbindungs: ~glied n. connecting link; ~linie f. line of communication; ~offizier m. liaison officer.
verbissen a. dogged, obstinate.
verbitten (sich) v.refl.st. to deprecate.
verbittern v.t. to embitter, to exasperate.
verblassen v.i. (s) to fade; to turn pale.
Verbleib m. (-[e]s, 0) place of abode.
verbleiben v.i.st. (s) to remain.
verblenden v.t. to delude.
Verblendung f. (-, 0) infatuation.
verblichen a. faded; deceased.
verblüffen v.t. (fam.) to dumbfound.
verblühen v.i. (s) to wither, to fade.
verblümt a. allusive; ~ adv. by innuendo.
verbluten (sich) v.refl. to bleed to death.

verbohren *v.t. sich in etwas* ~, to go mad about a thing; *ein verbohrter Mensch,* a crank, a faddist.

verborgen *a.* concealed, secret.

Verborgenheit *f.* (-, 0) retirement.

Verbot *n.* (-[e]s, -e) prohibition; (*amtlich*) ban.

verbrämen *v.t.* to border, to trim.

verbrannte Erde (*mil.*) scorched earth.

Verbrauch *m.* (-[e]s, 0) consumption, use; (*mil. Munitions*~) expenditure.

verbrauchen *v.t.* to consume.

Verbraucher *m.* (-s, -) consumer.

Verbrauchsgüter *pl.* consumer goods.

Verbrauchsteuer *f.* excise duty.

Verbrechen *n.* (-s, -) crime, offence.

verbrechen *v.t.st.* to commit, to perpetrate (a crime).

Verbrecher *m.* (-s, -) criminal, convict.

verbrecherisch *a.* criminal.

verbreiten *v.t.* to spread, to diffuse, to disseminate; (sich) ~ *v.refl.* to spread; (*fig.*) to enlarge upon.

verbreitern *v.t.* to widen.

Verbreitung *f.* (-, 0) propagation; diffusion.

verbrennbar *a.* combustible.

verbrennen *v.t.ir.* to burn; ~ *v.i.ir.* (*s*) to be burnt (down); (sich) ~ *v.refl.* to burn *or* scald oneself.

Verbrennung *f.* (-, 0) combustion.

verbriefen *v.t.* to promise by writ; *verbriefte Rechte pl.* vested rights *pl.*

verbringen *v.t.st.* to pass, to spend.

verbrüdern (sich) *v.refl.* to fraternize.

Verbrüderung *f.* (-, -en) fraternization.

verbrühen *v.t.* to scald.

verbuchen *v.t.* to book.

Verbum *n.* (-[s], -ba) (*gram.*) verb.

verbummeln *v.t.* (*fam.*) to idle away; to forget.

verbunden *a.* obliged; connected; *Operationen der* ~*en Waffen,* combined operations.

verbünden (sich) *v.refl.* to ally oneself (to *or* with).

Verbündete[r] *m.* (-n, -n) ally.

verbürgen *v.t.* to warrant; *sich* ~ *für,* to vouch for, to guarantee.

verbüssen *v.t.* to serve one's time.

verchromt *a.* chromium-plated.

Verdacht *m.* (-[e]s, 0) suspicion; *über allen* ~ *erhaben,* above suspicion.

verdächtig *a.* suspect, suspicious.

verdächtigen *v.t.* to cast suspicion on.

Verdächtigung *f.* (-, -en) aspersion; insinuation.

Verdachtsperson *f.,* **Verdächtiger** *m.* suspect.

verdammen *v.t.* to condemn; to damn.

verdammlich *a.* damnable.

Verdammnis *f.* (-, 0) damnation.

verdammt *adv.* (*vulg.*) confound it!

Verdammung *f.* (-, -en) damnation; condemnation.

verdampfen *v.i.* (*s*) to evaporate.

verdanken *v.t.* to owe, to be indebted for (a thing to one).

verdauen *v.t.* to digest.

verdaulich *a.* digestible.

Verdauung *f.* (-, 0) digestion.

Verdauungs: ~**beschwerden** *pl.* indigestion; ~**kanal** *m.* digestive tract; ~**system** *n.* digestive system.

Verdeck *n.* (-[e]s, -e) deck; covering.

verdecken *v.t.* to cover, to hide.

verdenken *v.t.ir.* to blame (one) for.

Verderb *m.* (-[e]s, 0) ruin.

verderben *v.t.st.* to spoil; to corrupt; ~ *v.i.st.* (*s*) to be spoiled, to go bad; *sich den Magen* ~, to upset one's stomach; *es mit einem nicht* ~ *wollen,* to be unwilling to disoblige one.

Verderben *n.* (-s, 0) ruin; deprivation.

verderblich *a.* pernicious; (*Waren*) perishable; fatal.

Verderbnis *n.* (-nisses, -nisse) corruption; perdition.

verderbt *a.* depraved, corrupt.

verdeutlichen *v.t.* to make plain.

verdeutschen *v.t.* to translate into German.

verdichten *v.t.* to condense.

verdienen *v.t.* to gain, to earn; to deserve, to merit; *sich verdient machen um,* to deserve well of.

Verdienst *m.* (-es, 0) gain, profit; earnings *pl.*

Verdienst *n.* (-es, -e) merit, desert.

verdienstlich *a.* meritorious, deserving.

verdienstvoll *a.* deserving, able.

verdient *a.* deserving, meritorious; (*Strafe*) condign.

Verdikt *n.* (-[e]s, -e) verdict.

verdingen *v.t.r. & st.* to hire (out).

verdolmetschen *v.t.* to interpret.

verdoppeln *v.t.* to double.

verdorben *a.* spoiled; depraved; ~*er Magen,* upset stomach.

verdorren *v.i.* (*s*) to dry up, to wither.

verdrängen *v.t.* to crowd out.

Verdrängung *f.* displacement; repression; suppression; inhibition.

verdrehen *v.t.* to twist; (*fig.*) to misrepresent, to distort.

verdreht *a.* distorted; (*fig.*) cracked, flighty.

Verdrehung *f.* (-, -en) distortion.

verdreifachen *v.t.* to treble.

verdriessen *v.t.imp.st.* to vex, to annoy, to grieve.

verdriesslich *a.* tiresome, annoying; vexed; peevish, morose.

verdrossen *a.* sullen, unwilling.

Verdruss *m.* (-drusses, 0) annoyance, trouble, chagrin.

verduften v.i. (s) (fam.) to take French leave.

verdummen v.t. to make stupid; ~ v.i. (s) to become stupid.

verdunkeln v.t. to darken; to obscure; (fig.) to eclipse.

Verdunkelung f. (-, -en) (Luftschutz) blackout.

verdünnen v.t. to dilute.

verdunsten v.i. (s) to evaporate.

verdursten v.i. (s) to perish from thirst.

verdüstert a. (fig.) gloomy.

verdutzt a. nonplussed.

veredeln v.t. to improve, to refine.

verehelichen v.t. & refl. (sich) to marry.

verehren v.t. to revere; to worship, to adore; to make a present of.

Verehrer m. (-s, -) worshipper; admirer.

Verehrung f. (-, 0) veneration; worship.

verehrungswürdig a. venerable.

vereiden, vereidigen v.t. to administer an oath to; to swear (in).

Vereidigung f. (-, -en) swearing-in.

Verein m. (-[e]s, -e) union, society, club; im ~ mit meinem Freunde, jointly with my friend.

vereinbar a. compatible, consistent.

vereinbaren v.t. to stipulate.

Vereinbarung f. (-, -en) agreement.

vereinen, vereinigen v.t. to unite; to reconcile; (sich) ~ v.refl. to unite; die Vereinigten Staaten, the United States.

vereinfachen v.t. to simplify.

vereinheitlichen v.t. to standardize.

Vereinigung f. (-, -en) association.

vereinnahmen v.t. to receive, to take.

vereinsamen v.i. to feel solitary.

Vereins- und Versammlungsfreiheit f. freedom of association and assembly.

vereinzelt a. sporadic.

Vereinzelung f. (-, 0) isolation.

vereisen v.i. to turn into ice.

vereiteln v.t. to frustrate.

verekeln v.t. to render loathsome.

verenden v.i. (s) to die.

verenge[r]n v.t. to narrow, to contract.

vererbbar a. inheritable.

vererben v.t. to bequeath, to leave; to transmit (disease); (sich) ~ v.refl. to be hereditary, to run in the family.

Vererbung f. (-, 0) heredity; hereditary transmission.

verewigen v.t. to perpetuate.

verfahren v.i.st. (s) to proceed, to go to work, to act; ~ v.t.st. to bungle.

Verfahren n. (-s, -) method, procedure; (chem.) process; (law) proceedings; beschleunigtes ~, summary proceedings.

Verfall m. (-[e]s, 0) decay, decline, ruin; forfeiture; (eines Wechsels) maturity.

verfallen v.i.st. (s) to decay; to decline; (von Wechseln) to fall due; (Rechte) to lapse; to expire; auf einen Gedanken ~,

to hit upon an idea; das Pfand ist ~, the pledge is forfeited; verfallene Güter, escheats pl.

Verfall: ~tag m. day of payment; ~zeit f. time of payment, maturity.

verfälschen v.t. to falsify; to adulterate.

verfangen v.i.st. to take effect, to tell; das verfängt bei mir nicht, you need not try that on (with) me; (sich) ~ v.refl. to get entangled.

verfänglich a. risky, awkward.

Verfänglichkeit f. (-, -en) captiousness.

verfärben (sich) v.refl. to change colour.

verfassen v.t. to compose, to write.

Verfasser m. (-s, -), Verfasserin f. (-, -nen) author; authoress.

Verfassung f. (-, -en) constitution.

verfassunggebend a. constituent.

verfassungsmässig a. constitutional.

Verfassungsrecht n. constitutional law.

verfassungswidrig a. unconstitutional.

verfaulen v.i. (s) to rot, to putrify.

verfechten v.t.st. to advocate.

verfehlen v.t. to miss.

verfehlt a. unsuccessful, abortive.

verfeinden v.t. to set (one) against (another); (sich) ~ v.refl. to fall out with.

verfeinern v.t. to refine, to polish.

verfemen v.t. to outlaw.

verfertigen v.t. to make, to manufacture.

Verfettung f. (-, 0) fatty degeneration.

verfilmen v.t. to film, to screen.

verfinstern v.t. to darken; to eclipse.

Verfinsterung f. (-, -en) eclipse.

verflachen v.t. to flatten, to level.

verflechten v.t.st. to interlace; to entangle in.

verfliegen v.i.st. (s) to evaporate, to vanish.

verfliessen v.i.st. (s) to elapse, to expire.

verfluchen v.t. to curse, to execrate.

verflucht a. cursed.

verflüchtigen v.i. (s) (sich) ~ v.refl. to evaporate, to vanish.

Verfolg m. (-[e]s, 0) pursuance, progress.

verfolgen v.t. to pursue; to persecute; (eine Sache) to follow up; gerichtlich ~, to prosecute at law.

politisch Verfolgter m. persecutee.

Verfolgung f. (-, -en) pursuit; persecution; prosecution.

Verfolgungswahn m. persecution mania.

verfrachten v.t. to freight; to load; to ship.

verfrüht a. premature.

verfügbar a. available.

verfügen v.t. to order; ~ v.i. to dispose (of); (sich) ~ v.refl. to betake oneself (to).

Verfügung f. (-, -en) disposition, disposal; order, decree, injunction; (gerichtlich) rule; ~srecht n. power of disposal.

verführen v.t. (fig.) to seduce.

verführerisch a. tempting, seductive.

verfüttern *v.t.* consume as fodder.
vergällen *v.t.* (*fig.*) to embitter.
vergangen *a.* past, last, bygone.
Vergangenheit *f.* (-, 0) the past, time past; (*gram.*) past tense.
vergänglich *a.* passing, perishable.
Vergaser *m.* (-s, -) carburettor.
vergeben *v.t.st.* to forgive, to pardon; to give away, to dispose of; *seiner Ehre etwas* ~, to compromise one's honour.
vergebens *adv.* in vain, vainly.
vergeblich *a.* vain, fruitless.
Vergebung *f.* (-, 0) forgiveness, pardon; bestowal; cession (of a right).
vergegenwärtigen *v.t.* to figure, to represent, to visualize; to realize.
vergehen *v.i.st.* (*s*) to pass away, to elapse; to vanish; *sich* ~, to offend; to violate.
Vergehen *n.* (-s, -) fault, offence; misdemeanour.
vergeistigen *v.t.* to spiritualize.
vergelten *v.t.st.* to requite, to return, to repay.
Vergeltung *f.* (-, 0) retribution; (*feindliche*) retaliation, reprisal.
Vergeltungs...retaliatory, *a.*; *als Vergeltungsmassnahme für*, in reprisal for.
vergessen *v.t.st.* to forget; (**sich**) ~ *v.refl.* to forget oneself.
Vergessenheit *f.* (-, 0) oblivion.
vergesslich *a.* forgetful.
vergeuden *v.t.* to squander, to dissipate.
Vergeudung *f.* (-, -en) wastage, waste.
vergewaltigen *v.t.* to offer violence (to); to violate; to commit rape on.
vergewissern (sich) ~ *v.refl.* to ascertain, to make sure of.
Vergewisserung *f.* (-, 0) confirmation.
vergiessen *v.t.st.* to spill; to shed.
vergiften *v.t.* to poison; (*fig.*) to envenom, to embitter.
vergilbt *a.* yellowed.
Vergissmeinnicht *n.* (-s, -) forget-me-not.
vergittern *v.t.* to grate (up), to lattice.
verglasen *v.t.* to glaze; to vitrify.
Vergleich *m.* (-[e]s, -e) comparison; arrangement, compromise, agreement.
vergleichbar *a.* comparable.
vergleichen *v.t.st.* to compare; *sich* ~ *mit*, to compound with.
Vergleichung *f.* (-, -en) comparison.
vergleich[ung]sweise *adv.* comparatively.
vergnügen *v.t.* to amuse; (**sich**) ~ *v.refl.* to enjoy oneself, to take pleasure in.
Vergnügen *n.* (-s, -) pleasure; diversion; ~ *finden an*, to delight in.
vergnügt *a.* pleased, cheerful.
Vergnügung *f.* pleasure, amusement.
Vergnügungssteuer *f.* entertainment tax.
vergolden *v.t.* to gild.
vergönnen *v.t.* to grant, to allow; not to grudge.

vergöttern *v.t.* to deify; (*fig.*) to idolize.
Vergötterung *f.* (-, -en) deification.
vergraben *v.t.st.* to bury.
vergrämt *a.* grief-worn, woe-begone.
vergreifen (sich) *v.refl.st.* to mistake; (*an Geld*) to embezzle.
vergriffen *a.* sold out; out of print.
vergrössern *v.t.* to magnify; (*phot.*) to enlarge.
Vergrösserung *f.* (-, -en) (*Mikroskop, etc.*) magnification; (*phot.*) enlargement.
Vergrösserungsglas *n.* magnifying-glass.
Vergünstigung *f.* (-, -en) favour, privilege.
vergüten *v.t.* to compensate; (*Auslagen*) to reimburse.
Vergütung *f.* (-, -en) remuneration; reimbursement.
verhaften *v.t.* to arrest.
Verhaftung *f.* (-, -en) arrest.
verhallen *v.i.* (*s*) to die away.
verhalten *v.t.st.* to retain, to keep back; (*das Lachen*) to restrain; (**sich**) ~ *v.refl.* to stand; to behave; *wie verhält sich die Sache?* how does the matter stand?; *sich ruhig* ~, to keep quiet.
Verhalten *n.* (-s, 0) conduct, behaviour.
Verhältnis *n.* (-nisses, -nisse) proportion, rate, ratio; circumstance; state, condition; love affair; mistress; *im* ~ *zu*, in proportion to.
verhältnismässig *a.* comparative.
verhältniswidrig *a.* disproportionate.
Verhältniswahl *f.* proportional representation.
Verhältniswort *n.* preposition.
Verhaltungs(mass)regeln *pl.* directions, instructions *pl.*
verhandeln *v.t.* & *i.* to negotiate, to treat; *gerichtlich* ~, to try, to hear a case; *erneut* ~, to retry.
Verhandlung *f.* (-, -en) negotiation; (*law*) trial, hearing; *nochmalige Verhandlung*, rehearing, retrial; ~*en aufnehmen*, to enter into negotiations.
verhängen *v.t.* (*Strafe*) to inflict; (**sich**) ~ *v.refl.* to become entangled.
Verhängnis *n.* (-nisses, -nisse) fate, destiny.
verhängnisvoll *a.* fatal, fateful.
verhärmt *a.* care-worn.
verharren *v.i.* to persist (in); to remain.
verharschen *v.i.* (*s*) to cicatrize, to close.
verhärten *v.t.* (*h*), *v.i.* (*s*) & (**sich**) ~ *v.refl.* to harden.
verhasst *a.* hated, odious.
verhätscheln *v.t.* to coddle, to spoil.
verhauen *v.t.* (*fam.*) to thrash; (**sich**) ~ *v.refl.st.* to blunder.
verheeren *v.t.* to devastate, to lay waste.
Verheerung *f.* (-, -en) devastation.
verhehlen *v.t.* to conceal, to hide.
verheilen *v.i.* (*s*) to heal up.

verheimlichen v.t. to keep (a thing) a secret.
Verheimlichung f. (-, -en) concealment.
verheiraten v.t. to give in marriage, to marry; (sich) ~ v.refl. to marry, to get married.
verheissen v.t.st. to promise.
Verheissung f. (-, -en) promise.
verhelfen v.i.st. to help to.
verherrlichen v.t. to glorify.
Verherrlichung f. (-, -en) glorification.
verhetzen v.t. to instigate, to set (against).
Verhetzung f. (-, -en) instigation.
verhexen v.t. to bewitch.
verhimmeln v.t. to idolize.
verhindern v.t. to prevent.
Verhinderung f. (-, -en) hindrance.
verhohlen a. & adv. secret(ly).
verhöhnen v.t. to deride, to jeer, to gibe.
Verhöhnung f. (-, -en) derision, mockery.
Verhör n. (-[e]s, -e) trial; cross-examination; ins ~nehmen, to cross-examine.
verhören v.t. to question, to interrogate; (sich) ~ v.refl. to mishear.
verhüllen v.t. to wrap up, to veil.
Verhüllung f. (-, -en) disguise.
verhundertfachen (sich) v.i. & refl. to increase a hundredfold.
verhungern v.i. (s) to starve.
verhunzen v.t. to spoil.
verhüten v.t. to prevent, to avert.
Verhütung f. (-, 0) prevention.
verirren (sich) v.refl. to lose one's way.
verirrt a. stray(ing), erring; misled.
Verirrung f. (-, -en) aberration.
verjagen v.t. to drive away.
verjähren v.i. (s) to be lost by limitation.
verjährt a. cancelled by the statute of limitations; (Schulden) superannuated.
Verjährung f. (-, -en) prescription, limitation; ~sfrist f. period of limitation; ~sgesetz n. statute of limitations.
verjüngen v.t. to rejuvenate; to reduce in size; (sich) ~ v.refl. to grow young again; to taper; in verjüngtem Masstab, on a reduced scale.
Verjüngung f. (-, -en) rejuvenation; reduction.
Verkalkung f. (-, -en) (Adern) arteriosclerosis.
verkannt a. misjudged, misunderstood.
verkappen v.t. to disguise, to mask.
Verkauf m. (-[e]s, -käufe) sale.
verkaufen v.t. to sell, to dispose of.
Verkäufer m. (-s, -) seller, (law) vendor; salesman, sales assistant, (Am.) salesclerk; ~in f. saleswoman.
verkäuflich a. sal(e)able; on or for sale.
Verkaufsgewandtheit f. salesmanship.
Verkaufspreis m. selling-price.
Verkaufssteuer f. purchase-tax.
Verkehr m. (-s, 0) intercourse; traffic; starker ~, heavy traffic .

verkehren v.t. to invert; (fig.) to pervert; ~ v.i. to associate (with); to frequent (a place).
Verkehrs: ~ampel f. traffic light; ~dienst (der Polizei), point-duty; ~flugzeug n. commercial or passenger plane; ~insel f. refuge; ~minister m. Minister of Transport; ~mittel n. means of communication; ~ordnung f. traffic regulations; ~regeln pl. traffic code; ~regelung f. traffic regulation; ~schild n. road-sign; ~schutzmann m. constable on point duty; ~stauung f. congestion; ~störung f. traffic hold-up, traffic jam; ~überlastet a. congested; ~zeichen n. traffic sign.
verkehrt a. inverted, upside down; wrong; perverse.
verkennen v.t.ir. to misjudge; to undervalue; to deny, to disbelieve.
Verkennung f. (-, -en) misconstruction; want of appreciation.
verketten v.t. to link together.
Verkettung f. (-, -en) concatenation.
verkitten v.t. to cement.
verklagen v.t. to sue, to bring an action against; to accuse.
verklären v.t. to glorify, to transfigure.
Verklärung f. (-, -en) transfiguration.
verklausuln, verklausulieren v.t. to guard by provisos, to provide against, to restrict.
verkleben v.a. to paste up or over.
Verkleiden v.t. to line; to disguise; (arch.) to face.
Verkleidung f. (-, -en) disguise.
verkleinern v.t. to diminish; to reduce; (fig.) to belittle, to derogate from.
Verkleinerung f. (-, -en) (phot.) reduction.
Verkleinerungswort n. diminutive.
verkleistern v.t. to paste up, to glue up.
verklingen v.i. (s) st. to die away.
Verknappung f. (-, 0) shortage.
verkneifen, sich etwas ~ v.refl.st. (vulg.) to forgo.
verknöchern v.i. to ossify.
verknüpfen v.t. to connect; to join, to combine.
Verknüpfung f. (-, -en) connection.
verkoken v.t. to coke; to carbonize.
verkommen v.i.st. (s) to be neglected, to perish, to decay.
verkoppeln v.t. to couple.
verkörpern v.t. to personify.
Verkörperung f. (-, -en) embodiment.
verkorxen v.t. to mishandle, to bungle.
verköstigen v.t. to board, to feed.
verkrachen v.i. to go smash, to fail.
verkriechen (sich) v.refl.st. to hide.
verkrümmt a. crooked.
verkrüppeln v.t. to cripple, to stunt.
verkümmern v.i. (s) to pine away, to fall away; to atrophy; to be stunted, to starve; ~ v.t. to embitter.

verkündigen *v.t.* to announce, to publish, to proclaim.

erkündigung *f.* (-, -en) announcement, proclamation; ~ *Mariä,* Annunciation-day, Lady-day.

verkuppeln *v.t.* to couple; to pander.

verkürzen *v.t.* to shorten; to abridge.

Verkürzung *f.* (-, -en) shortening; fore-shortening.

verlachen *v.t.* to deride, to laugh at.

verladen *v.t.st.* to load, to ship; *(Truppen)* to entrain.

Verlag *m.* (-[e]s, -lage) publication; publishing-firm.

Verlags: ~**buchhändler** *m.* publisher; ~**buchhandlung** *f.* publishing-house; ~**recht** *n.* copyright.

verlangen *v.t.* to demand; to desire.

Verlangen *n.* (-s, 0) request, demand.

verlängern *v.t.* to lengthen, to prolong; (sich) ~ *v.refl.* to lengthen out.

Verlängerung *f.* (-, -en) prolongation.

verlangsamen *v.t.* to slow down.

Verlangsamung *f.* (-, -en) slow-down.

Verlass *m. es ist auf ihn kein* ~, he is not to be relied on.

verlassen *v.t.st.* to leave; to desert; (sich) ~ *auf v.refl.st.* to rely *or* depend (on); ~ *a.* forlorn, forsaken.

Verlassenheit *f.* (-, 0) loneliness.

verlässlich *a.* reliable.

verlästern *v.t.* to slander, to calumniate.

Verlaub *m.* (-[e]s, 0) leave.

Verlauf *m.* (-[e]s, 0) course; expiration, lapse.

verlaufen *v.i.st.* (*s*) to expire, to elapse; (sich) ~ *v.refl.st.* to miss one's way; *wie ist die Sache* ~? how has the matter turned out?

verlautbaren *v.t.* to make known; ~ *v.imp.* to be divulged.

Verlautbarung *f.* (-, -en) pronounce-ment.

verlauten *v.imp.* to be reported.

verleben *v.t.* to spend, to pass.

verlegen *v.t.* to remove; to mislay; *(Weg)* to bar; *(aufschieben)* to put off; *(Buch)* to publish, to bring out; *sich* ~ *auf,* to go in for, to apply oneself to.

verlegen *a.* embarrassed.

Verlegenheit *f.* (-, -en) self-consciousness, embarrassment, dilemma.

Verleger *m.* (-s, -) publisher.

Verlegung *f.* (-, -en) removal, transfer; postponement.

verleiden *v.t.* to disgust (one) with.

verleihen *v.t.st.* to lend, to let out; to confer upon; to grant; to invest with.

verleiten *v.t.* to seduce.

verlernen *v.t.* to unlearn, to forget.

verlesen *v.t.st.* to read aloud; (sich) ~ *v.refl.* to read wrong.

verletzbar, verletzlich *a.* vulnerable.

verletzen *v.t.* to injure; to violate; to infringe; to offend.

Verletzung *f.* (-, -en) hurt, injury; *(med.)* lesion; violation, infraction.

verleugnen *v.t.* to deny, to disavow.

Verleugnung *f.* (-, 0) denial; abnegation.

verleumden *v.t.* to calumniate.

verleumderisch *a.* slanderous.

Verleumdung *f.* (-, -en) calumny, slander.

verlieben (sich) *v.refl.* to fall in love (with).

verliebt *a.* in love, enamoured; amorous.

verlieren *v.t.st.* to lose; *aus den Augen* ~, to lose sight of; ~ *v.i.* to be a loser; (sich) ~ *v.refl.* to lose one's way; to disappear gradually.

Verlies *n.* (-es, -e) dungeon.

verloben *v.t.* to betroth; (sich) ~ *v.refl.* to get engaged (to)

Verlöbnis *n.* (-nisses, -nisse) betrothal, engagement.

verlobt *a.* engaged (to be married); *seine Verlobte,* his fiancée.

Verlobung *f.* (-, -en) engagement; *die* ~ *auflösen,* to break off the engagement.

Verlobungsring *m.* engagement ring.

verlocken *v.t.* to entice, to allure.

Verlockung *f.* (-, -en) enticement.

verlogen *a.* given to lying, mendacious.

verlohnen *v.t. es verlohnt sich der Mühe,* it is worth while.

verloren *a. & p.* lost.

verlöschen *v.t.* to extinguish; ~ *v.i.st.* (*s*) to go out.

verlosen *v.t.* to raffle.

Verlosung *f.* (-, -en) lottery, raffle.

verlottern *v.i.* (*s*) to go to the bad.

verlumpen *v.t. & i.* = verlottern.

Verlust *m.* (-es, -e) loss; ~ **und Gewinn-konto** *n.* profit and loss account.

verlustig *a.* ~ *gehen,* to lose.

Verlustliste *f.* list of casualties.

vermachen *v.t.* to bequeath.

Vermächtnis *n.* (-nisses, -nisse) legacy, bequest.

vermählen (sich) *v.refl.* to marry, to get married.

Vermählung *f.* (-, -en) marriage.

vermauern *v.t.* to wall up; to close.

vermehren *v.t.* to augment, to increase; (sich) ~ *v.refl.* to multiply.

Vermehrung *f.* (-, -en) increase.

vermeiden *v.t.st.* to avoid, to shun.

vermeidlich *a.* avoidable.

Vermeidung *f.* (-, 0) avoidance.

vermeinen *v.t.* to suppose, to think.

vermeintlich *a.* supposed, pretended.

vermengen *v.t.* to mix, to intermingle; to confound.

Vermengung *f.* (-, -en) mingling; mixture, medley; confusion, mistake.

Vermerk *m.* (-[e]s, -e) entry, note.

vermerken *v.t.* to remark; to note down; *übel* ~, to take amiss.

vermessen—verschliessen 216

vermessen *v.t.st.* to measure; to survey; (sich) ~ *v.refl.st.* to presume; ~ *a.* audacious, presumptuous.
Vermessenheit *f.* (-, -en) presumption.
Vermessung *f.* (-, -en) measuring; survey.
vermieten *v.t.* to let (out), to lease; *zu ~*, on hire; *sich ~*, to hire oneself out.
Vermieter *m.* (-s, -) landlord; (*law*) lessor.
vermindern *v.t.* to diminish; to reduce; (sich) ~ *v.refl.* to decrease.
Verminderung *f.* (-, -en) diminution.
vermischen *v.t.* to (inter)mix, to mingle.
Vermischung *f.* (-, -en) mixture.
vermissen *v.t.* to miss.
Vermisste(r) *m.* (-ten, -ten) missing.
vermitteln *v.t.* to mediate; (*Zwist*) to make up; (*Frieden, Anleihen*) to negotiate.
vermittelst *pr.* by means of.
Vermitt(e)lung *f.* (-, -en) mediation.
Vermittler *m.* (-s, -) mediator.
vermodern *v.i.* (*s*) to moulder, to rot.
vermöge *pr.* by virtue of.
vermögen *v.t.ir.* to be able to do.
Vermögen *n.* (-s, -) ability, faculty; power; fortune, property; *über mein ~*, beyond my power *or* reach.
vermögend *a.* rich, wealthy.
Vermögens: ~abgabe *f.* capital levy; ~bestand *m.* assets *pl.*; ~einkommen *n.* unearned income; ~steuer *f.* property tax; ~umstände *pl.*, ~verhältnisse *n.pl.* financial circumstances.
vermummen *v.t.* to mask; to wrap up.
vermuten *v.t.* to conjecture, to surmise.
Vermuten *n.* (-s, 0) supposition; *wider ~*, unexpectedly.
vermutlich *a.* presumable; presumptive.
Vermutung *f.* (-, -en) supposition.
vernachlässigen *v.t.* to neglect.
Vernachlässigung *f.* (-, -en) neglect.
vernähen *v.t.* to sew up.
vernarben *v.i.* to cicatrize.
vernarrt *a.* infatuated (with).
vernehmen *v.t.st.* to understand, to hear; to interrogate, to examine; *sich ~ lassen*, to speak.
Vernehmen *n.* (-s, 0) intelligence.
vernehmlich *a.* audible, distinct.
Vernehmung *f.* (-, -en) interrogation, examination, trial.
verneigen (sich) *v.refl.* to bow.
Verneigung *f.* (-, -en) bow, curts(e)y.
verneinen *v.t.* to answer in the negative.
verneinend *a.* negative; *~ antworten*, to answer in the negative.
Verneinung *f.* (-, -en) negation; denial.
vernichten *v.t.* to annihilate, to destroy; (*mil.*) to wipe out.
Vernichtung *f.* (-, 0) annihilation.
vernickeln *v.t.* to nickel-plate.
vernieten *v.t.* to rivet, to clinch.
Vernunft *f.* (-, 0) reason; sense, judgment; *gesunde ~*, common sense.

vernunftbegabt *a.* endowed with reason.
vernunftgemäss *a.* reasonable, rational.
vernünftig *a.* reasonable; rational.
veröden *v.i.* (*s*) to become desolate.
Verödung *f.* (-, -en) desolation.
veröffentlichen *v.t.* to publish.
Veröffentlichung *f.* (-, -en) publication.
verordnen *v.t.* to decree, to ordain; (*med.*) to prescribe.
Verordnung *f.* (-, -en) decree; ordinance, regulations *pl.*; (*med.*) prescription.
verpachten *v.t.* to farm out.
verpacken *v.t.* to pack up.
Verpackung *f.* (-, -en) wrapping.
verpäp(p)eln *v.t.* to pamper.
verpassen *v.t.* to let slip, to miss, to lose.
verpesten *v.t.* to infect, to poison.
verpfänden *v.t.* to pawn, to pledge; to mortgage.
verpflanzen *v.t.* to transplant.
Verpflanzung *f.* (-, 0) transplantation.
verpflegen *v.t.* to feed, to board.
Verpflegung *f.* (-, -en) board and lodging, maintenance; (*mil.*) provisioning; *volle ~*, full board; *teilweise ~*, partial board; ~sgeld *n.* subsistence allowance.
verpflichten *v.t.* to oblige, to engage, to obligate; sich ~ *v.refl.* to pledge oneself, to undertake; *einen eidlich ~*, to bind one by oath; *zu Dank ~*, to lay under an obligation.
verpflichtend *a.* obligatory.
Verpflichtung *f.* (-, -en) obligation, engagement; (*Diplomatie*) commitment; (*Geld*)liability; *seinen ~en nachkommen*, to meet one's engagements; *eine ~ eingehen*, to incur an obligation.
verpfuschen *v.t.* to bungle.
verpichen *v.t.* to pitch.
verplappern, sich ~, to give oneself away.
verplempern *v.t.* (*fam.*) to waste.
verpönen *v.t.* to taboo.
verprassen *v.t.* to dissipate.
verproviantieren *v.t.* to victual.
verprügeln *v.t.* to beat up, to thrash.
verpuffen *v.t. & i.* (*fig.*) to squander; ~ *v.i.* (*s*) to be wasted, to vanish.
verpuppen (sich) *v.refl.* to change into a chrysalis.
Verputz *m.* (-es, 0) plaster.
verputzen *v.t.* to plaster (walls).
verquellen *v.i.st.* (*s*) to swell up (by moisture); (*Holz*) to warp.
verquicken *v.t.* to amalgamate.
verrammeln *v.t.* to barricade, to bar.
verrannt *a.* prejudiced, bigoted.
Verrat *m.* (-[e]s, 0) treason; treachery.
verraten *v.t.st.* to betray; to disclose.
Verräter *m.* (-s, -) traitor.
verräterisch *a.* treacherous; traitorous.
verrauchen *v.i.* (*s*) to go off in smoke, to evaporate; (*fig.*) to cool, to pass away.

verräuchern *v.t.* to fill with smoke; to blacken with smoke.

verrauschen *v.i.* (*s*) to pass away, to die away, to be hushed.

verrechnen *v.t.* to reckon up; (sich) ~ *v.refl.* to miscalculate; to be mistaken.

Verrechnung *f.* (-, -en) reckoning; miscalculation; *nur zur* ~, (*Scheck*) not negotiable; ~**sscheck** *m.* crossed cheque.

verrecken *v.i.* (*s*) (*von Tieren*) to die; (*vulg.*) to kick the bucket.

verregnen *v.t.* (*s*) to spoil by rain.

verreisen *v.i.* (*s*) to go on a journey.

verreist *a.* away on travel.

verrenken *v.t.* to dislocate, to sprain.

Verrenkung *f.* (-, -en) dislocation.

verrennen *v.t.ir. sich* ~ *in*, (*fig.*) to get stuck fast in.

verrichten *v.t.* to do, to perform, to execute, to achieve; *seine Notdurft* ~, to ease oneself; *sein Gebet* ~, to say one's prayers.

Verrichtung *f.* (-, -en) achievement; (discharge of) business.

verriegeln *v.t.* to bolt, to bar.

verringern *v.t.* to diminish, to lessen.

verrinnen *v.i.st.* (*s*) to run off *or* out.

verrohen *v.t. & i.* to brutalize; to grow brutal.

verrosten *v.i.* (*s*) to rust (all over).

verrostet *a.* rusty.

verrottet *a.* rotten.

verrucht *a.* infamous.

verrücken *v.t.* to displace, to remove.

verrückt *a.* deranged, crazy, mad.

Verrückte(r) *m.* lunatic, madman.

Verrücktheit *f.* (-, -en) craziness.

Verruf *m.* (-[e]s, 0) *in* ~ *sein*, to be in discredit.

verrufen *v.t.st.* to cry down, to decry; ~ *a.* ill reputed.

verrusst *a.* sooted up.

Vers *m.* (Verses, Verse) verse.

versagen *v.t. & i.* to deny, to refuse; ~ *v.i.* to miss fire; (*Stimme*) to fail.

versalzen *v.t.* to over salt.

versammeln *v.t.* to collect, to assemble; (sich) ~ *v.refl.* to assemble, to congregate, to meet.

Versammlung *f.* (-, -en) assembly, meeting; *eine* ~ *auf 10 Uhr einberufen*, to call a meeting for 10 o'clock.

Versand *m.* (-[e]s, 0) dispatch.

versanden *v.i.* (*s*) to get choked up with sand.

Versatz: ~**amt**, ~**haus** *n.* pawn shop; ~**stück** *n.* (*Pfand*) pawn, pledge.

versauen *v.t.* (*vulg.*) to make a mess of.

versauern *v.t.* to embitter.

versaufen *v.t.st.* to waste in drink.

versäumen *v.t.* to miss, to neglect.

Versäumnis *f.* (-, -nisse) omission; ~**urteil** *n.* judgment by default.

verschachern *v.t.* to barter away.

verschaffen *v.t.* to procure, to furnish with, to provide; (sich) ~ *v.refl.* to procure, to secure, to acquire.

verschalen *v.t.* to board over.

Verschalung *f.* (-, -en) wooden covering.

verschämt *a.* bashful, shamefaced.

verschandeln *v.t.* to disfigure, to spoil.

verschanzen *v.t.* to entrench, to fortify.

Verschanzung *f.* (-, -en) fortification.

verschärfen *v.t.* to aggravate.

verscharren *v.t.* to bury (without ceremony).

verscheiden *v.i.st.* (*s*) to expire, to die.

verschenken *v.t.* to give away.

verscherzen *v.t.* to forfeit, to lose.

verscheuchen *v.t.* to scare away.

verschicken *v.t.* to dispatch.

verschieben *v.t.st.* to shift, to displace; to delay, to put off, to postpone.

verschieden *a.* different; various; divers, sundry; deceased.

verschiedenartig *a.* various, heterogeneous.

verschiedenerlei *a.* of various kinds.

verschiedenfarbig *a.* in different colours.

Verschiedenheit *f.* (-, -en) diversity.

verschiedentlich *adv.* repeatedly.

verschiessen *v.t.st.* to spend in firing *or* shooting; ~ *v.i.st.* (*s*) to fade, to lose colour.

verschiffen *v.t.* to ship; to export.

verschimmeln *v.i.* (*s*) to get mouldy.

verschimmelt *a.* mouldy.

verschlafen *v.t.st.* to sleep away; (sich) ~ *v.refl.* to oversleep oneself.

Verschlag *m.* (-[e]s, -schläge) partition; box.

verschlagen *v.t.st.* to partition, to board; ~ *v.i.st.* (*s*) to grow lukewarm; *das Wasser* ~ *lassen*, to take the chill off the water; *das verschlägt nichts*, it's of no consequence.

verschlagen *a.* cunning, sly, crafty, subtle; lukewarm, with the chill off.

Verschlagenheit *f.* (-, 0) cunning.

verschlechtern *v.t.* to impair; (sich) ~ *v.refl.* to deteriorate.

verschleiern *v.t.* to veil; to screen.

Verschleimung *f.* (-, -en) stopping up with mucus.

Verschleiss *m.* (-es, -e) wear and tear; sale (by retail).

verschleissen *v.t.st.* to wear out; to sell (by retail).

verschleppen *v.t.* to mislay; to abduct; (*Krankheiten*) to spread; (*fig.*) to protract, to put off, to delay.

Verschleppung *f.* (-, -en) protraction.

verschleudern *v.t.* to waste; to sell dirt-cheap.

verschliessen *v.t.st.* to shut, to close; to lock; (sich)~*v.refl.st.* to lock oneself in *or* up.

verschlimmern *v.t.* to make worse; (sich)
~ *v.refl.* to get worse.
Verschlimmerung *f.* (-, 0) change for the
worse.
verschlingen *v.t.st.* to twist, to interlace;
to swallow (up), to devour.
verschlossen *a. & p.* locked up, shut; (*fig.*)
reticent, reserved, close.
Verschlossenheit *f.* (-, 0) (*fig.*) reserve.
verschlucken *v.t.* to swallow; (sich) ~
v.refl. to choke, to swallow the wrong
way.
Verschluss *m.* (-schlusses, -schlüsse) lock;
(*phot.*) shutter; (*Ware*) bond; unter ~,
under lock and key.
verschmachten *v.i.* (s) to pine away.
verschmähen *v.t.* to disdain, to scorn.
verschmelzen *v.t.st.* to blend; ~ *v.i.st.* (s)
to be blended.
verschmerzen *v.t.* to get over (a loss).
verschmieren *v.t.* to smudge, to blur.
verschmitzt *a.* cunning, sly, artful.
verschmutzen *v.t.* to dirty, to soil; *v.i.* to
get dirty.
verschnaufen (sich) *v.refl.* to recover one's
breath.
verschneiden *v.t.st.* to castrate; to adulterate (wine).
verschneien *v.t.* to snow up.
Verschnitt *m.* (-es, -e) blend.
Verschnittene[r] *m.* (-n, -n) eunuch.
verschnupfen *v.t.imp.* to offend; *ver-
schnupft sein*, to have a cold in one's
head; (*fig.*) to feel offended.
verschnüren *v.t.* to cord; to lace, to trim
with lace.
verschollen *a.* forgotten; presumed dead
or lost.
verschonen *v.t.* to spare.
verschönern *v.t.* to embellish.
verschossen *a.* faded, discoloured.
verschränken *v.t.* to cross (one's arms);
to interlace, to entwine.
verschreiben *v.t.st.* (*med.*) to prescribe;
(sich) ~ *v.refl.st.* to make a slip of the
pen.
Verschreibung *f.* (-, -en) prescription.
verschroben *a.* eccentric, queer.
verschroten *v.t.* to grind (up).
verschüchtern *v.t.* to intimidate.
verschulden *v.t.* to be guilty of, to commit; to involve in debt.
Verschulden *n.* (-s, 0) fault, guilt.
Verschuldung *f.* (-, -en) indebtedness;
offence, fault.
verschütten *v.t.* to spill; *verschüttet werden*, to be buried under (falling) earth
or stones.
Verschwägerung *f.* (-, -en) affinity.
verschweigen *v.t.st.* to keep (a thing) a
secret, to conceal; to suppress.
verschwenden *v.t.* to squander, to dissipate, to waste.

verschwenderisch *a.* prodigal, lavish;
(*reichlich*) profuse.
Verschwendung *f.* (-, -en) prodigality.
verschwiegen *a.* close, discreet, reticent.
Verschwiegenheit *f.* (-, 0) discretion.
verschwimmen *v.i.st.* (s) to become indistinct *or* blurred.
verschwinden *v.i.st.* (s) to disappear, to
vanish.
verschwommen *a.* indistinct, blurred.
verschwören *v.t.st.* to forswear; (sich) ~
v.refl.st. to plot, to conspire.
Verschwörer *m.* (-s, -) conspirator.
Verschwörung *f.* (-, -en) conspiracy,
plot.
versehen *v.t.* to provide, to supply;
(*Dienst*) to perform; (sich) ~ *v.refl.* to
make a mistake; *ehe ich mir's versehe*,
before I am aware of it.
Versehen *n.* (-s, -) oversight; *aus ~*, inad-
vertently.
versehren *v.t.* to injure, to hurt.
versenden *v.t.ir.* to dispatch, to ship.
Versendung *f.* (-, -en) dispatch.
versengen *v.t.* to singe, to scorch.
versenken *v.t.* to sink, to submerge;
(*Schiff*) to scuttle; (*Schraube*) to countersink.
versessen *a.* bent (upon).
versetzen *v.t.* to displace; to transplant;
to pawn; to promote (to a higher form);
to mix, to alloy; ~ *v.i.* to reply, to rejoin; *in die Notwendigkeit ~*, to lay
under the necessity of; *einem einen
Schlag, Hieb ~*, to deal someone a
blow, a cut; *einen in Anklagezustand ~*,
to put someone on trial, to indict.
Versetzung *f.* (-, -en) transfer (*eines Beam-
ten*); removal; promotion (school, etc.).
verseuchen *v.t.* to infect.
Versfuss *m.* (metrical) foot, metre.
versichern *v.t.* to assure, to affirm; to insure; *das Leben seiner Frau ~*, to take
out a policy on the life of one's wife;
(sich) ~ *v.refl.* to make sure of, to ascertain; to secure.
Versicherung *f.* (-, -en) assurance, affirmation; insurance; *eine ~ abschliessen*,
to effect a policy.
Versicherungs: ~anspruch *m.* insurance
claim; ~fähig *a.* insurable; ~makler
m. insurance broker; ~police, insurance policy; ~prämie *f.* insurance
premium.
versiegeln *v.t.* to seal (up).
versiegen *v.i.* (s) to dry up, to be drained.
versilbern *v.t.* to (silver-)plate; (*fig.*) to
convert into money.
Versilberung *f.* (-, -en) silver-plating; conversion.
versinken *v.i.st.* (s) to sink, to founder.
Version *f.* (-, -en) version.
Versmass *n.* metre.

versoffen a. besotted, sodden; drunken; (*Bergwerk*) flooded.
versöhnen v.t. to reconcile.
versöhnlich a. placable, conciliatory.
Versöhnung f. (-, -en) reconciliation.
versorgen v.t. to provide with, to supply; to provide for, to take care of, to maintain.
Versorger m. (-s, -) breadwinner (for).
Versorgung f. (-, -en) provision.
versorgungsberechtigt a. entitled to (parish-)relief.
verspäten (*sich*) v.t. v.refl. to be late.
verspätet a. behind time.
Verspätung f. (-, -en) delay, lateness.
verspeisen v.t. to eat (up).
verspekulieren v.t. to lose by speculation.
versperren v.t. to block up, to barricade.
verspielen v.t. to gamble away.
verspotten v.t. to deride, to scoff at.
Verspottung f. (-, -en) mockery, derision.
versprechen v.t.st. to promise; (sich) ~ v.refl.st. to make a slip of the tongue.
Versprechen n. (-s, -) promise.
versprengen v.t. to disperse.
verspüren v.t. to perceive, to feel.
verstaatlichen v.t. to nationalize.
Verstand m. (-[e]s, 0) understanding, intellect; (good) sense; *gesunder* ~, common sense; *den* ~ *verlieren*, to go out of one's mind.
verstandesmässig a. intellectual, rational.
verständig a. intelligent, sensible.
verständigen v.t. to inform; *sich mit einem* ~, to come to an understanding with someone.
Verständigung f. (-, -en) arrangement, agreement; information.
verständlich a. intelligible; *allgemein* ~, popular, within the reach (comprehension) of every one.
Verständnis n. (-nisses, -nisse) comprehension; understanding.
Verständnislosigkeit f. (-, 0) lack of appreciation.
verstärken v.t. to strengthen, to reinforce; to intensify; (*radio*) to amplify.
Verstärker (*röhre* f.), m. (*radio*) amplifier (valve).
Verstärkung f. (-, -en) reinforcement.
verstatten v.t. to permit, to allow.
verstauben v.i. (s) to get dusty.
verstauchen v.t. to sprain; to dislocate.
Verstauchung f. (-, -en) spraining; dislocation.
Versteck m. (-[e]s, -e) hiding-place; *~en spielen*, to play at hide-and-seek.
verstecken v.t. to hide, to conceal.
versteckt a. close; secretive.
verstehen v.t.st. to understand; to comprehend; to know (how); to mean; *falsch* ~, to misunderstand.
versteifen v.t. to strut, to prop; *sich* ~

v.refl. to stiffen (*Börse*); (*fig.*) to insist upon.
versteigen (sich) v.refl.st. *sich zu einer Behauptung* ~, to go so far as to maintain that...
versteigern v.t. to sell by auction.
Versteigerung f. (-, -en) auction, public sale.
versteinert a. petrified.
Versteinerung f. (-, -en) petrifaction, fossil.
verstellbar a. adjustable.
verstellen v.t. to displace; to shift; (*den Weg*) to bar; (sich) ~ v.refl. to dissemble, to feign.
Verstellung f. (-, -en) dissimulation.
versteuern v.t. to pay excise or duty on.
verstiegen a. high-flown, extravagant.
verstimmen v.t. to put out of humour.
verstimmt a. out of tune; (*fig.*) out of humour, put out.
Verstimmtheit, Verstimmung f. (-, -en) (*fig.*) ill-humour, ill-feeling.
verstocken v.t. to harden.
verstockt a. obdurate, hardened.
verstohlen a. surreptitious, stealthy.
verstopfen v.t. to block, to stop; (*med.*) to constipate.
Verstopfung f. (-, -en) stopping, obstruction; constipation.
verstorben a. deceased, defunct.
verstört a. troubled, haggard, wild.
Verstoss m. (-es, -stösse) fault, offence, mistake.
verstossen v.t.st. to cast off, to expel; ~ v.i.st. ~ *gegen*, to offend against, to transgress.
verstreichen v.i.st. (s) to elapse.
verstreuen v.t. to scatter, to disperse.
verstricken v.t. (*fig.*) to entangle, to ensnare.
verstümmeln v.t. to mutilate, to mangle.
Verstümmelung f. (-, -en) mutilation.
verstummen v.i. (s) to grow dumb.
Versuch m. (-[e]s, -e) experiment; trial, attempt.
versuchen v.t. to try, to attempt; to taste.
Versucherin f. (-, -nen) temptress.
Versuchs: ~**ballon** m. (*fig.*) kite; ~**fabrik** f. pilot plant.
versuchsweise adv. by way of experiment.
Versuchung f. (-, -en) temptation.
versündigen (sich) v.refl. to sin (against).
Versündigung f. (-, -en) grave offence.
Versunkenheit f. (-, 0) absorption; corruption, depravity.
versüssen v.t. to sweeten.
vertagen v.t. to adjourn; to prorogue (parliament); (sich) ~ v.refl. to adjourn.
Vertagung f. (-, -en) adjournment; prorogation.
vertändeln v.t. to trifle away.
vertauschen v.t. to exchange.

Vertauschung f. (-, -en) exchange, barter.

verteidigen v.t. to defend.

Verteidiger m. (-s, -) defender; (law) counsel for the defence; (Fussball) back.

Verteidigung f. (-, -en) defence.

verteilen v.t. to distribute, to apportion.

Verteiler m. (-s, -) (auf Akten) distribution list.

Verteilung f. (-, -en) distribution.

verteuern v.t. to make dearer.

verteufelt a. (fam.) devilish.

vertiefen v.t. to deepen; (sich) ~ v.refl. to be absorbed in.

vertieren v.i. to grow brutish.

vertikal a. vertical.

vertilgen v.t. to exterminate; to consume.

vertonen v.t. to set to music.

vertrackt a. odd, strange; confounded, intricate.

Vertrag m. (-[e]s, -träge) contract, agreement; (Staats~) treaty.

vertragen v.t. to bear, to stand, to endure; to digest; ich kann kein Bier ~, beer does not agree with me; (sich) ~ v.refl. to get on well (together); to square, to tally (with).

vertraglich a. contractual; stipulated.

verträglich a. sociable, peaceable; compatible.

vertragsmässig a. stipulated.

Vertrags: ~partei f. contracting party; ~recht n. law of contract.

vertragswidrig a. contrary to a contract or treaty.

vertrauen v.t. to entrust, to confide; ~ v.i. to confide, to rely upon.

Vertrauen n. (-s, 0) confidence; trust; im ~, privately, confidentially.

Vertrauensbruch m. breach of trust.

Vertrauensstellung f. position of trust.

vertrauens: ~selig a. quick to give one's confidence, gullible, rashly trustful; ~voll a. confiding, trusting, trustful; ~würdig a. trustworthy.

vertrauern v.t. to spend in sorrow.

vertraulich a. confidential, intimate.

Vertraulichkeit f. (-, -en) familiarity, intimacy.

verträumen v.t. to dream away.

vertraut a. intimate, familiar; conversant (with), versed (in); auf ~em Fusse stehen, to be on terms of intimacy.

Vertraute[r] m. & f. (-n, -n) confidant.

Vertrautheit f. (-, 0) familiarity.

vertreiben v.t. st. to drive away, to expel, to banish; to sell; to pass away (the time.

Vertreibung f. (-, -en) expulsion.

vertreten v.t.v.st. to represent.

Vertreter m. (-s, -) representative.

Vertretung f. (-, -en) representation; in ~ von, acting for or as representative of; by proxy.

Vertrieb m. (-[e]s, 0) sale, distribution.

vertrinken v.t.st. to spend in drinking.

vertrocknen v.i. to dry up, to wither.

vertrödeln v.t. to trifle or fritter away.

vertrösten v.t. to fob off, to put off (with fine words).

vertun v.t.st. to waste, to squander.

vertuschen v.t. to hush up; to suppress.

verübeln v.t. to take amiss.

verüben v.t. to commit, to perpetrate.

verulken v.t. to make fun of.

verunehren v.t. to dishonour, to disgrace.

verunglimpfen v.t. to defame, to revile.

verunglücken v.i. (s) to meet with an accident.

verunreinigen v.t. to soil, to contaminate; (Wasser) to pollute; (Luft) to infect; (fig.) to defile.

Verunreinigung f. (-, -en) defilement, contamination.

verunstalten v.t. to disfigure, to deface.

Verunstaltung f. (-, -en) disfigurement.

veruntreuen v.t. to embezzle.

Veruntreuung f. (-, -en) embezzlement.

verunzieren v.t. to disfigure, to mar.

verursachen v.t. to cause; to occasion.

Verursachung f. (-, -en) causation.

verurteilen v.t. to condemn; to convict, to sentence.

Verurteilung f. (-, -en) condemnation.

vervielfältigen v.t. to multiply; to duplicate, to mimeograph.

Vervielfältigung f. (-, -en) reproduction.

Vervielfältigungsapparat m. mimeograph.

vervierfachen v.t. to quadruple.

vervollkommnen v.t. to perfect.

vervollständigen v.t. to complete, to complement.

verwachsen v.i.st. (s) to grow together; ~ a. deformed, crippled.

verwahren v.t. to keep; sich gegen etwas ~, to protest against.

verwahrlost, neglected, unkempt.

Verwahrlosung f. (-, -en) neglect.

Verwahrung f. (-, -en) keeping, custody; protest; in ~ nehmen, to take into custody; ~ einlegen gegen, to enter a protest against.

verwaisen v.i. (s) to become an orphan.

verwaist a. orphan; (fig.) deserted.

verwalten v.t. to administer.

Verwalter m. (-s, -) administrator.

Verwaltung f. (-, -en) administration, management.

Verwaltungs: ~gericht n. administrative court; ~recht n. administrative law.

verwandeln v.t. to change, to transform, to convert, to turn; (Strafe) to commute; (sich) ~ v.refl. to be changed.

Verwandlung f. (-, -en) change, transformation; changing, turning.

verwandt a. related, akin to; (*Begriffe*) cognate.

Verwandte[r] m. & f. (-n, -n) relation, relative, kinsman, kinswoman; *nächste* ~, next-of-kin.

Verwandtschaft f. (-, -en) relationship; relations pl.; (*chem.*) affinity.

verwandtschaftlich a. suitable among relatives.

verwarnen v.t. to forewarn.

verwaschen a. washed-out, faded.

verwässern v.t. to dilute, to drown.

verweben v.t. to interweave.

verwechseln v.t. to mistake (for), to confound.

Verwechslung f. (-, -en) mistake, confusion.

verwegen a. audacious, daring, bold.

verwehen v.t. to blow away.

verwehren v.t. to hinder, to prohibit.

verweichlichen v.t. to render effeminate.

verweigern v.t. to refuse.

Verweigerung f. (-, -en) denial, refusal.

verweilen v.i. to stay, to stop, to abide, to tarry; to sojourn; (*fig.*) to dwell (on).

verweint a. red with weeping.

Verweis m. (-es, -e) rebuke, reprimand; (*in Buch*) cross-reference.

verweisen v.t.st. to refer (one) to; *einen des Landes* oder *aus dem Lande* ~, to exile, to banish someone; *einem etwas* ~, to rebuke someone for, to have someone up for.

Verweisung f. (-, -en) reference; banishment, exile; ~szeichen, reference.

verwelken v.i. (s) to wither, to fade.

verweltlichen v.t. to secularize.

verwendbar a. available; applicable.

verwenden v.t.ir. to apply (to), to spend (on), to employ (in); *sich ~ für*, to intercede on behalf of.

Verwendung f. (-, -en) application, use, employment; intercession.

verwendungsunfähig a. unemployable.

verwerfen v.t.st. to reject; to quash; to condemn.

verwerflich a. objectionable.

Verwerfung f. (-, -en) rejection; condemnation.

verwerten v.t. to utilize.

verwesen v.t. to administer; ~ v.i. (s) to rot, to decay.

verweslich a. perishable, corruptible.

Verwesung f. (-, -en) putrefaction.

verwickeln v.t. to entangle, to complicate, to implicate; to involve; (*sich*) ~ v.refl. to become complicated; to get involved.

verwickelt a. complicated, intricate.

Verwick(e)lung f. (-, -en) entanglement, complication; plot (of a play).

verwildern v.i. (s) to run wild.

verwirken v.t. to forfeit.

verwirklichen v.t. to realize; (*sich*) ~, to be or become realized, to materialize.

Verwirklichung f. (-, -en) realization.

verwirren v.t. to entangle; to embarrass, to perplex.

verwirrt a. confused; embarrassed.

Verwirrung f. (-, -en) confusion.

verwirtschaften v.t. to waste (by mismanagement).

verwischen v.t. to wipe out, to blot out; (*fig.*) to obliterate.

verwittern v.i. (s) to become disintegrated, dilapidated.

verwittert a. weather-beaten.

verwitwet a. widowed.

verwogen a. bold, daring, audacious.

verwöhnen v.t. to spoil, to pamper.

verworfen a. abandoned, depraved.

verworren a. intricate, confused.

verwundbar a. vulnerable.

verwunden v.t. to wound, to hurt.

verwunderlich a. strange, odd.

verwundern (sich) v.refl. to be surprised.

verwundert a. astonished, surprised.

verwunschen a. (*fam.*) enchanted.

verwünschen v.t. to curse, to execrate.

verwünscht a. confounded; ~! confound it!

verwüsten v.t. to devastate, to lay waste.

Verwüstung f. (-, -en) devastation.

verzagen v.i. to lose courage, to despair.

verzagt a. discouraged, despondent.

verzählen (sich) v.refl. to count wrong.

Verzahnung f. (-, -en) (*Holz*) dovetailing.

verzapfen v.t. to sell (liquor) by retail.

verzärteln v.t. to coddle, to pamper.

verzaubern v.t. to bewitch, to enchant.

Verzauberung f. (-, -en) enchantment.

verzehren v.t. to consume; to eat.

verzeichnen v.t. to note down; to specify, to distort.

Verzeichnis n. (-nisses, -nisse) list, catalogue; index.

verzeihen v.t.st. to pardon, to forgive.

verzeihlich a. pardonable; excusable.

Verzeihung f. (-, 0) pardon; forgiveness; *um ~ bitten*, to beg pardon.

verzerren v.t. to distort.

verzetteln v.t. to fritter away.

Verzicht m. (-[e]s, -e) renunciation; ~ *leisten auf*, to renounce.

verzichten v.i. to renounce, to resign.

Verzichtleistung f. renunciation.

verziehen v.t.st. to distort; ~ v.i. *ein Kind* ~, to spoil a child; *in die Stadt* ~, to move into town; (*sich*) ~ v.refl. to pass away.

verzieren v.t. to decorate, to adorn.

Verzierung f. (-, -en) decoration, ornament.

verzinnen v.t. to tin.

verzinsen v.t. to pay interest on; (*sich*) ~ v.refl. to bear or yield interest.

verzinslich a. bearing interest.

verzogen a. spoilt (child); removed (into another house).

verzögern *v.t.* to delay, to protract.
verzollbar *a.* dutiable, liable to pay duty.
verzollen *v.t.* to pay duty on.
verzuckern *v.t.* to sugar over.
verzückt *a.* in raptures *or* transports.
Verzückung *f.* (-, -en) ecstasy.
Verzug *m.* (-[e]s, 0) delay.
Verzugs: ~tage *pl.* days of grace; ~zeit *f.* delayed action; ~zinsen *pl.* interest on arrears.
verzweifeln *v.i.* (s) to despair (of).
verzweifelt *a.* desperate; despairing.
Verzweiflung *f.* (-, 0) despair, desperation.
verzweigen (sich) *v.refl.* to ramify.
verzwickt *a.* odd, strange; intricate.
Vesper *f.* (-, -n) vespers *pl.*
vespern *v.i.* to have one's tea or supper.
Vestalin *f.* (-, -nen) vestal.
Veteran *m.* (-en, -en) veteran.
Veterinär *m.* (-s, -e) veterinary surgeon.
Veto *n.* (-[s], -s) veto.
Vettel *f.* (-, -n) old woman.
Vetter *m.* (-s, -n) (male) cousin; ~ zweiten Grades, second cousin.
vexieren *v.t.* to tease, to banter; to quiz, to puzzle, to mystify.
Vexiererei *f.* (-, -en) teasing; quizzing.
via *pr.* via, by way (of).
Viadukt *m.* (-[e]s, -e) viaduct.
vibrieren *v.i.* to vibrate.
Vieh *n.* (-[e]s, 0) beast; cattle.
Vieh: ~futter *n.* fodder, provender; ~händler *m.* cattle dealer.
viehisch *a.* beastly, brutal, bestial.
Vieh: ~seuche *f.* cattle-plague, rinderpest; foot-and-mouth disease; ~zucht *f.* cattle-breeding; ~züchter *m.* stockfarmer, cattle-breeder.
viel *a. & adv.* much, a great deal; ~e *pl.* many; gleich viel, as many or much; no matter, just the same.
vielbändig *a.* in many volumes.
vielbeschäftigt *a.* busy, much occupied.
vieldeutig *a.* ambiguous.
Vieleck *n.* (-[e]s, -e) polygon.
vielerlei *a.* different, various.
vielfach, vielfältig *a. & adv.* manifold, multifarious; repeatedly.
Vielfrass *m.* (-es, -e) glutton.
vielgestaltig *a.* Protean, multiform.
Vielgötterei *f.* (-, 0) polytheism.
Vielheit *f.* (-, -en) multitude; plurality.
vielköpfig *a.* many-headed.
vielleicht *adv.* perhaps, maybe.
vielmals *adv.* many times, frequently.
vielmalig *a.* repeated, frequent.
vielmehr *adv.* rather; on the contrary.
vielsagend *a.* significant, expressive.
vielseitig *a.* multilateral; (*fig.*) many-sided, versatile.
Vielseitigkeit *f.* (-, 0) versatility.
vielsilbig *a.* polysyllabic.

vielstimmig *a.* (*mus.*) for many voices; many-voiced.
vielverheissend *a.* promising.
Vielweiberei *f.* (-, 0) polygamy.
vier *a.* four; auf allen ~en, on all fours; unter ~ Augen, in private, between you and me.
Vier *f.* (-, -en) the number *or* figure four.
vierbeinig *a.* four-footed, four-legged.
vierblätt(e)rig *a.* four-leaved.
Viereck *n.* (-[e]s, -e) square, quadrangle.
viereckig *a.* quadrangular, square.
viererlei *a.* of four sorts.
vierfach, vierfältig *a.* fourfold.
vierfüssig *a.* four-footed.
Vierfüssler *m.* (-s, -) quadruped.
vierhändig *a.* four-handed; ~ (*Klavier*) spielen, to play four-handed.
vierhundert *a.* four hundred.
vierjährig *a.* four years old.
Vierlinge *pl.* quadruplets.
viermal *adv.* four times; ~ so viel, four times as much, four times the number.
Viermächte...quadripartite *a.*
viermalig *a.* four times repeated.
viermotorig *a.* four-engine(d).
Vierradbremse *f.* four-wheel brake.
vierräd[e]rig *a.* four-wheeled.
vierschrötig *a.* square-built, robust.
Viersitzer *m.* four-seater.
viersitzig *a.* four-seated.
vierspännig *a.* four-horse(d).
vierstimmig *a.* for four voices *or* parts.
vierteilen *v.t.* to quarter.
Viertel *n.* (-s, -) fourth part; quarter; (*Stadt*) quarter; (*Villen~*) residential quarter; es ist ein ~ auf 2 (*Uhr*), it is a quarter past one.
Vierteljahr *n.* quarter.
vierteljährig *a.* quarterly.
vierteljährlich *adv.* every three months, quarterly.
Vierteljahrsschrift *f.* quarterly (review).
Viertel: ~note *f.* crotchet; ~stunde *f.* quarter of an hour.
viertelstündlich *a.* every quarter of an hour.
viertens *adv.* fourthly, in the fourth place.
Viervierteltakt *m.* (*mus.*) common time.
vierzehn *a.* fourteen; ~ Tage, a fortnight.
vierzig *a.* forty.
Vierziger *m.* (-s, -), -in, *f.* (-, -nen) quadragenarian; in den vierziger Jahren, in the forties.
Vikar *m.* (-s, -e) curate.
Viktualien *pl.* victuals, eatables *pl.*
Villa *f.* (-, Villen) residence; country-house, country-box.
Villenkolonie *f.* garden city.
vindizieren *v.t.* to claim; to vindicate.
Viola *f.* (-, -len) viola.
Viole *f.* (-, -n) viola.
violett *a.* violet(-coloured).

Violinbogen *m.* bow.
Violine *f.* (-, -n) violin.
Violinist *m.* (-en, -en) Violinspieler *m.*
   violinist; erster ~, leader.
Violin: ~saite *f.* fiddle-string; ~schlüssel
   m. treble-clef.
Violon *n.* (-s, -s) bass-viol.
Violoncell(o) *n.* (-[s], -cellos *u.* -cells)
   cello, violon-cello.
Viper *f.* (-, -n) viper.
Virtuose *m.* (-n, -n), virtuoso.
Virtuosität *f.* (-, -en) mastery.
Visier *n.* (-[e]s, -e) beaver, visor; (am
   Gewehr) sight.
visieren *v.t.* to aim; to gauge; (Pass) to
   visa, to vise.
Vision *f.* (-, -en) vision.
Visitation *f.* (-, -en) inspection.
Visite *f.* (-, -n) visit, call.
Visitenkarte *f.* (visiting-)card.
Visum *n.* (-s, -sa) visa; signature.
Vitamin *n.* (-s, -e) vitamin(e).
Vitriol *m. or n.* (-[e]s, -e) vitriol.
Vivisektion *f.* (-, -eu) vivisection.
Vize: *in Zusammensetzun en*, vice...;
   Vizekönig *m.* viceroy.
Vlies, Vliess *n.* (-es, -e) fleece.
Vogel *m.* (-s, Vögel) bird; (Huhn) fowl;
   einen ~ haben, (fig.) to have a bee in
   one's bonnet; den ~ abschiessen, to
   carry off the prize.
Vogel: ~bauer *m.* bird-cage; ~flinte *f.*
   fowling-piece.
vogelfrei *a.* outlawed, proscribed.
Vogel: ~haus *n.* aviary; ~perspektive *f.*
   bird's-eye view; ~schau *f.* bird's-eye
   view; aus der ~, a bird's-eye view of;
   ~scheuche *f.* scarecrow.
Vöglein *n.* (-s, -) little bird.
Vogt *m.* (-[e]s, Vögte) steward; bailiff.
Vokabel *f.* (-, -n) word.
Vokal *m.* (-[e]s, -e) vowel.
Vokalmusik *f.* vocal music, singing.
Vokativ *m.* (-s, -e) vocative.
Volk, *n.* (-[e]s, Völker) people, nation.
Völker: ~bund *m.* League of Nations;
   ~kunde *f.* ethnology; ~mord *m.* genocide; ~recht *n.* law of nations, international law.
völkerrechtlich *a.* relating to the law of
   nations; international.
Völkerschaft *f.* (-, -en) tribe, people.
Völkerwanderung *f.* migration of
   nations.
völkisch *a.* racial.
volkreich *a.* populous.
Volks... ethnic *a.*
Volks: ~abstimmung *f.* plebiscite, referendum; ~bibliothek *f.* free library;
   ~charakter *m.* national character;
   ~deutscher *m.* ethnic *or* racial German;
   ~entscheid (über) *m.* referendum (on);
   ~fest *n.* people's festival; ~front *f.*

popular front; ~hochschule *f.* university extension; ~kunde *f.* folklore;
   ~lied *n.* popular song, folk-song.
volksmässig *a.* popular.
Volks: ~menge *f.* multitude, throng;
   ~partei *f.* people's party; ~redner
   m. popular speaker, stump-orator;
   ~schule *f.* primary *or* elementary
   school; ~schullehrer *m.* elementary
   teacher; ~schulwesen *n.* system of
   national education; ~stamm *m.* tribe;
   ~tracht *f.* national dress *or* costume.
Volkstum *n.* (-s, 0) nation(ality); national
   character.
volkstümlich *a.* popular; national.
Volks: ~unterricht *m.* public instruction;
   ~versammlung *f.* public meeting; ~ver-
   treter *m.* representative of the people;
   ~vertretung *f.* popular representation;
   national assembly, parliament; ~wirt-
   schaft *f.* political economy; national
   economic structure.
volkswirtschaftlich *a.* politico-economical.
Volkszählung *f.* census.
voll *a.* full; entire; (vulg.) drunk; es war ~
   im Theater, the house was crowded;
   nicht für ~ ansehen, not to take seriously; das Mass ~machen, to fill up the
   measure, to crown all; um das Unglück
   ~zumachen, to make things worse;
   ~pfropfen, to cram, to stuff; aus dem
   Vollen wirtschaften, not to stint oneself.
vollauf *adv.* abundantly, plentifully; (fam.)
   galore.
voll ausgeschrieben *a.* in full.
Vollbart *m.* beard.
Vollbesitz *m.* full possession.
Vollblut, Vollblutpferd *n.* thoroughbred
   (horse).
vollbringen *v.t.st.* to accomplish.
Volldampf, *m.* full steam.
vollenden *v.t.* to finish; to accomplish.
vollendet *a.* perfect.
vollends *adv.* altogether, wholly; finally.
Vollendung *f.* (-, 0) completion, perfection.
Völlerei *f.* (-, 0) gluttony.
vollführen *v.t.* to execute; to accomplish.
Vollgefühl *n.* full consciousness.
Vollgehalt *m.* full *or* entire contents *pl.*
Vollgenuss *m.* full enjoyment.
vollgepfropft, vollgerüttelt *a.* crammed
   (with), chokefull.
vollgültig *a.* of full value.
völlig *a.* entire, whole; ~ *adv.* fully.
volljährig *a.* of full age.
Volljährigkeit *f.* (-, 0) full age, majority.
vollkommen *a.* perfect; consummate.
Vollkommenheit *f.* (-, -en) perfection.
Vollkraft *f.* (-, 0) full vigour, energy.
Vollmacht *f.* (-, -en) full power; power of
   attorney; letter of attorney.
Vollmatrose *m.* able seaman.

Vollmilch *f.* unskimmed milk.
Vollmond *m.* full moon.
Vollreifen *m.* solid tyre.
Vollsitzung *f.* plenary session.
vollständig *a.* complete, full, integral; ~ *adv.* completely, in full.
vollstreckbar *a.* executable; (*law*) enforceable.
vollstrecken *v.t.* to execute, to carry out.
vollstreckend *a.* executive.
Vollstreckungsbefehl *m.* writ of execution.
volltönend *a.* sonorous, full-toned.
Volltreffer *m.* direct hit.
Vollversammlung *f.* plenary meeting.
vollwertig *a.* of full value.
vollzählig *a.* complete (in number).
vollziehen *v.t.st.* to execute; to carry out; to consummate (marriage); (*Testament*) to administer; ~*de Gewalt*, executive (power).
Vollziehung *f.* (-, -en) **Vollzug** *m.* (-[e]s, 0) execution, consummation.
Volontär *m.* (-s, -s) unsalaried clerk *or* assistant.
Volt *n.* (-s, -) volt.
Voltmesser *m.* (-s, -) volt-meter.
Volumen *n.* (-s, -mina) volume.
vom = **von dem.**
von *pr.* of; from; by; upon, on; ~...*an*, since, from...upwards (downwards, forward); ~...*her*, from; ~...*herab*, from; ~ *selbst*, of itself, of its own accord, automatically.
vonnöten *a.* needful, necessary.
vonstatten gehen *v.i.* to proceed.
vor *pr.* before, in front of; above; prior to; since, ago; ~ *ago*; before; *nach wie* ~, now as before; ~ *allem*, above all; *vor 8 Tagen*, a week ago; *10 Minuten vor 8 Uhr*, ten minutes to eight; *Gnade* ~ *Recht ergehen lassen*, to let mercy overrule justice.
Vorabend *m.* eve.
Vorahnung *f.* misgiving, presentiment.
voran *adv.* before, in front; on, ahead.
vorangehen *v.i.* (*s*) to go before, to lead the way; to precede; *mit gutem Beispiel* ~, to set the example.
Voranschlag *m.* previous estimate.
Voranzeige *f.* previous announcement.
Vorarbeit *f.* preliminary work.
vorarbeiten *v.i.* to prepare the ground(for).
Vorarbeiter *m.* foreman.
voraus *adv.* before; beforehand, in advance; ahead of; *im* (*zum*) *voraus*, beforehand, in anticipation.
vorausbedingen *v.t.st.* (sich) ~ *v.refl.* to stipulate beforehand.
vorausbestellbar *a.* bookable in advance.
vorausbestellen *v.t.* to order in advance.
Vorausbestellung *f.* booking.
vorausbezahlen *v.t.* to pay in advance, to prepay.

vorauseilen *v.i.* to hurry on in advance.
vorausgehen *v.i.st.* to lead the way.
voraushaben *v.t.ir.* to have an advantage over; to have in advance.
vorausnehmen *v.t.st.* to anticipate.
voraussagen *v.t.* to foretell, to predict.
vorausschicken *v.t.* to send before or in advance; (*fig.*) to premise.
voraussehen *v.t.st.* to foresee.
voraussetzen *v.t.* to suppose, to presuppose, to presume; to take for granted.
Voraussetzung *f.* (-, -en) prerequisite; supposition; *unter der* ~ *dass*, on the understanding that.
Voraussicht *f.* foresight, prudence.
voraussichtlich *a.* presumptive; ~ *adv.* probably, presumably.
Vorauszahlung *f.* advance payment.
vorbauen *v.i.* (*fig.*) to prevent, to preclude, to guard against.
vorbedacht *a.* premeditated.
Vorbedacht *m.* (-[e]s, 0) premeditation; *mit bösem Vorbedacht*, with malice aforethought.
Vorbedeutung *f.* omen, portent.
Vorbedingung *f.* (-, -en) precondition.
Vorbehalt *m.* (-[e]s, -e) reservation; proviso; *unter* ~, with the proviso that.
vorbehalten *v.t.st.* to reserve; *alle Rechte* ~, all rights reserved; *sich* ~ *v.refl.* to reserve to oneself.
vorbehaltlich *a.* conditional; ~ *pr. & adv.* with the proviso that (of), subject to.
Vorbehaltsklausel *f.* saving clause.
vorbei *adv.* by, past; over; finished.
vorbeigehen *v.i.st.* (*s*) to pass by.
vorbeilassen *v.t.st.* to let pass.
Vorbeimarsch *m.* march-past.
vorbeischiessen *v.i.st.* to miss (one's mark); (*s*) to shoot past, to rush past.
Vorbemerkung *f.* preliminary notice.
vorbereiten *v.t.* to prepare.
vorbereitend *a.* preparatory.
Vorbereitung *f.* (-, -en) preparation.
Vorbestellung *f.* (-, -en) reservation.
vorbestraft *a.* previously convicted; *nicht* ~, no criminal record; *nicht* ~*er Verbrecher*, first offender.
vorbeten *v.t. & i.* to lead prayers.
vorbeugen *v.i.* (*fig.*) to prevent, to preclude, to guard against; (sich) ~ *v.refl.* to bend forward, to crane.
Vorbeugung *f.* prevention, preventing.
Vorbeugungsmittel *n.* preservative.
Vorbild *n.* model, standard; (proto-)type.
vorbildlich *a.* exemplary; model.
Vorbildung *f.* (-, 0) previous training.
Vorbote *m.* harbinger; forerunner.
vorbringen *v.t.ir.* to bring forward, to advance; to utter.
vorchristlich *a.* pre-Christian.
vordatieren *v.t.* to antedate.
vordem *adv.* formerly.

Vordemonstrieren *v.t.* to demonstrate.
vorder *a.* anterior, fore-, front-.
vorder: ~**ansicht** *f.* front-view; ~**arm** *m.* fore-arm; ~**fuss** *m.* fore-foot; ~**gebäude** *n.* front-building; ~**grund** *m.* fore-ground.
vorderhand *adv.* for the present.
Vorder: ~**mann** *m.* (*mil.*) man in front; ~**rad** *n.* front-wheel; ~**reihe** *f.* front rank; ~**satz** *m.* premise; ~**seite** *f.* front (face); ~**sitz** *m.* front-seat.
vorderst *a.* foremost.
Vorder: ~**teil** *n.* fore-part; ~**tür** *f.* front-door.
vordrängen *v.t.* (sich) ~ *v.refl.* to press or push forward.
vordringen *v.i.st.* (s) to advance.
vordringlich *a.* urgent.
Vordruck *m.* printed form.
voreilig *a.* hasty, forward, rash.
voreingenommen *a.* prejudiced, biased.
Voreingenommenheit *f.* (-, 0) bias.
vorenthalten *v.t.st.* to withhold (from).
Vorenthaltung *f.* (-, 0) detention.
vorerst *adv.* first of all; for the present.
vorerwähnt *a.* aforementioned.
Vorfahr[e] *m.* (-s *u.* -en, -en) ancestor.
vorfahren *v.i.st.* (s) to drive up to a house; (*Verkehr*) to pass.
Vorfall *m.* occurrence, incident; (*med.*) prolapse.
vorfallen *v.i.st.* (s) to occur, to happen.
vorfinden *v.t.st.* to find, to meet with.
Vorfrage *f.* preliminary question.
Vorfreude *f.* anticipated joy.
Vorführdame *f.* mannequin.
vorführen *v.t.* to produce.
Vorführraum *m.* (*Lichtbilder, etc.*) projection room.
Vorführung *f.* (-, -en) demonstration; (~ vor Gericht) arraignment.
Vorgabe *f.* (-, -n) handicap.
Vorgang *m.* occurrence, incident.
Vorgänger *m.* (-s, -) predecessor.
vorgängig *a.* previous, preliminary.
Vorgarten *m.* front garden.
vorgaukeln *v.t. einem etwas* ~, to deceive one by false promises.
vorgeben *v.t.st.* to pretend.
Vorgeben *n.* (-s, 0) pretence, pretext.
Vorgebirge *n.* promontory, cape.
vorgeblich *a.* pretended; would-be.
vorgeburtlich *a.* antenatal.
vorgefasst *a.* preconceived.
vorgefertigt *a.* prefabricated.
Vorgefühl *n.* presentiment, misgiving.
vorgehen *v.i.st.* (s) to go before; (*Uhr*) to be fast; to proceed, to act; to occur, to happen.
Vorgehen *n.* proceedings *pl.*
Vorgelegewelle *f.* (*mech.*) countershaft.
vorgenannt *a.* before-mentioned.
Vorgericht *n.* first course or dish, entrée.

Vorgeschichte *f.* primitive history; previous history; antecedents *pl.*
vorgeschichtlich *a.* prehistoric.
Vorgeschmack *m.* foretaste.
vorgesehen! *i.* look out!
Vorgesetzte[r] *m.* (-n, -n) superior.
vorgesetzte Stelle or **Behörde** *f.* superior authority, headquarters.
vorgestern *adv.* the day before yesterday.
vorgreifen *v.i.st.* to anticipate.
vorhaben *v.t.ir.* to intend, to purpose.
Vorhaben *n.* (-s, -) design, intention.
Vorhalle *f.* entrance-hall.
Vorhalt *m.* (-[e]s, -e) admonition, remonstrance; *einem* ~*e machen*, to expostulate or remonstrate with one.
vorhalten *v.t.st.* to reproach with, to rebuke; ~ *v.i.* to last, to hold out.
Vorhaltung *f.* remonstrance.
vorhanden *a.* at hand; on hand, in stock; ~ *sein*, to exist; to be at hand.
Vorhang *m.* (-[e]s, -hänge) curtain; *den* ~ *zuziehen*, to draw the curtain.
Vorhängeschloss *n.* padlock.
Vorhangsstange *f.* curtain-rail.
Vorhaut *f.* prepuce, foreskin.
vorher *adv.* before(hand), previously.
vorherbestimmen *v.t.* to predestine.
Vorherbestimmung *f.* predestination.
vorhergehen *v.i.st.* (s) to go before, to precede.
vorhergehend *a.* preceding, previous.
vorherig *a.* preceding.
vorherrschen *v.i.* to predominate.
vorhersagen *v.t.* to foretell, to predict.
vorhersehen *v.t.st.* to foresee.
vorherwissen *v.t.ir.* to know beforehand.
vorhin *adv.* before; a short time ago.
Vorhof *m.* (outer-)court, entry.
Vorhut *f.* (-, 0) vanguard.
vorig *a.* former, preceding, last; ~*e Woche*, last week.
Vorjahr *n.* preceding year.
vorjährig *a.* of last year.
Vorkämpfer *m.* champion; leader.
vorkauen *v.t.* (*fig.*) to repeat over and over again.
Vorkauf *m.* pre-emption.
Vorkaufsrecht *n.* right of pre-emption.
Vorkehrung *f.* (-, -en) preventive measure, precaution; preparation; ~*en treffen*, to make provisions.
Vorkenntnisse *f.pl.* preliminary knowledge; rudiments *pl.*
vorklassisch *a.* pre-classical.
vorkommen *v.i.st.* (s) to occur, to happen; to seem, to appear.
Vorkommen *n.* (-s, -) incidence.
Vorkommnis *n.* (-nisses, -nisse) occurrence.
Vorkriegs... pre-war.
vorladen *v.t.st.* to cite, to summon.
Vorladung *f.* citation, summons.

Vorladungsschreiben *n.* writ of summons, subpœna.

Vorlage *f.* draft, bill; model, pattern (for drawing *or* writing).

vorgelagert *a.* lying in front of.

vorlängst *adv.* some time ago.

vorlassen *v.t.st.* to let pass before, to admit.

Vorlassung *f.* (-, 0) admittance.

Vorläufer *m.* forerunner, precursor.

vorläufig *a.* provisional, preliminary.

vorlaut *a.* pert, forward.

Vorleben *n.* (-s, -) antecedents; *gutes, schlechtes ~*, good, bad record.

Vorlegemesser *n.* carving-knife.

vorlegen *v.t.* to lay before, to present to produce, to exhibit; to propose, to submit (a plan).

Vorlegeschloss *n.* padlock.

vorlesen *v.t.st.* to read (to).

Vorlesung *f.* (-, -en) lecture; course of lectures; *~en halten*, to lecture.

Vorlesungsraum *m.* lecture-room.

vorletzt *a.* last but one, penultimate.

vorleuchten *v.i.* to shine before.

vorliebnehmen *v.i.* to put up with.

Vorliebe *f.* predilection.

vorliegen *v.i.st.* to lie before.

vorliegend *a.* in question; present.

vorlügen *v.t.st.* (*einem etwas*) to tell lies *or* stories (to one).

vormachen *v.t.* to show how a thing is done; *einem etwas* oder *blauen Dunst ~*, to humbug someone, to impose upon someone.

Vormacht *f.* leading power; supremacy.

vormalig *a.* former.

vormals *adv.* formerly, heretofore.

Vormarsch *m.* advance.

vormerken *v.t.* to book.

Vormerkgebühr *f.* booking-fee.

vormilitärisch *a.* premilitary.

Vormittag *m.* forenoon.

vormittägig *a.* forenoon, in the forenoon.

vormittags *adv.* in the forenoon, a.m. (*ante meridiem*).

Vormund *m.* (-[e]s, -e *u.* -münder) guardian.

Vormundschaft *f.* guardianship; *unter ~ stellen*, to place under the care of a guardian.

vormundschaftlich *a.* custodial.

Vormundschaftsgericht *n.* Court of guardianship; (in England) Court of Chancery.

vorn *adv.* before, in front; (*nav.*) fore; *von ~*, facing, head . . .; from the beginning; over again, anew; *von vornherein*, from the first.

Vornahme *f.* (-, 0) taking up, doing, taking in hand.

Vorname *m.* Christian name, first name.

vornehm *a.* distinguished.

vornehmen *v.t.st.* to take in hand; to examine; (sich) *~ v.refl.* to resolve on, to intend.

Vornehmen *n.* (-s, 0) intention.

Vornehmheit *f.* (-, 0) rank, distinction.

vornehmlich *adv.* chiefly, principally.

vornherein, von ~ from the first.

Vorort *m.* suburb.

Vorortsferngespräch *n.* toll call.

Vorortsverkehr *m.* suburban traffic.

Vorortszug *m.* suburban train.

Vorplatz *m.* court (in front); hall; vestibule.

Vorposten *m.* outpost.

vorpredigen *v.t.* to preach to.

Vorprüfung *f.* preliminary examination.

Vorrang *m.* (-s, 0) precedence, priority.

Vorrat *m.* (-[e]s, -räte) store, stock, provision, supply; (*Am.*) stockpile; (*Erz*) resources.

vorrätig *a.* in stock, on hand.

Vorratskammer *f.* store-room; pantry.

vorrechnen *v.t.* to give an account of . . . to . . .

Vorrecht *n.* prerogative, privilege.

Vorrede *f.* preface, foreword; prologue.

vorreden *v.t.* to tell (tales).

Vorredner *m.* previous *or* last speaker.

vorrichten *v.t.* to prepare, to fit up.

Vorrichtung *f.* (-, -en) device.

vorrücken *v.t.* to advance; *~ v.i.* (*s*) to march on, to advance.

Vorrücken *n.* (-s, 0) advance.

Vorsaal *m.* anteroom, hall.

vorsagen *v.t.* to prompt.

Vorsaison *f.* early season.

Vorsänger *m.* precentor; leader of a choir.

Vorsatz *m.* (-es, -sätze) purpose, design, intention; *mit ~*, intentionally, on purpose.

vorsätzlich *a.* premeditated, wilful; *~ adv.* on purpose.

Vorschau *f.* (-, -en) preview.

Vorschein *m.* *zum ~ kommen*, to come forth, to appear.

vorschicken *v.t.* to send forward.

vorschieben *v.t.* to shove *or* push forward; to plead as an excuse; to slip (a bolt).

vorschiessen *v.t.st.* to advance (money).

Vorschlag *m.* proposal, offer.

vorschlagen *v.t.st.* to propose.

vorschneiden *v.t.st.* to carve (meat).

vorschnell *a.* precipitate, hasty, rash.

vorschreiben *v.t.st.* to prescribe.

vorschreiten *v.i.st.* (*s*) to advance.

Vorschrift *f.* direction, instruction.

vorschriftsmässig *a.* according to rule; regulation; *~es Verfahren n.* (*mil.*) standard operating procedure (SOP).

Vorschub *m.* (-[e]s, 0) (*mech.*) feed; *~ leisten*, to further, to abet, to assist.

Vorschule *f.* preparatory school.

Vorschuss *m.* payment in advance.

vorschützen v.t. (fig.) to pretend.
vorschweben v.i. to be (vaguely) before one's mind.
vorsehen (sich) v.refl.st. to take care, to guard (against); *vorgesehen!* look out! mind (your head, your hat, etc.)!
Vorsehung f. (-, 0) Providence.
vorsetzen v.t. to put before; (sich) ~ v.refl. to resolve.
Vorsicht f. (-, 0) caution; ~! (auf Kisten) with care!
vorsichtig a. cautious, careful; ~e Schätzung, conservative estimate.
Vorsichtsmassnahme f. precaution; ~n treffen, to take precautions.
Vorsilbe f. prefix.
vorsingen v.t.st. to sing to.
vorsintflutlich a. antediluvian.
Vorsitz m. (-es, 0) chair, chairmanship; den ~ führen, to be in the chair.
vorsitzen v.i.st. to be in the chair.
Vorsitzender m. (-n, -n) chairman; stellvertretender ~, vice-chairman.
Vorsorge f. foresight; precaution.
vorsorglich a. careful; provident.
vorspannen v.t. (Pferde) to put (horses) to.
vorspiegeln v.t. to make a false show of.
Vorspiegelung f. (-, -en) pretence; ~ falscher Tatsachen, false pretences.
Vorspiel n. prelude.
vorspielen v.t. to play to.
vorsprechen v.i.st. to call on.
vorspringen v.i.st. (s) to project.
Vorsprung m. (-[e]s, -sprünge) advantage, start, lead.
Vorstadt f. suburb.
Vorstand m. (-[e]s, -stände) (Firma) executive committee or board, management; (Krankenhaus, etc.) governing body; principal, head.
Vorstandssitzung f. board meeting.
vorstehen v.i.st. to preside over.
vorstehend a. preceding; ~ adv. above.
Vorsteher m. (-s, -) director, manager.
Vorstehhund m. pointer, setter.
vorstellbar a. imaginable.
vorstellen v.t. to introduce; to represent; to act; (eine Uhr) to put on; (sich) (Dativ) ~ v.refl. to imagine.
vorstellig a. ~ werden, to present a case.
Vorstellung f. (-, -en) introduction, presentation; performance; conception, idea; expostulation.
Vorstoss m. advance.
vorstossen v.t.st. to push forward.
Vorstrafe f. previous conviction.
vorstrecken v.t. to stretch forward, to thrust or poke out; (fig.) to advance, to lend (money).
Vorstufe f. first steps pl.; introduction.
vortäuschen v.t. to feign.
Vorteil m. (-[e]s, -e) advantage, profit.
vorteilhaft a. advantageous, profitable.

Vortrag m. (-[e]s, -träge) elocution; recitation; lecture; (Musik) recital; (com.) balance carried forward; einen ~ halten, to deliver a lecture, to read a paper.
vortragen v.t.st. to carry forward; to recite, to declaim; to lecture (on), to deliver (a speech); (mus.) to execute.
Vortragskunst f. elocution.
vortrefflich a. excellent, superior.
vortreten v.i.st. (s) to step forward.
Vortritt m. (-[e]s, 0) precedence.
vorüber adv. by; past, over, finished.
vorübergehen v.t.st. (s) to pass by.
vorübergehend a. transitory, temporary.
Vorübergehende[r] m. passer-by.
Vorübung f. preliminary exercise.
Voruntersuchung f. investigation before trial.
Vorurteil n. prejudice.
vorurteilslos a. unprejudiced.
Vorverhör n. preliminary examination.
Vorverkauf m. (theat.) booking in advance; advance sale.
Vorversammlung f. preliminary meeting.
vorvorig a. last but one, penultimate.
vorwalten v.i. to prevail.
Vorwand m. (-[e]s, -wände) pretence, pretext.
vorwärmen v.t. to preheat.
vorwärts adv. ahead, forward(s), on; ~ marsch! quick march!; ~ kommen, to get on, to make one's way.
vorweg adv. before(hand).
vorwegnehmen v.t.st. to anticipate.
vorweisen v.t.st. to produce.
Vorwelt f. (-, 0) prehistoric world.
vorwerfen v.t.st. (einem etwas) to upbraid or reproach with.
Vorwerk n. small outlying farm.
vorwiegen v.i. to prevail.
Vorwissen n. (-s, 0) (fore-)knowledge.
vorwitzig a. pert; prying.
Vorwort n. (-[e]s, -worte) foreword, preface; (-[e]s, -wörter) preposition.
Vorwurf m. (-[e]s, -würfe) reproach; object, subject.
vorwurfsfrei, vorwurfslos a. irreproachable.
vorwurfsvoll a. reproachful.
Vorzeichen n. omen, token, portent; (mus.) signature; (math.) sign.
vorzeichnen v.t. to trace out, to sketch (a plan).
vorzeigen v.t. to produce.
Vorzeit f. (-, 0) past ages pl.
vorzeitig a. premature; precocious.
vorziehen v.t. to prefer.
Vorzimmer n. anteroom, antechamber.
Vorzug m. preference; advantage, privilege; (rail.) special train.
vorzüglich a. superior, excellent, exquisite; ~ adv. chiefly, especially.
Vorzüglichkeit f. (-, -en) superiority, excellence.

Vorzugs...preferential *a*.
Vorzugs: ~aktie *f*. preference share, (*Am*.) preferred stock; ~behandlung *f*. preferential treatment; ~tarif *m*. preference; ~zoll *m*. preferential duty.
vorzugsweise *adv*. preferably.
votieren *v.t. & i*. to vote.
Votum *n*. (-[s], -ta *u*. -ten) vote, suffrage.
vulgär *a*. vulgar.
Vulkan *m*. (-[e]s, -e) volcano.
vulkanisch *a*. volcanic.
vulkanisieren *v.t*. to vulcanize.

W

Waage = Wage.
Wabe *f*. (-, -n) honey-comb.
wach, *a*. awake, astir; on the alert.
Wachdienst *m*. guard-duty.
Wache *f*. (-, -n) guard, watch; guard-room; sentry; *auf ~ sein*, to be on guard.
wachen *v.i*. to be awake; to watch over.
wachhabend *a*. on duty, on guard.
Wacholder *m*. (-s, -) juniper.
Wacholderbranntwein *m*. gin.
Wachs *n*. (Wachses, Wachse) wax.
wachsam *a*. watchful, vigilant.
wachsen *v.i.st*. (s) to grow; *einem gewachsen sein*, to be a match for someone; *einer Sache gewachsen sein*, to be equal to a task.
wächsern *a*. waxen, made of wax.
Wachs: ~figurenkabinett *n*. wax-works *pl*.; ~leinwand *f*. oil-cloth; ~tuch *m*. oil-cloth.
Wachstum *n*. (-[e]s, 0) growth; increase.
Wacht *f*. (-, -en) guard, watch.
Wachtel *f*. (-, -n) quail.
Wächter *m*. (-s, -) watchman; keeper.
Wachtposten *m*. post, sentinel, sentry.
wack(e)lig *a*. shaky, rickety, tottering.
wackeln *v.i*. to wobble, to totter.
wacker *a*. stout, gallant, brave, valiant.
Wade *f*. (-, -n) calf (of the leg).
Waffe *f*. (-, -n) weapon; arm.
Waffel *f*. (-, -n) waffle, wafer.
Waffenbruder *m*. brother in arms.
waffenfähig *a*. able *or* fit to bear arms.
Waffengattung *f*. branch of the service, arm.
waffenlos *a*. unarmed.
Waffen: ~ruhe *f*. cease-fire; ~schein *m*. gun licence; ~schmied *m*. armourer; ~schmuggel *m*. gun-running; ~stillstand *m*. armistice, truce.
waffnen *v.t*. to arm.
wägbar *a*. ponderable.
Wa(a)ge *f*. (-, -n) balance; (pair of) scales; *einem die ~ halten*, to counter-balance.
Wagehals *m*. dare-devil.

wagehalsig *a*. foolhardy, rash.
wagen *v.t*. to venture, to dare, to risk; *sich ~*, to venture.
Wagen *m*. (-s, -) (*Last~*) waggon, cart carriage, coach; vehicle.
wägen *v.t.st*. to weigh.
Wagen: ~heber *m*. jack; ~ladung *f*. cart-load, waggon-load; ~lenker *m*. charioteer; ~pflege *f*. car service; ~schlag *m*. carriage door.
wa(a)gerecht *a*. horizontal, level.
Waggon *m*. (-s, -s) railway-carriage; (*Güter~*) truck, van.
Wagner *m*. (-s, -) cartwright.
Wagnis, *n*. (-nisses, -nisse) venture.
Wa(a)gschale *f*. scale(-pan).
Wahl *f*. (-, -en) choice, selection, option; (*politisch*) election.
wählbar *a*. eligible.
Wählbarkeit *f*. (-, 0) eligibility.
wahlberechtigt *a*. entitled to vote.
Wahlbeteiligung *f*. poll.
Wahlbezirk *m*. electoral district.
wählen *v.t*. to choose; to select; (*politisch*) to elect; ~ *v.i*. (*politisch*) to vote; (*Telephon*) to dial.
Wähler *m*.(-s,-) voter, constituent, elector.
Wahlergebnis *n*. election returns *or* result.
wählerisch *a*. particular, fastidious.
Wählerschaft *f*. (-, 0) electoral body, constituency.
wahlfähig *a*. eligible; entitled to vote.
wahlfrei *a*. optional.
Wählscheibe *f*. (*tel*.) dial.
Wahl: ~freiheit *f*. free will; ~kampf *m*. electoral contest; ~kreis *m*. constituency; ~lokal *n*. polling station; ~recht *n*. right to vote, franchise; (*allgemeines*) universal suffrage; ~urne *f*. ballot-box; ~zettel *m*. ballot paper.
Wahn *m*. (-[e]s, 0) illusion, error.
Wahnbild *n*. phantasm, delusion.
wähnen *v.t*. to imagine.
Wahnsinn *m*. (-, 0) madness, frenzy.
wahnsinnig *a*. insane, mad, frantic.
Wahnsinnige[r] *m*. madman, lunatic.
Wahnwitz *m*. insanity, madness, frenzy.
wahnwitzig *a*. insane, mad, frantic.
wahr *a*. true; real; genuine; *so ~ ich lebe!* as sure as I live!; *~ machen*, to bear out; to prove, to fulfil; *nicht ~?* isn't it? don't you think so?
wahren *v.t*. to guard; *das Gesicht wahren*, to save one's face.
während *v.i*. to last.
während *pr*. during; ~ *c*. while.
wahrhaft *a*. true, veracious, truthful, real.
wahrhaftig *a*. genuine; ~ *adv*. truly.
Wahrhaftigkeit *f*. (-, 0) veracity.
Wahrheit *f*. (-, -en) truth; *einem die ~ sagen*, to tell a person off.
wahrheits: ~gemäss *a*. veracious; ~getreu *a*. truthful.

wahrlich *adv.* in truth, verily.

wahrnehmbar *a.* perceptible.

wahrnehmen *v.t.st.* to perceive, to observe.

Wahrnehmung *f.* (-, -en) perception, observation; care (of).

wahrsagen *v.i.* to tell fortunes.

Wahrsager *m.* (-s, -) fortune-teller, soothsayer.

wahrscheinlich *a.* likely, probable.

Wahrscheinlichkeit *f.* (-, -en) likelihood, probability.

Wahrspruch *m.* verdict.

Wahrung *f.* (-, 0) maintenance, defence.

Währung *f.* (-, -en) currency.

Währungsausgleichfonds *m.* exchange stabilization fund.

Wahrzeichen *n.* token, sign; omen.

Waise *f.* (-, -n) orphan(-child).

Waisenhaus *n.* orphan asylum.

Wal *m.* (-[e]s, -e) *m.* whale.

Wald *m.* (-[e]s, Wälder) wood, forest.

Wald: ~**brand** *m.* forest-fire; ~**horn** *n.* bugle-horn, French-horn.

waldig *a.* wooded, woody.

waldreich *a.* woody, wooded.

Waldung *f.* (-, -en) woodland; forest.

Waldweg *m.* wood-path.

Walfisch *m.* whale.

Walfischfänger *m.* whaler.

Walke *f.* (-, -n) fulling-machine; fulling.

walken *v.t.* to full.

Walküre *f.* (-, -n) Valkyrie.

Wall *m.* (-[e]s, Wälle) rampart; mound.

Wallach *m.* (-[e]s *u.* -en, -e *u.* -en) gelding.

wallen *v.i.* to boil (up), to bubble.

Wallfahrer *m.* (-s, -) pilgrim.

Wallfahrt *f.* pilgrimage.

wallfahrten *v.i.* (*s*) to go on a pilgrimage.

Wallung *f.* (-, -en) ebullition; agitation.

Wallnuss *f.* walnut.

Walross *n.* (-rosses, -rosse) walrus.

walten *v.i.* to rule, to manage; *seines Amtes* ~, to perform the duties of one's office, to officiate.

Walze *f.* (-, -n) roller, cylinder; (*Schreibmaschine*) platen.

walzen *v.t.* to roll; ~ *v.i.* to waltz.

wälzen *v.t.* to roll, to turn about; (sich) ~ *v.refl.* to wallow, to welter.

walzenförmig *a.* cylindrical.

Walzer *m.* (-s, -) waltz.

Walzwerk *n.* rolling-mill.

Wams *n.* (Wamses, Wämser) doublet.

Wand *f.* (-, Wände) wall, partition; *spanische* ~, folding-screen.

Wandbekleidung *f.* wainscot(ing).

Wandel *m.* (-s, 0) mutation; conduct.

wandelbar *a.* variable.

Wandehalle, lobby.

wandeln (sich) *v.refl.* to change.

Wanderer *m.* (-s, -) wanderer, tourist, hiker.

Wandergewerbe *f.* itinerant trade.

wandern *v.i.* (*s*) to wander, to hike.

Wanderschaft *f.* (-, 0) *auf der* ~ *sein*, to be travelling.

Wanderung *f.* (-, -en) walking tour.

Wandervogel *m.* Boy *or* Girl Scout.

Wand: ~**gemälde** *n.* wall-painting, mural; ~**karte**, wall-map; ~**schirm** *m.* folding-screen; ~**tafel** *f.* blackboard; ~**uhr** *f.* clock.

Wandlung *f.* (-, -en) change; (*Religion*) transubstantiation.

Wange *f.* (-, -n) cheek; side-piece.

Wankelmut *m.* fickleness, inconstancy.

wankelmütig *a.* fickle, inconstant.

wanken *v.i.* to totter, to stagger; to waver.

wann *adv.* when; *dann und* ~, now and then, occasionally.

Wanne *f.* (-, -n) bath tub, bath; tub.

Wanst *m.* (-es, Wänste) belly, paunch.

Wanze *f.* (-, -n) bug, (*Am.*) bedbug.

Wappen *n.* (-s, -) (coat of) arms.

wappnen *v.t.* to arm.

Ware *f.* (-, -n) merchandise, ware, goods *pl.*, commodity.

Waren: ~**haus** *n.* stores, (*Am.*) department store; ~**pass** *m.* (*nav.*) navicert; ~**lager** *n.* warehouse, stock-in-trade; ~**probe** *f.* sample; ~**sendung** *f.* shipment, consignment; ~**zeichen** *n.* trademark.

warm *a.* warm; hot.

warmblütig *a.* warm-blooded.

Wärme *f.* warmth, heat; *Blutwärme, Körperwärme*, etc., blood heat, body heat.

wärmen *v.t.* to warm, to heat.

wärmesicher *a.* heatproof.

Wärmflasche *f.* hot-water bottle.

warmherzig *a.* warm hearted.

warnen *v.t.* to warn.

Warnung *f.* (-, -en) warning, caution.

Warnungssignal *n.* danger signal.

Warte *f.* (-, -n) watch-tower; observatory.

Warteliste *f.* reservation list.

warten *v.t.* to tend, to nurse; ~ *v.i.* to wait, to stay; to attend to; ~*lassen*, to keep waiting.

Wärter *m.* (-s, -) attendant; keeper.

Wärterin *f.* (-, -nen) nurse; attendant.

Warte: ~**saal** *m.* waiting-room (at a station); ~**zimmer** *n.* (physician's) waiting-room.

Wartung *f.* (-, -en) nursing, attendance; (*Wagen*) maintenance.

warum *adv.* why.

Warze *f.* (-, -n) wart; (*Brust* ~) nipple.

was *pn.* what; which; something; ~ *immer*, whatever; ~ *für ein*, what (kind of).

Wasch: ~**anstalt** *f.* laundry; ~**becken** *n.* washing-(*or* hand)basin.

waschbar *a.* washable.

Wäsche *f.* (-, -n) washing, linen; laundry; *schmutzige* ~, soiled, dirty linen.

waschecht a. fast (colours); (*fig.*) thorough, genuine.

Wäsche: ~klammer f. clothes-peg; ~korb m. linen-basket; ~leine f. clothes-line; ~rolle f. mangle; ~schrank m. linen press.

waschen v.t. & i., sich ~ v.refl. to wash; (*Wäsche*) to launder.

Wäscherei f. (-, -en) laundry.

Wäscherin f. (-, -nen) washerwoman, laundress.

Wasch: ~fass n. wash-tub; ~haus n. wash-house, laundry; ~kessel m. copper; ~korb m. clothes-basket; ~küche f. scullery, laundry; ~lappen m. flannel, face-cloth; ~maschine f. washing machine; ~seide f. washing silk; ~seife f. laundry soap; ~tag m. washday; ~tisch m. washing-stand; ~zeug n. washing things.

Wasser n. (-s, -) water; ~abschlagen, to make water; *fliessendes* ~, running water; *unter* ~ *setzen*, to submerge, to flood; *zu* ~ *und zu Lande*, by sea and land.

wasserblau a. marine-blue, light-blue.

Wasserbombe f. depth-charge.

wasserdicht a. waterproof, tight.

Wasser: ~fall m. waterfall, cataract, cascade; ~farbe f. water-colour; ~glas n. water-glass; ~heilanstalt f. hydropathic (establishment).

wäss(e)rig a. watery; (*fig.*) insipid, flat.

Wasser: ~kopf m. hydrocephalus; ~kraft f. water-power; ~leitung f. water (-supply); ~leitungsröhre f. conduit-pipe; ~mann m. (*als Sternbild*) Aquarius.

Wasserkraftwerk n. hydroelectric station.

wässern v.t. to water, to irrigate.

Wasserpflanze f. aquatic plant.

wasserreich a. abounding in water.

Wasser: ~röhre f. water-pipe; ~scheide f. watershed.

wasserscheu a. afraid of water.

Wasser: ~spiegel m. surface of the water, water-level; ~sport m. aquatic sports pl.; ~stand m. height of the water, watermark; ~standmesser m. water-gauge; ~stoff m. hydrogen.

Wasserstoffsuperoxyd n. hydrogen peroxide.

Wasser: ~strasse f. waterway; ~sucht f. dropsy.

wassersüchtig a. dropsical.

Wasser: ~suppe f. gruel; slops; ~turm m. water-tower; ~versorgung f. water-supply; ~waage f. (spirit-) level; ~werk n. water-works; ~zeichen n. watermark.

waten v.i. (*s*) to wade.

watscheln v.i. (*s*) to waddle.

Watt n. (-[e]s, -e) muddy shallow, flat; (*elck.*) watt.

Watte f. (-, -n) wadding; cotton wool, (*Am.*) (absorbent) cotton.

wattieren v.t. to wad, to pad.

wauwau! i. bow-wow!

weben v.t.st. to weave.

Weber m. (-s, -) weaver.

Weber: -baum m. weaver's beam; ~schiffchen n. shuttle.

Webstuhl m. weaver's loom, frame.

Wechsel m. (-s, -) change, vicissitude; exchange; bill of exchange; (*auf Sicht*) bill payable at sight; (*gezogener*) draft; *auf einen einen* ~ *ziehen*, to draw on a person.

Wechsel: ~akzept n. acceptance (of a bill (of exchange)); ~balg m. changeling; ~beziehung f. mutual relation, correlation.

wechselfähig a. entitled to draw bills of exchange.

Wechsel: ~fall m. vicissitudes pl.; ~fieber n. intermittent fever; ~geld n. bankmoney; agio; change; ~geschäft n. exchange office, banking business; ~gläubiger m. holder or bearer of a bill of exchange; ~inhaber m. holder of a bill of exchange; ~klage f. action on or about a bill of exchange; ~konto n. account of exchange, bill-account; ~kredit m. paper-credit; ~kurs m. rate of exchange; ~makler m. bill-broker, exchange-broker.

Wechseljahre n.pl. climacteric.

wechseln v.t. to change, to exchange; ~ v.i. to alternate; *Briefe* ~, to correspond.

wechselnd a. alternating.

Wechsel: ~ordnung f. exchange regulations pl.; ~protest m. protest; ~provision f. bill-commission; ~recht n. laws (pl.) of exchange; ~reiter m. billjobber; ~reiterei f. bill-jobbing, kite-flying; ~schuld f. debt founded on a bill of exchange.

wechselseitig a. reciprocal, mutual.

Wechselseitigkeit f. reciprocity.

Wechsel: ~strom m. alternating current; ~verhältnis n. reciprocal relation or proportion.

wechsel: ~voll a. changeful, vicissitous; ~weise adv. alternately; mutually.

Wechselwirkung f. reciprocal action.

wecken v.t. to wake, to awaken, to rouse.

Wecken n. (-s, 0) waking, awaking; ~ m. (-s, 0) small loaf.

Wecker m. (-s, -) alarum.

Weckuhr f. alarum-clock.

wedeln v.i. to wag (the tail); to fan.

weder c. neither; ~ ..., noch..., neither ..., nor...

weg adv. away; gone; off; *das Buch ist* ~, the book is gone, missing; *über etwas* ~ (*hinweg*) *sein*, to be above a thing; *in einem* ~, at a stretch, at a sitting; *kurz-*

weg, briefly, curtly; *schlechtweg*, simply, unceremoniously.

Weg *m.* (-[e]s, -e) way, path; (*Gang*) road; course, errand; (*fig.*) manner, means; *auf gütlichem* ~, amicably; *auf halbem* ~*e*, halfway, midway; *verbotener* ~! no thoroughfare!; *sich auf den* ~ *machen*, to set out, to start; *auf bestem* ~ *sein*, to be in a fair way to; *im* ~*e sein, stehen*, to be in the way.

Wegarbeiter *m.* road-maker.

wegbegeben (sich) *v.refl.st.* to go away.

wegblasen *v.t.st.* to blow away.

wegbleiben *v.i.st.* (*s*) to stay away or out; to be omitted.

wegbringen *v.t.ir.* to remove.

wegdenken *v.t.ir.* to withdraw in thought.

wegdürfen *v.i.ir.* to be permitted to go.

Weg(e)bau *m.* road-making.

wegeilen *v.i.* (*s*) to hasten away.

Wegelagerer *m.* (-s, -) highwayman.

wegen *pr.* on account of, because of; *von Rechts* ~, by right.

Wegerecht *n.* right of way.

wegessen *v.t.st.* to eat away, to eat up.

wegfahren *v.t.st.* to carry away; ~ *v.i.st.* (*s*) to drive off, to start.

Wegfall *m.* omission; *in* ~ *kommen*, to be abolished or omitted, to cease.

wegfallen *v.i.st.* (*s*) to be omitted.

wegfangen *v.t.st.* to catch (away).

wegfliegen *v.i.st.* (*s*) to fly away or off.

wegführen *v.t.* to lead or carry away.

Weggang *m.* (-[e]s, 0) departure.

weggeben *v.t.st.* to give away.

weggehen *v.i.st.* (*s*) to go away, to leave; *über etwas* ~, to pass over.

weggetreten! dismissed!

weggiessen *v.t.st.* to pour away.

weghaben *v.t.ir.* to have one's share, to have got; to understand.

weghängen *v.t.st.* to hang somewhere else.

weghauen *v.t.st.* to cut off or away.

weghelfen *v.i.st.* to help to get away.

wegholen *v.t.* to fetch or carry away.

wegjagen *v.t.* to drive away.

wegkommen *v.i.st.* (*s*) to get away; to come off; to get lost.

wegkönnen *v.i.ir.* to be able to go or get away.

weglassen *v.t.st.* to let go; to leave out, to omit.

weglaufen *v.i.st.* (*s*) to run off or away.

weglegen *v.t.* to put away, to lay aside.

wegleugnen *v.t.* to deny flatly.

weglocken *v.t.* to entice away.

wegmachen (sich) *v.refl.* to be off.

wegmüssen *v.i.ir.* to be obliged to leave.

Wegnahme *f.* (-, 0) seizure; capture.

wegnehmen *v.t.st.* to take away, to seize.

wegraffen *v.t.* to sweep off.

wegräumen *v.t.* to clear away.

wegreisen *v.i.* (*s*) to depart.

wegreissen *v.t.st.* to tear or snatch away.

wegrücken *v.t.* to remove: ~ *v.i.* (*s*) to move aside.

wegrufen *v.t.st.* to call away.

wegschaffen *v.t.* to remove.

wegschenken *v.t.* to give away.

wegscheuchen *v.t.* to frighten away.

wegschicken *v.t.* to send away or off.

wegschieben *v.t.st.* to shove away.

wegschleichen (sich) *v.refl.st.* to steal or sneak away.

wegschleppen *v.t.* to drag or force away.

wegschmeissen *v.t.st.* to chuck away.

wegschnappen *v.t.* to snatch away.

wegschneiden *v.t.st.* to cut away or off.

wegsehen *v.i.st.* to look away; (*über etwas*) to overlook.

wegsehnen (sich) *v.refl.* to wish oneself away.

weg sein *v.i.ir.* (*s*) to be gone, to be absent; to be lost; *über etwas* ~, to be above (minding) a thing; *ganz* ~, to be enraptured with.

wegsenden *v.t.ir.* to send away.

wegsetzen *v.i.* (*s*) (*über etwas*) to leap (over), to clear; *sich über etwas* ~, not to mind a thing.

wegspringen *v.i.st.* (*s*) to leap away; to run away, to escape.

wegspülen *v.t.* to wash away.

wegstehlen *v.t.st.*(*sich*) *v.refl.* to steal away.

wegstellen *v.t.* to put away or aside.

wegsteuern *v.i.st.* (*s*) to die off.

wegstossen *v.t.st.* to push away.

wegstreichen *v.t.st.* to strike out.

wegtragen *v.t.st.* to bear or carry away.

wegtreiben *v.t.st.* to drive away.

wegtreten *v.i.st.* to step aside.

wegtun *v.t.st.* to put away, to remove.

wegwälzen *v.t.* to roll away.

Wegweiser *m.* (-s, -) road-sign.

wegwerfen *v.t.st.* to throw or cast away; (sich) ~ *v.refl.* to make oneself cheap.

wegwerfend *a.* disparaging.

wegwollen *v.i.ir.* to want to go.

wegwünschen *v.t.* to wish away.

wegzaubern *v.t.* to spirit away.

wegziehen *v.t.st.* to pull away; ~ *v.i.st.* (*s*) to march away; (*aus einer Wohnung*) to (re)move.

weh, wehe *i.* wo! woe!

weh *a.* painful, sore; ~*tun*, to cause pain; *sich* ~*tun*, to hurt oneself.

Weh *n.* (-[e]s, 0) woe, pain, grief; *Wohl und* ~, weal and woe.

Wehen *f.pl.* labour-pains.

wehen *v.t.* & *i.* to blow.

Wehgeschrei *n.* lamentations, wailings *pl.*

Wehklage *f.* lamentation, wailing.

wehklagen *v.i.* to lament, to wail.

wehleidig *a.* (*fam.*) woe-begone.

Wehmut *f.* sadness, (*sweet*) melancholy.

wehmütig *a.* sad, melancholy.

Wehr f. (-, -en) defence; *sich zur ~ setzen,* to offer resistance.

Wehr n. (-[e]s, -e) weir; dam, dike.

wehren v.t. & i. to restrain; to hinder; (sich) ~ v.refl. to defend oneself.

wehrfähig a. able or fit to bear arms.

wehrhaft a. =wehrfähig.

wehrlos a. defenceless, weak.

Wehr: ~**kreisbezirk** m. military district; ~**macht** f. the (fighting) services; ~**machtsangehöriger** m. service-man; ~**pflicht** f. compulsory military service, conscription, (Am.) draft.

wehrpflichtig a. liable to military service.

Weib n. (-es, -er) woman, female; wife.

Weibchen n. (-s, -) little woman; (von Tieren) female.

weiberhaft a. womanlike, womanish.

weibisch a. womanish; effeminate.

weiblich a. female; womanly, feminine.

Weiblichkeit f. (-, 0) womanhood; womanliness; female nature.

Weibsbild n. female, wench, hussy.

weich a. soft, mellow; tender(-hearted).

Weichbild n. boundary of a town.

Weiche f. (-, -n) softness; side; flank (rail.) points pl.; (elek.) switch, shunt.

weichen v.t. to steep, to soak, to soften; ~ v.i. (s) to soak, to soften.

weichen v.i.st. (s) to give way, to yield; *von der Stelle ~,* to budge, to stir.

weichherzig a. tender-hearted.

weichlich a. soft; weak, effeminate.

Weichling m. (-[e]s, -e) weakling.

Weichsel f. (-, -n), **Weichselkirsche** f. morello cherry.

Weichtier n. mollusc.

Weide f. (-, -n) pasture(-ground); pasturage; (Baum) willow.

Weideland n. pasture-land.

weiden v.t. to feed, to tend; ~ v.i. to pasture, to graze; *sich ~ (an etwas),* to delight (in), to gloat (over).

Weidengeflecht n. wicker-work.

weidlich adv. thoroughly.

Weidmann m. sportsman, huntsman.

weidmännisch a. sportsmanlike.

weigern (sich) v.refl. to refuse.

Weigerung f. (-, -en) refusal, denial.

Weih: ~**becken** n. holy-water font; ~**bischof** m. suffragan bishop.

Weihe f. (-, -n) consecration.

weihen v.t. to consecrate, to ordain; (fig.) to dedicate, to devote; *sich ~ lassen,* to take (holy) orders.

Weiher m. (-s, -) (fish-)pond.

weihevoll a. sacred, hallowed, solemn.

Weihnachten f.pl. Christmas, Xmas.

Weihnachts: ~**abend** m. Christmas eve; ~**baum** m. Christmas-tree; ~**(feier)tag** m. Christmas-day; ~**lied** n. Christmas carol or hymn; ~**mann** m. Father Christmas, Santa Claus.

Weihrauch m. (-[e]s, 0) (frank-)incense.

Weihrauchfass n. censer.

Weihwasser n. holy-water.

weil c. because, since, as.

weiland adv. formerly; late, deceased.

Weilchen n. (-s, 0) little while.

Weile f. (-, 0) while, time; leisure; *eine ~,* for a while.

weilen v.i. to tarry, to stay.

Weiler m. (-s, -) hamlet.

Wein m. (-[e]s, -e) wine; (bot.) vine; *einem reinen ~ einschenken,* to tell one the plain truth, not to mince matters; *wilder ~,* Virginia creeper.

Wein: ~**bau** m. viticulture; ~**berg** m. vineyard.

weinen v.i. to weep (for, at, over), to cry.

weinerlich a. lachrymose; whining.

Wein: ~**ernte** f.v intage; ~**essig** m. (wine-)vinegar; ~**geist** m. spirit of wine; ~**handel** m. wine-trade; ~**händler** m. wine-merchant; ~**jahr** n. *gutes ~,* good vintage; ~**karte** f. wine-list; ~**keller** m. wine-cellar; ~**kenner** m. connoisseur of wine; ~**laub** n. vine-leaves pl.; ~**säure** f. acidity of wine, tartaric acid; ~**stein** m. tartar; ~**stock** m. vine; ~**traube** f. (bunch of) grapes; ~**zwang** m. obligation to order wine with one's meal.

weise a. wise.

Weise[r] m. (-n, -n) sage, philosopher, wise man; *Stein der ~n,* philosopher's stone.

Weise f. (-, -n) manner, way; method, fashion; habit; tune, melody; *auf keine ~,* no ways, by no means.

weisen v.t.st. to point out, to show, to direct; *an einen ~,* to refer to one; *von sich ~,* to reject, to refuse; to repudiate; *etwas von der Hand ~,* to dismiss, to eject a thing.

Weisheit f. (-, -en) wisdom, prudence.

Weisheitszahn m. wisdom-tooth.

weislich adv. wisely, prudently.

weismachen to make one believe a thing.

weiss a. white; clean.

Weiss n. (-es, 0) white colour.

weissagen v.t. to prophesy, to foretell.

Weissager m. (-s, -) fortune-teller.

Weissagung f. (-, -en) prophecy.

Weiss: ~**blech** n. tin-plate, white metal; ~**brot** n. white bread; ~**buch** n. white paper; ~**dorn** m. hawthorn.

Weisse f. (-, 0) whiteness, white; white woman; (-n, -n) (fam.) glass of Berlin pale beer.

weissen v.t. to whiten; to whitewash.

Weissfisch m. whiting; whitebait.

weissglühend a. at a white heat.

Weissglühhitze f. white heat.

Weisskohl m. common cabbage.

weisslich a. whitish.

Weissmetall n. white metal.

Weiss: ~näherin *f.* seamstress; ~zeug *n.* linen.

Weisung *f.* (-, -en) direction, instruction.

weit *a.* distant, remote, far, far off, wide; large; ~ *adv.* far; widely; *zwei Meilen* ~, two miles off; *bei* ~*em*, by far; *von* ~*em*, from afar; ~ *und breit*, far and wide; *nicht* ~ *kommen*, to make no great progress; *mit etwas* ~ *sein*, to have got well into a thing; *die Sache ist noch lange nicht soweit*, the matter has not got nearly so far as that; *nicht* ~ *her sein*, (*fam.*) not much to speak of; *es* ~ *bringen*, to get on in the world; *das geht zu* ~, that is going too far; *es zu* ~ *treiben*, to carry things too far; *einen* ~ *ubertreffen*, far to surpass someone; ~ *gefehlt!*, very wide of the mark!; (*in*)*soweit*, so far; *soweit* (*als*), so far as; *des Weiten und Breiten erzählen*, to spin a long yarn about.

weitaus *adv.* by far.

weitberühmt *a.* far-famed.

weitblickend *a.* (*fig.*) far-sighted.

Weite *f.* (-, -n) width; distance; capacity.

weiten *v.t.* to widen; (sich) ~ *v.refl.* to widen, to expand.

weiter *adv.* further; forward, on; *und so* ~, and so on, etc.; ~ *nichts*, nothing else; ~! *i.e.* go on! proceed!; ~ *niemand*, no one else *or* besides; ~*lesen*, to go on reading; ~*kommen*, to get on, to proceed; *bis auf* ~*es*, until further notice, advice *or* orders; *ohne* ~*es*, without much ado.

Weiterbeförderung *f.* forwarding; *zur* ~ *an*, to be forwarded *or* sent on to...

Weiterbestand *m.* continued existence.

weitergehen *v.i.st.* (s) to proceed.

weiterhin *adv.* further.

weiterleiten *v.t.* to pass on.

Weiterreise *f.* progress, journey onwards.

Weiterungen *f.pl.* complications.

weitgehend *a.* far-reaching; extensive.

weitgreifend *a.* far-reaching.

weither *adv.* from afar; ~ *geholt*, far-fetched.

weithin *adv.* to a great distance, far off.

weitläuf[t]ig *a.* ample, spacious; detailed; *sie sind* ~ *verwandt*, they are distantly related.

weit: ~maschig *a.* with wide meshes; ~reichend *a.* far-reaching; ~schichtig *a.* extensive; long-winded; ~schweifig *a.* prolix, lengthy, tedious.

weitsichtig *a.* long-sighted; (*fig.*) far-sighted.

Weitsprung *m.* long jump.

weit: ~tragend *a.* far-reaching, portentous; ~umfassend *a.* comprehensive.

Weizen *m.* (-s, -) wheat.

welcher, welche, welches *pn.* who, which, that; some, any.

welcherlei *a.* of what kind.

welk *a.* withered, faded, flabby.

welken *v.i.* (s) to wither, to fade.

Wellblech *n.* corrugated iron.

Welle *f.* (-, -n) wave, billow; shaft, axle-tree.

wellen *v.t.* (*Haar*) to wave.

Wellen: ~band *n.* (*Radio*) waveband; ~brecher *m.* breakwater.

wellenförmig *a.* wavy, undulating.

Wellenlänge *f.* wavelength.

wellig *a.* wavy.

Wels *m.* (Welses, Welse) sheat-fish.

welsch *a.* Italian; French.

Welsche[r] *m.* (-n, -n) Italian; Frenchman.

Welt *f.* (-, -en) world; universe; people; *alle* ~, all the world, everybody; *zur* ~ *bringen*, to give birth to; *aus der* ~ *schaffen*, to do away with; *um alles in der* ~ *nicht*, not for the world.

Weltall, Weltenall *n.* (-s, 0) universe.

Welt: ~anschaulich *a.* ideological; ~anschauung *f.* ideology; ~ausstellung *f.* international exhibition.

welt: ~bekannt *a.* notorious; ~berühmt *a.* far-famed, of world-wide renown.

Weltbürger *m.* cosmopolite.

weltbürgerlich *a.* cosmopolitan.

Welt: ~bürgertum *n.* cosmopolitism; ~dame *f.* fashionable lady, woman of the world.

weltenfern *a.* & *adv.* worlds apart.

welterfahren *a.* experienced.

welterschütternd *a.* world-shaking.

weltfremd *a.* secluded from society.

Welt: ~friede(n) *m.* universal peace; ~geistliche[r] *m.* secular priest; ~geschichte *f.* universal history.

weltgeschichtlich, welthistorisch *a.* historical.

weltgewandt *a.* experienced in the world.

Welt: ~handel *m.* international trade; ~herrschaft *f.* world supremacy; ~karte *f.* map of the world; ~kenntnis *f.* knowledge of the world.

weltklug *a.* politic, worldly-wise.

Welt: ~körper *m.* heavenly body; ~krieg *m.* (1914–18) Great War; ~lage *f.* international situation; ~lauf *m.* course of the world.

weltlich *a.* worldly, mundane; temporal, secular.

Welt: ~literatur *f.* literature of the world; ~macht *f.* great power *or* empire; ~mann *m.* man of the world.

weltmännisch *a.* characteristic of a man of the world, gentlemanly.

Welt: ~markt *m.* international market; ~meer *n.* ocean, main; ~meister *m.* world-champion; ~meisterschaft *f.* world-championship.

weltmüde *a.* world-worn.

Welt: ~postverein *m.* (International)

Postal Union; ~priester *m.* secular priest; ~raum *m.* space; ~reich *n.* great empire; ~schmerz *m.* weariness of life, pessimistic melancholy; ~sprache *f.* universal language; ~stadt *f.* great and important city; ~stellung *f.* position in the world; ~teil *m.* part of the world; ~untergang *m.* end of the world; ~verkehr *m.* international traffic *or* commerce.

wem *pn.* to whom; he to whom.

wen *pn.* whom; he whom.

Wende *f.* (-, -n) turn, turning point.

Wendekreis *m.* tropic.

Wendeltreppe *f.* winding-stairs *pl.*, spiral staircase.

wenden *v.t. & i. ir. & reg.* to turn; (sich) ~ *v.refl.* to turn; (*an einen*) to address, to apply to; *bitte* ~*!* please turn over (PTO)!

Wendepunkt *m.* turning-point.

Wendung *f.* (-, -en) turn; *eine* ~ *zum Schlimmeren,* a change for the worse.

wendig *a.* nimble; easy to steer.

wenig *a. & adv.* little; some; ~*e,* few; *ein* ~, a little.

weniger *a.* less; fewer.

Wenigkeit *f.* (-, 0) *meine* ~, my humble self.

wenigstens *adv.* at least.

wenn *c.* when; if; ~ *anders,* ~ *nur,* provided that; *es ist als* ~, it is as if; *ausser* ~, unless, except when (if); ~ *auch,* though, although; *selbst* ~, *und* ~, even when (if); ~ *anders,* if. . .at all, if really; ~ *schon, denn schon,* (*fam.*) in for a penny, in for a pound; ~ *auch noch so,* if. . .ever so.

wenngleich, wennschon *c.* though, although, albeit.

wer *pn.* who; he who; which; whoever, whosoever; ~ *da?* who goes there?

Werbe . . .(*in Zus.*), advertising . . .

Werbefachmann *m.* publicity agent.

werben *v.i.st.* to apply for, to sue, to court; to canvass, to make propaganda; ~ *v.t.st.* to recruit; to enlist; ~ *um,* to court, to woo (a girl), to sue for.

Werber *m.* (-s, -) wooer, suitor.

Werbung *f.* (-, -en) recruiting; courtship; (*com.*) advertising, public relations.

Werdegang *m.* career.

werden *v.i.ir.* (*s*) to become; to grow, to turn, to get; *zuteil* ~, to fall to one's share; *was soll aus ihm* ~*?* what is to become of him? *die Sache wird,* the matter is in a fair way; *es wird schon!,* we are getting on well!; *wird's bald?* will you soon have done?

Werden *n.* (-s, 0) genesis; *im* ~ *sein,* to be in progress, to be preparing.

werfen *v.t.st.* to throw, to cast, to fling; (*von Tieren*) to bring forth; (sich) ~

v.refl.st. (*Holz*) to warp; *Verdacht* ~ *auf,* to cast suspicions on.

Werft *m.* (-[e]s, -e) ship-yard, dock-yard.

Werg *n.* (-es, 0) tow, oakum.

Werk *n.* (-[e]s, -e) work; action, deed; clockwork; mechanism; *ins* ~ *setzen,* to set going; *im* ~ *sein,* to be going on; *ans* ~ *gehen,* to go to work; *Hand ans* ~ *legen,* to set to work; *sich ans* ~ *machen,* to begin work; *zu* ~*e gehen,* to set about (a thing), to go (the right way) to work.

Werkbank *f.* work-bench, shop-counter.

Werk: ~führer *m.* foreman; ~führerin *f.* forewoman; ~meister *m.* foreman; ~schutz *m.* factory guard; ~statt, ~stätte *f.* workshop; ~stattauftrag *m.* work-order; ~stoff *m.* synthetic material, substitute; ~student *m.* working student; ~tag *m.* working-day.

werktäglich *a.* workaday, every-day.

Werktagskleid *n.* every-day dress.

werktätig *a.* active, industrious.

Werk: ~zeug *n.* instrument, tool; ~zeugmaschine *f.* machine tool.

Wermut *m.* (-[e]s, 0) wormwood; vermouth.

wert *a.* worth, worthy; valuable; dear; *der Mühe* ~, worth (our) while; ~*achten,* ~*schätzen,* to hold dear, to prize highly; *Ihr* ~*es Schreiben,* your favour.

Wert *m.* (-[e]s, -e) value, worth; rate, price; ~ *auf etwas legen,* to attach value to.

Wert: ~angabe *f.* declaration of value; ~bestimmung *f.* valuation; ~betrag *m.* value in money; ~brief *m.* money-letter.

wertbeständig *a.* of fixed value.

Wertgegenstand *m.* valuable.

wertlos *a.* worthless.

Wert: ~paket *n.* parcel registered with declaration of value; ~papiere *n.pl.* securities *pl.*; ~sachen *pl.* valuables.

wertschätzen *v.t.* to esteem highly.

Wertschätzung *f.* (-, 0) esteem, regard.

Wertsendung *f.* parcel containing money *or* valuables.

wertvoll *a.* valuable; precious.

Wertzuwachs *m.* increment value; ~steuer *f.* increment value tax.

Werwolf *m.* (-[e]s, -wölfe) wer(e)wolf.

wes *pn.* whose (*obs.* poet.).

Wesen *n.* (-s, -) being, entity; essence; substance, nature, character; ado, hubbub, noise; *sein* ~ *treiben,* to be at it (again); *viel* ~*s aus etwas machen,* to make a good deal of fuss *or* much ado about a thing; . . .*wesen,* (*in* (Zus.)) affairs, concerns *pl.*; *Finanzwesen,* finances; *Kriegswesen,* military affairs; *Schulwesen,* educational affairs.

Wesenheit *f.* (-, 0) essence, nature.

wesenlos *a.* unsubstantial, unreal.

wesentlich *a.* real, essential; substantial.
weshalb, weswegen *adv.* wherefore, why.
Wespe *f.* (-, -en) wasp.
wessen *pn.* whose.
Weste *f.* (-, -n) waistcoat; (*com.*) vest.
Westen *m.* (-s, 0) west, Occident.
Westentasche *f.* waistcoat pocket.
westlich *a.* western, westerly.
Westmächte *pl.* Western Powers.
Westseite *f.* western side.
westwärts *adv.* westward.
Westwind *m.* west wind.
wett *a.* equal, (*fam.*) quits; *etwas~ machen,* to quit scores.
Wettbewerb *m.* competition; contest.
Wettbewerber *m.* competitor.
Wettbüro *n.* betting office.
Wette *f.* (-, -n) bet, wager; *um die ~ laufen,* to race one another; *eine ~ eingehen, machen,* to lay a wager, to make a bet.
Wetteifer *m.* emulation.
wetteifern *v.i.* to vie, to contend with.
wetten *v.t.* to wager, to bet, to lay a wager; *es lässt sich 100 gegen eins ~,* you may bet *or* lay 100 to one; *auf etwas ~,* to back (a horse, a cock).
Wetter *n.* (-s, -) weather; *schlechtes ~,* bad weather; *schönes ~,* fine *or* fair weather; *bei gutem ~,* weather permitting.
Wetter: ~**aussichten** *pl.* weather outlook; ~**bericht** *m.* weather report; ~**dienst** *m.* meteorological service; ~**fahne** *f.* weather-cock, vane; (*fig.*) turn-coat.
wetterfest *a.* weather-proof.
Wetter: ~**karte** *f.* meteorological chart; ~**kunde** *f.* meteorology.
Wetterlage *f.* weather conditions.
Wetterleuchten *n.* sheet lightning.
wettern *v.i.* to storm, to swear.
Wetter: ~**vorhersage** *f.* weather forecast; ~**warte** *f.* weather bureau.
wetterwendisch *a.* changeable, fickle.
Wetterwolke *f.* thunder cloud.
Wett: ~**kampf** *m.* contest; prize fight, match; ~**lauf** *m.* race, running-match.
wettlaufen *v.i.st.* (*s*) to run a race; *~ gegen einen,* to race against one.
Wett: ~**läufer** *m.* prize runner; ~**rennen** *n.* horse race; racing; ~**rudern** *n.* boat race; ~**streit** *m.* contest, contention, match.
wetzen *v.t.* to whet, to sharpen.
Wetzstein *m.* whetstone.
Whist *n.* whist; ~**tournier** *n.* whist drive.
Wichs *m.* (Wichses, 0) (*Studentensprache*) full dress.
Wichse *f.* (-, -en) blacking, polish.
wichsen *v.t.* to black, to polish.
Wicht *m.* (-[e]s, -e) wight.
wichtig *a.* important.
Wichtigkeit *f.* (-, 0) importance.
Wichtigtuer *m.* busybody.

Wickel *m.* (-s, -) roll(er); curl-paper; cotton-winder; lap.
Wickel: ~**gamasche** *f.* puttee; ~**kind** *n.* child in swaddling clothes, baby.
wickeln *v.t.* to wind (up); to wrap up; to roll, to curl; to swathe, to swaddle; *auseinander ~,* to unwrap, to undo, to unfold.
Wickelung *f.* (-, -en) (*elek.*) winding.
Widder *m.* (-s, -) ram; (*Sternbild*) Aries.
wider *pr.* against, contrary to; versus; ~ *Willen,* unwillingly; *das Für und Wider,* the pros and cons.
widerfahren *v.i.st.* (*s*) to happen to, to befall; *einem Gerechtigkeit ~ lassen,* to do one justice.
widerhaarig *a.* refractory, cross-grained.
Widerhaken *m.* barbed hook; barb (of an arrow *or* hook).
Widerhall *m.* (-[e]s, -e) echo.
widerhallen *v.i.* to (re-)echo.
Widerlager *n.* (*arch.*) abutment; (*Pfeiler*) buttress.
widerlegen *v.t.* to refute, to disprove.
Widerlegung *f.* (-, -en) refutation.
widerlich *a.* disgusting, repulsive.
widernatürlich *a.* contrary to nature.
Widerpart *m.* (-[e]s, -e) opponent.
widerraten *v.t.st.* to dissuade (from).
widerrechtlich *a.* unlawful.
Widerrede *f.* contradiction.
Widerruf *m.* revocation; recantation.
widerrufen *v.t.st.* to revoke; to recant, to retract.
widerruflich *a.* revocable; ~ *adv.* on probation.
Widerrufung *f.* (-, -en) revocation.
Widersacher *m.* (-s, -) adversary.
Widerschein *m.* reflection, reflex.
widersetzen (sich) *v.refl.* to resist.
widersetzlich *a.* refractory.
Widersinn *m.* nonsense, absurdity.
widersinnig *a.* nonsensical, absurd.
widerspenstig *a.* refractory, obstinate.
widerspiegeln *v.t.* to reflect.
Widerspiel *n.* contrary, reverse.
widersprechen *v.i.st.* to contradict, to gainsay; (*sich*) ~ *v.refl.* to contradict oneself; *sich ~d,* contradictory.
Widerspruch *m.* contradiction.
Widerstand *m.* resistance, opposition; (*elek.*) resistance; ~ *leisten,* to offer resistance; ~**bewegung** *f.* underground movement; ~**smesser** *m.* (*elek.*) ohmmeter.
widerstandsfähig *a.* capable of resistance.
widerstandslos *a.* unresisting.
widerstehen *v.i.st.* to resist, to withstand; to be repugnant (to).
widerstreben *v.i.st.* to oppose, to resist; *das widerstrebt mir,* the thing jars upon me.
Widerstreit *m.* conflict, clash.
widerstreiten *v.i.* to conflict with.

widerwärtig *a.* repulsive.
Widerwille *m.* aversion, repugnance.
widerwillig *a.* reluctant, unwilling.
widmen *v.t.* to dedicate, to inscribe; to devote.
Widmung *f.* (-, -en) dedication.
widrig *a.* contrary; adverse; offensive.
widrigenfalls *adv.* else, failing this.
Widrigkeit *f.* (-, -en) adversity.
wie *adv.* how; ~ *c.* as, like; ~*so?* how do you mean?; ~ *wenn*, as if, as though; ~ *glücklich er auch sein mag*, however happy he may be; ~ *dem auch sei*, however this may be.
wieder *adv.* again, anew, afresh; back, in return; *hin und* ~, now and then; ~ *gut machen*, to redress.
wiederabdrucken *v.t.* to reprint.
Wiederaufbau *m.* reconstruction.
wiederaufbauen *v.t.* to rebuild.
wiederauffinden *v.t.st.* to recover.
Wiederauffindung *f.* recovery.
wiederaufleben *v.i.* (*s*) to revive.
Wiederaufnahme *f.* resumption.
Wiederaufnahmeverfahren *n.* (*law*) retrial.
wiederaufnehmen *v.t.st.* to resume.
wiederbekommen *v.t.st.* to recover.
wiederbeleben *v.t.* to revive, to resuscitate.
Wiederbelebungsversuch *m.* attempt to restore to life.
wiederbezahlen *v.t.* to repay.
wiederbringen *v.t.ir.* to restore, to return.
wiedereinbringen *v.t.ir.* to retrieve, to make up for.
wiedereinführen *v.t.* to re-introduce, to re-import.
wiedereinlösen *v.t.* to redeem.
Wiedereinreiseerlaubnis *f.* re-entry permit.
wiedereinsetzen *v.t.* to re-instate.
wiedererhalten *v.t.st.* to recover.
wiedererkennen *v.t.ir.* to recognize.
wiedererlangen *v.t.* to recover.
wiedererobern *v.t.* to reconquer.
wiedereröffnen *v.t.* to reopen.
wiederersetzen, wiedererstatten *v.t.* to restitute, to restore; to reimburse.
Wiedererstattung *f.* repayment.
wiedererzählen *v.t.* to recount.
Wiedergabe *f.* reproduction, rendering.
wiedergeben *v.t.st.* to give back; to re-produce, to render, to translate.
Wiedergeburt *f.* regeneration, new birth.
wiedergenesen *v.i.st.* (*s*) to recover (one's health).
wiedergewinnen *v.t.st.* to regain.
Wiedergutmachung *f.* reparation.
wiederhaben *v.t.* to have (got) back.
wiederherstellen *v.t.* to restore; to cure.
Wiederherstellung *f.* restoration.
wiederholen *v.t.* to repeat, to reiterate.
Wiederholung *f.* (-, -en) repetition.
Wiederholungsaufführung *f.* repeat performance.

Wiederholungskurs *m.* refresher course.
wiederkauen *v.i. & t.* (*auch fig.*) to ruminate, to chew the cud.
Wiederkäuer *m.* ruminant.
Wiederkehr *f.* (-, 0) return.
wiederkehren *v.i.* (*s*) to return.
wiederkommen *v.i.st.* (*s*) to come again *or* back, to return.
Wiederkunft *f.* (-, 0) return; second advent (of Christ).
wiedersehen *v.t.st.* to see *or* meet again.
Wiedersehen *n.* (-s, 0) meeting after a separation; *auf* ~! so long!, I'll be seeing you.
Wiedertäufer *m.* anabaptist.
wiederum *adv.* again, anew, afresh.
wiedervereinigen *v.t.* to reunite.
Wiedervereinigung *f.* reunion.
wiederverheiraten *v.t.* remarry.
Wiederverheiratung *f.* remarriage.
Wiederverkauf *m.* resale.
Wiederwahl *f.* re-election.
wiederwählbar *a.* re-eligible.
wiederwählen *v.t.* to re-elect.
Wiederzulassung *f.* re-admission.
Wiege *f.* (-, -n) cradle.
wiegen *v.t.* to rock; to mince; ~ *v.t. & i.st.* to weigh; *sich* ~ *in*, to lull oneself into.
Wiegen: ~druck *m.* incunabulum; ~fest *n.* birthday; ~lied *n.* lullaby.
wiehern *v.i.* to neigh.
Wiese *f.* (-, -n) meadow.
Wiesel *n.* (-s, -) weasel.
wieviel(s)te *a.* which of the number; *der* ~? what day of the month?
wiewohl *c.* though, although.
wild *a.* wild; savage, uncultivated; fierce, ferocious; turbulent; unmanageable; ~*e Ehe*, concubinage.
Wild *n.* (-[e]s, 0) game, deer; (*Wildbret*) venison.
Wild: ~bret *n.* venison, game; ~dieb *m.* poacher.
Wilde[r] *m.* (-n, -n) savage.
Wilderer *m.* (-s, -) poacher.
wildern *v.i.* to poach.
Wildfang *m.* (-[e]s, -fänge), romp.
wildfremd *a.* quite strange.
Wildheit *f.* (-, 0) wildness, savageness.
Wildleder *n.* deer-skin, doe-skin.
Wildnis *f.* (-, -nisse) wilderness.
Wildpark *m.* deer park.
Wildschwein *n.* wild boar.
wildwachsend *a.* growing wild.
Wille(n) *m.* (-ns, 0) will; mind, wish; design, intention, purpose; *letzter* ~, last will; *um...willen*, for the sake of; ~*s sein*, to intend, to have a mind; *einem zu Willen sein*, to do someone's will or pleasure; *aus freiem Willen*, of one's own accord, voluntarily; *wider Willen*, unwillingly.
willenlos *a.* irresolute, without energy.

Willensfreiheit f. freedom of will.
willfahren v.i. to comply with.
willfährig a. compliant, complaisant.
willig a. willing, docile, co-operative.
willigen(in) v.i. to consent (to).
willkommen a. & i. welcome; ~ heissen, to welcome.
Willkomm(en), m. (-s, 0) welcome.
Willkür f. (-, 0) arbitrariness; (Belieben) discretion; nach ~, at one's pleasure.
willkürlich a. arbitrary.
wimmeln v.i. to swarm (with).
wimmern v.i. to whimper, to whine.
Wimpel f. (-, -n) pennon, pennant.
Wimper f. (-, -n) eyelash.
Wind m. (-[e]s, -e) wind, breeze.
Windbeutel m. (Backwerk) cream puff; (fig.) swaggerer, humbug.
Winde f. (-, -n) windlass; reel.
Windel f. (-, -n) swaddling cloth, diaper.
windeln v.t. to swaddle, to swathe.
windelweich a. soft as velvet; einen ~ schlagen, to beat someone to a jelly.
winden v.t.st. to wind; to twist; (sich) ~ v.refl. to wind, to meander; to writhe.
Windeseile f. mit ~, on the wings of the wind.
Wind: ~fahne f. vane; ~hose f. water spout; ~hund m. greyhound.
windig a. windy; doubtful, shaky.
Wind: ~jacke f. trench jacket; ~mühle f. windmill; ~pocken pl. chicken-pox; ~rose f. compass-card.
Windscheibe f. (mot.) windscreen.
windschief a. warped, bent.
windstill a. calm.
Wind: ~stille f. calm; ~stoss m. gust, squall.
Windung f. (-, -en) winding, coil; spire, whorl (of a shell); worm (of a screw).
Wink m. (-[e]s, -e) sign, nod; (fig.) hint; tip; ~ mit einem Zaunpfahl, broad hint.
Winkel m. (-s, -) angle; corner; nook.
Winkeladvokat m. pettifogger.
winkelförmig a. angular.
wink(e)lig, a. angular; crooked.
Winkelmass n. (carpenter's) square, iron rule.
winken v.i. to beckon to, to nod; mit den Augen ~, to wink.
winseln v.i. to whimper, to whine.
Winter m. (-s, -) winter.
Winterhalbjahr n. winter-term.
winterlich a. wintry.
Winzer m. (-s, -) wine-grower; vintager.
winzig a. diminutive, tiny.
Wipfel m. (-s, -) top (of a tree).
wir pn. we.
Wirbel m. (-s, -) whirl, eddy, whirlpool; (phys.) vortex; crown (of the head); vertebra.
wirbelig a. whirling; vertiginous, giddy.
wirbellos a. invertebrate.

wirbeln v.i. to whirl, to eddy; mir wirbelt der Kopf, my head swims.
Wirbel: ~säule f. spine, vertebral column; ~sturm m. cyclone, tornado; ~tier n. vertebrate; ~wind m. whirlwind; tornado.
wirken v.t. to weave; to effect; to work, to produce; ~ v.i. to act (upon); to operate, to influence.
wirkend a. active, efficient, operative.
wirklich a. real, actual; effective; ~ adv. really, actually, positively; ~?, indeed?
Wirklichkeit f. (-, -en) reality.
wirksam a. efficacious, efficient, effectual; impressive; (med.) operative; ~ werden (law), to take effect.
Wirksamkeit f. (-, 0) efficacy, efficiency; (eines Gesetzes) operation.
Wirkstuhl m. loom.
Wirkung f. (-, -en) effect, operation, action; mit sofortiger ~, effective immediately; mit ~ vom 1. Juni, effective 1 June, with effect from 1 June.
Wirkungs: ~kraft f. efficiency; ~kreis m. sphere of action.
wirkungslos a. ineffectual.
wirkungsvoll a. effective.
wirr a. confused; ~es Haar, dishevelled head.
Wirren f.pl. disorders pl.
wirrköpfig a. muddle-headed.
Wirrnis f. (-nisses, -nisse), **Wirrsal** n. (-[e]s, -e) confusion, jumble.
Wirrwarr m. (-s, 0) confusion, jumble.
Wirsing m. (-s, 0), **Wirsingkohl** m. savoy.
Wirt m. (-[e]s, -e) host, landlord, innkeeper.
Wirtin f. (-, -nen) hostess, landlady.
wirtlich a. hospitable.
Wirtschaft f. (-, -en) economy; public house, inn; freie ~, private enterprise.
wirtschaften v.i. to manage, to keep house; to manage; to economize.
Wirtschafterin f. (-, -nen) housekeeper.
wirtschaftlich a. economic(al), thrifty.
Wirtschafts: ~betrieb m. (rail.) buffet; ~geld n. housekeeping money; ~krieg m. economic warfare; ~krise f. economic crisis; ~politik f. economic policy; ~ministerium n. Ministry of Economics, (in Eng.) Board of Trade.
Wirtshaus n. inn; tavern; public house; (Am.) saloon.
Wirts: ~leute pl. host and hostess; ~stube f. inn parlour; common room.
Wisch m. (-es, -e) clout; wisp (of straw); piece of waste paper.
wischen v.t. to wipe, to rub.
Wischer m. (-s, -) sponge.
Wischlappen m. dish cloth; duster.
Wismut m. (-[e]s, 0) bismuth.
wispern, v.i. to whisper.
Wissbegierde f. desire of knowledge.

wissbegierig *a.* eager for knowledge; curious.

wissen *v.t. & i.ir.* to know; to be aware of; *einem Dank ~,* to owe, to feel indebted to a person for; *er will von uns nichts ~,* he will have nothing to do with us.

Wissen *n.* (-s, 0) knowledge; learning; *meines ~s,* as far as I know, to my knowledge; *nach bestem ~ und Gewissen,* to the best of my knowledge and belief.

wissend, *a.* knowing.

Wissenschaft *f.* (-, -en) knowledge; science; learning; *die schönen ~en,* belles-lettres, the humanities.

Wissenschaftler *m.* scholar, savant, scientist.

wissenschaftlich *a.* scientific, learned.

Wissensdrang, Wissensdurst, Wissenstrieb *m.* desire of knowledge.

wissenswert *a.* worth knowing.

wissentlich *a.* knowing, wilful.

wittern *v.t.* to scent, to smell.

Witterung *f.* (-, -en) weather; scent.

Wittum *n.* (-[e]s, *and* -e *u.* -tümer) jointure.

Witwe *f.* (-, -n) widow; *(von Stande)* dowager.

Witwen: ~gehalt *m.* widow's pension, jointure; ~kasse *f.* fund for the support of widows.

Witwer *m.* (-s, -) widower.

Witz *m.* (-es, -e) joke, witticism.

Witzblatt *n.* comic paper.

Witzbold *m.* (-[e]s, -e) wit, wag.

Witzelei *f.* (-, -en) witticism.

witzeln *v.i.* to affect wit.

witzig *a.* witty; *~er Einfall,* flash of wit.

witzigen *v.t.* to make wiser.

Witzling *m.* (-[e]s, -e) wit, witling.

Witzwort *n.* sally, witticism.

wo *adv.* where; somewhere; when; *~ nicht,* if not, unless; *~ nur,* wherever.

wobei *adv.* at, by, in, with, which *or* what, in which case.

Woche *f.* (-, -n) week.

Wochen *pl.* childbed.

Wochen: ~besuch *m.* lying-in visit; ~bett *n.* childbed; ~bettfieber *n.* puerperal fever; ~ende *n.* week-end; ~schau *f.* (Film) newsreel; ~schrift *f.* weekly; ~tag *m.* week-day.

wochenlang *a. & adv.* for weeks together.

wochentags *adv.* on weekdays.

wöchentlich *a. & adv.* weekly.

Wöchnerin *f.* (-, -nen) woman lying-in.

wodurch *adv.* by which, through what *or* which.

wofern *c.* if, provided that; *~ nicht,* if not, unless.

wofür *adv.* for what *or* which.

Woge *f.* (-, -n) billow, wave.

wogegen *adv.* against what *or* which; (in return) for what *or* which.

wogen *v.i.* to wave; to fluctuate; to heave; to surge.

woher *adv.* whence, from what place.

wohin *adv.* whither; where.

wohl *adv.* well; indeed; possibly, probably; *wieder ~ sein,* to be all right again; *~ oder übel,* willy-nilly, 'whether or no'; *mir ist ~,* I feel comfortable.

Wohl *n.* (-[e]s, 0) welfare, good, benefit.

wohlan! *i.* now then! well!

wohl: ~anständig *a.* becoming, decent, decorous.

wohlauf! *i.* now then! up!; *er ist ~,* he is in good health.

wohlbedacht *a.* well-considered, well-advised.

Wohl: ~befinden *n.* good health; ~behagen *n.* comfort, ease.

wohl: ~behalten *a.* safe (and sound); ~bekannt *a.* well-known; ~beleibt *a.* corpulent, stout; ~beschaffen *a.* in good condition; ~besetzt *a.* well-filled, well-stored; ~betagt *a.* stricken in years; ~bewandert *a.* well-versed, well up (in).

wohlerfahren *a.* experienced, well skilled.

Wohlergehen *n.* (-s, 0) welfare.

wohl: ~erhalten *a.* in good condition, well-preserved, safe; ~erwogen *a.* well-considered; ~erworben *a.* duly acquired; ~erzogen *a.* well-bred.

Wohlfahrt *f.* (-, 0) welfare, weal, prosperity.

Wohlfahrtspflege *f.* welfare work.

wohlfeil *a.* cheap.

wohl: ~gebildet *a.* well-formed, well-shaped.

Wohlgefallen *n.* pleasure, delight; *sein ~ haben an,* to take delight in; *sich in ~ auflösen,* to end satisfactorily.

wohlgefällig *a.* pleasant; pleased, complacent.

wohl: ~gelitten *a.* popular; ~gemeint *a.* well-meant; ~gemut *a.* cheerful, merry ~ genährt *a.* well-fed, corpulent; ~ geordnet *a.* well-ordered; ~geraten *a.* well-done, perfect.

Wohl: ~geruch *m.* perfume, fragrance; ~geschmack *m.* flavour, relish.

wohl: ~gesinnt *a.* well-minded; ~gesittet *a.* well-mannered.

Wohlgestalt *f.* fine shape, beauty.

wohl: ~gestaltet *a.* well-shaped; ~gewogen *a.* well-affected, kind.

wohlgezogen *a.* well-bred, well-behaved.

wohlhabend *a.* well off, well-to-do.

Wohlhabenheit *f.* (-, 0) wealth, affluence.

wohlig *a.* comfortable, snug, cosy.

Wohlklang, Wohllaut *m.* euphony, harmony; harmonious sound.

wohlklingend *a.* sweet(-sounding), harmonious, euphonious.

Wohlleben *n.* life of luxury.

wohlmeinend *a.* well-meaning.
wohl: ~riechend *a.* sweet-scented, fragrant; ~schmeckend *a.* savoury, palatable.
Wohl: ~sein *n.* good health; ~stand *m.* prosperity, comfort; ~tat *f.* benefit; kindness, good action; ~täter *m.* benefactor.
wohltätig *a.* charitable, salutary.
Wohl: ~tätigkeit *f.* charity, benevolence; ~tätigkeitsverein *m.* charitable society.
wohltuend *a.* beneficial, salutary.
wohltun *v.i.st.* to do good, to benefit.
wohlverbürgt *a.* well authenticated.
wohlverdient *a.* well-deserved; condign (punishment); deserving.
Wohlverhalten *n.* good conduct.
wohlverstanden *a.* well understood.
wohlweislich *adv.* prudently.
wohlwollen *v.i.ir.* to wish (one) well.
Wohlwollen *n.* good-will, kindness.
wohlwollend *a.* benevolent, kind.
Wohn...residential, *a.*
wohnen *v.i.* to dwell, to live, to reside; to lodge, to stay.
Wohngebäude *n.* dwelling-house.
wohnhaft *a.* dwelling, residing.
Wohnhaus *n.* dwelling-house.
wohnlich *a.* comfortable.
Wohn: ~ort, ~platz *m.* place of residence, domicile; ~sitz *m.* domicile; abode.
Wohnschlafzimmer *n.* bed-sitting room.
Wohnung *f.* (-, -en) lodging, flat, apartments *pl.* (*Am.*) apartment; ~ mit Bedienung, service flat.
Wohnungs: ~amt *n.* housing office; ~mangel *m.*, ~not *f.* housing shortage; ~wechsel *m.* change of residence.
Wohn: ~viertel *n.* residential district; ~wagen *m.* caravan; ~zimmer *n.* sitting-room.
wölben *v.t.* to vault, to arch.
Wölbung *f.* (-, -en) vault(ing).
Wolf *m.* (-[e]s, Wölfe) wolf.
Wölfin *f.* (-, -nen) she-wolf.
wölfisch *a.* wolfish.
Wolfram *m.* (-s, 0) tungsten; ~erz *n.* wolfram.
Wolfs: ~hund *m.* Alsatian; ~hunger *m.* ravenous appetite.
Wölkchen *n.* (-s, -) cloudlet.
Wolke *f.* (-, -n) cloud.
Wolkenbruch *m.* cloudburst.
Wolkenkratzer *m.* sky scraper.
wolkenlos *a.* cloudless, serene.
wolkig *a.* cloudy, clouded.
Wolle *f.* (-, -n) wool.
wollen *a.* woollen; worsted; *v.i.ir.* to be willing, to intend, to wish, to want; *ich will,* I will; *lieber ~,* to prefer.
Wollen *n.* will; volition (*phil.*).
Woll[en]garn *n.* worsted.
Woll[en]stoffe *m.pl.* woollens *pl.*

Wollhändler *m.* woollen-draper.
wollig, *a.* woolly.
Wollust *f.* (-, -lüste) delight; lust, voluptuousness.
wollüstig *a.* voluptuous.
Wollüstling *m.* (-[e]s, -) voluptuary.
womit *adv.* wherewith, with which *or* what.
womöglich *adv.* if possible.
wonach *adv.* after what *or* which.
Wonne *f.* (-, -n) delight, bliss, rapture.
wonnesam, wonnevoll *a.* delightful.
wonnetrunken *a.* in raptures.
wonnig *a.* delightful, blissful.
woran *adv.* on what *or* which; ~ liegt es? how is it that?
worauf *adv.* whereupon.
woraus *adv.* wherefrom.
worein *adv.* in(to) what *or* which.
worin *adv.* wherein, in which *or* what.
Wort *n.* (-[e]s, Worte *or* Wörter) word, term; *mit anderen ~en,* in other words; *ich bitte ums Wort,* I request permission to speak; *sein ~ brechen, halten,* to break, keep one's word; *das ~ haben,* to be in possession of the House, (*Am.*) to have the floor; *ins ~ fallen,* to interrupt.
Wortbruch *m.* breach of faith.
wortbrüchig *a.* faithless.
Wörterbuch *n.* dictionary.
Wortführer *m.* spokesman.
wortgetreu *a.* literal.
wortkarg *a.* laconic.
Wortlaut *m.* wording, text.
wörtlich *a.* verbal, literal; ~ *adv.* literally, word for word, verbatim.
wortlos *a.* wordless.
wortreich *a.* verbose, wordy, voluble.
Wort: ~schatz *m.* vocabulary; ~schwall *m.* bombast; volley of words; ~sinn *m.* literal sense; ~spiel *n.* pun; ~stellung *f.* order of words; ~streit *m.* dispute (about words) quarrel; ~wechsel *m.* dispute, altercation; ~witz *m.* pun.
worüber *adv.* whereon.
worum *adv.* about what *or* which.
worunter *adv.* under *or* among which *or* what.
woselbst *adv.* where.
wovon *adv.* whereof; ~ leben sie? what do they live on?
wovor *adv.* before, of what *or* which.
wozu *adv.* whereto, what for.
Wrack *n.* (-[e]s, -e) wreck.
wringen *v.t.st.* to wring (out).
Wringmaschine *f.* wringing-machine.
Wucher *m.* (-s, 0) usury, profiteering.
Wucherer *m.* (-s, -) usurer.
wucherhaft, wucherisch *a.* usurious.
wuchern *v.i.* to practise usury; (*von Pflanzen*) to grow luxuriantly.
Wucherung *f.* (-, -en) growth.

Wuchs m. (Wuchses, Wüchse) growth; figure, stature, shape, size.

Wucht f. (-, 0) weight; force, impact.

wuchtig a. heavy, ponderous.

Wühlarbeit f. subversive activities pl.

wühlen v.i. & t. to rake, to dig (up); (fig.) to agitate, to stir up; to wallow.

Wulst m. (-s, Wülste) roll; pad.

wulstig a. padded, puffy; thick (lip).

wund a. sore, wounded, galled; mit ~en Füssen, footsore; ein ~er Punkt, a sore spot.

Wundarzt m. surgeon.

wundärztlich a: surgical.

Wunde f. (-, -n) wound, hurt.

Wunder n. (-s, -) wonder, marvel; miracle; es nimmt mich wunder, I wonder at it.

wunderbar a. wonderful, wondrous, miraculous, marvellous, strange.

Wunder: ~ding n. wondrous thing, prodigy; ~doktor m. quack.

wunderhübsch a. simply lovely.

Wunder: ~kind n. infant prodigy; ~kraft f. power of working miracles; ~kur f. miraculous cure.

wunderlich a. strange, odd, peculiar.

wundern (sich) v.refl. to wonder, to be amazed; es wundert mich, I wonder at it, I am surprised.

wundersam a. wonderful; miraculous.

wunderschön a. wondrous fair.

Wundertäter m. worker of miracles.

wundertätig a. working miracles.

Wundertier n. (fig.) lion.

wundervoll a. wonderful, marvellous.

Wunderwerk n. wonderful work.

Wundfieber n. wound fever.

wundgelaufen a. (foot) sore, galled.

Wundmal n. scar, cicatrice; stigma.

Wunsch m. (-es, Wünsche) wish, desire; auf ~, at the request of; nach ~ (according) to one's wish; ein frommer ~, a vain desire or wish.

Wünschelrute f. divining-rod.

Wünschelrutengänger m. dowser.

wünschen v.t. to wish (for); to desire, to long for; Glück ~, to congratulate.

wünschenswert a. desirable.

Wunschtraum m. pipe dream.

Wunschzettel m. list of things desired.

Würde f. (-, -n) dignity; honour; office.

würdelos a. undignified.

Würdenträger m. dignitary.

würdevoll a. dignified, grave.

würdig a. worthy; deserving (of).

würdigen v.t. to appreciate, to value.

Würdigung f. (-, -en) appreciation.

Wurf m. (-[e]s, Würfe) cast, throw; litter, brood.

Würfel m. (-s, -) die; (math.) cube.

Würfelbecher m. dice-box.

würfelförmig a. cubic(al).

würf[e]lig a. cubic (von Stoffen) chequered.

würfeln v.i. to play at dice; to chequer; durcheinander ~, to throw into confusion, to make a jumble of.

Würfel: ~spiel n. game at dice; ~zucker m. cube-sugar.

Wurf: ~geschoss n. missile, projection; ~linie f. trajectory; ~maschine f. catapult; ~speer, ~spiess m. javelin.

würgen v.t. to strangle, to throttle.

Würger m.(-s, -) murderer, cut-throat.

Wurm m. (-[e]s, Würmer) worm.

wurmartig a. vermicular, worm-like.

wurmen v.t. to vex, to annoy.

Wurmfortsatz m. (med.) appendix.

wurmig a. wormy; worm eaten.

wurmstichig a. worm eaten.

Wurst f. (-, Würste) sausage; (vulg.) das ist mir (ganz) ~, I don't care a fig.

Wursthändler m. pork-butcher.

Wurstigkeit f. (-, 0) (vulg.) utter indifference.

Würze f. (-, -n) spice, seasoning.

Wurzel f. (-, -n) root; carrot; ~ fassen (schlagen), to take root.

wurzeln v.t. to root, to be rooted.

Wurzelzeichen n. (math.) radical sign.

würzen v.t. to season, to spice.

würzhaft, würzig a. aromatic, spicy.

Wust m. (-es, -e) chaos.

wüst a. waste, desert, dissolute.

Wüste f. (-, -n) desert, wilderness.

wüsten v.i. (mit.) to waste.

Wüstenei f. (-, -en) desert, wilderness.

Wüstling m. (-[e]s, -e) libertine, rake.

Wut f, (-, 0) rage, fury.

wüten v.i. to rage, to rave.

wütend, wutentbrannt a. furious, enraged.

Wüterich m. (-s, -e) barbarous tyrant.

wütig a. outrageous mad.

wutschnaubend a. infuriated.

X

X n. einem ein X für ein U (vor-) machen, to bamboozle, to hoodwink, to humbug.

X-Beine n.pl. knock-knees pl.

x-beinig a. knock-kneed.

X-beliebig a. any...(you like).

x-mal adv. ever so many times.

Y

Yacht f. (-, -en) yacht.

Z

Z *n. von A bis Z*, from beginning to end
Zacke *f.* (-, -n), **Zacken** *m.* (-s, -) tooth
spike, prong; (*Felsen~*) jag.
zacken *v.t.* to tooth, to indent.
zackig *a.* pronged, indented; jagged.
zagen *v.i.* to hesitate; to be afraid.
zaghaft *a.* timorous.
zähe *a.* tough; sticky; tenacious.
zähflüss'g *a.* viscous.
Zähflüssigkeit *f.* (-, 0) viscosity.
Zahl *f.* (-, -en) number; figure, digit.
Zählapparat *m.* counter; meter (gas).
zahlbar *a.* payable, due.
zählbar *a.* numerable, countable.
zahlen *v.t.* to pay; *Kellner ~!* the bill,
please!
zählen *v.t.* to count, to number.
zahlender Gast *m.* paying guest.
Zahlenwert *m.* numerical value.
Zahler *m.* (-s, -) payer.
Zähler *m.* (-s, -) (*math.*) numerator; (*gas,
elek.*) meter.
Zahlkellner *m.* head-waiter.
zahllos *a.* numberless, innumerable.
Zahlmeister *m.* paymaster.
zahlreich *a.* numerous.
Zahl: ~**stelle** *f.* pay-office; ~**tag** *m.* pay-
day.
Zahlung *f.* (-, -en) payment; *als ~* in
settlement; *~en einstellen,* to stop *or*
suspend payment.
Zahlungs: ~**aufschub** *m.* moratorium;
~**bedingungen** *pl.* terms of payment;
~**befehl** *m.* payment order; ~**einstellung** *f.* suspension of payment; ~**empfänger** *m.* payee.
zahlungsfähig *a.* solvent, capable to pay.
Zahlungs: ~**fähigkeit** *f.* solvency; ~**frist** *f.*
time *or* respite of payment; ~**mittel** *n.*
(legal) tender; ~**ort** *m.* place of payment; ~**termin** *m.* time or term of payment.
zahlungsunfähig *a.* insolvent.
Zahlungs: ~**unfähigkeit** *f.* insolvency;
~**verbindlichkeit** *f.* liability (to pay).
Zahl: ~**wort** *n.* numeral; ~**zeichen** *n.*
figure; digit (0–9).
zahm *a.* tame, domesticated; (*fig.*) gentle.
zähmen *v.t.* to tame, to domesticate.
Zahn *m.* (-[e]s, **Zähne**) tooth; cog (of a
wheel); *Haare auf den Zähnen haben,* to
know what's what; to be a Tartar; an
awkward customer to deal with.
Zahnarzt *m.* dental surgeon.
Zahnbürste *f.* toothbrush.
Zähnefletschen *n.* (-s, 0) showing one's
teeth.
Zähn(e)klappern *n.* (-s, 0) chattering of
teeth.

Zähn(e)knirschen *n.* gnashing of teeth.
zahnen *v.i.* to teethe, to cut one's teeth;
~ *v.t.* to indent, to tooth, to notch.
Zahn: ~**fäule** *f.* caries; ~**fleisch** *n.* gums
pl.; ~**füllung** *f.* stopping; ~**heilkunde** *f.*
dentistry; ~**laut** *m.* dental (sound).
zahnlos *a.* toothless.
Zahnlücke *f.* gap between two teeth.
Zahn: ~**paste** *f.* tooth-paste; ~**pulver** *n.*
tooth-powder; ~**rad** *n.* gear, pinion, cog-
wheel; ~**radbahn** *f.* cog-wheel railway;
~**schmerzen** *m.* toothache; ~**stange** *f.*
rack; ~**stein** *m.* tartar; ~**stocher** *m.*
tooth-pick; ~**techniker** *m.* dental
mechanic; ~**weh** *n.* toothache.
Zähre *f.* (-, -n) tear.
Zange *f.* (-, -n) pincers; tongs; pliers *pl.*
Zangenbewegung *f.* (*mil.*) pincer movement.
Zank *m.* (-[e]s, 0) quarrel, altercation.
Zankapfel *m.* (*fig.*) bone of contention.
zanken *v.i.* to quarrel, to wrangle; (**sich**)
~ *v.refl.* to quarrel, to dispute.
zänkisch *a.* quarrelsome.
Zank: ~**lust,** ~**sucht** *f.* quarrelsomeness.
zanksüchtig *a.* quarrelsome.
Zäpfchen *n.* (-s, -) (*anat.*) uvula; (*med.*)
suppository.
Zapfen *m.* (-s, -) pin, peg; (*Fass*) tap.
zapfen *v.t.* to draw, to tap; to mortise.
Zapfenstreich *m.* tattoo.
zapp[e]lig *a.* fidgety, restless, fussy.
zappeln *v.i.* to sprawl, to kick, to struggle,
to flounder; to fidget.
Zar *m.* (-en, -en) czar, tsar.
zart *a.* tender; delicate; frail.
zartfühlend *a.* considerate, sensitive.
Zartgefühl *n.* delicacy of feeling.
Zartheit *f.* (-, -en) tenderness; delicacy.
zärtlich *a.* tender, amorous, fond.
Zärtlichkeit *f.* (-, -en) tenderness; fondness; ~**en** *pl.* caresses *pl.*
Zartsinn *m.* delicacy.
Zäsur *f.* (-, -en) caesura.
Zauber *m.* (-s, -) charm, enchantment,
spell, fascination.
Zauberei *f.* (-, -en) magic, witchcraft.
Zauberer *m.* (-s, -) magician, sorcerer:
zauberhaft *a.* magical, enchanting.
Zauberin *f.* (-, -nen) sorceress, witch.
zauberisch *a.* magic; enchanting.
Zauberkraft *f.* magic power.
zaubern *v.i.* to practise magic, to conjure.
zaudern *v.i.* to hesitate, to tarry.
Zaum *m.* (-[e]s, **Zäume**) bridle; *im ~e
halten,* to bridle, to check.
zäumen *v.t.* to bridle; (*fig.*) to restrain.
Zaumzeug *n.* horse's headgear.
Zaun *m.* (-[e]s, **Zäune**) hedge, fence.
Zaunkönig *m.* wren.
zausen *v.t.* to pull about, to touse.
Zebra *n.* (-[s], -s) zebra.
Zechbruder *m.* boon-companion; toper.

Zeche f. (-, -n) score, (tavern-) reckoning; (*Bergwerk*) mine, colliery; *die ~ bezahlen* (*fig.*) to pay the piper.

zechen *v.i.* to tipple, to drink hard, to carouse.

Zechgelage n. drinking-bout.

Zechkumpan m. boon companion.

Zech: ~**preller** m. person who shirks paying his score, bilk; ~**stein** m. dolomite.

Zeder f. (-, -n) cedar.

zedieren *v.t.* to cede, to surrender.

Zehe f. (-, -n) **Zeh** m. (-en, -en) toe; *die grosse ~,* the big toe; *auf den ~n gehen,* to walk on tiptoe.

Zehenspitze f. tiptoe; point of the toe.

zehn a. ten.

Zehner m. (-s, -) ten.

zehnerlei a. of ten sorts.

zehnfach, zehnfältig a. tenfold.

zehnjährig a. ten years old, of ten years.

zehnmal adv. ten times.

Zehnte m. (-n, -n) tithe.

zehntens adv. tenthly.

zehren *v.i.* (*an, von*) to live on, to feed on.

Zehrung f. (-, -en) (expenses of) living.

Zeichen n. (-s, -) sign, token, mark; (*com.*) reference(-number); ~*s ist er Schuster,* he is a shoemaker by trade.

Zeichen: ~**brett** n. drawing-board; ~**erklärung** f. references, legend; ~**sprache** f. sign-language; ~**tinte** f. marking ink.

zeichnen *v.t.* to draw, to design; to mark; to sign, to subscribe; (*Anleihe*) to subscribe for.

Zeichner m. (-s, -) draughtsman; subscriber.

Zeichnung f. (-, -en) drawing, design, sketch, diagram; subscription.

zeichnungsberechtigt a. authorized to sign.

Zeichnungsliste f. subscription list.

Zeigefinger m. forefinger, index.

zeigen *v.t.* to show, to point out, to demonstrate; (*sich*) ~ *v.refl.* to appear; *es muss sich zeigen,* it remains to be seen.

Zeiger m. (-s, -) hand (of a clock); pointer.

zeihen *v.t.st.* to accuse (of).

Zeile f. (-, -n) line; *in Einzeilenstellung,* single-spaced, a.; *in Zweizeilenstellung,* double-spaced, a.

Zeisig m. (-[e]s, -e) siskin.

Zeit f. (-, -en) time; season; age; era, period; tide; *zur ~,* at present; *bei ~en,* betimes; *mit der ~,* in the course of time; *vor ~en,* in former times; *zu rechter ~, zur rechten ~,* in (good) time; *zu ~en,* at times; *eine ~lang,* for a while, for some time; (*seines*) *Lebens,* (in) (all) his life; *sich ~ lassen,* to take (one's) time; *sich die ~ vertreiben,* to while away the time.

Zeit: ~**ablauf** m. lapse of time; ~**abschnitt** m. epoch, period; ~**alter** n. age, era; ~**bombe** f. time-bomb; ~**dauer** f. duration, lapse of time; ~**form** f. (*gram.*) tense; ~**geist** m. spirit of the age.

zeitgemäss a. seasonable, well-timed.

Zeitgenoss, Zeitgenosse m. contemporary.

zeitgenössisch a. contemporary.

zeitig a. early, timely; ripe; ~ adv. early, in (due) time.

zeitigen *v.t.* to mature; ~ *v.i.* (*s*) to ripen, to get ripe.

Zeitläuf(t)e pl. conjunctures, times pl.

zeitlebens adv. for life; during life.

zeitlich a. temporal, temporary, earthly.

Zeitlichkeit f. (-, 0) earthly life.

Zeit: ~**lupe** f. time lens; ~**lupenaufnahme** f. slow-motion picture; ~**punkt** f. moment.

zeitraubend a. requiring much time.

Zeit: ~**raum** m. space of time, period; ~**rechnung** f. chronology; era; ~**schrift** f. periodical, journal, magazine.

Zeitung f. (-, -en) newspaper, gazette.

Zeitungs: ~**ausschnitt** m. newspaper cutting *or* clipping; ~**ente** f. canard; ~**inserat** n. advertisement; ~**kiosk** m. newsstall; ~**papier** n. newsprint; ~**verkäufer** m. newsagent, newsvendor; ~**wesen** n. journalism, the press.

Zeitvergeudung f. waste of time.

Zeit: ~**verhältnisse** pl. circumstances; ~**verlauf** m. lapse of time; ~**verschwendung** f. waste of time; ~**vertreib** m. pastime, diversion.

zeitvertreibend a. diverting, amusing.

zeitweilig a. temporary; ~**er Dienst** m. (*mil.*) temporary duty (**TDY**).

zeitweise adv. at times.

Zeit: ~**wort** n. verb; ~**zeichen** n. (*Radio*) time signal.

Zeitzünder m. time-fuse.

Zelle f. (-, -n) cell.

zellenförmig a. cellular.

Zellengewebe n. cellular tissue.

Zellophan n. (-s, 0) cellophane.

Zellstoff m. cellulose; pulp.

Zelluloid n. (-s, 0) celluloid.

Zellulose f. (-, 0) cellulose; pulp.

Zellwolle f. cellulose wool.

Zelot m. (-en, -en) zealot.

Zelt n. (-[e]s, -e) tent, awning; pavilion.

Zeltdach n., **Zeltdecke** f. marquee.

Zelter m. (-s, -) ambler, palfrey.

Zeltlager n. tent camp.

Zement m. (-es, -) cement.

zementieren *v.t.* to cement.

Zenit m. (-[e]s, 0) zenith.

zensieren *v.t.* to criticize; to censure.

Zensor m. (-s, -en) censor; (*von Druckwerken auch*) licenser.

Zensoramt n. censorship.

Zensur censorship; (school-)report, marks *pl.*

Zensus *m.* (-, 0) census.

Zentigramm *n.* centigram.

Zentimeter *m.* or *n.* (-n) centimetre.

Zentner *m.* (-s, -) (German) hundred-weight (cwt.).

Zentnerlast *f.* heavy burden.

zentnerschwer *a.* very heavy, ponderous, oppressive.

zentral *a.* central.

Zentrale *f.* (-, -n) central office *or* station; headquarters.

Zentralheizung *f.* central heating; *mit ~,* centrally heated.

zentralisieren *v.t.* to centralize.

Zentrum *n.* (-s, -tren) centre; bull's eye; (Roman Catholic) Centre Party.

Zepter *n. & m.* (-s, -) sceptre; mace.

zerbeissen *v.t.st.* to bite into pieces.

zerbersten *v.i.st.* (s) to burst asunder.

zerbrechen *v.t.st.* to break (to pieces); *sich den Kopf ~,* to rack one's brains; *~ v.i.st.* (s) to break.

zerbrechlich *a.* fragile, brittle.

zerbröckeln *v.i.* (s) to crumble.

zerdrücken *v.t.* to crush; to bruise.

Zeremonie *f.* (-, -n) ceremony.

zeremoniell *n.* (-s, -e) ceremonial.

zeremoniös *a.* ceremonious.

zerfahren *a.* thoughtless, incoherent.

Zerfall *m.* (-[e]s, 0) ruin, decay.

zerfallen *v.i.st.* (s) to fall to pieces; to decay; (*fig.*) to fall out (with one).

zerfasern *v.t.* to ravel out.

zerfetzen *v.t.* to slash, to tatter.

zerfleischen *v.t.* to lacerate, to mangle.

zerfliessen *v.i.st.* (s) to dissolve, to melt.

zerfressen *v.t.st.* to corrode.

zergehen *v.i.st.* (s) to dissolve.

zergliedern *v.t.* to dissect, to dismember.

Zergliederung *f.* (-, -en) dissection; (*fig.*) analysis.

zerhacken *v.t.* to chop, to mince.

zerhauen *v.t.st.* to cut asunder, to cut up, to slash.

zerkauen *v.t.* to chew.

zerkleinern *v.t.* to chop (wood).

zerklüftet *a.* cleft, riven.

zerknirscht *a.* contrite.

Zerknirschung *f.* (-, 0) contrition.

zerknittern, zerknüllen *v.t.* to crumple.

zerkratzen *v.t.* to scratch.

zerlassen *v.t.st.* to dissolve, to melt.

zerlegbar *a.* dissectible.

zerlegen *v.t.* to take to pieces; to carve.

zerlumpt *a.* ragged, tattered.

zermahlen *v.t.st.* to grind (to powder).

zermalmen *v.t.* to bruise, to crush.

zermürben *v.t.* to wear down.

Zermürbung *f.* (-, 0) attrition.

zerpflücken *v.t.* to pick to pieces.

zerplatzen *v.i.* (s) to burst.

zerquetschen *v.t.* to bruise, to squash.

Zerrbild *n.* caricature.

zerreiben *v.t.st.* to grind to powder.

zerreissbar *a.* tearable.

zerreissen *v.t.st.* to tear, to rend; *~ v.i.st.* (s) to be torn.

zerren *v.t.* to pull, to tug.

zerrinnen *v.i.st.* (s) to dissolve, to melt.

Zerrissenheit *f.* (-, 0) dismemberment; (*fig.*) distraction.

zerrütten *v.t.* to unsettle, to ruin, to shatter; (*den Geist*) to unhinge.

Zerrüttung *f.* (-, -en) disorder, ruin; (*Geistes~*) derangement.

zersägen *v.t.* to saw to pieces.

zerschellen *v.i.* (s) to be dashed to pieces.

zerschlagen *v.t.st.* to shatter, to smash, to break (by striking); (*sich*) *~ v.refl.* to come to nothing; *~ a.* knocked up.

zerschmettern *v.t.* to crush, to shatter.

zerschneiden *v.t.st.* to cut to pieces.

zersetzen *v.t.* to decompose.

Zersetzung *f.* (-, -en) decomposition.

zerspalten *v.t.* to cleave, to split.

zersplittern *v.t.* to split, to shiver; to fritter away.

zersprengen *v.t.* to disperse, to scatter.

zerspringen *v.i.st.* (s) to burst; (*Glas*) to crack; (*Kopf*) to split.

zerstäuben *v.t.* to spray.

zerstieben *v.i.st.* (s) to vanish, to fly asunder.

zerstörbar *a.* destructible.

zerstören *v.t.* to destroy, to ruin.

Zerstörer *m.* (-s, -) (*nav.*) destroyer.

Zerstörung *f.* (-, -en) destruction.

zerstossen *v.t.st.* to pound, to triturate.

zerstreuen *v.t.* to scatter, to disperse; to dispel; (*sich*) *~ v.refl.* to divert oneself, to seek diversion.

zerstreut *a.* (*fig.*) absent-minded; (*Licht*) diffused.

Zerstreutheit *f.* (-, 0) absence of mind.

Zerstreuung *f.* (-, -en) dispersion; diversion.

zerstückeln *v.t.* to dismember; to cut up, to parcel out.

Zerstück[e]lung *f.* (-, -en) dismemberment, parcelling (out).

zerteilbar *a.* divisible.

zerteilen *v.t.* to divide, to disperse, to dismember; (*math.*) to resolve (into factors).

zertrennen *v.t.* to unstitch, to rip up.

zertreten *v.t.st.* to trample down.

zertrümmern *v.t.* to destroy, to wreck.

Zervelatwurst *f.* salami.

Zerwürfnis *n.* (-nisses, -nisse) difference, discord, quarrel, dissension.

zerzausen *v.t.* to dishevel, to tousle.

Zession *f.* (-, -en) transfer, cession.

zeter *i.* *~ über einen schreien,* to cry shame upon someone.

Zetergeschrei n. loud outcry.

zetern v.i. to clamour, to brawl.

Zettel m. (-s, -) slip of paper, note; label; poster; chain, warp.

Zeug n. (-[e]s, -e) stuff; matter; cloth; rubbish, trash; *das ~ haben zu etwas*, (fig.) to have in one the making of; *was das ~ hält* or *halten will*, with might and main; *sich ins ~ legen*, to launch out; *dummes ~*, stuff and nonsense.

Zeuge m. (-n, -n) witness; *einen ~n beibringen*, to produce a witness.

zeugen v.t. to beget, to generate; ~ v.i. to witness, to testify, to depose.

Zeugen: *~aussage* f. deposition (of a witness); *~beweis* m. evidence; *~bank* f. witness-box; *~stand* m. witness stand; *~verhör* n., *~vernehmung* f. examination of witnesses; *~vorladung* f. witness summons.

Zeughaus n. arsenal.

Zeugnis n. (-nisses, -nisse) testimony, evidence; character, certificate; (*Schul~*) report; *~ ablegen*, to give evidence; to bear witness.

Zeugniszwang m. compulsion to give evidence.

Zeugung f. (-, -en) begetting, procreation, generation.

zeugungsfähig a. able to beget.

zeugungsunfähig a. impotent.

Zichorie f. (-, -n) chicory.

Zicke f., **Zicklein** n. (-s, -) kid.

Zickzack m. (-[e]s, -e) zigzag.

Ziege f. (-, -n) goat, she-goat.

Ziegel m. (-s, -) tile; brick.

Ziegelbrenner m. brickmaker.

Ziegelbrennerei f. brickworks pl.

Ziegel: *~dach* n. tiled-roof; *~decker* m. tiler.

Ziegelei f. (-, -en) brick-works.

Ziegelstein m. brick.

Ziegen: *~bock* m. he-goat; *~fell* n. goat-skin; *~hirt* m. goat-herd; *~leder* n. suède.

Ziegenpeter m. (-s, -) (*fam.*) mumps pl.

Ziehbrunnen m. draw-well.

ziehen v.t.st. to draw; to pull; to cultivate, to grow, to breed; to rifle (a gun); (*Schiff*) to tow; to extract (a tooth, a root of a number); (sich) ~ v.refl. to extend; (*Holz*) to warp; ~ v.i. (h) (*im Schach*) to move; (*aus der Wohnung*) to move, to remove; *die Bilanz ~*, to draw up the balance-sheet; *Nutzen aus etwas ~*, to derive profit from; *in den Schmutz ~*, (fig.) to blacken, to asperse; *in Betracht, in Erwägung ~*, to take into consideration, to consider; *ins Geheimnis, ins Vertrauen ~*, to take (a person) into the secret, into one's confidence; *Gesichter ~*, to pull faces; *den kürzeren ~*, to get the worst of it; *in die Länge ~*, to

spin out; *in Zweifel ~*, to (call in) question, to doubt; *Folgen nach sich ~*, to entail consequences; *das Stück zieht*, the play draws large audiences; *der Tee muss noch ~*, the tea is not drawn yet; *es zieht hier*, there's a draught here; *sich in die Länge ~*, to be protracted.

Zieh: *~harmonika* f. accordion, concertina; *~kind* n. foster-child.

Ziehung f. (-, -en) drawing (of the lottery).

Ziel n. (-[e]s, -e) aim, goal, mark; (*Luftkrieg*) target, objective; (*Reise*) destination; *ein ~ setzen*, to aim at.

zielen v.i. to aim, to take aim, to sight; (*fig.*) to drive at.

ziellos a. aimless.

Zielscheibe f. target.

ziemen v.i. to become, to be suitable.

Ziemer m. (-s, -) loin, chine (of venison); penis.

ziemlich a. suitable, fit; fair, moderate, passable, middling.

Zier f. (-, -en) ornament.

Zierat m. (-[e]s, -en) ornament.

Zierbengel m. fop, coxcomb.

Zierde f. (-, -n) ornament.

zieren v.t. to adorn, to decorate; (sich) ~ v.refl. to affect shyness; **geziert** a. affected.

Ziererei f. (-, -en) affectation, airs pl.

zierlich a. elegant, neat.

Ziffer f. (-, -n) figure; digit; cipher; numeral.

Zifferblatt n. dial-plate, face.

ziffer(n)mässig a. by figures, in number.

Zigarette f. (-, -n) cigarette, fag.

Zigaretten: *~etui* n. cigarette-case; *~stummel* m. cigarette-end, (*Am.*) cigarette butt or stump.

Zigarre f. (-, -n) cigar.

Zigarren: *~spitze* f. cigar-holder; tip (of a cigar); *~tasche* f. cigar-case.

Zigeuner m. (-s, -) ~in f. (-, -nen) gipsy.

Zikade f. (-, -n) cicada, cigala.

Zimbel f. (-, -n) cymbal.

Zimmer n. (-s, -) room, chamber.

Zimmer: *~einrichtung* f. suite; *~herr* m. lodger; *~mädchen* n. chambermaid; *~mann* m. carpenter.

zimmern v.t. to construct (of wood).

Zimmervermieter(in) f. m. lodging-house keeper.

Zimmet, Zimt m. (-[e]s, -e) cinnamon.

zimperlich a. prim, prudish, mincing.

Zink n. (-[e]s, 0) zinc; spelter.

Zinke f. (-, -n) prong; (*mus.*) cornet.

Zinkgiesser m. zinc-founder.

Zinn n. (-[e]s, 0) tin; (*für Geräte*) pewter.

Zinnbergwerk n. tin-mine, stannary.

Zinne f. (-, -n) battlement; pinnacle.

Zinngeschirr n. pewter-utensils pl.).

Zinngiesser m. pewterer.

Zinnober m. (-s, 0) cinnabar, vermilion

zinnoberrot *a.* vermilion.
Zins *m.* (Zinses, Zinsen) rent; interest.
zinsbar *a.* tributary; bearing interest.
zinsbringend *a.* bearing interest.
Zinsen *f.pl.* interest; ~ tragen, to bear interest.
zinsen *v.i.* to pay rent *or* tribute.
Zinseszins *m.* compound interest.
zinsfrei *a.* rent-free.
Zinsfuss *m.* rate of interest.
Zinssatz *m.* rate of interest.
Zionismus *m.* zionism.
Zipfel *m.* (-s, -) tip, corner.
Zipfelmütze *f.* jelly-bag hat, tasselled cap.
Zipperlein *n.* (-s, 0) gout.
zirka *adv.* approximately.
Zirkel *m.* (-s, -) circle of people; pair of compasses *or* dividers.
zirkulieren *v.t. & i.* to circulate.
Zirkular *n.* (-s, -e) circular.
Zirkumflex *m.* (-es, -e) circumflex.
Zirkus *m.* (-, -. -u. -kusse) circus.
zirpen *v.i.* to chirp.
zischeln *v.i.* to whisper.
zischen *v.i.* to hiss; to whiz.
Zischlaut *m.* hissing sound; sibilant.
ziselieren *v.t.* to chase, to enchase.
Zisterne *f.* (-, -n) oriental well.
Zitadelle *f.* (-, -n) citadel.
Zitat *n.* (-[e]s, -e) quotation.
Zither *f.* (-, -n) zither.
zitieren *v.t.* to cite; to quote.
Zitrone *f.* (-, -n) lemon.
zitronengelb *a.* lemon-coloured.
Zitronen: ~saft *m.* lemon-juice; ~schale *f.* lemon-peel; ~wasser *n.* lemonade.
zittern *v.i.* to tremble, to shiver.
Zitze *f.* (-, -n) teat, dug, nipple.
zivil *a.* civil; Zivil *n.* (-s, 0) civilians; *in* ~, in plain clothes, in mufti.
Zivilehe *f.* civil marriage.
Zivilisation *f.* (-, -en) civilization.
zivilisatorisch *a.* civilizing.
zivilisieren *v.t.* to civilize.
Zivilist *m.* (-en, -en) civilian.
Zivil: ~klage *f.* (*law*) action; ~liste *f.* civil list; ~prozessordnung *f.* code of civil procedure; ~sache *f.* civil case.
Zobel *m.* (-s, -) sable.
Zobelpelz *m.* sable-cloak.
Zofe *f.* (-s, -n) (lady's) maid.
zögern *v.i.* to hesitate, to delay.
Zögerung *f.* (-, -en) delay.
Zögling *m.* (-[e]s, -e) pupil.
Zölibat *n.* (-es, 0) celibacy.
Zoll *m.* (-[e]s, -) inch; (*pl.* Zölle) duty, tariff, custom; (*fig.*) tribute.
Zollabfertigung *f.* customs clearance.
Zollamt *n.* custom house, customs station.
Zollbeamte[r] *m.* custom-house officer.
zollen *v.t.* to pay, to give.
Zolleinnehmer *m.* customs receiver.

Zollerklärung *f.* customs declaration.
zollfrei *a.* duty-free.
Zoll: ~grenze *f.* customs-frontier; ~haus *n.* custom-house; ~krieg *m.* tariff war.
zollpflichtig *a.* liable to duty.
Zollrevision *f.* customs examination *or* inspection.
Zoll: ~tarif *m.* tariff; ~verband, ~verein *m.* customs-union; ~verschluss *m.* customs-seal; *unter* ~, in bond.
Zollschranke *f.* tariff wall.
zollweise *adv.* by inches.
Zone *f.* (-, -n) zone.
Zonen...zonal, *a.*
Zonentarif *m.* zone-tariff.
Zoologe *m.* (-n, -n) zoologist.
Zoologie *f.* (-, 0) zoology.
zoologisch *a.* zoological.
Zopf *m.* (-[e]s, Zöpfe) pigtail; (*Mädchen*~) plait of hair; (*fig.*) pedantry, routine.
zopfig *a.* old-fashioned, old-world.
Zopfzeit *f.* Georgian era, pigtail age.
Zorn *m.* (-[e]s, 0) wrath, anger, ire.
Zornausbruch *m.* fit *or* burst of anger.
zornentbrannt *a.* angry.
zornig *a.* wrathful, angry.
Zote *f.* (-, -n) foul jest, obscenity.
zotenhaft, zotig *a.* obscene, ribald.
Zotte, Zottel *f.* (-, -n) tuft, lock.
zottig *a.* shaggy, ragged; matted.
zu *pr.* to, at, by, in, on, for; ~ *adv.* too; shut; ~ *Land*, by land on (dry) land; *zur See*, at sea; *zum Beispiel*, for instance; *zur Not*, if need be; ~ *zweien*, two of us (them, etc.); ~ *Hunderten*, by hundreds, in their hundreds; ~ *dritt*, three of them (us, etc.); *Tür* ~!, shut the door, please.
Zubehörteile *pl.* accessories.
zubeissen *v.i.st.* to bite *or* snap (at a thing).
zubenannt *a.* surnamed.
Zuber *m.* (-s, -) (two-handled) tub.
zubereiten *v.t.* to prepare, to cook.
zubilligen *v.t.* to grant.
zubinden *v.t.st.* to tie up; (*die Augen*) to blindfold.
zubleiben *v.i.st.* to remain closed.
zubringen *v.t.ir.* to bring into marriage (dowry, children); to pass, to spend (time); *das Zugebrachte*, the dowry.
Zucht *f.* (-, 0) breeding, breed; discipline, education; modesty.
Zuchtbuch *n.* stud-book.
züchten *v.t.* to breed; to grow, to cultivate; to train.
Züchter *m.* (-s, -) breeder (of animals); grower (of plants).
Zuchthaus *n.* penitentiary; (*Strafe*) penal servitude; *lebenslängliches* ~, penal servitude for life.
züchtig *a.* modest, chaste.
züchtigen *v.t.* to chastise, to correct.

Züchtigung f. (-, -en) chastisement.
zuchtlos a. undisciplined; disorderly.
Zuchtlosigkeit f. indiscipline.
Zuchtperle f. cultured pearl.
Zuchtpferd n. pedigree horse.
Züchtung f. (-, -en) breeding; (von Pflanzen) cultivation; training.
Zucht: ~vieh n. cattle for breeding; natürliche ~, natural selection.
zucken v.i. to be convulsed, to quiver; to wince; ~ v.t. to jerk, to tug; to shrug (one's shoulders).
zücken v.t. to draw, to flourish (a sword).
Zucker m. (-s, 0) sugar.
Zucker: ~bäcker m. confectioner; ~bäckerei f. confectioner's shop; ~dose f. sugar-basin; ~fabrik f. sugar-works pl., refinery; ~guss m. (sugar) icing, frosting; ~hut m. sugar loaf; ~kranker m. diabetic; ~krankheit f. diabetes.
zuckern v.t. to sugar (over).
Zucker: ~rohr n. sugar cane; ~rübe f. (weisse) sweet turnip; (rote) sugar-beet.
zuckersüss a. sweet as sugar.
Zucker: ~werk n. sweets pl., confectionery; ~zange f. sugar-tongs pl.
Zuckung f. (-, -en) convulsion.
zudecken v.t. to cover (up).
zudem adv. besides, moreover.
zudenken v.t.ir. to intend as a present, etc., for somebody.
zudiktieren v.t. to impose a punishment.
Zudrang m. (-[e]s, 0) rush, run (on).
zudrehen v.t. to shut off, to turn off; einem den Rücken ~, to turn one's back upon one.
zudringlich a. obtrusive.
zudrücken v.t. to close (by pressure); ein Auge bei etwas ~, to connive or wink at a thing.
zueignen v.t. to dedicate; (sich) ~ v.refl. to appropriate, to seize.
Zueignung f. (-, -en) dedication.
zueilen v.i. (s) to hasten (up) to.
zuerkennen v.t.ir. to award, to adjudicate; to sentence (one) to.
zuerst adv. first, at first.
zufahren v.i.st. (s) to drive on; auf einen ~, to rush upon, to make a dash at.
Zufall m. chance, hazard, accident.
zufallen v.i.st. (s) to shut of itself, to close; to fall to one's share.
zufällig a. casual, accidental.
zuflicken v.t. to patch or vamp up.
zufliegen v.i.st. (s) to fly to or towards; (Tür) to slam.
zufliessen v.i.st. (s) to flow to or towards; einem etwas ~ lassen, to make a thing come somebody's way.
Zuflucht f. (-, 0) refuge; recourse; seine ~ nehmen zu, to have recourse to

Zufluchtsort m. **Zufluchtsstätte** f. place of refuge, asylum.
Zufluss m. (-flusses, -flüsse) afflux, influx; supply; (Strom) affluent.
zuflüstern v.t. to whisper to.
zufolge pr. in consequence of, owing to.
zufrieden a. content(ed), satisfied; ~stellen, to satisfy, to content.
Zufriedenheit f. (-, 0) satisfaction.
zufriedenstellend a. satisfactory.
zufrieren v.i.st. (s) to freeze over or up.
zufügen v.t. to do, to inflict, to cause.
Zufuhr f. (-, -en) (mil.) provisions pl., supply.
zuführen v.t. to lead to, to bring to; to introduce; to import, to supply; (mech.) to feed.
Zug m. (-[e]s, Züge) pull; draught, current (of air); procession; (im Schach) move; (Eisenbahn..) train; feature, trait; (Feder..) stroke; (Neigung) bent, impulse; (mil.) platoon; ~ Pferde, team of horses; (Gebirgs..) mountain range; der Ofen hat keinen guten ~, the stove draws badly; in einem ~, auf einen ~, at one stroke; in den letzten Zügen liegen, to be breathing one's last.
Zugabe f. addition, adjunct; (com.) make-weight; (theat.) encore.
Zugang m. access, approach; entrance.
zugänglich a. accessible; (fig.) affable.
Zugbrücke f. drawbridge.
zugeben v.t.st. to give into the bargain, to add; to permit; to admit, to grant.
zugegen a. present.
zugehen v.i.st. (s) to shut; to go up to, to move towards; to come to hand; to come to pass, to happen; einem etwas ~ lassen, to send, to forward, to transmit a thing to someone.
zugehören v.i. to belong to.
zugehörig a. appertaining.
Zugehörigkeit f. (-, 0) membership (of a company, union, club, etc.).
zugeknöpft a. buttoned up.
Zügel m. (-s, -) rein, bridle.
zügellos a. (fig.) unbridled.
zügeln v.t. to bridle; to curb, to check.
zugesellen v.t. to associate, to unite.
zugestehen v.t.st. to concede, to grant, to admit.
zugetan a. attached.
Zugfestigkeit f. tensile strength.
zugiessen v.t.st. to pour more on, to add.
zugig a. draughty.
Zugkraft f. power of traction; (fig.) attractiveness.
zugkräftig a. attractive.
zugleich adv. at the same time, together.
Zugluft f. draught (of air).
zugreifen v.i.st. to seize, to fall to, to help oneself (at table).

zugrunde *adv.* ~ *gehen*, to perish; ~ *richten*, to ruin.
zugucken *v.i.* to look on.
zugunsten *adv.* in favour of.
zugute *adv.* ~ *halten*, not to put down to someone's account; ~ *kommen lassen*, to give the benefit of; *sich etwas auf eine Sache* ~ *tun*, to be proud of a thing.
zuguterletzt *adv.* finally, ultimately.
Zug: ~**vieh** *n.* draught-cattle; ~**vogel** *m.* bird of passage.
zuhalten *v.t.st.* to keep closed, to stop.
Zuhälter *m.* (-s, -) male companion of a prostitute, bully, fancy man.
zuhanden *adv.* at hand; to hand.
zuhängen *v.t.st.* to hang (curtain) over *or* in front of.
zuhauen *v.t.st.* to rough-hew, to shape; ~ *v.i.* to strike.
zuheilen *v.i.* (*s*) to heal up, to close.
Zuhilfenahme *f.* (-, 0) *unter oder mit* ~ *von*, with the aid of.
zuhorchen *v.i.* to listen to.
zuhören *v.i.* to give ear to, to listen.
Zuhörer *m.* (-s, -) hearer, auditor.
Zuhörerraum *m.* lecture room, auditorium.
Zuhörerschaft *f.* (-, 0) audience.
zujauchzen, zujubeln *v.i.* to cheer.
zukehren *v.t.* to turn (towards).
zukleben, zukleistern *v.t.* to glue *or* paste up.
zuknöpfen *v.t.* to button up.
zukommen *v.i.st.* (*s*) to come to hand; to belong to; to befit, to be due *or* suitable; to fall to one's share; *einem etwas* ~ *lassen*, to let...have.
Zukunft *f.* (-, 0) future, time to come; *in* ~, in future.
zukünftig *a.* future; next; intended.
Zukunftsmusik *f.* castles in the air.
zulächeln *v.i.* to smile on.
Zulage *f.* (-, -n) extra pay, allowance.
zulangen *v.i.* to fall to, to help oneself.
zulänglich *a.* sufficient.
zulassen *v.t.st.* to permit; to admit.
zulässig *a.* admissible, allowable.
Zulässigkeit *f.* propriety.
Zulassung *f.* (-, 0) admission, admittance; permission.
Zulauf *m.* (-[e]s, 0) run (of customers); *grossen* ~ *haben*, to be in vogue.
zulaufen *v.i.st.* (*s*) to run on; to run to; *spitz* ~, to taper.
zulegen *v.t.* to add, to increase; *sich etwas* ~, to provide oneself with.
zuleide *adv.* ~ *tun*, to do harm.
zuleiten *v.t.* to direct to.
zulernen *v.i. & t.* to enlarge one's knowledge, to live and learn.
zuletzt *adv.* (at) last, finally, after all.
zumachen *v.t.* to shut, to close, to fasten.

zumal *adv.* especially, chiefly; *c.* especially as.
zumauern *v.t.* to wall *or* brick up.
zumeist *adv.* for the most part, mostly.
zumessen *v.t.st.* to measure out (to).
zumuten *v.t.* to expect of a person.
Zumutung *f.* (-, -en) (unreasonable) demand; imputation.
zunächst *adv.* first, above all.
zunageln *v.t.* to nail up.
zunähen *v.t.* to sew up.
Zunahme *f.* (-, 0) increase, growth.
Zuname *m.* surname, family name.
zünden *v.i.* to catch fire; (*fig.*) to take, to catch on; ~ *v.t.* to kindle.
zündend *a.* stirring (speech).
Zunder *m.* (-s, 0) tinder.
Zünder *m.* (-s, -) fuse, match, igniter.
Zünd: ~**holz** *n.* match; *ein* ~*holz anzünden*, to strike a match; ~**hütchen** *n.* percussion-cap; ~**kerze** *f.* sparking plug, (*Am.*) spark plug; ~**schnur** *f.* fuse.
Zündung *f.* (-, -en) ignition.
zunehmen *v.i.st.* to increase, to grow; to put on weight.
zuneigen *v.t.* to bend *or* incline (towards).
Zuneigung *f.* inclination, affection.
Zunft *f.* (-, Zünfte) company, guild.
zünftig *a.* skilled, competent.
Zunge *f.* (-, -n) tongue.
züngeln *v.i.* (*von Flammen*) to lick; (*Schlange*) to hiss.
züngelnd *a.* lambent.
zungenfertig *a.* voluble.
Zungenspitze *f.* tip of the tongue.
zunichte *adv.* undone, ruined.
zunicken *v.i.* to nod to.
zunutzemachen *v.t.* to turn to account.
zuoberst *adv.* at the top, uppermost.
zuordnen *v.t.* to classify with.
zupfen *v.t.* to pull, to tug, to pluck, to pick.
zuraten *v.t.st.* to advise.
zuraunen *v.t.* to whisper (into one's ear).
zurechnen *v.t.* to impute, to attribute.
zurechnungsfähig *a.* of sound mind.
zurecht *adv.* in time; ready.
zurechtbringen *v.t.ir.* to put to rights, to restore, to adjust.
zurechtfinden (sich) *v.refl.st.* to find *or* see one's way.
zurechtkommen *v.i.st.* (*s*) to succeed, to get on well; (*mit einem*) to get on (with), to agree (with); (*der Zeit nach*) to arrive in (the nick of) time.
zurechtlegen *v.t.* to arrange, to lay out in order; *sich* ~, to explain to oneself.
zurechtmachen *v.t.* to prepare; (**sich**) ~ *v.refl.* to get ready.
zurechtschneiden *v.t.st.* to trim.
zurechtsetzen *v.t.* to set *or* put right.
zurechtweisen *v.t.st.* to reprimand.
Zurechtweisung *f.* reprimand.

Zurede *f.* persuasion; encouragement; *gutes Zureden n.* moral suasion.
zureden *v.i.* to persuade, to encourage.
zureichen *v.i.* to suffice.
zureichend *a.* sufficient.
zureiten *v.t.st.* to break in (a horse).
Zureiter *m.* trainer, rough-rider.
zurichten *v.t.* to prepare, to dress.
zuriegeln *v.t.* to bolt.
zürnen *v.i.* to be angry.
Zurschaustellung *f.* exhibition, display.
zurück *adv.* back, backwards; ~ *sein (fig.)* to be backward *or* behindhand; ~! stand back!; *ich werde bald ~ sein,* I shan't be long.
zurückbeben *v.i.* (*s*) to shrink (back) (from), to start back (from).
zurückbegeben (sich) *v.refl.st.* to go back, to return.
zurückbehalten *v.t.st.* to keep back.
zurückbekommen *v.t.st.* to get back.
zurückberufen *v.t.st.* to recall.
zurückbezahlen *v.t.* to repay, to' reimburse.
zurückbleiben *v.i.st.* (*s*) to remain behind; to lag behind.
zurückblicken *v.i.* to look back.
zurückbringen *v.t.ir.* to bring back, to return.
zurückdatieren *v.t.* to antedate; ~ *v.i.* to date back.
zurückdenken *v.i.st.* (*an*) to think back.
zurückdrängen *v.t.* to repress.
zurückerbitten *v.t.st.* to ask back.
zurückerhalten *v.t.st.* to get back.
zurückerstatten *v.t.* to give back, to return.
zurückfahren *v.i.st.* to drive back; (*fig.*) to start back.
zurückfinden¹ (sich) *v.refl.* to find one's way back.
zurückfordern *v.t.* to demand back.
Zurückforderung *f.* reclamation.
zurückführen *v.t.* to lead back; (*ar.*) to reduce (to); to trace (back) (to).
zurückgeben *v.t.st.* to give back, to return, to restore.
zurückgehen *v.i.st.* (*s*) to go back; to fall off, to decrease; (*Preis*) to decline.
zurückgezogen *a.* retired.
Zurückgezogenheit *f.* (-, 0) retirement.
zurückgreifen *v.i.st.* (*auf*) to fall back (upon).
zurückhaben *v.t.ir.* to have back.
zurückhalten *v.t.st.* to hold back, to restrain; *mit etwas ~,* to be reserved as regards.
zurückhaltend *a.* reserved; cautious.
Zurückhaltung (-, 0) *f.* reserve.
zurückkaufen *v.t.* to buy back, to buy in.
zurückkehren *v.i.* (*s*) to return.
zurückkommen *v.i.st.* (*s*) to come back, to return.

zurückkönnen *v.i.ir.* to be able to return.
zurücklassen *v.t.st.* to leave (behind).
zurücklegen *v.t.* to put by, to save; (*Weg*) to travel.
Zurücknahme *f.* revocation, withdrawal.
zurücknehmen *v.t.st.* to take back; to withdraw, to retract.
zurückprallen *v.i.* (*s*) to rebound.
zurückrufen *v.t.st.* to call back.
zurückschaudern *v.i.* (*s*) to recoil (from).
zurückschlagen *v.t.st.* to beat back, to repulse.
zurückschrecken *v.i.st.* (*s*) to shrink (from).
zurücksetzen *v.t.* to put back; to reduce the price of; to slight; neglect.
Zurücksetzung *f.* (-, -en) neglect, slight.
zurücksinken *v.i.st.* (*s*) to relapse (into).
zurückspringen *v.i.st.* (*s*) to rebound.
zurückstehen *v.i.st.* to be inferior (to).
zurückstellen *v.t.* to put back; to shelve; (*mil.*) to defer.
Zurückstellung *f.* (-, -en) (*mil.*) deferment.
zurückstrahlen *v.t.* to reflect, to throw back.
zurücktreiben *v.t.st.* to drive back, to thrust back, to repulse, to repel.
zurücktreten *v.i.st.* (*s*) to step back; (*vom Amt*) to resign office.
zurückübersetzen *v.t.* to retranslate.
zurückverlangen *v.t.* to demand *or* ask back; ~ *v.i.* to desire to go back (to).
zurückversetzen, *sich in eine Zeit ~,* to go back to a time.
zurückweichen *v.i.st.* (*s*) to fall back, to recede, to give way, to yield.
zurückweisen *v.t.st.* to reject, to repel, to decline.
Zurückweisung *f.* (-, -en) repulse, repudiation.
zurückwerfen *v.t.st.* to throw back.
zurückzahlen *v.t.* to pay back, to repay.
zurückziehen *v.t.st.* to withdraw; (sich) ~ *v.refl.* to withdraw (from); to retreat; to retire.
Zuruf *m.* (-[e]s, -e) acclamation; call.
zurufen *v.i.st.* to call to, to shout to; *Beifall ~,* to cheer, to applaud.
Zurüstung *f.* (-, -en) preparation.
zurzeit *adv.* for the time being.
Zusage *f.* (-, -n) promise; assent.
zusagen *v.t.* to promise; ~ *v.i.* to promise to come; to suit, to please.
zusammen *adv.* together; jointly.
zusammenarbeiten *v.i.* to collaborate, to co-operate.
Zusammenarbeit *f.* co-operation.
zusammenballen *v.t.* to conglomerate.
zusammenbeissen *v.t.st.* to set (one's teeth).
zusammenberufen *v.t.st.* to convene.
zusammenbinden *v.t.st.* to bind *or* tie together.

zusammenbrechen *v.i.st.* (*s*) to break down, to collapse.

zusammenbringen *v.t.ir.* to collect.

Zusammenbruch *m.* collapse.

zusammendrängen *v.t.* to compress; to condense; (sich) ~ *v.refl.* to crowd together.

zusammendrücken *v.t.* to compress.

zusammenfahren *v.i.st.* (*s*) to start, to wince.

zusammenfallen *v.i.st.* (*s*) to fall in, to collapse; to coincide.

zusammenfalten *v.t.* to fold (together, up), to double up.

zusammenfassen *v.t.* to collect; to sum up, to summarize.

zusammenfinden (sich) *v.refl.st.* to meet.

zusammenflicken *v.t.* to patch together, to botch up.

Zusammenfluss *m.* (-flusses, -flüsse) confluence; concourse, crowd.

zusammenfügen *v.t.* to join, to unite.

zusammengehen *v.i.st.* (*s*) to coincide; ~ mit, to be attended with.

zusammengehören *v.i.* to belong together, to be of the same kind.

zusammengesetzt *a.* composed, compound; composite.

Zusammenhalt *m.* (-[e]s, 0) cohesion.

zusammenhalten *v.t.* to hold together; ~ *v.i.st.* to assist one another.

Zusammenhang *m.* (-[e]s, -hänge) connection, coherence; ohne ~, incoherent; aus dem ~, detached from the context.

zusammenhängen *v.i.st.* to cohere; to be connected (with).

zusammenhangslos *a.* incoherent.

zusammenhauen *v.t.st.* to cut to pieces.

zusammenkauern (sich) *v.refl.* to huddle up.

zusammenkaufen *v.t.* to buy up.

zusammenketten *v.t.* to chain together.

zusammenkitten *v.t.* to cement together.

Zusammenklang *m.* accord, harmony.

zusammenklappen *v.t.* to fold together, to shut; ~ *v.i.* (fig.) to break down.

zusammenkommen *v.i.st.* (*s*) to meet.

Zusammenkunft *f.* (-, -künfte) meeting.

zusammenlaufen *v.i.st.* (*s*) to flock together; to shrink; to curdle; (math.) to converge.

Zusammenleben *n.* (-s, 0) social life; (eheliches) cohabitation.

zusammenlegbar *a.* folding, collapsible.

zusammenlegen *v.t.* to lay together, to fold up; (Geld) to club together.

zusammenleimen *v.t.* to stick together.

zusammennehmen *v.t.st.* to summon; ~(sich) *v.refl.st.* to pull oneself together; seine Gedanken gehörig ~, to collect one's thoughts.

zusammenpacken *v.t.* to pack up.

zusammenpassen *v.i.* to agree, to be well matched.

zusammenpferchen *v.t.* to pen up.

zusammenraffen *v.t.* to collect hurriedly; (sich) ~ *v.refl.* to muster courage; seine Kräfte ~, to collect all one's strength.

zusammenrechnen *v.t.* to add up.

zusammenreimen (sich) *v.refl.* to agree.

zusammenrotten (sich) *v.refl.* to band together, to form a mob.

zusammenrücken *v.t.* to join together, to put close together; ~ *v.i.* (*s*) to draw together.

zusammenschiessen *v.t.st.* to club (money).

zusammenschlagen *v.t.st.* to fold; die Hände über dem Kopf ~, to throw up one's arms in astonishment; ~ *v.i.* (*s*) die Wogen schlugen über ihm zusammen, the waves closed over him.

zusammenschliessen *v.t.st.* to amalgamate; (sich) ~ *v.refl.st.* to amalgamate; to line up (against).

Zusammenschluss *m.* amalgamation, fusion, merger, combine.

zusammenschmelzen *v.i.st.* (*s*) to melt away; ~ *v.t.st.* (fig.) to fuse, to weld.

zusammenschnüren *v.t.* das Herz ~, to wring the heart.

zusammenschrecken *v.i.* (*s*) to startle.

zusammenschrumpfen *v.i.* (*s*) to shrivel up, to dwindle; to wrinkle.

zusammensetzen *v.t.* to compose; (mech.) to assemble; (sich) ~ *v.refl.* to consist of.

Zusammensetzung *f.* (-, -en) composition; compound.

zusammensinken *v.i.st.* (*s*) to collapse.

Zusammenspiel *n.* (-[e]s, -e) (sport) team work.

zusammenstecken *v.t.* die Köpfe ~, to lay (their) heads together.

zusammenstellen *v.t.* to put together; to make up, to compile.

Zusammenstellung *f.* (-, -en) combination; (fig.) compilation.

zusammenstimmen *v.t.* to accord, to chime in, to agree; to harmonize.

zusammenstoppeln *v.t.* to compile carelessly.

Zusammenstoss *m.* (-es, -stösse) collision; (mil.) encounter; (fig.) clash, conflict.

zusammenstossen *v.i.st.* (*s*) to collide; to adjoin each other; ~ *v.t.* to knock together; (Gläser) to clink.

zusammenströmen *v.i.* (*s*) to flock together.

zusammenstürzen *v.i.* (*s*) to tumble down; to collapse.

zusammentreffen *v.i.st.* (*s*) to meet; to coincide; to clash; to encounter.

zusammentreten *v.i.st.* (*s*) to meet.

Zusammentritt *m.* meeting.

zusammentrommeln *v.t.* (fam.) to drum up; (Geld) to raise by hook and by crook.

zusammentun *v.refl.* to combine.

zusammenwachsen *v.i.st.* (*s*) to coalesce.

zusammenwerfen *v.t.st.* to jumble *or* throw together, to pool, to confound.

zusammenwürfeln *v.t.* to mix up confusedly.

zusammenwirken *v.i.* to co-operate.

zusammenzählen *v.t.* to add up.

zusammenziehen *v.t.st.* to draw together, to contract; to gather, to concentrate; to abridge; to astringe; (sich) ~ *v.refl.* to shrink up; to gather.

zusammenziehend *a.* astringent.

Zusatz *m.* (-es, -sätze) addition, supplement; alloy, admixture; codicil; postscript.

zusätzlich *a.* additional.

zuschanzen *v.t.* (*fam.*) einem etwas ~, to make a thing come somebody's way.

zuschauen *v.i.* to look on.

Zuschauer *m.* (-s, -) spectator, looker-on.

Zuschauerraum *m.* (*Theater*) house.

zuschicken *v.t.* to send (to).

zuschieben *v.t. st.* to push towards; shut gently.

zuschiessen *v.t.st.* to contribute.

Zuschlag *m.* (-[e]s -schläge) knocking down (to the highest bidder); extra-payment; excess fare; (*Steuer*) surtax; *Teuerungs*~, bonus.

zuschlagen *v.t.st.* to slam (a door); to knock down (to a bidder); ~ *v.i.st.* to strike hard, to hit away.

Zuschlagporto *n.* surcharge.

zuschliessen *v.t.st.* to lock (up).

zuschmeissen *v.t.st.* (vulg.) to bang.

zuschneiden *v.t.st.* to cut out.

Zuschneider *m.* (-s, -) cutter.

Zuschnitt *m.* (-[e]s, -e) cut; style.

zuschnüren *v.t.* to lace; to throttle.

zuschrauben *v.t.* to screw up.

zuschreiben *v.t.st.* to ascribe, to impute; (*com.*) to put to one's credit.

zuschreiten *v.i.st.* (*s*) to step up to.

Zuschrift *f.* (-, -en) letter, favour.

Zuschuss *m.* (-schusses, -schüsse) additional allowance; grant.

zuschütten *v.t.* to fill up; to pour on.

zusehen *v.i.st.* to look on; to suffer; to see to, to take care.

zusehends *adv.* visibly.

zusenden *v.t.ir.* to send (to).

zusetzen *v.t.* to add; ~ *v.i.* (*einem*) to press hard.

zusichern *v.t.* to promise.

Zusicherung *f.* (-, -en) assurance.

zusperren *v.t.* to lock, to bar.

zuspitzen *v.t.* to point; (sich) ~ *v.refl.* to taper; (*fig.*) to come to a crisis.

Zusprache *f.* (-, -n) encouragement.

zusprechen *v.i.st.* to exhort; to comfort, to encourage; ~ *v.t.st.* to award, to adjudge; to do justice to (a dish).

Zuspruch *m.* (-[e]s, -sprüche) encouragement; run of customers.

Zustand *m.* (-[e]s, -stände) condition, situation, state (of affairs).

zustande *adv.* ~ bringen, to accomplish, to bring about; ~ kommen, to come about, to be realized.

zuständig *a.* appertaining; competent.

Zuständigkeit *f.* (-, 0) competence.

zustatten kommen *v.i.* to prove useful.

zustecken *v.t.* to pin up; einem etwas ~, to convey a thing secretly to one.

zustehen *v.i.st.* to be due; to belong; (*law*) to be vested in.

zustellen *v.t.* to deliver, to hand to.

Zustellung *f.* writ, service; delivery.

zustimmen *v.t.* to agree to.

Zustimmung *f.* (-, -en) consent, assent, concurrence.

zustopfen *v.t.* to stop up; to darn.

zustossen *v.i.st.* (*s*) to happen, to befall.

zuströmen *v.i.* (*s*) to flow towards; to crowd in (upon one).

zustutzen *v.t.* to trim, to fashion.

zutage *adv.* to light.

Zutat *f.* (-, -en) ingredient, addition; (*Schneiderei*) trimmings *pl.*

zuteilen *v.t.* to allot, to apportion.

zuteil *adv.* ~ werden, to fall to one's share; ~ werden lassen, to allot to.

Zuteilung *f.* (-, -en) quota, allowance.

Zuteilungsperiode *f.* ration period.

zutragen *v.t.st.* to carry to; to report; (sich) ~, *v.refl.* to happen.

zuträglich *a.* wholesome; conducive (to).

zutrauen *v.t.* (*einem etwas*) to believe someone capable of.

Zutrauen *n.* (-s, 0) trust, confidence, faith.

zutraulich *a.* confiding, trustful.

zutreffen *v.i.st.* to prove right; to come true.

zutreiben *v.t.st.* to drive towards; ~ *v.i.st.* (*s*) to drift towards.

zutrinken *v.i.st.* to drink to, to pledge.

Zutritt *m.* (-[e]s, -e) access, admittance; ~ verboten, no entrance, no entry; *Unbeschäftigten* ~ verboten, no admittance except on business.

Zutun *n.* (-s, 0) aid, interference.

zutun *v.t.st.* einem zugetan sein, to be devoted to someone.

zuunterst *adv.* at the (very) bottom.

zuverlässig *a.* reliable, trustworthy, dependable.

Zuverlässigkeit *f.* (-, 0) reliability.

Zuversicht *f.* (-, 0) confidence, trust.

zuvor *adv.* before(hand), previously.

zuvörderst *adv.* first and foremost.

zuvorkommen *v.i.st.* (*s*) to be beforehand with, to get the start of; to obviate, to prevent; to anticipate.

zuvorkommend *a.* obliging.

zuvortun *v.t.st.*, es einem ~, to outdo.

Zuwachs *m.* (-wachses, 0) accretion.
Zuwanderung *f.* (-, -en) immigration.
zuwarten *v.i.* to wait.
zuwege bringen *v.t.ir.* to bring about.
zuweilen *adv.* sometimes.
zuweisen *v.t.st.* to send to, to direct to.
zuwenden *v.t.ir.* to turn *or* direct towards; to procure (for).
zuwider *a.* repugnant, odious.
zuwiderhandeln *v.i.* to contravene.
Zuwiderhandelnder *m.* (-n, -n) offender.
Zuwiderhandlung *f.* (-, 0) non-compliance.
zuwiderlaufen *v.i.st.* (*s*) to run counter to.
zuwinken *v.i.* to beckon to.
zuzahlen *v.t.* to pay extra.
zuziehen *v.t.st.* to draw together *or* tight; to draw (a curtain); to call in (another physician); (**sich**) ~ *v.refl.* to incur; to catch.
Zuzug *m.* (-[e]s, -züge) (increase of population by) new-comers *pl.*
Zwang *m.* (-[e]s, 0) constraint, compulsion, coercion; force.
Zwangs-: **~anleihe** *f.* forced loan; **~arbeit** *f.* forced *or* hard labour; **~jacke** *f.* strait jacket *or* waistcoat; **~kurs** *m.* forced rate of exchange; **~massnahme** *f.* **~mittel** *n.* coercive measure; **~verkauf** *m.* forced sale; **~verschleppter** *m.* displaced person (DP); **~versteigerung** *f.* forced sale; **~verwaltung** *f.* sequestration; **~vollstreckung** *f.* (*law*) distress, distraint.
zwängen *v.t.* to force, to press (into).
zwanglos *a.* unconstrained; informal.
Zwangs..., compulsory.
zwangsläufig *a.* automatic.
Zwangswirtschaft *f.* government control.
zwangsweise *adv.* by compulsion *or* force.
zwanzig *a.* twenty; a score; *in den Zwanzige[r]n sein, stehen*, to be between twenty and thirty (years of age).
zwar *adv.* it is true, no doubt.
Zweck *m.* (-[e]s, -e) aim, purpose, object, end; *es hat keinen ~*, there is no point in.
zweckdienlich *a.* expedient.
Zwecke *f.* (-, -n) hob-nail, tack.
zweckentsprechend *a.* suitable.
zwecklos *a.* useless; purposeless, aimless.
zweckmässig *a.* expedient, suitable.
zwei: **~armig** *a.* two-armed; **~beinig** *a.* two-legged.
zwecks *pr.* for the purpose of.
zweckwidrig *a.* unsuitable, inexpedient.
zwei *a.* two.
Zwei *f.* (-, -en) number *or* figure of two; (*im Spiel*) deuce.
zweibettiges Zimmer *n.* double room.
Zweidecker *m.* (-s, -) (*avi.*) biplane.
zweideutig *a.* ambiguous, equivocal.
Zweideutigkeit *f.* (-, -en) ambiguity.
zweierlei *a.* of two sorts; different.

zweifach *a.* double, twofold; *in ~er Ausfertigung*, in duplicate.
Zweifel *m.* (-s, -) doubt.
zweifelhaft *a.* doubtful.
zweifellos *a.* indubitable, doubtless.
zweifeln *v.i.* to doubt, to question.
Zweifelsfall *m.* case of doubt; *im ~ zu eines Gunsten entscheiden*, to give a person the benefit of the doubt.
zweifelsohne *adv.* doubtless.
zweifelsüchtig *a.* (morbidly) sceptical.
Zweifler *m.* (-s, -) sceptic, doubter.
zweifüssig *a.* two-footed, biped.
Zweig *m.* (-[e]s, -e) branch, bough; twig.
Zweigbahn *f.* branch-line.
Zweigespann *n.* team of two (horses).
Zweiggeschäft *n.* branch (establishment).
zweigleisig *a.* double track (*rail.*).
zweihändig *a.* two handed.
zweijährig *a.* two years old, of two years.
Zweikammersystem *n.* two-chamber system of government.
Zweikampf *m.* single combat, duel.
zweimal *adv.* twice.
zweimalig *a.* done twice.
zweimonatlich *a.* bimonthly.
zweimotorig *a.* (*avi.*) twin engined.
Zweirad *n.* bicycle; (*sl.*) bike.
zweiräd[e]rig *a.* two wheeled.
zweireihig *a.* double-breasted (coat).
zweischläf(e)rig *a.* double (bed).
zweischneidig *a.* double edged.
zweiseitig *a.* two-sided, bilateral.
zweisilbig *a.* dissyllabic.
zweisitzig *a.* having two seats.
zweispaltig *a.* in double columns.
zweispännig *a.* drawn by two horses.
zweisprachig *a.* bilingual.
zweistimmig *a.* for two voices.
zweistündig *a.* (lasting) two hours.
zweite[r] *a.* second; *jeden zweiten Tag*, every other day; **~s Gesicht** *n.* second sight; *der zweitbeste*, the second-best; *der zweitletzte*, the last but one.
zweiteilig *a.* **~er Anzug** *m.* two-piece suit.
zweitens *adv.* secondly.
zweitjüngst *a.* youngest but one.
Zweiunddreissigstelnote *f.* demi-semi-quaver.
zweiwöchentlich *a.* biweekly.
Zwerchfell *n.* diaphragm.
Zwerg *m.* (-[e]s, -e) dwarf, pygmy, midget.
zwergartig, zwerghaft *a.* dwarfish.
Zwetsche, Zwetschge *f.* (-, -n) plum.
Zwickel *m.* (-s, -) clock (of a stocking); gusset (of a shirt); (*arch.*) spandrel.
zwicken *v.t.* to pinch, to nip.
Zwicker *m.* (-s, -) pince-nez.
Zwickmühle *f.* (*Spiel*) double-mill; (*fig.*) dilemma.
Zwieback *n.* (-[e]s, -e) biscuit.

Zwiebel *f.* (-, -n) onion; (*Blumen~.*) bulb.
zwiefach, zwiefältig *a.* twofold.
Zwiegespräch *n.* dialogue, colloquy.
Zwielicht *n.* twilight.
Zwiespalt *m.* (-[e]s, -e) dissension, discord.
zwiespältig *a.* (*fig.*) discordant.
Zwietracht *f.* (-, 0) discord.
Zwillich *m.* (-[e]s, -e) tick(ing).
Zwilling *m.* (-[e]s, -e) twin.
zwingen *v.t.st.* to constrain, to compel, to force; *~de Gründe*, cogent, forcible reasons; *gezwungen*, forced, constrained.
Zwinger *m.* (-s, -) keep, donjon.
Zwingherrschaft *f.* despotism, tyranny.
zwinkern *v.i.* to twinkle, to blink.
Zwirn *m.* (-[e]s, -e) thread; twine.
Zwirnfaden *m.* thread.
zwischen *pr.* between.
Zwischen: ~akt *m. entr' acte*; ~bemerkung *f.* incidental remark; digression; ~deckspassagier *m.* steerage-passenger; ~ding *n.* cross.
zwischendurch *adv.* at intervals, betweenwhiles.
Zwischen: ~fall *m.* incident, episode; ~gericht *n.* entrée; ~glied *n.* connecting link; ~handel *m.* carrying trade; ~händler *m.* middleman.
zwischenliegend *a.* intermediate.

Zwischen: ~landung *f.* (*avi.*) intermediate landing; ~raum *m.* interval, interstice, intermediate space; ~ruf *m.* interruption; ~satz *m.* parenthesis; ~spiel *n.* interlude; ~zeit *f.* intervening time, meantime.
Zwischenurteil *n.* (*law*) interlocutory judgment.
Zwischenzonen... interzonal, *a.*
Zwist *m.* (-[e]s, -e) dispute, quarrel.
Zwistigkeit *f.* (-, -en) discord, quarrel.
zwitschern *v.i.* to twitter, to warble.
Zwitter *m.* (-s, -) hermaphrodite; (*bot.*) hybrid.
zwitterhaft *a.* androgynous.
zwo *a.* two.
zwölf *a.* twelve.
zwölferlei *a.* of twelve sorts.
Zwölffingerdarm *m.* duodenum.
zwölfjährig *a.* twelve years old.
zwölftens *adv.* twelfthly.
Zyankali *n.* (-s, -) cyanide of potassium.
Zyklon *m.* (-s, -e) cyclone.
Zyklus *m.* (-, -len) cycle.
Zylinder *m.* (-s, -) cylinder; (*Hut*) silk hat, top hat.
zylindrisch *a.* cylindrical.
Zyniker *m.* cynic.
zynisch *a.* cynical.
Zynismus *m.* (-, -men) cynicism.
Zypresse *f.* (-, -n) cypress.

Table of the more important modern Geographical Proper Names not identical in both languages*

Aachen *n.* Aix-la-Chapelle.
Abessinien *n.* Abyssinia.
Abruzzen *pl.* Abruzzi.
Admiralitätsinseln *f.pl.* the Admiralty Islands.
Adrianopel *n.* Adrianople.
Adriatische(s) Meer *n.* Adriatic (Sea).
Afrika *n.* Africa.
Afrikaner(in) *m.* (& *f.*), afrikanisch *a.* African.
Ägäische(s) Meer *n.* Ægean Sea.
Ägypten *n.* Egypt.
Ägypter(in) *m.* (& *f.*), ägyptisch, *a.* Egyptian.
Akko *n.* Acre.
Albanese *m.* Albanian.
Albanien *n.* Albania.
Algier *n.* Algeria (*Land*); Algiers (*Stadt*).
Alpen *pl.* Alps.
Älpler *m.*, alpinisch *a.* Alpine.
Amazonenstrom *m.* Amazon (river).
Amerika *n.* America.
Amerikaner(in) *m.* (& *f.*), amerikanisch *a.* American.
Anatolien *n.* Anatolia.
Andalusien *n.* Andalusia.
Andalusier(in) *m.* (& *f.*), andalusisch *a.* Andalusian.
Anden *pl.* Andes.
Angelsachse *m.* Anglo-Saxon.
Ansbach *n.* Anspach.
Antillen *pl.* Antilles.
Antwerpen *n.* Antwerp.
Apenninen *pl.* Apennines.
Apulien *n.* Apulia.
Araber(in) *m.* (& *f.*) Arab.
Arabien *n.* Arabia; *das glückliche* ~, Araby the Blest.
Aragonien *n.* Aragon.
Aragonier(in) *m.* (& *f.*), aragonisch *a.* Aragonese.
Ardennen *pl.* Ardennes.
Armenien *n.* Armenia.

Armenier(in) *m.* (& *f.*), armenisch *a.* Armenian.
Asiat(in) *m.* (& *f.*), asiatisch *a.* Asiatic.
Asien *n.* Asia.
Asowsche(s) Meer *n.* Sea of Azov.
Athen *n.* Athens.
Athener(in), Athenienser(in) *m.* (& *f.*), athen(iens)isch *a.* Athenian.
Atlantische(s) Meer *n.* Atlantic.
Ätna (der) Mount Etna.
Australien *n.* Australia.
Azoren, azorische(n) Inseln (die) *pl.* Azores.

Balte *m.*, Baltin *f.* native of the Baltic States.
baltisch *a.* Baltic.
Baltische(s) Meer *n.* the Baltic.
Balearen *pl.* the Balearic Isles.
Basel *n.* Basle, Bâle.
Baske *m.* Baskin *f.*, baskisch *a.* Basque.
Bayer(in) *m.* (& *f.*) (-n, -n), bayrisch *a.* Bavarian.
Bayern *n.* Bavaria.
Beduine *m.* Bedouin.
Behringstrasse *f.* Behring's Strait.
Belgien *n.* Belgium.
Belgier(in) *m.* (& *f.*), belgisch *a.* Belgian.
Belgrad *n.* Belgrade.
Bengale *m.*, Bengalin *f.*, bengalisch *a.* Bengali.
Bengalen *n.* Bengal.
Berberei *f.* (-) Barbary States *pl.*
Bessarabien *n.* Bessarabia.
Birma *n.* Burmah; Birmane *m.*, birmanisch *a.* Burmese.
Biskaya, Biscay.
Blindheim *n.* Blenheim.
Bodensee *m.* (-s) Lake Constance.
Böhme *m.*, Böhmin *f.*, böhmisch *a.* Bohemian.
Böhmen *n.* Bohemia.
Böotien *n.* Bœotia.

* Names of Countries, Places, and Peoples in -er, generally take -s (or -[e]s) in the Gen. Sing. [*Asien, Asiens; Athen, Athens; Afrika, Afrikas; Gent, Gents; Russland, Russlands; Hessen, Hessens;* also: *der Holländer, des Holländers*] (Nom. Sing. and Plur. always alike). Names of Peoples in -e take -n in the Gen. Sing. and Nom. Plur.; Feminine Names in -in take -nen in the Nom. Plur. [*der Pole,* Gen. Sing. *des Polen* Nom. Plur. *die Polen; die Polin, die Polinnen*] (Masc. Gen. Sing. always like the Nom. Plur.).

Bosnien *n.* Bosnia.
Bosporus *m.* (-) Bosphorus.
Bottnische(r) Meerbusen *m.* Gulf of Bothnia.
Brasilier(in) *m.* (& *f.*), brasilianisch *a.* Brazilian.
Brasilien *n.* Brazil.
Braunschweig *n.* Brunswick.
Bretagne *f.* (-) Brittany.
Britannien *n.* Britain.
britannisch, britisch *a.* British.
Brite *m.*, Britin *f.* Briton.
Brügge *n.* Bruges.
Brüssel *n.* Brussels.
Bukarest *n.* Bucharest.
Bulgare *m.*, Bulgarin *f.*, bulgarisch *a.* Bulgarian.
Bulgarien *n.* Bulgaria.
Burgund *n.* Burgundy.
Burgunder(in) *m.* (& *f.*), burgundisch *a.* Burgundian.
Byzanz *n.* Byzantium.

Cadix *n.* Cadiz.
Chaldäer *m.*, chaldäisch *a.* Chaldean.
Chilene *m.*, Chilenin *f.* Chilian.
Chinese *m.*, Chinesin *f.*, chinesisch *a.* Chinese.

Dahome *n.* Dahomey.
Dalmatien *n.* Dalmatia.
Dalmatiner(in) *m.* (& *f.*), dalmatinisch *a.* Dalmatian.
Däne *m.*, Dänin *f.* Dane.
Dänemark *n.* Denmark.
dänisch *a.* Danish.
Danzig *n.* Dantzig, Danzig.
Dardanellenstrasse (Straits of) the Dardanelles.
Dauphiné *f.* (-) Dauphiny.
Delphi *n.* Delphos.
deutsch *a.*, Deutsche[r] *m.* & *f.* German.
Deutschland *n.* Germany.
Dnjeper *m.* Nieper, Dnieper.
Dnjester *m.* Niester, Dniester.
Donau *f.* (-) Danube.
Donaufürstentümer *pl.* Danubian Principalities.
Drau *f.* River Drave.
Düna *f.* River Dwina.
Dünkirchen *n.* Dunkirk.

Eismeer *n.* Polar Sea; *Nördliches* ~, Arctic Sea; *Südiches* ~, Antarctic Sea.
Elsass *n.* (- or asses) Alsace.
Elsässer(in) *m.* (& *f.*), elsässisch *a.* Alsatian.
Engländer(in) *m.* (& *f.*) Englishman; Englishwoman.
englisch *a.* English.
Epirus *m.* (-) Epiros.
Esthland *n.* Est(h)onia.
Etsch *f.* (-) Adige.

Euphrat *m.* Euphrates.
Europa *n.* Europe.
Europäer(in) *m.* (& *f.*), europäisch *a.* European.

Felsengebirge *n.* Rocky Mountains *pl.*
Feuerland *n.* Tierra del Fuego.
Fidschiinseln *pl.* Fiji Islands.
Finnland *n.* Finland.
Finnländer(in), Finne *m.* (& *f.*) Finlander.
Flame *m.*, Flämin *f.* Fleming; flam-(l)ändisch, flämisch *a.* Flemish.
Flandern *n.* Flanders.
Florentiner(in) *m.* (& *f.*), florentinisch *a.* Florentine.
Florenz *n.* Florence.
Franke *m.*, fränkisch *a.* Franconian, Frank.
Franken *n.* Franconia.
Frankfurt *n.* Frankfort.
Frankreich *n.* France.
Franzose *m.* Frenchman; *die* ~*n,* the French.
Französin *f.* Frenchwoman.
französisch *a.* French.
Freiburg *n.* Friburg.
Freundschaftsinseln *pl.* Friendly Islands.
Friese *m.*, Friesin *f.*, Friesländer(in) *m.* (& *f.*) Frieslander, Frisian; friesisch *a.* Frisian.

Galiläa *n.* Galilee.
gälisch *a.* Gaelic.
Galizien *n.* Galicia.
Gallen, St. *n.* St. Gall.
Gascogne *f.* (-) Gascony.
Geldern *n.* Guilderland.
Genf *n.* Geneva.
Genfer(in) *m.* (& *f.*), genferisch *a.* Genevese.
Gent *n.* Ghent.
Genua *n.* Genoa.
Genuese(rin) *m.* (& *f.*). genuesisch *a.* Genoese.
Germane *m.* Teuton; Germanin *f.* Teuton woman; germanisch, Germanic, Teutonic.
Golgatha *n.* Golgotha.
Gote *m.* Goth; gotisch *a.* Gothic.
Graubünden *n.* the Grisons *pl.*
Grieche *m.*, Griechin *f.* Greek; griechisch *a.* Greek, Hellenic.
Griechenland *n.* Greece.
Grönland *n.* Greenland.
Grönländer(in) *m.* (& *f.*) Greenlander.
Grossbritannien *n.* Great Britain.
Grosse[r] Ozean *m.* Pacific (Ocean).

Haag *m.* The Hague.
Hameln *n.* Hamelin.
Hannover *n.* Hanover.
Hansastädte *pl.* Hanse Towns, Hanseatic Towns *pl.*

Harz *m.* (-es) Hartz Mountains *pl.*
Havanna *n.* Havana.
Hebräer *m.*, hebräisch *a.* Hebrew.
Hebriden *pl.* Hebrides.
Helgoland *n.* Heligoland.
Helsingör *n.* Elsinore.
Hennegau *m.* Hainault.
Hesse *m.*, Hessin *f.*, hessisch *a.* Hessian.
Hessen *n.* Hesse.
Hinterindien *n.* Indo-China.
Hochland, schottische(s) *n.* the Highlands *pl.*
Holländer(in) *m.* (& *f.*) Dutchman; Dutchwoman.
holländisch *a.* Dutch.

Illyrien *n.* Illyria.
Inder(in) *m.* (& *f.*) Indian.
Indianer(in) *m.* (& *f.*) Red Indian.
Indien *n.* India.
indisch *a.* Indian.
indo: ~europäisch *a.* Indo-European; ~germanisch *a.* Indo-Germanic.
Ingermanland *n.* Ingria.
Ionisch *a.* Ionian.
Ire = Irländer.
irisch, irländisch *a.* Irish.
Irland *n.* Ireland.
Irländer(in) *m.* (& *f.*) Irishman; Irishwoman.
Island *n.* Iceland.
Isländer(in) *m.* (& *f.*) Icelander; isländisch *a.* Icelandic.
Istrien *n.* Istria.
Italien *n.* Italy.
Italiener(in) *m.* (& *f.*), italienisch *a.* Italian.

Japaner *m.*, Japanerin *f.*, japan[es]isch, Japanese.
Joppe *n.* Jaffa.
Judäa *n.* Judæa.
Jude *m.* Jew, Jüdin *f.* Jewess, jüdisch *a.* Jewish.
Jugoslavien *n.* Jugoslavia.

Kaffer *m.* Kaffir.
Kaffernland *n.* Kaffraria.
Kalabrien *n.* Calabria.
Kalifornien *n.* California.
Kalmücke *m.* Calmuck.
Kalvarienberg *m.* Mount Calvary.
Kamerun *n.* the Cameroons *pl.*
Kanada *n.* Canada.
Kanadier(in *f.*) *m.*, kanadisch *a.* Canadian.
Kanal *m.* the Channel.
Kanarische(n) Inseln *f.pl.* Canaries *pl.*
Kandiote *m.* Candian.
Kärnten *n.* Carinthia.
Karpathen *pl.* Carpathians.
Kaschmir *n.* Cashmere.
Kaspische(s) Meer *n.* Caspian Sea.
Kastilien *n.* Castile.

Kaukasus *m.* (-s) Caucasus.
Kelte *m.* Kelt, Celt; keltisch *a.* Keltic, Celtic.
Kirchenstaat *m.* States (*pl.*) of the Church.
Kleinasien *n.* Asia Minor.
Kleve *n.* Cleves.
Köln *n.* Cologne.
Korse *m.*, Korsin *f.*, korsisch *a.* Corsican.
Kosak *m.* (-en, -en) Cossack.
Krain *f.* Carniola.
Krakau *n.* Cracow.
Kreta *n.* Crete.
Krim *f.* (-) the Crimea.
Kroate *m.*, Kroatin *f.*, kroatisch *a.* Croatian.
Kroatien *n.* Croatia.
Kurland *n.* Courland.

Lakedämon *n.* Lacedæmon.
Lakedämonier(in), *m.* (& *f.*), lakedämonisch *a.* Lacedæmonian.
Lappe, Lappländer(in) *m.* (& *f.*) Laplander; lappländisch *a.* Lapp.
Lausitz *f.* Lusatia.
Lausitzer(in) *m.* (& *f.*), lausitzisch *a* Lusatian.
Lazedämon = Lakedämon.
Leipzig *n.* Leipsic.
Levante *f.* Levant.
Libanon *m.* Lebanon.
libysch *a.* Libyan.
Lille *n.* Lisle.
Liparische Inseln *pl.* Lipari Islands.
Lissabon *n.* Lisbon.
Litauen *n.* Lithuania.
Litauer(in) *m.* (& *f.*), litauisch *a.* Lithuanian.
Livland *n.* Livonia.
Livländer(in) *m.* (& *f.*), livländisch *a.* Livonian.
Livorno *n.* Leghorn.
Lofoten *pl.* Lofoden Islands.
Lombarde *m.*, Lombardin *f.*, lombardisch *a.* Lombard.
Lombardei *f.* (-) Lombardy.
Lothringen *n.* Lorraine.
Löwen *n.* Louvain.
Ludwigsburg *n.* Lewisburg.
Luganer See *m.* Lake Lugano.
Lüttich *n.* Liege.
Luzern *n.* Lucerne.
Lyon *n.* Lyons.

Maas *f.* Meuse.
Mähre *m.*, Mährin *f.*, mährisch *a.* Moravian.
Mähren *n.* Moravia.
Mailand *n.* Milan.
Mainz *n.* Mayence.
Malaie *m.* Malay; malaiisch *a.* Malayan.
Malteser(in) *m.* (& *f.*) maltesisch *a.* Maltese.

Mandschurei *f.* Manchuria.
Mark *f.* (-) the March.
Marmarameer *n.* Sea of Marmora.
Marokko *n.* Morocco.
Marseille *n.* Marseilles.
Maure *m.* Moor; (*in Spanien*) Moresco.
maurisch *a.* Moorish.
Mazedonien *n.* Macedonian.
Mazedonier(in) *m.* (*& f.*), mazedonisch *a.* Macedonian.
Mecheln *n.* Malines.
Meerbusen: der Arabische ~, the gulf of Arabia; *der Bengalische* ~, the bay of Bengal; *der Finnische* ~, the gulf of Finland; *der Persische* ~, the Persian gulf.
Meissner *a.* Misnian; ~*Porzellan*, Dresden china.
Mittel..., Central...
Mittelländische(s) Meer, Mittelmeer *n.* Mediterranean.
Moldau *f.* (-) (*Land*) Moldavia.
Molukken, molukkische(n) Inseln (die) *pl.* the Moluccas.
Mongole *m.*, Mongolin *f.*, mongolisch, Mongol.
Mongolei *f.* (-) *n.* Mongolia.
Mosel *f.* (-) Moselle.
Moskau *n.* Moscow.
Mulatte *m.* Mulatto; Mulattin *f.* Mulattress.
Mülhausen *n.* Mulhouse.
München *n.* Munich.
Muselman *m.* Moslem.

Neapel *n.* Naples.
Neapolitaner(in) *m.* (*& f.*), neapoanischlit *a.* Neapolitan.
Neuenburg *n.* New(f)chatel.
Neufundland *n.* Newfoundland.
Neuschottland *n.* Nova Scotia.
Neuseeland *n.* New Zealand.
Niederlande *pl.* the Netherlands.
Niederländer(in) *m.* (*& f.*) Dutchman; Dutchwoman.
niederländisch *a.* Dutch.
Niederrhein *m.* Lower Rhine.
Nil *m.* Nile.
Nimwegen *n.* Nimeguen.
Nizza *n.* Nice.
Nordamerika *n.* North America; Nordamerikanische Union, *f.* the United States *pl.*
nordisch *a.* Norse; Nordic.
Nordsee *f.* German Ocean, North Sea.
Normandie *f.* (-) Normandy.
Normanne *m.*, normannisch *a.* Norman.
Norwegen *n.* Norway.
Norweger(in) *m.* (*& f.*), norwegisch *a.* Norwegian.
Nubien *n.* Nubia.
Nubier(in), *m.* (*& f.*), nubisch *a.* Nubian.
Nürnberg *n.* Nuremberg.

Ober..., Upper...
Ofen *n.* Buda.
Olymp *m.* Olympus.
Oranien *n.* Orange.
Oranjefreistaat *m.* Orange River Colony.
Orkaden (*Inseln*) *pl.* the Orkneys.
Osmanische(s) Reich *n.* Ottoman Empire.
Ostasien *n.* Eastern Asia, Far East.
Ostende *n.* Ostend.
Ostfriesland *n.* East Frisia.
Ostindien *n.* the East Indies *pl.*
Ostindische(r) Archipel *m.* the Malay Archipelago.
Österreich *n.* Austria.
Österreicher(in) *m.* (*& f.*), österreichisch *a.* Austrian.
Ostsee *f.* Baltic (Sea).
Otahaitier(in) *m.* (*&f.*), otahaitisch *a.* Tahitian.
Ozeanien *n.* Australasia.
Ozeanier *m.* South Sea Islander.

Palästina *n.* Palestine.
Parnass *m.* (-nasses) Parnassus.
Peking *n.* Pekin.
Peloponnes *m.* (-) Peloponnese.
Perser(in) *m.* (*& f.*), persisch *a.* Persian.
Persien *n.* Persia.
Pfalz *f.* (-) the Palatinate.
Pfälzer(in) *m.* (*& f.*), pfälzisch *a.* Palatine.
Pforte *f.*, *die Hohe* oder *ottomanische* ~, the Sublime Porte.
Philippinen *pl.* Philippines.
Phönizien *n.* Phenicia.
Piemont *n.* Piedmont.
Piemontese(rin) *m.* (*& f.*), piemontesisch *a.* Piedmontese.
Pole *m.* Pole.
Polen *n.* Poland.
polnisch *a.* Polish.
Pommern *n.* Pomerania.
Portugiese *m.*, Portugiesin *f.*, portugiesisch *a.* Portuguese.
Prag *n.* Prague.
Preusse *m.*, Preussin *f.*, preussich *a.* Prussian.
Preussen *n.* Prussia.
Pyrenäen *pl.* the Pyrenees.

Regensburg *n.* Ratisbon.
Rhein *m.* Rhine.
rheinisch, rheinländisch *a.* Rhenish.
Rhodier(in) *m.* (*&f.*), Rhodian.
Rhodus *n.* Rhodes.
Rom *n.* Rome.
Römer(in) *m.* (*& f.*), römisch *a.* Roman.
Rumäne *m* = Rumänier.
Romanen *pl.* Romance Nations.
romanisch *a.* Romance; (*arch.*) Norman, Romanesque.
Rumänien *n.* Roumania & Rumania.
Rumänier(in) *m.* (*& f.*), rumänisch *a.* Roumanian & Rumanian.

Rumelien *n.* Roumelia.
Russe *m.*, Russin *f.*, russisch *a.* Russian.
Russland *n.* Russia.

Sachse *m.*, Sächsin *f.*, sächsisch *a.* Saxon.
Sachsen *n.* Saxony.
Saloniki *n.* Thessalonica.
Samojede *m.*, Samojedin *f.*, samojedisch *a.* Samoied.
Sansibar *n.* Zanzibar.
Sarazene *m.*, sarazenisch *a.* Saracen.
Sarde *m.*, Sardinier(in) *m.* (& *f.*), sardinisch *a.* Sardinian.
Sardinien *n.* Sardinia.
Sauerland *n.* Southern Westphalia.
Savoyarde *m.*, Savoyer(in) *m.* (& *f.*), savoyisch *a.* Savoyard.
Savoyen *n.* Savoy.
Schelde *f.* Scheldt.
Schlesien *n.* Silesia.
Schlesier(in) *m.* (& *f.*), schlesisch *a.* Silesian.
Schonen *n.* Scania.
Schotte *m.*, Schottin *f.*, Scotsman; Scotswoman.
schottisch *a.* Scotch, Scottish.
Schottland *n.* Scotland.
Schottländer etc.=Schotte etc.
Schwabe *m.*, Schwäbin *f.*, schwäbisch *a.* Swabian.
Schwaben *n.* Swabia.
Schwarze(s) Meer *n.* Black Sea.
Schwarzwald *m.* Black Forest.
Schwede *m.*, Schwedin *f.* Swede.
Schweden *n.* Sweden.
schwedisch *a.* Swedish.
Schweiz *f.* Switzerland.
Schweizer(in) *m.* (& *f.*), schweizerisch *a.* Swiss.
Seeland *n.* Zealand.
Serbe *m.*, Serbin *f.*, serbisch *a.* Servian.
Serbien *n.* Serbia.
Sevilla *n.* Seville.
Sibirien *n.* Siberia.
sibirisch *a.* Siberian.
Siebenbürgen *n.* Transylvania.
Sizili[an]er(in) *m.* (& *f.*), sizil[ian]isch *a.* Sicilian.
Sizilien *n.* Sicily.
Skandinavien *n.* Scandinavia.
Slave *m.*, Slavin *f.* Slav.
slavisch *a.* Slavonic, Slav.
Slavonien *n.* Slavonia.
Slavonier(in), Slavone *m.* (& *f.*), slavonisch *a.* Slavonian.
Slowake *m.*, Slowakin *f.*, slowakisch *a.* Slovak.
Slowene *m.*, Slowenin *f.*, slowenisch *a.* Slovenian.
Sowjets *pl.* Soviets.
Spanien *n.* Spain.
Spanier(in) *m.* (& *f.*) Spaniard.
spanisch *a.* Spanish.

Spartaner(in) *m.* (& *f.*), spartanisch *a.* Spartan.
Speyer *n.* Spire(s), Speyer.
Stambul *n.* Constantinople.
Steiermark *f.* Styria.
Steiermärker(in) *m.* (&*f.*), steiermärkisch, steirisch *a.* Styrian.
Stille(r) Ozean *m.* Pacific.
Südafrika *n.* South Africa.
Südamerika *n.* South America.
Sudeten *pl.* Sudetes.
Südsee *f.* South Sea.
Sund *m.* The Sound.
Syrakus *n.* (0) Syracuse.
Syrien *n.* Syria, syrisch, (*a.*) Syrian.
Syrte *f.* Syrtis; *Grosse* ~, Syrtis Major, *Kleine* ~, Syrtis Minor.

Tafelberg *m.* Table Mountain.
Tajo *m.* Tagus.
Tanger *n.* Tangier.
Tarent *n.* Tarentum.
Tartare *m.*, tartarisch *a.* Tartar.
Tartarei *f.* (-) Tartary.
Taurien, Tauris *n.* Taurie Chersonese.
Teutone *m.* Teuton; teutonisch *a.* Teutonic.
Themse *n.* Thames.
Thermopylen *pl.* Thermopylæ.
Thessalien *n.* Thessaly.
Thessal(i)er(in) *m.* (& *f.*), thessalisch *a.* Thessalian.
Thrazien *n.* Thrace.
Thüringen *n.* Thuringia.
Thüringer(in) *m.* (& *f.*) thüringisch *a.* Thuringian.
Thüringer Wald *m.* Thuringian Mountains.
Tirol *n.* the Tyrol.
Tiroler(in) *m.* (&*f.*), tirolisch *a.* Tyrolese.
Toskana *n.* Tuscany.
Tote(s) Meer *n.* Dead Sea.
Trapezunt *n.* Trebizond.
Trient *n.* Trent.
Trier *n.* Treves.
Tripolis *n.* Tripoli.
Troja *n.* Troy.
Trojaner(in) *m.* (&*f.*), trojanisch *a.* Trojan.
Tscheche *m.*, tschechisch *a.* Czech.
Tschechoslovakei *f.* Czechoslovakia.
Türke *m.*, Türkin *f.* Turk.
Türkei *f.* (-) Turkey.
türkisch *a.* Turkish.
Tyrrhenische(s) Meer *n.* Tyrrhenian Sea

Ungar(in) *m.* (& *f.*), ungarisch *a.* Hungarian.
Ungarn *n.* Hungary.

Veltlin *n.* Valtelline.
Venedig *n.* Venice.

Venetianer(in) *m.* (& *f.*) venetianisch *a.* Venetian.
Vereinigte Staaten *pl.* United States.
Vesuv *m.* Vesuvius.
Vierwaldstätter See *m.* Lake of Lucerne.
Vlame *m.* = Flame.
Vliessingen *n.* Flushing.
Vogesen *pl.* Vosges.
Voralpen *pl.* Lower Alps.
Vorderasien *n.* Anterior Asia.
Vorderindien *n.* India.

Waadt *n.* Vaud.
Walache *m.*, Walachin *f.*, walachisch *a.* Wallachian.
Walachei *f.* (-) Wallachia.
Wallis *n.* Valais.
Walliser *m.* Welshman.
wallisisch *a.* Welsh.

Wallone *m.* Walloon.
Warschau *n.* Warsaw.
Wasgau, Wasgenwald *m.* the Vosges *pl.*
Weichsel *f.* (-) Vistula.
welsch *a.* Italian, French, Spanish.
Welschland *n.* Italy, France, Spain.
Westfalen *n.* Westphalia; Westfale *m.*, westfälisch *a.* Westphalian.
Westindien *n.* West Indies *pl.*
Wien *n.* Vienna.
Wiener(in) *m.* (& *f.*), wienerisch *a.* Viennese.
Württemberg *n.* Würtemberg.

Zabern *n.* Saverne.
Zante *n.* Sante, Cephalonia.
Zürich *n.* Zurich.
Zweibrücken *n.* Deux-Ponts.
Zypern *n.* Cyprus; zyprisch *a.* Cyprian.

Table of Christian Names not identical in both languages*

Adele f. Adela.
Adelheid f. Adelaide.
Adolf m. Adolphus.
Ägidius m. (0) Giles.
Alberich m. Alberic, Aubrey.
Alexander m. Alexander, Sandy.
Alfons m. (0) Alphonso.
Alwine f. Albina.
Amalie f. Amelia.
Ambros, Ambrosius m. (0) Ambrose.
Andreas m. Andrew.
Anna f. Anne, Anna, Ann.
Ännchen n. Nancy, Nan, Annie.
Anton m. Anthony.
August m. Augustus.
Auguste f. Augusta.
Augustin m. Austin.

Balduin m. Baldwin.
Barthel (-s), Bartholomäus (0) m. Bartholomew.
Beatrix f. (0) Beatrice.
Benedikt m. Benedict, Bennet.
Bernhard m. Bernard.
Bianka f. Blanche.
Bonifaz m. Boniface.
Brigitte f. Bridget, Biddy.

Cäcilie f. Cicely, Cis.
Carl = Karl.
Chlodwig m. Clovis.
Christoph, Christopher, Kit.
Christus, (Christi), Christ.
Cyrill(us) m. Cyril.

Dietrich m. Derrick, Theodoric.
Dina f. Dinah.
Dionys(ius) m. Dennis.
Dorchen n. Doll(y).
Dorothea f. Dorothy.

Eberhard m. Everard.
Eduard m. Edward, Ted.
Eleonore f. Eleanor.
Elisabeth f. Elizabeth, Betsey, Betty.
Elise f. Elsie, Eliza.

Else f. Elsa, Alice.
Emil m. Emile, Emilius.
Emilie f. Emily.
Ernst m. Ernest, Ernie.
Eugen m. Eugene.
Eugenie f. Eugenia.
Eva f. Eve.

Florentia f. Florence, Flossie, Flo.
Franz m. (-ens) Frank, Francis.
Franziska f. Frances, Fanny.
Frida f. Freda, Freddie.
Friederike f. Frederica, Freda.
Friedrich m. (-s), **Fritz** m. (-ens) Frederic(k), Fred(dy).

Georg m. George, Georgie.
Gertrud f. Gertrude, Gerty.
Gervasius m. Gervase, Jarvis.
Gottfried m. Godfrey, Geoffrey, Jeffry.
Gotthard m. Goddard.
Gregor m. Gregory.
Gretchen n., **Grete** f. Madge, Margery, Meg, Peggy.
Guido m. Guy.
Gustav m. Gustavus.

Hannchen n. **Hanne** f. Hannah, Jane, Jenny.
Hans m. (-ens) John, Jack.
Hänschen n., **Hänsel** m. Johnny.
Hedwig f. Hedwiga.
Heinrich m. Henry, Harry, Hal.
Heinz m. (-ens) Hal, Harry.
Helene f. Helen, Ellen, Nellie.
Henriette f. Henrietta, Harriet, Hettie.
Hieronymus m. Jerome.
Hinz m. Hal.
Hiob m. Job.
Horatius m. 0), **Horaz** m. (-ens), Horace.
Hugo m. Hugh.
Humfried m. Humphrey.

Ignaz m. (-ens) Ignatius.
Ilse f. Alice, Lizzie, Elsie.

*Most male Christian Names take -s in the genitive, when used without the definite article, and similarly female names in -e, -s or -ns. Names marked 0 do not change, — a. at the end of a Christian Name is either long or short, according to its position.
Ex.: *Anna von England* (short); *Anna*, alone (*long*).

Jakob *m.* James, Jem(my), Jim(my).
Jettchen *n.*, **Jette** *f.* Harriet, Hetty.
Johann(es) *m.* John, Johnnie, Jack(ie).
Johanna, Johanne *f.* Jane, Joan, Janet.
Julchen *n.* Juliet, Gilian, Gil(l).
Julie *f.* Julia.
Jürg *m.* = Georg.
Justus *m.* (0) Jocelyn.

Karl *m.* Charles, Charlie.
Kaspar *m.* Jasper.
Katharina *f.* Katherine, Kate, Kit(ty), Kathleen.
Käthchen *n.*, **Käthe** *f.* Kate, Kitty.
Klara *f.* **Klärchen** *n.* Clara, Clar(ri)e.
Klaus *m.* Nick.
Klemens *m.* Clement.
Klementine *f.* Clementina.
Konstantin *n.* Constantine.
Konstanze *f.* Constance, Connie.
Kunigunde *f.* Cunegund.
Kunz, Kurt *m.* Conrad.

Laurenz *m.* Lawrence.
Lenchen *n.*, **Lene** *f.* Maud; Nellie.
Leonhard *m.* Leonard, Len(nie).
Leonore *f.* Eleanor.
Lieschen *n.*, **Liese, Lisbeth,** *f.* Lizzie, Lizzy.
Lil(l)i, *f.* Lilian, Lil(l)y.
Linchen *n.* Carry.
Lolo *f.* Lottie.
Lorchen *n.* Nell, Nelly.
Lorenz *m.* (-ens) Laurence.
Lottchen *n.*, **Lotte** *f.* Charlotte, Lottie.
Lucia, Luzie *f.* Luey.
Ludovika *f.* Louisa.
Ludwig *m.* Lewis, Louis.
Luischen *n.*, **Luise** *f.* Loo.

Magdalena *f.* Magdalen, Maud(lin).
Malchen *n.* Amelia.
Margarethe *f.* Margaret, Margery, Marjory, Mag(gie), Madge, Peg(gy).
Marie *f.* Mary; **Mariechen** *n.* May, Moll, Molly, Poll, Polly.
Markus *m.* (0) Mark.
Martha *f.* Martha, Matty.
Mathilde *f.* Matilda, Tilly.
Matthäus *m.* (0) Matthew, Mat.
Meta *f.* Peggie.
Michael *m.* Michael, Mike.
Mieke, Mieze = **Mariechen.**
Mimi *f.* Millie.
Moritz *m.* (-ens) Maurice, Morris.

Nannchen *n.*, **Nannette** *f.* Nan, Nancy.
Nikolaus *m.* (0) Nicholas, Nick.
Noa(h) *m.* Noah.

Parzival *m.* Percival.
Patrizius *m.* Patrick, Pat, Paddy.
Paula, Pauline *f.* Paulina.
Pepi *m.* Joe.
Peter (-s), Petrus (0) *m.* Peter.
Philipp *m.* Philip.
Philippine *f.* Philippa.
Pompejus *m.* (0) Pompey.

Rahel *f.* Rachel.
Raimund *m.* Raymond.
Reinhold *m.* Reynold, Reginald, Reggie.
Richard *m.* Richard, Dick.
Rieke = **Friederike.**
Robert *m.* Robert, Bob.
Roland *m.* Ro(w)land.
Röschen *n.*, **Rose** *f.* Ros(i)e.
Rüdiger *m.* Roger, Hodge.
Rudolf *m.* Ralph, Rodolphus.
Ruprecht *m.* Rupert.

Salchen *n.* Sal, Sally.
Salomo(n) *m.* Solomon.
Sara *f.* Sarah.
Sepp(i), Sepperl *m.* Joe(y).
Simson *m.* Samson.
Sophie *f.* Sophia, Sophy.
Stephan *m.* Stephen, Steve.
Susanna, Susanne *f.*, **Suschen** *n.* Susannah, Susan, Sukey, Sue.

Theodor *m.* Theodore, Theo.
Therese *f.* Theresa.
Tilde *f.* Tilda, Tilly.
Timotheus *m.* Timothy, Tim(my).
Tinchen *n.* Tina, Tinie.
Tobias *m.* Tobiah, Toby.
Toni *f.* Tony.
Trine *f.* **Trinchen** *n.* Kitty.
Trudchen *n.* Gerty.
Tullius *m.* (0) Tully.

Ursel *f.* Ursula, Ursly.

Valentin *m.* Valentine.
Veit *m.* Vitus, Guy.
Vrenel *f.* Veronica.

Walt(h)er *m.* Walter, Wat.
Wenzel *m.* Wenceslas.
Wilhelm *m.* William, Willy, Bill(y).
Wilhelmine *f.* Wilhelmina.
Willi, Willy *m.* Bill(y).

Xaver *m.* Xavier.

Zacharias *m.* (0) Zachary.

Table of German Strong and Irregular Verbs

Tenses enclosed in [ ] are used, but not to be recommended. Those enclosed in ( ), though less often used, are admissible.

Infinitive	Present Indicative	Imperfect	Subjunctive Imperfect	Imperative	Past Participle
backen	ich backe, du bäckst [backst], er bäckt [backt]	ich buk*	ich büke*	back(e)***	gebacken
bedingen	ich bedinge	ich bedang, bedingte	ich bedingte, bedinge**	beding(e)	bedungen*†
befehlen	ich befehle, du befiehlst, er befiehlt	ich befahl	ich beföhle [befähle]**	befiehl	befohlen
befleissen, sich†	ich befleisse mich, du befleissest u. befleisst dich, er befleisst sich	ich befliss mich, du beflissest dich	ich beflisse mich	befleisse dich	beflissen
beginnen	ich beginne	ich begann	ich begönne [begänne]	beginn(e)	begonnen
beissen	ich beisse, du beissest u. beisst, er beisst etc.	ich biss, du bissest	ich bisse	beiss(e)	gebissen
bergen	ich berge, du birgst, er birgt	ich barg	ich bürge (u. bärge)	birg	geborgen
bersten	ich berste, du berstest u. birst, er birst (berstet)	ich barst, borst	ich bärste, börste	birst (berste)	geborsten
besinnen sich	ich besinne mich	ich besann mich	ich besänne u. besönne mich	besinn(e) dich	besonnen
besitzen	ich besitze, du besitzest u. besitzt	ich besass	ich besässe	besitz(e)	besessen
betrügen	ich betrüge	ich betrog	ich betröge	betrüg(e)	betrogen
bewegen††	ich bewege	ich bewog	ich bewöge**	beweg(e)	bewogen
biegen	ich biege	ich bog	ich böge**	bieg(e)	gebogen
bieten	ich biete	ich bot	ich böte	biet(e)	geboten

* The German verbs and tenses marked by one asterisk (*) are more commonly used in their regular form.
** The Imperfects of the Subjunctive marked by two asterisks (**) are used in the literary language only; in spoken German the Conditional is, though incorrectly, used instead, e.g. 'Ich würde befehlen' instead of 'Ich beföhle'.
*** The Imperative forms ending in e are grammatically incorrect, although they are generally used.
† The verb 'sich befleissen' is not in use; in its stead use the regular verb 'sich befleissigen'.
†† The verb 'bewegen', 'to move' is regular; 'bewegen', 'to induce' strong.
*† 'bedingt' is also adj.

Table of German Strong and Irregular Verbs—*continued*

Infinitive	Present Indicative	Imperfect	Subjunctive Imperfect	Imperative	Participle Past
binden	ich binde	ich band, du band(e)st	ich bände	bind(e)	gebunden
bitten	ich bitte	ich bat, du bat(e)st	ich bäte	bitte	gebeten
blasen	ich blase, du bläst, er bläst	ich blies, du bliesest	ich bliese	blas u. blase	geblasen
bleiben	ich bleibe	ich blieb, du bliebst	ich bliebe	bleib(e)	geblieben
braten	ich brate, du brätst, er brät	ich briet	ich briete**	brat(e)	gebraten
brechen	ich breche, du brichst, er bricht	ich brach	ich bräche	brich	gebrochen
brennen	ich brenne	ich brannte	ich brennte**	brenn(e)	gebrannt
bringen	ich bringe	ich brachte	ich brächte	bring(e)	gebracht
denken	ich denke	ich dachte	ich dächte	denk(e)	gedacht
dingen	ich dinge	ich dang	ich dingte, ich dünge**, dänge	ding(e)	gedungen*
dreschen	ich dresche, du drisch(e)st, er drischt	ich drosch (drasch)	ich drösche***	drisch	gedroschen
dringen	ich dringe	ich drang	ich dränge	dring(e)	gedrungen
dünken	mich dünkt, däucht	mich däuchte, dünkte	mich däuchte, dünkte	dünke	gedäucht
dürfen	ich darf, du darfst, er darf; wir dürfen	ich durfte	ich dürfte	—	gedurft (dürfen)
empfangen	ich empfange, du empfängst, er empfängt	ich empfing	ich empfinge	empfang(e)	empfangen
empfehlen	ich empfehle, du empfiehlst, er empfiehlt	ich empfahl	ich empföhle (empfähle)	empfiehl	empfohlen
empfinden	ich empfinde	ich empfand	ich empfände	empfind(e)	empfunden
erbleichen	ich erbleiche	ich erblich	ich erbliche**	erbleich(e)	erblichen
erfrieren	ich erfriere	ich erfror	ich erfröre	erfrier(e)	erfroren
erlöschen	ich erlösche, du erlischest [erlöschest], er erlischt [erlöscht]	ich erlosch [erlöschte]*	ich erlösche**	erlösche(e), erlisch	erloschen
erschallen	es erschallt*	es erschallte**	es erschölle**	erschall(e)	erschallt, erschollen
erscheinen	ich erscheine	ich erschien	ich erschiene	erschein(e)	erschienen
erschrecken†	ich erschrecke, du erschrickst, er erschrickt	ich erschrak	ich erschräke	erschrick	erschrocken

† The verb '*erschrecken*' in its transitive sense '*einen erschrecken*' is regular.

Table of German Strong and Irregular Verbs—continued

Infinitive	Present (Indicative)	Imperfect	Subjunctive Imperfect	Imperative	Past Participle
ertrinken	ich ertrinke	ich ertrank	ich ertränke	ertrink(e)	ertrunken
erwägen	ich erwäge	ich erwog	ich erwöge**	erwäg(e)	erwogen
essen	ich esse, du [issest] u. isst, er isst	ich ass	ich ässe	iss	gegessen
fahren	ich fahre, du fährst, er fährt	ich fuhr, du fuhr(e)st	ich führe	fahr(e)	gefahren
fallen	ich falle, du fällst, er fällt	ich fiel	ich fiele	fall(e)	gefallen
fangen	ich fange, du fängst, er fängt	ich fing	ich finge	fang(e)	gefangen
fechten	ich fechte, du fichtst, er ficht	ich focht	ich föchte**	ficht (fechte)	gefochten
finden	ich finde	ich fand	ich fände	find(e)	gefunden
flechten	ich flechte, du flichtst*, er flicht*	ich flocht	ich flöchte	flicht*	geflochten
fliegen	ich fliege	ich flog	ich flöge	flieg(e)	geflogen
fliehen	ich fliehe	ich floh	ich flöhe	flieh(e)	geflohen
fliessen	ich fliesse	ich floss	ich flösse	fliess(e)	geflossen
fragen	ich frage, du fragst, er fragt [frägst, frägt]	ich fragte (frug)	ich fragte** (früge)	frag(e)	gefragt
fressen	ich fresse, du [frissest] u. frisst, er frisst	ich frass	ich frässe	friss	gefressen
frieren	ich friere	ich fror	ich fröre	frier(e)	gefroren
gären	ich gäre	ich gor u. gärte	ich göre u. gärte	gär(e)	gegoren, gegärt
gebären	ich gebäre, du gebierst [gebärst], er gebiert [gebärt]	ich gebar	ich gebäre**	gebier(e)	geboren
geben	ich gebe, du gibst, er gibt	ich gab	ich gäbe	gib	gegeben
gebieten	ich gebiete	ich gebot	ich gebäte	gebiet(e)	geboten
gedeihen	ich gedeihe	ich gedieh	ich gediehe	gedeih(e)	gediehen
gefallen	ich gefalle, du gefällst, er gefällt	ich gefiel	ich gefiele	gefall(e)	gefallen
gehen	ich gehe, du gehst	ich ging	ich ginge	geh(e)	gegangen
gelingen	es gelingt	es gelang	es gelänge	geling(e)	gelungen
gelten	ich gelte, du giltst, er gilt	ich galt, du galt(e)st	es gölte (gälte)	gilt	gegolten
genesen	ich genese, du genesest u. genest, er genest	ich genas, du genasest	ich genäse**	genese	genesen
geniessen	ich geniesse	ich genoss	ich genösse	geniess(e)	genossen
geraten	ich gerate, du gerätst, er gerät	ich geriet	ich geriete	gerat(e)	geraten
geschehen	es geschieht, sie geschehen	es geschah	es geschähe	gescheh(e)	geschehen
gewinnen	ich gewinne	ich gewann, du gewann(e)st	ich gewönne (gewänne)	gewinn(e)	gewonnen

Table of German Strong and Irregular Verbs—continued

Infinitive	Present Indicative	Imperfect	Subjunctive Imperfect	Imperative	Participle Past
giessen	ich giesse, du giessest u. giesst	ich goss	ich gösse	giess(e)	gegossen
gleichen	ich gleiche	ich glich, du glich(e)st	ich gliche	gleich(e)	geglichen
gleiten	ich gleite	ich glitt	ich glitte	gleit(e)	geglitten
glimmen	ich glimme	ich glomm*	ich glömme**	glimm(e)	geglommen*
graben	ich grabe, du gräbst, er gräbt	ich grub, du grub(e)st	ich grübe	grab(e)	gegraben
greifen	ich greife	ich griff, du griff(e)st	ich griffe	greif(e)	gegriffen
haben	ich habe, du hast, er hat, wir haben, ihr habt, sie haben	ich hatte	ich hätte	hab(e)	gehabt
halten	ich halte, du hältst, er hält	ich hielt	ich hielte	halt(e)	gehalten
hangen, hängen†	ich hange u. hänge, du [hang(e)st] u. hängst, [er hangt] u. hängt	ich hing(e)st	ich hinge	häng(e)	gehangen*
hauen	ich haue, du haust	ich hieb, (haute) du hiebst	ich hiebe (haute)	hau(e)	gehauen
heben	ich hebe	ich hob	ich höbe (du hübest)	heb(e)	gehoben
heissen	ich heisse, du heissest u. heisst, er heisst	ich hiess	ich hiesse, du hiessest	heiss(e)	geheissen
helfen	ich helfe, du hilfst, er hilft	ich half	ich hülfe (hälfe)	hilf	geholfen
kennen	ich kenne	ich kannte	ich kennte**	kenn(e)	gekannt
kiesen	ich kiese, du kiesest u. kiest	ich kor u. kieste	ich köre u. kieste	kiese	gek'est u. gekoren
klimmen	ich klimme	ich klomm*	ich klömme**	klimm(e)	geklommen
klingen	es klingt	es klang	es klänge	kling(e)	geklungen
kneifen	ich kneife	ich kniff, du kniffst	ich kniffe, du kniffst	kneif(e)	gekniffen
kommen	ich komme	ich kam	ich käme	komm(e)	gekommen
können	ich kann, du kannst, er kann	ich konnte	ich könnte	—	gekonnt (können)
kriechen	ich krieche	ich kroch	ich kröche	kriech(e)	gekrochen
laden	ich lade, du ladest u. lädst, er ladet u. lädt	ich lud	ich lüde**	lad(e)	geladen
lassen	ich lasse, du [lässest] u. lässt, er lässt	ich liess	ich liesse	lass (lasse)	gelassen (lassen)

† **hängen** *v.i.* is regular.

Table of German Strong and Irregular Verbs—continued

Infinitive	Present Indicative	Imperfect	Subjunctive Imperfect	Imperative	Participle Past
laufen	ich laufe, du läufst, er läuft	ich lief	ich liefe	lauf(e)	gelaufen
leiden	ich leide	ich litt	ich litte	leid(e)	gelitten
leihen	ich leihe	ich lieh	ich liehe	leih(e)	geliehen
lesen	ich lese, du [liesest] u. liest, er liest	ich las	ich läse	lies	gelesen
liegen	ich liege	ich lag	ich läge	lieg(e)	gelegen
lügen	ich lüge	ich log	ich löge	lüg(e)	gelogen
mahlen	ich mahle	ich mahlte	ich mahlte	mahl(e)	gemahlen
meiden	ich meide	ich mied	ich miede	meid(e)	gemieden
melken	ich melke	ich molk*	ich mölke**	melk(e)*	gemolken
messen	ich messe, du [missest] u. misst, er misst	ich mass	ich mässe**	miss	gemessen
missfallen	ich missfalle, du missfällst, er missfällt	ich missfiel	ich missfiele	missfall(e)	missfallen
mögen	ich mag, du magst, er mag, wir mögen, ihr mög(e)t, sie mögen	ich mochte	ich möchte	—	gemocht (mögen)
müssen	ich muss, du musst, er muss; wir müssen, ihr müsst, sie müssen	ich musste	ich müsste	—	gemusst (müssen)
nehmen	ich nehme, du nimmst, er nimmt	ich nahm	ich nähme	nimm(e)	genommen
nennen	ich nenne	ich nannte	ich nennte**	nenn(e)	genannt
pfeifen	ich pfeife	ich pfiff	ich pfiffe	pfeif(e)	gepfiffen
pflegen†	ich pflege	ich pflog*	ich pflöge*	pfleg(e)*	gepflogen*
preisen	ich preise	ich pries	ich priese	preis(e)	gepriesen
quellen	ich quelle, du quillst, er quillt	ich quoll	ich quölle	quill*	gequollen
raten	ich rate, du rätst, er rät	ich riet	ich riete	rat(e)	geraten
reiben	ich reibe	ich rieb	ich riebe	reib(e)	gerieben
reissen	ich reisse	ich riss	ich risse	reiss(e)	gerissen
reiten	ich reite	ich ritt	ich ritte	reit(e)	geritten
rennen	ich renne	ich rannte	ich rennte**	renn(e)	gerannt
riechen	ich rieche	ich roch	ich röche	riech(e)	gerochen
ringen	ich ringe	ich rang	ich ränge	ring(e)	gerungen
rinnen	ich rinne	ich rann	ich ränne	rinn(e)	geronnen
rufen	ich rufe	ich rief	ich riefe	ruf(e)	gerufen
salzen	ich salze	ich salzte	ich salzte**	salz(e)	gesalzen, gesalzt††

† The verb 'pflegen' in the sense of *to nurse, to attend to*, is regular.
†† In compounds and fig. use only (ver)salzen.

Table of German Strong and Irregular Verbs—*continued*

Infinitive	Present Indicative	Imperfect	Subjunctive Imperfect	Imperative	Participle Past
saufen†	ich saufe, du säufst, er säuft	ich soff	ich söffe**	sauf(e)	gesoffen
saugen	ich sauge	ich sog [saugte]	ich söge, sauge	saug(e)	gesogen [gesaugt]
schaffen†	ich schaffe	ich schuf, du schufst	ich schüfe**	schaff(e)	geschaffen
schallen	es schallt	schallte u. scholl	schallte u. schölle	schall(e)	geschallt
scheiden	ich scheide	ich schied	ich schiede	scheid(e)	geschieden
scheinen	ich scheine	ich schien	ich schiene	schein(e)	geschienen
schelten	ich schelte, du schiltst, er schilt	ich schalt, du schalt(e)st	ich schölte [schälte]	schilt	gescholten
scheren	ich schere, du scher(e)st u. schierst, er schert u. schiert	ich schor u. [scherte]	ich schöre** (scherte)	scher(e)	geschoren
schieben	ich schiebe	ich schob	ich schöbe**	schieb(e)	geschoben
schiessen	ich schiesse, du schiessest u. schiesst	ich schoss, du schossest	ich schösse**	schiess(e)	geschossen
schinden	ich schinde	ich schund*, du schund(e)st*	ich schünde	schind(e)	geschunden
schlafen	ich schlafe, du schläfst, er schläft	ich schlief	ich schliefe	schlaf(e)	geschlafen
schlagen	ich schlage, du schlägst, er schlägt	ich schlug	ich schlüge	schlag(e)	geschlagen
schleichen	ich schleiche	ich schlich	ich schliche	schleich(e)	geschlichen
schleifen	ich schleife	ich schliff	ich schliffe	schleif(e)	geschliffen
schliessen	ich schliesse, du schliessest u. schliesst	ich schloss	ich schlösse	schliess(e)	geschlossen
schlingen	ich schlinge	ich schlang	ich schlänge	schling(e)	geschlungen
schmeissen	ich schmeisse, du schmeissest u. schmeisst	ich schmiss	ich schmisse	schmeiss(e)	geschmissen
schmelzen††	ich schmelze, du schmilzt, er schmilzt; schmilzt u. schmelzt	ich schmolz, du schmolzest	ich schmölze	schmilz	geschmolzen
schnauben	ich schnaube	ich schnob*	ich schnöbe*	schnaub(e)	geschnoben
schneiden	ich schneide	ich schnitt	ich schnitte	schneid(e)	geschnitten
schreiben	ich schreibe	ich schrieb	ich schriebe	schreib(e)	geschrieben
schreien	ich schreie	ich schrie	ich schriee	schrei(e)	geschrie[e]n

† '*schaffen,*' when used in the sense of *arbeiten* is regular.
†† The verb *schmelzen* is regular in its transitive sense.

Table of German Strong and Irregular Verbs—*continued*

Infinitive	Indicative Present	Imperfect	Subjunctive Imperfect	Imperative	Participle Past
schreiten	ich schreite	ich schritt	ich schritte	schreit(e)	geschritten
schweigen	ich schweige	ich schwieg	ich schwiege	schweig(e)	geschwiegen
schwellen	ich schwelle, du schwillst, er schwillt	ich schwoll	ich schwölle	schwill	geschwollen
schwimmen	ich schwimme	ich schwamm	ich schwömme [schwämme]**	schwimm(e)	geschwommen
schwinden	ich schwinde	ich schwand	ich schwände	schwind(e)	geschwunden
schwingen	ich schwinge	ich schwang	ich schwänge	schwing(e)	geschwungen
schwören	ich schwöre	ich schwor (schwur)	ich schwüre [schwöre]	schwöre	geschworen
sehen	ich sehe, du siehst, er sieht	ich sah	ich sähe	sieh(e)	gesehen
sein	ich bin, du bist, er ist; wir sind, ihr seid, sie sind, Konj. ich sei, du seist, er sei; wir seien, ihr seiet, sie seien	ich war	ich wäre	sei	gewesen
senden	ich sende	ich sandte*	ich sendete**	sende	gesandt (gesendet)
sieden	ich siede	ich sott*	ich sötte*	sied(e)	gesotten
singen	ich singe	ich sang	ich sänge	sing(e)	gesungen
sinken	ich sinke	ich sank	ich sänke	sink(e)	gesunken
sinnen	ich sinne	ich sann	ich sänne** (sönne)	sinn(e)	gesonnen
sitzen	ich sitze	ich sass	ich sässe	sitze	gesessen
sollen	ich soll, du sollst, er soll	ich sollte	ich sollte	—	gesollt (sollen)
spalten	ich spalte, du spaltest	ich spaltete	ich spaltete	spalt(e)	gespalten
speien	ich speie	ich spie	ich spie(e)	spei(e)	gespie(e)n
spinnen	ich spinne	ich spann	ich spänne**	spinn(e)n	gesponnen
spleissen	ich spleisse, du spleissest u. spleisst	ich spliss	ich splisse**	spleiss(e)	gesplissen
sprechen	ich spreche, du sprichst, er spricht	ich sprach	ich spräche	sprich	gesprochen
spriessen	ich spriesse, du spriessest u. spriesst	ich spross	ich sprösse	spriess(e)	gesprossen
springen	ich springe	ich sprang	ich spränge	spring(e)	gesprungen
stechen	ich steche, du stichst, er sticht	ich stach	ich stäche	stich	gestochen
stecken†	ich stecke	ich stak u. steckte	ich stäke u. steckte	steck(e)	gesteckt
stehen	ich stehe, du steh(e)st	ich stand, du stand(e)st	ich stände (stünde)	steh(e)	gestanden

Table of German Strong and Irregular Verbs—continued

Infinitive	Present	Imperfect	Subjunctive Imperfect	Imperative	Participle Past
stehlen	ich stehle, du stiehlst, er stiehlt	ich stahl	ich stöhle**, (stähle)	stiehl	gestohlen
steigen	ich steige	ich stieg	ich stiege	steig(e)	gestiegen
sterben	ich sterbe, du stirbst, er stirbt	ich starb	ich stürbe	stirb	gestorben
stieben	ich stiebe	ich stob	ich stöbe**	stieb(e)	gestoben
stinken	ich stinke	ich stank	ich stänke	stink(e)	gestunken
stossen	ich stosse, du [stössest] u. stösst, er stösst	ich stiess, du stiessest	ich stiesse	stoss(e)	gestossen
streichen	ich streiche	ich strich	ich striche	streich(e)	gestrichen
streiten	ich streite	ich stritt	ich stritte	streit(e)	gestritten
tragen	ich trage, du trägst, er trägt	ich trug	ich trüge	trag(e)	getragen
treffen	ich treffe, du triffst, er trifft	ich traf	ich träfe	triff	getroffen
treiben	ich treibe	ich trieb	ich triebe	treib(e)	getrieben
treten	ich trete, du trittst, er tritt	ich trat	ich träte	tritt	getreten
triefen	ich triefe, du triefst	ich troff, triefte	ich tröffe**, triefte	trief(e)	getroffen, getrieft
trinken	ich trinke	ich trank	ich tränke	trink(e)	getrunken
trügen	ich trüge	ich trog	ich tröge	trüg(e)	getrogen
tun	ich tue, du tust, er tut	ich tat	ich täte	tu(e)	getan
verbergen	ich verberge, du verbirgst er verbirgt	ich verbarg	ich verbürge u. (verbärge)	verbirg	verborgen
verbieten	ich verbiete	ich verbot	ich verböte	verbiet(e)	verboten
verbleiben	ich verbleibe	ich verblieb	ich verbliebe	verbleib(e)	verblieben
verbleichen	ich verbleiche	ich verblich	ich verbliche	verbleich(e)	verblichen
verderben††	ich verderbe, du verdirbst, er verdirbt	ich verdarb	ich verdürbe	verdirb	verdorben
verdriessen	es verdriesst	es verdross	es verdrösse	—	verdrossen
vergessen	ich vergesse, du [vergissest] u. vergisst, er vergisst	ich vergass	ich vergässe	vergiss	vergessen
verlieren	ich verliere	ich verlor	ich verlöre	verlier(e)	verloren
verlöschen	ich verlösche, du verlischest u. verlischt [verlöschest, verlöschst], er verlischt [verlöscht]	ich verlosch [verlöschte]	ich verlösche**	verlösch(e), u. verlisch	verloschen

† The verb 'stecken' meaning to put to, to fix, is regular and transitive.
†† The verb 'verderben' is irregular in the sense of to spoil, but its Participle is regular when used in the sense of to corrupt.

Table of German Strong and Irregular Verbs—*continued*

Infinitive	Present Indicative	Imperfect	Subjunctive Imperfect**	Imperative	Participle Past
verschallen	ich verschalle	verschallte verschollte	verschölle**	verschall(e)	verschollen
verschwinden	ich verschwinde	ich verschwand	ich verschwände	verschwind(e)	verschwunden
verzeihen	ich verzeihe	ich verzieh	ich verziehe	verzeih(e)	verziehen
wachsen	ich wachse, du [wächsest] u. wächst er wächst	ich wuchs	ich wüchse	wachs u. wachse	gewachsen
wägen	ich wäge, du wägst, er wägt	ich wog	ich wöge**	wäg(e)	gewogen
wiegen†	ich wiege, du wiegst, er wiegt			wieg(e)	
weben	ich webe, du webst	ich webte (wob)	webte (wöbe)	web(e)	gewebt (gewoben)
waschen	ich wasche, du wasch(e)st, er wäscht	ich wusch	ich wüsche	wasche(e)	gewaschen
weichen††	ich weiche	ich wich	ich wiche	weich(e)	gewichen
weisen	ich weise, du weisest u. weist	ich wies, du wiesest	ich wiese	weis, weise	gewiesen
wenden	ich wende	ich wandte*	ich wendete**	wend(e)	gewandt*
werben	ich werbe, du wirbst, er wirbt	ich warb	ich würbe	wirb	geworben
werden	ich werde, du wirst, er wird	ich wurde u. ward, du wurdest u. ward, er wurde u. ward	ich würde	werde	geworden (worden)
werfen	ich werfe, du wirfst, er wirft	ich warf	ich würfe	wirf	geworfen
wiegen = wägen					
winden	ich winde	ich wand	ich wände	wind(e)	gewunden
wissen	ich weiss, du weisst, er weiss, wir (sie) wissen, ihr wisst	ich wusste	ich wüsste	wisse	gewusst
wollen	ich will, du willst, er will	ich wollte	ich wollte	wolle	gewollt (wollen)
zeihen	ich zeihe	ich zieh	ich ziehe	zeih(e)	geziehen
ziehen	ich ziehe	ich zog	ich zöge	zieh(e)	gezogen
zwingen	ich zwinge	ich zwang	ich zwänge	zwing(e)	gezwungen

† '*Wiegen*' in the sense of *to rock a cradle* or *to mince*, is regular.
†† Compounds meaning *to soften*, *to mollify*, are regular.

Some Current German Abbreviations

a.a.O., *am angeführten Orte,* in the above-mentioned place.
Abh., *Abhandlung,* treatise.
a.c., *anni currentis,* of this year.
a.Ch., *ante Christum,* before Christ, B.C.
a.D., *ausser Dienst,* retired, on half-pay.
A.G., *Aktien-Gesellschaft,* Limited Company.
A.H., *Alter Herr,* past member of a students' society.
ahd., *althochdeutsch,* Old High German, O.H.G.
a.d.L., *an der Lahn,* on the Lahn.
a.M., *am Main,* on the Main.
a.d.O., *an der Oder,* on the Oder.
a.Rh., *am Rhein,* on the Rhein.
a.d.S., *an der Saale,* on the Saale.
A.T., *Altes Testament,* Old Testament.
Aufl., *Auflage,* edition.

b., *bei,* near.
B. (com.) *Brief,* offered.
Bd., *Band,* volume.
Bde., *Bände,* volumes.
bed., *bedeutet,* signifies.
beif., *beiflgd., beifolgend,* herewith.
beil., *beiliegend,* enclosed
bez., *bezüglich,* with reference to.
bezw., bzw., *beziehungsweise,* respectively.
B.G.B., *Bürgerliches Gesetzbuch,* Civil Code.

ca., *circa,* about.
Ch., Chr., *Christus.*
cr., *currentis,* current.

das., *daselbst,* in the same place.
dgl., *dergleichen, desgleichen,* things like that, likewise.
d.Gr., *der Grosse,* the Great.
d.h., *das heisst,* that is, i.e.
d.J., *dieses Jahres,* of this year.
d.M., *dieses Monats,* of this month, inst.
d.O., *der Obige,* the above.
D.R.P., *Deutsches Reichspatent,* Imperial Patent.
Dr. phil., *Doctor philosophiae,* Ph.D.
dtsch., *deutsch,* German.
Dtz., *Dutzend,* dozen.
d.Vf., *der Verfasser,* the author.
D-Zug, *Durchgangszug,* corridor train.

ebd., ebds., *ebendaselbst,* in the same place.
E.E., Ew.E., *Euer Ehrwürden,* Your Reverence.
eig., eigtl., *eigentlich,* properly.
Em., *Eminenz,* Eminence.
engl., *englisch,* English.
entspr., *entsprechend,* corresponding.
ev., *eventuell,* eventually, possibly.
Ew., *Euer,* Your.
exkl., *exklusive,* not included.

F.D-Zug, *Fern-D-Zug,* long distance corridor train.
ff., *folgende,* following; *fein-fein,* extra fine.
fg., flgd., *folgend,* following.
Fol., fol., *Folio,* page, folio.
Forts., *Fortsetzung,* continuation.
fr., *franko,* post-free.
Fr., *Frau,* Mrs.
franz., *französisch,* French.
frdl., *freundlich,* kind.
Frl., *Fräulein,* Miss.
Frz., Frzbd., *Franzband,* calf binding.

G. (com.) *Geld,* buyers.
g, *Gramm,* gramme.
geb., *geboren,* born.
gef., *gefälligst,* kindly.
geh., *geheftet,* stitched, in sheets.
Geh.R., *Geheimer Rat,* Privy Councillor.
gen., *genannt,* mentioned; surnamed.
gest., *gestorben,* died.
gez., *gezeichnet,* signed.
GM., *Goldmark,* goldmark.
G.m.b.H., *Gesellschaft mit beschränkter Haftung,* limited liability company, Ltd.
Gr., *Grad,* degree.

H., *Haben,* cr it; **HH.,** *Herren,* Messrs.; **H.,** *Hoheit,* Highness; **H.H.,** *Hoheiten;* **h., hl.,** *heil., heilig,* saint, holy.
hd., *hochdeutsch,* High German, H.G.
Hfrzbd., *Halbfranzband,* half calf (binding).
holl., *holländisch,* Dutch.
Hr., *Herr,* Mr.
hrsg., hsgb., *herausgegeben,* edited.
Hs., *Handschrift,* manuscript, MS.; **Hss.,** *Handschriften,* MSS.
Hsgbr., *Herausgeber,* editor.

I., *Ihre,* Her, Your, Their.
i.A., *im Auftrage,* by order.
I.H. (on address), *Ihre Hochwohlgeboren,* Miss *or* Mrs.
i.J., *im Jahre,* in the year.
I.K.H., *Ihre Königliche Hoheit,* Her Royal Highness.
I.M., *Ihre Majestät,* Her Majesty.
inkl., *inklusive,* included.
i.R., *im Ruhestand,* retired.
i.V., *in Vertretung,* on behalf of, by order

kais., *kaiserlich,* Imperial.
Kap., *Kapitel,* chapter.
kgl., *königlich,* Royal.
k.J., *kommenden Jahres,* of next year.
Kl., *Klasse,* class.
km., *Kilometer,* kilometre.
k.M., *kommenden Monats,* of next month.

l, *Liter,* litre.
l., *lies,* read.
l.c., *loco citato,* in the place quoted.
Ldrb., *Lederband,* calf (binding).
Lfrg., *Lieferung,* delivery; part.
l.J., *laufenden Jahres,* of this year.
l.M., *laufenden Monats,* of this month.
l.S., *lange Sicht,* long sight.
L.S., *loco sigilli,* instead of a seal.
Lwd., *Leinwand,* cloth (binding).
L-Zug, *Luxuszug,* saloon train.

M., *Mark,* mark.
m, *Meter,* metre.
M.d.L., *Mitglied des Landtags,* Member of the Diet.
M.d.R., *Mitglied des Reichstags,* M.P.
m.E., *meines Erachtens,* in my opinion.
M.E.Z., *Mitteleuropäische Zeit,* Central European Time.
mg, *Milligramm,* milligramme.
mhd., *mittelhochdeutsch,* Middle High German, M.H.G.
m.H., *Meine Herren,* Gentlemen.
mm, *Millimeter,* millimetre.

N., *Nachmittag(s),* afternoon; *Nacht(s),* night.
Nachm., *Nachmittags,* in the afternoon, P.M.
näml., *nämlich,* that is to say, viz.
namtl., *namentlich,* especially.
N.B., *nördliche Breite,* northern latitude.
n.Chr., *nach Christus,* after Christ, A.D.
nhd., *neuhochdeutsch,* new High German, N.H.G.
N.N., *nescio nomen,* name unknown, so-and so.
no., ntto., *netto,* net.
No., Nr., *Numero,* number.
N.T., *Neues Testament,* New Testament.

o., *oben,* above.
o.J., *ohne Jahr,* no date.
ö.L., *östliche Länge,* east longitude.
o.O., *ohne Ort,* no place (of publication).

p., *per,* per, by.
p.A., p.Adr., *per Adresse,* care of, c/o.
p.Ct., *Prozent,* per cent.
Pf., *Pfennig(e).*
Pfd., *Pfund,* pound.
P.P., *praemissis praemittendis,* omitting titles, Sir, Madam.
p.p., the aforesaid.
Prof. Ord., *Professor Ordinarius,* Professor.
P.S., *Pferdestärke f.* horse-power; *Nachschrift,* postscript.
p.t., *pro tempore,* for the time being.

qkm.,*Quadratkilometer,* square kilometre.
qm., *Quadratmeter,* square metre.

R., *Réaumur.*
Rab., *Rabatt,* discount.
Rbl., *Rubel,* rouble.
Ref., *Referent,* referee.
resp., *respektive,* respectively.
Rh., *Rhein,* the Rhine.
R.M., *Reichsmark,* reichsmark.
R.W., *Reichswährung,* Imperial currency.

S., *Seite,* page.
s., *siehe,* see.
s.d., *siehe dort,* see above *or* there.
Se., *Seine,* His.
sel., *selig,* late, deceased.
sg., sog., *sogenannt,* so-called.
S.H. (on addresses), *Seiner Hochwohlgeboren,* Esq.
s.l., *seinem lieben,* to his dear friend.
S.M., *Seine Majestät,* His Majesty.
s.o., *siehe oben,* see above.
spr., *sprich,* pronounce.
Sr., *Seiner,* of His.
St., *Sankt,* Saint; *Stück,* piece.
s.u., *siehe unten,* see below.
s.Z., *seiner Zeit,* in due time, at the time.

t., *Tonne,* ton.
teilw., *teilweise,* partly.

u., *und,* and.
u.a., *unter anderm,* amongst other things; *und andere,* and others.
u.a.m., *und anderes mehr,* and other things; *und andere mehr,* and others.
u.A.w.g., *um Antwort wird gebeten,* R.S.V.P.
u.dergl.m., *und dergleichen mehr,* and more of the kind.
ult., *ultimo,* of the last month; on the last day of the month.
u.ö., *und öfter,* and in other places.

urspr., *ursprünglich,* originally.
usf., usw., *und so fort, und so weiter,* and so forth, etc.

V.v., *Vers,* line; *vormittags,* in the fore-noon, A.M.
v., *von,* of.
Verf., Vf., *Verfasser,* author.
vgl., *vergleiche,* compare, cf.
v.H., *vom Hundert,* per cent.
v.J., *vorigen Jahres,* of last year.
v.M., *vorigen Monats,* of last month.
v.o., *von oben,* from the top.
Vorm., *Vormittag,* forenoon, A.M.
v.u., *von unten,* from the bottom.

w., *wenden,* turn over, T.O.

w.o., *wie oben,* as above.
W.S.g.u., *wenden Sie gefälligst um,* please turn over, P.T.O.
Ww., Wwe., *Witwe,* widow.
Wz., *Wurzel,* root.

Z., *Zeile,* line; *Zoll,* inch.
z.B., *zum Beispiel,* for instance.
z.D., *zur Disposition,* on half-pay.
z.E., *zum Exempel,* for instance.
z.H., *zu Händen,* at or on hand; care of.
z.S., *zur See,* naval.
Ztschr., *Zeitschrift,* periodical.
z.T., *zum Teil,* partly.
Ztr., *Zentner,* German hundredweight, cwt.
z.Z., *zur Zeit,* at the time being.

ENGLISH AND GERMAN

A

a(n) *art.* ein, eine, ein.
A 1 *a. & adv.* erster Klasse, vorzüglich.
aback *adv.*; taken ~, bestürzt, verblüfft.
abandon *v.t.* aufgeben; verlassen, preisgeben.
abandon *s.* das Sichgehenlassen.
abandoned *p. & a.* verlassen; liederlich.
abandonment *s.* Aufgeben *n.*; Verlassenheit *f.*; Hingabe *f.*
abase *v.t.* erniedrigen.
abasement *s.* Erniedrigung *f.*
abash *v.t.* beschämen; verlegen machen.
abate *v.t. & i.* vermindern, herabsetzen; nachlassen; fallen (vom Preise).
abatement *s.* Verminderung *f.*; Abnahme *f.*; Rabatt *m.*, Abzug *m.*
abbess *s.* Äbtissin *f.*
abbey *s.* Abtei *f.*
abbot *s.* Abt *m.*
abbreviate *v.t.* abkürzen.
abbreviation *s.* Abkürzung *f.*
abdicate *v.t. & i.* aufgeben; abdanken.
abdication *s.* Abdankung *f.*
abdomen *s.* Unterleib *m.*; Bauch *m.*
abdominal *a.* Unterleibs...
abduct *v.t.* entführen, wegführen.
abduction *s.* Wegführung, Entführung *f.*
abed *adv.* im, zu Bette.
aberration *s.* Abirrung *f.*; (*opt.*) Abweichung *f.*
abet *v.t.* aufhetzen; unterstützen.
abetment *s.* Aufhetzung *f.*; Vorschub *m.*
abettor *s.* Anstifter, Mitschuldige *m.*
abeyance *s. in* ~, herrenlos (von Ländereien); (*fig.*) in der Schwebe.
abhor *v.t.* verabscheuen.
abhorrence *s.* Abscheu *m.*
abhorrent *a.* widerlich; unvereinbar.
abide *v.t. & i.st.* bleiben, warten; (*vulg.*) aushalten; *to* ~ *by,* befolgen (Gesetze).
abiding, dauernd.
ability *s.* Fähigkeit *f.*; *abilities pl.* Geisteskräfte *f.pl.*; *to the best of one's* ~, nach bestem Vermögen.
abject *a.*, ~ly *adv.* verworfen, verächtlich.
abjuration *s.* Abschwörung *f.*
abjure *v.t.* abschwören; entsagen.
ablative *s.* Ablativ *m.*
ablaze *adv.* lodernd.

able *a.* fähig, geschickt; *to be* ~, imstande sein; ~-bodied, rüstig, dienstfähig.
able(-bodied) seaman *s.* Vollmatrose *m.*
ablution *s.* Abwaschung *f.*
abnegate *v.t.* ableugnen.
abnormal *a.* abnorm, äregelwidrig.
abnormity *s.* Abnormität *f.*
aboard *pr. & adv.* an Bord.
abode *s.* Wohnort *m.*; Aufenthalt *m.*
abolish *v.t.* abschaffen, vernichten
abolition *s.* Abschaffung *f.*
abominable *a.*, ~bly *adv.* abscheulich.
abominate *v.t.* verabscheuen.
abomination *s.* Abscheu *f.*; Greuel *m.*; *to hold in* ~, verabscheuen.
aboriginal *a.* ursprünglich.
aborigines *s.pl.* Ureinwohner *m.pl.*
abortion *s.* Fehlgeburt *f.*; Missgeburt *f.*; Abtreibung *f.*; *to procure* ~, abtreiben.
abortive, ~ly *a.* unzeitig (von der Geburt); misslungen.
abound *v.i.* Überfluss haben an, reichlich vorhanden sein.
about *pr. & adv.* um, herum; (*fig.*) über; etwa, ungefähr, bei, an, auf; wegen; *to be* ~, im Begriffe sein; *round* ~, ringsumher; *to see* ~ *a thing,* eine Sache erledigen; ~ *turn,* ~ *face,* linksum kehrt; *right* ~ *turn,* rechtsum kehrt.
above *pr. & adv.* oben, über, mehr als; ~ *all,* vor allem; ~ *board,* frank und frei, ehrlich; ~-mentioned, obenerwähnt; *over and* ~, ausser, über; obendrein.
abrasion *s.* Abschabung *f.*
abrasive *s.* Schleifmittel.
abreast *adv.* nebeneinander.
abridge *v.t.* abkürzen.
abridgment *s.* Abkürzung *f.*
abroad *adv.* draussen; im Ausland; *to get* ~, bekannt werden.
abrogate *v.t.* abschaffen; aufheben (Gesetz).
abrupt *a.*, ~ly *adv.* jäh; barsch.
abscess *s.* Geschwür *n.*
abscond *v.i.* durchbrennen; sich verstecken.
absence *s.* Abwesenheit *f.*: ~ *of mind,* Zerstreutheit *f.*; *leave of* ~, Urlaub *m.*
absent *a.* abwesend; ~ *without leave,* abwesend ohne Urlaub; ~-minded, geistesabwesend, zerstreut.

absent *v.refl.* sich entfernen, ausbleiben.
absentee *s.* Abwesender (bes. von der Arbeit).
absolute *a.*, ~ly *adv.* unbeschränkt, unbedingt; schlechthin.
absolution *s.* Lossprechung *f.*
absolutism *s.* Absolutismus *m.*
absolve *v.t.* freisprechen.
absorb *v.t.* einsaugen; in Anspruch nehmen.
absorbent *a.* einsaugend; ~ *s.* aufsaugende Mittel *n.*
absorption *s.* Aufsaugen *n.*
abstain *v.i.* sich enthalten.
abstainer *s.* Abstinenzler *m.*; *total* ~, Temperenzler *m.*
abstemious *a.*, ~ly *adv.* enthaltsam.
abstention *s.* Enthaltung *f.*
abstinence *s.* Enthaltsamkeit *f.*; *day of* ~, Fasttag *m.*
abstinent *a.*, ~ly *adv.* enthaltsam, mässig.
abstract *v.t.* abziehen; entwenden.
abstract *a.* abstrakt; abgesondert; ~ *s.* Auszug *m.*; *in the* ~, theoretisch.
abstraction *s.* Abstraktion *f.*; abstrakter Begriff *m.*; Zerstreutheit *f.*
abstruse *a.*, ~ly *adv.* dunkel.
absurd *a.*, ~ly *adv.* vernunftwidrig.
absurdity *s.* Ungereimtheit *f.*
abundance *s.* Überfluss *m.*, Menge *f.*
abundant *a.*, ~ly *adv.* überflüssig, reichlich.
abuse *v.t.* missbrauchen; betrügen; schmähen; schänden, verführen; ~ *s.* Missbrauch *m.*; Beschimpfung *f.*
abusive *a.*, ~ly *adv.* missbräuchlich; schimpfend.
abysmal *a.* grundlos.
abyss *s.* Abgrund *m.*
A.C. (*ante Christum*), vor Christi Geburt.
A/c = *account.*
acacia *s.* Akazie *f.*
academic(al) *a.*, ~ly *adv.* akademisch.
academy *s.* Akademie *f.*
accede *v.i.* beitreten, beipflichten.
accelerate *v.t.* beschleunigen.
accelerator *s.* (*mot.*) Gasfusshebel *m.*, Gaspedal *n.*
accent *s.* Betonung *f.*; Tonzeichen *n.*; Nachdruck *m.*, Aussprache *f.*; ~ *v.t.* betonen, hervorheben.
accentuate *v.t.* betonen.
accept *v.t.* annehmen; (einen Wechsel) akzeptieren.
acceptable *a.*, ~bly *adv.* annehmbar.
acceptance *s.* Annahme *f.*; Akzept (eines Wechsels) *n.*; Abnahme (von Maschinen) *f.*
access *s.* Zugang *m.*; Zuwachs, *m.*; *easy of* ~, leicht zugänglich.
accessary *s.* Teilnehmer, Mitschuldige *m.*; ~ *before the fact*, Teilnehmer an einem

Verbrechen vor Begehung desselben; ~ *after the fact*, Hehler, *m.*
accessible *a.* zugänglich.
accession *s.* Thronbesteigung *f.*
accessory *a.* hinzukommend; Neben-; ~ *s.* Mitschuldige *m.*; *accessories* pl. Beiwerk, Zubehör *n.*
accidence *s.* Formenlehre *f.*
accident *s.* Unfall *m.*; Zufall *m.*; *by* ~, zufällig; ~ *insurance*, Unfallversicherung *f.*
accidental *a.*, ~ly *adv.* zufällig; Neben-.
acclaim *v.t.* (einem) Beifall zurufen.
acclamation *s.* Zuruf, Beifall *m.*
acclimatize *v.t.* akklimatisieren.
accommodate *v.t.* anpassen; schlichten; unterbringen, versorgen; Geld leihen.
accommodating *a.* willfährig, gefällig.
accommodation *s.* Anpassung *f.*; Vergleich *m.*; Unterkommen (für die Nacht) *n.*; ~-**bill** *s.* Gefälligkeitswechsel *m.*
accompaniment *s.* (*mus.*) Begleitung *f.*
accompanist *s.* (*mus.*) Begleiter *m.*
accompany *v.t.* begleiten; mitspielen.
accomplice *s.* Mitschuldige *m.*
accomplish *v.t.* vollenden, erreichen.
accomplished *a.* gebildet.
accomplishment *s.* Ausführung *f.*; Fertigkeit *f.*; ~s *pl.* Talente *n.pl.*
accord *s.* Eintracht *f.*; Vergleich *m.*; ~ *v.t.* & *i.* übereinstimmen.
accordance *s.* Übereinstimmung *f.*
according (to), *pr.* gemäss.
accordingly *adv.* demgemäss, folglich.
accordion *s.* Ziehharmonika *f.*
accoucheur (*frz.*) *s.* Geburtshelfer *m.*
account *s.* Rechnung *f.*; Rechenschaft *f.*; Bericht *m.*; Rücksicht *f.*; Konto *n.*; ~-**book**, Kontobuch *n.*; ~-**holder**, Kontoinhaber *m.*; *current* ~, laufende Rechnung *f.*, laufendes Konto *n.*; *deposit* ~, Depositenkonto *n.*; *fictitious* ~, fiktives Konto *n.*; *on* ~, auf Rechnung; *on* ~ *of*, wegen; *to call to* ~, zur Rechenschaft ziehen; *to keep* ~, Buch führen; *to open an* ~, ein Konto eröffnen; *to turn to* ~, gehörig verwerten; ~ *v.t.* schätzen; halten für; *to* ~ *for*, Rechenschaft ablegen von; erklären; **accounting** *s.* Buchhaltung *f.*
accountant *s.* Bücherrevisor *m.*
accredit *v.t.* beglaubigen.
accrue *v.i.* zuwachsen; zufallen; *accrued interest*, anfallende Zinsen *m.pl.*
accumulate *v.t.* & *i.* aufhäufen; sich häufen; *accumulated interest*, aufgelaufene Zinsen *m.pl.*
accumulative *a.* sich anhäufend.
accumulator *s.* Akkumulator *m.*
accuracy *s.* Genauigkeit, Pünktlichkeit *f.*
accurate *a.*, ~ly *adv.* genau, sorgfältig.
accursed *p.* & *a.* verflucht, fluchwürdig.

accusation *s.* Anklage, Beschuldigung *f.*
accusative *s.* Akkusativ *m.*
accuse *v.t.* anklagen; beschuldigen.
accused *s. (law)* Angeklagte *m.*
accustom *v.t.* gewöhnen.
accustomed *a.* gewohnt.
ace *s.* As, *n.*; Eins (auf Würfeln) *f.*; *(avi.)* Fliegerheld.
acetylene Azetylen *n.*
ache *s.* Schmerz *m.*; ~ *v.i.* schmerzen.
achieve *v.t.* zustande bringen; erwerben.
achievement, Vollendung *f.*; Leistung *f.*
acid *a.* sauer; ~ *s.* Säure *f.*; ~-**proof**, säurefest.
acidity *s.* Säure, Schärfe *f.*
acknowledge *v.t.* anerkennen; bestätigen; *to* ~ *receipt*, den Empfang bestätigen.
acknowledgment *s.* Anerkennung *f.*; Empfangsbestätigung *f.*
acme *s.* Gipfel, höchste Punkt *m.*
acorn *s.* Eichel *f.*
acoustic *a.* akustisch.
acoustics *s.pl.* Schallehre, Akustik *f.*
acquaint *v.t.* bekannt machen, melden.
acquaintance *s.* Bekanntschaft *f.*; Bekannte *m.*
acquiesce *v.i.* sich beruhigen, einwilligen.
acquiescence *s.* Einwilligung, Fügung *f.*
acquire *v.t.* erwerben, erlangen.
acquirement *s.* Erwerbung *f.*; Fertigkeit *f.*; ~**s** *pl.* Kenntnisse *f.pl.*
acquisition *s.* Erwerbung, *f.*; Errungenschaft *f.*
acquisitive *a.*, ~**ly** *adv.* habsüchtig.
acquit *v.t.* freisprechen; quittieren; *refl.* (gut, schlecht) machen.
acquittal *s.* Freisprechung *f.*
acre *s.* Acker *m.* (ungefähr 0,4 Hektar).
acreage *s.* Ackerfläche *f.*
acrimonious *a.*, ~**ly** *adv.* scharf, beissend.
acrimony *s.* Schärfe *f.*
acrobat *s.* Akrobat *m.*
across *adv.* kreuzweise; ~ *pr.* quer durch, quer hinüber; *to come* ~, zufällig finden, begegnen.
act *v.t.* spielen, darstellen; ~ *v.i.* handeln; ~ *s.* Handlung, Tat *f.*; *(theat.)* Aufzug, Akt *m.*; Gesetz *n.*; *Act of God*, höhere Gewalt *f.*; *Act of Parliament*, Parlamentsakte *f.*; *in the very* ~, auf frischer Tat; *Acts of the Apostles*, Apostelgeschichte *f.*
acting *p. & a. (mil. & nav.)* stellvertretend.
action *s.* Handlung, Wirkung *f.*; Klage *f.*; Gefecht *n.*; *to bring an* ~ *against a person*, gegen einen eine Klage anstrengen, einen verklagen; *to put out of* ~ *(mil.)* ausser Gefecht setzen, *(mech.)* ausser Betrieb setzen; *to take* ~, Massnahmen ergreifen, *(law)* klagen.
active *a.*, ~**ly** *adv.* tätig, wirksam, lebhaft, rührig; *(com.)* gesucht, belebt; *(mil.)* aktiv; ~ *voice*, *(gram.)* Aktivum *n.*

activity *s.* Wirksamkeit *f.*; Lebhaftigkeit *f.*
actor *s.* Schauspieler *m.*
actress *s.* Schauspielerin *f.*
actual *a.*, ~**ly** *adv.* wirklich; faktisch; ~ *stock*, Istbestand *m.*; ~ *strength*, *(mil.)* Iststärke.
acumen *s.* Scharfsinn *m.*
acute *a.*, ~**ly** *adv.* scharf, spitzig; scharfsinnig; *(med.)* akut, hitzig; ~-**angled**, spitzwink[e]lig.
A.D. = *Anno Domini*.
adamant *a.*, ~**ly** *adv.* fest, unerbittlich.
Adam's apple *s.* Adamsapfel *m.*
adapt *v.t.* anpassen; adaptieren.
adaptability *s.* Anpassungsfähigkeit *f.*
adaptable *a.* anpassungsfähig.
adaptation *s.* Anpassung *f.*
add *v.t. & i.* hinzutun; addieren.
addendum *s.* Nachtrag *m.*
adder *s.* Natter *f.*
addict *v.refl.* sich ergeben; ~ *s.* Süchtige *m.*; *drug* ~, Rauschgiftsüchtige *m.*
adding machine *s.* Rechenmaschine *f.*
addition *s.* Hinzusetzung *f.*; *(ar.)* Addition *f.*; Zusatz *m.*; *sign of* ~, Additionszeichen *n.*
additional *a.* weiter, zusätzlich, Neben-, Zusatz-; ~ *claim*, ~ *charge*, Nachforderung *f.*
address *s.* Anrede *f.*; Adresse *f.*; Bittschrift *f.*; Geschicklichkeit *f.*
address *v.t.* anreden; richten, adressieren; *to* ~ *oneself to a person*, sich an einen wenden.
addressee *s.* Adressat, Empfänger *m.*
adduce *v.t.* anführen.
adept *a.* erfahren; ~ *s.* erfahrene Mann *m.*; Eingeweihte *m.*
adequacy *s.* Angemessenheit *f.*
adequate *a.*, ~**ly** *adv.* angemessen.
adhere *v.i.* anhangen; ankleben.
adherence *s.* Anhänglichkeit *f.*
adherent *a.*, ~**ly** *adv.* anhangend; ~ *s.* Anhänger *m.*
adhesion *s.* Anhaften *n.*
adhesive *a.*, ~**ly** *adv.* anhaftend; klebrig; ~ *dressing*, Heftverband *m.*; ~ *envelopes* *s.pl.* gummierte Briefumschläge; ~ *plaster* *s.* Heftpflaster *n.*
adieu *i.* lebe wohl!; ~ *s.* Lebewohl *n.*
adjacent *a.* anliegend, angrenzend.
adjective *s.* Eigenschaftswort *n.*
adjoin *v.t.* anfügen; *v.i.* angrenzen.
adjourn *v.t. & i.* vertagen; sich vertagen.
adjournment *s.* Vertagung *f.*
adjudicator *s.* Preisrichter *m.*
adjure *v.t.* beschwören.
adjust *v.t.* ordnen; berichtigen; einstellen; ausgleichen; eichen.
adjustable *a.* einstellbar, verstellbar, anpassbar.
adjustment *s.* Ausgleich *m.*; Beilegung *f.*
adjutant *s.* Adjutant *m.*

administer *v.t.* verwalten; darreichen; (Verweis) erteilen; *to ~ an oath*, (einem) einen Eid abnehmen; *to ~ a will*, ein Testament vollziehen.

administration *s.* Verwaltung, Regierung *f.*; Austeilung (der Sakramente); *~ of justice*, Rechtspflege *f.*

administrative *a.* verwaltend; *~ court*, Verwaltungsgericht *n.*; *~ law*, Verwaltungsrecht *n.*

administrator *s.* Verwalter *m.*; Testamentsvollstrecker *m.*

admirable *a.* bewunderungswürdig.

admiral *s.* Admiral *m.*; *rear ~*, Konteradmiral *m.*

admiralty *s.* Marineministerium *n.*

admiration *s.* Bewunderung *f.*

admire *v.t.* bewundern.

admissible *a.*, *~bly adv.* zulässig.

admission *s.* Zulassung *f.*, Eintritt *m.*; Zugeständnis *n.*; *~ ticket*, Eintrittskarte *f.*

admit *v.t.* zulassen, zugeben.

admittance *s.* Zulassung *f.*; *no ~!* verbotener Eingang!

admittedly *adv.* zugestandenermassen.

admixture *s.* Beimischung *f.*

admonish *v.t.* ermahnen, warnen.

admonition *s.* Erinnerung, Warnung *f.*

ado *s.* Getue *n.*; Aufheben *n.*

adobe *s.* Luftstein.

adolescence *s.* Jünglingsalter *n.*

adolescent *a.* heranwachsend.

adopt *v.t.* annehmen; adoptieren.

adoption *s.* Adoption *f.*; Annahme *f.*

adoptive *a.* adoptiert.

adorable *a.*, *~bly adv.* anbetungswürdig; bezaubernd.

adoration *s.* Anbetung *f.*

adore *v.t.* anbeten.

adorn *v.t.* schmücken.

adrift *adv.* treibend, schwimmend; *turned ~*, in die weite Welt gestossen.

adroit *a.*, *~ly adv.* gewandt.

adulation *s.* Schmeichelei *f.*

adult *a.* erwachsen.

adulterate *v.t.* verfälschen.

adulterate *a.* ehebrecherisch; verfälscht.

adulterer *s.* Ehebrecher *m.*

adulteress *s.* Ehebrecherin *f.*

adulterous *a.* ehebrecherisch.

adultery *s.* Ehebruch *m.*

adumbrate *v.t.* flüchtig skizzieren.

ad valorem, *an ~ ~ duty*, Wertzoll *m.*

advance *s.* Fortschritt *m.*; Vorschuss *m.*; Steigen (der Preise), *n.*; *in ~*, im voraus; *~s pl.* Auslagen *f.pl.*; *~ v.t. & i.* vorrücken; befördern; vorschiessen; Fortschritte machen; im Preise steigen; *to ~ a claim*, eine Forderung geltend machen; *to ~ an opinion*, eine Meinung vorbringen; *advanced pupil, ~ student*, Fortgeschrittene *m.*

advancement *s.* Beförderung *f.*

advantage *s.* Vorteil, Vorzug *m.*; Überlegenheit *f.*; *to take ~ of*, sich etwas zunutze machen; betrügen.

advantageous *a.*, *~ly adv.* vorteilhaft.

advent *s.* Advent *m.*; (*poet.*) Herannahen *n.*

adventitious *a.*, *~ly adv.* zufällig.

adventure *s.* Abenteuer *n.*; *~ v.t. & i.* wagen.

adventurer *s.* Abenteurer *m.*

adventuress *s.* Abenteuerin *f.*

adventurous *a.*, *~ly adv.* abenteuerlich.

adverb *s.* Umstandswort *n.*, Adverb *n.*

adversary *s.* Gegner *m.*

adverse *a.*, *~ly adv.* widrig; (Bilanz) passiv.

adversity *s.* Schwierigkeit *f.*, Unglück *n.*

advertise *v.t.* ankündigen, annoncieren.

advertisement *s.* Anzeige *f.*; Reklame *f.*; Inserat *n.*

advertising *s.* *~ agent* *s.* Inhaber eines Annoncenbüros *m.*

advice *s.* Rat *m*; Bericht *m.*

advisable *a.* rätlich.

advise *v.t.* raten; benachrichtigen; *~ v.i.* sich beraten.

adviser *s.* Ratgeber *m.*

advisory board, *~ council* *s.* Beirat *m.*

advocacy *s.* Befürwortung *f.*

advocate *s.* Verteidiger, Anwalt *m*; *~ v.t.* verteidigen; befürworten.

advowson *s.* Patronatrecht *n.*

ægis *s.* Schutz *m.*

aerated *a.* kohlensauer.

aerial *a.* luftig; Luft ...; *~ s.* (*radio*) Antenne *f.*; *~ photograph*, Luftbild *n.*, Luftaufnahme *f.*

aerodrome *s.* Flugplatz *m.*

aeronautics *s.* Aeronautik *f.*

aeroplane *s.* Aeroplan, Flugzeug *n.*

æsthetic *a.*, *~ally adv.* ästhetisch.

æsthetics *s.* Ästhetik *f.*

afar *adv.* fern, von fern.

affability *s.* Leutseligkeit *f.*

affable *a.*, *~bly adv.* leutselig, gesprächig.

affair *s.* Geschäft *n.*; Angelegenheit *f.*

affect *v.t.* betreffen; begehren; affektieren.

affectation *s.* Ziererei *f.*

affected *p. & a.* gerührt; geziert.

affecting *a.* rührend, ergreifend.

affection *s.* Gemütsbewegung *f.*; Zuneigung *f.*; Erkrankung *f.*

affectionate *a.* liebend zugetan.

affidavit *s.* schriftliche eidliche (eidesstattliche) Versicherung *f.*; *to make an ~*, eine eidliche Versicherung abgeben.

affiliation *s.* Angliederung *f.*

affinity *s.* Verschwägerung, Verwandtschaft *f.*; (*chem.*) Affinität *f.*

affirm *v.t.* bestätigen, behaupten.

affirmation *s.* Bekräftigung *f.*

affirmative *a.*, *~ly adv.* bejahend; *~ s.* Bejahung *f.*; *in the ~*, bejahend.

affix *v.t.* anheften.
afflict *v.t.* betrüben; plagen.
affliction *s.* Kummer *m.*, Missgeschick *n.*
affluence *s.* Reichtum *m.*; Überfluss *m.*
affluent *a.*, **~ly** *adv.* reich.
afflux *s.* Zufluss *m.*
afford *v.t.* sich leisten können; liefern.
aforementioned *a.* vorerwähnt.
afforest *v.t.* aufforsten.
affray *s.* Schlägerei *f.*; Auflauf *m.*
affront *s.* Beleidigung *f.*, Schimpf *m.*
affront *v.t.* beleidigen.
afield *adv.* auf dem Felde; ins Feld.
aflame *adv.* in Flammen.
afloat *adv.* schwimmend, flott.
afoot *adv.* zu Fuss; im Gange.
afraid *a.* besorgt, bange.
afresh *adv.* von neuem.
after *pr.* nach, hinter; zufolge; **~** all, am Ende, alles wohl erwogen, schliesslich; **~** after, hinterher, darauf; **~** c. nachdem.
after-birth *s.* Nachgeburt *f.*
after-effect *s.* Nachwirkung *f.*
aftermath *s.* Spätheu *n.*; Grummet *f.* & *n.*; (*fig.*) Nachwirkungen *f.pl.*
afternoon *s.* Nachmittag *m.*
aftertaste *s.* Nachgeschmack *m.*
afterthought *s.* nachträgliche Einfall *m.*
afterwards *adv.* nachher.
again *adv.* wieder, zurück; **~** and **~**, immer wieder.
against *pr.* wider, gegen.
agape *adv.* gaffend.
agate *s.* Achat *m.*
age *s.* Alter *n.*; Zeitalter *n.*; to be of **~**, mündig sein; **~-class**, **~-group** (*mil.*) Altersklasse *f.*; **~-limit**, Altersgrenze *f.*; old **~**, Greisenalter *n.*; under **~**, unmündig; not seen for ages, seit einer Ewigkeit nicht gesehen; **~** *v.i.* altern, alt werden.
aged *a.* bejahrt; **~** 9 years, neun Jahre alt.
agency *s.* Wirkung *f.*; Vermittelung *f.*; Agentur *f.*; Dienststelle *f.*
agenda *s.pl.* Tagesordnung *f.*
agent *s.* Agent *m.*; Mittel *n.*
agglomerate *v.i.* sich klumpen.
agglutinate *v.t.* zusammenleimen.
aggrandizement *s.* Vergrösserung *f.*
aggravate *v.t.* erschweren; ärgern.
aggravating *a.* ärgerlich; **~** circumstances, (*law*) erschwerende Umstände *m.pl.*
aggregate *s.* Haufen *m.*; Ganze *n.*; Aggregat *n.*; **~** *a.*, **~ly** *adv.* gehäuft; **~** amount, aufgelaufene Summe *f.*; **~** *v.t.* zusammenhäufen.
aggression *s.* Angriff, Anfall *m.*
aggressive *a.* angreifend; **~** war, Angriffskrieg *m.*
aggressor *s.* Angreifer *m.*
aggrieve *v.t.* kränken.
aghast *a.* erschrocken, bestürzt.
agile *a.* behend, flink.

agitate *v.t.* aufregen, beunruhigen.
agitation *s.* Bewegung; Hetzerei *f.*
agitator *s.* Volksaufwiegler *m.*
agnate *a.* verwandt (von väterlicher Seite).
agnostic *s.* Agnostiker *m.*
ago *adv.* vor; a year **~**, vor einem Jahre; long **~**, lange her.
agog *adv.*, all **~**, ganz erpicht.
agonize *v.t.* martern, quälen.
agony *s.* Todeskampf *m.*; Pein *f.*
agrarian *s.* Agrarier *m.*; **~** *a.* agrarisch.
agree *v.i.* übereinstimmen; sich vergleichen; vereinbaren; zuträglich sein; zustimmen; that does not **~** with me, das bekommt mir nicht.
agreeable *a.* angenehm; gemäss; einverstanden.
agreement *s.* Übereinstimmung *f.*; Vergleich *m.*; Vertrag *m.*; to come to an **~**, sich verständigen, sich vergleichen; to enter into an **~**, to make an **~**, ein Übereinkommen treffen.
agricultural *a.* landwirtschaftlich.
agriculture *s.* Landwirtschaft *f.*
agriculturist *s.* Landwirt *m.*
aground *adv.* gestrandet; to go **~**, to run **~**, auf Grund laufen.
ague *s.* kalte[s] Fieber *n.*
ahead *adv.* voran; go **~**! vorwärts!
aid *v.t.* helfen; to **~** and abet, (*law*) Beihilfe leisten; **~** *s.* Hilfe *f.*
aide-de-camp (*frz.*) Adjutant *m.*
aider *s.* **~** and abettor, Helfershelfer *m.*
ail *v.t.* what **~** you? Was fehlt dir?
ailing *a.* kränklich.
ailment *s.* Unpässlichkeit *f.*
aim *v.i.* & *t.* zielen, trachten; richten; **~** *s.* Ziel *n.*, Richtung *f.*; Absicht *f.*
aimless *a.*, **~ly** *adv.* ziellos.
ain't (*vulg.*)=is not, am not, are not.
air *v.t.* lüften; **~** *s.* Luft *f.*; Luftzug, Wind *m.*; Melodie *f.*; Miene *f.*; Schein *m.*; by **~**, auf dem Luftwege; open **~**, freie Luft.
airborne troops *s.pl.* (*mil.*) Luftlandetruppen *f.pl.*
aircraft *s.* Flugzeug *n.*
aircraft carrier *s.* (*nav.*) Flugzeugträger *m.*
airfield *s.* Flugplatz *m.*
air-gun *s.* Luftgewehr *n.*
airing *s.*, to take an **~**, frische Luf schöpfen.
airline *s.* Luftfahrtgesellschaft *f.*
airliner *s.* Passagierflugzeug *n.*
air-mail *s.* Luftpost; by **~**, mit Luftpost.
airman *s.* Flieger *m.*
air-marshal *s.* General der Flieger *m.*
airplane=aeroplane.
airpocket (*avi.*) Luftloch *n.*
airport, Flughafen *m.*
air-raid *s.* Luftangriff *m.*
air-raid protection (ARP) *s.* Luftschutz *m.*

air-raid warden s. Luftschutzwart m.
air-raid warning s. Fliegeralarm m.
air-reconnaissance s. (mil.) Luftaufklärung f.
airship s. Luftschiff n.
air-speed indicator s. (avi.) (Luft-) Geschwindigkeitsmesser m.
air-tight a. luftdicht.
airy a. luftig; leicht, flüchtig.
aisle s. Seitenschiff n.; Chorgang m.
ajar adv. halb offen, angelehnt.
akimbo adv. mit eingestemmten Armen.
akin a. verwandt.
alabaster s. Alabaster m.
alack i. ach! o weh!
alacrity s. Bereitwilligkeit f.
alarm v.t. alarmieren; beunruhigen; ~s. Lärm, Aufruhr m.;. Besorgnisf.; Wecker (in der Uhr) m.
alarm-clock s. Weckuhr f.
alarmist s. Bangemacher m.
alas i. ach! o weh! leider!
albatross s. Albatross m.
albeit c. obschon.
albino s. Albino m.
album s. Stammbuch n.
albumen s. Eiweiss n.
alchemy s. Goldmacherkunst f.
alcohol s. Alkohol m.
alcoholic a. alkoholisch, spiritusartig.
alcove s. Alkoven m.; Nische f.
alder s. Erle f.
alderman s. Ratsherr m., Stadtrat m.
ale s. helle englische Bier n.
alert a., ~ly adv. wachsam, flink; on the ~, auf der Hut, wach.
algebra s. Algebra f.
algebraic a. algebraisch.
alias s. falsche[r] Name m.
alibi s. (law) Alibi n.; to prove one's ~, sein Alibi nachweisen.
alien a. fremd; ~ s. Ausländer m.
alienate v.t. entfremden, veräussern.
alienist s. Irrenarzt m.
alight v.i. sich niederlassen; aussteigen; ~ a. brennend, angezündet.
align v.t. in eine Linie bringen, richten.
alignment s. Aufstellung in einer Linie f.; Richtung f.
alike a. & adv. gleich, ähnlich; ebenso.
alimentary a. Nahrungs..., nahrhaft.
alimentation s. Unterhalt m.
alimony s. Unterhaltsgeld m.
alive a. lebendig; (fig.) munter; (elek.) geladen.
alkali s. Laugensalz n.; Alkali n.
alkaline a. laugensalzig.
all a. aller, alle, alles; ~ adv. gänzlich; at ~, überhaupt; ~ at once, auf einmal; ~ but, fast; by ~ means, auf jeden Fall; on ~ fours, auf allen Vieren; not at ~ ganz und gar nicht; once for ~, ein für allemal; ~ the better, desto besser; ~ the

same, trotzdem, doch; ~ right!, ganz recht! in Ordnung; ~ of a sudden, urplötzlich; ~ along, die ganze Zeit.
allay v.t. lindern, beruhigen.
all-clear signal s. (mil.) Entwarnung f.
allegation s. Angabe f.; Behauptung f.
allegiance s. Lehenspflicht f.; Gehorsam m.; to swear ~, den Treueid schwören.
allege v.t. angeben, behaupten.
allegoric(al) a. sinnbildlich.
allegory s. bildliche Rede f.
alleviate v.t. erleichtern.
alley s. Gässchen n.
All-Hallows, Allerheiligen n.
alliance s. Bündnis n.
allied a. verbündet; verwandt.
alliteration s. Stabreim m.
allocate v.t. zuteilen; anweisen.
allocation s. Anweisung, Zuteilung f.
allocution a. Andrede f.
allot v.t. zuteilen, zuerkennen.
allotment s. Anteil m.; Zuteilung f.; Landparzelle f.; Schrebergarten m.
allow v.t. erlauben, bewilligen; zugestehen; vergüten; abrechnen.
allowable a. zulässig.
allowance s. Erlaubnis f.; Taschengeld, Kostgeld m.; Ration f.; Nachsicht f.; Abzug m.; Zulage f.; family ~, Familienzulage f.
alloy s. Legierung f.; to ~ v.t. (Metalle) beschicken, legieren.
All Saints' Day s. Allerheiligen n.
All Souls' Day s. Allerseelen n.
allude (to) v.i. anspielen (auf).
allure v.t. anlocken.
allurement s. Anlockung f.
allusion a. Anspielung f.
allusive a. anspielend.
alluvial a. angeschwemmt.
all-wool a. Ganzwolle...
ally s. Bundesgenosse m.; ~ v.t. verbünden; verbinden (mit).
almanac s. Almanach m., Kalender m.
almighty a. allmächtig.
almond s. Mandel f.
almoner s. Almosenpfleger m.; lady ~, Fürsorgebeamtin (im Krankenhaus) f.
almost adv. beinahe, fast.
alms s.pl. Almosen n.
alms-house s. Armenhaus n.
aloe s. Aloë f.
aloft adv. hoch, erhaben.
alone a. & adv. allein; to let ~, in Ruhe lassen.
along pr. längs, an...entlang; adv. entlang; weiter.
alongside adv. längsseits, Bord an Bord.
aloof adv. weit ab; to keep ~ from, sich fernhalten von.
aloofness s. Zurückhaltung f.
aloud adv. laut.
alphabet s. Alphabet n.

alphabetical *a.* alphabetisch.
Alpine *a.* von den Alpen, alpinisch.
alpinist *s.* Bergsteiger *m.*
already *adv.* schon, bereits.
also *adv.* auch, ebenfalls.
altar *s.* Altar *m.*
altar-cloth *s.* Altardecke *f.*
altar-piece *s.* Altargemälde *n.*
alter *v.t. & i.* ändern; sich ändern.
alterable *a.* veränderlich.
alteration *s.* Änderung *f.*
altercate *v.i.* streiten.
altercation *s.* Zank *m.*
alternate *v.t. & i.* abwechseln; ~ *a.,* ~ly *adv.* abwechselnd.
alternative *s.* Alternative *f.;* ~ *a.* abwechselnd.
although *c.* obgleich.
altimeter *s.* (*avi.*) Höhenmesser *m.*
altitude *s.* Höhe (*Luft, geographisch*).
alto *s.* Alt *m.*
altogether *adv.* gänzlich, ganz und gar.
altruism *s.* Nächstenliebe *f.*
alum *s.* Alaun *m.*
aluminium *s.* Aluminium *n.*
aluminium acetate *s.* essigsaure Tonerde *f.*
aluminum *s.* (*Am.*) Aluminium *n.*
always *adv.* immer.
a.m. (= ante meridiem), vormittags.
amalgam *s.* Amalgam *n.*
amalgamate *v.t. & i.* verschmelzen.
ambulance *s.* Feldlazarett *n.;* Krankenwagen *m.;* ~-column Sanitätskolonne *f.*
amass *v.t.* anhäufen.
amateur *s.* Liebhaber, Dilettant *m.*
amatory *a.* die Liebe betreffend.
amaze *v.t.* in Erstaunen setzen.
amazement *s.* Erstaunen *n.*
amazing *a.,* ~ly erstaunlich.
Amazon *s.* Amazone *f.*
ambassador *s.* Botschafter *m.*
amber *s.* Bernstein *m.*
ambidextrous *a.* mit der rechten wie linken Hand gleich geschickt.
ambiguity *s.* Zweideutigkeit *f.*
ambiguous *a.,* ~ly *adv.* zweideutig.
ambition *s.* Ehrsucht *f.,* Ehrgeiz *m.*
ambitious *a.,* ~ly *adv.* ehrgeizig, begierig.
amble *s.* Passgang *m.;* ~ *v.i.* passgehen.
ambrosia *s.* Götterspeise *f.*
ambulatory *a.* herumziehend.
ambuscade, ambush *s.* Hinterhalt *m.;* to ambush *v.t.* im Hinterhalt auflauern.
ameliorate *v.t.* verbessern.
amen *adv.* amen; *s.* Amen *n.*
amenable *a.* verantwortlich; willfährig.
amend *v.t. & i.* bessern; (Gesetzentwurf) ändern od. ergänzen; sich bessern.
amendment *s.* Verbesserung *f.;* Verbesserungsantrag *m.*
amends *s.pl.* Ersatz *m.*
amenity *s.* Annehmlichkeit *f.*

amiable *a.,* ~bly *adv.* liebenswürdig.
amicable *a.,* ~bly *adv.* freundschaftlich.
amid(st) *pr.* mitten in, mitten unter.
amidships *adv.* mittschiffs.
amiss *adv.* unrecht, verkehrt, fehlerhaft; to take ~, übelnehmen.
amity *s.* gute Einvernehmen *n.*
ammeter *s.* (*elek.*) Strommesser, Ampèremeter *m.*
ammonia *s.* Ammoniak; *liquid* ~, Salmiakgeist *m.*
ammonite *s.* Ammonshorn *n.*
ammunition *s.* Munition *f.,* Kriegsvorrat *m.;* ~-bread, Kommissbrot *n.*
amnesty *s.* Amnestie *f.;* ~ *v.t.* begnadigen.
among(st) *pr.* unter, zwischen.
amorous *a.,* ~ly *adv.* verliebt.
amorphous *a.* amorph, gestaltlos.
amortization *s.* Tilgung (einer Schuld) *f.*
amortize *v.t.* tilgen, amortisieren.
amount *s.* Betrag *m.;* ~ *v.i.* sich belaufen (auf).
amour *s.* Liebschaft *f.*
ampere *s.* (*elek.*) Ampère *n.; ampere-hour,* Ampèrestunde *f.*
amphibian, amphibious *a.* auf dem Lande und im Wasser lebend; ~ tank, (*mil.*) Schwimmpanzer *m.*
amphitheatre *s.* Amphitheater *n.*
ample *a.* gross, weit; reichlich.
amplification *s.* Erweiterung *f.*
amplifier *s.* (*radio, elek.*) Verstärker *m.*
amplify *v.t.* erweitern.
amplitude *s.* Umfang *m.*
amputate *v.t.* amputieren.
amuck *adv.,* to run ~ (*against* or at), Amok laufen.
amulet *s.* Amulett *n.*
amuse *v.t.* unterhalten, ergötzen.
amusement *s.* Unterhaltung *f.*
amusing *a.,* ~ly *adv.* ergötzlich.
an *art.* ein, eine, ein.
anabaptist *s.* Wiedertäufer *m.*
anachronism *s.* Anachronismus *m.*
anæmia *s.* (*med.*) Anämie.
anæmic *a.* anämisch, blutarm.
anæsthesia *s.* Unempfindlichkeit *f.*
anæsthetic *a.* (*med.*) (Schmerz) betäubend; ~ *s.* Betäubungsmittel *n.*
anagram *s.* Anagramm *n.*
analogous *a.,* ~ly *adv.* ähnlich.
analogy *s.* Ähnlichkeit.
analyse *v.t.* analysieren.
analysis *s.* Analyse, Auflösung *f.*
analytic(al) *a.,* ~ly *adv.* analytisch.
anarchic(al) *a.* anarchisch.
anarchist *s.* Anarchist *m.*
anarchy *s.* Anarchie *f.,* Gesetzlosigkeit *f.*
anatomical *a.* anatomisch.
anatomist *s.* Anatom, Zergliederer *m.*
anatomize *v.t.* zergliedern.
anatomy *s.* Anatomie *f.*
ancestor *s.* Ahnherr *m.,* Vorfahr *m.*

ancestral *a.* ererbt, angestammt.
ancestry *s.* Ahnen *m.pl.*
anchor *s.* Anker *m.*; *to cast ~*, vor Anker gehen; *to weigh ~*, Anker lichten; *~ v.t. & i.* vor Anker legen; vor Anker liegen.
anchorage *s.* Ankerplatz *m.*
anchoret, anchorite *s.* Einsiedler *m.*
anchovy *s.* Sardelle, Anschovis *f.*
ancient *a.* alt; *~ly adv.* vor alters; *the ancients*, die Alten.
ancillary *a.* dienstbar, untergeordnet.
and *c.* und.
anecdote *s.* Anekdote *f.*
anemone *s.* Anemone *f.*
anew *adv.* von neuem.
angel *s.* Engel *m.*
angelic *a.* engelgleich.
anger *v.t.* erzürnen, ärgern; *~ s.* Zorn, Ärger *m.*
angina *s.* Halsentzündung *f.*
angle *s.* Winkel *m*; *right ~*, rechte Winkel *m*; *v.i.* angeln.
Anglican *a.* anglikanisch.
anglicize *v.t.* anglisieren.
anglicism *s.* englische Spracheigenheit *f.*
angling-line *s.* Angelschnur *f.*
angling-rod *s.* Angelrute *f.*
anglomania *s.* Engländerei *f.*
anglophil *s.* Englandfreund *m.*
anglophobe *s.* Englandfeind *m.*
angry *a.* zornig.
anguish *s.* Seelenangst *f.*; Qual *f.*
angular *a.*, *~ly adv.* winkelig, eckig.
animadversion *s.* Verweis *f.*
aniline *s.* Anilin *n.*
animal *s.* Tier *n.*; *~ a.* animalisch, tierisch; *~ fat*, tierisches Fett *n.*; *~ spirits*, die Lebensgeister *m.pl.*, Lebenskraft *f.*
animate *v.t.* beseelen; *~ a.* beseelt.
animation *s.* Lebhaftigkeit *f.*
animosity *s.* Erbitterung *f.*
animus *s.* Absicht *f.*; Groll *m.*
aniseed *s.* Aniskorn *n.*
ankle *s.* Fussknöchel *m.*, Enkel *m.*
annals *s.pl.* Jahrbücher *n.pl.*
anneal *v.t.* ausglühen; kühlen (Glas).
annex *v.t.* anhängen; annektieren; *~ s.* Anhang *m.*; Nebengebäude *n.*
annexation *s.* Einverleibung, Annexion *f.*
annihilate *v.t.* vernichten, anschaffen.
anniversary *s.* Jahrestag *m.*
annotate *v.t.* mit Anmerkungen versehen.
announce *v.t.* ankündigen.
announcement *s.* Ankündigung *f.*
announcer *s.* Ansager *m.*
annoy *v.t.* ärgern, belästigen.
annoyance *s.* Plage *f.*; Verdruss *m.*
annual *a.*, *~ly adv.* jährlich; *~ leave*, Jahresurlaub *m.*; *~ report*, Jahresbericht *m.*
annuity *s.* Jahresrente *f.*
annul *v.t.* ungültig machen, vernichten.

annular *a.* ringförmig.
annunciation *s.* Verkündigung *f.*; Mariä Verkündigung *f.*
anode *s.* Anode *f.*
anodyne *a.* schmerzstillend; *~ s.* (*med.*) schmerzstillendes Mittel, (*fig.*) Linderungsmittel *n.*
anoint *v.t.* salben.
anointment *s.* Salbung *f.*
anomalous *s.* abweichend, unregelmässig.
anomaly *s.* Anomalie *f.*
anon *adv.* sogleich.
anonymity *s.* Anonymität *f.*
anonymous *a.*, *~ly adv.* anonym.
another *a.* ein anderer; *one another*, einander.
answer *s.* Antwort *f.*; Resultat (einer Rechnung), *n.*; *~ v.t. & i.* antworten; verantwortlich sein für; entsprechen; (*com.*) sich rentieren; *to ~ for*, bürgen; *to ~ the bell* (*door*), nach der Tür sehen; *to ~ the telephone*, ans Telephon gehen; *to ~ to a name*, auf einen Namen hören.
answerable *a.* verantwortlich.
ant *s.* Ameise *f.*
antagonize *v.t.* sich einen zum Gegner machen.
antagonism *s.* Widerstreit *m.*
antagonist *s.* Gegner *m.*
antarctic *a.* südlich, am Südpol.
antecedent *a.*, *~ly adv.* vorhergehend; *~ s.* Vorhergehender *m.*; *antecedents pl.* frühere Lebensumstände.
antechamber *s.* Vorzimmer *n.*
antedate *v.t.* vordatieren; *~ s.* Vordatierung *f.*
antelope *s.* Antilope *f.*
antenatal *a.* vorgeburtlich; *~ care s.* Schwangerenfürsorge *f.*
antenna *s.* (*radio*) Antenne *f.*
anterior *a.* vorherig; älter.
anthem *s.* Hymne *f.*
ant-hill *s.* Ameisenhaufen *m.*
anthology *s.* Blumenlese *f.*
anthracite *s.* Anthrazit *m.*
anthrax *s.* Milzbrand *m.*
anthropologist *s.* Anthropolog[e] *m.*
anthropology *s.* Anthropologie.
anti (in Zus.) Gegen...
anti-aircraft Fliegerabwehr...
antic *a.*, *~ly adv.* lächerlich; *~ s.* Posse *f.*; Possenreisser *m.*
anticipate *v.t.* vorwegnehmen; zuvorkommen; voraussehen.
anticipation *s.* Vorwegnahme *f.*; Erwartung *f.*; Vorgeschmack *m.*
anticlockwise *adv.* gegen die Richtung des Uhrzeigers.
antidote *s.* Gegengift *n.*
antimony *s.* Antimon *n.*, Spiessglanz *m.*
antipathetic *a.* antipathisch, zuwider.
antipathy *s.* natürliche Abneigung *f.*
antipodes *s.pl.* Gegenfüssler *m.pl.*

antiquarian *a.* antiquarisch.
antiquary *s.* Altertumsforscher *m.*
antiquated *a.* veraltet, abgekommen.
antique *a.* altertümlich; ~ *s.* Antiquität *f.*; ~-dealer, Antiquitätenhändler *m.*; ~ furniture, antike Möbel.
antiquity *s.* Vorzeit *f.*, Altertum *n.*
antisemite *s.* Antisemit *m.*
antisemitic *a.* antisemitisch.
antiseptic *a.* & *s.* Fäulnis verhindernd; Mittel wider die Fäulnis *n.*
antisocial *a.* asozial.
antitank *a.* Antitank...; ~-ditch, Panzergraben *m.*; ~-gun, Panzerabwehrkanone; ~-troops, Panzerjäger *m.pl.*
antithesis *s.* Entgegenstellung *f.*
antitoxin *s.* Gegengift *n.*
antler *s.* Sprosse *f.* (am Hirschgeweih).
anvil *s.* Amboss *m.*
anxiety *s.* Angst *f.*; Beklemmung *f.*
anxious *a.*, ~ly *adv.* ängstlich; begierig.
any *a.* jeder, jede; irgendein, -eine, -ein; *anybody,* ~ *one,* irgend jemand; *anything,* etwas, irgend etwas; *anyhow,* irgendwie, immerhin; jedenfalls; *anywhere,* irgendwo.
apace *adv.* hurtig, zusehends.
apart *adv.* beiseite, für sich; ~ *from,* abgesehen von.
apartment *s.* Zimmer *n.*; (*Am.*) Wohnung *f.*
apathetic *a.* apathisch, stumpf.
apathy *s.* Gleichgültigkeit *f.*, Apathie *f.*
ape *s.* Menschenaffe *m.*; Nachäffer *m.*; ~ *v.t.* nachäffen.
aperient *a.* (*med.*) abführend.
aperture *s.* Öffnung *f.*
apex *s.* Spitze *f.*, Gipfel *m.*
aphorism *s.* Aphorismus *m.*
apiece *adv.* für das Stück.
apish *a.*, ~ly *adv.* affenartig.
aplomb (*frz.*) *s.* Sicherheit in der Haltung, im Auftreten *f.*
apocryphal *a.* apokryph.
apodictic(al) *a.*, ~ly *adv.* apodiktisch.
apologetic(al) *a.*, ~ly *adv.* bereit sich zu entschuldigen.
apologize *v.i.* sich entschuldigen.
apology *s.* Verteidigung *f.*; Entschuldigung *f.*
apoplectic(al) *a.* schlagflüssig.
apoplexy *s.* Schlagfluss *m.*
apostasy *s.* Abtrünnigkeit *f.*
apostate *a.* abtrünnig.
apostatize *v.i.* abtrünnig werden.
apostle *s.* Apostel *m.*
apostolic(al) *a.* apostolisch.
apostrophe *s.* Anrede *f.*; Apostroph *m.*
apothecary *s.* Apotheker *m.*
apotheosis *s.* Vergötterung, Apotheose *f.*
appal *v.t.* erschrecken.
apparatus *s.* Gerät *n.*; Apparat *m.*
apparel *s.* Kleidung *f.*; ~ *v.t.* ankleiden.

apparent *a.*, ~ly *adv.* augenscheinlich; *heir* ~, rechtmässige Thronerbe *m.*
apparition *s.* Erscheinung *f.*; Gespenst *n.*
appeal *v.i.* appellieren, Berufung einlegen; gefallen; ~ *v.t.* anrufen; ~ *s.* Ruf *m.*, Bitte *f.*; Anziehungskraft *f.*; Reklamewirkung *f.*; (*law*) Berufung *f.*, Rechtsmittel *n.*; *court of* ~, Berufungsgericht *n.*; *to allow an* ~, einer Berufung stattgeben; *to dismiss an* ~, eine Berufung zurückweisen; *to lodge an* ~, Berufung einlegen.
appear *v.i.* erscheinen, scheinen.
appearance *s.* Erscheinung *f.*; Anschein *m.*; *to keep up* ~*s*, den Schein wahren; *to put in an* ~, sich blicken lassen.
appease *v.t.* besänftigen.
appeasement *s.* Beruhigung *f.*
appellant *s.* Berufungskläger *m.*
appendage *s.* Anhang *m.*, Zubehör.
appendicitis *s.* Blinddarmentzündung *f.*
appendix *s.* Anhang *m.*; Blinddarm *m.*
appertain *v.i.* gehören.
appetite *s.* Esslust *f.*, Verlangen *n.*
appetizing *a.* appetitlich.
applaud *v.t.* Beifall spenden.
applause *s.* Beifall *m.*
apple *s.* Apfel *m.*
apple-pie *s.* Apfelpastete *f.*
apple-sauce *s.* Apfelmus *n.*
appliance *s.* Vorrichtung, Anwendung *f.*; Gerät *n.*
applicable *a.* anwendbar.
applicant *s.* Bewerber *m.*
application *s.* Anwendung *f.*; Gesuch *n.*; (*surg.*) Verband *m.*; Fleiss *m.*; Aufmerksamkeit *f.*; *to make an* ~, ein Gesuch einreichen; *to grant an* ~, ein Gesuch bewilligen; ~ *form,* Antragsformular *n.*
apply *v.t.* & *i.* anwenden; sich auf etwas verlegen; sich bewerben um; sich wenden an; *for particulars* ~ *to* ..., Näheres zu erfragen bei...
appoint *v.t.* bestimmen, ernennen; *at the appointed time,* zur verabredeten Zeit, zur festgesetzten Zeit.
appointment *s.* Festsetzung *f.*; Verabredung *f.*; Ausrüstung *f.*; Ernennung *f.*; *by* ~, nach Verabredung; *to make an* ~, eine Verabredung treffen.
apportion *v.t.* verhältnismässig verteilen.
apposition *s.* Zusatz *m.*
appraisal *s.* Beurteilung *f.*
appraise *v.t.* abschätzen, taxieren.
appreciable *a.* nennenswert.
appreciate *v.t.* schätzen, zu würdigen wissen.
appreciation *s.* Würdigung, Schätzung *f.*
apprehend *v.t.* ergreifen; begreifen; fürchten.
apprehensible *a.* begreiflich.
apprehension *s.* Verhaftung *f.*; Besorgnis *f.*

apprehensive *a.*, ~ly *adv.* besorgt.
apprentice *s.* Lehrling *m.*; ~ *v.t.* in die Lehre tun.
apprenticeship *s.* Lehrzeit *f.*
apprise *v.t.* benachrichtigen, belehren.
approach *v.t. & i.* nähern; sich nähern; sich wenden an; ~ *s.* Annäherung *f.*; Zutritt *m.*; Auffahrt *f.*
approbation *s.* Billigung *f.*, Beifall *m.*
appropriate *v.t.* sich aneignen; zu einem Zwecke bestimmen; *appropriated funds,* bewilligte Gelder; ~ *a.* angemessen.
appropriation *s.* Aneignung *f.*; Bewilligung (von Geldern) *f.*; ~s *s.pl.* bewilligte Gelder *n.pl.*
approval *s.* Billigung *f.*
approve *v.t.* billigen, loben.
approximate *v.t. & i.* nahe bringen; sich nahen; ~, annähernd.
approximation *s.* Annäherung *f.*
appurtenance *s.* Zubehör *n.*
apricot *s.* Aprikose *f.*
April *s.* April *m.*
apron *s.* Schürze *f.*; Schurzfell *n.*
apron-string *s.* Schürzenband *n.*
apropos *adv.* beiläufig.
apse, apsis *s.* (*arch.*) Apsis *f.*
apt *a.*, ~ly *adv.* geschickt; geneigt; fähig.
aptitude, aptness *s.* Tauglichkeit.
aquarium *s.* Aquarium *n.*
aquatic *a.* wasser; ~s *s.pl.* Wassersport *m.*
aqueduct *s.* Wasserleitung *f.*
Arab *s.* Araber *m.*; *street* ~, Strassenjunge *m.*
arabesque *a.* arabesk; ~ *s.* Arabeske *f.*
arabic *a.* arabisch; ~ numerals *s.pl.* arabische Ziffern *f.pl.*
arable *a.* pflügbar.
arbiter *s.* Schiedsrichter *m.*; Gebieter *m.*
arbitrament *s.* Entscheidung *f.*
arbitrary *a.*, ~ily *adv.* willkürlich.
arbitrate *v.t. & i.* schlichten.
arbitration *s.* Schiedsspruch *m.*; (*com.*) Arbitrage *f.*; *court of* ~, Schiedsgericht *n.*, Schlichtungsausschuss *m.*
arbitrator *s.* Schiedsrichter *m.*; ~'s award, Schiedsspruch *m.*
arbor *s.* Spindel, Welle *f.*, Drehbaum *m.*
arbour *s.* Laube *f.*
arc *s.* (*geom.*) Bogen *m.*; ~-lamp, Bogenlampe; ~-welding, Lichtbogenschweissung *f.*
arcade *s.* Bogengang *m.*
Arcadian *a.* idyllisch, ländlich, einfach.
arcanum *s.* Geheimnis *n.*
arch *a.*, ~ly *adv.* schlau; schalkhaft; ~ *a.* (in Zus.) Erz...; ~ *v.t.* wölben; ~ *s.* Bogen *m.*; Gewölbe *n.*; ~-support, Plattfusseinlage *f.*
archæologic(al) *a.* archäologisch.
archæologist *s.* Altertumsforscher *m.*
archæology *s.* Altertumskunde *f.*

archaic *a.* archaistisch, altertümlich.
archaism *s.* veraltete Sprachwendung *f.*
archangel *s.* Erzengel *m.*
archbishop *s.* Erzbischof *m.*
archduke *s.* Erzherzog *m.*
archer *s.* Bogenschütze *m.*
archery *s.* Bogenschiessen *n.*
archiepiscopal *a.* erzbischöflich.
archipelago *s.* Archipel *m.*, Inselmeer *n.*
architect *a.* Baumeister *m.*
architecture *s.* Baukunst *f.*
archives *s.pl.* Archiv *n.*
archway *s.* Bogengang *m.*
arctic *a.* nördlich, Polar...
ardent *a.*, ~ly *adv.* heiss; inbrünstig.
ardour *s.* Hitze *f.*, Eifer *m.*
arduous *a.* schwierig; steil.
area *s.* Fläche *f.*, Flächenraum *m.*; Bezirk *m.*
arena *s.* Kampfplatz *m.*, Arena *f.*
argue *v.i.* Gründe anführen; streiten; ~ *v.t.* beweisen.
argument *s.* Beweisgrund *m.*; Streitfrage *f.*; Inhalt *m.*
argumentation *s.* Beweisführung *m.*
argumentative *a.* beweisend; streitsüchtig.
aria *s.* Arie *f.*
arid *a.* dürr.
aright *adv.* gerade, richtig.
arise *v.i.st.* aufsteigen; entstehen.
aristocracy *s.* Aristokratie *f.*
aristocrat *s.* Aristokrat *m.*
aristocratic *a.*, ~ally *adv.* aristokratisch.
arithmetic *s.* Rechenkunst *f.*; *mental* ~, Kopfrechnen *n.*
arithmetical *a.*, ~ly *adv.* arithmetisch.
ark *s.* Arche *f.*
arm *s.* Arm *m.*; *to keep at arm's length,* in gehöriger Entfernung halten; ~ *v.t. & i.* bewaffnen; sich rüsten.
arm of service *s.* (*mil.*) Waffengattung *f.*
armament *s.* Kriegsmacht *f.*, Rüstung *f.*
armature *s.* Rüstung *f.*; Armatur *f.*; Anker (*elek.*) *m.*
arm-chair *s.* Lehnsessel *m.*
armistice *s.* Waffenstillstand *m.*
armorial *a.* Wappen...
armour *s.* Rüstung *f.*; Panzer *m.*
armoured *a.* Panzer...; ~troops, Panzertruppen *f.pl.*
armourer *s.* Waffenschmied *m.*
arm-pit *s.* Achselgrube *f.*
arms *s.pl.* Waffen *f.pl.*; (*her.*) Wappen *n.*; *small* ~, Handwaffen *f.*; *under* ~, gerüstet.
army *s.* Heer *m.*
army-list *s.* Rangliste der Offiziere *f.*
army post office (APO) *s.* Feldpostamt *n.*
aroma *s.* Wohlgeruch *m.*
aromatic(al) *a.* würzig.
around *adv.* ringsherum.
arouse *v.t.* wecken, aufwecken.
arrack *s.* Reisbranntwein *m.*, Arrak *m.*
arraign *v.t.* anklagen, vor Gericht stellen.

arraignment s. (law) öffentliche Anklage f., Vorführung vor Gericht f.

arrange v.t. ordnen, einrichten; anordnen (Stühle usw.); schlichten.

arrangement s. Beilegung f., Vergleich m.; Anordnung f.

arrant a., ~ly adv. schändlich.

array s. Reihe f.; Anzug m.; ~ v.t. anordnen; ankleiden.

arrear s. (Zahlungs-)Rückstand m.; in arrears, rückständig; interest on arrears, Verzugszinsen m.pl.

arrest s. Verhaftung f.; Hemmung f.; under ~, in Verhaft, in Gewahrsam; ~ v.t. hemmen; verhaften; (fig.) fesseln.

arrival s. Ankunft f.; Ankömmling m.

arrive v.i. ankommen; gelangen.

arrogance s. Anmassung f.; Dünkel m.

arrogant a., ~ly adv. anmassend.

arrogate v.t. sich anmassen.

arrow s. Pfeil m.

arse s. Arsch m.

arsenal s. Zeughaus n.

arsenic s. Arsenik n.

arson s. Brandstiftung f.

art s. Kunst f.; List f.; ~-dealer, Kunsthändler m.

arterial a. Pulsader...; ~ road, Hauptverkehrsstrasse f.

artery s. Pulsader f.

artesian a. artesisch.

artful a., ~ly adv. listig; künstlich.

arthritis Gicht f.

artichoke a. Artischocke f.

article s. Artikel m.

articulate a., ~ly adv. gegliedert; vernehmlich; ~ v.t. klar und deutlich aussprechen; zusammenfügen.

artifice s. Kunstgriff m.; List f.

artificial a., ~ly adv. künstlich.

artillery s. Artillerie f.; long-range ~, Fernkampfartillerie f.

artillery-man s. Artillerist, Kanonier m.

artisan s. Handwerker m.

artist s. Künstler m.

artistic a. künstlerisch.

artless a. kunstlos; naiv.

as c. als, da, so, sowie, sofern, wenn; wie; weil; indem; ~ ... ~ ..., (eben) so..., wie; ~ for, ~ to, was betrifft; ~ it were, sozusagen; as if, as though, als ob, wie wenn; ~ far ~, soweit als; ~ long ~, solange; ~ soon ~, sobald (als); ~ yet, noch, bisher.

asbestos s. Asbest m.

ascend v.t. & i. hinaufsteigen; ersteigen.

ascendancy s. Übergewicht n.

ascendant a. aufsteigend; überlegen.

ascension s. Aufsteigen n., Besteigung f.; ~-day s. Himmelfahrtstag m.

ascent s. Aufstieg m.

ascertain v.t. festellen, ermitteln.

ascetic a. asketisch; ~ s. Asket m.

ascribe v.t. zuschreiben.

aseptic a. keimfrei.

ash s. Esche f.; Asche f.

ash-can s. (Am.) Müllkasten m.

ashes s.pl. Asche f.

ashamed a. beschämt.

ashlar s. Quaderstein m.

ashore adv. am Ufer; to get ~, landen.

ash-tray s. Aschenbecher m.

Ash-Wednesday s. Aschermittwoch m.

aside adv. beiseite, abseits; ~ s. beiseite gesprochene Worte n.pl.

asinine a. eselhaft; Esel...

ask v.t. & i. fordern, fragen, bitten; to be had for the asking, umsonst zu bekommen.

askance adv. schief, schräg.

askew adv. seitwärts, überzwerch.

aslant adv. schräg, quer.

asleep adv. schlafend; to fall ~, einschlafen.

asparagus s. Spargel m.

aspect s. Anblick m.; Aussicht f.

asperity s. Rauheit, Roheit f.

asperse v.t. besprengen; verleumden.

aspersion s. Verleumdung f.

asphalt s. Asphalt m.

asphyxiate v.t. ersticken.

aspirant s. Bewerber m.

aspirate v.t. aspirieren.

aspiration s. Streben n.; Sehnsucht f.

aspire v.i. streben, heftig verlangen.

ass s. Esel m.

assail v.t. anfallen, angreifen.

assailant s. Angreifer m.

assassin s. Meuchelmörder m.

assassinate v.t. meuchlings ermorden.

assault s. Angriff, Sturm m.; (law) tätliche Beleidigung f.; ~ and battery, schwere tätliche Beleidigung f.; indecent ~, Sittlichkeitsvergehen n.; ~ v.t. angreifen, anfallen.

assay s.v.t. prüfen, probieren.

assemblage s. Zusammenkunft f.

assemble v.t. & i. sammeln; sich versammeln; (mech.) zusammensetzen, montieren.

assembly s. Versammlung f.; ~-plant s. Montagewerkstatt f.; ~-line Montagefliessband n.

assent s. Genehmigung f.; ~ v.i. beipflichten.

assert v.t. behaupten, verfechten.

assertion s. Behauptung f.

assess v.t. abschätzen, besteuern.

assessable a. steuerbar.

assessment s. Einschätzung f.

asset s. Aktivposten m.; (fig.) Vorteil m.; ~s pl. (com.) Activa pl.

asseveration s. Beteuerung f.

assiduity s. Emsigkeit f.

assiduous a., ~ly adv. emsig.

assign v.t. anweisen; abtreten; to ~ to a unit, (mil.) einer Einheit unterstellen.

assignment s. Anweisung f.; (mil.) Auftrag m.

assimilate v.t. angleichen; in sich aufnehmen; ~ v.i. ähnlich werden.

assimilation s. Angleichung f.

assist v.t. beistehen; ~ v.i. zugegensein, teilnehmen (an).

assistance s. Beistand m.

assistant a. behilflich; ~ s. Helfer, Gehilfe m.; ~ master, Studienrat m.

assize s. Gerichtssitzung f.; Taxe f.

associate s. Genosse m.; Teilhaber m.; Mitarbeiter m.; ~ v.t. & i. zugesellen; umgehen mit.

association s. Vereinigung, Verband m.

assort v.t. aussuchen, sortieren; ~ v.i. übereinstimmen.

assortment s. Auswahl f.; Sortiment n.

assuage v.t. besänftigen.

assume v.t. annehmen, sich anmassen; to ~ duty, Dienst antreten.

assumption s. Annahme f.; (law) ~ of authority, Dienstanmassung f.

assurance s. Vertrauen n.; Versicherung, Assekuranz f.; Dreistigkeit f.

assure v.t. versichern, sicher stellen.

assured a., ~ly adv. gewiss; dreist.

asterisk s. Sternchen n.

astern adv. achteraus.

asthma s. (med.) Asthma n.

asthmatic(al) a. engbrüstig.

astir adv. rege, wach.

astonish v.t. in Erstaunen setzen.

astonishment s. Erstaunen n.

astound v.t. in Staunen versetzen.

astraddle adv. rittlings.

astral a. gestirnt, Stern...

astray adv. to go ~, irregehen.

astride adv. sperrbeinig, rittlings.

astringent a. (med.) zusammenziehend.

astrologer s. Sterndeuter m.

astrology s. Sterndeuterei f.

astronomer s. Astronom m.

astronomical a. astronomisch.

astronomy s. Sternkunde f.

astute a. schlau.

asunder adv. auseinander, entzwei.

asylum s. Zufluchtsort m.; lunatic ~ s. Irrenhaus n.

at pr. an, zu, bei, auf, in, gegen; ~ first, zuerst; ~ last, endlich; ~ least, wenigstens; ~ length, schliesslich; ~ once, auf einmal.

atheism s. Gottesleugnung f.

athirst adv. durstig.

athlete s. Athlet m.

athletic a. athletisch; kraftvoll.

athletics s.pl. Leichtathletik f.

athwart pr. querüber.

atlas s. Atlas m.

atmosphere s. Atmosphäre f.

atmospheric(al) a. atmosphärisch, Luft ...; ~ pressure, Luftdruck m.

atmospherics s.pl. (radio) Luftstörungen f.pl.

atom s. Atom n.

atomic a. Atom....

atone v.i. sühnen; büssen.

atonement s. Sühne f.; Versöhnung f.

atrocious a., ~ly adv. abscheulich.

atrocity s. Abscheulichkeit, Grässlichkeit f.; Greueltat f.

atrophy s. Abzehrung, Verkümmerung f.

attach v.t. anhängen, anheften; belegen; fesseln; verhaften; ~ v.i. verknüpft sein mit.

attaché s. Attaché m.; ~-case s. kleiner Handkoffer.

attached a. beiliegend.

attachment s. Anhänglichkeit, Ergebenheit f.; Anhängsel n.

attack v.t. angreifen; ~ s. Angriff m.; Anfall m.

attain v.t. & i. erreichen, erlangen.

attainable a. erreichbar.

attaint v.t. beflecken, verunehren.

attempt s.Versuch m.; Angriff m.; Attentat n.; ~ v.t. versuchen; angreifen.

attend v.t. begleiten; aufmerken; aufwarten, pflegen; ~ v.i. achthaben; besorgen; zugegen sein; besuchen; to ~ to, bearbeiten (Angelegenheit).

attendance s. Bedienung f.; Gefolge n.

attendant a. begleitend; ~ s. Diener m.; Aufwärter m.

attention s. Aufmerksamkeit f.; to call (draw) a person's ~ to a thing, einen auf etwas aufmerksam machen; attention Mr. Smith, zu Händen Herrn Smith; attention!, stillgestanden! to stand to ~, stramm stehen.

attentive a., ~ly adv. aufmerksam.

attenuate v.t. verdünnen, vermindern.

attest v.t. bezeugen; beglaubigen.

attic a. attisch; ~ s. Dachstube f.

attire s. Anzug, Putz m.; ~v.t. ankleiden, putzen.

attitude s. Stellung f., Haltung f.

attorney s. Bevollmächtigte, Anwalt m.; power of ~, schriftliche Vollmacht f.; ~-general s. Oberstaatsanwalt m.

attract v.t. anziehen, reizen.

attraction s. Anziehung f.; Reiz m.

attractive a., ~ly adv. anziehend.

attribute v.t. beilegen, beimessen; ~ s. Abzeichen n.; Merkmal n.

attributive a. zueignend.

attrition s. Zermürbung f.; Zerknirschung f.

auburn a. nussbraun, kastanienbraun.

auction s. Versteigerung f.; to sell by ~, versteigern; ~ v.t. versteigern.

auctioneer s. Auktionator m.

audacious a., ~ly adv. kühn.

audacity s. Kühnheit f.

audible a., ~bly adv. hörbar.

audience *s.* Audienz *f.*; Gehör, *n.*; Zuhörer *m.pl.*

audit, Prüfung von Rechnungen *f.*; ~ *v.t.* Rechnungen prüfen.

auditor *s.* Bücherrevisor *m.*

auditorium *s.* Zuhörer *m.pl.*; Zuhörerraum *m.*

aught *pn.* irgend etwas.

augment *v.t.* vermehren.

augmentation *s.* Vermehrung.

augury *s.* Wahrsagung *f.*; Vorzeichen *n.*

august *a.* erhaben, hehr.

August *s.* August (Monat) *m.*

aunt *s.* Tante *f.*

aura *s.* Fluidum *n.*

auricula *s.* Aurikel *f.*

auricular *a.*, ~ly *adv.* Ohren...; ~ confession *s.* Ohrenbeichte *f.*

aurora *s.* Morgenröte *f.*; ~ borealis, Nordlicht *n.*

auspices *s.* Vorbedeutung *f.*; (*fig.*) Schutz *m.*

auspicious *a.*, ~ly *adv.* günstig.

austere *a.*, ~ly *adv.* herb, streng.

austerity *s.* Strenge *f.*

authentic(al) *a.*, ~ly *adv.* glaubwürdig, echt.

authenticate *v.t.* beurkunden.

authenticity *s.* Echtheit *f.*

author *s.* Verfasser *m.*, Urheber *m.*; Schriftsteller *m.*

authoress *s.* Verfasserin *f.*

authoritative *a.*, ~ly *adv.* gebieterisch; bevollmächtigt; massgebend.

authority *s.* Ansehen *n.*; Glaubwürdigkeit *f.*; Gewährsmann *m.*, Autorität *f.*; Befugnis, Vollmacht *f.*; authorities *pl.* Behörden *f.pl.*

authorization *s.* Bevollmächtigung *f.*

authorize *v.t.* bevollmächtigen.

authorship *s.* Autorschaft *f.*

autobiography *s.* Selbstbiographie *f.*

autocracy *s.* Selbstherrschaft *f.*

autocrat *s.* Selbstherrscher *m.*

autocratic(al) *a.* selbstherrlich.

autograph *s.* eigene Handschrift.

autographic *a.* eigenhändig.

automatic *a.* automatisch, selbsttätig; ~ telephone, Selbstanschlusstelephon *n.*

automaton *s.* Automat *m.*

automobile *s.* Automobil *n.*

autonomous *a.* autonom.

autonomy *s.* Selbstregierung, Autonomie *f.*

autopsy *s.* Leichenschau *f.*

autumn *s.* Herbst *m.*

autumnal *a.* herbstlich.

auxiliaries *s.pl.* Hilfstruppen *f.pl.*

auxiliary *a.* Hilfs...

avail *s.* Vorteil *m.*; *of no* ~, vergeblich; ~ *v.t. & i.* helfen, nützen; *to* ~ *oneself of a thing*, sich etwas zunutze machen.

available *a.* gültig; verfügbar

avalanche *s.* Lawine *f.*

avarice *s.* Geiz *m.*, Habsucht *f.*

avaricious *a.*, ~ly *adv.* geizig, habsüchtig.

avenge *v.t.* rächen.

avenue *s.* Allee *f.*; Zugang *m.*

aver *v.t.* behaupten.

average *s.* Durchschnitt *m.*; Havarie *f.*; *on an* ~, durchschnittlich; ~ *v.t. & i.* durchschnittlich fertig bringen, liefern, betragen.

averse *a.*, ~ly *adv.* abgeneigt.

aversion *s.* Widerwille *m.*

avert *v.t.* abwenden, wegwenden.

aviary *s.* Vogelhaus *n.*

aviation *s.* Fliegen *n.*, Flugwesen *n.*

aviator *s.* Flieger *m.*

avitaminosis *s.* (*med.*) Avitaminose *f.*

avocation *s.* Berufsgeschäft *n.*

avoid *v.t.* vermeiden.

avoidable *a.* vermeidlich.

avoidance *s.* Vermeidung *f.*

avoir-du-pois *s.* Handelsgewicht *n.* (~ *pound*=16 Unzen).

avouch *v.t.* behaupten, bekräftigen.

avow *v.t.* anerkennen, eingestehen.

avowal *s.* Geständnis *n.*

avowedly *adv.* eingestandenermassen.

await *v.t.* erwarten.

awake *v.t.st.* aufwecken; ~ *v.i.st.* aufwachen; ~ *a.* wach.

awaken *v.t.* erwecken.

award *s.* Urteil *n.*, Spruch *m.*; Prämie *f.* ~ *v.t.* zuerkennen; gewähren.

aware *a.* gewahr, bewusst; *I am* ~ *of it*, ich weiss es.

away *adv.* weg, fort; abwesend.

awe *s.* Ehrfurcht *f.*; Scheu *f.*; ~ *v.t.* in Furcht halten; Ehrfurcht einflössen.

awe-struck *a.* von Ehrfurcht ergriffen.

awful *a.* schauerlich; (*fam.*) schrecklich.

awhile *adv.* eine Zeitlang.

awkward *a.*, ~ly *adv.* linkisch; ungelegen.

awl *s.* Ahle, Pfriem *m.*

awning *s.* Markise *f.*; Zeltdecke *f.*

awry *adv.* schief; verkehrt.

axe *s.* Axt *f.*; Beil *n.*

axiom *s.* Axiom *n.*, Grundsatz *m.*

axiomatic(al) *a.* unumstösslich.

axis *s.* (*math.*) Achse *f.*

axle *s.* Achse *f.*; ~-tree *s.* Radachse *f.*

ay *adv.* ja, gewiss.

azalea *s.* (*bot.*) Azalee *f.*

azure *a.* himmelblau.

B

B.A.=Bachelor of Arts.

b flat (*mus.*) H=Moll; *b sharp*, H=dur.

babble *v.i.* schwatzen; ~ *s.* Geschwätz *n.*

baboon *s.* Pavian *m.*

baby *s.* kleines Kind *n.*

baby-carriage *s.* Kinderwagen *m.*

babyhood *s.* erste Kindheit *f.*

baby-linen *s.* Kinderwäsche *f.*

bachelor *s.* Junggeselle *m.*; ~ *of Arts*, Bakkalaureus Artium (erster akademischer Grad) *m.*

bachelorhood *s.* Junggesellentum *n.*

back *s.* Rücken *m.*; Rückseite *f.*; Rücksitz (Wagen) *m.*; (Fussball) Verteidiger *m.*; ~ *of*, (*Am.*) hinter; ~ *v.t.* unterstützen; *to ~ a horse*, auf ein Rennpferd wetten; *gold-backing*, Golddeckung *f.*; *dollar-backed instruments*, Zahlungsmittel mit Dollardeckung; ~ *adv.* hinterwärts, zurück.

backbencher *s.* Parlamentarier ohne Sitz in der Regierung oder Oppositionsführung.

backbite *v.t.st.* verleumden.

backbone *s.* Rückgrat *n.*

back-door *s.* Hintertür *f.*

backer *s.* Unterstützer *m.*

backgammon *s.* Tricktrack *n.*

background *s.* Hintergrund *m.*

backlash *s.* (*mech.*) Flankenspiel *n.*; totes Spiel *n.*

back-number *s.* frühere Nummer (*f.*) einer Zeitschrift oder Zeitung.

backside *s.* Rückseite *f.*; Hintere *m.*

backslide *v.i.* rückfällig werden.

backstairs *s.pl.* Hintertreppe *f.*

backstitch *s.* Steppstich *m.*

backstroke *s.* Rückenschwimmen *n.*

backward *adv.* zurück, rücklings; ~ *a.*, ~ly *adv.* langsam; rückständig; spät.

backwater *s.* Stauwasser *n.*; totes Wasser *n.*

backwoodsman *s.* Hinterwäldler *m.*

bacon *s.* Speck *m.*

bacterium *s.* Bakterie *f.*

bacteriological *a.* Bakterien...

bad *a.*, ~ly *adv.* schlecht; böse; schlimm; *to be badly off*, übel daran sein; ~ *debt*, faule Schuld *f.*

badge *s.* Abzeichen, Ehrenzeichen *n.*

badger *s.* Dachs *m.*; ~ *v.t.* hetzen.

baffle *v.t.* vereiteln; verwirren; vor ein Rätsel stellen.

bag *s.* Sack, Beutel *m.*; Handtasche *f.*; ~ *v.t.* einsacken; ~ *v.i.* bauschen.

bagatelle *s.* Kleinigkeit, Lappalie *f.*

baggage *s.* Gepäck *n.*

bagpipe *s.* Dudelsack *m.*

bail *s.* Bürgschaft *f.*; Bürge *m.*; *to allow ~*, Bürgschaft zulassen; *to give ~*, einen Bürgen stellen; *to release on ~*, gegen Bürgschaft freilassen; ~ *v.t.* sich verbürgen für; freibürgen.

bailable *a.* bürgschaftsfähig.

bailiff *s.* Gerichtsdiener *m.*

bail out (bale out) *v.i.* (*avi.*) mit Fallschirm abspringen.

bairn *s.* Kind *n.*

bait *s.* Köder *m.*; ~ *v.t. & i.* ködern; hetzen.

baiting *s.* Hetze *f.*

bake *v.t. & i.* backen (im Ofen).

baker *s.* Bäcker *m.*

bakery *s.* Bäckerei *f.*

baking powder *s.* Backpulver *n.*

balance *s.* Wage *f.*; Gleichgewicht *n.*; Bilanz *f.*; Bankguthaben *n.*; (*Am.*) Rest *m.*; Saldo *m.*; (*fig.*) Unschlüssigkeit *f.*; Unruhe (in der Uhr) *f.*; ~ *of power s.* politische Gleichgewicht der Mächte; ~ *of trade s.* Handelsbilanz *f.*; ~-sheet *s.* Bilanz *f.*; ~ *v.t.* wägen, wägen; balanzieren; erwägen; ~ *v.i.* sich ausgleichen, sich balanzieren.

balcony *s.* Balkon, Altan *m.*

bald *a.*, ~ly *adv.* kahl.

balderdash *s.* dummes Zeug *n.*

bale *s.* Ballen *m.*

baleful *a.*, ~ly *adv.* unheilvoll.

balk *s.* Balken *m.*; (*fig.*) Querstrich *m.*; ~ *v.t.* vereiteln; ~ *v.i.* scheuen (vor).

ball *s.* Ball *m.*; Kugel *f.*; Tanzfest *n.*; ~-joint, ~ and socket joint *s.* Kugelgelenk *n.*; ~ *of wool s.* Wollknäuel *m.*; ~ *v.i.* sich ballen.

ballad *s.* Ballade *f.*, Volkslied *n.*

ballast *s.* Ballast *m.*

ball-bearing *s.* Kugellager *n.*

ballet *s.* Ballett *n.*

balloon *s.* Luftballon *m.*

ballot *s.* Wahlkugel *f.*; Wahl durch Stimmzettel; ~ *v.t. & i.* ballotieren.

ballot-box *s.* Wahlurne *f.*

ballot-paper *s.* Stimmzettel *m.*

ballroom *s.* Ballsaal *m.*

balm *s.* Balsam *m.*; Salböl *n.*; ~ *v.t.* balsamieren.

balsam *s.* Balsam *m.*; Balsamine *f.*

balsamic *a.* balsamisch.

balustrade *s.* Geländer *n.*

bamboo *s.* Bambus *m.*

bamboozle *v.t.* hintergehen.

ban *s.* öffentliche Ächtung *f.*; Bann *m.*; amtliches Verbot *n.*; ~ *v.t.* in den Bann tun, verbieten.

banality *s.* Trivialität *f.*

banana *s.* Banane *f.*

band *s.* Band *n.*; Binde *f.*; Bande *f.*; Musikkapelle *f.*; ~ *v.t.* binden, sich verbinden.

bandage *s.* Verband *m.*

bandit *s.* Bandit *m.*

bands *s.pl.* Bäffchen *n.pl.*

bandy *v.t.* (den Ball) schlagen; wechseln; *to ~ about*, (Gerücht) verbreiten; ~ *v.i.* wettstreiten.

bandy-legs *s.pl.* O-Beine *n.pl.*; ~-legged *a.* o-beinig.

bane *s.* Gift *n.*, Verderben *n.*

baneful *a.* giftig; verderblich.

bang *s.* Schlag, Stoss *m.*, Knall *m.*; *i.* bums!; *to go ~*, explodieren, zuschlagen; ~ *v.t.* knallen, schlagen; zuschlagen.

banish v.t. verbannen.
banishment s. Verbannung f.
banisters pl. Geländer n.
banjo. s. Banjo n.
bank s. Ufer n.; Damm m.; Bank f.;
~-bill s. Bankwechsel, (Am.) Banknote; ~ of issue, Zettelbank, Notenbank; ~ v.t. eindämmen.
banker s. Bankier m.
bank holiday s. bürgerlicher Feiertag m.
bank-note s. Banknote f.
bank-rate s. Bankdiskont m.
bankrupt a. bankrott; to go ~, become ~, Konkurs machen; ~ s. Bankrottierer m.; ~'s estate s. Konkursmasse f.; ~ v.t. (einen) bankrott machen.
bankruptcy s. Bankrott m.; fraudulent ~, betrügerischer Bankrott.
banns s.pl. Aufgebot (n.) (vor der Heirat).
banquet s. Festmahl n.
bantam s. Zwerghuhn n.; ~-weight s. Bantamgewicht (Boxen).
banter v.t. zum besten haben; ~ s. Scherz, Spott m.
baptism s. Taufe f.; certificate of ~, Taufschein m.
baptismal a., ~ font, Taufstein m.
baptize v.t. taufen.
bar s. Barre, Stange f.; Riegel, Balken, Schlagbaum m.; Schranken f.pl.; Schenktisch m.; Gericht n.; Anwaltschaft f.; Taktstrich m.; Takt (eines Musikstücks) m.; to practise at the ~, als Anwalt tätig sein; to call to the ~, zum Anwalt berufen; ~ v.t. verriegeln; hindern, schliessen.
barb s. Widerhaken m.
barbarian a. barbarisch; ~ s. Barbar m.
barbaric a. barbarisch.
barbarism s. sprachwidrige Ausdruck m., Barbarei f.
barbarity s. Grausamkeit f.
barbarous a., ~ly adv. roh, grausam.
barbed a. ~ wire s. Stacheldraht m.
barber s. Barbier m.
bard s. Barde, Dichter m.
bare a., ~ly adv. bloss; dürftig; kaum; ~ v.t. entblössen.
barefaced a. (fig.) unverschämt.
barefooted a. barfüssig.
bareheaded a. barhäuptig.
bargain s. Handel m.; Kauf m.; Gelegenheitskauf m.; into the ~, obendrein.
bargain v.t. & i. handeln, feilschen.
barge s. Barke f.; Boot n.
bargeman s. Bootsmann m.
bark s. Baumrinde f.; Borke f.; (Schiff) Barke f.; ~ v.t. abrinden; ~ v.i. bellen; ~ s. Bellen n.
barley s. Gerste f.
barley-corn s. Gerstenkorn n.
barmaid s. Schenkmädchen n.
barman s. (Büfett-)Kellner m.

barmy a. hefig; blödsinnig, verdreht.
barn s. Scheune f.
barn-floor s. Dreschtenne f.
barnacle s. Nasenknebel (des Pferdes) m.; Bernikelgans f.; ~s pl. Brille f.
barometer s. Barometer n.
baron s. Freiherr, Baron m.
baroness s. Baronin f.
baronet s. Baronet m.
baronetcy s. Baronetswürde f.
baronial a. freiherrlich.
barony s. Freiherrschaft f.
baroque s. (in der Kunst) Barock n.
barouche s. viersitzige Wagen m.
barrack s. Hütte f.; ~s pl. Kaserne f.
barrage s. Damm m., Wehr n.; (mil.) Sperrfeuer n.
barrel s. Fass n.; Flintenlauf m.
barrel-organ s. Drehorgel f.
barren a., ~ly adv. unfruchtbar.
barricade s. Barrikade f.; ~ v.t. verrammeln; hindern.
barrier s. Schlagbaum m.; Barriere f.; Grenze f.; (fig.) Hindernis n.; ~s s.pl. Schranken f.pl.
barrister s. (vor Gericht auftretender) Rechtsanwalt m.
barring, ausgenommen.
bar-room s. Schenkstube f.
barrow s. Trage f.; Schiebkarren m.
barter v.t. & i. tauschen; ~ s. Tauschhandel m.
barytone s. Bariton m.
basalt s. Basalt m.
base a., ~ly adv. niedrig; verächtlich; (von Metallen) unedel; ~ s. Grundfläche f.; Grundlinie (des Dreiecks), f.; Grund m.; Fussgestell n.; (mil.) Stützpunkt m.; (mus.) Bass m.; (chem.) Basis f.
baseball s. Grundballspiel n.
baseless a. grundlos.
basement s. Kellergeschoss n.
bashful a., ~ly adv. schamhaft.
basic a. basisch; ~ salary s. Grundgehalt n.
basilica s. Basilika f.
basin s. Becken n.; Schale f.
basis s. Grundlage f.
bask v.t. & i. sonnen; sich sonnen.
basket s. Korb m.
basque s. Baske m.; ~ a. baskisch.
bas-relief s. halberhabene Relief n.
bass s. Bass m.; ~ s. Bast m., Matte f.
bassoon s. Fagott n.
bast s. Bast m.
bastard s. Bastard m.; ~ a., ~ly adv. unehelich, unecht.
bastardize v.t. im Ehebruche zeugen.
bastardy s. uneheliche Geburt f.
bastion s. Bollwerk n.
bat s. Fledermaus f.; Knüttel m.; Schlagholz n., Schläger, (im Kricket) m.

batch *s.* Partie, Sendung *f.*

bate *v.t.* (Preis) ablassen, verringern; (Atem) verhalten.

bath *s.* Bad *n.*; Badewanne *f.*; ~-cap *s.* Badehaube *f.*; ~-room *s.* Badezimmer *n.*; ~-sheet *s.* Badetuch *n.*; ~-tub (*Am.*) Badewanne *f.*

bath-chair *s.* Rollstuhl *m.*

bathe *v.t.* baden; ~ *v.i.* ein Bad nehmen; ~ *s.* Bad (Handlung) *n.*

bathing-suit *s.* Badeanzug *m.*

batiste *s.* Batist *m.*

baton *s.* Taktstock *m.*, Stab *m.*

batsman *s.* Schläger *m.*

battalion *s.* Bataillon *n.*

batten *v.t.* mästen; düngen; ~ *v.i.* sich mästen.

batter *v.t.* schlagen, zerschlagen.

battery *s.* Angriff *m.*; Batterie *f.*

battle *s.* Schlacht *f.*; Schlägerei *f.*; ~ *v.i.* ein Treffen liefern.

battle-cruiser *s.* (*nav.*) Schlachtkreuzer *m.*

battledore *s.* Rakett *n.*, Brotschieber *m.*

battlefield *s.* Schlachtfeld *n.*

battlement *s.* Zinne *f.*

battleship *s.* (*nav.*) Schlachtschiff *n.*

battue *s.* Treibjagd *f.*

bauble *s.* Spielzeug *n.*; Tand *m.*

baulk = balk.

bauxite *s.* Bauxit *m.*

bawd *m.* Kupplerin *f.*

bawl *v.t. & i.* laut schreien; ausrufen.

bay *s.* rotbraun; ~ horse *s.* Braune *m.*; ~ *s.* Bucht *f.*; Fach *m.*; Nische, Abteilung *f.*, Erker *m.*; Lorbeer *m.*; *to stand at* ~, gestellt sein, in Bedrängnis; ~ *v.i.* bellen; blöken; ~ *v.t.* jagen.

bayonet *s.* Bajonett *n.*; ~ *v.t.* mit dem Bajonett erstechen.

bay-window *s.* Erkerfenster *n.*

bazaar *s.* Basar *m.*

be *v.i.ir.* sein; (*pass.*) werden; *to* ~ *off*, sich fortmachen; *to* ~ *in*, zuhause sein.

beach *s.* Gestade *n.*; ~ *v.t.* auf den Strand setzen.

beacon *s.* Leuchtfeuer *n.*; Bake *f.*

bead *s.* Kügelchen *n.*; Perle *f.*; ~s *pl.* Rosenkranz *m.*

beadle *s.* Pedell *m.*; Büttel *m.*

beak *s.* Schnabel *m.*

beam *s.* Balken *m.*; Strahl *m.*; Deichsel *f.*; ~ *v.i.* strahlen.

beam-ends *s.pl. to be on one's* ~, (finanziell) ruiniert sein.

bean *s.* Bohne *f.*; *French* ~, grüne Bohne *f.*; *broad* ~, Saubohne *f.*

bear *s.* Bär *m.*; Baissier *m.*; ~ *v.t. & i.st.* tragen, bringen; dulden; gebären; *to* ~ *company*, Gesellschaft leisten; *to* ~ *in mind*, nicht vergessen; *to* ~ *on*, Bezug haben, wirken auf; *to* ~ *out*, bestätigen; *to* ~ *witness*, Zeugnis ablegen.

beard *s.* Bart *m.*; Widerhaken *m.*

bearer *s.* Träger *m.*; Wechselinhaber *m.*

bearer-share *s.* Inhaberaktie *f.*

bearing *s.* Tragweite *f.*; Lage, Haltung *f.*; Stütze, Höhe *f.*; Peilung *f.*; *to take the* ~s, sich orientieren.

beast *s.* Vieh, Tier *n.*

beastly *a.* viehisch; (*fig.*) scheusslich, niederträchtig.

beat *v.t. & i.st.* schlagen; zerstossen; besiegen; klopfen; *to* ~ *off*, zurückschlagen; *to* ~ *time*, den Takt schlagen; *to* ~ *up*, Eier schlagen; verprügeln; ~ *s.* Schlag *m.*; Revier *n.*, Runde *f.*

beatification *s.* Seligsprechung *f.*

beatify *v.t.* seligmachen.

beatitude *s.* Seligkeit *f.*

beau *s.* Stutzer *m.*

beauteous *a.*, ~ly *adv.* schön.

beautiful *a.*, ~ly *adv.* schön.

beautify *v.t.* verschönern.

beauty *s.* Schönheit *f.*

beauty-parlour *s.* Schönheitssalon *m.*

beaver *s.* Biber *m.*; Kastorhut *m.*

becalm *v.t.* besänftigen.

because *c.* weil; ~ *of*, wegen.

beck *s.* Wink *m.*; kleine Bach *m.*; *at a person's* ~ *and call*, auf jemandes Wink.

beck, beckon *v.t. & i.* winken; locken.

becloud *v.t.* umwölken.

become *v.i. & t.st.* werden; sich schicken; anstehen.

becoming *a.*, ~ly *adv.* anständig.

bed *s.* Bett *n.*; Beet *n.*; Schicht *f.*; (*mech.*) Bett *n.*, Unterbau *m.*; ~ *v.t.* betten.

bedaub *v.t.* besudeln.

bedbug *s.* (*Am.*) Wanze *f.*

bed-clothes *s.* Bettzeug *n.*

bedding *s.* Bettzeug *n.*

bedfellow *s.* Schlafkamerad *m.*

bedizen *v.t.* bunt kleiden.

bed-jacket *s.* Bettjacke *f.*

bedlam *s.* Tollhaus *n.*

bedlamite *s.* Tollhäusler *m.*

bed-ridden *a.* bettlägerig.

bedroom *s.* Schlafzimmer *n.*

bed-sitting room *s.* Wohnschlafzimmer *n.*

bed-slip *s.* Bettbezug *m.*

bedspread *s.* Bettbelag *m.*

bedstead *s.* Bettstelle *f.*

bee *s.* Biene *f.*

beech *s.* Buche *f.*

beechen *a.* buchen.

beech-nut *s.* Buchecker *f.*

beef *s.* Rindfleisch *n.*; Rind *n.*; ~-cattle, Mastvieh *n.*

beef-eater *s.* Wächter im Tower *m.*

beef-steak *s.* Beefsteak *n.*

bee-hive *s.* Bienenstock *m.*

beekeeper *s.* Imker *m.*

beer, Bier *n.*; *small* ~, Dünnbier *n.*

beeswax *s.* Bienenwachs *n.*

beet *s.* (rote) Rübe *f.*

beetle *s.* Käfer *m.*

beetle-brows *s.pl.* überhängende Augenbrauen *f.pl.*
beet: ~**root** *s.* Runkelrübe *f.*; ~ **sugar**, Rübenzucker *m.*
befall *v.t.st.* zustossen, widerfahren; ~ *v.i.* sich ereignen.
befit *v.t.* sich schicken.
before *pr.* vor; ~ *c.* bevor, ehe; ~ *adv.* vorn; früher; schon einmal.
beforehand *adv.* voraus, im voraus.
befoul *v.t.* besudeln.
befriend *v.t.* unterstützen.
beg *v.t.* bitten, betteln; *to* ~ *the question*, die Streitfrage als bewiesen voraussetzen; *I* ~ *your pardon?*, wie beliebt?; ~ *v.i.* betteln gehen; sich erlauben.
beget *v.t.st.* zeugen, erzeugen.
beggar *s.* Bettler *m.*; Lump *m.*; ~ *v.t.* zum Bettler machen.
beggarly *a.* bettelhaft.
beggary *s.* Bettelei *f.*; *to reduce to* ~, an den Bettelstab bringen.
begin *v.t. & i.st.* anfangen.
beginner *s.* Anfänger *m.*
beginning *s.* Anfang *m.*; ~**s** *pl.* Anfangsgründe *m.pl.*
begone *i.* fort! packe dich!
begonia *s.* Begonie *f.*, Schiefblatt *s.*
begrime *v.t.* beschmutzen.
begrudge *v.t.* missgönnen.
beguile *v.t.* betrügen, hintergehen.
behalf *s. on* ~, im Namen, behufs, wegen; *in* ~ *of*, im Interesse von, für.
behave *v.i.* sich betragen.
behaviour *s.* Betragen *n.*
behead *v.t.* enthaupten.
behest *s.* Befehl *m.*
behind *pr. & adv.* hinter, zurück; ~ *s.* Hintern *m.*
behindhand *a.* im Rückstande.
behold *v.t.st.* erblicken, betrachten.
beholden *a.* verpflichtet.
behoof *s.* Vorteil, Nutzen *m.*
behove *v.t.* sich ziemen.
being *s.* Dasein *n.*; Wesen, Geschöpf *n.*
belated *a.* verspätet.
belch *v.i. & t.* rülpsen; ~ *s.* Rülps *m.*
beldam *s.* alte Hexe *f.*
beleaguer *v.t.* belagern.
belfry *s.* Glockenturm *m.*
belie *v.t.* Lügen strafen; belügen.
belief *s.* Glaube *m.*
believe *v.t. & i.* glauben, vertrauen; *to* ~ *in*, glauben an.
believer *s.* Gläubige *m.*
belittle *v.t.* (boshaft) verkleinern.
bell *s.* Glocke *f.*; Klingel *f.*; *to ring the* ~, klingeln; *to answer the* ~, auf vorheriges Klingeln öffnen.
bell-circuit *s.* (*elek.*) Klingelleitung *f.*
bell-founder *s.* Glockengiesser *m.*
bell-foundry *s.* Glockengiesserei *f.*
belligerent *a.* kriegführend.

bell-metal *s.* Glockenspeise *f.*
bellow *v.i.* brüllen.
bellows *s.pl.* Blasebalg *m.*
bell-rope *s.* Klingelzug *m.*
belly *s.* Bauch *m.*; ~ *v.t.* schwellen.
belong *v.i.* gehören; betreffen.
belongings *s.pl.* Habe *f.*
beloved *a.* geliebt.
below *pr.* unter; ~ *adv.* unten.
belt *s.* Gürtel *m.*; Gehenk *n.*; Treibriemen *m.*; ~ *v.t.* umgürten.
bemoan *v.t.* beklagen, beweinen.
bench *s.* Bank *f.*; Gerichtsbank *f.*; Arbeitsbank *f.*; Richter *m.pl.*
bend *v.t.ir* biegen; ~ *v.i.* sich biegen; ~ *s.* Biegung *f.*
beneath *pr.* unter; ~ *adv.* unten.
benediction *s.* Segen *m.*
benefactor *s.* Wohltäter *m.*
benefactress *s.* Wohltäterin *f.*
benefice *s.* Pfründe *f.*
beneficence *s.* Wohltätigkeit *f.*
beneficent *a.* wohltätig.
beneficial *a.*, ~**ly** *adv.* heilsam, dienlich.
beneficiary *s.* Pfründner *f.*; Tutzniesser.
benefit *s.* Wohltat *f.*; Vorteil *m.*; Benefizvorstellung *f.*; Vorrecht *m.*; (Versicherung) Unterstützung, Geld; ~ *v.t. & i.* Vorteil bringen; heilsam sein; *to* ~ *by*, Nutzen ziehen von.
benevolence *s.* Wohlwollen *n.*; Gunst *f.*
benevolent *a.*, ~**ly** *adv.* wohlwollend.
benevolent fund *s.* Unterstützungskasse *f.*
benighted, in Unwissenheit versunken.
benign *a.*, ~**ly** *adv.* gütig, mild; (*med.*) gutartig.
benignant *a.* gütig, wohltätig.
benignity *s.* Güte, Milde *f.*
bent *a.* gebogen; ~ *on*, versessen auf; ~ *s.* Biegung *f.*; Neigung *f.*
benumb *v.t.* betäuben, erstarren.
benzene (-ine) *s.* Benzin *n.*
benzole (-line) *s.* Benzol *n.*
bequeath *v.t.* vermachen.
bequest *s.* Vermächtnis *n.*
bereave *v.t.st. & r.* berauben.
bereavement *s.* Verlust *m.*
beret *s.* Baskenmütze *f.*
bergamot *s.* Bergamotte *f.* (Birne).
berry *s.* Beere *f.*; (Kaffee)bohne *f.*
berth *s.* Ankerplatz *m.*; (*nav.*) Koje *f.*, Schiffsbett *n.*, Kajütenbett *n.*; Posten *m.*
beseech *v.t.ir.* bitten, anflehen.
beseechingly *adv.* flehentlich.
beseem *v.t.* sich schicken.
beset *v.t.st.* umgeben.
besetting sin Gewohnheitssünde *f.*
beside *pr.* neben; ~ *oneself*, ausser sich ~ *the mark*, weit vom Ziel.
besides *pr.* ausser; ~ *adv.* ausserdem
besiege *v.t.* belagern.
besmear *v.t.* beschmieren.

besmirch *v.t.* besudeln.

besotted *a.* versoffen, verdummt.

bespatter *v.t.* bespritzen; verleumden.

bespeak *v.t.st.* bestellen.

bespoke tailor *s.* Masschneider *m.*

besprinkle *v.t.* besprengen.

best *a. & adv.* best; aufs beste; am besten; ~ *s.* Beste *n.*; *to make the* ~ *of*, mit etwas tun was man kann; *to do one's* ~, tun was man kann; *as* ~ *he could*, so gut er konnte; *to the* ~ *of one's abilities*, nach besten Kräften.

bestial *a.*, **~ly** *adv.* viehisch.

bestiality *s.* viehische Wesen *n.*

bestir *v.refl.* sich rühren, sich regen.

best-man *s.* Brautführer *m.*

bestow *v.t.* verleihen.

bestowal *s.* Verleihung *f.*

bestrew *v.t.st.* bestreuen.

bestride *v.t.* reiten auf; beschreiten.

bestseller *s.* Reisser (Buch) *m.*

bet *s.* Wette *f.*; ~ *v.t.* wetten um.

betake *v.refl.st.* sich wohin begeben.

bethink *v.refl.st.* sich besinnen auf.

betimes *adv.* bei Zeiten, bald; früh.

betray *v.t.* verraten; verführen.

betrayal *s.* Verrat *m.*

betroth *v.t.* verloben.

betrothal *s.* Verlobung *f.*

better *a. & adv.* besser; lieber; mehr; *so much the* ~, desto besser; *you had* ~ *go*, Sie tun wohl am besten, hinzugehen; *to think* ~ *of it*, sich eines Bessern besinnen; ~ *s.* Vorteil; *to get the* ~ *of a person*, einem den Vorteil abgewinnen; ~s *pl.* Vorgesetzte *m.pl.*; ~ *v.t. & i.* verbessern; besser werden.

betterment *s.* Verbesserung *f.*

between, betwixt *pr.* zwischen; *they did it* ~ *them*, sie taten es zusammen; ~ *you and me*, unter uns.

bevel *a.* schräg, schief; ~ *s.* Schräge *f.*, schräger Anschnitt *m.*, *(mech.)* Fase *f.*; **~-gear** *s.* *(mech.)* Kegelrad *n.*; ~ *v.t.* abschrägen, facettieren.

beverage *s.* Getränk *n.*

bevy *s.* Schar *f.*; Gesellschaft *f.*

bewail *v.t.* betrauern.

beware *v.i.* sich hüten.

bewilder *v.t.* verwirren, bestürzt machen.

bewitch *v.t.* behexen, bezaubern.

beyond *pr.* über, jenseits; ~ *adv.* darüber hinaus.

bias *s.* Neigung *m.*; Vorurteil *n.*; ~ *v.t.* auf eine Seite neigen.

bib *s.* (Geifer)lätzchen *n.*

Bible *s.* Bibel *f.*

biblical *a.* biblisch.

bibliographer *s.* Bücherkenner *m.*

bibliophile *s.* Bücherfreund *m.*

bibulous *a.* aufsaugend; trunkliebend.

bicarbonate, ~ *of soda*, doppeltkohlensaures Natron *n.*

bicker *v.i.* streiten, zanken; glitzern.

bickerings *s.pl.* Gezänk *n.*

bicycle *s.* Zweirad *n.*

bid *v.t.ir.* befehlen; einladen; wünschen, bieten; (Kartenspiel) ansagen; *to* ~ *fair*, Aussicht geben auf; ~ *s.* (Auktions-) Gebot; *no* ~, ich passe (Kartenspiel).

bidder *s.* Bieter *m.*; **highest** ~ *s.* Meistbietende *m.*

bidding *s.* Befehl *m.*; *(com.)* Gebot *n.*

bide *v.t.* ertragen; ~ *v.i.* abwarten.

biennial *a.* zweijährig.

bier *s.* Totenbahre *f.*

bifurcated *a.* gabelförmig gespalten.

big *a.*, **~ly** *adv.* gross, stark, dick; *to talk* ~, prahlen.

bigamist *s.* Bigamist *m.*

bigamy *s.* Doppelehe *f.*

bight *s.* Bai, Bucht *f.*

bigot *s.* blinder Anhänger; Frömmler *m.*

bigoted *a.* blind eingenommen für.

bigotry *s.* Frömmelei *f.*

big-wig *s.* grosse Tier *(fig.)* *n.*

bilateral *a.* zweiseitig.

bilberry *s.* Heidelbeere *f.*

bile *s.* Galle *f.*

bilingual *a.* zweisprachig.

bilious *a.* gallig.

bilk *v.t.* beschwindeln, betrügen.

bill *s.* Schnabel *m.*; Hippe *f.*; Rechnung *f.*; Wechsel *m.*; Zettel *n.*; Gesetzentwurf *m.*; ~ *of exchange*, Wechsel *m.*; ~ *of lading*, Konnossement *n.*, Frachtbrief *m.*

bill-broker *s.* Wechselmakler *m.*

billet *s.* Quartierzettel *n.*; Quartier *n.*; Scheit *n.*; ~ *v.t.* einquartieren.

bill-holder *s.* Wechselinhaber *m.*

billiard-cue *s.* Queue *m.*

billiards *s.pl.* Billard(spiel) *n.*

billiard-table *s.* Billard *n.*

billow *s.* Welle *f.*; ~ *v.i.* anschwellen.

bill-sticker *s.* Zettelankleber *m.*

bimonthly *a.* zweimonatlich.

bin *s.* Behälter *m.*, Kasten *m.*

bind *v.t.* binden; verpflichten; *to* ~ *over*, *(law)* durch Gerichtsbeschluss verpflichten; *to be bound over for two years*, zwei Jahre Bewährungsfrist erhalten; **clothbound** *a.* in Leinen (Kaliko) gebunden (Buch); **leatherbound** *a.* in Leder gebunden.

binder *s.* (Buch)Binder *m.*, Binde *f.*

binding *s.* Einband *m.*; ~ *a.* bindend.

binocular *a.* für beide Augen; **~s** *s.pl.* Operngucker *m.*

biographer *s.* Biograph *m.*

biographical *a.* biographisch.

biography *s.* Lebensbeschreibung *f.*

biology *s.* Biologie *f.*

bipartite *a.* zweiteilig; Zweimächte...

biplane *s.* Doppeldecker *m.*

birch *s.* Birke *f.*; Rute *f.*; ~ *v.t.* peitschen.

bird *s*. Vogel *m*.; ~ *of passage*, Zugvogel *m*.

bird-cage *s*. Vogelbauer *m*.

bird's eye *s*. aus der Vogelschau gesehen; ~ view *s*. Vogelperspektive *f*.

birth *s*. Geburt *f*.

birth-certificate *s*. Geburtsschein *m*.

birth-control *s*. Geburtenkontrolle, Geburtenbeschränkung *f*.

birthday *s*. Geburtstag *m*.

birth-mark *s*. Muttermal *n*.

birthplace *s*. Geburtsort *m*.

birth-rate *s*. Geburtenziffer *f*.

biscuit *s*. Kek(s) *m*.

bisect *v.t.* halbieren.

bishop *s*. Bischof *m*.; Läufer (im Schach) *m*.

bishopric *s*. Bistum *n*.

bismuth *s*. Wismut *m*.

bissextile *a*. Schalt...; *s*. Schaltjahr *n*.

bit *s*. Bissen *m*.; Bisschen *n*.; Pferdegebiss *n*.; Schlüsselbart *m*.

bitch *s*. Hündin *f*.

bite *v.t.st.* beissen; ~ *v.i.st.* greifen; ~ *s*. Biss *m*.

bitter *a*., ~ly *adv*. bitter; erbittert.

bittern *s*. Rohrdommel *f*.

bitterness *s*. Bitterkeit *f*.; Gram *m*.

bitumen *s*. Erdpech *n*.

bituminous *a*. bituminös.

bivouac *s*. Biwak *n*., Beiwacht *f*.; ~ *v.i.* biwakieren.

biweekly *a*. zweiwöchentlich.

bizarre *a*. bizarr.

blab *v.t.* & *i*. ausschwatzen.

black *a*. schwarz, dunkel; finster; ~ *s*. Schwärze *f*.; Trauer *f*.; Neger *m*.; ~ *v.t.* schwärzen; (Stiefel) wichsen.

blackamoor *s*. Neger *m*.

blackball *s*. schwarze Wahlkugel *f*.; ~ *v.t.* hinausballotieren.

black-beetle *s*. Schabe *f*.

blackberry *s*. Brombeere *f*.; ~ *v.t.* Brombeeren pflücken.

blackbird *s*. Amsel *f*.

black-board *s*. Wandtafel *f*.

blacken *v.t.* & *i*. schwärzen; schwarz werden.

blackguard *s*. Lump.

blackish *a*. schwärzlich.

blackleg *s*. Gauner *m*.; Streikbrecher *m*.

black-letter *s*. Fraktur *f*.

blacklist *s*. schwarze Liste *f*.; ~ *v.t.* auf die schwarze Liste setzen.

blackmail *s*. Erpressung *f*.; ~ *v.t.* Geld erpressen von.

black market *s*. schwarzer Markt *m*.

blackout *s*. (Luftschutz) Verdunkelung *f*.

black-pudding *s*. Blutwurst *f*.

blacksmith *s*. Grobschmied *m*.

blackthorn *s*. Schlehdorn *m*.

bladder *s*. Blase *f*.

blade *s*. Blatt, Halm *m*.; Klinge *f*.

blame *v.t.* tadeln; ~ *s*. Tadel *m*.; Schuld *f*.

blameable *a*., ~bly *adv*. tadelhaft.

blameless *a*., ~ly *adv*. untadelhaft.

blameworthy *a*. tadelnswürdig.

blanch *v.t.* weiss machen, bleichen.

blanc-mange *s*. Flammeri *m*.

bland *a*. sanft, gütig; glattzüngig.

blandishment *s*. Schmeichelei.

blank *a*., ~ly *adv*. weiss; unbeschrieben, leer; verwirrt; reimlos; (*com*.) Blanko; ~ *s*. Weisse *n*.; leere Blatt *n*.; leere Raum *m*.; Niete *f*.; ~ *cartridge*, Platzpatrone *f*.; ~ *cheque*, Blankoscheck *m*.; ~ *verse*, reimloser Vers *m*.

blanket *s*. Wolldecke *f*.; ~ *v.t.* bedecken.

blare *v.i.* blöken, brüllen; schmettern.

blaspheme *v.t.* (Gott) lästern.

blasphemous *a*., ~ly *adv*. gotteslästerlich.

blasphemy *s*. Gotteslästerung *f*.

blast *s*. Windstoss *m*.; Schall, Trompetenstoss *m*.; Explosion *f*.; ~ *v.t.* sprengen; versengen; zerstören.

blast-furnace *s*. Hochofen *m*.

blast-pipe *s*. Dampfauslassrohr (der Lokomotive) *n*.

blatant *a*. lärmend, schreiend.

blaze *s*. Lichtstrahl *m*.; Flamme *f*.; weisser Fleck, Blesse *f*.; ~ *v.i.* flammen, leuchten; ~ *v.t.* ausposaunen.

blazer *s*. farbige Flanelljacke *f*.

blazon *s*. Wappenschild *n*.; ~ *v.t.* schildern; ausposaunen.

blazonry *s*. Wappenkunde *f*.; Zurschaustellung *f*.

bleach *v.t.* & *i*. bleichen; weiss werden.

bleak *a*., ~ly *adv*. öde; rauh, kalt.

blear *a*. trübe; ~ *v.t.* trüben.

blear-eyed *a*. triefäugig.

bleat *v.i.* blöken; ~ *s*. Blöken *n*.

bleed *v.i.ir.* bluten; ~ *v.t.st.* zur Ader lassen.

blemish *s*. Schandfleck *m*.; Schande *f*.; ~ *v.t.* verunstalten, entehren.

blend *v.t.* & *i*. vermischen; sich mischen; ~ *s*. Mischung (*f*.) von Tee, Kaffee, Tabaken, etc.

bless *v.t.* segnen, beglücken.

blessed *a*. gesegnet, selig; verwünscht.

blessing *s*. Segen *m*.

blight *s*. Meltau *m*.; ~ *v.t.* verderben.

blind *a*. blind; ~ *alley*, Sackgasse *f*.; ~ *s*. Blende *f*.; Vorwand *m*.; Rouleau *n*.; *Venetian* ~, Jalousie *f*.; ~ *v.t.* blind machen; blenden.

blindfold *a*. & *adv*. blindlings; ~ *v.t.* die Augen verbinden.

blindman's-buff *s*. Blindekuh(spiel) *n*.

blindness *s*. Blindheit *f*.

blindworm *s*. Blindschleiche *f*.

blink *s*. Blinken *n*.; ~ *v.i.* blinzeln; ~ *v.t.* nicht sehen wollen.

blinker *s*. Scheuleder *n*.

bliss *s*. Wonne, Seligkeit *f*.

blissful *a.*, ~ly *adv.* wonnevoll, selig.

blister *s.* Blatter *f.*; Bläschen *f.*; ~ *v.t. & i.* Blasen bekommen.

blithe *a.*, ~ly *adv.* munter, lustig.

blizzard *s.* Schneesturm *m.*

bloat *v.t. & i.* aufschwellen.

bloated *a.* aufgedunsen; (*fig.*) aufgeblasen.

block *s.* Block, Klotz *m.*; Häuserviereck *n.*; Versperrung, Stockung *f.*; ~ of flats *s.* Etagenwohnungsbau *m.*; ~ *v.t.* versperren, blockieren, verstopfen; *blocked account*, Sperrkonto *n.*

blockade *s.* Blockade *f.*; *to run the* ~, die Blockade brechen; ~runner *s.* Blockadebrecher *m.*; ~ *v.t.* blockieren.

blockhead *s.* Dummkopf *m.*

blockish *a.*, ~ly *adv.* tölpisch.

block letters *s.pl.* grosse Buchstaben in Druckschrift.

bloke *s.* (*fam.*) Kerl *m.*

blond(e) *a.* blond; ~ *s.* Blondine *f.*

blood *s.* Blut *n.*; *related by* ~, blutsverwandt; ~ *v.t.* blutig machen; zur Ader lassen.

blood-donor *s.* Blutspender *m.*

blood-group *s.* (*med.*) Blutgruppe *f.*

bloodhorse *s.* Vollblutpferd *m.*

bloodhound *s.* Schweisshund *m.*

bloodless *a.* blutlos; unblutig.

blood-orange *s.* Blutorange *f.*

blood-poisoning *s.* Blutvergiftung *f.*

blood-pressure *s.* Blutdruck *m.*

blood-relation *s.* Blutsverwandte *m.*

blood-relationship *s.* Blutsverwandtschaft *f.*

bloodshed *s.* Blutvergiessen *n.*

bloodshot *a.* blutunterlaufen (Augen).

bloodthirsty *a.* blutdürstig.

blood-transfusion *s.* Blutübertragung, Bluttransfusion *f.*

bloodvessel *s.* Blutgefäss *n.*

bloody *a.* blutig; blutdürstig; (*vulg.*) verdammt!

bloom *s.* Blüte, Blume *f.*; ~ *v.i.* blühen.

bloomer *s.* (*sl.*) Schnitzer, Fehler *m.*

blooming *a.* blühend; verflixt.

blossom *s.* Blüte *f.*; *to be in* ~, in Blüte sein, blühen; ~ *v.i.* blühen.

blot *s.* Klecks *m.*; Schandfleck *m.*; ~ *v.t.* klecksen; *to* ~ *out*, auslöschen.

blotch *s.* Blatter *f.*; ~ *v.t.* schwärzen.

blotter, blotting-pad *s.* Löscher *m.*

blotting-paper *s.* Löschpapier *n.*

blouse *s.* Bluse *f.*

blow *s.* Schlag, Stoss *m.*; Blüte *f.*; ~ *v.i.st.* wehen; schnauben; schallen; blühen; ~ *v.t.* blasen, hauchen; *to* ~ *one's nose*, sich schneuzen; *to* ~ *over*, vorübergehen; sich legen; *to* ~ *up*, sprengen; *to* ~ *a kiss*, eine Kusshand zuwerfen.

blown *a.* aufgeblüht; ausser Atem.

blowpipe *s.* Blaserohr, Lötrohr *n.*

blowzy *a.* rotbäckig, pausbäckig.

blubber *s.* Wallfischspeck *m.*; ~ *v.i.* plärren, schluchzen.

bludgeon *s.* Knüttel *m.*

blue *a.*, ~ly *adv.* blau; ~ *s.* Blau *n.*; the blues *s.pl.* Trübsinn *m.*; *out of the* ~, aus heiterem Himmel; ~ *v.t.* blau färben.

blueberry *s.* Blaubeere *f.*

blue-book *s.* Blaubuch *n.*

blue-devils *s.pl.* Trübsinn *m.*

bluejacket *s.* Blaujacke *f.*, Matrose *m.*

blueness *s.* Bläue *f.*

blue pencil *s.* Blaustift.

blue print *s.* Blaupause *f.*, technische Zeichnung *f.*

bluestocking *s.* (*fig.*) Blaustrumpf *m.*

bluff *a.* grob; steil; barsch; ~ *s.* Irreführung *f.*; ~ *v.t.* irreführen.

bluish *a.* bläulich.

blunder *s.* Fehler *m.*, Schnitzer *m.*; ~ *v.i.* einen Schnitzer machen.

blunt *a.*, ~ly *adv.* stumpf; grob, plump; ~ *v.t.* abstumpfen.

blur *s.* Klecks, Flecken *m.*; ~ *v.t.* besudeln; verwischen.

blurb *s.* Reklamestreifen auf Büchern.

blurt *v.t.* (*out*) unbesonnen heraussagen.

blush *v.i.* erröten; ~ *s.* Schamröte *f.*

bluster *v.i.* toben; grosstun; ~ *s.* Ungestüm *m.*; Prahlerei *f.*

boa *s.* Riesenschlange *f.*; Pelzboa *f.*

boars Eber *m.*, Keiler *m.*

board *s.* Brett *n.*; Bohle *f.*; Bord *m.*; Tafel, Kost *f.*; Behörde *f.*; Direktorium *n.*; Kostgeld *n.*; *full* ~, volle Verpflegung *f.*; *partial* ~, teilweise Verpflegung *f.*; ~ *of directors*, Aufsichtsrat *m.*; ~-meeting, Aufsichtsratssitzung, Vorstandssitzung *f.*; ~ *of Trade*, Handelsministerium *n.*; ~ *v.t.* dielen; in die Kost tun, beköstigen; entern; *to* ~ *up*, mit Brettern verschlagen; ~ *v.i.* in der Kost sein.

boarder *s.* Kostgänger *m.*; Enterer *m.*

boarding-house *s.* Pension *f.*

boarding-school *s.* Internat *m.*

board-wages *pl.* Kostgeld (für Dienstboten) *n.*

boast *v.i. & t.* prahlen; stolz sein auf.

boastful *a.* prahlerisch.

boat *s.* Boot *n.*; Schiff *n.*, Dampfer *m.*

boatswain *s.* (Hoch)bootsmann *m.*

bob *s.* Gehänge *n.*; Ruck *m.*; Büschel *n.*; Schilling *m.*; ~ *v.i.* baumeln; mit dem Kopfe nicken; ~ *v.t.* stutzen; *bobbed hair*, Bubikopf *m.*

bobbin *s.* Spule *f.*; Klöppel *m.*

bobbinet *s.* Tüll *m.*

bobby *s.* (*vulg.*) Polizist *m.*

bobtail *s.* Stutzschwanz *m.*

bode *v.t.* vorbedeuten, ahnen.

bodice *s.* Schnürbrust *f.*, Mieder *n.*

bodiless *a.* unkörperlich.

bodily *a.* körperlich; wirklich, ganz und gar; ~ *harm*, ~ *injury*, Körperverletzung *f.*
bodkin *s.* Pfrieme *f.*; Haarnadel *f.*
body *s.* Leib, Körper *m.*; Körperschaft *f.*; Wagenkasten *m.*, (*mot.*) Karosserie *f.*; (*mil.*) Abteilung *f.*; ~ *corporate*, juristische Person *f.*; *in a* ~, geschlossen, sämtlich; ~ *v.t.* formen; verkörpern.
body-guard *s.* Leibgarde *f.*
Boer *s.* Bur *m.*
bog *s.* Sumpf, Moor *m.*
boggy *a.* sumpfig.
bogie *s.* bewegliches Radgestell *n.*
bogus *a.* unecht.
bogy *s.* Kobold *m.*, Popanz *m.*
Bohemia *s.* Boheme *f.*
bohemian *s.* Bohemien *m.*
boil *s.* Furunkel, *m.*; Geschwür *n.*; ~ *v.t. & i.* kochen, wallen; *boiled beef*, Suppenfleisch *n.*; *boiled egg*, gekochtes Ei (*hard-boiled, soft-boiled*), hartgekocht, weichgekocht); *boiled shirt*, Hemd mit steifem Einsatz.
boiler *s.* Kochkessel *m.*; Dampfkessel *m.*
boiler-maker *s.* Kesselschmied *m.*
boiling-point *s.* Siedepunkt *m.*
boisterous *a.*, ~**ly** *adv.* ungestüm, heftig.
bold *a.*, ~**ly** *adv.* kühn; dreist; *to make* ~, sich erkühnen.
boldface *a.* (*typ.*) Fettdruck *m.*
bolster *s.* Kissen *n.*; Kompresse *f.*; ~ *v.t.* polstern; unterstützen.
bolt *s.* Bolzen *m.*; Pfeil *m.*; Riegel, *m.*; Sieb *n.*; Blitzstrahl *m.*; ~ *v.t.* verriegeln; beuteln, sieben; gierig hinunterschlingen; ~ *v.i.* davonlaufen, durchgehen.
bolter *s.* Mehlbeutel *m.*; Sieb *n.*
bomb *s.* Bombe *f.*; ~ *v.t.* mit Bomben belegen.
bombard *v.t.* bombardieren.
bombardment *s.* Bombardieren *n.*
bombast *s.* Schwulst *m.*
bombastic *a.* schwülstig.
bomber *s.* Bombenflugzeug *m.*, Kampfflugzeug *n.*
bomb-proof *a.* bombenfest.
bomb-rack *s.* (*avi.*) Bombenschacht *m.*
bombshell *s.* Bombe *f.*
bomb-sight *s.* (*avi.*) Bombenzielgerät *n.*
bona fide (*law*) in gutem Glauben, gutgläubig.
bond *s.* Band, Seil *n.*; Fessel *f.*; Schuldverschreibung; *in* ~, unter Zollverschluss.
bondage *s.* Knechtschaft *f.*
bonded goods *s.pl.* Güter unter Zollverschluss *n.pl.*
bonded warehouse *s.* Zollspeicher *m.*
bondholder *s.* Schuldscheininhaber *m.*
bondman *s.* Höriger, Fröner *m.*
bone *s.* Knochen *m.*; Gräte *f.*; ~ *v.t.* entknochen, entgräten; (*med.*) ~**-grafting**, Knochenübertragung *f.*

bone-dust *s.* Knochenmehl *n.*
bonelace *s.* Spitzen *f.pl.*
bonfire *s.* Freudenfeuer *n.*
bonnet *s.* Mütze *f.*; Barett *n.*; Frauenhut *m.*; (*mot.*) Haube *f.*; *to have a bee in one's* ~, einen Vogel haben.
bonny *a.*, ~**ily** *adv.* munter; hübsch.
bonus *s.* Zulage *f.*, Zuschlag *m.*
bony *a.* knochig.
booby *s.* Tölpel *m.*
book *s.* Buch *n.*, Heft *n.*; *to keep the* ~*s*, die Bücher führen; ~ *v.t.* eintragen, buchen; ~ *v.i.* (einen Platz) bestellen; eine Fahrkarte lösen (auf der Eisenbahn); *bookable in advance*, vorausbestellbar; **booking** *s.* Vorausbestellung *f.*; **booking-fee** *s.* Bestellgebühr *f.*
bookbinder *s.* Buchbinder *m.*
book-case *s.* Bücherschrank *m.*
booking-office *s.* Fahrkartenausgabe *f.*
bookish *a.* auf Bücher versessen.
bookkeeper *s.* Buchhalter *m.*
book-keeping *s.* Buchführung *f.*; ~ *by double* (*single*) *entry*, doppelte (einfache) Buchführung *f.*
book-maker *s.* Buchmacher (Sport) *m.*
book-post *s.* (auf Kreuzband) 'Drucksachen'.
bookseller *s.* Buchhändler *m.*
book-shelf *s.* Regal, Bücherbrett *n.*
book-stall *s.* Bücherstand (an den Bahnhöfen) *m.*
book-trade *s.* Buchhandel *m.*
book-worm *s.* Bücherwurm *m.*
boom *s.* Stange *f.*; Aufschwung *m.*, Hausse *f.*; ~ *v.i.* dumpf dröhnen; in die Höhe treiben; anpreisen.
boomerang *s.* Bumerang *m.* (australische Schleuder).
boon *s.* Gabe, Wahltat *f.*; ~**-companion** *m.* Zechkumpan *m.*
boor *s.* Lümmel *m.*
boorish *a.*, ~**ly** *adv.* bäuerisch.
boost *v.t.* anpreisen, verstärken.
boot *s.* Stiefel *m.*; *to* ~, überdies, obendrein.
boot-black *s.* Stiefelputzer *m*
booted *a.* gestiefelt.
bootee *s.* Damenhalbstiefel *m.*
booth *s.* Bude *f.*
boot-jack *s.* Stiefelknecht *m.*
bootlegger *s.* Alkoholschmuggler *m*
bootless *a.* unnütz, vergeblich.
bootmaker *s.* Schuster *m.*
boots *s.* Hausknecht *m.*
boot-tree *s.* Leisten *m.*
booty *s.* Beute *f.*
booze *v.i.* zechen.
borax *s.* Borax *m.* (*chem.*).
border *s.* Rand, Saum *m.*; Grenze *f.*; ~ *v.i.* grenzen; ~ *v.t.* einfassen.
borderer *s.* Grenzbewohner *m.*
borderline case *s.* Grenzfall *m.*

bore—brim 294

bore *v.t.* bohren, eindringen; langweilen; ~ *s.* Bohrer *m.*; Bohrloch *n.*; Kaliber *n.*; langweilige Person *f.*
boreal *a.* nördlich.
borer *s.* Bohrer *m.*
boring machine *s.* Bohrmaschine *f.*
born *p. & a.* geboren.
borough *s.* Stadtgemeinde *f.*
borrow *v.t.* borgen; leihen.
bosh *s.* Unsinn *m.*
bosom *s.* Busen *m.*; (*fig.*) Schoss *m.*
boss *s.* Buckel, Knopf *m.*; ~ *s.* Meister, Herr, Prinzipal, Chef *m.*; ~ *v.t.* leiten; veranstalten.
botanic(al) *a.* botanisch.
botanist *s.* Botaniker *m.*
botany *s.* Botanik *f.*
botch *v.t.* flicken; verpfuschen; ~ *s.* Flickfleck *m.*; Pfuscherei *f.*
botcher *s.* Flickschneider *m.*; Pfuscher *m.*
both *a.* beide; beides; both...and *c.* sowohl...als auch.
bother *v.t.* plagen, quälen; ~ *s.* Last, Plage.
bottle *s.* Flasche *f.*; Bündel *n.*; ~ *v.t.* auf Flaschen füllen; *bottled beer,* Flaschenbier *n.*
bottleneck *s.* Flaschenhals *m.*; Engpass *m.* (übertragen)
bottom *s.* Boden *m.*; Grund *m.*; Schiff *n.*; Ende *s.*, Steiss *m.*; *at the ~,* unten, am unteren Ende, im Grunde; ~ *a.* untere.
bottomless *a.* bodenlos.
bottomry *s.* Bodmerei *f.*
bough *s.* Ast *m.*
bouillon cube *s.* Bouillonwürfel *m.*
bounce *s.* Knall *m.*; Rückprall *m.*; Prahlerei *f.*; ~ *v.i.* aufspringen; anprallen; prahlen.
bouncing *a.* stramm.
bound *s.* Sprung *m.*; Prall *m.*; ~ *v.i.* springen, prallen; ~ *s.* Grenze *f.*; *out of ~s,* gesperrt, Zutritt verboten; ~ *v.t.* begrenzen, einschränken; ~ *a.* bestimmt, auf der Reise (nach); *northbound,* in nördlicher Richtung fahrend.
boundary *s.* Grenze *f.*
boundless *a.* grenzenlos.
bounteous, bountiful *a.* freigebig.
bounty *s.* Freigebigkeit *f.*; Prämie *f.*
bouquet *s.* Strauss *m.*, Blume (des Weins) *f.*
bourn *s.* Bach *m.*
bout *s.* Gelage *m.*; (*fenc.*) Gang *m.*
bovine *a.* zum Rind gehörig, Rind...
bow *v.t. & i.* biegen, bücken; sich verbeugen; ~ *s.* Verbeugung *f.*
bow *s.* Bogen *m.*; Schleife *f.*; Bug *m.*
bowdlerize *v.t.* Buchtext verstümmeln.
bowels *s.pl.* Eingeweide *n.pl.*
bower *s.* Laube *f.*; Gemach *n.*
bowie-knife lange Dolchmesser *n.*
bowl *s.* Becken *n.*; Pfeifenkopf *m.*; Schüs-

sel *f.*; Kugel *f.*; *to play at ~s,* Kegel schieben; ~ *v.i.* kegeln, rollen.
bow-legs *s.pl.* O-Beine *n.pl.*
bowler hat *s.* niedriger steifer Filzhut.
bowling-green *s.* Kugelspielrasen *m.*
bowsprit *s.* Bugspriet *m.*
bow-string *s.* Bogensehne *f.*
bow-window *s.* Bogenfenster, vorspringende Fenster *n.*
bow-wow *s.* Wauwau *m.*
box *s.* Büchse *f.*; Kasten *m.*; Schachtel *f.*; Verschlag *m.*; Schliessfach *n.*; Kutschersitz, Bock *m.*; Loge *f.*; Koffer *m.*; Buchsbaum *m.*; Schlag *m.*; (*Am.*) Dollar *m.*; ~ *on the ear,* Ohrfeige *f.*
box *v.t.* ohrfeigen; ~ *v.i.* boxen.
box-car *s.* (*rail.*) Güterwagen *m.*
boxer *s.* Boxer *m.*
Boxing-day *s.* zweite Weihnachtstag *m.*
box-keeper *s.* Logenschliesser *m.*
box-office *s.* Kartenausgabe *f.*, Kasse *f.*
box-wood *s.* Buchsbaumholz *n.*
boy *s.* Knabe *m.*, Junge *m.*
boycott *v.t.* boykottieren, in Verruf erklären; ~ *s.* Boykott *m.*
boyhood *s.* Knabenalter *n.*
boyish *a.*, ~ly *adv.* knabenhaft, kindisch.
brace *s.* Strebe *f.*; Klammer *f.*; Stütze *f.*; (*nav.*) Brasse; (Federwild) Paar *n.*; (*mus.*) Ligaturbogen *m.*; ~ *v.t.* schnüren, spannen, anschnallen; erfrischen.
bracelet *s.* Armband *n.*
braces *s.pl.* Hosenträger *m.pl.*
brachial *a.* Arm...
bracing *a.* stärkend, gesund.
bracken *s.* Farnkraut *n.*
bracket *s.* Klammer *f.*; Wandarm *m*; Gasarm *m.*; (*arch.*) Träger *m.*; *in the lower brackets,* in den unteren Einkommensklassen.
bracket *v.t.* einklammern.
brackish *a.* salzig (vom Wasser).
brad-awl *s.* Spitzbohrer *m.*
brag *v.i.* prahlen; ~ *s.* Prahlerei *f.*
braggart *s.* Prahler *m.*; ~ *a.* prahlerisch.
brahmin, brahman *s.* Brahmane *m.*
braid *v.t.* flechten; ~ *s.* Flechte *f.*; Litze *f.*
braille *s.* Blindenschrift *f.*
brain *s.* Gehirn *n.*; ~ *s,* Verstand *m.*
brainless *a.* unbesonnen.
brainwave *s.* Eingebung *f.*, Geistesblitz *m.*
brainy *a.* gescheit.
braise *v.t.* schmoren.
brake *s.* Farnkraut *n.*; Bremse *f.*; ~ *v.t.* brechen (Flachs); bremsen.
bramble *s.* Brombeerstrauch *m.*
bran *s.* Kleie *f.*
branch *s.* Zweig *m.*; Abschnitt *m.*; Fach *n.*; Filiale *f.*, Zweigstelle *f.*
branch *v.t.* in Zweige teilen; ~ *v.i.* Zweige treiben; abzweigen.
branch-line *s.* Zweigbahn *f.*

brand s. Feuerbrand m.; Brandmal n.; Sorte f.; Handelsmarke f.; ~ v.t. brandmarken.

brandish v.t. schwingen.

brand-new a. funkelnagelneu.

brandy s. Kognak m.

brass s. Erz n.; Messing n.; Unverschämtheit f.

brass-band s. Blechmusikkapelle f.

brass-founder s. Gelbgiesser m.

brassiere s. Büstenhalter m.

brass-plate s. Namensschild (n.)

brat s. Balg m., Kind n.

brave a. tapfer, edel; stattlich; ~ v.t. herausfordern, trotzen.

bravery s. Tapferkeit f.; Pracht f.

bravo s. Bandit m.; bravo.

brawl v.i. zanken; ~ s. Zank m.

brawn s. Muskelstärke f.; Pressülze f.

brawny a. fleischig; muskelstark.

bray s. Eselsgeschrei n.; ~ v.i. schreien, schmettern.

braze v.t. hartlöten.

brazen a., ~ly adv. ehern; unverschämt.

brazen-faced a. unverschämt.

brazier s. Kupferschmied m.; Kohlenbecken n.

breach s. Bruch m.; Bresche f.; Uneinigkeit f.; ~ of promise, Bruch des Eheversprechens m.

bread s. Brot n.; ~ and butter, Butterbrot n.; ~ and cheese, Käsebrot n.

breadspread s. Brotaufstrich m.

breadth s. Breite f.; Weite f.

break v.t. & i. brechen; bersten; anbrechen; vernichten; bankerott werden; umschlagen (Wetter); (ein Pferd) zureiten; to ~ down, zusammenbrechen, versagen, nicht funktionieren (Maschine), eine Panne haben (Motor); klassifizieren; to ~ in, anlernen; to ~ off, abbrechen; to ~ out, ausbrechen; to ~ up, zersprengen (bes. mil.), sich auflösen, auseinandergehen; ~ s. Bruch m.; Lücke f.; Absatz m.; Pause f.; Anbruch m.; ~ of the weather, Witterungsumschlag m.; breaking of the voice, Stimmbruch m.

breakable a. zerbrechlich.

breakage s. Bruch (der Waren), m.

breakdown s. Zusammenbruch m.; (Betriebs)störung, f.; Panne f.; Klassifizierung f.

breakfast v.i. frühstücken; ~ s. Frühstück n.; to lay ~, das Frühstück anrichten.

breakneck a. halsbrecherisch.

breakthrough s. (mil.) Durchbruch m.

break-up s. Auflösung f.

breakwater s. Wellenbrecher m.

bream s. Brassen m. (Fisch).

breast s. Brust f.; Busen m.; ~ v.t. die Stirn bieten.

breast-pin s. Busennadel f.

breaststroke s. Brustschwimmen m.

breast-work s. Brustwehr f.

breath s. Atem m.; Hauch m.; to hold one's ~, den Atem anhalten; out of ~, ausser Atem.

breathe v.t. & i. atmen; äussern.

breathing space s. Atempause f.

breathless s. atemlos.

breeches s.pl. Kniehosen, f.pl.

breed v.t. & i. zeugen; wachsen; aushecken; züchten; ~ s. Zucht f.; Schlag m.; Tierrasse f.; ~-dog, Rassehund m.

breeder s. Erzeuger m.; Züchter m.

breeding s. Züchten n.; Erziehung f.

breeze s. frische Wind m.; Streit m.

breezy a. windig, luftig; jovial.

brethren s.pl. (Bibl.) Brüder m.pl.

breviary s. Brevier n.

brevity s. Kürze f.

brew v.t. brauen; mischen; ~ s. Gebräu n.

brewer s. Brauer m.

brewery s. Brauerei f.

briar = brier.

bribe s. Bestechung f.; ~ v.t. bestechen.

bribery s. Bestechung f.

brick s. Backstein m.; (fam.) Prachtkerl m.; ~ v.t. mit Ziegelsteinen mauern; to ~ up, zumauern.

bricklayer s. Maurer m.

bridal a. hochzeitlich, bräutlich.

bride s. Braut (am Hochzeitstag) f.

bridegroom s. Bräutigam m.

bridesmaid s. Brautjungfer f.

bridesman s. Brautführer m.

bridge s. Brücke f. (auch Zahnbrücke); Steg m. (der Geige); Bridge n.; ~ v.t. überbrücken.

bridgehead s. (mil.) Brückenkopf m.

bridle s. Zaum, Zügel m.; ~ v.t. aufzäumen; bändigen.

bridle-path s. Reitweg m.

brief a., ~ly adv. kurz; knapp; ~ s. Aktenauszug m.; schriftliche Auftrag m.; (law) Schriftsatz m.

brief-case s. Aktentasche f.

briefing s. (mil.) Befehlsausgabe f.

brier s. Dornstrauch m., wilde Rose f., (Stummel-) Pfeife f.

brig s. Zweimaster m., Brigg f.

brigade s. Brigade f.

brigadier s. Brigadeführer m.

brigand s. Strassenräuber m.

brigandage s. Räuberwesen n., Räuberei f.

bright a., ~ly adv. hell; gescheit.

brighten v.i. hell werden, glänzen; ~ v.t. glänzend machen; aufheitern.

brightness s. Glanz m.; Scharfsinn m.

brill s. Glattbutt m. (Fisch).

brilliance, brilliancy s. Glanz m.

brilliant a., ~ly adv. glänzend; hervorstehend; ~ s. Brilliant m.

brim s. Rand m.; Krempe f.; ~ v.t. bis an den Rand füllen; ~ v.i. voll sein.

brimful a., ~ly adv. ganz voll.
brimstone s. Schwefel m.
brindled a. scheckig, gestreift.
brine s. Salzwasser n.; Sole f.
bring v.t. ir. bringen; to ~ about, zustande bringen; to ~ forth, hervorbringen, gebären; to ~ round, wieder zu sich bringen; to ~ to bear, anwenden, zur Wirkung bringen; to ~ up, erziehen, aufziehen; (mil.) heranführen; to ~ up the subject, den Gegenstand zur Sprache bringen.
brink s. Rand m.
briny a. salzig.
briquette, briquet s. Presskohle, Brikett n.
brisk a., ~ly adv. frisch, lebhaft, feurig, stark; ~ v.t. (up), aufmuntern.
brisket s. Bruststück (Speise) n.
bristle s. Borste f.; ~ v.t. (die Borsten) aufrichten; ~ v.i. starren.
Britisher s. (fam.) Brite m.
brittle a. zerbrechlich; spröde.
broach s. Bratspiess m.; Busennadel f.; ~ v.t. anspiessen; (ein Fass) anzapfen; (fig.) vorbringen; anfangen.
broad a., ~ly adv. breit, gross; grob; schlüpfrig; derb; ~ day, helle Tag m.
broad bean s. Saubohne f.
broadcast a. weit verbreitet; ~ v.t. rundfunken; **broadcasting** n., Rundfunk m.
broad-cloth s. feine Tuch n.
broaden v.t. weiten.
broadside s. (nav.) Breitseite, volle Lage f.; bedruckte Papierbogen m.
broad-sword s. Säbel m.
brocade s. Brokat m.
broccoli s. Sprossenkohl m.
brochure s. Broschüre (eines Hotels u.dgl.) f.
brogue s. starke Schuh m.; irländische Aussprache f.
broil s. Lärm, Aufruhr m.; ~ v.t. & i. vor dem Feuer rösten.
broke a. bankerott.
broken p. & a. gebrochen (auch fig.); zerrissen; unterbrochen; ~ stones s. Schotter m.; ~ ground s. unebenes Gelände f.; ~-hearted gebrochenen Herzens, gramvoll.
broker s. Makler m.; Trödler m.
brokerage s. Maklerlohn m.
bromine s. Brom n.
bronchial a. zur Luftröhre gehörig.
bronchitis s. Luftröhrenentzündung f.
bronze s. Bronze f.; ~ v.t. bronzieren.
brooch s. Busennadel, Brosche f.
brood v.i. brüten; ~ v.t. ausbrüten; ~ s. Brut f.
brook s. Bach m.; ~ v.t. ertragen.
broom s. Ginster m.; Besen m.
broomstick s. Besenstiel m.
broth s. Fleischbrühe f.
brothel s. Bordell n.

brother s. Bruder m.
brotherhood s. Brüderschaft f.
brother-in-law s. Schwager m.
brotherly a. brüderlich.
brow s. Augenbraue f.; Stirn f.
browbeat v.t. st. einschüchtern.
brown a. braun.
browned off a. deprimiert.
brownie s. Heinzelmännchen n.
brownish a. bräunlich.
brown-paper s. Packpapier n.
browse s. junge Spross m.; ~ v.t. abweiden; ~ v.i. weiden; flüchtig lesen.
bruise v.t. quetschen, zerstossen; ~ s. Quetschung f.; Stoss m.
brunette a. brünett; ~ s. Brünette f.
brunt s. Stoss, Anprall m.: (fig.) Hitze f.
brush s. Bürste f.; Pinsel m.; Schwanz (m.) des Fuchses; ~ v.t. bürsten; fegen; streifen.
brushwood s. Gestrüpp, Buschholz n.
brusque a. barsch, trotzig.
Brussels sprouts s.pl. Rosenkohl m.
brutal a., ~ly adv. viehisch; roh.
brutalize v.t. verrohen.
brutality s. rohe Wesen n.
brute a. tierisch, wild; ~ s. Vieh n.; rohe Kerl m., (fam.) Scheusal n.
brutish a., ~ly adv. viehisch, grob.
bubble s. Wasserblase f; leere Schein m.; Betrug, Schwindel m; ~ v.i. sprudeln.
buccaneer s. Seeräuber m.
buck s. Bock m.; männliches Tier n.; Stutzer m.; to pass the ~ (Am.) einem andern die Schuld zuschieben; ~ v.i. bocken; to ~ up, Mut machen, anfeuern.
bucket s. Eimer m.
buckle s. Schnalle f.; Locke f.; ~ v.t. schnallen; sich biegen.
buckram s. Steifleinwand f.
buckskin s. Hirschleder n.; (Stoff) Buckskin m.
buckwheat s. Buchweizen m.
bucolic a. hirtenmässig, Hirten...
bud s. Knospe f.; ~ v.i. sprossen, blühen; ~v.t. pfropfen.
budge v.i. sich regen.
budget s. Brieftasche f.; Vorrat m.; Haushaltsplan m., Etat m.; ~ estimate, Haushaltsvoranschlag m.
buff s. Büffelleder n.; Lederzeug n.; ~ a. mattgelb.
buffalo s. Büffel m.
buffer s., Puffer m., Stosskissen n.
buffet s. Anrichte(tisch) f.; Schenktisch m.; Wirtschaftsbetrieb m., Buffet n.; ~ v.t. puffen, schlagen.
buffoon s. Possenreisser m.
buffoonery s. Possen f.pl.
bug s. Wanze f.
bugbear s. Popanz m.
buggy s. leichte, zweirädrige Wagen m.
bugle s. Wald-, Signalhorn n.

bugs *s.pl.* (*Am.*) Ungeziefer *n.*
build *v.t. & i.* bauen; ~ *s.* Bauart *f.*
builder *s.* Bauunternehmer *m.*
building *s.* Bauen *n.*; Gebäude *n.*
building society *s.* Bausparkasse *f.*
built-up *a.* bebaut.
bulb *s.* Zwiebel *f.*; Thermometerkugel *f.*; *light* ~, Glühlampe *f.*, Birne *f.*
bulge *s.* Anschwellung *f.*; ~ *v.i.* anschwellen, vorragen.
bulk *s.* Umfang *m.*; Masse *f.*; Hauptteil *m.*; ~ *v.i.* vorragen.
bulkhead *s.* (*navi.*) Schott *n.*
bulk-purchase *s.* Grosseinkauf *m.*
bulky *a.* gross, schwer.
bull *s.* Bulle, Stier *m.*; Schnitzer *m.*; Haussier *m.*; päpstliche Bulle *f.*
bulldog *s.* Bullenbeisser *m.*, Bulldogge *f.*
bulldozer *s.* Pflugbagger *m.*
bullet *s.* Kugel *f.*
bullet-proof *a.* kugelfest; ~ *glass s.* Panzerglas *n.*
bulletin *s.* Tagesbericht *m.*; ~-board *s.* schwarze Brett *n.*
bull-fight *s.* Stierkampf *m.*
bull-frog *s.* Ochsenfrosch, Brüllfrosch *m.*
bullion *s.* Gold- oder Silberbarren *m.*
bullock *s.* Ochse *m.*
bull's-eye *s.* Schwarze (in der Scheibe) *n.*
bully *s.* (feige) Tyrann *m.*; grober Flegel *m.*; ~ *v.t.* einschüchtern; tyrannisieren.
bully-beef *s.* Büchsenfleisch *n.*
bulrush *s.* glatte Binse *f.*
bulwark *s.* Bollwerk *n.*; ~ *v.t.* befestigen.
bumble-bee *s.* Hummel *f.*
bump *s.* Schlag *m.*; Beule *f.*; ~ *v.t.* puffen, (*boat*) überholen.
bumper *s.* Humpen *m.*; ~ *a.* ungewöhnlich gross.
bumptious *a.* aufgeblasen, anmassend.
bun *s.* Korinthenbrötchen *n.*
bunch *s.* Bündel *n.*; Büschel *m.*; Strauss *m.*; ~ *of grapes*, Weintraube *f.*; ~ *of keys*, Schlüsselbund *m.*; ~ *v.i.* schwellen, strotzen.
bundle *s.* Bündel *n.*; (*fig.*) Bürde *f.*; ~ (*up*), *v.t.* einpacken.
bung *s.* Spund *m.*; ~ *v.t.* zuspunden.
bungalow *s.* einstöckiges (Sommer)haus *n.*
bungle *v.t. & i.* verpfuschen; stümpern.
bunion *s.* Schwellung (am Fuss) *f.*
bunk *s.* (*nav.*) Bettgestell *n.*; (*Am.*) Blech *n.*, Unsinn *m.*
bunker *s.* (*nav.*) Bunker *m.*, Kohlenbehälter *m.*
bunting *s.* Flaggentuch *n.*
buoy *s.* Boje, Bake *f.*; ~ *v.t. & i.* schwimmen.
buoyancy *s.* Schwimmkraft *f.*, Auftrieb *m.*; (*fig.*) Schwungkraft *f.*
buoyant *a.* schwimmend; (*fig.*) leicht, heiter.

bur *s.* Klette *f.*
burden *s.* Bürde *f.*; Ladung *f.*; (*fig.*) Last *f.*; Refrain *m.*, Kehrreim *m.*; ~ *of proof*, (*law*) Beweislast *f.*; ~ *v.t.* aufbürden.
burdensome *a.* beschwerlich.
bureau *s.* Büro *n.*, Geschäftszimmer *f.*; Schreibtisch *m.*; (*Am.*) Kommode *f.*
bureaucracy *s.* Bürokratie *f.*
burgeon *s.* Knospe *f.*; *v.* knospen.
burgess *s.* Bürger *m.*
burgh *s.* Flecken *m.*
burgher *s.* Bürger *m.*
burglar *s.* Einbrecher *m.*
burglary *s.* Einbruch *m.*
burgomaster *s.* Bürgermeister *m.*
Burgundy *s.* Burgunder *m.*
burial *s.* Begräbnis *n.*
burlesque *a.* possenhaft; ~ *s.* Burleske *f.*; ~ *v.a.* lächerlich machen.
burly *a.* stämmig.
burn *v.t. & i.ir.* brennen; strahlen; ~ *s.* Brand, Brandschaden *m.*
burner *s.* Brenner *m.*
burnish *v.a.* polieren; ~ *s.* Glanz *m.*
burnous *s.* Burnus *m.*
burr *s.* Hof(um den Mond) *m.*; (*mech.*) Grat *m.*; gerollte R *n.*
burrow *s.* Kaninchenbau *m.*; ~ *v.n.* sich eingraben, wühlen.
bursar *s.* Kassenwart *m.*; Stipendiat *m.*
burst *v.i.* bersten; ~ *v.t.* sprengen; ~ *s.* Riss *m.*; Ausbruch *m.*
bury *v.t.* begraben; vergraben.
bus *s.* Omnibus *m.*
bush *s.* Busch *m.*, Strauch *m.*; (*mech.*) Metallfutter *n.*
bushel *s.* Bushel *m.* (36 Liter).
bushy *a.* buschig.
business *s.* Geschäft *n.*; Handel *m.*; (*fam.*) Geschichte *f.*; *small* ~, Handwerk *n.*; *line of* ~, Geschäftszweig *m.*; *to do* (*transact*) ~ *with*, in geschäftlicher Verbindung stehen mit; *to go into* ~, Kaufmann werden; *mind your own* ~, kümmere dich um deine eigenen Angelegenheiten; *what* ~ *have you to...*, wie kommst du dazu...?; ~*like a.* geschäftsmässig.
buskin *s.* Kothurn *m.*, Halbstiefel *m.*
bus-stop *s.* Omnibushaltestelle *f.*
bust *s.* Büste *f.*
bustle *s.* Lärm, Auflauf *m.*; ~ *v.i.* sich rühren, geschäftig sein.
busy *a.* geschäftig; unruhig; ~ *v.t.* beschäftigen; *to be* ~, zu tun haben; *the line is busy*, (*tel.*) die Verbindung ist besetzt.
busybody *s.* Wichtigtuer *m.*
but *c.* aber, sondern; doch; nur; als; wenn nur; ~ *pr.* ausser.
butcher *s.* Fleischer *m.*; ~ *v.t.* schlachten.
butchery *s.* Metzelei *f.*
butler *s.* oberste Diener *m.*

butt s. dicke Ende n.; Stoss m.; Ziel-scheibe f.; ~ v.t. stossen.
butt-end s. Gewehrkolben m.
butter s. Butter f.; ~ v.t. buttern.
buttercup s. Butterblume f.
butterfly s. Schmetterling m.
butter-milk s. Buttermilch f.
buttery s. Speisekammer f.
buttock s. Hinterteil n.
button s. Knopf m.; ~ v.t. zuknöpfen.
button-hole s. Knopfloch n.; Sträusschen (fürs Knopfloch) n.; ~ v.t. (fig.) am Rock festhalten.
buttress s. Strebepfeiler m.
buxom a., ~ly adv. gesund, kräftig, drall.
buy v.t.ir. kaufen.
buyer s. Käufer m.
buzz v.i. summen, flüstern; ~ s. Gesumse, Geflüster n.
buzzard s. Bussard m.
by pr. von, zu, nach, auf, neben, bei; ~ adv. nahe, vorbei; ~ and ~, nach und nach; ~ the bye, nebenbei gesagt; ~ no means, keinesfalls, keineswegs; ~ all means, freilich, auf jeden Fall; ~ my-self, ~ yourself, etc., allein; ~ nine o' clock, bis neun Uhr; ~ that time, bis dahin.
by-election s. Ersatzwahl f.
bygone a. vergangen.
by-law s. Ortstatut n.; Verordnung f.
by-name s. Beiname, Spitzname m.
by-pass s. Entlastungs-, Umgehungs-strasse f.; ~ v.t. umgehen.
by-product s. Nebenprodukt n.
bystander s. Zuschauer m.
by-way s. Nebenweg, Umweg m.
by-word s. Sprichwort n.; Beispiel n.

C

cab s. Droschke f.; Autodroschke f.; (rail.) Führerstand m.; ~-rank s. Auto-haltestelle f., Droschkenstand m.
cabal s. Kabale f.; ~ v.i. Ränke schmie-den.
cabaret s. Kabarett n.
cabbage s. Kohl m.
cabdriver s. Taxichauffeur m.
cabin s. Kajüte f.; Hütte f.; Badezelle f.; ~ v.t. einsperren.
cabin-boy s. Schiffsjunge m.
cabinet s. Kabinett n.; Schrank m.
cabinet-maker s. Kunsttischler m.
cable s. Kabel n.; ~ v.t. kabeln.
cablegram s. Kabeldepesche f.
cabman s. Droschkenkutscher m.
caboose s. Schiffsküche f., Kombüse f.
cabriolet s. Kabriolett n.
cab-stand s. Droschkenhaltestelle f.

cacao s. Kakao m.
cackle v.i. gackern; kichern; ~ s. Ge-schnatter n.
cactus s. Kaktus m.
cad s. gemeine Kerl, Knote m.
cadastral a. katastral, Grundbuch...
cadaverous a. leichenhaft.
caddie s. Junge (beim Golfspiel) m.
caddy s. Teekästchen n.
cadence s. Tonfall m.
cadet s. Kadett m.; jüngere Sohn m.
Caesarian operation s. (med.)Kaiserschnitt m.
café a. Kaffeehaus n.
cafeteria s. Imbissraum mit Selbstbedien-ung m.
caffeine s. Koffein n.
cage s. Käfig m.; ~ v.t. einsperren.
caitiff a. niederträchtig, feig, elend.
cajole v.t. liebkosen.
cajolery s. Liebkosung f.; Schmeichelei f.
cake s. Kuchen m.; ~ of soap, Stück Seife n.; ~ v.t. zusammenbacken.
calamitous a. unheilvoll.
calamity s. Unglück n.; Trübsal f.
calcareous a. kalkartig.
calcium s. Kalzium n.
calcium cyanamide s. Kalkstickstoff m.
calculable a. berechenbar.
calculate v.t. berechnen; ~ v.i. rechnen.
calculating machine s. Rechenmaschine f.
calculation s. Berechnung f.
calculus s. (math.) Rechnung f.
calendar s. Kalender m.
calender s. Tuchpresse f.; ~ v.t. warm pressen.
calf s. Kalb n.; Kalbleder n.; Wade f.; in ~ trächtig (Kuh).
calibre s. Kaliber n.; Beschaffenheit f.; Befähigung f.
calico s. Kattun m.
caliph s. Kalif m.
call v.t. & i. rufen, nennen; wecken; (tel.) anrufen; anlegen (Schiff); heissen; be-suchen; to ~ for ... abholen; erfordern; to ~ to account, zur Rechenschaft ziehen; to ~ to mind, sich erinnern; to ~ up, (Am.) anrufen (tel.); ~ s. Ruf m.; Aufforderung f.; Besuch m.; Tele-phongespräch n.; local ~, Ortsgespräch; trunk ~, long-distance ~, Ferngespräch; on~, auf Abruf, auf tägliche Kündigung.
call-box s. Telephonzelle f.
caller s. Besucher m.
calligraphy s. Schönschreibekunst f.
calling s. Rufen n.; Beruf, Stand m.
callipers s.pl. (mech.) Kaliberzirkel, Tast-zirkel m.pl.
call-money s. tägliches Geld n., Geld auf Abruf n.
callosity s. Schwiele, Hautverhärtung f.
callous a. schwielig; (fig.) unempfindlich.
callow a. nicht flügge; jung, unreif.

calm *a.*, ~ly *adv.* ruhig; ~ *s.* Windstille, Ruhe *f.*; ~ *v.t.* besänftigen.
calomel *s* Kalomel *n.*
calorie *s.* Wärmeeinheit *f.*
calorific *a.* wärmeerzeugend.
calumniate *v.t.* verleumden.
calumny *s.* Verleumdung *f.*
calve *v.i.* kalben.
cam *s.* (*mech.*) Nocken *m.*; ~-shaft Nockenwelle *f.*
cambric *s.* Batist *m.*
camel *s.* Kamel *n.*
cameo *s.* Kamee *f.*
camera *s.* Kamera *f.*, photographischer Apparat *m.*; (*law*) *in* ~, unter Ausschluss der Öffentlichkeit.
cami-knickers *s.pl.* Hemdhose *f.*
camomile *s.* Kamille *f.*
camouflage *s.* (*mil.*) Tarnung *f.*; ~ *v.t.* tarnen.
camp *s.* Lager *n.*; ~ *v.i.* kampieren.
campaign *s.* Feldzug *m.*
campaigner *s.* alte Soldat *m.*
camp-bed *s.* Feldbett *n.*; ~-stool *s.* Klappstuhl *m.*
camp-followers *s.pl.* Trosspersonen *f.pl.*
camphor *s.* Kampfer *m.*
can *s.* Kanne *f.*; (*Am.*) Konservenbüchse *f.*; ~ *v.t.* (*Am.*) in Büchsen einmachen; ~ *v.i.ir.*, I ~, ich kann.
canal *s.* Kanal *m.*; Rinne *f.*
canalization *s.* Kanalisierung *f.*
canalize *v.t.* kanalisieren.
canard *s.* Zeitungsente *f.*
canary *s.* Kanarienvogel *m.*
cancel *v.t.* ausstreichen, tilgen; ungültig machen; widerrufen.
cancellation *s.* Aufhebung *f.*; Widerruf *m.*; Tilgung *f.*
cancer *s.* (*med.*) Krebs *m.*
cancerous *a.* krebsartig.
candelabrum *s.* Armleuchter *m.*
candid *a.*, ~ly *adv.* aufrichtig, bieder.
candidate *s.* Kandidat *m.*; Bewerber *m.*
candidature *s.* Kandidatur *f.*
candle *s.* Licht *n.*; Kerze *f.*
Candlemas *s.* Lichtmess *f.*
candle-power *s.* Kerzenstärke *f.*
candlestick *s.* Leuchter *m.*
candour *s.* Redlichkeit, Offenheit *f.*
candy *s.* überzuckern; ~ *s.* Kandiszucker *m.*; Zuckerwerk *n.*
cane *s.* Rohr *n.*; Stock *m.*; ~ *v.t.* durchprügeln.
cane-bottom chair *s.* Rohrstuhl *m.*
canine *a.* hündisch; Hunds...
canister *s.* Körbchen *n.*; Büchse *f.*
canker *s.* Krebs (an Bäumen) *m.*; ~ *v.t.* anfressen.
cankerous *a.* krebsartig.
cannibal *s.* Menschenfresser *m.*; ~ *a.* kannibalisch.
cannibalism *s.* Kannibalismus *m.*

cannon *s.* Kanone *f.*; Carambolage *f.*
cannonade *s.* Kanonade *f.*
cannon-ball *s.* Kanonenkugel *f.*
cannot = can not.
canny *a.* schlau, vorsichtig.
canoe *s.* Paddelboot *n.*
canon *s.* Regel *f.*; Kanon *m.*; Domherr *m.*
canonical *a.* kanonisch, kirchlich.
canonize *v.t.* heiligsprechen.
canon-law *s.* kanonische Recht *n.*
canonry *s.* Domherrnwürde *f.*
canopy *s.* Traghimmel *m.*; ~ *v.t.* mit einem Baldachin bedecken.
cant *s.* Schrägung *f.*; Zunftsprache *f.*; Heuchelei *f.*; ~ *v.i.* kanten; kauderwelschen; scheinheilig reden.
can't = cannot.
cantankerous *a.* rechthaberisch.
cantata *s.* Kantate *f.*
canteen *s.* Feldflasche *f.*; Kantine *f.*; ~ *o cutlery*, Messerwarenkoffer *m.*
canter *s.* kurze Galopp *m.*; ~ *v.i* in kurzen Galopp reiten.
cantilever *s.* (*arch.*) Dielenkopf *m.*
canto *s.* Gesang *m.*
canton *s.* Kanton *m.*; ~ *v.i.* kantonieren, einquartieren.
cantonment *s.* Kantonierung *f.*
canvas *s.* Kanevas *m.*; Segeltuch *n.*; Gemälde *n.*; *under* ~, in Zelten.
canvass *s.* Bewerbung (um Wahlstimmen) *f.*; ~ *v.t.* prüfen, erörtern; ~ *v.i.* sich bewerben, Stimmen sammeln.
canyon *s.* Felsental *n.*, Klamm *f.*
caoutchouc *s.* Kautschuk *m.* or *n.*
cap *s.* Mütze, Kappe *f.*; Deckel *m.*; ~ *v.t.* mit einer Kappe bedecken; übertreffen.
capability *s.* Fähigkeit *f.*; *enemy capabilities*, (*mil.*) Feindmöglichkeiten *f.pl.*
capable *a.* fähig; ~ *of work*, arbeitsfähig.
capacious *a.*, ~ly *adv.* geräumig.
capacitate *v.t.* befähigen.
capacity *s.* Umfang *m.*; Fähigkeit *f.*; Eigenschaft *f.*; Inhalt *m.*; Leistungsfähigkeit *f.*; Aufnahmefähigkeit *f.*; *legal* ~, Rechtsfähigkeit, Geschäftsfähigkeit *f.*; ~ *measures*, Hohlmasse *n.pl.*
caparison *s.* Pferdedecke *f.*; ~ *v.t.* die Decke auflegen; schmücken.
cape *s.* Vorgebirge *n.*; Cape *n.*
caper *s.* Kaper *f.*; Luftsprung *m.*; ~ *v.i.* Luftsprünge machen.
capillary *a.* haarfein.
capital *a.*, ~ly *adv.* Haupt...; vorzüglich; ~ *punishment s.* Todesstrafe *f.*; ~ *s.* Hauptstadt *f.*; Kapital *n.*; Kapitäl *n.*; grosse Buchstabe *m.*
capital levy *s.* Kapitalabgabe *f.*
capital ship *s.* (*nav.*) Grosskampfschiff *n.*
capitalism *s.* Kapitalmacht *f.*
capitalist *s.* Kapitalist *m.*
capitalize *v.t.* kapitalisieren; mit grossen Buchstaben schreiben.

capitation s. Kopfsteuer f.

capitulate v.n. kapitulieren.

capon s. Kapaun m.; ~ v.t. verschneiden.

caprice s. Grille f.; Eigensinn m.

capricious a., ~ly adv. launenhaft.

Capricorn s. (astr.) Steinbock m.

capriole s. Luftsprung, Gaukelsprung m.

capsize v.t. (nav.) umwenden; ~ v.i. kentern.

capstan s. (nav.) Gangspill n.

captain s. Hauptmann m.; (Schiffs-)kapitän m.; ~ of horse, Rittmeister m.

captaincy, captainship s. Hauptmanns-, Kapitänsstelle f.

caption s. (Am.) Überschrift f.

captious a., ~ly adv. trügerisch, spitzfindig; tadelsüchtig.

captivate v.t. (fig.) einnehmen, fesseln.

captive a. gefangen; ~ balloon, Fesselballon m.; ~ s. Gefangene m.

captivity s. Gefangenschaft f.

capture s. Raub m.; Beute f.; Kapern n., Prise f.; ~ v.t. erbeuten; kapern.

capuchin s. Kapuziner m.

car s. Auto; n.; Karren m.; Wagen m.; (Am.) Eisenbahnwagen m.

caracole s. (mil.) halbe Schwenkung f.; ~ v.i. schwenken.

carafe s. Wasserflasche f.

caramel s. gebrannte Zucker m.; Karamelle f.

carat s. Karat n.

caravan s. Karawane f.; (grosse) Wohnwagen m.

caraway s. Kümmel (Pflanze) m.

carbide s. Karbid n.

carbine s. Karabiner m.

carbohydrate s. Kohlehydrat n.

carbolic acid, Karbolsäure f.

carbon s. Kohlenstoff m.

carbonaceous a. kohlenstoffhaltig, kohleführend.

carbonate s. kohlensaure Salz n.

carbon-copy s. Durchschlag m.; ~-paper s. Kohlepapier n.

carbonic acid s. Kohlensäure f.

carbonize v.t. verkohlen.

carbuncle s. Karfunkel m.; (med.) Karbunkel m.

carburettor, -ter s. Vergaser m.

carcase s. Gerippe n.; tote Körper m.

card s. Karte f.; Visitenkarte f.; Seekarte f.; Wollkratze f.; ~ v.t. krempeln, aufkratzen; house of ~s, Kartenhaus n.

card-index s. Kartothek f., Kartei f.

cardboard s. Pappendeckel m., Pappe f.

carder s. Wollkrempler m.

cardiac a. Herz...

cardigan s. Wollweste f.

cardinal a. vornehmst, Haupt...; hochrot; ~ s. Kardinal m.

cardinal numbers s.pl. Grundzahlen f.pl.

cardinalate s. Kardinalswürde f.

card-party s. Spielgesellschaft f.

card-sharper s. Betrüger im Kartenspiel m.

card-table s. Spieltisch m.

care s. Sorge f.; Vorsicht, Pflege f.; ~ of (c/o) Mrs. S., (auf Briefen) per Adresse, bei; to take ~ (to), dafür sorgen, dass; to take ~ (of), sich einer Sache oder Person annehmen; ~ v.i. sorgen; to ~ for, gern haben.

career s. Laufbahn f.; Lauf m.; ~ v.i. rennen.

career-diplomat s. Berufsdiplomat m.

careful a., ~ly adv. besorgt, sorgfältig; vorsichtig; to be ~, sich in Acht nehmen.

careless a., ~ly adv. sorglos; unvorsichtig.

caress v.t. liebkosen; ~ s. Liebkosung f.

caretaker s. Aufseher, Wächter m.

care-worn a. abgehärmt.

cargo s. Schiffsladung f.; ~-steamer s. Frachtdampfer m.

caricature s. Zerrbild n.; ~ v.t. lächerlich darstellen, karikieren.

caricaturist s. Karikaturenzeichner m.

caries s. Knochenfrass m.

carman s. Fuhrmann m.

carmelite s. Karmeliter m.

carmine s. Karmin m.

carnage s. Blutbad n.; Gemetzel n.

carnal a., ~ly adv. fleischlich.

carnation s. Fleischfarbe f.; Gartennelke f.

carnival s. Karneval, Fasching m.

carnivorous a. fleischfressend.

carol s. Lobgesang m.; ~ v.t. & i. lobsingen, jubeln.

carotid a., ~ artery s. Halsschlagader f.

carousal s. Gelage, Fest n.

carouse v.i. zechen; ~ s. Gelage n.

carp s. Karpfen m.; ~ v.i. bekritteln.

carpenter s. Zimmermann m.

carpentry s. Zimmerhandwerk n.

carper s. Bekrittler, Splitterrichter m.

carpet s. Teppich m.

carpet-sweeper s. Teppichkehrmaschine .

carriage s. Fuhre f.; Fracht f.; Wagen m.; Eisenbahnwagen m.; (mech.) Schlitten m.; Lafette f.; Fuhrlohn m.; Haltung f., Benehmen n.

carriage-free, carriage-paid a. frachtfrei.

carrier s. Fuhrmann; Überbringer m.; Träger m.; Gepäckhalter (Fahrrad) m.

carrier-pigeon s. Brieftaube f.

carrier-wave s. (radio) Trägerwelle f.

carrion s. Aas n.

carrot s. gelbe Rübe, Möhre f.

carroty a. möhrenfarbig; rothaarig.

carry v.t. & i. führen, fahren, fortbringen; befördern; tragen; sich betragen; to ~ forward, (com.) übertragen; to ~ a motion, einen Antrag durchbringen; to

~ on, treiben, weiterführen; to ~ on the person, bei sich tragen; to ~ out, ausführen, durchführen; to ~ through, durchführen; to ~ on v.i. sein Wesen treiben, sich wild gebärden; fortfahren.

cart s. Fuhrwerk n.; Karren m.; ~ v.t. karren, auf dem Karren fahren.

cartage s. Fuhrlohn m.; Fahren n.

cartel s. Kartell n.

carter s. Fuhrmann m.

cart-horse s. Zugpferd n.

carthusian s. Kartäusermönch m.

cartilage s. Knorpel m.

cart-load s. Karrenladung f.

carton s. Kartonschachtel f.

cartoon s. Karton m., (gedruckte) Vollbild n., politische Karikatur f.

cartoon-film s. Trickfilm m.

cartoonist s. Karikaturist m.

cartridge s. Patrone f.; Kartätsche f. ~-box Patronentasche f.

cartwright s. Stellmacher m.

carve v.t. aushauen, in Kupfer stechen; schnitzen; vorschneiden.

carving s. Schnitzwerk n.; Stich m.

cascade s. Wasserfall m.; Kaskade f.

case s. Fall m.; Futteral, Gehäuse n.; Kiste f.; Schriftkasten m.; Rechtsfall m.; (gram.) Fall m.; glass-~, Glaskasten m.; civil ~, (law) Zivilsache f.; criminal ~, Strafsache f.; the ~ for, die Argumente zu Gunsten; in ~, im Falle, falls; in any case, auf jeden Fall.

case-harden v.t. (mech.) einsatzhärten, oberflächenhärten.

case-knife s. Messer in einer Scheide n.

casemate s. Kasematte f.

casement s. Fensterflügel m.

case-shot s. Kartätsche f.

cash s. Kasse f.; bare Geld n.; for ~, gegen bar; ~ on delivery, Nachnahme; ~ v.t. einlösen (Scheck); einkassieren; ~ register s. Kontrollkasse f.

cash book s. Kassabuch n.

cashier s. Kassierer m.; ~ v.t. absetzen; kassieren.

cashmere s. Kaschmirschal, -stoff m.

casing s. Futteral, Gehäuse n.

cask s. Fass n.

casket s. Schmuckkästchen n.

casserole s. kleiner Kochtopf (aus feuerfestem Ton), Kasserolle f.

cassia s. Kassia f., Zimt m.

cassock s. lange Priesterrock m.

cast v.t.ir. (aus-, ent-, weg-) werfen; ausrechnen; giessen; (Rollen) verteilen; to ~ up, addieren; to ~ one's skin, sich häuten; to ~ a vote, eine Stimme abgeben; ~ down a. niedergeschlagen; ~ s. Wurf, Guss m.; Form f.; Gattung f.; Probe f.; angeborene Manier f.; Blick m.; Rollenverteilung, Rollenbesetzung f.

castaway a. verworfen; ~ s. Verworfene m.; Schiffbrüchige m.

caste s. (in Indien) Kaste f.; to lose ~, seinen gesellschaftlichen Rang verlieren.

castellan s. Kastellan m.

castellated a. zinnengekrönt.

castigate v.t. züchtigen.

casting-vote s. entscheidende Stimme f.

cast-iron s. Gusseisen n.

castle s. Burg f., Schloss n.; Turm (im Schach) m.

cast-off a. abgeworfen, abgelegt.

castor s. Biber m.; Kastorhut m.; Streubüchse; ~-oil, Rizinusöl n.

castor sugar s. Streuzucker m.

castrate v.t. entmannen; verstümmeln.

castration s. Kastration f.

cast-steel s. Gusstahl m.

casual a., ~ly adv. zufällig; ~ labourer, Gelegenheitsarbeiter m.

casualty s. Unfall m.; (mil.) Verlust m.

casuistic a. kasuistisch.

casuistry s. Kasuistik f.

cat s. Katze f.; ~ o' nine tails s. Schiffspeitsche f.; ~ burglar, Fassadenkletterer m.

cataclysm s. Sündflut f.

catacomb s. Katakombe f.

catalepsy s. Katalepsie, Starrsucht f.

cataleptic a. starrsüchtig.

catalogue s. Katalog m. Verzeichnis n.; ~ v.t. katalogisieren.

catalyst s. (chem.) Katalysator m.

catapult s. Katapulte f.

cataract s. Wasserfall m.; Star (im Auge) m.

catarrh s. Schnupfen m.; Katarrh m.

catarrhal a. katarrhalisch.

catastrophe s. Katastrophe f.

catastrophic a. katastrophal.

cat call s. schrille Pfeifen (als Missbilligung) n.

catch v.t. & i.ir. fangen, überfallen; einnehmen; anstecken; to ~ cold, sich erkälten; to ~ the train, den Zug erreichen; to ~ up with, aufholen.

catch s. Fang m.; Beute f.; Rundgesang m.; Kniff m.

catching a. ansteckend; 'packend'.

catchword s. Schlagwort n.

catechise v.t. katechisieren.

catechism s. Katechismus m.

categorical a., ~ly adv. kategorisch.

category s. Kategorie f.; Klasse f.

cater v.i. Lebensmittel anschaffen.

caterer s. Lieferant, Einäufer m.

caterpillar s. Raupe f.

caterwaul v.i. miauen; ~ s. Katzengeschrei n.

cat-gut s. Darmsaite f.

cathedral a. Dom...; ~ s. Dom(kirche f.) m.

catheter—charlatan 302

catheter *s.* (*med.*) Katheter *m.*
cathode *s.* Kathode *f.*; ~-rays *s.pl.* Kathodenstrahlen *m.pl.*; ~-ray tube *s.* Braunsche Röhre *f.*
catholic *a.* katholisch; ~ *s.* Katholik *m.*
catholicism *s.* katholische Glaube *m.*
cat's-paw, catspaw *s.* Werkzeug (übertr.) *n.*, Strohmann (übertr.) *m.*
cattle *s.* Vieh, Rindvieh *n.*
cattle-dealer *s.* Viehhändler *m.*
cattle-plague *s.* Rinderpest *f.*
cattle-show *s.* Tierschau *f.*
caucus *s.* örtliche Wahlausschuss *m.*
cauldron *s.* Kessel *m.*
cauliflower *s.* Blumenkohl *m.*
caulk *v.t.* kalfatern.
causal *a.*, ~ly *adv.* ursächlich.
causation *s.* Verursachung *f.*
cause *s.* Ursache *f.*; Rechtssache *f.*; Sache, Umstand *m.*; ~ *v.t.* verursachen.
causeless *a.*, ~ly *adv.* grundlos.
causeway *s.* Dammweg *m.*
caustic *a.* ätzend; ~ *s.* Ätzmittel *n.*
cauterize *v.t.* ätzen, ausbrennen.
cautery *s.* Brenneisen *n.*
caution *s.* Vorsicht *f.*; Bürgschaft, Warnung *f.*; ~ *v.t.* warnen.
cautionary *a.* warnend.
cautious *a.*, ~ly *adv.* vorsichtig.
cavalcade *s.* Reiterzug *m.*
cavalier *s.* Reiter *m.*; Ritter *m.*
cavalry *s.* Reiterei *f.*
cave *s.* Höhle *f.*; ~ *v.i.* (*in*), einsinken.
cavern *s.* Höhle *f.*
cavernous *a.* voll Höhlen.
caviar(e) *s.* Kaviar *m.*
cavil *v.i.* spitzfindig tadeln; ~ *s.* Spitzfindigkeit, Schikane *f.*
cavity *s.* Höhlung, Höhle *f.*
caw *v.i.* krächzen, schreien.
Cayenne-pepper *s.* spanische Pfeffer *m.*
cease *v.i.* aufhören, nachlassen; ~ *v.t.* aufhören machen, einstellen.
cease-fire *s.* (*mil.*) Waffenruhe *f.*
ceaseless *a.* unaufhörlich.
cedar *s.* Zeder *f.*
cede *v.t. & i.* abtreten; nachgeben.
ceiling *s.* Zimmerdecke *f.*; Höchstgrenze *f.*
celebrate *v.t.* preisen; feiern.
celebrated *a.* berühmt.
celebration *s.* Feier *f.*
celebrity *s.* Berühmtheit *f.*
celerity *s.* Geschwindigkeit *f.*
celery *s.* Stangensellerie *m. & f.*
celestial *a.*, ~ly *adv.* himmlisch.
celibacy *s.* ehelose Stand *m.*
celibate *a.* unverheiratet.
cell *s.* (*elek.*) Element *n.*; Zelle *f.*
cellar *s.* Keller *m.*
cellophane *s.* Zellophanpapier *n.*
cellular *a.* zellig.

cellulose *s.* Zellstoff *m.*; ~-wool *s.* Zellwolle *f.*
celtic *a.* keltisch.
cement *s.* Zement *m.*, Kitt *m.*; (*fig.*) Band *n.*; ~ *v.t. & i.* verkitten.
cemetery *s.* Friedhof *m.*
cenotaph *s.* Ehren(grab)mal *n.*
censer *s.* Rauchfass *n.*
censor *s.* Zensor *m.*; to ~ *v.t.* der Zensur unterwerfen, prüfen; censored *a.* geprüft.
censorious *a.*, ~ly *adv.* tadelsüchtig.
censorship *s.* Zensur *f.*
censure *s.* Verweis *m.*; Tadel *m.*; *vote of* ~, Misstrauensantrag *m.*; ~ *v.t.* tadeln, verurteilen.
census *s.* Volkszählung *f.*; Schätzung *f.*
cent *s.* (*Am.*) Cent *m.* (hundertste Teil eines Dollars) *m.*; *per* ~, Prozent *n.*
centaur *s.* Kentaur *m.*
centenarian *s.* Hundertjährige *m.*
centenary *s.* Hundertjahrfeier *f.*
centigrade *a.* hundertgradig.
centimetre *s.* Zentimeter *m.* or *n.*
centipede *s.* Tausendfuss *m.*
central *a.*, ~ly *adv.* im Mittelpunkte befindlich.
central heating *s.* Zentralheizung *f.*; *centrally heated*, mit Zentralheizung.
centralize *v.t.* zentralisieren.
centre *s.* Mittelpunkt *m.*; ~ *of gravity*, Schwerpunkt *m.*; ~ *v.t.* in den Mittelpunkt stellen; ~ *v.i.* im Mittelpunkte zusammenlaufen.
centric(al) *a.* im Mittelpunkte befindlich.
centrifugal *a.* vom Mittelpunkte wegstrebend.
centripetal *a.* zum Mittelpunkte hinstrebend.
centuple *a.* hundertfältig.
century *s.* Jahrhundert *n.*; Hundert *n.*
ceramic *a.* Töpfer..., keramisch.
cereal *a.* Getreide...; ~s *s.pl.* Getreidearten *pl.*; ~ *s.* (*Am.*) Frühstücksspeise aus Getreide.
cerebral *a.* Gehirn...
ceremonial *a.*, ~ly *adv.* förmlich, umständlich; ~ *s.* Zeremoniell *n.*
ceremonious *a.*, ~ly *adv.* feierlich.
ceremony *s.* Feierlichkeit *f.*
certain *a.* gewiss, zuverlässig; *for* ~, bestimmt.
certainly *adv.* gewiss, allerdings, freilich.
certainty *s.* Gewissheit *f.*
certificate *s.* Bescheinigung *f.*; Zeugnis *n.*; ~ *of good conduct*, Führungszeugnis *n.*; ~ *v.t.* ein Zeugnis ausstellen; bescheinigen.
certify *v.t.* bescheinigen; certified *a.* staatlich anerkannt od. geprüft; *certified true copy*, die Richtigkeit der Abschrift wird bezeugt.
certitude *s.* Gewissheit *f.*

cerulean *a.* himmelblau.

cervical *a.* Hals..., Nacken...

cessation *s.* Aufhören *n.*

cession *a.* Abtretung *f.*

cesspool *s.* Senkgrube *f.*

chafe *v.t.* wund reiben; erzürnen; ~ *v.i.* toben, wüten.

chaff *s.* Spreu *f.*; Neckerei *f.*; ~ *v.t.* necken, foppen.

chaffinch *s.* Buchfink *m.*

chagrin *s.* Verdruss, Ärger *m.*

chain *s.* Kette *f.*; Kettenglied *n.*; ~ *of command*, (*mil.*) Befehlsweg *m.*; ~ *of reasoning*, Schlusskette *f.*; ~ *v.t.* anketten.

chain-store *s.* (*Am.*) Reihengeschäft *n.*

chair *s.* Stuhl *m.*; Lehrstuhl *m.*; Vorsitz *m.*; ~ *!* zur Ordnung!; *to take the* ~, die Sitzung eröffnen; *to be in the* ~, den Vorsitz führen (in einer Versammlung).

chair-bottom *s.* Stuhlsitz *m.*

chairman *s.* Vorsitzender *m.*

chairmanship *s.* Vorsitz *m.*

chaise *s.* Chaise *f.*, Halbkutsche .

chalice *s.* Kelch *m.*

chalk *s.* Kreide *f.*; ~ *v.t.* entwerfen.

challenge *v.t.* herausfordern; (Richter od. Geschworene) ablehnen; ~ *s.* Herausforderung *f.*; (*mil.*) Anruf *m.*; Verwerfung, Ablehnung (von Richtern od. Geschworenen) *f.*

chamber *s.* Zimmer *n.*; Kammer *f.*

chamber of commerce *s.* Handelskammer *f.*

chamber-concert *s.* Kammerkonzert *n.*; ~-music *s.* Kammermusik *f.*

chamberlain *s.* Kammerherr *m.*

chamber-maid *s.* Kammermädchen *n.*

chameleon *s.* Chamäleon *n.*

chamfer *s.* Auskehlung *f.*

chamois *s.* Gemse *f.*; Gemsleder *n.*

champ *v.t. & i.* kauen; verschlingen.

champagne *s.* Champagner *m.*

champaign *s.* flache Land *n.*

champion *s.* Kämpe, Vorkämpfer *m.*; (Sport) Meister *m.*; preisgekrönte Rassetier *n.*; ~ *v.t.* verteidigen.

championship *s.* (Sport) Meisterschaft *f.*

chance *s.* Zufall *m.*; Schicksal *n.*; Glück *n.*; Aussicht *f.*; gute Gelegenheit *f.*; *by* ~, von ungefähr; *to give a person a* ~, einem Gelegenheit geben sich zu bewähren; *to take a* ~, es darauf ankommen lassen; *to take no* ~s, es nicht darauf ankommen lassen; ~ *v.i.* sich zutragen.

chancellery *s.* Kanzlei *f.*

chancellor *s.* Kanzler *f.*; ~ *of the Exchequer*, britische Finanzminister *m.*

chancery *s.* Kanzlei *f.*

chandelier *s.* Armleuchter *m.*

chandler *s.* Lichtzieher *m.*; Krämer *m.*

change *v.t.* ändern, wechseln, tauschen; herausgeben (auf); ~ *v.i.* sich ändern; sich umziehen; (Eisenbahn) umsteigen; ~ *s.* Veränderung *f.*; Tausch, Wechsel *m.*; Kleingeld *f.*; Agio *n.*; Börse *f.*; ~ *of clothes* (linen), Anzug (Wäsche) zum Wechseln; *small* ~, Kleingeld *n.*; *a* ~ *for the worse*, eine Wendung zum Schlimmeren *f.*; *for a* ~, zur Abwechslung.

changeable *a.*, -ly *adv.* veränderlich.

changeful *a.* unbeständig.

changeless *a.* unveränderlich.

changeling *s.* Wechselbalg *m.*

changeover *s.* Umstellung *f.*

channel *s.* Kanal *m.*; Rinne *f.*; Flussbett *n.*; (*fig.*) Weg, *m.*; *through official* ~s, im Instanzenweg; ~ *v.t.* aushöhlen, kannellieren.

chant *s.* Gesang *m.*; ~ *v.t.* singen.

chaos *s.* Chaos *n.*, Wirrwarr *m.*

chaotic *a.* chaotisch.

chap *s.* Spalte *f.*; Riss *m.*; Kinnbacken von Tieren *m.*; Kerl, Bursche *m.*

chapel *s.* Kapelle *f.*

chaperon *s.* Anstandsdame *f.*; ~ *v.t.* Damen öffentlich begleiten.

chaplain *s.* Kaplan, Feldprediger *m.*

chaplet *s.* Kranz *m.*; Rosenkranz *m.*

chapter *s.* Kapitel *n.*; Domkapitel *n.*

char *v.t.* verkohlen; *v.i.* um Tagelohn dienen; ~ *s.* Tagearbeit *f.*

char-a-banc *s.* Gesellschaftswagen *m.*

character *s.* Merkmal *n.*; Schriftzug *m.*; Charakter *m.*; Original *n.*, Sonderling *m.*; Stand *m.*; Rolle *f.*; Zeugnis *n.*; *the characters*, die handelnden Personen (in einem Stück oder Roman).

characterize *v.t.* charakterisieren.

characteristic *a.* charakteristisch; ~ *s.* Kennzeichen *n.*

charade *s.* Silbenrätsel *n.*

charcoal-burner *s.* Köhler.

charge *v.t.* laden, beladen; beauftragen; beschuldigen; angreifen; anrechnen; debitieren; einschärfen; ~ *s.* Last *f.*; Ladung *f.*; Auftrag *m.*; Beschwerde *f.*; Aufsicht *f.*; Amt *n.*; Kosten *pl.*; Mündel *n.*; Ermahnung *f.*; Beschuldigung, Anklage *f.*; Angriff *m.*; ~s *pl.* Spesen *pl.*; *to be in* ~ *of*, die Leitung von etwas haben; *to take* ~ *of*, die Sorge für etwas übernehmen; *free of* ~, kostenfrei.

chargeable *a.*, -ly *adv.* lästig; kostspielig; zurechenbar.

chargé d'affaires, Geschäftsträger *m.*

charger *s.* Schlachtross *n.*

chariot *s.* (Triumph-, Kriegs-) Wagen *m.*

charitable *a.*, -bly *adv.* wohltätig.

charity *s.* christliche Liebe *f.*; Mildtätigkeit *f.*; Wohltätigkeitseinrichtung *f.*; milde Gabe *f.*, Almosen *n.*

charlatan *s.* Marktschreier *m.*

charlatanism s. Marktschreierei f.

charm v.t. bezaubern; ~ s. Zauber.

charming a. bezaubernd, reizend.

charnel-house s. Beinhaus n.

chart s. Seekarte f.; Tabelle f.; Übersichtstafel f.

charter s. Gründungsbrief m.; Urkunde f.; ~ v.t. privilegieren; (ein Schiff) mieten.

chartered accountant s. beeidigter Bücherrevisor m.

charwoman s. Scheuerfrau f.

chary a. sorgsam; karg.

chase v.t. jagen, verfolgen; ziselieren; einfassen; ~ s. Jagd f.; to give ~, Jagd machen.

chasm s. Kluft f., Schlund m.

chassis s. Rahmen (m.) (eines Wagens).

chaste a., ~ly adv. keusch.

chasten v.t. züchtigen, reinigen.

chastise v.t. züchtigen.

chastisement s. Züchtigung f.

chastity s. Keuschheit f.

chat s. Plauderei f.; ~ v.i. plaudern.

chattels s. bewegliche Habe f.

chatter v.i. plaudern; klappern; ~ s. Geschnatter n.; Gezwitscher n.

chatter-box s. Plappermaul m.

chauffeur s. Chauffeur, Führer m.

cheap a., ~ly adv. wohlfeil, billig.

cheapen v.t. verbilligen.

cheat s. Betrug m.; Betrüger m.; ~ v.t. betrügen.

check s. Anstoss m.; Einhalt m.; Hindernis n.; Kontrolle f.; Gepäckschein m.; Kontrollmarke f.; (Am.) Scheck m.; ~ v.t. zurückhalten, hemmen; kontrollieren; nachprüfen; ~ v.i. Schach bieten; to ~ out, (Am.) Hotel verlassen, (Buch) ausleihen; ~-room (Am.) Gepäckaufbewahrung f.

check-book s. Scheckbuch n.

checkmate s. Schachmatt n.; ~ v.t. matt setzen.

cheek s. Backe, Wange f.; (fam.) Unverschämtheit f.

cheeky a. frech.

cheek-bone s. Backenknochen m.

cheer s. Bewirtung f.; Frohsinn m.; Beifallsruf m.; of good ~, gutes Mutes; ~ v.t. & i. erheitern; mit lautem Ruf begrüssen.

cheerful a., ~ly adv. fröhlich.

cheerfulness, cheeriness, Heiterkeit f.

cheerless a. mutlos; freudlos.

cheery a. heiter, lustig.

cheese s. Käse m.

cheesemonger s. Käsehändler m.

cheeseparing a. knauserig.

chef s. Küchenchef, Koch, m.

chemical a. chemisch; ~ action, chemische Wirkung f.; (mil.) ~ warfare, Gaskrieg, chemische Krieg m.; ~-warfare agent,

Kampfstoff m.; ~s s.pl. Chemikalien f.pl.

chemise s. (Frauen-) Hemd n.

chemist s. Drogist m.; Chemiker m.

chemistry s. Chemie f.

cheque s. Scheck, Bankschein m.

chequer v.t. karrieren, bunt machen; ~ s. gewürfeltes Muster n.

cherish v.t. pflegen, hegen; liebkosen.

cherry s. Kirsche f.

cherry-brandy s. Kirschwasser n.

cherub s. Cherub m.

chess s. Schach(spiel) n.

chess-board s. Schachbrett n.

chess-man s. Schachfigur f.

chest s. Lade, Kiste f.; Brust f.; ~ of drawers, Kommode f.

chestnut s. Kastanie f.; ~ a. kastanienbraun.

cheviot s. Cheviot m.

chevron s. (mil.) Unteroffiziersstreifen m.

chew v.t. & i. kauen; (fig.) überlegen.

chewing gum s. Kaugummi m.

chewing tobacco s. Kautaback m.

chicane s. Schikane f.; ~ v.t. schikanieren.

chicanery s. Schikanieren n.

chick, Küken n.

chicken s. (junges) Huhn n.

chicken-hearted a. feig.

chicken-louse s. Hühnerstall m.

chicken-pox s. Windpocken pl.

chicory s. Cichorie f.

chide v.t. & i.st. schelten.

chief a., ~ly adv. vornehmst; hauptsächlich; ~ s. Erste m.; Oberhaupt n.; ~ of staff, Generalstabschef m.

chieftain s. Anführer, Häuptling m.

chilblain s. Frostbeule f.

child s. Kind n.; ~-welfare Kinderfürsorge f.

childbed s. Wochenbett n.

childbirth s. Gebären n.

childhood s. Kindheit f.

childish a., ~ly adv. kindisch.

childless a. kinderlos.

childlike a. kindlich.

children pl. von child.

chill a. frostig; ~ s. Kälte f.; Verkühlung f.; to take the ~ off, ganz wenig anwärmen; to ~ v.t. kühlen; mutlos machen.

chilly a. etwas kalt, frostig.

chime s. Glockenspiel n.; ~ v.t. Glocken läuten; ~ v.i. einstimmig sein.

chimera s. Hirngespinst n.

chimerical a., ~ly adv. schimärisch.

chimney s. Schornstein m.

chimney-piece s. Kaminsims m.

chimney-sweep(er) s. Schornsteinfeger m.

chimpanzee s. Schimpanse m.

chin s. Kinn n.

china s. Porzellan n.

Chink s. (sl.) Chinese m.

chink s. Ritze f.; Spalt m.; ~ v.t. & i. klimpern; sich spalten.

chintz s. Zitz m., Möbelkattun m.

chip v.t. schnitzeln; abraspeln; ~ s. Span m.; Schnitzel n.

chiromancy s. Handlesen n.

chiropodist s. Hühneraugenschneider m.

chirp v.i. zwitschern; ~ s. Gezwitscher n.

chirrup s. Zwitschern n.

chisel s. Meissel m.; ~ v.t. meisseln.

chit s. Schein m., Schriftstück n.

chit-chat s. Geschwätz n.

chivalrous a. ritterlich.

chivalry s. Ritterschaft f.; Tapferkeit f.

chive s. Schnittlauch m.

chloride s. Chlorid n.

chlorine s. Chlor n.

chloroform s. Chloroform n.; ~ v.t. chloroformieren.

chlorosis s. (med.) Bleichsucht f.

chock s. Holzkeil m.

chock-full a. gestopft voll.

chocolate s. Schokolade f.; ~s s.pl. Pralinen f.pl.; box of ~s s. Pralinenschachtel f.

choice s. Wahl f.; Auswahl f.; ~ a., ~ly adv. auserlesen, sehr schön.

choir s. Chor m.

choke v.t. ersticken; verstopfen.

cholera s. Cholera f.

choleric a. cholerisch; hitzig.

choose v.t. & i.st. wählen, vorziehen.

chop v.t. & i. spalten; ~ s. Schnitt m.; Stück n.; Röstrippchen, Kotelett n.

chopping-block s. Hackblock m.

chopping-knife s. Hackmesser n.

choppy a. unstet; hohl (sea).

choral a. chorartig, Chor...

chord s. Saite f.; Akkord m.

chore s. (Am.) Hausarbeit f.; to ~ v.i. Hausarbeit tun.

chorister s. Chorsänger m.

chorus s. Chor m.

chrestomathy s. Blütenlese f.

chrism s. Salböl n.

Christ s. Christus m.

christen v.t. taufen.

Christendom s. Christenheit f.

Christening s. Taufe f.

Christian a., ~ly adv. christlich; ~ s. Christ m.; ~ name s. Vorname m.

christianize v.t. zum Christen machen.

Christianity s. Christentum n.

Christmas, (Xmas) s. Weihnachten.

Christmas-box s. Weihnachtsgeschenk n.

Christmas-carol s. Weihnachtslied n.

chromatic a. chromatisch.

chrome s. chromgelb.

chromium s. Chrom n.; ~-plated a. verchromt.

chronic a. chronisch; langwierig.

chronicle s. Chronik f.; ~ v.t. aufzeichnen.

chronicler s. Chronist m.

chronological a., ~ly adv. chronologisch.

chronology s. Zeitrechnung f.

chrysalis s. (Insekten) Puppe f.

chub s. Kaulbarsch m.

chubby a. kurz und dick; pausbäckig.

chuck v.i. glucken; sanft stossen; (fam.) wegwerfen; ~ s. Glucken n; ~ s.(mech.) Spannfutter n.

chuckle v.i. schmunzeln, kichern.

chum s. Stubengenosse m.; Kamerad.

chump s. Klotz m.

chunk s. Kloben, Klumpen m.

church s. Kirche f.; ~-attendance, Kirchenbesuch m.

churching s.Kirchgang einer Wöchnerin m.

churchman s. Mitglied (n) der anglikanischen Kirche.

churchwarden s. Kirchenvorsteher m.

churchy a. kirchlich (gesinnt).

churchyard s. Kirchhof m.

churl s. Bauer m.; Grobian m.

churlish a., ~ly adv. grob; mürrisch.

churn v.t. buttern; ~ s. Butterfass n.

chute s. Gleitbahn f.

chyme s. Speisebrei m.

cicada s. Zikade, Baumgrille f.

cicatrice s. Narbe f.

cicatrize v.i. vernarben.

cider s. Apfelwein m.

cigar s. Zigarre f.

cigar-case s. Zigarrentasche f.

cigarette s. Zigarette f.; ~-case s. Zigarettenetui n.; ~-end (Am. ~-butt, ~-stump) s. Zigarettenstummel m.

cigar-holder s. Zigarrenspitze f.

cincture s. Gurt, Gürtel m.

cinder s. Löschkohle f.; Schlacke f.

cinderella s. Aschenbrödel n.

cinder-sifter s. Aschensieb n.

cinema s. Kino n.

cinerary a. Aschen...

cinnabar s. Zinnober m.

cinnamon s. Zimt m.

cipher s. Ziffer f.; Null f.; Geheimschrift f.; ~ v.i. rechnen; ~ v.t. mit Chiffern schreiben.

circle s. Kreis m.; Kreislinie f.; ~ v.t. einschliessen; ~ v.i. umkreisen.

circuit s. Umkreis m.; (elek.) Stromkreis m.; short ~, Kurzschluss m.; Bezirk m.; Rundreise der Richter f.

circuitous a. weitschweifig, Um...

circular a., ~ly adv. kreisförmig; ~ s. Rundschreiben n.

circularize v.t. Zirkulare herumschicken an.

circular-tour ticket s. Rundreisebillet n.

circulate v.t. in Umlauf bringen; ~ v.i. umlaufen; circulating library s. Leihbibliothek f.

circulation s. Kreislauf, Umlauf m.; Auflage (einer Zeitung) f.

circulatory a. Kreislauf...

circumcise *v.t.* beschneiden.
circumcision *s.* Beschneidung *f.*
circumference *s.* Umfang *m.*
circumflex *s.* Zirkumflex (Akzent) *m.*
circumlocution *s.* Umschweif *m.*
circumnavigate *v.t.* umschiffen.
circumscribe *v.t.* umschreiben; einschränken.
circumscriptions *s.* Begrenzung *f.*
circumspect *a.*, ~ly *adv.* umsichtig.
circumspection *s.* Umsicht, Vorsicht *f.*
circumstance *s.* Umstand, Zufall *m.*
circumstanced *a.* beschaffen.
circumstantial *a.*, ~ly *adv.* zufällig; eingehend; ~ evidence *s.* (*law*) Indizienbeweis *m.*
circumvent *v.t.* umgehen; überlisten.
circus *s.* Zirkus *m.*
cirrus *s.* Federwolke *f.*
Cistercian *a.* zisteriensich.
cistern *s.* Wasserbehälter *m.*
citadel *s.* Festung *f.*, Zitadelle *f.*
citation *s.* Vorladung *f.*; Zitat *n.*
cite *v.t.* vorladen; (Stellen) anführen.
citizen *s.* Bürger *m.*
citizenship *s.* Bürgerrecht *n.*
citric *a.*, ~ acid *s.* Zitronensäure *f.*
citrine *a.* zitronengelb.
citron *s.* Limone *f.*
city *s.* (grosse) Stadt *f.*; Altstadt *f.*
city-page *s.* Handelsteil der Zeitung.
civic *a.* bürgerlich.
civil *a.*, ~ly *adv.* bürgerlich; höflich; ~ action *s.* (*law*) Zivilklage *f.*; ~ code *s.* bürgerliches Gesetzbuch; ~ list *s.* Zivilliste *f.*; ~ rights *s.pl.* Bürgerrechte *n.pl.*; ~ servant *s.* Staatsbeamte *m.*; ~ service *s.* Staatsdienst *m.*; ~ war *s.* Bürgerkrieg *m.*
civilian *s.* Zivilist; Bürger *m.*
civility *s.* Artigkeit *f.*, Höflichkeit *f.*
civilization *s.* Kultur, Zivilisation *f.*
civilize *v.t.* verfeinern, gesittet machen.
clack *s.* Geklapper *n.*; Geplauder *n.*; ~ *v.i.* klappern; plaudern.
clad *p.* gekleidet.
claim *v.t.* Anspruch machen, fordern; ~ *s.* Anspruch *m.*; Forderung *f.*
claimant *s.* Forderer *m.*
clairvoyant (*frz.*), *s.* Hellseher, *m.*
clamber *v.i.* klettern.
clammy *a.* kleberig.
clamorous *a.* schreiend, tobend.
clamour *s.* Geschrei, *n.*; ~ *v.i.* schreien.
clamp *s.* Balken *m.*; Klammer *f.*; ~ *v.t.* verklammern, verzapfen.
clan *s.* Stamm *m.*; Sippschaft *f.*
clandestine *a.*, ~ly *adv.* heimlich.
clang *s.* Schall *m.*; ~ *v.i.* schallen.
clangour *s.* Geklirr *n.*
clank *s.* Geklirr *n.*; ~ *v.i.* klirren.
clannish *a.* eng zusammenhaltend (von Personen).

clap *v.t.* klappern; beklatschen; ~ *v.i.* zusammenschlagen; ~ *s.* Klaps, Schlag *m.*; Klatschen *n.*
claptrap *s.* Getue *n.*; Windbeutelei *f.*
claret *s.* Rotwein, Bordeaux *m.*
clarification *s.* Abklärung *f.*
clarify *v.t.* abklären; aufhellen; ~ *v.i.* sich aufklären.
clarion *s.* Trompete *f.*
clari(o)net *s.* Klarinette *f.*
clash *v.t.* & *i.* zusammenstossen; rasseln; widerstreiten; ~ *s.* Stoss *m.*; Geklirr *n.*; Widerspruch *m.*; (*mil.*) Zusammenstoss *m.*
clasp *s.* Haken *m.*; Schnalle *f.*; Spange *f.*; Umarmung *f.*; ~ *v.t.* zuhaken; sich anklammern, umarmen.
clasp-knife *s.* Taschenmesser *n.*
class *s.* Klasse *f.*; ~ *v.t.* klassifizieren.
classic(al) *s.* mustergiltig, klassisch; classic *s.* Klassiker *m.*
classification *s.* Einteilung in Klassen *f.*
classify *v.t.* klassifizieren, einordnen.
class-war *s.* Klassenkampf *m.*
clatter *v.t.* & *i.* klappern; ~ *s.* Getöse *n.*
clause *s.* Klausel *f.*; (*gram.*) Satzglied *n.*, (Neben-)Satz *m.*
claustral *a.* klösterlich.
clavicle *s.* Schlüsselbein *n.*
claw *s.* Klaue, Pfote *f.*; ~ *v.t.* kratzen.
clay *s.* Ton, Lehm *m.*; ~ *v.t.* mit Tonerde mischen, düngen.
clayey, clayish *a.* tonig, lehmig.
clean *a.*, ~ly *adv.* rein, sauber, blank; ~ *adv.* gänzlich; ~ *v.t.* reinigen.
cleanly *a.* rein, sauber; unschuldig; ~ *adv.* reinlich.
cleanse *v.t.* reinigen, scheuern.
clean-shaven *a.* glattrasiert.
clear *a.*, ~ly *adv.* klar, rein, hell; deutlich; schuldlos; netto; gänzlich; *in* ~, im Klartext; ~ *v.t.* reinigen; aufklären; befreien; abräumen; springen über; ~ *v.i.* hell, frei werden.
clearance *s.* Freilegung, Räumung *f.*; Abfertigung *f.*; ~-sale, Ausverkauf *m.*
clear-headed *a.* klardenkend.
clearing *s.* Lichtung *f.*; Abrechnung *f.*; ~-House *s.* Abrechnungskontor *n.*
clear-sighted *a.* scharfsichtig.
cleat *s.* Klampe *f.*
cleavage *s.* Spaltung *f.*
cleave *v.i.st.* ankleben; ~ *v.t.st.* spalten.
clef *s.* (*mus.*) Schlüssel *m.*
cleft *s.* Spalte *f.*
clemency *s.* Gnade, Milde *f.*; ~-plea, *petition for* ~, (*law*) Gnadengesuch *n.*
clement *a.* sanft, mild.
clench *see* clinch.
clergy *s.* Geistlichkeit *f.*
clergyman *s.* Geistliche *m.*
cleric(al) *a.* geistlich; Schreib...; clerical

error *s.* Schreibfehler *m.*; **clerical staff** *s.* Büropersonal *n.*
clerk *s.* Kommis *m.*; Sekretär *m.*
clerkship *s.* Schreiberstelle.
clever *a.*, ~ly *adv.* gewandt, gescheit.
clew *s.* Knäuel *m.*
cliché *s.* Block *m.*; abgedroschene Redewendung *f.*
click *s.* Ticken (einer Uhr) *m.*; Türklinke *f.*; ~ *v.i.* ticken.
client *s.* Klient *m.*, Kunde *m.*; (*law*) Mandant *m.*
cliff *s.* Klippe *f.*
climacteric *a.* zu den Wechseljahren gehörg; ~ *s.* Wechseljahr *n.*
climate *s.* Himmelsstrich *m.*; Klima *n.*
climatic *a.* klinatisch.
climax *s.* Gipfelpunkt *m.*
climb *v.i.* klettern; ~ *v.t.* ersteigen.
clime *s.* Klima *n.*
clinch *v.t.* anpacken; (die Faust) ballen; nieten; befestigen; entscheiden, erledigen; ~ *s.* Vernietung *f.*; Klinke *f.*
clincher *s.* Haken *m.*; Klammer *f.*
cling *v.i.st.* anklammern, ankleben.
clinic(al) *a.* klinisch.
clink *v.i.* & *t.* klingen, klirren; (Gläser) anstossen; ~ *s.* Geklirr *n.*
clinker *s.* Klinker(stein) *m.*
clip *v.t.* beschneiden; (Billette) lochen; ~ *s.* Zwicke *f.*; Hosenklammer *f.*
clipper *s.* Schnellsegler *m.*
clippings *s.pl.* Abfälle *m.pl.*
clique *s.* Clique *f.*, Klüngel *m.*
cloak *s.* Mantel *m.*; (*fig.*) Deckmantel *m.*; ~-room *s.* (Eisenbahn) Gepäckaufbewahrung *f.*; Garderobe *f.*; ~ *v.t.* bemänteln.
clock *s.* Uhr *f.*; Schlaguhr *f.*; Wanduhr.
clockwise *adv.* in der Richtung des Uhrzeigers.
clock-work *s.* Uhrwerk *n.*
clod *s.* Erdkloss, Klumpen *m.*
clog *v.t.* beladen; hemmen; ~ *v.i.* gerinnen; ~ *s.* Last *f.*; Hindernis *n.*; Klotz *m.*; Holzschuh *m.*
cloister *s.* Kloster *n.*; Kreuzgang *m.*
close *v.t.* verschliessen; beschliessen; vereinigen; handgemein werden; *to ~ up*, aufschliessen; *to ~ down*, (Betrieb) einstellen, stillegen; ~ *v.i.* sich schliessen; übereinkommen; ~ *s.* Einzäunung *f.*; Schluss, Beschluss *m.*; Ruhepunkt *m.*; ~ *a.* verschlossen; verschwiegen: knapp; dicht, steif; bündig, trübe; drückend (Luft); einsam; geizig; ~ *prisoner*, strengbewachter Gefangene *m.*; ~ *quarters*, Handgemenge *n.*; ~ *season*, Schonzeit (Jagd) *f.*; **close-up** *s.* (*Film*) Nahaufnahme *f.*
closely *adv.* geschlossen; genau, strenge; verborgen; sparsam.
closet *s.* Kabinett *n.*; Verschlag *m.*; Abort

m. (*W.C.*=*water closet*); (*Am.*) Schrank *m.*; ~ *v.t.* einschliessen.
closure *s.* Einschliessung *f.*; Schliessung *f.*; Schluss der Debatte *m.*
clot *a.* Klumpen *m.*; ~ *v.i.* gerinnen.
cloth *s.* Zeug, Tuch *n.*; Tischtuch *n.*; Leinwand *f.*; geistliche Stand *m.*; *bound in ~*, in Leinwand gebunden.
clothe *v.t.* bekleiden; ~ *v.i.* sich kleiden.
clothes *s.pl.* Kleider *n.pl*; Wäsche *f.*
clothes-basket *s.* Wäschekorb *m.*
clothes-brush *s.* Kleiderbürste *f.*
clothes-line *s.* Wäscheleine *f.*
clothes-peg *s.* Wäscheklammer *f.*
clothes-press *s.* Kleiderschrank *m.*
clothing *s.* Kleidung *f.*
cloth-worker *s.* Tuchwirker *m.*
cloud *s.* Wolke *f.*; (*fig.*) Gewühl *n.*; ~ *v.t.* bewölken, verdunkeln; ~ *v.i.* sich unwölken.
cloudburst *s.* Wolkenbruch *m.*
cloudless *a.* unbewölkt.
cloudy *a.*, ~ily *adv.* wolkig.
clout *s.* Lappen *m.*
clove *s.* Gewürznelke *f.*
cloven *a.* gespalten.
clover *s.* Klee *m.*; (*fig.*) in ~, üppig.
clown *s.* Clown, Hanswurst *m.*
clownish *a.*, ~ly *adv.* bäuerisch, grob.
cloy *v.t.* überladen; sättigen.
club *s.* Keule *f.*; Kreuz, Treff (der Karte) *n.*; Klub *m.*, Verein *m.*; ~ *v.t.* & *i.* beitragen; sich vereinigen.
club-foot *s.* Klumpfuss *m.*
club-law *s.* Faustrecht *n.*
cluck *v.i.* glucken.
clue *s.* Leitfaden *m.*; (*fig.*) Schlüssel *m.*; Anhaltspunkt *m.*
clump *s.* Klumpen *m.*; Gruppe *f.*
clumsy *a.*, ~ily *adv.* plump, ungeschickt.
cluster *s.* Büschel *m.*; Traube *f.*; Haufen *m.*; ~ *v.t.* häufen; ~ *v.i.* in Büscheln wachsen.
clutch *v.t.* greifen; packen; umspannen; ~ *s.* Griff *m.*; Kuppelung *f.*
clutter *s.* Verwirrung *f.*; ~ *v.i.* verworren rennen.
coach *s.* Kutsche; Eisenbahnwagen *m.*; Überlandomnibus *m.*; (*pers.*) Einpauker *m.*; (*Sport*) Trainer *m.*; *a ~ and four*, vierspännige Kutsche *f.*; ~ *v.t.* einpauken; trainieren.
coach-box *s.* Kutschbock *m.*
coach-house *s.* Schuppen *m.*
coachman *s.* Kutscher *m.*
coadjutor *s.* Mitgehilfe *m.*
coagulate *v.t.* gerinnen machen; ~ *v.i.* gerinnen.
coal *s.* Kohle *f.*; ~ *v.i.* zu Kohle werden; Kohlen einnehmen.
coal-dust *s.* Kohlenstaub *m.*
coalesce *v.i.* verschmelzen.
coalfield *s.* Kohlenlager *n.*; Kohlenfeld *n.*

coalition s. Vereinigung f.
coal-mine, coal-pit s. Kohlengrube f.
coal-shed s. Kohlenschuppen m.
coarse a., **~ly** adv. grob, gemein.
coast s. Küste f.; ~ v.i. längs der Küste hinfahren; einen Abhang hinabfahren.
coastal a. Küsten...
coat s. Rock m.; Fell, n.; Rinde f.; ~ of arms, Wappenschild n.; ~ of mail, Panzerhemd n.; ~ v.t. bekleiden.
coating s. Schicht; Anstrich m.
coax v.t. schmeicheln; beschwatzen.
cob s. Kolben m.; grosse Haselnuss.
cobalt s. Kobalt m.
cobble v.t. Kieselstein m.; to ~, flicken.
cobbler s. Schuhflicker m.
cobweb s. Spinngewebe n.
cocaine s. Kokain n.
cock s. Hahn m.; Heuschober m.; Dampfhahn m.; ~ v.t. (den Hahn) spannen; aufstutzen; ~ v.i. stolzieren.
cockade s. Kokarde f.
cock-a-doodle-doo kikeriki!
cockatoo s. Kakadu m.
cockatrice s. Basilisk m.
cock-chafer s. Maikäfer m.
cocked a. ~ hat s. dreieckige Hut m.
cockerel s. junge Hahn m.
cock-eyed a. schief.
cock-horse adv. rittlings, zu Pferde.
cockle v.t. runzeln; ~ s. Herzmuschel f.
cockney s. Londoner m.
cockpit s. Kampfplatz für Hähne m.; (avi.) Führersitz m.
cock-roach s. Schabe f.
cock-sure a. totsicher.
coco, cocoa s. Kokospalme f.
cocoa s. Kakao m.
cocktail s. Parvenü m.; Cocktail m.
cocoa-nut s. Kokosnuss f.
cocoon s. Seidenraupenpuppe f.
cod s. Kabeljau m.; ~-liver oil, Lebertran m.
coddle v.t. verhätscheln.
code s. Gesetzbuch n.; (Telegramm) Schlüssel m.; ~ of civil procedure, Zivilprozessordnung f.; ~ of criminal procedure, Strafprozessordnung f.; commercial ~, Handelsgesetzbuch n.; **~-name** s. Deckname m.; to ~ v.t. chiffrieren.
codicil s. Kodizill n.
codification s. Kodifizierung f.
codify v.t. kodifizieren.
coeducation s. gemeinsame Erziehung (f.) der Knaben und Mädchen.
coefficient a. mitwirkend; ~ s. Koefficient m.
coerce v.t. zwingen.
coercion s. Zwang m.
coercive a. zwingend, Zwangs...
coeval a. gleichalt, gleichzeitig.
coexist v.i. zugleich da sein.

coexistent a. gleichzeitig.
coffee s. Kaffee m.
coffee-bean s. Kaffeebohne f.
coffee-grounds s.pl. Kaffeesatz m.
coffee-mill s. Kaffeemühle f.
coffee-pot s. Kaffeekanne f.
coffee-roaster s. Kaffeebrenner f.
coffee-room s. Gastzimmer im Hotel.
coffee-shop s. Imbissraum m.
coffer s. Kasten, Koffer m.
coffin s. Sarg m.
cog s. Zahn (am Rade) m.
cogency s. zwingende Kraft f.
cogent a., **~ly** adv. zwingend, triftig.
cogitate v.i. denken, erwägen.
cogitation s. Denken n.; Gedanke m.
cognate a. verwandt.
cognition s. (Er)kenntnis, Kunde f.
cognizance s. Kenntnis f.
cognizant a. wissend.
cogwheel s. Zahnrad, Kammrad m.
cohabit v.i. bei(sammen)wohnen.
cohabitation s. (eheliche) Beiwohnung f.; Beisammenwohnen n.
co-heir s. Miterbe m.
co-heiress s. Miterbin f.
cohere v.i. zusammenhängen.
coherence s. Zusammenhang m.
coherent s. zusammenhängend.
cohesion s. Kohäsion f.; Zusammenhang m.
cohesive a. zusammenhaltend.
cohort s. Kohorte f.
coign s. Ecke f.; ~ of vantage, Aussichtspunkt m.
coil v.t. aufwickeln; ~ s. (Draht) Rolle, f.; Windung f.; Schlinge f.
coin s. Münze f.; false ~, falsche Geld n.; ~ v.t. münzen; erdichten.
coinage s. Geld n.; Gepräge n.
coincide v.i. zusammentreffen.
coincidence s. Zusammentreffen n.
coincident a. übereinstimmend; zusammentreffend.
coiner s. Falschmünzer m.
coke s. Koks m.; ~ v.t. verkoken.
cold a., **~ly** adv. kalt; ~ s. Kälte, Erkältung f.; to catch ~, sich erkälten, einen Schnupfen bekommen.
coldness s. Kälte f.
cold storage s. Kühlraum m.
colic s. Bauchkrampf m., Kolik f.
collaborate v.i. zusammenarbeiten.
collaboration s. Mitarbeiterschaft f.
collaborator s. Mitarbeiter m.
collapse v.i. zusammenfallen.; ~ s. Zusammenbruch m.
collapsible a. zusammenlegbar, zusammenklappbar; ~ boat s. Faltboot m.
collar s. Halsband m.; Kragen m.; Halfter f.; **~-bone** s. Schlüsselbein n.; ~ v.t. beim Kragen fassen.
collate v.t. vergleichen; verleihen.

collateral *a.*, **~ly** *adv.* Seiten..., neben; gleichlaufend; **~s** *s.pl.* Seitenverwandte *m. & f.pl.*

collation *s.* Imbiss *m.*

colleague *s.* Kollege, Amtsgenosse *m.*

collect *v.t.* sammeln; einkassieren; **~** *s.* kurze Gebet *n.*, Kollekte *f.*

collected *a.* ruhig, gefasst.

collection *s.* Sammlung *f.*; Abholung *f.*; Leerung der Briefkästen *f.*

collective *a.* gesammelt; Kollektiv...; **~** *agreement*, Tarifvertrag *m.*; **~** *security*, kollektive Sicherheit *f.*

collector *s.* Sammler *m.*

college *s.* Kollegium *n.*; höhere Bildungsanstalt *f.*; Studenteninternat *n.*

collegiate *a.* Kollegiat...

collide *v.i.* zusammenstossen (von Schiffen etc.).

collier *s.* Kohlenarbeiter *m.*; Kohlenschiff *n.*

colliery *s.* Kohlenbergwerk *n.*, Zeche *f.*

collision *s.* Zusammenstoss *m.*

collocation *s.* Stellung, Ordnung *f.*

collodion *s.* Kollodium *n.*

collop *s.* Fleischschnitte *f.*

colloquial *a.* in der Umgangssprache üblich.

colloquialism *s.* Ausdruck der Umgangssprache *m.*

colloquy *s.* Gespräch *n.*

collotype *s.* Lichtdruck *m.*

collusion *s.* heimliche Einverständnis *n.*; Durchstecherei *f.*

collusive *a.*, **~ly** *adv.* abgekartet.

colon *s.* Doppelpunkt *m.*

colonel *s.* Oberst *m.*

colonelcy *s.* Oberstenstelle *f.*

colonial *a.* Kolonial...

colonize *v.t.* besiedeln, kolonisieren.

colonist *s.* Kolonist, Ansiedler *m.*

colonnade *s.* Säulengang *m.*

colony *s.* Kolonie *f.*

colophony *s.* Geigenharz *n.*

coloration *s.* Färbung *f.*

colossal *a.* kolossal, riesig.

colossus *s.* Koloss *m.*

colour *s.* Farbe *f.*; Schein *m.*; Vorwand *m.*; **~s** *pl.* Fahne *f.*; *to show a person in his true ~,* jemand nach dem Leben malen; **~** *v.t.* färben; beschönigen; *v.i.* erröten.

colour-blind *a.* farbenblind.

colour-box *s.* Malkasten *m.*

coloured *a.* farbig (von Personen).

colouring *s.* Färben, Beschönigen *n.*

colourless *a.* farblos.

colours *s.pl.* Fahne *f.*; *with the ~,* bei der Wehrmacht.

colt *s.* Füllen *n.*; (*fig.*) Wildfang *m.*

columbine *s.* (*bot.*) Akelei *f.*

column *s.* Säule *f.*; (*print.*) Spalte *f.*; Kolonne *f.*

columnar *a.* säulenförmig.

columnist *s.* Kommentator (in der Presse) *m.*

coma *s.* Lethargie, Scheintod *m.*

comatose *a.* schlafsüchtig.

comb *s.* Kamm *m.*; Striegel *m.*; **~** *v.t.* kämmen, striegeln.

combat *s.* Kampf *m.*; Gefecht *n.*; *single ~,* Zweikampf *m.*; **~** *v.i.* kämpfen; **~** *v.t.* bekämpfen.

combatant *s.* Kombattant *m.*

combative *a.* streitsüchtig.

comber *s.* Wollkämmer *m.*

combination *s.* Verbindung *f.*; **~** *s.pl.* Hemdhose *f.*

combine *v.t.* verbinden; (*mil.*) *combined operations,* Operationen der verbundenen Waffen; **~** *v.i.* sich verbinden; **~** *s.* Zusammenschluss, Verband, Konzern *m.*

combustible *a.* verbrennlich; **~** *s.* Brennmaterial *n.*

combustion *s.* Verbrennung *f.*

come *v.i.st.* kommen; werden; *to ~ about,* sich wenden; sich zutragen; *to ~ at,* erlangen; *to ~ by,* etwas erlangen; *to ~ for,* holen kommen, kommen um...; *to ~ off,* zustande kommen; davonkommen; loskommen; *to ~ of age,* mündig werden; *to ~ round,* sich anders besinnen; sich erholen; *to ~ to pass,* geschehen, sich ereignen.

comedian *s.* Komödiant *m.*

comedy *s.* Lustspiel *n.*

comely *a.* hübsch; artig.

comestibles *pl.* Nahrungsmittel *m.pl.*

comet *s.* Komet *m.*

comfort *v.t.* trösten; erquicken; **~** *s.* Trost *m.*; Erquickung *f.*; Bequemlichkeit *f.*; Behaglichkeit *f.*; *cold ~,* schwache Trost *m.*

comfortable *a.*, **~bly** *adv.* tröstlich, erfreulich; bequem, behaglich.

comforter *s.* Halstuch *m.*

comic(al) *a.*, **~ly** *adv.* komisch; **~** *strip s.* Karikaturstreifen *m.*; *comics s.pl.* komische Zeitschrift od. Vorträge.

comity *s.* gute Einvernehmen *n.*

comma *s.* Komma *n.*; *inverted ~,* Anführungszeichen *n.*

command *v.t. & i.* befehlen; anführen, herrschen; bestellen; **~** *s.* Befehl *m.*; Beherrschung *f.*; Herrschaft *f.*; Bestellung *f.*

commandant *s.* Befehlshaber *m.*

commander *s.* Befehlshaber *m.*; (*nav.*) Fregattenkapitän *m.*; Handramme *f.*; *~-in-chief,* Oberbefehlshaber *m.*

commandeer *v.t.* requirieren.

commandment *s.* Befehl *m.*; Gebot *n.*

commemorate *v.t.* feiern, gedenken.

commemoration *s.* Gedächtnisfeier *f.*

commemorative *a.* erinnernd, Erinnerungs...

commence v.t. & i. anfangen; werden.
commencement s. Anfang m.
commend v.t. empfehlen, loben.
commendable a., ~bly adv. empfehlenswert.
commendation s. Empfehlung f.; Lob n.
commendatory a. empfehlend.
commensurable a. kommensurabel.
commensurate a., ~ly adv. von gleichem mass.
comment v.i. erläutern, auslegen; ~ s. Auslegung f.; comments s.pl. Bemerkungen f.pl.; Stellungnahme f.
commentary s. Kommentar m.
commentator s. Erklärer m.
commerce s. Handel, Verkehr m.; Gewerbe n.
commercial a. kaufmännisch, Handels ...; ~ directory, Handelsadressbuch n.; ~ law, Handelsrecht n.; ~ papers s.pl. Geschäftspapiere n.pl. (Post); ~ traveller, Handlungsreisende m.; ~ treaty, Handelsvertrag m.
commingle v.t. & i. vermischen.
commiserate v.t. bemitleiden.
commissariat s. Militärintendantur f.
commissary s. Kommissar m.; Intendanturbeamter m.
commission s. Auftrag m.; Vollmacht f.; Ausschuss m.; Begehung (von Sünden); Offizierspatent n.; Provision f.; Indientstellung (eines Schiffes) f.; ~ v.t. einen Auftrag geben, bevollmächtigen; in Dienst stellen.
commissionaire s. Dienstmann m.
commissioner s. Bevollmächtigte, Kommissär m.
commit v.t. übergeben, anvertrauen; verüben; verpflichten, festlegen; (mil.) einsetzen (Truppen); to ~ oneself, sich binden; to ~ to prison, einsperren.
commitment s. Verpflichtung f.; (mil.) Einsatz m.; without any ~, unverbindlich.
committee s. Ausschuss m.; to be on the ~, dem Ausschuss angehören.
commixture s. Vermischung f.
commode s. Kommode f.
commodious a., ~ly adv. bequem, nützlich; geräumig.
commodity s. Ware f.
commodore s. Kommodore m.
common a., ~ly adv. gemein, gewöhnlich; gemeinschaftlich; ~ law, Gewohnheitsrecht n.; ~ room, Konversationszimmer m.; ~ time s. (mus.) gerade Takt m.; ~ s. Gemeindeweide f.; ~s pl. Gemeinen m.pl.; Volk n.; Kost f.; House of Commons, Unterhaus (in England) n.
common stock s. (Am.) Stammaktien f.pl.
commonalty s. Gemeinschaft f.; gemeine Volk n.

commoner s. Bürgerliche m.; Mitglied des Unterhauses n.
commonplace s. Gemeinplatz m.; ~ a. abgedroschen.
common sense s. gesunde Menschenverstand m.
commonwealth s. Gemeinwesen n.; Republik f.
commotion s. Erschütterung f.; Aufruhr m.
communal a. Gemeinde...
commune s. Gemeinde f., Kommune .
communicable a. mitteilbar.
communicant s. Kommunikant m.
communicate v.t. mitteilen; ~ v.i. Gemeinschaft haben; kommunizieren.
communication s. Mitteilung f.; Umgang m.; Verbindung f.; (rail.) ~ cord, Notbremse f.; (mil.) ~-zone, Etappe f.
communicative s. mitteilsam.
communion s. Gemeinschaft f.; Umgang m.; heilige Abendmahl n.
communism s. Kommunismus m.
communist s. Kommunist m.
community s. Gemeinschaft, Gemeinde f.; Allgemeinheit f., Staat m.; ~ of goods, (law) Gütergemeinschaft f.
commutable a. vertauschbar.
commutation s. Vertauschung f.; Auswechslung f.; ~ of a sentence, (law) Strafumwandlung f.
commute v.t. umtauschen, auswechseln; ersetzen; (law) (Strafe) umwandeln od. mildern; (Am.) täglich in die Stadt fahren.
compact s. Vertrag m.; ~ a., ~ly adv. dicht, gedrängt, bündig; ~ v.t. fest verbinden.
companion s. Gefährte m.
companionable a., ~bly adv. gesellig, umgänglich.
companionship s. Gesellschaft f.
company s. Gesellschaft f.; (mil.) Kompanie; Zunft f.; Trupp m.
comparable a., ~bly adv. vergleichbar; vergleichungsweise.
comparative a., ~ly adv. vergleichend; verhältnismässig; ~ s. (gram.) Komparativ m.
compare v.t. vergleichen.
comparison s. Vergleichung f.; (gram) Steigerung f.
compartment s. Abteilung f.; Fach n.; (rail.) (Wagen-) Abteil m.
compass v.t. umgeben, einschlissen; erreichen; ~ s. Bereich m.; Umfang m.; Kompass m.; (pair of) compasses pl. Zirkel m.
compassion s. Mitleid n.
compassionate a. mitleidig; ~ v.t. Mitleid haben mit; ~ leave s. Familienurlaub m.
compatible a., ~bly adv. Vereinbar.

compatriot *s.* Landsmann *m.*
compeer *s.* Genosse, Gevatter *m.*
compel *v.t.* zwingen, nötigen.
compendious *a.*, **~ly** *adv.* kurz, gedrängt.
compendium *s.* Auszug *m.*; Kompendium *n.*
compensate *v.t.* ersetzen, entschädigen.
compensation *s.* Ersatz *m.*; Entschädigung *f.*; (*elek.*) Ausgleich *m.*; *to make* ~ *for*, Entschädigung leisten für...
compensatory *a.* ausgleichend.
compete *v.i.* sich mitbewerben, konkurrieren.
competence, competency *s.* behagliche Auskommen *n.*; Befugnis, Kompetenz *f.*; Befähigung *f.*
competent *a.* hinlänglich; kompetent.
competition *s.* Mitbewerbung, Konkurrenz *f.*; Preisausschreiben *n.*, Wettbewerb *m.*; *unfair* ~, unlauterer Wettbewerb *m.*
competitive *a.* wetteifernd; Konkurrenz...; ~ *examination*, Konkurrenzprüfung *f.*; ~ *price*, konkurrenzfähige Preis *m.*
competitor *s.* Mitbewerber, Konkurrent *m.*
compilation *s.* Zusammenstellung *f.*
compile *v.t.* zusammentragen.
compiler *s.* Kompilator *m.*
complacence, complacency *s.* Wohlgefallen *n.*; Gefälligkeit *f.*
complacent *a.* gefällig, selbstzufrieden.
complain *v.i.* sich beklagen.
complainant *s.* Beschwerdeführer *m.*
complaint *s.* Beschwerde *f.*; Unpässlichkeit *f.*; *to lodge a* ~, eine Beschwerde einlegen.
complaisance *s.* Nachgiebigkeit *f.*
complaisant *a.* gefällig, höflich.
complement *s.* Ergänzung *f.*; volle Zahl, volle Besetzung (Schiff, Einheit) *f.*; *to* ~ *v.t.* vervollständigen.
complete *a.*, **~ly** *adv.* vollständig, vollendet; gänzlich; ~ *v.t.* vervollständigen, ergänzen; *to* ~ *a form*, ein Formular ausfüllen.
completion *s.* Ergänzung *f.* Vollendung *f.*
complex *s.* Komplex *m.*; *a.*, **~ly** *adv.* zusammengesetzt, verwickelt.
complexion *s.* Aussehen *n.*; Gesichtsfarbe *f.*
complexity *s.* Verwickeltheit *f.*
compliance *s.* Willfährigkeit *f.*
compliant *a.*, **~ly** *adv.* willfährig.
complicate *v.t.* verwickeln.
complicated *a.* kompliziert, verwickelt.
complication *s.* Verwick(e)lung *f.*
complicity *s.* Mitschuld *f.*
compliment *s.* Gruss *f.*; ~ *v.t.* grüssen; beglückwünschen; einem Komplimente machen.
complimentary *a.* höflich; schmeichlerisch; löblich; ~ *dinner*, Festessen *n.*

comply *v.i.* sich fügen; *to* ~ *with* (Gesetze) befolgen.
component *s.* Bestandteil *m.*; ~ *a.* Teil...
compose *v.t.* zusammensetzen, verfassen; kompieren; (*print.*) setzen; beruhigen, ordnen; schlichten, beilegen; *to* ~ *oneself*, sich fassen, sich beruhigen.
composed *a.*, **~ly** *adv.* ruhig, gesetzt.
composer *s.* Komponist *m.*
composite *a.* zusammengesetzt.
composition *s.* Zusammensetzung *f.*; Aufsatz *f.*; Schriftsatz *m.*; Tonsatz *m.*; Vergleich *m.*; Abfindungssumme *f.*; Übereinkunft *f.*; Natur *f.*
compositor *s.* Schriftsetzer *m.*
compost *s.* Dünger *m.*; ~ *v.t.* düngen.
composure *s.* Gemütsruhe, Fassung *f.*
compound *v.t.* zusammensetzen; beilegen; ~ *v.i.* sich vergleichen.; ~ *a.* zusammengesetzt; ~ *interest* *s.* Zinseszins *m.*; ~ *fraction* *s.* (*math.*) Doppelbruch *m.*; (*med.*) ~ *fracture* *s.* komplizierte Bruch *m.*; ~ *s.* Mischung *f.*; (*chem.*) Verbindung *f.*; Zusammensetzung *f.*; Einzäunung *f.*
comprehend *v.t.* zusammenfassen; begreifen.
comprehensible *a.*, **~bly** *adv.* begreiflich.
comprehension *s.* Inbegriff *m.*; Fassungskraft *f.*; Umfang *m.*
comprehensive *a.*, **~ly** *adv.* umfassend; gedrängt.
compress *v.t.* zusammendrücken.
compressible *a.* zusammendrückbar.
compression *s.* Zusammendrückung *f.*
compressor *s.* (*mot.*) Kompressor, Verdichter *m.*
comprise *v.t.* in sich fassen, enthalten.
compromise *s.* Kompromiss *n.*; ~ *v.t.* durch Vergleich beilegen; *to* ~ *oneself*, sich kompromittieren.
compulsion *s.* Zwang *m.*
compulsory *a.*, **~ily** *adv.* Zwangs...
compunction *s.* Gewissensangst *f.*
computation *s.* Berechnung *f.*
compute *v.t.* rechnen, berechnen.
comrade *s.* Gefährte *m.*, Kamerad *m.*
con *v.t.* auswendig lernen, wiederholen.; ~ *adv. pro and* ~, für und wider.
concatenation *s.* Verkettung *f.*
concave *a.*, **~ly** *adv.* hohlrund, konkav.
concavity *s.* Hohlrundung *f.*
conceal *v.t.* verhehlen.
concealment *s.* Verhehlung *f.*
concede *v.t.* einräumen, gestatten.
conceit *s.* Einbildung, Dünkel *m.*; Witzelei *f.*
conceited *a.* eingebildet, dünkelhaft.
conceivable *a.*, **~bly** *adv.* denkbar.
conceive *v.t. & i.* begreifen; erdenken; meinen; empfangen, schwanger werden
concentrate *v.t.* zusammenziehen, konzentrieren.

concentration s. Zusammenziehung, Konzentrierung f.; ~-camp Konzentrationslager n.
concentric a. konzentrisch.
concept s. Begriff m.
conception s. Empfängnis f.; Auffassung f.; Begriff m.; Meinung f.
conceptual a. begrifflich.
concern v.t. betreffen; beunruhigen; to ~ oneself about, sich kümmern um; ~ s. Angelegenheit f.; Belang m.; Unternehmen n.; Anteil m.; Unruhe f.; Geschäft n.
concerned p. & a. bekümmert; interessiert; those ~, die Beteiligten m.pl.; ~ly adv. angelegentlich.
concerning pr. betreffend.
concernment s. Sorge, Teilnahme f.
concert s. Einverständnis n.; Verabredung f.; (mus.) Konzert n.; ~ v.t. verabreden.
concert-hall s. Konzertsaal m.
concertina s. Ziehharmonika f.
concession s. Zugeständnis n., Vergünstigung f.
concessionaire s. Inhaber einer Vergünstigung m.
concessive a. einräumend; Konzessiv...
conciliate v.t. versöhnen; für sich gewinnen.
conciliation s. Versöhnung f.; ~-board, Schlichtungsamt n.; ~-proceedings s.pl. (law) Sühneverfahren n.
conciliator s. Vermittler m.
conciliatory a. vermittelnd, versöhnlich.
concise a., ~ly adv. kurz, gedrängt.
conclave s. Konklave n.; geheime Beratung f.
conclude v.t. & i. folgern, schliessen; sich entschliessen; beschliessen.
conclusion s. Schluss m.; Beschluss m.; Ende n.; Folgerung f.; Abschluss (eines Vertrags) m.
conclusive a., ~ly adv. entscheidend; endgültig; schlüssig, überzeugend.
concoct v.t. schmieden, anzetteln.
concoction s. Gebräu n.; Ausbrütung f.
concomitant a., ~ly adv. begleitend.
concord s. Eintracht f.; (gram.) Übereinstimmung f.
concordance s. Übereinstimmung f.; Konkordanz f.
concordant a. übereinstimmend.
concordat s. Konkordat n.
concourse s. Zusammenlauf m.
concrete v.i. sich verdichten; ~ly adv. konkret, bestimmt; ~ s. Beton m.
concretion s. Verdichtung f.
concubinage s. Konkubinat n., wilde Ehe f.
concubine s. Konkubine n.
concupiscence s. Begierde, Wollust f.
concur v.i. zusammentreffen; übereinstimmen; mitwirken.

concurrence s. Zusammentreffen n.; Mitwirkung f.; Einverständnis n.
concurrent a. mitwirkend; begleitend; übereinstimmend. •
concussion s. Erschütterung f.; (med.) Prellung f., Quetschung f.
condemn v.t. verdammen, verurteilen; tadeln; verwerfen; (Ware) beschlagnahmen, (Ware) für untauglich erklären.
condemnation s. Verurteilung f.
condemnatory a. verdammend.
condensation s. Verdichtung f.
condense v.t. verdichten; einen Auszug machen von; ~ v.i. sich verdichten.
condensed milk s. kondensierte Milch f.
condenser s. Kondensator (Dampfmaschine od. elek.) m.
condescend v.t. sich herablassen; ~ingly adv. herablassend, gefällig.
condescension s. Herablassung f.
condign a. gehörig, verdient.
condiment s. Würze f.
condition s. Zustand m.; Beschaffenheit f.; Bedingung f.; Stand m.; Stellung f.; ~ v.t. bedingen; (mech.) in guten Zustand bringen (Maschinen usw.).
conditional (on) a. bedingt (durch).
conditionally adv. bedingungsweise, unter Bedingungen.
conditioned a. beschaffen, geartet.
condole v.t. & i. Beileid bezeigen.
condolence s. Beileid n.
condonation s. Vergebung f.
condone v.t. vergeben, verzeihen.
conduce v.i. dienlich sein, fördern.
conducive a. förderlich, behilflich.
conduct s. Führung f.; Geleit n.; Aufführung f.; Verwaltung f.; ~ v.t. führen; verwalten; (mus.) dirigieren; (phys.) leiten; to ~ oneself, sich aufführen; conducted tour s. Gesellschaftsreise f.
conductivity s. (elek.) Leitfähigkeit f.
conductor s. Schaffner, Kondukteur m.; Leiter m.; (mus.) Dirigent m.
conduit s. Röhre f.; Wasserleitung f.
cone s. Kegel m.; Tannenzapfen m.
coney s. = cony.
confabulation s. vertrauliche Gespräch.
confection s. Zuckerwerk n.; Konfekt n.; Konfektionsartikel (für Damen) m.
confectioner s. Konditor m.
confectionery s. Zuckerwerk n.; Konditorei f.
confederacy s. Bündnis n.
confederate v.t. & i. (sich) verbünden; ~ a. verbündet; ~ s. Bundesgenosse m.
confederation s. Bündnis n., Bund m.
confer v.t. vergleichen; verleihen; ~ v.i. verhandeln.
conference s. Verhandlung, Beratschlagung f., Konferenz f.
confess v.t. & i. bekennen, gestehen; beichten; Beichte hören; kundgeben.

confession s. Geständnis n.; Bekenntnis n.; Beichte f.
confessional s. Beichtstuhl m.
confessor s. Bekenner m.; Beichtvater m.
confidant s. Vertraute m. & f.
confide v.t. & i. anvertrauen; vertrauen.
confidence s. Vertrauen n.; Zuversicht f.; ~-trickster s. Bauernfänger m.
confident a., ~ly adv. vertrauend.
confidential a. vertraulich.
configuration s. Gestaltung, Bildung f.
confine s. Grenze f.; ~ v.t. begrenzen; beschränken; einsperren; to be confined, in den Wochen liegen; confined to barracks, unter Kasernenarrest.
confinement s. Haft f.; Wochenbett n.; Niederkunft f.; solitary ~, Einzelhaft f.
confirm v.t. bestätigen, bewähren; einsegnen, konfirmieren.
confirmation s. Bestätigung f.; Konfirmation f.; Firmung f.
confirmatory a. bekräftigend.
confirmed a. unverbesserlich.
confiscate v.t. einziehen; ~ a. verfallen.
confiscation s. Beschlagnahme f.
conflagration s. grosse Brand m.
conflict s. Kampf, Streit m., Konflikt m.; ~ v.i. kämpfen; widerstreiten.
confluence s. Zusammenfluss m.
confluent a. zusammenfliessend.
conform a. gleichförmig, gemäss; ~ v.t. gleichförmig machen; ~ v.i. sich richten.
conformable a., ~bly adv. übereinstimmend.
conformist s. Mitglied (n.) der anglikanischen Kirche.
conformity s. Übereinstimmung f.; in ~ with, gemäss; gleichlaufend.
confound v.t. verwirren; verwechseln; zerstören; ~ it! verwünscht!
confounded a. bestürzt; verwünscht.
confraternity s. Brüderschaft f.
confront v.t. & i. gegenüberstellen; gegenüberstehen.
confrontation s. Gegenüberstellung f.
confuse v.t.verwirren; verwechseln.
confused a., ~ly adv. verworren.
confusion s. Verwirrung f.; Verwechslung f.
confutation s. Widerlegung f.
confute v.t. widerlegen.
congeal v.t. gefrieren machen; ~ v.i. gefrieren.
congelation s. Gefrieren n.
congenial a. sympathisch, zusagend; geistesverwandt.
congenital a. angeboren.
congeries s. Masse f., Gemenge n.
congested a. überfüllt (Strassenverkehr, Bevölkerung); (med.) mit Blut überfüllt.
congestion s. Überfüllung f.; Blutandrang m.

conglomeration s. Zusammenhäufung f.
congratulate (on) v.t. & i. gratulieren, Glück wünschen (zu).
congratulation s. Glückwunsch m.
congratulatory a. beglückwünschend.
congregate v.t. & i. (sich) versammeln.
congregation s. Gemeinde f.
congress s. Kongress m.
congruence s. Übereinstimmung f.
congruent a. übereinstimmend.
congruity s. Übereinstimmung f.
congruous a., ~ly adv. übereinstimmend, angemessen.
conic(al), a., ~ly adv. konisch; kegelförmig; ~ section s. Kegelschnitt m.
conifer s. Nadelholzbaum m.
coniferous a. Nadelholz...
conjectural a., ~ly adv. mutmasslich.
conjecture s. Mutmassung f.; ~ v.t. mutmassen.
conjoin v.t. & i. verbinden.
conjoint a., ~ly adv. vereinigt.
conjugal a., ~ly adv. ehelich.
conjugate v.t. konjugieren.
conjugation s. Konjugation f.
conjunction s. Verbindung f.; Bindewort n.
conjunctiva s. Bindehaut f.
conjunctive a., ~ly adv. verdindend; ~ s. (gram.) Konjunktiv m.
conjunctivitis s. Bindehautentzündung f.
conjuncture s. Zusammentreffen n.
conjuration s. Beschwörung f.
conjure v.t. & i. beschwören; bezaubern; zaubern; bannen.
conjurer s. Zauberer m.; Taschenspieler m.
connate, connatural a.,~ly adv. angeboren.
connect v.t. verbinden, verknüpfen; ~ v.i. verbunden sein; well-connected a. mit guten Beziehungen.
connecting-rod s. (mech.) Pleuelstange f.
connection, connexion s. Zusammenhang m.; Verbindung f.; (rail.) Anschluss m.; (tel.) Anschluss m.; Praxis (Arzt, Rechtsanwalt) f.; (elek.) Schaltung f.; Anschluss m.; ~-box (elek.) Anschlussdose f.
conning tower s. Kommandoturm m.
connivance s. Nachsicht f.; stillschweigende Einwilligung f.
connive (at) v.i. stillschweigend dulden.
connoisseur s. Kenner m.
connotation s. Mitbezeichnung f.
connote v.t. mitbezeichnen.
connubial a. ehelich.
conquer v.t. & i. erobern, (be)siegen.
conqueror s. Eroberer, Sieger m.
conquest s. Eroberung f.; Sieg m.
consanguineous a. blutsverwandt.
consanguinity s. Blutsverwandtschaft f.
conscience s. Gewissen n.
conscientious a., ~ly adv. gewissenhaft.

conscientious objector s. Kriegsdienstverweigerer m.
conscientiousness s. Gewissenhaftigkeit f.
conscious a., **~ly** adv. bewusst; wissentlich.
consciousness s. Bewusstsein n.
conscript s. ausgehobene Rekrut; **~** a. ausgehoben.
conscription s. (Zwangs-)Aushebung f; allgemeine Wehrpflicht f.
consecrate v.t. weihen; einsegnen.
consecration s. Einsegnung.
consecutive a., **~ly** adv. aufeinander folgend; folglich; konsekutiv.
consensus s. Übereinstimmung f.
consent s. Einwilligung f.; age oj ~ (law) Mündigkeitsalter n.; **~** v.i. einwilligen, einstimmen.
consentient a. einstimmig.
consequence s. Folge f.; Einfluss m.; Wichtigkeit f.
consequent a., **~ly** adv. folgend; folglich; konsequent; **~** s. Folge f.
consequential a. wichtigtuend, anmassend; folgerecht.
conservation s. Erhaltung f.
conservative a. erhaltend; konservativ; **~** estimate, vorsichtige Schätzung f.
conservator s. Erhalter, Konservator m.
conservatory a. erhaltend; **~** s. Gewächshaus n.; Konservatorium n.
conserve v.t. erhalten.
consider v.t. & i. betrachten; überlegen; achten.
considerable a., **~bly** adv. ansehnlich.
considerate a., **~ly** adv. bedächtig; rücksichtsvoll.
consideration s. Betrachtung, Überlegung f.; Rücksicht f.; Preis m.
considering pr. in Erwägung (dass).
consign v.t. übertragen; zusenden.
consignee s. Warenempfänger m.
consignment s. Übersendung f.; Warensendung, Konsignation f.
consignor s. Warenabsender m.
consist v.i. bestehen.
consistence, consistency s. Festigkeit f.; Folgerichtigkeit f.
consistent a., **~ly** adv. dicht, fest; übereinstimmend; konsequent.
consistory s. Konsistorium n.
consolation s. Trost m.
consolatory a. tröstlich.
console v.t. trösten; **~** s. Kragstein, m., Konsole f.
consolidate v.t. befestigen; **~** v.i. sich verbinden; zuheilen; sich befestigen.
consolidation s. Verdichtung f.; Verbindung f.; Zusammenlegung f.
consols s.pl. fundierte englische Staatsschuld f.
consonance s. Einklang m.
consonant a., **~ly** adv. einstimmig; gemäss; **~** s. Konsonant m.

consort s., Gefährte m.; Gatte m.; Gattin f.; **~** v.i. sich gesellen, umgehen; übereinstimmen.
conspicuous a., **~ly** adv. sichtbar; auffallend; hervorragend.
conspiracy s. Verschwörung f.
conspirator s. Verschwörer m.
conspire v.i. sich verschwören.
constable s. Polizist, Schutzmann m.; Chief **~**, Polizeipräsident m.
constabulary s. Schutzpolizei, Schupo f.
constancy s. Beständigkeit.
constant a., **~ly** adv. standhaft, zuverlässig; dauernd; **~** hot water, fliessendes warmes Wasser n.
constellation s. Sternbild n.
consternation s. Bestürzung f.
constipate v.t. verdichten, verstopfen.
constipation s. Verstopfung f.
constituency s. Wahlkreis m.
constituent a. ausmachend, wesentlich; Wahl...; verfassunggebend; **~** body, Wählerschaft f.; **~** s. Vollmachtgeber m.; Bestandteil m.; Wähler m.
constitute v.t. ausmachen; bilden, errichten; ernennen.
constitution s. Einrichtung f.; Verfassung f.; Körperbeschaffenheit f.
constitutional a., **~ly** adv. verfassungsmässig; **~** s. Spaziergang zur Verdauung m.
constitutional law s. Verfassungsrecht n.
constitutive a. verordnend; wesentlich.
constrain v.t. zwingen.
constraint s. Zwang m., Haft f.
constrict v.t. zusammenziehen.
constriction s. Zusammenziehung f.
constrictor s. boa **~**, Riesenschlange f.
constringent a. zusammenziehend.
construct v.t. errichten, bauen; konstruieren; ersinnen.
construction s. Zusammensetzung f.; Bau m.; Deutung f.; under **~**, im Bau; **~-battalion** (mil.) Baubataillon n.
constructive a. Bau...; aufbauend.
construe v.t. konstruieren; auslegen.
consuetudinary a. gewohnheitsmässig.
consul s. Konsul m.; **~** General, Generalkonsul m.
consular a. konsularisch.
consulate, consulship s. Konsulat n.
consult v.i. sich beraten; **~** v.t. um Rat fragen.
consultation s. Beratung, Beratschlagung f.; Rücksprache f.
consultative a. beratend.
consulting engineer s. technische Berater m.
consulting hours s.pl. Sprechstunden (Arzt), f.pl.
consume v.t. verzehren; verbrauchen.
consumer s. Verbraucher, Konsument m.; Abnehmer m.; **~-goods** Verbrauchsgüter n.pl.

consummate a. vollendet.
consummation s. Vollendung f.
consumption s. Verzehrung f.; Verbrauch m.; Schwindsucht f.
consumptive a. schwindsüchtig.
contact s. Berührung f.; (elek.) Kontakt m.; ~ v.t. sich in Verbindung setzen mit.
contactor s. (elek.) Schütz m.
contagion s. Ansteckung, Seuche f.
contagious a. ansteckend.
contain v.t. in sich fassen, enthalten; (mil.) Kräfte binden; to ~ oneself, sich beherrschen.
container s. Behälter m.
contaminate v.t. besudeln.
contamination s. Befleckung f.
contango (com.) Report m.
contemn v.t. verachten.
contemplate v.t. betrachten; beabsichtigen; ~ v.i. nachdenken.
contemplation s. Betrachtung f.
contemplative a., ~ly adv. beschaulich.
contemporaneous a. gleichzeitig.
contemporary a. gleichzeitig, zeitgenössisch; ~ s. Zeitgenosse m.
contempt s. Verachtung f.; ~ of court, (law), Missachtung des Gerichts f.
contemptible a., ~bly adv. verächtlich.
contemptuous a., ~ly adv. verachtend.
contend v.i. streiten; streben; behaupten.
content a. zufrieden; ~ s. Zufriedenheit f.; Umfang m.; Inhalt m.; ~ v.t. befriedigen.
contented a., ~ly adv. zufrieden.
contention s. Streit m.; Wetteifer m.; Behauptung f.; Argument n.
contentious a., ~ly adv. streitig.
contentment a. Zufriedenheit f.
contents s.pl. Inhalt m.
contest v.t. streiten; bestreiten, anfechten; to ~ a seat, in einem Wahlkreis kandidieren; ~ v.i. wetteifern; ~ s. Streit m.; Wettbewerb, Wettkampf m.
contestable a. anfechtbar, streitig.
contestant s. Teilnehmer an einem Wettbewerb od. Wettkampf.
context s. Zusammenhang m.
contexture s. Bau m.; Gewebe n.
contiguity s. Aneinanderstossen n.
contiguous a., ~ly adv. anstossend, nahe.
continence s. Enthaltsamkeit f.
continent a., ~ly adv. enthaltsam, mässig; ~ s. Festland n.
continental a. festländisch.
contingency s. Zufall m., Möglichkeit f.
contingent a. möglich; abhängig von; (mil.) Kontingent n.
continual a., ~ly adv. fortwährend.
continuance s. Fortdauer f.
continuation s. Fortsetzung f.; ~ school, Fortbildungsschule f.
continue v.t. & i. fortsetzen; fortdauern, beharren.

continuity s. Zusammenhang m.
continuous a. zusammenhängend.
contort v.t. zusammendrehen, verdrehen.
contortion s. Verdrehung, Verzerrung f.
contour s. Umriss m.
contra pr. gegen, wider.
contraband a. Schmuggel...; ~ s. Schmuggelware f.
contraception s. Empfängnisverhütung f.
contraceptive a. empfängnisverhütend; ~ s. empfängnisverhütende Mittel n.
contract s. Vertrag m.; Akkord m.; law o ~, Vertragsrecht n.; to make a ~, einen Vertrag eingehen; under ~ to, einem kontraktlich verpflichtet; ~ v.t. zusammenziehen; sich zuziehen; erlangen; to ~ debts, Schulden eingehen; ~ v.i. einschrumpfen; einen Vertrag schliessen; sich verpflichten; contracting party, Vertragspartei f.
contraction s. Zusammenziehung f.; Krampf m.
contractor s. Kontrahent m.; Lieferant m.; Unternehmer m.
contractual a. vertragsmässig.
contradict v.t. widersprechen.
contradiction s. Widerspruch m.
contradictory a., ~ily adv. widersprechend.
contradistinction s. Gegensatz m.
contralto s. tiefe Altstimme f.
contrariety s. Widerwärtigkeit f.
contrariwise adv. umgekehrt.
contrary a. entgegengesetzt, zuwider; widerspenstig; ~ s. Gegenteil n.; ~ to, im Gegensatz zu; on the ~, im Gegenteil.
contrast s. Kontrast m.; Gegensatz m.
contrast v.t. & i. gegenüberstellen; abstechen von.
contravene v.t. zuwiderhandeln.
contravention s. Übertretung f.
contribute v.t. & i. beitragen.
contribution s. Beitrag m., Beisteuer.
contributor s. Beitragende m.; Mitarbeiter (an einer Zeitung) m.
contributory a. beitragend.
contrite a., ~ly adv. zerknirscht.
contrition s. Zerknirschung f.
contrivance s. Vorrichtung f.
contrive v.t. & i. ersinnen; veranstalten, fertigbringen; worauf ausgehen.
control s. Einschränkung f.; Aufsicht f.; Gewalt f.; Kontrolle f.; Überwachung f.; (mech.) Steuerung, Kontrolvorrichtung f.; ~-office, Überwachungsstelle f.; ~ v.t. beaufsichtigen, überwachen; beherrschen; kontrollieren.
controllable a. kontrollierbar.
controller s. Kontrolleur, Aufseher m. Leiter; Rechnungsprüfer m.
controversial a. streitig.
controversy s. Streitfrage f.; Streit m.; matter in ~, (law) Streitgegenstand m.

controvert v.t. bestreiten.

controvertible a. bestreitbar, streitig.

contumacious a., ~ly adv. widerspenstig.

contumacy s. Widerspenstigkeit f.

contumelious a., ~ly adv. schimpflich.

contumely s. Schimpf m.; Schmach f.

contuse v.t. quetschen.

contusion s. Quetschung f.

conundrum s. Wortspiel, Scherzrätsel n.

convalescence s. Genesung f.

convalescent a. genesend; ~-home, Genesungsheim n.

convene v.t. zusammenberufen; vorladen; ~ v.i. zusammenkommen.

convenience s. Schicklichkeit, Gelegenheit, Bequemlichkeit f.; at your earliest ~, umgehend; with all modern ~s, mit allem Komfort.

convenient a., ~ly adv. bequem.

convent s. (Nonnen-)Kloster n.

conventicle s. Zusammenkunft f.

convention s. Zusammenkunft, Versammlung f.; Vergleich m.; Bund m.; (Am.) Tagung f., Kongress m.

conventional a. verabredet, vertragsmässig; herkömmlich.

conventionalism, conventionality s. Festhalten (n.) am Herkömmlichen.

conventual a. klösterlich.

converge v.i. zusammenlaufen.

convergence s. Zusammenlaufen.

convergent a. konvergierend.

conversant a. vertraut, bewandert.

conversation s. Unterhaltung f.; Umgang m.

conversational a. Unterhaltungs...

converse a. umgekehrt; ~ v.i. Umgang haben, sich unterhalten.

conversely adv. umgekehrt.

conversion s. Umwandlung f.; Bekehrung f.; Schwenkung f.; Konvertierung (von Staatspapieren) f.; Versilberung f.; fraudulent ~, (law) betrügerische Verwendung anvertrauten Geldes.

convert s. Bekehrte m.; ~ v.t. umändern; bekehren, umkehren; ~ v.i. sich verwandeln.

converter s. (elek.) Umformer m.

convertible a. umwandelbar; umsetzbar, vertauschbar; (com.) konvertierbar.

convex a. konvex.

convexity s. Konvexheit f.

convey v.t. führen; befördern; übertragen.

conveyance s. Beförderung f.; Abtretung f.; Fuhrwerk n.

conveyancer s. Notar m.

conveyor s. laufende Band n.

convict v.t. für schuldig erklären; überführen; ~ s. Zuchthäusler, Verbrecher m.

conviction s. Überzeugung f.; Überführung f.; (law) Schuldigerklärung f.

convince v.t. überzeugen.

convivial a. gastlich, festlich.

convocation s. Zusammenberufung f. Versammlung, Synode f.

convoke v.t. zusammenberufen.

convoy v.t. geleiten; ~ s. Geleit n.; Bedeckung f.; (nav.) Geleitzug m.

convulsion s. Zuckung f.; Krampf m.

convulsive a. zuckend, krampfhaft.

cony s. Kaninchen n.

coo v.i. girren.

cook s. Koch m.; Köchin f.; ~ v.t. kochen; zurechtstutzen.

cookbook s. (Am.) Kochbuch n.

cooker s. Kochapparat, Kochherd m.

cookery s. Kochkunst f.; ~-book Kochbuch n.

cool a. kühl; kaltblütig; unverfroren; ~ v.t. kühlen, erfrischen; besänftigen; ~ v.i. erkalten.

coolant s. (mech.) Kühlflüssigkeit f.

coolie s. Kuli m.

coolly adv. kaltblütig.

cooper s. Böttcher m., Küfer m.

co-operate v.i. mitwirken, teilnehmen.

co-operation s. Mitwirkung f.

co-operative a. mitwirkend; zur Mitarbeit bereit, willig; ~ society s. Konsumverein m.

co-operator s. Mitarbeiter m.

co-opt v.t. kooptieren.

co-ordinate a., ~ly adv. beigeordnet; ~ v.t. beiordnen; gleichordnen, koordinieren.

copartner s. Teilhaber m.

cope s. Decke, Kuppel f.; Chorrock m.; ~ v.t. bedecken; ~ v.i. to ~ with, es mit einem aufnehmen, einer Sache gewachsen sein.

coping s. Sims m.; ~ stone, Deckstein m.

copious a., ~ly adv. reichlich.

copper s. Kupfer n.; Kupfergeschirr n.; Kupfermünze f.; (slang) Schupo m.

copper-plate s. Kupferplatte f.; Kupferstich m.

coppice, copse s. Unterholz n.

copulate v.i. sich begatten.

copulation s. Begattung f.

copulative a. verbindend, Binde...

copy s. Abschrift f.; Abdruck m.; Durchschlag m.; Exemplar n.; Nachahmung f.; fair ~, clean ~, Reinschrift f.; rough ~, Konzept n.; ~ v.t. kopieren; nachzeichnen, nachahmen; to ~ out, ins Reine schreiben.

copyist s. Abschreiber, Kopist m.

copyright s. Verlagsrecht, Urheberrecht n.; ~ in designs, Musterschutz m.

coquet v.i. kokettieren.

coquetry s. Gefallsucht f.

coquette s. Kokette f.

coquettish a. gefallsüchtig, kokett.

coral s. Koralle f.

cord s. Strick m., Schnur f.; Tau n.;

gerippte Stoff *m.*; ~ *v.t.* mit Stricken befestigen.

cordage *s.* Tauwerk *n.*

cordial *a.*, ~ly *adv.* herzlich; ~ *s.* Herzstärkung *f.*; Magenlikör *m.*

cordiality *s.* Herzlichkeit *f.*

cordon *s.* Truppenkette *f.*; *to* ~ *off v.t.* (polizeilich) absperren.

corduroy *s.* gerippte Stoff *m.*

core *s.* Mark *n.*; Herz *n.*; Kern *m.*

co-religionist *s.* Glaubensgenosse *m.*

co-respondent *m.* Mitbeklagte im Scheidungsprozess *m.*

cork *s.* Kork *m.*; ~ *v.t.* verkorken; *the wine is* ~*ed*, der Wein schmeckt nach dem Korke.

corkscrew *s.* Korkzieher *m.*

cork-tree *s.* Korkeiche *f.*

cormorant *s.* Kormoran *m.*, Scharbe *f.*

corn *s.* Korn *n.*; Getreide *n.*; (*Am.*) Mais *m.*; Hühnerauge *n.*; ~*ed beef*, Büchsenrindfleisch *n.*

cornea *s.* Hornhaut (Auge) *f.*

corner *s.* Winkel *m.*; Ecke *f.*; ~*-stone*, Eckstein *m.*; ~ *v.t.* in eine Ecke treiben.

cornet *s.* Zinke *f.*

corn-factor *s.* Kornmakler *m.*

corn-flower *s.* Kornblume *f.*

cornice *s.* Karnies *n.*; Fries *m.*

cornucopia *s.* Füllhorn *m.*

corollary *s.* Zusatz *m.*, Folgesatz *m.*

coronation *s.* Krönung *f.*

coroner *s.* Leichenbeschauer (bei gewaltsamen od. rätselhaftem Tode); ~*'s inquest*, gerichtliche Leichenschau *f.*

coronet *s.* Adelskrone *f.*

corporal *a.*, ~ly *adv.* körperlich, leiblich; ~ *s.* Korporal *m.*

corporal punishment *s.* Prügelstrafe *f.*

corporate *a.*, ~ly *adv.* körperschaftlich, Gesellschafts…

corporation *s.* Gemeinde, Innung, Körperschaft *f.*; ~ *profits tax*, Körperschaftssteuer *f.*

corporeal *a.* körperlich.

corps *s.* Armeekorps *n.*

corpse *s.* Leichnam *m.*

corpulence *s.* Wohlleibtheit *f.*

corpulent *a.* wohlbeleibt.

Corpus Christi *s.* Fronleichnamsfest *n.*

corpuscle *s.* Blutkörperchen *n.*

correct *v.t.* verbessern; tadeln; strafen; (Zahlen) abrunden; ~ *a.*, ~ly *adv.* fehlerfrei, richtig.

correction *s.* Verbesserung *f.*, Berichtigung *f.*; Bestrafung *f.*; *house of* ~, Besserungsanstalt *f.*; ~ *of the press*, Korrektur *f.*

corrective *a.* verbessernd; ~ *s.* Besserungsmittel *n.*

corrector *s.* Verbesserer *m.*; Korrektor *m.*

correlate *v.t. & i.* in Wechselwirkung bringen od. stehen.

correlate *s.* Korrelat *n.*

correlation *s.* Wechselbeziehung *f.*

correlative *a.* in Wechselbeziehung.

correspond *v.i.* in Briefwechsel stehen; entsprechen.

correspondence *s.* Briefwechsel *m.*; Übereinstimmung *f.*; ~*-course*, schriftliche Lehrkurs *m.*

correspondent *s.* Korrespondent *m.*

corresponding *a.*, ~ly *adv.* entsprechend.

corridor *s.* Gang *m.*; ~ *train*, D-Zug, (Durchgangszug) *m.*

corrigible *a.* verbesserlich.

corroborate *v.t.* stärken; bestätigen.

corroboration *s.* Bestätigung *f.*

corroborative *a.* bestätigend.

corrode *v.t.* zernagen, zerfressen.

corrosion *s.* Zerfressung *f.*

corrosive *a.*, ~ly *adv.* zerfressend, ätzend; ~ *s.* Ätzmittel *n.*

corrugated *a.* gewellt; ~ *iron*, Wellblech *n.*

corrupt *v.t.* verderben; verführen; bestechen; ~ *v.i.* verderben; verfaulen; ~ *a.*, ~ly *adv.* verfault; lasterhaft; verderbt; bestechlich.

corruptible *a.*, ~bly *adv.* verderblich; verweslich; bestechlich.

corruption *s.* Verdorbenheit, Fäulnis *f.*; Bestechung *f.*

corruptive *a.* verderbend.

corsair *s.* Seeräuber *m.*; Raubschiff *n.*

cors(e)let *s.* Leibchen *n.*

corset *s.* Schnürleib *m.*, Korsett *n.*

coruscate *v.t.* schimmern.

coruscation *s.* Schimmern *n.*, Lichtglanz *m.*

corvette *s.* Korvette *f.*

cosine *s.* (*math.*) Kosinus *m.*

cosmetic *a.* kosmetisch; ~ *s.* Schönheitsmittel *n.*

cosmic(al) *a.* kosmisch, Welt…

cosmopolitan, cosmopolite *s.* Weltbürger *m.*; ~ *a.* weltbürgerlich.

Cossack *s.* Kosak *m.*

cost *s.* Kosten, Unkosten *pl.*; Preis *m.*; Aufwand *m.*; Schaden *m.*; *cost of living*, Lebenshaltungskosten *pl.*; *prime cost*, Gestehungspreis *m.*; ~*s pl.* Gerichtskosten *pl.*; *to dismiss with* ~ (*law*) kostenpflichtig abweisen; ~ *v.i.* kosten, zustehen kommen.

costermonger *s.* Strassenhändler (mit Gemüse, Obst, Fisch, etc.) *m.*

costly *a.* kostspielig, kostbar.

costume *s.* Kostüm *n.*

cosy *a.* behaglich; ~ *s.* Teemütze *f.*

cot *s.* Hütte *f.*; Kinderbett *n.*

coterie *a.* Clique, Sippschaft *f.*

cottage *s.* Hütte *f.*; Landhäuschen *n.*

cotton *s.* Baumwolle *f.*; Kattun *m.*; Garn *n.*; (*Am.*) (*absorbent*) ~, Watte *f.*; ~ *v.t.* in Baumwolle packen; ~ *v.i.* sich vertragen, anpassen.

cotton-gin s. Egreniermaschine f.
cotton-mill s. Baumwollspinnerei f.
cotton-wool s. rohe Baumwolle, Watte f.
couch s. Lager n.; Liegesofa n.; v.t. lagern; (in Worte) fassen; den Staar stechen; ~ v.i. sich niederlegen.
cough s. Husten m.; ~ v.i. husten.
council s. Ratsversammlung f.; Rat m.; Common ~, Stadtrat m.
councillor s. Ratsmitglied n., Ratsherr m.; Stadtverordnete m.
counsel s. Rat m.; Beratschlagung f.; Vorhaben n.; Anwalt m.; die juristischen Berater im Prozess, m.pl.; ~ for the defence, Verteidiger; ~ for the prosecution, Staatsanwalt, Staatsanwaltschaft f., Anklagevetreter m.; to keep one's ~, seine Gedanken bei sich behalten; ~ v.t. raten.
counsellor s. Ratgeber; ~ of legation, Gesandtschaftsrat m.
count s. Graf m.; ~ s. Zahl f.; Rechnung f.; Anklagepunkt m.; ~ v.t. zählen, rechnen; dafür halten; ~ v.i rechnen, sich verlassen; gelten.
countenance s. Antlitz n.; Miene f.; Fassung f.; Schutz m.; ~ v.t. unterstützen, verteidigen.
counter s. Spielmarke f.; Zahltisch m.; Ladentisch m.; ~ v.t. entgegenwirken; ~ adv. zuwider; entgegen.
counteract v.t. entgegenwirken.
counteraction s. Gegenwirkung f.
counter-attack s. Gegenangriff m.
counterbalance s. Gegengewicht n.; ~ v.t. aufwiegen, ausgleichen.
counter-charge s. Gegenbeschuldigung f.
counter-check s. Kontrazettel m.
counter-claim s. Gegenforderung f.
counterclockwise adv. gegen die Richtung des Uhrzeigers.
counter-espionage s. Spionageabwehr f.
counterfeit s. nachgemachte Sache f.; Betrüger m.; ~ a. nachgemacht; ~ v.t. fälschen.
counterfoil s. Kontrollabschnitt m.
counter-intelligence s. (mil.) Abwehr f.
countermand v.t. abbestellen, widerrufen.
countermine s. Gegenmine f.
countermove s. Gegenschlag m.
counter-order s. Gegenbefehl m.
counterpane s. Steppdecke f.
counterpart s. Gegenstück n.
counterpoint s. Kontrapunkt m.
counterpoise s. Gegengewicht n.; ~ v.t. das Gleichgewicht halten.
counter-security s. Rückbürgschaft f.
countershaft s. (mech.) Vorgelegewelle f.
countersign v.t. gegenzeichnen.
countersink v.t. (mech.) versenken; countersunk screw, Senkschraube f.
countervail v.t. ausgleichen, aufwiegen.
countess s. Gräfin f.

counting-house s. Kontor n.
countless a. unzählbar.
country s. Land n.; Gegend, Landschaft f.; Vaterland n.; ~ a. ländlich, Land...
country-dance s. Volkstanz m.
country-house s. Landhaus n.
countryman s. Landsmann m.; Landmann m.
country-seat s. Landsitz m.
countryside s. Gegend f.; Landschaft f.
county s. Grafschaft f.
coup s. Schlag, Streich m.
couple s. Paar n.; ~ v.t. koppeln.
couplet s. Verspaar n.
coupling s. Kuppelung f.
coupon s. Coupon, Zinsschein m.
courage s. Mut m.; Tapferkeit f.
courageous a., ~ly adv. mutig, tapfer.
courier s. Kurier, Eilbote m.
course s. Lauf, Gang m., Fahrt f.; Kurs m.; Gang (beim Essen) m.; a ~ of bricks, eine Lage Ziegel; in due ~, zur gehörigen Zeit; in (the) ~ of time, mit der Zeit, nach und nach; out of ~, ausser Kurs (Geld, Briefmarke); the fever has run its ~, das Fieber hat seinen Verlauf gehabt; of ~, natürlich, versteht sich; ~ v.i. laufen, rennen; ~ v.t. jagen, hetzen.
court s. Hof m.; Gerichtshof m.; criminal ~, Strafgericht n.; commercial ~, Handelsgerichts n.; ~-house, Gerichtsgebäude n.; ~-room, Gerichtssaal m.; out of ~, aussergerichtlich; to pay ~ to, den Hof machen; ~ v.t. den Hof machen; freien; huldigen; sich bewerben um.
courteous a., ~ly adv. höflich, gefällig.
courtesan s. Buhlerin f.
courtesy s. Artigkeit, Höflichkeit f.; by ~ of, mit gütiger Erlaubnis von; ~ v.i. sich verneigen.
courtier s. Höfling m.
courtly a. höfisch; höflich.
court-martial s. Kriegsgericht n.; ~ v.t. vor ein Kriegsgericht stellen.
court-plaster s. englische Pflaster n.
courtship s. Freien n.; Werbung f.
courtyard s. Hof, Hofraum m.
cousin s. Vetter m.; Base, Kusine f.; first ~, Vetter ersten Grades; second ~, Vetter zweiten Grades.
cove s. Bucht f.; Wölbund f.; Obdach n.; (vul.) Kerl m.; ~ v.t. wölben.
covenant s. Vertrag m.; Bündnis n.; ~ v.i. übereinkommen; geloben.
cover s. v.t. decken, bedecken; bemänteln; schützen; (Weg) zurücklegen; (Gelände) bestreichen; brüten; ~ s. Decke f.; Deckel m.; Umschlag m.; Kuvert n.; Schutzrücken (eines Buches) m.; Gehege n.; Dickicht n.; Schutz m.; (mil.) Deckung f.; ~ of a tyre, Schlauch-

mantel *m.*; ~*(ing) letter*, Begleitbrief *m.*; ~ *address*, Deckadresse *f.*

covert *s.* Dickicht *n.*; ~ *a.* bedeckt, verborgen; ~ly *adv.* heimlich.

coverture *s.* Schutz *m.*; Stellung einer verheirateten Frau *f.*

covet *v.t.* begehren, gelüsten.

covetous *a.*, ~ly *adv.* habsüchtig.

covey *s.* Flug *m.*; Brut *f.*; Volk (*n.*) Rebhühner.

cow *s.* Kuh *f.*; ~ *v.t.* einschüchtern.

coward *s.* Feigling *m.*; ~ *a.* feig.

cowardice *s.* Feigheit *f.*

cowardly *a. & adv.* feig(e).

cowboy *s.* Kuhjunge, Rinderhirt *m.*

cower *v.i.* niederkauern.

cowherd *s.* Kuhhirt *m.*

cowhide *s.* Ochsenziemer *m.*

cowhouse *s.* Kuhstall *m.*

cowl *s.* Kapuze *f.*, Kutte *f.*

cowling *s.* (*mot.*) Motorhaube *f.*

cow-pox *s.* Kuhpocken *f.pl.*

cowslip *s.* (wilde) Schlüsselblume *f.*

coxcomb *s.* Stutzer, Narr *m.*

coxswain *s.* Bootsführer *m.*

coy *a.*, ~ly *adv.* schüchtern; spröde.

cozen *v.t.* täuschen; prellen.

cozenage *s.* Betrug.

crab *s.* Taschenkrebs *m.*; wilde Apfel *m.*; Murrkopf *m.*

crabbed *a.*, ~ly *adv.* herbe; mürrisch, schwierig; unleserlich.

crack *s.* Knall *m.*; Riss *m.*; Spalte *f.*; ~ *v.t.* sprengen, aufbrechen, zerreissen; knallen; ~ *v.i.* krachen, bersten, springen, zerplatzen; ~ *a.* ausgezeichnet, prächtig, Haupt...; ~ brained *a.* verrückt; ~ *troops pl.* Elitetruppen *pl.*

crack-brained *a.* verrückt.

cracked *a.* geborsten; nicht recht gescheit.

cracker *s.* knusprige Keks *m.*; Knallbonbon *m.*

crackle *v.i.* krachen; knistern.

crackling *s.* Geknister *n.*; Kruste (*f.*) des Schweinebratens.

crackpot *s.* (*Am.*) verschrobene Mensch *m.*

cradle *s.* Wiege *f.*; ~ *v.t.* einwiegen.

craft *s.* Fertigkeit *f.*; Gewerbe, Handwerk *n.*; List *f.*; Schiff *n.*

craftsman *s.* (Kunst-) Handwerker *m.*

craftsmanship *s.* fachmännische Arbeit *f.*

crafty *a.*, ~ily *adv.* listig.

crag *s.* Klippe *f.*; Fels *m.*

craggy *a.* schroff, felsig.

cram *v.t. & i.* stopfen, nudem; mästen; einpauken.

crammer *s.* Einpauker *m.*

cramp *s.* Krampf *m.*; Klammer *f.*; ~ *v.i.* verklammern; verzerren.

cramped *a.* krampfhaft; steif.

cranberry *s.* Preisselbeere, Kronsbeere *f.*

crane *s.* Kranich *m.*; Kran *m.*; ~ *v.t.* aufwinden.

cranial *s.* Schädel...

cranium *s.* Hirnschale *f.*

crank *s.* Kurbel *f.*; Krummzapfen *m.*; grillenhafter Mensch *m.*

crankiness *s.* Verdrehtheit *f.*

crankshaft *s.* (*mech.*) Kurbelwelle *f.*

cranny *s.* Riss, Spalt *m.*

crape *s.* Flor *m.*, Krepp *m.*

crash *v.i.* krachen, platzen; ~ *s.* Bruch *m.*; Krach *m.*; (*avi.*) Absturz *m.*; *crash-landing*, Bruchlandung *f.*

crass *a.* dick, krass; dumm.

crate *s.* Packkorb *m.*

crater *s.* Krater *m.*

crave *v.t.* dringend bitten, verlangen.

craven *s.* Memme *f.*; ~ *a.* feig.

craving *s.* Begierde *f.*; ~ *a.* begehrlich, gierig.

crawl *v.i.* kriechen, schleichen; *to ~ with*, wimmeln von.

crayfish *s.* Krebs *m.*

crayon *s.* Farbstift *m.*

craze *v.t.* verrückt machen; ~ *s.* Grille *f.*, Manie *f.*

crazy *a.* baufällig; wahnsinnig.

creak *v.n.* knarren.

cream *s.* Rahm *m.*; Sahne *f.*; (*fig.*) Beste *n.*; ~ *v.t.* abrahmen.

creamery *s.* Butterei *f.*; Milchgeschäft *n.*

crease *s.* Falte, Bügelfalte *f.*; Eselsohr (im Buche) *n.*; ~-resisting, nicht knitternd; ~ *v.t.* umbiegen, kniffen; ~ *v.i.* knittern.

create *v.t.* erschaffen; ernennen.

creation *s.* Schöpfung *f.*; Ernennung *f.*

creative *a.* schöpferisch.

creator *s.* Schöpfer *m.*

creature *s.* Geschöpf *n.*; Wesen *n.*

crèche *s.* Kleinkinderbewahranstalt *f.*

credence *s.* Glaube *m.*; Beglaubigung *f.*

credentials *s.pl.* Beglaubigungsschreiben *n*

credibility *s.* Glaubwürdigkeit *f.*

credible *a.*, ~bly *adv.* glaubwürdig.

credit *s.* Glaube *m.*; Glaubwürdigkeit *f.*; Zeugnis *n.*; Einfluss *m.*; Ehre *f.*; Kredit *m.*; *to his ~*, zu seinen Gunsten; *open ~*, Blankokredit *f.*; *letter of ~*, Kreditbrief *m.*; ~-balance, Guthaben *n.*; ~-restriction, Kreditbeschränkung *f.*; ~-voucher, Kreditkassenschein *m.*; *on ~*, auf Kredit; *to enter to a person's ~*, einem gutschreiben; ~ *v.t.* glaubentrauen; kreditieren, gutschreiben.

creditable *a.*, ~bly *adv.* lobenswert.

creditor *s.* Gläubiger *m.*

credulity *s.* Leichtgläubigkeit *f.*

credulous *a.* leichtgläubig.

creed *s.* Glaubensbekenntnis *n.*

creek *s.* kleine Bucht *f.*; (*Am.*) kleine Fluss *m.*

creep *v.i.* kriechen, schleichen; *my flesh creeps*, mich überläuft eine Gänsehaut.

creeper *s.* Schlingpflanze *f.*

creepy *a.* kribbelnd; gruselich.
cremate *v.t.* einäschern.
cremation *s.* Leichenverbrennung *f.*
crematorium, crematory *s.* Krematorium *n.*
crenellated *a.* mit Zinnen, gezackt.
creosote *s.* Kreosot *n.*
crepuscular *a.* dämmerig.
crescent *s.* zunehmende Mond *m.*; Halb-mond *m.*; ~ *a.* halbmondförmig; ~ *s.* halbmondförmige Strasse *f.*
cress *s.* Kresse *f.*
crest *s.* Kamm *m.*; Federbusch *m.*; Mähne *f.*; Bergrücken *m.*; Helm-schmuck (im Wappen) *m.*
crestfallen *a.* niedergeschlagen.
crevice *s.* Riss *m.*
crew *s.* Besatzung (Schiff, Panzer) *f.*; (*Am.*) Mannschaft *f.*, Personal *n.*
crib *s.* Krippe *f.*; Wiege *f.*; (*fig.*) Esels-brücke *f.*; ~ *v.t.* abschreiben.
cribbage *s.* ein Kartenspiel *n.*
cricket *s.* Grille *f.*, Heimchen *n.*; Kricket, Schlagballspiel *n.*
crier *s.* Ausrufer *m.*
crime *s.* Verbrechen *n.*; *capital* ~, Kapital-verbrechen *n.*
criminal *a.*, ~**ly** *adv.* verbrecherisch; *Straf...*; ~ *code*, Strafgesetzbuch *n.*; ~ *investigation department*, Kriminal-abteilung *f.*; ~ *justice*, Strafrechtspflege *f.*; ~ *procedure*, Strafprozess *m.*; ~ *register*, Strafregister *n.*; ~ *s.* Ver-brecher *m.*; *habitual* ~, Gewohnheits-verbrecher *m.*
criminality *s.* Strafbarkeit.
criminate *v.t.* eines Verbrechens be-schuldigen.
criminologist *s.* Kriminologe *m.*
crimson *s.* Karmesin *n.*; ~ *a.* karmesinrot; ~ *v.t.* rot färben.
cringe *s.* tiefe Verbeugung *f.*; ~ *v.i.* sich krümmen; kriechen.
crinkle *v.i.* sich krümmen; ~ *s.* Krüm-mung, Falte *f.*
crinoline *s.* Krinoline *f.*
cripple *s.* Krüppel *m.*; ~ *a.* krüpplig; ~ *v.t.* verstümmeln; lähmen.
crisis *s.* Krise *f.*, Wendepunkt *m.*
crisp *a.* kraus; knusperig; frisch; ~ *v.t.* kräuseln; braun rösten.
criss-cross *s.* Gewirr (von Strassen, Kanälen, usw.) *n.*
criterion *s.* Kriterium, Merkmal *n.*
critic *s.* Kritiker *m.*
critical *a.* kritisch; bedenklich; entscheid-end; *in a* ~ *condition*, lebensgefährlich verwundet od. krank; ~ *goods* *s.pl.* Mangelware *f.*
criticize *v.t.* & *i.* beurteilen, tadeln.
criticism *s.* Kritik *f.*; *open to* ~, anfecht-bar.
critique *s.* Kritik *f.*

croak *v.i.* quaken, krächzen.
croaker *s.* Unglücksprophet *m.*
crochet *s.* Häkelarbeit *f.*; ~ *v.i.* häkeln.
crock *s.* Krug, Topf *m.*
crockery *s.* Töpferware *f.*
crocodile *s.* Krokodil *n.*
crocus *s.* Krokus *m.*
crofter *s.* kleine Pächter (im Norden Schottlands) *m.*
cromlech *s.* Kromlech *m.* (Hünengrab).
crone *s.* alte Frau *f.*; Hexe *f.*
crony *s.* alte Bekannte *m.*
crook *s.* Haken *m.*; Kunstgriff *m.*; Schwindler *m.*; ~ *v.t.* krümmen.
crooked *a.*, ~**ly** *adv.* krumm, verdreht, schief; verbrecherisch.
croon *v.i.* leise singen; wimmern.
crooner *s.* (*Am.*) Sänger *m.*
crop *s.* Kropf (der Vögel) *m.*; Ernte *f.*; kurze Haar *n.*; Jagdpeitsche, Reitgerte *f.*; ~ *v.t.* stutzen, verschneiden; ab-pflücken, einsammeln, ernten; ~ (*up*) *v.i.* auftauchen.
croquet *s.* Krocket, Kugelschlagspiel *n.*
crosier *s.* Bischofsstab *m.*
cross *s.* Kreuz *n.*; Leiden *n.*; (Rassen-) Kreuzung *f.*; ~ *a.* & *adv.* kreuzweise; zuwider, widrig; störrisch, mürrisch; böse; querdurch; ~ *v.t.* kreuzen; über-schreiten, gehen über; widersprechen, widerstehen; ~ *v.i.* sich kreuzen; *to* ~ *out*, ausstreichen; *your letter crossed mine*, unsere Briefe haben sich ge-kreuzt; *crossed cheque*, Verrechnungs-scheck *m.*
cross-bar *s.* Querholz *n.*
crossbow *s.* Armbrust *f.*
cross-bred *a.*, ~ *horse* *s.* Halbblut *n.*
cross-examination *s.* Kreuzverhör *n.*
cross-examine *v.t.* einem Kreuzverhör unterziehen.
crossing *s.* Übergang (auf der Strasse) *m.*, Kreuzung *f.*; Überfahrt *f.*; *pedes-trian* ~, Übergang für Fussgänger; *vehicle* ~, Übergang für Fahrzeuge.
cross-over *s.* Überleitung (Strasse).
cross-reference *s.* Verweis (im Buch) *m.*
cross-roads *s.pl.* Strassenkreuzung *f.*
cross-purpose *s.* Missverständnis *n.*
cross-section *s.* Querschnitt *m.*
crosswise *adv.* kreuzweise.
crotchet *s.* Haken *m.*; Klammer *f.*; Vier-telnote *f.*; Grille *f.*
crouch *v.i.* kriechen, sich schmiegen.
croup *s.* Kreuz (eines Pferdes) *n.*; Bräune (Krankheit) *f.*
crow *s.* Krähe *f.*; *distance as the* ~ *flies*, Luftlinie *f.*, Kartenentfernung *f.*; ~**-bar** *s.* Brecheisen *n.*, Hebestange *f.*; ~ *v.i.* krähen.
crowd *s.* Haufen *m.*; Gedränge *n.*; ~ *v.t.* drängen; vollstopfen; ~ *v.i.* sich drängen.

crown s. Krone f.; Kranz m.; Scheitel, Gipfel m.; Kopf (des Hutes) m.; ~ v.t. krönen.

crown-prince s. Kronprinz m.

crucial a. entscheidend; kritisch.

crucible s. Schmelztiegel m.

crucifix s. Kruzifix n.

crucifixion s. Kreuzigung f.

cruciform a. kreuzförmig.

crucify v.t. kreuzigen.

crude a., ~ly adv. roh, unreif; ~ oil s. Rohöl n.; ~ rubber s. Rohgummi m.

crudity s. Roheit, Unreife f.

cruel a., ~ly adv. grausam.

cruelty s. Grausamkeit f.; ~ to animals, Tierquälerei f.

cruet-stand s. Plattmenage f.

cruise v.n. hin- und herfahren; ~ s. Kreuzen n.; Seefahrt f.

cruiser s. (nav.) Kreuzer m.

crumb s. Krume f.; ~ v.t. & i. krümeln, zerbröckeln.

crumble v.i. zerbröckeln.

crumple v.t. zerknittern; ~ v.i. einschrumpfen.

crunch v.t. & i. knirschen; zerkauen.

crusade s. Kreuzzug m.

crusader s. Kreuzfahrer m.

crush s. Stoss m.; Quetschung f.; ~ v.t. quetschen; unterdrücken.

crust s. Rinde f.; Schale f.; Brotkruste f.; ~ v.t. mit einer Kruste überziehen.

crusty s., ~ily adv. krustig, rindig; mürrisch.

crutch s. Krücke f.

crux s. Kreuz n., Schwierigkeit f.

cry v.i. & a. schreien; weinen; rufen; ~ s. Geschrei n.; Zuruf m.

crypt s. Gruft, Krypta f.

cryptic a. geheim, undurchsichtig.

crystal s. Kristall m.; ~ a. kristallen.

crystalline a. kristallen.

crystallize v.t. & i. kristallisieren.

cub s. Junge n.; ~ v.t. Junge werfen.

cube s. Kubus m.; ~ (-number) s. Kubikzahl f.; ~ root s. Kubikwurzel f.

cubic a. kubisch; ~ metre, Kubikmeter m.

cubicle s. Schlafsaalabteil m.

cubit s. Unterarm m.; Elle f. (1½ Fuss).

cuckold s. Hahnrei m.

cuckoo s. Kuckuck m.

cucumber s. Gurke f.; pickled ~, saure Gurke f.

cud s. Futter (n.) im Vormagen der Tiere; to chew the ~, wiederkäuen.

cuddle v.t. hätscheln, umarmen.

cudgel s. Prügel m.; ~ v.t. prügeln.

cue s. Schwanz m.; Queue n., Billardstock m.; Stichwort n.; Wink m.

cuff s. Puff m.; Manschette f.; ~ v.t. & i. puffen; sich schlagen.

cuirass s. Brustharnisch m.

cuirassier s. Kürassier m.

cuisine s. Küche (Art zu kochen) f.

culinary a. zur Küche gehörig.

cull v.t. aussuchen.

culminate v.i. kulminieren; gipfeln.

culmination s. Gipfelpunkt m.

culpability s. Strafbarkeit, Schuld f.

culpable a., ~bly adv. strafbar, schuldig.

culprit s. Schuldige m.; Verbrecher m.

cult s. Kultus m.

cultivate v.t. anbauen; (Pflanzen, Pilze) züchten; ausbilden; pflegen.

cultivation s. Anbau m.; Pflege f.

cultivator s. Pflanzer m.

culture s. Anbau m.; Bildung f.; Kultur f.; cultured pearl s. Zuchtperle f.

culvert s. Abzugsgraben m.

cumber v.t. überhäufen.

cumbersome a., ~ly adv. lästig, hinderlich; unbehilflich.

cumbrous see cumbersome.

cumulative a. aufhäufend.

cuneiform a. keilförmig; Keilschrift...

cunning a., ~ly adv. listig; kundig; ~ s. List f.; Geschicklichkeit f.

cup s. Becher; Tasse f.; Schröpfkopf m.; ~ v.t. schröpfen.

cupboard s. Schrank m.

cupidity s. Begierde f., Habgier f.

cupola s. Kuppel f.

cur s. Köter m.; Schurke m.

curable a. heilbar.

curate s. Hilfsgeistlicher m.

curative a. heilend.

curator s. Aufseher, Kurator m.

curb s. Kinnkette f.; Hindernis n.; ~ v.t. bändigen; einfassen.

curd s. Quark m.

curdle v.t. & i. gerinnen machen; gerinnen; erstarren.

cure s. Kur f.; ~ of souls, Seelsorge f.; ~ v.t. heilen; einpökeln; räuchern.

curfew s. Abendglocke f.; Ausgehverbot n.; to lift the ~, das Ausgehverbot aufheben.

curio s. Rarität f.

curiosity s. Neugierde f.; Kuriosität f.

curious a., ~ly adv. neugierig; sorgfältig; zierlich; seltsam.

curl s. Locke f.; Wallung f.; ~ v.t. kräuseln; winden; ~ v.i. sich locken.

curling s. Eisstockschiessen n.

curling-iron s. Brenneisen n.

curl-paper s. Haarwickel m.

curly a. gekräuselt.

curmudgeon s. Geizhals, Knicker m.

currant s. Korinthe f.; Johannisbeere f.

currency s. Lauf, Umlauf m.; Währung f.; Kurs m.; Umlaufsmittel n.; hard ~, feste Währung; soft ~, unstabile Währung.

current a., ~ly adv. (um)laufend; gangbar; geläufig; ~ s. Lauf, Strom m.; Zug m.; elektrische Strom m.; alternat-

ing ~ (AC), Wechselstrom *m.*; *direct* ~ (DC), Gleichstrom *m.*
curriculum *s.* Lehrplan *m.*
curry *v.t.* striegeln; prügeln; *to ~ favour,* die Gunst erschleichen; ~ *s.* Curry *m.* (ostindische Mischgewürz).
curry-comb *s.* Pferdestriegel *m.*
curse *s.* Fluch *m.*; Verwünschung *f.*; ~ *v.i. & t.* fluchen; verwünschen.
cursive *a.* laufend, Kursiv...
cursory *a.* flüchtig, oberflächlich.
curt *a.,* ~ly *adv.* kurz, kurz angebunden.
curtail *v.t.* stutzen, abkürzen; verstümmeln; (*fig.*) einschränken.
curtailment *s.* Beschränkung, Kürzung *f.*
curtain *s.* Vorhang *m.*; (*mil.*) Zwischenwall *m.*; *to draw the* ~, den Vorhang zuziehen; ~ *v.t.* mit Vorhängen versehen, verhüllen.
curtain-fire *s.* (*mil.*) Sperrfeuer *n.*; ~-**lecture** *s.* Gardinenpredigt *f.*
curtain-rod *s.* Vorhangsstange *f.*
curtsy *s.* Verneigung *f.*; Knicks *m.*; ~ *v.i.* sich verneigen, knicksen.
curvature *s.* Krümmung *f.*
curve *s.* Krümmung *f.*; ~ *v.t.* krümmen, biegen.
cushion *s.* Kissen *n.*; Polster *m.*
cussedness *s.* Widerhaarigkeit *f.*
custard *s.* Eierrahm *m.*
custodial *a.* vormundschaftlich.
custodian *s.* Hüter, Kustos *m.*
custody *s.* Verwahrung *f.*; Haft *f.*; Aufsicht *f.*; Bedeckung *f.*; *protective* ~, Schutzhaft *f.*; *to take into* ~, verhaften.
custom *s.* Gebrauch *m.*; Gewohnheit *f.*; Kundschaft *f.*; Zoll *m.*
customary *a.,* ~ily *adv.* gebräuchlich.
customer *s.* Kunde *m.*; *regular* ~, Stammkunde, Stammgast *m.*
custom-house *s.* Zollamt *n.*   •
customs *s.pl.* Zoll *m.*; ~-**clearance**, Zollabfertigung *f.*; ~-**declaration**, Zollerklärung *f.*; ~-**examination**, ~-**inspection**, Zollrevision *f.*; ~-**station** Zollamt *n.*
cut *v.t. & i.ir.* schneiden, hauen; schnitzen; spalten; verstümmeln; kürzen; abheben (Karten); *to ~ a person,* einen nicht sehen wollen, schneiden; *to ~ out,* (*mech.*) ausschalten; (*com.*) unterbieten; *to ~ prices,* Preise herabsetzen; *to ~ teeth,* Zähne bekommen; ~ *and dried,* fix und fertig; ~ *s.* Schnitt, Einschnitt *m.*; Stich, Hieb *m.*; Kürzung *f.*; *short* ~, Abkürzungsweg *m.*
cutaneous *a.* zur Haut gehörig.
cute *a.* (*fam.*) schlau.
cuticle *s.* Oberhaut *f.*, Häutchen *n.*
cutlass *s.* Entermesser *n.*
cutler *s.* Messerschmied *m.*
cutlery *s.* Messerwaren *f.pl.*
cutlet *s.* Kotelett *n.*

cutter *s.* Steinschneider *m.*; Schneidezeug *n.*; Zuschneider *m.*; (*mech.*) Schneider *m.*; Kutter (Schiff) *m.*
cut-throat *s.* Meuchelmörder *m.*
cutting *s.* Einschnitt; Zeitungsausschnitt *m.*; ~ *a.* schneidend, scharf.
cuttle *s.* Tintenfisch *m.*
cwt. = hundredweight, Zentner (112 engl. Pfund) *m.*
cycle *s.* Kreis; Fahrrad *n.*; Zyklus *m.*; ~-**inflator** *s.* Fahrradpumpe *f.*
cycling *s.* Radfahren *n.*
cyclist *s.* Radfahrer; ~ *s' path,* Radfahrweg *m.*
cyclone *s.* Wirbelsturm *m.*
cyclopedia *s.* Enzyklopädie *f.*
cygnet *s.* junge Schwan *m.*
cylinder *s.* Zylinder *m.*; Walze *f.*
cylindrical *a.* zylindrisch.
cymbal *s.* Schallbecken *n.,* Zimbel *f.*
cynic *a.* zynisch; schamlos; ~ *s.* Zyniker.
cypress *s.* Zypresse *f.*
cyst *s.* Blase *f.*; Eitersack *m.*
czar *s.* Zar *m.*

D

dab *v.t.* betupfen; besudeln; ~ *s.* Berührung *f.*; Klecks *m.*
dabble *v.i.* planschen; stümpern; ~ *v.t.* bespritzen, besudeln.
dachshund *s.* Dachshund *m.,* Dackel *m.*
dad, daddy *s.* Papa, Vater *m.*; ~-**longlegs** *s.* langbeinige Mücke *f.*; Weberknecht *m.*
daffodil *s.* gelbe Narzisse *f.*
dagger *s.* Dolch *m.*
dahlia *s.* Dahlie *f.,* Georgine *f.*
daily *a. & adv.* täglich; ~ *s.* Tageszeitung *f.*
dainty *a.,* ~ily *adv.* lecker; niedlich; zierlich, fein; geziert; heikel; ~ *s.* Leckerbissen *m.,* Naschwerk *n.*
dairy *s.* Milchkammer, Milchwirtschaft *f.*; ~-**farm** Meierei *f.*
dairy-maid *s.* Milchmagd *f.*
dais *s.* Estrade *f.*
daisy *s.* Gänseblümchen *n.*
dale *s.* Tal *n.*
dalliance *s.* Tändelei *f.*; Trödelei *f.*; Verzögerung *f.*
dally *v.i.* tändeln, trödeln.
dam *s.* Damm *m.*; Talsperre *f.*; Muttertier *f.*; ~ *v.t.* dämmen.
damage *s.* Schaden, Verlust *m.*; Beschädigung *f.*; ~ *to property,* Sachbeschädigung *f.*; ~ *v.t.* beschädigen.
damageable *a.* leicht zu beschädigen.
damages *s.pl.* Schadenersatz *m.*
damask *s.* Damast *m.*; ~ *a.* damasten; ~ *v.t.* damaszieren.
damn *v.t.* verdammen; verwerfen.

damnable *a.*, **~bly** *adv.* verdammlich.
damnation *s.* Verdammung *f.*
damnatory *a.* verdammend.
damp *a.* feucht, dumpfig; **~** *s.* Feuchtigkeit *f.*; Schwaden *m.*; **~** *v.t.* befeuchten; dämpfen.
dampcourse *s.* vor Nässe schützende Schicht *f.*
damper *s.* Dämpfer *m.*
damp-proof *a.* feuchtigkeitssicher.
damsel *s.* Mädchen *n.*; Jungfer *f.*
damson *s.* Damaszenerpflaume *f.*
dance *s.* Tanz *m.*; **~** *v.i.* tanzen; *ballroom dancing*, Gesellschaftstanz *m.*
dancer *s.* Tänzer *m.*; Tänzerin *f.*
dancing-master *s.* Tanzlehrer *m.*
dandelion *s.* (*bot.*) Löwenzahn *m.*
dandle *v.t.* schaukeln, hätscheln.
dandruff *s.* Kopfschuppen *f.pl.*
dandy *s.* Stutzer *m.*
danger *s.* Gefahr *f.*
dangerous *a.*, **~ly** *adv.* gefährlich.
dangle *v.i.* baumeln; anhängen.
dapper *a.* flink, gewandt; nett.
dapple *a.* gefleckt, scheckig; **~** *s.* Apfelschimmel *m.*; **~** *v.t.* sprenkeln.
dare *v.i.* & *ir.* dürfen; wagen; *I ~say*, ich denke; **~** *v.t.* trotzen.
daredevil *a.* waghalsig; **~** *s.* Wagehals, Teufelskerl *m.*
daring *a.*, **~ly** *adv.* vermessen, verwegen; **~** *s.* Kühnheit *f.*
dark *a.* dunkel, trübe; **~ room** *s.* Dunkelkammer *f.*; *after ~*, nach Eintritt der Dunkelheit; **~** *s.* Finsternis *f.*
darken *v.t.* & *i.* verdunkeln; dunkel werden.
dark(e)y *s.* Neger *m.*
darkish *a.* etwas dunkel.
darkness *s.* Dunkelheit *f.*; Verborgenheit *f.*; Unwissenheit *f.*
darling *a.* teuer; **~** *s.* Liebling *m.*
darn *v.t.* stopfen, ausbessern.
dart *s.* Wurfgeschoss *n.*; Pfeil *m.*; **~** *v.t.* werfen, schiessen; **~** *v.i.* hinschiessen, stürzen; **darts** *s.pl.* Pfeilwurfspiel *n.*
dash *v.t.* schmeissen, stossen; vermischen; zerschmettern; vereiteln; **~** *v.i.* stossen; stürmen, stürzen, jagen; dahinrauschen; scheitern; *~ it!*, verwünscht!; **~** *s.* Klatsch, Schlag, Stoss *m.*; Federzug *m.*; Gedankenstrich *m.*; Aufguss *m.*; Stückchen, Bischen *n.*; Wagemut *m.*, Schneid *f.*
dash-board *s.* Spritzleder *n.*
dashing *a.* schneidig, flott.
dastard *s.* feige Memme *f.*; **~** *a.*, **~ly** *adv.* feig; abscheulich.
data *s.pl.* Angaben *f.pl.*
date *s.* Datum *n.*; Frist *f.*; Dattel *f.*; *what is the ~?*, den wievielten haben wir?; *up-to-~*, zeitgemäss, modern; *out of ~*, aus der Mode; **~** *v.t.* datieren.

dative *s.* (*gram.*) Dativ *m.*
daub *v.t.* überschmieren, sudeln.
daughter *s.* Tochter *f.*; **~-in-law**, Schwiegertochter *f.*
daunt *v.t.* entmutigen.
dauntless *a.* unerschrocken.
davit *s.* Jütte *f.*, Davit *m.*
dawdle *v.i.* trödeln; schlendern.
dawdler *s.* Tagedieb *m.*
dawn *v.i.* dämmern, tagen; **~** *s.* Dämmerung *f.*
day *s.* Tag *m.*; *by ~*, untertags; *the other ~*, neulich; *~s of grace pl.* Verzugstage *m.pl.*
day-boarder *s.* Schüler (*m.*), der nicht in der Pension wohnt.
daybreak *s.* Tagesanbruch *m.*
daylight *s.* Tageslicht; (*avi.*) **~-attack**, Tagesangriff *m.*
day-nursery *s.* Kinderhort *m.*
day-time *s.* Tageszeit *f.*; *in the ~*, bei Tage.
daze *v.t.* blenden; betäuben.
dazzle *v.t.* blenden.
deacon *s.* Diakon(us) *m.*
dead *a.* tot; dumpf, schal; (*elek.*) spannungslos; *~ against*, gerade entgegen; *~ bargain*, Spottpreis *m.*; **~-wall** *s.* blinde Mauer *f.*; **~-letter** *s.* unbestellbare Brief *m.*; **~** *adv.* ganz, völlig; **~** *s.* Totenstille *f.*; *the ~*, die Toten *pl.*
deaden *v.t.* abstumpfen, schwächen.
deadline *s.* Termin *m.*
dead-lock *s.* Stockung *f.*, Stillstand *m.*
deadly *a.* & *adv.* tödlich.
deaf *a.*, **~ly** *adv.* taub; dumpf; *~ and dumb*, taubstumm.
deafen *v.t.* betäuben.
deafness *s.* Taubheit *f.*
deal *s.* Teil *m.*; Anzahl *f.*; Geschäft *f.*; Kartengeben *n.*; Fichtenholz, Brett *n.*; *a good ~, a great ~*, viel, sehr; **~** *v.t.* austeilen, ausstreuen; Karten geben; **~** *v.i.* handeln, verfahren; vermitteln; *to ~ with*, behandeln.
dealer *s.* Händler *m.*; Kartengeber *m.*
dealing *s.* Verfahren *n.*; Austeilen *n.*; Umgang *m.*; *to have ~s with*, mit einem zu tun haben.
dean *s.* Dechant, Dekan *m.*
deanery *s.* Dekanat *n.*
dear *a.* teuer, wert; innig; **~** *s.* Geliebte *m.* & *f.*; *~ me!*, verwünscht!
dearth *s.* Teuerung *f.*; Mangel *m.*
death *s.* Tod *m.*; Todesfall *m.*; *to put to ~*, hinrichten.
death-bed *s.* Sterbebett *n.*
death-duty *s.* Erbschaftssteuer *f.*
deathless *a.* unsterblich.
deathly *a.* totenähnlich, Todes...
death-penalty *s.* Todesstrafe *f.*
death-rate *s.* Sterblichkeitsziffer *f.*
death's head *s.* Totenkopf *m.*
death-warrant *s.* Todesurteil *n.*

debar *v.t.* ausschliessen; verhindern.

debase *v.t.* erniedrigen; verfälschen.

debasement *s.* Erniedrigung *f.*

debatable *a.* streitig.

debate *s.* Debatte *f.*; ~ *v.t.* bestreiten, erörtern.

debauch *v.t.* verführen, verderben.

debauchee *s.* Schwelger, Wüstling *m.*

debauchery *s.* Ausschweifung *f.*

debenture *s.* Schuldschein *m.*; (*com.*) Obligation *f.*

debilitate *v.t.* schwächen, entkräften.

debility *s.* Schwachheit.

debit *v.t.* belasten, debitieren; ~ *s.* Debet *n.*; Lasten *f.pl.*

debonair *a.* gutlaunig, aufgeräumt.

debouch *v.i.* hervorbrechen; einmünden.

débris *s.* Trümmer *pl.*

debt *s.* Schuld *f.*; *to run into* ~, in Schulden geraten.

debtor *s.* Schuldner *m.*

decade *s.* Jahrzehnt *n.*

decadence *s.* Verfall *m.*

decadent *a.* dekadent.

decalogue *s.* die zehn Gebote *n.pl.*

decamp *v.i.* aufbrechen, ausreissen.

decant *v.t.* abgiessen; umfüllen.

decanter *s.* Karaffe *f.*

decay *v.i.* verfallen; verwelken; ~ *s.* Verfall *m.*; Abnahme *f.*

decease *s.* Ableben *n.*; ~ *v.i.* sterben, verscheiden.

deceit *s.* Betrug *m.*; List *f.*

deceitful *a.*, ~ly *adv.* betrügerisch.

deceive *v.t.* betrügen, täuschen.

December *s.* Dezember *m.*

decency *s.* Anstand *m.*; Schicklichkeit *f.*

decennial *a.* zehnjährig.

decent *a.*, ~ly *adv.* sittsam, anständig.

decentralize *v.t.* dezentralisieren.

deception *s.* Betrug *m.*

deceptive *a.* trügerisch.

decide *v.t.* entscheiden, bestimmen.

decided *adv.* entschieden, bestimmt.

decimal *a.* dezimal; ~ *s.* Dezimale *f.*

decimate *v.t.* zehnten, dezimieren.

decipher *v.t.* entziffern.

decision *s.* Entscheidung *f.*; Entschlossenheit *f.*

decisive *a.*, ~ly *adv.* entscheidend.

deck *s.* Deck, Verdeck *n.*; ~ *v.t.* bekleiden; schmücken.

deck-chair *s.* Liegestuhl *m.*

declaim *v.t.* deklamieren; eifern.

declamation *s.* Deklamation *f.*

declamatory *a.* deklamatorisch.

declaration *s.* Erklärung *f.*

declaratory *a.*, ~ily *adv.* erklärend.

declare *v.t.* erklären, behaupten; (Zoll) deklarieren; ~ *v.i.* sich erklären.

declension *s.* (*gram.*) Deklination *f.*

declination *s.* Abweichung *f.*; Abnahme *f.*; Deklination *f.*

decline *v.i.* abweichen; abnehmen; sich weigern; fallen (im Preise); ~ *v.t.* ablehnen; deklinieren; ~ *s.* Abnahme *f.*; Verfall *m.*

declivity *s.* Abhang *m.*

decoction *s.* Absud *m.*, Absieden *n.*

decode *v.t.* entziffern.

decompose *v.t.* zerlegen.

decomposition *s.* Zersetzung *f.*

decontrol *v.t.* freigeben.

decorate *v.t.* verzieren, schmücken.

decoration *s.* Dekoration *f.*, Schmuck *m.*; Ordenszeichen *n.*

decorative *a.* schmückend.

decorator *s.* Dekorateur *m.*

decorous *a.*, ~ly *adv.* anständig.

decorum *s.* Anstand *m.*

decoy *v.t.* locken, ködern; ~ *s.* Köder *m.*

decrease *v.t.* vermindern; ~ *v.i.* abnehmen; ~ *s.* Abnahme *f.*

decree *v.t.* beschliessen; ~ *s.* Beschluss *m.*, Verordnung *f.*; ~ *nisi*, (*law*) vorläufiges Urteil (Ehescheidungsprozess); ~ *absolute*, endgültiges Urteil (Ehescheidungsprozess).

decrepit *a.* abgelebt.

decrepitude *s.* Abgelebtheit *f.*

decry *v.t.* verrufen, tadeln.

dedicate *v.t.* widmen, zueignen.

dedication *s.* Widmung, Zueignung *f.*

dedicatory *a.* Widmungs...

deduce *v.t.* abietten; schliessen, folgern.

deducible *a.* ableitbar.

deduct *v.t.* abziehen, abrechnen.

deduction *s.* Abzug, Rabatt *m.*; Schlussfolge *f.*

deductive *a.*, ~ly *adv.* deduktiv, folgernd.

deed *s.* Tat, Handlung *f.*; Urkunde *f.*; ~ *of gift*, Schenkungsurkunde *f.*; ~ *of partnership*, Gesellschaftsvertrag *m.*; ~ *of sale*, Kaufkontrakt *m.*

deem *v.t.* halten für, erachten.

deep *a.*, ~ly *adv.* tief; geheim; schlau; ~ *s.* Tiefe *f.*; Meer *n.*

deepen *v.t.* vertiefen; ~ *v.i.* sich vertiefen; stärker werden.

deep-laid *a.* tief, schlau angelegt.

deer *s.* Rotwild *n.*; Hirsch *m.*

deerskin *s.* Wildleder *n.*

deer-stalking *s.* Pirschen *n.*

deface *v.t.* verunstalten, entstellen.

defalcate *v.i.* (Gelder) unterschlagen.

defamation *s.* Verleumdung *f.*

defamatory *a.* verleumderisch.

defame *v.t.* verleumden; verlästern.

default *s.* Versäumnis *n.*; Zahlungseinstellung *f.*; Nichterscheinen *n.*; *in* ~ *of*, mangels; *judgment by* ~, (*law*) Versäumnisurteil *n.*; ~ *v.i.* unterlassen; fehlen; im Verzug sein, Verpflichtungen nicht erfüllen.

defaulter *s.* säumiger Zahler *m.*; zum Termin nicht Erscheinende(r) *m.*

defeat v.t. schlagen; vereiteln; ~ s. Niederlage, Vereitelung f.

defeatism s. Miesmacherei f., Defaitismus m.

defect s. Mangel m.; Gebrechen n.; ~ of speech, Sprachfehler m.

defection s. Mangel m.; Abtrünnigkeit f.; Abfall m.

defective a. mangelhaft, unvollständig.

defence s. Verteidigung (auch law) f.; (mil.) Widerstand m.; witness for the ~, Entlastungszeuge m.

defenceless a., ~ly adv. wehrlos.

defend v.t. verteidigen.

defendant s. Verteidiger m.; (law) Angeklagte, Beklagte m.

defensible a. zu verteidigen, haltbar.

defensive a., ~ly adv. Verteidigungs...; ~ s. (mil.) Defensive f.; to be on the ~, in der Defensive sein.

defer v.t. aufschieben, vorenthalten; (mil.) zurückstellen; ~red shares, Verzugsaktien pl.; ~ v.i. sich beugen, nachgeben.

deference s. Ehrerbietung f.; Nachgiebigkeit f.

deferential a., ~ly adv. ehrerbietig.

deferment s. Zurückstellung f. (mil.)

defiance s. Herausforderung f.; Trotz m.

defiant a. herausfordernd.

deficiency s. Mangel m.

deficient a. unzulänglich, mangelhaft.

deficit s. Fehlbetrag m., Defizit n.

defile v.t. beflecken; ~ v.i. defilieren ~ s. Engpass m.

defilement s. Befleckung f.

define v.t. festsetzen; definieren.

definite a. festgesetzt, bestimmt.

definition s. Begriffsbestimmung f.

definitive a., ~ly adv. endgültig.

deflate v.t. Luft herauslassen (aus Reifen, etc.)

deflation s. Entleerung f.; Deflation f.

deflect v.t. & i. ablenken; abweichen.

deflection s. Abweichung f.

deflower v.t. entjungfern; schänden.

deform v.t. verunstalten, entstellen.

deformity s. Ungestaltheit f., Gebrechen n.

defraud v.t. betrügen; to ~ the revenue, Steuern hinterziehen.

defraudation s. Betrug m.

defray v.t. bestreiten, bezahlen.

deft a., ~ly adv. geschickt, gewandt.

defunct a. verstorben.

defy v.t. herausfordern, trotzen.

degeneracy s. Entartung f.

degenerate v.i. entarten; ~ a., ~ly adv. ausgeartet, schlecht, entartet.

degradation s. Erniedrigung f.

degrade v.t. herabsetzen, erniedrigen, herabwürdigen; vermindern.

degree s. Grad m.; Stufe f.; Gattung, Ordnung, Klasse f.

dehydrate v.t. Wasser entziehen; ~d food, Trockennahrung f.

deify v.t. vergöttern.

deign v.t. geruhen; belieben.

deity s. Gottheit f.

deject v.t. entmutigen.

dejection s. Niedergeschlagenheit f.

delate v.t. anklagen, denunzieren.

delay v.t. aufschieben, hinhalten; hindern; ~ed action,; Verzugszeit f.; ~ v.i. zaudern; ~ s. Aufschub m., Verzug m.

delectable a., ~bly adv. f. angenehm.

delegacy s. Abordnung .

delegate v.t. abordnen; übertragen; to ~ authority, Befugnis übertragen; ~ s. Abgeordnete.

delegation s. Abordnung f.

delete v.t. auslöschen, tilgen.

deleterious a. schädlich.

deliberate v.i. beratschlagen; ~ a. absichtlich.

deliberation s. Beratschlagung f.

deliberative a. beratschlagend.

delicacy s. Schmackhaftigkeit f.; Leckerbissen m.; Zartheit n.

delicate a., ~ly adv. zart; fein; heikel

delicatessen pl. Delikatessen f.pl.

delicious a., ~ly adv. köstlich.

delight s. Vergnügen n.; Wonne f.; ~ v.t. ergötzen, vergnügen; ~ v.i. Vergnügen finden.

delightful a., ~ly adv. entzückend.

delimit v.t. abgrenzen.

delimitation s. Abgrenzung f.

delineate v.t. zeichnen, entwerfen.

delinquency s. Pflichtvergessenheit f., Vergehen n.; Kriminalität f.

delinquent s. Verbrecher m.

delirious a. wahnsinnig.

delirium s. (Fieber-) Wahnsinn m.

deliver v.t. überliefern; befreien; vortragen; entbinden; abliefern; (Angriff) ausführen.

deliverance s. Befreiung f.

delivery s. Lieferung f.; Befreiung f.; Vortrag m.; Entbindung f.; Briefbestellung f.

delivery-note s. Lieferschein m.

delta s. Delta n.

delude v.t. betrügen, täuschen.

deluge s. Überschwemmung f.; Sündflut f.; ~ v.t. überschwemmen.

delusion s. Täuschung f.; Wahn m.

delusive a., ~ly adv. täuschend.

de-luxe a. Luxus...

delve v.t. graben.

demagogic a. demagogisch.

demagogue s. Aufwiegler m.

demand v.t. fordern; fragen; verlangen; ~ s. Forderung f.; Frage f.; Anspruch m.; Nachfrage f.

demarcate v.t. abgrenzen.

demarcation s. Grenzlinie f.

demean *v.r.* sich erniedrigen.
demeanour *s.* Betragen *n.*
demented *a.* toll, verrückt.
dementi *s.* Dementi *n.*, Richtigstellung *f.*
demerit *s.* Mangel *m.*; Verschuldung *f.*
demi -(*prefix*) halb.
demise *s.* Übertragung *f.*; Ableben *n.*; ~ *v.t.* vermachen; verpachten.
demisemiquaver *s.* Zweiunddreissigstelnote *f.*
demobilize *v.t.* abrüsten, demobilisieren.
democracy *s.* Demokratie *f.*
democrat *s.* Demokrat *m.*
democratic *a.* demokratisch.
demolish *v.t.* niederreissen, abtragen.
demolition *s.* Niederreissen *n.*
demon *s.* Dämon *m.*; Teufel *m.*
demoniac *s.* Besessene *m.*; ~ *a.* dämonisch.
demonstrable *a.*, ~bly *adv.* erweislich.
demonstrate *v.t.* beweisen.
demonstration *s.* Beweis *m.*; Äusserung (des Gefühls) *f.*; Vorführung *f.*; Demonstration *f.*
demonstrative *a.*, ~ly *adv.* beweisend; auffällig; (*gram.*) hinweisend. ;
demoralize *v.t.* entsittlichen.
demur *v.i.* Einwendungen machen.
demure *a.*, ~ly *adv.* sittsam.
demurrage *s.* (*nav.*) Liegegeld *n.*
demurrer *s.* Rechtseinwand *m.*
demy *s.* Briefpapierformat *n.* (15½ × 20 Zoll).
den *s.* Höhle, Grube *f.*; (*slang*) Bude *f.*
denial *s.* Verneinung, Verweigerung *f.*
denizen *s.* Bewohner *m.*
denomination *s.* Benennung *f.*; Klasse *f.*; Nennwert (Banknote, Scheck) *m.*; Konfession *f.*
denominational *a.* konfessionell, Sekten ...
denominative *a.* benennend.
denominator *s.* (*ar.*) Nenner *m.*
denote *v.t.* bezeichnen, bedeuten.
denounce *v.t.* drohend ankündigen; verklagen, anklagen; aufkündigen.
dense *a.* dicht, fest; dumm.
density *s.* Dichtheit *f.*
dent *s.* Kerbe *f.*, Einschnitt *m.*
dental *a.* Zahn...
dental surgeon *s.* Zahnarzt *m.*
dentifrice *s.* Zahnpulver *n.*
dentist *s.* Zahnarzt *m.* Zahntechniker *m.*
dentistry *s.* Zahnheilkunde *f.*
denture *s.* künstliches Gebiss *n.*
denude *v.t.* entblössen.
denunciate *v.t.* denunzieren.
denunciation *s.* Anzeige; Anklage *f.*
deny *v.t.* verneinen; abschlagen; (ver)leugnen.
deodorant *s.* geruchtilgende Mittel *n.*
deodorize *v.t.* geruchlos machen.
depart *v.i.* abreisen; abweichen.

department *s.* Abteilung *f.*; Bezirk *m.*; Geschäftskreis *m.*; Behörde *f.*
department store *s.* (*Am.*) Warenhaus *n.*
departure *s.* Abreise *f.*; Abweichung *f.*; (*fig.*) Tod *m.*; *a new* ~, eine neue einführung *f.*
depend *v.i.* abhängen; *to* ~ *on*, sich verlassen auf; *it* ~*s*, das kommt darauf an, je nachdem.
dependable *a.* zuverlässig.
dependence *s.* Vertrauen *n.*; Abhängigkeit *f.*
dependency *s.* Besitzung, Kolonie *f.*
dependent *a.* abhängig; dependant, ~ *s.* Untergebene *m.*; abhängige Angehörige *m.*
depict *v.t.* abmalen, schildern.
deplete *v.t.* entleeren; erschöpfen.
depletion *s.* Entleerung *f.*
deplorable *a.*, ~bly *adv.* beklagenswert.
deplore *v.t.* beklagen, bemängeln.
deploy *v.t.* aufmarschieren, Truppen entwickeln.
deployment *s.* Aufmarsch *m.*
deponent *s.* vereidigte Zeuge *m.*
depopulate *v.t.* entvölkern.
deport *v.t.* fortschaffen, deportieren; *to* ~ *oneself*, sich betragen.
deportation *s.* Deportation *f.*
deportee *s.* Deportierte *m.*
deportment *s.* Haltung *f.*; Anstand *m.*
depose *v.t.* & *i.* niedersetzen; entsetzen; bezeugen; sich absetzen.
deposit *v.t.* niederlegen; ablegen; deponieren; ausleihen; anlegen; ~ *s.* Unterpfand, Pfand *n.*; Einlage *f.*; Depot *n.*, Einzahlung *f.*, Depositum *n.*; anvertraute Gut *n.*; Niederschlag *m.*; (Erz-) Lager *n.*
depositary *s.* Verwahrer *m.*
deposition *s.* Absetzung *f.*; Zeugenaussage *f.*
depositor *s.* Einzahler, Hinterleger *m.*
depository *s.* Gewahrsam *m.*; Niederlage *f.*; Verwahrungsort *m.*
depot *s.* Lagerhaus *n.*
deprave *v.t.* verderben.
depravity *s.* Verdorbenheit *f.*
deprecate *v.t.* abbitten; flehen, um etwas abzuwenden; sehr missbilligen.
deprecatory *a.* abbittend; missbilligend.
depreciate *v.t.* herabsetzen, verkleinern; entwerten; abschreiben.
depredation *s.* Plünderung *f.*; Räuberei *f.*
depress *v.t.* niederdrücken.
depressed area *a.* Notstandsgebiet *n.*
depression *s.* Tief *n.*; Niedergeschlagenheit *f.*; Erniedrigung *f.*; Sinken (im Preise) *n.*
deprivation *s.* Beraubung *f.*
deprive *v.t.* berauben; entziehen.
depth *s.* Tiefe *f.*; ~ *charge*, Unterwasserbombe *f.*

deputation *s.* Abordnung *f.*

depute *v.t.* abordnen.

deputy *s.* Abgeordnete, Stellvertreter *m.*

derail *v.t.* entgleisen (lassen).

derailment *s.* Entgleisung *f.*

derange *v.t.* zerrütten.

derangement *s.* Unordnung *f.*; Geisteszerrüttung *f.*

deration *v.t.* von der Rationierung absetzen.

derelict *a.* verlassen, herrenlos.

dereliction *s.* Verlassen *n.*; ~ of duty, Pflichtvergessenheit *f.*

derequisition *v.t.* Beschlagnahme aufheben.

deride *v.t.* verlachen.

derision *s.* Verspottung *f.*

derisive *a.* spöttisch, höhnisch.

derivation *s.* Ableitung, Herleitung *f.*

derivative *a.*, ~ly *adv.* hergeleitet; abgeleitet; ~ *s.* abgeleitete Wort *n.*, Ableitung *f.*; (chem.) Derivat *n.*

derive *v.t.* ableiten; herleiten.

derogate *v.i.* Abbruch tun.

derogation *s.* Schmälerung *f.*

derogatory *a.* verletzend.

derrick *s.* Hebekran *m.*

descant *s.* Diskantstimme *f.*

descend *v.i. & t.* herabsteigen; sich senken; landen; abstammen.

descendant *s.* Nachkomme *m.*

descent *s.* Herabsteigen *n.*; Senkung *f.*; Abstammung *f.*

describe *v.t.* beschreiben, schildern.

description *s.* Beschreibung *f.*; Sorte *f.*

descriptive *a.* beschreibend.

descry *v.t.* ausspähen, entdecken.

desecrate *v.t.* entweihen.

desert *a.* öde, wüst; ~ *s.* Wüste.; ~ *s.* Verdienst *n.*; ~ *v.t. & i.* verlassen entlaufen, desertieren.

deserter *s.* Fahnenflüchtiger.

desertion *s.* Fahnenflucht *f.*

deserve *v.t.* verdienen; ~ *v.i.* sich verdient machen.

deservedly *adv.* nach Verdienst.

deserving *a.*, ~ly *adv.* verdienstvoll.

deshabille *s.* leichte Hauskleid *n.*

desideratum *s.* Wünschenswerte *n.*

design *v.t. & i.* bestimmen; entwerfen, zeichnen; planen; ~ *s.* Absicht *f.*; Entwurf *m.*; Zeichnung *f.*; Muster *n.*

designate *v.t.* bezeichnen; ernennen.

designation *s.* Bezeichnung, Bestimmung *f.*

designer *s.* Erfinder *m.*; Musterzeichner *m.*

designing *a.* hinterlistig.

desirable *a.* wünschenswert.

desire *s.* Verlangen *n.*; Wunsch *m.*; ~ *v.t.* wünschen, verlangen; bitten.

desirous *a.*, ~ly *adv.* wünschend, begierig.

desist *v.i.* abstehen.

desk *s.* Pult *n.*; Schultisch *m.*

desk-clerk *s.* Hotelportier *m.*

desolate *a.*, ~ly *adv.* öde; wüst; betrübt; ~ *v.t.* verwüsten.

desolation *s.* Verwüstung, Einöde *f.*

despair *s.* Verzweiflung *f.*; ~ *v.i.* verzweifeln.

despatch *see* dispatch.

desperado *s.* Wagehals *m.*

desperate *a.*, ~ly *adv.* verzweifelt; verwegen.

despicable *a.*, ~bly *adv.* verächtlich.

despise *v.t.* verachten, verschmähen.

despoil *v.t.* plündern.

despond *v.i.* verzagen, verzweifeln.

despondency *s.* Kleinmut *m.*

despondent *a.* verzagend, verzweifelnd.

despot *s.* Gewaltherrscher, Despot *m.*

despotic(al) *a.*, ~ly *adv.* despotisch.

despotism *s.* Gewaltherrschaft *f.*

dessert *s.* Nachtisch *m.*

destination *f.* Bestimmung *f.*; Ziel *n.*

destine *v.t.* bestimmen.

destiny *s.* Schicksal, Verhängnis *n.*

destitute *a.* verlassen, hilflos; entblösst.

destitution *s.* Hilflosigkeit, Not *f.*

destroy *v.t.* zerstören, verwüsten.

destroyer *s.* Zerstörer *m.* (auch Schiff.).

destruction *s.* Zerstörung *f.*

destructive *a.*, ~ly *adv.* zerstörend.

desuetude *s.* Abkommen (eines Gebrauchs) *n.*; Entwöhnung *f.*

desultory *a.* sprunghaft; oberflächlich.

detach *v.t.* absondern; auf Kommando ausschicken.

detachable *a.* abtrennbar.

detachment *s.* Detachement, Absonderung *f.*; (mil.) Abteilung *f.*, Trupp *m.*

detail *v.t.* umständlich erzählen; (mil.) abordnen; ~ *s.* Einzelheit *f.*; ~ed *a.* in die Einzelheiten gehend; in ~ ausführlich.

detain *v.t.* zurückhalten; abhalten; in Haft halten.

detainee *s.* Häftling *m.*

detect *v.t.* entdecken, aufdecken.

detection *s.* Entdeckung *f.*

detective *s.* Geheimpolizist, Detektiv *m.*

detector *a.* (radio) Detektor.

detention *s.* Haft *m.*

deter *v.t.* abschrecken.

detergent *s.* Reinigungsmittel *n.*

deteriorate *v.t.* verschlimmern.

deterioration *s.* Verschlimmerung.

determent *s.* Hindernis *n.*

determinate *a.*, ~ly *adv.* bestimmt.

determination *s.* Bestimmung; Entschlossenheit *f.*; Beschluss *m.*

determinative *a.*, ~ly *adv.* bestimmend.

determine *v.t.* festsetzen; festellen; beendigen; ~ *v.i.* sich entschliessen.

deterrent *s.* Abschreckungsmittel *n.*

detest *v.t.* verabscheuen.

detestable *a.*, ~bly *adv.* abscheulich.

detestation *s.* Abscheu *m.*

dethrone *v.t.* entthronen.

dethronement *s.* Entthronung *f.*

detonate *v.i.* explodieren, verpuffen.

detonator *s.* Zünder *m.*; Sprengkapsel *f.*

detonation *s.* Knall *m.*

detour *s.* Umweg *m.*; ~ *v.t.* umleiten.

detract *v.t.* schmälern; verleumden.

detraction *s.* Verleumdung *f.*

detrain *v.t.* (*mil.*) (Truppen) ausladen; ~ *v.i.* aussteigen.

detriment *s.* Schaden, Nachteil *m.*

detrimental *a.*, ~ly *adv.* nachteilig.

deuce *s.* Teufel *m.*

devaluation *s.* Abwertung *f.*

devalue *v.t.* abwerten.

devastate *v.t.* verwüsten.

devastation *s.* Verwüstung *f.*

develop *v.t.* entwickeln, enthüllen.

development *s.* Entwicklung *f.*

deviate *v.i.* abweichen.

deviation *s.* Abweichung, Verirrung *f.*

device *s.* Kunstgriff *m.*; Vorrichtung *f.*; Wahlspruch *m.*

devil *s.* Teufel *m.*

devilish *a.* teuflisch.

devilry *s.* Teufelei *f.*

devious *a.* abwegig.

devise *v.i.* ersinnen; (*by will*) vermachen.

devoid *a.* bar, frei; ~ *of*, ohne.

devolution *s.* Heimfall *m.*; Abwälzung von Aufgaben *f.*

devolve *v.t.* (*fig.*) übertragen; ~ (*upon*) *v.i.* zufallen, heimfallen.

devote *v.t.* widmen; aufopfern.

devoted *a.*, ~ly *adv.* ergeben, fromm.

devotee *s.* Verehrer *m.*; Frömmler *m.*

devotion *s.* Aufopferung, Hingabe *f.*; Widmung *f.*; Andacht *f.*

devotional *a.*, ~ly *adv.* andächtig.

devour *v.t.* verschlingen.

devout *a.*, ~ly *adv.* andächtig.

dew *s.* Tau *m.*; ~ *v.t.* betauen.

dexterity *s.* Gewandtheit, Fertigkeit *f.*

dexterous *a.*, ~ly *adv.* gewandt, geschickt.

diabetes *s.* (*med.*) Zuckerkrankheit *f.*

diabetic *a.* zuckerkrank; ~ *s.* Zuckerkranke *m.*, Diabetiker *m.*

diabolic(al) *a.*, ~ly *adv.* teuflisch.

diadem *s.* Diadem *n.*

diæresis *s.* Trema *n.*, Trennpunkte *pl.*, *m.*

diagnose *v.t.* diagnostizieren.

diagnosis *s.* Diagnose *f.*

diagonal *a.*, ~ly *adv.* schräg; diagonal; ~ *s.* Diagonale *f.*

diagram *s.* (*geom.*) Riss *m.*; Figur *f.*; graphische Darstellung *f.*

dial *s.* Zifferblatt *n.*; Wählscheibe *f.*; ~ *v.t.* (*tel.*) wählen.

dialect *s.* Mundart *f.*

dialectical *a.*, ~ly *adv.* dialektisch.

dialogue *s.* Zwiegespräch *n.*

diameter *s.* Durchmesser *m.*

diametrical *a.*, ~ly *adv.* diametrisch; ~ *opposed*, gerade entgegengesetzt.

diamond *s.* Diamant *m.*; Karo, Rot (der Karte) *n.*

diapason *s.* (*mus.*) Zusammenklang *m.*; Mensur (der Orgel) *f.*

diaper *s.* geblümte Leinwand, *f.*; Windel *f.*; Binde *f.*; ~ *v.t.* (Zeug, Getäfel) rautenförmig mustern.

diaphragm *s.* Zwerchfell *n.*; (*tel.*) Membran *f.*; (*optics*) Blende *f.*

diarrhœa *s.* Durchfall *m.*

diary *s.* Tagebuch *n.*

diatribe *s.* heftige Angriff, Tadel *m.*

dice *s.* (*pl.* von *die*) Würfel *m.pl.*; ~ *v.i.* würfeln.

dice-box *s.* Würfelbecher *m.*

dickens *s.* *what the ~!* was zum Kuckuck!

dick(e)y *s.* Hintersitz am Wagen *m.*

dictate *v.t.* diktieren; ~ *s.* Vorschrift *f.*

dictation *s.* Diktat *n.*; Geheiss *n.*

dictator *s.* Diktator *m.*

dictatorial *a.* gebieterisch.

dictatorship *s.* Diktatur *f.*

diction *s.* Sprechweise *f.*, Stil *m.*

dictionary *s.* Wörterbuch *n.*

didactic *a.* lehrhaft; Lehr...

diddle *v.t.* beschwindeln.

die *s.* Würfel *m.*; Stempel *m.*; Matrize *f.*; ~ *v.i.* sterben; umkommen; verwelken; sich verlieren.

die-hard *s.* Unentwegte *m.*

diet *s.* Diät *f.*; Kost *f.*; Landtag *m.*; ~ *v.t.* beköstigen.

dietary *a.* diätetisch.

dietetics *s.pl.* Ernährungswissenschaft *f.*, Diätetik *f.*

dietitian *s.* Diätkoch *m.*, Diätköchin *f.*; Diätiker *m.*

differ *v.i.* verschieden sein, abweichen; streiten, sich unterscheiden.

difference *s.* Unterschied *m.*; Streit *m.*

different *s.*, ~ly *adv.* verschieden, anders.

differential tariff *s.* Staffeltarif *m.*

differentiate *v.t.* & *i.* (sich) unterscheiden; dfferenzieren.

difficult *a.* schwierig.

difficulty *s.* Schwierigkeit *f.*

diffidence *s.* Misstrauen *n.*

diffident *a.*, ~ly *adv.* misstrauisch; schüchtern.

diffuse *v.t.* ausgiessen; verbreiten; zerstreuen; ~ *a.* weitläufig.

diffusion *s.* Verbreitung *f.*

dig *v.t.* & *i.st.* graben; bohren.

digest *v.t.* verdauen; überdenken; ertragen; ~ *s.* Auszug, Abriss *m.*; Übersicht *f.*; Gesetzessammlung *f.*

digestible *a.* verdaulich.

digestion *s.* Verdauung *f.*; Überlegung *f.*

digestive system *s.* Verdauungssystem *n.*

digger *s.* Gräber *m.*

digging *s.* Graben *n.*; ~s *pl.* Goldgräberei *f.*; (*slang*) Bude *f.*

digit *s.* Fingerbreite *f.*; Ziffer *f.* (unter Zehn).

dignified *a.* würdevoll.

dignitary *s.* Würdenträger *m.*

dignity *s.* Würde *f.*; Rang *m.*

digress *v.t.* abschweifen.

digression *s.* Abschweifung *f.*

digressive *a.* abweichend, abschweifend.

dike *s.* Graben *m.*; Damm *m.*

dilapidate *v.t.* niederreissen; zerstören.

dilapidated *a.* baufällig.

dilate *v.t.* erweitern, ausdehnen.

dilatory *a.*, ~ily *adv.* aufschiebend.

dilemma *s.* Dilemma *n.*

diligence *s.* Fleiss *m.*; Sorgfalt *f.*

diligent *a.*, ~ly *adv.* fleissig, emsig.

dill *s.* (*bot.*) Dille *f.*, Dill *m.*

dilute *v.t.* verdünnen; mildern.

dilution *s.* Verdünnung *f.*

dim *a.*, ~ly *adv.* dunkel, trübe, matt; ~ *v.t.* verdunkeln, trüben; (*mot.*) abblenden.

dime *a.* (*Am.*) Münze von zehn Cents *f.*

dimension *s.* Ausdehnung *f.*; Mass *n.*

diminish *v.t.* vermindern; ~ *v.i.* abnehmen.

diminution *s.* Verkleinerung *f.*; Abnahme *f.*

diminutive *a.*, ~ly *adv.* vermindernd; winzig; ~ *s.* Verkleinerungswort *n.*

dimple *s.* Grübchen *n.*

din *s.* Gerassel, Getöse *n.*; ~ *v.t.* & *i.* schallen; rasseln; betäuben.

dine *v.i.* zu Mittag speisen.

ding-dong *s.* Klingklang *m.*; ~ *fight*, schwankende, heissumstrittene Kampf *m.*

dingey, dinghy *s.* flaches Boot *n.*

dingy *a.* schmutzig; schwarzbraun.

dining-car *s.* Speisewagen *m.*; ~ *attendant s.* Speisewagenschaffner *m.*

dining-room *s.* Speisesaal *m.*; Esszimmer *n.*

dinner *s.* Hauptmahlzeit *f.*; ~-jacket, Smoking *m.*; ~-set Ess-Service *n.*

dint *s.*, *by* ~ *of*, mittels, kraft.

diocese *s.* Diözese *f.*

diorama *s.* Diorama *n.*; Guckkasten *m.*

dip *v.t.* eintauchen; ~ *v.i.* sich senken; ~ *s.* Eintauchen *n.*; Neigung *f.*

diphtheria *s.* Diphtheritis *f.*

diphthong *s.* Diphthong *m.*

diploma *s.* Diplom *n.*

diplomacy *s.* Diplomatie *f.*

diplomatic(al) *a.* diplomatisch.

diplomatist *s.* Diplomat *m.*

dipsomania *s.* Trunksucht *f.*

dire *a.* grässlich.

direct *a.* gerade, unmittelbar; ausdrücklich; ~ly *adv.* geradezu, sogleich, direkt; ~ *v.t.* richten, anweisen; adressieren.

direction *s.* Richtung *f.*; Leitung, Anordnung *f.*; Adresse *f.*

directional aerial *s.* (*radio*) Richtstrahler *m.*; Richtantenne *f.*

direction-finding *s.* (*radio*) Peilung, Funkpeilung *f.*

directions for use *pl.* Gebrauchsanweisung *f.*

directive *s.* Anweisung *f.*; ~s *pl.* Richtlinien *f.pl.*

director *s.* Direktor *m.*, Leiter *m.*

directorate *s.* Präsidium *n.*

directory *s.* Adressbuch *n.*

direful *see* dire.

dirge *s.* Trauergesang *m.*

dirk *s.* Dolch *m.*

dirt *s.* Kot, Schmutz *m.*; ~-cheap, spottbillig.

dirty *a.*, ~ily *adv.* schmutzig; ~ *v.t.* besudeln.

disability *s.* Unvermögen *n.*; Unfähigkeit *f.*

disable *v.t.* unfähig machen.

disabled *a.* unfähig, untauglich; invalid.

disablement *s.* Arbeitsunfähigkeit *f.*

disabuse *v.t.* aufklären.

disaccustom *v.t.* abgewöhnen.

disadvantage *s.* Nachteil *m.*

disadvantageous *a.*, ~ly *adv.* nachteilig.

disaffect *v.t.* abgeneigt machen.

disaffected *a.* unzufrieden.

disaffection *s.* Abneigung *f.*

disagree *v.i.* nicht übereinstimmen; nicht gut bekommen (von Speisen).

disagreeable *a.*, ~bly *adv.* unangenehm.

disagreement *s.* Misshelligkeit *f.*

disallow *v.t.* & *i.* nicht gestatten; in Abrede stellen.

disappear *v.i.* verschwinden.

disappearance *s.* Verschwinden *n.*

disappoint *v.t.* vereiteln, enttäuschen.

disappointment *s.* Enttäuschung *f.*

disapprobation *s.*, disapproval *s.* Missbilligung *f.*

disapprove *v.t.* & *i.* missbilligen.

disarm *v.t.* entwaffnen; ~ *v.i.* abrüsten.

disarmament *s.* Abrüstung *f.*

disarrange *v.t.* verwirren.

disarray *v.t.* in Unordnung bringen; ~ *s.* Verwirrung *f.*

disaster *s.* Unglück *n.*, Unfall *m.*, Katastrophe *f.*

disastrous *a.*, ~ly *adv.* unheilvoll.

disavow *v.t.* nicht anerkennen.

disband *v.t.* verabschieden; (*mil.*) (Einheit) auflösen; ~ *v.i.* sich auflösen.

disbelief *s.* Unglaube, Zweifel *m.*

disburse *v.t.* auszahlen, vorschiessen.

disbursement *s.* Auszahlung *f.*

disc *s.* = disk.

discard *v.t.* entfernen; verabschieden, abdanken; abwerfen (eine Karte); ablegen (Kleider).

discern *v.t.* & *i.* unterscheiden, erkennen.

discernible *a.*, ~bly *adv.* unterscheidbar.

discharge *v.t.* ausladen, löschen; abfeuern; loslassen; entlassen; entlasten; entrichten; ~ *v.i.* sich entladen; eitern.; ~ *s.* Entladung *f.*; Entlassung, Befreiung *f.*; Entlastung *f.*; Abfeuern *n.*; Abfluss, Ausfluss *m.* (*med.*).
disciple *s.* Schüler, Jünger *m.*
disciplinarian *s.* Zuchtmeister *m.*
disciplinary *a.* disziplinarisch; ~ *action*, Disziplinarverfahren *n.*; ~ *power*, Disziplinargewalt *f.*; ~ *proceedings pl.* Disziplinarverfahren *n.*
discipline *s.* Unterweisung, Zucht *f.*; Mannszucht *f.*; ~ *v.t.* züchtigen.
disclaim *v.t.* leugnen; entsagen.
disclaimer *s.* Verzicht *m.*; Widerruf *m.*
disclose *v.t.* erschliessen; offenbaren.
disclosure *s.* Enthüllung, Mitteilung *f.*
discoloration *a.* Verfärbung *f.*; Verschiessen *n.*
discolour *v.t.* entfärben; entstellen.
discomfit *v.t.* vereiteln.
discomfiture *s.* Niederlage.
discomfort *s.* Missbehagen *n.*
discompose *v.t.* beunruhigen.
discomposure *s.* Verwirrung, Verlegenheit *f.*; Verdriesslichkeit *f.*
disconcert *v.t.* ausser Fassung bringen.
disconnect *v.t.* trennen; (*mech.*) entkuppeln, ausschalten.
disconnected *a.* zusammenhangslos.
disconsolate *a.*, ~ly *adv.* trostlos, betrübt.
discontent *a.* missvergnügt; ~ *s.* Unzufriedenheit *f.*; ~ *v.t.* missvergnügt machen.
discontinuance *s.* Unterbrechung *f.*; Aufhören *n.*; Trennung *f.*
discontinue *v.t.* unterbrechen; ~ *v.i.* aufhören.
discord *s.* Missklang *m.*; Zwietracht *f.*
discordance *s.* Uneinigkeit *f.*
discordant *a.* missklingend; verschieden; misshellig.
discount *v.t.* abziehen, diskontieren; ~ *s.* Abzug *m.*; Diskonto *n.*
discountenance *v.t.* ausser Fassung bringen, entmutigen; missbilligen.
discourage *v.t.* entmutigen; abraten.
discouragement *s.* Entmutigung *f.*
discourse *s.* Gespräch *n.*; Vortrag *m*; Abhandlung *f.*; ~ *v.i.* sich unterreden; sprechen.
discourteous *a.* unhöflich.
discourtesy *s.* Unhöflichkeit *f.*
discover *v.t.* entdecken, offenbaren.
discovery *s.* Entdeckung *f.*
discredit *s.* Schimpf *m.*; üble Ruf *m.*; ~ *v.t.* in schlechten Ruf bringen; bezweifeln.
discreditable *a.*, ~bly *adv.* schimpflich.
discreet *a.*, ~ly *adv.* vorsichtig; klug; verschwiegen.
discrepancy *s.* Widerspruch *m.*

discrepant *a.* widersprechend.
discretion *s.* Besonnenheit, Klugheit, Verschwiegenheit *f.*; Takt *m.*; Belieben, *n.*; *to surrender at* ~, sich auf Gnade und Ungnade ergeben.
discretionary *a.* willkürlich.
discriminate *v.t.* unterscheiden; unterschiedlich behandeln; ~ *a.*, ~ly *adv.* unterschieden; genau, deutlich.
discrimination *s.* Unterscheidung *f.*; Unterschied *m.*; Scharfsinn *m.*
discriminative *a.* unterscheidend.
discursive *a.* folgernd, Urteils...
discuss *v.t.* erörtern; verzehren.
discussion *s.* Erörterung *f.*; Diskussion *f.*
disdain *s.* Verachtung *f.*; ~ *v.t.* verschmähen, verächtlich herabsetzen.
disdainful *a.*, ~ly *ad.* geringschätzig.
disease *s.* Krankheit *f.*
diseased *a.* krank.
disembark *v.t. & i.* ausschiffen, landen.
disembarkation *s.* Ausschiffung *f.*
disembarrass *v.t.* aus der Verlegenheit bringen.
disembody *v.t.* entkörpern.
disembowel *v.t.* ausweiden.
disenchant *v.t.* entzaubern; ernüchtern.
disenchantment *s.* Ernüchterung *f.*
disencumber *v.t.* befreien; entbinden.
disengage *v.t.* losmachen, befreien; ~ *v.i.* (*mil.*) sich absetzen.
disengaged *a.* frei, unbeschäftigt.
disengagement *s.* Entbindung *f.*; (*mil.*) Absetzungsbewegung *f.*
disentangle *v.t.* entwirren, losmachen.
disfavour *s.* Ungnade *f.*; Missfallen *n.* ~ *v.t.* nicht begünstigen.
disfigure *v.t.* entstellen.
disfigurement *s.* Entstellung *f.*
disfranchise *v.t.* das Wahlrecht entziehen.
disgorge *v.t.* wieder herausgeben.
disgrace *s.* Ungnade *f.*; Schande *f.*; ~ *v.t.* die Gunst entziehen; entehren.
disgraceful *a.*, ~ly *adv.* schimpflich.
disgruntled *a.* unzufrieden.
disguise *v.t.* vermummen; verbergen; ~ *s.* Verkleidung, Verstellung *f.*
disgust *s.* Ekel, Widerwille *m.*; ~ *v.t.* Ekel verursachen; verdriessen.
disgusting *a.* ekelhaft, widrig.
dish *s.* Schüssel *f.*; Napf *m.*; Gericht *n.*; ~ *v.t.* (*up*) anrichten, auftragen.
dish-cover *s.* Speisestürze *f.*
dishearten *v.t.* verzagt machen.
dishevel *v.t.* zerzausen.
dishonest *a.*, ~ly *adv.* unehrlich.
dishonesty *s.* Unredlichkeit *f.*
dishonour *s.* Schande *f.*; ~ *v.t.* verunehren; nicht honorieren (Wechsel).
dishonourable *a.*, ~bly *adv.* ehrlos.
dish-water *s.* Spülwasser *n.*
disillusion *s.* Ernüchterung *f.*; ~ *v.t.* ernüchtern.

disinclination s. Abneigung f.
disincline v.t. abgeneigt machen.
disinfect v.t. desinfizieren.
disinfectant s. Desinfizierungsmittel n.
disinfection s. Desinfizierung f.
disingenuous a. falsch, unaufrichtig.
disinherit v.t. enterben.
disintegrate v.t. & i. (sich) (in Bestandteile) auflösen.
disinter v.t. wieder ausgraben.
disinterested a., ~ly adv. uneigennützig.
disjoin v.t. trennen.
disjoint v.t. verrenken; zerstückeln.
disk s. (Wurf)scheibe f.; Platte f.
dislike s. Abneigung f.; Missfallen n.; ~ v.t. missbilligen, nicht mögen.
dislocate v.t. verrenken.
dislocation s. Verrenkung f.; Verrückung f.; Störung f.
dislodge v.t. vertreiben.
disloyal a., ~ly adv. ungetreu.
disloyalty s. Treulosigkeit f.
dismal a. trübe; schrecklich; traurig.
dismantle v.t. entblössen; niederreissen; demontieren; abtakeln.
dismantling s. Demontage f.
dismay v.t. erschrecken; ~ s. Bangigkeit f.; Bestürzung f.
dismember v.t. zerstückeln.
dismemberment s. Aufteilung f.
dismiss v.t. entlassen; abweisen; ~ed! (mil.) weggetreten!
dismissal s. Entlassung, Abdankung f.
dismount v.i. absitzen.
disobedience s. Ungehorsam m.
disobedient a., ~ly adv. ungehorsam.
disobey v.t. nicht gehorchen.
disoblige v.t. ungefällig begegnen.
disorder s. Unordnung f.; Störung f.; Unpässlichkeit f.
disordered p. & a., disorderly a. unordentlich; liederlich.
disorderly a. gesetzwidrig; liederlich; ~ conduct, ordnungswidrige Betragen n.
disorganize v.t. auflösen, zerrütten.
disown v.t. verleugnen, verwerfen.
disparage v.t. herabsetzen, schmälern.
disparagement s. Herabsetzung f.; Beeinträchtigung f.
disparity s. Ungleichheit f.
dispassionate a., ~ly adv. leidenschaftslos.
dispatch v.t. abfertigen; befördern; erledigen; ~ s. Absendung f.; Eile f.; Depesche f.; ~-box Depeschenmappe f.; ~-rider (mil.) Meldegänger m.
dispel v.t. vertreiben.
dispensary s. Apotheke f.
dispensation s. Austeilung f.; Erlassung f.; Dispens f.; Fügung (der Vorsehung) f.
dispense v.t. austeilen; dispensieren; to ~ with, erlassen; entbehren können, nicht

missen; dispensing chemist s. Apotheker m.
dispersal s. Zerstreuung f.; ~ of industry, Industrieauslagerung f.
disperse v.t. zerstreuen; verteilen; ~ v.i. sich zerstreuen.
dispersion s. Zerstreuung f.
dispirit v.t. entmutigen.
displace v.t. absetzen; verdrängen.
displaced person s. Zwangsverschleppte m.
displacement s. Verschiehlung f.; Verrückung f.; Absetzung f.; Wasserverdrängung f.
display v.t. entfalten; zur Schau stellen; ~ s. Schaustellung f.; Darstellung f.; Pomp m.; on ~, ausliegend.
displease v.t. & i. missfallen.
displeased p. & a. ungehalten.
displeasure s. Missfallen n.; Verdruss m.
disposal s. Anordnung, Verfügung f.; Beseitigung f.; Leitung f.; power of ~, (law) Verfügungsrecht n.
dispose v.t. anordnen, einrichten, anwenden; geneigt, bereit machen; verfügen; ~ of, beseitigen; absetzen.
disposed p. & a. gesinnt; gelaunt.
disposition s. Einrichtung, Anordnung f.; Zustand m.; Neigung, Gemütsart f.; (mil.) Aufstellung f.
dispossess v.t. aus dem Besitze treiben.
dispossession s. Vertreibung aus dem Besitze f.
disproof s. Widerlegung f.
disproportion s. Missverhältnis n.
disproportionate a., ~ly adv. unverhältnismässig.
disprove v.t. widerlegen.
disputable a. streitig.
disputant s. Streiter, Gegner m.
disputation s. gelehrte Streit m.
disputatious a. streitsüchtig.
dispute v.i. streiten, disputieren; ~ v.t. bestreiten; ~ s. Streit m.
disqualify v.t. untauglich machen; unfähig erklären; aus der Liste streichen.
disquiet s. Unruhe f.; ~ v.t. beunruhigen.
disquisition s. Untersuchung f.
disregard s. Nichtachtung f.; ~ v.t. unbeachtet lassen.
disrelish s. Ekel m.; Abneigung f.; ~ v.t. nicht leiden können.
disrepair s. Baufälligkeit f.
disreputable a. verrufen; schimpflich.
disrepute s. üble Ruf m.; Ehrlosigkeit f.
disrespect s. Geringschätzung, Unehrerbietigkeit f.
disrespectful a. unehrerbietig.
disrupt v.t. spalten; auseinanderreissen.
dissatisfaction s. Unzufriedenheit f.
dissatisfy v.t. nicht befriedigen.
dissect v.t. zergliedern; sezieren.
dissecting-room s. Präparierboden m.
dissection s. Zergliederung f.

dissemble v.i. sich verstellen, heucheln; ~ v.t. verhehlen.

dissembler s. Heuchler m.

disseminate v.t. aussäen, ausstreuen.

dissension s. Uneinigkeit f., Zwist m.

dissent v.i. anderer Meinung sein; ~ing opinion, (law) abweichende Meinung f.; ~ s. Abweichung f.

dissenter s. Dissenter (nicht der englischen Landeskirche angehörige Protestant) m.

dissentient a. andersdenkend.

dissertation s. Abhandlung f.

disservice s. schlechte Dienst m.

dissever v.t. absondern, trennen.

dissidence s. Uneinigkeit f.

dissident a. verschieden.

dissimilar a. ungleichartig.

dissimilarity s. Ungleichheit.

dissimulate v.i. sich verstellen.

dissipate v.t. zerstreuen; verschwenden.

dissipated a. ausschweifend.

dissipation s. Zerstreuung f.; Ausschweifung f.

dissociate v.t. trennen.

dissoluble a. löslich.

dissolute a., ~ly adv. ausschweifend.

dissolution s. Auflösung f.

dissolve v.t. auflösen, schmelzen; ~ v.t. zergehen.

dissonance s. Missklang m.; Dissonanz f.

dissuade v.t. abraten.

dissuasion s. Abraten n.

dissuasive a., ~ly adv. abratend.

distaff s. Spinnrocken m.

distance s. Entfernung, Weite f.; Abstand m.; Entfremdung, Kälte f.; ~ v.t. hinter sich lassen.

distant a. entfernt; zurückhaltend, kalt.

distaste s. Widerwille m.; Ärger m.

distasteful a., ~ly adv. ärgerlich, widrig.

distemper s. (Branntwein-) Brennerei f.

distend v.t. ausdehnen, ausstrecken.

distich s. Distichon n.

distil v.i. & a. destillieren.

distillery s. (Branntwein-) Brennerei f.

distinct a., ~ly adv. unterschieden; deutlich.

distinction s. Unterscheidung f.; Unterschied m.; Auszeichnung f.

distinctive a. unterscheidend; ~ly adv. deutlich.

distinguish v.t. unterscheiden; auszeichnen.

distinguishable a. unterscheidbar.

distort v.t. verdrehen; verzerren.

distortion s. Verdrehung, Verzerrung f.

distract v.t. ablenken, zerstreuen; beunruhigen, stören, zerrütten.

distraction s. Zerstreuung f.; Kummer m.; Zerrüttung f.; Wahnsinn m.

distrain v.t. in Beschlag nehmen.

distraint s. Beschlagnahme f.

distress s. Elend n., Not f.; Seenot f.; Beschlagnahme, Pfändung f.; ~-signal (nav.) Notzeichen n.; ~-warrant, Pfändungsbefehl m.; ~ v.t. auspfänden; in Verlegenheit, in Not bringen.

distribute v.t. verteilen, austeilen.

distribution s. Verteilung f.; ~-list, Verteiler (auf Akten) m.

district s. Bezirk m.; Landstrich m.

distrust v.t. misstrauen; ~ s. Misstrauen n.

distrustful a., ~ly adv. misstrauisch.

disturb v.t. stören.

disturbance s. Störung, Verwirrung f.; Aufruhr m.

disunion s. Trennung, Uneinigkeit f.

disunite v.t. trennen, entzweien.

disuse s. Nichtgebrauch m.

ditch s. Graben m.; ~ v.t. & i. graben, Gräben machen.

ditto adv. desgleichen.

ditty s. Liedchen n., Gesang m.

diurnal a. täglich.

divan s. Diwan m.

dive v.i. untertauchen; eindringen.

divebomber s. Sturzkampfflieger m.

diver s. Taucher m.

diverge v.i. auseinanderlaufen; abweichen.

divergence s. Abweichen n.

divergent a., divergierend, abweichend.

diverse a., ~ly adv. verschieden, mannigfaltig.

diversify v.t. verschieden machen.

diversion s. Ablenkung f.; Zeitvertreib m.

diversity s. Verschiedenheit f.; Mannigfaltigkeit f.

divert v.t. ablenken; belustigen.

divest v.t. entkleiden; berauben.

divide v.t. teilen, trennen; dividieren; ~ v.i. sich trennen; namentlich abstimmen.

dividend s. (com.) Dividende f.; (ar.) Dividend m.

dividers s.pl. Zirkel m.

divine v.t. weissagen, erraten; ahnen; ~ a., ~ly adv. göttlich; ~ s. Geistliche m.

diving-bell s. Taucherglocke f.

divining-rod s. Wünschelrute f.

divinity s. Gottheit f.; Theologie f.

divisible a. teilbar.

division s. Teilung f.; Trennung f.; Abteilung f.; Division f.; namentliche Abstimmung im Parlament f.

divisor s. (ar.) Divisor m., Teiler m.

divorce s. Ehescheidung f.; v.t. scheiden; verstossen.

divorcee s. geschiedene Frau od. Mann.

divulge v.t. verbreiten; ausschwatzen.

dizzy a. schwindlig; unbesonnen; ~ v.t. schwindlig machen.

do *v.t.* & *i.st.* tun, machen; ausführen; *that will* ~, das genügt; *that won't* ~, das geht nicht; *I cannot* ~ *without it*, ich kann es nicht entbehren; *to* ~ *away with*, abschaffen; *to* ~ *up*, instand setzen; einpacken; *to* ~ *ill*, schlecht fortkommen; *to* ~ *well*, gut fortkommen.

docile *a.* gelehrig.

dock *s.* (*nav.*) Dock *n.*; Stutzschwanz *m*; Anklagebank *f.*; ~ *v.t.* stutzen; in ein Dock bringen, docken.

docket *s.* Liste *f.*; Zettel *m.*

dockyard *s.* Schiffswerft *n.* & *f.*

doctor *s.* Doctor *m.*; Arzt *m.*; ~ *v.t.* ärztlich behandeln; zustutzen; fälschen; (Tier) kastrieren.

doctorate *s.* Doktorwürde *f.*

doctrine *s.* Lehre *f.*

document *s.* Urkunde *f.*

documentary *a.* urkundlich; ~ *evidence*, Urkundenbeweis *m.*; ~ *film*, Kulturfilm *m.*

documentation *s.* Urkundenbelege *m.pl.*

dodder *s.v.i.* schlottern.

dodge *v.i.* ausweichen; Kniff, Schlich *m.*

doe *s.* Reh *n.*; Hindin *f.*

dog *s.* Hund *m.*; Gestell *n.*; Kerl *m.*

dogdays *s.pl.* Hundstage *m.pl.*

dogfight *s.* Handgemenge *n.*; (*avi.*) Kurvenkampf *m.*

dogged *a.*, **~ly** *adv.* verbissen.

doggerel *a.*, *s.* ~ *rhymes s.pl.* Knüttelverse *m.pl.*

dogma *s.* Glaubenssatz, Lehrsatz *m.*

dogmatic *a.*, **~ally** *adv.* dogmatisch.

dogmatize *v.i.* Behauptungen aufstellen.

dog-rose *s.* Heckenrose, wilde Rose *f.*

dog's ear *s.* Eselsohr (im Buche) *n.*

doing *s.* Begebenheit *f.*

doit *s.* Deut. Pfifferling *m.*

doldrums *s.pl.* Niedergeschlagenheit *f.*

dole *s.* Spende *f.*; Erwerbslosenunterstützung *f.*; ~ *v.t.* spenden.

doleful *a.*, **~ly** *adv.* kummervoll, kläglich.

doll *s.* Puppe *f.*

dolomite *s.* Dolomit, Bitterspat *m.*

dolorous *a.* schmerzhaft.

dolphin *s.* Delphin *m.*

dolt *s.* Tölpel *m.*

doltish *a.*, **~ly** *adv.* tölpisch, plump.

domain *s.* Gebiet *n.*; Staatsgut *n.*

dome *s.* Kuppel *f.*; Wölbung *f.*

domestic *a.* häuslich; inländisch: zahm, ~ *fuel*, Hausbrand *m.*; ~ *offices pl.* Nebengelass *n.*; ~ *politics*, Innenpolitik *f.*; ~ *subjects pl.* Haushaltskunde *f.*; ~ *s.* Dienstbote *m.*

domesticate *v.t.* heimisch machen; zähmen.

domesticity *s.* Häuslichkeit *f.*

domicile *s.* Wohnsitz *m.*

domiciled *a.* wohnhaft.

domiciliary *a.* Haus...

dominant *a.* herrschend.

dominate *v.t.* & *i.* (be)herrschen.

domination *s.* Herrschaft *f.*

domineer *v.i.* den Herrn spielen.

Dominican *s.* Dominikaner *m.*

dominion *s.* Herrschaft *f.*; Dominium (Kolonie (*f.*) mit Selbstverwaltung) *m.*

domino *s.* Domino *m.*

dominoes *s.* Domino(spiel) *n.*

don *s.* an einer Universität angestellte Graduierte *m.*; ~ *v.t.* anziehen.

donation *s.* Schenkung *f.*

donkey *s.* Esel *m.*

donor *s.* Geschenkgeber *m.*

doom *s.* Urteilsspruch *m.*; Schicksal *n.*; Verderben *n.*; ~ *v.t.* verurteilen.

doomsday *s.* Jüngste Tag *m.*

door *s.* Tür *f.*; *within* ~*s*, im Hause; *out o* ~*s*, aus dem Hause.

door-keeper *s.* Pförtner *m.*

door-plate *s.* Türschild *n.*

doorpost *s.* Türpfosten *m.*

doorway *s.* Eingang, Türöffnung *f.*

dope *s.* zähe Flüssigkeit *f.*; Betäubungstrank *m.*; **to** ~ *v.t.* betäuben.

dormant *a.* schlafend; unbenutzt.

dormer *s.* Dachfenster *n.*

dormitory *s.* Schlafsaal *m.*

dormouse *s.* Haselmaus *f.*

dorsal *a.* Rücken...

dose *s.* Dosis *f.*; ~ *v.t.* eingeben.

doss-house *s.* Obdachlosenasyl *n.*

dossier *s.* Akte, Personalakte *f.*

dot *s.* Punkt *m.*; ~ *v.t.* punktieren.

dotage *s.* kindische Greisenalter *n.*

dote *v.i.* kindisch werden; vernarrt sein.

double *a.* & *adv.* doppelt; **~-barrelled** *gun s.* Doppelflinte *f.*; **~-breasted** *coat s.* zweireihige Rock *m.*; ~ *room*, zweibettige Zimmer *n.*; ~ *time*, Laufschritt *m.*; **~-track** *a.* zweigleisig; ~ *window*, Doppelfenster *n.*; ~ *s.* Doppelte *n.*; Doppelgänger *m.*; ~ *v.t.* verdoppeln; (Faust) ballen; umschiffen; ~ *up*, zusammenklappen, zusammenfalten; ~ *v.i.* sich verdoppeln.

doublecross *v.t.* (*Am.*) betrügen.

double-dealer *s.* Betrüger *m.*

double-quick *a.* im Geschwindschritt.

doublet *s.* Paar *m.*; Wams *n.*

doubt *v.t.* & *i.* (be)zweifeln; ~ *s.* Zweifel *m.*; *to give a person the benefit of the* ~, im Zweifelsfall zu jemandes Gunsten entscheiden.

doubtful *a.*, **~ly** *adv.* zweifelhaft.

doubtless *a.* & *adv.* ohne Zweifel, gewiss.

douche *s.* Dusche *f.*

dough *s.* Teig *m.*

doughnut *s.* Krapfen *m.*

doughty *a.*, **~ily** *adv.* beherzt, tapfer.

dove *s.* Taube *f.*

dove-cot *s.* Taubenschlag *m.*

dovelike *a.* sanft wie eine Taube.

dovetail *v.t.* keilförmig befestigen; innig verbinden; ~ *s.* Schwalbenschwanz *m.*
dowager *s.* Witwe von Stande *f.*
dowdy *a.* schlampig; ~ *s.* Schlampe *f.*
dower *s.* Ausstattung, Mitgift *f.*
down *s.* Flaum *m.*, Daune *f.*; Düne *f.*; ~ *pr. & adv.* nieder, hinab, herunter, zu Boden; *the second* ~, der zweite von oben; ~ *under*, bei den Antipoden; ~ *a.* niedergeschlagen; to ~ *v.t.* niederlegen.
down-cast *a.* niedergeschlagen.
downfall *s.* Sturz, Untergang *m.*
downgrade *v.t.* (*Am.*) in niederen Rang versetzen; *on the* ~, auf dem absteigenden Ast.
downhearted *a.* mutlos.
down-hill *a.* abschüssig; bergab.
down-payment *s.* Anzahlung *f.*
downpour *s.* Regenguss *m.*
downright *a.* offen, bieder; ~ *adv.* geradezu; gänzlich.
down-stairs *adv.* treppab; unten, (die Treppe) hinunter.
downstream *adv.* stromabwärts.
down-train *s.* Zug (*m.*) von Endstation in die Provinz.
downward(s) *adv.* abwärts, hinab.
dowry *s.* Mitgift *f.*
dowser *m.* Wünschelrutengänger *m.*
doze *v.i.* schläfrig sein; schlummern.
dozen *s.* Dutzend *n.*
drab *s.* hellbraun.
drachm *see* dram.
draft *s.* Tratte *f.*; Skizze *f.*; Mannschaft *f.*; Aushebung *f.*; (*Am.*) Wehrpflicht *f.*; ~ *a.* zum Ziehen bestimmt; ~ *v.t.* zeichnen, entwerfen; detachieren.
drag *v.t. & i.* ziehen; schleppen; ~ *s.* Schleife *f.*; Hemmung *f.*
draggle *v.t.* im Kote schleifen.
dragoman *s.* Dolmetscher *m.*
dragon *s.* Drache *m.*; ~-**fly**, Wasserjungfer (Insekt) *f.*, Libelle *f.*
dragoon *s.* Dragoner *m.*
drain *v.t.* ablassen; austrocknen; ~ *s.* Abzugsgraben *m.*
drainage *s.* Entwässerung *f.*
dram *s.* Quentchen *n.*; Schluck *m.*
drama *s.* Schauspiel *n.*, Drama *n.*
dramatic *a.*, ~**ally** *adv.* dramatisch.
dramatist *s.* Schauspieldichter *m.*
drape *v.t.* drapieren, einhüllen.
draper *s.* Tuchhändler *m.*
drapery *s.* Tuchhandel *m.*; Draperie *f.*; Faltenwurf *m.*
drastic *a.* wirksam, durchschlagend.
draught *s.* Zug *m.*; Luftzug *m.*; (Schiff) Tiefgang *m.*; Schluck *m.*; Rinne *f.*; Entwurf *m.*; Zeichnung *f.*; Tratte *f.*; *beer on* ~, Bier vom Fass; ~**s** *pl.* Damenspiel *n.*, Dame *f.*
draught-board *s.* Damenbrett *n.*

draughtsman *s.* Zeichner *m.*
draught-horse *s.* Zugpferd *n.*
draw *v.t. & i.st.* ziehen; spannen; abzapfen; zeichnen; trassieren; herleiten; locken; (Pension, Lohn) beziehen; (Geld) abheben; *to* ~ *up*, anhalten; aufsetzen, entwerfen, abfassen; *to* ~ *six feet*, sechs Fuss Tiefgang haben; *to* ~ *on a person*, einen Wechsel auf einen ziehen; ~ *s.* Ziehen *n.*; Los *n.*; unentschiedene Spiel *n.*; Zugstück *n.*
drawback *s.* Rückzoll *m.*; Rabatt *m.*; Übelstand *m.*, Schattenseite *f.*
drawbridge *s.* Zugbrücke *f.*
drawee *s.* Trassat, Bezogene *m.*
drawer *s.* Trassant *m.*; Schublade *f.*; ~**s** *pl.* Unterhosen *f.pl.*
drawing *s.* Ziehen *n.*; Zeichnung *f.*
drawing-board *s.* Reissbrett *n.*
drawing-office *s.* Konstruktionsbüro *n.*
drawing-pin *s.* Reissnagel *m.*
drawing-room *s.* Gesellschaftszimmer *n.*
drawl *v.i.* dehnen; (die Worte)schleppen.
drawn *s.* gezogen; unentschieden, remis.
dray-cart *s.* niedrige Lastwagen *m.*
dread *s.* Schrecken *m.*; ~ *a.* schrecklich; ~ *v.t.* erschrecken; ~ *v.i.* sich fürchten.
dreadful *a.* schrecklich.
dream *s.* Traum *m.*; ~ *v.i.r. & ir.* träumen.
dreary *a.*, ~**ily** *adv.* öde; traurig.
dredge *s.* Schleppnetz *n.*; ~ *v.t.* ausbaggern.
dredger *s.* Bagger *m.*
dregs *s.pl.* Hefen *f.pl.*; Bodensatz *m.*
drench *v.t.* tränken; durchnässen.
dress *s.* Anzug *m.*; Kleidung *f.*; Kleid *n.*; ~-**boots**, Lackstiefel *m.pl.*; ~-**circle**, erste Rang (im Theater) *m.*; ~-**rehearsal** *s.* Hauptprobe *f.*; ~-**shirt**, Frackhemd *n.*: ~ *v.t.* ankleiden; putzen; zurichten; anrichten; verbinden; ~ *v.i.* sich ankleiden; (*mil.*) richt euch!; ~ *left*, ~*!*, nach links, richt euch!; ~ *right*, ~*!*, richt euch!
dresser *s.* Anrichtetisch *m.*
dressing *s.* Ankleiden *n.*; Anzug *m.*; Verband *m.*; Füllung (Braten) *f.*; Haarsalbe *f.*; *salad* ~, Salatkreme *f.*
dressing-gown *s.* Schlafrock *m.*
dressing-station *s.* Verbandplatz *m.*, Verbandstelle *f.*
dressing-table *s.* Toilette *f.*
dressmaker *s.* Schneiderin *f.*
dribble *v.t. & i.* tröpfeln, geifern.
driblet *s.* Kleinigkeit *f.*
drift *s.* Trieb, Antrieb *m.*; Tendenz *f.*; Schneewehe *f.*; ~ *v.i.* sich aufhäufen.
drill *s.* Drillbohrer *m.*; Exerzieren *n.*; Furche *f.*; Drillich *m.*; ~ *v.t. & i.* drillen, bohren; einexerzieren.
drink *s.* Getränk *n.*; ~ *v.t.st.* trinken.
drinkable *a.* trinkbar.

drinking straw s. Trinkhalm m.; **drinking water** s. Trinkwasser n.
drip v.t. & i. tröpfeln; ~ s. Traufe f.
dripping s. Bratenfett n.
dripping wet a. tropfnass.
drive v.t.st. treiben; fahren; ~ v.i. fahren; *what he is driving at,* worauf er hinauswill; *driving-belt,* (mech.) Treibriemen m.; *driving-licence,* Führerschein m.; *driving-test,* Führerprüfung f.; ~ s. (tennis) Treibschlag m.; Spazierfahrt f.; Fahrweg m.; Schwung m., Energie f.; Aktion f.
drivel v.i. geifern; faseln; ~ s. Geifer m.; Gefasel f.
driver s. Fuhrmann, Kutscher m.; Lokomotivführer m.; Chauffeur m.
driveway s. Autostrasse f.
driving-box s. Kutschbock m.
drizzle v.t. & i. rieseln; ~ s. Sprühregen, Staubregen m.
droll possierlich, drollig.
drollery s. Posse, Schnurre f.
dromedary s. Dromedar n.
drone s. Drohne f.; Faulenzer m.; ~ v.i. summen; faulenzen.
droop v.t. sinken lassen; v.i. niederhangen; schmachten; den Kopf hängen lassen.
drop s. Tropfen m.; (Zucker, etc.) Plätzchen n.; Rückgang, Fall m.; ~ v.i. tropfen; fallen; sinken; ~ v.t. tropfen; fallen lassen; fahren lassen.
drophammer s. Fallhammer m.
dropsical a. wassersüchtig.
dropsy s. Wassersucht f.
dross s. Schlacke f.; Schaum, Unrat m.
drought s. Trockenheit, Dürre f.
drove s. Herde f.; Haufen m.; Trift f.
drover s. Viehtrieber m.
drown v.t. ertränken; überschwemmen; *he was ~ed,* er ertrank.
drowsy a., ~ily adv. schläfrig.
drub v.t. schlagen, prügeln.
drubbing s. Tracht, Schläge f.
drudge s. Knecht m.; *to ~* v.i. schwere Arbeit verrichten, sich placken.
drudgery s. Plackerei f.
drug s. Droge, Apothekerware f.; Rauschgift n.; Ladenhüter f.; ~ v.t. mit Arznei versetzen, Arznei eingeben, vergiften.
druggist s. Drogist m.
drum s. Trommel f.; ~ v.t. trommeln.
drum: ~-fire, Trommelfeuer n.; ~-head s. Fell der Trommel n.; ~-stick s. Trommelstock m.
drunk a. betrunken.
drunkard s. Trunkenbold m.
drunkenness s. Trunkenheit f.
dry a., ~ly adv. trocken, dürr; durstig; (Wein) herb; ~ v.t. trocknen; ~ v.i. dürr werden.
dry cell s. Trockenbatterie f.

dry cleaning s. chemische Reinigung f.
dry dock s. Trockendock n.
dry-goods s. Kurz-, Schnittwaren f.pl.
dry-salter s. Materialwarenhändler m.
dry-shod a. trockenen Fusses.
dual a. Zwei..., doppelt.
dub v.t. zum Ritter schlagen; ernennen.
dubious a., ~ly adv. zweifelhaft.
ducal a. herzoglich.
ducat s. Dukaten m.
duchess s. Herzogin f.
duchy s. Herzogtum n.
duck s. Ente f.; ~ v.t. untertauchen; ~ v.i. sich ducken.
duckling s. junge Ente f.
duct s. Gang m., Röhre f.
ductile a. dehnbar.
ductless gland s. Hormondrüse f.
dud s. Blindgänger (Granate, Bombe) m.
dudgeon s. Groll, Unwille m.
due a. & adv. schuldig, gebührend; fällig; recht, pünktlich; *to become ~,* fällig werden (Wechsel, etc.); *in ~ course,* zur gehörigen Zeit; ~ s. Gebühr, Pflicht f.; Gerechtsame f.; Abgabe f.
duel s. Zweikampf m; ~ v.i. sich duellieren.
duellist s. Duellant m.
duet s. Duett n.
dug s. Zitze f.
dug-out s. Unterstand m. (mil.)
duke s. Herzog m.
dukedom s. Herzogtum n.
dull a. matt; stumpf; einfältig, dumm; plump, langweilig, dumpf; (com.) flau; ~ v.t. abstumpfen; dumm machen.
dullard s. Dummkopf m.
dullness s. Stumpfheit, Stumpfsinnigkeit f.; Flauheit f.
duly adv. gehörig, richtig.
dumb a., ~ly adv. stumm; (Am.) dumm.
dumb-bells s.pl. Hanteln f.pl.
dumbfound v.t. sprachlos machen.
dumb-show s. Gebärdenspiel n.
dumb-waiter s. Drehtisch m.
dummy s. Attrappe f.; (mil.) Blindgänger m.; Strohmann (im Kartenspiele) m.; Schein..., Schwindel...
dump s. Abladestelle f.; Munitionslager n.; ~ v.t. hinwerfen; umkippen, (Waren ins Ausland) schleudern.
dumping s. Schleuderausfuhr f.
dumping-ground s. (Schutt-) Abladeplatz m.
dumpling s. Mehlkloss m.
dumps s.pl. Unmut m.
dumpy a. kurz und dick.
dun a. schwarzbraun; dunkel; ~ s. ungestüme Mahner m.; ~ v.t. ungestüm mahnen.
dunce s. Dummkopf m.
dune s. Düne f.
dung s. Mist, Dünger m.; ~ v.t. düngen.

dungeon s. Kerker m.
dungfork s. Mistgabel f.
dunghill s. Misthaufen m.
dupe s. Gimpel, Narr m.; ~ v.t. prellen.
dupery s. Täuschung f.
duplicate a. doppelt; ~ s. Duplikat n.;
~ v.t. verdoppeln; vervielfältigen.
duplicity s. Falschheit, Zweideutigkeit f.
durability s. Dauerhaftigkeit f.
durable a., ~bly adv. dauerhaft.
duration s. Dauer f.
duress s. Zwang m.; Haft f.; under ~, (law)
durch Nötigung.
during pr. während.
dusk a. dämmerig, dunkel; ~ s. Dämmerung, Dunkelheit f.
dust s. Staub m.; ~ v.t. abstäuben.
dust-bin s. Müll-, Kehrichtkasten m.
dust-cart s. Müll-, Kehrichtwagen m.
dust-cover s. Schutzumschlag (Buch) m.
duster s. Wischlappen m.; Staubbesen m.
dustman s. Müllkutscher m.
dustpan s. Kehrichtschaufel f.
Dutch a. holländisch.
duteous, dutiful a., ~ly adv. pflichttreu.
dutiable a. zollpflichtig, steuerpflichtig.
duty s. Pflicht, Schuldigkeit f.; Abgabe f.;
Zoll m.; Dienst m.; free of ~, zollfrei;
on ~, im Dienst; off ~, ausser Dienst;
~-hours pl. Dienststunden f.pl.; breach
of ~, Pflichtverletzung f.
dwarf s. Zwerg m.; ~ v.t. am Wachstum
hindern.
dwarfish a., ~ly adv. zwergartig.
dwell v.i.r. & ir. wohnen; verweilen.
dwelling s. Wohnort, Aufenthalt m.
dwindle v.i. einschrumpfen, abnehmen.
dye s. Farbstoff m.; ~-works s.pl. Farb-
werke n.pl.; ~stuff, Farbstoff m.; ~ v.t.
färben.
dyer s. Färber m.
dying a. sterbend.
dynamic(al) a. dynamisch.
dynamics s.pl. Dynamik f.
dynamite s. Dynamit n.
dynamo s. Dynamo(maschine f.) m.
dynastic a. dynastisch.
dynasty s. Dynastie f.
dysentery s. Ruhr f.
dyspepsia s. Dyspepsie f.

E

each pn. jeder, jede, jedes; ~ other, einander.
eager a., ~ly adv. eifrig; erpicht.
eagerness s. Eifer m.; Begierde f.
eagle s. Adler m.
eaglet s. junge Adler m.
ear s. Ohr n.; Gehör n.; Öhr n.; Henkel
m.; Ähre f.

earl s. (englischer) Graf m.
ear-lobe s. Ohrläppchen n.
earldom s. Grafenwürde f.
early a. & adv. früh, zeitig.
ear-mark s. Ohrenzeichen (bei Schafen)
n.; ~ v.t. vormerken.
earn v.t. erwerben, gewinnen.
earnest a., ~ly adv. ernstlich; dringend;
~ s. Ernst m.; Eifer m.; Handgeld n.;
Unterpfand n.; in good ~, in vollem
Ernste.
earnings s.pl. Verdienst, Lohn m.
earphone s. Kopfhörer m.
ear-ring s. Ohrring m.
ear-shot s. Hörweite f.
earth s. Erde f.; (radio) Erdung f.; ~ v.t.
(radio) erden.
earthen a. irden.
earthenware s. Steingut n.
earthly a. irdisch, sinnlich.
earthquake s. Erdbeben n.
earthworm s. Regenwurm m.
earthy a. erdig; irdisch.
ear-trumpet s. Hörrohr n.
ear-wax s. Ohrenschmalz n.
earwig s. Ohrwurm m.
ear-witness s. Ohrenzeuge m.
ease s. Ruhe, Gemächlichkeit f.; Erleichterung f.; at ~, gemächlich; stand at ~,
(mil.) rührt euch!; ~ v.t. erleichtern;
beruhigen; lindern.
easel s. Staffelei f.
easement s. (law) Servitut f.
east s. Osten m.; Orient m.; ~ a. östlich.
Easter s. Ostern n. or pl.; ~-day, Oster-
sonntag m.
easterly a. & adv. östlich.
eastern a. östlich; morgenländisch.
eastward adv. ostwärts.
easy a., ~ly adv. leicht, bequem; frei;
willig, gefällig; stand ~!, (mil.) rührt
euch!
easy-chair s. Lehnstuhl m.
easy-going a. lässig, gemütlich.
eat v.t. & i.st. essen; fressen; zerfressen.
eatable a. essbar; ~s pl. Esswaren f.pl.
eating-apple s. Essapfel m.
eating-house s. Speisehaus n.
eaves s.pl. Dachtraufe f.
eavesdropper s. Horcher m.
ebb s. Ebbe f.; ~ v.i. abfliessen.
ebonite s. Hartgummi n.
ebony s. Ebenholz n.
ebullient a. sprudelnd.
ebullition s. Aufwallung f.
eccentric a. exzentrisch; überspannt.
ecclesiastic(al) a. kirchlich, geistlich; ~
s. Geistliche m.
echelon s. Staffel f.; in ~ formation, (mil.)
gestaffelt.
echo s. Wiederhall m.; Echo n.; ~ v.i. & t.
wiederhallen; wiederholen.
eclectic a. eklektisch, auswählend.

eclecticism s. Eklektizismus m.
eclipse s. Finsternis f.; ~ v.t. verfinstern, verdunkeln.
eclogue s. Hirtengedicht n.
economic(al) a. wirtschaftlich; sparsam.
economic warfare s. Wirtschaftskrieg m.
economist s. Nationalökonom m.
economics s.pl. Volkswirtschaftslehre f.
economize v.t. haushälterisch verwalten; sparen.
economy s. Sparsamkeit f.; Anordnung f., Bau m.; Haushaltung f.; Wirtschaft, Volkswirtschaft f.; ~-measures pl. Sparmassnahmen f.pl.; planned ~, Planwirtschaft f.; political ~, Volkswirtschaft, Nationalökonomie f.
ecstasy s. Verzückung f.
ecstatic a. verzückt.
eczema s. Hautausschlag m.
eddy s. Wirbel m.; ~ v.i. wirbeln.
edge s. Schärfe, Schneide f.; Ecke f.; Kante f.; Rand m.; on ~, hochkant adv.; to be on ~ over, nervös sein über; cutting-~ s. Schneide f.; ~ v.t. schärfen; säumen, einfassen; drängen; ~ v.i. vordringen.
edgeways, edgewise adv. hochkantig.
edging s. Saum m., Einfassung f.
edible a. essbar; ~s, Esswaren f.pl.
edict s. Verordnung f.
edification s. (fig.) Erbauung f.
edifice s. Gebäude n.
edify v.t. (fig.) erbauen.
edit v.t. herausgeben (ein Buch); edieren.
edition s. Ausgabe, Auflage f.
editor s. Herausgeber m.; Redakteur m.; ~-in-chief, Hauptschriftleiter m.
editorial s. Leitarikel m.; ~ a. Redaktions...
editorialist s. Leitartikler m.
educate v.t. erziehen.
education s. Erziehung f.
educational a. Erziehungs...
educator s. Erzieher m.
eel s. Aal m.
eerie a. gespenstisch, unheimlich.
efface v.t. auslöschen, austreichen; in den Schatten stellen.
effect s. Wirkung f.; in ~, in Wirklichkeit; to take ~, to go into ~, wirksam werden (Verordnung etc.); with ~ from, mit Wirkung von; to the ~, des Inhalts; ~ v.t. ausführen, bewirken; to ~ a policy, eine Versicherung abschliessen.
effective a., ~ly adv. wirksam, kräftig; wirklich vorhanden; ~ 1 June, mit Wirkung vom 1. Juni; ~ immediately, mit sofortiger Wirksamkeit.
effectual a., ~ly adv. wirklich, wirksam.
effectuate v.t. bewerkstelligen.
effeminacy s. Verweichlichung f.
effeminate a., ~ly adv. weibisch, weich-

lich; üppig; ~ v.t. verweichlichen; ~ v.i. sich verweichlichen.
effervesce v.i. aufbrausen; ~ powder s. Brausepulver n.
effervescence s. Aufbrausen n.
effete a. entkräftet; abgenutzt.
efficacious a., ~ly adv. wirksam.
efficacy s. Wirksamkeit f.
efficiency s. Wirksamkeit f.; (mech.) Nutzeffekt m.; Tüchtigkeit, Brauchbarkeit f.; ~-rating, (mil.) Beurteilung f.
efficient a. wirksam, leistungsfähig; tüchtig, brauchbar.
effigy s. Bild n.
efflorescent a. aufblühend; sich beschlagend.
effort s. Anstrengung f.
effulgence s. Glanz, Schimmer m.
effulgent a. glänzend.
effuse v.t. ausgiessen.
effusion s. Ausgiessung f.; Verschwendung f.; (fig.) Erguss f.
effusive a. überschwenglich.
egg s. Ei n.; dried ~, Trockenei n.; newlaid ~, frisch gelegte Ei n.; bad ~, übler Bursche m.; to ~ on, v.t. anhetzen.
egg-cup s. Eierbecher m.
egg-shell s. Eierschale f.
egoism s. Egoismus m., Selbstsucht f.
egotism s. Selbstsucht f.
egotist s. Egoist m.
egotistical a. egoistisch, selbstisch.
egregious a., ~ly adv. ausgezeichnet, ungemein; gewaltig.
egress s. Ausgang m.
eh i. he? ho!
eiderdown s. Daunendecke f.
eight a. acht.
eighteen a. achtzehn.
eightfold a. achtfach.
eighty a. achtzig.
either pn. einer von beiden; beide; ~ c. entweder...; not...either, auch nicht; nor...either, und...auch nicht.
ejaculate v.t. ausstossen.
ejaculation s. Ausstossen n.; Stosseufzer m.
eject v.t. ausstossen, vertreiben.
ejection s. Ausstossung f.; Absetzung f.
eke v.t. to ~ out, dehnen, verlängern; ergänzen; sich durchhelfen.
elaborate v.t. ausarbeiten; verfeinern; ~ a., ~ly adv. ausgearbeitet; verfeinert, umständlich.
elapse v.i. verfliessen, verlaufen.
elastic a. elastisch; ~ s. Gummiband n.
elasticity s. Spring-, Federkraft f.
elation s. gehobene Stimmung f.; Stolz m.
elbow s. Ellbogen m.; (mech.) Knie n.; ~ v.t. wegstossen; verdrängen.
elbow-room s. Spielraum m.

elder *a.* älter; ~ *s.* Kirchenälteste *m.*;
~ *s.* Holunder *m.*
elderly *a.* ältlich, bejahrt.
eldest *a.* älteste.
elect *v.t.* (er)wählen; ~ *a.* erwählt.
election *s.* Erwählung *f.*, Wahl *f.*; *general*
~, Parlamentswahl *f.*
electioneering *a.* Wahl...; *s.* Wahlarbeit *f.*
elective *a.*, ~ly *adv.* wählend; Wahl...
elector *s.* Wähler *m.*; Kurfürst *m.*
electoral *a.* Wahl...; kurfürstlich.
electoral district *s.* Wahlbezirk *m.*
electorate *s.* Wählerschaft *f.*, Kurfür-
stentum *n.*
clectric *a.* elektrisch; ~ arc *s.* Lichtbogen
m.; ~ heater *s.* elektrische Heizvorrich-
tung *f.*
electrical *a.*, ~ *adv.* elektrisch; ~ contractor, elekttysche Installateur *m.*; ~
engineer, Elekrirotechniker *m.*
electricity *s.* Elektrizität *f.*
electrify *v.t.* elektrisieren; elektrifizieren.
electrocute *v.t.* elektrisch hinrichten.
electrode *s.* Elektrode *f.*
electrolyse *v.a.* durch Elektrizität zersetzen.
electrolysis *s.* Elektrolyse *f.*
electrolyte *s.* Elektrolyt *m.*
electroplating *s.* Galvanostegie *f.*
electrotype *s.* galvanische Druck *m.*
electuary *s.* Latwerge *f.*
eleemosynary *a.* Almosen...; Almosen
spendend.
elegance *s.* Zierlichkeit, Eleganz *f.*
elegant *a.*, ~ly *adv.* zierlich; geschmackvoll; elegant.
elegiac *a.* elegisch.
elegy *s.* Elegie *f.*, Trauergedicht *n.*
element *s.* Urstoff *m.*; Bestandteil *m.*; ~s
pl. Anfangsgründe *m.pl.*
clementary *a.* elementar, Anfangs...
elephant *s.* Elefant *m.*
elephantine *a.* elefantenartig.
elevate *v.t.* erhöhen, erheben.
elevated *p.* & *a.* hoch, erhaben; stolz.
elevation *s.* Erhöhung, Erhabenheit *f.*;
Höhe *f.*; Polhöhe *f.*; Aufriss *m.*
elevator *s.* (avi.) Höhensteuer *m.*; (*Am.*)
Aufzug *m.*
eleven, elf.
elf *s.* Elf, Kobold *m.*
elfin *a.* Elfen...
elicit *v.t.* hervorlocken.
eligibility *s.* Wählbarkeit *f.*
eligible *a.* wählbar; wünschenswert.
eliminate *v.t.* ausscheiden, entfernen.
elision *s.* Weglassung *f.*; Ausstossung *f.*
elk *s.* Elch *m.*; Elentier *n.*
ell *s.* Elle *f.*
ellipsis *s.* Ellipse *f.*
elliptical *a.* elliptisch.
elm *s.* Ulme *f.*
elocution *s.* Vortrag *m.*, Vortragsweise *f.*;
Vortragskunst *f.*

elongate *v.t.* verlängern.
elope *v.i.* sich entführen lassen; (*with*)
entführen.
elopement *s.* Entführung *f.*
eloquence *s.* Beredsamkeit *f.*
eloquent *a.*, ~ly *adv.* beredt.
else *adv.* anders, sonst, ausserdem.
elsewhere *adv.* anderswo.
elucidate *v.t.* erläutern.
elude *v.t.* entwischen, ausweichen; entgehen; (Gesetz) umgehen.
elusive *a.* ausweichend; flüchtig.
emaciate *v.t.* ausmergein, abmagern; ~ *a.*
abgezehrt.
emanate *v.i.* ausströmen; herrühren.
emancipate *v.t.* freimachen; bürgerlich
gleichstellen.
emasculate *v.t.* entmannen.
embalm *v.t.* einbalsamieren.
embank *v.t.* eindeichen, dämmen.
embankment *s.* Eindämmung *f.*; (*rail.*)
Damm *m.*; Kai *m.*; Ufereinfassung *f.*
embarcation *see* embarkation.
embargo *s.* Beschlag (auf Schiffe) *m.*;
Hafensperre *f.*; Handelsverbot *n.*
embark *v.t.* (*v.i.* sich) einschiffen; ~ *v.i.*
sich einlassen (auf).
embarkation *s.* Einschiffung *f.*
embarrass *v.t.* verwirren; verlegen machen.
embarrassment *s.* Verlegenheit *f.*
embassy *s.* Botschaft *f.*
embattle *v.t.* in Schlachtordnung stellen.
embed *v.t.* betten, lagern, legen.
embellish *v.t.* verschönern.
embellishment *s.* Verschönerung *f.*
Ember Day *s.* Quatember *m.*
embers *s.pl.* glühende Kohle, Glut *f.*
embezzle *v.t.* unterschlagen, veruntreuen.
embezzlement *s.* Unterschlagung *f.*
embitter *v.t.* verbittern.
emblazon *v.t.* glänzend machen.
emblem *s.* Sinnbild *n.*
emblematic *a.*, ~ally *adv.* sinnbildlich.
embodiment *s.* Verkörperung *f.*
embody *v.t.* verkörpern; enthalten.
embolden *v.t.* anfeuern, kühn machen.
emboss *v.t.* bossieren.
embrace *v.t.* umarmen; enthalten; ergreifen; ~ *s.* Umarmung *f.*
embrasure *s.* Schiessscharte *f.*
embrocation *s.* (*med.*) Einreibungmittel
n.
embroider *v.t.* sticken; ausschmücken.
embroidery *s.* Stickerei *f.*
embroil *v.t.* verwirren, verwickeln.
embryo *s.* Fruchtkeim *m.*, Embryo *m.*
emendation *s.* Verbesserung *f.*
emerald *s.* Smaragd *m.*
emerge *v.i.* auftauchen, emporkommen.
emergency *s.* unerwartete Ereignis *n.*;
Notfall *m.*; Not...; ~-exit Notaus-
gang *m.*

emergent *a.* emporkommend.

emery *s.* Schmirgel *m.*

emetic *s.* Brechmittel *n.*

emigrant *s.* Auswanderer *m.*

emigrate *v.i.* auswandern.

emigration *s.* Auswanderung *f.*

eminence *s.* Höhe, Anhöhe *f.*; Auszeichnung *f.*; Eminenz (Titel) *f.*

eminent *a.*, **~ly** *adv.* hervorragend.

emissary *s.* Sendling, Kundschafter *m.*

emission *s.* Aussendung *f.*; Ausgabe *f.*

emit *v.t.* aussenden; äussern; ausgeben.

emollient *a.* erweichend.

emolument *s.* Vorteil, Nutzen *m.*; (Neben-) Einkünfte *f.pl.*

emotion *s.* Gemütsbewegung *f.*

emotional *a.* erregbar, leicht zu erregen.

empanel *v.t.* (die Geschworenen) eintragen.

emperor *s.* Kaiser *m.*

emphasis *s.* Nachdruck *m.*; **~ added**, Unterstreichung zugefügt.

emphasize *v.t.* betonen, hervorheben.

emphatic(al) *a.*, **~ly** *adv.* nachdrücklich.

empire *s.* Reich *n.*

empiric *s.* Empiriker; Quacksalber *m.*

empirical *a.* erfahrungsmässig.

emplacement *s.* Geschützstand *m.*

employ *v.t.* anwenden; beschäftigen.

employee *s.* Arbeitnehmer *m.*

employer *s.* Arbeitgeber *m.*

employment *s.* Amt *n.*; Beschäftigung *f.*; Gebrauch *m.*; **~-exchange** *s.* Arbeitsamt *n.*; *creation of* **~**, Arbeitsbeschaffung *f.*

emporium *s.* Handelsplatz, Stapelplatz *m.*; Warenhaus *n.*

empower *v.t.* ermächtigen.

empress *s.* Kaiserin *f.*

empty *a.* leer, ledig; nichtig; vergeblich; **~** *v.t.* ausleeren.

emulate *v.t.* wetteifern mit.

emulation *s.* Nacheiferung *f.*; Wetteifer *m.*

emulous *a.*, **~ly** *adv.* nacheifernd.

enable *v.t.* fähig machen.

enabling act *s.* Ermächtigungsgesetz *n.*

enact *v.t.* verordnen, verfügen; (Gesetz) erlassen.

enactment *s.* Verordnung, Verfügung *f.*

enamel *s.* Schmelz *m.*, Emaille *f.*; **~** *v.t.* in Schmelz arbeiten, emaillieren.

enamoured *a.* verliebt.

encamp *v.t. & i.* (sich) lagern.

encampment *s.* Lagern *n.*; Lager *n.*

encash *v.t.* einkassieren.

encashment *s.* Einkassierung *f.*

encaustic *a.* enkaustisch.

enchain *v.t.* fesseln; verketten.

enchant *v.t.* bezaubern.

enchantress *s.* Zauberin *f.*

encircle *v.t.* umringen.

encirclement *s.* (*mil.*) Einkreisung *f.*

enclave *s.* Enklave *f.*

enclose *v.t.* einhegen; einschliessen; enthalten; (einem Brief) beilegen.

enclosure *s.* Einhegung *f.*; Einlage, Anlage (in Briefen) *f.*

encomiastic *a.*, **~ly** *adv.* lobpreisend.

encomium *s.* Lobrede *f.*

encompass *v.t.* umgeben.

encore (*frz.*), *s.* Zugabe *f.*

encounter *s.* Zusammentreffen *n.*; Gefecht *n.*; **~** *v.t.* zusammentreffen mit; **~** *v.i.* sich begegnen.

encourage *v.t.* ermutigen; fördern.

encouragement *s.* Ermutigung *f.*; Unterstützung *f.*

encroach *v.i.* Eingriff tun; übergreifen.

encroachment *s.* Eingriff, Übergriff *m.*

encumber *v.t.* verwickeln; belasten.

encumbrance *s.* Beschwerde, Last *f.*; Hindernis *n.*; (*law*) Grunddienstbarkeit *f.*

encyclic(al) *s.* Enzyklika *f.*

encyclopedia *s.* Konversationslexikon *n.*

end *s.* Ende, Ziel *n.*; Absicht *f.*; Stückchen *n.*; *at an* **~**, am Ende; *no* **~** *of* . . ., eine Unzahl von . . .; *on* **~** aufrechtstehend, hochkant; *in itself*, Selbstzweck *m.*; **~** *v.t.* beendigen; **~** *v.i.* aufhören.

endanger *v.t.* gefährden.

endear *v.t.* wert machen, teuer machen.

endearment *s.* Zärtlichkeit *f.*

endeavour *s.* Bestreben *n.*; **~** *v.i.* sich bestreben.

endemic *a.* endemisch, einheimisch.

ending *s.* Ende *n.*; Schluss *m.*; Endung *f.*

endive *s.* Endivie *f.*

endless *a.*, **~ly** *adv.* unendlich, endlos.

endorse *v.t.* indossieren; gutheissen.

endorsement *s.* Indossierung *f.*, Giro *n.*

endow *v.t.* begaben, ausstatten.

endowment *s.* Begabung, Ausstattung *f.*; **~-insurance**, abgekürzte Lebensversicherung *s.*

endue *v.t.* bekleiden; begaben.

endurable *a.* erträglich.

endurance *s.* Beharrlichkeit *f.*

endure *v.t. & i.* erdulden; dauern.

enema *s.* Einlauf *m.*; Klistierspritze *f.*

enemy *s.* Feind *m.*; **~** *alien*, feindliche Ausländer *m.*

energetic *a.* kräftig, nachdrücklich.

energy *s.* Tatkraft *f.*, Energie *f.*

enervate *v.t.* entnerven; schwächen.

enfeeble *v.t.* schwächen.

enforce *v.t.* erzwingen; einschärfen.

enforcement *s.* Durchsetzung *f.*

enfranchise *v.t.* befreien; einbürgern; das Stimmrecht verleihen.

engage *v.t.* verpflichten; anwerben; beschäftigen; angreifen; **~** *v.i.* fechten; sich einlassen; sich verloben.

engaged *p. & a.* verlobt; bestellt, besetzt; beschäftigt.

engagement *s.* Verpfändung *f.*; Verpflichtung f.; Verbindlichkeit f.; Beschäftigung f.; Verlobung f.; Einladung f.; Gefecht n.; to meet one's engagements, seinen Verpflichtungen nachkommen; to break off the ~, die Verlobung auflösen.

engaging a. verbindlich, einnehmend.

engender v.t. erzeugen.

engine s. Maschine f.; Motor m.; Lokomotive f.; Feuerspritze f.

engine-driver s. Lokomotivführer m.

engineer s. Ingenieur m.; Techniker, Maschinenbauer m.; (mil.) Pioneer m.

engineering s. Ingenieurwesen n.; Maschinenbaukunst f.; electrical ~,Elektrotechnik f.

English a. englisch; ~ s. Englisch n.; ~man, Engländer m.

engraft v.t. pfropfen; einprägen.

engrain v.t. tief färben; einprägen.

engrave v.t. stechen, gravieren.

engraver s. Graveur m.; Bildstecher m.

engraving s. Kupferstich, Steindruck m.

engross v.t. ganz in Anspruch nehmen.

engulf v.t. versenken, verschlingen.

enhance v.t. erhöhen, steigern.

enigma s. Rätsel n.

enigmatic(al) a., ~ly adv. rätselhaft.

enjoin v.t. einschärfen, anbefehlen.

enjoy v.t. geniessen; to ~ oneself, sich gut unterhalten.

enjoyable a. genussreich, erfreulich.

enjoyment s. Genuss m.

enlarge v.t. erweitern, vergrössern; ~ v.i. sich verbreiten.

enlargement s. Erweiterung f.; (phot.) Vergrösserung f.

enlighten v.t. aufklären, erleuchten.

enlist v.t. anwerben; ~ v.i. Dienste nehmen.

enlistment s. (mil.) Einstellung f.

enliven v.t. beleben, ermuntern.

enmesh v.t. umgarnen, verstricken.

enmity s. Feindschaft f.

ennoble v.t. adeln; veredeln.

enormity s. Ungeheuerlichkeit f.

enormous a., ~ly adv. ungeheuer.

enough a. & adv. genug; ganz.

enounce v.t. verkünden; aussprechen.

enquire v.i. & t. see inquire.

enrage v.t. in Wut versetzen.

enrapture v.t. entzücken.

enrich v.t. bereichern.

enrol(l) v.t. einschreiben; anwerben.

enshrine v.t. einschliessen; (als Heiligtum) aufbewahren.

ensign s. Fahne f.; Fähnrich m.

ensilage s. Konservierung von Grünfutter (im Silo) f.

enslave v.t. zum Sklaven machen.

ensnare v.t. verstricken, verführen.

ensue v.i. folgen; sich ergeben.

entablature s. Gebälk n.

entail s. Art Fideikommiss; ~ v.t. zu einem Fideikommiss machen; zur Folge haben.

entangle v.t. verwickeln; to become ~d, sich verhängen.

entanglement s. Verwirrung, Verwicklung f., Verstrickung f.

enter v.t. & i. eintreten; hineingehen; einführen; einschreiben, eintragen.

enteric a. enterisch, Darm...

enterprise s. Unternehmung f.; Unternehmungsgeist m.

enterprising a. unternehmend.

entertain v.t. unterhalten; bewirten; hegen (Hoffnung).

entertainment s. Unterhaltung f.

entertainment tax s. Vergnügungssteuer f.

enthral v.t. knechten; fesseln.

enthrone v.t. auf den Thron setzen.

enthusiasm s. Begeisterung f.

enthusiast s. Schwärmer m.

enthusiastic a. schwärmerisch, begeistert.

entice v.t. reizen, anlocken.

enticement s. Anlockung f.; Reiz m.

entire a., ~ly adv. ganz, ungeteilt.

entirety s. Ganzheit, Gesamtheit f.

entitle v.t. betiteln; berechtigen.

entity s. Wesen n.

entomb v.t. begraben.

entombment s. Begräbnis n.

entomology s. Insektenkunde f.

entourage s. Umgebung, Begleitung f.

entrails s.pl. Eingeweide n.pl.

entrain v.t. & i. (Truppen in einen Zug) laden; einsteigen.

entrance s. Eingang m.; Antritt m.; ~-examination, Aufnahmeprüfung f.; ~-fee, Aufnahmegebühr f.; ~-hall s. Diele f.; Vorsaal m.; no ~, Eintritt verboten.

entrance v.t. entzücken.

entrant s. Beitretender (zu einem Verein) m.; Bewerber m.; Teilnehmer eines Wettbewerbs m.

entreat v.t. anflehen, beschwören.

entreaty s. Bitte f.; Gesuch n.

entree s. Zwischengericht n.

entrench v.t. mit Gräben versehen; ~ (upon) v.i. sich einen Übergriff erlauben.

entrenchment s. Verschanzung f.

entrust v.t. anvertrauen.

entry s. Eingang m.; Eintragung f.; Meldung f. (Sport); gebuchte Posten m.; ~-permit, Einreiseerlaubnis f.; no ~, Eintritt verboten, Einfahrt verboten.

enumerate v.t. aufzählen.

enunciate v.t. aussagen, berichten.

envelop v.t. einhüllen, einwickeln; (mil.) umfassen.

envelope s. Hülle f.; (Brief)umschlag m.

envelopment s. (mil.) Umfassung f.

envenom v.t. vergiften; erbittern.

enviable *a.* beneidenswert.
envious *a.*, **~ly** *adv.* neidisch.
environ *v.t.* umgeben.
environment *s.* Umgebung *f.*
environs *s.pl.* Umgebung *f.*
envisage *v.t.* ins Auge fassen.
envoy *s.* Gesandte *m.*; Bote *m.*
envy *s.* Neid *m.*; ~ *v.t.* beneiden.
epaulet(te) *s.* Epaulette *f.*
ephemeral *a.* eintägig.
epic *a.* episch; ~ Epos *n.*
epicure *s.* Epikuräer, Genussmensch *m.*
epicurean *a.* üppig lebend, epikuräisch.
epidemic *a.* epidemisch; ~ *s.* Seuche *f.*
epigram *s.* Sinngedicht *n.*
epilepsy *s.* Fallsucht *f.*
epileptic *a.* fallsüchtig.
epilogue *s.* Nachwort *n.*
Epiphany *s.* Dreikönigsfest *n.*
episcopal *a.* bischöflich.
episcopate *s.* Episkopat *n.*
episode *s.* Episode *f.*; Einschaltung *f.*
epistle *s.* Brief *m.*; Epistel *f.*
epistolary *a.* brieflich.
epitaph *s.* Grabschrift *f.*
epithet *s.* Beiwort *n.*
epitome *s.* Auszug *m.*
epitomize *v.t.* abkürzen.
epoch *s.* Epoche *f.*
equal *a.*, **~ly** *adv.* gleich; gewachsen; **to ~**
  v.i. gleichen, gleichkommen.
equality *s.* Gleichheit *f.*; *sign of* ~, *(at)*
  Gleichheitszeichen *n.*
equalize *v.t.* gleichmachen.
equanimity *s.* Gleichmut *m.*
equation *s.* Gleichung *f.*
equator *s.* Äquator *m.*
equatorial *a.* äquatorial.
equestrian *a.* reitend; Reiter...
equilateral *a.* (*geom.*) gleichseitig, gleich-
  schenkelig (Dreieck).
equilibrium *s.* Gleichgewicht *n.*
equinox *s.* Tag- und Nachtgleiche *f.*
equip *v.t.* ausrüsten.
equipment *s.* Ausrüstung *f.*
equipoise *s.* Gleichgewicht *n.*
equitable *a.*, **~bly** *adv.* billig.
equity *s.* Billigkeit, Unparteilichkeit *f.*
equivalent *a.*, **~ly** *adv.* gleichbedeutend;
  ~ *s.* Gegenwert *m.*, Äquivalent *n.*
equivocal *a.*, **~ly** *adv.* zweideutig.
equivocate *v.i.* zweideutig reden; Ausflüchte gebrauchen.
equivocation *s.* Ausflucht *f.*
equivoque *s.* Zweideutigkeit *f.*
era *s.* Zeitrechnung *f.*; Ära, Zeit *f.*
eradicate *v.t.* ausrotten.
erase *v.t.* ausstreichen; ausradieren.
erasure *s.* Ausradierung.
ere *conj. & pr.* ehe, eher, bevor; vor.
erect *v.t.* aufrichten; errichten; ~ *a.*
  aufrecht.
erection *s.* Aufrichtung *f.*; Erhebung *f.*

eremite *s.* Einsiedler *m.*
ermine *s.* Hermelin *n. & m.*
erosion *s.* Zerfressung *f.*
erotic *a.* Liebes..., erotisch.
err *v.i.* sich verirren; abweichen; irren.
errand *s.* Botengang *m.*
errand-boy *s.* Laufbursche *m.*
errant *a.* herumirrend (Ritter) fahrend.
erratic *a.* irrend; erratisch.
erratum *s.* Druckfehler *m.*
erroneous *a.*, **~ly** *adv.* irrig, irrtümlich.
error *s.* Irrtum, Fehler *m.*
erudite *a.*, **~ly** *adv.* gelehrt.
erudition *s.* Gelehrsamkeit *f.*
eruption *s.* Ausbruch *m.*
erysipelas *s.* Rotlauf *m.*; Rose *f.*
escalator *s.* Rolltreppe *f.*
escapade *s.* Seitensprung *m.*
escape *v.t. & i.* entrinnen, entlaufen; entweichen; vermeiden; ~ *s.* Entkommen
  n.; Ausflucht *f.*; ~ *of gas,* Ausströmen
  von Gas *n.*; *to have a narrow* ~, mit
  knapper Not davonkommen.
escarp(ment) *s.* Böschung *f.*
escheat *v.i.* heimfallen.
eschew *v.t.* meiden, scheuen.
escort *v.t.* geleiten, decken; ~ *s.* Bedeckung
  f., Geleit *a.*, Begleit ...; ~ *plane,*
  Begleitflugzeug *n.*
escutcheon *s.* Wappenschild *m. & n.*
esoteric *a.* esoterisch, geheim.
espalier *s.* Spalier *n.*
especial *a.*, **~ly** *adv.* besonders.
espionage *s.* Spionage *f.*
espouse *v.t.* verheiraten; sich einer Sache
  annehmen, verteidigen.
esquire *s.* (*obs.*)=*squire.* Abbr. Esq.
  =Hochwohlgeboren. Titel auf Adres-
  sen sofort nach dem Namen, ohne vor-
  hergehendes Mr.
essay *v.t.* versuchen; prüfen; ~ *s.* Versuch
  m.; Aufsatz *m.*
essence *s.* Wesen *n.*; Essenz *f.*
essential *a.*, **~ly** *adv.* wesentlich; ~ *s.*
  Hauptsache *f.*; wesentlicher Umstand *m.*
establish *v.t.* errichten, einsetzen; ansiedeln; bestätigen; festsetzen.
Established Church *s.* Staatskirche *f.*
establishment *s.* Einrichtung *f.*; Niederlassung *f.*; Anlage (von Fabriken, etc.)
  f.; (*mil.*) Mannschaftsbestand *m.*
  Etablissement *n.*, Firma *f.*
estate *s.* Stand *m.*; Vermögen *n.*; Grundstück *n.*; Landgut *n.*; Nachlass *m.*
estate-duty *s.* Nachlasssteuer *f.*
esteem *v.t.* achten, schätzen; erachten;
  ~ *s.* Hochschätzung *f.*
estimable *a.* schätzbar, achtbar.
estimate *v.t.* schätzen; veranschlagen, berechnen; ~ *s.* Schätzung *f.*; Veran-
  schlag *m.*; *rough* ~, ungefähre Überschlag *m.*; *budget estimates,* Haushaltsvoranschlag *m.*

estimation s. Schätzung f.; Achtung f.
estrange v.t. entfremden; entwenden.
estrangement s. Entfremdung f.
estuary s. Mündung f.; Seebucht f.
etch v.t. ätzen, radieren.
etching s. Radierung f.
eternal a., **~ly** adv. ewig.
eternity s. Ewigkeit f.
ether s. Äther m.
ethereal a. ätherisch.
ethical a., **~ly** adv. sittlich, ethisch; **ethics** s.pl. Sittenlehre f., Ethik f.
ethnic a. Volks...; ~ German, Volksdeutscher m.
ethnography s. Völkerkunde f.
etiquette s. (feine) Sitte, Etikette f.
etymology s. Wortforschung f.
eugenics s.pl. Eugenik f.
eulogize v.t. loben.
eulogy s. Lobrede f.
eunuch s. Verschnittene m.
euphemism s. Euphemismus m.
euphonic a. wohlklingend.
euphony s. Wohlklang m.
euthanasia s. Euthanasie f.
evacuate v.t. ausleeren; (med.) abführen; (mil.) räumen.
evacuation s. Ausleerung f.; Stuhlgang m.; Räumung f.
evade v.t. & i. ausweichen; umgehen.
evaulate v.t. zahlenmässig berechnen.
evanescent a. verschwindend.
evangelical a. evangelisch.
evaporate v.i. verdunsten, verdampfen; ~ v.t. verdampfen; evaporated milk, Trockenmilch f.
evasion s. Umgehung f. (eines Gesetzes).
evasive a. Ausflüchte suchend.
eve s. Abend m.; Vorabend m.
even a., **~ly** adv. eben, glatt; gerade; unparteiisch; quitt; ~ adv. sogar; not ~, nicht einmal; ~ now, eben jetzt; ~ though, selbst wenn.; ~ v.t. gleichmachen, ebnen.
even-handed a. unparteiisch.
evening s. Abend m.; **~-dress**, Gesellschaftsanzug m.
evensong s. Abendgottesdienst m.
event s. Begebenheit f.; Vorfall m.; at all ~s, auf alle Fälle.
eventful a. ereignisvoll.
eventual a. etwaig; zufällig; **~ly** adv. schliesslich.
eventuality s. Möglichkeit f., Fall m.
eventuate v.i. endigen, ausgeben.
ever adv. je, jemals; immer; noch so.
evergreen a. immergrünend; ~ s. Immergrün n.
everlasting a., **~ly** adv. immerwährend.
every a. jeder, jede, jedes; ~ one, jeder(mann), alle pl.; **~thing**, alles; **~where**, allenthalben.
evict v.t. aus dem Besitz vertreiben.

eviction s. gerichtliche Austreibung f.
evidence s. Zeugnis n.; Beweis m.; to admit in ~, als Beweis zulassen; to give ~, aussagen; to produce ~, Beweis antreten; to turn king's ~, Kronzeuge werden; ~ v.t. beweisen.
evident a., **~ly** adv. augenscheinlich, klar.
evil a., **~ly** adv. übel, böse; ~ s. Übel, Verbrechen n.; Unglück n.
evince v.t. zeigen, an den Tag legen.
evocation s. Hervorrufung f.
evoke v.t. hervorrufen; beschwören.
evolution s. Entwicklung f.; Bewegung, Schwenkung f.
evolve v.t. entwickeln; ~ v.i. sich entwickeln.
ewe s. Mutterschaf n.
ewer s. (Wasch-) Wasserkanne f.
exacerbate v.t. erbittern.
exact a., **~ly** adv. genau, gewissenhaft; ~ v.t. fordern, erpressen.
exacting a. strenge, genau.
exaction s. Eintreibung f.
exactitude, exactness s. Genauigkeit f.
exaggerate v.t. übertreiben.
exalt v.t. erhöhen, erheben.
exaltation s. Erhöhung, Erhebung f.; Überschwang m.
examination s. Prüfung f., Examen´ n.; Untersuchung f.; (law) Verhör n., Vernehmung f.; to be under ~, erwogen werden; **~-board**, Prüfungskommission f.; final ~, Schlussexamen n.; **~-papers** pl. Prüfungsaufgaben f.pl.
examine v.t. prüfen; verhören.
examiner s. Untersucher, Examinator m.
examining magistrate s. Untersuchungsrichter m.
example s. Beispiel, Muster n.; for ~, zum Beispiel.
exasperate v.t. reizen.
excavate v.t. aushöhlen; ausgraben.
excavation s. Ausgrabung f.
exceed v.t. überschreiten, übertreffen.
exceeding a., **~ly** adv. ausserordentlich, überaus; not ~, nicht mehr als.
excel v.t. übertreffen; ~ v.i. hervorstechen, sich auszeichnen.
excellence(cy) s. Vortrefflichkeit, Erhabenheit f.; (Titel) Excellenz f.
excellent a., **~ly** adv. vortrefflich.
except v.t. ausnehmen; Einwendungen machen; ~ pr. ausgenommen, ausser.
exception s. Ausnahme f.; Einwendung f.; to admit of no ~, keine Ausnahme zulassen; to take ~ to, sich stossen an.
exceptionable a. tadelnswert; streitig.
exceptional a. aussergewöhnlich, ausnahmsweise.
excerpt v.t. exzerpieren; ~ s. Auszug m.
excess s. Übermass n.; Ausschweifung f.; ~ fare s. Zuschlag m.; ~ luggage s. Übergewicht n.

excessive *a.*, ~ly *adv.* übermässig.
exchange *v.t.* wechseln, tauschen; ~ *s.* Tausch, Wechsel *m.*; Börse *f.*; ~-rate *s.* Wechselkurs *m.*; *foreign* ~, Devisen *f.pl.*; *foreign* ~ *control*, Devisenzwangswirtschaft *f.*
exchequer *s.* Schatzkammer *f.*; Staatskasse *f.*; Schatzamt *n.*; *Chancellor of the* ~, (englische) Schatzkanzler *m.*
excise *s.* Akzise *f.* (Verbrauchs-) Steuer *f.*; ~ *v.t.* besteuern; ausschneiden.
excision *s.* Ausschneidung *f.* (*med.*).
excitable *a.* reizbar.
excite *v.t.* erregen, anfeuern, reizen.
excitement *s.* Anregung *f.*; Aufregung *f.*
exclaim *v.t.* ausrufen.
exclamation *s.* Ausruf *m.*; ~-mark, ~-point Ausrufungszeichen *n.*
exclamatory *a.*, ausrufend, Ausrufungs...
exclude *v.t.* ausschliessen.
exclusion *s.* Ausschluss *m.*
exclusive *a.* ausschliesslich.
excommunicate *v.t.* in den Kirchenbann tun.
excommunication *s.* Kirchenbann *m.*
excrement *s.* Auswurf, Kot *m.*
excrescence *s.* Auswuchs *m.*
excretion *s.* Absonderung *f.*
excretory *a.* Ausscheidungs...
excruciate *v.t.* martern.
exculpate *v.t.* entschuldigen.
excursion *s.* Ausflug *m.*; ~-train (Vergnügungs-) Sonderzug *m.*
excursionist *s.* Tourist, Ausflügler *m.*
excursive *a.* abschweifend.
excusable *a.* verzeihlich.
excuse *v.t.* entschuldigen, verzeihen; *excused from appearing*, vom Erscheinen befreit; ~ *s.* Entschuldigung *f.*
execrable *a.*, ~ly *adv.* abscheulich.
execrate *v.t.* verwünschen, verabscheuen.
execration *s.* Verwünschung *f.*
execute *v.t.* ausführen, vollziehen; vortragen, spielen (Musik, Theater); hinrichten; *to* ~ *a deed*, eine Urkunde ausfertigen.
execution *s.* Ausführung, Vollziehung *f.*; Vortrag *m.*, Vortragsweise *f.*; Pfändung *f.*; Hinrichtung *f.*; Verheerung *f.*; *writ of* ~, (*law*) Vollstreckungsbefehl *m.*
executioner *s.* Scharfrichter *m.*
executive *a.* vollziehend; ~ *committee*, Vorstand *m.*; ~ *regulation*, Ausführungsbestimmung *f.*; ~ *s.* vollziehende Gewalt *f.*; geschäftsführender Beamter *m.*
executor *s.* Testamentsvollstrecker *m.*
executrix *s.* Vollstreckerin *f.*
exemplary *a.*, ~ily *adv.* vorbildlich.
exemplify *v.t.* durch Beispiele erläutern.
exempt *a.* frei, ausgenommen; ~ *v.t.* ausnehmen, verschonen.

exemption *s.* Befreiung *f.*
exercise *s.* Übung, Ausübung *f.*; Beweg; ung *f.*; ~ *v.t.* ausüben; ~ *v.i.* sich üben; exerzieren.
exercise-book *s.* Schreibheft *n.*, Schulheft *n.*
exert *v.t.* ausüben; geltend machen; sich anstrengen.
exertion *s.* Anstrengung, Bemühung *f.*
exhalation *s.* Ausdünstung *f.*
exhale *v.t.* ausdünsten, verdampfen.
exhaust *v.t.* erschöpfen; auspumpen; ~ *s.* Auslass, Auspuff *m.*
exhausted *p.* vergriffen (von Büchern).
exhausting *a.* ermüdend, anstrengend.
exhaustion *s.* Erschöpfung *f.*
exhibit *v.t.* darstellen; aufweisen; ausstellen; ~ *s.* ausgestellte Gegenstand *m.*
exhibition *s.* Darstellung *f.*; Ausstellung *f.*; Stipendium *n.*
exhibitioner *s.* Stipendiat *m.*
exhilarate *v.t.* aufheitern.
exhort *v.t.* ermahnen.
exhortation *s.* Ermahnung *f.*
exhumation *s.* Wiederausgrabung *f.*
exhume *v.t.* wieder ausgraben.
exigence(cy) *s.* Erfordernis *n.*; Not *f.*
exile *s.* Verbannung *f.*; Verbannte *m.f.*; ~ *v.t.* verbannen.
exist *v.i.* existieren.
existence *s.* Dasein *n.*
existent *a.* vorhanden.
existing *a.* wirklich; bestehend.
exit *s.* Ausgang *m.*; Abtreten *n.*; ~-permit, Ausreiseerlaubnis *f.*
exodus *s.* Auszug *m.*
ex officio *a.* & *adv.* von Amts wegen, amtlich.
exonerate *v.t.* entladen; entlasten.
exorbitant *a.*, ~ly *adv.* masslos.
exorcise *v.t.* (böse Geister) bannen.
exorcism *s.* Geisterbeschwörung *f.*
exordium *s.* Eingang *m.*, Einleitung *f.*
exotic *a.* ausländisch, exotisch.
expand *v.t.* erweitern; ~ *v.i.* sich ausdehnen.
expanse *s.* weite Raum *m.*
expansible *s.* ausdehnbar.
expansion *s.* Ausdehnung, Vergrösserung *f.*
expansive *a.* ausgedehnt; mitteilsam, überschwänglich.
expatiate *v.i.* sich weitläufig verbreiten.
expatriate *v.t.* verbannen.
expatriation *s.* Verbannung *f.*; Auswanderung *f.*; Ausbürgerung *f.*
expect *v.t.* erwarten; denken, vermuten.
expectance(cy) *s.* Erwartung *f.*; Anwartschaft *f.*
expectant *a.* erwartend; ~ *mother*, werdende Mutter *f.*; ~ *s.* Anwärter *m.*
expectation *s.* Erwartung *f.*; ~ *of life*, mutmassliche Lebensdauer *n.*

expectorate *v.t.* spucken.
expedience(cy) *s.* Zweckmässigkeit *f.*
expedient *a.*, ~ly *adv.* zweckmässig; ~ *s.* Mittel *n.*, Ausweg *m.*
expedite *v.t.* beschleunigen; abfertigen.
expedition *s.* Geschwindigkeit *f.*; Abfertigung *f.*; Feldzug *m.*; Forschungsreise *f.*
expeditionary *a.* zu einem Feldzuge gehörig.
expeditious *a.*, ~ly *adv.* hurtig, förderlich.
expel *v.t.* vertreiben; verstossen.
expend *v.t.* ausgeben; aufwenden.
expenditure *s.* Kosten *pl.*; Ausgabe *f.*; Aufwand *m.*; (*mil.*) Verbrauch (von Munition) *m.*
expense *s.* Ausgabe *f.*; Preis *m.*; Kosten *pl.*; *to bear the ~s*, die Kosten tragen.
expensive *a.*, ~ly *adv.* teuer, kostspielig.
experience *s.* Erfahrung *f.*; Erlebnis *n.*; ~ *v.t.* erfahren; erleben.
experienced *a.* erfahren; erleben.
experiment *s.* Versuch *m.*; ~ *v.i.* Versuche anstellen.
experimental *a.* erfahrungsmässig.
expert *a.*, ~ly *adv.* erfahren, kundig; ~ *s.* Sachverständige, Fachmann *m.*; ~'*s opinion*, ~ *evidence*, Gutachten *n.*
expiate *v.t.* sühnen.
expiation *s.* Sühnung *f.*
expiration *s.* Ablauf *m.*; Verfallzeit *f.*
expire *v.i.* ablaufen; fällig werden.
explain *v.t.* erklären, erläutern.
explanation *s.* Erklärung *f.*
explanatory *a.* erklärend.
expletive *s.* Fluch *m.*
explicable *a.* erklärbar.
explicit *a.*, ~ly *adv.* ausdrücklich.
explode *v.t.* sprengen; ~ *v.i.* platzen, ausbrechen.
exploded *a.* überlebt, veraltet.
exploit *s.* Heldentat *f.*; ~ *v.t.* ausbeuten.
exploitation *s.* Ausbeutung *f.*
exploration *s.* Erforschung *f.*
explore *v.t.* erforschen, untersuchen.
explorer *s.* Erforscher *m.*; Forschungsreisende *m.*
explosion *s.* Explosion *f.*, Ausbruch *m.*
explosive *a.* explosiv; ~ *s.* Sprengstoff *m.*
exponent *s.* Exponent *m.*
export *s.* Ausfuhr *f.*; ~ *control office*, Ausfuhrstelle *f.*; ~-*duty*, Ausfuhrzoll *m.*; ~-*trade*, Ausfuhrhandel *m.*; ~ *v.t.* ausführen.
exporter *s.* Exporteur *m.*
expose *v.t.* blossstellen; belichten.
exposition *s.* Erklärung *f.*; Ausstellung *f.*
expostulate *v.i.* zur Rede stellen.
exposure *s.* Blossstellung *f.*; (*phot.*) Belichtung *f.*
expound *v.t.* auslegen.
express *v.t.* ausdrücken; äussern; ~ *a.*, ~ly *adv.* deutlich, ausdrücklich; ~

letter, Eilbrief *m.*; ~ *train* *s.* Schnellzug *m.*; *to send* ~, durch Eilboten schicken; ~ *s.* Eilbote *m.*; ~ *company s.* (*Am.*) Paketfahrtgesellschaft *f.*
expression *s.* Ausdruck *m.*; Redensart *f.*
expressive *a.*, ~ly *adv.* ausdrucksvoll.
expropriate *v.t.* enteignen.
expulsion *s.* Vertreibung *f.*
expunge *v.t.* ausstreichen, tilgen.
expurgate *v.t.* reinigen, ausmerzen.
expurgation *s.* Reinigung *f.*
exquisite *a.*, ~ly *adv.* auserlesen.
ex-service man *s.* ehemalige Soldat *m.*
extant *a.* noch vorhanden.
extemporaneous, extemporary *a.*, ~ily *adv.* unvorbereitet, aus dem Stegreif.
extempore *adv.* aus dem Stegreif.
extend *v.t.* ausdehnen; erweisen; ~ *v.i.* sich erstrecken; *extending table*, Ausziehtisch *m.*
extension *s.* Ausdehnung *f.*; (*tel.*) Nebenanschluss *m.*; *University* ~, Volkshochschulkurse *pl.*
extensive *a.*, ~ly *adv.* ausgedehnt.
extent *s.* Ausdehnung, Weite *f.*; Umfang *m.*; Grad *m.*
extenuate *v.t.* verdünnen; schwächen; beschönigen; *extenuating circumstances s.pl.* mildernde Umstände *m.pl.*
exterior *a.*, ~ly *adv.* äusserlich; ~ *s.* Äussere *n.*
exterminate *v.t.* ausrotten.
extermination *s.* Ausrottung *f.*
external *a.*, ~ly *adv.* äusserlich; ~ *s.* Äussere *n.*; *for* ~ *use only*, äusserlich! (von Medizinen).
extinct *a.* erloschen; ausgestorben.
extinction *s.* Auslöschung, Tilgung *f.*
extinguish *v.t.* auslöschen; vertilgen.
extirpate *v.t.* ausrotten, vertilgen.
extol *v.t.* erheben, preisen.
extort *v.t.* entwinden; erpressen.
extortion *s.* Erpressung, Plackerei *f.*
extortionate *a.* erpressend.
extra *s.* Extra..., Sonder..., Neben...; *coffee will be an* ~, Kaffee wird besonders berechnet; ~s *s.pl.* Nebenkosten *pl.*; *no* ~s, keine Kosten ausserdem; **film**—~ *s.* Filmstatist *m.*
extract *v.t.* ausziehen; ableiten; ~ *s.* Auszug *m.*
extraction *s.* Herkunft *f.*
extradite *v.t.* ausliefern.
extradition *s.* Auslieferung (von Verbrechern) *f.*
extraneous *a.* ausländisch, fremd; nicht zur Sache gehörig.
extraordinary *a.*, ~ily *adv.* ausserordentlich.
ex(tra)territorial *a.* exterritorial.
ex(tra)territoriality *s.* Exterritorialität *f.*
extravagance *s.* Verschwendung *f.*; Übertriebenheit *f.*; Extravaganz *f.*

extravagant *a.*, **~ly** *adv.* verschwenderisch; übermässig hoch; extravagant.
extreme *a.*, **~ly** *adv.* äusserst, höchst; radikal; **~** *s.* Äusserste *n.*; höchste Grad *m.*
extremity *s.* Äusserste *n.*; Unglück *n.*; **~ies** *pl.* Gliedmassen *pl.*
extricate *v.t.* herauswickeln.
extrinsic *a.*, **~ally** *adv.* äusserlich, auswendig; von aussen.
exuberance *s.* Überfülle *f.*
exuberant *a.*, **~ly** *adv.* üppig; überschwenglich.
exude *v.t.* ausschwitzen.
exult *v.i.* frohlocken.
exultant *a.* frohlockend.
exultation *s.* Frohlocken *n.*
eye *s.* Auge *n.*; (Nadel-) Öhr *n.*; Knospe *f.*; *eyes front!* (*mil.*) Augen gerade aus!; *eyes right!* (*mil.*) Augen rechts!; **~** *v.t.* ansehen.
eyeball *s.* Augapfel *m.*
eyebrow *s.* Augenbraue *f.*; **~-pencil**, Augenbrauenstift *m.*
eye-glass *s.* Zwicker'*m.*, Brille *f.*
eyelash *s.* Augenwimper *f.*
eyelid *s.* Augenlid *n.*
eye-sight *s.* Sehkraft *f.*
eye-socket *s.* Augenhöhle *f.*
eyesore *s.* hässlicher Anblick *m.*; Dorn im Auge *m.*
eyewash *s.* Humbug *m.*
eye-witness *s.* Augenzeuge *m.*

F

fable *s.* Fabel *f.*; **~** *v.i.* fabeln; **~** *v.t.* erdichten.
fabric *s.* Bau *m.*; Gewebe *n.*; Stoff *m.*
fabricate *v.t.* erbauen; verfertigen; fälschen; erdichten.
fabrication *s.* Erdichtung, Fälschung *f.*
fabulous *a.*, **~ly** *adv.* fabelhaft.
façade *s.* Fassade *f.*
face *s.* Gesicht *n.*; Vorderseite *f.*; Uhrblatt *n.*; Fläche, Oberfläche *f.*; *in the ~ of*, angesichts; **~** *v.t.* ansehen; gegenüber liegen od. stehen; Trotz bieten; einfassen; (*arch.*) verkleiden; (*mech.*) glätten; *to ~ about* v.i. sich umdrehen.
facet *s.* geschliffene Ecke *f.*, Facette *f.*
facetious *a.*, **~ly** *adv.* drollig, scherzhaft.
facial *a.* Gesichts . . .
facile *a.* leicht; gefällig.
facilitate *v.t.* erleichtern.
facility *s.* Leichtigkeit *f.*; Erleichterung *f.*; **facilities** *s.pl.* Anlagen, Einrichtungen *f.pl.*
facing *adv.* gegenüber; (Fenster) hinaus liegend; **~** *s.* Vorderseite *f.*; Aufschlag *m.*; Einfassung *f.* (Kleid).

facsimile *s.* genaue Nachbildung *f.*
fact *s.* Tat *f.*; Tatsache *f.*
faction *s.* Partei *f.*
factious *a.* parteisüchtig; aufrührerisch.
factor *s.* Geschäftsführer *m.*; Faktor *m.*
factory *s.* Fabrik *f.*; Faktorei *f.*; **~-guard**, Werkschutz *m.*; **~-hand**, Fabrikarbeiter *m.*
faculty *s.* Fähigkeit *f.*; Fakultät *f.*
fad *s.* (Umgangsspr.) Steckenpferd *n.*
faddist *s.* Prinzipienreiter *m.*
fade *v.i.* verwelken; verschiessen; vergehen; (*radio*) schwinden.
fag *s.* Fuchs (auf der Schule) *m.*; (*sl.*) Zigarette *f.*; **~** *v.i.* sich abarbeiten; als *fag* dienen.
fag-end *s.* letzte (schlechte) Ende *n.*
fagot, faggot *s.* Reisigbündel *n.*; **~** *v.t.* zusammenbinden.
fail *v.i.* fehlen, mangeln; versiegen; fehlschlagen; durchfallen; bankerott werden; **~** *v.t.* verlassen, unterlassen; **~** *s.* Mangel *m.*
failing *s.* Mangel, Fehler *m.*; **~** *pr.* in Ermangelung von.
failure *s.* Mangel *m.*; Misserfolg, Fehlschlag *m.*; Bankerott *m.*; *~ to do a thing*, Unterlassen etwas zu tun.
fain *a.* froh, geneigt; gezwungen; **~** *adv.* mit Vergnügen, gern.
faint *v.i.* vergehen; in Ohnmacht fallen; **~** *a.*, **~ly** *adv.* schwach.
fair *a.*, **~ly** *adv.* hübsch; rein; hell; günstig; ehrlich, aufrichtig; blond; billig; **~** *play* *s.* ehrliche Spiel *n.*; anständige Handeln *n.*; **~** *adv.* mässig, gefällig, höflich; **~** *s.* Schöne *f.*; Jahrmarkt *m.*
fairly *adv.* ziemlich, leidlich; gehörig.
fairness *s.* Schönheit *f.*; Ehrlichkeit *f.*; Freundlichkeit *f.*; Billigkeit *f.*
fair-spoken *a.* einnehmend.
fairway *s.* Fahrwasser *n.*
fairy *s.* Fee *f.*; Zauberin *f.*
faith *s.* Glaube *m.*; Treue *f.*; *breach of ~*, Treubruch *m.*; *in good ~*, in gutem Glauben, gutgläubig.
faithful *a.*, **~ly** *adv.* gläubig, treu; ehrlich; *yours ~ly*, hochachtungsvoll.
faithless *a.* ungläubig; treulos.
fake *v.t.* Betrug, Schwindel *m.*; **~** *v.t.* betrügen.
falcon *s.* Falke *m.*
falconer *s.* Falkner *m.*
fall *v.i.st.* fallen; abnehmen; sich ereignen; geraten; *to ~ away*, abmagern; abfallen; *to ~ due*, fällig, zahlbar werden; *to ~ in*, (*mil.*) antreten; *to ~ into*, münden in (Fluss); *to ~ off*, abfallen; vergehen; *to ~ out with*, sich verkrachen mit; *to ~ over*, umfallen; *to ~ short of*, zurückbleiben hinter; **~** *s.* Fall *m.*; Abnahme *f.*; Senkung *f.*; (*Am.*) Herbst *m.*; Wasserfall *m.*

fallacious *a.*, ~ly *adv.* trüglich.
fallacy *s.* Täuschung *f.*; Betrug *m.*; Trugschluss *m.*
fallible *a.*, ~bly *adv.* fehlbar.
falling-sickness *s.* Fallsucht *f.*
fallow *a.* falb; brach; ~ *deer*, Damwild *n.*; ~ *s.* Brache *f.*; ~ *v.t.* brachen.
false *a.*, ~ly *adv.* falsch, unecht; ~ *alarm*, blinde Alarm *m.*; ~ *key*, Nachschlüssel *m.*
falsehood *s.* Lüge *f.*; Falschheit *f.*
falsetto *s.* Fistelstimme *f.*
falsification *s.* Verfälschung *f.*
falsify *v.t.* verfälschen; verdrehen.
falsity *s.* Falschheit *f.*
falter *v.i.* straucheln; stammeln.
fame *s.* Ruhm, Ruf *m.*
familiar *a.*, ~ly *adv.* vertraulich; vertraut; ~ *s.* Vertraute *m.* & *f.*
familiarity *s.* Vertraulichkeit *f.*
familiarize *v.t.* vertraut machen.
family *s.* Familie *f.*, Weib und Kinder; Gattung *f.*; *in the* ~ *way*, schwanger.
family-doctor *s.* Hausarzt *m.*
famine *s.* Hungersnot *f.*
famish *v.t.* aushungern.
famous *a.*, ~ly *adv.* berühmt.
fan *s.* Fächer *m.*; Ventilator *m.*; ~ *v.t.* fächeln; anfachen.
fanatic(al) *a.*, ~ally *adv.* eifervoll; ~ *s.* Eiferer, Fanatiker *m.*
fanaticism *s.* Fanatismus *m.*
fancier *s.* Liebhaber, Züchter (von Vögeln, Pflanzen, etc.) *m.*
fanciful *a.*, ~ly *adv.* phantastisch.
fancy *s.* Einbildung, Phantasie *f.*; Vorliebe *f.*; Grille *f.*; ~ *v.i.* sich einbilden; ~ *v.t.* Gefallen finden an; lieb haben; ~ *going...*, denken Sie sich nur, man geht...
fancy-dress *s.* Maskenanzug *m.*; ~ *ball*, Maskenball, Kostümball *m.*
fancy-goods *s.pl.* Modeartikel *m.pl.*, Galanteriewaren *pl.*
fancy-price *s.* Liebhaberpreis *m.*
fanfare *s.* Fanfare *f.*
fang *s.* Fangzahn, Hauer *m.*; Klaue *f.*
fantastic(al) *a.*, ~ally *adv.* eingebildet, sonderbar, wunderlich, fantastisch.
fantasy *s.* Phantasie *f.*
far *adv.* weit, fern; ~ *a.* fern, entfernt; *by* ~, bei weitem.
farce *s.* Posse *f.*; ~ *v.t.* stopfen.
farcical *a.*, possenhaft.
fare *v.i.* essen, trinken; sich befinden; ~ *s.* Fahrt, Reise *f.*; Fuhre *f.*; Kost *f.*; Fahrgast *m.*; Fahrpreis *m.*, Fahrgeld *n.*; *at half fares*, zum halben Fahrpreis.
farewell *adv.* lebe wohl; ~ *s.* Lebewohl *n.*, Abschied *m.*
farm *s.* Pachtgut *n.*; Bauernhof *m.*; (*Am.*) Landgut *n.*; ~-**yard**, Gutshof *m.*;

~-**manager**, landwirtschaftliche Betriebsleiter *m.*; ~ *v.t.* (ver)pachten.
farmer *s.* Pächter *m.*; Landwirt *m.*
farrago *s.* Gemengsel *n.*
farrier *s.* Hufschmied *m.*; Rossarzt *m.*
farrow *s.* Ferkel *n.*; ~ *v.i.* ferkeln.
far-sighted *a.* weitsichtig; weitblickend.
farther *a.* & *adv.* weiter, ferner.
farthest *a.* & *adv.* am weitesten.
farthing *s.* ¼ Penny *m.*
fascinate *v.t.* bezaubern.
fascination *s.* Zauber, Reiz *m.*
fascist *s.* Faschist *m.*
fashion *s.* Form, Gestalt *f.*; Mode *f.*; ~ *v.t.* gestalten.
fashionable *a.*, ~bly *adv.* elegant, modisch; modern; standesmässig.
fast *v.i.* fasten; ~ *s.* Fasten *n.*; Fasttag *m.*; ~ *a.* & *adv.* fest; stark, sehr; geschwind; flott, leichtlebig; *the clock is* ~, die Uhr geht vor.
fasten *v.t.* befestigen; verbinden.
fastener *s.* Verschluss *m.*, Zwecke *f.*; patent ~ *s.* Druckknopf (Kleid).
fastidious *a.*, ~ly *adv.* wählerisch.
fastness *s.* Festigkeit, Stärke *f.*; Festung *f.*
fast-train *s.* Schnellzug *m.*
fat *a.* fett, plump, dick; reichlich; ~ *s.* Fett *n.*
fatal *a.*, ~ly *adv.* verhängnisvoll; tödlich.
fatalism *s.* Fatalismus *m.*
fatalist *s.* Fatalist *m.*
fatality *s.* Verhängnis *n.*; (tödliche) Unglücksfall *m.*
fate *s.* Schicksal *n.*, Verhängnis *n.*
fateful *a.* verhängnisvoll.
father *s.* Vater *m.*; Stammvater *m.*
fatherhood *s.* Vaterschaft *f.*
father-in-law *s.* Schwiegervater *m.*
fatherland *s.* Vaterland *n.*
fatherless *a.* vaterlos.
fatherly *a.* väterlich.
fathom *s.* Faden *m.*; Klafter *f.*; ~ *v.t.* umklaftern; ergründen.
fathomless *a.* unergründlich.
fatigue *s.* Müdigkeit, Mühseligkeit *f.*; ~ *v.t.* ermüden.
fatigue-dress *s.* Drillichanzug *m.*
fatigue-party *s.* (*mil.*) Arbeitskommando *n.*
fatness *s.* Fettigkeit *f.*; Fett *n.*
fatten *v.t.* mästen; ~ *v.i.* fett werden.
fatty *a.* fettig, ölig; Fett...; ~ **acid** *s.* Fettsäure *f.*
fatuity *s.* Albernheit *f.*
fatuous *a.* albern.
fault *s.* Fehler, Mangel *m.*; *to find* ~ *with*, etwas auszusetzen finden an..., tadeln.
faultless *a.* fehlerfrei.
faulty *a.*, ~ily *adv.* fehlerhaft.
favour *s.* Gunst, Gewogenheit *f.*; Gefallen; *your* ~, Ihr Geehrtes (Schreiben); *in* ~ *of*, zu Gunsten; *to do a person a* ~,

einem einen Gefallen erweisen; ~s *pl.*
Gunstbezeigungen *f.pl.*; ~ *v.t.* begünstigen, beehren.

favourable *a.*, ~bly *adv.* günstig.

favourite *s.* Günstling *m.*; ~ *a.* Lieblings...

fawn *s.* Rehkalb *n.*; Rehfarbe *f.*; ~ *a.* hellbraun; ~ *v.i.* kriechend schmeicheln.

fealty *s.* Lehnstreue *f.*

fear *s.* Furcht *f.* Scheu *f.*; ~ *v.t.* & *i.* fürchten; sich fürchten.

fearful *a.*, ~ly *adv.* furchtsam; fürchterlich.

fearless *a.*, ~ly *adv.* furchtlos.

feasibility *s.* Möglichkeit *f.*; Ausführbarkeit *f.*

feasible *a.*, ~bly *adv.* tunlich, möglich.

feast *s.* Fest *n.*; Schmauserei *f.*; ~ *v.i.* schmausen; ~ *v.t.* bewirten.

feat *s.* Tat *f.*; Kunststück *n.*

feather *s.* Feder *f.*; ~ *v.t.* mit Federn schmücken.

feature *s.* Gesichtszug *m.*; Merkmal *n.*; ~ *v.t.* (*film*) darstellen.

febrile *a.* fieberhaft.

February *s.* Februar *m.*

fecundate *v.t.* befruchten.

fecundity *s.* Fruchtbarkeit *f.*

federal *a.* bundesmässig; Bundes...

federalism *s.* Föderalismus *m.*

federate *a.* verbündet.

federation *s.* Bund *m.*

fee *s.* Lohn *m.*, Honorar *n.*; Gebühr *f.*; Lehen *n.*; *to charge a ~ for,* ein Honorar berechnen, eine Gebühr erheben; ~ *v.t.* bezahlen, besolden.

feeble *a.*, ~bly *adv.* schwach; ~ minded *a.* geistesschwach.

feed *v.t.ir.* füttern; weiden; ~ *v.i.* essen; (*mech.*) Material zuführen, vorschieben; sich nähren; ~ *s.* Futter *n.*; Nahrung *f.*; (*mech.*) Vorschub *m.*

feeder, Zufluss *m.*

feeding-bottle *s.* Saugflasche *f.*

feeding-stuffs *pl.* Futtermittel *n.pl.*

feel *v.t.* & *i.ir.* (sich) fühlen, befühlen, empfinden; ~ *s.* Gefühl *n.*

feeler *s.* Fühler *m.*, Fühlhorn *n.*

feeling *p.* & *a.*, ~ly *adv.* fühlend, gefühlvoll; ~ *s.* Gefühl *n.*

feet *s.pl.* (von *foot*) Füsse *m.pl.*

feign *v.t.* & *i.* erdichten; heucheln, vorgeben.

feint *s.* Verstellung, Finte *f.*; (*mil.*) Scheinangriff *m.*

felicitate *v.t.* beglückwünschen.

felicitous *a.* glücklich.

felicity *s.* Glückseligkeit *f.*; Glück *n.*

feline *a.* katzenartig.

fell *a.* grausam; ~ *s.*, Fell *n.*; Haut *f.*; ~ *v.t.* fällen, hinstrecken.

felloe *s.* Felge *f.*

fellow *s.* Genosse *m.*; Mitglied *n.*; Bursche *m.*; (in Zusammensetzungen) Mit...

fellow-citizen *s.* Mitbürger *m.*

fellow-creature *s.* Mitmensch *m.*

fellow-feeling *s.* Mitgefühl *n.*

fellowship *s.* Gemeinschaft, Genossenschaft *f.*; Mitgliedschaft (eines Kollegs) *f.*, Stipendium *n.*

felly *s.* Radfelge *f.*

felon *s.* Verbrecher *m.*

felonious *a.* verbrecherisch; treulos.

felony *s.* schwere Verbrechen *n.*

felspar *s.* Feldspat *m.*

felt *s.* Filz *m.*; ~ *v.t.* filzen.

female *a.* weiblich; ~ *s.* weibliche Person *f.*; Weibchen (von Tieren).

feminine *a.* weiblich; weibisch; ~ *s.* (*gram.*) Femininum *n.*

fen *s.* Sumpf *m.*, Moor *n.*

fence *s.* Zaun *m.*; Schutzwehr *f.*; ~ *v.t.* einhegen; verteidigen; ~ *v.i.* fechten; abwehren.

fencer *s.* Fechter *m.*

fencing *s.* Einhegung *f.*; Fechtkunst *f.*

fend *v.t.* abwehren; parieren.

fender *s.* Kaminvorsetzer *m.*

fennel *s.* Fenchel *m.*

ferment *v.i.* gären; ~ *s.* Gärungsmittel *n.*

fermentation *s.* Gärung *f.*

fern *s.* Farnkraut *n.*

ferocious *a.*, ~ly *adv.* wild, grimmig.

ferocity *s.* Wildheit, Grausamkeit *f.*

ferret *s.* Frettchen *n.*; ~ *v.t.* durchsuchen, verfolgen.

ferrous *a.* Eisen...

ferruginous *a.* eisenhaltig; rostig.

ferrule *s.* Zwinge *f.*

ferry *s.* Fähre *f.*; ~ *v.t.* übersetzen.

ferryman *s.* Fährmann *m.*

fertile *a.*, ~ly *adv.* fruchtbar.

fertility *s.* Fruchtbarkeit *f.*

fertilize *v.t.* befruchten.

ferule *s.* (grosse) Lineal *n.*

fervency *s.* Inbrunst *f.*; Eifer *m.*

fervent *a.*, ~ly *adv.* heiss, inbrünstig.

fervid *a.* heiss, glühend; eifrig.

fervour *s.* Hitze *f.*; Inbrunst *f.*

festal, festive *a.* festlich.

fester *v.i.* schwären, eitern.

festival *a.* festlich; ~ *s.* Festtag *m.*

festivity *s.* Festlichkeit *f.*

festoon *s.* Girlande *f.*

fetch *v.t.* holen, beibringen.

fetid *a.* stinkend.

fetish, fetich *s.* Fetisch *m.*

fetlock *s.* Fussfessel der Pferde *f.*

fetter *v.t.* fesseln; ~ *s.* Fessel *f.*

feud *s.* Fehde *f.*; Lehen *n.*

feudal *a.* lehnbar, Lehns...

feudalism *s.* Lehnswesen *n.*

feudatory *s.* Lehnsmann *m.*

fever *s.* Fieber *n.*

feverish *a.* fieberhaft.

few a. wenig pl. wenige; a ~, einige.

fiancé s. Verlobte, Bräutigam m.

fiancée s. Verlobte. Braut f.

fiat s. Machtspruch m.; Befehl m.

fib s. kleine Lüge, Schwindelei f.; ~ v.i. flunkern.

fibre s. Fiber f.

fibreboard s. Faserbrett n.

fibrous a. faserig.

fickle a. veränderlich, unbeständig.

fiction s. Erdichtung f.; Romandichtung f., Unterhaltungsliteratur.

fictitious a., ~ly adv. erdichtet; ~ transaction, Scheingeschäft n.

fiddle s. Geige, Fiedel f.; ~ v.i. geigen.

fiddle-stick s. Fiedelbogen m.; ~s! i. Unsinn! Larifari!

fiddle-string s. Violinsaite f.

fidelity s. Treue f.

fidget v.i. sich ruhelos bewegen, zappeln; ~ s. nervöse Unruhe f.

fidgety a. unruhig, nervös.

fiduciary a. Vertrauens...; ~ issue, ungedeckte Notenausgabe f.; ~ s. Treuhänder m.

fie i. pfui!

fief s. Lehen n.

field s. Feld n.; Schlachtfeld n.; Arbeitsgebiet n.; ~-glass, Feldstecher m.; ~-marshal s. Feldmarschall m.; ~-kitchen s. Feldküche f.; field(grade) officer, Stabsoffizier m.; fieldpost s. Feldpost f.

fiend s. Teufel m.; Unhold m.

fierce a., ~ly adv. wild, grimmig.

fiery a. feurig; jähzornig.

fife s. Querpfeife f.

fifteen a. fünfzehn.

fifth column s. fünfte Kolonne f.

fifty a. fünfzig.

fig, s. Feige f.; (fig.) Pfifferling m.

fight v.t. & i.st. kämpfen, streiten; ~ s. Gefecht n.; Kampf m.

fighter s. Jagdflugzeug n.

figment s. Erdichtung f.

figurative a., ~ly adv. bildlich.

figure s. Gestalt f.; Ziffer f.; Zahl, Summe f.; ~-head Gallionsbild n.; (fig.) Strohpuppe f.; ~ of speech, Redewendung f.; ~ v.i. bilden, formen; vorstellen; ~ v.i. eine Rolle spielen, auftreten.

figured a. gemustert.

figurine s. kleine Figur f.

filament s. Faser f.; Faden (m.) der Glühlampe.

filch a. mausen.

file s. Faden m.; Glied n.; Liste f.; Reihe f., (mil.) Rotte f.; Briefordner m.; Feile f.; Akt m., Aktenbündel n.; single ~, Gänsemarsch m.; ~ v.t. aufreihen; einordnen; feilen; to ~ a petition, ein Gesuch einreichen.

file-cutter s. Feilenhauer m.

file-leader s. Flügelmann m.

filial a., ~ly adv. kindlich.

filibuster s. Freibeuter m.

filigree s. Filigranarbeit f.

filing-cabinet s. Kartothek f.

filings s.pl. Feilspäne m.pl.

fill v.t. füllen; einschenken; stopfen; to ~ out, to ~ up, ausfüllen (Formular); ~ s. Fülle, Genüge f.

fillet s. Kopfbinde f.; Lendenbraten m.

fillip s. Nasenstüber m.; Anreiz m.

filly s. Stutenfüllen n.; lose Mädchen n.

film s. Häutchen n. (phot.) Film, m.; ~ v.t. & i. (ver) filmen.

filter v.t. Filter m & n.; ~ v.t. filtern.

filth s. Schmutz, Kot m.

filthy a., ~ily adv. kotig; unflätig.

filtrate v.t. & i. filtrieren.

fin, Flosse f.

final a., ~ly adv. endlich; endgültig; ~ s. (Sport) Schlussrunde f.

finance s. Finanzwesen n.; ~ v.t. finanzieren; ~s.pl. Finanzen pl.

financial a. finanziell; ~ year, Haushaltsjahr n.

financier s. Finanzmann m.

finch s. Fink m.

find v.t. & i.st. finden, antreffen; bemerken; to ~ out, herausfinden, ausfindig machen; the jury found him guilty, die Geschworenen sprachen ihn schuldig; ~ s. Fund m.

finding s. Befund m., Gerichtsspruch m.

fine a., ~ly adv. fein, schön; zart; kostbar; schlau; ~ s. Geldbusse f.; ~ v.t. klären; eine Geldstrafe auflegen.

fine arts pl. schöne Künste f.pl.

finery s. Staat, Putz m.

finger s. Finger m.; ~ v.t. betasten.

finger-bowl s. Fingerglas n.

fingering s. (mus.) Fingersatz m.

finger-print s. Fingerabdruck m.

fingertip s. Fingerspitze f.; to have a thing at one's ~s, etwas am Schnürchen haben.

finical a., ~ly adv. geziert.

finicking, finicky a. zimperlich, geziert.

finish v.t. endigen, vollenden; ~ s. letzte Hand; Schluss m.; Appretur f.

finished goods f.pl. Fertigwaren f.pl.

finite a., ~ly adv. endlich.

fir s. Tanne, Kiefer f.

fire s. Feuer n.: Feuersbrunst f.; Leidenschaft f.; to set on ~, anzünden; ~ v.t. anzünden; anfeuern; abfeuern; (Am.) entlassen, herauswerfen; ~ v.i. Feuer fangen; schiessen.

fire-alarm s. Feuermelder m.

fire-arms s.pl. Feuerwaffen f.pl.

fire-brand s. Feuerbrand m.; Aufwiegler m.

fire-brick s. feuerfeste Ziegel m.

fire-brigade s. Feuerwehr f.

fire-damp s. schlagende Wetter n.

fire-eater s. Eisenfresser m.
fire-engine s. Feuerspritze f.
fire-escape s. Rettungsleiter f.
fire-extinguisher s. Feuerlöschapparat m.
fire-fighting s. Feuerbekämpfung f.
firefly s. Leuchtkäfer m.
fire-guard s. Feuergitter (Kamin) n.
fire-insurance s. Feuerversicherung f.
fireman s. Feuerwehrmann m.
fire-place s. Kamin, Herd m.
fire-power s. (mil.) Feuerkraft f.
fire-proof a. feuerfest.
fireside s. Herd, Kamin m.
fire-station s. Feuerwache f.
fire-watcher s. Brandwächter (im Luftschutz) m.
fire-wood s. Brennholz n.
fire-works s.pl. Feuerwerk n.
firing-range s. (mil.) Schussweite f.; Schiessstand m.
firm a., ~ly adv. fest, derb; entschlossen; ~ s. Firma f.
firmament s. Himmelsgewölbe n.
first a. & adv. ~ly adv. der, die, das erste; erstlich; at ~, anfänglich, zuerst, zunächst; ~ of all, vor allen Dingen; ~ of exchange s. Primawechsel m.; ~ come, ~ served, wer zuerst kommt, mahlt zuerst.
first aid s. erste Hilfe bei Unglücksfällen f.; ~ outfit s. Notverbandskasten m.
first-rate a. erstklassig, vorzüglich.
fiscal a. fiskalisch; ~year, Haushaltsjahr n.
fish s. Fisch m.; ~ v.t. fischen.
fish-bone s. Fischgräte f.
fisher s. Fischer m.
fisherman s. Fischer m.
fishery s. Fischfang m., Fischerei f.
fishing-boat s. Fischerboot n.
fishing-hook s. Fischangel f.
fishing-line s. Angelschnur f.
fishing-rod s. Angelrute f.
fishing-tackle s. Angelgerät n.
fishmonger s. Fischhändler m.
fishy a. fischartig; verdächtig.
fission s. Spaltung (Zelle, Atomkern) f.
fissure s. Spalte f.; ~ v.t. spalten.
fist s. Faust f.
fisticuffs pl. Faustkampf m.
fistula s. Fistel f.
fit s. Anwandlung f.; Anfall m.; ~ a., ~ly adv. passend; bequem, tauglich; in guter Form; ~ v.t. anpassen, versehen; zurechtmachen; to ~ on, anprobieren; ~ up, montieren; ~ v.i. sich schicken.
fitful a. launisch.
fitness s. Tauglichkeit; Schicklichkeit f.
fitter s. Zubereiter m.; Monteur m.
fitting a., ~ly adv. schicklich, passend; ~ s.pl. Zubehörteile f.pl.; Einrichtung f.; ~ s. Anprobe f. (beim Schneider).
five a. fünf.
fix v.t. befestigen, anbringen; festsetzen;

bestimmen; (Am.) in Ordnung bringen; (phot.) fixieren; ~ v.i. festwerden; ~ s. Verlegenheit, Klemme f.
fixation s. Festsetzung, Befestigung f.
fixed p. & a., ~ly adv. festgesetzt, unverwandt; (mil.) ortsfest.
fixing solution s. (phot.) fixierbad n.
fixture s. unbewegliche Hausgerät n.
fizzle v.i. zischen, sprühen.
flabbergast v.t. völlig verblüffen.
flabby a. schlaff, welk.
flaccid a. schlapp, schlaff.
flag s. Flagge f.; Steinfliese f.; ~ v.i. erschlaffen.
flagellate v.t. geisseln.
flageolet s. Flageolett n.
flagitious a. schändlich, lasterhaft.
flagon s. (Deckel-)Kanne f.; Flasche f.
flagrant a., ~ly adv. offenkundig; berüchtigt; abscheulich.
flag-ship s. Flaggenschiff n.
flag-staff s. Flaggenstange f.
flail s. Dreschflegel m.
flake s. Flocke f.; ~ v.i. sich flocken; abblättern.
flame s. Flamme f.; ~ v.i. flammen.
flamethrower s. (mil.) Flammenwerfer m.
flan s. Torte f., Törtchen n.
flange s. Flansche f.
flank s. Seite, Weiche f.; Flanke f.; ~ v.t. in die Flanke fallen, flankieren.
flannel s. Flanell m.; Flanelltuch n.; ~ Waschlappen m.; ~s pl. wollene Unterzeug n.; Flanellhosen pl.
flap s. Lappen m.; Klaps m.; Rockschoss m.; ~ v.t. klapsen.
flapper s. Klappe f.; (fig.) Backfisch m.
flare v.i. flackern; ~ s. Lohe f., Geflacker n.
flare-path s. (avi.) Leuchtpfad m.
flash s. schnelle Flamme f.; Blitz m.; ~ v.i. aufblitzen, auflodern.
flashlight s. (Am.) Taschenlampe f.
flashy a. schimmernd; oberflächlich anziehend.
flask s. Flasche f.; Reiseflasche, Feldflasche f.; Pulverhorn n.
flat a., ~ly adv. platt, flach, schal; matt; rundheraus; (com.) flau; (mus.) um halben Ton erniedrigt; ~ rate, (com.) Einheitssatz m.; ~ tire, (Am.) Reifenpanne f.; ~ s. Plattheit; Fläche f.; Untiefe f.; Stockwerk n.; Etagenwohnung f.; (mus.) das B n.
flat-foot s. Plattfuss; flatfooted a. plattfüssig.
flat-iron s. Bügeleisen n.
flatten v.t. flach machen; ~ v.i. schal werden.
flatter v.t. schmeicheln.
flattery s. Schmeichelei f.
flatulence s. Blähung f.; Nichtigkeit f.
flatulent a. blähend; schwülstig.

flaunt *v.i. & t.* prunken; ~ *s.* Prunk *m.*

flavour *s.* Geschmack *m.*; Aroma *n.*; Blume (des Weines) *f.*

flaw *s.* Riss *m.*; Fehler *m.*

flawless *a.* ohne Risse; (*fig.*) fehlerfrei.

flax *s.* Flachs *m.*

flaxen *a.* flachsen.

flay *a.* (die Haut) abziehen, schinden.

flea *s.* Floh *m.*; ~ bite *s.* (*fig.*) Kleinigkeit *f.*

fleck *s.* Fleck *m.*; ~ *v.t.* sprenkeln.

fledge *v.t.* befiedern.

fledged *a.* flügge, befiedert.

flee *v.i.i.r.* fliehen.

fleece *s.* Vlies *n.*; ~ *v.t.* scheren; (*fig.*) prellen.

fleecy *a.* wollig.

fleet *s.* Flotte *f.*; ~ *a.* flüchtig; schnellfüssig; ~ *v.i.* verfliegen.

flesh *s.* Fleisch *n.*

fleshless *a.* mager.

fleshy *a.* fleischig.

flex *s.* (*elek.*) Litze *f.*, Litzendraht *m.*

flexible *a.*, ~bly *adv.* biegsam.

flexion *s.* Biegung *f.*; (*gram.*) Beugung *f.*

flick *v.t.* schnippen, schnellen.

flicker *v.i.* flackern; flimmern (Film).

flier *s.* Flieger *f.*; Renner *m.*

flight *s.* Flucht *f.*; Flug *m.*; Schwarm *m.*; (*avi.*) Kette *f.*; ~ (*of stairs*) *s.* Treppe *f.*

flighty *a.* flüchtig, schnell; faselnd.

flimsy *a.* locker, dünn; schwach.

flinch *v.i.* zurückschaudern.

fling *v.t. st.* werfen, schleudern; ~ *s.* Wurf, Schlag *m.*; Austoben *n.*

flint *s.* Feuerstein, Kiesel *m.*

flip *v.t. & i.* schnellen; ~ *s.* Schneller, Klaps *m.*

flippancy *s.* Leichtfertigkeit.

flippant *a.* leichtfertig, frivol.

flirt *v.t.* schnellen; ~ *v.i.* liebeln, kokettieren; ~ *s.* Kokette *f.*

flirtation *s.* Liebelei *f.*, Flirt *m.*

flit *v.i.* flattern; huschen; ausrücken.

flitch *s.* Speckseite *f.*

flitter *v.i.* flattern.

float *s.* Floss *m.*; Schwimmer *m.*; (*avi.*) Schwimmgestell, Floss *n.*; ~ *v.i.* obenauf schwimmen; dahintreiben; ~ *v.t.* flössen; überfluten; flott machen; ins Leben rufen; *to* ~ *a loan*, eine Anleihe auflegen.

floating *a.* schwimmend; unsicher, schwebend; ~ debts *pl.* schwebende Schulden *f.pl.*; ~ dock *s.* Schwimmdock *n.*

flock *s.* Herde *f.*; Haufen *m.*; (Woll-) Flocke *f.*; ~ *v.i.* in Haufen ziehen, strömen, sich scharen.

flocky *a.* flockig.

flog *v.t.* peitschen.

flogging *s.* Prügelstrafe *f.*

flood *s.* Flut *f.*; Hochwasser *n.*; ~ *v.t.* überschwemmen.

floodlight *s.* Scheinwerferlicht *n.*; ~ *v.t.* mit Scheinwerfer beleuchten.

floor *s.* Fussboden, Boden *m.*; Tenne *f.*; Stockwerk *n.*; ~ *v.t.* dielen; zu Boden schlagen.

floorshow *s.* Tanzvorführung, Tanzeinlage *f.*

flop *v.i.* plumpsen; ~ *s.* Versager.

floral *a.* Blüten..., Blumen...

floral tribute *s.* Blumenspende *f.*

florid *a.*, ~ly *adv.* verschnörkelt.

florin *s.* Gulden *m.*; englische Zweischillingstück *n.*

florist *s.* Blumenhändler *m.*

flotation, floatation *s.* Auflegen (einer Anleihe) *n.*

flotilla *s.* Flotille *f.*

flotsam *s.* treibende Wrackgut *n.*

flounce *s.* Falbel *f.*; ~ *v.t.* mit Falbeln versehen; ~ *v.i.* auffahren, sich heftig bewegen.

flounder *s.* Flunder *m.* or *f.*; ~ *v.i.* zappeln; sich abmühen; Fehler machen.

flour *s.* feine Mehl *n.*

flourish *v.i.* blühen; prahlen; ~ *v.t.* schwingen; verzieren; ~ *s.* Schnörkel *m.*; Verzierung *f.*; Gepränge *m.*; Trompetenstoss *m.*

flout *s.* Spott *m.*; ~ *v.i. & t.* verspotten.

flow *v.i.* fliessen; fluten; ~ *s.* Flut *f.*; Redefluss *m.*

flower *s.* Blume, Blüte *f.*; Beste *n.*; ~ *v.i.* blühen.

flowered *a.* geblümt.

flower-pot *s.* Blumentopf *m.*

flowery *a.* blumig.

fluctuate *v.i.* schwanken.

fluctuation *s.* Schwankung *f.*

flue *s.* Heizröhre *f.*, Ofenrohr *m.*

flu(e) *s.* Grippe *f.*, Influenza *f.*

fluency *s.* Fluss (der Rede) *m.*

fluent *a.*, ~ly *adv.* flüssig; geläufig.

fluff *s.* Staubflocke, Flause *f.*; Flaum *m.*

fluid *a.* flüssig; ~ *s.* Flüssigkeit *f.*

fluke *s.* (*fam.*) glückliche Zufall *m.*

flummery *s.* Haferbrei *m.*; Pudding *m.*; (*fig.*) leere Geschwätz *n.*

flunkey *s.* Lakai *m.*

fluorescence *s.* Fluoreszenz *f.*

fluorescent *a.* fluoreszierend.

flurry *s.* Windstoss *m.*; Unruhe *f.*; ~ *v.t.* beunruhigen.

flush *s.* fliegende Röte *f.*; Aufwallung *f.*; kurze Regenguss *m.*; ~ *a.* blühend, frisch; auf derselben Ebene; (*Am.*) freigebig; ~ *v.t.* ausspülen; erröten machen; ~ *v.i.* erröten.

fluster *v.t.* aufregen; verwirren.

flute *s.* Flöte *f.*; Hohlkehle *f.*; ~ *v.t.* riefeln.

flutist *s.* Flötenspieler *m.*

flutter *v.i.* flattern; unruhig sein; ~ *v.t.* scheuchen, beunruhigen; ~ *s.* Geflatter *n.*; Unruhe *f.*

flux *s.* Fluss *m.*; Abfluss *m.*

fly *v.i. & t.* *st.* fliegen; fliehen; jagen; ~ *s.* Fliege *f.*; offene Droschke *f.*

flyer=flier.

fly-fishing *s.* Angeln mit künstlichen Fliegen als Lockspeise *n.*

flying *a.* fliegend; ~ **boat** *s.* Flugboot *n.*; ~ **bomb** *s.* Flugbombe *f.*; ~ **squad** *s.* Überfallkommando *n.*; ~ **suit** *s.* Fluganzug *m.*

fly-leaf *s.* Vorsetzblatt *n.*; loses Blatt *n.*

fly-paper *s.* Fliegenpapier *n.*

fly-wheel *s.* Schwungrad *n.*

foal *s.* Fohlen *n.*; ~ *v.i.* fohlen.

foam *s.* Schaum *m.*; ~ *v.i.* schäumen.

fob *v.t.* foppen, anführen.

focal *a.* im Brennpunkt.

focus *s.* Brennpunkt *m.*; ~ *v.t.* (*phot.*) einstellen.

fodder *s.* Viehfutter *n.*; ~ *v.t.* füttern.

foe *s.* Feind *m.*

fog *s.* dicke Nebel; Wintergras *n.*; ~-**signal** *s.* Nebelsignal *n.*

fog(e)y *s.* alte Philister *m.*

foggy *a.*, ~**ily** *adv.* nebelig, dunkel.

fog-signal *s.* Nebelhorn *n.*

foible *s.* Schwäche *f.*; schwache Stelle *f.*

foil *v.t.* vereiteln; ~ *s.* Folie *f.*; Laubwerk *n.*; Rapier *n.*; Metallblättchen *n.*; Einfassung *f.*

foist *v.t.* unterschieben, zuschieben.

fold *s.* Falte *f.*; Falz *m.*; Schafhürde *f.*; ~ *v.t.* falten; pferchen; ~ *v.i.* sich schliessen.

folder *s.* Falzbein *n.*; Broschüre *f.*; (*Am.*) Aktendeckel *m.*, Mappe *f.*

folding *a.* zusammenklappbar; ~ **doors** *pl.* Doppeltüre *f.*

folding-knife *s.* Taschenmesser *n.*

folding-screen *s.* spanische Wand *f.*

foliage *s.* Laubwerk *n.*

folio *s.* Folio *n.*; Foliant *m.*

folk *s.* Volk *n.*; Leute *pl.*

folklore *s.* Volkskunde *f.*

follow *v.t. & i.* (be-, nach-, ver-)folgen; *to ~ suit*, bedienen, Farbe bekennen (in der Karte); jemandes Beispiel folgen.

follower *s.* Nachfolger *m.*; Anhänger *m.*

folly *s.* Torheit *f.*; Ausschweifung *f.*

foment *v.t.* bähen; pflegen, Aufruhr erregen.

fond *a.*, ~**ly** *adv.* vernarrt; zärtlich; *to be ~ of*, gern haben, gern tun.

fondle *v.t.* liebkosen, verzärteln.

fondness *s.* Zärtlichkeit *f.*; Vorliebe *f.*

font *s.* Taufstein *m.*; ~ *s.* (*Am.*), see **fount** (Schriftguss).

food *s.* Speise *f.*, Essen *n.*; Futter *n.*; *to go without ~*, ohne Nahrung sein.

food-hoarder *s.* Hamsterer *m.*

fool *s.* Narr *m.*; ~ *v.t.* zum besten haben.

foolery *s.* Narrheit *f.*

fool-hardy *a.* tollkühn.

foolish *a.*, ~**ly** *adv.* töricht, närrisch.

foolproof *a.* kinderleicht; betriebssicher.

foolscap *s.* Kanzleipapier *n.*

foot *s.* Fuss *m.*; Tritt *m.* Fussvolk *n.*; *on ~*, zu Fuss; ~ *v.t. & i.* treten, fussen; zu Fuss gehen; ~ *the bill*, zahlen.

foot-and-mouth disease *s.* Maul-und Klauenseuche *f.*

foot-ball *s.* Fussball (spiel) *n.*

football-pool *s.* Fussballtoto *n.*

footbridge *s.* Steg *m.*; Brücke für Fussgänger *f.*

footfall *s.* Geräusch eines Schrittes *n.*

Foot-guards *s.pl.* Gardeinfanterie *f.*

foothold *s.* fester Stützpunkt *m.*

footing *s.* Halt; Stützpunkt *m.*; war-~, Kriegsstand *m.*

foot-lights *s.pl.* Rampenlichter *n.pl.*

foot-locker *s.* verschliessbare Truhe *f.*

footman *s.* Lakai, Bediente *m.*

foot-note *s.* Fussnote *f.*

foot-pace *s.* langsame Schritt *m.*

foot-path *s.* Fussweg *m.*

foot-print *s.* Fusstapfe *f.*

footsore *a.* mit wunden Füssen.

foot-step *s.* Schritt *m.*; Fusstritt *m.*

foot-stool *s.* Fusschemel *m.*

foot-support *s.* Schuheinlage *f.*

foot-wear *s.* Schuhwerk, -zeug *n.*

fop *s.* Geck *m.*

foppery *s.* Narrheit *f.*; Ziererei *f.*

foppish *a.* geziert, geckenhaft.

for *pr. & c.* für, mit, nach, wegen, um... willen; aus, an, auf, zu, zufolge; denn, deswegen; ~ *all that*, trotzdem; ~ *and on behalf of*, per procura (p.p.).

forage *s.* Futter *n.*; ~ *v.t.* fouragieren; stöbern.

foray *s.* Raubzug *m.*; ~ *v.t.* plündern.

forbear *v.i. st.* unterlassen; Geduld haben; ~ *v.t.* sich enthalten; ~ *s.* Ahne *m.*, Vorfahre *m.*

forbearance *s.* Vermeidung, Unterlassung; Nachsicht *f.*

forbid *v.t. st.* verbieten, verhindern; *God ~!* Gott behüte!

force *s.* Kraft, Gewalt, Gültigkeit *f.*; Mannschaft *f.*; ~**s** *pl.* Truppen *f.pl.*; *to be in ~*, in Kraft sein; *to come into ~*, in Kraft treten; ~ *v.t.* zwingen; Gewalt brauchen, notzüchtigen; erstürmen; ~**d labour** *s.* Zwangsarbeit *f.*; ~**d loan** *s.* Zwangsanleihe *f.*; ~**d march** *s.* Eilmarsch *m.*; ~**d rate of exchange** *s.* Zwangskurs *m.*; ~**d sale**, Zwangsverkauf *m.*

forceful *a.* wirkungsvoll.

forcible *a.*, ~**bly** *adv.* kräftig, gewaltsam.

ford *s.* Furt *f.*; ~ *v.t.* durchwaten.

fore *a.* vorder; vorherig; ~ *adv.* vorn.

forebode *v.t.* vorbedeuten, ahnen.

forecast *v.t.* & *i.st.* voraussehen; ~ *s.* Voraussage *f.*

forecastle *s.* (*nav.*) Back *f.*, Vorderdeck *n.*

foreclose *v.i.* ein Pfand für verfallen erklären.

foreclosure *s.* Verfallserklärung *f.*

foredoom *s.* Vorherbestimmung *f.*; ~ *v.t.* zum Untergang bestimmen.

forefather *s.* Vorfahr *m.*

forefinger *s.* Zeigefinger *m.*

forefront *s.* vorderste Reihe *f.*

forego *v.i.st.* vorhergehen; ~=forgo.

foregone *a.* von vornherein bestimmt; ~ *conclusion*, ausgemachte Sache *f.*

foreground *s.* Vordergrund *m.*

forehead *s.* Stirn *f.*

foreign *a.* ausländisch; fremd; ~ *bill*, Auslandswechsel *m.*; ~ **Office** *s.* Auswärtige Amt *n.*

foreigner *s.* Ausländer *m.*

foreknowledge *s.* Vorherwissen *n.*

foreland *s.* Vorgebirge *n.*

forelock *s.* Stirnhaar *n.*; Schopf *m.*

foreman *s.* Werkmeister *m.*

foremast *s.* Fockmast *m.*

foremost *a.* vorderste, vornehmste.

forenoon *s.* Vormittag *m.*

forensic *a.* gerichtlich.

forerunner *s.* Vorbote *m.*

foresee *v.t.st.* vorhersehen.

foreshadow *v.t.* vorher andeuten.

foreshorten *v.t.* in Verkürzung zeichnen.

foresight *s.* Voraussicht *f.*

forest *s.* Forst, Wald *m.*; ~-fire *s.* Waldbrand *m.*

forestall *v.t.* vorwegnehmen, vorkaufen; zuvorkommen.

forester *s.* Förster *m.*

forestry *s.* Forstwirtschaft *f.*

foretaste *s.* Vorgeschmack *m.*; ~ *v.t.* einen Vorschmack haben.

foretell *v.t.st.* vorhersagen.

forethought *s.* Vorbedacht *m.*

forewarn *v.t.* vorher warnen.

forewoman *s.* Werkführerin *f.*

foreword *s.* Vorwort *n.*

forfeit *s.* Verwirkung *f.*; Geldbusse *f.*; Pfand (im Pfänderspiel) *n.*; ~ *v.t.* verwirken, verscherzen; ~ *a.* verwirkt, verfallen.

forfeiture *s.* Verwirkung *f.*

forge *s.* Schmiede *f.*; ~ *v.t.* schmieden; ersinnen; fälschen; ~ *ahead*, vorwärtsdrängen.

forger *s.* Schmieder *m.*; Verfälscher *m.*

forgery *s.* Fälschung *f.*

forget *v.t.st.* vergessen.

forgetful *a.* vergesslich.

forget-me-not *s.* Vergissmeinnicht *n.*

forgive *v.t.st.* vergeben, verzeihen.

forgo *v.t.* verzichten auf, aufgeben.

fork *s.* Gabel, Zinke *f.*

forked *a.* gabelförmig.

forlorn *a.* verzweifelt; verlassen.

form *s.* Form, Gestalt *f.*; Formular *f.*; Formel *f.*; Vordruck *m.*; Bank *f.*; (Schul-)Klasse *f.*; good ~ *s.* feine Ton *m.*; (*sport*) Form *f.*; *it is bad* ~, es gehört sich nicht; ~ *v.t.* bilden, einrichten; *to* ~ *a company*, (*com.*) eine Gesellschaft gründen.

formal *a.*, ~ly *adv.* förmlich; scheinbar.

formality *s.* Förmlichkeit *f.*

formation *s.* Bildung *f.*, Gestaltung *f.*

formative *a.* formend, bildend.

former *a.*, ~ly *adv.* vorig; vormalig; früher, ehemals.

formic acid *s.* Ameisensäure *f.*

formidable *a.*, ~bly *adv.* furchtbar.

form-master *s.* Klassenlehrer *m.*

formula *s.* Formel *f.*

formulate *v.t.* formulieren.

fornication *s.* Hurerei *f.*

forsake *v.t.st.* verlassen; entsagen.

forsooth *adv.* wahrlich, wirklich.

forswear *v.t.* & *refl.st.* abschwören; verschwören.

fort ~. Schanze *f.*, Fort *n.*

forth *adv.* vorwärts, fort, ferner, heraus, hinaus, draussen; fortan.

forthcoming *a.* bevorstehend; bereit.

forthwith *adv.* sogleich.

fortification *s.* Befestigung *f.*; *permanent* ~, ständige Befestigung *f.*

fortify *v.t.* befestigen; stärken.

fortitude *s.* Tapferkeit, Stärke *f.*

fortnight *s.* vierzehn Tage *pl.*

fortnightly *a.* & *adv.* alle vierzehn Tage (erscheinend).

fortress *s.* Festung *f.*

fortuitous *a.*, ~ly *adv.* zufällig.

fortunate *a.*, ~ly *adv.* glücklich.

fortune *s.* Glück *n.*; Schicksal *n.*; Vermögen *n.*; Mitgift *f.*

fortune-hunter *s.* Mitgiftjäger *m.*

fortune-teller *s.* Wahrsager(in) *m.* (& *f.*).

forty *a.* vierzig.

forward *a.*, ~ly *adv.* vordere; voraus; hastig, vorlaut; eifrig; frühzeitig; vorwärts; fortschriftlich; ~ *s.* Stürmer (Fussball) *m.*; ~ *v.t.* befördern; absenden; (Brief) nachsenden; *please* ~, bitte nachsenden!

forwarding *s.* Versendung *f.*; ~ *agent s.* Spediteur *m.*

forwards *adv.* vorwärts, weiter.

fossil *a.* fossil; ~ *s.* Fossil *n.*

foster *v.t.* nähren, aufziehen; pflegen.

foster-brother *s.* Milchbruder *m.*

foster-child *s.* Pflegekind *n.*

fosterer, foster-father *s.* Pflegevater *m.*

foster-home *s.* Pflegefamilie *f.*

foster-mother *s.* Pflegemutter *f.*

foul *a.*, ~ly *adv.* unrein; verdorben; widrig; ruchlos; ~ *v.t.* verunreinigen.

found *v.t.* giessen; gründen; stiften.

foundation s. Gründung f.; Fundament n.; Stiftung f.; Anstalt f.; **~-stone**, Grundstein f.

founder s. Giesser m.; Gründer m.; ~ v.i. scheitern; lahmen.

foundling s. Findelkind n.; **~-hospital**, Findelhaus n.

foundress s. Gründerin f.

foundry s. Giesserei f.

fount s. Schriftguss m.; = fountain.

fountain s. Quelle f.; Springbrunnen m.; **~-head** s. Urquell m.; **~-pen** s. Füllfeder f.

four a. vier; ~ s. (sport) Vierer m.

four-engine(d) a. (avi.) viermotorig.

fourfold a. vierfach.

four-in-hand s. Vierspänner m.

fourposter s. Himmelbett n.

fourteen a. vierzehn.

fowl s. Vogel m.; Huhn n.; Geflügel n.; ~ v.i. Vögel fangen.

fowler s. Vogelsteller m.

fowling-piece s. Vogelflinte f.

fox s. Fuchs m.

fox-glove s. (bot.) Fingerhut m.

fox-hunt s. Fuchsjagd f.

fraction s. (ar.) Bruch; Bruchteil m.; vulgar ~, common ~, gemeine Bruch m.; **~-line**, Bruchstrich m.

fractional a. gebrochen, Bruch...

fracture s. (Knochen-) Bruch m.; ~ v.t. brechen.

fragile a. zerbrechlich, schwach.

fragility s. Zerbrechlichkeit f.; Gebrechlichkeit f.

fragment s. Bruchstück n.

fragmentary a. fragmentarisch.

fragrance s. Wohlgeruch m., Duft m.

fragrant a., **~ly** adv. wohlriechend.

frail a. gebrechlich; schwach.

frailty s. Gebrechlichkeit f.; Fehltritt m.; Schwachheit f.

frame s. Rahmen m.; Gerüst, Gestell n.; Gestalt, Form f.; Einfassung f.; ~ v.t. einfassen; bilden; erfinden.

framework s. Fachwerk n.; (fig.) Bau m., Rahmen; within the ~ of, im Rahmen von.

franchise s. Wahlrecht n.; Gerechtsame f.

Francophil a. frankreichfreundlich.

frank a., **~ly** adv. frei; aufrichtig.

frankincense s. Weihrauch m.

frankness s. Offenheit f.

frantic a., **~ally** adv. wahnsinnig.

fraternal a., **~ly** adv. brüderlich.

fraternity s. Brüderschaft f.; Brüderlichkeit f.

fraternization s. Verbrüderung f.

fraternize v.i. sich verbrüdern.

fratricidal a. brudermörderisch.

fratricide s. Brudermord m.; Brudermörder m.

fraud s. Betrug m.; Enttäuschung f.

fraudulent a., **~ly** adv. betrügerisch.

fraught p. befrachtet; voll.

fray s. Schlägerei f.; ~ v.t. ausfransen; durchscheuern.

freak s. Einfall m.; Grille f.

freckle s. Sommersprosse f.

freckled, **freckly** a. sommersprossig.

free a., **~ly** adv. frei; offenherzig; ohne Kosten; gutwillig; ~ on board (f.o.b.), frei Schiff; ~ on rail, frei Eisenbahn; of my ~ will, freiwillig; ~ v.t. befreien; freigeben.

freebooter s. Freibeuter m.

freedom s. Freiheit f.; Bürgerrecht n.; ~ of association and assembly, Koalitions- und Versammlungsfreiheit.

freehand-drawing s. Freihandzeichnen n.

freehold s. Freigut n.

freeholder s. Grundeigentümer m.

freelance s. freier Ausüber eines Berufes; ~ journalist, freier Journalist m.

freeman s. Ehrenbürger m.

freemason s. Freimaurer m.

freemasonry s. Freimaurerei f.

freeport s. Freihafen m.

freestone s. Sandstein m.

freethinker s. Freigeist m.

free-trade s. Freihandel m.

freewheel s. Freilauf m.

freeze v.i.s.t. frieren, gefrieren; to ~ to death, erfrieren; ~ v.t. gefrieren machen; to ~ promotions, wages, Beförderungen aussetzen, Löhne nicht erhöhen.

freezing-point s. Gefrierpunkt m.

freight s. Fracht f.; **~-car** s. (Am.) Güterwagen m.; **~-train** s. (Am.) Güterzug; **~-yard** s. (Am.) Güterbahnhof.

French a. französisch; Franzosen n.pl.; ~ polish s. Schellackpolitur f.; ~ window s. Flügelfenster, Verandatür f.

frenchify v.t. französisch machen.

frenzied a. wahnsinnig.

frenzy s. Raserei f.

frequency s. Häufigkeit f.; (elek., radio) Frequenz f.; high ~, Hochfrequenz f.

frequent a., **~ly** adv. häufig, zahlreich.; ~ v.t. oft besuchen.

fresh a., **~ly** adv. frisch; kühl; neu.

freshen v.t. erfrischen; ~ v.i. frisch, kühl werden.

freshman s. 'Fuchs', m.

freshwater s. Süsswasser n.

fret s. Ärger, Verdruss m.; Griff(brett) n.; ~ v.t. abreiben; zerfressen; erzürnen; ~ v.i. sich grämen, ärgern.

fretful a., **~ly** adv. ärgerlich.

fret-saw s. Laubsäge, Stichsäge f.

fretwork s. Gitterwerk, feine Schnitzwerk n., Laubsägearbeit f.

friable a. zerreibbar.

friar s. Mönch, Frater m.

friction s. Reibung f.

Friday s. Freitag m.; *Good* ~, Karfreitag m.
friend s. Freund(in) m. (& f.).
friendly a. freundschaftlich; ~ **society** s. Unterstützungsverein m.
friendship s. Freundschaft f.
frieze s. Fries m.
frigate s. Fregatte f.
fright s. Entsetzen n.; Schreckbild n
frighten v.t. erschrecken.
frightful a., ~ly adv. schrecklich.
frigid a., ~ly adv. kalt, frostig.
frigidity s. Kälte f.; Kaltsinn m.
frill s. Krause f.
fringe s. Franse f.; Rand m.; ~ v.t. befransen; säumen.
frippery s. Trödelkram m.
frisk s. Sprung m.; ~ v.i. hüpfen.
frisky a. lustig, munter.
fritter v.t. zerstückeln; vertändeln.
frivolity s. Leichtfertigkeit f.
frivolous a., ~ly adv. frivol.
frizz(le) s. Haarlocke f.; ~ v.t. kräuseln.
fro adv., *to and* ~, hin und her.
frock s. Rock m. Frauenkleid.
frog s. Frosch m.
frolic a. fröhlich; ~ s. Scherz m.; ~ v.i. spassen.
frolicsome a., ~ly adv. lustig.
from pr. von, aus, nach, wegen; vor.
front s. Stirn f.; Vorderseite f., Front f.; Vorder...; ~**-door** s. Vordertür f.; ~**-room** s. Vorderzimmer; ~**-view** s. Vorderansicht f.; ~ v.t. gegenüberstehen.
frontage s. Vorderseite f.
frontal a. Stirn..., Front...; ~ **attack** s. (mil.) Stirnangriff m.
frontier s. Grenze f.; ~**-readjustments** pl. Grenzberichtigungen f.pl.
frontispiece s. Vorderseite (eines Gebäudes) f.; Titelbild n.
frost s. Frost m.; Reif m.
frostbite s. Frostbeulen f.pl.
frost-bitten a. vom Froste beschädigt.
frosted a. (Silber) matt; (cook.) glasiert; ~ **glass** s. Mattglas n.
froth s. Schaum m.; ~ v.t. & i. schäumen.
frown s. gerunzelte Stirn f.; ~ v.i. die Stirn runzeln; finster blicken.
frozen p. gefroren; ~ **meat** s. Gefrierfleisch n.
fructify v.t. befruchten.
frugal a., ~ly adv. sparsam; mässig.
frugality s. Sparsamkeit, Mässigkeit f.
fruit s. Frucht f.; Obst n.; Ertrag m.
fruiterer s. Obsthändler m.
fruitful a., ~ly adv. fruchtbar.
fruition s. Genuss m.; Verwirklichung f.
fruitless a., ~ly adv. fruchtlos.
fruit-salad s. Fruchtsalat m.
fruity a. blumig, geschwollen (Ausdrucksweise).

frustrate v.t. vereiteln, vernichten.
frustration s. Vereitlung f.
fry s. Fischbrut f.; *small* ~, kleine Volk n.; ~ v.t. rösten, braten; backen (Fisch); **fried egg** s. Spiegelei n.
frying-pan s. Bratpfanne f., Pfanne f.
fuchsia s. (bot.) Fuchsie f.
fuddle v.t. (v.i. *sich*) berauschen.
fudge s. Unsinn m.; ~ v.t. pfuschen.
fuel s. Brennmaterial n.; Feuerung f.
fuel oil s. Heizöl n.
fuel-tanker s. Kesselwagen m.
fugitive a. flüchtig; leicht verschwindend (Farbe); ~ s. Flüchtling m.
fugue s. (mus.) Fuge f.
fulcrum s. Stützpunkt m.
fulfil v.t. erfüllen, vollziehen.
fulfilment s. Erfüllung, Vollziehung f.
full a. voll; gänzlich; ~ adv. völlig, genau, recht, gerade; in ~, vollständig, voll ausgeschrieben; ~ **face** s. Vorderansicht (des Gesichts) f.; ~ **powers** f.pl. Vollmacht f.; ~ **stop** s. Punkt (Interpunktion) m.; ~ s. Fülle f.; ~ v.t. walken.
full-blown a. ganz aufgeblüht; richtig.
full-dress s. Galauniform f.
fuller s. Walker m.
fulling-mill s. Walkmühle f.
full-length a. in Lebensgrösse.
full-moon s. Vollmond m.
fulminate v.i. donnern; schelten.
fullness s. Fülle f.
fulsome a., ~ly adv. ekelhaft, widrig.
fumble v.i. & t. tappen, betasten; stümpern.
fume s. Rauch m.; Dunst m.; Zorn m.; ~ v.i. rauchen, verdampfen; zornig sein; ~ v.t. räuchern.
fumigate v.t. räuchern.
fun s. Scherz, Spass m.; *to make* ~ *of*, zum besten haben.
function s. Amt n.; Dienst m.; Tätigkeit f.; Funktion f.; gesellige Veranstaltung f.; ~ v.i. funktionieren; tätig sein.
fund s. Kapital n.; Fonds m.pl.; Vorrat m.; **public** ~ s pl. Staatsschulden f.pl.; ~ v.t. Kapitalien anlegen; fundieren.
fundamental s., ~ly adv. grundlegend.
funereal a. Trauer..., traurig.
funeral s. Begräbnis n.
fungible a. fungibel.
fungous a. schwammig.
fungus s. Schwamm m., Pilz u...
funicular a. Drahtseil...
funk s. grosse Angst f.; ~ v.t. & i. sich drücken.
funnel s. Trichter m.; Schornstein m.
funny a. spasshaft, komisch.
fur s. Pelz m.; Belag (auf der Zunge) m.; Kesselstein m.; ~ v.t. mit Pelz füttern.
furbelow s. Falbel f.; ~ v.t. verbrämen.
furbish v.t. polieren; putzen.

355 **Friday—garish**

furious *a.*, ~ly *adv.* wütend, rasend.
furl *v.t.* aufrollen; (die Segel) aufziehen.
furlong *s.* ein Achtel engl. Meile, 201 m.
furlough *s.* Urlaub *m.*
furnace *s.* Ofen, Schmelzofen *m.*
furnish *v.t.* versehen, ausstatten, (aus-)möblieren.
furnishing *s.* Ausrüstung *f.*; ~s *pl.* Ausrüstungsgegenstände, Einrichtungsgegenstände *m.pl.*
furniture *s.* Möbel *n.pl.*; Hausgerät *m.*
furred *a.* belegt (Zunge).
furrier *s.* Kürschner *m.*
furrow *s.* Furche *f.*; Runzel *f.*; ~ *v.t.* furchen.
furry *a.* pelzig.
further *a. & adv.* ferner, weiter; überdies; ~ to, in weiterer Bezugnahme auf (in Briefen); ~ *v.t.* befördern.
furtherance *s.* Förderung *f.*
furthermore *adv.* ferner, ausserdem.
furthest *a. & adv.* weitest; am weitesten.
furtive *a.*, ~ly *adv.* verstohlen.
fury *s.* Tollheit, Wut, *f.*
furze *s.* Stechginster *m.*
fuse *v.t. & i.* (ver)schmelzen; to ~ mines, Minen schärfen; ~ *s.* Zünder *m.*; (*elek.*) Sicherung *f.*
fuselage *s.* Rumpf (*m.*) des Flugzeuges.
fusible *a.* schmelzbar.
fusilier *s.* Füselier *m.*
fusion *s.* Schmelzen *n.*; (*fig.*) Verschmelzung *f.*
fuss *s.* Lärm *m.*, Getue *n.*
fussy *a.* unruhig, übertrieben geschäftig.
fustian *s.* Barchent *m.*; (*fig.*) Schwulst *m.*
futile *a.* nichtig, wertlos.
futility *s.* Nichtigkeit *f.*
future *a.* künftig; ~ *s.* Zukunft *f.*; ~s *pl.* Termingeschäfte *n.pl.*
futurity *s.* Zukunft *f.*
fuzz *s.* leichter Flaum.
fy *i.* pfui!

G

gab *s.* Mundwerk *n.*; (*fam.*) Geschwätzigkeit *f.*
gabble *v.i.* schnattern; plaudern; ~ *s.* Geschnatter, Geschwätz *n.*
gaberdine *s.* Gabardine (Stoff) *m.*
gable *s.* Giebel *m.*
gad *i.* wahrhaftig; ~ *v.i.* herumstreichen.
gad-fly *s.* Bremse *f.*
gadget *s.* technische Vorrichtung *f.*
gaff *s.* Fischhaken *m.*; Gaffel *f.*
gag *s.* Knebel *m.*; Improvisation (auf dem Theater) *f.*; ~ *v.i.* knebeln.
gage *s.* Unterpfand *n.*; ~ *v.t.* verpfänden.
gaiety *s.* Fröhlichkeit *f.*; Schmuck *m.*
gain *s.* Gewinn, Vorteil *m.*; ~ *v.t.* gewinnen, erlangen.

gainful *a.*, ~ly *adv.* einträglich.
gainsay *v.t.st.* widersprechen; leugnen.
gait *s.* Gangart, Gehart *f.*
gaiter *s.* Gamasche *f.*
gala *s.* (Gala) Fest *n.*
galaxy *s.* Milchstrasse *f.*; (*fig.*) glänzende Versammlung *f.*
gale *s.* frische Wind *m.*; Sturm *m.*; ~-warning *s.* Sturmwarnung *f.*
gall *s.* Galle *f.*; Gallapfel *m.*; Bitterkeit *f.*; ~ *v.t.* wund reiben; ärgern.
gallant *a.*, ~ly *adv.* tapfer, stattlich; ~ *a.*, *adv.* höflich; galant, artig (gegen Frauen); ~ *s.* Stutzer *m.*; Liebhaber *m.*
gallantry *s.* Tapferkeit *f.*; Artigkeit *f.*
gallery *s.* Galerie *f.*; Kombüse *f.*; Stollen (Bergwerk) *m.*
galley *s.* Galeere *f.*; Kombüse *f.*
galley(-proof) *s.* Fahnenabzug *m.* (*typ.*)
gallon *s.* Gallone (4½ Liter) *f.*
gallop *v.i.* galoppieren; ~ *s.* Galopp *m.*
gallows *s.* Galgen *m.*
gall-stone *s.* Gallenstein *m.*
galore *s.* *adv.* (in) Menge *f.*
galosh *s.* Überschuh, Gummischuh *m.*
galvanic *a.* galvanisch.
galvanize *v.t.* galvanisieren.
gamble *v.i.* (hoch) spielen; ~ *s.* Glückspiel *n.*
gambler *s.* Spieler *m.*
gambol *s.* Luftsprung *m.*; lustige Streich *m.*; ~ *v.i.* springen, hüpfen.
game *s.* Spiel *n.*; Scherz *m.*; jagdbare Tier *n.*; Wildbret *m.*; ~ of chance *s.* Glücksspiel *n.*; ~-law *s.* Jagdgesetz *n.*; ~ *a.* mutig; ~ *v.i.* spielen.
game-keeper *s.* Wildhüter *m.*
gamesome *a.*, ~ly *adv.* scherzhaft.
gamester *s.* Spieler *m.*
gammon *s.* (geräucherte) Schinken *m.* Schwindelei *f.*; ~ *v.t.* betrügen.
gamut *s.* Tonleiter *f.*
gander *s.* Gänserich *m.*
gang *s.* Bande *f.*; Trupp *m.*
gangrene *s.* (kalte) Brand *m.*
gangway *s.* Durchgang *m.*; (*nav.*) Laufplanke *f.*
gaol *s.* Gefängnis *n.*; ~-bird *s.* Gewohnheitsverbrecher *m.*
gaoler *s.* Kerkermeister *m.*
gap *s.* Lücke *f.*; Bresche *f.*; Riss *m.*
gape *v.i.* gaffen; gähnen; klaffen.
garage *s.* Garage *f.*
garb *s.* Gewand *n.*, Kleidung *f.*
garbage *s.* Dreck *m.*; Unrat *m.*
garble *v.t.* auslesen; entstellen.
garden *s.* Garten *m.*; ~ *v.i.* Gartenbau treiben.
gardener *s.* Gärtner *m.*
gardening *s.* Gärtnerei *f.*
gargle *v.t.* gurgeln.
gargoyle *s.* Wasserspeier *m.*, Abtraufe *f.*
garish *a.*, ~ly *adv.* grell; prunkend.

garland s. Girlande f.
garlic s. Knoblauch m.
garment s. Gewand n.
garner s. Kornboden m.; ~ v.t. aufspeichern.
garnish v.t. schmücken; versorgen; garnieren, ~ s. Verzierung f.
garniture s. Zubehör n., Schmuck m.; Garnierung f.
garret s. Dachstube f.
garrison s. Besatzung f.; ~ v.t. Besatzung einlegen.
garrulity s. Schwatzhaftigkeit f.
garrulous a. schwatzhaft.
garter s. Strumpfband n.; Hosenband n.; ~ v.t. aufbinden.
gas s. Gas n.
gas-bracket s. Gasarm m.
gas-burner s. Gasbrenner m.
gaseous a. gasförmig.
gas-fitter s. Gasrohrleger m.
gash s. Hieb m.; Schmarre f.; ~ v.t. tief verwunden.
gas-jet s. Gasflamme f.
gasket s. (mech.) (Flach-)Dichtung f.
gas-lighting s. Gasbeleuchtung f.
gas-meter s. Gasmesser m.
gasoline s. (Am.) Benzin n.; ~-station s. Tankstelle f.
gasometer s. Gasometer m.
gasp v.i. keuchen; schnappen.
gas-pipe s. Gasrohr n.
gastric a. gastrisch, Magen...
gastronomer s. Feinschmecker m.
gastronomy s. Feinschmeckerei f.
gas-works s.pl. Gasanstalt f.
gate s. Tor n.; Pforte f.
gateway s. Torweg m.
gather v.t. sammeln; pflücken, ernten; ~ v.i. sich versammeln; eitern.
gathering s. Sammeln n.; Versammlung f.; Kräuseln n., Geschwür n.
gaudy a., ~ly adv. geputzt, bunt.
gauge v.t. eichen; ausmessen; abschätzen; ~ s. Eichmass n.; Spurweite (der Eisenbahn) f.; (mech.) Lehre f.; **narrow-~ railway** s. Schmalspurbahn, Kleinbahn f.
gaunt a., ~ly adv. dürr, hager.
gauntlet s. Fehdehandschuh m.; to run the ~, Spiessruten laufen; to take up the ~, die Herausforderung annehmen.
gauze s. Gaze f.
gawk s. Tölpel m.
gawky a. ungeschickt, albern.
gay a., ~ly adv. munter, lustig; bunt.
gaze v.i. anstaunen, anstarren; ~ s. starrer Blick m.
gazelle s. Gazelle f.
gazette s. Zeitung f., Amtsblatt n.; ~ v.t. amtlich veröffentlichen.
gazetteer s. geographische Lexikon n.
gear s. Pferdegeschirr n.; Zeug n.; Trieb-

werk n.; (mech.) Zahnrad n.; (mech.) Übersetzung f., Gang m.; to put in another ~, einen anderen Gang einschalten; **high** ~, grosse Übersetzung (am Fahrrad) f.; **low** ~, kleine Übersetzung f.
gearbox s. (mech.) Getriebe(-kasten) m.
gearing s. Getriebe n.; Übersetzung f.
gelatine s. Gallerte f.
gelatinous a. gallertartig.
geld v.t. verschneiden.
gelding s. Wallach m.
gem s. Edelstein m.
gender s. Gattung f.; (gram.) Geschlecht n.
genealogical a. genealogisch, Stamm...
genealogy s. Genealogie f.
general a. allgemein; ~ s. General m.; Mädchen für alles n.
generality s. Allgemeinheit f.
generalize v.t. verallgemeinern.
generally adv. im allgemeinen.
general meeting s. Generalversammlung f.
generalship s. Feldherrnkunst f.
generate v.t. erzeugen.
generation s. Erzeugung f.; Geschlecht n.; Zeitalter n.
generator s. Erzeuger m.; Dampfkessel m.; Dynamomaschine f.
generic a. Gattungs...
generosity s. Edelmut m.; Freigebigkeit f.
generous a., ~ly adv. grossmütig; freigebig.
genesis s. Entstehung f.
genial a., ~ly adv. heiter; traulich.
genitals s.pl. Geschlechtsteile m.pl.
genitive s. Genitiv m.
genius s. Schutzgeist m.; Genie n.
genocide s. Völkermord m.
genteel a., ~ly adv. fein, vornehm.
gentian s. Enzian m.
gentile s. Heide m.; ~ a. heidnisch.
gentle a. vornehm; artig, fein; gütig; fromm (von Pferden).
gentleman s. Herr, Mann von Stande, feine Mann m.; Gentleman m.; gentlemen's agreement, freundschaftliche Übereinkommen n.
gentlemanlike a. wohlgesittet, anständig.
gentleness s. Artigkeit, Sanftmut f.
gentlewoman s. Dame aus gutem Hause f.
gentry s. obere Bürgerstand m.; Leute pl.
genuflexion s. Kniebeugung f.
genuine a., ~ly adv. echt, rein.
geographer s. Geograph m.
geographical a., ~ly adv. geographisch.
geography s. Erdkunde f.
geological a. geologisch.
geologist s. Geologe, Erdkundige m.
geology s. Erdkunde f.
geometric a. geometrisch.
geometrician s. Geometer m.

geometry s. Geometrie f.; plane ~, ebene Geometrie f.; solid ~, Stereometrie f.
geranium s. Geranium n.
germ s. Keim m.
german(e) a. verwandt; zugehörig; German a. deutsch; ~ silver, Neusilber n.
germicide s. bazillentötende Mittel n.
germinal a. Keim...
germinate v.i. keimen, sprossen.
gerund s. Gerundium n.
gestation s. Trächtigkeit f.
gesticulate v.i. Gebärden machen.
gesture s. Gebärde, Stellung f.
get v.t.st. erhalten, bekommen; veranstalten; besorgen; erzeugen; ~ v.i. werden; wohin geraten; sich wohin begeben; to ~ into, geraten; to ~ off, wegschaffen, entkommen; aussteigen; to ~ on, anziehen; vorwärts kommen; Erfolg haben; to ~ out, herausbringen; heraus(be)kommen; aussteigen; to ~ one's own back, sich rächen; to ~ over, überwinden; to ~ through, durchkommen; fertig bringen; to ~ together, zusammenbringen; zusammenkommen; to ~ up, aufsteigen; sich erheben; aufstehen.
get-at-able a. erreichbar, zugänglich.
get-up s. Aufmachung f.
gewgaw s. Tand m.
geyser s. Geiser, Badeofen m.
ghastly a. grässlich; geisterhaft.
gherkin s. (kleine) Essiggurke f.
ghost s. Geist m.; Gespenst n.
giant s. Riese m.
gibberish s. Kauderwelsch n.
gibbet s. Galgen m.; ~ v.t. hängen.
gibe v.t. & i. spotten, verhöhnen; ~ s. Hohn m.
giblets s.pl. Gänseklein n.
giddy a., ~ily adv. schwind[e]lig; leichtsinnig.
gift s. Gabe f.; Geschenk n.
gifted a. begabt.
gig s. Kabriolett n.; leichte Boot n.
gigantic a. riesenhaft.
giggle v.i. kichern.
gild v.t.ir. vergolden.
gilding, gilt s. Vergoldung f.
gill s. Kieme f.; Viertelpinte f.
gillyflower s. Goldlack m.; Levkoje f.
gilt-edged a. mündelsicher.
gimcrack s. Spielwerk n.; Tand m.
gimlet s. (Zwick)bohrer m.
gin s. Schlinge f.; Hebekran m.; Wacholderbranntwein m., Gin m.
ginger s. Ingwer m.; ~-beer, Ingwerbier n.
gingerbread s. Ingwerkuchen m.
gingerly a. sachte, zimperlich.
gipsy s. Zigeuner(in) m. (& f.).
giraffe s. Giraffe f.
gird v.t. & i.r. & ir. gürten; sticheln, schmähen.

girder s. Bindebalken m.; Träger m.
girdle s. Gürtel m.; ~ v.t. umgürten.
girl s. Mädchen n.
girlhood s. Mädchenjahre n.pl.; Mädchentum n.
girlish a., ~ly adv. mädchenhaft.
girth s. Gurt m.; Umfang m.
gist s. Hauptpunkt m.
give v.t.st. geben; schenken; to ~ away, verschenken; to ~ birth to, gebären; to ~ in, to ~ way, nachgeben; to ~ up, abgeben; aufgeben; to ~ oneself up, sich freiwillig stellen; ~ v.i. nachgeben; sich werfen (vom Holze); to ~ out, ausgehen.
given p. bestimmt, festgesetzt.
give-and-take s. gegenseitige Entgegenkommen n.
gizzard s. (Vogel-, Fisch-) Magen m.
glacial a. eisig; Gletscher..., Eis...
glacier s. Gletscher m.
glad a., ~ly adv. heiter, froh; angenehm.
gladden v.t. erfreuen, erheitern.
glade s. Lichtung f.
gladiator s. Fechter m.
gladiolus s. Gladiole f.
gladsome a. heiter, fröhlich.
glamour s. Zauber m., Blendwerk n.
glamorous a. bezaubernd.
glance s. Schimmer, Blitz m., Blick m.; ~ v.t. flüchtig anschauen; abgleiten; ~ v.i. schimmern; strahlen.
gland s. Drüse f.
glanders s.pl. Rotz (m.) (der Pferde).
glare s. Glanz, Schimmer m.; durchdringende Blick m.; ~ v.i. blendenden Glanz werfen; starr ansehen.
glaring a. grell; offenkundig.
glass s. Glas m.; Spiegel m.; Fernglas n.; ~ a. gläsern; ~ v.t. überglasen, verglasen.
glasses pl. Brille f.
glass-blower s. Glasbläser m.
glass-works s.pl. Glashütte f.
glassy a. gläsern, glasartig.
glaze v.t. verglasen; glätten; mit Glasscheiben versehen.
glazed paper s. Glanzpapier n.
glazier s. Glaser m.
gleam s. Strahl, Glanz m.; ~ v.i. strahlen, glänzen.
glean v.t. nachlesen, sammeln.
gleaner s. Ährenleser m.
glebe s. Erdscholle f.; Pfarrland n.
glee s. Fröhlichkeit f.; Scherz m.
glib a., ~ly adv. glatt; zungenfertig.
glide v.i. gleiten, schleichen; (avi.) einen Gleitflug (oder Segelflug) machen; ~ s. Gleitflug m.
glider s. Segelflugzeug m.
glimmer v.i. schimmern; ~ s. Schimmer m.; Glimmer m.
glimpse s. Schimmer m.; ~ v.i. schimmern.

glint s. Lichtschein m.; ~ v.i. glänzen.
glisten, glister v.i. glitzern, glänzen.
glitter v.i. glänzen, glitzern.
gloaming s. Zwielicht n.
gloat v.i. glotzen; to ~ over, sich weiden an.
globe s. Kugel f.; Globus m.; ~ trotter, Weltbummler m.
globular a. kugelförmig.
globule s. Kügelchen n.
gloom, gloominess s. Dunkelheit f.; Trübsinn m.
gloomy a., ~ily adv. düster; traurig.
glorification s. Verherrlichung f.
glorify v.t. verherrlichen; glorified messenger boy, bessere Briefträger m.
glorious a., ~ly adv. glorreich; herrlich.
glory s. Ruhm m.; Herrlichkeit f.; Stolz m.; ~ v.i. sich rühmen.
gloss s. Glanz m.; Politur f.; Glosse f.; ~ v.t. polieren; Glossen machen; to ~ over, beschönigen, bemänteln.
glossary s. Glossar, Wörterbuch n.
glossy a. glänzend, glatt.
glove s. Handschuh m.
glover s. Handschuhmacher m.
glow v.i. glühen; ~ s. Glut f.
glow-worm s. Glühwürmchen n.
gloze v.i. schmeicheln, beschönigen.
glue s. Leim m.; ~ v.t. leimen.
glum a. finster, mürrisch.
glut v.t. überladen; ~ s. Überfluss m.
glutton s. Fresser m.; Vielfrass m.
gluttonous a., ~ly adv. gefrässig.
gluttony s. Gefrässigkeit f.
glycerine s. Glyzerin n.
gnarled a. knorrig, ästig.
gnash v.t. knirschen.
gnat s. Mücke f.
gnaw v.t. nagen, zerfressen.
gnome s. Gnom, Erdgeist m.
go v.i.st. gehen; fahren; gelten; the sirens ~, die Sirenen gehen an; it goes without saying, es versteht sich von selbst; to ~ back on one's word, sein Versprechen nicht erfüllen od. zurücknehmen; to ~ down, fallen (Preise); to ~ fishing, zum Fischen gehen; to ~ in for, sich auf etwas legen; to ~ off, explodieren; to ~ on, weitermachen, fortfahren; to ~ sour, sauer werden; to ~ through, durchsehen; durchmachen; to ~ up, steigen (Preise); to ~ to law, eine Klage anstrengen; ~ s. Gang, Lauf m.; Bewegung f., Schwung, Schneid m.
goad s. Treibestachel m.; ~ v.t. stacheln; quälen.
go-ahead a. rührig, strebsam.
goal s. Mal n.; Grenzpfahl m.; Ziel n.; (Fussball) Tor n.
goal-keeper s. Torwächter m.
goat s. Ziege f.; he-goat, Ziegenbock m.
gobble v.t. gierig verschlingen.

go-between s. Vermittler m.
goblet s. Becher m.
goblin s. Kobold m.
God s. Gott m.
godchild s. Patenkind n.
goddess s. Göttin f.
godfather s. Pate m.
godhead s. Gottheit f.
godless a. gottlos.
godlike a. göttlich.
godly a. gottselig, fromm.
godmother s. Patin f.
godsend s. gute Fund, wahre Segen m.
goggle v.i. glotzen; die Augen verdrehen; ~s s.pl. Schutzbrille f.
goitre s. Kropf m.
gold s. Gold n.
golden a. golden.
goldfinch s. Stieglitz m.
goldfish s. Goldfisch m.
gold-leaf s. Goldblatt, Blattgold n.
goldsmith s. Goldschmied m.
gold-standard s. Goldstandard m.
golf s. Golf n.; ~-course, ~-links, Golfplatz m.; ~-club s. Golfschläger; Golf Klub m.
golfer s. Golfspieler m.
golliwog s. Groteskpuppe f.
gondola s. Gondel f.
gondolier s. Gondolier m.
gone p. & a. weg, fort; vergangen.
gong s. Gong m. & n.
good a. gut, wohl; recht; ~-Friday, Karfreitag m.; be ~ enough, seien Sie so freundlich; to make ~, vergüten, (Versprechen) erfüllen; sich durchsetzen, sich bewähren; ~ s. Gut n.; this is no ~, das ist nichts wert; ~s pl. Güter pl.; Habe f.; Waren pl.
good-bye adv. & s. lebe wohl!; Lebewohl n.
good-looking a. hübsch, schön.
goodly a. schön; beträchtlich.
good-natured a. gutmütig.
goodness s. Güte, Gütigkeit f.; for ~ sake, um Himmels willen!; ~ gracious, gütiger Himmel!; thank ~, Gott sei Dank!
goods station s. Güterbahnhof m.
goods train s. Güterzug m.
goodwill s. gute Ruf einer Firma m.
goose s. Gans f.
gooseberry s. Stachelbeere f.
goose-step s. Paradeschritt m.
Gordian a. gordisch, verwickelt.
gore s. geronnene Blut n.; Zwickel m.
gorge s. Kehle, Gurgel f.; Felsenschlucht f.; ~ v.t. verschlucken; vollstopfen.
gorgeous a., ~ly adv. glänzend, prächtig.
gorilla s. Gorilla m.
gormandize v.i. fressen.
gorse s. Stechginster m.
gory a. blutig, mörderisch.

gosling s. Gänschen n.
Gospel s. Evangelium n.
gossamer s. Sommerfäden m.pl.
gossip s. Gevatter m.; Klatschbase f.; Klatsch m.; ~ v.i. klatschen.
Gothic a. gotisch; roh; **Gothic letters** pl. (typ.) Fraktur f.
gourd s. Kürbis m.
gourmand s. Fresser, Feinschmecker m.
gout s. Gicht f.
gouty a. gichtisch.
govern v.t. regieren, lenken, beherrschen; ~ v.i. herrschen.
governess s. Erzieherin f.
governing body s. Vorstand (Krankenhaus, Schule) m.
government s. Regierungsform, Regierung f.; ~-**property**, Behördeneigentum n.
governor s. Gouverneur m.; (fam.) Chef, Vater m.; Prinzipal m.
gown s. Talar m.; Frauenkleid n.; Abendtoilette f.
grab v.t. plötzlich greifen, packen; ~ s. (fig.) Räuberei f.
grace s. Gnade f.; Anmut f.; Tischgebet n.; Your ~, (Titel) Euer Gnaden; ~ v.t. begünstigen; schmücken.
graceful a., ~**ly** adv. anmutig.
gracious a., ~**ly** adv. gnädig, anmutig.
gradation s. Steigerung f.; Abstufung f.; Ablaut m.
grade s. Grad, Rang m.; ~ v.t. abstufen, einteilen.
gradient s. Steigung f.
gradual a., ~**ly** adv. allmählich.
graduate v.t. in Grade teilen; abstufen; ~ v.i. einen Grad erlangen; ~ s. Person (f.), mit akademischem Grad.
graduation s. Stufengang m.; Promotion f.
graft s. Pfropfreis n.; ~ v.t. pfropfen; (fig.) Schiebung f.
grain s. Korn, Samenkorn n.; Gran m. & n.; Holzfaser f.
grain-elevator s. Getreidespeicher m.
grammar s. Grammatik f.
grammar-school s. höhere Schule f.
grammarian s. Grammatiker m.
grammatical a., ~**ly** adv. grammatisch.
gramme, gram s. Gramm n.
gramophone s. Grammophon n.
granary s. Kornboden m.; Kornkammer (bes. übertr.) f.
grand a. gross, erhaben; grossartig.
grand-child s. Enkel m.
granddaughter s. Enkelin f.
grandduke s. Grossherzog m.
grandee s. Grande (in Spanien) m.; hohe Herr m.
grandeur s. Grösse f.; Pracht f.
grandfather s. Grossvater m.
grandiloquent a. grossprecherisch.
grandiose a. hochtrabend; grossartig.

grandmother s. Grossmutter f.
grandson s. Enkel m.
grange s. Meierhof m.; Scheune f.
granite s. Granit m.
granny s. (fam.) Grossmütterchen n.
grant v.t. zugestehen; bewilligen, verleihen; ~ s. Bewilligung f.
grantee s. Privilegierte m.
grant-in-aid s. Hilfsunterstützung, Notunterstützung f.
granulate v.t. (v.i. sich) körnen.
granulated sugar s. Griesszucker m.
grape s. Weinbeere f.; bunch of ~s, Weintraube f.
grape-shot s. Kartätsche f.
graphic a. graphisch, genau; anschaulich; ~ representation, graphische Darstellung f., Kurvenbild n.
graphite s. Graphit m.
grapple v.t. packen, ergreifen; ~ v.i. ringen (mit).
grasp s. Griff m.; Bereich m.; Fassungskraft f.; ~ v.t. greifen, fassen; ~ v.i. haschen; streben.
grasping a. gierig, habsüchtig.
grass s. Gras n.
grasshopper s. Heuschrecke f.
grassplot s. Rasenplatz m.
grass-widow s. Strohwitwe f.
grate s. Feuerrost m.; ~ v.t. vergittern; raspeln; kränken; ~ v.i. knirschen.
grateful a., ~**ly** adv. dankbar; angenehm.
grater s. Reibeisen n.
gratification s. Befriedigung f.
gratify v.t. befriedigen; willfahren.
gratifying a. erfreulich.
grating s. Gitter n.; ~ a., ~**ly** adv. verdriesslich, widrig.
gratis a. unentgeltlich.
gratitude s. Dankbarkeit f.
gratuitous a., ~**ly** adv. unentgeltlich.
gratuity s. Trinkgeld n.
grave a. feierlich, ernst; tief (vom Tone); ~ s. Grab n.; ~ v.t. graben.
grave-digger s. Totengräber m.
gravel s. Kies m.
gravestone s. Grabstein m.
gravitate v.i. gravitieren, zuneigen.
gravitation s. Schwerkraft f.
gravity s. Ernst m.; Schwere f.; Wichtigkeit f.
gravy s. Sauce f., Bratentunke f.; Saft des Fleisches m.; ~ boat s. Sauciere f.
graze v.i. weiden, grasen; ~ v.t. abweiden; streifen.
grazier s. Viehmäster m.
grease s. Fett n., Wagenschmiere f.; ~ v.t. schmieren; bestechen.
greaseproof paper s. Butterbrotpapier n.
greasy a., ~**ly** adv. fett, schmierig.
great a. gross; ~-**grandfather, etc.** s. Urgrossvater, etc.
great coat s. Überrock m., Überzieher m.

greatly *adv.* sehr.
greatness *s.* Grösse, Macht *f.*
greed, greediness *s.* Gier(igkeit) *f.*
greedy *a.*, ~ily *adv.* gierig.
green *a.*, ~ly *adv.* grün; frisch; unreif; unerfahren; ~ *s.* Rasenplatz *m.*; ~s *s.pl.* Gemüse *n.*
greengage *s.* Reineclaude (Pflaume) *f.*
greengrocer *s.* Gemüsehändler *m.*
greenhorn *s.* grüne Junge *m.*
greenhouse *s.* Gewächshaus *n.*
green-sickness *s.* Bleichsucht *f.*
greet *v.t.* grüssen.
greeting *s.* Begrüssung *f.*, Grüss *n.*
gregarious *a.*, ~ly *adv.* gesellig.
grenade *s.* Granate *f.*
grenadier *s.* Grenadier *m.*
grey *a.* grau; ~ *s.* Grau *n.*; Grauschimmel *m.*
greyhound *s.*, Windhund *m.*
greyish *a.* etwas grau, gräulich.
grid, gridiron *s.* Bratrost *m.*
grief *s.* Gram, Kummer *m.*
grievance *s.* Beschwerde *f.*
grieve *v.t.* kränken; ~ *v.i.* sich grämen.
grievous *a.*, ~ly *adv.* schmerzlich.
griffin *s.* Greif *m.*
grill *v.t.* rösten; ~ *s.* Bratrost *m.*
grille *s.* Gitter *n.*
grim *a.*, ~ly *adv.* grimmig.
grimace *s.* Fratze, Grimasse *f.*
grimalkin *s.* alte Katze *f.*
grime *s.* Schmutz *m.*; ~ *v.t.* beschmutzen.
grimy *a.* schmutzig, russig.
grin *s.* Grinsen *n.*; ~ *v.i.* grinsen.
grind *v.t.st.* mahlen; (Orgel) drehen; (teeth) knirschen; schleifen; quälen.
grindstone *s.* Schleifstein *m.*
grip *s.* Griff; ~ *v.t.* fest greifen.
gripe *v.t.* greifen, kneipen; ~ *s.* Griff *m.*; ~s *pl.* Bauchgrimmen *n.*
grisly *a.* scheusslich.
grist *s.* Mahlkorn *n.*; (fig.) Unterhalt *m.*
gristle *s.* Knorpel *m.*
grit *s.* Griess *m.*; (fig.) Festigkeit *f.*
grizzled, grizzly *a.* grau; ~ bear *s.* graue Bär *m.*
groan *v.i.* seufzen, stöhnen; ~ *s.* Seufzer *m.*; Murren *n.*
grocer *s.* Kolonialwarenhändler *m.*
groceries *s.pl.* Kolonialwaren *f.*
grog *s.* Grog *m.*
groin *s.* Schamleiste *f.*; Gewölbrippe *f.*; ~ed arch, Kreuzbogen *m.*
groom *s.* Aufwärter *m.*; Stallknecht *m.*; ~ *v.t.* ein Pferd warten.
groove *s.* Rinne *f.*; Nut *f.*; (fig.) Gleis *n.*; ~ *v.t.* auskehlen, falzen.
grope *v.i. & t.* tappen, tasten.
gross *a.*, ~ly *adv.* dick; dumm; grob; zotig; Brutto; ~ weight *s.* Bruttogewicht *n.*; ~ *s.* Ganze *n.*; Masse *f.*; Gros *n.*

grotesque *a.*, ~ly *adv.* grotesk.
grotto *s.* Grotte *f.*
ground *s.* Grund, Boden *m.*; (Beweis-) Grund *m.*; (elek.) Erde *f.*; ~s *pl.* Bodensatz; ~ *v.t.* gründen; (elek.) erden.
ground-floor *s.* Erdgeschoss *n.*
ground-forces *pl.* (mil.) Erdtruppen, Erdwaffen *pl.*
ground glass, ground disc *s.* (phot.) Mattscheibe *f.*
grounding *s.* Anfangsgründe *m.pl.*
ground-landlord *s.* Grundeigentümer *m.*
groundless *a.*, ~ly *adv.* grundlos.
groundnut *s.* Erdnuss *f.*
ground-plan *s.* Grundriss *m.*
ground-rent *s.* Grundzins *m.*
groundwork *s.* Grundlage *f.*
group *s.* Gruppe *f.*; (avi.) Gruppe *f.*; ~-captain *s.* Gruppenkommandeur *m.*; ~ *v.t.* gruppieren.
grouping *s.* Gruppierung *f.*
grouse *s.* schottische Moorhuhn *n.*
grove *s.* Hain *m.*, Gehölz *n.*
grovel *v.i.* kriechen.
grow *v.i.st.* wachsen; werden; ~ *v.t.* bauen, kultivieren.
growl *v.i.* brummen, knurren; ~ *s.* Brummen *n.*
grown-up *a.* erwachsen.
growth *s.* Wachstum *n.*, Wuchs *m.*; Erzeugnis *n.*; Gewächs *n.*
grub *s.* Larve, Made *f.*; Wurm *m.*; Futter *n.*; (sl.) Essen *n.*; ~ *v.t.* wühlen; futtern.
grudge *v.i.*; ~ *v.t.* missgönnen, ungern tun; ~ *s.* Groll, Neid *m.*
gruel *s.* Haferschleim *m.*, Grütze *f.*
gruelling *a.* erschöpfend, aufreibend.
gruesome *a.* grausig.
gruff *a.*, ~ly *adv.* mürrisch.
grumble *v.i.* murren, brummen.
grumpy *a.* mürrisch, böse.
grunt *v.i.* grunzen.
guarantee *s.* Bürge *m.*; Bürgschaft, Pfandsumme *f.*; ~ *v.t.* verbürgen.
guaranty *s.* Bürgschaft *f.*
guard *s.* Wache *f.*; Schutz *m.*; Stichblatt (Degen) *n.*; Garde *f.*; Schaffner *m.*; ~ of honour *s.* Ehrenwache *f.*; on one's ~, auf der Hut; to be on ~, Wache stehen; ~s *pl.* Leibwache *f.*; ~ *v.t.* bewachen, beschützen; ~ *v.i.* auf der Hut sein.
guarded *adv.* behutsam.
guardian *s.* Aufseher *m.*; Vormund *m.*; Beschützer *m.*; ~-angel Schutzengel *m.*; to place under the care of a ~, unter Vormundschaft stellen.
guardianship *s.* Vormundschaft *f.*
guardsman *s.* Gardist *m.*
gudgeon *s.* Gründling (Fisch) *m.*; Tölpel *m.*
guerdon *s.* Lohn *m.*
guerilla *s.* Freischärler, Partisan *m.*

guess *v.i.* & *t.* mutmassen, (er)raten; ~ *s.*
Vermutung *f.*
guest *s.* Gast *m.*
guffaw *s.* rohe Gelächter *n.*
guidance *s.* Führung, Leitung *f.*
guide *v.t.* leiten, führen; ~ *s.* Führer *m.*;
girl ~, Mädchenwandervogel *m.*
guide-book *s.* Reiseführer *m.*
guided missile *s.* (*mil.*) Fernsteuerwaffe *f.*
guild *s.* Gilde, Innung *f.*
guilder *s.* holländische Gulden *m.*
guile *s.* Betrug *m.*; Arglist *f.*
guileless *a.* arglos, ehrlich.
guillotine *s.* Guillotine *f.*, Fallbeil *n.*
guilt *s.* Schuld *f.*
guilty *a.*, ~ily *adv.* schuldig.
guinea *s.* Guinee *f.* (=21 shillings).
guinea-pig *s.* Meerschweinchen *n.*
guise *s.* Gewand *n.*; Maske *f.*
guitar *s.* Gitarre *f.*
gulf *s.* Meerbusen *m.*; Abgrund *m.*
gull *s.* Möwe *f.*; Tropf *m.*; ~ *v.t.* betrügen.
gullet *s.* Gurgel *f.*; Schlund *m.*
gullible *a.* leichtgläubig.
gully *s.* Abfluss, Graben *m.*
gulp *s.* Schluck, Zug *m.*; ~ *v.t.* schlucken.
gum *s.* Gummi *n.*; Zahnfleisch *n.*; ~ *v.t.*
gummieren.
gumption *s.* Verstand *m.*
gun *s.* Geschütz *n.*; Kanone *f.*; Flinte *f.*,
Gewehr *n.*; (*Am.*) Revolver *m.*; ~-
licence *s.* Waffenschein *m.*; ~-running
s. Waffenschmuggel *m.*
gun-boat *s.* Kanonenboot *n.*
gun-carriage *s.* Lafette *f.*
gun-cotton *s.* Schiessbaumwolle *f.*
gunner *s.* Kanonier *m.*
gunpowder *s.* Schiesspulver *n.*
gun-shot *s.* Schussweite *f.*
gunsmith *s.* Büchsenmacher *m.*
gunwale *s.* (*nav.*) Schanzdeck *n.*
gurgle *v.i.* gurgeln; rieseln.
gush *v.i.* strömen; ~ *s.* Guss *m.*
gust *s.* Windstoss *m.*; Bö *f.*
gustation *s.* Schmecken *n.*
gusto *s.* Eifer *m.*, Vergnügen *n.*
gut *s.* Darm *m.*; Eingeweide *n.*; ~ *v.t.* ausweiden; ausbrennen (ein Haus); gutted
p. ausgebrannt.
gutter *s.* Rinne, Gosse *f.*
guttural *a.* Kehl...; ~ *s.* Kehllaut *m.*
guzzle *v.i.* schlemmen, schwelgen; ~ *v.t.*
verschlingen.
gymkhana *s.* Sportfest *n.*
gymnasium *s.* Turnhalle *f.*
gymnastic(al) *a.*, ~ly *adv.* gymnastisch.
gymnastics *s.pl.* Turnkunst *f.*
gym-shoe *s.* Turnschuh *m.*
gynæcologist *s.* Frauenarzt *m.*
gypsum *s.* Gips *m.*
gyrate *v.i.* wirbeln, kreiseln.
gyroscope *s.* Kreiselkompass *m.*
gyve *s.* Fessel *f.*

H

haberdasher *s.* Kurzwarenhändler *m.*
haberdashery *s.* Kurzwaren *m.*
habit *s.* Gewohnheit *f.*; Zustand *m.*;
Anzug *m.*; *by* ~, aus Gewohnheit.
habitable *a.* bewohnbar.
habitation *s.* Wohnung *f.*
habitual *a.*, ~ly *adv.* gewohnt.
habituate *v.t.* gewöhnen.
hack *v.t.* hacken; ~ *s.* Hacke *f.*; Einschnitt
m.
hackle *s.* Hechel *f.*; ~ *v.t.* hecheln.
hackney-coach *s.* Mietskutsche *f.*
hackneyed *a.* abgedroschen.
hack-saw *s.* Metallsäge *f.*
hack-writer *s.* Lohnschreiber *m.*
haddock *s.* Schellfisch *m.*
hæmorrhage *s.* Blutsturz *m.*
hæmorrhoids *s.pl.* Hämorrhoiden *f.pl.*
haft *s.* Stiel *m.*; Heft *n.*
hag *s.* Hexe *f.*
haggard *a.*, ~ly *adv.* wild; hager.
haggle *v.i.* streiten; feilschen.
hail *s.* Hagel *m.*; ~ *v.i.* hageln; ~ *s.* Ruf
m.; *within* ~, in Rufweite; ~! *i.* Glück!
Heil!; ~ *v.t.* grüssen; anrufen; stammen;
to ~ *a taxi,* ein Auto herbeirufen.
hailstone *s.* Hagelkorn *n.*
hair *s.* Haar *n.*; *to do one's* ~, sich die
Haare machen; ~-style, ~-do, Frisur
f.; long-~ed *a.* langhaarig; short-~ed
a. kurzhaarig.
hair-dresser *s.* Haarkünstler, Friseur *m.*
hairpin *s.* Haarnadel *f.*; ~-bend S-Kurve
f.
hair-splitting *s.* Wortklauberei *f.*
hair-tonic *s.* Haarwuchsmittel *n.*
hairy *a.* haarig, hären.
halberd *s.* Hellebarde *f.*
halcyon *s.* Eisvogel *m.*; ~ *a.* still, friedlich.
hale *a.* heil, frisch, gesund.
half *a.* halb; ~-bound, in Halbfranzband;
~ *past five,* halb sechs; ~ *s.* Hälfte *f.*
half-back *s.* (Fussball) Läufer *m.*
half-blood *s.* Halbblut *n.*
half-breed *s.* Mischling *m.*
half-calf *s.* Halbfranzband *m.*
half-cast *s.* Halbblut *n.*
half-hearted *a.* mutlos, verzagt.
half-pay *s.* Halbsold *m.*
halfpenny *s.* halbe Penny *m.*
halfway *adv.* auf halbem Wege.
half-witted *a.* einfältig.
halibut *s.* Heilbutte *f.*
hall *s.* Saal *m.*; Halle *f.*; (Guts-) Herrenhaus *n.*; Hausflur *f.*
hall-mark *s.* Feingehaltstempel *m.*
halloo! *i.* hallo!; ~ *v.t.* anrufen.
hallow *v.t.* weihen, heiligen.
hall-porter *s.* Hotelportier *m.*
hallucination *s.* Halluzination *f.*

halo *s.* Hof (um Sonne oder Mond), *m.*; Heiligenschein *m.*

halt *i.* halt!; *s.* Halt *m.*; ~ *v.i.* anhalten; hinken; zögern.

halter *s.* Strick *m.*; Halfter *f. & m.*

halve *v.t.* halbieren.

ham *s.* Schenkel *m.*; Schinken *m.*

hamlet *s.* Weiler *m.*, Dörfchen *n.*

hammer *s.* Hammer *m.*; Hahn (am Gewehr) *m.*; ~ *v.t.* hämmern, schmieden.

hammock *s.* Hängematte *f.*

hamper *v.t.* belästigen, behindern.

hamster *s.* Hamster *m.*

hamstring *s.* Flechse *f.*; ~ *v.t.* die Fussflechsen durchschneiden.

hand *s.* Hand *f.*; Handschrift *f.*; Uhrzeiger *m.*; Richtung, Seite *f.*; Arbeiter *m.*; Karten (*f.pl.*) eines Spielers; *at* ~, zur Hand, nah; *at the* ~*s of*, von Seiten; *by* ~, mit der Hand; *signed in his own* ~, eigenhändig unterschrieben; *on* ~, vorrätig, auf Lager; *to give (lend) a* ~, helfen, zugreifen; *to have on one's* ~*s*, auf dem Hals haben; *on the one* ~, *on the other* ~, einerseits, andererseits; *out of* ~, unlenkbar; *off* ~, aus dem Stegreif; *the upper* ~, die Oberhand ~ *v.t.* einhändigen; reichen; *to* ~ *down (order, decision)*, (Entscheidung) erlassen; *to* ~ *over*, übergeben, überstellen.

hand-bag *s.* Handtasche *f.*

hand-bill *s.* (Werbe-) Zettel *m.*

hand-book *s.* Handbuch *n.*

hand-camera *s.* Handkamera *f.*

handcuff *s.* Handfessel *f.*

handful *s.* Handvoll *f.*

hand-grenade *s.* Handgranate *f.*

handicap *s.* Vorgabe *f.*; Belastung *f.*; (*fig.*) Behinderung *f.*; Vorgaberennen; *to* ~, *v.t.* belasten; hemmen.

handicraft *s.* Handwerk *n.*

handiwork *s.* Handarbeit *f.*

handkerchief *s.* Taschentuch *n.*

handle-bar *s.* Lenkstange *f.*

hand-made paper *s.* Büttenpapier *n.*

handmaid *s.* Magd *f.*

hand-rail *s.* Geländer *n.*

handsel *s.* Handgeld *n.*

hand-shake *s.* Händedruck *m.*

handsome *a.*, ~ly *adv.* schön, artig.

hand-tailored *a.* handgeschneidert.

hand-to-hand fighting *s.* Handgemenge *n.*

handle *s.* Stiel *m.*; Türknopf *m.*; Handhabe *f.*; Griff *m.*; Kurbel *f.*; ~ *v.t.* handhaben, angreifen; behandeln; bearbeiten.

handwriting *s.* Handschrift *f.*

handy *a.*, ~ily *adv.* geschickt; handlich.

hang *s.* Abhang *m.*; Fall, Sitz (von Kleidern) *m.*; Sinn *m.*, Bedeutung *f.*; *to get the* ~ *of it*, hinter etwas kommen, etwas loskriegen; ~ *v.t.* hängen, behängen; *to* ~ *oneself*, sich aufhängen; ~ *v.i.* hängen, schweben.

hangar *s.* Flugzeughalle *f.*

hanger *s.* Henkel, Haken *m.*

hanger-on *s.* Schmarotzer *m.*

hangman *s.* Henker *m.*

hangover *s.* Katzenjammer *m.*

hanker *v.i.* sich sehnen, trachten.

haphazard *s.* Ungefähr *n.*; Zufall *m.*

hapless *a.* unglücklich.

happen *v.i.* sich ereignen; *I* ~*ed to be there*, ich war zufällig da.

happiness *s.* Glückseligkeit *f.*; Glück *n.*

happy *a.*, ~ily *adv.* glücklich.

harangue *s.* Ansprache *f.*; ~ *v.t.* anreden.

harass *v.t.* quälen, abmatten.

harbinger *s.* Vorbote *m.*

harbour *s.* Hafen *m.*; Zufluchtsort *m.*; ~-dues *pl.* Hafengebühren *f.pl.*; ~ *v.t.* beherbergen; hegen; ~ *v.i.* vor Anker gehen.

hard *a. & adv.* hart; mühsam; ~up, in Not, ohne Geld; ~ *cash s.* klingende Münze *f.*; ~ *coal s.* Steinkohle *f.*; ~ *drinks pl.* (*Am.*) alkoholische Getränke *n. pl.*; ~ *rubber s.* Hartgummi *m.*

harden *v.t.* härten; ~ *v.i.* hart werden, sich verhärten; (Preise) anziehen.

hardihood *s.* Unerschrockenheit *f.*

hardly *adv.* kaum.

hardness *s.* Härte *f.*

hardship *s.* Beschwerde *f.*; Ungemach *n.*

hardware *s.* Metallwaren *f.pl.*

hardy *a.*, ~ily *adv.* hart, fest, stark; tapfer kühn; abgehärtet.

hare *s.* Hase *m.*

hare-bell *s.* Glockenblume *f.*

hare-brained *a.* albern.

hare-lip *s.* Hasenscharte *f.*

harem *s.* Harem *m.*

haricot *s.* weisse Bohne *f.*

hark *v.i.* horchen; ~! *i.* horch!

harlequin *s.* Harlekin *m.*

harlot *s.* Hure *f.*

harm *s.* Unrecht, Leid *n.*; Schaden *m.*; *to do* ~, schaden; ~ *v.t.* verletzen. beeinträchtigen.

harmful *a.*, ~ly *adv.* schädlich.

harmless *a.* unschädlich, arglos, harmlos; unverletzt; *to render* ~, (Granate) blind machen.

harmonic *a.* wohlklingend.

harmonics *s.pl.* Harmonielehre *f.*

harmonious *a.* harmonisch.

harmonize *v.t.* in Einklang bringen; ~ *v.i.* übereinstimmen, harmonieren.

harmonium *s.* Harmonium *n.*

harmony *s.* Einklang *m.*

harness *s.* Pferdegeschirr *n.*; Harnisch *m.*; ~ *v.t.* anschirren.

harp *s.* Harfe *f.*; ~ *v.i.* auf der Harfe spielen; anspielen; berühren.

harpist *s.* Harfenspieler(in) *m.* (& *f.*).
harpoon *s.* Harpune *f.*; ~ *v.t.* harpunieren.
harpy *s.* Harpyie *f.*
harridan *s.* alte Vettel *f.*
harrow *s.* Egge *f.*; ~ *v.t.* eggen; quälen, heimsuchen.
harry *v.t.* plündern, verheeren; quälen.
harsh *a.*, ~ly *adv.* herbe, rauh; barsch.
hart *s.* Hirsch *m.*
hartshorn *s.* Hirschhorn *n.*
harum-scarum *a.* Hals über Kopf, hastig.
harvest *s.* Ernte *f.*; ~ *v.t.* ernten.
harvester *s.* Schnitter *m.*; Gnitze *f.*
harvest-home *s.* Erntefest *n.*
hash *v.t.* zerhacken; ~ *s.* gehackte Fleisch *n.*, Haschee *n.*
hasp *s.* Haspe *f.*
haste *s.* Eile, Hast *f.*; Eifer *m.*
hasten *v.n.* eilen; ~ *v.t.* beschleunigen.
hasty *a.*, ~ily *adv.* eilig; hastig; hitzig.
hat *s.* Hut *m.*; ~-box *s.* Hutschachtel *f.*; *to raise one's ~ to a person*, vor einem den Hut abnehmen.
hatch *v.t.* brüten, ausbrüten; schraffieren; ~ *v.i.* im Werke sein; ~ *s.* Brut *f.*; Schutzbrett *n.*, Luke *f.*
hatchet *s.* Beil *n.*; Axt *f.*
hatchway *s.* Luke *f.*
hate *s.* Hass *m.*; ~ *v.t.* hassen.
hateful *a.*, ~ly *adv.* verhasst, gehässig.
hatred *s.* Hass *m.*
hatter *s.* Hutmacher *m.*
haughty *a.*, -ily *adv.* stolz, hochmütig.
haul *v.t.* ziehen, schleppen; ~ *s.* Zug *m.*; Schleppen *n.*
haulage *s.* Transport *m.*; ~-contractor *s.* Transportunternehmer *m.*
haunch *s.* Hüfte *f.*; Schenkel *m.*; ~ of venison *s.* Keule *f.*
haunt *s.* Aufenthalt *m.*; Lager, Nest *n.*; ~ *v.t.* oft besuchen; beschweren, plagen; umgehen, spuken in.
haunted *p.* & *a.* nicht geheuer; *a ~ house*, ein Haus, in welchem es spukt.
hautboy *s.* Hoboe *f.*
have *v.t.ir* haben; halten; handeln; bekommen; lassen; ~ *to*, müssen.
haven *s.* Hafen *m.*; Freistätte *f.*
haversack *s.* Brotbeutel *m.*
havoc *s.* Verwüstung, Zerstörung *f.*
haw *s.* Hagebutte *f.*
hawk *s.* Habicht *m.*; Falke *m.*; ~ *v.i.* mit Falken jagen; hausieren.
hawker *s.* Hausierer *m.*
hawser *s.* (*nav.*) Kabeltau *n.*, Trosse *f.*
hawthorn *s.* Hagedorn *m.*
hay *s.* Heu *n.*
hay-cock *s.* Heuschober *m.*
hay-fever *s.* Heuschnupfen *m.*
hay-loft *s.* Heuboden *m.*
hay-rick *s.* Heufeime *f.*
hay-stack *s.* Heuschober *m.*

hazard *s.* Ungefähr *n.*; Gefahr *f.*; ~ *v.t.* aufs Spiel setzen.
hazardous *a.*, ~ly *adv.* gefährlich.
haze *s.* leichte Nebel *m.*
hazel *s.* Haselstaude *f.*; ~ *a.* nussbraun, Hasel...
hazel-nut *s.* Haselnuss *f.*
hazy *a.* nebelig; dunstig; unbestimmt.
he *pn.* er; ~ *s.* Männchen *n.*
head *s.* Haupt *n.*; Kopf *m.*; Spitze (einer Kolonne etc.) *f.*; Gipfel *m.*; Schiffschnabel *m.*; Kapitel *n.*; Punkt *m.*; Titel (Buch, Abschnitt) *m.*; Stück *n.*; Vorsteher *m.*; Ober...; *to bring to a ~*, zur Entscheidung bringen; *he could not make ~ or tail of it*, er konnte daraus nicht klug werden; ~ *v.t.* & *i.* anführen, befehligen; mit einer Überschrift versehen; (*nav.*) einen Kurs nehmen.
headache *s.* Kopfweh *n.*
head-dress *s.* Kopfputz *m.*
header *s.* Kopfsprung.
heading *s.* Überschrift *f.*
headland *s.* Vorgebirge *n.*
headless *a.* kopflos, unbesonnen.
headlights *pl.* Scheinwerferlicht (*Auto*) *n.*
headlong *a.* & *adv.* kopfüber.
headmaster *s.* Schuldirektor *m.*
headmistress *s.* Schulvorsteherin *f.*
headphone *s.* Kopfhörer *m.*
headquarters *pl.* Hauptgeschäftsstelle, Zentrale *f.*; Hauptquartier *n.*; vorgesetzte Stelle *f.*
headstrong *a.* halsstarrig.
head-waiter *s.* Oberkellner *m.*
headway *s.* Fortschritt *m.*
head-wind *s.* Gegenwind *m.*
heady *a.* hastig; starrköpfig.
heal *v.t.* & *i.* heilen, zuheilen.
health *s.* Gesundheit *f.*
health-insurance *s.* Krankenversicherung *f.*
health resort *s.* Kurort *m.*
healthy *a.*, ~ily *adv.* gesund.
heap *s.* Haufen *m.*; ~ *v.t.* häufen.
hear *v.t.* & *i.ir.* hören, anhören; erfahren; verhören; *to ~ a case*, (*law*) einen Fall verhandeln.
hearing *s.* Hören *n.*; Gehör *n.*; Verhör *n.*, Verhandlung *f.* (*law*); Hörweite *f.*; *hard of ~*, schwerhörig; ~-aids *pl.* Gehörhilfen *f.pl.*; *to fix a ~*, (*law*) einen Termin anberaumen.
hearken *v.i.* zuhören, horchen.
hearsay *s.* Hörensagen *n.*; *by ~*, vom Hörensagen.
hearse *s.* Leichenwagen *m.*, Bahre *f.*
heart *s.* Herz *n.*; Gemüt *n.*; *at ~*, im Grunde; *by ~*, auswendig; *to take ~*, Mut fassen; ~s *pl.* Coeur (in der Karte).
heartbreaking *a.* = heartrending.
heart-burn(ing) *s.* Sodbrennen *n.*; Groll *m.*

heart-felt a. innig empfunden, herzlich.
hearth s. Boden (m.) des Kamins; ~ **rug** s. Kaminvorleger m.
heartless a., ~**ly** adv. grausam; zaghaft.
heartrending a. herzzerreissend.
hearty a., ~**ily** adv. herzlich, aufrichtig.
heat s. Hitze f.; Lauf m., Rennen n.; Brunst(zeit) f.; (phys.) Wärme; Blutwärme; ~ s. Blutwärme; **body**~ s. Körperwärme f.; ~**proof** a., wärmesicher; ~ v.t. heizen; erhitzen.
heath s. Heide f.
heathen s. Heide m.; ~ a. heidnisch.
heather s. Heidekraut n., Heide f.
heating s. Heizung f.; ~**-unit** s. Heizkörper m.
heave v.t. & r.st. heben; erheben; (nav.) lichten; ~ v.i. schwellen; ~ s. Heben n.; Seufzer m.
heaven s. Himmel m.
heavenly a. & adv. himmlisch.
heavy a., ~**ily** adv. schwer; träge; ~ **artillery**, schwerste Artillerie f.; ~ **smoker**, starker Raucher; ~ **type**, (typ.) Fettdruck m.; ~ **traffic**, starker Verkehr m.
heavyweight s. Schwergewicht (Boxen) n.
hebdomadal a. wöchentlich.
Hebrew a. hebräisch; ~ s. Hebräer.
hecatomb s. Hekatombe f.
heckle v.t. (einen Redner) durch Zwischenrufe unterbrechen.
hectic a. schwindsüchtig; hektisch.
hector v.i. & t. prahlen; einschüchtern.
hedge s. Hecke f.; Zaun m.; ~ v.t. einhegen; to ~ v.i. Ausflüchte machen.
hedgehog s. Igel m.; ~**-position** s. (mil.) Igelstellung f.
hedgerow s. Baumhecke f.
heed s. Aufmerksamkeit f.; ~ v.t. beachten.
heedful a., ~**ly** adv. vorsichtig.
heedless a., ~**ly** adv. unachtsam.
heel s. Ferse f.; Absatz m.; Hug m.; ~ v.t. mit einem Absatz versehen; ~ v.i. sich auf die Seite legen (nav.).
hefty a. handfest, unentwegt, stramm.
hegemony s. Vorherrschaft f.
heifer s. junge Kuh f.
height s. Höhe f.; Gipfel m.
heighten v.t. erhöhen, verbessern.
heinous a., ~**ly** adv. abscheulich.
heir s. Erbe m.; ~**-apparent** s. rechtmässige Erbe; ~**-at-law** s. gesetzliche Erbe; ~**-presumptive** s. mutmassliche Erbe.
heiress s. Erbin f.
heirloom s. Erbstück n.
helical a. schraubenförmig, Spiral...
heliotrope s. (bot.) Sonnenwende f.; Heliotropfarbe f.
heliogravure s. Kupferlichtdruck m.
hell s. Hölle f.
hellish a., ~**ly** adv. höllisch.

helm s. Steuerruder n.
helmet s. Helm m.
helmsman s. Steuermann m.
help s. Hilfe f.; ~ v.t. & i. helfen; (bei Tische) bedienen; ~ **yourself**! langen Sie zu!; I cannot ~, ich kann nicht umhin; I cannot ~ it, ich kann es nicht ändern.
helpful a. behilflich, heilsam, nützlich.
helping s. Portion (Essen), f.; **second** ~, zweite Portion f.
helpless a., ~**ly** adv. hilflos.
helpmate s. Gehilfe m.; Gehilfin f.
helter-skelter adv. Hals über Kopf.
hem s. Saum m.; Räuspern n.; ~ v.t. säumen; ~ v.i. sich räuspern.
hemisphere s. Halbkugel f.
hemlock s. Schierling m.
hemostatic a. blutstillend.
hemp s. Hanf m.
hempen a. hänfen.
hem-stitch s. Hohlsaum m.; to ~ v.t. mit Hohlsaum nähen.
hen s. Henne f.
hence adv. von hier; von nun an; daher.
henceforth adv. von nun an; von da an.
henchman s. Anhänger m.
henpecked p. unter dem Pantoffel stehend.
hen-roost s. Hühnerstange f.
her pn. sie, ihr.; (poss.) ihr.
herald s. Herold m.; ~ v.t. verkünden.
heraldry s. Wappenkunde f.
herb s. Kraut n.; Gras n.
herbalist s. Kräuterkenner m.
herd s. Herde f.
herdsman s. Hirt m.
here adv. hier; her.
hereafter adv. künftig.
hereat adv. hierbei.
hereby adv. hierdurch; hiermit.
hereditary a., ~**ily** adv. erblich.
heredity s. Erblichkeit f.
herein adv. hierin; hier hinein.
hereinafter adv. im Folgenden.
hereof adv. hiervon.
hereon adv. hieran, hierauf, hierüber.
heresy s. Ketzerei f.
heretic s. Ketzer m.
heretical a., ~**ly** adv. ketzerisch.
heretofore adv. ehemals.
herewith adv. hiermit.
heritage s. Erbgut n., Erbschaft f.
hermaphrodite s. Zwitter m.
hermetic a., ~**ally** adv. luftdicht.
hermit s. Einsiedler m.
hermitage s. Einsiedelei f.
hernia s. (med.) Bruch (m.)
hero s. Held m.
heroic a., ~**ally** adv. heldenhaft, heroisch.
heroine s. Heldin f.
heroism s. Heldenmut m.
heron s. Reiher m.
herring s. Hering m.

hers *pn.* der, die, das ihrige.
herself *pn.* sie selbst, ihr selbst, sich.
hesitate *v.i.* zögern.
hesitation *s.* Unschlüssigkeit *f.*
heterodox *a.* irrgläubig.
heterogeneous *a.* verschiedenartig.
hew *v.t.* hauen, hacken, fällen.
hexagon *s.* Sechseck *n.*
hexameter *s.* Hexameter *m.*
heyday *s.* Höhepunkt *m.*, Blüte *f.*
hibernate *v.i.* überwintern.
hiccup, hiccough *v.i.* Schlucken *m.*; ~ *v.i.* den Schlucken haben.
hickory *s.* weisse Walnussbaum *m.*
hide *s.* Haut *f.*; Hufe Land *f.*; Fell *n.*; ~ *v.t.st.* verstecken; ~ *v.i.* sich verstecken; ~ **and seek** *s.* Versteckenspiel *n.*
hidebound *a.* mager; engherzig.
hideous *a.*, **~ly** *adv.* scheusslich.
hiding-place *s.* Schlupfwinkel *m.*
hierarchy *s.* Hierarchie *f.*
hieroglyphic *a.* hieroglyphisch; **~s** *s.pl.* Hieroglyphen *f.pl.*
high *a.*, **~ly** *adv.* hoch, erhaben; **(Wild) angegangen;** ~ **life** *s.* vornehme Welt *f.*; **highly strung** *a.* nervös, reizbar; ~ *s.* Hoch (Wetterkunde) *n.*
high-angle fire *s.* (*mil.*) Steilfeuer *n.*
highbrow *s.* Intellektuelle *m.*; ~ *a.* intellektuell.
High Church *s.* Hochkirche *f.*
high command *s.* (*mil.*) Oberkommando *n.*
high explosive *s.* Sprengstoff *m.*
high-flown *a.* schwülstig.
high-grade *a.* hochwertig.
highland *s.* Hochland *n.*
highness *s.* Höhe *f.*; Hoheit *f.* (Titel).
high pressure *s.* Hochdruck *m.*
highroad, highway *s.* Landstrasse *f.*
high seas *pl.* hohe See *f.*
high tension, high voltage *s.* (*elek.*) Hochspannung *f.*; ~ **cable** *s.* Hochspannungsleitung *f.*
highwayman *s.* Strassenräuber *m.*
highway robbery *s.* Strassenraub *m.*
hike *v.i.* wandern; **to hitchhike** *v.i.* in fremden Autos mitfahren.
hiker *s.* Wanderer *m.*
hilarious *a.* heiter, aufgeheitert.
hilarity *s.* Fröhlichkeit *f.*
hill *s.* Hügel *m.*, Berg *m.*
hillock *s.* kleine Hügel *m.*
hilly *a.* hügelig.
hilt *s.* Heft *n.*; Degengefäss *n.*
him *pn.* ihn, ihm; den, dem.
himself *pn.* er selbst, ihn selbst, ihm selbst; sich.
hind *a.* hinter; ~ *s.* Hirschkuh *f.*; Bauer, Tagelöhner *m.*
hinder *v.t.* hindern, stören.
hindmost *a.* hinterst.

hindrance *s.* Hindernis *n.*
hind-quarters *s.pl.* Hinterbeine (des Pferdes), *n.pl.*
hinge *s.* Türangel *f.*; Scharnier *n.*; ~ *v.i.* sich um etwas drehen.
hint *s.* Wink, Fingerzeig *m.*; Anspielung *f.*; ~ *v.t.* zu verstehen geben.
hip *s.* Hüfte *f.*
hip-bath *s.* Sitzbad *n.*
hippodrome *s.* Rennbahn *f.*
hippopotamus *s.* Nilpferd *n.*
hire *s.* Miete *f.*; Lohn *m.*; **on** ~, zu vermieten; ~ *v.t.* mieten, vermieten; anwerben.
hireling *s.* Mietling *m.*
hire-purchase *s.* Anzahlung, Ratenzahlung *f.*
hirsute *a.* haarig, rauh.
his *pn.* sein; der, die, das seinige.
hiss *v.i.* zischen; ~ *v.t.* auszischen.
historian *s.* Geschichtsforscher *m.*
historical *a.*, **~ly** *adv.* geschichtlich.
historiographer *s.* Geschichtsschreiber *m.*
history *s.* Geschichte *f.*
histrionic *a.* schauspielerisch.
hit *v.t.ir.* schlagen, stossen; treffen; ~ *v.i.* anstossen; zusammenstossen; ~ *s.* Schlag, Stoss *m.*; Treffer, Zufall *m.*; (*theat.*) Schlager *m.*; (*mil.*) **direct** ~, Volltreffer *m.*
hitch *v.t.* & *i.* festmachen; (*sich*) ruckweise bewegen; ~ *s.* Ruck *m.*; (*nav.*) Knoten *m.*; Schwierigkeit *f.*
hither *adv.* hierher; ~ *a.* diesseitig.
hitherto *adv.* bisher.
hive *s.* Bienenstock, Schwarm *m.*; ~ *v.i.* beisammen wohnen.
hoard *s.* Vorrat, Schatz *m.*; ~ *v.t.* & *i.* aufhäufen, sammeln; hamstern.
hoarding *s.* Bretterzaun *m.*
hoar-frost *s.* Reif *m.*
hoarse *a.*, **~ly** *adv.* heiser.
hoary *a.* eisgrau; bereift.
hoax *s.* Fopperei *f.*; ~ *v.t.* foppen.
hobble *v.i.* humpeln.
hobbledehoy *s.* Knabe (*m.*) in den Flegeljahren; Schlaks *m.*
hobby *s.* Steckenpferd *n.*
hobgoblin *s.* Kobold *m.*
hobnail *s.* Nagel *m.*; **hobnailed boots** *pl.* genagelte Schuhe *m.pl.*
hob-nob *v.i.* vertraulich zusammen trinken (anstossen).
hobo *s.* (*Am.*) Landstreicher *m.*
hock *s.* Rheinwein *m.*
hockey *s.* Hockey *n.*
hocus-pocus *s.* Taschenspielerei *f.*
hodge-podge *s.* Mischmasch *m.*
hodman *s.* Handlanger *m.*
hoe *s.* Hacke *f.*; ~ *v.t.* hacken.
hog *s.* Schwein *n.*
hoggish *a.*, **~ly** *adv.* schweinisch.
hogshead *s.* Oxhoft *n.*

hoist *v.t.* in die Höhe heben; hissen; ~ *s.* (Personen) Aufzug *m.*

hoity-toity *a.* mutwillig; ~ *i.* potztausend!

hold *v.t.st.* halten; behalten; enthalten; meinen, schätzen; besitzen; ~ *v.i.* sich halten; beharren; *to ~ forth*, darstellen; hinreichen; vortragen; *to ~ good*, sich bestätigen; gültig sein; *to ~ off*, abhalten, ausweichen; ~ *on!*, ~ *the line!*, bleiben Sie am Telephon!; *to ~ on to*, (*mil.*) (eine Stellung) halten; *to ~ out*, ausstrecken; aushalten; anbieten; *to ~ up*, in die Höhe halten; aufrecht erhalten, unterstützen; ~*.!* halt!; ~ *s.* Halten, Fassen *n.*; Griff *m.*; Gewalt *f.*; Schiffsraum *m.*; Lager *n.*; *to get ~ of*, habhaft werden; ~*-all s.* Reisekoffer *m.*

holder *s.* Inhaber *m.*; Halter *m.*

holding *s.* Pachtgut *n.*; Besitz *m.*; ~ **company** *s.* Dachgesellschaft *f.*; (*mil.*) ~**line** *s.* Auffanglinie *f.*

hold-up *s.* Verkehrsstockung *f.*

hole *s.* Loch *n.*; (*fig.*) Klemme *f.*

holiday *s.* Feiertag *m.*; ~ *of obligation*, gebotene Feiertag *m.*; *public* ~, gesetzliche Feiertag *m.*; *on* ~, in den Ferien; ~*s pl.* Ferien *pl.*; ~*s with pay*, bezahlte Urlaub *m.*

holiness *s.* Heiligkeit *f.*

hollow *a.* hohl; falsch; ~ *s.* Höhle *f.*; ~ *v.t.* aushöhlen.

holly *s.* Stechpalme *f.*

hollyhock *s.* Stockrose *f.*

holm *s.* Holm, Werder *m.*; Uferland *n.*

holocaust *s.* Brandopfer *n.*

holograph *s.* eigenhändig geschriebene Dokument *n.*

holster *s.* Halfter *f.* & *m.*

holy *a.*, ~**ly** *adv.* heilig; ~ *Saturday*, Karsamstag *m.*

holy-water *s.* Weihwasser *n.*

holy-week *s.* Karwoche *f.*

homage *s.* Huldigung *f.*; *to do* ~, huldigen.

home *s.* Heimat *f.*; Wohnung *f.*; ~ *a.* heimisch; ~**-address** *s.* Heimatadresse *f.*; ~ *for the aged* *s.* Altersheim *n.*; ~ **Office** *s.* Innenministerium *n.*; ~**rule** *s.* Selbstverwaltung *f.*; ~**-trade** *s.* Binnenhandel *m.*; ~ *adv.* heim; nach Hause; tüchtig, derb; *at* ~, zu Hause.

homeless *a.* obdachlos, heimatlos.

homely *a.* & *adv.* einfach, schmucklos.

home-made *a.* zu Hause hergestellt.

homesick *a.* Heimweh habend.

homesickness *s.* Heimweh *n.*

homestead *s.* Heimstätte *f.*; Gehöft *n.*

homeward(s) *adv.* heimwärts; ~ *bound*, auf der Rückreise.

homework *s.* Hausarbeiten (des Schülers) *f.pl.*

homicide *s.* Totschlag *m.*; Mörder *m.*

homily *s.* Predigt *f.*

homœopathic *a.* homöopathisch.

homœopathy *s.* Homöopathie *f.*

homogeneous *a.* gleichartig.

hone *s.* Wetzstein *m.*

honest *a.*, ~**ly** *adv.* anständig; redlich.

honesty *s.* Ehrlichkeit, Ehrbarkeit *f.*

honey *s.* Honig *m.*; Süssigkeit *f.*

honey-comb *s.* Honigwabe *f.*

honeycombed *a.* zellig, löcherig; ~ *with*, durchsetzt mit.

honeyed *a.* honigsüss.

honeymoon *s.* Flitterwochen *f.pl.*

honeysuckle *s.* Geissblatt *m.*

honorary *a.* Ehren...

honour *s.* Ehre, Würde *f.*; ~ *v.t.* ehren, beehren; honorieren (Wechsel).

honourable *a.*, ~**bly** *adv.* ehrenvoll.

hood *s.* Haube *f.*

hoodwink *v.t.* täuschen.

hoof *s.* Huf *m.*; Klaue *f.*

hook *s.* (Angel-)Haken *m.*; Gartenmesser *n.*; *by ~ or by crook*, so oder so; ~ *v.t.* anhaken.

hooked *p.* & *a.* gebogen, gekrümmt.

hooligan *s.* Strassenlümmel *m.*

hoop *s.* Reif *m.*; Reifrock *m.*; Schrei *m.*; ~ *v.t.* (ein Fass) binden; ~ *v.i.* laut rufen.

hooper *s.* Böttcher *m.*

hoopoe *s.* Wiedehopf *m.*

hoot *v.i.* tuten.

hop *v.i.* hüpfen; ~ *v.t.* hopsen; ~ *s.* Hüpfen *n.*; Sprung *m.*; Hopsen *m.*; Hopfen *m.*; ~*s pl.* (*com.*) Hopfen.

hope *s.* Hoffnung *f.*; ~ *v.i.* hoffen.

hopeful *a.*, ~**ly** *adv.* hoffnungsvoll.

hopeless *a.* hoffnungslos.

horde *s.* Horde *f.*

horizon *s.* Horizont *m.*; (*avi.*) *artificial* ~, künstliche Horizont *m.*

horizontal *a.*, ~**ly** *adv.* waagerecht.

horizontal bar *s.* Reck (Turnen) *m.*

hormone *s.* Hormon *n.*

horn *s.* Horn *n.*; Fühlhorn *n.*; ~**-signal** *s.* Hupsignal *n.*

hornet *s.* Hornisse *f.*

hornpipe *s.* Matrosentanz *m.*

horoscope *a.* Horoskop *n.*

horrible *a.*, ~**bly** *adv.* abscheulich.

horrid *a.* schrecklich.

horrific *a.* schreckenerregend.

horrify *v.t.* entsetzen.

horror *s.* Entsetzen *n.*; Greuel *m.*

horse *s.* Pferd *n.*; Reiterei *f.*; *on* ~**-back**, zu Pferde; ~**-riding** *s.* Reiten *n.*

horse-breaker *s.* Bereiter *m.*

horse-dealer *s.* Pferdehändler *m.*

horsedrawn *a.* (*mil.*) Pferde..., bespannt; ~ *artillery*, bespannte Artillerie *f.*; ~ *vehicle*, Pferdefuhrwerk *n.*

horsehair *s.* Rosshaar *n.*

horseman *s.* Reiter *m.*

horsemanship *s.* Reitkunst *f.*

horse-play *s.* rohe, grobe Scherz *m.*

horse-pond *s.* Pferdeschwemme *f.*
horse-power *s.* Pferdekraft *f.*
horse-race *s.* Pferderennen *n.*
horse-radish *s.* Meerrettich *m.*
horse-shoe *s.* Hufeisen *n.*
horsewoman *s.* Reiterin *f.*
horticultural *a.* zum Gartenbau gehörig.
horticulture *s.* Gartenbau *m.*
hose *s.* Strumpf *m.*; Spritzenschlauch *m.*
hosier *s.* Strumpfwarenhändler *m.*
hosiery *s.* Strumpfwaren *f.pl.*
hospitable *a.*, **~ly** *adv.* gastfrei.
hospital *s.* Hospital, Krankenhaus *n.*; **~-ship** *s.* Lazarettschiff *n.*; **~-train** *s.* Lazarettzug *m.*
hospitality *s.* Gastlichkeit *f.*
host *s.* Wirt *m.*; Heer *n.*, Schwarm *m.*
hostage *s.* Geisel *m.*
hostel *s.* Herberge *f.*
hostess *s.* Wirtin *f.*; Gastgeberin *f.*
hostile *a.*, **~ly** *adv.* feindlich.
hostility *s.* Feindseligkeit *f.*
hot *a.*, **~ly** *adv.* heiss; scharf (gewürzt).
hotbed *s.* Mistbeet *m.*; Brutstätte *f.*
hot-blooded *a.* heissblütig, hitzig.
hotchpotch *s.* Mischmasch *m.*
hotel *s.* Gasthof *m.*, Hotel *n.*
hot-house *s.* Treibhaus *n.*
hot plate *s.* Heizplatte *f.*
hot-water bottle *s.* Wärmflasche *f.*
hough *s.* Kniekehle *f.*
hound *s.* Tagdhund, Hetzhund *m.*
hour *s.* Stunde *f.*
hour-glass *s.* Sanduhr *f.*
hour-hand *s.* Stundenzeiger *m.*
hourly *a.* & *adv.* stündlich.
house *s.* Haus *n.*; (*theat.*) Zuschauerraum *m.*; **~** *v.t.* beherbergen; **~** *v.i.* hausen.
house-agent *s.* Häusermakler *m.*
housebreaker *s.* Einbrecher *m.*
household *s.* Haushalt *m.*, Haushaltung *f.*; **~** *a.* häuslich, einfach.
householder *s.* Haushaltsvorstand *m.*
housekeeper *s.* Haushälterin *f.*
housekeeping *s.* Haushalten *n.*; **~** *a.* Haushalts...
house of correction *s.* Besserungsanstalt *f.*
house-search *s.* Haussuchung *f.*
house-warming *s.* Einzugsschmaus *m.*
housewife *s.* Hausfrau *f.*; Nähtäschchen *n.*
housing *s.* Obdach *n.*; Lagern *n.*; Satteldecke *f.*; **~-department**, **~-office** *s.* Wohnungsamt *n.*; **~-shortage** *s.* Wohnungsnot *f.*
hovel *s.* Schuppen *m.*; Hütte *f.*
hover *v.i.* schweben, ungewiss sein.
how *adv.* wie.
however *adv.* wie dem auch sei, dennoch; aber, trotzdem; *c.* wie...auch.
howitzer *s.* Haubitze *f.*; Mörser *m.*
howl *v.i.* heulen; **~** *s.* Geheul *n.*
howler *s.* (*sl.*) grobe Fehler *m.*

howsoever *adv.* dessenungeachtet.
hoyden *s.* ausgelassene, wilde Mädchen *n.*, Wildfang *m.*
hub *s.* Radnabe *f.*; Mittelpunkt *m.*
hubbub *s.* Tumult, Lärm *m.*
huckster *s.* Höker *m.*; **~** *v.i.* hökern.
huddle *s.* Verwirrung, Unordnung *f.*; **~** *v.t.* eilfertig verrichten, hudeln; **~** *v.i.* sich drängen; *to* **~** *oneself up*, sich zusammenkauern.
hue *s.* Farbe *f.*, Farbton *m.*; **~** *and cry*, Zetergeschrei *n.*; Hetze *f.*
huff *s.* plötzliche Zorn *m.*; **~** *v.i.* poltern, toben.
hug *s.* Umarmung *f.*; **~** *v.t.* umarmen, liebkosen.
huge *a.* sehr gross, ungeheuer.
hulk *s.* Rumpf (des Schiffes) *m.*
hull *s.* Schale, Hülse *f.*; Rumpf (des Schiffes) *m.*; Wanne (eines Panzers) *f.*; **~** *v.t.* hülsen.
hullabaloo *s.* Spektakel, Klamauk *m.*
hullo *i.* hallo!
hum *s.* Gesumme, Gemurmel *n.*; **~!** *i.* hm!; **~** *v.i.* summen, brummen.
human *a.*, **~ly** *adv.* menschlich.
humane *a.*, **~ly** *adv.* liebreich, menschenfreundlich.
humanity *s.* Menschheit *f.*; Menschlichkeit *f.*; **~ties** *pl.* klassische Wissenschaft *f.*
humanize *v.t.* gesittet machen.
humanitarian *s.* Menschenfreund *m.*
humankind *s.* Menschengeschlecht *n.*
humble *a.*, **~bly** *adv.* bescheiden, unterwürfig; demütig; **~** *v.t.* demütigen.
humble-bee *s.* Hummel *f.*
humbug *s.* Schwindel *m.*; Schwindler *m.*; **~** *v.t.* betrügen.
humdrum *a.* langweilig; dumm.
humid *a.* feucht, nass.
humidity *s.* Feuchtigkeit *f.*
humiliate *v.t.* erniedrigen.
humiliation *s.* Demütigung *f.*
humility *s.* Unterwürfigkeit *f.*
humorist *s.* Humorist *m.*
humorous *a.*, **~ly** *adv.* humoristisch; launig.
humour *s.* Feuchtigkeit (im Körper) *f.*; (Gemüts)stimmung *f.*; Laune *f.*; Humor *m.*; **~** *v.t.* willfahren.
hump, **hump-back** *s.* Höcker, Buckel *m.*
hump-backed *a.* buck[e]lig.
hunch *s.* Buckel *m.*; **~** *v.t.* krümmen.
hunch-back *s.* Buck[e]lige *m.*
hundred *a.* hundert; **~** *s.* Hundert *n.*
hundred-weight *s.* (englischer) Zentner *m.* (112 Pfund; 50.8 kg.).
hunger *s.* Hunger *m.*; **~** *v.i.* hungern.
hungry *a.*, **~ily** *adv.* hungrig.
hunt *v.t.* & *i.* hetzen, jagen; nachspüren; **~** *s.* (Hetz-) Jagd *f.*
hunter *s.* Jäger *m.*; Jagdpferd *n.*

hunting s. (Hetz-) Jagd f.
hunting-box s. Jagdhäuschen n.
hunting-licence s. Jagdschein m.
huntsman s. Jäger m.
hurdle s. Hürde f.
hurl v.t. werfen, schleudern.
hurly-burly s. Wirrwarr m.
hurrah i. hurra!
hurricane s. Orkan m.
hurry s. Eile, Unruhe f.; ~ v.t. beschleunigen, treiben; ~ v.i. eilen.
hurt s. Verletzung f.; Nachteil m.; ~ v.t.ir. verletzen; ~ v.i. schmerzen, wehtun.
hurtful a., ~ly adv. schädlich, nachteilig.
husband s. Gatte, Ehemann m.; ~ v.t. wirtschaftlich verfahren mit.
husbandry s. Landwirtschaft f.; Haushaltung, Wirtschaftlichkeit f.
hush! i. still!; ~, stillen, beruhigen; to ~ up, vertuschen; ~ v.i. schweigen.
hush-money s. Schweigegeld n.
husk s. Hülse f.; ~ v.t. aushülsen.
husky a. hülsig; heiser.
hussar s. Husar m.
hussy s. Weibsbild n.; Range f.
hustle v.t. stossen, drängen; eilen.
hut s. Hütte; Baracke f.
hyacinth s. Hyazinthe f.
hybrid s. Bastardtier n., Bastardpflanze f.; ~ a. Zwitter...
hydrant s. Wasserhahn m.; Hydrant m.
hydraulic a. hydraulisch.
hydrocarbon s. Kohlenwasserstoff m.
hydrocephalus s. Wasserkopf m.
hydrochloric acid s. Salzsäure f.
hydroelectric station s. Wasserkraftwerk n.
hydrogen s. Wasserstoff m.
hydrogenation s. Kohleverflüssigung f.
hydrogen peroxide s. Wasserstoffsuperoxyd n.
hydrophobia s. Hundswut f.
hyena s. Hyäne f.
hygiene s. Hygiene f.
hymen s. Jungfernhäutchen n.
hymn s. Loblied n., Hymne f.; Church-~, Kirchenlied n.; ~-book s. Gesangsbuch n.
hyperbole s. Hyperbel f.
hyperbolical a., ~ly adv. übertrieben.
hypercritical a. übertrieben kritisch.
hyphen s. Bindestrich m.
hyphenated a. Bindestrich...
hypnotic a. einschläfernd.
hypnotize v.t. hypnotisieren.
hypnotism s. Hypnotismus m.
hypochondriac a. schwermütig.
hypocrisy s. Heuchelei f.
hypocrite s. Heuchler m.
hypothecary a. hypothekarisch.
hypothesis s. Hypothese f.; Annahme f.
hypothetical a. hypothetisch.
hysteria s. Hysterie (bes. übertragen) f.

hysterical a. hysterisch.
hysterics s.pl. Hysterie f.; hysterischer Anfall.

I

I pn. ich; it is ~, ich bin's.
iambic a. iambisch.
ibex s. Steinbock m.
ice s. Eis n.; Gefrorne n.; ~ v.t. mit Eis kühlen; überzuckern.
iceberg s. Eisberg m.
ice-bound a. eingefroren.
ice-breaker s. Eisbrecher m.
ice-cream s. Eis n., Gefrorene n.; ~ parlour s. Eisdiele f.
icicle s. Eiszapfen m.
iconoclast s. Bilderstürmer m.
icy a. eisig.
idea s. Begriff m.; Idee f.; Vorstellung f.; Gedanke m.
ideal a., ~ly adv. ideal; ~ s. Ideal n.
idealist s. Idealist m.
idealize v.t. idealisieren.
idealism s. Idealismus m.
identic(al) a. identisch.
identification, identification-card s. Ausweis m.
identify v.t. identifizieren.
identity s. Identität f.; ~-card s. Kennkarte f.; certificate of ~, Ausweispapier n.; ~-papers pl. Ausweispapiere pl.; to prove one's ~, sich ausweisen.
ideological a. ideologisch, weltanschaulich.
ideology s. Ideologie, Weltanschauung f.
idiocy s. Blödsinn m.
idiom s. Mundart f.; Redewendung f.
idiomatic a. einer Sprache eigen.
idiosyncrasy s. Eigentümlichkeit f.
idiot s. Dummkopf m.; Blödsinnige m.f.
idiotic a. blödsinnig; einfältig.
idle a. faul; unnütz; müssig, träge; ~ capital s. tote Kapital n.; ~ factory s. stilliegende Fabrik f.; ~ gear, ~ motion s. Leerlauf m.; ~ v.i. müssig gehen; to ~ away v.t. vertändeln.
idleness s. Müssiggang m.; Trägheit f.
idol s. Abgott m.; Götzenbild n.
idolatrous a., ~ly adv. abgöttisch.
idolatry s. Götzendienst m.
idolize v.t. vergöttern.
idyl s. Idylle f.
idyllic a. idyllisch.
if c. wenn, falls; ob.
igneous a. feurig.
ignis-fatuus s. Irrlicht n.
ignite v. anzünden, sich entzünden.
igniter s. Zünder m.
ignition s. Entzündung f.; Zündung f.
ignoble a., ~bly adv. unedel, gemein.

ignominious *a.*, ~**ly** *adv.* schimpflich.
ignominy *s.* Schmach, Schande *f.*
ignoramus *s.* Unwissende *m.*
ignorance *s.* Unwissenheit *f.*
ignorant *a.*, ~**ly** *adv.* unwissend.
ignore *v.t.* nicht wissen; unbeachtet lassen.
ill *a. & adv.* krank; unwohl; übel, böse; ~ *at ease*, unbehaglich; ~ *s.* Übel *n.*
ill-advised *a.* übelberaten; unbedacht.
ill-bred *a.* schlecht erzogen, unmanierlich.
illegal *a.*, ~**ly** *adv.* gesetzwidrig.
illegality *s.* Gesetzwidrigkeit *f.*
illegible *a.* unleserlich.
illegitimacy *s.* uneheliche Geburt *f.*
illegitimate *a.*, ~**ly** *adv.* unrechtmässig; unehelich.
ill-fated *a.* unglücklich.
ill-feeling *s.* Abneigung, Verstimmung *f.*
illiberal *a.*, ~**ly** *adv.* engherzig; karg.
illicit *a.* unerlaubt.
illiteracy *s.* Analphabetentum *n.*
illiterate *a.* ungelehrt; ~ *s.* Analphabet *m.*
ill-luck *s.* Unglück *n.*, Pech *n.*
ill-natured *a.* bösartig.
illness *s.* Krankheit *f.*
illogical *a.*, ~**ly** *adv.* unlogisch.
ill-timed *a.* zur unrechten Zeit.
illtreat *v.t.* misshandeln.
ill-treatment *s.* Misshandlung *f.*
illuminate *v.t.* erleuchten; illuminieren.
illumination *s.* Festbeleuchtung *f.*; Erleuchtung *f.*
ill-usage *s.* Misshandlung *f.*
illusion *s.* Täuschung *f.*
illusive, illusory *a.* täuschend, trüglich.
illustrate *v.t.* erläutern; illustrieren.
illustration *s.* Erläuterung *f.*; Illustration, Abbildung *f.*
illustrative *a.*, ~**ly** *adv.* erläuternd.
illustrious *a.*, ~**ly** *adv.* erlaucht.
ill-will *s.* Übelwollen *n.*, Groll *m.*
image *s.* Bild *n.*
imagery *s.* bildhafte Sprache *f.*
imaginable *a.* denkbar.
imaginary *a.* eingebildet.
imagination *s.* Phantasie *f.*
imaginative *a.* erfinderisch.
imagine *v.t.* sich einbilden; ersinnen.
imbecile *a.* schwachsinnig.
imbibe *v.t.* einsaugen.
imbroglio *s.* Verwick(e)lung *f.*
imbrue *v.t.* durchnässen; beflecken.
imbue *v.t.* tränken; erfüllen.
imitate *v.t.* nachahmen, nachbilden.
imitation *s.* Nachahmung *f.*
imitative *a.* nachahmend.
imitator *s.* Nachahmer *m.*
immaculate *a.*, ~**ly** *adv.* unbefleckt.
immanent *a.* innewohnend.
immaterial *a.*, ~**ly** *adv.* unkörperlich; unwesentlich.
immature *a.*, ~**ly** *adv.* unreif; unzeitig.

immeasurable *a.*, ~**bly** *adv.* unermesslich.
immediate *a.* unmittelbar; unverzüglich; ~**ly** *adv.* sogleich.
immemorial *a.* undenkbar.
immense *a.*, ~**ly** *adv.* unermesslich.
immensity *s.* Unermesslichkeit *f.*
immerse *v.t.* eintauchen, versenken.
immersion *s.* Eintauchen *n.*
immigrant *s.* Einwanderer *m.*
immigrate *v.i.* einwandern.
immigration *s.* Einwanderung *f.*
imminence *s.* Bevorstehen *n.*
imminent *a.* bevorstehend, drohend.
immobile *a.* unbeweglich.
immobility *s.* Unbeweglichkeit *f.*
immobilize *v.t.* unbeweglich machen; festlegen.
immoderate *a.*, ~**ly** *adv.* unmässig.
immodest *a.*, ~**ly** *adv.* unbescheiden; unanständig.
immolate *v.t.* opfern.
immoral *a.* unsittlich; unmoralisch.
immorality *s.* Unsittlichkeit *f.*
immortal *a.*, ~**ly** *adv.* unsterblich.
immortality *s.* Unsterblichkeit *f.*
immortalize *v.t.* unsterblich machen.
immovable *a.*, ~**bly** *adv.* unbeweglich; ~**s** *s.pl.* unbewegliche Güter *n.pl.*
immune *a.* geschützt (gegen).
immunity *s.* Freiheit *f.*; Befreiung *f.*; Vorrecht *n.*; Immunität *f.*
immunization *s.* Schutzimpfung *f.*
immure *v.t.* einmauern.
immutable *a.*, ~**bly** *adv.* unveränderlich.
imp *s.* Kobold *m.*; kleine Schelm *m.*
impact *s.* Stoss, Anprall *m.*
impair *v.t.* vermindern, beeinträchtigen.
impale *v.t.* pfählen; aufspiessen.
impart *v.t.* mitteilen; verleihen.
impartial *a.*, ~**ly** *adv.* unparteiisch.
impartiality *s.* Unparteilichkeit *f.*
impassable *a.* ungangbar.
impasse *s.* Sackgasse *f.*
impassible *a.* gefühllos; unverletzlich.
impassioned *p.* leidenschaftlich bewegt.
impassive *a.* unempfindlich.
impatience *s.* Ungeduld *f.*
impatient *a.*, ~**ly** *adv.* ungeduldig.
impeach *v.t.* anfechten; anklagen.
impeachment *s.* Anklage *f.*
impecunious *a.* geldlos.
impede *v.t.* verhindern.
impediment *s.* Hindernis *n.*; **marriage-~** *s.* Ehehindernis *n.*; ~ **in one's speech** *s.* Sprachhemmung *f.*
impel *v.t.* antreiben.
impend *v.i.* (drohend) bevorstehen.
impenetrable *a.*, ~**bly** *adv.* undurchdringlich; unerforschlich.
impenitent *a.*, ~**ly** *adv.* unbussfertig.
imperative *a.*, ~**ly** *adv.* gebieterisch; dringend nötig; ~ *s.* Imperativ *m.*
imperceptible *a.*, ~**bly** *adv.* unmerklich.

imperfect *a.*, **~ly** *adv.* unvollkommen; **~** *s.* (*gram.*) Imperfekt(um) *n.*
imperfection *s.* Unvollkommenheit *f.*
imperial *a.*, **~ly** *adv.* kaiserlich; Reichs...
Imperialism *s.* Imperialismus *m.*
imperil *v.t.* gefährden.
imperious *a.*, **~ly** *adv.* gebieterisch.
imperishable *a.* unvergänglich.
impermeable *a.* undurchdringlich.
impersonal *a.*, **~ly** *adv.* unpersönlich.
impersonate *v.t.* verkörpern; darstellen.
impertinence *s.* Anmassung *f.*
impertinent *a.* frech.
imperturbable *a.* unerschütterlich.
impervious *a.* undurchdringlich.
impetuous *a.*, **~ly** *adv.* ungestüm.
impetus *s.* Antrieb *m.*; Drang *m.*
impiety *s.* Gottlosigkeit *f.*
impinge *v.i.* anstossen; sich vergehen.
impious *a.*, **~ly** *adv.* gottlos.
implacable *a.*, **~bly** *adv.* unversöhnlich.
implant *v.t.* einpflanzen; einprägen.
implement *s.* Zubehör *n.*; Gerät *n.*; **~** *v.t.* durchführen, erfüllen.
implicate *v.t.* verwickeln.
implication *s.* Verwick(e)lung *f.*; Folgerung *f.*, Voraussetzung *f.*
implicit, *a.*, **~ly** *adv.* unbedingt; stillschweigend einbegriffen.
implore *v.t.* anflehen.
imply *v.t.* in sich schliessen; besagen; stillschweigend einschliessen.
impolite *a.* unhöflich.
impolitic *a.*, **~ly** *adv.* unklug.
imponderable *a.* unwägbar; **~s** *pl.* unwägbare Dinge *n.pl.*
import *s.* Einfuhr *f.*; Wichtigkeit *f.*; **~** *v.t.* einführen; bedeuten.
importance *s.* Wichtigkeit *f.*
important *a.*, **~ly** *adv.* wichtig.
importation *s.* Einfuhr *f.*
importer *s.* Einführer (von Waren) *m.*
importunate *a.*, **~ly** *adv.* zudringlich.
importune *v.t.* beschweren, belästigen.
importunity *s.* Zudringlichkeit *f.*
impose *v.t.* auferlegen, verhängen (Strafe); *to ~ upon,* imponieren; täuschen, hintergehen; oktroyieren.
imposing *a.* imponierend.
imposition *s.* Auflegung *f.*; Auflage *f.*; Betrügerei *f.*
impossibility *s.* Unmöglichkeit *f.*
impossible *a.*, **~bly** *adv.* unmöglich.
impost *s.* Steuer, Abgabe *f.*
impostor *s.* Betrüger *m.*
imposture *s.* Betrug *m.*
impotence *s.* Unvermögen *n.*; Impotenz *f.*
impotent *a.*, **~ly** *adv.* unvermögend, schwach; impotent.
impound *v.t.* beschlagnahmen; sperren.
impoverish *v.t.* arm machen.
impracticable *a.* untunlich; unlenksam.

imprecate *v.t.* verfluchen, verwünschen.
imprecation *s.* Verwünschung *f.*
impregnable *a.*, **~bly** *adv.* uneinnehmbar.
impregnate *v.t.* schwängern; sättigen; imprägnieren.
impress *v.t.* eindrücken, einprägen.
impression *s.* Eindruck *m.*; Abdruck, Abzug *m.*; Auflage *f.*
impressionable *a.* eindrucksfähig.
impressive *a.*, **~ly** *adv.* eindringlich.
imprint *v.t.* prägen; einprägen; **~** *s.* Stempel *m.*
imprison *v.t.* gefangen setzen.
imprisonment *s.* Haft *f.*; *false ~,* ungesetzliche Gefangensetzung *f.*; *sentence of ~,* Gefängnisstrafe, Freiheitsstrafe *f.*; *one year's ~,* ein Jahr Gefängnis; *~ on remand,* Untersuchungshaft *f.*
improbability *s.* Unwahrscheinlichkeit *f.*
improbable *a.*, **~ly** *adv.* unwahrscheinlich.
improbity *s.* Unredlichkeit *f.*
impromptu *s.* Stück (*n.*) aus dem Stegreif; **~** *a.* aus dem Stegreif.
improper *a.*, **~ly** *adv.* uneigentlich; unpassend, unanständig; *~ assault,* (*law*) Sittlichkeitsvergehen *n.*; *~ use,* Missbrauch *m.*
impropriety *s.* Unrichtigkeit *f.*; Unschicklichkeit *f.*
improvable *a.*, **~bly** *adv.* verbesserungsfähig.
improve *v.t.* verbessern; **~** *v.i.* besser werden; Fortschritte machen.
improvement *s.* Verbesserung *f.*
improvident *a.*, **~ly** *adv.* unbedachtsam.
improvise *v.t.* improvisieren.
imprudence *s.* Unklugheit *f.*
imprudent *a.*, **~ly** *adv.* unklug.
impudence *s.* Unverschämtheit *f.*
impudent *a.*, **~ly** *adv.* unverschämt.
impugn *v.t.* anfechten; bestreiten.
impulse, impulsion *s.* Antrieb *m.*; Stoss *m.*
impulsive *a.*, erregbar; antreibend.
impunity *s.* Straflosigkeit *f.*; *with ~,* ungestraft.
impure *a.*, **~ly** *adv.* unrein, unkeusch.
impurity *s.* Unreinigkeit *f.*; Unkeuschheit *f.*
imputable *a.* zurechenbar.
imputation *s.* Anschuldigung *f.*; Zurechnung, Beimessung *f.*
impute *v.t.* Schuld geben; beimessen; unterstellen.
in *pr.* in, an, zu, bei, mit, auf; unter, während; *~ itself,* an und für sich; **~** *adv.* hinein, herein, drinnen; *I am not ~ for anyone,* ich bin für niemanden zu sprechen.
inability *s.* Unfähigkeit *f.*; *~ to pay,* Zahlungsunfähigkeit *f.*
inaccessible *a.*, **~bly** *adv.* unzugänglich.
inaccuracy *s.* Ungenauigkeit *f.*

inaccurate *a.* ungenau.
inaction *s.* Untätigkeit *f.*
inactive *a.*, ~ly *adv.* untätig.
inactivity *s.* Untätigkeit *f.*
inadequacy *s.* Unzulänglichkeit *f.*
inadequate *a.* unzulänglich.
inadmissible *a.* unzulässig.
inadvertence *s.* Unachtsamkeit *f.*
inadvertent *a.* unachtsam, ~ly *adv.* aus Versehen.
inalienable *a.* unveräusserlich.
inalterable *a.* unveränderlich.
inane *a.* leer, nichtig.
inanimate *a.* unbeseelt; leblos; flau.
inanition *s.* Leere *f.*; Kraftlosigkeit *f.*
inapplicable *a.* unanwendbar.
inappreciable *a.* unbemerkbar.
inapproachable *a.* unzugänglich.
inappropriate *a.* unpassend.
inapt *a.* unpassend; ungeschickt.
inaptitude *s.* Untauglichkeit *f.*
inarticulate *a.*, ~ly *adv.* undeutlich.
inasmuch *adv.* insofern, weil.
inattention *s.* Unaufmerksamkeit *f.*; Nichtbeachten (einer Vorschrift) *n.*
inattentive *a.*, ~ly *adv.* unaufmerksam.
inaudible *a.* unhörbar.
inaugural *a.* einweihend; ~ address *s.* Antrittsrede *f.*
inaugurate *v.t.* einweihen.
inauspicious *a.*, ~ly *adv.* ungünstig.
inborn *a.* angeboren.
inbred *a.* angeboren.
incalculable *a.* unberechenbar.
incandescent *a.* weissglühend; ~ light (Gas-) Glühlicht *n.*
incantation *s.* Bezauberung *f.*
incapability *s.* Unfähigkeit *f.*
incapable *a.* unfähig, untauglich.
incapacitate *v.t.* unfähig machen.
incapacity *s.* Unfähigkeit *f.*
incarcerate *v.t.* einkerkern.
incarnate *a.* fleischgeworden.
incarnation *s.* Menschwerdung *f.*; Verkörperung *f.*
incautious *a.*, ~ly *adv.* unvorsichtig.
incendiarism *s.* Brandstiftung *f.*
incendiary *s.* Brandstifter *m.*; Aufwiegler *m.*; ~ *a.* brandstifterisch; ~ bomb *s.* Brandbombe *f.*
incense *s.* Weihrauch *m.*; ~*v.t.* entzünden; erzürnen.
incentive *a.* anreizend; ~ *s.* Anreiz *m.*
inception *s.* Anfang *m.*
inceptive *a.* Anfangs...
incertitude *s.* Ungewissheit *f.*
incessant *a.*, ~ly *adv.* unaufhörlich.
incest *s.* Blutschande *f.*
incestuous *a.*, ~ly *adv.* blutschänderisch.
inch *s.* Zoll *m.* (2.54 cm.)
incidence *s.* Vorkommen *n.*; (*phys.*) Einfall *m.*
incident *s.* Ereignis *n.*; Nebenumstand *m.*

incidental *a.* zufällig, ~ to, gehörig zu, verbunden mit; ~s *pl.* Nebenausgaben *f.pl.*; ~ly *adv.* übrigens, nebenbei bemerkt.
incipient *a.* anfangend.
incision *s.* Einschnitt *m.*
incisive *a.* einschneidend.
incisor *s.* Schneidezahn *m.*
incite *v.t.* anreizen, antreiben.
incitement *s.* Anreizung *f.*
incivility *s.* Unhöflichkeit *f.*
inclemency *s.* Unbarmherzigkeit *f.*
inclement *a.* unbarmherzig, rauh.
inclination *s.* Neigung *f.*
incline *v.t.* neigen; ~ *v.i.* sich neigen, geneigt sein; ~d plane *s.* schiefe Ebene *f.*; ~ *s.* Neigung *f.*; Abhang *m.*
inclose *v.t.* einschliessen; to ~ in inverted commas, in Anführungszeichen setzen.
include *v.t.* einschliessen.
inclusion *s.* Einschliessung *f.*; Einbeziehung *f.*
inclusive *a.*, ~ly *adv.* einschliesslich; alles einbegriffen; *both dates,* beide Tage einbegriffen; ~ terms *pl.* Pensionspreis mit Licht und Bedienung *m.*
incoherence *s.* Mangel an Zusammenhang *m.*
incoherent *a.*, ~ly *adv.* unzusammenhängend.
incombustible *a.* unverbrennlich.
income *s.* Einkommen *n.*; *earned* ~, Einkommen durch Arbeit; *unearned* ~, Einkommen aus Vermögen.
income-tax *s.* Einkommensteuer *f.*; ~ return *s.* Einkommensteuererklärung *f.*
incoming *a.* einlaufend, eingehend; neu eintretend; ~s *s.pl.* Eingänge *m.pl.*
incommensurable *a.* inkommensurabel.
incommode *v.t.* belästigen.
incomparable *a.*, ~bly *adv.* unvergleichlich.
incompatible *a.*, ~bly *adv.* unvereinbar.
incompetence, incompetency *s.* Unbefugtheit *f.*; Unzulänglichkeit *f.*
incompetent *a.*, ~ly *adv.* unzuständig; unfähig: unbefugt; unzulänglich.
incomplete *a.* unvollständig.
incomprehensible *a.*, ~bly *adv.* unbegreiflich.
incomprehension *f.* Unverständnis *n.*
inconceivable *a.*, ~bly *adv.* unbegreiflich.
inconclusive *a.* nicht überzeugend.
incongruity *s.* Ungereimtheit *f.*
incongruous *a.*, ~ly *adv.* nicht passend.
inconsequence *s.* Folgewidrigkeit *f.*
inconsequent *a.*, ~ly *adv.* folgewidrig.
inconsiderable *a.*, ~bly *adv.* unbedeutend, unwichtig.
inconsiderate *a.*, ~ly *adv.* unbedachtsam, rücksichtslos.
inconsistency *s.* Inkonsequenz *f.*

G.D.   N

inconsistent *a.*, ~ly *adv.* unvereinbar, ungereimt, widersinnig; inkonsequent.

inconsolable *a.*, ~bly *adv.* untröstlich.

inconspicuous *a.* unauffällig.

inconstant *a.* unbeständig.

incontestable *a.*, ~bly *adv.* unbestreitbar.

incontinence *s.* Unkeuschheit *f.*

incontinent *a.* unkeusch, unenthaltsam; ~ly *adv.* sogleich.

incontrovertible *a.* unwidersprechlich.

inconvenience *s.* Unbequemlichkeit, Lästigkeit *f.*; ~ *v.t.* belästigen.

inconvenient *a.*, ~ly *adv.* unbequem, ungelegen; unpassend.

incorporate *v.t.* einverleiben; (*law*) zu einer Gesellschaft machen; ~ *a.* einverleibt; ~d company *s.* (*Am.*) (eingetragene) Aktiengesellschaft *f.*

incorporation *s.* Einverleibung *f.*

incorporeal *a.*, ~ly *adv.* unkörperlich.

incorrect *a.*, ~ly *adv.* fehlerhaft; ungenau.

incorrigible *a.*, ~bly *adv.* unverbesserlich.

incorruptible *a.*, ~bly *adv.* unbestechlich; unverderblich.

increase *v.i.* wachsen, zunehmen; ~ *v.t.* vergrössern; ~ *s.* Zunahme *f.*

incredible *a.*, ~bly *adv.* unglaublich.

incredulity *s.* Unglaube *m.*

incredulous *a.*, ~ly *adv.* ungläubig.

increment *s.* Zuwachs *m.*, Zunahme *f.*; ~ value *s.* Wertzuwachs *m.*

incriminate *v.t.* beschuldigen; ~ing *a.* belastend.

incubate *v.t.* brüten.

incubator *s.* Brutapparat *m.*

incubus *s.* Alpdrücken *n.*

inculcate *v.t.* einschärfen, einprägen.

inculpate *v.t.* beschuldigen, tadeln.

incumbent *a.* obliegend; ~ *s.* Pfründner *m.*

incunabula *s.pl.* Wiegendrucke *m.pl.*

incur *v.t.* auf sich laden, sich zuziehen; to ~ debts, Schulden machen; to ~ a fine, in eine Geldstrafe verfallen; to ~ an obligation, eine Verpflichtung eingehen.

incurable *a.*, ~bly unheilbar.

incursion *s.* Einfall, Streifzug *m.*

indebted *p. & a.* verschuldet; verpflichtet.

indebtedness *s.* Verschuldung *s.*

indecency *s.* Unanständigkeit *f.*

indecent *a.*, ~ly *adv.* unanständig.

indecision *s.* Unentschlossenheit *f.*

indecisive *a.* unschlüssig; nicht entscheidend.

indecorous *a.* unanständig.

indeed *adv.* in der Tat, allerdings.

indefatigable *a.*, ~bly *adv.* unermüdlich.

indefensible *a.* unhaltbar.

indefinable *a.* unbestimmbar.

indefinite *a.*, ~ly *adv.* unbestimmt, unbeschränkt.

indelible *a.*, ~bly *adv.* unauslöschlich.

indelicacy *s.* Mangel (*m.*) an Zartgefühl.

indemnification *s.* Entschädigung *f.*

indemnify *v.t.* schadlos halten.

indemnity *s.* Straflosigkeit *f.*; Schadenersatz *m.*

indent *v.t.* auszacken; einkerben; (Zeile) einrücken.

indentation *s.* Kerbe *f.*; Einschnitt *m.*

indenture *s.* Vertrag *m.*; Lehrbrief *m.*; ~ *v.t.* verdingen.

independence *s.* Unabhängigkeit *f.*

independent *a.*, ~ly *adv.* unabhängig.

indescribable *a.* unbeschreiblich.

indestructible *a.* unzerstörbar.

indeterminate *a.*, ~ly *adv.* unbestimmt.

index *s.* Anzeiger *m.*; Zeigefinger *m.*; Register *n.*; Index *m.*; ~ *v.t.* registrieren.

Indian corn *s.* Mais *m.*

Indian summer *s.* (*Am.*) Nachsommer *m.*

india-rubber *s.* Gummi *m.* or *n.*, Kautschuk *m.*; Radiergummi *m.* or *n.*

indicate *v.t.* anzeigen.

indication *s.* Anzeichen *n.*

indicative *a.*, ~ly *adv.* anzeigend; ~ *s.* (*gram.*) Indikativ *m.*

indicator *s.* Anzeiger *m.*

indict *v.t.* schriftlich anklagen, belangen.

indictable *a.* (*law*) klagbar.

indictment *s.* Anklage vor der grossen Jury *f.*

indifference *s.* Gleichgültigkeit *f.*

indifferent *a.*, ~ly *adv.* gleichgültig; unparteiisch; leidlich; mässig.

indigence *s.* Armut, Dürftigkeit *f.*

indigenous *a.* eingeboren.

indigent *a.*, ~ly *adv.* dürftig; arm.

indigestible *a.* unverdaulich.

indigestion *s.* Verdauungsbeschwerde *f.*

indignant *a.*, ~ly *adv.* unwillig.

indignation *s.* Entrüstung *f.*

indignity *s.* Unwürdigkeit *f.*

indirect *a.* mittelbar, indirekt.

indiscernible *a.* nicht zu unterscheiden.

indiscipline *s.* Zuchtlosigkeit *f.*

indiscreet *a.*, ~ly *adv.* unbedachtsam; unbescheiden; indiskret.

indiscretion *s.* Unbedachtsamkeit *f.*; Unbescheidenheit, Indiskretion *f.*

indiscriminate *a.*, ~ly *adv.* nicht unterschieden, unbedingt; ohne Unterschied.

indispensable *a.*, ~bly *adv.* unentbehrlich, unerlässlich.

indisposed *a.* unpässlich, abgeneigt.

indisposition *s.* Unpässlichkeit *f.*

indisputable *a.*, ~bly *adv.* unbestreitbar.

indissoluble *a.*, ~bly *adv.* unauflöslich.

indistinct *a.*, ~ly *adv.* undeutlich; ohne Unterschied.

indistinguishable *a.* ununterscheidbar.

indite *v.t.* abfassen, schreiben.

individual *a.*, ~ly *adv.* einzeln, persönlich; ~ *s.* Individuum *n.*, Person *f.*

individuality s. Individualität f.
indivisible a., ~**bly** adv. unteilbar.
indocile a. ungelehrig.
indolence s. Trägheit f.
indolent a., ~**ly** adv. träge.
indomitable a. unbezähmbar.
indoor a. im Hause befindlich; ~**s** adv.
   im Hause, drinnen.
indoors adv. im Hause, drinnen.
indubitable a., ~**bly** adv. unzweifelhaft.
induce v.t. bewegen, veranlassen; (elek.)
   induzieren.
inducement s. Beweggrund, Anlass m.
induction s. Einführung f.; Induktion f.
inductive a., ~**ly** adv. bewegend; folger-
   ungsmässig; Induktions...
indulge v.t. nachsichtig sein, nachgeben;
   ~ v.i. frönen.
indulgence s. Nachsicht f.; Ablass m.;
   plenary ~, vollkommene Ablass m.
indulgent a., ~**ly** adv. nachsichtig.
industrial a. industriell, Gewerbe...;
   ~ court, Arbeitsgericht n.; ~ dispute,
   Arbeitsstreit m.; ~ exhibition, Gewer-
   beausstellung f.
industrious a., ~**ly** adv. fleissig.
industry s. Fleiss m.; Industrie f.
inebriate v.t. berauschen.
inebriety s. Trunkenheit f.
ineffable a., ~**bly** adv. unaussprechlich.
ineffective, ineffectual a., ~**ly** adv. unwirksam.
inefficiency s. Unfähigkeit f.
inefficient a. unwirksam, untüchtig.
ineligible a. nicht wählbar.
ineptitude s. Albernheit f.
inequality s. Ungleichheit f.
inequitable a. unbillig.
inert a., ~**ly** adv. träge.
inertia s. (phys.) Trägheit f.
inestimable a., ~**bly** adv. unschätzbar.
inevitable a., ~**bly** adv. unvermeidlich.
inexact a. ungenau.
inexcusable a., ~**bly** adv. nicht zu entschuldigen.
inexhaustible a. unerschöpflich.
inexorable a., ~**bly** adv. unerbittlich.
inexpediency s. Unzweckmässigkeit f.
inexpedient a. unzweckmässig, unpassend.
inexpensive a. nicht kostspielig.
inexperience s. Unerfahrenheit f.
inexperienced a. unerfahren.
inexpert a. unerfahren, ungeübt.
inexpiable a., ~**bly** adv. unsühnbar.
inexplicable a., ~**bly** adv. unerklärlich.
inexpressible a. unaussprechlich.
inextinguishable a. unauslöschlich.
inextricable a. unentwirrbar.
infallibility s. Unfehlbarkeit f.
infallible a., ~**bly** adv. unfehlbar.
infamous a., ~**ly** adv. verrufen, ehrlos.
infamy s. Ehrlosigkeit, Schande f.
infancy s. Kindheit f.; Unmündigkeit f.

infant s. (kleines) Kind n.; Unmündige m.;
   ~ mortality, Säuglingssterblichkeit f.
   ~-school, Kleinkinderschule f.
infanta s. Infantin f.
infanticide s. Kindesmord m.
infantile a. kindlich; kindisch; ~ paralysis,
   spinale Kinderlähmung f.
infantry s. Infanterie f., Fussvolk n.
infatuate v.t. betören.
infatuation s. Verblendung, Betörung f.
infeasible a. unausführbar.
infect v.t. anstecken.
infection s. Ansteckung f.
infectious a., ~**ly** adv. ansteckend.
infer v.t. folgern, herleiten.
inference s. Folgerung f.
inferior a. untergeordnet; niedriger;
   minderwertig; ~ s. Untergebene m.
inferiority s. Minderwertigkeit f.
infernal a. höllisch.
infertile a. unfruchtbar.
infest v.t. plagen; wimmeln.
infidel a. ungläubig; ~ s. Ungläubige m.
infidelity s. Untreue f.; Unglaube m.
infiltrate v.i. einsickern.
infinite a., ~**ly** adv. unendlich.
infinitive s. (gram.) Infinitiv m.
infinitude, infinity s. Unendlichkeit f.
infirm a. kraftlos, schwach; gebrechlich.
infirmary s. Krankenstube f.
infirmity s. Schwäche f.
inflame v.t. anzünden.
inflammable a. entzündlich.
inflammation s. Entzündung f.
inflammatory a. entzündend; aufreizend.
inflate v.t. aufblasen, aufblähen.
inflation s. Aufblähung f.; Aufgeblasen-
   heit f.; Inflation f.
inflect v.t. biegen; deklinieren; konjugieren.
inflection s. Biegung f.; Beugung f.
inflexible a., ~**bly** adv. unbeugsam.
inflict v.t. auferlegen, verhängen.
influence s. Einfluss m.; ~ v.t. Einfluss
   üben auf, einwirken, beeinflussen.
influential a. einflussreich.
influenza s. Influenza, Grippe f.
influx s. Einfliessen n.; Zufluss m.
inform v.t. benachrichtigen; ~ v.i.
   (against) angeben, denunzieren.
informal a., ~**ly** adv. formlos.
informant s. Gewährsmann m.
information s. Unterweisung f.; Nachricht f.; Auskunft f.; for (your) information, zur Kenntnisnahme.
informer s. Angeber, Ankläger m.
infraction s. Bruch m.; Verletzung f.
infrequent a. selten, ungewöhnlich.
infringe v.t. übertreten, verletzen.
infringement s. Übertretung f.
infuriate v.t. wütend machen.
infuse v.t. hineingiessen, einflössen.
infusion s. Eingiessung f.; Aufguss (Tee)
   m.

ingenious *a.*, ~ly *adv.* sinnreich.
ingenuity *s.* Scharfsinn *m.*
ingenuous *a.* unbefangen; offen; bieder.
inglorious *a.*, ~ly *adv.* unrühmlich.
ingot *s.* Metallbarren *m.*
ingrained *a.* eingefleischt.
ingratiate *v.t.* beliebt machen.
ingratitude *s.* Undankbarkeit *f.*
ingredient *s.* Bestandteil *m.*
inhabit *v.t.* bewohnen.
inhabitable *a.* bewohnbar.
inhabitant *s.* Einwohner *m.*
inhale *v.t.* einatmen; inhalieren.
inharmonious *a.* unharmonisch.
inhere *v.i.* anhaften, innewohnen.
inherent *a.* anhaftend; eigen.
inherit *v.t.* erben; bekommen.
inheritable *a.* vererbbar.
inheritance *s.* Erbschaft *f.*; Erbgut *n.*; *law of* ~, Erbrecht *n.*
inhibit *v.t.* hindern; verbieten.
inhospitable *a.*, ~bly *adv.* ungastlich.
inhuman *a.*, ~ly *adv.* unmenschlich.
inhumanity *s.* Unmenschlichkeit *f.*
inimical *a.* feindselig.
inimitable *a.*, ~bly *adv.* unnachahmlich.
iniquitous *a.* unbillig, frevelhaft.
iniquity *s.* Bosheit, Ungerechtigkeit *f.*
initial *a.*, ~ly *adv.* anfänglich; ~ *s.* Anfangsbuchstabe *m.*; ~ *v.t.* paraphieren.
initiate *v.t.* einführen, einweihen; einleiten (Massnahmen).
initiative *a.* einleitend; ~ *s.* Initiative *f.*
inject *v.t.* einspritzen.
injection *s.* Einspritzung *f.*
injudicious *a.*, ~ly *adv.* unverständig.
injunction *s.* Einschärfung; Vorschrift; Verfügung *f.*
injure *v.t.* verletzen, beeinträchtigen; schädigen; *the* ~*d person,* (*law*) der Geschädigte *m.*
injurious *a.*, ~ly *adv.* nachteilig.
injury *s.* Nachteil *m.*; Verletzung *f.*
injustice *s.* Ungerechtigkeit *f.*
ink *s.* Tinte *f.*; Druckerschwärze *f.*
ink-lines *pl.* Linienblatt *n.*
inkling *s.* Ahnung *f.*; Wink *m.*
inkstand *s.* Tintenfass *n.*, Schreibzeug *n.*
inlaid *a.* eingelegt.
inland *a.* inländisch; ~ *s.* Binnenland *n.*; ~ *harbour,* ~ *port,* Binnenhafen *m.*
inlay *v.t.ir.* einlegen.
inlet *s.* Zugang *m.*; Bucht *f.*; Einlage *f.*
inmate *s.* Insasse *m.*; Hausgenosse *m.*
inmost *a.* innerst.
inn *s.* Gasthof *m.*; Wirtshaus *n.*
innate *a.*, ~ly *adv.* angeboren.
inner *a.*, ~ly *adv.* innerlich; geheim.
innkeeper *s.* Gastwirt *m.*
innocence *s.* Unschuld *f.*
innocent *a.*, ~ly *adv.* unschuldig.
innocuous *a.*, ~ly *adv.* unschädlich.
innovate *v.i.* Neuerungen machen.

innovation *s.* Neuerung *f.*
innovator *s.* Neuerer *m.*
innuendo *s.* Wink, Fingerzeig *m.*
innumerable *a.*, ~bly *adv.* unzählig.
inoculate *v.t.* einimpfen.
inoffensive *a.*, ~ly *adv.* unanstössig, arglos.
inoperative *a.* unwirksam.
inopportune *a.* ungelegen.
inordinate *a.*, ~ly *adv.* ausschweifend.
inorganic *a.*, ~ally *adv.* unorganisch.
in-patient *s.* Anstaltskranke *m.* & *f.*
inquest *s.* Leichenschau *f.*
inquietude *s.* Unruhe *f.*
inquire *v.i.* sich erkundigen; untersuchen; fragen.
inquiry *s.* Untersuchung *f.*; Nachfrage, Erkundigung *f.*
inquisition *s.* Untersuchung *f.*; Ketzergericht *n.*; Inquisition *f.*
inquisitive *a.*, ~ly *adv.* neugierig.
inroad *s.* Einfall *m.*; Eingriff *m.*
insane *a.*, geisteskrank, wahnsinnig.
insanitary *a.* gesundheitsschädlich, unhygienisch.
insanity *s.* Wahnsinn *m.*
insatiable *a.*, ~bly *adv.* unersättlich.
inscribe *v.t.* einschreiben; widmen.
inscription *s.* Inschrift *f.*; Aufschrift *f.*; Einschreibung *f.*
inscrutable *a.*, ~bly *adv.* unerforschlich.
insect *s.* Insekt *n.*; ~-powder *s.* Insektenpulver *n.*
insecticide *s.* Insektenpulver *n.*
insecure *a.*, ~ly *adv.* unsicher.
insecurity *s.* Unsicherheit *f.*
insensate *a.* unvernünftig.
insensible *a.*, ~bly *adv.* unempfindlich; unmerklich.
inseparable *a.*, ~bly *adv.* unzertrennlich.
insert *v.t.* einfügen, einschalten.
insertion *s.* Einfügung, Einschaltung *f.*
inset *s.* Einsatz *m.*; Einsatzbild *n.*, Einsatzkarte *f.*
inshore *adv.* nahe der Küste.
insidious *a.*, ~ly *adv.* hinterlistig.
insight *s.* Einsicht *f.*
insignia *s.pl.* Insignien *pl.*; Abzeichen *n.pl.*
insignificance *s.* Geringfügigkeit *f.*
insignificant *a.*, ~ly *adv.* unbedeutend.
insincere *a.*, ~ly *adv.* nicht aufrichtig.
insincerity *s.* Unaufrichtigkeit *f.*
insinuate *v.t.* zu verstehen geben; ~ *v.refl.* & *i.* sich einschmeicheln.
insinuation *s.* Einschmeichelung *f.*; Unterstellung *f.*; Wink *m.*
insipid *a.*, ~ly *adv.* geschmacklos, fad.
insist *v.i.* auf etwas bestehen.
insistence *s.* Beharren, Bestehen *n.*
insole *s.* Schuheinlage *f.*
insolence *s.* Frechheit *f.*
insolent *a.* unverschämt, frech.
insoluble *a.* unlöslich.

insolvency s. Zahlungsunfähigkeit f.
insolvent a. zahlungsunfähig.
insomnia s. Schlaflosigkeit f.
inspect v.t. besichtigen.
inspection s. Besichtigung f.
inspector s. Aufseher m., Inspektor m.
inspectorate s. Inspektorat n.; Aufsichtsbehörde f.
inspiration s. Eingebung f.
inspire v.t. einhauchen, einflössen; begeistern; einatmen.
instability s. Unbeständigkeit f.
install v.t. einsetzen.
installation s. Bestallung f.; Anlage f.
instalment s. Teilzahlung f.; Rate f.; by ~s, in Raten.
instance s. dringende Bitte f.; Gelegenheit f.; Fall m.; Instanz f.; for ~, zum Beispiel; ~ v.t. als Beispiel anführen.
instant a., ~ly adv. dringend; augenblicklich, sogleich; ~ s. Augenblick m.; the 10th inst., der 10. dieses Monats.
instantaneous a., ~ly adv. augenblicklich.
instead pr. anstatt; ~ adv. stattdessen.
instep s. Spann, Rist m.
instigate v.t. aufhetzen, anstiften.
instigator s. Anstifter m.
instil v.t. einflössen.
instinct s. Instinkt m.; ~ a. belebt.
instinctive a., ~ly adv. unwillkürlich.
institute v.t. einsetzen, verordnen, stiften; ~ s. Anstalt f.
institution s. Einsetzung f.; Verordnung f.; Anstalt f.; Einrichtung f.
instruct v.t. unterrichten; unterweisen; beauftragen.
instruction s. Unterweisung f.; Unterricht m.; Vorschrift f.; Auftrag m.
instructional pamphlet s. Merkblatt n.
instructions pl. Gebrauchsanweisung f.
instructive a. lehrreich.
instructor s. Lehrer m.
instrument s. Werkzeug n.; Urkunde f.; Zahlungsmittel n.
instrumental a., ~ly adv. als behilflich.
insubordination s. Ungehorsam m.
insufferable a., ~bly adv. unerträglich.
insufficiency s. Unzulänglichkeit f.
insufficient a., ~ly adv. unzulänglich.
insular a. Insel...
insularity s. insulare Lage f.; Beschränktheit f.
insulate v.t. absondern, isolieren; (elek.) ~ing tape, Isolierband n.
insulator s. Isolator m.
insult v.t. beschimpfen, beleidigen; ~ s. Beleidigung, Beschimpfung f.
insuperable a. unüberwindlich.
insurable a. versicherungsfähig.
insurance s. Versicherung f.; **~-broker** s. Versicherungsmakler m.; **~-claim** s. Versicherungsanspruch m.; **~-policy** s. Versicherungspolice f.

insure v.t. versichern; sichern.
insurgents s.pl. Aufrührer m.pl.
insurmountable a. unübersteiglich.
insurrection s. Aufstand m.
intact a. unberührt; unversehrt.
intaglio s. geschnittene Stein m.
intake s. Zustrom m.; Einlassöffnung f.
intangible a. unfühlbar.
integral a. ganz, vollständig.
integrate v.t. zusammenfassen.
integrity s. Vollständigkeit f.; Rechtschaffenheit f.
intellect s. Verstand m.
intellectual a. Verstandes...; geistig; verständig; ~s pl. Gebildeten pl.
intelligence s.; Verstand m., Verständnis n.; Einsicht f.; Nachricht f.
intelligence-service s. Nachrichtendienst m.
intelligent a., ~ly adv. verständig, einsichtig: intelligent.
intelligible a., ~bly adv. verständlich.
intemperance s. Unmässigkeit f.
intemperate a., ~ly adv. unmässig.
intend v.t. beabsichtigen.
intendant s. Aufseher, Verwalter m.
intending a. angehend; künftig.
intense a., ~ly adv. heftig.
intensify v.t. steigern, verstärken.
intensity s. Heftigkeit f.
intensive a., ~ly adv. angestrengt.
intent a., begierig; ~ s. Vorhaben n.
intention s. Absicht f.
intentional a. absichtlich.
inter v.t. beerdigen.
interact v.i. sich gegenseitig beeinflussen.
interaction s. Wechselwirkung f.
intercede v.i. dazwischen treten, vermitteln.
intercept v.t. abfangen; auffangen; unterbrechen.
intercession s. Fürsprache f.
interchange v.t. & i. tauschen; abwechseln; ~ s. Tausch, Verkehr m.; Abwechselung f., Tauschhandel m.
intercourse s. Verkehr, Umgang m.
interdict v.t. untersagen.
interdiction s. Untersagung f.
interest v. Anteil m.; Nutzen m.; Zins m., Zinsen pl.; Interesse n., Belang m.; rate of ~, Zinssatz m.; to bear ~, Zinsen tragen; ~ v.t. angehen, beteiligen, interessieren.
interested p. & a. interessiert (an); eigennützig.
interesting a. interessant.
interfere v.i. sich einmengen; stören.
interference s. Dazwischenkunft f.; Einmischung f.; (phys.) Interferenz f.
interim s. Zwischenzeit f.; ~ a. adv. vorläufig, Zwischen...
interior a., ~ly adv. innerlich; ~ s. Innere n.; **~ decoration** s. Innendekoration f.

interjection s. (*gram.*) Interjektion f.
interlock v.i. ineinandergreifen.
interlope v.i. sich eindrängen.
interloper s. Eindringling m.
interlude s. Zwischenspiel n.
intermarriage s. Wechselheirat f.
intermarry v.i. eine Wechselheirat schliessen.
intermeddle v.i. sich einmischen.
intermediary a. dazwischen befindlich; ~ s. Vermittler m.
intermediate a., ~ly adv. in der Mitte befindlich, Zwischen..., Mittel...
interment s. Beerdigung f.
intermezzo s. (*mus.*) Intermezzo; (*fig.*) Zwischenspiel, Intermezzo n.
interminable a. unbegrenzt.
intermingle v.t. untermischen; ~ v.i. sich vermischen.
intermission s. Aussetzen n., Pause f.
intermittent a. aussetzend.
intern v.t. internieren.
internal a., ~ly adv. innerlich; ~ combustion engine s. Explosionsmotor, Verbrennungsmotor m.
international a. international, zwischenstaatlich; Welt..., Völker...; ~ call, (*tel.*) Auslandsgespräch n.; ~ law, Völkerrecht n.; ~ relations pl. auswärtige Beziehungen f.pl.
internee s. Internierte m.
internment s. Internierung f.
interpellation s. Anfrage (f.) im Parlament.
interplay s. Ineinanderspiel n.
interpolation s. Einschiebung f.
interpose v.i. dazwischen treten.
interposition s. Dazwischenkunft.
interpret v.t. auslegen.
interpretation s. Auslegung f.
interpreter s. Dolmetscher.
interrogate v.t. & i. befragen.
interrogation s. Frage f.; Befragen n.; Verhör n.; ~-mark s. Fragezeichen n.
interrogative a. fragend; ~ s. Fragewort n.
interrogatory a. fragend; ~ s. Verhör n.
interrupt v.t. unterbrechen.
interruption,s. Unterbrechung f.
intersect v.t. & i. (sich) durchschneiden, sich kreuzen.
intersection s. Schnittpunkt m.; Strassenkreuzung f.
intersperse v.t. einstreuen.
interstate a. (*Am.*) zwischenstaatlich.
interstice s. Zwischenraum m.
interval s. Zwischenraum m.; Pause f.; Abstand m.; Intervall n.
intervene v.i. sich einmischen; eintreten.
intervention s. Dazwischenkunft, Vermittlung f.; Einmischung, Intervention f.
interview s. Zusammenkunft f., Unterredung f.; ~ v.t. bei einem Besuch ausfragen, interviewen; interviewing hours pl. Sprechstunden (von Stellen und Behörden).
interweave v.t.st. verweben.
interzonal a. Zwischenzonen...
intestacy s. Sterben ohne Testament n.
intestate adv. ohne Testament.
intestine a. inner; ~s s.pl. Eingeweide n., Darm m.
intimacy s. Vertraulichkeit f.
intimate s., ~ly adv. innig; vertraut; ~ v.t. andeuten, anzeigen.
intimation s. Andeutung f.; Wink m.
intimidate v.t. einschüchtern.
into pr. in; hinein.
intolerable a., ~bly adv. unerträglich.
intolerance s. Unduldsamkeit f.
intolerant a. unduldsam.
intonation s. Tonfall m.
intoxicate v.t. berauschen; *intoxicating liquors*, berauschende Getränke n.pl.
intoxication s. Rausch m.
intractable a. unlenksam, unbändig.
intransigent a. unnachgiebig.
intransitive a. intransitiv.
intravenous a. intravenös.
intrazonal a. Innerzonen...
intrepid a., ~ly adv. unerschrocken.
intricacy s. Verwicklung, Verlegenheit f.
intricate a., ~ly adv. verworren, schwierig.
intrigue s. Verwicklung f.; Intrige f.; ~ v.i. Ränke schmieden.
intrinsic a., ~ally adv. inner, wesentlich.
introduce v.t. einführen; vorstellen.
introduction s. Einführung, Einleitung f.; Vorstellung f.
introductory a. einleitend.
introspection s. Selbstprüfung f.
introspective a. nach innen gerichtet.
introversion f. Nachinnengerichtetsein n.
introvert s. nach innen gerichtete Mensch m.
intrude v.i. sich eindrängen; ~ v.t. eindrängen.
intruder s. Eindringling m.
intrusion s. Eindringen n.
intuition s. Intuition f.
intuitive a., ~ly adv. intuitiv.
inundate v.t. überschwemmen.
inundation s. Überschwemmung f.
inure v.t. gewöhnen, abhärten.
invade v.t. einfallen; angreifen.
invalid a. kränklich; dienstunfähig; ungültig; ~ s. Invalide m.
invalidate v.t. ungültig machen.
invalidity s. Ungültigkeit f.
invaluable a. unschätzbar.
invariable a., ~bly adv. unveränderlich.
invasion s. Einfall, Angriff m.
invective s. Schmähung f.
inveigh v.i. losfahren, schmähen.
inveigle v.t. verleiten, verführen.

invent *v.t.* erfinden.
invention *s.* Erfindung *f.*
inventive *a.* erfinderisch.
inventor *s.* Erfinder *m.*
inventory *s.* Verzeichnis; Inventar *n.*
inverse *a.*, ~ly *adv.* umgekehrt.
inversion *s.* Umkehrung *f.*
invert *v.t.* umkehren; ~ed commas *pl.* Anführungszeichen *n.*
invest *v.t.* bekleiden; erteilen; (eine Summe) anlegen; einschliessen.
investigate *v.t.* erforschen.
investigation before trial *s.* (law) Voruntersuchung *f.*
investiture *s.* Belehnung, Einsetzung *f.*
investment *s.* (Geld-) Anlage *f.*
investor *s.* Geldgeber *m.*
inveterate *a.* eingewurzelt.
invidious *a.*, ~ly *adv.* hasserregend.
invigorate *v.t.* stärken; beleben.
invincible *a.*, ~bly *adv.* unüberwindlich.
inviolable *a.*, ~bly *adv.* unverletzlich.
inviolate *a.* unverletzt.
invisible *a.*, ~bly *adv.* unsichtbar.
invisible mending *s.* Kunststopferei *f.*
invitation *s.* Einladung *f.*
invite *v.t.* einladen; auffordern.
invocation *s.* Anrufung *f.*
invoice *s.* Warenrechnung, Faktura *f.*
invoke *v.t.* anrufen; sich berufen auf.
involuntary *a.*, ~ily *adv.* unfreiwillig; unwillkürlich.
involve *v.t.* in sich schliessen; verwickeln.
invulnerable *a.* unverwundbar.
inward *a. & adv.*, ~ly *adv.* innerlich; einwärts; ~ *s.* Innere *n.*
inwards *adv.* einwärts.
iodine *s.* Jod *n.*
ionize *v.t.* (*elek.*) ionisieren.
I.O.U.=I owe you *s.* Schuldschein *m.*
irascible *a.* jähzornig; reizbar.
irate *a.* erzürnt, zornig.
ire *s.* Zorn *m.*
iris *s.* Regenbogenhaut *f.*; Schwertlilie *f.*
irksome *a.* ärgerlich; lästig.
iron *s.* Eisen *n.*; Bügeleisen *n.*; ~ *a.* eisern; fest; ~ *v.t.* bügeln.
ironclad *a.* gepanzert (von Schiffen).
ironic(al) *a.*, ~ally *adv.* ironisch.
ironmonger *s.* Eisenhändler *m.*
iron-works *s.pl.* Eisenhütte *f.*
irony *s.* Ironie *f.*
irradiate *v.t.* bestrahlen, bescheinen.
irrational *a.*, ~ly *adv.* unvernünftig.
irreclaimable *a.* unwiederbringlich, unverbesserlich.
irreconcilable *a.*, ~bly *adv.* unversöhnlich; unvereinbar.
irrecoverable *a.*, ~ly *adv.* unwiederbringlich; unersetzlich; ~ debts *pl.* uneinbringliche Forderungen.*f.pl.*
irredeemable *a.* unablöslich, nicht tilgbar, nicht rückzahlbar; unverbesserlich.

irreducible *a.* nicht zu verringern; nicht zu verwandeln.
irrefutable *a.*, ~bly *adv.* unwiderleglich.
irregular *a.*, ~ly *adv.* unregelmässig.
irregularity *s.* Unregelmässigkeit *f.*
irrelevant *a.*, ~ly *adv.* unerheblich.
irreligion *s.* Unglaube *m.*
irreligious *a.*, ~ly *adv.* ungläubig.
irremediable *a.*, ~bly *adv.* unheilbar, unersetzlich.
irremovable *a.* unabsetzbar.
irreparable *a.*, ~bly *adv.* unersetzlich.
irreplaceable *a.*, ~ly *adv.* unersetzlich.
irreprehensible *a.*, ~bly *adv.* untadelhaft.
irrepressible *a.* ununterdrückbar.
irreproachable *a.*, ~bly *adv.* untadelhaft.
irresistible *a.*, ~bly *adv.* unwiderstehlich.
irresolute *a.*, ~ly *adv.* unschlüssig.
irrespective *a.*, ~ly *adv.* ohne Rücksicht auf; ~ *of*, ungeachtet.
irresponsibility *s.* Unverantwortlichkeit *f.*
irresponsible *a.* unverantwortlich.
irretrievable *a.*, ~bly *adv.* unersetzlich.
irreverent *a.*, ~ly *adv.* unehrerbietig.
irrevocable *a.*, ~bly *adv.* unwiderruflich.
irrigate *v.t.* bewässern.
irrigation *s.* Bewässerung *f.*
irritable *a.* reizbar.
irritant *s.* Reizmittel *n.*
irritate *v.t.* reizen; erbittern.
irritation *s.* Erbitterung *f.*
irruption *s.* Einbruch *m.*
isinglass *s.* Hausenblase *f.*; Gelatine .
island *s.* Insel *f.*; Schutzinsel *f.*
islander *s.* Inselbewohner *m.*
isle *s.* Insel *f.*
isolate *v.t.* absondern.
isolation *s.* Isolierung *f.*
issuance *s.* (*Am.*) Ausgabe *f.*
issue *s.* Ausgang *m.*; Erfolg *m.*; Notenausgabe, Emission *f.*; Nacnkommen *pl.*; streitige Frage *f.*; ~ *of a paper*, Zeitungsausgabe *f.*; ~ *v.i.* herrühren, entspringen; endigen; ~ *v.t.* ergehen lassen; ausgeben, ausstellen (Wechsel).
isthmus *s.* Landenge *f.*
it *pn.* es, das; *with* ~, damit.
Italian warehouse *s.* Kolonialwaren-, Südfruchthandlung *f.*
italics *s.pl.* Kursivschrift *f.*
itch *s.* Jucken *n.*; Krätze *f.*; Gelüst *n.*; ~ *v.i.* jucken; verlangen.
item *adv.* desgleichen; ferner; ~ *s.* Posten *m.*; Stück *m.*; Punkt *m.*
itemize *v.t.* detaillieren.
itinerant *a.* wandernd.
itinerary *a.* reisend, wandernd; ~ *s.* Reiseroute *f.*; Reisebuch *n.*
its *pn.* sein, dessen.
itself *pn.* es selbst, selbst, sich.
ivory *s.* Elfenbein *n.*; ~ *a.* elfenbeinern.
ivy *s.* Epheu *m.*

J

jabber *v.i.* schwatzen.
jack *s.* Kerl, Matrose *m.*; Bube *m.* (Karte); (*nav.*) Gösch *f.*; Sägebock *m.*; (Hand-)Winde *f.*; Bratenwender *m.*; Stiefelknecht *m.*; Flaschenzug *m.*; (*mech.*) Hebebock, Wagenheber *m.*
jackal *s.* Schakal *m.*
jackanapes *s.* Naseweis, Schlingel *m.*
jack-boots *s.pl.* hohe Stiefel *m.pl.*
jackdaw *s.* Dohle *f.*
jacket *s.* Jacke *f.*; Schutzumschlag (eines Buches) *m.*
Jack-of-all-trades *s.* Hans in allen Gassen.
jade *s.* Schindmähre *f.*; Weibsbild *n.*; Beilstein *m.*; ~ *v.t.* abmatten.
jag *v.t.* kerben; ~ *s.* Kerbe *f.*; Felszacken *m.*; Zahn *m.*
jagged *a.* zackig.
jail *s.* Gefängnis *n.*; ~ *v.t.* einkerkern.
jailer *s.* Gefangenwärter *m.*
jam *s.* Marmelade *f.*; ~ *v.t.* zusammenpressen; (*radio*) stören.
janitor *s.* (*Am.*) Türhüter, Pförtner *m.*
January *s.* Januar *m.*
japan *s.* lackierte Arbeit *f.*; ~ *v.t.* lackieren.
jar *v.i.* knarren; misstönen; ~ *s.* Misshelligkeit *f.*; Krug *m.*
jargon *s.* Kauderwelsch *n.*
jasmine *s.* Jasmin *m.*
jasper *s.* Jaspis *m.*
jaundice *s.* Gelbsucht *f.*
jaundiced *a.* gelbsüchtig.
jaunt *v.i.* herumstreifen.
jaunty *a.*, ~ily *adv.* leicht, munter.
javelin *s.* Wurfspeer *m.*
jaw *s.* Kinnbacken, Kiefer *m.*; (*mech.*) Backen; ~s *s.pl.* Rachen *m.*; ~ *v.t.* schimpfen.
jay *s.* Häher *m.*
jazz *s.* Jazzmusik *f.*; ~-band *s.* Jazzbande *f.*
jealous *a.*, ~ly *adv.* eifersüchtig.
jealousy *s.* Eifersucht *f.*; Argwohn *m.*
jeer *v.t. & i.* spotten; ~ *s.* Spott *m.*
jejune *a.* nüchtern; fade, trocken.
jelly *s.* Gallerte *f.*; Gelee *n.*
jelly-fish *s.* Qualle, Meduse *f.*
jeopardize *v.t.* aufs Spiel setzen.
jeopardy *s.* Gefahr *f.*
jerk *s.* Stoss *m.*; ~ *v.t.* stossen.
jerry-built *a.* unsolide gebaut.
jersey *s.* Wolljacke *f.*
jessamine *s.* Jasmin *m.*
jest *s.* Scherz *m.*; ~ *v.i.* scherzen.
jester *s.* Spassvogel *m.*; Hofnarr *m.*
jesuit *s.* Jesuit *m.*
jesuitical *a.*, ~ly *adv.* jesuitisch.
jet *s.* Jet *n.*; Pechkohle *f.*; Wasser(Gas-)-

strahl *m.*; ~-fighter *s.* (*avi.*) Düsenjäger *m.*
jet-black *a.* pechschwarz.
jetsam *s.* Strandgut *n.*
jettison *v.t.* über Bord werfen; ~able *tank*, (*avi.*) abwerfbare Tank *m.*
jetty *s.* Hafendamm.
Jew *s.* Jude *m.*
jewel *s.* Juwel *n.*
jeweller *s.* Juwelier *m.*
jewellery *s.* Juwelen *pl.*
Jewess *s.* Jüdin *f.*
Jewish *a.* jüdisch.
Jewry *s.* Judenschaft *f.*; Judenviertel *n.*
jiff(y) *s. in a* ~, augenblicklich.
jig *s.* Gigue (Tanz) *f.*; (*mech.*) (Bohr) Schablone, (Bohr) Lehre *f.*
jilt *s.* Kokette *f.*; ~ *v.i. & t.* (den Liebhaber) sitzen lassen.
jingle *v.t. & i.* klingeln, klimpern; ~ *s.* Geklingel *n.*
jingo *s.* Hurrapatriot, Chauvinist *m.*
job *s.* (geringe) Arbeit *f.*; Arbeitsstück *n.*; odd ~s *pl.* Gelegenheitsarbeiten *pl.*; ~ *v.t.* (ver)mieten; ramschen; Schiebungen machen; ~ *v.i.* Lohnarbeit tun; ~bing gardener, Lohngärtner *m.*
jobber *s.* Stückarbeiter, Handlanger, Makler *m.*; Aktienhändler *m.*
jobbery *s.* abgekartete Geschichte *f.*; Schiebung, Korruption *f.*
jobless *a.* arbeitslos.
jockey *s.* Jockei, Reitknecht *m.*; Betrüger *m.*; ~ *v.t.* prellen.
jocose *a.*, ~ly *adv.* scherzhaft.
jocular *a.*, ~ly *adv.* spasshaft, lustig.
jocund *a.*, ~ly *adv.* lustig, munter.
jog *v.t.* stossen; schütteln; ~ *v.i.* traben; ~ *s.* Schupp *m.*; Rütteln *n.*
joggle *v.t.* rütteln; verzahnen; ~ *v.i.* sich schütteln.
join *v.t.* zusammenfügen, verbinden, zugesellen; ~ *v.i.* sich berühren; sich verbinden; sich beteiligen; sich anschliessen; *to* ~ *issue with*, nicht übereinstimmen mit.
joiner *s.* Tischler *m.*
joinery *s.* Tischlerei *f.*
joint *a.* vereinigt; ~ *s.* Gelenk *n.*; Fuge *f.*; Knoten *m.*; Bratenstück *n.*; ~ *v.t.* zusammenfügen; zergliedern.
joint-heir *s.* Miterbe *m.*
jointly *adv.* gemeinsam.
joint owner *s.* Mitinhaber *m.*
joint-stock company *s.* Aktiengesellschaft *f.*
jointure *s.* Wittum *n.*
joist *s.* Querbalken *m.*
joke *s.* Spass, Scherz, Witz *m.*; ~ *v.i.* spassen.
jollity *s.* Lustigkeit *f.*
jolly *a.*, ~ily *adv.* fröhlich, lustig; (*sl.*) famos; ~ *adv.* sehr.

jolt *v.t. & i.* rütteln; ~ *s.* Stoss *m.*
jostle *v.t.* stossen, anrennen.
jot *s.* Iota, Pünktchen *n.*; **to ~ down** *v.t.* kurz niederschreiben.
journal *s.* Tagebuch *n.*; Zeitschrift *f.*; Zeitung *f.*
journalism *s.* Zeitungswesen *n.*
journalist *s.* Journalist *m.*
journey *s.* Reise *f.*; ~ *v. .* reisen.
journeyman *s.* Geselle *m.*
Jove *s. by ~!*, bei Gott!
jovial *a.*, ~**ly** *adv.* frohsinnig.
joviality *s.* Frohsinnigkeit *f.*
jowl *s.* Backe *f.*; *cheek by ~*, dicht zusammen.
joy *s.* Freude, Fröhlichkeit *f.*; ~ *v.i.* sich freuen.
joyless *a.*, ~**ly** *adv.* freudlos.
joyous *a.*, ~**ly** *adv.* fröhlich, erfreulich.
jubilant *a.* frohlockend.
jubilation *s.* Jubel *m.*
jubilee *s.* Jubeljahr *n.*
Judaism *s.* Judentum *n.*
judge *s.* Richter *m.*; Kenner *m.*; *associate ~*, Beisitzer (bei Gericht) *m.*; ~ *v.i. & t.* richten; (be)urteilen; entscheiden.
judg(e)ment *s.* Urteil *n.*; Urteilskraft *f.*; *to pronounce (pass) ~ on*, ein Urteil fällen.
judicature *s.* Gerichtswesen; ~**-act** *s.* Gerichtsverfassungsgesetz *n.*
judicial *a.*, ~**ly** *adv.* gerichtlich.
judiciary *s.* Gerichtswesen; Richterstand *m.*
judicious *a.*, ~**ly** *adv.* scharfsinnig, klug.
jug *s.* Krug *m.*
juggle *s.* Gaukelei *f.*; ~ *v.i.* gaukeln.
juggler *s.* Gaukler *m.*
jugular *a.* Hals...; ~ *s.* Halsader *f.*
juice *s.* Saft *m.*
juicy *a.* saftig.
July *s.* Juli *m.*
jumble *v.t.* vermengen, verwirren; ~ *s.* Mischmasch *m.*; ~ *sale s.* Ramschverkauf *m.*
jump *v.i.* springen, hüpfen; stossen (vom Wagen) ~ *v.t.* überspringen; ~ *s.* Sprung *m.*; *high ~*, Hochsprung *m.*; *long ~*, Weitsprung *m.*
jumper *s.* Schlüpfbluse *f.*
jumpy *a.* nervös.
junction *s.* Vereinigung *f.*; Knotenpunkt (*m.*) mehrerer Eisenbahnen.
juncture *s.* Verbindung *f.*; Gelenk *n.*; Fuge *f.*; (kritische) Zeitpunkt *m.*
June *s.* Juni *m.*
jungle *s.* Dschungel *m.* or *f.*
junior *a.* jünger; Unter...
juniper *s.* Wacholder *m.*
junk *s.* alte Tauwerk *n.*; Dschonke *f.*
junket *s.* süsse Speise *f.*) aus Quark und Molken; ~ *v.i.* schmausen.
juridical *a.*, ~**ly** *adv.* gerichtlich.
jurisdiction *s.* Gerichtsbarkeit *f.*; Rechts-

sprechung, Zuständigkeit *f.*; *contentious ~*, streitige Gerichtsbarkeit; *lack of ~*, Unzuständigkeit (des Gerichts).
jurisdictional *a.* Gerichtsbarkeits..., Zuständigkeits...
jurisprudence *s.* allgemeine Rechtswissenschaft *f.*
jurist *s.* Rechtsgelehrte *m.*; Jurist *m.*
juror *s.* Geschworne *m.*
jury *s.* Geschworene *m.pl.*; ~**-box**, Geschworenenbank *f.*; ~**man** *s.* Geschworenen *m.*
just *a.* gerecht; rechtschaffen; richtig, gehörig; vollständig; ~ *adv.* eben, bloss, gerade, fast.
justice *s.* Gerechtigkeit *f.*; Richter *m.*; *to administer (dispense) ~*, Recht sprechen.
justifiable *a.*, ~**bly** *adv.* zu rechtfertigen.
justification *s.* Rechtfertigung *f.*
justify *v.t.* rechtfertigen.
justly *adv.* mit Recht; genau.
justness *s.* Rechtmässigkeit *f.*
jut *v.i.* hervorragen, überhangen.
jute *s.* Jute *f.*
juvenile *a.* jung, jugendlich; ~ *s.* Jugendliche; ~ *court s.* Jugendgericht *n.*
juxtaposition *s.* Nebeneinanderstellung *f.*

K

kaleidoscope *s.* Kaleidoskop *n.*
kali *s.* Salzkraut *n.*, Kali *n.*
kangaroo *s.* Känguruh *n.*
keel *s.* Kiel *m.*; Kielraum *m.*
keen *a.*, ~**ly** *adv.* scharf, spitzig; eifrig; heftig; scharfsinnig; ~ *edge*, scharfe Schneide *f.*; ~ *on a thing*, hinter etwas her, auf etwas erpicht.
keep *v.t.ir.* halten; behalten; erhalten; aufbewahren; führen (Laden); hüten; unterhalten; beobachten; feiern; fortfahren; ~ *v.i.* sich halten, dauerhaft sein; sich aufhalten, bleiben; *he ~s repeating*, er wiederholt dauernd; *to ~ well*, sich weiter gut befinden; *to ~ away*, abhalten, sich fern halten; *to ~ house*, den Haushalt führen; *to ~ in touch*, in Verbindung bleiben; *to ~ off*, abhalten; davonbleiben; *to ~ on*, dabei bleiben, fortfahren; aufbehalten (*hat*); anbehalten (*dress*); *to ~ up*, aufrecht erhalten; unterhalten, sich erhalten; Schritt halten; ~ *s.* Obhut, Pflege *f.*; Weide *f.*; Burgverliess *n.*
keeper *s.* Aufseher *m.*; Verwalter *m.*
keeping *s.* Gewahrsam *m.*
keepsake *s.* Andenken *n.*
keg *s.* Fässchen *n.*
ken *s.* Gesichtskreis *m.*
kennel *s.* Hundestall *m.*; Gosse *f.*
kerbstone *s.* Prellstein *m.*; Randstein *m.*

kerchief s. Kopf-, Halstuch n.
kernel s. Kern m.
kerosene s. Kerosin (Brennöl) n.
ketchup s. Pikante Sauce f.
kettle s. Kessel m.
kettle-drum s. Kesselpauke f.
key s. Schlüssel m.; Tonart f.; Taste f.; (mech.) Keil m.; ~-position, Schlüsselstellung f.; ~ way, s. (mech.) Nute f.
keyboard s. Tastatur f.; Klaviatur f.
key-hole s. Schlüsselloch n.
key-note s. Grundton m.
key-stone s. Schlussstein m.
kick v.t. & i. mit dem Fusse stossen, treten, ausschlagen; strampeln; ~ s. Tritt, Stoss m.
kid s. Zicklein n.; Kind n.
kid-gloves s.pl. Glacéhandschuhe m.pl.
kidnap v.t. (Kinder) entführen, Menschen rauben.
kidney s. Niere f.
kill v.t. töten, schlachten; to ~ weeds, Unkraut vernichten.
kill-joy s. Spielverderber m.
kiln s. Brenn-, Darrofen m.
kin s. Verwandtschaft f.; ~ a. verwandt.
kind s. Art f.; Gattung f.; payment in ~, Naturalleistung, f.; ~ a., ~ly adv. gütig, liebreich.
kindle v.t. anzünden; ~ v.i. sich entzünden.
kindly a. gütig, sanft.
kindness s. Güte, Freundlichkeit f.
kindred s. Verwandtschaft, Schwägerschaft f.; ~ a. verwandt.
king s. König m.
kingdom s. Königreich n.; Reich n.
kingfisher s. Eisvogel m.
kink s. Schleife (f.) im Tau; (fig.) Schrulle f., Sparren m.
kinsfolk s. Sippe f., Verwandten pl.
kinship s. Verwandtschaft f.
kinsman s. Verwandte m.
kipper s. geräucherter Bückling m.
kirk s. schottische Kirche f.
kiss v.t. küssen; ~ s. Kuss m.
kit s. Ausrüstung f.; ~-bag s. Tornister m.
kitchen s. Küche f.; ~-appliances pl. Küchenartikel m.pl.; ~-garden, Gemüsegarten m.; ~-maid, Küchenmädchen n.
kitchenette s. kleine Küche f.
kite s. Gabelweih m.; Papierdrache m.; (fig.) Versuchsballon.
kith s. ~ and kin, Freunde und Verwandte.
kitten s. Kätzchen n.
knack s. Kunstgriff m.; Geschick n.
knacker s. Rosschlächter, Abdecker m.
knapsack s. Tornister m., Ränzel n.
knave s. Schurke m.; Bube (in der Karte) m.
knavish a., ~ly adv. schurkisch.
knead v.t. kneten.

knee s. Knie n. ~-cap s. Kniescheibe f.; Knieleder n.
kneel v.i.ir. knie[e]n.
knell s. Totenglocke f.
knicker-bockers s.pl. Kniehosen f.pl.
knickers s.pl. Schlüpfer m.
knick-knacks s.pl. Nippsachen f.pl.
knife s. Messer n.
knife-rest s. Messerbänkchen n.
knight s. Ritter m.; Springer (im Schach) m.
knight-errant s. fahrende Ritter m.
knighthood s. Ritterwürde f.
knit v.t.r. & ir. stricken; knüpfen; runzeln.
knitting s. Strickzeug n.
knitting-needle s. Stricknadel f.
knitwear s. Strickwaren f.pl.
knob s. Knopf, Knorren m.; Quaste f.
knock v.t. & i. klopfen, pochen; schlagen, stossen; to ~ about, sich umhertreiben; to ~ down m., zuschlagen (bei Versteigerungen); ~-down price, äusserster Preis, Taxe (bei Versteigerungen) ~-kneed a. x-beinig; ~-knees pl. X-Beine n.pl.; to ~ off, mit der Arbeit aufhören; ~ s. Schlag m.; Anklopfen n.
knocker s. Türklopfer m.
knoll s. kleine Hügel m.
knot s. Knoten m.; Schleife f.; Baumast, Baumknorren m.; Schwierigkeit f.; Seemeile f.; ~ v.t. verknüpfen; verwirren.
knotty a., ~ily adv. knotig; verwickelt.
knout s. Knute f.; ~ v.t. knuten.
know v.t. & i.st. wissen, kennen; erkennen; können; to let me ~, mich benachrichtigen; to get to ~, erfahren.
know-how s. (Am.) Kenntnisse f.pl.
knowing p. & a. bewusst, kundig, bewandert; schlau; ~ s. Wissen n.; Kenntnis f.
knowingly adv. wissentlich.
knowledge s. Wissen n.; Wissenschaft f.; Erkenntnis f.; Bekanntschaft f.; to the best of my ~ and belief, nach bestem Wissen und Gewissen; it is common ~, es ist allgemein bekannt.
knuckle s. Knöchel m.; ~ of veal s. Kalbshaxe f.
knuckle-duster s. Schlagring m.
knur(l) s. Knorren m.; to knurl v.t. (mech.) rändeln.
kodak s. Kodak m.; ~ v.t. mit einem Kodak photographieren.

L

label s. Zettel m.; Aufschrift f.; ~ v.t. mit Zettel versehen, mit Aufschrift versehen.
labial s. Lipenlaut m.
laboratory s. Laboratorium n.

laborious *a.*, ~ly *adv.* arbeitsam, mühsam; umständlich.
labour *s.* Arbeit *f.*; Mühe *f.*; Geburts-wehen *pl.*; hard ~ *s.* Zwangsarbeit *f.*; ~ *v.i.* arbeiten sich abmühen; in Not sein; in Kindesnöten sein; ~ *v.t.* bearbeiten, durcharbeiten.
labourer *s.* Arbeiter *m.*; Hilfsarbeiter *m.*; landwirtschaftliche Arbeiter, Tagelöhner *m.*
labour-exchange *s.* Arbeitsamt *n.*
labour-service *s.* Arbeitsdienst *m.*; *compulsory* ~, Arbeitsdienstpflicht *f.*
laburnum *s.* (*bot.*) Goldregen *m.*
labyrinth *s.* Labyrinth *n.*
lace *s.* Schnur *f.*; Spitze, Tresse *f.*; ~ *v.t.* zuschnüren; besetzen.
lace-bobbins *s.pl.* Spitzenklöppel *m.pl.*
lace-boots *s.pl.* Schnürstiefel *m.pl.*
lacerate *v.t.* zerreissen.
lachrymose *a.* weinerlich.
lack *v.i.* bedürfen, nicht haben; fehlen; ~ *s.* Mangel *m.*
lackadaisical *a.* schmachtend; geziert.
lackey *s.* Lakai *m.*
laconic *a.* lakonisch.
lacquer *s.* Lack *m.*; *v.t.* lackieren.
lacuna *s.* Lücke *f.*
lad *s.* Knabe, Junge *m.*
ladder *s.* Leiter *f.*; Laufmasche (*f.*) im Strumpf.
lade *v.t.r. & st.* laden, befrachten.
lading *s.* Ladung, Fracht *f.*
ladle *s.* Schöpflöffel *m.*; ~ *v.t.* ausschöpfen, auslöffeln.
lady *s.* Dame *f.*; Gemahlin *f.*, Herrin *f.*; ~-bird, Marienkäfer *m.*; ~'s maid, Zofe *f.*
ladylike *a.* damenhaft; wohlerzogen.
lag *v.i.* zögern; zurückbleiben.
lager *s.* Lagerbier *n.*
laggard *a.* träge, langsam; ~ *s.* Zauderer *m.*
lagoon *s.* Lagune *f.*
laic(al) *a.* weltlich; ~ *s.* Laie *m.*
lair *s.* Lager (des Wildes) *n.*
laird *s.* Gutsherr (in Schottland) *m.*
laity *s.* Laienstand *m.*
lake *s.* See *m.*
lamb *s.* Lamm *n.*; ~ *v.i.* lammen.
lambent *a.* lodernd; funkelnd.
lamblike *a.* lammartig; fromm, sanft.
lame *a.*, lahm; ~ *v.t.* lähmen.
lameness *s.* Lähmung *f.*
lament *v.i.* klagen, jammern; ~ *s.* Wehklage *f.*
lamentable *a.*, ~bly *adv.* kläglich.
lamentation *s.* Wehklage *f.*
lamina *s.pl.* Plättchen *n.*, Lamelle *f.*
lamp *s.* Lampe *f.*
lampholder *s.* (Glüh-) Birnenfassung *m.* (*elek.*).
lampoon *s.* Schmähschrift *f.*
lamp-post *s.* Laternenpfahl *m*

lamprey *s.* Neunauge *n.*
lampshade *s.* Lampenschirm *m.*
lance *s.* Lanze *f.*; ~ corporal *s.* Gefreite *m.*; ~ *v.t.* aufstechen.
lancet *s.* Lanzette *f.*; Spitzbogen *m.*
land *s.* Land *n.*; Landschaft, Länderei *f.*; Boden *m.*; Grundstück *n.*; ~ *v.t. & i.* landen.
landed *a.* Land..., Grund...
land-forces *s.pl.* Landmacht *f.*
landing *s.* Landung *f.*; Treppenabsatz *m.*; ~-stage *s.* Landungsbrücke *f.*; *forced* ~, (*avi.*) Notlandung *f.*
landlady *s.* Hauswirtin; Gastwirtin *f.*
landlord *s.* Gutsbesitzer *m.*; Gastwirt *m.*; Hauswirt *m.*
land-lubber *s.* Landratte *f.*
land-mark *s.* Grenzstein *m.*; Markstein *m.*
landowner *s.* Grundbesitzer *m.*
land-register *s.* Grundbuch *n.*
land-registry *s.* Grundbuchamt *n.*
landscape *s.* Landschaft *f.*
land-service *s.* Landhilfe *f.*
land-slide *s.* Erdrutsch *m.*; politische Umschwung *m.*
landslip *s.* Erdrutsch *m.*
land-tax *s.* Grundsteuer *f.*
lane *s.* Heckengang *m.*; Gasse *f.*
language *s.* Sprache *f.*; Ausdruck *m.*
languid *a.*, ~ly *adv.* matt, langsam.
languish *v.i.* schmachten; (*fig.*) danieder liegen; ~ *s.* Schmachten *n.*
languor *s.* Mattigkeit *f.*; Sehnen *n.*
lank, lanky *a.*, ~ly *adv.* schlank; dünn.
lantern *s.* Laterne *f.*; Türmchen *n.*; dark-~ Blendlaterne *f.*
lantern-lecture *s.* Lichtbildervortrag *m.*
lantern-slide *s.* Lichtbild *n.*
lap *s.* Schoss *m.*; Runde *f.*; ~ *v.t.* wickeln, einwickeln; lecken.
lap-dog *s.* Schosshund *m.*
lapel *s.* Aufschlag (*m.*) an einem Rocke.
lapse *s.* Gleiten *n.*; Fehltritt *m.*; Versehen *n.*; Verlauf *m.*; ~ *of time*, Zeitablauf *m.*; ~ *v.i.* fallen; verfliessen; verfallen.
lapwing *s.* Kiebitz *m.*
larceny *s.* Diebstahl *m.*
larch *s.* Lärche *f.*
lard *s.* Schmalz, Schweinefett *n.*; ~ *v.t.* spicken.
larder *s.* Speisekammer *f.*
large *a.*, ~ly *adv.* gross; weit, breit; stark; reichlich; *at* ~, in Freiheit.
lark *s.* Lerche *f.*; Schabernack *m.*
larva *s.* Larve, Puppe *f.*
larynx *s.* Kehlkopf *m.*
lascivious *a.*, ~ly *adv.* wollüstig, geil.
lash *s.* (Peitschen) Hieb *m.*; Schnur *f.*; Geissel *f.*; Rute *f.*; Augenwimper *f.*; ~ *v.t.* peitschen; schlagen; ~ *v.i.* ausschlagen; ausschweifen.
lass *s.* Mädchen *n.*
lassitude *s.* Mattigkeit *f.*

last *a.* letzte, äusserste; vorig; *at* ~, endlich; ~ly *adv.* zuletzt; schliesslich; ~ *s.* Leisten *m.*; (Gewichts-) Last *f.*; ~ *v.i.* währen, dauern; sich halten.

lasting *p. & a.* ~ly *adv.* dauernd.

latch *s.* Klinke *f.*; ~ *v.t.* zuklinken.

latch-key *s.* Drücker *m.*

late *a. & adv.* spät, letzt; (von Zügen) verspätet; ehemalig; neulich; verstorben; *of* ~, neulich.

lately *adv.* neulich, kürzlich.

latent *a.* verborgen, latent; ~ *heat s.* gebundene Wärme *f.*

lateral *a.*, ~ly *adv.* seitlich; Quer...

lath *s.* Latte *f.*; ~ *v.t.* belatten.

lathe *s.* Drehbank *f.*

lather *s.* Seifenschaum *m.*; ~ *v.i.* schäumen; ~ *v.t.* einseifen; prügeln.

Latin *a.* lateinisch; ~ *s.* Latein *n.*

latitude *s.* Breite *f.*; Spielraum *m.*

latitudinarian *a.* freisinnig.

latter *a.* [der] letztere (von zweien), spätere; *the* ~, dieser, diese (*f. & pl.*).

lattice *s.* Gitter *n.*; ~ *v.t.* vergittern.

laudable *a.*, ~bly *adv.* lobenswert.

laudanum *s.* Opiumtinktur *f.*

laudatory *a.* lobend.

laugh *v.i.* lachen; ~ *s.* Gelächter *n.*

laughable *a.* lächerlich.

laughing-stock *s.* Gegenstand des Gelächters *m.*

laughter *s.* Gelächter *m.*

launch *v.t.* schleudern; loslassen; vom Stapel lassen; in Gang setzen; ~ *v.i.* sich aufmachen; ~ *s.* Stapellauf *m.*; Barkasse *f.*

launder *v.t.* (Wäsche) waschen.

laundress *s.* Wäscherin *f.*

laundry *s.* Waschanstalt *f.*; Wäsche *f.*

laundry-bill *s.* Waschzettel *m.*

Laureate, *poet* ~, Hofdichter *m.*

laurel *s.* Lorbeer, Lorbeerbaum *m.*

lava *s.* Lava *f.*

lavatory *s.* Toilette *f.*

lavender *s.* Lavendel *m.*

lavish *a.*, ~ly *adv.* verschwenderisch; ~ *v.t.* verschwenden.

law *s.* Gesetz *n.*; Recht *n.*; Prozess *m.*; Rechtswissenschaft *f.*

law-court *s.* Gerichtshof *m.*

lawful *a.*, ~ly *adv.* gesetzmässig; erlaubt.

lawless *a.*, ~ly *adv.* gesetzlos.

lawn *s.* Rasenplatz *m.*; Batist *m.*

lawn-tennis *s.* Tennis *n.*

lawsuit *s.* Rechtsstreit, Prozess *m.*

lawyer *s.* Rechtsgelehrte, Anwalt *m.*

lax *a.*, ~ly *adv.* schlaff, locker.

laxative *s.* Abführmittel *n.*

laxity *s.* Schlaffheit *f.*

lay *v.t.* legen, stellen; lindern, dämpfen; *to* ~ *at*, (Schaden) taxieren auf; *to* ~ *by*, zurücklegen (Geld); *to* ~ *in*, sich eindecken; *to* ~ *out*, anlegen (Garten); *to* ~

the table, den Tisch decken;` *to* ~ *up*, abtakeln; *to be laid up*, krank im Bett liegen; ~ *s.* Lage, Richtung *f.*; Ballade *f.*; ~ *a.* weltlich, Laien...; ~-brother, Laienbruder *m.*

layer *s.* Lage, Schicht *f.*; Ableger *m.*

layette *s.* Babywäsche *f.*

lay-figure *s.* Gliederpuppe *f.*

layman *s.* Laie *m.*

layout *s.* Anlage (Garten, etc.) *f.*

lazaret(to) *s.* Lazarett *n.*

laze *v.i.* faulenzen.

laziness *s.* Faulheit *f.*

lazy *a.*, ~ily *adv.* faul, träge.

lea *s.* Wiese, Fläche *f.*; Garnmass *n.*

lead *s.* Blei *n.*; Lot, Senkblei *n.*

lead *v.t.ir.* führen, leiten; verleiten; ~ *v.i.* vorangehen; leading *a.* führend, erste, vornehmste, Haupt...; ~ *s.* Führung, Leitung *f.*; Vorsprung *m.*; *leading article, leader, Leitartikel m.*

leaden *a.* bleiern.

leader *s.* Führer *m.*; Leitartikel *m.*

leadership *s.* Führerschaft, Leitung *f.*; ~-principle, Führerprinzip *n.*

leader-writer *s.* Leitartikler *m.*

leading-strings *s.pl.* Gängelband *n.*

leading case *s.* (*law*) Präzedenzfall *m.*

leaf *s.* Blatt *n.*; Türflügel *m.*; gold-~, Blattgold *n.*; ~ *v.i.* Blätter bekommen.

leafless *s.* blätterlos.

leaflet *s.* Blättchen *n.*, Zettel *m.*

leafy *a.* belaubt.

league *s.* Bündnis *n.*; Meile *f.* (4.8 km.); ~ *v.i.* sich verbünden.

leak *s.* Leck *m.*; Durchsickern von Geheimnissen *n.*; ~ *v.i.* leck sein; (*fig.*) *to* ~ *out*, durchsickern.

leakage *s.* Lecksein *n.*; Verlust *m.*

leaky *a.* leck.

lean *v.i.r. & ir.* (sich) lehnen; ~ *v.t.* anlehnen; ~ *a.*, ~ly *adv.* mager.

leaning *s.* Neigung, Richtung *f.*

leap *v.i.st.* springen, hüpfen; ~ *s.* Sprung *m.*

leap-frog *s.* Bockspringen *n.*

leap-year *s.* Schaltjahr *n.*

learn *v.i. & t.* lernen; erfahren.

learned *a.*, ~ly *adv.* gelehrt; erfahren.

learning *s.* Gelehrsamkeit *f.*; Lernen *n.*

lease *s.* Pacht *f.*; Miete *f.*; ~ *v.t.* verpachten.

lease-hold *s.* Pachtung *f.*; Pacht...

leash *s.* (Koppel)leine *f.*; Koppel *f.*; ~ *v.t.* koppeln.

least *a.* kleinste, wenigste; ~ *adv.* am wenigsten; *at* ~, wenigstens.

leather *s.* Leder *m.*

leave *s.* Erlaubnis *f.*; Urlaub, Abschied *m.*; *to beg* ~, so frei sein; ~ *v.t.ir.* lassen; verlassen; hinterlassen; ~ *v.i.ir.* abstehen von etwas, aufhören; abreisen, weggehen; *leaving certificate,*

Abgangszeugnis *n.*; *leaving examination*, Schlussexamen, Abitur *n.*

leaven *s.* Sauerteig *m.*; ~ *v.t.* säuern.

lectern *s.* Lesepult *n.*

lecture *s.* Vorlesung *f.*; Strafpredigt *f.*, Vortrag *m.*: ~ *v.t.* abkanzeln; ~ *v.i.* Vorlesungen, Vorträge halten; **~-room**, Vorlesungsraum *m.*

lecturer *s.* Vortragender *m.*; Dozent *m.*

ledger *s.* (*com.*) Hauptbuch *n.*

lee *s.* (*nav.*) Leeseite *f.*

leech *s.* Blutegel *m.*

leek *s.* Lauch *m.*

leer *s.* Seitenblick *m.*; ~ *v.i.* schielen.

lees *s.pl.* Hefen *f.pl.*

leeway *s.* Abtrift *f.*

left *p.* von *to leave*, übrig; *to be ~ till called for*, zur Aufbewahrung; postlagernd; ~ *a.* link; *lefthand side*, linke Seite; ~ *s.* Linke (in der Politik) *f.*

left-handed *a.* linkshändig.

leg *s.* Bein *n.*; Keule *f.*; Stiefelschaft *m.*; ~ *of mutton, veal, etc.*, Hammelkeule, Kalbskeule *f.*; *three-legged, four-legged, etc.*, dreibeinig, vierbeinig.

legacy *s.* Vermächtnis *n.*

legal *a.*, **~ly** *adv.* gesetzlich; ~ *remedy*, Rechtsmittel *n.*, Rechtshilfe *f.*: ~ *status*, Rechtsstellung *f.*; ~ *tender*, gesetzliche Zahlungsmittel *n.*

legalize *v.t.* rechtskräftig machen.

legality *s.* Gesetzlichkeit *f.*

legate *s.* (päpstliche) Legat *m.*

legatee *s.* Vermächtnisnehmer, Erbe *m.*

legation *s.* Gesandtschaft *f.*

legend *s.* Legende *f.*; Sage *f.*; Zeichenerklärung *f.*

legendary *a.* sagenhaft; legendhaft

legerdemain *s.* Taschenspielerei *f.*

leggings *s.pl.* Gamaschen *f.pl.*

legible *a.*, **~bly** *adv.* leserlich.

legion *s.* Legion *f.*; Menge *f.*

legislation *s.* Gesetzgebung *f.*

legislative *a.* gesetzgebend; ~ *body*, gesetzgebende Körperschaft *f.*

legislator *s.* Gesetzgeber *m.*

legislature *s.* Gesetzgebung *f.*

legitimacy *s.* eheliche Geburt *f.*

legitimate *a.*, **~ly** *adv.* zulässig, richtig; ehelich.

legitimation *s.* Ehelicherklärung *f.*; Gültigmachung *f.*; Ausweis *m.*

leisure *s.* Musse *f.*

leisurely *a. & adv.* mit Musse, gemächlich.

lemon *s.* Zitrone *f.*

lemonade *s.* Limonade *f.*

lend *v.t.ir.* leihen, borgen.

lending library *s.* Leihbibliothek *f.*

length *s.* Länge *f.*; Strecke *f.*; *at ~*, zuletzt, endlich; *a ~ of carpet*, ein Stück Teppich; *a trouser-~*, eine Hosenlänge (von Stoff).

lengthen *v.t.* (*v.i. sich*) verlängern.

lengthwise *adv.* der Länge nach.

lengthy *a.* weitschweifig.

leniency *s.* Milde, Nachsicht *f.*

lenient *a.* nachsichtig, mild.

lenitive *a.* lindernd; ~ *s.* Linderungsmittel *n.*

lenity *s.* Gelindigkeit *f.*; Nachsicht *f.*

lens *s.* (Glas) Linse *f.*

Lent *s.* Fastenzeit *f.*

lentil *s.* Linse *f.*

leopard *s.* Leopard *m.*

leper *s.* Aussätzige *m.*

leprosy *s.* Aussatz *m.*

leprous *a.* aussätzig.

lesion *s.* (*med.*) Verletzung *f.*

less *a. & adv.* kleiner, weniger, geringer.

lessee *s.* Pächter *m.*

lessen *v.t. & i.* vermindern; abnehmen.

lesser *a.* kleiner, weniger.

lesson *s.* Lektion, Stunde *f.*; Lehre *f.*

lessor *s.* Verpächter *m.*

lest *c.* damit nicht; dass.

let *v.t.ir.* lassen; gestatten; vermieten, verpachten; *rooms to ~*, Zimmer zu vermieten; ~ *alone*, geschweige denn; ~ *down v.t.* im Stiche lassen.

lethal *a.* tödlich, Toten...

lethargic *a.* schlafsüchtig.

lethargy *s.* Schlafsucht *f.*

letter *s.* Buchstabe *f.*; (*print.*) Type *f.*; Brief *m.*; *by ~*, brieflich; **~s** *s.pl.* Wissenschaft *f.*; Literatur *f.*

letter-balance *s.* Briefwaage *f.*

letter-box *s.* Briefkasten *m.*

letter-press *s.* Druckpresse *f.*

letterpress *s.* Druck, Text *m.*

letter-weight *s.* Briefbeschwerer *m.*

lettuce *s.* Kopfsalat *m.*

levee *s.* Morgenempfang beim König *m.*; (*Am.*) Schutzdamm (*m.*) an Flüssen.

level *a.* gleich, eben, flach; waagerecht; ~ *s.* Fläche *f.*; Niveau *n.*, Höhenlage *f.*; Wasserwaage *f.*; Pegel *m.*; *on top ~*, an höchster Stelle; ~ *v.t.* gleichmachen; dem Boden gleichmachen; ebnen; nivellieren; richten.

level-crossing *s.* schienengleicher Bahnübergang *m.*

lever *s.* Hebel *m.*

leverage *s.* Hebelkraft *f.*

levity *s.* Leichtigkeit *f.*; Leichtsinn *m.*

levy *v.t.* heben; erheben; ausheben; ~ *s.* Hebung; Aushebung *f.*; Erhebung (von Steuern).

lewd *a.*, **~ly** *adv.* liederlich, unzüchtig.

lexicon *s.* Wörterbuch *n.*

liability *s.* Verantwortlichkeit *f.*; Hang *m.*; Verbindlichkeit *f.*; Haftpflicht *f.*;

limited ~ *s.* beschränkte Haftung *f.*;

liabilities *pl.* Passiva *s.pl.*; ~ *of kin*, Sippenhaftung *f.*

liable *a.* unterworfen, ausgesetzt; haftbar; *to be ~*, haften; ~ *to duty*, zollpflichtig;

to render oneself ~ *to prosecution*, sich strafbar machen.
liaison *s.* (*mil.*) Verbindung *f.*; ~-**officer** *s.* Verbindungsoffizier *m.*
liar *s.* Lügner *m.*
libel *s.* Klageschrift *f.*; Verleumdung *f.*; ~ *v.t.* beschimpfen; verleumden.
libellous *s.* ehrenrührig.
liberal *a.*, ~**ly** *adv.* freisinnig; freigebig; edeldenkend; liberal (*polit.*).
liberality *s.* Freigebigkeit *f.*
liberate *v.t.* befreien.
liberation *s.* Befreiung *f.*
libertine *a.* ausschweifend; ~ *s.* Wüstling *m.*
liberty *s.* Freiheit *f.*
libidinous *a.* unzüchtig.
librarian *s.* Bibliothekar *m.*
library *s.* Bibliothek *f.*, Bücherei *f.*
licence *s.* Freiheit, Erlaubnis *f.*; Zügellosigkeit *f.*; Konzession *f.*; Schankgerechtigkeit *f.*; *under ~ from the Government*, mit Regierungskonzession; *to take our a* ~, sich eine Konzession verschaffen; ~**d** *p.* mit Konzession; ~**d victualler** *s.* konzessionierte Gastwirt *m.*
license *v.t.* genehmigen.
licensee *s.* Lizenz-, Konzessionsinhaber, Lizenzträger *m.*
licentious *a.*, ~**ly** *adv.* ausschweifend.
lichen *s.* Flechte *f.*; Leberkraut *n.*
lick *v.t.* lecken; prügeln.
licking *s.* Tracht Prügel *f.*
lid *s.* Deckel *m.*; Augenlid *n.*
lie *s.* Lüge *f.*; Lage *f.*; ~ *v.i.* lügen; ~ *v.i.st.* liegen; ruhen.
liege *s.* Lehnsherr *m.*; Lehnsmann *m.*
lien *s.* Pfandrecht *n.*
lieu *s.*, *in* ~ *of*, statt, anstatt.
lieutenant *s.* Leutnant *m.*; ~-**colonel** *s.* Oberstleutnant *m.*
life *s.* Leben *n.*; Lebensbeschreibung *f.*; Lebhaftigkeit *f.*; Lebensdauer (eines Abkommens, einer Maschine, etc.); *for* ~, auf Lebenszeit; ~-**interest** (*law*) lebenslängliche Niessbrauch *m.*
life-annuity *s.* Lebensrente *f.*
life-belt *s.* Rettungsgürtel *m.*
life-boat *s.* Rettungsboot *n.*
life-guard *s.* Leibwache *f.*
life-insurance *s.* Lebensversicherung *f.*
lifeless *a.*, ~**ly** *adv.* leblos.
life-jacket *s.* Schwimmweste *f.*
life-size *a.* lebensgross.
life-time *s.* Lebenszeit *f.*
lift *v.t.* heben, aufheben; entwenden; ~ *v.i.* sich heben, sich heben lassen; ~ *s.* Heben *n.*; Hebewerkzeug *n.*; **Aufzug**, Fahrstuhl *m.*
ligament *s.* Band *n.*; Flechse *f.*
ligature *s.* Band *n.*; Bindung *f.*
light *s.* Licht *n.*; Beleuchtung *f.*; *will you*

give me a ~?, kann ich Feuer haben?; ~ *v.t.r. & ir.* leuchten, erleuchten, anzünden; beleuchten; *to* ~ *on v.i.* sich niederlassen auf; geraten auf; ~ *a. & adv.*, ~**ly** *adv.* leicht; unbedeutend; licht, hell; leichtsinnig; ~**-blue**, ~**-brown**, hellblau, hellbraun, etc.
lighten *v.t.* erleuchten; erleichtern; lichten; löschen; ~ *v.i.* blitzen.
lighter *s.* Anzünder *m.*; Lichterschiff *n.*
light-hearted *a.* wohlgemut, fröhlich.
light-house *s.* Leuchtturm *m.*
lighting *s.* Beleuchtung *f.*
light metal *s.* Leichtmetall *n.*
lightning *s.* Blitz *m.*; ~-**war** *s.* Blitzkrieg *m.*
lightning-conductor, lightning-rod *s.* Blitzableiter *m.*
lights *pl.* Lunge (der Tiere als Speise) *f.*
lightsome *a.* licht, hell; heiter.
lightweight *s.* Leichtgewicht (Boxen) *n.*
ligneous *a.* hölzern; holzig.
lignite *s.* Braunkohle *f.*
like *a. & adv.* gleich, ähnlich; fast; *it's just* ~ *him*, das sieht ihm ähnlich; ~ *s.* Gleiche, Ebenbild *n.*; ~ *v.t. & i.* mögen, gefallen, belieben; gern haben.
likelihood *s.* Wahrscheinlichkeit *f.*
likely *a. & adv.* wahrscheinlich.
liken *v.t.* vergleichen.
likeness *s.* Gleichheit *f.*; Ebenbild *n.*
likewise *adv.* gleichfalls.
liking *s.* Gefallen *n.*, Belieben *n.*
lilac *s.* Flieder *m.*; ~ *a.* lila.
lily *s.* Lilie *f.*; ~ *of the valley*, Maiglöckchen *n.*
limb *s.* Glied *n.*; Ast *m.*
limber *s.* Protze *f.*
limbo *s.* Vorhölle *f.*; Gefängnis *n.*; Vergessenheit *f.*
lime *s.* Leim *m.*; Kalk *m.*; Linde *f.*; Limone *f.*; ~-**juice** Limonensaft *m.*
lime-kiln *s.* Kalkofen *m.*
lime-light *s.* Kalklicht *n.*; *in the* ~, in aller Munde.
limestone *s.* Kalkstein *m.*
limerick *s.* Klapphornvers *m.*
limit *s.* Grenze *f.*; Schranke *f.*; (*com.*) Limite *f.*; *off* ~*s*, (*Am.*) für Zutritt gesperrt; *that is the* ~, das ist die Höhe; ~ *v.t.* beschränken; ~**ed company**, Gesellschaft mit beschränkter Haftung; ~**ed in scope**, von beschränktem Umfang.
limitation *s.* Einschränkung *f.*; (*law*) Verjährung *f.*; *period of* ~, Verjährungsfrist *f.*; *statute of* ~*s*, Verjährungsgesetz *n.*
limitless *a.* grenzenlos.
limp *a.* schlapp; matt; ~ *s.* Hinken *n*; ~ *v.i.* hinken.
limpid *a.* klar, durchsichtig.
linch-pin *s.* Lünse *f.*

line *s.* Linie, Zeile *f.*; Eisenbahnlinie *f.*; Telephonleitung, elektrische Leitung *f.*; Leine *f.*; Reihe *f.*; Vers *m.*; Geschäftszweig *m.*; Äquator *m.*; Stamm *m.*; Art und Weise *f.*; *in the direct* ~, in gerader Linie (verwandt); *in the ascending* ~, in aufsteigender Linie; *in the descending* ~, in absteigender Linie; ~ *of communications*, (*mil.*) Zufuhrstrasse, Verbindungslinie *f.*; ~'*v.t.* liniieren; einfassen, füttern; *to* ~ *up*, sich in einer Reihe aufstellen, sich zusammenschliessen; ~*-up* *s.* Formierung *f.*, Zusammenschluss *m.*

lineage *s.* Geschlecht *n.*

lineal *a.*, ~**ly** *adv.* in gerader Linie; linienweise.

lineament *s.* Gesichtszug *m.*

linear *a.* aus Linien bestehend, linear.

linen *s.* Leinwand *f.*; Wäsche *f.*; ~ *a.* leinen.

linendraper *s.* Weisswarenhändler *m.*

linen-press *s.* Wäscheschrank *m.*

liner *s.* Passagierboot *n.*

linger *v.i.* säumen, zögern.

lingo *s.* Kauderwelsch *n.*

lingual *a.* Zungen...

linguist *s.* Sprachkundige *m.*

linguistic *a.* sprachwissenschaftlich.

liniment *s.* Salbe *f.*

lining *s.* (Unter-)Futter *n.*; Verschalung *f.*

link *s.* (Ketten)glied *n.*; Band *n.*; Kette *f.*; ~ *v.t.* verketten; *to* ~ *up with* *v.i.* Verbindung herstellen mit (bes. mil.).

linnet *s.* Hänfling *m.*

linseed *s.* Leinsamen *n.*

linseed-oil *s.* Leinöl *n.*

linsey-woolsey *s.* Halbwollenzeug *m.*

lint *s.* Flachs *m.*; Scharpie *f.*

lintel *s.* (obere) Türschwelle *f.*

lion *s.* Löwe *m.*

lioness *s.* Löwin *f.*

lip *s.* Lippe *f.*; Rand *m.*

lipstick *s.* Lippenstift *m.*

liquefy *v.t.* & *i.* verflüssigen.

liqueur *s.* Liqueur *m.*, Likör *m.*

liquid *a.* flüssig; klar, erwiesen; ~ *s.* Flüssigkeit *f.*

liquidate *v.t.* (*com.*) liquidieren, bezahlen; abwickeln.

liquidation *s.* (*com.*) Liquidation.

liquor *s.* Flüssigkeit *f.*; alkoholisches Getränk *n.*; *in* ~, betrunken.

liquorice *s.* Süssholz *n.*

lisp *v.i.* lispeln; ~ *s.* Lispeln *n.*

lissom(e) *a.* geschmeidig, gelenkig.

list *s.* Liste *f.*; Musterrolle *f.*; Saum *m.*; Salleiste *f.*; Schranke *f.*; Neigung *f.*; (*nav.*) Schlagseite *f.*; ~ *v.t.* einschreiben; aufführen; ~ *v.i.* gelüsten.

listen *v.i.* zuhören; lauschen.

listener *s.* Horcher *m.*; Hörer *m.*

listless *a.*, ~**ly** *adv.* verdrossen.

litany *s.* Litanei *f.*

literacy *s.* Kenntnis (*f.*) des Lesens und Schreibens.

literal *a.*, ~**ly** *adv.* buchstäblich.

literary *a.* literarisch; ~ *award* *s.* Literaturpreis *m.*; ~ *historian* *s.* Literarhistoriker *m.*

literate *a.* des Lesens und Schreibens kundig.

literature *s.* Literatur *f.*

lithe *a.* biegsam, geschmeidig.

lithograph *s.* Steindruck *m.*; ~ *v.t.* lithographieren.

lithographer *s.* Steindrucker *m.*

lithography *s.* Steindruck *m.*

litigant *s.* streitende Partei *f.*

litigate *v.t.* & *i.* streiten; prozessieren.

litigation *s.* Prozess *m.*

litigious *a.*, ~**ly** *adv.* streitsüchtig.

litmus *s.* Lackmus *n.*

litter *s.* Sänfte *f.*; Wurf *m.*; Abfälle *m.pl.*; Streu *f.*; ~ *v.t.* (Junge) werfen; umherstreuen.

little *a.* & *adv.* klein, wenig; gering; ~ *by* ~, nach und nach.

littoral *a.* Ufer...; ~ *s.* Küstenland *n.*

liturgy *s.* Liturgie *f.*

live *v.i.* leben; verleben; am Leben bleiben; wohnen; dauern; ~*a.* lebendig; (*elek.*) geladen; (Patrone) scharf; ~*-stock*, Viehbestand *m.*; ~ *coal* *s.* glühende Kohle *f.*

livelihood *s.* Unterhalt *m.*

livelong *a.*, *the* ~ *day*, der liebe lange Tag.

lively *a.* lebhaft, munter.

liver *s.* Lebende *m.*; Leber *f.*

livery *s.* Livree *f.*

livid *a.* bleifarbig, fahl.

living *s.* Leben *n.*; Unterhalt *m.*; Pfarrstelle, Pfründe *f.*; *to earn a* ~, sich sein Leben verdienen; ~ *room* *s.* Wohnzimmer *n.*; ~*-wage* *s.* Existenzminimum *n.*

lizard *s.* Eidechse *f.*

llama *s.* Lama *n.*; Lamawolle *f.*

load *s.* Ladung, Last *f.*; (*elek.*) Belastung *f.*; ~ *v.t.* laden, aufladen; ~*-line*, Ladelinie *f.*; ~*ing ramp*, Laderampe *f.*

loadstone *s.* Magnet *m.*

loaf *s.* Laib *m.*, Brot *n.*; (Zucker) Hut *m.*; ~ *v.i.* umherlungern.

loam *s.* Lehm *m.*

loan *s.* Anleihe *f.*; ~ *v.t.* leihen.

loath *a.* unwillig, abgeneigt.

loathe *v.t.* Ekel haben, verabscheuen.

loathing *s.* Ekel *m.*

loathsome *a.*, ~**ly** *adv.* ekelhaft.

lobby *s.* Vorsaal *m.*; Wandelgang *m.*; *to* ~ *v.t.* Abgeordnete bearbeiten.

lobe *s.* Lappen *m.*

lobster *s.* Hummer *m.*

local *a.* örtlich, Orts...; ~ *authorities* *pl.* Kommunalbehörden *f.pl.*; ~ *govern-*

ment, Kommunalverwaltung *f.*; ~ *traffic*, Nahverkehr *m.*
locality *s.* Örtlichkeit *f.*
localize *v.t.* lokalisieren.
locate *v.t.* setzen, stellen, verlegen; einen Ort bestimmen.
location *s.* Setzen *n.*; Standort *m.*; Feststellung (*f.*) eines Ortes.
loch *s.* See *m.*; Bucht *f.*
lock *s.* Schloss *n.*; Locke *f.*; Schleuse *f.*; Verschluss *m.*; Hemmung *f.*; *under* ~ *and key*, hinter Schloss und Riegel; ~ *v.t.* verschliessen; hemmen (ein Rad); ~ *v.i.* ineinander greifen.
locker *s.* Schliessfach *f.*; Schrank *m.*
locket *s.* Schlösschen *n.*; Medaillon *n.*
lockjaw *s.* Mundsperre *f.*
lock-out *s.* Aussperrung *f.*
locksmith *s.* Schlosser *m.*
lock-up *s.* verschliessbare Raum *m.*
locomotion *s.* Ortsveränderung *f.*
locomotive *a.* (sich) fortbewegend; ~ (*engine*) *s.* Lokomotive *f.*
locust *s.* (afrikanische) Heuschrecke *f.*
locution *s.* Redensart *f.*; Ausdruck *m.*
lode *s.* Wasserlauf *m.*; Erzgang *m.*; ~**-star**, Leitstern, Polarstern *m.*
lodge *v.i.* wohnen; ~ *v.t.* beherbergen; ~ *s.* Häuschen *n.*; Loge *f.*
lodger *s.* Mieter(in), *m. & f.*
lodging *s.* Obdach *n.*
lodgings *s.pl.* möblierte Zimmer *n.pl.*
loft *s.* Boden, Dachboden *m.*
lofty *a.*, ~**ily** *adv.* hoch, erhaben; stolz.
log *s.* Klotz *m.*; (*nav.*) Log *n.*
loganberry *s.* Kreuzung von Himbeere und Brombeere.
logarithm *s.* Logarithmus *m.* (*math.*)
log-book *s.* Schiffstagebuch *n.*
log-cabin *s.* Blockhaus *n.*
loggerhead *s.*, *to be at* ~*s*, sich in den Haaren liegen.
logic *s.* Logik *f.*
logical *a.*, ~**ly** *adv.* logisch.
logician *s.* Logiker *m.*
logistics *s.pl.* (*Am. mil.*) Nachschubwesen *n.*
loin *s.* Lendenbraten *m.*; ~**s** *s.pl.* Lenden *f.pl.*
loiter *v.i.* zaudern, trödeln, herumlungern.
loll *v.i.* sich dehnen; träge liegen.
lollipop *s.* Zuckerwerk, Naschwerk *n.*
lone *a.*, ~**ly** *adv.* einsam; allein.
lonely, lonesome *a.* einsam.
long *a. & adv.* lang; lange; ~**-term** langfristig; *I shan't be* ~, ich werde nicht lange brauchen; *so* ~*!*, auf Wiedersehen!; ~ *v.t.* sich sehnen.
longevity *s.* Langlebigkeit *f.*
longhand *s.* gewöhnliche Schrift (nicht Kurzschrift) *f.*
longing *s.* Sehnsucht *f.*

longitude *s.* geographische Länge *f.*
longitudinal *a.*, ~**ly** *adv.* der Länge nach; Längen . . .
long-lived *a.* langlebig; von langer Lebensdauer (Material).
long-shoreman *s.* Werftarbeiter *m.*
long-sighted *a.* weitsichtig.
long-suffering *a.* langmütig.
long wave *s.* Langwelle *f.* (*radio*).
long-winded *a.* langatmig.
look *v.t. & i.* sehen, hinsehen; aussehen; *to* ~ *after*, betreuen; *to* ~ *for*, suchen; *to* ~ *over*, sich anschauen; *to* ~ *through*, durchsehen, durchlesen.
looker-on *s.* Zuschauer *m.*
looking-glass *s.* Spiegel *m.*
look-out *s.* Ausguck *m.*; Wache *f.*
loom *s.* Webstuhl *m.*; ~ *v.i.* sichtbar werden.
loop *s.* Schlinge *f.*; Schnürloch *n.*
loop-hole *s.* Ausflucht *f.*
loose *a.*, ~**ly** *adv.* lose, los; locker; liederlich; frei; ~**-leaf** *notebook* *s.* Loseblätterbuch *n.*
loosen *v.t.* lösen, locker machen.
loot *s.* Beute *f.*; ~ *v.t.* plündern.
lop *v.t.* ausästen; herabhängen.
lop-sided *a.* schief, einseitig.
loquacious *a.* schwatzhaft.
loquacity *s.* Schwatzhaftigkeit *f.*
lord *s.* Lord *m.*; Herr *m.*; Gott *m.*; ~ *v.i.* herrschen.
lordly *a.* vornehm, stolz.
lordship *s.* Herrschaft, Macht *f.*; *Your Lordship* (Titel), Ew. Gnaden.
lore *s.* Kunde *f.*; Lehre *f.*
lorry *s.* Lori, Lore *f.*; Lastwagen *m.*
lose *v.t. ir.* verlieren; *to* ~ *one's way*, sich verlaufen.
loss *s.* Verlust *m.*; *at a* ~, ratlos.
lost-property office *s.* Fundbüro *n.*
lot *s.* Los *n.*; Schicksal *n.*; Anteil *m.*; Menge *f.*; Posten *m.*; Partie *f.*; (*Am.*) Stück Land *n.*; ~ *v.t.* verlosen.
loth *see* loath.
lotion *s.* Abwaschung *f.*; Waschmittel *n.*; Hautwasser *n.*
lottery *s.* Lotterie *f.*; ~**-ticket** *s.* Lotterielos *n.*
loud *a.*, ~**ly** *adv.* laut; grell (Farben).
loudspeaker *s.* (*radio*) Lautsprecher *m.*; ~**-van**, Lautsprecherwagen *m.*
lounge *v.i.* faulenzen; ~ *s.* Halle (zum müssigen Ruhen).
lounge-suit *s.* Sakkoanzug *m.*
lour *v.i.* finster aussehen; die Stirn runzeln.
louse *s.* Laus *f.*
lout *s.* Lümmel *m.*
loutish *a.*, ~**ly** *adv.* plump, tölpisch.
lovable *a.* liebenswert.
love *v.t. & i.* lieben, gern haben, Vergnügen finden; *s.* ~, Liebe *f.*; Liebchen

n.; Gruss *m.*; *in ~,* verliebt; *to fall in ~ with,* sich verlieben in.
love-affair *s.* Liebesverhältnis *n.*
lovely *a.* liebenswürdig; lieblich; herrlich.
love-match *s.* Liebesheirat *f.*
lover *s.* Liebhaber *m.*
low *a. & adv.* niedrig; leise; niedergeschlagen; ~ dress *s.* ausgeschnittene Kleid *n.*; *in a ~ voice,* leise; ~ *s.* Tief (Wetterkunde); ~ *v.i.* brüllen.
lower *a.* niedriger; ~ House *s.* Unterhaus, *n.*; lower deck *s.* Zwischendeck *n.*; *v.t.* niederlassen; verringern; *to ~ a boat,* ein Boot aussetzen; *to ~ one's voice,* leiser reden; ~ *v.i.* abnehmen; ~ *v.i.* =lour.
low-grade *a.* geringwertig.
lowland *s.* Niederung *f.*; Tiefland *n.*
lowly *a. & adv.* niedrig, demütig.
low-pressure *s.* Niederdruck *m.*
low-spirited *a.* niedergeschlagen, mutlos.
loyal *a.*, ~ly *adv.* treu, pflichttreu.
loyalty *s.* Treue *f.*
lozenge *s.* Raute *f.*; Pastille *f.*
lubber *s.* Tölpel, Grobian *m.*
lubricant *s.* Schmierstoff *m.*
lubricate *v.t.* einölen, schmieren.
lucern(e) *s.* Luzerne *f.*
lucid *a.* leuchtend; klar, licht, durchsichtig.
lucifer *s.* Streichholz *n.*
luck *s.* Glück *n.*; Zufall *m.*; *good ~,* Glück *n.*; *ill ~, bad ~,* Unglück *n.*
luckless *a.* unglücklich.
lucky *a.*, ~ily *adv.* glücklich; glücklicherweise.
lucrative *a.* einträglich.
lucre *s.* Gewinn *m.*
lucubration *s.* nächtliche Studium *n.*; ~s *pl.* gelehrte Abhandlungen *f.pl.*
ludicrous *a.*, ~ly *adv.* lächerlich, albern.
luggage *s.* Gepäck *n.*; hand-~, Handgepäck *n.*; *heavy ~,* grosse Gepäck *n.*; ~-office, Gepäckabfertigung *f.*; left-~ office, Gepäckaufbewahrungsstelle *f.*; ~-van, Gepäckwagen *m.*
lugubrious *a.* kläglich, traurig.
lukewarm *a.*, ~ly, *adv.* lau.
lull *v.t.* einlullen; ~ *v.i.* sich legen (vom Winde).
lullaby *s.* Wiegenlied *n.*
lumbago *s.* Hexenschuss *m.*
lumber *s.* Gerümpel *n.*, Plunder *m.*; (*Am.*) Bauholz *n.*
luminary *s.* Lichtkörper *m.*; (*fig.*) Leuchte *f.*
luminous *a.* leuchtend; lichtvoll; ~ watch *s.* Leuchtuhr *f.*
lump *s.* Klumpen *m.*; Masse *f.*; *in the ~,* in Bausch und Bogen; ~-sugar, Stückzucker *m.*; ~ sum, Pauschalsumme *f.*; ~ *v.t.* im ganzen nehmen; *to ~ together,* in einen Topf werfen.

lumpy *a.* klumpig.
lunacy *s.* Irrsinn, Wahnsinn *m.*
lunar *a.* Mond...
lunatic *a.* irrsinnig; ~ *s.* Irre *m. & f.*; ~ asylum *s.* Irrenhaus *n.*
lunch, luncheon *s.* Mittags-Imbiss *m.*; zweite Frühstück *n.*; ~-basket *s.* Imbisskorb *m.*; ~ *v.i.* leichtes Mittagessen einnehmen.
lung *s.* Lunge *f.*
lunge *s.* Ausfall (beim Fechten) *m.*
lupin *s.* Lupine *f.*
lurch *s. leave in the ~,* im Stiche lassen; ~ *v.i.* taumeln.
lure *s.* Lockspeise *f.*; ~ *v.t.* ködern.
lurid *a.* fahl; finster, trübe.
lurk *v.i.* lauern.
luscious *a.*, ~ly *adv.* übersüss; widerlich.
lush *a.* üppig.
lust *s.* Begierde *f.*; Trieb *m.*; Wollust *f.*; ~ *v.i.* gelüsten.
lustre *s.* Glanz *m.*; Kronleuchter *m.*
lustrous *a.* glänzend.
lusty *a.*, ~ily *adv.* munter; kräftig.
lute *s.* Laute *f.*; Kitt *m.*; ~ *v.t.* verkitten.
Lutheran *a.* lutherisch; ~ *s.* Lutheraner *m.*.
luxuriance *s.* Üppigkeit *f.*
luxuriant *a.*, ~ly *adv.* üppig, reichlich.
luxuriate *v.i.* üppig wachsen; schwelgen.
luxurious *a.*, ~ly *adv.* üppig; wollüstig.
luxury *s.* Üppigkeit *f.*; Luxus *m.*
lye *s.* Lauge *f.*
lying-in *s.* Wochenbett *n.*; ~-hospital, Entbindungsanstalt *f.*
lymph *s.* Lymphe *f.*; Quellwasser *n.*
lynch *v.t.* lynchen.
lynch-law *s.* Pöbeljustiz, Lynchjustiz *f.*
lynx *s.* Luchs *m.*
lyre *s.* Leier *f.*; Lyra *f.*
lyric *a.* lyrisch; ~ *s.* lyrische Gedicht *n.*

M

macadamize *v.t.* makadamisieren, beschottern.
macaroni *s.* Makkaroni *f.pl.*
macaroon *s.* Makrone *f.*
mace *s.* Keule *f.*; Amtsstab *m.*
macerate *v.t.* abzehren; kasteien.
machination *s.* Anschlag *m.*
machine *s.* Maschine *f.*; ~ *v.t.* maschinell bearbeiten od. herstellen; ~-gun *s.* Maschinengewehr *n.*; ~-tool *s.* Werkzeugmaschine *f.*
machinery *s.* Maschinerie *f.*
machinist *s.* Maschinist *m.*
mackerel *s.* Makrele *f.*
mackintosh *s.* Gummimantel *m.*
mad *a.*, ~ly *adv.* wahnsinnig, toll.
madam *s.* gnädige Frau *f.*

madcap *s.* Tollkopf *m.*

madden *v.t.* toll machen.

madhouse *s.* Tollhaus *n.*

madman *s.* Wahnsinnige *m.*

madness *s.* Wahnsinn *m.*, Tollheit *f.*

magazine *s.* Lagerhaus *n.*; Pulvermagazin *n.*; Vorratsbehälter *m.*; Zeitschrift *f.*; ~-rifle *s.* Mehrladegewehr *n.*

maggot *s.* Made *f.*; (*fig.*) Grille *f.*

magic *s.* Zauberkunst *f.*; ~ *a.* zauberartig, Zauber...

magician *a.* Zauberer *m.*

magisterial *a.*, ~ly *adv.* behördlich.

magistracy *s.* obrigkeitliche Stand *m.*

magistrate *s.* Friedensrichter *m.*; obrigkeitliche Person *f.*

magnanimity *s.* Grossmut *f.*

magnanimous *a.*, ~ly *adv.* grossmütig.

magnate *s.* Magnat *m.*, Grosse *m.*

magnesia *s.* Magnesia *f.*

magnet *s.* Magnet *m.*

magnetic *a.* magnetisch.

magnetism *s.* Magnetismus *m.*

magnetize *v.t.* magnetisieren.

magneto *s.* Zündapparat *m.*

magnification *s.* Vergrösserung *f.* (Mikroskop, etc.).

magnificence *s.* Grösse, Pracht *f.*

magnificent *a.*, ~ly *adv.* prachtvoll.

magnify *v.t.* vergrössern, verherrlichen.

magnitude *s.* Grösse *f.*

magpie *s.* Elster *f.*

mahogany *s.* Mahagoni(holz) *n.*

maid *s.* Jungfer *f.*; Mädchen *n.*; Dienstmädchen *n.*; *old* ~, alte Jungfer.

maiden *s.* Jungfer *f.*; Magd *f.*; ~ *a.* jungfräulich; ~ *name s.* Mädchenname *m.*; ~ *speech s.* Jungfernrede *f.*

maidenhead, maidenhood *s.* Jungfernschaft *f.*

mail *s.* Panzer *m.*; Briefpost *f.*; ~ *v.t.* bepanzern; mit der Post schicken.

mail-bag *s.* Briefbeutel *m.*

mail-train *s.* Postzug *m.*

maim *v.t.* lähmen, verstümmeln.

main *a.* hauptsächlich; Haupt...; gross; ~ *s.* Hauptteil *m.*; Hauptrohr *n.*; Hauptleitung *f.*; Ganze *n.*; Weltmeer *n.*; Festland *n.*; *in the* ~, hauptsächlich, im allgemeinen; *the* ~ *chance,* der eigene Vorteil; ~-land *s.* Festland *n.*; ~ *line s.* Haupteisenbahnlinie *f.*; ~-stay *s.* Uhrfeder *f.*; Triebfeder *f.*; ~ *subject,* Hauptfach *n.*

mainly *adv.* hauptsächlich.

maintain *v.t.* erhalten, unterhalten; ernähren; behaupten; verfechten.

maintenance *s.* Unterhalt *m.*; (*mil.*) Instandhaltung, Unterhaltung, Wartung *f.*

maisonette *s.* Wohnung (*f.*) mit eigenem Eignang.

maize *s.* Mais *m.*

majestic *a.*, ~ally *adv.* majestätisch.

majesty *s.* Majestät *f.*

major *a.* grösser; mündig; (*mus.*) Dur; ~ *s.* Major *m.*; Obersatz *m.*

majority *s.* Mehrheit *f.*; Mündigkeit *f.*

make *v.t.ir.* machen; (veran)lassen; *to* ~ *good,* Erfolg haben, sich bewähren; *to* ~ *out,* ausschreiben, ausstellen; *to* ~ *up,* verarbeiten; ~ *v.i.* sich wenden, wohin gehen; sich stellen; *to* ~ *for,* lossteuern auf; *to* ~ *out,* ausmachen; *to* ~ *up for,* entschädigen; ~ *s.* Machwerk *n.*; Gestalt *f.*; Sorte, Art *f.*

make-believe *s.* Vorwand *m.*

maker *s.* Verfertiger *m.*; Schöpfer *m.*

makeshift *s.* Notbehelf *m.*

make-up *s.* Schminke *f.*

makeweight *s.* Zugabe *f.*

maladministration *s.* Misswirtschaft *f.*

malady *s.* Krankheit *f.*

malaise *s.* Unbehagen *n.*

malaria *s.* Sumpffieber *n.*, Malaria *f.*

malcontent *a.*, ~ly *adv.* unzufrieden.

male *a.* männlich; ~ *s.* Mann *m.*; Männchen *n.*

malediction *s.* Fluch *m.*

malefactor *s.* Übeltäter *m.*

male nurse *s.* Krankenwärter *m.*

malevolence *s.* Bosheit *f.*

malevolent *a.*, ~ly *adv.* böswillig.

malformation *s.* Missbildung *f.*

malformed *a.* missbildet.

malice *s.* Bosheit *f.*, Groll *m.*; *with* ~ *aforethought,* (*law*) mit bösem Vorbedacht.

malicious *a.*, ~ly *adv.* boshaft, tückisch.

malign *a.* schädlich; ~ *v.t.* verlästern.

malignancy *s.* Bösartigkeit *f.*

malignant *a.*, ~ly *adv.* bösartig.

malignity *s.* Bosheit, Schadenfreude *f.*

malinger *v.i.* simulieren.

malleable *a.* hämmerbar.

mallet *s.* Schlegel *m.*, Holzhammer *m.*

mallow *s.* Malve *f.*

malnutrition *s.* Unterernährung *f.*

malpractice *s.* Amtsvergehen *n.*

malt *s.* Malz *n.*; ~ *v.i.* malzen.

maltreat *v.t.* misshandeln.

maltreatment *s.* Misshandlung *f.*

malversation *s.* Amtsmissbrauch, Unterschleif *m.*

mam(m)a *s.* Mama *f.*

mammal *s.* Säugetier *n.*

mammoth *s.* Mammut *n.*; *a.* riesig.

man *s.* Mensch *m.*; Mann *m.*; ~ *of war,* Kriegsschiff *m.*; ~ *v.t.* bemannen.

manacle *s.* Handschelle *f.*; ~ *v.t.* fesseln.

manage *v.t.* handhaben; verwalten; einrichten; leiten; fertig bringen; zureiten; ~ *v.i.* die Aufsicht führen; sich behelfen.

manageable *a.* handlich; lenksam.

management s. Verwaltung f., Leitung f., Direktion f.; Behandlung f.

manager s. Verwalter, Leiter m.; Direktor m.; a good ~, ein guter Haushalter; general ~, Generaldirektor m.; works ~, Betriebsleiter m.

manageress s. Direktrice f.

managing a. geschäftsführend, Betriebs...

mandatary s. Bevollmächtigte m.

mandate s. Mandat n., Auftrag m.

mandatory a. befehlend; Mandats...

mandolin s. Mandoline f.

mandrake s. Alraun(e) m. (f.).

mandrel s. (mech.) Spindel, Docke f.

mane s. Mähne f.

manful a., ~ly adv. mannhaft, tapfer.

manganese s. Mangan n.

mange s. Räude f.

manger s. Krippe f., Trog m.; dog in the ~, Neidhammel m.

mangle s. Mangel, Rolle f.; ~ v.t. verstümmeln; mangeln, rollen.

mangold s. Mangold m., Runkelrübe f.

manhandle v.t. rauh anfassen.

manhole s. Einsteigloch n.

manhood s. Mannheit f.; Tapferkeit f.; Mannesalter n.

manhour s. Arbeitsstunde (f.) pro Arbeitskraft.

mania s. Wahnsinn m.; Sucht f.

maniac a. wahnsinnig; ~ s. Wahnsinnige m.

manicure s. Maniküre f.; to ~ v.t. maniküren.

manifest a., ~ly adv. offenbar; ~ s. Ladungsverzeichnis n.; ~ v.t. offenbaren.

manifestation s. Bekanntmachung f.

manifesto s. Kundgebung f.

manifold a., ~ly adv. vielfältig.

manikin s. Männlein n.; Gliederpuppe f.

manipulate v.t. handhaben.

mankind s. Menschengeschlecht n.

manlike a. männlich.

manly a. männlich; mannhaft.

manner s. Art f.; ~s pl. Sitten f.pl.; in a ~, gewissermassen.

mannerism s. Manieriertheit f.

mannerly a. & adv. artig.

manœuvre s. Manöver n.; Kunstgriff m.; ~ v.t. manövrieren.

manometer s. Druckmesser m.

manor s. Rittergut n.

manor-house s. Herrenhaus n.

manpower s. Menschenmaterial n.; ~ allocation, Arbeitseinsatz m.

man-servant s. Diener m.

mansion s. Wohnhaus n.

manslaughter s. Totschlag m.

mantel s. Kaminverkleidung f.

mantelpiece s. Kaminsims m.

mantle s. Umhang m.; Hülle f.

man-trap s. Fussangel f.

manual a. eigenhändig, Hand... ;~ s* Handbuch n.

manufacture s. Fabrikation f.; Fabrikat n.; ~ v.t. fabrizieren; verarbeiten; ~ed articles pl. Fertigwaren f.pl.

manufacturer s. Fabrikant m.

manure v.t. düngen; ~ s. Dünger m.

manuscript s. Handschrift f.

many a. viele, mancher, manche, manches; as ~ as, soviele als or wie.

map s. Landkarte f., Stadtplan m.; ~ v.t. in Kartenform darstellen; (mil.) ~-exercise s. Planspiel n.; (mil.) ~-manœuvre s. Kriegspiel n.; ~-scale s. Kartenmasstab m.

maple s. Ahorn m.

mar v.t. verderben; beschädigen.

marauder s. Plünderer m.

marble s. Marmor m.; Murmel f.; ~ a. marmorn.

March s. März m.

march s. Marsch; Zug m.; Mark f., Grenzland n.; ~ v.i. marschieren; ~ v.t. marschieren lassen; ~ past s. Vorbeimarsch m.

marchioness s. Markgräfin f.

mare s. Stute f.; Alp m.; ~'s nest, (fig.) Hirngespinst n.

margarine s. Margarine f.

margin s. Rand m.; Spielraum m.; Überschuss m.

marginal a. am Rande; Rand...; ~ note s. Randbemerkung f.

marigold s. Dotterblume f.

marine a. See...; ~ s. Marine f.; Seesoldat m.

mariner s. Seemann m.

marital a. ehelich.

maritime a. zur See gehörig; ~ law, Seerecht n.

marjoram s. Majoran m.

Mark s. Marke f.; Kennzeichen n.; Spur f.; Schutzmarke f.; (Zeugnis) Note m.; Ziel n.; not quite up to the ~, nicht ganz auf der Höhe; ~ v.t. & i. zeichnen; aufmerken; markieren; to ~ off, abstreichen; to ~ out, abstecken; to ~ out for, ausersehen für; to ~ time, auf der Stelle treten (mil. & fig.).

market s. Markt m.; Absatz m.; ~-research s. Konjunkturforschung f.; ~-gardener s. Handelsgärtner m.; ~ v.t. auf den Markt bringen; ~ing association s. Absatzgenossenschaft f.; to come into the ~, auf den Markt kommen; to place on the ~, auf den Markt bringen.

marketable a. verkäuflich, gangbar.

marking s. Musterung f., Zeichnung (eines Fells) f.; (mil.) Hoheitsabzeichen n.; ~-ink s. (unauslöschliche) Zeichentinte f.; ~-iron s. Brenneisen n.

marksman s. Schütze m.

marksmanship s. Schiessfertigkeit, Zielsicherheit f.
marl s. Mergel m.
marmalade s. Apfelsinenmarmelade f.
maroon a. kastanienbraun.
marquee s. Zeltdach n., Markise f.
marquess, marquis s. Marquis m.
marquetry s. eingelegte Arbeit f.
marriage s. Ehe, Heirat f.; ~-certificate, Trauschein m.; ~-settlement, Ehevertrag m.
marriageable a. heiratsfähig.
marrow s. Mark n.; vegetable ~, Kürbis m.; ~-bone s. Markknochen m.
marry v.t. heiraten; verheiraten; trauen; ~ v.i. heiraten.
marsh s. Marsch f., Sumpf m.
marshal s. Marschall m.; ~ v.t. ordnen; anführen.
marshalling yard s. Verschiebebahnhof m.
marsupial s. Beuteltier n.
mart s. Markt m.; Stapelplatz m.
marten s. Marder m.
martial a. kriegerisch, militärisch; ~ law s. Standrecht n.
martinet s. strenge Offizier m.
martyr s. Märtyrer m.; ~ v.t. martern.
martyrdom s. Märtyrertum m.
marvel s. Wunder n.; ~ v.i. staunen.
marvellous a., ~ly adv. wunderbar.
mascot s. Glücksbringer, Maskott m.
masculine a. männlich; ~, (gram. Maskulinum n.
mash s. Gemisch n.; Maische f.; ~ v.t. mengen, maischen, zerdrücken.
mask s. Maske f.; Vorwand m.; ~ v.t. & i. maskieren; sich verstellen.
mason s. Maurer m.; Freimaurer m.
masonic a. freimaurerisch.
masonry s. Maurerei f.; Mauerwerk n.
masquerade s. Maskenball m.; Verkleidung f.; ~ v.i. maskiert gehen.
mass s. Masse, Menge f.; Messe f.; high ~ s. Hochamt n.; low ~ s. stille Messe; ~ v.t. & i. (sich) anhäufen, sich sammeln.
massacre s. Metzelei f.; ~ v.t. niedermetzeln.
massage v.t. massieren.
massive a. dicht, fest, massiv.
mast s. Mast(baum) m.; Mast f.
master s. Meister m.; Herr m.; Magister, Lehrer m.; ~ v.t. meistern.
master-builder s. Baumeister m.
masterful a. herrisch; meisterhaft.
master-key s. Hauptschlüssel m.
masterly a. & adv. meisterhaft.
master-piece s. Meisterstück n.
mastery s. Herrschaft f.; Geschicklichkeit f.; (Sprache) Beherrschung f.
masticate v.t. & i. kauen.
mastiff s. Bullenbeisser m

mat s. Matte f.; ~ v.t. mit Matten bedecken; sich verwirren; mattieren.
match s. Lunte f.; Streichholz n.; Gleiche n.; Wette f.; Heirat f.; (Spiel)partie f.; Wettspiel n.; ~ v.t. zusammenpassen, zusammenbringen; vergleichen; aufwiegen; ~ v.i. passen; sich verheiraten.
matchless a., ~ly adv. unvergleichlich.
mate s. Gefährte, Gehilfe m.; Geselle m.; Maat m.; Steuermann m.; Gatte m., Gattin f.; ~ adv. (schach)matt; ~ v.t. & i. (sich) paaren.
material a., ~ly adv. körperlich; wesentlich; materiell; ~ s. Material n., Stoff m.; Kleiderstoff m.; raw ~, Rohstoff m.
materialism s. Materialismus m.
materialist, Materialist m.
materialistic a. materialistisch.
materialize v.t. verwirklichen; ~ v.i. sich verwirkliche, zu Stande kommen.
matériel s. (Am. mil.) Gerät n., Kriegsmaterial n.
maternal a., ~ly adv. mütterlich.
maternity s. Mutterschaft f.; ~ hospital, Entbindungsanstalt f.
mathematical a., ~ly adv. mathematisch.
mathematician s. Mathematiker m.
mathematics s.pl. Mathematik f.
matinée s. Nachmittagsvorstellung f.
matins s.pl. Frühmette f.
matricide s. Muttermord m.
matriculate v.t. einschreiben, immatrikulieren.
matrimonial a., ~ly adv. ehelich.
matrimony s. Ehe f.
matrix s. Matrize f.
matron s. Matrone; Vorsteherin f.
matter s. Stoff m.; Sache m.; Gegenstand m.; Eiter m.; (typ.) Satz m.; ~ of course s. Selbstverständlichkeit; as a ~ of fact, tatsächlich; matter-of-fact a. sachlich, nüchtern; ~ of opinion, Ansichtssache f.; what is the ~?, was ist los? no ~ how, gleichgültig, wie ...; ~ v.i. daran liegen, etwas ausmachen; it does not ~, es macht nichts.
mattock s. Hacke f.
mattress s. Matratze f.
mature a., ~ly adv. reif; fällig; reiflich; ~ v.t. reifen; ~d a. abgelagert.
maturity s. Reife f.; Verfallzeit f.
maudlin a. (betrunken) weinerlich.
maul v.t. stampfen; schlagen; verletzen.
maunder v.i. dahindösen; faseln.
Maundy-Thursday s. Gründonnerstag m.
mausoleum s. Mausoleum n.
mauve a. lila, hellviolett.
maw s. Magen (der Tiere) m.; Kropf m.
mawkish a. widerlich; (fig.) empfindsam.
maxim s. Grundsatz m.
maximum s. Höchstmass n.; Höchst...; ~ price, Höchstpreis m.

may *v.i.ir.* dürfen, mögen, können; ~ *s.* Weissdorn *m.*

May *s.* Mai *m.*

May-day *s.* erste Mai *m.*

mayor *s.* Bürgermeister *m.*

mayoralty *s.* Bürgermeisteramt *n.*

mayoress *s.* Bürgermeisterin *f.*

May-pole *s.* Maibaum *m.*

maze *s.* Labyrinth *n.;* Wirrwarr *m.*

me *pn.* mich, mir.

mead *s.* Met *m.;* Wiese *f.*

meadow *s.* Wiese *f.*

meagre *a.,* ~ly *adv.* mager; dürftig.

meal *s.* Mehl *n.;* Mahlzeit *f.*

mealy *a.* mehlig.

mealy-mouthed *a.* schüchtern, zimperlich.

mean *a.,* ~ly *adv.* niedrig, gemein; verächtlich; mittler, Durchschnitts..., mittelmässig; *in the* ~ *time,* inzwischen; ~ *s.* Mittel *n.;* Mitte *f.;* ~ *v.t. & i.ir.* meinen, bedeuten; beabsichtigen.

meander *s.* Windung *f.;* ~ *v.i.* sich schlängeln.

meaning *s.* Sinn *m.;* Bedeutung *f.*

meanness *s.* Gemeinheit *f.;* Filzigkeit *f.*

means *s.pl.* Mittel *n.;* Vermögen *n.;* ~ *of production,* Produktionsmittel *n.pl.*

meanwhile *adv.* inzwischen.

measles *s.pl.* Masern *f.pl.;* German ~, Röteln *pl.*

measurable *a.,* ~bly *adv.* messbar.

measure *s.* Mass *n.;* Masstab *m.;* (*mus.*) Takt *m.;* (*ar.*) Teiler, Faktor *m.;* Massregel *f.; to* ~, nach Mass; made-to~ *a.* massgearbeitet; *to take* ~*s,* Massnahmen ergreifen; ~ *v.t. & i.* messen, abmessen; enthalten; fassen.

measurement *s.* Messung *f.;* Mass *n.; to take a person's* ~, einem Mass nehmen.

meat *s.* Fleisch *n.;* Speise *f.;* ~ *safe,* Fliegenschrank *m.*

meat-pie *s.* Fleischpastete *f.*

mechanic *s.* Mechaniker *m.;* ~*s s.pl.* Mechanik *f.*

mechanical *a.,* ~ly *adv.* mechanisch.

mechanism *s.* Getriebe *n.* ◆

medal *s.* Denkmünze *f.;* Medaille *f.*

meddle *v.i.* sich mischen; sich abgeben.

meddlesome *a.* sich einmischend.

mediæval, medieval *a.* mittelalterlich.

mediate *v.i.* vermitteln.

mediation *s.* Vermittlung *f.*

mediator *s.* Vermittler, Fürsprecher *m.*

medical *a.,* ~ly *adv.* medizinisch; ~ *care,* ärztliche Betreuung *f.;* ~ *certificate,* ärztliche Attest *n.;* ~ *opinion,* ärztliche Gutachten *n.;* ~ *practitioner s.* praktische Arzt; (*mil.*) ~ *service,* Sanitätsdienst *m.*

medicament *s.* Arzneimittel *n.*

medicate *v.t.* mit Arznei versetzen; medizinisch behandeln.

medicinal *a.,* ~ly *adv.* medizinisch, Heil...

medicine *s.* Arznei *f.;* Medizin *f.*

mediocre *a.* mittelmässig.

mediocrity *s.* Mittelmässigkeit *f.*

meditate *v.t. & i.* nachsinnen, überlegen.

meditation *s.* Betrachtung *f.*

Mediterranean *a.* Mittelmeer *n.;* ~ *a.* Mittelmeer..., mittelländisch.

medium *s.* Mittel, *n.;* Bindemittel (Malerei) *n.;* Mittelding *n.;* Medium *n.;* ~ *a.* Mittel..., mittlere; ~ *artillery,* (*mil.*) schwere Artillerie *f.;* ~*-sized a.* mittelgross; ~ *wave s.* (*radio*) Mittelwelle.

medley *s.* Gemenge *n.,* Mischmasch *m.*

meek *a.,* ~ly *adv.* sanftmütig; demütig.

meet *v.t. & i.ir.* treffen; begegnen; entgegenkommen; versammeln; (Schuld) bezahlen; erleiden; ~ *a.,* ~ly *adv.* schicklich; brauchbar.

meeting *s.* Zusammentreffen *n.;* Versammlung, Sitzung *f.; to call a* ~ *for 10 o'clock,* eine Sitzung auf 10 Uhr einberufen.

meeting-house *s.* Bethaus.

megacycle *s.* (*radio*) Megahertz *n.*

megalomania *s.* Grössenwahn *m.*

megaphone *s.* Megaphon *n.*

melancholic *a.* schwermütig.

melancholy *s.* Schwermut *f.;* ~ *a.* schwermütig.

mellow *a.* mürbe; mild; ~ *v.t.* zur Reife bringen; mürbe machen; ~ *v.i.* mürbe werden; sich mildern.

melodious *s.,* ~ly *adv.* wohlklingend.

melodrama *s.* Melodrama *n.*

melody *s.* Singweise, Melodie *f.*

melon *s.* Melone *f.*

melt *v.t.* schmelzen; ~ *v.i.* schmelzen, zerfliessen; melting point *s.* Schmelzpunkt *m.*

member *s.* Glied *n.;* Mitglied *n.*

membership *s.* Mitgliedschaft *f.;* ~*-card s.* Mitgliedskarte *f.;* ~*-subscription s.* Mitgliedsbeitrag *m.*

membrane *s.* Häutchen *n.,* Membran *f.*

memento *s.* Andenken *n.*

memoir *s.* Denkschrift *f.;* ~*s pl.* Denkwürdigkeiten *f.pl.*

memorable *a.,* ~bly *adv.* denkwürdig.

memorandum *s.* Note, Anmerkung *f.;* Denkschrift *f.*

memorial *s.* Denkmal *n.;* Denkschrift, Bittschrift *f.;* ~ *a.* Gedächtnis...; ~*-celebration s.* Gedenkfeier *f.;* ~*-day s.* Totengedenktag *m.*

memorialize *v.t.* eine Bittschrift einreichen an.

memorize *v.t.* auswendig lernen.

memory *s.* Gedächtnis *n.;* Andenken *n.*

menace *v.t.* drohen; ~ *s.* Drohung *f.*

mend *v.t.* (aus)bessern; ~ *v.i.* sich bessern.

mendacious *a.* lügenhaft.

mendacity *s.* Lügenhaftigkeit *f.*

mendicancy *s.* Bettelei *f.*

mendicant *a.* bettelnd; ~ *s.* Bettler, Bettelmönch *m.*

menial *a.* Gesinde...; niedrig; gemein; ~ *s.* Diener *m.*

meningitis *s.* Hirnhautentzündung *f.*

menstruation *s.* Monatsfluss *m.*

mensuration *s.* Ausmessung *f.*

mental *a.*, ~ly *adv.* geistig, innerlich; ~ly **defective** *a.* schwachsinnig; ~ **deficiency** *s.* Schwachsinn *m.*; ~ **hospital** *s.* psychiatrische Klinik *f.*; ~ **patient,** ~ **case** *s.* Geisteskranker *m.*

mention *s.* Erwähnung *f.*; ~ *v.t.* erwähnen; *don't* ~ *it!*, bitte!; *not to* ~, geschweige denn.

mentor *s.* Mentor, weise Ratgeber *m.*

menu *s.* Speisenfolge *f.*, Speisekarte *f.*

men working! Baustelle!

mercantile *a.* kaufmännisch, Handels...

mercenary *a.* feil; gedungen; ~ *s.* Mietling *m.*

mercer *s.* Schnittwaren-, Seidenhändler *m.*

merchandise *s.* Ware *f.*

merchant *s.* Kaufmann *m.*; ~-**ship** *s.* Kauffahrteischiff *n.*; ~ **navy** *s.* Handelsmarine *f.*

merchantman *s.* Kauffahrteischiff *n.*

merciful *a.*, ~ly *adv.* barmherzig.

merciless *a.*, ~ly *adv.* unbarmherzig.

mercurial *a.* Quecksilber...; lebhaft.

mercury *s.* Quecksilber *n.*

mercy *s.* Barmherzigkeit, Gnade *f.*

mere *a.* bloss; lauter; ~ly *adv.* nur.

meretricious *a* , ~ly *adv.* prunkhaft.

merge *v.t.* eintauchen; verschmelzen; ~ *v.i.* aufgehen(in).

merger *s.* Zusammenlegung, Fusion *f.*

meridional *a.*, ~ly *adv.* südlich.

meringue *s.* Schaumgebäck *n.*

merit *s.* Verdienst *n.*; Wert *m.*; ~ *v.t.* verdienen.

meritorious *a.*, ~ly *adv.* verdienstlich.

mermaid *s.* Seejungfer *f.*

merriment *s.* Fröhlichkeit, Belustigung *f.*

merry *a.*, ~ily *adv.* lustig, fröhlich, munter; ~-**go-round** *s.* Karussell *n.*

mesh *s.* Masche *f.*; Netz *n.*; ~ *v.t.* bestricken, fangen; (*mech.*) in Eingriff bringen; ~ *v.i.* (*mech.*) ineinandergreifen.

mesmerize *v.t.* magnetisieren.

mess *s.* Offizierstisch *m.*; Unordnung *f.*, Sauerei *f.*; ~ *v.i.* zusammen speisen; ~ *v.t.* verpfuschen.

message *s.* Botschaft *f.*; *to give a* ~ ausrichten; *to leave a* ~ etwas ausrichten lassen; ~-**centre** *s.* (*mil.*) Nachrichtenstelle, Meldesammelstelle *f.*

messenger *s.* Bote *m.*; ~ **dog** *s.* Meldehund *m.*

Messiah *s.* Messias *m.*

messmate *s.* Tischgenosse *m.*

Messrs. *s.pl.* = **Messieurs,** die Herren.

metabolism *s.* Stoffwechsel *m.*

metal *s.* Metall *n.*; Kiesfüllung *f.*

metallic *a.* metallisch.

metallurgy *s.* Hüttenkunde *f.*

metamorphose *v.t.* umgestalten.

metamorphosis *s.* Verwandlung *f.*

metaphor *s.* Metapher *f.*

metaphorical *a.* bildlich, übertragen.

metaphysical *a.* metaphysisch.

metaphysics *s.pl.* Metaphysik *f.*

mete *s.* messen; ~ **out** *v.t.* zumessen.

meteor *s.* Meteor *n.*

meteorological *a.* wetterkundlich; ~ **service** *s.* Wetterdienst *m.*

meteorology *s.* Wetterkunde *f.*

meter *s.* Messer; (*elek.*) Zähler *m.*

method *s.* Verfahren *n.*; Ordnung *f.*; Lehrweise *f.*, Methode *f.*

methodical *a.* methodisch.

Methodist *s.* Methodist *m.*

methylated *a.* denaturiert.

meticulous *a.* peinlich genau.

metre *s.* Versmass *n.*; Meter *n. & m.*

metric *a.* metrisch, Meter...; ~ **system** *s.* metrische System *n.*

metrical *a.*, ~ly *adv.* metrisch, Vers...

metropolis *s.* Hauptstadt *f.*

metropolitan *a.* hauptstädtisch.

mettle *s.* Naturanlage *f.*; Mut, Eifer *m.*; ~s *pl.* Beste, Möglichste *m.*

mettlesome *a.* mutig, feurig.

mew *s.* Käfig *m.*; Möve *f.*; ~s *pl.* Stallungen *f.pl.*; ~ *v.i.* miauen.

mezzotint *s.* Schabkunst *f.*; Schabkunstblatt *n.*

miasma *s.* Ansteckungshauch *m.*

mica *s.* Glimmer *m.*; Marienglas *n.*

microbe *s.* Mikrobe *f.*

micrometer *s.* Mikrometer *n.*

microphone *s.* Mikrophon *n.*

microscope *s.* Mikroskop *n.*

mid *a.* mitten, mittel; **in** ~-**air,** mitten in der Luft; ~-**June,** Mitte Juni.

midday *s.* Mittag *m.*

middle *s.* Mitte *f.*; ~ *a.* Mittel....

middleman *s.* Zwischenhändler *m.*

middling *a.* mittelmässig.

midge *s.* Mücke *f.*

midget *s.* Zwerg *m.*

midnight *s.* Mitternacht *f.*; ~ *a.* mitternächtlich.

midship *s.* Mitte (*f.*) des Schiffs.

midshipman *s.* Seekadett *m.*

midst *s.* Mitte *f.*

midsummer *s.* Sommersonnenwende *f.*

midway *adv.* auf halben Wege.

midwife *s.* Hebamme *f.*

midwifery *s.* Geburtshilfe *f.*

midwinter *s.* Wintersonnenwende *f.*

mien *s.* Miene *f.*

might *s.* Macht, Gewalt *f.*

mighty *a.*, ~ily *adv.* mächtig, wirksam.

migrant *s.* Wanderer *m.*, Wandertier *n.*;
~ *a.* Wander...

migrate *v.i.* wandern, fortziehen.

migration *s.* Wanderung *f.*

migratory *a.* wandernd, Zug...

milch *a.*, melk, Milch...

mild *a.*, ~ly *adv.* sanft, mild.

mild steel *s.* weiche Stahl *m.*

mildew *s.* Meltau *m.*; Stockfleck *n.*

mile *s.* (englische) Meile *f.*; 1609 m.

mileage *s.* Meilenzahl *f.*

militarism *s.* Militarismus *m.*

militant *a.* streitend, kriegführend.

military *a.* militärisch; ~ bridge *s.*
Kriegsbrücke *f.*; ~ code *s.* Militär-
strafgesetzbuch *n.*; ~ district *s.* Wehr-
(kreis)bezirk *m.*; ~ law *s.* Kriegsrecht
n.; ~ government *s.* Militärregierung *f.*;
~ post *s.* Standort *m.*; ~ target, ~
objective *s.* kriegswichtige Ziel *n.*; ~ *s.*
Soldatenstand *m.*

militate (against) *v.i.* sprechen gegen.

militia *s.* Land-, Bürgerwehr *f.*

milk *s.* Milch *f.*; ~ *v.t.* melken.

milkbar *s.* Milchhalle *f.*

milk-maid *s.* Milchmädchen *n.*

milk-sop *s.* Schwächling *m.*

milktooth *s.* Milchzahn *m.*

milky-way *s.* Milchstrasse *f.*

mill *s.* Mühle *f.*; Fabrik *f.*; ~ *v.t.* mahlen;
(Münzen) rändeln; walken.

miller *s.* Müller *m.*

millennium *s.* tausendjährige Reich (*n.*).

millet *s.* Hirse *f.*

milliner *s.* Putzmacherin *f.*

millinery *s.* Putzwaren *f.pl.*

milling machine *s.* Fräsmaschine *f.*

million *s.* Million *f.*

millionaire *s.* Millionär *m.*

milt *s.* Milch (der Fische) *f.*; Milz *f.*

mimeograph *s.* Vervielfältigungsapparat
m.; ~ *v.t.* vervielfältigen.

mimic *a.* mimisch, Schein...; ~ *s.* Mime;
~ *v.t.* nachäffen.

mimicry *s.* Mimikrie *f.*

minatory *a.* drohend.

mince *v.t.* kleinhacken; *to* ~ *matters*, sich
ein Blatt vor den Mund nehmen; ~ *v.i.*
sich zieren; ~d meat *s.* Hackfleisch *n.*

mincemeat *s.* Füllungsmasse des *mince-
pie* (Fett, Rosinen, Zitrone, etc.).

mince-pie *s.* Pastetchen (*n.*) mit *mincemeat* gefüllt.

mincingly *adv.* geziert, affektiert.

mincing-machine *s.* Hackmaschine *f.*

mind *s.* Gemüt *m.*; Geist, Verstand, Sinn
m.; Neigung *f.*; *to make up one's* ~, sich
entschliessen; *to bear in* ~, sich merken;
to change one's ~, sich anders besinnen;
~ *v.t.* merken; achten; sich bekümmern
um; *v.i.* willens sein; *never* ~!, es tut
nichts!

minded *a.* gesinnt, geneigt.

mindful *a.*, ~ly *adv.* achtsam; eingedenk.

mine *pn.* mein, meinige; ~s. Bergwerk *n.*;
Grube *f.*; Mine *f.*; ~ *v.t.* graben; Minen
legen.

minefield *s.* (*mil.*) Minenfeld *n.*

minelayer *s.* Minenleger *m.*

miner *s.* Bergmann *m.*

mineral *s.* Mineral *n.*; ~ *a.* mineralisch;
~ *water*, Sauerbrunnen *m.*

mineralogy *s.* Mineralogie *f.*

minesweeper *s.* Minensucher *m.*

mingle *v.t.* & *i.* mischen; sich mischen.

miniature *s.* Miniaturgemälde *n.*

minim *s.* (*mus.*) halbe Note *f.*

minimize *v.t.* möglichst klein machen.

minimum *s.* Mindestmass, Minimum *n.*

mining *s.* Bergbau *m.*; ~-academy *s.* Berg-
akademie *f.*; ~-bureau *s.* Bergamt *n.*;
~-industry *s.* Montanindustrie *f.*; ~-
share *s.* Kux *f.*

minion *s.* Günstling *m.*

minister *s.* Diener *m.*; Minister, Gesandte *m.*; Geistliche *m.*; ~ *v.t.* darreichen; ~ *v.i.* dienen.

ministerial *a.*, ~ly *adv.* ministeriell;
geistlich.

ministration *s.* Dienst *m.*; Amt *n.*

ministry *s.* Dienst *m.*; Predigtamt *n.*;
Ministerium *n.*

mink *s.* Nerz *m.*

minor *a.* kleiner, geringer; jünger; unmündig; (*mus.*) Moll.

minority *s.* Minderheit *f.*; Unmündigkeit
f.

minster *s.* Münster *m.* or *n.*

minstrel *s.* Spielmann *m.*

mint *s.* Münze *f.*; Fundgrube *f.*; Minze
(Pflanze) *f.*; ~ *v.t.* münzen, prägen.

mintage *s.* Prägen *n.*; Münzgebühr *f.*

mint-sauce *s.* Minzsosse *f.*

minuet *s.* Menuett *f.*

minute *a.* klein; umständlich.; ~ *s.* Minute
f.; Entwurf *m.*, Notiz *f.*; ~s *pl.* Protokoll
n.; *to keep the* ~s, das Protokoll führen.

minutiæ *s.pl.* Einzelheiten *f.pl.*

minx *s.* schelmische Mädchen *n.*

miracle *s.* Wunder *n.*

miraculous *a.*, ~ly *adv.* wunderbar.

mirage *s.* Luftspiegelung *f.*

mire *s.* Schlamm, Kot *m.*

mirror *s.* Spiegel *m.*; ~ *v.t.* spiegeln.

mirth *s.* Fröhlichkeit, Freude, Lust *f.*

miry *a.* schlammig, kotig.

misadventure *s.* Missgeschick *n.*

misalliance *s.* Missheirat *f.*

misanthrope *s.* Menschenfeind *m.*

misapplication *s.* falsche Anwendung *f.*

misapply *v.t.* falsch anwenden.

misapprehend *v.t.* missverstehen.

misapprehension *s.* Missverständnis *n.*

misappropriate *v.t.* sich mit Unrecht an
eignen; widerrechtlich verwenden.

misbehave *v.i.* sich schlecht aufführen.

miscalculate *v.t.* falsch berechnen.

miscarriage *s.* Misslingen *n.*; Fehlgeburt *f.*; Verlust (von Briefen) *f.*; ~ *of justice*, Fehlurteil *n.*

miscarry *v.i.* misslingen; verlorengehen; fehlgebären.

miscegenation *s.* Rassenmischung *f.*

miscellaneous *a.* gemischt.

miscellany *s.* Gemisch *n.*; vermischte Schriften *f.pl.*

mischance *s.* Unfall *m.*

mischief *s.* Unglück *n.*; Unfug *m.*

mischief-maker *s.* Unheilstifter *m.*

mischievous *a.*, ~ly *adv.* nachteilig; boshaft; mutwillig.

misconceive *v.t.* unrecht verstehen.

misconception *s.* Missverständnis *n.*

misconduct *s.* Fehltritt *m.*; schlechte Verwaltung *f.*; (*law*) Ehebruch *m.*

misconstruction *s.* Missdeutung *f.*

misconstrue *v.t.* missdeuten.

miscount *v.t.* falsch rechnen.

miscreant *s.* Bösewicht *m.*

misdeed *s.* Missetat *f.*; Verbrechen *n.*

misdemeanour *s.* Vergehen *n.*

misdirect *v.t.* falsch leiten; falsch adressieren.

miser *s.* Geizhals *m.*

miserable *a.*, ~bly *adv.* elend.

miserly *a.* karg, geizig.

misery *s.* Elend *n.*, Not *f.*

misfire *v.i.* versagen (Gewehr); fehlzünden (motor).

misfit *s.* nichtpassende Kleid *or* Schuhwerk *n.*

misfortune *s.* Unglück *n.*

misgiving *s.* Befürchtung *f.*

misgovern *v.t.* schlecht regieren.

misguide *v.t.* verleiten.

mishandle *v.t.* schlecht handhaben, verkorxen.

mishap *s.* Unfall *m.*

mishear *v.t. & i.* (sich)verhören.

misinform *v.t.* falsch berichten.

misinterpret *v.t.* missdeuten.

misinterpretation *s.* falsche Auslegung *f.*

misjudge *v.i. & t.* falsch urteilen, verkennen.

mislay *v.t.st.* verlegen.

mislead *v.t.st.* verleiten; irreführen.

mismanage *v.t.* übel verwalten.

misnomer *s.* falsche Name *m.*

misogynist *s.* Weiberhasser *m.*

misplace *v.t.* unrecht stellen.

misprint *v.t.* verdrucken; ~ *s.* Druckfehler *m.*

mispronounce *v.t.* falsch aussprechen.

misquotation *s.* falsche Anführung *f.*

misquote *v.t.* falsch anführen.

misread *v.t.* falschlesen; falsch deuten.

misrepresent *v.t.* falsch darstellen.

misrepresentation *s.* Verdrehung *f.*

misrule *s.* schlechte Regierung *f.*

miss *v.t.* missen, vermissen; verfehlen, verpassen; versäumen; übersehen; auslassen; ~ *s.* Fehl-stoss, -wurf, -schuss *m.*; ~ *s.* Fräulein *n.*

missal *s.* Messbuch *n.*

misshapen *a.* missgestaltet.

missile *s.* Wurfgeschoss *n.*

missing *a.* verloren, abwesend; (*mil.*) vermisst.

mission *s.* Sendung *f.*; Gesandtschaft *f.*; Mission *f.*; (*mil.*) Auftrag *m.*

missionary *s.* Missionär *m.*

misspell *v.t.r. & st.* falsch buchstabieren, unrichtig schreiben.

misstate *v.t.* falsch angeben, falsch darstellen.

misstatement *s.* falsche Angabe *f.*

mist *s.* Nebel *m.*

mistake *v.t.st.* missverstehen; ~ *v.i.* sich irren; ~ *s.* Irrtum *m.*; Versehen *n.*

mistaken *a.* irrig.

Mister (Mr.) *s.* Herr (Titel) *m.*

mistimed *a.* unzeitig.

mistletoe *s.* Mistel *f.*

mistranslate *v.t.* falsch übersetzen.

mistreat *v.t.* (*Am.*) misshandeln.

mistress *s.* Gebieterin *f.*; Lehrerin *f.*; Herrin; Meisterin *f.*; Geliebte *f.*; ~, (*Mrs.*), Frau (als Titel) *f.*

mistrust *s.* Misstrauen *n.*; ~ *v.t.* misstrauen.

mistrustful *a.*, ~ly *adv.* misstrauisch.

misty *a.*, ~ily *adv.* neb(e)lig, trübe.

misunderstand *v.t.st.* missverstehen.

misunderstanding *s.* Missverständnis *n.*

misuse *v.t.* missbrauchen; ~ *s.* Missbrauch *m.*

mite *s.* Scherflein *n.*; kleine Kind *n.*

mitigate *v.t.* lindern, mildern.

mitre *s.* Bischofsmütze *f.*

mitten *s.* Fausthandschuh *m.*

mix *v.t.* mischen, vermischen; (Salat) anmachen; ~ *v.i.* sich vermischen, verkehren; *to ~ up*, durcheinanderbringen, verwechseln; ~ed double *s.* (*tennis*) gemischte Doppelspiel *n.*; *a good ~er*, ein umgänglicher Mensch.

mixture *s.* Mischung *f.*

moan *v.i.* stöhnen; ~ *v.t.* beklagen; ~ *s.* Stöhnen *n.*

moat *s.* Burggraben *m.*

mob *s.* Pöbel *m.*; ~ *v.t.* lärmend angreifen, belästigen.

mobile *a.* fahrbar, beweglich.

mobility *s.* Beweglichkeit *f.*

mobilize *v.t.* mobil machen (Truppen).

moccasin *s.* Mokassin *m.*

mock *s.* Spott *m.*; ~ *a.* nachgemacht; ~-turtle *s.* falsche Schildkrötensuppe *f.*; ~ *v.i.& t.* verspotten, täuschen.

mockery *s.* Spötterei *f.*; Schein *m.*

mode *s.* Art und Weise, Sitte *f.*

model *s.* Muster, Modell *n.*; Vorbild *n.*;
   ~ *v.t.* modellieren, entwerfen; modeln.
moderate *a.*, ~ly *adv.* mässig; gemässigt;
   mittelmässig; ~ *v.t.* mässigen.
moderation *s.* Mässigung, Mässigkeit *f.*
modern *a.* neu, modern.
modernize *v.t.* modernisieren.
modest *a.*, ~ly *adv.* bescheiden, sittsam.
modesty *s.* Sittsamkeit; Bescheidenheit *f.*
modicum *s.* geringe Menge *f.*
modification *s.* Abänderung *f.*; Einschränkung *f.*; (*gram.*) Umlaut *m.*
modify *v.t.* abändern, einschränken,
   mildern; (*gram.*) umlauten.
modulate *v.t.* modulieren; anpassen.
mohair *s.* Zeug (*n.*) aus Angorahaar.
moiety *s.* Hälfte *f.*
moist *a.* feucht.
moisten *v.t.* befeuchten.
moisture *s.* Feuchtigkeit *f.*
molar *s.* Backenzahn *m.*
molasses *s.* Melasse *f.*; Sirup *m.*
mole *s.* Maulwurf *m.*; Steindamm *m.*;
   Muttermal *n.*
molecule *s.* Molekül *n.*
molest *v.t.* belästigen, beschweren.
molestation *s.* Belästigung *f.*
mollify *v.t.* erweichen; besänftigen.
mollusc *s.* Molluske *f.*, Weichtier *n.*
molly-coddle *s.* Weichling *m.*; ~ *v.t.* verzärteln.
molten *a.* geschmolzen, gegossen.
molybdenum *s.* Molybdän *n.*
moment *s.* Augenblick *m.*; Wichtigkeit *f.*
momentary *a.*, ~ily *adv.* einen Augenblick dauernd.
momentous *a.* wichtig, von Bedeutung.
momentum *s.* Triebkraft *f.*; Moment *n.*
monarch *s.* Monarch *m.*
monarchical *a.* monarchisch.
monarchy *s.* Monarchie *f.*
monastery *s.* (Mönchs-) Kloster *n.*
monastic *a.*, ~ally *adv.* klösterlich.
Monday *s.* Montag *m.*
monetary *a.* Geld...; ~ standard *s.*
   Münzfuss *m.*; ~ unit, Geld-, Münzeinheit *f.*
money *s.* Geld *n.*; ready ~, ~ in hand, bares
   Geld.
money-changer *s.* Geldwechsler *m.*
money-order *s.* Postanweisung *f.*
mongrel *s.* Mischling, Bastard *m.*
monitor *s.* Ermahner *m.*; Schüler als Gehilfe des Lehrers *m.*; Panzerschiff *n.*; ~
   v.t. abhören, mithören.
monk *s.* Mönch *m.*
monkey *s.* Affe *m.*
monkish *a.* mönchisch.
monogamy *s.* Einehe, Monogamie *f.*
monogram *s.* Namenszug *m.*
monograph *s.* Monographie *f.*
monologue *s.* Selbstgespräch *n.*
monomania *s.* fixe Idee *f.*

monomaniac *s.* Irrsinnige *m.* & *f.*
monoplane *s.* Eindecker *m.*
monopolize *v.t.* Alleinhandel treiben; ganz
   in Besitz nehmen.
monopolist *s.* Alleinhändler *m.*
monopoly *s.* Alleinhandel *m.*, Monopol *n.*
monosyllabic *a.* einsilbig.
monosyllable *s.* einsilbige Wort *n.*
monotonous *a.* eintönig.
monotony *s.* Eintönigkeit *f.*
monsoon *s.* Monsun *m.*
monster *s.* Ungeheuer *n.*; Riesen...
monstrance *s.* Monstranz *f.*
monstrosity *s.* Ungeheuerlichkeit *f.*
monstrous *a.*, ~ly *adv.* ungeheuer;
   scheusslich.
month *s.* Monat *m.*
monthly *a.* & *adv.* monatlich; ~ *s.*
   Monatsschrift *f.*
monument *s.* Denkmal *n.*
monumental *a.*, ~ly *adv.* Denkmal...
   monumental; erstaunlich.
mood *s.* Stimmung, Laune *f.*; (*gram.*)
   Modus *m.*; (*mus.*) Tonart *f.*
moody *a.*, ~ily *adv.* mürrisch, launisch.
moon *s.* Mond *m.*; Monat *m.*; once in a
   blue ~, alle Jubeljahre.
moon-calf *s.* Mondkalb *n.*
moonlight *s.* Mondschein *m.*
moonshine *s.* Schwindel *m.*
moon-struck *a.* mondsüchtig.
moor *s.* Mohr *m.*; Haideland *n.*; Moor *n.*;
   ~ *v.t.* (*nav.*) vermooren.
mooring *s.* Ankerplatz *m.*
moor-hen *s.* Wasserhuhn *n.*
moorish *a.* maurisch; moorig.
moot *v.t.* & *i.* disputieren, streiten.
moot-point *s.* streitige Punkt *m.*
mop *s.* Wisch *m.* Scheuertuch *n.*
mope *v.i.* Trübsal blasen.
moraine *s.* Moräne *f.*
moral *a.*, ~ly *adv.* sittlich; gut, moralisch;
   ~ *s.* Nutzanwendung *f.*; ~s *pl.* Sitten
   f.pl.; Moral *f.*
morale *s.* (*mil.*) Moral, Stimmung *f.*
moralize *v.i.* Sittlichkeit predigen.
morality *s.* Sittenlehre, Sittlichkeit *f.*
morass *s.* Morast *m.*
moratorium *s.* (*com.*) Moratorium *n.*,
   Schuldenstundung *f.*, Zahlungsauf-
   schub *m.*
morbid *a.* krankhaft.
mordant *a.*, ~ly *adv.* beissend, sarkastisch.
more *a.* & *adv.* mehr; ferner, noch; once ~,
   noch einmal.
moreover *adv.* überdies.
moribund *a.* im Sterben (liegend).
morning *s.* Morgen *m.*; ~-coat *s.* Cut *m.*;
   ~-dress *s.* Strassenanzug *m.*
morocco *s.* Maroquin, Saffian *m.*
morose *a.*, ~ly *adv.* mürrisch.
morphia, morphine *s.* Morphium *n.*

morrow *s.* Morgen *n.*; *to-morrow*, morgen.
morsel *s.* Bissen *m.*
mortal *a.*, **ly~** *adv.* sterblich, tödlich; ~ *sin*, Todsünde *f.*; ~ *s.* Sterbliche, Mensch *m.*
mortality *s.* Sterblichkeit, Sterblichkeitsziffer *f.*; **~-rate** Sterblichkeitsziffer *f.*
mortar *s.* Mörser *m.*; Mörtel *m.*; (*mil.*) Granatwerfer *m.*
mortgage *s.* Hypothek *f.*; *to foreclose a ~*, eine Hypothek für verfallen erklären; *debt on ~*, Hypothekenschuld *f.*; **~-bond, ~-deed** *s.* Pfandbrief *m.*; ~ *credit bank*, Bodenkreditbank *f.*; ~ *v.t.* mit einer Hypothek belasten, verpfänden.
mortgagee *s.* Pfandgläubiger *m.*
mortgager *s.* Pfandschuldner *m.*
mortification *s.* Kränkung *f.*, Ärger *m.*
mortify *v.t.* abtöten; demütigen.
mortmain *s.* (*law*) tote Hand *f.*
mortuary *a.* Begräbnis…
mosaic *s.* Mosaik *n.*
moselle *s.* Mosel *f.*; Moselwein *m.*
mosque *s.* Moschee *f.*
mosquito *s.* Moskito *m.*
moss *s.* Moos *n.*
most *a.* meist, die meisten; ~ *adv.* meistenteils; höchst; ~ *s.* Meiste *n.*; *at ~*, höchstens.
most-favoured-nation clause *s.* Meistbegünstigungsklausel *f.*
mostly *adv.* meistenteils, meist, meistens.
moth *s.* Motte *f.*; **~-eaten** *a.* von Motten zerfressen; **~-powder** *s.* Mottenpulver *n.*; **~-proof** *a.* mottensicher.
mother *s.* Mutter *f.*; ~ *of pearl*, Perlmutter *f.*; ~ *v.t.* bemuttern.
motherhood *s.* Mutterschaft *f.*
mother-in-law *s.* Schwiegermutter *f.*
motherly *a.* mütterlich.
motion *s.* Bewegung *f.*; Gang *m.*; Trieb *m.*; Antrag *m.*
motionless *a.* unbeweglich.
motion-picture *s.* (*Am.*) Film *m.*
motivate *v.t.* motivieren, begründen.
motive *a.* bewegend; ~ *s.* Motiv *n.*
motley *a.* scheckig, bunt.
mottled *a.* gesprenkelt, gescheckt.
motor *a.* bewegend; ~ *s.* Motor *m.*, Kraftmaschine *f.*; **~-ambulance** *s.* Krankenkraftwagen *m.*; **~-bicycle, ~-bike** *s.* Motorrad *n.*; **~-bus** *s.* Autobus *m.*; **~-car** *s.* Automobil *n.*, Kraftwagen *m.*; **~-coach** *s.* Reiseomnibus *m.*; **~-corps** *a.* (*mil.*) Kraftfahrkorps *n.*; **~-highway** *s.* Autobahn *f.*; **~-launch** *s.* (*nav.*) Motorbarkasse *f.*; **~-lorry** *s.* Lastauto *n.*; **~-pool** *s.* Kraftfahrpark *m.*; ~ *transport service* *s.* (*mil.*) Kraftfahrwesen *n.*; **~-vehicle** *s.* Motorfahrzeug *n.*; *to ~* *v.i.* mit dem Auto fahren.
motorist *s.* Motorfahrer *m.*

motorize *v.t.* motorisieren.
motto *s.* Wahl- Sinnspruch *m.*
mould *s.* Form *f.*; Giessform *f.*; Schablone *f.*; Schimmel *m.*; ~ *v.t.* formen; giessen; ~ *v.i.* schimmeln.
moulder *v.i.* vermodern; zerbröckeln.
moulding *s.* Fries *m.*, Simswerk *n.*
mouldy *a.* schimm(e)lig, moderig.
moult *v.i.* (sich) mausern; ~ *s.* Mauser *f.*
mound *s.* Erdhügel *m.*; Reichsapfel *m.*
mount *s.* Berg, Hügel *m.*; Reitpferd *n.*; (*mil.*) Lafette *f.*; ~ *v.i.* (hinauf)steigen; ~ *v.t.* erheben; besteigen; beschlagen (mit Silber, etc.); montieren; (Bilder) aufziehen; (Edelsteine) fassen; *to ~ guard*, auf Wache ziehen.
mountain *s.* Berg *m.*; **~-ash**, Eberesche *f.*
mountaineer *s.* Bergbewohner *m.*; Bergsteiger *m.*
mountainous *a.* gebirgig.
mountebank *s.* Marktschreier *m.*
mounted *a.* beritten.
mourn *v.t.* & *i.* trauern.
mourner *s.* Leidtragende *m.*
mournful *a.*, **~ly** *adv.* traurig.
mourning *s.* Trauer *f.*
mouse *s.* Maus *f.*
mouse-hole *s.* Mäuseloch *n.*
mouse-trap *s.* Mäusefalle *f.*
moustache *s.* Schnurrbart *m.*
mouth *s.* Mund *m.*; Mündung *f.*; ~ *v.t.* in den Mund nehmen.
mouthful *s.* Mundvoll *m.*
mouth-organ *s.* Mundharmonika *f.*
mouth-piece *s.* Mundstück *n.*; Wortführer *m.*
mouthwash *s.* Mundwasser *n.*
movable *a.*, **~bly** *adv.* beweglich; ~ *property*, bewegliche Habe *f.*; **~s** *pl.* bewegliche Güter *n.pl.*
move *v.t.* bewegen, fortbewegen; anregen; beantragen; überreden, erregen; ~ *v.i.* sich bewegen, sich fortbewegen, vorrücken; umziehen; *to ~ into a house*, ein Haus beziehen; *to ~ up*, (*mil.*) heranführen; nachrücken; ~ *s.* Bewegung *f.*; Zug (beim Spiele) *m.*; Massregel *f.*
movement *s.* Bewegung *f.*; Gangwerk (Uhr) *n.*; (*mus.*) Satz *m.*, Tempo *n.*
mover *s.* Anreger *m.*; Antragsteller *m.*
movies *s.* Kino *n.* (*vulg.*) Kientopp *m.*
mow *v.t.* mähen.
mower *s.* Mäher, Schnitter *m.*
much *a.* & *adv.* viel; sehr.
mucilage *s.* Pflanzenschleim *m.*; (*Am.*) Klebstoff *m.*
muck *s.* Mist, Dünger *m.*; Dreck *m.*
mucous *a.* schleimig.
mucus *s.* Nasenschleim *m.*
mud *s.* Schlamm, Lehm *m.*; **~-guard** *s.* Kotflügel *m.*

muddle *v.t.* verwirren; verpfuschen; ~ *v.i.* wursteln; ~ *s.* Verwirrung *f.*
muddy *a.*, ~ily *adv.* schlammig; trübe.
muff *s.* Muff *m.*
muffin *s.* dünne Butterkuchen *m.*
muffle *s.* (*mech.*) Muffel *f.*; ~ *v.t.* umwickeln; dämpfen (Trommel).
mufti *s.* Zivil *n.*; Kleidung *f.*
mug *s.* Krug, Becher *m.*; Fratze *f.*
mulatto *s.* Mulatte *m.*
mulberry *s.* Maulbeere *f.*
mule *s.* Maultier *n.*
muleteer *s.* Maultiertreiber *m.*
mulish *a.* störrig.
mull *s.* Mull *m.*
mullion *s.* Fensterpfosten *m.*
multifarious *a.*, ~ly *adv.* mannigfaltig.
multiform *a.* vielförmig.
multiple *a.* vielfach; ~ *s.* Vielfaches *n.*
multiplicand *s.* Vervielfältigungszahl *f.*
multiplication *s.* Vervielfältigung, Multiplikation *f.*
multiplication-table *s.* Einmaleins *n.*
multiplicity *s.* Menge, Mannigfaltigkeit *f.*
multiply *v.t.* multiplizieren, vervielfältigen.
multitude *s.* Vielheit *f.*, Menge *f.*
mum *a.* still; ~! *i.* still! st!
mumble *v.i. & t.* murmeln.
mummer *s.* Schauspieler *m.*
mummy *s.* Mumie *f.*; Baumwachs *n.*
mummy, mum *s.* Mama *f.*
mump *v.i. & t.* grämlich sein; betteln.
mumps *s.pl.* üble Laune; (*med.*) Ziegenpeter *m.*
munch *v.t. & i.* bedächtig kauen.
mundane *a.* weltlich.
municipal *a.* Stadt..., Gemeinde...; ~ *board*, Magistrat *m.*
municipality *s.* Stadtbezirk *m.*; Stadtrat *m.*
munificence *s.* Freigebigkeit *f.*
munificent *a.*, ~ly *adv.* äusserst freigebig.
munition *s.* Kriegsvorrat *m.*
mural *a.* Mauer...
murals *s.pl.* Wandgemälde *n.*, Fresko *n.*
murder *s.* Mord *m.*; ~ *with robbery*, Raubmord *m.*; ~ *v.t.* ermorden.
murderer *s.* Mörder *m.*
murderous *a.*, ~ly *adv.* mörderisch.
muriatic *a.* ~ *acid*, Salzsäure *f.*
murky *a.* dunkel, trübe.
murmur *s.* Gemurmel *n.*; ~ *v.i.* murmeln; murren.
murrain *s.* Viehseuche *f.*
muscle *s.* Muskel *m.*
muscular *a.* muskelhaft.
muse *s.* Muse *f.*; ~ *v.i.* nachdenken.
museum *s.* Museum *n.*
mushroom *s.* Pilz *m.*
music *s.* Musik *f.*; Noten *f.pl.*
musical *a.*, ~ly *adv.* musikalisch.
musical comedy *s.* Operette *f.*
music-hall *s.* Tingeltangel *m.*, Varieté *n.*

musician *s.* Musiker *m.*
music-stand *s.* Notenpult *n.*
musk *s.* Bisam *m.*, Moschus *m.*
musket *s.* Flinte, Muskete *f.*
musketeer *s.* Musketier *m.*
muslin *s.* Musselin *m.*
Mussulman *s.* Muselmann *m.*
must *v.i.ir.def.* müssen, muss; ~ *s.* Most *m.*
mustard *s.* Senf *m.*
muster *v.t.* mustern; einstellen; aufbringen; ~ *s.* Musterung, Musterrolle *f.*; Trupp *m.*
musty *a.*, ~ily *adv.* dumpfig, muffig.
mutable *a.* veränderlich.
mutation *s.* Veränderung *f.*
mute *a.*, ~ly *adv.* stumm.
mutilate *v.t.* verstümmeln.
mutineer *s.* Meuterer *m.*
mutinous *a.*, ~ly *adv.* aufrührerisch.
mutiny *s.* Meuterei *f.*; ~ *v.i.* sich empören.
mutter *v.i. & t.* murren; murmeln; ~ *s.* Gemurmel *n.*
mutton *s.* Hammelfleisch *n.*; ~-chop Hammelrippchen *n.*
mutual *a.* gegenseitig.
muzzle *s.* Maulkorb *m.*; Mündung (eines Gewehrs) *f.*; ~ *v.t.* den Maulkorb anlegen.
my *pn.* mein, meine.
myopic *a.* kurzsichtig.
myriad *s.* Myriade *f.*
myrrh *s.* Myrrhe *f.*
myrtle *s.* Myrte *f.*
myself *pn.* (ich) selbst; mich, mir.
mysterious *a.*, ~ly *adv.* geheimnisvoll.
mystery *s.* Geheimnis *n.*
mystic(al) *a.*, ~ly *adv.* mystisch; dunkel; ~ *s.* Mystiker *m.*
mystification *s.* Fopperei *f.*
mystify *v.t.* foppen; irreführen.
myth *s.* Mythe *f.*; Erdichtung *f.*
mythological *a.* mythologisch.
mythology *s.* Mythologie *f.*

N

nadir *s.* Nadir, Tiefpunkt *m.*
nag *s.* Klepper *m.*; ~ *v.t. & i.* nörgeln.
nail *s.* Nagel *m.*; ~ *v.t.* nageln.
nail-scissors *s.pl.* Nagelschere *f.*
naïve *a.* unbefangen, naiv.
naïveté *s.* Unbefangenheit *f.*
naked *a.*, ~ly nackt, bloss; wehrlos; offen; ~ *light*, ungeschützte Licht; ~ *eye*, blosse Auge *n.*
nakedness *s.* Nacktheit, Blösse *f.*
name *s.* Name *m.*; (gute) Ruf *m.*; *Christian* ~, *first* ~, Vorname *m.*; *family* ~, Familienname *m.*; *proper* ~, Eigenname *s.*; *of the* ~ N., N. *by* ~, namens N.; *in* ~ *only*, nur dem Namen nach; *to*

send in one's ~, sich anmelden; ~ *v.t.* nennen, ernennen.

nameday *s.* Namenstag *m.*

nameless *a.* namenlos.

namely *adv.* nämlich.

nameplate *s.* Namensschild *n.*

namesake *s.* Namensvetter *m.*

nankeen *s.* Nanking *m.*

nap *s.* Noppe *f.*; Schläfchen *n.*

nape *s.* Genick *n.*, Nacken *m.*

napkin *s.* Serviette *f.*

narcosis *s.* Narkose *f.*

narcotic *a.* betäubend, narkotisch; ~ *s.* Betäubungsmittel *n.*

narcotize *v.t.* narkotisieren.

narrate *v.t.* erzählen.

narration *s.* Erzählung *f.*

narrative *a.*, ~ly *adv.* erzählend; ~ *s.* Erzählung *f.*

narrow *a.* eng[e]; schmal; ~ly *adv.* mit genauer Not; ~ *gauge*, Schmalspur...; ~ *s.* Meerenge *f.*; ~ *v.t. & i.* (sich) verengen.

narrow-minded *a.* beschränkt.

nasal *a.* Nasen..., nasal; ~ *s.* Nasenlaut *m.*

nascent *a.* entstehend, werdend.

nasty *a.*, ~ily *adv.* schmutzig; bösartig; ungünstig, unfreundlich.

natal *a.* Geburts...

nation *s.* Volk *n.*, Nation *f.*

national *a.*, ~ly *adv.* national, Volks...; ~ *s.* Staatsangehöriger *m.*; ~ *debt s.* Staatsschuld *f.*

nationalize *v.t.* verstaatlichen.

nationality *s.* Staatsangehörigkeit *f.*, Nationalität *f.*

native *a.*, ~ly *adv.* natürlich; angeboren; einheimisch; ~ *country s.* Heimat *f.*; ~ *language s.* Muttersprache *f.*; ~ *s.* Eingeborener *m.*

nativity *s.* Geburt *f.*

natural *a.*, ~ly *adv.* natürlich; ~ *s.* Idiot, Blödsinnige *m.*

naturalize *v.t.* einbürgern.

naturalist *s.* Naturforscher *m.*

nature *s.* Natur *f.*; Beschaffenheit *f.*; *law of* ~, *natural law s.* Naturrecht, Naturgesetz *n.*

natured *a.* geartet.

naught *s.* Nichts *n.*; Null *f.*; *to set at* ~, missachten, in den Wind schlagen.

naughty *a.*, ~ily *adv.* unartig.

nausea *s.* Übelkeit *f.*

nauseate *v.t.* mit Ekel zurückweisen.

nauseous *a.*, ~ly *adv.* ekelhaft.

nautical *a.* nautisch, See...; ~ *mile s.* Seemeile *f.*

naval *a.* Schiffs..., See...; ~ *base s.* Kriegshafen *m.*

nave *s.* Schiff (einer Kirche) *n.*; Nabe *f.*

navel *s.* Nabel *m.*

navicert *s.* (*nav.*) Warenpass *m.*

navigable *a.* schiffbar; lenkbar.

navigate *v.i.* schiffen; ~ *v.t.* befahren.

navigation *s.* Seemannskunst *f.*; Schiffahrt *f.*; ~ *light*, Positionslicht, Kennlicht *n.*

navigator *s.* Seefahrer *m.*

navvy *s.* Erdarbeiter *m.*

navy *s.* (Kriegs-) Flotte *f.*; Marine *f.*; ~-yard *s.* Marinewerft *f.*

nay *adv.* nein; vielmehr.

near *pr.* neben, in der Nähe von; ~ *a.* nahe; verwandt; ~ *adv.* beinahe; ~ *v.t. & i.* sich nähern.

nearly *adv.* nahe, beinahe; genau, karg.

near-sighted *a.* kurzsichtig.

neat *a.*, ~ly *adv.* nett, sauber.

nebulous *a.* neblig, wolkig.

necessaries *s.pl.* Bedürfnisse *n.pl.*

necessary *a.*, ~ily *adv.* notwendig.

necessitate *v.t.* erfordern; zwingen.

necessitous *a.* dürftig.

necessity *s.* Notwendigkeit *f.*; Bedürfnis *n.*

neck *s.* Hals *m.*; Busen *m.*

neckerchief *s.* Frauenhalstuch *n.*

necklace *s.* Halsband *n.*

necktie *s.* Binde, Kravatte *f.*

necromancy *s.* schwarze Kunst *f.*

necrosis *s.* (*med.*) Nekrose *f.*

nectar *s.* Nektar, Göttertrank *m.*

need *s.* Not *f.*, Mangel *m.*; *in case of* ~, im Notfall; ~ *v.t.* nötig haben, bedürfen; brauchen; ~ *v.i.* nötig sein.

needful *a.* notwendig.

needle *s.* Nähnadel *f.*; Nadel *f.*

needless *a.* ~ly *adv.* unnötig; ~ *to say*, selbstverständlich.

needle-woman *s.* Näherin *f.*

needlework *s.* Näharbeit *f.*

needs *adv.* notwendigerweise.

needy *a.*, ~ily *adv.* dürftig, arm.

nefarious *a.* schändlich.

negation *s.* Verneinung *f.*

negative *a.*, ~ly *adv.* verneinend; ~ *s.* Verneinung *f.*; (*phot.*) Negativ *n.*; *to answer in the* ~, verneinend antworten; ~ *v.t.* verneinen, verwerfen; unwirksam machen.

neglect *v.t.* vernachlässigen; ~ *s.* Vernachlässigung *f.*; *gross* ~, (*law*) grobe Fahrlässigkeit *f.*; ~ *of duty*, Pflichtversäumnis *f.*

negligence *s.* Nachlässigkeit *f.*

negligent *a.*, ~ly *adv.* nachlässig.

negotiable *a.* verkäuflich; begebbar; *not* ~, nur zur Verrechnung (auf Schecks).

negotiate *v.i.* handeln; unterhandeln; ~ *v.t.* verhandeln; (Wechsel) begeben; (Hindernis) nehmen.

negotiation *s.* Handel *m.*; Unterhandlung *f.*; *to enter into* ~s, Verhandlungen aufnehmen.

negotiator *s.* Unterhändler *m.*

negress *s.* Negerin *f.*

negro *s.* Neger *m.*

neigh *v.i.* wiehern; ~ *s.* Wiehern *n.*
neighbour *s.* Nachbar *m.*; Nächste *m.*; ~ *v.t. & i.* angrenzen.
neighbourhood *s.* Nachbarschaft *f.*
neighbourly *a.* nachbarlich, gefällig.
neither *pn.* keiner (von beiden); ~ *c.* weder; auch nicht.
neon *s.* Neon (Edelgas) *n.*; ~-lamp *s.* Neonlampe; ~-tube *s.* Neonröhre *f.*
neophyte *s.* Neubekehrte *m. & f.*
nephew *s.* Neffe *m.*
nephritis *s.* Nierenentzündung *f.*
nepotism *s.* Vetternwirtschaft *f.*
nerve *s.* Nerv *m.*; Sehne *f.*; (*fig.*) Kraft *f.*; to lose one's ~, die Nerven verlieren; ~ *v.t.* stärken.
nerveless *a.* kraftlos.
nervous *a.*, ~ly *adv.* nervig; nervös.
nescient *a.* unwissend.
nest *s.* Nest *n.*; ~-egg *s.* Sparpfenning, Notpfennig *m.*; to ~ *v.i.* nisten.
nestle *v.i.* nisten; ~ *v.t.* sich schmiegen.
nestling *s.* Nestling *m.*
net *s.* Netz *n.*; ~ *v.t.* häkeln; einfangen; ~ *a.* netto.
nether *a.* untere, niedere.
nettle *s.* Nessel *f.*; ~-rash, Nesselfieber *n.*; ~ *v.t.* erbittern.
network *s.* Netzwerk, Netz *n.*
neuralgia *s.* Nervenschmerz *m.*
neuritis *s.* Nervenentzündung *f.*
neurotic *a.* nervenkrank.
neuter *a.* geschlechtslos; (*gram.*) sächlich; ~ *s.* Neutrum *n.*
neutral *a.*, ~ly *adv.* neutral.
neutralize *v.t.* neutralisieren.
neutrality *s.* Neutralität *f.*
never *adv.* nie, niemals.
nevertheless *adv.* nichtsdestoweniger.
new *a.* neu.
newcomer *s.* Ankömmling, Fremde *m.*
newfangled *a.* neumodisch.
newly *adv.* kürzlich; neu.
new moon *s.* Neumond *m.*
newness *s.* Neuheit *f.*; Unerfahrenheit *f.*
news *s.* Neuigkeit *f.*; Nachricht; ~-medium *s.* Mittel der Nachrichtenverbreitung *n.*
news-agent *s.* Zeitungsverkäufer *m.*
newspaper *s.* Zeitung *f.*; ~-clipping, ~-cutting, Zeitungsausschnitt *m.*
newsprint *s.* Zeitungspapier *n.*
newsreel *s.* Filmwochenschau *f.*
news-stall, news-stand *s.* Zeitungskiosk *m.*
news-vendor *s.* Zeitungsverkäufer *m.*
newt *s.* Sumpfeidechse *f.*
New-year's eve *s.* Silvester (abend) *m.*
next *a.* nächst, folgend; ~ *adv.* gleich darauf, hernach; ~ door, nebenan; ~ of kin, die nächsten Verwandten *pl.*
nib *s.* Spitze (besonders einer Schreibfeder); Stahlfeder *f.*; ~ *v.t.* mit einer Spitz versehen.

nibble *v.i. & t.* benagen; anbeissen (von Fischen); kritteln.
nice *a.*, ~ly *adv.* fein, nett; wählerisch; genau.
niceness, nicety *s.* Feinheit.
nicety *s.* Feinheit *f.*; Genauigkeit *f.*
niche *s.* Nische *f.*
nick *s.* Kerbe *f.*; rechte Augenblick *m.*; Old Nick, der Teufel; ~ *v.t.* kerben.
nickel *s.* Nickel *m.*
nickname *s.* Spitzname *m.*
nicotine *s.* Nikotin *n.*
niece *s.* Nichte *f.*
niggard *s.* Filz, Knicker *m.*
niggardly *a.* karg, geizig.
nigger *s.* (*vulg.*) Neger, *m.*
nigh *a.* nahe; ~ *adv.* nahe, beinahe.
night *s.* Nacht *f.*; by ~, nachts; last ~, gestern Abend; ~-cap, Schlafmütze *f.*; first ~, Erstaufführung *f.*
nightblindness *s.* Nachtblindheit *f.*
nightclub *s.* Nachtklub *m.*, Kabarett *n.*
nightdress *s.* Nachtkleid *n.*
nightfighter *s.* (*avi.*) Nachtjäger *n.*
nightfall *s.* Einbruch (*m.*) der Nacht.
night-gown *s.* Nachtkleid *n.*
nightingale *s.* Nachtigall *f.*
nightly *a.* nächtlich; ~ *adv.* nachts; alle Nächte.
nightmare *s.* Alpdrücken *n.*
night-service *s.* Nachtdienst *m.*
nightshade *s.* Nachtschatten *m.*
nil *s.* nichts.
nimble *a.*, ~bly *adv.* hurtig, flink.
nimbus *s.* Strahlenkranz.
nine *a.* neun; ~ *s.* Neun *f.*
ninefold *a.* neunfach.
nine-pins *s.pl.* Kegelspiel *n.*
nineteen *a.* neunzehn.
nincompoop *s.* Einfaltspinsel, Trottel *m.*
ninety *a.* neunzig.
ninny *s.* Tropf, Dummkopf *m.*
nip *v.t.* kneifen; schneiden (von der Kälte); to ~ in the bud, im Keim ersticken; ~ *s.* Kniff *m.*, Kneifen *n.*
nippers *s.pl.* Kneifzange *f.*
nipple *s.* Brustwarze *f.*; Saughütchen *n.*
nitrate *s.* salpetersauer.
nitre *s.* Salpeter *m.*
nitric acid *s.* Salpetersäure *f.*
nitrogen *s.* Stickstoff *m.*
nitrous *a.* salpetrig.
no *adv.* nein, nicht; ~ *a.* kein.
nobility *s.* Adel *m.*
noble *a.*, ~bly *adv.* adlig; edel; trefflich; ~ *s.* Adlige *m.*
nobleman *s.* Edelmann *m.*
nobody *s.* niemand, keiner.
nocturnal *a.* nächtlich, Nacht...
nod *v.i. & t.* nicken, winken; schlummern; ~ *s.* Nicken *n.*; Wink *m.*
nodal *a.* Knoten...
node *s.* Knoten *m.*; Überbein *n.*

noise s. Lärm m.; Gerücht n.; ~ v.t. & i. lärmen.

noiseless a. geräuschlos.

noisome a., ~ly adv. schädlich; widrig.

noisy a. geräuschvoll, laut.

nomad s. Nomade m.

nomadic a. nomadisch.

nomenclature s. Terminologie f.

nominal a., ~ly adv. dem Namen nach; Namen..., Nenn..., Titular...; sehr gering, unwesentlich; ~ capital, Stammkapital n.; ~ value, Nennwert m.

nominate v.t. ernennen; vorschlagen.

nomination s. Ernennung, Vorwahl f.; Aufstellung eines Wahlkandidaten f.

nominative s. (gram.) Nominativ m.

nominee s. Vorgeschlagene m.

non-acceptance s. Nichtannahme f.

non-aggression s. Nichtangriff m.

non-attendance s. Nichterscheinen n.

non-belligerent s. Nichtkriegführender m.; ~ a. nichtkriegführend.

nonce s., for the ~, für dies eine Mal.

nonchalance s. Sichgehenlassen n.; Gleichgültigkeit f.

non-combatant a. nichtkämpfend; ~ s. Nichtkämpfender.

non-commissioned a., ~ officer, Unteroffizier m.

non-committal a. sich nicht bindend.

non-compliance s. Nichterfüllung s.

nonconformist s. Dissident m.

nondescript a. unklassifizierbar, seltsam.

none a. keiner, keine, keines; ~ the less adv. nichtsdestoweniger.

nonentity s. Nichtsein n.; (fig.) Null f.

non-fulfilment s. Nichterfüllung s.

non-intervention s. Nichteinmischung s.

non-member s. Nichtmitglied n.

non-observance s. Nichtbeachtung f.

non-party a. parteilich nicht gebunden.

non-payment s. Nichtzahlung f.

non-plus v.t. in Verlegenheit setzen.

non-profitmaking organization s. gemeinnützige Unternehmen n.

non-resident a. nichtansässig; ~ s. Nichtansässiger m.

nonsense s. Unsinn m.

nonsensical a., ~ly adv. unsinnig, albern.

non-smoker s. Nichtraucher m.

non-stop a. durchgehend (Zug).

non-suit s. (law) Zurücknahme, Sistierung einer Klage; to ~ v.t. (Prozess) sistieren.

noodle s. Dummkopf m.

nook s. Winkel m.; Ecke f.

noon, noontide s. Mittag m.

noose s. Schlinge f.; ~ v.t. verstricken.

nor c. noch; auch nicht; weder.

norm s. Regel f.; Muster n.

normal a. regelrecht; senkrecht; normal.

north s. Norden m.; a. & adv. nördlich.

north-and-south line s. Nordsüdlinie f.

north-east s. Nordost(en) m.; ~ a. nordöstlich.

northerly, northern a. nördlich.

nose s. Nase f.; ~ v.t. auswittern.

nose-dive s. (avi.) Sturzflug m.

nosegay s. Blumenstrauss m.

nose-landing, nose-over s. (avi.) Kopfstand m.

nostalgia s. Heimweh n.

nostalgic a. heimwehverursachend; heimwehkrank.

nostril s. Nasenloch n., Nüster f.

nostrum s. Geheimmittel n.

not adv. nicht.

notable a., ~bly adv. bemerkenswert; ~, angesehene Bürger m.

notary s. Notar m.

notation s. Bezeichnung f.

notch s. Kerbe f.; ~ v.t. einkerben.

note s. Zeichen, Merkmal n.; Note f.; Schein m.; Anmerkung f.; Zettel m.; Briefchen n.; Rechnung f.; Wichtigkeit f.; ~ of hand, Schuldschein m.; ~ v.t. aufzeichnen; bemerken; be it ~d, wohlgemerkt.

noted a., ~ly adv. berühmt, bekannt.

note-paper s. Briefpapier n.

noteworthy a. beachtenswert.

nothing pn. nichts; for ~, umsonst; ~ s. Nichts n.

nothingness s. Nichts n.; Nichtigkeit f.

notice s. Bemerkung f.; Kenntnis f.; Bekanntmachung f.; Nachricht f.; Kündigung f.; to give ~, kündigen; until further ~, bis auf weiteres; at (subject to) a month's ~, auf monatliche Kündigung; period of ~, Kündigungsfrist f.; ~ v.t. bemerken, Acht geben auf.

noticeable a. bemerklich.

notice-board s. schwarze Brett n.

notifiable a. meldepflichtig.

notification s. Benachrichtigung f.

notify v.t. (an)melden; benachrichtigen, formell anzeigen.

notion s. Begriff m.; Meinung f.

notoriety s. Offenkundigkeit f.

notorious a., ~ly adv. allbekannt; offenkundig; berüchtigt.

notwithstanding c. & pr. ungeachtet; dennoch.

nought see naught.

noun s. Hauptwort n., Substantiv n.

nourish v.t. & i. (er)nähren, unterhalten.

nourishment s. Nahrung f.

novel s. Roman m.; ~ a. neu, ungewöhnlich.

novelist s. Romanschreiber m.

novelty s. Neuheit f.

November s. November m.

novice s. Neuling m.; Novize m. & f.

novitiate s. Probezeit f.

now *adv.* jetzt, nun; **~-a-days,** heutzutage; ~ **and then,** zuweilen.

nowhere *adv.* nirgends.

nowise *adv.* keineswegs.

noxious *a.,* **~ly** *adv.* schädlich.

nozzle *s.* Tülle *f.*; Düse *f.*; Öffnung einer Röhre *f.*

nuclear *a.* (*phys.*) Kern...; ~ *fission,* Kernteilung *f.*; ~ *physics,* Kernphysik *f.*

nucleus *s.* Kern *m.*

nude *a.* nackt, bloss.

nudge *v.t.* leise anstossen.

nudity *s.* Nacktheit *f.*

nugatory *a.* läppisch, ungültig.

nuisance *s.* Unfug *m.*; Plage *f.*; Verdruss *m.*; Schaden *m.*; *commit no* ~*!* Verunreinigung dieses Ortes ist verboten!; **~-raid** (*avi.*) Störungsangriff *m.*

null *a.* nichtig, ungültig; ~ *and void,* null und nichtig.

nullify *v.t.* ungültig machen.

nullity *s.* Nichtigkeit *f.*; (*law*) ~ *action,* Nichtigkeitsklage *f.*; **~-appeal,** Nichtigkeitsbeschwerde *f.*

numb *a.* starr.

number *s.* Zahl *f.*; Nummer *f.*; Lieferung *f.*; ~ *v.t.* zählen, rechnen.

numberless *a.* unzählbar.

number-plate *s.* Nummernschild *n.*

numeral *a.* Zahl...; ~ *s.* Zahlwort *n.*; Zahlzeichen *n.*; Ziffer (des Uhrblatts) *f.*

numerator *s.* Zähler *m.*

numerical *a.,* **~ly** *adv.* numerisch.

numerous *a.* zahlreich.

numismatics *s.pl.* Münzkunde *f.*

nun *s.* Nonne *f.*

nuncio *s.* Nuntius *m.*

nunnery *s.* Nonnenkloster *n.*

nuptial *a.* hochzeitlich, ehelich.

nurse *s.* Amme *f.*; Krankenpfleger (*m.*) (-in, *f.*); Kindermädchen *n.*; ~ *v.i.* säugen; pflegen, warten; hegen.

nursemaid *s.* Kindermädchen *n.*

nursery *s.* Kinderstube *f.*; Pflanzschule *f.*

nurseryman *s.* Kunstgärtner *m.*

nursery rhymes *s.pl.* Kinderlieder *n.pl.*

nursing *s.* (Kranken-)Pflege *f.*; ~ **home** *s.* Privatklinik *f.*

nursling *s.* Pflegekind *n.*

nurture *v.t.* nähren, aufziehen; ~ *s.* Nahrung *f.*; Erziehung *f.*

nut *s.* Nuss *f.*; Schraubenmutter *f.*

nutcracker *s.* Nussknacker *m.*

nutmeg *s.* Muskatnuss *f.*

nutriment *s.* Nahrung *f.*; Futter *m.*

nutrition *s.* Ernährung *f.*; Fütterung *f.*

nutritious *a.* nährend, nahrhaft.

nutritive *a.* Nähr...; ~ **value** *s.* Nährwert *m.*

nutshell *s.* Nusschale *f.*

nylon *s.* Nylon *n.*

nymph *s.* Nymphe *f.*

O

o *i.* o, ach.

oaf *s.* Tölpel *m.*; Wechselbalg *m.*

oak *s.* Eiche *f.*

oaken *a.* eichen.

oakum *s.* Werg *n.*

oar *s.* Ruder *n.*; Riemen *m.*

oarsman *s.* Ruderer *m.*

oasis *s.* Oase *f.*

oath *s.* Eid, Schwur *m.*; Fluch *m.*; *upon* ~, eidlich, unter Eid; *in lieu of an* ~, eidesstattlich, an Eides Statt; *to take an* ~, einen Eid leisten.

oatmeal *s.* Hafer-mehl (*n.*), -grütze *f.*

oats *s.pl.* Hafer *m.*

obduracy *s.* Verstocktheit *f.*

obdurate *a.,* **~ly** *adv.* verstockt.

obedience *s.* Gehorsam *m.*

obedient *a.,* **~ly** *adv.* gehorsam.

obeisance *s.* Verbeugung *f.*

obelisk *s.* Obelisk *m.*

obese *a.* fettleibig, feist.

obesity *s.* Fettleibigkeit *f.*

obey *v.t.* gehorchen.

obituary *s.* Totenliste *f.*; Todesanzeige *f.*; Nachruf *m.*; ~ *a.* Todes..., Toten...

object *s.* Gegenstand *m.*; Zweck *m.*; Objekt *n.*; *that is no* ~, das ist nebensächlich, das spielt keine Rolle; ~ *v.t.* entgegensetzen; einwenden.

objection *s.* Einwand *m.*; *no* ~, nichts dagegen; *to make an* ~ *to,* einen Einwand erheben gegen.

objectionable *a.* verwerflich, anstössig.

objective *a.,* **~ly** *adv.* sachlich; ~ *s.* Ziel *n.*; (*opt.*) Objektiv *n.*

obligation *s.* Verpflichtung *f.*; Schuldverschreibung *f.*

object-lesson *s.* Anschauungsunterricht *m.*

obligate *v.t.* verpflichten.

obligatory *a.* verpflichtend, verbindlich.

oblige *v.t.* verpflichten, verbinden.

obliging *a.,* **~ly** *adv.* verbindlich.

oblique *a.,* **~ly** *adv.* schief, schräg; mittelbar.

obliterate *a.* auslöschen, ausstreichen.

oblivion *s.* Vergessenheit *f.*; (*law*) Strafer-lass *m.*; *Act of* ~, Gnadenerlass *m.*

oblivious *a.* vergesslich, vergessend.

oblong *a.,* **~ly** *adv.* länglich.

obloquy *s.* Schmähung *f.*; Tadel *m.*

obnoxious *a.,* **~ly** *adv.* anstössig, verrufen.

oboe *s.* Oboe *f.*

obscene *a.,* **~ly** *adv.* unzüchtig.

obscenity *s.* Unzüchtigkeit *f.*

obscure *a.,* **~ly** *adv.* dunkel; niedrig; verborgen; ~ *v.t.* verdunkeln.

obscurity *s.* Dunkelheit *f.*; Niedrigkeit *f.*

obsequies *s.pl.* Leichenbegängnis *n.*

obsequious *a.,* **~ly** *adv.* kriechend.

observance s. Beobachtung f.; Innehaltung f.; Vorschrift f.; Regel f.
observant a. beobachtend, achtsam.
observation s. Beobachtung f.
observatory s. Sternwarte f.
observe v.t. beobachten; bemerken.
obsessed a. (with) besessen (von).
obsession s. Besessenheit f.
obsolete a. veraltet.
obstacle s. Hindernis n.
obstinacy s. Hartnäckigkeit f.
obstinate a., ~ly adv. hartnäckig.
obstreperous a., ~ly adv. lärmend; widerspenstig.
obstruct v.t. verstopfen; hemmen.
obstruction s. Verstopfung f.; Hindernis n.; Hemmung f.
obtain v.t. erlangen; ~ v.i. herrschen, in Gebrauch sein.
obtainable a. erlangbar, erhältlich.
obtrude v.t. aufdrängen.
obtrusive a. aufdringlich.
obtuse a., ~ly adv. stumpf; dumm; ~-angled a. (geom.) stumpfwinklig.
obviate v.t. begegnen; vorbeugen.
obvious a. augenfällig, deutlich; einleuchtend; ~ly adv. selbstverständlich.
occasion s. Gelegenheit f.; Veranlassung f.; on this ~, dabei; ~ v.t. verursachen, veranlassen.
occasional a., ~ly adv. gelegentlich.
occident s. Abendland n.
occidental a. westlich; abendländisch.
occult a., ~ly adv. verborgen, geheim.
occupant s. Inhaber m.; Insasse (m.) (Zimmer, Abteil).
occupation s. Besitzergreifung f.; Besetzung f.; Besatzung f.; Beschäftigung f.
occupational a. beruflich; Berufs...; Besatzungs...
occupier s. Besitzer m.; Inhaber m.
occupy v.t. in Besitz nehmen; beschäftigen; innehaben, bewohnen; bekleiden (Amt); besetzen.
occur v.i. sich ereignen; einfallen.
occurrence s. Ereignis n.; Vorfall m.
ocean s. Weltmeer n.; Ozean m.
o'clock s.=of the clock, Uhr.
ochre s. Ocker m.
octagon s. Achteck n.
octane s. Oktan n.; ~-rating s. Oktanzahl f., Klopfwert m. (mot.).
octave s. Oktave f.
octavo s. Oktavformat n.
October s. Oktober m.
octogenarian s. achtzigjährige Greis m.; ~ a. achtzigjährig.
ocular a., ~ly adv. Augen...; augenscheinlich.
oculist s. Augenarzt m.
odd a., ~ly adv. ungerade; überzählig; übrig; einzeln; wunderlich; ungefähr, etwas über; a hundred ~, einige hundert.

oddity, oddness s. Seltsamkeit f.
odds s. Ungleichheit f.; Wahrscheinlichkeit f.; Vorgabe f.; Streit m.
ode s. Ode f.
odious a., ~ly adv. verhasst, widerlich.
odium s. Tadel m., Vorwurf m.
odorous a. duftig.
odour s. Geruch, Wohlgeruch m.
of pr. von, aus, vor, um, in Betreff.
off adv. & pr. von, ab, weg, davon; entfernt; (nav.) auf der Höhe von; ~! i. weg! fort!
offal s. Abfall m.; Aas n.
off-duty hours pl. Ausserdienststunden f.pl.
offence s. Beleidigung f.; Verdruss m.; Ärgernis n.; Vergehen n.; Anstoss m.; to give ~ to, Anstoss, erregen; einen beleidigen; to take ~ at a thing, etwas übelnehmen.
offend v.t. beleidigen, ärgern; verletzen; the ~ed party, der Beleidigte m.; ~ v.i. sich vergehen; verstossen.
offender s. Beleidiger m.; Zuwiderhandelnder m.; Missetäter m.; first ~, nicht vorbestrafte Verbrecher m.
offensive a., ~ly adv. anstössig; beleidigend; Angriffs...; ~ s. Offensive f.
offer v.t. anbieten, darbringen, opfern; ~ v.i. sich erbieten; ~ s. Anerbieten n.; Antrag m.; Offerte f.
offhand a. aus dem Stegreif.
office s. Amt n.; Dienst m.; Gottesdienst m.; Bureau n.; head ~, main ~, Hauptbüro n., Hauptgeschäftsstelle f.; to resign ~, vom Amt zurücktreten; discharge from ~, Amtsenthebung f.; oath of ~, Diensteid m.; term of ~, Amtszeit; ~-appliances pl. Büroartikel m.pl.; ~-holder, Amtsinhaber m.; ~-hours pl. Amtsstunden, Geschäftsstunden f.pl.
officer s. Beamte m.; Offizier m.; ~ candidate, Offiziersanwärter m.; ~s' mess, Kasino n.
official a., ~ly adv. amtlich, offiziell; ~ authority, Amtsgewalt f.; ~ journey s. Dienstreise f.; ~ s. Beamte m.; senior ~, höhere Beamte m.
officialdom s. Beamtentum n.; Bürokratie f.
officiate v.i. amtieren.
officious a., ~ly adv. diensteifrig; zudringlich.
offset s. Gegenrechnung f.; (arch.) Absatz m.; ~ v.t. ausgleichen.
offshoot s. Spross, Ausläufer m.
offspring s. Nachkommenschaft f.
oft, often adv. oft, öfters.
ogle v.t. (lieb)äugeln.
ogre s. Menschenfresser m.
oh! i. oh! ach!
ohm s. (elek.) Ohm n.; ohmmeter s. Widerstandsmesser m.

oil s. Öl n.; ~ v.t. einölen.
oilcake s. Ölkuchen m.
oil-cloth s. Wachstuch n.
oil-gauge s. (mot., avi.) Ölstandzeiger m.
oil-level s. (mot., avi.) Ölstand m.
oil-painting s. Ölgemälde n.
oil-refinery s. Ölraffinerie f.
oil-tanker s. Öltankschiff n.
oily a. ölig, fett; schmierig.
ointment s. Salbe f.
old a. alt.
old age s. Alter n., Greisenalter n.; ~ insurance s. Altersversicherung f.; ~ pension s. Alterspension f.
old-fashioned a. altmodisch.
oleander s. Oleander m.
oleograph s. Öldruck m.
olfactory a. Geruchs...
oligarchy s. Oligarchie f.
olive s. Olive f.; Ölbaum m.
olive-oil s. Baumöl n., Olivenöl n.
omelet s. Omelett n.
omen s. Vorbedeutung f., Vorzeichen n.
ominous a., ~ly adv. von übler Vorbedeutung, unheilvoll.
omission s. Unterlassung f.; Auslassung f.
omit v.t. auslassen; unterlassen.
omnibus s. Omnibus m.
omnipotence s. Allmacht f.
omnipotent a., ~ly adv. allmächtig.
omnipresent a., allgegenwärtig.
omniscient a. allwissend.
on pr. & adv. an, auf; in, zu, mit, bei, unter, von; zufolge; weiter, fort; and so ~ und so weiter.
once adv. einmal; einst, dereinst; ~ more, ~ again, noch einmal.
one a. & pn. einer, eine, ein(s); man; jemand; any ~, irgend jemand, jeder; ~ another, einander, sich; every ~, jeder; one's self, oneself, sich selbst; ~ by ~, einer nach dem andern.
one-armed a. einarmig; **one-eyed** a. einäugig.
onerous a. lästig, beschwerlich.
one-sided a. einseitig.
one-way street s. Einbahnstrasse f.; **one-way traffic** s. Einbahnverkehr m.
onion s. Zwiebel f.
onlooker s. Zuschauer m.
only a. einzig; ~ adv. allein, nur; erst.
onset s. Angriff, Anfall m.
onslaught s. Angriff m.
onus s. Last f.
onward a. & adv. vorwärts.
ooze s. Schlamm m.; ~ v.i. sickern.
opal s. Opal m.
opaque a. dunkel, undurchsichtig.
open a. ~ly adv. offen; öffentlich; freimütig; aufrichtig; zugänglich; in the ~ air, im Freien; ~ drive, (mot.) freie Fahrt f.; ~ v.t. offnen, eröffnen; er-

schliessen; ~ v.i. sich öffnen; to ~ out, aufgehen.
opencast mining s. (min.) Tagbau m.
opener s. Öffner m.
open-handed a. freigebig.
opening s. Öffnung f.; Eröffnung f.; (com.) Absatzweg m.; Gelegenheit, Aussicht f.; ~-hours pl. Öffnungszeiten f.pl.
open season s. Jagdsaison f.
opera s. Oper f.
opera-glass s. Operngucker m.
opera-hat s. Klapphut m.
opera-house s. Opernhaus n.
operate v.t. wirken, operieren; (mil.) operieren, vorgehen; (mech.) handhaben, bedienen (Maschine); ~ v.i. (mech.) arbeiten, in Betrieb sein (Fabrik); in operating condition, in arbeitsfähigem Zustand; to be ~d on, sich operieren lassen.
operatic a. opernmässig.
operation s. Wirkung f.; Operation s.; (chem.) Verfahren n.; (mech.) Arbeitsgang m.; Betrieb (einer Fabrik) m.; (mil.) Unternehmen n., Operation f.; to be in ~, in Kraft sein; railways in ~, in Betrieb befindliche Eisenbahnen.
operational a. (mil.) operativ.
operative a. wirksam, tätig; ~ s. Arbeiter m.
operator s. Operateur m.; Telephonfräulein n.
ophthalmia s. Augenentzündung f.
ophthalmic a. Augen...; augenärztlich.
opiate s. Opiat n.; ~ a. einschläfernd.
opine v.i. meinen.
opinion s. Meinung; Ansicht f.; (law) Urteilsbegründung f.
opinionated, opinionative a. starrsinnig.
opium s. Opium m.
opponent a. widerstreitend; ~ s. Gegner m.
opportune a., ~ly adv. günstig, gelegen.
opportunist s. Opportunist m.
opportunity s. (gute) Gelegenheit, bequeme Zeit f., günstige Augenblick m.; to take an ~, eine Gelegenheit ergreifen.
oppose v.t. entgegenstellen, sich widersetzen; ~ v.i. Widerstand leisten; einwenden.
opposite a., ~ly adv. entgegengesetzt; widerstreitend; ~ number, der entsprechende Beamte (eines anderen Staates); ~ pr. gegenüber; ~ adv. gegenüber; ~ s. Gegenteil n.
opposition s. Entgegensetzung f.; Gegensatz m.; Opposition(spartei) f.; Widerstand m.
oppress v.t. unterdrücken, bedrücken.
oppression s. Unterdrückung f.
oppressive a., ~ly adv. drückend.
oppressor s. Bedrücker m.
opprobrious a., ~ly adv. schimpflich.

opprobrium *s.* Schimpf *m.*; Schande *f.*

optic(al) *a.* optisch, Seh...

optician *s.* Optiker *m.*

optics *s.pl.* Optik *f.*

optimism *s.* Optimismus *m.*

option *s.* Wahl *f.*; *first* ~, Vorkaufsrecht *n.*, Vorhand *f.*

optional *a.* freigestellt, wahlfrei.

opulence *s.* Wohlhabenheit *f.*

opulent *a.* wohlhabend.

or *c.* oder; entweder; ~ *else*, sonst.

oracle *s.* Orakel *n.*

oracular *a.* orakelhaft.

oral *a.*, ~ly *adv.* mündlich.

orange *s.* Orange *f.*; Apfelsine *f.*

orangeade *s.* Orangenlimonade *f.*

oration *s.* Rede *f.*

orator *s.* Redner *m.*

oratorical *a.* rednerisch.

oratorio *s.* Oratorium *n.*

oratory *s.* Redekunst *f.*

orb *s.* Kugel *f.*; Augapfel *m.*

orbit *s.* Augenhöle *f.*; Bereich *m.*; Planetenbahn *f.*

orchard *s.* Obstgarten *m.*

orchestra *s.* Orchester *n.*

orchestral *a.* Orchester...; ~ *music s.* Orchestermusik *f.*

orchid *s.* Orchidee *f.*

ordain *v.t.* verordnen; einsetzen; *to* ~ *priest,* zum Priester weihen.

ordeal *s.* Gottesurteil *n.*; Heimsuchung *f.*

order *s.* Ordnung *f.*; Verordnung *f.*; Befehl *m.*; Bestellung *f.*; Auftrag *m.*; Anweisung *f.*; Gattung *f.*; Rang *m.*; Orden *m.*; Reihenfolge *f.*; *in* ~ *to,* um zu; *by* ~ *of,* auf Befehl von: *out of* ~, defekt, kaputt; *to* ~, auf Bestellung, nach Mass; *to call to* ~, zur Ordnung rufen; *to establish* ~, Ordnung schaffen; *to take* ~s, Aufträge, Bestellungen entgegennehmen; sich zum Priester weihen lassen; ~-blank *s.* Bestellungsformular *n.*; ~-form *s.* Bestellschein *m.*; ~ *of* battle *s.* (*mil.*) Kriegsgliederung *f.*; ~s *pl.* geistliche Stand *m.*; ~ *v.t.* ordnen, anordnen, befehlen; bestellen; *to* ~ *again,* nachbestellen.

orderly *a. & adv.* ordentlich, regelmässig; gesittet; diensttuend; ~ *s.* Ordnonnanzoffizier *m.*; ~ *room s.* (*mil.*) Schreibstube *f.*

ordinal *s.* Ordnungszahl *f.*

ordinance *s.* Verordnung, Regel *f.*

ordinary *a.*, ~ily *adv.* gewöhnlich, regelmässig; gebräuchlich, gemein; ~ *share,* Stammaktie *f.*; ~ *s.* Bischof *m.*

ordination *s.* (Priester-) Weihe *f.*

ordnance *s.* schwere Geschütz *n.*; ~ survey map *s.* Generalstabskarte *f.*

ordure *s.* Kot, Schmutz *m.*

ore *s.* Erz, Metall *n.*; *high-grade* ~, hoch-

wertige Erz; *low-grade* ~, geringwertige Erz.

organ *s.* Werkzeug *n.*; Organ *n.*; Orgel *f.*; ~-stop *s.* Orgelregister *n.*

organ-grinder *s.* Orgeldreher *m.*

organic *a.*, ~ally *adv.* organisch.

organization *s.* Organisation *f.*; Bau *m.*, Bildung *f.*; Vereinigung *f.*; (*mil.*) Gliederung *f.*, Truppenteil *m.*

organizational *a.*, ~ly *adv.* organisatorisch.

organize *v.t.* einrichten, organisieren.

organism *s.* Organismus *m.*

organist *s.* Orgelspieler *m.*

orgy *s.* Orgie *f.*

oriel *s.* Erkerfenster *n.*

orient *a.* östlich; ~ *s.* Osten *m.*, Morgenland *n.*; *to* ~ *oneself v.* sich orientieren.

oriental *a.* östlich; ~ *s.* Morgenländer *m.*

orientate *v.t.* orientieren.

orientation *s.* Orientierung *f.*; *general* ~, Einführungsbesprechung *f.*

orifice *s.* Öffnung *f.*; Loch *n.*

origin *s.* Ursprung *m.*; Herkunft *f.*

original *a.*, ~ly *adv.* ursprünglich, eigenartig; ~ *sin s.* Erbsünde *f.*; ~ *s.* Urbild *n.*; Urschrift *f.*; Original *n.*

originality *s.* Ursprünglichkeit *f.*

originate *v.t.* ins Leben rufen; ~ *v.i.* entstehen, entspringen.

originator *s.* Urheber, Schöpfer *m.*

ornament *s.* Verzierung *f.*; Putz *m.*; Zier, Schmuck *m.*; Schmuckstück *n.*

ornamental *a.*, ~ly *adv.* zierend, Zier...

ornate *a.* geziert, zierlich; schmuckreich.

ornithology *s.* Vogelkunde *f.*

orphan *s.* Waise *m. & f.*

orphanage *s.* Waisenhaus *n.*

orthodox *a.* rechtgläubig; üblich, landläufig.

orthodoxy *s.* Rechtgläubigkeit *f.*

orthographic(al) *a.* orthographisch.

orthography *s.* Rechtschreibung *f.*

orthopædic *a.* orthopädisch.

oscillate *v.i.* schwingen; schwanken.

oscillation *s.* Schwingung *f.*

osier *s.* Korbweide *f.*

ossify *v.i.* zu Knochen werden.

ostensible *a.* scheinbar, vorgeblich.

ostentation *s.* Gepränge *n.*; Prahlerei *f.*

ostentatious *a.*, ~ly *adv.* prahlerisch.

osteology *s.* Knochenlehre *f.*

osteopath *s.* Osteopath, Knochenheilkundige *m.*

ostler *s.* Hausknecht *m.*

ostracize *v.t.* verbannen.

ostracism *s.* Ächtung *f.*

ostrich *s.* Strauss (Vogel) *m.*

other *a.* ander.

otherwise *adv.* anders, sonst.

otter *s.* Fischotter *f.*

ottoman *s.* Ruhebett *n.*

ought *v.i.ir.def.* sollte, müsste.

ounce *s.* Unze *f.* (28,35 g.).

our *pn.* unser, unsere.

ours *pn.* unser, der unsrige.

ourself *pn.* (wir) selbst, wir.

ourselves *pn. pl.* (wir) selbst, uns.

oust *v.t.* ausstossen, verdrängen.

out *adv.* aus; draussen, ausserhalb; heraus, hinaus; erloschen; ~ *of*, aus, aus ...hinaus; *to be* ~ *for*, bedacht sein auf, trachten nach.

outbid *v.t.st.* überbieten.

outboard motor *s.* Aussenbordmotor *m.*

outbreak *s.* Ausbruch *m.*

outbuilding *s.* Nebengebäude *n.*

outburst *s.* Ausbruch *m.*

outcast *p. & a.* verworfen; verbannt; ~ *s.* Verstossene *m.*

outcome *s.* Ergebnis *n.*

outcry *s.* Ausruf, Schrei *m.*

outdo *v.t.st.* übertreffen.

outdoor *a.* im Freien; Aussen...; *out of doors*, im Freien.

outer *a.* äusser.

outermost *a.* äusserst.

outface *v.t.* Trotz bieten.

outfit *s.* Ausrüstung *f.*; Ausstattung *f.*

outfitter *s.* Inhaber (*m.*) eines Herrenaustattunggeschäfts.

outflank *v.t.* überflügeln.

outgo *v.t.st.* zuvorkommen.

outgoing *s.* Ausgang *m.*; ~s *s.pl.* Ausgaben *f.pl.*; ~ *a.* abgehend; *the* ~ *president*, der ausscheidende Präsident *m.*

outgrow *v.t.st.* entwachsen.

outhouse *s.* Nebengebäude *n.*

outing *s.* Ausflug *m.*

outlandish *a.* ausländisch.

outlast *v.t.* überdauern.

outlaw *s.* Geächtete *m.*; ~ *v.t.* ächten.

outlawry *s.* Acht *f.*

outlay *s.* Auslage *f.*; Ausgabe *f.*

outlet *s.* Ausgang *m.*; Abfluss *m.*; Absatzmarkt *m.*

outline *s.* Umriss, Abriss *m.*; ~ *v.t.* kurz darstellen, umreissen.

outlive *v.t.* überleben.

outlook *s.* Ausblick *m.*, Aussicht *f.*

outlying *a.* fernliegend; abgelegen.

outnumber *v.t.* an Zahl übertreffen.

outpatient *s.* ambulante Kranke *m.*

outpost *s.* Vorposten *m.*

output *s.* Ertrag *m.*; Produktion *f.*

outrage *v.t.* schmählich behandeln; vergewaltigen; ~ *s.* Beleidigung *f.*; Schimpf *m.*; Gewalttätigkeit *f.*

outrageous *a.*, ~ly *adv.* übertrieben; heftig; abscheulich.

outright *adv.* gänzlich, völlig.

outrun *v.t.st.* im Laufen übertreffen.

outset *s.* Anfang *m.*; Aufbruch *m.*

outshine *v.t.st.* überstrahlen.

outside *s.* Aussenseite *f.*; ~ *adv. & pr.*

aussen; ausserhalb; draussen; äusserst; hinaus.

outsider *s.* Aussenseiter *m. & f.*

outsize *a. & s.* (Damenkonfektion) starke Figur *f.*

outskirts *s.pl.* Grenze *f.*; Vorstadt *f.*

outspoken *a.* freimütig, offen.

outstanding *a.* unbezahlt; hervorragend.

outstep *v.t.* überschreiten.

outstretched *p. & a.* ausgestreckt.

outstrip *v.t.* überholen.

outvote *v.t.* überstimmen.

outward *a.* der, die, das äussere, äusserlich; ~ *adv.* aussen, auswärts.

outwardly *adv.* äusserlich.

outward(s) *adv.* nach aussen; **outward-bound** *a.* nach auswärts fahrend.

outweigh *v.t.* überwiegen.

outwit *v.t.* überlisten.

outwork *s.* Aussenwerk *n.*

oval *a.* eirund; ~ *s.* Oval *n.*

ovary *s.* Eierstock *m.*

ovation *s.* Ehrenbezeigung *f.*

oven *s.* Backofen, Ofen *m.*

over *pr. & adv.* über, darüber, hinüber, überhin; vorüber, vorbei, zu sehr, allzu; *all* ~, über und über; ganz vorbei; ~ *again*, noch einmal; *continued* ~, Fortsetzung umseitig; ~ *there*, da drüben.

overall *s.* Überkleid *n.*; ~ *size*, Grösse über alles; ~s *pl.* Arbeitsanzug *m.*

overawe *v.t.* in Furcht halten.

overbalance *v.t.* überwiegen.

overbear *v.t.st.* überwältigen.

overbearing *a.* anmassend, stolz.

overbid *v.t.st.* überbieten.

overboard *adv.* über Bord.

overburden *v.t.* überladen.

overcast *v.t.st.* überziehen; ~ *a.* bewölkt.

overcharge *v.t.* überladen; überfordern.

overcloud *v.t.* überwölken.

overcoat *s.* Überzieher *m.*, Mantel *m.*

overcome *v.t.st.* überwältigen.

overconfidence *s.* Vermessenheit *f.*

overcrowded *a.* überfüllt.

overdo *v.t.st.* zu viel tun, übertreiben.

overdose *v.t.* überdosieren.

overdraft, overdraught *s.* überzogene Konto *n.*

overdraw *v.t.* zu viel trassieren; das Bankguthaben überschreiten.

overdress *v.t.* zu sehr putzen.

overdrive *v.t.* abhetzen, treiben; ~ *s.* (*mot.*) Schnellgang *m.*

overdue *a.* fällig; überfällig.

overeat *v.i.* zu viel essen.

overestimate *v.t.* überschätzen.

overexpose *v.t.* überbelichten.

overexposure *s.* (*phot.*) Überbelichtung *f.*

overflow *v.i. & v.t.st.* überfliessen; ~ *s.* Überlauf *m.*, Ausflussröhre *f.*; ~ **meeting**, Parallelversammlung *f.*

overgrow *v.t.st.* überwachsen.
overgrown *p. & a.* überwachsen; zu sehr gewachsen.
overgrowth *s.* zu üppige Wuchs *m.*
overhang *v.t.st.* überhängen.
overhaul *v.t.* gründlich prüfen; (*nav.*) überholen.
overhead *adv. & a.* oben, Ober...; ~ *cable,* ~ *line,* ~ *wire,* (*elek.*) Freileitung, Oberleitung *f.*; ~ *clearance,* lichte Höhe *f.*; ~ *expenses pl.* laufende Ausgaben *f.pl.*; ~ *railway,* Hochbahn *f.*
overhear *v.t.ir.* zufällig hören; behorchen.
overjoy *v.t.* entzücken.
overland *a.* Überland...
overlap *v.t.* übereinander greifen, teilweise zusammenfallen.
overlay *v.t.ir.* darüber legen.
overleaf *adv.* umseitig.
overleap *v.t.st.* überspringen.
overload *v.t.* überladen.
overlook *v.t.* überblicken; durchsehen, prüfen; Nachsicht haben; übersehen.
overmuch *a.* zu viel.
overnight *adv.* übernacht; ~ *accommodation,* Übernachtungsunterkunft *f.*
overpay *v.t.* zu reichlich bezahlen.
overpower *v.t.* überwältigen.
overproduction *s.* Überproduktion *f.*
overrate *v.t.* überschätzen.
overreach *v.t.* überragen; übervorteilen; *to ~ oneself,* zu weit gehen.
override *v.t.* umstossen; *of overriding importance,* von überwiegender Wichtigkeit.
overrule *v.t.* als ungültig verwerfen.
overrun *v.t.st.* überlaufen, überrennen.
oversea *a. & adv.,* **overseas** *adv.* überseeisch.
oversee *v.t.st.* beaufsichtigen.
overseer *s.* Aufseher *m.*
overshadow *v.t.* überschatten.
overshoe *s.* Überschuh *m.*
overshoot *v.t.ir.* über das Ziel hinausschiessen.
oversight *s.* Versehen *n.*
oversleep *v.refl.ir.* sich verschlafen.
overspend *v.refl.* sich verausgaben.
overspread *v.t.st.* überdecken.
overstate *v.t.* zu hoch angeben.
overstatement *s.* Übertreibung *f.*
overstay *v.t.* (Zeit) überschreiten; *to ~ a date,* über einen Termin hinaus ausbleiben; *~ing of leave,* Urlaubsüberschreitung *f.*
overstep *v.t.* überschreiten.
overstrain *v.t.* (*v.refl. sich*) überanstrengen.
oversubscribe *v.t.* überzeichnen.
overt *a.,* ~**ly** *adv.* offenbar, öffentlich.
overtake *v.t.st.* überholen, ereilen.
overtax *v.t.* zu hoch besteuern; überbürden; überschätzen.

overthrow *v.t.st.* umwerfen; umstürzen, vernichten; ~ *s.* Umsturz *m.*
overtime *s.* Überstunden *f.pl.*; *to work* ~, Überstunden machen.
overture *s.* Vorschlag, Antrag *m.*; Ouvertüre *f.*
overturn *v.t.* umwerfen; zerstören; ~ *v.i.* umkippen, umfallen; ~ *s.* Umsturz *m.*
overvalue *v.t.* zu hoch schätzen.
overweening *a.,* ~**ly** *adv.* anmassend.
overweight *s.* Übergewicht *n.*
overwhelm *v.t.* überwältigen.
overwork *v.t. & i.* (sich) überarbeiten; ~ *s.* übermässige Arbeit *f.*
oviparous *a.* eierlegend.
owe *v.t.* schuldig sein, verdanken.
owing *p.* schuldig; ~ *to pr.* dank..., infolge; *how much is ~ to you?,* wieviel ist an Sie zu zahlen?
owl *s.* Eule *f.*
own *a.* eigen; *on one's* ~, selbstständig, für sich; *to come into one's* ~, zu seinem Rechte kommen.
owner *s.* Eigentümer *m.*; *at* ~'s *risk,* auf eigene Gefahr.
ownership *s.* Eigentum(srecht) *n.*
ox *s.* Ochs[e] *m.*; Rindvieh *n.*
oxide *s.* Oxyd *n.*
oxidize *v.t. & i.* oxydieren.
oxygen *s.* Sauerstoff *m.*; ~**-apparatus** *s.* Sauerstoffapparat *m.*
oyster *s.* Auster *f.*
ozone *s.* Ozon *n.*

P

pace *s.* Schritt, Gang *m.*; ~ *v.i.* schreiten; passgehen; ~ *v.t.* abschreiten; *to keep* ~ *with,* Schritt halten mit.
pacific *a.* friedlich, friedsam.
pacification *s.* Befriedung *f.*
pacifist *s.* Pazifist, Friedensfreund *m.*
pacify *v.t.* Frieden stiften; beruhigen.
pack *s.* Packen, Ballen *m.*; Päckchen *n.*; Rudel *n.,* Meute *f.*; Spiel Karten *n.*; Tornister *m.*; ~**-horse** *s.* Packpferd *n.*; ~ *radio set,* Tornisterempfänger *m.*; ~ *receiver,* Tornisterempfänger *m.* (*radio*); ~**-saddle** *s.* Packsattel *m.*; ~ *v.t.* packen; parteiisch zusammensetzen; ~ *v.i.* einpacken; sich packen.
package *s.* Verpackung *f.* Paket *n.*
packet *s.* Päckchen *n.*
packet-boat *s.* Postschiff *n.*
packing *s.* Verpackung *f.*; Dichtung (*f.*) bei Maschinen.
pack-thread *s.* Bindfaden *m.*
pact *s.* Vertrag *m.*
pad *s.* Block (*m.*) Papier; Polster *n.,* Kissen *n.*; Bausch, Wulst *m.*; Unterlage *f.*; ~ *v.t.* polstern, wattieren.

paddle s. Paddel n.; Rührholz n.; Schaufel f.; ~ v.i. paddeln; plätschern, waten.
paddle-steamer s. Raddampfer m.
paddle-wheel s. Schaufelrad n.
paddock s. Gehege n.
padlock s. Vorlegeschloss n.
padre s. Feldgeistlicher m.
pagan s. Heide m.; ~ a. heidnisch.
paganism s. Heidentum n.
page s. Page m.; Diener m.; (Buch)seite f.; ~ v.t. mit Seitenzahlen bezeichnen; (Am.) (durch einen Hotelpagen) suchen (lassen).
pageant s. Prunkaufzug, Festzug m.
pageantry s. Prunk m.; Gepränge n.
paginate v.t. paginieren.
pail s. Eimer m.
pain s. Schmerz m.; ~s pl. Mühe f.; Leiden n.pl.; ~ v.t. Schmerzen machen, peinigen.
painful a., ~ly adv. schmerzhaft; mühsam.
painless a. schmerzlos.
painstaking a. äusserst sorgsam.
paint v.t. malen; anstreichen; ~ v.i. sich schminken; ~ s. Farbe f.; Schmink f.
paint-box s. Malkasten m.
painter s. Maler m.; Fangleine f.
painting s. Malerei f.; Gemälde n.
pair s. Paar n.; ~ v.t. (v.i. sich) paaren.
pajamas s.pl. (Am.) see pyjamas.
pal s. (sl.) Kamerad, Genosse m.
palace s. Palast m.
palatable a. schmackhaft.
palatal a. Gaumen...
palate s. Gaumen m.
palaver s. Gespräch, Geschwätz n.
pale a., ~ly adv. blass, bleich; ~-ale s. helle Bier n.; ~ s. Pfahl m.; Bezirk m.; ~ v.t. pfählen; bleich werden (v.i.).
palette s. Palette f.
palfrey s. Zelter m.
palisade s. Pfahlwerk n.
pall s. Bahrtuch n.; Pallium n.; Mantel m.; ~ v.t. schal machen; (fig.) langweilen; ~ v.i. schal werden.
pallet s. Strohsack m.
palliasse s. Strohsack m.
palliate v.t. bemänteln; lindern.
palliative a. beschönigend, lindernd; ~ s. Linderungsmittel n.
pallid a., ~ly adv. blass, bleich.
pallor s. Blässe f.
palm s. Palme f.; Handfläche f.; ~ v.t. betrügen; ~ off, aufschwindeln.
palmistry s. Handwahrsagerei f.
palmy a. palmenreich; (fig.) siegreich; glücklich.
palpable a., ~bly adv. handgreiflich.
palpitate v.i. pochen (vom Herzen).
palpitation s. Herzklopfen n.
palsied a. gelähmt
palsy s. Lähmung f.
paltry a. armselig, erbärmlich.

pamper v.t. mästen; versärteln.
pamphlet s. Flugschrift f.
pamphleteer s. Verfasser von Flugschriften m.
pan s. Kochtopf m.; Pfanne f.
panacea s. Allheilmittel n.
pancake s. Pfannkuchen m.
pandemonium s. Heidenlärm m.
pander s. Kuppler m.; ~ v.i. kuppeln; Vorschub leisten.
pane s. Glasscheibe f.
panegyrist s. Lobredner m.
panel s. (Tür-) Füllung f.; Fach, Feld n.; Geschworenenliste f.; Kassenarztliste, Krankenkasse f.; Ausschuss m.; ~-doctor, Kassenarzt m.; ~-patient, Kassenpatient m.
panelling s. Täfelung f.
pang s. Stich, Schreck m.
panic s. Panik f.
panicky a. beunruhigend; unruhig.
panoply s. völlige Rüstung f.
pansy f. (bot.) Stiefmütterchen n.
pant v.i. schnappen (nach Luft); keuchen; lechzen; pochen.
panther s. Panther m.
pantomime s. Pantomime f.; (Weihnachts-) Ausstattungsstück n.
pantry s. Speisekammer f.
pants s.pl. (Herren-) Unterhosen f.pl.; (Am.) Hosen f.pl.
pap s. Kinderbrei m.; Fleisch (der Früchte) n.
papa s. Papa m.
papacy s. Papsttum n.
papal a. päpstlich.
paper s. Papier n.; Zettel m.; Abhandlung f.; Zeitung f.; ~s pl. Schriften f.pl.; Akten, Legitimationspapiere pl.; to read a ~, einen Vortrag halten; to commit to ~, zu Papier bringen; ~-bag s. Tüte f.; ~-clamp s. (grosse) Papierklammer f.; ~-clip s. (kleine) Papierklammer f.; ~-credit s. Wechselkredit m.; ~-napkin s. Papierserviette f.; ~-work s. Büroarbeit f.; ~-bound a. broschiert; ~ a. papieren; ~ v.t. tapezieren.
paper-chase s. Schnitzeljagd f.
paper-hanger s. Tapezier m.
paper-mill s. Papiermühle f.
paper-weight s. Briefbeschwerer m.
papier-maché s. Papiermaché n.
Papist s. Papist m.
par s. Gleichheit f.; Pari n.; at ~, pari.
parable s. Parabel f.; Gleichnis n.
parabola s. (geom.) Parabel f.
parabolic a. gleichnisweise; parabolisch.
parachute s. Fallschirm m.; ~-flare s. Fallschirmleuchtbombe f.
parachutist s. Fallschirmabspringer m.
parade s. Gepränge n.; Parade f.; ~ v.i. aufziehen; ~ v.t. prunken mit.

paradigm s. Beispiel n., Paradigma n.

Paradise s. Paradies n.

paradox s. Paradox n.

paradoxical a., **~ly** adv. paradox.

paraffin s. Paraffin n.; Petroleum n.

paragon s. Muster, Urbild n.

paragraph s. Abschnitt m.

parallel a. parallel, gleichlaufend; entsprechend; **~ bars** pl. Barren (Turnen) m.; (elek.) **~ connection** s. Nebeneinanderschaltung f.; **~ s.** Parallelinie f.; Ähnlichkeit, Vergleichung f.; **~ v.t.** gleichmachen; gleichkommen, vergleichen.

paralyse v.t. lähmen.

paralysis s. Lähmung f.; Schlagfluss m.

paralytic a. gelähmt; **~ s.** Gelähmte m. & f.

paramount a. oberst, hervorragend.

paramour s. Liebhaber m.; Geliebte m. & f.

parapet s. Brustwehr f.; Geländer n.

paraphernalia s. Drum und Dran n.

paraphrase s. Umschreibung f.; **~ v.t.** umschreiben.

parasite s. Schmarotzer m.

parasol s. Sonnenschirm m.

paratroops s.pl. Fallschirmtruppen f.pl.

paratyphoid s. Paratyphus m.

parboil v.t. halb sieden; überhitzen.

parcel s. Stück n.; Teil m.; Partie, Anzahl f., Posten (Ware) m.; Paket n., Päckchen n.; **~ of land**, Parzelle f.; **~ post** Paketpost f.; **~s company** s. Paketfahrtgesellschaft f.; **~s office** (rail.), Gepäckabfertigung f.; **~ v.t.** teilen, zerstückeln.

parch v.t. dörren; austrocknen; **~ v.i.** verdorren.

parchment s. Pergament n.

pardon s. Verzeihung, Begnadigung f.; beg your **~?** was beliebt?; wie, bitte?; **~ v.t.** verzeihen, begnadigen.

pardonable a., **~bly** adv. verzeihlich.

pare v.t. beschneiden; schälen.

parent s. Vater m.; Mutter f.; **~ company** s. Muttergesellschaft; **~s** pl. Eltern pl.

parentage s. Abstammung f.

parental a. elterlich.

parenthesis s. Einschaltung f.; Klammer f., Parenthese f.

parenthetical a. eingeschaltet, beiläufig.

paring s. Schale f.; Abfall m.

parish s. Kirchspiel n.; Pfarre f.; **~ a.** Gemeinde...; **~-register** s. Kirchenbuch n.

parishioner s. Pfarrkind n.

parity s. Gleichheit f.; Umrechnungskurs m.

park s. Park m.; **~ v.t.** einhegen; (Autos) parken; No parking! Parken verboten! **~-lot**, **~-space** s. Parkplatz m.

parlance s. Redeweise f.

parley s. Unterredung; v.t. & i. verhandeln; parlamentieren.

parliament s. Parlament n.

parliamentary a. Parlaments..., parlamentarisch; **~ division**, Wahlbezirk m.

parlour s. Wohnzimmer n.; Privatzimmer n.; **~ maid** Stubenmädchen n.

parochial a. Pfarr..., Gemeinde...; (fig.) Kirchturms...

parody s. Parodie f.; **~ v.t.** parodieren.

parole s. Ehrenwort n.; Losung f.

paroxysm s. heftige Anfall m.

parquet s. Parkett n.

parricide s. Vatermord m.; Vatermörder m.

parrot s. Papagei m.; **~ v.t.** nachplappern.

parry v.t. & i. abwehren, parieren.

parsimonious a., **~ly** adv. sparsam.

parsimony s. Sparsamkeit f.

parsley s. Petersilie f.

parsnip s. Pastinake f.

parson s. Pfarrer m.; Pfaffe m.

parsonage s. Pfarre f.; Pfarrhaus n.

part s. Teil, Anteil m.; Rolle f.; Schuldigkeit f.; Gegend f.; **~s** pl. Anlagen pl., Talent n.; Gegenden f.pl.; in **~** teilweise; to take in good **~** gut aufnehmen; on my **~**, meinerseits; **~-payment**, Teilzahlung, Abschlagszahlung f.; **~ v.t.** teilen; trennen; **~ v.i.** sich trennen; abreisen.

partake v.i.st. teilnehmen, teilhaben.

partial a., **~ly** adv. teilweise; parteiisch.

partiality s. Vorliebe, Parteilichkeit f.

participant s. Teilnehmer m.

participate v.i. teilnehmen, teilhaben.

participle s. (gram.) Partizip.

particle s. Teilchen n.; Partikel f.

parti-coloured a. buntfarbig.

particular a., **~ly** adv. besonder; einzeln; sonderbar; seltsam; wählerisch, genau, heikel; **~ s.**, Einzelheit f.; besondere Umstand m.; further **~s**, Näheres n.

particularity s. Besonderheit f.; Umständlichkeit f.

parting s. Scheiden n.; Scheitel m.; **~ a.** Scheide...

partisan s. Parteigänger m.; Guerillakrieger, Partisan m.

partition s. Teilung f.; Scheidewand f.; **~ v.t.** teilen, abteilen.

partitive a., **~ly** adv. teilend, partitiv.

partly adv. teils, zum Teil.

partner s. Teilnehmer m.; Gefährte m.; Teilhaber m.; Tanzpartner(in) m. (f.); Spielgegner m.; silent **~**, stille Teilhaber m.

partnership s. Genossenschaft f.; Handelsgesellschaft f.; Teilhaberschaft f.; general **~**, offene Handelsgesellschaft f.; to enter into **~ with**, sich assoziieren mit.

partridge s. Rebhuhn n.

part-song s. mehrstimmige Lied n.
party s. Partei f.; Gesellschaft, Partie f.; Teilnehmer m.; *to be a* ~ *to*, beteiligt sein an; *contracting* ~, Kontrahent m.; **~official** s. Parteifunktionär m.
parvenu s. Emporkömmling m.
paschal a. Oster...
pasquinade s. Schmähschrift f.
pass v.i. gehen, vorübergehen; vergehen; fahren; gelten; geschehen; *to* ~ *away*, sterben; *to* ~ *in the opposite direction*, (mot.) kreuzen; ~ v.t. verbringen; übertragen; überschicken; gehen lassen; bestätigen; (Gesetz) annehmen; verleben; passieren; überschreiten; (mot.) überholen; *to* ~ *an examination*, eine Prüfung bestehen; *to* ~ *on*, weiterleiten; *to be* ~ed *as fit*, für tauglich befunden werden; ~ s. Pass, Weg, Durchgang m.; Passierschein, Ausweis m.; Stoss (im Fechten) m.; Zustand m.; Lage f.
passable a., **~bly** adv. gangbar; mittelmässig.
passage s. Durchgang m.; Durchfahrt f.; Hausflur f.; Gang m.; Überfahrt f.; (Buch) Stelle f.; Inkrafttreten (eines Gesetzes) n.
pass-book s. Privatkontobuch n.
passenger s. Reisende, Passagier m.; ~ *train*, Personenzug m.; ~ *traffic*, Personenverkehr m.
passer-by s. Vorübergehende m.
passing a. vorübergehend, flüchtig; ~, **~ly** adv. sehr, äusserst; in ~, im Vorübergehen.
passing-bell s. Totenglocke f.
passion s. Leidenschaft f.; Zorn m.; *to fly into a* ~, zornig werden; *Passion of Christ*, Leiden Christi n.
passionate a., **~ly** adv. leidenschaftlich.
passive a., **~ly** adv. leidend; untätig; passiv; ~ s. (gram.) Passivum n.
Passover s. Passah(fest) n.
passport s. Pass m.
password s. Losung f.; Kennwort n.
past a. & pr. vergangen, vorbei, über... hinaus; ~ *master*, Altmeister m.; ~ s. Vergangenheit f.
paste s. Teig m.; Kleister m.; Paste f.; künstliche Diamant m.; ~ v.t. kleistern, pappen.
paste-board s. Pappendeckel m.
pastel s. (bot.) Waid m.; Pastell n.
pastern s. Fessel am Pferdefuss f.
pasteurize v.t. pasteurisieren.
pastil(le) s. Räucherkerzchen n.
pastime s. Zeitvertreib m.
pastor s. Hirt m.; Pfarrer m.
pastoral a. Hirten...; pastoral; ~ *letter* s. Hirtenbrief m.; ~ s. Schäfergedicht n.
pastry s. Backwerk n., Kuchen m.
pastrycook s. Konditor m.

pasture s. Weide f.; ~ v.t. & i. weiden.
pasty s. Wildpastete f.; ~ a. teigig.
pat s. Schlag, Patsch m.; Scheibchen n.; ~ a. bequem, passend; ~ v.t. patschen, streicheln; klopfen.
patch s. Fleck m.; Stück n.; Flicken m.; Schönheitspflästerchen n.; ~ v.t. flicken, ausbessern.
patchy a. ungleich, zusammengestoppelt.
pate s. Schädel m.
patent a. offen; patentiert; *letters* ~, Freibrief m.; ~ s. Vorrecht, Patent n.; *to take out a* ~ *for a thing*, sich etwas patentieren lassen; *pending* ~, angemeldete Patent; *renewal of a* ~, Patentverlängerung f.; ~ *agent*, ~ *lawyer* s. Patentanwalt m.; **~grant**, Patenterteilung s.; **~holder** s. Patentinhaber m.; **~holding company**, Patentinhabergesellschaft f.; ~ **Office**, Patentamt n.; ~ v.t. patentieren.
patentee s. Patentinhaber m.
patent-fastener s. Druckknopf m.
patent-leather s. Lackleder n.
paternal a. väterlich.
paternity s. Vaterschaft f.
path s. Pfad, Fussteig m.; Weg m.
pathetic a., **~ally** adv. rührend, traurig.
pathological a., **~ly** adv. pathologisch.
pathology s. Krankheitslehre f.
pathos s. Feierlichkeit f.; Rührung f.
pathway s. Fussweg m.
patience s. Geduld f.
patient a., **~ly** adv. geduldig; ~ s. Kranke m., Patient m.
patriarch s. Erzvater m.
patriarchal a. patriarchalisch.
patrician s. Patrizier m.; ~ a. patrizisch.
patrimony s. Erbgut, Erbteil n.
patriot s. Vaterlandsfreund m.
patriotic a. patriotisch.
patriotism s. Vaterlandsliebe f.
patrol s. Patrouille f., Spähtrupp m.; **~activity**, Spähtrupptätigkeit f.; ~ v.i. patrouillieren.
patron s. Gönner, Schutzherr m.; Schutzheilige m.
patronage s. Gönnerschaft f.; Schutz m.; Kundschaft f.
patroness s. Gönnerin f.
patronize v.t. beschützen, begünstigen; als Kunde besuchen; gönnerhaft behandeln.
patten s. Holzschuh, Überschuh m.
patter v.i. platschen; trippeln.
pattern s. Muster n.; Schnitt m., Schnittmuster n.
patty s. Pastetchen n.
paucity s. Wenigkeit f.
paunch s. Wanst m.
pauper s. Arme m.
pauperism s. Massenarmut f.
pause s. Ruhepunkt, Absatz m.; Pause f.; ~ v.i. pausieren; sich bedenken.

pave *v.t.* pflastern; bahnen.

pavement *s.* Pflaster *n.*; Bürgersteig *m.*

pavilion *s.* Zelt *n.*; Pavilion *m.*

paving-stone *s.* Pflasterstein *m.*

paw *s.* Pfote, Tatze *f.*; ~ *v.t.* scharren; streicheln; tölpisch angreifen.

pawn *s.* Pfand *n.*; Bauer (im Schach) *m.*; ~ *v.t.* verpfänden.

pawnbroker *s.* Pfandleiher *m.*

pawnshop *s.* Pfandhaus *n.*

pawn-ticket *s.* Pfandschein *m.*

pay *v.t.ir.* zahlen; abstatten; *to ~ for*, bezahlen; *to ~ down*, bar bezahlen; *to ~ in*, einzahlen; *to ~ off*, abzahlen (Schuld); *to ~ in advance*, pränumerando bezahlen; *to ~ after receipt*, postnumerando bezahlen; *to ~ attention*, achtgeben; *to ~ a call, visit*, einen Besuch abstatten; *to ~ the piper*, die Zeche bezahlen; ~ *v.t.* sich lohnen, rentieren; ~ *s.* Bezahlung *f.*; Lohn *m.*; ~-day *s.* Zahltag *m.*; ~-envelope *s.* Lohntüte *f.*

payable *a.* zahlbar, fällig.

payee *s.* Zahlungsempfänger *m.*; Wechselinhaber *m.*

payer *s.* Zahler *m.*; Bezogene *m.*

paying guest *s.* zahlende Gast *m.*; *to take paying guests*, zahlende Gäste aufnehmen.

paymaster *s.* Zahlmeister *m.*

payment *s.* Bezahlung *f.*; *against ~*, gegen Bezahlung; *payment order*, Zahlungsbefehl *m.*; *action for ~*, Schuldklage *f.*; ~ *on account*, Abschlagszahlung *f.*; *to stop, suspend ~*, Zahlungen einstellen.

payroll *s.* (*mil.*) Soldliste *f.*

pea *s.* Erbse *f.*; *sweet ~*, Edelwicke *f.*

peace *s.* Friede *m.*; Ruhe *f.*; *to keep the ~*, Ruhe halten; ~-maker *s.* Friedensstifter *m.*; ~-treaty *s.* Friedensvertrag *m.*

peaceful *a.*, ~ly *adv.* friedlich, ruhig.

peach *s.* Pfirsich *m.*

peacock *s.* Pfau *m.*

peahen *s.* Pfauhenne *f.*

pea-jacket *s.* (*nav.*) Tuchjacke *f.*

peak *s.* Gipfel *m.*; Spitze *f.*; Höhepunkt *m.*; Mützenschirm *m.*

peal *s.* Schall *m.*; Geläut *n.*; Gekrach *n.*; ~ *v.i.* schallen, krachen.

pear *s.* Birne *f.*

pearl *s.* Perle *f.*; Perlschrift *f.*; *real ~*, echte Perle; ~-barley *s.* Perlgraupen *pl.*

pear-tree *s.* Birnbaum *m.*

peasant *s.* Bauer *m.*

peasantry *s.* Landvolk *n.*

peat *s.* Torf *m.*

pebble *s.* Kiesel *m.*

peccadillo *s.* kleine Sünde *f.*; Fehler *m.*

peck *s.* Viertelscheffel *m.* (9,09 Liter); Menge *f.*; ~ *v.t.* picken, hacken.

pectoral *a.* Brust...

peculation *s.* Unterschleif *m.*

peculiar *a.* eigen, eigentümlich; ~ly *adv.* besonders.

peculiarity *s.* Eigentümlichkeit *f.*

pecuniary *a.* Geld...

pedagogue *s.* Erzieher *m.*

pedal *s.* Trittbrett *n.*, Pedal *n.*

pedant *s.* Pedant, Schulfuchs *m.*

pedantic *a.* pedantisch.

pedantry *s.* Pedanterie *f.*

peddle *v.i.* hausieren.

pedestal *s.* Fussgestell *n.*; Säulenfuss *m.*

pedestrian *a.* zu Fuss; ~ *s.* Fussgänger *m.*

pedigree *s.* Stammbaum *m.*; ~-dog, Rassehund, Zuchthund *m.*

pedlar *s.* Hausierer *m.*

peel *s.* Schale, Rinde *f.*; ~ *v.t.* (*v.i.* sich schälen.

peep *v.i.* zum Vorschein kommen, hervorgucken; piepen.

peep-hole *s.* Guckloch *n.*

peer *s.* Gefährte *m.*; Ebenbürtige *m.*; Pair, Hochadlige *m.*

peerage *s.* Pairswürde *f.*; Pairs *m.pl.*; Handbuch des englischen Adels *n.*

peeress *s.* Gemahlin eines Pairs *f.*

peerless *a.*, ~ly *adv.* unvergleichlich.

peevish *a.*, ~ly *adv.* verdriesslich.

peg *s.* Pflock; Wirbel *m.*; Holzstift *m.*; ~ *v.t.* festpflöcken; sich abmühen.

Pekingese *s.* chinesische Schosshund *m.*

pelican *s.* Pelikan *m.*

pelisse *s.* Überwurf (für Frauen und Kinder) *m.*

pellet *s.* Kügelchen *n.*

pell-mell *adv.* durcheinander.

pellucid *a.* durchsichtig.

pelt *s.* Fell *n.*; Haut *f.*; ~ *v.t.* werfen, bewerfen; ~ *v.i.* dicht fallen, stark regnen; *~ing rain*, Platzregen *m.*

pelvis *s.* (*anat.*) Becken *n.*

pen *s.* Schreibfeder *f.*; Schafhürde *f.*; ~ *v.t.* niederschreiben; einpferchen.

penal *a.* Straf..., strafbar; ~ *clause*, (*law*) Strafklausel *f.*; ~ *administration*, Strafvollzug *m.*; ~ *code s.* Strafgesetzbuch *n.*; ~ *law s.* Strafgesetz *n.*; ~ *reform*, Strafrechtsreform *f.*; ~ *servitude s.* Zuchthausstrafe *f.*; ~ *servitude for life*, lebenslängliche Zuchthaus *n.*

penalize *v.t.* büssen lassen, bestrafen.

penalty *s.* Strafe, Busse *f.*; ~ *envelope s.* frankierte Dienstumschlag *m.*

penance *s.* Busse *f.*

pence *pl.* (von *penny*), Pennies *pl.*

pencil *s.* Griffel, Stift *m.*; Bleistift *m.*

pencil sharpener *s.* Bleistiftspitzer *m.*

pendant *s.* Anhänger (*m.*) an Kette; Wimpel *m.*; Gegenstück *n.*

pendent *a.* hängend, schwebend.

pending *a.* schwebend, unentschieden; ~ *case*, (*law*) anhängige Sache *f.*

pendulum *s.* Pendel *m.*

penetrable *a.* durchdringlich.
penetrate *v.t. & i.* durchdringen; ergründen; (*mil.*) eindringen.
penetration *s.* Durchdringung *f.*; Scharfsinn *m.*; (*mil.*) Einbruch *m.*
penguin *s.* Pinguin *m.*, Fettgans *f.*
pen-holder *s.* Federhalter *m.*
penicillin *s.* Penizillin *n.*
peninsula *s.* Halbinsel *f.*
penitence *s.* Busse, Reue *f.*
penitent *a.*, ~ly *adv.* bussfertig; ~ *s.* Büsser *m.*
penitentiary *s.* Besserungsanstalt *f.*; (*Am.*) Zuchthaus *n.*
pen-knife *s.* Federmesser *m.*
penmanship *s.* Schreibekunst *f.*
pen-name *s.* Schriftstellername *m.*
pennant, pennon *s.* Fähnchen *n.*, Wimpel *m.*
penniless *a.* ohne Geld.
penny *s.* Penny *m.*
pennyweight *s.* englische Gewicht (*n.*) von 24 Gran Troy.
penny-wise *a.* verkehrt sparsam.
pennyworth *s.* für einen Penny *m.*
pension *s.* Kostgeld *n.*; Ruhegehalt *n.*; ~, Pension *f.*; ~ *v.t.* pensionieren.
pensionable *a.* pensionsberechtigt, pensionsfähig.
pensioner *s.* Pensionierte *m.*; Rentenempfänger *m.*; Veteran *m.*
pensive *a.*, ~ly *adv.* gedankenvoll schwermütig.
pent *a.* ~ *up*, aufgestaut, verhalten.
pentagon *s.* Fünfeck *n.*
Pentecost *s.* Pfingsten *pl.*
penthouse *s.* Wetterdach *n.*
penumbra *s.* Halbschatten *m.*
penurious *a.*, ~ly *adv.* karg; dürftig.
penury *s.* Dürftigkeit *f.*; Mangel *m.*
peony *s.* Päonie *f.*, Pfingstrose *f.*
people *s.* Volk *n.*; Leute *pl.*, man; ~ *v.t.* bevölkern.
pepper *s.* Pfeffer *m.*; ~ *v.t.* pfeffern.
peppermint *s.* Pfefferminze *f.*
per *pr.* durch; *as* ~, laut; ~ *annum*, pro Jahr; ~ *cent*, Prozent *n.*; ~ *diem allowance*, Tagegeld *n.*; ~ *pound*, pro Pfund; ~ *rail*, per Bahn.
perambulator *s.* Kinderwagen *m.*
perceive *v.t.* wahrnehmen; merken.
percentage *s.* Prozentsatz *m.*
perceptible *a.*, ~bly *adv.* wahrnehmbar.
perception *s.* Empfindung *f.*; Wahrnehmung *f.*; Anschauung, Vorstellung *f.*
perch *s.* Barsch *m.*; Rute *f.* (5,029 m.); Hühnerstange *f.*; ~ *v.i.* aufsitzen (von Vögeln); ~ *v.t.* setzen.
percolate *v.t.* durchseihen, durchsickern.
percolator *s.* Filtriertrichter *m.*
percussion *s.* Schlag *m.*; Erschütterung *f.*
percussion-cap *s.* Zündhütchen *n.*
perdition *s.* Verderben *n.*

peregrination *s.* Reise, Wanderschaft *f.*
peremptory *a.*, ~ily *adv.* bestimmt; endgültig; herrisch; dogmatisch.
perennial *a.* (Pflanzen) ausdauernd; dauernd.
perfect *a.*, ~ly *adv.* vollkommen, vollendet; ~ *s.* (*gram.*) Perfekt(um) *n.*; ~ *v.t.* vervollkommnen.
perfection *s.* Vollkommenheit *f.*
perfidious *a.* treulos.
perfidy *s.* Treulosigkeit *f.*
perforate *v.t.* durchbohren.
perforator *s.* Locher, Lochapparat *m.*
perforce *adv.* notgedrungen.
perform *v.t.* vollziehen, erfüllen, verrichten, vollenden; durchführen, ausführen; ~ *v.i.* wirken; spielen (eine Rolle), aufführen; vortragen.
performance *s.* Leistung, Vollziehung *f.*; Aufführung *f.*
perfume *s.* Wohlgeruch *m.*; Parfüm, *n.*; ~ *v.t.* durchduften.
perfumery *s.* Parfümerie(n) *f.pl.*
perfunctory *a.* oberflächlich, sorglos.
perhaps *adv.* vielleicht.
peril *s.* Gefahr *f.*; *at your* ~, auf eigene Gefahr.
perilous *a.*, ~ly *adv.* gefährlich.
perimeter *s.* Umkreis *m.*
period *s.* Zeitraum *m.*; Periode *f.*; Absatz *m.*; Punkt (Interpunktion) *m.*; ~ *furniture* *s.* Stilmöbel *pl.*
periodical *a.* periodisch; ~ *s.* Zeitschrift *f.*
periodicity *s.* regelmässige Wiederkehr *f.*
periphery *s.* Peripherie *f.*
periphrastic(al) *a.* umschreibend.
periscope *s.* Sehrohr, Periskop *n.*
perish *v.i.* umkommen.
perishable *a.* leicht verderblich.
peristyle *s.* Säulengang *m.*
peritonitis *s.* Bauchfellentzündung *f.*
periwig *s.* Perücke *f.*
periwinkle *s.* Singrün *n.*
perjure *v.refl.* falsch schwören.
perjured *a.* meineidig.
perjury *s.* Meineid *m.*
perk *v.i.* sich vordrängen; sich brüsten; *to* ~ *up*, sich emporstrecken; ~ *v.t.* herausputzen; aufrichten.
permanence *s.* Fortdauer *f.*
permanent *a.*, ~ly *adv.* (fort)dauernd, beständig; planmässig (Beamte); ~ *waves* *pl.* Dauerwellen *f.pl.*
permeable *a.* durchdringlich.
permeate *v.t.* durchdringen.
permissible *a.* zulässig.
permission *s.* Erlaubnis; *to ask* ~, um Erlaubnis bitten; *by* ~ *of*, mit Erlaubnis von; *by special* ~, mit besonderer Genehmigung.
permit *v.t.* gestatten; ~ *s.* Erlaubnisschein *m.*
permutation *s.* Umstellung *f.*

pernicious *a.*, ~ly *adv.* verderblich.
pernicious anaemia *s.* perniziöse Anaemie *f.*
peroration *s.* Redeschluss *m.*
perpendicular *a.*, ~ly *adv.* senkrecht; ~ *s.* senkrechte Linie *f.*, Lot *n.*
perpetrate *v.t.* verüben.
perpetrator *s.* (*law*) Täter *m.*
perpetual *a.*, ~ly *adv.* immerwährend.
perpetuate *v.t.* verewigen; fortsetzen.
perpetuity *s.* Ewigkeit *f.*; Fortdauer *f.*; *in* ~, auf ewig, für immer.
perplex *v.t.* bestürzt machen, verwickeln.
perplexity *s.* Bestürzung *f.*; Verwirrung *f.*
perquisite *s.* Sporteln *f.pl.*
persecute *v.t.* verfolgen.
persecutes *s.* (politisch) Verfolgter *m.*
persecution *s.* Verfolgung *f.*
persecutor *s.* Verfolger *m.*
perseverance *s.* Beharrlichkeit *f.*
persevere *v.i.* beharren, ausdauern.
persist *v.i.* beharren, bestehen.
persistence *s.* Beharrlichkeit *f.*
persistent *a.* beharrlich.
person *s.* Person *m.*; Mensch *m.*; Rolle *f.*; *in* ~, persönlich.
personage *s.* Persönlichkeit *f.*
personal *a.*, ~ly *adv.* persönlich; ~ *estate*, bewegliche Habe; ~ *property*, bewegliche Vermögen *n.*; ~ *files* *pl.* Handakten *pl.*
personality *s.* Persönlichkeit *f.*; Anzüglichkeit *f.*
personalty *s.* persönliche Eigentum *n.*
personate *v.t.* vorstellen, darstellen; sich ausgeben für.
personify *v.t.* verkörpern.
personnel *s.* (*Am.*) Personal *n.*; (*mil.*) ~-carrier *s.* Mannschaftstransportwagen *m.*; ~-file, Personalakten *pl.*; ~-section, Personalabteilung *f.*
perspective *s.* Perspektive, Aussicht, Fernsicht(zeichnung) *f.*; ~ *a.*, ~ly *adv.* perspektivisch.
perspicacious *a.* scharfsichtig.
perspicacity *s.* Scharfblick *m.*
perspicuity *s.* Deutlichkeit *f.*
perspicuous *a.*, ~ly *adv.* durchsichtig; verständlich.
perspiration *s.* Schweiss *m.*
perspire *v.i.* ausdünsten, schwitzen.
persuade *v.t.* überreden, überzeugen.
persuasion *s.* Überredung *f.*; Überzeugung *f.*
persuasive *a.*, ~ly *adv.* überredend.
pert *a.*, ~ly *adv.* keck; vorlaut.
pertain *v.i.* gehören, betreffen.
pertinacious *a.*, ~ly *adv.* halsstarrig.
pertinacity *s.* Halsstarrigkeit *f.*
pertinency *s.* Angemessenheit *f.*
pertinent *a.*, ~ly *adv.* angemessen, passend; treffend; einschlägig.
perturb *v.t.* verwirren, stören; beunruhigen.

perturbation *s.* Beunruhigung *f.*
perusal *s.* Durchlesen *n.*; Durchsicht *f.*
peruse *v.t.* durchlesen; prüfen.
Peruvian bark *s.* Fieberrinde *f.*
pervade *v.t.* durchdringen.
perverse *a.*, ~ly *adv.* verkehrt; verstockt; verdorben; pervers.
perversion *s.* Verdrehung *f.*; Abkehr *f.*
perversity *s.* Verkehrtheit *f.*; Eigensinn *m.*; Verdorbenheit *f.*
pervert *v.t.* verdrehen; verführen.
pervious *a.* zugänglich; wegsam.
pessimist *s.* Pessimist *m.*
pest *s.* Plage *f.*, Plagegeist *m.*; Pflanzenschädling *m.*
pester *v.t.* belästigen, plagen.
pestiferous *a.* ansteckend; verpestet.
pestilence *s.* Seuche *f.*; Pest *f.*
pestilent *a.* verderblich; lästig.
pestilential *a.*, ~ly *adv.* pestartig.
pestle *s.* Mörserkeule *f.*, Stössel *m.*
pet *s.* Ärger *m.*; Liebling *m.*; ~ *a.* Lieblings . . .; ~ *v.t.* hätscheln.
petal *s.* Blütenblatt *n.*
petard *s.* Sprengbüchse *f.*
peter out *v.i.* allmählich aufhören.
petition *s.* Gesuch *n.*; Bittschrift *f.*; ~ *v.t.* bitten, anhalten.
petitioner *s.* Bittsteller *m.*
petrel *s.* Sturmvogel *m.*
petrifaction *s.* Versteinerung *f.*
petrify *v.i.* versteinern.
petrol *s.* Benzin; ~ *station*, (*mot.*) Tankstelle *f.*
petroleum *s.* Steinöl *n.*, Petroleum *n.*
petticoat *s.* Unterrock *m.*
pettifogging *s.* Schikane *f.*
petty *a.* klein; gering; kleinlich.
petulance *s.* Mutwille *m.*; Verdriesslichkeit *f.*
petulant *a.*, ~ly *adv.* mutwillig, ärgerlich; (verdriesslich).
pew *s.* Kirchenstuhl *m.*
pewit *s.* Kiebitz *m.*; Lachmöve *f.*
pewter *s.* Schüsselzinn *n.*
phantasm *s.* Traumbild, Trugbild *n.*
phantom *s.* Phantom *n.*; Gespenst *n.*
Pharisee *s.* Pharisäer *m.*
pharmaceutics *s.pl.* Arzneikunde *f.*
pharmacy *s.* Pharmazie *f.*
phase *s.* Phase *f.*
pheasant *s.* Fasan *m.*
phenomenal *a.* phänomenal; Erscheinungs . . .; ausserordentlich gross, etc.
phenomenon *s.* Phänomen *n.*
phial *s.* Fläschchen *n.*
philander *v.i.* liebeln.
philanthropic *a.* menschenfreundlich.
philanthropist *s.* Menschenfreund *m.*
philanthropy *s.* Menschenliebe *f.*
philatelist *s.* Briefmarkensammler *m.*
Philistine *s.* Philister *m.*, Spiesser *m.*
philological *a.* sprachwissenschaftlich.

philologist *s.* Sprachforscher *m.*

philology *s.* Sprachwissenschaft *f.*

philosopher *s.* Philosoph, Weltweise *m.*; ~'s stone, Stein der Weisen *m.*

philosophical *a.*, ~ly *adv.* philosophisch.

philosophy *s.* Philosophie *f.*

phlebitis *s.* Venenentzündung *f.*

phlegm *s.* Schleim *m.*; Phlegma *n.*

phlegmatic(al) *a.* phlegmatisch.

phonetic *a.*, ~ally *adv.* phonetisch.

phonetics *s.pl.* Phonetik *f.*

phonograph *s.* (*Am.*) Grammophon *n.*

phosphate *s.* Phosphat *n.*

phosphorus *s.* Phosphor *m.*

photo *s.* Photographie *f.*

photoelectric cell *s.* Photozelle *f.*

photoengraving *s.* Photogravüre *f.*

photograph *s.* Photographie *f.*, Lichtbild *n.*; ~ *v.t.* photographieren.

photographer *s.* Photograph *m.*

photographic *s.* photographisch.

photography *s.* Photographie *f.*

photogravure *s.* Lichtkupferätzung *f.*

photostatic copy *s.* Photokopie *f.*

phrase *s.* Redensart *f.*; Satz *m.*; ~ *v.t.* ausdrücken, nennen.

phraseology *s.* Redeweise *f.*

physic *s.*, ~s *pl.* Physik, Naturkunde *f.*

physical *a.*, ~ly *adv.* physikalisch, physisch; körperlich, Körper...; ~ peculiarities *pl.* besondere Merkmale *n.pl.*

physician *s.* Arzt *m.*

physicist *s.* Physiker *m.*

physiognomy *s.* Miene *f.*

physiology *s.* Physiologie *f.*

physique *s.* Körperbeschaffenheit *f.*, Körperbau *m.*

pianist *s.* Klavierspieler *m.*

piano *s.* Klavier *n.*; grand ~, Flügel *m.*; cottage ~, Pianino *n.*

pick *v.t. & i.* picken; hacken; stochern, stechen; pflücken; auflesen; wählen; zupfen; to ~ out, auswählen; to ~ up, aufheben, auflesen; (Passagiere) aufnehmen; (ab)holen; to ~ on a person, an einem herumkritisieren; to ~ a quarrel, mit einem anbinden; to ~ a person's pockets, Taschendiebstahl verüben; ~ *s.* Auswahl *f.*; Spitzhammer *m.*; the ~ of, das Beste von.

pickaback *adv.* huckepack.

pickaxe *s.* Spitzhaue *f.*

picked *a.* auserlesen.

picket *s.* Streikposten *m.*

pickle *s.* Salzeingemachte *n.*; missliche Lage *f.*; ~ *v.t.* einpökeln.

picklock *s.* Dietrich *m.*

pick-me-up *s.* Stärkungsmittel *n.*

pickpocket *s.* Taschendieb *m.*

picnic *s.* Picknick *n.*, Landpartie *f.*

pictorial *a.* illustriert; ~ representation, bildliche Darstellung *f.*

picture *s.* Bild *n.*; ~s Kino *n.*; ~ *v.t.* malen; schildern.

picturesque *a.* malerisch.

pie *s.* Pastete *f.*; Elster *f.*

piebald *a.* scheckig.

piece *s.* Stück *n.*; Kanone, Flinte *f.*; a ~, pro Stück; pro Person; ~-goods *pl.* Stückgüter *n.pl.*; by the ~, stückweise; in the ~, im Stück; to take to ~s, auseinandernehmen; ~ *v.t.* stücken; flicken.

piecemeal *a. & adv.* stückweise.

piecework *s.* Akkordarbeit *f.*; to do ~, im Akkord arbeiten; ~-(work) rates *pl.* Akkordlöhne *f.*

pier *s.* Pfeiler *m.*; Steindamm *m.*; Abfahrtsplatz *m.*, Landungsbrücke *f.*

pierce *v.t.* durchstechen; durchbohren; ~ *v.i.* eindringen; rühren.

piety *s.* Frömmigkeit, kindliche Liebe *f.*

pig *s.* Ferkel, Schwein *n.*; Metallbarren *m.*

pigeon *s.* Taube *f.*; ~-hole, Fach *n.*

pig-headed *a.* dickköpfig.

pig-iron *s.* Roheisen *n.*

pigment *s.* Farbstoff *m.*

pigmy *s.* see pygmy.

pigskin *s.* Schweinsleder *n.*

pigsty *s.* Schweinestall *m.*

pig-tail *s.* Haarzopf *m.*

pike *s.* Pike *f.*; Hecht *m.*

pilaster *s.* Wandpfeiler *m.*

pilchard *s.* kleine Sardellenart *f.*

pile *s.* Pfahl *m.*; Haufen, Stoss (Papier) *m.*; ~s *pl.* Hämorrhoiden *f.pl.*; ~ *v.t.* aufhäufen.

pile-dwelling *s.* Pfahlbau *m.*

pilfer *v.t. & i.* stehlen, mausen.

pilgrim *s.* Pilger *m.*

pilgrimage *s.* Pilgerfahrt *f.*

pill *s.* Pille *f.*

pillage *s.* Plünderung *f.*; ~ *v.t.* plündern.

pillar *s.* Pfeiler *m.*

pillar-box *s.* (Säulen)Briefkasten *m.*

pillar-drill *s.* (mech.) Säulenbohrmaschine *f.*

pillbox *s.* (mil.) Bunker *m.*, Maschinengewehrnest *n.*

pillory *s.* Pranger *m.*; ~ *v.t.* an den Pranger stellen, anprangern.

pillow *s.* Kopfkissen *n.*

pillow-case *s.* Kissenüberzug *m.*

pilot *s.* Lotse *m.*; (avi.) Pilot *m.*; ~-plant, Versuchsfabrik *f.*; ~-jet, Stichflamme *f.*; ~ *v.t.* steuern, lotsen.

pilotage *s.* Lotsengeld *n.*

pimp *s.* Kuppler *m.*; ~ *v.i.* kuppeln.

pimpernel *s.* Pimpernelle *f.*

pimple *s.* Finne *f.*; Bläschen *n.*

pimpled *a.* finnig, pickelig.

pin *s.* Stecknadel *f.*; Stift, Pflock *m.*; Bolzen *m.*; (Instrumenten-)Wirbel *m.*; (Spiel-)Kegel *m.*; ~-money *s.* (law) Nadelgeld *n.*; ~ *v.t.* anstecken; an-

nageln; to ~ down, festnageln (fig.); to
~ up, anstecken.
pinafore s. Schürzchen n.
pincers s.pl. Kneifzange f.; pincer-move-
ment s. (mil.) Zangenbewegung f.
pinch v.t. kneifen, zwicken; drücken
(Schuh); bedrücken, quälen; (fam.)
klauen, stibitzen; ~ v.i. knausern;
darben; ~ s. Zwick m.; Prise (Tabak)
f.; Druck m.; Not, Verlegenheit f.
pinchbeck s. Tombak m.; ~ a. falsch,
unecht.
pin-cushion s. Nadelkissen n.
pine s. Kiefer f.; ~ v.i. schmachten; sich
anhärmen.
pine-apple s. Ananas f.
ping-pong s. Tischtennis s.
pinhead s. Stecknadelkopf m.
pinion s. Flügelspitze f.; Schwungfeder f.,
Schwinge f.; Getriebe n.; Zahnrad n.;
~ v.t. fesseln (an).
pink s. Nelke f.; Gipfel m.; Höchste n.;
~ a. blassrot, rosa.
pinnacle s. Zinne f.; Gipfel m.
pinpoint bombing s. (avi.) Bombenpunkt-
wurf m.
pin-prick s. Nadelstich m.
pint s. Pinte f. (0,57 Liter).
pioneer s. Pionier m.; Bahnbrecher m.
pious a., ~ly adv. fromm; zärtlich.
pip s. Pips m.; Auge (in der Karte) n.;
Obstkern m.
pipe s. Röhre f.; Pfeife f.; Pipe f. (572,4
Liter); ~ v.i. pfeifen, kreischen.
pipe-clay s. Pfeifenerde f.
pipe-cleaner s. Pfeifenreiniger m.
pipe-dream s. Wunschtraum m.
pipe-line s. Röhrenleitung f.
piper s. Pfeifer m.
pipette s. Stechheber m.; Pipette f.
piping s. Zierstreifen (an Kleidern),
Litzenbesatz m.; ~ hot a. siedend heiss.
piquancy s. Schärfe f.
piquant a., ~ly adv. beissend; pikant.
pique s. Groll m.; ~ v.t. aufreizen; ~
v.refl. sich brüsten.
piracy s. Seeräuberei f.
pirate s. Seeräuber m.; Nachdrucker m.;
v.t. rauben; nachdrucken.
piratical a., ~ly adv. räuberisch.
pish! i. pfui!
piss s. Harn m.; ~ v.i. pissen.
pistol s. Pistole f.
piston s. Kolben m.; ~-rod s. Kolbenstange f.
pit s. Grube f.; Graben m.; (theat.) Parterre n.; ~ v.t. eingraben; gegenein-
ander hetzen.
pitch s. Pech n.; Wurf m.; Grad m.;
Tonhöhe f.; Steigung f.; ~ v.t. verpichen; befestigen; werfen; aufstellen;
ordnen; (mus.) abstimmen; ~ v.i.
herabstürzen; aufschlagen (Ball); sich

niederlassen; stampfen (Schiff); high-
pitched a. in hohem Ton.
pitch-dark a. pechschwarz, stockfinster.
pitcher s. Krug m.
pitchfork s. Heugabel f.; Stimmgabel f.
piteous a., ~ly adv. kläglich, erbärmlich.
pitfall s. Fallgrube, Falle f.
pith s. Mark n.; Kern m.; Kraft f.; Vor-
züglichste n.
pithy a., ~ily adv. markig, kräftig.
pitiable a. erbärmlich.
pitiful a., ~ly adv. erbärmlich, mitleidig.
pitiless a., ~ly adv. unbarmherzig.
pittance s. kärgliche (An-)Teil m.
pity s. Mitleid n.; it is a ~, es ist schade; ~
v.t. bemitleiden, bedauern.
pivot s. Zapfen; Drehpunkt m.; to ~ on
v.i. sich drehen um.
placable a. versöhnlich.
placard s. (öffentliche) Anschlag m.,
Plakat n.; ~ v.t. bekanntmachen.
placate v.t. besänftigen.
place s. Platz m., Stelle f.; Ort m.; Amt, n.;
to take ~, stattfinden; ~s of interest pl.
Sehenswürdigkeiten pl.; ~ v.t. stellen,
setzen; unterbringen (Kapital).
placement s. Stellenbesetzung f.
placid a., ~ly adv. gelassen, sanft.
plagiarism s. Plagiat n.; Ausschreiberei f.
plagiarist s. Plagiator m.
plagiary s. Plagiat n.
plague s. Seuche f.; Plage f.; ~-spot s.
Pestbeule f.; Schandfleck m.
plaice s. Scholle f.
plaid s. gewürfelte schottische Wollen-
zeug n.
plain a. eben, flach; einfach, schlicht;
aufrichtig; deutlich; hässlich; ~ly adv.
deutlich; ~ s. Fläche, Ebene f.
plain clothes pl. Zivil(anzug) n.
plain-dealing s. ehrliche Handlungsweise
f.
plain-spoken a. ehrlich, aufrichtig.
plaint s. Klage f.; Beschwerde f.
plaintiff s. Kläger(in) m. (& f.).
plaintive a., ~ly adv. klagend, kläglich.
plait s. Falte f.; Flechte f., Zopf m.; ~ v.t.
falten; verflechten.
plaited a. geflochten.
plan s. Plan, Grundriss m.; ~ v.t. entwerfen, modeln.
plane s. Fläche f.; Hobel m.; Platane f.;
~ v.t. ebnen, hobeln; abwärts gleiten.
planer s. Hobelmaschine f.
planet s. Planet, Wandelstern m.
planetary a. planetarisch.
plank s. Planke, Bohle f.; Programm-
punkt m.; ~ v.t. bohlen, dielen.
plant s. Pflanze f.; Gerätschaften f.pl.
Maschinen pl.; Betriebsanlage f.; ~ v.t.
& i. pflanzen, stiften.
plantation s. Pflanzung, Pflanzschule f.;
Plantage f.

planter s. Pflanzer m.

plaque s. Platte f.; Plakette f.

plash v.i. plätschern.

plaster s. Pflaster n.; Mörtel m., Verputz m.; ~ of Paris, Gips m.; ~ v.t. bepflastern; verputzen.

plasterer s. Gipsarbeiter m.

plastic a. plastisch, bildsam.

plastic surgery s. plastische Chirurgie f.

plate s. Metallplatte f.; Kupferstich, Stahlstich m.; (phot.) Platte f.; Teller m.; Silbergeschirr n.; ~ v.t. plattieren; panzern.

plate-glass s. Tafelglas n.

plate-layer s. Streckenarbeiter m.

platen s. Walze (der Schreibmaschine) f.

platform s. (rail.) Bahnsteig m.; Rednerbühne f.; politisches Programm n.; ~ ticket s. Bahnsteigkarte f.

platinum s. Platin n.

platitude s. Gemeinplatz m.

platoon s. (mil.) Zug m.

platter s. (Am.) Schüssel f.

plaudit s. laute Beifall m.

plausibility s. Glaubwürdigkeit f.

plausible a., ~bly adv. scheinbar richtig, annehmbar; einnehmend.

play s. Spiel n.; Schauspiel n., Stück n.; Spielraum m.; ~ v.t. spielen; to ~ off against, ausspielen gegen; ~ v.i. spielen; Scherzen.

play-bill s. Theaterzettel m.

player s. Spieler m.; Schauspieler m.

playfellow, playmate s. Spielkamerad m.

playful a. spielend; scherzend.

play-ground s. Spielplatz m.

play-pen s. Laufställchen n.

plaything s. Spielzeug n.

playwright s. Dramatiker m.

plea s. Prozess m.; Rechtsgrund m.; Einrede f.; Vorwand m.; dringende Vorstellung f.

plead v.i. vor Gericht reden; ~ guilty, sich schuldig bekennen; ~ v.t. als Beweis anführen, vorschützen; erörtern; verteidigen.

pleadings s.pl. Prozessakten f.pl.

pleasant a., ~ly adv. angenehm; munter, lustig.

pleasantry s. Lustigkeit f.; Scherz m.

please v.t. & i. gefallen; belieben; befriedigen, besänftigen; ~!, bitte!; ~ yourself!, wie Sie wünschen!

pleasing a., ~ly adv. gefällig, angenehm.

pleasurable a., ~bly adv. angenehm.

pleasure s. Vergnügen n.; Belieben n.

pleat s. Falte f.; ~ v.t. fälteln, falten.

plebeian a. pöbelhaft; ~ s. gemeine Mensch m.; Plebejer m.

plebiscite s. Volksentscheid m.

pledge s. Pfand n.; Bürgschaft f.; Bescheid (beim Trinken) m.; ~ v.t. verpfänden, verpflichten; zutrinken.

pledger s. Pfandschuldner m.

plenary a., ~ily adv. vollständig, Voll...

plenary session s. Plenarsitzung f.

plenipotentiary a. bevollmächtigt; ~ s. Bevollmächtigte m.

plenitude s. Fülle f.

plentiful a., ~ly adv. reichlich, ergiebig.

plenty s. Fülle f.; Überfluss m.; ~ of, vollauf, reichlich, mehr als genug.

pleonasm s. Pleonasmus m.

plethora s. Vollblütigkeit f.; Überfülle f.

pleurisy s. Brustfellentzündung f.

pliable a., ~bly adv. biegsam.

pliant a., ~ly adv. biegsam, geschmeidig.

pliers s.pl. Drahtzange f.

plight s. Zustand m.; Treuversprechen n.; ~ v.t. verpfänden.

plod v.i. sich anstrengen; ochsen.

plot s. Stück (Land) n.; Fleck m.; Plan m.; Anschlag, Putsch m.; Verwicklung, Handlung f.; ~ v.i. sich verschwören; ~ v.t. aussinnen, anzetteln; to ~ the course, den Kurs abstecken.

plough s. Pflug m.; ~ v.t. pflügen; durchfallen lassen.

ploughshare s. Pflugschar f.

plover s. Regenpfeifer m.

pluck s. Zug, Ruck m.; (fig.) Mut m., Schneid m.; ~ v.t. pflücken, rupfen; to ~ up courage, Mut fassen.

plucky a. mutig, schneidig.

plug s. Pflock, Stöpsel, Zapfen, Dübel m.; (elek.) Stecker m.; ~ v.t. zustopfen.

plum s. Pflaume; Rosine.

plumage s. Gefieder n.

plumb s. Bleilot n.; ~ adv. senkrecht; ~ v.t. sondieren; Klempnerarbeit machen.

plumbago s. Graphit m.

plumber s. Klempner, Rohrleger m.

plumbline s. Senkblei n.

plume s. (Schmuck-)Feder f.; ~ v.t. mit Federn schmücken; rupfen; ~ v.refl. sich brüsten.

plummet s. Bleilot n.

plump a., ~ly adv. fleischig, dick; derb, gerade heraus; ~ v.i. & t. schwellen; plumpsen; mästen.

plum-tree s. Pflaumenbaum m.

plunder s. Beute f.; Raub m.; ~ v.t. plündern.

plunge v.t. & i. untertauchen; hinabstürzen; (Pferd) ausschlagen; ~ s. Untertauchen n.; Sturz m. (fig.) Wagnis n.

pluperfect s. (gram.) Plusquamperfekt(um) n.

plural s. (gram.) Mehrzahl f.

plurality s. Vielheit; Mehrzahl f.

plus a. (ar.) plus; (adv.) zusammen mit; ~ fours pl. lange Kniehosen f.pl.

plush s. Plüsch m.

ply s. Falte f.; ~wood, Sperrholz n.; four ~, (Wolle) vierfach; ~ v.t. handhaben, treiben; ~ *v.t.* trachten; hin und her fahren.

pneumatic *a.* Luft..., pneumatisch; ~ *s.* Luftreifen *m.*

pneumonia *s.* Lungenentzündung *f.*

poach *v.t.* im Wasserbad kochen; wildern; ~ *v.i.* wildern; ~ed eggs *s.pl.* verlorene Eier *n.pl.*

poacher *s.* Wilddieb *m.*

pock *s.* Pocke, Blatter *f.*

pocket *s.* Tasche *f.*; (*mil.*) Kessel *m.*; ~ *v.t.* einstecken.

pocket-book *s.* Brieftasche *f.*, Taschenbuch *n.*

pod *s.* Hülse, Schale, Schote *f.*

poem *s.* Gedicht *n.*

poet *s.* Dichter *m.*

poetic(al) *a.*, ~ly *adv.* dichterisch.

poetics *s.pl.* Poetik *f.*

poetry *s.* Dichtkunst *f.*; Gedichte *n.pl.*

poignancy *s.* Schärfe *f.*

poignant *a.*, ~ly *adv.* beissend, scharf; durchdringend.

point *s.* Punkt *m.*; Spitze *f.*; Auge (in der Karte) *n.*; Zweck *m.*; Kompasstrich *m.*; ~s *pl.* (*rail.*) Weiche *f.*; ~-blank *adv.* & *a.* direkt, gerade heraus; *the'case in* ~ der betreffende Fall; *on the* ~, im Begriff; *in* ~ *of fact*, tatsächlich; *there is no* ~ *in doing that*, es hat keinen Zweck das zu tun; *that is beside the* ~, das hat damit nichts zu tun; ~ *of view s.* Gesichtspunkt *m.*; ~ *v.t.* hinweisen; *to* ~ *out*, hinweisen auf, anführen.

pointed *a.*, ~ly *adv.* zugespitzt; spitz; punktiert; beissend.

pointer *s.* Zeiger, Weiser *m.*; Vorstehhund *m.*

pointless *a.* stumpf.

points *pl.* Rationspunkte *m.pl.*; *to come off* ~, nicht mehr auf Punkten sein; *to go on* ~, auf Punkte kommen.

poise *s.* Gewicht, Gleichgewicht *n.*; Haltung *f.*; ~ *v.t.* wägen; im Gleichgewicht erhalten.

poison *s.* Gift *n.*; ~ *v.t.* vergiften.

poisonous *a.*, ~ly *adv.* giftig.

poke *s.* Tasche *f.*; Beutel *m.*; Puff *m.*; ~ *v.t.* tappen; schüren; stossen.

poker *s.* Schüreisen *n.*; Poker *n.*

polar *a.* polar, Pol...

polarity *s.* Polarität *f.*

pole *s.* Pol *m.*; Stange *f.*; Mast *m.*; Pfahl *m.*

pole-axe *s.* Streitaxt *f.*

pole-cat *s.* Iltis *m.*

pole-star *s.* Polarstern *m.*

polemic(al) *a.* Streit...; ~ *s.* Polemiker *m.*; ~s *pl.* Polemik *f.*

police *s.* Polizei *f.*; ~-headquarters *pl.* Polizeipräsidium *n.*; ~-informer *s.* Polizeispitzel *m.*

police-court *s.* Polizeigericht *n.*

policeman *s.* Polizist, Schutzmann *m.*

police-station *s.* Polizeiwache *f.*

policy *s.* Politik *f.*; Diplomatie *f.*; Versicherungspolice *f.*; ~-making *a.* politisch massgebend; ~-holder *s.* Policeinhaber *m.*; *to take out a* ~ *on the life of his wife*, das Leben seiner Frau versichern.

polish *v.t.* glätten; zieren; ~ *s.* Glätte, Politur *f.*; Glanz *m.*; Schliff *m.*

polite *a.*, ~ly *adv.* fein, höflich.

politic *a.* weltklug, politisch; schlau.

political *a.*, ~ly *adv.* politisch, staatskundig, Staats...; ~ science *s.* Staatswissenschaft *f.*

politician *s.* Staatsmann, Politiker *m.*

politics *s.pl.* Politik, Staatskunst *f.*

polity *s.* Verfassung, Regierungsform *f.*

poll *s.* Abstimmung *f.*; ~ *v.t.* Stimmen erhalten; ~ *v.i.* stimmen.

pollard *s.* gekappte Baum *m.*

pollen *s.* Blütenstaub *m.*

polling-station *s.* Wahllokal *n.*

poll-*ax *s.* Kopfsteuer *f.*

pollute *v.t.* beflecken; entweihen.

pollution *s.* Befleckung, Entweihung *f.*

poltroon *s.* Feigling *m.*

polygamy *s.* Vielweiberei *f.*

polyglot *a.* vielsprachig.

polygon *s.* Vieleck *n.*

polygonal *a.* vieleckig.

polyp(e) *s.* Polyp *m.*

polypus *s.* (*med.*) Polyp *m.*

polysyllabic *a.* vielsilbig.

polytechnic *a.* polytechnisch; ~ *s.* Gewerbeschule *f.*

polytheism *s.* Vielgötterei *f.*

pomade, pomatum *s.* Pomade *f.*

pomegranate *s.* Granatapfel *m.*; Granatbaum *m.*

pommel *s.* (Degen-, Sattel-)Knopf *m.*; ~ *v.t.* prügeln, knuffen.

pomp *s.* Pracht *f.*; Gepränge *n.*

pomposity *s.* Prahlerei *f.*; Schwulst *m.*

pompous *a.*, ~ly *adv.* hochtrabend.

pond *s.* Teich *m.*

ponderable *a.* wägbar.

ponderous *a.*, ~ly *adv.* schwer.

poniard *s.* Dolch *m.*; ~ *v.t.* erdolchen.

pontiff *s.* Hohepriester *m.*; Papst *m.*

pontifical *a.*, ~ly *adv.* päpstlich.

ponton *s.* (*Am.*) *see* pontoon.

pontoon *s.* Brückenkahn *m.*

pony *s.* kleine Pferd, Pony *n.*

poodle *s.* Pudel *m.*

pooh! oho! pah!

pooh-pooh *v.t.* (*fig.*) verächtlich ablehnen, nichts wissen wollen von.

pool *s.* Pfuhl, Teich *m.*; (Spiel-)Einsatz *m.*; (*com.*) Kartell *n.*; gemeinsame Fonds *m.*; ~ *v.t.* zusammenlegen, zusammenwerfen.

poop *s.* Hinterschiff *f.*; Achterhütte *f.*

poor *a.*, ~ly *adv.* arm, dürftig; gering.
poorly *a.* & *adv.* ärmlich; unpässlich.
poor-relief *s.* Armenfürsorge *f.*
pop *s.* Puff, Knall *m.*; ~ *v.i.* knallen, paffen; huschen;~ *v.t.* schnell bewegen, schnellen.
Pope *s.* Papst *m.*
popery *s.* Papisterei *f.*
pop-gun *s.* Knallbüchse *f.*
popish *a.*, ~ly *adv.* papistisch.
poplar *s.* Pappel *f.*
poplin *s.* wollseidene Zeug *n.*, Poplin *m.*
poppy *s.* Mohn *m.*
populace *s.* Pöbel *m.*
popular *a.* volkstümlich, beliebt, volksmässig; Volks...
popularize *v.t.* gemeinfasslich machen.
popularity *s.* Volkstümlichkeit *f.*
populate *v.t.* bevölkern.
population *s.* Bevölkerung *f.*
populous *a.*, ~ly *adv.* volkreich.
porcelain *s.* Porzellan *n.*
porch *s.* Vorhalle *f.*; Portal *n.*
porcupine *s.* Stachelschwein *n.*
pore *s.* Pore *f.*; ~ *v.i.* brüten.
pork *s.* Schweinefleisch *n.*
pork-butcher *s.* Schweineschlächter, Wursthändler *m.*
pornographic *a.* pornographisch, Schmutz...
porous *a.* porös.
porphyry *s.* Porphyr *m.*
porridge *s.* Haferbrei *m.*
port *s.* Hafen *m.*, Hafenstadt *f.*; (*nav.*) Pfortluke *f.*; Backbord *n.*; Portwein *m.*; ~ *of arrival,* Ankunftshafen *m.*; ~ *of call,* Anlegehafen *m.*; ~ *of destination,* Bestimmungshafen *m.*; ~ *of registry,* Heimathafen *m.*; ~-charges, ~-dues *pl.* Hafengebühren *f.pl.*
portable *a.* tragbar.
portal *s.* Portal *n.*
portcullis *s.* Fallgatter *n.*
portend *v.t.* vorbedeuten, deuten auf.
portent *s.* (üble) Vorbedeutung *f.*
portentous *a.* verhängnisvoll, fürchterlich.
porter *s.* Träger, Dienstmann *m.*; Portier *m.*
porterage *s.* Trägerlohn *m.*
portfolio *s.* Mappe *f.*; Portefeuille *n.* (*fig.*)
porthole *s.* (*nav.*) Stückpforte *f.*
portico *s.* Säulengang *m.*
portion *s.* Teil, Anteil *m.*; Portion *f.* Heiratsgut *n.*; ~ *v.t.* austeilen.
portly *a.* stattlich; wohlbeleibt.
portmanteau *s.* Reisekoffer *m.*
portrait *s.* Bildnis, Porträt *n.*
portraitist *s.* Porträtmaler *m.*
portray *v.t.* abmalen; schildern.
pose *s.* Pose, Stellung *f.*; ~ *v.t.* (eine Frage, Behauptung) aufstellen.
position *s.* Stellung, Lage *f.*; Stand *m.*;

Standpunkt *m.*; ~-warfare *s.* (*mil.*) Stellungskrieg *m.*; *to hold a* ~, ein Amt bekleiden.
positive *a.*, ~ly *adv.* ausdrücklich; sicher; bestimmt; rechthaberisch; positiv.
posse *s.* (Polizei-) Aufgebot *n.*
possess *v.t.* besitzen; besetzen.
possession *s.* Besitz *m.*; Besitzung *f.*; *to be in* ~ *of,* im Besitz von etwas sein.
possessive *a.* Besitz...; (*gram.*) besitzanzeigend.
possessor *s.* Besitzer *m.*
possibility *s.* Möglichkeit *f.*
possible *a.* möglich.
possibly *adv.* möglicherweise, vielleicht.
post *s.* Pfosten, Pfahl *m.*; Posten *m.*; Stelle *f.* Anstellung *f.*; Post *f.*; *by* ~, mit der Post; *Ministry of* ~, Postministerium *m.*; ~ *v.t.* anschlagen; hinstellen; auf die Post geben, (Brief) einstecken; ~ *v.i.* mit der Post reisen, eilen.
postage *s.* Porto *n.*, Postgebühr *f.*; ~ *due,* Strafporto *n.*, Nachgebühr *f.*; ~ *free,* franko.
postage-stamp *s.* Briefmarke *f.*
postal *a.* Post...; ~-order (P.O.), Postanweisung *f.*; ~ *cheque s.* Postscheck *m.*; ~ *expenses pl.* Portospesen *pl.*
postcard *s.* Postkarte *f.*; *colour* ~, farbige Postkarte; *picture* ~, *view* ~, Ansichtspostkarte.
post-date *v.t.* nachdatieren.
poste restante *adv.* postlagernd; ~ *s.* Briefaufbewahrungsstelle *f.*
poster *s.* Anschlagzettel *m.*; Plakat *n.*
posterior *a.* später; Hintere *m.*
posterity *s.* Nachwelt *f.*
post-haste *adv.* in grosser Eile.
posthumous *a.* nachgeboren, hinterlassen.
posting-box *s.* Briefkasten *m.*
postman *s.* Briefträger *m.*
post-mark *s.* Poststempel *m.*
post-master *s.* Postmeister *m.*
post-mortem *s.* Leichenschau *f.*
post-office *s.* Postamt *n.*; ~-box (P.O. box) *s.* Postfach *n.*; ~ *savings bank,* Postsparkasse *f.*
postpone *v.t.* verschieben; aufschieben.
postponement *s.* Aufschub *m.*
postscript *s.* Nachschrift *f.*
postulate *s.* Postulat *n.*, Forderung *f.*; ~ *v.t.* fordern; als richtig annehmen.
posture *s.* Stellung, Lage *f.*; (körperliche) Haltung *f.*
post-war Nachkriegs...
posy *s.* Blumenstrauss *m.*
pot *s.* Topf, Krug *m.*; Kanne *f.*; ~ *boiler,* Brotarbeit *f.*
potable *a.* trinkbar.
potash *s.* Pottasche *f.*; Kali *n.*
potassium *s.* Kalium *n.*
potato *s.* Kartoffel *f.*; boiled ~es *pl.* Salzkartoffeln *pl.*; chipped ~es, chips *pl.*

pommes frites; **fried ~es** pl. Bratkartoffeln; **mashed ~es,** Kartoffelbrei m.; **~-blight,** Kartoffelkrankheit f.; **~-haulms** pl. Kartoffelkraut n.; **~es in jackets** pl. Pellkartoffeln pl.

potency s. Kraft f.

potent a., **~ly** adv. mächtig, stark.

potentate s. Machthaber m.

potential a., **~ly** adv. möglich, potentiell; **military ~** s. Kriegspotential n.

potentialities pl. Möglichkeiten f.pl.

pother s. Lärm m.; **~** v.i. lärmen, poltern; **~** v.t. aufregen.

potion s. (Arznei-)Trank m.

potter s. Töpfer m.

pottery s. Töpferei f.; Töpferwaren f.pl.

pouch s. Tasche f.; Beutel m.; **~** v.t. einstecken.

poulterer s. Geflügelhändler m.

poultice s. Breiumschlag m.

poultry s. Federvieh, Geflügel n.

pounce s. Klaue f.; Glättpulver n.; v.i. herfallen über.

pound s. Pfund n. (lb.=453,6 g.); Pfund Sterling n.; **~** v.t. zerstossen; (Vieh) einsperren; (mil.) belegen mit, bombardieren.

poundage s. Pfandgeld n.; Provision (f.) auf das Pfund.

pounder s. Stössel m.; ...pfünder m.

pour v.t. giessen; **~** v.i. strömen.

pout s. üble Laune f.; **~** v.i. schmollen.

poverty s. Armut f.; Mangel m.

powder s. Pulver n.; Puder, Staub m.; v.t. pudern; bestreuen.

power s. Macht, Gewalt f.; Kraft f.; Vollmacht f.; (math.) Potenz f.; (elek.) Starkstrom m.; **~ station** s. Kraftwerk n.

powerful a., **~ly** adv. mächtig, kräftig.

powerless a. kraftlos, ohnmächtig.

powerloom s. mechanische Webstuhl m.

practicable a., **~bly** adv. tunlich; ausführbar; gangbar.

practical a., **~ly** adv. ausübend, praktisch; tatsächlich; **~ joke,** grober, handgreiflicher Scherz m.

practice s. Ausübung f.; Übung f.; Praxis f.

practise v.t. üben; anwenden; **~** v.i. sich üben; treiben.

practitioner s. praktische Arzt m.

pragmatic a., **~ally,** adv. pragmatisch.

prairie s. Prärie f.

praise s. Lob n.,; **~** v.t. loben.

praiseworthy s., **~ily** adv. lobenswürdig.

pram s. Prahm m.; **~** s. (=perambulator) Kinderwagen m.

prance v.i. bäumen; prunken.

prank s. Possen, Streich m.; **~** v.t. schmücken.

prate v.i. schwatzen; **~** s. Geschwätz n.

prattle v.t. schwatzen; **~** s. Geschwätz n.

prawn s. Garnele f.

pray v.i. & t. beten; bitten.

prayer s. Gebet n.; Bitte f.; **the Lord's ~,** das Vaterunser.

prayer-book s. Gebetbuch n., Agende f.

preach v.t. & i. predigen.

preacher s. Prediger m.

preamble s. Einleitung, Vorrede f.

prearrange v.t. vorher anordnen.

prebend s. Pfründe f.

prebendary s. Pfründner m.

precarious a., **~ly** adv. unsicher; abhängig; aufkündbar.

precaution s. Vorsicht, Vorsichtsmassregel f.; **to take ~s,** Vorsichtsmassnahmen treffen.

precautionary a., vorbeugend, Vorsichts ...

precede v.t. vorhergehen.

precedence s. Vortritt, Vorrang m.

precedent s. Präzedenzfall m.

precentor s. Vorsänger m.

precept s. Vorschrift, Regel f.

preceptor s. Lehrer m.

precinct s. Bezirk, Umfang m.

precious a., **~ly** adv. kostbar; recht.

precipice s. Abgrund m.

precipitate v.t. hinabstürzen; (chem.) fällen; überstürzen; heraufbeschwören; **~** v.i. herabstürzen; sich übereilen; vorschnell sein; **~** a., **~ly** adv. übereilt; voreilig; **~** s. (chem.) Niederschlag m.

précis s. kurze Inhaltsangabe f.

precise a., **~ly** adv. genau; steif.

precision s. Bestimmtheit f.; (mech.) **~ worker** s. Präzisionsarbeiter m.; **~ tool** s. Präzisionswerkzeug n.

preclude v.t. ausschliessen.

precocious a. frühreif; altklug.

precocity s. Frühreife f.

preconceive v.t. sich vorher denken.

preconception s. Vorurteil n.

precursor s. Vorläufer, Vorbote m.

predatory a. räuberisch.

predecessor s. Vorgänger m.

predestinate v.t. vorherbestimmen.

predestination s. Vorherbestimmung f.; Gnadenwahl f.

predestine v.t. vorherbestimmen.

predicament s. (missliche) Lage f.

predicate v.t. aussagen; **~** s. (gram.) Prädikat n.

predication s. Aussage f.

predict v.t. vorhersagen.

prediction s. Weissagung f.

predictor s. (avi.) Kommandogerät n.

predilection s. Vorliebe f.

predispose v.t. geneigt machen.

predisposition s. Geneigtheit f.

predominance s. Übergewicht n.

predominant a., **~ly** adv. vorherrschend.

predominate v.i. vorherrschen.

pre-eminence s. Vorrang m.

pre-eminent *a.*, **~ly** *adv.* hervorragend.
pre-emption *s.* Vorkauf *m.*; Vorkaufsrecht *n.*
pre-exist *v.i.* vorher da sein.
prefabricated *a.* vorgefertigt.
preface *s.* Vorrede *f.*; **~** *v.t.* einleiten.
prefatory *a.* einleitend.
prefect *s.* Präfekt.
prefer *v.t.* vorziehen.
preferable *a.* vorzuziehen.
preference *s.* Vorzug *m.*; Vorzugstarif *m.*; **~ share**, Vorzugsaktie *f.*
preferential *a.*, **~ly** *adv.* bevorzugt, Vorzugs...; **~ duty**, Vorzugszoll *m.*; **~ treatment**, Vorzugsbehandlung *f.*
preferred stock *s.* (*Am.*) Vorzugsaktie *f.*
preferment *s.* Beförderung *f.*
prefigure *v.t.* sich ausmalen.
prefix *v.t.* vorsetzen; **~** *s.* Vorsilbe *f.*
pregnancy *s.* Schwangerschaft *f.*
pregnant *a.*, **~ly** *adv.* schwanger; (*fig.*) fruchtbar; inhaltsschwer; treffend.
prejudge *v.t.* absprechen.
prejudice *s.* Vorurteil *n.*; Nachteil *m.*; **without ~ to**, unbeschadet; **~** *v.t.* einnehmen (gegen); benachteiligen.
prejudicial *a.*, **~ly** *adv.* schädlich.
prelacy *s.* Prälatenwürde *f.*
prelate *s.* Prälat *m.*
preliminary *a.* vorläufig, Vor...; (*law*) **~ examination**, Vorverhör *n.*; **~** *s.* Vorbereitung *f.*; **~ies** *pl.* Vorverhandlungen *f.pl.*
prelude *s.* Vorspiel *n.*, Auftakt *m.*
premature *a.*, **~ly** *adv.* vorschnell.
premeditate *v.t.* vorher überlegen; **~d** *p.* vorbedacht, vorsätzlich.
premeditation *s.* Vorbedacht *m.*
premier *s.* Premierminister *m.*
premilitary *a.* vormilitärisch.
premise *v.t.* vorausschicken.
premises *s.pl.* Vordersätze *m.pl.*; Haus (*n.*) mit Zubehör; Grundstücke *n.pl.*
premium *s.* Preis *m.*; Versicherungsprämie *f.*; **at a ~**, über pari; sehr gesucht.
premonition *s.* Warnung, Vorahnung *f.*
preoccupation *s.* Vorurteil *n.*; Vertieftsein *n.*
preoccupy *v.t.* ganz in Anspruch nehmen.
preparation *s.* Vorbereitung, Zubereitung *f.*; Präparat *n.*
preparedness *s.* Bereitschaft *f.*
preparatory *a.* vorbereitend; vorläufig.
prepare *v.t.* vorbereiten; zubereiten; **~** *v.i.* sich vorbereiten.
prepay *v.t.* vorausbezahlen; frankieren.
prepayment *s.* Vorausbezahlung.
prepense *a.* vorbedacht.
preponderance *s.* Übergewicht *n.*
preponderant *a.* überwiegend.
preponderate *v.i.* überwiegen.
preposition *s.* (*gram.*) Präposition *f.*

prepossess *v.t.* vorher einnehmen.
prepossessing *a.* einnehmend, anziehend.
prepossession *s.* Voreingenommenheit *f.*
preposterous *a.* verkehrt; unsinnig.
prerequisite *s.* Bedingung, Voraussetzung *f.*
prerogative *s.* Vorrecht *n.*
presage *s.* Vorbedeutung *f.*
presage *v.t.* anzeigen.
presbyterian *a.* presbyterianisch; **~ s.** Presbyterianer *m.*
prescience *s.* Vorherwissen *n.*
prescribe *v.t. & i.* vorschreiben; verschreiben.
prescription *s.* Vorschrift *f.*; Rezept *n.*; Verjährung *f.*
prescriptive right *s.* (*law*) ersessene Recht *n.*
presence *s.* Gegenwart *f.*; **~ of mind**, Geistesgegenwart *f.*
present *a.* gegenwärtig; bereit; **at ~**, gegenwärtig; **~ s.** (*Zeit*) Gegenwart *f.*; (*gram.*) Präsens *n.*; Geschenk *n.*
present *v.t.* vorlegen, unterbreiten; (Gesuch) einreichen; beschenken; vorschlagen, präsentieren; **to ~ a play**, ein Stück zeigen.
presentable *a.* präsentierbar.
presentation *s.* Darstellung *f.*; Vorzeigung *f.*; **~ copy**, Freiexemplar *n.*
presentiment *s.* Vorgefühl *n.*, Ahnung *f.*
presently *adv.* gleich; bald; nachher.
preservation *s.* Erhaltung, Bewahrung *f.*
preservative *a.* bewahrend; **~ s.** Schutzmittel *n.*; Einmachemittel *n.*
preserve *v.t.* bewahren; einlegen, einmachen; **~ s.** Eingemachte *n.*
preside *v.i.* den Vorsitz führen.
presidency *s.* Vorsitz *m.*
president *s.* Präsident *m.*
press *s.* Presse *f.*; Druck, Drang *m.*; Gedränge *n.*; **in the ~**, in der Presse; **~ conference**, Pressebesprechung *f.*; **~-service**, Pressekorrespondenz *f.*; **clothes-~**, Wäscheschrank *m.*; **~** *v.t.* pressen; keltern; drängen; **~** *v.i.* drücken; dringen, drängen.
press-gallery *s.* Pressetribüne *f.*
pressing *a.*, **~ly** *adv.* dringend.
pressure *s.* Druck *m.*; **under ~**, unter Druck (arbeiten); **to put ~ on**, auf jemand Druck ausüben.
prestige *s.* Ansehen *n.*, Geltung *f.*
presumable *a.* mutmasslich.
presume *v.t. & i.* mutmassen; sich anmassen; sich verlassen; **~d dead**, verschollen.
presumption *s.* Mutmassung *f.*; Dünkel *m.*; Vermessenheit *f.*
presumptive *a.*, **~ly** *adv.* mutmasslich.
presumptuous *a.*, **~ly** *adv.* anmassend.
presuppose *v.t.* voraussetzen.

pretence s. Vorwand m.; Schein m.; false ~s, Vorspiegelung falscher Tatsachen f.

pretend v.t. vorgeben; erheucheln; ~ v.i. sich stellen; beanspruchen.

pretender s. (Thron-) Prätendent, Beansprucher m.

pretension s. Anmassung f.

pretentious a., ~ly adv. anspruchsvoll.

preterite s. (gram.) Präteritum n.

preternatural a., ~ly adv. aussergewöhnlich; übernatürlich.

pretext s. Vorwand m.

pretty a. & adv. niedlich, nett; ziemlich.

prevail v.i. (vor-) herrschen.

prevalence s. Verbreitung f.

prevalent a., ~ly adv. vorherrschend.

prevaricate v.i. Ausflüchte suchen.

prevarication s. Verdrehung, Ausflucht f.

prevent v.t. zuvorkommen; vorbeugen.

preventative s. Schutzmittel n.

prevention s. Verhütung f.

preventive a., ~ly adv. vorbeugend; ~ s. Verhütungsmittel n.

preview s. Vorschau f.

previous a., ~ly adv. vorig, früher.

pre-war a. Vorkriegs...

prey s. Raub m.; Beute f.; ~ v.i. rauben, plündern.

price s. Preis m.; Wert m.; ~-control, Preisüberwachung f.; low ~d, in niedriger Preislage.

priceless a. unschätzbar.

prick v.t. stechen, anstechen; spornen; spitzen; to ~ one's ears, die Ohren spitzen; ~ v.i. stechen, prickeln; ~ s. Stachel m.; Spitze f.; Stich m.

prickle s. Stachel m.

pride s. Stolz m.; Pracht f.; ~ v.refl. stolz sein auf.

priest s. Priester m.

priestcraft s. Pfaffentrug m.

priestess s. Priesterin f.

priesthood s. Priesteramt n.; Geistlichkeit f.

priestly a. priesterlich.

priest-ridden a. von Pfaffen regiert.

prig s. eingebildete, lehrhafte Mensch m.

priggish a. pedantisch.

prim a. geziert, förmlich; gesetzt.

prima facie, beim ersten Anschein.

primacy s. Primat m.; Vorrang m.

primary a. ursprünglich, Anfangs..., Haupt...; ~ily adv. vornehmlich.

primate s. Primas m.

prime a., ~ly adv. Haupt...; vortrefflich; ~-cost s. Gestehungskosten pl.; ~ Minister, Ministerpräsident m.; ~ s. Blüte, Vollendung f.; Beste n.; ~ v.t. grundieren; unterrichten.

primer s. Fibel f., Elementarbuch n.

primeval a. ursprünglich, uralt.

primitive a., ~ly adv. ursprünglich; einfach, primitiv.

primogeniture s. Erstgeburt f.

primrose s. Primel f.

prince s. Fürst, Prinz m.

princely a. & adv. prinzlich, fürstlich.

princess s. Prinzessin, Fürstin f.

principal a., ~ly adv. vorzüglich, Haupt ..., hauptsächlich; ~ s. Haupt n.; (law) Haupttäter m.; Direktor m.; Hauptsache f.; Kapital n.

principality s. Fürstentum n.

principle s. Prinzip n.; Grundursache f.; Grundsatz m.; to lay down a ~, einen Grundsatz aufstellen.

print v.t. drucken, abdrucken; in grossen Buchstaben schreiben; (phot.) abziehen; einprägen; ~ s. Druck m.; Abdruck m.; (phot.) Abzug m., Kopie f.; Spur f.; (Stahl)Stick m.; out of ~, vergriffen; ~s pl. gedruckte Kattunstoffe m.pl.

printed matter, printed paper s. Drucksache f.

printer s. Buckdrucker m.

printing: -house s. Buchdruckerei f.; ~ ink, Druckerschwärze f.

prior a. früher; ~ to, vor; ~ s. Prior m.

prioress s. Priorin f.

priority s. Priorität f.; Vorrang m.

prism s. Prisma n.

prison s. Gefängnis m.

prisoner s. Gefangene m.; ~ of war s. Kriegsgefangene m.

pristine a. ehemalig, alt.

privacy s. Verborgenheit f.

private a., ~ly adv. privat; geheim; nicht öffentlich; nicht amtlich; persönlich, Privat..., eigen; (tel.) ~ call, Privatgespräch; ~ enterprise, freie Wirtschaft f.; ~ s. gemeine Soldat m.; in ~, unter vier Augen.

privateer s. Kaper m.

privation s. Beraubung f.; Mangel m.

privilege s. Vorrecht n.; ~ v.t. bevorrechten.

privy a. geheim, besonder; mitwissend; ~ council, Staatsrat m.; Lord Privy Seal, Geheimsiegelbewahrer; ~ s. Abort m.

prize s. Preis m.; Belohnung f.; Prise, Beute f.; ~ v.t. würdigen, schätzen; (mit Gewalt) öffnen.

prize-court s. Prisengericht n.

prize-fighter s. Boxer m.

probability s. Wahrscheinlichkeit f.

probable a., ~ly adv. wahrscheinlich.

probate s. Testamentsbestätigung f.

probation s. Prüfung f.; Probezeit f.; Bewährungsfrist f.; on ~, auf Probe, widerruflich.

probationary a. Probe ...; ~ service s. Probedienst m.

probationer s. Prüfling m.; Anwärter m.

probe *s.* Sonde *f.*; ~ *v.t.* sondieren.

probity *s.* Redlichkeit *f.*

problem *s.* Aufgabe *f.*, Problem *n.*

problematic *a.*, ~ally *adv.* zweifelhaft.

proboscis *s.* Rüssel *m.*

procedure *s.* Verfahren *n.*; *legal* ~, Prozessverfahren *n.*

proceed *v.i.* hervorgehen, herrühren; fortfahren; verfahren; vorgehen; weitergehen; *to* ~ *to*, sich begeben nach, reisen nach.

proceeding *s.* Verfahren; (legal) ~s *pl.* Prozess, gerichtliche Verfahren *n.*; *to take* ~s *against*, gerichtlich vorgehen gegen.

proceeds *s.pl.* Ertrag, Gewinn *m.*

process *s.* Fortschritt, Vorgang *m.*; Verfahren *n.*; Prozess *m.*; *to* ~ *v.t.* behandeln, bearbeiten (*chem.*) Verwaltungsdienst.

procession *s.* Prozession *f.*

proclaim *v.t.* öffentlich bekanntmachen.

proclamation *s.* Verkündigung *f.*

proclivity *s.* Neigung *f.*, Hang *m.*

procrastinate *v.t. & i.* verschieben.

procreate *v.t.* zeugen, erzeugen.

proctor *s.* Universitätsrichter *m.*

procuration *s.* Beschaffung *f.*; Vollmacht .; Prokura *f.*; *per* ~, (p.p.), per Prokura.

procurator *s.* Bevollmächtigte *m.*

procure *v.t.* besorgen; verschaffen, liefern; ~ *v.i.* kuppeln.

procurement *s.* Beschaffung *f.*

procurer *s.* Kuppler *m.*

procuress *s.* Kupplerin *f.*

prod *s.* Stachel *m.*; ~ *v.t.* stacheln.

prodigal *a.*, ~ly *adv.* verschwenderisch; ~ *s.* Verschwender *m.*

prodigality *s.* Verschwendung *f.*

prodigious *a.*, ~ly *adv.* ungeheuer.

prodigy *s.* Wunderding, Ungeheuer *n.*

produce *v.t.* vorführen; hervorbringen; vorstellen; vorzeigen; *to* ~ *a play*, ein Stück einstudieren; *to* ~ *a witness*, einen Zeugen beibringen; ~ *s.* Erzeugnis *n.*; Ertrag *m.*; Produkte *n.pl.*; ~ *exchange* *s.* Produktenbörse *f.*

producer *s.* Erzeuger *m.*; Regisseur *m.*; ~ *gas* *s.* Generatorgas, Holzgas *n.*

product *s.* Erzeugnis, Produkt *n.*

production *s.* Vorführung *f.*; Etzeugnis *n.*; Vorlegung *f.*; Produktion *f.*; Erzeugung *f.*

productive *a.* fruchtbar; schöpferisch.

profanation *s.* Entweihung *f.*

profane *a.*, ~ly *adv.* ungeweiht; gottlos; weltlich; ~ *v.t.* entweihen.

profanity *s.* Gottlosigkeit, Ruchlosigkeit *f.*; Fluchen *n.*

profess *v.t.* bekennen; ausüben.

professedly *adv.* erklärtermassen, eingestandenermassen.

profession *s.* Bekenntnis *n.*; Beruf *m.*; *the* ~s, die freien Berufe *m.pl.*

professional *a.* berufsmässig, Berufs...; Fach...; ~ *man*, Angehörige der freien Berufe *m.*; ~ *s.* Berufsspieler (*Sport*) *m.*

professor *s.* Bekenner *m.*; Professor *m.*

professorship *s.* Professur *f.*

proffer *v.t.* anbieten; ~ *s.* Anerbieten *n.*

proficiency *s.* Tüchtigkeit *f.*

proficient *a.* tüchtig, bewandert.

profile *s.* Seitenansicht *f.*; Durchschnitt *m.*

profit *s.* Gewinn *m.*; Vorteil *m.*; *at a* ~, mit Gewinn; ~ *and loss*, Gewinn und Verlust; ~ *sharing* *s.* Gewinnbeteiligung *f.*; ~ *v.t. & i.* Vorteil bringen; Nutzen ziehen; nutzen; Fortschritte machen.

profitable *a.*, ~bly *adv.* einträglich.

profiteer *v.i.* (Kriegs-) Wucher treiben; ~ *s.* Kriegsgewinnler *m.*

profligacy *s.* Liederlichkeit *f.*

profligate *a.*, ~ly *adv.* ruchlos; liederlich.

profound *a.*, ~ly *adv.* tief, dunkel; (*fig.*) gründlich.

profundity *s.* Tiefe *f.*

profuse *a.*, ~ly *adv.* verschwenderisch.

profusion *s.* Überfluss *m.*

progenitor *s.* Vorvater, Ahn *m.*

progeny *s.* Nachkommenschaft *f.*

prognostic *s.* Vorzeichen *n.*

prognosticate *v.t.* vorhersagen.

program(me) *s.* Programm *n.*

progress *s.* Fortschritt, Gang *m.*; *to be in* ~, im Gange sein; ~ *v.i.* fortschreiten.

progression *s.* Fortschritt *m.*; Zunahme *f.*; Progression *f.*

progressive *a.* fortschreitend; ~ly *adv.* nach und nach.

prohibit *v.t.* verbieten, verhindern.

prohibition *s.* Verbot *n.*; Prohibition *f.*

prohibitive, prohibitory *a.* verbietend; ~ *duty*, Sperrzoll *m.*; ~ *price*, unerschwingliche Preis *m.*

project *v.t.* entwerfen; ~ *v.i.* vorspringen; ~ *s.* Entwurf, Plan *m.*; Unternehmen *n.*; Aktion *f.*

projectile *a.* Wurf...; ~ *s.* Geschoss *n.*

projection *s.* Wurf *m.*; Entwurf, Riss *m.*; (*arch.*) Vorsprung *m.*; Projektion *f.*; ~-**room** *s.* Vorführraum *m.* (für Lichtbilder).

projector *s.* Erfinder *m.*; Plänemacher *m.*; Projektionsapparat *m.*

proletarian *a.* proletarisch; Arbeiter...

proletariat(e) *s.* Proletariat *n.*

prolific *a.*, ~ally *adv.* fruchtbar.

prolix *a.*, ~ly *adv.* weitläufig, langwierig.

prolixity *s.* Weitschweifigkeit *f.*

prologue *s.* Eröffnungsrede *f.*

prolong *v.t.* verlängern; (*com.*) prolongieren.

prolongation *s.* Verlängerung *f.*

promenade s. Spaziergang m.; Spazierweg m.; ~ v.i. spazieren(gehen).
prominence s. Hervorragen n., Wichtigkeit f.
prominent a. hervorragend.
promiscuous a., ~ly adv. vermischt; gemeinsam; unterschiedslos.
promise s. Versprechen n.; ~ v.t. versprechen.
promissory a. versprechend; ~ note s. Eigen(Sola)wechsel m., Promesse f.
promontory s. Vorgebirge n.
promote v.t. befördern; gründen.
promoter s. Förderer m.; Gründer m.
promotion s. Beförderung f.; Förderung f.; (Schule) Versetzung f.
prompt a., ~ly adv. bereit; schnell; ~ v.t. vorsagen; anreizen; souffliieren.
prompt-book s. Souffleurbuch n.
prompter s. Anreger m.; Souffleur m.
promptitude, promptness s. Pünktlichkeit f.
promulgate v.t. verkünden; verbreiten.
prone a., ~ly adv. geneigt, hingestreckt.
prong s. Gabel f.; Zinke f.
pronominal a. fürwörtlich.
pronoun s. Fürwort n.
pronounce v.t. aussprechen· feierlich erklären.
pronouncement s. Verlautbarung, Äusserung f.; (Urteils-) Verkündigung f.
pronunciation s. Aussprache f.
proof s. Beweis m.; Probe f.; Korrekturbogen m.; in ~ of, zum Beweis von; burden of ~, Beweislast f.; to furnish ~, Beweis liefern; ~ a. probehaltig, bewährt, fest.
proofed a. imprägniert.
proof-sheet s. Korrekturbogen m.
prop s. Stütze f., Pfahl m.; Grubenklotz m.; ~ v.t. stützen; to ~ up, aufstützen.
propaganda s. Propaganda f.
propagate v.t. (v.i. sich) fortpflanzen; ausbreiten.
propel v.t. vorwärtstreiben.
propeller s. (Schiffs-, Luft-)Schraube f.; Propeller m.; ~-blade s. Luftschraubenblatt n.; ~-hub s. Propellernabe f.
propensity s. Neigung f.; Hang m.
proper a., ~ly adv. eigen, eigentümlich; schicklich; eigentlich; tauglich.
property s. Eigentum n.; Eigenschaft f.; (chem.) Eigenschaft f.; Vermögen n.; law of ~, Sachenrecht n.
prophecy s. Prophezeiung f.
prophesy v.t. prophezeien.
prophet s. Prophet m.
prophetic a., ~ally adv. prophetisch.
prophylactic a. vorbeugend; ~ s. Vorbeugungsmittel n.
propitiate v.t. geneigt machen, versöhnen.
propitious a., ~ly adv. gnädig, günstig.

proportion s. Verhältnis n.; Ebenmass n.; Anteil m.; ~ v.t. ins Verhältnis bringen, anpassen; inversely ~ed, umgekehrt proportionell.
proportional a. verhältnismässig, im Verhältnis stehend; ~ representation, Verhältniswahl f.
proportionate a., ~ly adv. entsprechend, im Verhältnis.
proposal s. Vorschlag m.; Antrag m.
propose v.t. vorschlagen; sich vornehmen; ~ v.i. vorhaben; anhalten um.
proposition s. Vorschlag m.; Antrag m.; (math.) Satz m.; (log.) Aussage f.
propound v.t. vorschlagen, vortragen.
proprietary a. eigentümlich; gesetzlich geschützt; ~ article, Markenartikel m.; ~ right, Schutzrecht n.; ~ s. Eigentümer m.pl.
proprietor s. Eigentümer m.; Inhaber m.
proprietress s. Eigentümerin f.
propriety s. Schicklichkeit, Zulässigkeit f.
proscription s. Ächtung f.; Verbot n.
propulsion s. Antrieb m.
prorogation s. Vertagung f.
prorogue v.t. vertagen.
prosaic a. prosaisch.
proscribe v.t. ächten.
prose s. Prosa f.
prosecute v.t. verfolgen; verklagen.
prosecution s. Verfolgung, Anklage f.; (law) Anklagebehörde; ~ witness, Belastungszeuge m.
prosecutor s. Kläger m.; Verfolger m.; public ~, Staatsanwalt m.
proselyte s. Neubekehrte m.
prosody s. Prosodie f.
prospect s. Ansicht, Aussicht f.; ~ v.i. sich umschauen; schürfen.
prospective a. zu gewärtigen, bevorstehend.
prospectus s. Prospekt m.
prosper v.i. gedeihen, gelingen; ~ v.t. begünstigen; segnen.
prosperity s. Wohlstand m., Glück n.
prosperous a., ~ly adv. glücklich, günstig.
prostitute v.t. schänden; ~ s. Dirne f.
prostitution s. Feilbieten n.; gewerbsmässige Unzucht f.; Entehrung f.
prostrate a. hingestreckt, fussfällig; ~ v.t. niederwerfen.
prostration s. Niedergeschlagenheit f.
prosy a. langweilig, weitschweifig.
protect v.t. schützen, bewahren.
protection s. Schutz m.; Aufnahme f. (Wechsel); Zollschutz m.
protectionist s. Schutzzöllner m.
protective a. beschützend; ~ duty, Schutzzoll m.
protector s. Beschützer m.
protectorate s. Protektorat n.
protest v.i. & t. beteuern; sich verwahren, protestieren; zurückweisen; ~ s. Protest

m.; Gegenerklärung *f.*; Verwahrung *f.*; *to enter a* ~ *with,* bei einem Verwahrung einlegen.
Protestant *a.* protestantisch; ~ *s.* Protestant *m.*
protestation *s.* Beteuerung *f.*; Verwahrung *f.*
protocol *s.* Protokoll *n.*
protoplasm *s.* Protoplasma *n.*
prototype *s.* Urbild, Muster *n.*
protract *v.t.* in die Länge ziehen.
protraction *s.* Verzögerung *f.*
protractor *s.* Gradbogen *m.*
protrude *v.i.* vordringen, hervorragen.
protuberance *s.* Auswuchs *m.*; Beule *f.*
protuberant *a.* (her)vorstehend.
proud *a.*, **~ly** *adv.* stolz.
prove *v.t.* beweisen; prüfen; ~ *v.i.* sich bewähren, erweisen.
proven *p.* (*Am.*) bewiesen.
provender *s.* Viehfutter *n.*
proverb *s.* Sprichwort *m.*
proverbial *a.*, **~ly** *adv.* sprichwörtlich.
provide *v.t.* versehen; verschaffen, versorgen; festsetzen, bedingen, verordnen; ~ *v.i.* sich vorsehen; sorgen für; *to* ~ *against,* unmöglich machen; *to be* ~*d for,* versorgt sein.
provided *c.*, ~ *that,* vorausgesetzt dass.
providence *s.* Vorsehung *f.*
provident *a.*, **~ly** *adv.* vorsichtig.
providential *a.*, **~ly** *adv.* von der Vorsehung herrührend.
province *s.* Gebiet *n.*; Provinz *f.*
provincial *a.*, **~ly** *adv.* provinziell.
provision *s.* Vorsorge, Vorkehrung *f.*; Vorrat *m.*; Bestimmung *f.*; ~**s** *pl.* Lebensmittel *n.pl.*, Proviant *m.*; ~ *v.t.* mit Lebensmitteln versorgen.
provisional *a.*, **~ly** *adv.* vorläufig.
proviso *s.* Vorbehalt *m.*
provisory *a.* vorläufig.
provocation *s.* Herausforderung *f.*
provocative *a.* aufreizend.
provoke *v.t.* herausfordern.
provoking *a.*, **~ly** *adv.* empörend.
provost *s.* Vorsteher *m.*; Profoss *m.*
provost marshal *s.* (*mil.*) Chef der Feldpolizei *m.*
prow *s.* Bug, Vorderteil (eines Schiffes) *n.*
prowess *s.* Tapferkeit *f.*
prowl *v.i.* umherstreichen.
proximate *a.*, **~ly** *adv.* nächst, zunächst.
proximity *s.* Nähe, Nachbarschaft *f.*
proxy *s.* Vollmacht *f.*; Stellvertreter, Geschäftsträger *m.*; *by* ~, in Vertretung, per procura.
prude *s.* Spröde *f.*
prudence *s.* Klugheit *f.*
prudent *a.*, **~ly** *adv.* klug, vorsichtig.
prudential *a.* klug, Klugheits...
prudery *s.* Sprödigkeit *f.*

prune *s.* Backpflaume *f.*; ~ *v.t.* (Bäume) beschneiden; putzen.
pruning-hook, pruning-knife, Hippe *f.*, Baummesser *n.*
prurience *s.* Jucken *n.*; Geilheit *f.*
prurient *a.* juckend, kitzlig; lüstern.
Prussian blue *a.* preussischblau.
prussic acid *s.* Blausäure *f.*
pry *v.i.* spähen, ausforschen.
psalm *s.* Psalm *m.*
psalmist *s.* Psalmist *m.*
psalter *s.* Psalmbuch *n.*
pseudonym *s.* Deckname *m.*
pseudonymous *a.* pseudonym.
pshaw! *i.* pah!
psoriasis *s.* Schuppenflechte *f.*
psychic *a.* psychisch.
psychological *a.* psychologisch.
psychology *s.* Psychologie *f.*
pub *s.* Kneipe *f.*
puberty *s.* Entwicklungsalter *n.*, Pubertät *f.*
pubescent *a.* mannbar werdend.
public *a.*, **~ly** *adv.* öffentlich, allgemein; Staats...; ~ *convenience,* öffentliche Bedürfnisanstalt *f.*; ~ *relations pl.* Presse und Propaganda, Werbung *f.*; ~ *utility,* gemeinnütziges Unternehmen *n.*; ~ *s.* Publikum *n.*, Leute *pl.*
publican *s.* Zöllner *m.*; Gastwirt *m.*
publication *s.* Bekanntmachung *f.*; Herausgabe *f.*; Veröffentlichung, Schrift *f.*; ~ *price,* Ladenpreis (eines Buches) *m.*
public-house *s.* Wirtshaus *n.*
publicity *s.* Öffentlichkeit; Reklame *f.*; ~ *agent s.* Werbefachmann *m.*
publish *v.t.* herausgeben, verlegen.
publisher *s.* Verleger, Herausgeber *m.*
pucker *v.t.* runzeln, falten; ~ *v.i.* sich falten; ~ *s.* Bausch *m.*; Falte *f.*
pudding *s.* Pudding *m.*
puddle *s.* Pfütze *f.*; ~ *v.t.* puddeln.
puddling-furnace *s.* Puddelofen *m.*
puerile *a.* kindisch.
puerperal fever *s.* Kindbettfieber *n.*
puff *s.* Windstoss *m.*; Bausch *m.*; Reklame *f.*; ~ *v.i.* blasen, schnauben; aufschwellen; ~ *v.t.* aufblasen; stolz machen; anpreisen.
puffy *a.* bauschig; schwülstig.
pug *s.* Mops *m.*
pugilist *s.* Boxer *m.*
pugnacious *a.* kampfsüchtig.
pugnacity *s.* Kampflust *f.*
puisne *a.* jünger; Unter...
puissant *a.* mächtig.
pule *v.i.* piepen; winseln, plärren.
pull *v.t.* ziehen; reissen; rudern; ~ *through,* durchkommen; ~ *up,* anhalten; ~ *s.* Zug, Ruck, Stoss *m.*
pullet *s.* Hühnchen *n.*
pulley *s.* Rolle *f.*, Kloben *m.*
pull-over *s.* Pullover *m.*
pullulate *v.i.* sprossen, keimen.

pulmonary a. Lungen...
pulp s. Brei m.; Zellstoff m.; Fleisch (vom Obste), Mark n.
pulpit s. Kanzel f.
pulsation s. Pulsschlag n.
pulse s. Puls m.; Hülsenfrucht f.
pulverize v.t. zu Staub machen.
pumice s. Bimsstein m.
pump s. Pumpe f.; ~ room, Trinkhalle f.; ~ v.t. & i. pumpen; (fig.) ausforschen.
pumpkin s. Kürbis m.
pun s. Wortspiel n.; ~ v.i. witzeln.
punch s. Stoss m.; Pfrieme f.; Punze f.; Locheisen n.; Punsch m.; Hanswurst m.; ~ and Judy show, Kasperletheater; ~ v.t. lochen; puffen, schlagen.
punchy a. kurz und dick.
punctilio s. übertriebene Genauigkeit f.
punctilious a. ängstlich genau.
punctual a., ~ly adv. pünktlich.
punctuality s. Pünktlichkeit f.
punctuate v.t. interpunktieren.
punctuation s. Interpunktion f.
puncture s. Stich m.; Punktur f.; Loch n., Reifenpanne f.; Punktion f.; ~ v.t. stechen.
pundit s. Pandit, gelehrte Hindu m.; gelehrte Haupt n.
pungency s. Schärfe f.
pungent a., ~ly adv. stechend; scharf.
punish v.t. strafen, bestrafen.
punishable a. strafbar.
punishment s. Strafe, Bestrafung f.
punitive a. Straf...
punster s. Wortspieler m.
punt s. flache Kahn m., Schauke f.; ~ v.t. staken.
puny a. winzig; schwach.
pup s. junge Hund m.; in ~, trächtig (von Hunden); ~ v.i. junge Hunde werfen, welpen.
pupil s. Pupille f.; Mündel n.; Zögling m.
pupilage s. Minderjährigkeit f.
pupillary a. Pupillen...
puppet s. Puppe f., Marionette f.
puppet-show s. Puppenspiel n.
puppy s. junge Hund m.; Laffe m.
purblind a. halbblind; schwachsichtig.
purchase s. Kauf m.; ~-tax, Verkaufssteuer f.; ~ v.t. kaufen; erwerben; purchasing power, Kaufkraft f.
purchaser s. Käufer m.
pure a., ~ly adv. rein, echt; lauter.
purgation s. Reinigung f.
purgative a. reinigend; ~ s. Abführmittel n.
Purgatory s. Fegefeuer n.
purge v.t. reinigen; läutern; abführen; ~ s. politische Säuberung f.
purify v.t. reinigen, klären.
purist s. Sprachreiniger m.
Puritan s. Puritaner m.
purity s. Reinheit f., Keuschheit f.

purl s. Geriesel n.; Gekräusel n.; ~ v.i. rieseln.
purlieu s. Grenze f.; Umgebung f.
purloin v.t. entwenden.
purple s. Purpur m.; ~ a. purpurn.
purport s. Inhalt m.; ~ v.t. zum Inhalt haben; scheinbar besagen; ~ed, angeblich.
purpose s. Absicht f.; Zweck m.; Inhalt m.; Tendenz f.; on ~, absichtlich; to the ~, zweckdienlich; to no ~, vergebens; novel with a ~, Tendenzroman m.; ~ v.i. sich vornehmen.
purposeless a. zwecklos.
purposely adv. vorsätzlich.
purr v.i. schnurren (von Katzen).
purse s. Geldtäschchen n.; Börse f.; ~ v.t. rümpfen, runzeln.
purser s. Zahlmeister m.
pursuance s. Verfolgung f., Verfolg m.; in ~ of, zufolge, gemäss.
pursuant to pr. zufolge, gemäss.
pursue v.t. verfolgen; fortsetzen; fortfahren; (Beruf) betreiben.
pursuit s. Verfolgung f.; Trachten n.; ~s pl. Geschäfte n.pl.
purulent a. eitrig.
purvey v.t. versorgen, liefern; ~ v.i. Vorrat anschaffen.
purveyor s. Lieferant m.
purview s. Verfügung f.; Bereich m.
pus s. Eiter m.
push v.t. & i. stossen, schieben; beschleunigen; ~ s. Stoss, Schub m.
pushing a. aufdringlich, streberhaft.
pusillanimity s. Kleinmut m.
pusillanimous a., ~ly adv. kleinmütig.
puss, pussy s. Mieze (Katze) f.
pustule s. Bläschen n., Blatter f.
put v.t.ir. setzen, stellen, legen; stecken; to ~ at, schätzen auf; to ~ by, beiseitelegen; to ~ down, aufschreiben; to ~ forward, vorbringen; to ~ in, in den Hafen einlaufen; to ~ into operation, effect, ausführen; to ~ on, anlegen; aufsetzen; anziehen; umbinden; (fig.) annehmen, erheucheln; (Uhr) vorstellen; to ~ on flesh, Fleisch ansetzen; to ~ on weight, zunehmen; to ~ off, weglegen, hinhalten, aufschieben ; to ~ out, auslöschen; ärgern; ausfahren (Flotte); ausstrecken; to ~ up, hinzufügen; anspannen; to ~ together, zusammenstellen; to ~ up, aufstellen, errichten, aufschlagen (Bett), einsetzen (Pflanze), heraufsetzen (Preis), verpacken; unterbringen; absteigen, einkehren; to ~ up for sale, meistbietend verkaufen; to ~ up with, sich abfinden mit; ~-up job, abgekartete Sache f.; to ~ through to, (tel.) Verbindung herstellen mit.
putative a. vermeintlich.
putrefaction s. Fäulnis f.

putrefy *v.i.* faul werden.
putrescent *a.* faulend.
putrid *a.* faul, verfault.
puttee *s.* Wickelgamasche *f.*
putty *s.* Glaserkitt *m.*
puzzle *v.t.* verwirren, in Verlegenheit bringen; ~ *s.* Verwirrung; Rätsel *n.*
pygmy *s.* Zwerg *m.*; Pygmäe *m.*
pyjamas *s.pl.* Schlafanzug *m.*
pyramid *s.* Pyramide *f.*
pyre *s.* Scheiterhaufen *m.*
pyrotechnics *s.pl.* Feuerwerkskunst *f.*
pyx *s.* Monstranz *f.*

Q

quack *v.i.* quaken; marktschreierisch anpreisen; ~ *s.* Quacksalber *m.*; Marktschreier *m.*
quackery *s.* Quacksalberei *f.*
quadrangle *s.* Viereck *n.*; Hof *m.*
quadrille *s.* Quadrille *f.*; Kontretanz *m.*
quadripartite *a.* Viermächte...
quadroon *s.* Viertelneger *m.*
quadruped *a.* vierfüssig; ~ *s.* Vierfüsser *m.*
quadruple *a.*, ~**ply** *adv.* vierfach; ~ *s.* Vierfache *n.*; ~ *v.t.* vervierfachen.
quadruplets *pl.* Vierlinge *pl.*
quaff *v.i.* & *t.* zechen.
quagmire *s.* Sumpf, Moorboden *m.*
quail *s.* Wachtel *f.*; ~ *v.i.* verzagen.
quaint *a.*, ~**ly** *adv.* seltsam; niedlich.
quake *v.i.* zittern, beben.
Quaker *s.* Quäker *m.*
qualification *s.* Eigenschaft *f.*; Befähigung *f.*; Beschränkung *f.*
qualified *a.* geeignet; berechtigt; bestimmt; bedingt, eingeschränkt.
qualify *v.t.* befähigen; einschränken; bestimmen; ~ *v.i.* seine Befähigung nachweisen; *to* ~ *for,* Befähigung erwerben für; ~*ing date,* Stichtag *m.*; ~*ing period,* Probezeit *f.*
qualitative *a.* qualitativ.
quality *s.* Eigenschaft, Beschaffenheit *f.*; Qualität *f.*; (hohe) Stand, Rang *m.*; ~ *papers,* Qualitätspapiere *pl.*
qualm *s.* Gewissenszweifel *m.*
quandary *s.* Ungewissheit *f.*; Verlegenheit *f.*
quantitative *a.* der Menge nach.
quantity *s.* Menge, Anzahl *f.*; (*math.*) Grösse *f.*; Quantität *f.*
quantum *s.* Menge, Grösse *f.*; Betrag *m.*
quarantine *s.* Liegezeit, Quarantäne *f.*
quarrel *s.* Zank *m.*; Streit *m.*; ~ *v.i.* sich zanken, streiten.
quarrelsome *a.*, ~*ly adv.* zänkisch.
quarry *s.* Steinbruch *m.*; verfolgte Wild *n.*; ~ *v.t.* Steine brechen.

quart *s.* Viertelmass *n.* (1,136 l.).
quartan *s.* viertägige Fieber *n.*
quarter *s.* Viertel *n.*; Stadtviertel *n.*; Vierteljahr *n.*; Wohnung *f.*; Quartier *n.*; Pardon *m.*; Gnade *f.*; Malter *n.* (2,908 hl.); ~**s** *pl.* (*mil.*) Unterkunft *f.*; ~ *v.t.* vierteilen; beherbergen; einquartieren.
quarter-day *s.* Quartalstag *m.*
quarter-deck *s.* Achterdeck, Halbdeck *n.*
quarterly *a. & adv.* vierteljährlich; ~ *s.* Vierteljahrsschrift *f.*
quarter-master *s.* Quartiermeister *m.*
quartet(te) *s.* Quartett *n.*
quarto *s.* Quartformat *n.*
quartz *s.* Quarz *m.*
quash *v.t.* unterdrücken; vernichten; (Urteil) aufheben.
quasi *a. & adv.* gewissermassen, Halb..., scheinbar.
quaver *v.i.* zittern; trillern; ~ *s.* Triller *m.*; Achtelnote *f.*
quay *s.* Kai *m.*, Schiffslände *f.*
quean *s.* Frauenzimmer *n.*
queasy *a.* übel, ekel; überempfindlich.
queen *s.* Königin *f.*
queer *a.*, ~*ly adv.* wunderlich, seltsam; verdächtig; unwohl, schwindlig.
quell *v.t.* dämpfen; unterdrücken.
quench *v.t.* löschen; (den Durst) stillen.
querulous *a.*, ~*ly adv.* klagsüchtig.
query *s.* Frage *f.*; ~ *v.t.* fragen, bezweifeln.
quest *s.* Suchen *n.*; Untersuchung *f.*; *in* ~ *of,* auf der Suche.
question *s.* Frage *f.*; Streitfrage *f.*; Untersuchung *f.*; Zweifel *m.*; *in* ~, fraglich, vorliegend; ~*!,* zur Sache!; ~ *v.i. & t.* fragen, befragen; verhören, vernehmen; bezweifeln.
questionable *a.* zweifelhaft, fraglich; fragwürdig.
question-mark *s.* Fragezeichen *n.*
questionnaire *s.* Fragebogen *m.*
queue *s.* Zopf *m.*; Schlange (von Menschen) *to* ~ *up v.i.* Schlangestehen.
quibble *s.* Wortspiel *n.*; Zweideutigkeit *f.*; Ausflucht *f.*; ~ *v.i.* (spitzfindig) witzeln; ausweichen.
quick *a. & adv.*, ~*ly adv.* schnell; lebendig; lebhaft; hurtig; scharfsinnig; ~**-acting** *a.* schnellwirkend; ~ *march!,* vorwärts marsch!; ~ *step,* Geschwindschritt *m.*
quicken *v.t.* beleben, aufeuern, beschleunigen; ~ *v.i.* lebendig werden.
quicklime *s.* ungelöschte Kalk *m.*
quicksand *s.* Flugsand *m.*
quickset hedge *s.* lebendige Hecke *f.*
quicksilver *s.* Quecksilber *n.*
quid *s.* Priemchen *n.*; Pfund (*n.*) Sterling.
quid-pro-quo *s.* Gegenleistung *f.*
quiescence *s.* Ruhe *f.*
quiescent *a.* ruhend.

quiet *a.*, ~ly *adv.* ruhig, gelassen; ~ *s.*
Ruhe *f.*; ~ *v.t.* beruhigen.
quietness, quietude *s.* Ruhe *f.*
quill *s.* Federkiel *m.*; Feder *f.*; Weber-
spule *f.*; ~ *v.t.* spulen; fälteln.
quill-driver *s.* Federfuchser *m.*
quilt *s.* Steppdecke *f.*; ~ *v.t.* steppen.
quince *s.* Quitte *f.*
quinine *s.* Chinin *n.*
quinquennial *a.* fünfjährig.
quinsy *s.* Bräune (Halskrankheit) *f.*
quint *s.* Quinte *f.*
quintessence *s.* Quintessenz *f.*
quintet(te) *s.* Quintett *n.*
quintuple *a.* fünffach.
quintuplets *s.pl.* Fünflinge *pl.*
quip *s.* Stichelei *f.*
quire *s.* Buch Papier *n.*
quirk *s.* Stichelei *f.*; Kniff *m.*; Schnörkel
m.
quit *a.* quitt, los, frei; ~ *v.t.* verlassen;
lossprechen; fahren lassen; *notice to* ~,
Kündigung *f.*
quite *adv.* völlig, gänzlich.
quits *adv.* quitt, abgemacht.
quiver *s.* Köcher *m.*; ~ *v.i.* zittern.
Quixotic *a.* donquichottisch.
quiz *v.t.* necken, ausfragen; ~ *s.* Examen.
quoin *s.* Ecke (eines Hauses) *f.*; Keil (*m.*)
des Setzers.
quondam *adv.* ehemalig.
quorum *s.* beschlussfähige Anzahl *f.*
quota *s.* Anteil *m.*, Quote *f.*; Zuteilung *f.*,
Kontingent *n.*
quotation *s.* Anführung *f.*; Zitat *n.*;
Preisangabe *f.*; Notierung *f.*; ~ **marks**
pl. Anführungszeichen *n.*
quote *v.t.* (Stellen) anführen; (einen
Preis) notieren, berechnen.
quotient *s.* Quotient, Teilzähler *m.*

R

rabbet *s.* Fuge *f.*; Falz *m.*; Nuthobel *m.*;
~ *v.t.* einfugen; abhobeln.
rabbi *s.* Rabbiner *m.*
rabbit *s.* Kaninchen *n.*; **Welsh** ~ *s.*
geröstete Käse (*m.*) auf Brot.
rabble *s.* Pöbel, Janhagel *m.*
rabid *a.* wütend, rasend.
rabies *s.* Tollwut *f.*
race *s.* Rasse *f.*, Geschlecht *n.*; Wettlauf
m.; ~s *pl.* Pferde(wett)-rennen *n.*; ~
v.i. wettrennen.
race-course *s.* Rennbahn *f.*
race-meeting *s.* Rennen *n.*
racial *a.*, ~ly *adv.* rassisch, völkisch;
Rassen...; ~ **German**, Volksdeutsche
m.
rack *s.* Folterbank *f.*; Raufe *f.*; *luggage* ~,
Gepäcknetz *n.*; Gestell *n.*; Zahnstange

f.; ~ *and ruin*, gänzlich zu Grunde; ~
v.t. strecken, foltern; *to* ~ *one's brains*,
sich den Kopf zerbrechen.
racket *s.* Schläger *m.* (Sport); Lärm *m.*;
Erpressung, Schiebung *f.*; **racketeer** *s.*
Schieber *m.*
rack-rent *s.* wucherische Miete *f.*
racy *a.* rassig; kräftig; geistreich.
radar *s.* (*mil.*) Funkmessgerät *n.*
radial *a.*, ~ly *adv.* strahlenförmig; ~ *drill*,
(*mech.*) Radialbohrmaschine *f.*
radiance *s.* Glanz *m.*
radiant *a.* strahlend.
radiate *v.t. & i.* ausstrahlen, strahlen.
radiation *s.* Ausstrahlung *f.*
radiator *s.* Heizkörper *m.*; (*mot.*) Kühler
m.
radical *a.*, ~ly *adv.* Grund...; eingewurzelt; radikal; ~ *s.* Wurzel *f.*, Grund-
stoff *m.*; Radikale *m.*
radio *s.* Radio *n.*, Funk *m.*; ~ **direction-
finding** *s.* (*mil.*) Funkpeilung *f.*; ~
intelligence *s.* Funkaufklärung *f.*; ~
operator *s.* Funker, Bordfunker *m.*;
~-**set** *s.* Radioapparat *m.*; ~-**station** *s.*
Rundfunksender *m.*; ~-**telegram** *s.*
Funktelegramm *n.*
radioactive *a.* radioaktiv.
radiograph *s.* Röntgenbild *n.*
radiotherapeutics *pl.* Radiotherapie *f.*
radish *s.* Radieschen *n.*
radium *s.* Radium *n.*
radius -*s.* Halbmesser *m.*; Strahl *m.*;
Umkreis *m.*
raffle *s.* Lotterie *f.*; ~ *v.i.* auslosen.
raft *s.* Floss *n.*
rafter *s.* Dachsparren *m.*
rag *s.* Lumpen *m.*; Budenulk *m.*; ~-**time**
s. (*mus.*) Negerrhythmus *m.*
ragamuffin *s.* Lumpenkerl *m.*
rage *s.* Wut, Raserei *f.*; Entzückung *f.*;
~ *v.i.* rasen.
ragged *a.* zerlumpt; rauh.
rag-picker *s.* Lumpensammler *m.*
ragout *s.* Ragout *n.*
raid *s.* Überfall *m.*; Beutezug *m.*
raider *s.* Plünderer *m.*
rail *s.* Riegel *m.*; Querholz *n.*; Geländer
n.; Schiene *f.*; (*nav.*) Reling *f.*; *by* ~, mit
der Eisenbahn; ~ *v.t.* mit einem Gitter
versehen; ~ *v.i.* spotten, schmähen.
railhead *s.* Ausladebahnhof *m.*, Eisen-
bahnendpunkt *m.*
railing *s.* Geländer *n.*
raillery *s.* Spötterei *f.*
railway, railroad *s.* Eisenbahn *f.*; ~-**network** *s.* Eisenbahnnetz *n.*; ~-**shop** *s.*
Eisenbahnwerkstatt *f.*
railway-guide *s.* Kursbuch *n.*
raiment *s.* Kleidung *f.*
rain *s.* Regen *m.*; ~ *v.i.imp.* regnen; ~-
coat *s.* Regenmantel *m.*; ~**fall** *s.*
Niederschlagsmenge *f.*; ~-**soaked** *a.*

vom Regen durchnässt; ~storm s.
Regenguss m.; ~wear s. Regen-
kleidung f.
rainbow s. Regenbogen m.
rain-gauge s. Regenmesser m.
rainy a. regnerisch, Regen...; for a ~ day,
für eine Notzeit.
raise v.t. aufheben, erheben; errichten;
erhöhen; erregen, veranlassen; aufziehen; werben; auftreiben (Geld).
raisin s. Rosine f.
rake s. Rechen m.; Wüstling m.; ~ v.t.
harken; zusammenschüren, scharren;
durchstöbern; (nav.) überhangen, der
Länge nach bestreichen.
rakish a., ~ly adv. liederlich.
rally v.t. wider sammeln; verspotten; ~
v.i. sich wieder sammeln; sich erholen;
~ s. Sammlung f.; Tagung, Treffen,
Versammlung f.; (Autosport) Sternfahrt f.
ram s. Widder m.; Ramme f.; ~ v.t. ein-
rammen.
ramble v.i. umherschweifen; abschweifen;
~ s. Ausflug m.
rambling a. zusammenhanglos; (von Ge-
bäuden) unregelmässig.
ramification s. Verzweigung f.
ramify v.t. (v.i. sich) verzweigen.
rammer s. Ramme f.; Ladestock m.
ramp v.i. sich drohend aufrichten (vom
Löwen); toben; ~ s. Rampe f.; Schwindelei f.
rampant a. dreist; überhandnehmend;
wuchernd; steigend (Wappentier).
rampart s. Wall m.
ramshackle a. wack[e]lig, baufällig.
ranch s. Viehwirtschaft f.
rancid a. ranzig.
rancidity s. Ranzigkeit f.
rancorous a., ~ly adv. voll Groll.
rancour s. Groll m.; Erbitterung f.
random a. zufällig, Zufalls...; at ~, aufs
Geradewohl, ins Blaue.
range s. Reihe f.; Ordnung f.; Küchen-
herd m.; Umfang m.; Bereich m.; Spielraum m.; Schussweite f.; ~ of prices,
Preislage f.; to get the ~, sich einschiessen (Artillerie); ~ v.i. sich reihen;
herumstreifen; sich erstrecken; ~ v.t.
ordnen; schweifen über.
rangefinder s. (phot.) Entfernungsmesser
m.
rank s. Reihe f.; Linie f.; Glied n.; Rang
m.; to serve in the ~s, (mil.) als gemeiner
Soldat dienen; ~ v.t. & i. reihen, sich
reihen; zugehören; it ~s third, es
steht an dritter Stelle; ~ a., ~ly adv.
üppig, übermässig; ranzig; arg; Erz...,
rein.
rankle v.i. sich entzünden; schmerzen;
(fig.) nagen.
ransack v.t. plündern; durchstöbern.

ransom s. Lösegeld n.; ~ v.t. loskaufen.
rant s. Schwulst m.; ~ v.i. schwülstig
reden; eifern; wüten.
ranter s. Grossprecher m.
rap v.t. & i. schlagen, klopfen; ~ s. Schlag
m.; Klopfen n.; Nasenstüber m.
rapacious a., ~ly adv. raubgierig.
rapacity s. Raubgier f.
rape s. Raub m.; Notzucht f.; Rübsamen
m.; ~ v.i. rauben, notzüchtigen.
rape-seed s. Rübsamen m.
rapid a., ~ly adv. schnell, reissend; ~s
s.pl. Stromschnellen f.pl.
rapidity s. Schnelligkeit f.
rapier s. Stossdegen m.
rapine s. Raub m.
rapt a. hingerissen, entzückt.
rapture s. Entzückung f.
rapturous a. hinreissend; leidenschaftlich.
rare a., ~ly adv. selten; kostbar; dünn;
(Am.) nicht durchgebraten.
rarebit see (Welsh) rabbit.
raree-show s. Guckkasten m.
rarefy v.t. verdünnen.
rareness, rarity s. Seltenheit f.; Dünnheit
f.
rascal s. Schurke m.
rascality s. Schurkerei f.
rash a., ~ly adv. übereilt, unbesonnen;
~ s. Hautausschlag m.
rasher s. Schnitte (Speck) f.
rasp v.t. raspeln; wehtun; ~ s. Raspel f.
raspberry s. Himbeere f.
rat s. Ratte f.; Überläufer m.
rat(e)able a., steuerpflichtig.
ratch, ratchet s. Sperrstange f.; Sperrad n.
rate s. Preis m.; Taxe f.; Anteil m., Satz
m.; Rate (statistisch) f.; bestimmte
Mass n.; Verhältnis n.; Grad, Rang m.;
Klasse f.; (Gemeinde-)Steuer f.; at any
~, auf jeden Fall; ~ v.t. schätzen, einschätzen; tadeln; ~ v.t. rangieren,
einen bestimmten Wert haben; to ~
highly, einen hohen Wert haben.
rate-payer s. Steuerzahler m.
rather adv. vielmehr, lieber; ziemlich; I
had ~, ich wollte lieber.
ratification s. Bestätigung f.; Ratifizierung
f.
ratify v.t. bestätigen.
rating s. (bes. nav.) Dienstklasse f.,
Dienstgrad m.; naval ~s pl. Marine-
angehörige unter Offiziersrang.
ratio s. Verhältnis n.
ration s. Ration f.; ~-period s. Zuteilungsperiode f.; ~-book s. Lebensmittel-
karten pl.; to come off the ~, nicht mehr
rationiert sein; to go on ~s, rationiert
werden; ~ v.t. rationieren; ~ing,
Rationierung f.
rational a., ~ly adv. vernünftig.
rationalization s. Rationalisierung f.
ratsbane s. Rattengift n.

rattle *s.* Geklapper *n.*; Knarre *f.*; Geschnatter *n.*; Röcheln *n.*; ~ *v.t. & i.* rasseln; knarren; plappern.
rattle-snake *s.* Klapperschlange *f.*
rattling *a.* rasselnd; grossartig; rüstig.
raucous *a.* heiser, rauh.
ravage *v.t.* verwüsten, verheeren; ~ *s.* Verwüstung *f.*
rave *v.i.* rasen, wüten; schwärmen.
ravel *v.t.* verwickeln; auflösen, auftrennen; (*v.i. sich*) fasern.
raven *s.* Rabe *m.*
ravenous *a.*, ~ly *adv.* gefrässig; gierig.
ravine *s.* Schlucht *f.*
raving *a.*, ~ly *adv.* rasend; faselnd.
ravish *v.t.* rauben, entführen; notzüchtigen; hinreissen, entzücken.
ravishment *s.* Raub *m.*; Entführung *f.*; Entzückung *f.*
raw *a.*, ~ly *adv.* roh; unreif; rauh; neu, unerfahren; wund; unverdünnt (von Spirituosen).
ray *s.* Strahl *m.*; ~ *v.t.* strahlen.
rayon *s.* Kunstseide *f.*
raze *v.t.* schleifen, zerstören; radieren.
razor *s.* Rasiermesser *n.*
razor-strop *s.* Streichriemen *m.*
razzia *s.* Razzia *f.*
re *pr.* betreffend.
reach *v.t.* reichen, langen; erreichen; ~ *v.i.* sich erstrecken; streben; ~ *s.* Reichweite *f.*; Strecke *f.*; Flussabschnitt, Stromabschnitt *m.*; Raum, Bereich *m.*; Hörweite, Schussweite *f.*; Fassungskraft *f.*
react *v.i.* rückwirken, gegenwirken, (*chem.*) reagieren.
reaction *s.* Rückwirkung *f.*; Reaktion *f.*; (*elek.*) Rückkopplung *s.*
reactionary *a.* reaktionär; ~ *s.* Reaktionär *m.*
read *v.t. & i.ir.* lesen, vorlesen; (fürs Examen) studieren; sich lesen, lauten, klingen; anzeigen (von Messapparaten).
readable *a.* lesbar.
reader *s.* Leser *m.*; Vorleser *m.*; Korrektor *m.*; Dozent *m.*
readiness *s.* Bereitwilligkeit *f.*
reading *s.* Lektüre *f.*; Belesenheit *f.*; Lesart *f.*; Stand *m.*, Ablesung *f.* (eines Messapparates).
reading-room *s.* Lesezimmer *n.*
readjust *v.t.* wieder in Ordnung bringen.
readmission *s.* Wiederzulassung *f.*
readmit *v.t.* wieder zulassen.
ready *a.*, ~ily *adv.* bereit; fertig; bar.
ready-made *a.* gebrauchsfertig; **ready-to-serve** *a.* servierfertig; **ready-to-wear** *a.* tragfertig (Anzug).
reagent *s.* Reagens *n.*
real *a.*, ~ly *adv.* echt (auch Perle, Diamant, etc.); in der Tat, wesentlich, wirklich.

real estate *s.* Grundbesitz ; ~ **register** *s.* (*Am.*) Grundbuch, *n.*
realization *s.* Verwirklichung *f.*; Verwertung *f.*
realize *v.t.* verwirklichen; erzielen; sich vorstellen; zu Geld machen.
realism *s.* Realismus *m.*
reality *s.* Wirklichkeit, Wesenheit *f.*
really *adv.* wirklich, in der Tat.
realm *s.* Königreich, Reich *n.*
realty *s.* Grundbesitz *m.*
ream *s.* Ries (Papier) *n.*; ~ *v.t.* (*mech.*) ausweiten, ausbohren.
reamer *s.* (*mech.*) Ausbohrwerkzeug *n.*, Aufräumer *m.*
reanimate *v.t.* wieder beleben.
reap *v.t. & i.* Korn schneiden; einernten.
reaper *s.* Schnitter *m.*; Mähmaschine *f.*
reappear *v.i.* wieder erscheinen.
reappearance *s.* Wiedererscheinen *n.*
rear *s.* Nachhut *f.*; Hintergrund *m.*; Hinter... (*mil.*) rückwärtig; ~ **area** *s.* rückwärtiges Heeresgebiet *n.*; ~ **cover** *s.* Rückendeckung *f.*; ~ **lamp**, ~ **light** *s.* (*mot. und cycling*) Schlusslicht, Katzenauge *n.*; ~ **wheel** *s.* Hinterrad *n.*; ~ *v.t.* aufrichten; erziehen, aufziehen; ~ *v.i.* sich bäumen.
rear-admiral *s.* Konteradmiral *m.*
rear-guard *s.* Nachhut *f.*
rearm *v.i.* aufrüsten.
rearmament *s.* Aufrüstung *f.*
reason *s.* Vernunft *f.*; Ursache *f.*; Grund *m.*; *it stands to* ~, es ist klar; ~ *v.i.* schliessen; nachdenken; streiten; ~ *v.t.* durchdenken; erörtern.
reasonable *a.*, ~ly *adv.* vernünftig; billig; ziemlich; ~ *prices*, mässige Preise *pl.*
reasoning *s.* Urteilskraft, Beweisführung *f.*; *line of* ~, Gedankengang *m.*
reassemble *v.t.* (*v.i. sich*) wieder versammeln.
reassert *v.t.* wieder behaupten.
reassure *v.t.* beruhigen.
rebate *s.* Rabatt *m.*, Abzug *m.*
rebel *v.i.* sich empören; ~ *s.* Rebell, Empörer *m.*
rebellion *s.* Empörung *f.*
rebellious *a.*, ~ly *adv.* aufrührerisch.
rebirth *s.* Wiedergeburt *f.*
rebound *v.i.* zurückprallen.
rebuff *s.* Rückstoss *m.*; Abweisung *f.*; ~ *v.t.* zurückstossen; abweisen.
rebuild *v.t.r. & st.* wieder aufbauen.
rebuke *v.t.* tadeln; auszanken; ~ *s.* Tadel Verweis *m.*
rebut *v.t.* widerlegen, zurückweisen.
rebuttal *s.* Widerlegung *f.*, Gegenbeweis *m.*
recalcitrant *a.* widerstrebend, störrig.
recall *s.* Zurückberufung *f.*; Widerruf *m.*; ~ *v.t.* zurückrufen; sich erinnern; kündigen.

recant *v.t. & i.* widerrufen.

recantation *s.* Widerruf *m.*

recapitulate *v.t.* kurz wiederholen.

recapture *s.* Wieder(gefangen)nahme *f.*; ~ *v.t.* wieder(gefangen)nehmen.

recast *v.t.* umschmelzen; umarbeiten.

recede *v.i.* zurückweichen, abstehen.

receipt *s.* Empfang *m.*; Entgegennahme *f.*; Einnahme *f.*; Quittung *f.*; Aufnahme *f.*; Rezept *n.*; ~-stamp *s.* Quittungsmarke *f.*, Quittungsstempel *m.*; ~ *v.t.* quittieren.

receive *v.t.* empfangen, annehmen.

receiver *s.* Empfänger *m.* (auch radio); (*tel.*) Hörer *m.*; Einnehmer *m.*; ~ *of stolen goods*, Hehler *m.*; *official* ~, Konkursverwalter *m.*

receiving-office *s.* Annahmestelle *f.*

recent *a.* neu; frisch; ~ly *adv.* neulich.

receptacle *s.* Behälter *m.*

reception *s.* Aufnahme *f.*; Empfang *m.*

receptionist *s.* Empfangsdame *f.*

receptive *a.* empfänglich.

recess *s.* Zurückgehen *n.*; Falte *f.*; Nische *f.*; Einbuchtung *f.*; Versteck *m.*; Ferien *pl.*; zeitweilige Vertagung (einer Sitzung) *f.*

recession *s.* Zurückweichen, Abstehen *n.*

recipe *s.* Rezept *n.*

recipient *s.* Empfänger *m.*

reciprocal *a.*, ~ly *adv.* wechselseitig.

reciprocate *v.t. & i.* abwechseln; erwidern.

reciprocity *s.* Gegenseitigkeit *f.*

recital, recitation *s.* Vortrag *m.*; Musikvortrag *m.*; Hersagen *n.*; Erzählung *f.*

recite *v.t.* vortragen; hersagen.

reck *v.t. & i.* sich kümmern.

reckless *a.* unbekümmert, tollkühn; rücksichtslos.

reckon *v.t. & i.* rechnen, schätzen, achten; meinen; *to* ~ *up*, zusammenrechnen; *to* ~ *over again*, nachrechnen.

reckoning, Rechnen *n.*; Rechnung *f.*

reclaim *v.t.* zurückfordern; bekehren; urbar machen.

reclamation *s.* Zurückforderung *f.*

recline *v.t.* (*v.i.* sich) lehnen.

recluse *a.*, ~ly *adv.* verschlossen; zurückgezogen; ~ *s.* Einsiedler *m.*

recognize *v.t.* wiedererkennen; anerkennen.

recognizance *s.* schriftliche Verpflichtung *f.* (vor Gericht).

recognition *s.* Wiedererkennung, Anerkennung *f.*

recoil *v.i.* zurückprallen; zurückschrecken; ~ *s.* Rückstoss *m.*

recollect *v.t.* wieder sammeln; ~ sich besinnen, sich erinnern.

recollection *s.* Erinnerung *f.*; Fassung *f.*

recommend *v.t.* empfehlen.

recommendation *s.* Empfehlung *f.*

recompense *v.t.* vergelten; entschädigen; belohnen; ~ *s.* Vergeltung *f.*; Belohnung *f.*; Ersatz *m.*

reconcilable *a.* versöhnbar; vereinbar.

reconcile *v.t.* versöhnen; vereinigen.

reconciliation *s.* Versöhnung *f.*

recondite *a.* verborgen; dunkel.

recondition *v.t.* neu instandsetzen, überholen.

reconnaissance *s.* (*mil.*) Aufklärung *f.*; *close* ~, Nahaufklärung *f.*; *long-range* ~, Fernaufklärung *f.*

reconnoitre *v.t.* auskundschaften.

reconquer *v.t.* wiedererobern.

reconsider *v.t.* von neuem erwägen.

reconstruct *v.t.* wieder aufbauen.

record *v.t.* eintragen; ~ *s.* Verzeichnis *n.*; Urkunde *f.*; Protokoll *n.*; Bericht *m.*; Ruf *m.*; Höchstleistung *f.*; (Grammophon-) Platte *f.*; *good* ~, gute Vorleben *n.*; *bad* ~, schlechte Vorleben *n.*; *no criminal* ~, nicht vorbestraft; *the worst on* ~, der nachweisbar schlechteste; *to place on* ~, zu Protokoll geben; *electric* ~-*player*, elektrische Plattenspieler *m.*; ~s *pl.* Akten *pl.*; Archiv *n.*; Chronik *f.*

recorder *s.* (Stadt-)Richter *m.*; Registrator *m.*; Registrierapparat *m.*

recount *v.t.* erzählen.

recoup *v.t.* entschädigen; wieder einbringen.

recourse *s.* Zuflucht *f.*; (*law*) Regress, Rekurs *m.*; *to have* ~ *to*, sich an einen halten; *to have* ~, Regress nehmen; *person liable to* ~, Regresspflichtige *m.*

recover *v.t.* wiederbekommen; wieder gut machen; eintreiben; ~ *v.i.* sich erholen.

recoverable *a.* wiederlangbar; *debts* ~ *by law*, klagbare Schulden.

recovery *s.* Wiedererlangung, Wiederherstellung *f.*; Genesung *f.*

recreant *a.* feigherzig; treulos, ruchlos; ~ *s.* Bösewicht *m.*; Abtrünnige *m.*

recreate *v.t.* (*v.i.* sich) erquicken.

recreation *s.* Erholung *f.*; Erquickung *f.*

recreational *a.* Unterhaltungs..., Erholungs...

recreative *a.* erquickend, ergötzlich; Unterhaltungs...

recrimination *s.* Gegenbeschuldigung *f.*

recrudescence *s.* Wiederaufbrechen (einer Wunde) *n.*

recruit *v.t. & i.* sich erholen; erneuern; ersetzen; rekrutieren; ~ *s.* Rekrut *m.*; Neuling *m.*

rectangle *s.* Rechteck *n.*

rectangular *a.* rechtwinklig, rechteckig.

rectification *s.* Berichtigung *f.*

rectifier *s.* Gleichrichter *m.* (*elek. und radio*).

rectify *v.t.* berichtigen, verbessern.

rectilinear *a.* geradlinig.

rectitude *s.* Biederkeit, Redlichkeit *f.*

rector s. Rektor m.; Pfarrer m.
rectory s. Pfarre f.; Pfarrhaus n.
rectum s. Mastdarm m.
recumbent a. zurückgelehnt, liegend.
recuperate ..t. wiederherstellen; ~ v.i. sich erholen.
recur v.i. zurückkommen; sich wiederholen.
recurrence s. Wiederkehr f.
recurrent a. wiederkehrend.
red a. rot; ~ beet s. rote Rübe f.; ~ currant s. (rote) Johannisbeere f.; ~ herring s. Bückling; (fig.) Ablenkungsversuch m.; ~ tape, Bürokratie f.; bürokratisch; ~ s. Rot n.; ~ Riding-hood, Rotkäppchen n.
redaction s. Abfassung, Neubearbeitung f.
redbreast s. Rotkehlchen n.
Red Cross s. Rote Kreuz n.
redden v.t. röten; ~ v.i. erröten.
reddish a. rötlich.
redecorate v.t. neu dekorieren.
redeem v.t. loskaufen, auslösen, erlösen; büssen; entschädigen; einlösen; amortisieren, tilgen.
redeemable a. ablöslich, austilgbar.
redeemer s. Erlöser m.; Heiland m.
redemption s. Loskaufung f.; Erlösung f.; Tilgung f.; Einlösung f.; Ablösung f.
redesignate v.t. neu bezeichnen, neu benennen.
red-handed a. auf frischer Tat.
red-hot a. rotglühend.
redintegrate v.t. wiederherstellen.
redirect v.t. (Brief) umadressieren.
red-lead s. Mennig m.
red-letter, ~ day, s. Glückstag m.
redness s. Röte f.
redolent a. starkriechend; (fig.) einen Anstrich habend.
redouble v.t. (v.i. sich) verdoppeln.
redoubt s. Schanze f.
redoubtable a. furchtbar.
redound v.i. gereichen, beitragen.
redress v.t. bessern; abhelfen; ~ s. Abhülfe f.; Verbesserung f.; Ersatz m.; right of ~, Ersatzanspruch m.
reduce v.t. herunterbringen; verkleinern; herabsetzen; bezwingen; verwandeln; (mil.) to ~ to the ranks, zum gemeinen Soldaten degradieren; at ~d rates, zu ermässigten Preisen; (mech.) ~d gear, Untersetzungsgetriebe n.
reducible a. zurückführbar.
reduction s. Zurückführung f.; Herabsetzung f.; Bezwingung f.; Verminderung f.; Rabatt m.; (phot.) Verkleinerung f.; ~ of staff, Personalabbau m.
redundant a., ~ly adv. überflüssig.
reduplicate v.t. verdoppeln.
re-echo v.t. & i. widerhallen.
reed s. Schilfrohr n.; Flöte f.
reef s. Riff n.; Reff n.; ~ v.t. reffen.

reek s. Rauch, Dampf m.; ~ v.i. rauchen`
reel s. Haspel m. or f.; (Garn-) Rolle f.; (Art) Tanz m.; ~ v.t. haspeln; (Film) kurbeln; ~ v.i. taumeln.
re-election s. Wiedererwählung f.
re-eligible a. wieder wählbar.
re-embark v.t. & i. (sich) wieder einschiffen; to ~ upon, erneut beginnen.
re-enact v.t. wieder in Kraft setzen.
re-engage v.t. wieder beginnen; wieder anstellen; ~ v.i. wieder Dienste nehmen.
re-enter v.t. wieder eintreten.
re-entry permit s. Wiedereinreiseerlaubnis f.
re-establish v.t. wiederherstellen.
re-examine v.t. nachprüfen.
re-export v.t. wieder ausführen.
refectory s. Speisezimmer (im Kloster) n.
refer v.t. verweisen; beziehen; ~ v.i. sich beziehen, sich berufen.
referee s. Schiedsrichter m.
reference s. Verweisung, Bezugnahme, Beziehung f.; Auskunftsgeber m.; ~ (-number) s. Aktenzeichen n., Aktennummer f., Geschäftsnummer f., Verweisungszeichen n.; ~s pl. Referenzen, Empfehlungen f.pl.; Zeichenerklärung f.; ~-date s. Stichtag m.; ~-book s. Nachschlagewerk n.; ~-library s. Handbücherei, Nachschlagebibliothek f.
referendum (on) s. Volksentscheid (über) m.
refill v.t. neu füllen; ~ s. Ersatzteil (für den Bleistifthalter); ~-battery s. Ersatzbatterie f.
refine v.t. raffinieren, reinigen; verfeinern; ~ v.i. sich verfeinern; klügeln.
refinement s. Verfeinerung f.
refinery s. Zuckerraffinerie f.
refit v.t. wiederherstellen; ausbessern.
reflect v.t. zurückwerfen; ~ v.i. zurückfallen; zurückprallen; betrachten, nachdenken; tadeln.
reflection s. Zurückstrahlung f.; Widerschein m.; Betrachtung, Überlegung f.; Tadel m.
reflective a. nachdenkend.
reflector s. Reflektor m.
reflex s. Widerschein m.; Reflex m.
reflexive a. zurückwirkend; (gram.) reflexiv.
refloat v.t. wieder flott machen.
reflux s. Rückfluss m.
reform v.t. umändern; verbessern; reformieren; ~ v.i. sich bessern; ~ s. Verbesserung, Reform f.
reformation s. Umänderung f.; Besserung f.; Reformation f.
reformatory s. Besserungsanstalt f.
reformer s. Verbesserer, Reformator m.
refract v.t. (Strahlen) brechen.

refraction s. Strahlenbrechung f.

refractory a., ~ily adv. widerspenstig.

refrain v.t. zügeln; ~ v.i. sich enthalten; ~ s. Kehrreim m.

refresh v.t. erfrischen; aufrischen.

refresher s. Zuschlagsgebühr (f.) des Anwalts; ~ course s. Wiederholungskurs m.

refreshment s. Erfrischung f.; ~-room, Restauration ´.; Erfrischungsraum m.

refrigerate v.t. kühlen.

refrigerator s. Eisschrank m.

refuel v.t. & i. nachtanken; wieder mit Brennstoff füllen.

refuge s. Zuflucht f.; Rettungsinsel f. (auf der Strasse).

refugee s. Flüchtling m.

refulgence s. Glanz m.

refulgent a. glänzend.

refund v.t. zurückzahlen; ~ s. Rückerstattung f.

refusal s. Verweigerung f.; Vorkaufsrecht n.

refuse v.t. verweigern, abschlagen; verwerfen; ~ a. verworfen, schlecht; ~ s. Abfall m., Ausschuss m., (fig.) Auswurf m.; ~-clearance s. Müllabfuhr f.

refutation s. Widerlegung f.

refute v.t. widerlegen.

regain v.t. wiedergewinnen.

regal a., ~ly adv. königlich.

regard v.t. ansehen; achten; beobachten; Rücksicht nehmen; sich beziehen; betrachten als; ~ s. Blick m.; Achtung f.; Ansicht f.; Rücksicht, Beziehung f.; ~s pl. Empfehlungen, Grüsse pl.

regarding prep. hinsichtlich, betreffend.

regardless adv. ohne Rücksicht auf.

regency s. Regentschaft f.

regenerate v.t. wiedergebären; neu beleben; ~ a. wiedergeboren.

regeneration s. Wiedergeburt f.

regent a. regierend; ~ s. Regent m.

regicide s. Königsmord, Königsmörder m.

regime s. Regierungssystem n.; Lebensführung f.; (law) Güterrecht n.

regimen s. Lebensordnung, Diät f.

regiment s. Regierung f.; Regiment n.

region s. Gegend f.

regional a., ~ly adv. örtlich, Landes...

register s. Verzeichnis n.; Register n.; (Orgel-) Register n.; ~ v.t. eintragen; (einen Brief) einschreiben; (Gepäck) aufgeben.

registered a. "eingeschrieben" (Brief); gesetzlich geschützt; ~ share s. Namensaktie f.

registrar s. Registrator m.; Standesbeamte m.; ~'s office s. Standesamt n.

registration s. Eintragung f.; ~ slip s. Gepäckaufgabeschein m.

registry s. Einschreibung f., Registratur f.; ~ office s. Standesamt n.

regret s. Bedauern n.; Kummer m.; ~ v.t. bedauern; bereuen.

regretful a. mit, voll Bedauern.

regrettable a. bedauerlich.

regroup v.t. & i. (bes. mil.) (sich) neugruppieren; ~ing s. Umgruppierung f.

regular a., ~ly adv. regelmässig, ordentlich; ~ s. Ordensgeistliche m.; ~s pl. Linientruppen pl.

regularity s. Regelmässigkeit f.

regulate v.t. ordnen, regeln.

regulation s. Einrichtung, Vorschrift f.; ~ a. vorschriftsmässig; ~s pl. Satzungen, Ausführungsbestimmungen pl.

rehabilitate v.t. wieder in den vorigen Stand setzen.

rehabilitation s. Wiedereinsetzung in den vorigen Stand f.; (mil.) Auffrischung f.

rehear v.t. (law) erneut verhandeln.

rehearsal s. Aufsagen n.; Wiederholung f.; Theaterprobe f.

rehearse v.t. wiederholen; hersagen; proben.

rehouse v.t. neu unterbringen.

reign v.i. herrschen, regieren; ~ s. Regierung, Macht f.

reimburse v.t. zurückerstatten; entschädigen.

reimbursement s. Entschädigung, Wiedererstattung f.

reimport v.t. wiedereinführen.

reimportation s. Wiedereinfuhr f.

rein s. Zügel m.; ~ v.t. zügeln.

reindeer s. Renntier n.

reinforce v.t. verstärken; ~d concrete, Eisenbeton m.

reinforcement s. Verstärkung f.

reinstate v.t. wieder einsetzen.

reinsurance s. Rückversicherung f.

reinsure v.t. rückversichern.

reinvest v.t. (Geld) wiederanlegen.

reissue s. neue Abdruck m.

reiterate v.t. wiederholen.

reject v.t. verwerfen; ausschlagen.

rejection s. Verwerfung f.

rejoice v.i. sich freuen; ~ v.t. erfreuen.

rejoicings s.pl. Freudebezeugungen f.pl.

rejoin v.t. wieder vereinigen; sich wieder vereinigen mit; ~ v.i. erwidern.

rejoinder s. Erwiderung.

rejuvenate v.t. verjüngen.

relapse v.i. zurückfallen, einen Rückfall bekommen; ~ s. Rückfall m.

relate v.t. erzählen, berichten; ~ v.i. sich beziehen.

related a. verwandt.

relation s. Bericht m.; Beziehung f.; Verwandtschaft f.; Verwandte m. & f.

relationship s. Verwandtschaft f.

relative a., ~ly adv. sich beziehend, bezüglich; verhältnismässig; relativ; ~ s. Verwandte m. & f.

relativity s. Relativität f.

relax v.t. lockern, entspannen; ~ v.i. erschlaffen; sich entspannen.
relaxation s. Erschlaffung f.; Erholung f.; Nachlassen n.; Erleichterung f.
relay s. Pferdewechsel m.; (elek.) Relais n.; Ablösungen...; ~ race, Stafettenlauf m.; to ~ to v.t. übertragen nach (radio).
release v.t. befreien; loslassen, entlassen; (Bomben) abwerfen; ~ s. Freilassung, Befreiung f.; Entbindung, Entlastung f.; Freigabe f. (für Veröffentlichung); (Bomben-)·Abwurf m.; (phot.) Auslösung f.; press ~ s. Veröffentlichung in der Presse.
relegate v.t. verweisen.
relent v.i. weich werden; nachgeben.
relentless a. unerbittlich, unbarmherzig.
relevance s. Erheblichkeit, Bedeutung f.
relevant a. erheblich; zur Sache gehörig.
reliability s. Zuverlässigkeit f.
reliable a. verlässlich, zuverlässig.
reliance s. Zuversicht f.; Vertrauen n.
relic s. Überrest m.; Reliquie f.
relict s. Witwe f.
relief s. Erleichterung f.; Unterstützung f.; Ablösung f.; (mil.) Entsatz m.; rechte Licht n.; Relief n.; low ~, Flachrelief n.; ~-fund s. Hilfsfond m.; ~-train s. Vorzug, Entlastungszug m.
relieve v.t. erleichtern; unterstützen; ablösen; entsetzen; beruhigen; (hervor) heben.
religion s. Religion f.
religious a., ~ly adv. religiös, Religions...; Ordens...; gewissenhaft.
relinquish v.t. verlassen; aufgeben.
relinquishment s. Verzicht m.
relish s. Geschmack m.; Beigeschmack m.; Würze f.; Genuss m.; ~ v.t. Geschmack finden an; schmackhaft machen; ~ v.i. schmecken, gefallen.
reluctance s. Widerstreben n.
reluctant a., ~ly adv. widerstrebend.
rely v.i. sich verlassen, vertrauen.
remain v.i. bleiben; übrigbleiben, verharren; it ~s to be seen, es muss sich zeigen.
remainder s. Rest m.; Rückstand m.
remains s.pl. (sterbliche) Reste; Überbleibsel pl.
remand v.t. (in Untersuchungshaft) zurückschicken.
remark v.t. bemerken; wahrnehmen; ~ s. Anmerkung f.
remarkable a., ~bly adv. bemerkenswert; hervorragend.
remarriage s. Wiederverheiratung f.
remedial a. heilend.
remedy s. Heilmittel, Hilfsmittel n.; Ersatz m.; ~ v.t. heilen, abhelfen.
remember v.t. sich erinnern; empfehlen, grüssen; gedenken; (fam.) behalten; to

~ a person in one's will, einen im Testament bedenken.
remembrance s. Erinnerung f.; Andenken n.
remind v.t. erinnern, mahnen.
reminder s. Mahnung f.
reminiscence s. Erinnerung f.
reminiscent (of) a. erinnernd (an).
remiss a., ~ly adv. schlaff; lässig.
remission s. Nachlassen n.; Milderung f., Erlassung, Vergebung f.; ~ of taxes, Steuernachlass m.
remit v.t. remittieren, übersenden; vermindern, nachlassen; erlassen.
remittance s. Überweisung f.; Rimesse.
remitter s. Remittent m.
remnant a. Überrest, Rest m.
remodel v.t. umbilden; umfassonieren (Hut, Mantel).
remonstrance s. Einwendung f.
remonstrate v.i. Einwendungen machen.
remorse s. Gewissensbiss m.
remorseless a., ~ly adv. hartherzig.
remote a., ~ly adv. entlegen, entfernt.
remote control s. (mech.) Fernsteuerung f.; ~led a. ferngesteuert.
remount v.t. wieder besteigen; ~ s. frische Reitpferd n.; Remonte f.
removal s. Wegschaffung, Absetzung f.; Umzug m.; Entlassung f.
remove v.t. wegräumen; versetzen; absetzen; entfernen; ~ v.i. sich entfernen; umziehen, ausziehen; ~ s. Abstand m.; Grad m., Stufe f.
remunerate v.t. belohnen, vergüten.
remuneration s. Belohnung, Vergütung f.
remunerative a. gewinnbringend.
renaissance s. Renaissance f.
renascence s. Wiedergeburt f.; Renaissance f.
rend v.t. & i.st. zerreissen.
render v.t. zurückgeben; überliefern; darstellen; übersetzen; leisten; machen; to ~ account, Rechenschaft ablegen; to ~ judgment, Urteil fällen; to ~ service, Dienst leisten; per account ~ed, laut erhaltener Rechnung.
rendering s. Wiedergabe f.; Übertragung f.
rendezvous s. Stelldichein n.
renegade s. Abtrünnige m.
renew v.t. erneuern; wiederholen.
renewal s. Erneuerung f.
renounce v.t. entsagen, abschwören, verzichten auf; verleugnen.
renovate v.t. erneuern.
renovation s. Erneuerung f.
renown s. Ruf, Ruhm m.
renowned a. berühmt.
rent s. Riss m.; Rente, Miete f.; Pacht f.; ~ v.t. (ver)mieten, (ver)pachten.
rental s. Miete f.; Mietsumme, Pachtsumme f.

rent-tribunal s. Mieteinigungsamt n.

renunciation s. Entsagung f.; Verzicht m.

reopen v.t. wieder eröffnen; ~ v.i. wieder eröffnet werden.

reorganize v.t. neugestalten.

rep, repp s. Rips m.

repair v.t. ersetzen; ausbessern; ~ v.i. sich wohin begeben; ~ s. Ausbesserung f.; Zustand m.; to keep in ~, in gutem Zustand halten; out of ~, baufällig; ~ shop s. Reparaturwerkstatt f.

reparable a., ~bly adv. ausbesserungsfähig; ersetzbar.

reparation s. Ausbesserung f.; Ersatz m.; Entschädigung f.

repartee s. schnelle, treffende Antwort f.

repast s. Mahlzeit f.

repatriate v.t. in die Heimat zurückbringen.

repatriation s. Rückführung, Repatriierung, f.

repay v.t.st. zurückzahlen; vergelten.

repayment s. Rückzahlung f.

repeal v.t. widerrufen; aufheben; ~ s. Aufhebung f.; Widerruf m.

repeat v.t. wiederholen; hersagen; ~ order, Nachbestellung f.; ~ performance, Wiederholung einer Aufführung f.

repeatedly adv. wiederholt.

repel v.t. zurückstossen; abstossen; zurückschlagen.

repellent a. abstossend.

repent v.t. & i. bereuen, Busse tun.

repentance s. Reue, Busse f.

repentant a. reuig, bussfertig.

repeople v.t. wieder bevölkern.

repercussion s. Widerhall m.

repertory s. Sachregister n.; Fundgrube f.; Repertoire n.; ~ theatre, Theater mit wechselndem Spielplan.

repetition s. Wiederholung f.; Hersagen n.; sign of ~, Tilde f.

repine v.i. sich grämen; murren, klagen.

replace v.t. wieder hinstellen; ersetzen.

replacement s. Ersatz m.; ~ army, Ersatzarmee f.

replant v.t. umpflanzen.

replenish v.t. (wieder)anfüllen.

replete a. angefüllt, voll.

repletion s. Überfülle f.

replica s. Nachbildung f.; Abbild n.

reply v.i. erwidern; ~ s. Antwort f.; ~ card, Postkarte (f.) mit Antwort; ~ coupon s. Antwortschein m.

repolish v.t. wieder polieren.

report v.t. berichten, erzählen; melden, anzeigen; ~ v.i. sich melden; to ~ out, sich abmelden; to ~ to the police, sich bei der Polizei melden; ~ s. Gerücht n.; Ruf m.; Nachricht f.; Knall m.; Bericht m.; Schulzeugnis n.

reporter s. Berichterstatter m.

repose v.t. setzen, legen; ~ v.i. ruhen,

beruhen; vertrauen auf; ~ s. Ruhe f.

repository s. Behältnis n.; Niederlage f.; Warenlager n.

repossess v.refl. wieder in Besitz nehmen.

reprehend v.t. tadeln; rügen.

reprehensible a., ~bly adv. tadelnswert.

reprehension s. Tadel m.; Rüge f.

reprehensive a. tadelsüchtig; tadelnd.

represent v.t. darstellen, vorstellen; vertreten; zu Gemüt führen.

representation s. Vorstellung f.; Darstellung f.; Stellvertretung f.

representative a., ~ly adv. vorstellend; stellvertretend; ~ s. Vertreter m.

repress v.t. unterdrücken; Einhalt tun.

repression s. Unterdrückung f.

repressive a. unterdrückend.

reprieve v.t. Frist geben; ~ s. Frist f.; Begnadigung f.

reprimand s. Verweis, Tadel m.; ~ v.t. tadeln.

reprint v.t. wieder drucken; ~ s. Neudruck m.

reprisal s. Wiedervergeltung f.; in ~ for, als Vergeltungsmassnahme für.

reproach v.t. vorwerfen; ~ s. Vorwurf m.; Schmach f.

reproachful a., ~ly adv. vorwurfsvoll.

reprobate a. verworfen, ruchlos; ~ s. Verworfene m.; ~ v.t. verwerfen.

reproduce v.t. & i. wieder hervorbringen; nachbilden; sich fortpflanzen.

reproduction s. Nachbildung, Wiederholung f.; Fortpflanzung f.

reproductive a. wiedererzeugend; Fortpflanzungs...

reproof s. Vorwurf, Verweis m.

reprove v.t. tadeln, verweisen; schelten.

reptile a. kriechend; ~ s. Reptil n.

republic s. Republik f., Freistaat m.

republican a. republikanisch; ~ s. Republikaner m.

republish v.t. (ein Buch) wieder auflegen.

repudiate v.t. zurückweisen, verstossen; Schulden nicht anerkennen.

repugnance s. Widerwille m.

repugnant a. widerspenstig; zuwider; ~ly adv. mit Widerwillen.

repulse v.t. zurückschlagen; abschlagen; ~ s. Zurücktreibung f.

repulsion s. Zurückstossung f.; Abweisung f.; (phys.) Abstossung f.

repulsive a. abstossend, widerwärtig.

repurchase v.t. wiederkaufen; ~ s. Rückkauf m.

reputable a., ~bly adv. angesehen.

reputation s. gute Ruf m.

repute v.t. halten für, achten; ~ s. Ruf m.

reputed a. vermeintlich.

request s. Bitte f.; Gesuch n.; Nachfrage f.; in ~ gesucht, begehrt; ~ v.t. bitten, ersuchen.

require v.t. verlangen, fordern; brauchen.
requirement s. Forderung f.; Bedarf m.
requisite a., ~ly adv. erforderlich; ~ s. Erfordernis n.; Bedarfsartikel m.
requisition s. Ersuchen n.; Forderung f.; Beschlag m.; (mil.) Requisition, Anforderung f.; ~ v.t. anfordern, requirieren, beitreiben.
requital s. Vergeltung f.
requite v.t. vergelten.
resale s. Wiederverkauf m.
rescind v.t. aufheben; abschaffen.
rescission s. Umstossung, Aufhebung (einer Verordnung) f.
rescript s. Erlass m.; Bescheid m.
rescue v.t. befreien, retten; ~ s. Befreiung, Rettung f.; to come to the ~ of, einem zu Hilfe kommen.
research s. Untersuchung f., Forschung f.; ~ v.i. Forschung treiben.
resemblance s. Ähnlichkeit f.; Ebenbild n.
resemble v.t. ähnlich sein, gleichen.
resent v.t. übelnehmen.
resentful a. empfindlich; rachgierig.
resentment s. Zorn m.; Verdruss m.; Groll m.
reservation s. Aufbewahrung f.; Vorbehalt m.; Zurückhaltung f.; Vorbestellung f.; ~-list s. Warteliste f.
reserve v.t. vorbehalten, aufbewahren; reservieren; ~ s. Rückhalt m., Reserve f.; Vorrat m.; Vorsicht f.; Zurückhaltung f.
reserved a., ~ly adv. zurückhaltend; vorsichtig; belegt.
reservist s. Reservist m.
reservoir s. Talsperre f.; Behälter m.
reset v.t. wieder setzen; neu einfassen.
resettlement s. Umsiedlung f.
reshape v.t. neugestalten, neuformen.
reshuffle s. Umbildung (der Regierung) f.
reside v.i. wohnen, sich aufhalten.
residence s. Aufenthalt, Wohnsitz m.; Wohnung f.; Residenz f.; place of ~, Aufenthaltsort m.
resident s. wohnhaft, ansässig; ~ s. Bewohner m.; Resident m.; British ~s, ansässige Briten.
residential a. Wohn...; ~ club s. Wohnklub m.; ~ district s. Wohnviertel n., Wohnbezirk m.
residual a. zurückbleibend.
residuary a. ~ legatee, Haupterbe m.
residue a. Rest, Rückstand m.
residuum s. Rückstand m.
resign v.t. entsagen, abtreten; aufgeben, sich ergeben in; ~ v.i. seine Stelle aufgeben.
resignation s. Abtretung, Entsagung, Verzichtleistung f.; (Amt.) Niederlegung f., Rücktritt m.; Ergebung f
resigned a. ergeben; ~ly adv. mit Ergebung.

resilience s. Schnellkraft, Spannkraft f.
resilient a. spannkräftig, elastisch.
resin s. Harz n.
resinous a. harzig.
resist v.t. & i. widerstehen.
resistance s. Widerstand m. (auch elek).
resistant, resisting a. . . . fest; oil-~, ölfest; shock-~, stossfest.
resolute a., ~ly adv. entschlossen.
resolution s. Auflösung f.; Entschlossenheit f.; Vorsatz m.; Beschluss m., Entschliessung f.
resolve v.t. auflösen; aufklären; beschliessen; ~ v.i. sich entschliessen; schmelzen; ~ s. Entschluss m.
resonance s. Widerhall m.; Nachhall m.; Resonanz f.
resonant a. widerhallend.
resonate v.i. mitklingen, mitschwingen.
resorption s. Aufsaugung f.
resort v.i. sich begeben; oft besuchen; seine Zuflucht nehmen; ~ s. Zusammenkunftsort m.; Zuflucht f.; health ~, Kurort m.
resound v.i. widerhallen.
resource s. Hilfsmittel n.; Zuflucht f.; ~s pl. Geldmittel n.pl.; (Erz-) Vorräte pl.; Fähigkeiten f.pl.
resourceful a. findig.
respect v.t. berücksichtigen; sich beziehen; (hoch)achten; ~ s. Rücksicht, Hinsicht, Beziehung f.; Hochachtung f.; ~s pl. Empfehlung f.
respectability s. Achtbarkeit f.
respectable a., ~bly adv. achtbar; ansehnlich; anständig; leidlich.
respectful a., ~ly adv. ehrerbietig, höflich.
respecting pr. hinsichtlich.
respective a. bezüglich; besonder, eigen, respektiv; ~ly adv. beziehungsweise.
respiration s. Atmen n.
respiratory a. Atmungs...
respire v.t. & i. atmen, einatmen.
respite s. Frist f.; Aufschub, Stillstand m.; ~ v.t. Frist geben.
resplendent a., ~ly adv. glänzend.
respond v.i. entsprechen; antworten.
respondent s. Beklagte m.
response s. Antwort f.
responsibility s. Verantwortlichkeit f., Verantwortung f.
responsible a., ~bly adv. verantwortlich.
responsive a. (be)antwortend; geneigt zu antworten, empfänglich.
rest s. Ruhe, Rast f.; Ruhepunkt m.; Pause f.; Rest m.; ~-centre s. Erholungsstätte f.; ~-cure s. Liegekur f.; die übrigen pl.; ~ v.i. ruhen, rasten; übrigbleiben; sich beruhigen; sich verlassen; bleiben, sein; liegen; ~ v.t. legen, stützen, lehnen.
restate v.t. neu formulieren.

restaurant s. Restaurant n.
restaurant-car s. Speisewagen m.
resting-place s. Ruheplatz m.
restitution s. Wiedererstattung f.; Wiederherstellung f.; **~-law** s. Wiedergutmachungsgesetz n.
restive a. störrisch, widerspenstig.
restless a., **~ly** adv. ruhelos.
restoration s. Wiederherstellung f.; Zurückerstattung f.
restorative a. stärkend; **~** s. kräftigende Heilmittel n.
restore v.t. wiedergeben; wiederherstellen.
restrain v.t. zurückhalten, einschränken.
restraint s. Einschränkung f.; Zurückhaltung f.; Zwang m.; under **~**, in Gewahrsam.
restrict v.t. einschränken; **~ed** p. nur für Dienstgebrauch.
restriction s. Einschränkung f.
restrictive a., **~ly** adv. einschränkend.
result v.i. hervorgehen, folgen, sich ergeben; **~** s. Ergebnis n., Folge f.
resume v.t. zurücknehmen; wieder aufnehmen; wieder anfangen; zusammenfassen.
resumption s. Zurücknahme f.; Wiederaufnahme f.
resurrection s. Auferstehung f.
resuscitate v.t. wieder erwecken; wiederbeleben.
retail v.t. im Kleinhandel verkaufen; **~** s. Einzelverkauf m.; **~-trade** s. Einzelhandel m.; **~-price** s. Ladenpreis m.
retailer s. Kleinhändler m.
retain v.t. behalten, beibehalten.
retainer s. Anhänger m.; Vorschuss (m.) für den Anwalt.
retake v.t.st. wieder nehmen.
retaliate v.i. wieder vergelten.
retaliation s. Wiedervergeltung f.
retaliatory a. Vergeltungs...
retard v.t. aufhalten; verzögern.
retardation s. Verzögerung f.
retch v.i. sich erbrechen wollen.
retention s. Zurückhalten n.; Beibehaltung f.; Verhaltung f.
retentive a. festhaltend.
reticence s. Verschwiegenheit f.
reticent a. verschwiegen, schweigsam.
reticule s. Pompadour m.
retina s. Netzhaut (des Auges) f.
retinue s. Gefolge n.
retire v.i. sich zurückziehen; zu Bett gehen; in den Ruhestand treten; **~** v.t. in den Ruhestand versetzen.
retired p. & a., **~ly** adv. zurückgezogen, eingezogen; pensioniert, im Ruhestand; **~ list**, Liste der Pensionierten.
retirement s. Zurückgezogenheit f.; Ausscheiden n.; Pensionierung f.
retort v.t. & i. erwidern; zurückgeben; **~** s. Erwiderung f.; Retorte f.

retouch v.t. überarbeiten; (phot.) retuschieren.
retrace v.t. wieder zeichnen; zurückgeben; zurückverfolgen.
retract v.t. & i. zurückziehen.
retraction s. Widerruf m.
retraining s. Umschulung f.
retread v.t. einen Reifen mit neuer Lauffläche versehen.
retreat s. Rückzug m.; Zufluchtsort m.; Eingezogenheit f.; Zapfenstreich m.
retrench v.t. einschränken; **~** v.i. seine Ausgaben einschränken.
retrenchment s. Einschränkung f.; Ersparung f.
retrial s. (law) nochmalige Verhandlung f.; Wiederaufnahmeverfahren n.
retribution s. Vergeltung f.
retrieve v.t. wiederbekommen; wieder ersetzen; (hunt.) apportieren.
retriever s. Stöberhund m.
retroactive a. rückwirkend; with **~** effect, mit rückwirkender Kraft.
retrograde a. rückläufig.
retrogression s. Rückgang m.
retrospect s. Rückblick m.
retrospective a. rückwirkend; zurückblickend.
retry v.t. (law) von neuem verhandeln.
return v.i. umkehren, wiederkommen; antworten; **~** v.t. erstatten; erwidern; zurückschicken, wiederbringen; melden, berichten; wählen; **~** s. Rückkehr f.; Rückgabe f.; Gewinn m.; Rückzahlung f.; Erwiderung f.; Gegendienst m.; Bericht, Wahlbericht m.; **~s** pl. statistische Angaben f.pl.; Einnahme f.; many happy returns of the day, Geburtstagsglückwunsch m.; in **~**, dafür, dagegen; by **~** of post, postwendend; **~** address s. Absenderadresse, Rückanschrift f.; **~** flight s. Rückflug m.; **~** journey s. Rückreise f.; **~** postage s. Rückporto n.
return-ticket s. Rückfahrkarte f.
reunion s. Wiedervereinigung f.
reunite v.t. (v.i. sich) wieder vereinigen.
revalorize, revalue v.t. aufwerten.
revaluate v.t. aufwerten, umwerten.
reveal v.t. offenbaren; enthüllen.
reveille s. (mil.) Morgensignal n.
revel v.i. schwärmen, schwelgen; **~** s. Gelage n.
revelation s. Offenbarung f.
reveller s. Nachtschwärmer m.
revelry s. Saus und Braus m.
revenge s. Rache f.; **~** v.t. rächen.
revengeful a., **~ly** adv. rachgierig.
revenue s. Einkommen n.; Ertrag m.; Staatseinnahmen f.pl.; **~** and expenditure, Einnahmen und Ausgaben pl.; **~-stamp** s. Banderole f.
reverberate v.i. wiederhallen.

reverberation s. Widerhall m.
revere v.t. ehren, verehren.
reverence s. Ehrerbietung f.; Verneigung
f.; Ehrwürden (Titel).
reverend a. ehrwürdig (Titel der Geist-
lichen, auch Right ~, Most ~).
reverent a., ~ly adv. ehrerbietig.
reverential a., ~ly adv. ehrerbietig.
reverie s. Träumerei f.
reversal s. Umstossung (eines Urteils) f.;
Umkehrung f.; Umsteuerung f.
reverse v.t. umkehren; umstossen; um-
steuern; ~ s. Wendung f., Umschlag
m., Wechsel m.; Gegenteil n.; Rückseite f.; Schlappe f.; ~ a. Rückwärts
...; ~-gear s. (mech.) Rückwärtsgang
m.
reversible a. umstösslich; umkehrbar.
reversion s. Umkehrung f.; Heimfall m.;
Anwartschaft f.
reversionary a. anwartschaftlich.
revert v.t. umkehren; zurückwerfen; ~
v.i. zurückkehren; heimfallen.
revertible a. heimfallend.
revetment s. Verkleidung f.
review v.t. wieder durchsehen; mustern;
rezensieren; revidieren; ~ s. Übersicht,
Durchsicht, Rezension f.; kritische
Zeitschrift, Rundschau f., (law) Revision f.
reviewer s. Rezensent m.
revile v.t. schmähen, schimpfen.
revise v.t. durchsehen.
revision s. Durchsicht, Revision f.
revisit v.t. wieder besuchen.
revival s. Wiederbelebung f.
revive v.i. wieder aufleben; ~ v.t. wieder
beleben.
revocable a. widerruflich.
revocation s. Zurückrufung f.; Widerruf m.
revoke v.t. widerrufen.
revolt v.i. sich empören; ~ s. Abfall m.;
Empörung f.
revolting a. abstossend.
revolution s. Umwälzung f.; Umlauf m.;
Umdrehung f.
revolutionary a. revolutionär.
revolutionize v.t. (gänzlich) umgestalten.
revolve v.t. umwälzen; erwägen; ~ v.i.
sich drehen, umlaufen.
revolver s. Revolver m.
revue s. Revue f.
revulsion s. Umschwung, Umschlag m.
reward v.t. vergelten, belohnen; ~ s.
Belohnung f.
rewrite v.t. umarbeiten.
rhapsody s. Rhapsodie f.; Überschweng-
lichkeit f.
rhetoric s. Redekunst f.
rhetorical a., ~ly adv. rednerisch.
rhetorician s. Rhetoriker m.
rheumatic a. rheumatisch.
rheumatism s. Rheumatismus m.

rhinoceros s. Nashorn n.
rhomb s. (geom.) Raute f.; Rhombus m.
rhomboidal a. rautenförmig.
rhubarb s. Rhabarber m.
rhyme s. Reim m.; Vers m.; ~ v.t. & i.
reimen.
rhythm s. Rhythmus m.
rhythmical a. rhythmisch.
rib s. Rippe f.; (nav.) Inholz n.; Schirm-
stange f.; ~ v.t. rippen.
ribald a. frech, zotig.
ribaldry s. unzüchtige Sprache f.
riband, ribbon s. Band, Ordensband n.;
Farbband n.; Streifen m.
rice s. Reis m.
rich a., ~ly adv. reich; kostbar; nahrhaft,
fett; (Kuchen) schwer.
riches s. Reichtum m.
richness s. Reichtum m.; Fülle f.
rick s. Schober m.
rickets s.pl. englische Krankheit f.
rickety a. rachitisch; wack[e]llig.
ricochet v.i. (mil.) abprallen; ~ s. Abpraller m.
rid v.t.st. befreien; wegschaffen; ~ a. ent-
ledigt; to get ~ of, loswerden.
riddance s. Befreiung, Entledigung f.
...ridden... geplagt; bed ~, bettlägerig.
riddle s. Rätsel n.; grobe Sieb n.; ~ v.t.
sieben; durchlöchern.
ride v.i. & st. reiten; fahren; to ~ at anchor,
vor Anker liegen; ~ s. Ritt m.; Fahrt f.;
Reitweg m.
rider s. Reiter m.; Bereiter m.; Zusatz-
klausel f.
ridge s. Grat m., Rücken m.; Erhöhung f.,
First m. or f.; Furche f.; Bergkette f.;
~ v.t. furchen.
ridicule s. Spott m.; Lächerlichkeit f.; ~
v.t. lächerlich machen.
ridiculous a., ~ly adv. lächerlich.
riding s. Reiten n.; ~ a. Reit...; ~
breeches pl. Reithosen pl.; ~-habit s.
Reitkleid n.
rife a., ~ly adv. herrschend, allgemein.
riffraff s. Gesindel n.
rifle v.t. rauben, plündern; riefeln; s. (ge-
zogene) Büchse f.
rifleman s. (mil.) Schütze m.; rifle-regi-
ment s. Schützenregiment n.
rifle-range s. Schiessstand m.
rift s. Riss m.; Spalte f.; ~ v.i. sich spalten.
rig s. Streich m.; Takelung f.; Putz m.; ~
v.t. putzen; auftakeln, ausrüsten.
rigging s. Takelwerk n.
right a. & adv., ~ly adv. gerade; recht;
richtig; sehr; echt, rechtmässig; to be ~,
recht haben; all ~!, alles in Ordnung!;
schon gut; ~ hand side, rechte Seite; ~
s. Recht n.; rechte Seite f.; by ~, von
Rechts wegen; all ~s reserved, alle
Rechte vorbehalten; ~ v.t. Recht verschaffen; berichtigen.

rightangled *a.* rechtwinkelig.

righteous *a.* gerecht, rechtschaffen.

righteousness *s.* Rechtschaffenheit *f.*

rightful *a.*, **~ly** *adv.* rechtmässig, gerecht.

rigid *a.*, **~ly** *adv.* steif; starr; streng.

rigidity *s.* Steifheit *f.*, Unbiegsamkeit *f.*

rigmarole *s.* Salbaderei *f.*

rigorous *a.*, **~ly** *adv.* streng; genau.

rigour *s.* Strenge *f.*

rill *s.* Bach *m.*; **~** *v.i.* rinnen, rieseln.

rim *s.* Rand *m.*; Reifen *m.*, Radkranz *m.*; Einfassung *f.*

rime *s.* Reif *m.*; **~** *v.i.* reifen.

rind *s.* Rinde, Schale *f.*

ring *s.* Ring *m.*; Clique *f.*; Schall *m.*; Geläute *n.*; **~** *v.t.* klingeln; **~** *v.i.* läuten; erschallen; *to* **~** *up*, anklingeln, anrufen.

ringleader *s.* Rädelsführer *m.*

ringlet *s.* Ringelchen *n.*; Ringellocke *f.*

rinse *v.t.* spülen, ausschwenken.

riot *s.* Schwelgerei *f.*; Tumult *m.*; Aufruhr *m.*; **~** *v.i.* schwärmen, schwelgen; Aufruhr stiften.

rioter *s.* Schwelger *m.*; Aufrührer *m.*

riotous *a.*, **~ly** *adv.* schwelgerisch; ausgelassen; aufrührerisch.

rip *v.t.* auftrennen, aufreissen; enthüllen; **~** *s.* Riss *m.*

ripe *a.*, **~ly** *adv.* reif, zeitig.

ripen *v.t. & i.* reifen.

riposte *s.* Gegenstoss *m.*

ripping *a.* (*sl.*) famos, tadellos.

ripple *v.i.* sich kräuseln; **~** *v.t.* riffeln; **~** *s.* Kräuseln *n.*; Flachsriffel *f.*

rise *v.i.* sich erheben, aufstehen; aufsteigen; aufgehen; heranwachsen; entstehen; steigen; **~** *s.* Anhöhe *f.*; Steigung *f.*; Ursprung *m.*; Steigen (im Preis) *n.*; Lohnerhöhung *f.*

rising *s.* Aufstand *m.*; Auferstehung *f.*; Aufbruch *m.*; Anschwellung *f.*

risk *s.* Gefahr *f.*; Wagnis *n.*; **~** *v.t.* wagen.

risky *a.* gewagt; gefährlich.

rite *s.* feierliche Brauch *m.*, Ritus *m.*

ritual *a.*, **~ly** *adv.* feierlich; rituell.

rival *s.* Nebenbuhler *m.*; Konkurrent *m.*; **~** *a.* nebenbuhlerisch; **~** *v.t. & i.* wetteifern.

rivalry *s.* Wetteifer *m.*; Konkurrenz *f.*

rive *v.t.st.* (*v.i. sich*) spalten.

river *s.* Fluss *m.*; Strom *m.*; **~** *crossing*, Flussübergang *m.*

rivet *s.* Niet *n.*; Klammer *f.*; **~** *v.t.* nieten, vernieten; befestigen.

rivulet *s.* Bach *m.*

roach *s.* Rotauge *n.* (Fisch).

road *s.* Strasse, Landstrasse *f.*; **~s** *pl.* Reede *f.*; **~-bed** *s.* Strassenunterbau *m.*; **~-block** *s.* (*mil.*) Strassensperre *f.*; **~-hog** *s.* rücksichtslose Fahrer *m.*; **~-sign** *s.* Verkehrsschild *n.*

roadstead *s.* (*nav.*) Reede *f.*

roam *v.i.* umherstreifen; **~** *v.t.* durchwandern.

roan *a.* scheckig, gefleckt; **~** *s.* Schecke *f.*

roar *v.i.* brüllen; lärmen; brausen; **~** *s.* Gebrüll *n.*; Brausen *n.*

roast *v.t.* braten, rösten; **~** *a.* gebraten; **~** *s.* Braten *m.*; **~** *mutton* *s.* Hammelbraten; **~** *chicken* *s.* Hühnerbraten.

roastbeef *s.* Rinderbraten *m.*

rob *v.t.* rauben, berauben, bestehlen.

robber *s.* Räuber *m.*

robbery *s.* Räuberei *f.*; Raub *m.*

robe *s.* lange Rock *m.*; Talar *m.*; Staatskleid *n.*; **~** *v.t. & i.* das Staatskleid anlegen, kleiden.

robin *s.* Rotkehlchen *n.*

robust *a.* stark, rüstig; derb.

rock *s.* Felsen *m.*; **~** *v.t. & i.* rütteln; einwiegen; schaukeln.

rocket *s.* Rakete *f.*; (*mil.*) **~-launcher**, **~-projector**, Raketenwurfmaschine *f.*

rocking-chair *s.* Schaukelstuhl *m.*

rocking-horse *s.* Schaukelpferd *n.*

rocky *a.* felsig; felsenhart.

rococo *s.* Rokoko *n.*

rod *s.* Rute *f.*; Stange *f.*; Messrute *f.*

rodent *s.* Nagetier *n.*

rodomontade *s.* Prahlerei *f.*

roe *s.* Reh *n.*; Hirschkuh *f.*; Fischrogen *m.*

roebuck *s.* Rehbock *m.*

rogue *s.* Schelm *m.*; Schurke *m.*

roguery *s.* Spitzbüberei, Schelmerei *f.*

roguish *a.*, **~ly** *adv.* spitzbübisch.

roister *v.i.* lärmen, poltern.

roll *v.t.* rollen, wälzen; walzen, strecken; **~** *v.i.* sich wälzen, sich drehen; schlingern; **~** *s.* Rollen *n.*; Rolle, Walze *f.*; Brötchen *n.*, Semmel *f.*; Wirbel (auf der Trommel) *m.*; Urkunde, Liste *f.*; **~** *and butter*, Butterbrötchen; *to* **~** *up* *v.t.* (*mil.*) aufrollen.

roll-call *s.* Namensaufruf *m.*, (*mil.*) Appell *m.*

roller *s.* Rolle *f.*; Walze *f.*; Wickelband *n.*; **~** *skate*, Rollschuh *m.*

roller-bearing *s.* (*mech.*) Rollenlager *n.*

roller-blind *s.* Rollvorhang *m.*

rollfilm *s.* (*phot.*) Rollfilm *m.*

rollick *v.i.* ausgelassen sein.

rolling-mill *s.* Walzwerk *n.*

rolling-pin *s.* Nudelholz *n.*, Teigrolle *f.*

rolling-stock *s.* (*rail.*) rollende Material *n.*

roman *a.* römisch; **~** *numerals* *pl.* römische Zahlen; **~** *type*, Antiquaschrift *f.*

romance *s.* Romanze *f.*; Roman *m.*; Erdichtung *f.*; **~** *v.i.* erdichten; aufschneiden; **~** *a.* romanisch.

Romanesque *a.* (*arch.*) romanisch.

Romanist *s.* Katholik *m.*

romantic *a.*, **~ally** *adv.* romantisch.

Romish *a.* römisch, katholisch.

romp s. Range f.; Wildfang m.; ~ v.i. ausgelassen sein, sich balgen.

rood s. Rute f. (¼ acre=10,117 a.); Kruzifix n., Kreuz...; Lettner m.

roof s. Dach n.; Decke f.; ~-garden s. Dachgarten m.; ~ v.t. bedachen.

roofing s. Bedachung f.; ~-felt s. Dachpappe f.

rook s. Saatkrähe f.; Turm (im Schach) m.; Gauner m.

rookery s. Krähenhorst m.

room s. Raum m.; Platz m.; Zimmer n.

roomy a. geräumig.

roost s. Hühnerstange f.

root s. Wurzel f.; Ursprung m.; ~-crops pl. Hackfrüchte f.pl.; ~ v.i. (ein)wurzeln; ~ out v.t. ausrotten; ausjäten, (Rüben) ausziehen.

rooted a. & p. eingewurzelt, fest.

rope s. Seil n.; Tau n.; Strick m.; ~ v.t. anseilen.

rope-dancer, rope-walker s. Seiltänzer m.

rope-ladder s. Strickleiter f.

rope-maker s. Seiler m.

rope-walk s. Seilerbahn f.

ropy a. klebrig, zähe.

rosary s. Rosenbeet n.; Rosenkranz m.

rose s. Rose f.; Rosette f.; Brause (an der Giesskanne) f.

roseate a. rosig, rosenfarben.

rosebud s. Rosenknospe f.

rosemary s. Rosmarin m.

rosette s. Rosette f. (Verzierung).

rosin s. Harz n.; Kolophonium n.

roster s. (mil.) Dienstliste, Namensliste f.

rosy a. rosig.

rot v.i. faulen, modern; ~ s. Fäulnis f.; Schund m.; Unsinn m.

rota s. Dienstturnus m.

rotary a. rotierend; Rotations...; ~ machine s. Rotationsmaschine f.; ~ switch s. (elek.) Dosenschalter, Drehschalter m.

rotate v.i. & t. (sich) drehen, rotieren.

rotation s. Kreislauf m.; Umdrehung f.; Wechsel m.; ~ of crops, Fruchtwechsel m.; in ~, abwechselnd.

rote s. by ~, auswendig.

rotten a. verfault; verdorben; verfallen; scheusslich, übel; ~ egg, faule Ei n.

rotter s. Nichtsnutz m.

rotund a. rund, kreisförmig.

rotundity s. Rundheit f.

rouble s. Rubel m.

rouge s. Schminke f.

rough a., ~ly adv. rauh, holprig, roh; ungebildet, grob; heftig; ~ draft, erste Entwurf m.; ~ notes pl. flüchtige Notizen f.pl.; ~ calculation, grobe Berechnung f.; ~ s. rohe Geselle, Flegel m.; ~ v.t. roh bearbeiten; to ~ it, sich mühsam durchschlagen.

rough-cast s. rohe Entwurf m.; Rohputz m.; ~ v.t. entwerfen.

roughen v.t. rauh machen.

rough-shod a. rücksichtslos.

round a. rund; unverhohlen, offen; volltönend; a ~ sum, eine runde Summe f.; ~ adv. & pr. um, herum, rings; geradeheraus; ~ s. Runde f.; Leitersprosse f.; Salve f.; (Patrone) Schuss m.; ~-up s. Razzia f.; ~ v.t. rundmachen; umfahren; ~ v.i. sich runden; to ~ up, v.t. zusammentreiben, umgingeln.

roundabout a. weitschweifig; umgebend Um...; ~ adv. rundherum; ~ s. Karussell n.; Umschweif m.

roundelay s. Rundgesang m.

roundly adv. rund; geradeheraus.

roundness s. Rundung f.; Offenheit f.

rouse v.t. aufwecken; aufregen, auftreiben; ~ v.i. aufwachen.

rout s. Aufruhr m.; Rotte f.; grosse Abendgesellschaft f.; wilde Flucht f.; ~ v.t. in die Flucht schlagen.

route s. Weg m.; Marschroute f.; en ~, unterwegs; ~ v.t. die Route bestimmen, leiten.

routine s. Routine f.; Schlendrian m.; ~ work, laufende Arbeiten pl.

rove v.i. herumschwärmen, wandern; ~ v.t. durchwandern.

rover s. Herumstreicher m.

row s. Reihe f.; ~ v.t. & i. rudern; ~ s. Lärm m.; Auflauf, Streit m.

rowan s. Eberesche f.

rowdy s. rohe, liederliche Kerl m.; ~ a. roh, lärmend.

rowel s. Spornrädchen n.

rowing-match s. Wettrudern n.

royal a., ~ly adv. königlich; prächtig.

royalist m. s. Royalist m.

royalty s. Königtum n.; Mitglied (n.) der Königsfamilie; Ertragsanteil m. (im Urheberrecht), Tantieme f.

rub v.t. reiben, scheuern, abwischen; ~ v.i. sich durchschlagen; ~ s. Reibung f.; Hindernis n.; to ~ one's hands together, sich die Hände reiben.

rubber s. Reibelappen m.; Robber (im Whistspiel) m.; Kautschuk n. or m., Gummi m.; Radiergummi m.; ~s pl. Gummischuhe m.pl.; ~-dinghy s. Schlauchboot n.; ~-truncheon s. Gummiknüppel m.

rubbish s. Unsinn m.; Schutt m.; Kehricht m. & n.

rubble s. Steinschutt m.

rubicund a. rot, rötlich.

rubric s. Rubrik f.

ruby s. Rubin m.; Pariser Schrift f.

rudder s. (Steuer)ruder n.; Steuer n.

ruddle s. Rötel m.

ruddy a. rötlich.

rude *a.*, **~ly** *adv.* roh, rauh; unhöflich.

rudiment *s.* Grundlage *f.*; (*bot.*) Ansatz *m.*; **~s** *pl.* Anfangsgründe *m.pl.*

rudimentary *a.* rudimentär, Anfangs...

rue *s.* Raute (Pflanze) *f.*; **~** *v.t.* bereuen; beklagen.

rueful *a.*, **~ly** *adv.* reuig, kläglich.

ruff *s.* Halskrause *f.*; Trumpfspielen *n.*

ruffian *s.* rohe Kerl *m.*; Raufbold *m.*

ruffianly *a.* wüst, brutal, bübisch.

ruffle *v.t.* kräuseln; zerknüllen; fälteln; aus der Fassung bringen; **~** *v.i.* rauh werden; flattern; **~** *s.* Krause, Rüsche *f.*; Gekräusel *n.*; Unruhe *f.*

rug *s.* Bettvorleger, Kaminvorleger *f.*; kleiner Teppich *m.*

rugby *s.* Rugby *n.*

rugged *a.*, **~ly** *adv.* rauh, holp[e]rig; struppig; mürrisch.

rugger *s.* = rugby.

ruin *s.* Einsturz *m.*; Ruine *f.*; Untergang *m.*; Verderben *n.*; **~** *v.t.* zerstören; zu Grunde richten.

ruinous *a.*, **~ly** *adv.* baufällig; verderblich.

rule *s.* Regel *f.*; (gerichtliche) Verfügung *f.*; Ordnung *f.*; Lineal *n.*; Masstab *m.*; Herrschaft *f.*; ~ of thumb, Erfahrungs-regel *f.*; ~ of the road, Strassenverkehrs-ordnung, Fahrordnung *f.*; **~** *v.t.* lin(i)-ieren; regeln; verordnen; beherrschen; **~** *v.i.* herrschen; *to* ~ out, ausschliessen.

ruler *s.* Herrscher *m.*; Lineal *n.*

ruling *s.* Gerichtsentscheidung *f.*

rum *s.* Rum *m.*; **~** *a.* altväterisch.

rumble *v.i.* rumpeln, rasseln.

ruminant *s.* Wiederkäuer *m.*

ruminate *v.t. & i.* wiederkäuen; nach-sinnen.

rummage *v.t.* durchstöbern; **~** *s.* Rest-waren *f.pl.*; ~ sale, Ramschverkauf *m.*

rumour *s.* Gerücht *n.*; **~** *v.t.* (ein Ge-rücht) verbreiten, aussprengen.

rump *s.* Steiss *m.*; Rumpf *m.*

rumple *s.* Runzel *f.*; Falte *f.*; **~** *v.t.* run-zeln, zerknittern.

rump-steak *s.* Rumpsteak *n.*

rumpus *s.* (*sl.*) Spektakel, Lärm *m.*

run *v.i. & t.st.* laufen; eilen; verstreichen; strömen; lauten; sich erstrecken; leiten; hetzen; *to* ~ down, niederrennen; ab-hetzen; heruntermachen; *to* ~ into, hin-einfahren in, anfahren; *to* ~ into debt, Schulden machen; *to* ~ off, davon-laufen; *to* ~ on, fortschreiten, fort-setzen; *to* ~ out, auslaufen; zu Ende gehen; sich erschöpfen; *to* ~ over, über-fahren; *to* ~ short, ausgehen; *to* ~ to, sich belaufen auf; *to* ~ up, in die Höhe laufen; anwachsen lassen; hinauf-treiben, steigern; errichten, aufbauen; **~** *s.* Laufen *n.*; Lauf, Gang *m.*; An-drang, Ansturm; Weidegrund *m.*; starke Nachfrage *f.*; Aufführungs-periode (*f.*) eines Stücks; *the common* ~, Durchschnittstyp *m.*; ~ *on a bank*, Ansturm (*m.*) auf eine Bank; *in the long* ~, auf die Dauer.

runaway *s.* Flüchtling *m.*; Ausreisser *m.*

rune *s.* Rune *f.*

rung *s.* (Leiter-)Sprosse *f.*

runic *a.* runisch, Runen...

runner *s.* Läufer *m.*; Bote *m.*; Kufe *f.*; **~-beans** *pl.* grüne Bohnen *f.pl.*; **~-up**, zweite Preisträger *m.*

running *a.*, **~ly** *adv.* laufend; fliessend; hintereinander; ~ water, laufende Wasser *n.*; **~-board** *s.* (*mot.*) Trittbrett *n.*

runway *s.* (*avi.*) Startbahn *f.*

rupee *s.* Rupie *f.* (etwa 2 M.).

rupture *s.* Bruch *m.*; Uneinigkeit *f.*; **~** *v.i.* brechen, bersten.

rural *a.*, **~ly** *adv.* ländlich.

ruse *s.* List, Kriegslist *f.*

rush *s.* Binse *f.*; Ansturm *m.*; Hetzerei, Hetze *f.*; Andrang *m.*, Gedränge *n.*; Sturz *m.*; ~ hours *pl.* Hauptgeschäfts-stunden *f.pl.*; **~** *v.i.* stürzen, schiessen, rennen; rauschen; **~** *v.t.* (durch)hetzen, durchpeitschen.

rusk *s.* Zwieback *m.*

russet *a.* braunrot; **~** *s.* Reinette *f.* (Apfel).

Russia-leather *s.* Juchtenleder *n.*

rust *s.* Rost *m.*; Schimmel *m.*; **~** *v.i.* rosten, schimmeln.

rustic *a.*, **~ally** *adv.* ländlich, bäu[e]risch; **~** *s.* Bauer *m.*

rusticity *s.* Ländlichkeit *f.*; Plumpheit *f.*

rustle *v.i.* rauschen; säuseln; rascheln.

rusty *a.*, **~ily** *adv.* rostig, schimmlig; ver-driesslich, mürrisch; eingerostet.

rut *s.* Spur *f.*; Geleise *n.*; Brunst *f.*, Brunft *f.*; **~** *v.i.* brunsten.

ruthless *a.*, **~ly** *adv.* unbarmherzig.

rutting-season *s.* Brunftzeit *f.*

rye *s.* Roggen *m.*; **~-grass**, Lolch *m.*

S

Sabbath *s.* Sabbat *m.*; Ruhetag *m.*

sable *s.* Zobel *m.*; Zobelpelz *m.*; **~** *a.* schwarz.

sabotage *s.* Sabotage *f.*; **to** **~** *v.t.* sabot-ieren.

sabre *s.* Säbel *m.*; **~** *v.t.* niedersäbeln.

saccharin(e) *s.* Sa[c]charin *n.*

sacerdotal *a.* priesterlich.

sack *s.* Sack *m.*; Plünderung *f.*; Laufpass *m.*; **~** *v.t.* einsacken; plündern; ent-lassen.

sackcloth *s.* Sackleinwand *f.*

sacrament *s.* Sakrament *n.*; heilige Abend-mahl *n.*; *to take the* ~, zum Abendmahl gehen.

sacred *a.*, ~ly *adv.* heilig; ehrwürdig.
sacrifice *v.t.* & *i.* opfern; widmen; ~ *s.* Opfer *n.*
sacrificial *a.* Opfer...
sacrilege *s.* Kirchenraub, Frevel *m.*
sacrilegious *a.*, ~ly *adv.* kirchenräuberisch; ruchlos.
sacristan *s.* Kirchner, Küster *m.*
sacristy *s.* Sakristei *f.*
sad *a.*, ~ly *adv.* dunkel; traurig; trübe, ernst; schlimm, arg.
sadden *v.t.* betrüben.
saddle *s.* Sattel *m.*; Rückenstück (*n.*); ~-horse, Reitpferd *n.*; ~ *v.t.* satteln; belasten.
saddler *s.* Sattler *m.*
sadness *s.* Traurigkeit, Schwermut *f.*; Ernst *m.*
safe *a.*, ~ly *adv.* sicher; unversehrt; ~ *s.* Speiseschrank; Geldschrank *m.*
safe-conduct *s.* sichere Geleit *n.*; Schutzbrief *m.*
safe-custody, safe-keeping *s.* sichere Gewahrsam *m.*
safeguard *s.* Schutzwache *f.*; Schutz *m.*; ~ *v.t.* schützen, sichern.
safety *s.* Sicherheit *f.*; ~-curtain *s.* eiserne Vorhang *m.*; ~-glass *s.* Plexiglas *n.*; ~-match *s.* Sicherheitszündholz *n.*; ~-pin *s.* Sicherheitsnadel *f.*; ~-razor *s.* Rasierapparat *m.*
saffron *s.* Safran *m.*; ~ *a.* safrangelb.
sag *v.i.* sich senken, sacken; durchhängen.
sagacious *a.*, ~ly *adv.* scharfsinnig.
sagacity *s.* Scharfsinn *m.*
sage *a.*, ~ly *adv.* weise, klug; ~ *s.* Weise *m.*; Salbei *f.*
sago *s.* Sago *m.*
sail *s.* Segel *n.*; Schiff *n.*; Windmühlenflügel *m.*; ~ *v.i.* segeln; abfahren (vom Schiff); ~ *v.t.* durchsegeln; ~ing-boat *s.* Segelboot *n.*
sailor *s.* Matrose *m.*; *to be a good* ~, seefest sein.
saint *a.*, ~ly *adv.* heilig; ~ *s.* Heilige *m.*
saintly *a.* fromm, heilig.
sake *s. for God's* ~, um Gotteswillen; *for the* ~ *of*, um... willen; *for my* ~, um meinetwillen.
salable *a.* verkäuflich, gangbar.
salacious *a.*, ~ly *adv.* wollüstig, geil.
salad *s.* Salat *m.*; ~-dressing Salatsauce *f.*
salamander *s.* Salamander *m.*
salame *s.* Salami (wurst) *f.*
salary *s.* Gehalt *n.*; ~-scale *s.* Gehaltsskala *f.*; salaried *a.* besoldet.
sale *s.* Verkauf, Absatz *m.*; Ausverkauf *m.*; ~s assistant *s.* Verkäufer(in) *m.*, *f.*; ~s clerk *s.* (*Am.*) Verkäufer(in) *m.*, *f.*; ~sgirl *s.* (*Am.*) Ladenmädchen *n.*; ~slady *s.* Verkäuferin *f.*; ~sman *s.* Verkäufer *m.*; ~smanship *s.* Verkauf-

stüchtigkeit, Verkaufsgewandtheit *f.*; *for* ~, verkäuflich.
saleable *see* salable.
salient *a.* springend; hervorragend; ~ *s.* vorspringende Ecke *f.*
saline *a.* salzartig; ~ *s.* Salzquelle *f.*
saliva *s.* Speichel *m.*
sallow *a.* blass; gelblich; ~ *s.* Salweide *f.*
sally *s.* Ausfall *m.*; Vorsprung *m.*; witzige Einfall *m.*; ~ *v.i.* sich aufmachen; hervorbrechen.
salmon *s.* Lachs, Salm *m.*
saloon *s.* Saal, Salon *m.*; (*Am.*) Kneipe *f.*; erste Klasse *f.* (Schiff); ~-car *s.* (*mot.*) Limousine *f.*, (rail.) Luxuswagen *m.*
salt *s.* Salz *n.*; (*fig.*) Seebär *m.*; Würze *f.*; Witz *m.*; ~ *a.*, ~ly *adv.* salzig; ~ *v.t.* (ein)salzen.
salt-cellar *s.* Salzfass *n.*
salter *s.* Salzhändler *m.*
saltpetre *s.* Salpeter *m.*
salt-shaker *s.* (*Am.*) Salzfass *n.*
salt-works *s.pl.* Saline *f.*
salty *a.* etwas salzig.
salubrious *a.* heilsam, gesund.
salubrity *s.* Heilsamkeit *f.*
salutary *a.* heilsam.
salutation *s.* Gruss *m.*; Anrede (Brief) *f.*
salute *v.t.* grüssen; ~ *s.* Gruss *m.*
salvage *s.* Bergung *f.*; Bergelohn *m.*; ~ *v.t.* bergen.
salvation *s.* Rettung, Seligkeit *f.*; ~-army, 'Heilsarmee,' *f.*
salve *s.* Salbe *f.*; ~ *v.t.* salben; lindern; bergen.
salver *s.* Präsentierteller *m.*
salvo *s.* Vorbehalt *m.*; Salve *f.*
sal-volatile *s.* Riechsalz *n.*
same *pn.* derselbe, dieselbe, dasselbe; einerlei; *all the* ~, trotzdem.
sameness *s.* Einerleiheit *f.*
sample *s.* Probe *f.*, Muster *n.*; *according to* ~, nach Muster; ~ *v.t.* eine Probe nehmen.
sampler *s.* Stick(muster)tuch *n.*
sanatorium *s.* Heilanstalt *f.*
sanctification *s.* Heiligung, Einsegnung *f.*
sanctify *v.t.* heiligen.
sanctimonious *a.*, ~ly *adv.* scheinheilig.
sanction *s.* Bestätigung *f.*, Genehmigung *f.*; Sanktion *f.*; Zwangsmassnahme *f.*; Gesetzeskraft *f.*; ~ *v.t.* bestätigen; genehmigen.
sanctity *s.* Heiligkeit, Reinheit *f.*
sanctuary *s.* Heiligtum *n.*; Freistätte *f.*
sand *s.* Sand *m.*; ~s *pl.* Sandwüste; Strand *m.*; Sandbank *f.*
sandal *s.* Sandale *f.*
sandal wood *s.* Sandelholz *n.*
sandbag *s.* Sandsack *m.*
sandpaper *s.* Sandpapier *n.*
sandstone *s.* Sandstein *m.*

sandwich *s.* belegte Butterbrot *n.*; ~ *v.t.* einklemmen; ~ man *s.* Plakatträger *m.*

sandy *a.* sandig; gelblichrot.

sane *a.* gesund (an Geist), vernünftig.

sangfroid *s.* Kaltblütigkeit *f.*

sanguinary *a.* blutig; blutdürstig.

sanguine *a.*, ~ly *adv.* hoffnungsvoll.

sanitary *a.* gesundheitlich, Gesundheits . . . ; ~ towel *s.* Monatsbinde *f.*

sanitation *s.* Hygiene *f.*

sanity *s.* Gesundheit *f.*; gesunde Verstand *m.*

sap *s.* Saft (der Bäume) *m.*; Splint *m.*; ~ *v.t. & i.* untergraben, sappen.

sapience *s.* Weisheit *f.*

sapient *a.* weise, (ironisch) 'hochgelahrt'.

sapless *a.* saftlos.

sapling *s.* junge Baum *m.*

sapper *s.* Sappeur *m.*

sapphire *s.* Saphir *m.*

sappy *a.* saftig; weich; munter.

sarcasm *s.* beissende Spott *m.*

sarcastic *a.* beissend, sarkastisch.

sarcenet *s.* Taffet *m.*

sarcophagus *s.* Steinsarg *m.*

sardine *s.* Sardine *f.*

sardonic *a.* sardonisch, bitter, grimmig.

sartorial *a.* Schneider. . .

sash *s.* Schärpe *f.*; Fensterrahmen *m.*; (~window) Schiebefenster *n.*

satanic *a.*, ~ally *adv.* teuflisch.

satchel *s.* Schulmappe *f.*; Tasche, *f.*

sate *v.t.* sättigen.

sateen *s.* Satin *m.*

satellite *s.* Trabant *m.*; Anhänger *m.*

satiate *v.t.* sättigen.

satiety *s.* Sättigung *f.*; Überdruss *m.*

satin *s.* Atlas *m.*

satin-wood *s.* Atlasholz *n.*

satire *s.* Satire *f.*

satirical *a.*, ~ly *adv.* satirisch.

satirist *s.* Satiriker *m.*

satirize *v.t.* bespötteln.

satisfaction *s.* Genugtuung *f.*; Befriedigung, Freude *f.*

satisfactory *a.*, ~ily befriedigend.

satisfied *p. & a.* zufrieden.

satisfy *v.t. & i.* genugtun, genügen; befriedigen; überzeugen.

saturate *v.t.* (chem.) sättigen.

Saturday *s.* Sonnabend, Samstag *m.*

saturnine *a.* mürrisch, finster.

sauce *s.* Sauce, Tunke *f.*; Würze *f.*; ~-boat *s.* Sauciere *f.*

saucepan *s.* Kochtopf *m.*, Tiegel *m.*

saucer *s.* Untertasse *f.*

saucy *a.*, ~ily *adv.* unverschämt; keck.

saunter *v.i.* schlendern.

saurian *s.* Saurier *m.*

sausage *s.* Wurst *f.*

savage *a.*, ~ly *adv.* wild, grausam; ~ *s.* Wilde *m.*

savagery *s.* Wildheit, Barbarei *f.*

savanna(h) *s.* offene Weide, Grasfläche *f.*

save *v.t.* retten, bergen; schonen; sparen, ersparen; aufheben; ~ *pr.* ausser, ausgenommen.

saveloy *s.* Zervelatwurst *f.*

saving *a.*, ~ly *adv.* sparsam; ~ *s.* Rettung *f.*; Vorbehalt *m.*; Ersparnis *f.*; ~ *pr.* ausser; ~ clause, (*law*) Vorbehaltsklausel *f.*; ~s-bank *s.* Sparkasse *f.*; ~s-certificate *s.* Spargutschein *m.*

Saviour *s.* Heiland *m.*; Retter *m.*

savour *s.* Geschmack *m.*; Geruch, Duft *m.*; ~ *v.i. & t.* schmecken, riechen; nach etwas aussehen.

savoury *a.*, ~ily *adv.* schmackhaft; wohlriechend; scharfgewürzt; ~ *s.* Vorspeise *f.*

savoy *s.* Wirsing(kohl) *m.*

saw *s.* Säge *f.*; Spruch *m.*; ~ *v.t.* sägen.

sawdust *s.* Sägespäne *m.pl.*

sawing-horse *s.* Sägebock *m.*

saw-mill *s.* Schneidemühle *f.*

saxifrage *s.* (*bot.*) Steinbrech *m.*

saxophone *s.* Saxophon *n.*

say *v.t & i.st.* sagen; hersagen; erzählen; *I ~!*, hören Sie mal!

saying *s.* Rede *f.*; Redensart *f.*; *it goes without* ~, es versteht sich von selbst.

scab *s.* Schorf *m.*; Krätze *f.*

scabbard *s.* Säbelscheide *f.*

scabby *a.* krätzig; schäbig.

scabies *s.* Krätze *f.*

scabious *a.* krätzig, räudig.

scabrous *a.* heikel, schlüpfrig.

scaffold *s.* Gerüst, Schafott *n.*; ~ *v.t.* ein Gerüst aufschlagen; stützen.

scaffolding *s.* Gerüst *n.*; Bühne *f.*

scald *s.* Verbrühung *f.*; Brandwunde *f.*; Skalde *m.*; ~ *v.t.* brühen, verbrennen; (Milch) abkochen.

scalding-hot *a.* brühheiss.

scale *s.* Waagschale *f.*; Schuppe *f.*; Kesselstein *m.*; Masstab *m.*; Tonleiter *f.*; Stufenleiter *f.*; Gradeinteilung *f.*; *pair of* ~s, Waage *f.*; *on a large* ~, im Grossen, auf grossem Fusse; ~ *v.t.* erklettern, stürmen; abschiefern, schuppen; ~ *v.i.* abblättern.

scaled *a.* schuppig.

scaling-ladder *s.* Sturmleiter *f.*; Feuerleiter *f.*

scallop *s.* Zacke *f.*, Langette *f.*; Muschel *f.*; ~ *v.t.* ausbogen.

scalp *s.* Kopfhaut *f.*; ~ *v.t.* skalpieren.

scalpel *s.* Skalpell *n.*

scaly *a.* schuppig, geschuppt.

scamp *s.* Taugenichts *m.*; Lausbub *m.*; ~ *v.t.* verpfuschen.

scamper *v.i.* rennen; ~ *s.* Durchhetzen *n.*; Galoppritt *m.*

scan *v.t.* skandieren (Verse); genau ansehen, erwägen.

scandal *s.* Ärgernis *n.* Skandal *m.*; Lästerung *f.*; Schmach *f.*
scandalize *v.t.* ärgern, Anstoss geben.
scandalous *a.*, ~ly *adv.* schändlich.
scansion *s.* Skandieren *n.*
scant *a.* knapp; sparsam.
scanty *a.* sparsam, karg, knapp; gering.
scape-goat *s.* Sündenbock *m.*
scape-grace *s.* Taugenichts *m.*
scapula(ry) *s.* Skapulier *n.*
scar *s.* Narbe *f.*; ~ *v.t.* schrammen; ~ *v.i.* vernarben.
scarab *s.* Käfer *m.*; Skarabäus *m.*
scarce *a.* spärlich, knapp.
scarcely *adv.* kaum.
scarcity *s.* Seltenheit, Spärlichkeit *f.*; Knappheit *f.*
scare *v.t.* scheuchen, schrecken; ~ *s.* leere Schreck *m.*; Panik *f.*
scarecrow *s.* Vogelscheuche *f.*
scarf *s.* Halsbinde *f.*; Halstuch *n.*
scarf-pin *s.* Busennadel *f.*
scarify *v.t.* einritzen; (Boden) lockern.
scarlet *s.* Scharlach *m.*; ~ *a.* scharlachfarben; ~-fever *s.* Scharlachfieber *n.*; ~-runner *s.* Feuerbohne *f.*
scarp *s.* Böschung *f.*
scathe *v.t.* vernichten, versehren; ~ *s.* Schaden *m.*
scatter *v.t.* zerstreuen, verbreiten; ~ *v.i.* sich zerstreuen.
scatterbrained *a.* konfus.
scavenger *s.* Strassenkehrer *m.*
scene *s.* Bühne *f.*; Schauplatz *m.*; Szene *f.*; Begebenheit *f.*; Kulisse *f.*; Auftritt *m.*; ~ *of action*, Schauplatz *m.*
scenery *s.* Landschaft, Gegend, Szenerie *f.*; Gemälde *n.*; Bühnengerät *n.*
scenic(al) *a.* bühnenmässig; landschaftlich, Landschafts...
scent *s.* Geruch *m.*; Witterung *f.*; Fährte *f.*; ~ *v.t.* riechen, wittern; durchduften.
sceptic *a.* zweifelsüchtig; ~ *s.* Zweifler *m.*
scepticism *s.* Zweifelsucht *f.*
sceptre *s.* Zepter *n.*
schedule *s.* Zettel *m.*; Verzeichnis *n.*, Liste *f.*; (*Am.*) Fahrplan *m.*; ~ *v.t.* aufzeichnen; ~ *p.* planmässig, fahrplanmässig.
scheme *s.* Plan, Entwurf *m.*; Figur *f.*, Schema *n.*; ~ *v.i.* & *t.* Pläne machen, entwerfen; Ränke schmieden.
schemer *s.* Ränkeschmied *m.*
schism *s.* Kirchenspaltung *f.*
schismatic *a.*, ~ally *adv.* schismatisch.
scholar *s.* Schüler *m.*; Gelehrte *m.*
scholarship *s.* Gelehrsamkeit *f.*; Stipendium *n.*
scholastic *a.*, ~ally *adv.* schulmässig; Schul...; scholastisch; ~ *degree*, Schulabgangszeugnis *n.*
school *s.* Schule *f.*; Schulhaus *n.*; ~-age, schulpflichtige Alter *n.*; ~-attendance,

Schulbesuch *m.*; ~-leaving age, Schulentlassungsalter *n.*; ~ *v.t.* schulen, unterrichten.
school-board *s.* Schulbehörde *f.*
schoolboy *s.* Schuljunge *m.*
school-fellow *s.* Schulkamerad *m.*
schoolmaster *s.* Schullehrer *m.*
schoolmistress *s.* Lehrerin *f.*
schooner *s.* Schoner (Fahrzeug) *m.*
sciatica *s.* Ischias *f.*
science *s.* Wissenschaft *f.*; Naturwissenschaft *f.*; Kenntnis *f.*
scientific *a.*, ~ally *adv.* wissenschaftlich.
scientist *s.* Naturwissenschaftler *m.*
scintillate *v.i.* funkeln.
scion *s.* Spross *m.*, Sprössling *m.*
scissors *s.pl.* Schere *f.*
scoff *v.t.* verspotten; ~ *s.* Hohn *m.*
scold *v.t.* & *i.* schelten, zanken; ~ *s.* Keiferin *f.*
scon, scone *s.* Mürbekuchen *m.*
sconce *s.* Laterne *f.*; Wandleuchter *m.*; Bollwerk *n.*; Kopf *m.*
scoop *s.* Schaufel; Spatel *m.*; ~ *v.t.* schaufeln, schöpfen, aushöhlen.
scope *s.* Spielraum *m.*, Umfang *m.*; Gesichtskreis *m.*; Zweck *m.*
scorch *v.t.* sengen, brennen; ~ *v.i.* ausdorren; *scorched earth*, (*mil.*) verbrannte Erde (Verwüstung des eigenen Landes durch eine zurückgehende Armee).
score *s.* Kerbholz *n.*, Kerbe *f.*; Zeche *f.*; Schuld *f.*; Partitur *f.*; Grund *m.*; Stiege (= 20) *f.*; (in Spielen) markierte Punkte *m.pl.*; ~ *v.t.* einkerben; anschreiben; Punkte machen; (*mus.*) instrumentieren; gewinnen.
scorn *s.* Spott *m.*; Geringschätzung *f.*; ~ *v.t.* & *i.* verspotten; verachten.
scornful *a.*, ~ly *adv.* höhnisch.
scorpion *s.* Skorpion *m.*
scotch *v.t.* einschneiden, kerben; hemmen; ~ *s.* Einschnitt *m.*
scotch fir *s.* Föhre, Kiefer *f.*
scotch tape *s.* Klebestreifen *m.*
scot-free *a.* unversehrt, straflos.
Scotland Yard *s.* Kriminalpolizei *f.*
scoundrel *s.* Schurke *m.*
scour *v.t.* & *i.* scheuern, reinigen; streifen, durchstreifen; hineilen.
scourge *s.* Geissel *f.*; Strafe *f.*; ~ *v.t.* geisseln, züchtigen.
scout *s.* Späher, Kundschafter *m.*; boy ~ *s.* Pfadfinder *m.*; ~ *v.i.* ausspähen; ~ *v.t.* zurückweisen, verspotten.
scowl *s.* finstere Gesicht *n.*; ~ *v.i.* finster aussehen.
scraggy *a.*, ~ily *adv.* mager.
scramble *v.i.* sich reissen; klettern; ~ *s.* Raffen, Gereisse *n.*; Gedränge *n.*
scrambled eggs *s.pl.* Rühreier *n.pl.*
scrap *s.* Stückchen *n.*; Fetzen *m.*; ~s *pl.*

Überbleibsel *n.pl.*; ~-iron Schrott *m.*; ~ *v.t.* verschrotten; zum alten Eisen werfen.

scrape *v.t. & i.* schaben, kratzen, zusammenscharren; ~ *s.* Kratzfuss *m.*; Klemme, Verlegenheit *f.*

scraper *s.* Kratzeisen, Schabeisen *n.*; Kratzbürste *f.*; Kratzer *m.*

scrappy *a.*, ~ily *adv.* zusammengestückelt.

scratch *v.t.* kratzen; ritzen, kritzeln; ~ *s.* Riss, Ritz *m.*; Schramme *f.*

scrawl *v.t.* kritzeln; ~ *s.* Gekritzel *n.*

scream *v.i.* kreischen, schreien; ~ *s.* Schrei *m.*

screech *v.i.* schreien, kreischen.

screen *s.* Schirm *m.*; (Kino) Leinwand *f.*; (*mil.*) Schützenschleier *m.*; Sandsieb *n.*; ~ *v.t.* schützen; sieben; (Licht) abblenden; (*fig.*) auf politische Einwandfreiheit prüfen.

screw *s.* Schraube *f.*; ~ *v.t.* schrauben; quetschen, drücken.

screw-driver *s.* Schraubenzieher *m.*

screw-propeller *s.* Schiffsschraube *f.*

screw-steamer *s.* Schraubendampfer *m.*

scribble *v.i. & t.* kritzeln; ~ *s.* Gekritzel *n.*

scribbler *s.* Schmierer, Sudler *m.*

scribe *s.* Schriftgelehrte *m.*

scriber *s.* (*mech.*) Reissnadel *f.*

scrimmage *s.* Handgemenge *n.*

scrip *s.* Zettel, Interimsschein *m.*; ~-money, Schwundgeld, Notgeld *n.*

script *s.* (*typ.*) Schrift *f.*; Schriftart *f.*; Schreibschrift *f.*; (*Film, Radio*) Drehbuch, Manuskript *n.*

Scriptural *a.* schriftmässig, biblisch.

Scripture *s.* Heilige Schrift *f.*

scrivener *s.* Notar *m.*; Geldmakler *m.*

scrofula *s.* Skrofeln *f.pl.*

scrofulous *a.* skrofulös.

scroll *s.* Rolle *f.*; Schnörkel *m.*

scrounge *v.t.* stehlen, klauen, schnorren.

scrub *v.t.* scheuern; ~ *v.i.* sich placken; ~ *s.* Gestrüpp *n.*; Schrubber *m.*

scrunch *v.t.* zermalmen; ~ *v.i.* knirschen.

scruple *s.* Bedenklichkeit *f.*, Skrupel *m.*; ~ *v.i.* Bedenken tragen.

scrupulous *a.*, ~ly *adv.* bedenklich, gewissenhaft, ängstlich.

scrutinize *v.t. & i.* forschen; prüfen.

scrutiny *s.* genaue Untersuchung *f.*; Wahlprüfung *f.*

scud *v.i.* fortlaufen; rennen; (*nav.*) lenzen.

scuffle *s.* Balgerei *f.*; Handgemenge *n.*; ~ *v.i.* sich balgen.

scull *s.* kurze Ruder *n.*; ~ *v.i.* (mit zwei Rudern) rudern; ~ing-boat *s.* Ruderboot *n.*

scullery *s.* Aufwaschraum *m.*

scullion *s.* Küchenjunge *m.*

sculptor *s.* Bildhauer *m.*

sculpture *s.* Bildhauerkunst *f.*; Skulptur *f.*; *v.t.* schnitzen.

scum *s.* Schaum *m.*; Abschaum, Auswurf *m.*; ~ *v.t.* abschäumen.

scurf *s.* Schorf *m.*; Kruste *f.*

scurrility *s.* grobe Spass *m.*

scurrilous *a.*, ~ly *adv.* possenhaft; gemein, grob, zotig.

scurry *v.i.* dahineilen; ~ *s.* Hasten *n.*

scurvy *s.* Skorbut *m.*; ~ *a.* skorbutisch; gemein.

scut *s.* kurze Schwanz *m.*

scutcheon *s.* Wappenschild *n.*

scuttle *s.* Kohlenkasten *m.*; Luke *f.*; hastige Flucht *f.*; ~ *v.t.* (ein Schiff) durchlöchern, versenken; ~ *v.i.* flüchten.

scythe *s.* Sense *f.*

sea *s.* See *f.*; Meer *n.*; *at* ~, (*fig.*) ratlos.

seabed *s.* Meeresboden *m.*

seaboard *s.* Seeküste *f.*

sea-chart *s.* Seekarte *f.*

sea-coast *s.* Meeresküste *f.*

seafaring *a.* seefahrend.

sea-fight *s.* Seeschlacht *f.*

sea-going *a.* die See befahrend.

sea-green *s.* Meergrün *n.*

sea-gull *s.* Möwe *f.*

sea-horse *s.* Seepferdchen *n.*

seal *s.* Siegel, Petschaft *n.*; Bestätigung *f.*; Robbe *f.*, Seehund *m.*; *under my hand and* ~, unter Brief und Siegel; ~ *v.t. & i.* besiegeln, siegeln.

sea-level *s.* Meeresspiegel *m.*

sealing-wax *s.* Siegellack *m.*

sealskin *s.* Seehundsfell *n.*

seam *s.* Saum *m.*; Naht *f.*; Fuge *f.*; Flöz *n.*

seaman *s.* Seemann *m.*

seamanship *s.* Seemannskunst *f.*

seamstress *s.* Näh[t]erin *f.*

seamy *a.* mit Nähten; ~ *side*, Schattenseite *f.*

sea-piece *s.* Seestück *n.*

sea-plane *s.* Wasserflugzeug *n.*

seaport *s.* Seehafen *m.*

sear *v.t.* brennen, sengen; brandmarken; verhärten.

search *v.t. & i.* suchen, untersuchen, prüfen; ~ *s.* Suchen, Durchsuchen, Nachforschen *n.*; Prüfung *f.*; ~-warrant *s.* Haussuchungsbefehl *m.*

search-light *s.* Scheinwerfer *m.*

seasick *a.* seekrank.

sea-sickness *s.* Seekrankheit *f.*

sea-side *s.* Strand *m.*; Küste *f.*; Seebad *n.*; *to the* ~, an die See.

season *s.* Jahreszeit *f.*; rechte Zeit *f.*; Saison *f.*; *to be in* ~, *out of* ~, gegessen werden, nicht gegessen werden, saisongemäss, nichtsaisongemäss sein; ~ *v.t. & i.* reifen; trocknen; gewöhnen, abhärten; würzen; mildern.

seasonable *a.* schicklich, zeitgemäss.

seasoned *a.* reif, abgelagert; gewürzt.

seasoning *s.* Würze *f.*

season-ticket *s.* (*rail.*) Dauerkarte *f.*

seat *s.* Sitz (auch Hosensitz) *m.*; Stuhl *m.*; Lage *f.*; Schauplatz *m.*; Landsitz *m.*; Platz (Bahn, Omnibus) *m.*; corner-~, Eckplatz *m.*; ~ *v.t.* setzen; *to be ~ed,* sitzen; *take a ~,* nehmen Sie Platz!

seaward *a. & adv.* nach der See zu gelegen; seewärts.

seaweed *s.* Tang *m.*, Alge *f.*

seaworthy *a.* seetüchtig.

secede *v.i.* sich trennen.

secession *s.* Spaltung *f.*; Trennung *f.*

secessionist *s.* Abtrünnige *m.*; Sonderbündler *m.*

seclude *v.t.* ausschliessen, absondern.

seclusion *s.* Absonderung *f.*; Zurückgezogenheit *f.*

second *a.* der, die, das zweite; nächste; geringer; ~ *cousin,* Vetter (Base) zweiten Grades; ~ *sight,* zweite Gesicht *n.*; *on ~ thoughts,* bei nochmaliger Überlegung; ~ *s.* Sekundant *m.*; Sekunde *f.*; ~ *v.t.* beistehen, (Antrag) unterstützen.

secondary *a.,* ~ily *adv.* nächstfolgend; untergeordnet; Neben...; ~ *circuit,* (*elek.*) Nebenstromkreis *m.*; ~ *school,* höhere Schule *f.*

second-hand *a.* aus zweiter Hand; gebraucht; antiquarisch.

secondly *adv.* zweitens.

secrecy *s.* Heimlichkeit *f.*; Verschwiegenheit *f.*; Eingezogenheit *f.*

secret *a.,* ~ly *adv.* geheim, verborgen; verschwiegen; ~ *police,* Geheimpolizei *f.*; ~ *service,* Geheimdienst *m.*; ~ *s.* Geheimnis *n.*; *official ~,* Amtsgeheimnis *n.*

secretarial *a.* Sekretärs...

secretariat *s.* Sekretariat *n.*

secretary *s.* Schriftführer *m.*; Sekretär *m.*; Sekretärin *f.*

secrete *v.t.* absondern.

secretion *s.* Absonderung *f.*

secretive *a.* verschwiegen; geheimtuerisch.

sect *s.* Sekte *f.*

sectarian *a.* zu einer Sekte gehörig; ~ *s.* Sektierer *m.*

section *s.* Zerschneiden *n.*; Abteilung *f.*; Abschnitt *m.*; (*rail.*) Strecke *f.*; Durchschnitt *m.*

sector *s.* Kreisausschnitt *m.*; (*mil.*) Geländeabschnitt *m.*

secular *a.,* ~ly *adv.* hundertjährig; weltlich.

secularize *v.t.* verweltlichen; säkularisieren.

secure *a.,* ~ly *adv.* sicher; sorglos; ~ *v.t.* sichern, versichern; befestigen; sich verschaffen.

security *s.* Sicherheit, Sorglosigkeit *f.*; Schutz *m.*; Bürgschaft *f.*; securities *pl.* Wertpapiere *n.pl.*

sedan *s.* Sänfte *f.*; (*mot.*) Limousine *f.*

sedate *a.,* ~ly *adv.* ruhig, gesetzt.

sedative, *a.* stillend, beruhigend.

sedentary *a.* viel sitzend, sesshaft.

sedge *s.* Schilfgras *n.*, Binse *f.*

sediment *s.* Bodensatz *m.*; Ablagerung *f.*

sedition *s.* Aufstand *m.*; Empörung *f.*

seditious *a.,* ~ly *adv.* aufrührerisch.

seduce *v.t.* verführen, verleiten.

seducer *s.* Verführer *m.*

seduction *s.* Verführung *f.*

seductive *a.* verführerisch.

sedulous *a.,* ~ly *adv.* emsig, fleissig.

see *v.t. & i.st.* sehen; besuchen; *to ~ through,* durchschauen; *to ~ a thing through,* etwas bis ans Ende durchhalten; *to ~ to it,* dafür sorgen; (*Am.*) *I'll be seeing you,* auf Wiedersehen! ~ *s.* Bischofsstuhl *m.*

seed *s.* Same *m.*; Saat *f.*; ~ *v.i.* in Samen schiessen, ausfallen.

seedy *a.* samenreich; schäbig; elend.

seek *v.t. & i.st.* suchen, trachten; aufsuchen.

seem *v.i.* scheinen, erscheinen.

seeming *s.* Anschein *m.*; ~ *a.,* ~ly *adv.* scheinbar; dem Anscheine nach.

seemly *a.* anständig, schicklich.

seer *s.* Seher, Prophet *m.*

see-saw *s.* Wippe *f.*; ~ *v.i.* schwanken.

seethe *v.t. & i.r. & st.* sieden, kochen.

segment *s.* Abschnitt *m.*

segregate *v.t. & i.* absondern.

seismometer *s.* Erdbebenmesser *m.*

seizable *a.* ergreifbar; mit Beschlag belegbar.

seize *v.t.* ergreifen; wegnehmen; beschlagnahmen; *to be ~d of,* im Besitz sein von.

seizure *s.* Ergreifung *f.*; Verhaftung *f.*; Beschlagnahme *f.*; Krankheitsanfall *m.*

seldom *adv.* selten.

select *v.t.* auswählen, auslesen; ~ *a.* auserlesen.

selection *s.* Auswahl *f.*; Zuchtwahl *f.*

selectivity *s.* (*radio*) Trennschärfe *f.*

selenium *s.* Selen *n.*

self *n. & pref.* Selbst, Ich *n.*; selbst.

self-acting *a.* automatisch.

self-command *s.* Selbstbeherrschung *f.*

self-conceit *s.* Eigendünkel *m.*

self-confidence *s.* Selbstvertrauen *n.*

self-conscious *a.,* ~ly *adv.* befangen.

self-contained *a.* verschlossen; in sich vollständig.

self-control *s.* Selbstbeherrschung *f.*

self-defence *s.* Notwehr *f.*

self-denial *s.* Selbstverleugnung *f.*; ~ *Sunday,* Opfersonntag *m.*

self-evident *a.* selbstverständlich.

self-explanatory *a.* selbsterklärend; *it is ~,* es erklärt sich selbst.

self-governing *a*. autonom.
self-government *s*. Autonomie *f*.; Selbstregierung *f*.; Selbstverwaltung *f*.
self-help *s*. Selbsthülfe *f*.
self-indulgent *a*. seinen Neigungen nachlebend.
self-interest *s*. Eigennutz *m*.
selfish *a*., **~ly** *adv*. selbstsüchtig.
self-made *a*. selbstgemacht; durch eigene Kraft emporgekommen.
self-possession *s*. Selbstbeherrschung *f*.
self-preservation *s*. Selbsterhaltung *f*.
self-propelled *a*. (*mil.*) Selbstfahr...
self-raising flour *s*. Backpulvermehl *n*.
self-respect *s*. Selbstachtung *f*.
self-respecting *a*. mit Selbstachtung.
self-righteous *a*. selbstgerecht.
selfsame *a*. ebenderselbe.
self-styled *a*. sich selbst (so) nennend.
self-sufficiency *s*. Autarkie *f*.
self-taught *a*. selbstunterrichtet.
self-will *s*. Eigenwille, Eigensinn *m*.
sell *v.t.st.* verkaufen; (*fig.*) hereinlegen; **~** *v.i.* Absatz finden, gehen; *to be sold out*, ausverkauft sein; **~** *s*. Reinfall *m*.
seller *s*. Verkäufer *m*.
semaphore *s*. optische Telegraph *m*.
semblance *s*. Ähnlichkeit *f*.; Anschein *m*.
semibreve *s*. ganze Note *f*.
semicircle *s*. Halbkreis *m*.
semicircular *a*. halbkreisförmig.
semicolon *s*. Strichpunkt *m*.
semi-detached *a*. halbfreistehend, an das Nachbarhaus angebaut.
semi-final *s*. Vorschlussrunde *f*.
semi-finished *a*. halbfertig.
seminary *s*. Seminar *n*.
semiquaver *s*. Sechzehntelnote
semistiff *a*. halbsteif (Kragen)
semitone *s*. Halbton *m*.
semolina *s*. Griess *m*.
sempiternal *a*. immerwährend.
sempstress *s*. Näherin *f*.
senate *s*. Senat, Rat *m*.
senator *s*. Senator, Ratsherr *m*.
senatorial *a*., **~ly** *adv*. ratsherrlich.
send *v.t. & i.st.* schicken, senden; *to ~ for*, holen lassen.
sender *s*. Absender *m*.
senile *a*. greisenhaft; altersschwach.
senility *s*. Altersschwäche *f*.
senior *s*. Ältere, Älteste *m*.; **~** *a*. dienstälteste, rangälteste, Ober...
seniority *s*. höhere Alter *n*.; Dienstalter *n*.; Altersfolge *f*.
sensation *s*. Aufsehen *n*.; Eindruck *m*.; Empfindung *f*.; Sensation *f*.
sensational *a*. Aufsehen erregend.
sense *s*. Sinn, Verstand *m*.; Bedeutung *f*.; Gefühl *n*.; *common ~*, gesunde Menschenverstand *m*.
senseless *a*., **~ly** *adv*. sinnlos; unvernünftig; gefühllos, bewusstlos.

sensibility *s*. Empfindlichkeit *f*.; Empfindsamkeit *f*.
sensible *a*., **~bly** *adv*. empfindlich, fühlbar, merkbar; reizbar; empfindsam; vernünftig, klug.
sensitive *a*., **~ly** *adv*. empfindsam, reizbar; **~** *plant* *s*. Sinnpflanze *f*.
sensory *a*. Sinnes...
sensual *a*., **~ly** *adv*. sinnlich; wollüstig.
sensualist *s*. Wollüstling *m*.
sensuality *s*. Sinnlichkeit *f*.
sensuous *a*. sinnlich, die Sinne betreffend.
sentence *s*. Richterspruch, Urteil *n*.; Satz *m*.; *~ of death*, Todesurteil *n*.; *to pass ~*, das Urteil fällen; *to serve one's ~*, seine Strafe absitzen; **~** *v.t.* verurteilen.
sententious *a*., **~ly** *adv*. spruchreich; bündig.
sentient *a*. empfindend.
sentiment *s*. Empfindung *f*.; Gefühl *n*.; Gesinnung *f*.; Meinung *f*.
sentimental *a*., **~ly** *adv*. empfindsam, sentimental; **~** *value*, persönliche Wert *m*.
sentimentality *s*. Rührseligheit *f*.
sentinel, **sentry** *s*. Schildwache *f*.; **~-box**, Schilderhaus *n*.; *line of sentries*, Postenkette *f*.
separable *a*. trennbar.
separate *v.t.* trennen; **~** *v.i.* sich trennen; **~** *a*. getrennt, geschieden, einzeln; **~ly** *adv*. besonders.
separation *s*. Trennung *f*.; (*chem.*) Scheidung *f*.; Ehetrennung *f*.; *~ allowance*, Scheidungsalimente *n.pl.*; (*mil.*) Familienunterstützung.
sepoy *s*. indische Soldat *m*.
September *s*. September *m*.
septennial *a*. siebenjährig; siebenjährlich.
septic *a*. septisch, Fäulnis...
septuagenarian *s*. Siebzigjährige *m*. & *f*.
sepulchral *a*. Grab..., Begräbnis...
sepulchre *s*. Grabmal *n*.; Gruft *f*.
sepulture *s*. Beerdigung *f*.; Begräbnis *n*.
sequel *s*. Folge *f*.
sequence *s*. (Reihen)folge, Ordnung *f*.
sequester, **sequestrate** *v.t.* einziehen.
sequestration *s*. Absonderung *f*.; Beschlagnahme *f*.; Zwangsverwaltung *f*.
seraglio *s*. Serail *n*.
seraph *s*. Seraph *m*.
seraphic *a*. seraphisch.
sere *a*. dürr, trocken.
serenade *s*. Ständchen *n*.
serene *a*., **~ly** *adv*. heiter; ruhig.
serenity *s*. Heiterkeit, Gemütsruhe *f*.
serf *s*. Leibeigene *m*.
serfdom *s*. Leibeigenschaft *f*.
serge *s*. Sersche *f*., Serge *f*.
sergeant *s*. Sergeant *m*.; (Polizei-) Wachtmeister *m*.; Gerichtsdiener *m*.; **~-major** *s*. Feldwebel *m*.
serial *a*. periodisch, Lieferungs...; **~**

number, laufende Nummer *f.*; ~ *s.* Lieferungswerk *n.*, Zeitschrift *f.*

seriatim *adv.* der Reihe nach.

series *s.* Reihe, Folge *f.*; (*elek.*) ~ *connection*, Reihenschaltung *f.*

serious *a.* ernsthaft; wichtig; ~ly *adv.* im Ernst; *to take a thing seriously*, etwas ernst nehmen.

sermon *s.* Predigt *f.*

serpent *s.* Schlange *f.*

serpentine *a.* schlangenförmig, geschlängelt.

serrated *a.* (*bot.*) gesägt, zackig.

serried *a.* dicht zusammengedrängt.

serum *s.* Blutwasser *n.*; Heilserum *n.*

servant *s.* Diener, Bediente *m.*; Magd *f.*; (Dienst)mädchen *n.*

serve *v.t. & i.* dienen; aufwarten, servieren; auftragen; dienlich sein; genügen; zustellen; (*tennis*) angeben, aufschlagen; ~*s him right!*, geschieht ihm recht!

service *s.* Dienst *m.*; Bedienung *f.*; Dienstpflicht *f.*; Zustellung *f.*; Gefälligkeit *f.*; Nutzen *m.*; Gottesdienst *m.*; Tafelservice *n.*; (*tennis*) Aufschlag *m.*, Angabe *f.*; Verkehrsdienst *m.*; *steamship* ~ *f.*; Dampferverkehr; *500 hours of* ~, 500 Stunden Arbeitsleistung (einer Maschine); *car* ~, Wagenpflege *f.*; ~ *station*, Tankstelle *f.*; ~ *flat*, Wohnung mit Bedienung *f.*; ~ *man*, Wehrmachtsangehöriger *m.*; ~ *s pl.* öffentliche Dienste, Betriebe (auch privater Gesellschaften), öffentliche Behörden; *the* (*fighting*) ~*s pl.* die Wehrmacht *f.*; *old* ~*s*, Gas, Elektrisch, etc.; *to* ~ *v.t.* bedienen (von öffentlichen Diensten, etc.).

serviceable *a.*, ~ly *adv.* nützlich, brauchbar, verwendungsfähig.

servile *a.*, ~ly *adv.* knechtisch.

servility *s.* Unterwürfigkeit *f.*

servitude *s.* Knechtschaft, Sklaverei *f.*

session *s.* Sitzung *f.*; Schuljahr *n.*

set *v.t.* setzen, stellen; ordnen; (Uhr) stellen; (Edelsteine) fassen; pflanzen; *to* ~ (*to music*), komponieren; ~ *v.i.* untergehen (Sonne); gerinnen; *to* ~ *about*, an etwas gehen, anfangen; *to* ~ *aside* (Urteil) aufheben; *to* ~ *down*, niedersetzen; aufschreiben; *to* ~ *forth*, dartun; ausdrücken; *to* ~ *in*, einsetzen; pflanzen; anfangen, eintreten; *to* ~ *off*, hervorheben; abreisen; *to* ~ *off against*, anrechnen gegen; *to* ~ *on*, anhetzen; angreifen; *to* ~ *out*, bestimmen, festsetzen; hervorheben; beginnen; aufbrechen; *to* ~ *to*, anfangen, sich legen (auf); *to* ~ *up*, aufrichten; festsetzen; sich niederlassen; *to* ~ *up for*, sich ausgeben für; ~ *s.* Satz *m.*; Reihe *f.*; Gespann, Paar *n.*; Spiel *n.*; Besteck *n.*; Gattung; Bande *f.*; Garnitur *f.*; Ser-

vice *n.*; ~ *p. & a.* festgesetzt, bestimmt; geordnet; starr; versessen auf.

setback *s.* Rückschlag *m.*

set-down *s.* derbe Verweis *m.*, Abfuhr *f.*

set-off *s.* Gegensatz *m.*; Schmuck *m.*; Gegenforderung *f.*

settee *s.* Ruhebank *f.*; Art Sofa *n.*

setter *s.* Vorstehhund *m.*; Setzer *m.*

setting *s.* Einfassung *f.*; Ordnen *n.*; Untergang (der Sonne) *f.*; Musikbegleitung *f.*

settle *v.t.* erledigen; festsetzen; einrichten, bestimmen; regeln; schlichten; bezahlen; (eine Summe) aussetzen; *to* ~ *an annuity on a person*, einem eine Leibrente aussetzen; ~ *v.i.* sich setzen, sich senken; sich ansiedeln; *to* ~ *down*, sich niederlassen (als Arzt, etc.), sich verheiraten; ~ *s.* Bank, Truhe *f.*; *settling day*, Abrechnungstag (Börse) *m.*

settlement *s.* Festsetzung, Anordnung, Einrichtung *f.*; Versorgung *f.*; Leibrente *f.*, Vermächtnis *n.*, Familienstiftung *f.*; Niederlassung, Ansiedlung *f.*; Vergleich *m.*; Rechnungsabschluss *m.*; Schlichtung *f.*; Regelung *f.*; *in* ~, als Bezahlung.

settler *s.* Ansiedler *m.*, Gnadenstoss *m.*

seven, sieben.

sevenfold *a. & adv.* siebenfach.

seventeen, siebzehn.

seventy, siebzig.

sever *v.t.* (*v.i. sich*) trennen, abschneiden.

several *a.* verschieden; getrennt, einzeln; mehrere; ~ly *adv.* besonders, einzeln.

severance *s.* Trennung *f.*

severe *a.*, ~ly *adv.* streng; heftig.

severity *s.* Strenge, Härte *f.*; Ernst *m.*

sew *v.t. & i.* nähen, heften; *sewing kit*, Nähzeug *n.*; *sewing silk*, Nähseide *f.*

sewage *s.* Kloakenwasser *n.*

sewer *s.* Abzugskanal *m.*; Kloake *f.*

sewerage *s.* Kanalwesen *n.*; abfliessende Wasser *n.*; Kanalbau *m.*

sewing-machine *s.* Nähmaschine *f.*

sewing-needle *s.* Nähnadel *f.*

sex *s.* Geschlecht *n.*

sexagenarian *s.* Sechzigjährige *m. & f.*

sextant *s.* Sextant *m.*

sexton *s.* Küster *m.*; Totengräber *m.*

sexual *a.* geschlechtlich.

shabby *a.*, ~ly *adv.* schäbig.

shackle *v.t.* fesseln; ~ *s.* Kettenglied *n.*; ~*s s.pl.* Fesseln *f.pl.*

shade *s.* Schatten *m.*; Schattierung *f.*; (*fig.*) Schirm *m.*; Glasglocke *f.*; Abtönung *f.*; ~ *v.t.* beschatten, schattieren; schützen.

shadow *s.* Schatten *m.*; ~ *v.t.* beschatten; schattieren; schützen; heimlich folgen.

shadowy *a.* schattig, dunkel.

shady *a.* schattig; anrüchig.

shaft *s.* Schaft *m.*; Pfeil; Deichsel *f.*; Schacht *m.*; (*mech.*) Welle, Spindel *f.*

shag *s.* Zotte *f.*; Krülltabak *m.*

shagged, shaggy *a.* zottig; buschig.

shake *v.t.st.* (ab)schütteln, rütteln; erschüttern; *to ~ hands,* sich die Hände geben; *to ~ off,* abschütteln; ~ *v.i.* beben, wanken; *(mus.)* trillern; ~ *s.* Erschütterung *f.*; Stoss *m.*; Triller *m.*; Schütteln *n.*; (Hände-)Druck *m.*

shakedown *s.* Notlager *n.*

shaky *a.* wacklig, gebrechlich.

shall *v.i. def.st.* soll, werde.

shallop *s.* Schaluppe *f.*

shallow *a.,* ~ly *adv.* seicht, matt; schwach, albern; ~ *s.* Untiefe *f.*

sham *a.* unecht, nachgemacht; Schein...; ~ *s.* Täuschung *f.*, Schein *m.*; ~ *v.t. & i.* vortäuschen, betrügen.

shamble *v.i.* schlenkern.

shambles *s.pl.* Schlachthaus *n.*

shame *s.* Scham *f.*;|Schande *f.*; *for ~!,* pfui; ~ *v.t.* beschämen; schänden.

shamefaced *a.,* ~ly *adv.* schamhaft.

shameful *a.,* ~ly *adv.* schändlich.

shameless *a.,* ~ly *adv.* unverschämt.

shampoo *v.t.* massieren, kneten; den Kopf waschen, schampunieren.

shamrock *s.* weisse Klee *m.*

shank *s.* Schenkel *m.*; Stengel *m.*; *(mech.)* Stiel, Schaft *m.*

shanty *s.* Hütte, Bude *f.*

shape *s.* Form, Gestalt *f.*; Modell *n.*; Wuchs *m.*; *in good ~,* in guter Verfassung; ~ *v.t.* bilden, gestalten; ~ *v.i.* sich gestalten.

shapeless *a.* unförmlich, ungestalt.

shapely *a.* wohlgebildet.

shaper, shaping machine *s. (mech.)* Shapingmaschine *f.*

share *s.* Teil, Anteil *m.*; Aktie *f.*, Anteilschein *m.*; *ordinary ~,* Stammaktie *f.*; *preference ~,* Vorzugsaktie *f.*; Pflugschar *f.*; *in equal ~s,* zu gleichen Teilen; ~ *v.t.* verteilen; ~ *v.i.* teilhaben, teilnehmen.

shareholder *s.* Aktionär *m.*

shark *s.* Haifisch *m.*; Gauner *m.*; ~ *v.i.* gaunern.

sharp *a.,* ~ly *adv.* scharf; spitzig; streng; heftig; hitzig; beissend; spitzfindig; pfiffig; genau; *(mus.)* um einen halben Ton erhöht; *to look ~,* aufpassen; *at 10 o'clock ~,* pünktlich um 10 Uhr; ~ *s. (mus.)* Kreuz *n.*

sharpen *v.t.* schärfen, wetzen, zuspitzen.

sharper *s.* Bauernfänger, Spitzbube *m.*

shatter *v.t.* zerschmettern, zerstreuen; zerrütten; ~ *v.i.* zerfallen.

shatterproof glass *s.* Sicherheitsglas *n.*

shave *v.t.r. & st.* schaben; scheren; rasieren; placken; leicht streifen; ~ *v.i.* sich rasieren.

shaving *s.* Rasieren *n.*; Schabsel, Schnitzel *n.*; ~s *pl.* Hobelspäne *m.pl.*; ~ *cream s.*

Rasierkreme *f.*; *brushless ~ cream,* Rasierkreme ohne Pinsel; ~ *soap,* ~ *stick,* Rasierseife *f.*; ~ *things pl.* Rasiersachen *f.pl.*

shaving-brush *s.* Rasierpinsel *m.*

shawl *s.* Umschlagetuch *n.*, Schal *m.*

she *pn.* sie; ~ *s.* Weibchen *n.*

sheaf *s.* Garbe *f.*

shear *v.t.st.* scheren; rupfen; ~ *s.* Schur *f.*; ~s *pl.* grosse Schere *f.*

sheath *s.* Scheide *f.*

sheathe *v.t.* in die Scheide stecken; überziehen.

sheave *s.* Rolle *f.*

shed *s.* Schuppen *m.*; Schirmdach *n.*; ~ *v.t.* vergiessen, ausschütten; abwerfen; verbreiten.

sheen *s.* Schimmer, Glanz *m.*; ~ *a.* schimmernd, glänzend.

sheep *s.* Schaf *n.*; Dummkopf *m.*

sheep-cot, sheep-fold *s.* Schafhürde *f.*

sheepish *a.,* ~ly *adv.* einfältig.

sheep-pen *s.* Schafhürde *f.*

sheep-walk *s.* Schafweide *f.*

sheer *a.* lauter, rein; senkrecht; ~ *adv.* völlig; ~ *v.i. (nav.)* gieren, abweichen.

sheet *s.* Stück Leinwand *n.*; Bettuch *n.*; Fläche, Platte *f.*; Bogen (Papier) *m.*; *in ~s,* un(ein-)gebunden (von Büchern); ~ *v.t.* überziehen.

sheet-anchor *s.* Notanker *m.*

sheet-glass *s.* Tafelglas *n.*

sheeting *s.* Bettleinwand *f.*

sheet-iron *s.* Eisenblech *n.*

sheet-lightning *s.* Wetterleuchten *n.*

sheet-metal *s.* Blech *n.*

shelf *s.* Fach *n.*, Brett *n.*; Regal *n.*; Sims *m.* (*& n.*); Sandbank *f.*

shell *s.* Schale, Hülse, Muschel *f.*; Gehäuse *n.*; Granate *f.*; ~ *v.t.* (*v.i. sich*) schälen, abschuppen; beschiessen.

shellac *s.* Schellack *m.*

shell-fish *s.* Schaltier *n.*

shell-proof *a.* bombensicher.

shelter *s.* Obdach *n.*; Schutz *m.*; Schutzraum (Luftschutz) *m.*; ~ *v.t.* decken; schützen, bergen, beherbergen; ~ *v.i.* Schutz suchen.

shelve *v.t.* auf ein Regal stellen; abschieben; auf die lange Bank schieben; ~ *v.i.* sich neigen.

shelving *a.* abschüssig.

shepherd *s.* Schäfer, Hirt *m.*

shepherdess *s.* Schäferin, Hirtin *f.*

sherbet *s.* Sorbett *n.*

sherry *s.* Sherry(wein) *m.*

shield *s.* Schild *n.*; ~ *v.t.* bedecken; beschirmen.

shift *v.t.* wechseln; ausziehen; umkleiden; versetzen, wegschieben, wegschaffen; ~ *v.i.* sich fortbewegen; ausweichen; sich verändern; sich umkleiden; sich heraushelfen; (für sich) sorgen; (Bal-

last) überschiessen; ~ s. Wechsel m.;
Ausflucht f.; List f.; Schicht f., Tagewerk m.; to make ~, sich behelfen.
shifting a., ~ly adv. listig, schlau; beweglich.
shiftless a. hilflos, ungewandt.
shifty a. unstet; ränkevoll.
shilling s. Schilling m.; a ~ in the pound,
zu 5 Prozent.
shilly-shally n. Unentschlossenheit f.; ~
v.i. schwanken.
shin s. Schienbein n.
shindy s. Radau, Krach m.
shine v.i. scheinen, leuchten, funkeln; ~ s.
Schein, Glanz m.
shingle s. Schindel f.; Steingeröll n.; ~s
s.pl. Gürtelrose f.; ~ v.t. (Haar) kurz
schneiden.
shining, shiny, a. hell, glänzend.
ship s. Schiff n.; ~ v.t. schiffen; einschiffen; verschiffen; versenden.
shipboard s. Schiffsbord m.
ship-boy s. Schiffsjunge m.
ship-broker s. Schiffsmakler m.
shipmate s. Schiffsmaat m.
shipment s. Verschiffung f.; Warensendung f.
shipowner s. Reeder m.
shipping s. Einschiffung f.; Schiffsbestand
m.; Schiffahrt f.; ~ agent s. Schiffs-
spediteur m.; ~-space s. Schiffsraum
m.
shipper s. Versender, Verlader m.
shipshape a. nach Schiffsart; in guter
Ordnung.
shipwreck s. Schiffbruch m.; ~ v.t. & i.
scheitern, stranden.
shipwright s. Schiffbauer m.
ship-yard s. Werft f.
shire (in Zus.) s. Grafschaft f.
shirk v.t. & i. vermeiden; sich drücken.
shirker s. Drückeberger m.
shirt s. (Manns)hemd n.; ~ blouse s.
Hemdbluse f.
shirt-front s. Vorhemdchen n.
shirting s. Hemdentuch n.
shirtsleeve s. Hemdsärmel m.
shiver v.t. zerbrechen; zertrümmern; ~
v.i. zersplöttern, frösteln, zittern; ~ s.
Splitter m.; Schauer m.
shivery a. brüchig; zitternd.
shoal s. Schwarm m.; Menge f.; Untiefe f.;
~ a. seicht; ~ v.i. wimmeln; seicht
werden.
shock s. Stoss m.; Angriff m.; Anstoss m.;
Ärgernis m.; Schock (Garben) n.;
Haarschopf m.; elektrische Schlag m.;
~ troops, (mil.) Stosstruppen pl.; ~ v.t.
anstossen; erschüttern; Anstoss geben,
verletzen, entsetzen.
shocking a., ~ly adv. anstössig.
shoddy s. schlechte Tuch n.; Lumpen-
wolle f.; ~ a. schlecht, Schund ...

shoe s. Schuh m.; Hufeisen n.; ~ v.t.st.
beschuhen; beschlagen (ein Pferd).
shoe-horn s. Schuhanzieher m., Schuh-
löffel m.
shoeing s. Beschlagen; ~ forge s. Huf-
schmiede f.
shoe-lace s. Schuhlitze f.
shoe-maker s. Schuhmacher m.
shoe-polish s. Schuhwichse f.
shoeshine s. Schuhglanz m.
shoe-stretcher, shoetree s. Schuhleisten m.
shoe-strings pl. (Am.) Schuhbänder n.pl.
shoot v.t.st. schiessen; abfeuern; to ~
down, (avi.) abschiessen; to ~ dead, to ~
to death, totschiessen; to ~ a film, einen
Film aufnehmen; ~ v.t. hervorschiess-
en; sprossen; daherschiessen; ~ s.
Schössling m.; Gleitbahn f.
shooting s. Jagd f.; Schuss m.; ~-box,
Jagdhütte f.; ~-gallery, Schiesstand
m.
shooting-star s. Sternschnuppe f.
shop, s. Laden m.; Werkstatt f.; to talk ~,
fachsimpeln; ~ v.i. einkaufen (gehen).
shop-front s. Schaufenster m.
shop-girl s. Ladenmädchen n.
shop-keeper s. Ladeninhaber m.
shop-lifter s. Ladendieb m.; ~-lifting s.
Ladendiebstahl m.
shopping s. Einkaufen n.; ~ centre Ge-
schäftsgegend f., Ladengebäude n.
shop-steward s. Arbeitervertrauensmann
m.
shop-walker s. Rayonchef m.
shore s. Gestade n.; Strand m.
short a. kurz; eng; beschränkt; ~ly adv. in
kurzem, bald; in ~, kurzum; to cut ~,
unterbrechen; in ~ supply, beschränkt
verfügbar; to be ~ of, an etwas Mangel
haben.
shortage s. Mangel m., Knappheit f.
shortbread s. Mürbegebäck n.
short-circuit s. (Am.) short s. Kurzschluss
m.
shortcoming s. Mangel m., Unzulänglichkeit f.
short-cut s. Abkürzungsweg m.
shorten v.t. abkürzen, verkürzen; ~ v.i.
kürzer werden.
shorthand s. Stenographie f.
short-handed a. mit zu wenig Arbeits-
kräften versehen.
short-lived a. kurzlebig.
shortness s. Kürze f.
short-sighted a. kurzsichtig.
short story s. Kurzgeschichte f.
short-term a. kurzfristig.
short-wave s. (radio) Kurzwelle f.
short-winded a. kurzatmig.
shot s. Schuss m.; Schussweite f.; Schrot
m. or n.; Kugel f.; Zeche f.; Schütze m.;
~ a. schillernd.¡
shotgun s. Jagdflinte. Schrotflinte f.

shot-proof *a.* kugelfest.

shoulder *s.* Schulter, Achsel *f.*; Vorsprung *m.*; *to turn a cold ~ on a person, to cold-~ a person,* einem die kalte Schulter zeigen; ~ *v.t.* auf die Schulter nehmen, schultern; drängen, stossen.

shoulder-bag *s.* (Damen)Schultertasche *f.*

shoulder-blade *s.* Schulterblatt *n.*

shoulder-strap *s.* Achselklappe *f.*

shout *v.t.* laut rufen; jauchzen; schreien; ~ *s.* Geschrei *n.*; Zuruf *m.*

shove *v.t.* schieben, stossen; ~ *s.* Schub, Stoss *m.*

shovel *s.* Schaufel *f.*; Schüppe *f.*; ~ *v.t.* schaufeln.

show *v.t.r. & st.* sehen lassen, zeigen; beweisen; *to ~ round,* herumführen; *on your own ~ing,* nach Ihrer eigenen Aussage; ~ *v.i.* sich zeigen, erscheinen; *to ~ off,* prahlen; ~ *s.* Schau *f.*; Schauspiel *n.*, Gepränge *n.*; Anschein *m.*; Ausstellung *f.*; *by ~ of hands,* durch Heben der Hände (bei Wahlen); dumb~ *s.* Pantomime *f.*; flower-~ *s.* Blumenausstellung *f.*; ~-case *s.* Schaukasten *m.*; ~man *s.* Schaubudenbesitzer, Aussteller *m.*; ~room *s.* Ausstellungsraum *m.*

showdown *s.* endgültige Kraftprobe *f.*

shower *s.* Regenschauer *m.*; Fülle *f.*; ~ *v.i.* schauern, regnen; ~ *v.t.* überschütten.

shower-bath *s.* Brausebad *n.*

showery *a.* regnerisch, Regen...

showy *a.* prunkend, Aufsehen erregend.

shrapnel *s.* Schrapnell *n.*

shred *v.t.st.* zerfetzen; schroten; ~ *s.* Abschnitzel *n.*; Fetzen *m.*

shrew *s.* zänkische Weib *n.*; Spitzmaus *f.*

shrewd *a.* ~ly *adv.* schlau, verschlagen.

shrewdness *s.* Schlauheit *f.*

shrewish *a.* ~ly *adv.* zänkisch.

shriek *v.i.* kreischen; ~ *s.* Schrei *m.*

shrift *s. short ~,* kurze Frist *f.*

shrill *a.* gellend.

shrimp *s.* Garnele *f.*, Krabbe *f.*; Knirps *m.*

shrine *s.* Schrein *m.*

shrink *v.i.st.* einschrumpfen; zurückbeben; einlaufen (Stoffe); zittern, schaudern; ~ *v.t.* zusammenziehen.

shrinkage *s.* Einschrumpfen *n.*

shrive *v.t.st.* Beichte hören; ~ *v.refl.* beichten.

shrivel *v.t.* runzeln, zusammenziehen; ~ *v.i.* einschrumpfen, sich runzeln.

shroud *s.* Hülle *f.*; Leichentuch *n.*; ~ *v.t.* bergen, beschützen; einhüllen.

Shrove-tide *s.* Fastenzeit *f.*

Shrove-Tuesday *s.* Fastnacht(sdienstag *m.*) *f.*

shrub *s.* Staude *f.*, Strauch *m.*

shrubbery *s.* Gebüsch *n.*

shrug *v.t.* die Achseln zucken; *to ~ one's shoulders,* mit den Achseln zucken; ~ *s.* Achselzucken *n.*

shudder *s.* Schauder *m.*; ~ *v.i.* schaudern.

shuffle *v.t.* mischen (Karten), mengen; *to ~ off,* abstreifen; ~ *v.i.* schlürfend gehen, Ausflüchte suchen, sich drehen und wenden; ~ *s.* Ausflucht *f.*; Unredlichkeit *f.*

shuffling *a.* wankend; unredlich, ausweichend.

shun *v.t.* meiden, fliehen, scheuen.

shunt *s.* Nebengleis *n.*; Nebenanschluss *f.*; ~ *v.t.* (einen Zug) auf ein Seitengeleise schieben, rangieren.

shut *v.t.* zumachen, schliessen; *to ~ down,* (Fabrik) stillegen; *to ~ up,* einsperren; ~ *v.i.* sich schliessen, zugehen; ~ *up,* halts Maul!

shutdown *s.* Stillegung *f.*

shutter *s.* Fensterladen *m.*; (*phot.*) Verschluss *m.*

shuttle *s.* (Weber-)schiffchen *n.*; ~-train *s.* Pendelzug *m.*; ~-service *s.* Pendelverkehr *m.*

shuttlecock *s.* Federball *m.*

shy *a.* ~ly *adv.* scheu, schüchtern; ~ *v.i.* scheuen (von Pferden).

sibilant *a.* zischend; ~ *s.* Zischlaut *m.*

sibyl *s.* Sibylle, Prophetin *f.*

sibylline *a.* sibyllinisch.

sick *a.* krank; übel; überdrüssig; (*mil.*) ~-bay, ~-ward *s.* Revier *n.*; ~-call *s.* (*mil.*) Krankenappell *m.*; *to go on ~-call,* sich krank melden; ~-leave *s.* Krankenurlaub *m.*

sicken *v.t.* krank machen; ~ *v.i.* krank werden; Ekel empfinden.

sickle *s.* Sichel *f.*

sickly *a.* kränklich, schwächlich, siech.

sickness *s.* Krankheit, Übelkeit *f.*

side *s.* Seite *f.*; Rand *m.*; Partei *f.*; (*geom.*) Schenkel (des Dreiecks); ~ *of bacon,* Speckseite *f.*; *to take ~s,* Partei nehmen; *to ~ with, v.i.* jemandes Partei ergreifen.

side-arms *s.pl.* Seitengewehr *n.*

sideboard *s.* Anrichte *f.*

side-car *s.* Beiwagen (*m.*) (des Motorrades).

side-light *s.* Streiflicht *n.*

sideline *s.* Nebenverdienst *m.*, Nebenbranche *f.*

sidelong *a. & adv.* seitwärts.

sidereal *a.* Sternen..., gestirnt.

side-saddle *s.* Damensattel *m.*

sideshow *s.* Nebenattraktion *f.*

sidestep *v.i.* (*Am.*) ausweichen (*fig.*).

sidetrack *v.t.* ablenken; *to ~ the issue,* von der wirklichen Frage ablenken.

sidestroke *s.* Seitenschwimmen *n.*

side-walk *s.* Bürgersteig *m.*

sideways *adv.* seitwärts.

siding *s.* Parteinahme *f.*; (*rail.*) Nebengleis *n.*

sidle *v.i.* seitwärts gehen.

siege s. Belagerung f.

sieve s. Sieb n.

sift v.t. sieben; sichten, prüfen.

sigh v.i. seufzen; ~ v.t. ausseufzen, beseufzen; ~ s. Seufzer m.

sight s. Gesicht n.; Sehkraft f.; Anblick m.; Visier n.; at first ~, auf den ersten Blick; 10 days after ~, (com.) 10 Tage nach Sicht; by ~, vom Sehen; in ~, in Sicht; to lose ~ of, aus dem Gesicht verlieren; bill at ~, Sichtwechsel m.; ~s pl. Sehenswürdigkeiten pl.; ~ v.t. sichten, zielen.

sightly a. wohlgestalt, schön.

sight-seeing s. Besichtigung (f.) von Sehenswürdigkeiten.

sign s. Zeichen n.; Kennzeichen n.; Aushängeschild n.; ~ v.t. & i. unterschreiben, unterzeichnen; winken; to ~ on, sich anwerben lassen; authorized to ~, zeichnungsberechtigt; ~ed 'gezeichnet' (gez.).

signal s. Zeichen n.; Signal n.; ~ box s. (rail.) Stellwerk n.; ~ centre s. (mil.) Nachrichtenzentrale f.; ~ communications pl. (mil.) Nachrichtenwesen n.; ~man s. (rail.) Signalwärter m.; ~ troops pl. (mil.) Nachrichtentruppen pl.; ~ a., ~ly adv. ausgezeichnet, vorzüglich; ~ v.t. signalisieren.

signalize v.t. auszeichnen.

signatory s. Unterzeichner m.; ~ a. unterzeichnend; ~ powers pl. Signatarmächte f.pl.

signature s. Zeichen, Kennzeichen n.; Unterschrift f.

sign-board s. Aushängeschild n.

signet s. Siegel n.; ~ ring s. Siegelring m.

significance s. Bedeutung f.; Sinn m.

significant a., ~ly adv. bezeichnend; bedeutsam.

signification s. Bedeutung f.

signify v.t. & i. anzeigen; bedeuten.

sign-post s. Wegweiser m.

silence s. Ruhe f., Stillschweigen n.; Verschwiegenheit f.; to keep ~, schweigen; ~!, i. still!; ~ v.t. zum Schweigen bringen.

silent a., ~ly adv. schweigend; stumm; verschwiegen; to be ~, schweigen; ~ film, stumme Film m.

silica s. Kieselerde f.

silk s. Seide f.; Seidenzeug n.; shot ~ Schillerseide f.; ~s pl. Seidenstoffe m.pl.; ~ a. seiden.

silken a. seiden; seidenartig, weich.

silk-growing s. Seidenzucht f.

silkworm s. Seidenraupe f.

silky a. seiden; seidenartig.

sill s. Schwelle, Brüstung f.; Fensterbrett n.

silly a., ~ily adv. einfältig, albern; ~ season, Sauregurkenzeit f.

silo s. Kornkeller m.; Kornlagerhaus n.

silt v.i. verschlammen; ~ s. Schlamm m.

silver s. Silber n.; Silbergeld n.; ~ lining, Silberstreifen; ~-plated a. versilbert; ~ a. silbern; ~ v.t. versilbern.

silver-plate s. Silbergerät n.

silversmith s. Silberarbeiter m.

silvery a. silbern; silberhell.

similar a., ~ly adv. gleichartig, ähnlich.

similarity s. Ähnlichkeit f.

simile s. Gleichnis n.

similitude s. Ähnlichkeit f.

simmer v.i. gelind kochen, brodeln.

simper v.i. einfältig lächeln; ~ s. gezierte Lächeln n.

simple a., **simply** adv. einfach, einzeln; einfältig.

simple-minded a. arglos.

simpleton s. Tropf m., Dummkopf m.

simplicity s. Einfachheit, Einfalt f.

simplify v.t. vereinfachen.

simulate v.t. & i. nachahmen; (er-) heucheln; vorschützen.

simulation s. Verstellung f.

simultaneous a., ~ly adv. gleichzeitig.

sin s. Sünde f.; ~ v.i. sündigen.

since pr. & adv. seit, seitdem; long ~, schon lange; ~ c. da; seit.

sincere a., ~ly adv. aufrichtig; yours ~ly, Ihr ergebener.

sincerity s. Aufrichtigkeit, Offenheit f.

sine s. (math.) Sinus m.

sinecure s. Sinekur f.; Ruheamt n.

sinew s. Sehne f.; Nerv m.

sinewy a. sehnig; stark.

sinful a., ~ly adv. sündig, sündhaft.

sing v.t. & i.st. singen, besingen.

singe v.t. ansengen, versengen.

singer s. Sänger(in) m. (& f.).

single a., ~ly adv. einfach; ledig; ~-breasted a. einreihig (Anzug); ~ combat s. Zweikampf m.; ~-handed a. ohne Hilfe; ~ journey s. Hinreise f.; ~ room s. einbettige Zimmer n.; ~ track a. (rail.) eingleisig; ~ s. (tennis) Einzelspiel n.; ~ out v.t. absondern; aussuchen.

singleness s. Einzelheit f.; Einfachheit f., Aufrichtigkeit f.

sing-song s., Singsang m.

singular a., ~ly adv. einzigartig; ungewöhnlich; ~ s. (gram.) Einzahl f.

singularity s. Einzigartigkeit f., Sonderbarkeit f.

sinister a., ~ly adv. (her.) link; unheilvoll; schlimm, boshaft.

sink v.i.st. (ver)sinken; fallen; abnehmen; umkommen; ~ v.t. (ver)senken; abteufen; unterdrücken, niederschlagen; in den Grund bohren; (Schuld) tilgen; ~ s. Abzug m.; Gusstein, Ausguss m.; Senkgrube f.

sinking-fund s. Tilgungsfonds m.

sinless *a.* sündlos, unschuldig.

sinner *s.* Sünder *m.*

sinuous *a.* geschlängelt, gewunden.

sinus *s. (anat.)* Höhlung *f.*

sip *v.t.* nippen; schlürfen; ~ *s.* Schlückchen *n.*

siphon *s.* (Saug-) Heber *m.*; Siphonflasche *f.*

sir *s.* Herr (als Anrede) *m.*; Sir (Titel eines Baronets und Ritters) *m.*

sire *s.* Vater *m.*; Sire *m.*

siren *s.* Sirene *f.*

siren-suit *s.* Luftschutzanzug *m.*

sirloin *s.* Lendenbraten *m.*

siskin *s.* Zeisig *m.*

sister *s.* Schwester *f.*; Nonne *f.*; Oberschwester (Krankenpflegerin) *f.*; ~-**in-law** *s.* Schwägerin *f.*

sisterhood *s.* Schwesternschaft *f.*

sisterly *a.* schwesterlich.

sit *v.i.s.t.* sitzen; brüten; ~ *v.t.* to ~ *oneself*, sich setzen; *to* ~ *down*, sich setzen; *to* ~ *for an examination*, sich einer Prüfung unterziehen; ~**down strike** *s.* Sitzstreik.

site *s.* Lage *f.*, Platz *m.*

sitter *s.* Portraitmodell *n.*

sitting *s.* Sitzen *n.*; Sitzung *f.*

sitting-room *s.* Wohnzimmer *n.*

situated *a.* liegend, gelegen.

situation *s.* Lage *f.*; Zustand *m.*; Stellung, Stelle *f.*; ~ *estimate*, (*mil.*) Lagebeurteilung *f.*, ~ *map*, Lagekarte *f.*, ~ *report*, Lagemeldung *f.*

six, sechs; *at* ~*es and sevens*, in Verwirrung.

sixteen, sechzehn.

sixty, sechzig.

sizable, sizeable *a.*, ~**ly** *adv.* ansehnlich.

size *s.* Grösse *f.*; Mass *n.*; Format *n.*; ~ *v.t.* grundieren.

sized *a.* von gewisser Grösse; geleimt.

skate *s.* Schlittschuh *m.*; Roche[n] (Fisch) *m.*; ~ *v.i.* Schlittschuh laufen.

skater *s.* Schlittschuhläufer *m.*

skating-rink *s.* Rollschuhbahn; Eisbahn *f.*

skedaddle *v.i.* davonlaufen.

skein *s.* Strähne *f.*

skeleton *s.* Gerippe *n.*; Gestell *n.*; Rodelschlitten *m.*; ~ *key*, Nachschlüssel *m.*; ~ *staff*, (*mil.*) Stammpersonal, Kader *n.*

sketch *s.* Entwurf *m.*; Skizze *f.*; ~ *v.t.* entwerfen, skizzieren.

sketchy *a.* flüchtig.

skewer *s.* Speiler *m.*; ~ *v.t.* aufspeilern.

ski *s.* Ski *m.* (*pl.* Skier), Schi, Schneeschuh *m.*; ~ *v.i.* skilaufen, schilaufen.

skid *s.* Hemmschuh *m.*; Kufe *f.*; ~ *v.t.* hemmen; ~ *v.i.* ausrutschen.

skiff *s.* Nachen *m.*

skilful *a.*, ~**ly** *adv.* geschickt, erfahren.

skill *s.* Geschicklichkeit *f.*; Fertigkeit *f.*

skilled *a.* geschickt; ausgebildet; ~ *worker*, gelernte Arbeiter *m.*

skim *v.t.* abschäumen, (Milch) entrahmen; ~ *v.i.* flüchtig hingleiten; ~-**milk** *s.* Magermilch *f.*

skimp *v.t.* knapp halten.

skin *s.* Haut *f.*; Balg *m.*; Schale, Hülse *f.*; ~ *v.t.* häuten, abdecken; ~ *v.i.* zuheilen.

skinner *s.* Lederhändler *m.*; Kürschner *m.*

skinny *a.* häutig; sehr mager.

skip *v.i.* springen, hüpfen; ~ *v.t.* überhüpfen; übergehen; ~ *s.* Sprung *m.*

skipper *s.* Schiffer *m.*; Hüpfer *m.*

skirmish *s.* Scharmützel *n.*; ~ *v.i.* plänkeln.

skirt *s.* Saum *m.*; Rockschoss *m.*; Einfassung *f.*; Frauenrock, Rock *m.*; ~ *v.t.* einfassen, besetzen; am Rande entlang gehen.

skit *s.* Stichelei, Satire, Spottschrift *f.*

skittish *a.*, ~**ly** *adv.* scheu, unstet; leichtfertig, flüchtig.

skittle *s.* Kegel *m.*; ~ *alley s.* Kegelbahn *f.*

skulk *v.i.* lauern, herumlungern, heimlich umherschleichen.

skull *s.* Schädel *m.*; ~-**cap** Hausmütze *f.*

skunk *s.* Stinktier *n.*; Schuft *m.*

sky *s.* (Wolken) himmel *m.*, Himmel *m.*

skylark *s.* Feldlerche *f.*; ~ *v.i.* Possen treiben.

skylight *s.* Oberlicht *n.*

skyline *s.* Kontur (einer Stadt) *f.*

skyscraper *s.* Wolkenkratzer *m.*

skywriting *s.* Himmelsschrift *f.*

slab *s.* Platte, Steinplatte *f.*; Rinde *f.*; Tafel *f.*

slack *a.*, ~**ly** *adv.* schlaff, locker; flau.

slacken *v.t.* schlaff machen, abspannen; nachlassen; verringern; (Kalk) löschen; ~ *v.i.* erschlaffen.

slacker *s.* Drückeberger *m.*

slacks *pl.* weite Hosen *f.pl.*

slag *s.* Schlacke *f.*

slake *v.t.* (Kalk) löschen; stillen; dämpfen.

slam *v.t.* zuschmeissen; ~ *s.* Klatsch, Schlag *m.*

slander *s.* Verleumdung *f.*; ~ *v.t.* verleumden, verunglimpfen.

slanderous *a.*, ~**ly** *adv.* verleumderisch.

slang *s.* lässige Umgangssprache; standessprachliche Ausdruck *m.*

slangy *a.* Slang; Slang redend.

slant *a.*, ~**ly** *adv.* schief, schräg; abschüssig; ~ *v.t.* seitwärts wenden; ~ *v.i.* abfallen (von der horizontalen Linie); ~ *s.* Tendenz.

slantwise *a.* schief, schräg.

slap *v.t. & i.* schlagen, klapsen; *to* ~ *a man's face*, einem ins Gesicht schlagen; ~ *s.* Klaps *m.*

slapdash *a.* heftig; nachlässig.

slash *v.t.* hauen; (auf)schlitzen; ~ *s.* Hieb *m.*; Schlitz *m.*; Schmarre *f.*

slate s. Schiefer m.; Schiefertafel f.; ~ v.t. mit Schiefer decken; abkanzeln; *slated for (Am.)*, festgesetzt, eingesetzt für...

slate-pencil s. Griffel, Schieferstift m.

slater s. Schieferdecker m.

slattern s. Schlampe f.

slaughter s. Metzelei f., Blutbad n.; ~ v.t. schlachten, morden.

slaughter-house s. Schlachthaus n.

slave s. Sklave m.; Sklavin f.; ~ v.i. sich placken.

slave-driver s. Leuteschinder m.

slaver s. Speichel m.; ~ v.i. geifern.

slavery s. Sklaverei f.

slavish a., ~ly adv. sklavisch.

slay v.t.st. erschlagen, töten.

sled s. Schlitten m.; Schleife f.

sledge s. Schlitten m.; Schleife f.

sledgehammer s. Schmiedehammer m.

sleek a., ~ly adv. glatt; weich; ~ v.t. glätten.

sleep v.i.st. schlafen; ~ s. Schlaf m.; *to go to ~*, einschlafen; *to put to ~*, einschläfern.

sleeper s. Schläfer m.; *(rail.)* Schwelle f.

sleeper s. Schlafwagen m.

sleeping-bag s. Schlafsack m.

sleeping-car s. (Eisenbahn) Schlafwagen m.

sleeping partner s. stille Teilhaber m.

sleeping sickness s. Schlafkrankheit f.

sleepless a., ~ly adv. schlaflos.

sleep-walker s. Schlafwandler m.

sleepy a., ~ily adv. schläfrig, verschlafen; (Obst) überreif, mehlig.

sleet s. Schneeregen m.; ~ v.i. regnen und schneien.

sleeve s. Ärmel m.; *to laugh in one's ~*, sich ins Fäustchen lachen; *to have a plan up one's ~*, einen Plan in petto haben.

sleeveless a. ärmellos.

sleevelink s. Manschettenknopf m.

sleigh s. Schlitten m.

sleight s. List f.; Kunststück n.; *~ of hand*, Taschenspielerstückchen n.

slender a., ~ly adv. schlank; dünn; spärlich, karg; schwach.

sleuth s. Bluthund m.; Detektiv m.

slice s. Schnitte, Scheibe f.; Spatel m.; ~ v.i. (in Scheiben) zerschneiden.

slick a. glatt, flott.

slide v.i.st. gleiten, ausgleiten; schlüpfen; ~ v.t. hineinschieben; ~ s. Gleitbahn f.; *(mech.)* Schlitten (Drehbank, etc.); *lantern ~*, Lichtbild; *~ fastener (Am.)* Reissverschluss m.; *~ valve* s. Schiebeventil n.

sliding-door s. Schiebetür f.; **~-scale** s. bewegliche Skala f.; *~ seat*, Rollsitz m.

slight a., ~ly adv. klein, gering; unwichtig, schwach, dünn; ~ s. Gering-

schätzung f.; Verachtung f.; ~ v.t. geringschätzig behandeln.

slim a. schlank, schmächtig.

slime s. Schleim m.; Schlamm m.

slimy a. schleimig; schlammig.

sling s. Schlag, Wurf m.; Schleuder f.; Schlinge, Binde f.; ~ v.t.st. schleudern; über die Schulter hängen.

slink v.i.st. schleichen.

slip v.i. gleiten, ausgleiten; (ent-) schlüpfen; sich verschnappen; entfallen; ~ v.t. schlüpfen lassen, abreissen; loslassen; anziehen; ~ s. Ausgleiten n.; Entwischen n.; Versehen n.; Stückchen, Streifchen s.; Zettel m.; Unterkleid n.; (Kissen-)überzug m.; (nav.) Helling f.; *~ of a boy*, schmächtige Junge m.; Fangleine f.; *~ of the pen*, Schreibfehler m.; *to give the ~*, entwischen.

slipper s. Pantoffel m.

slippery a. schlüpfrig, glatt.

slip-shod a. latschig; nachlässig.

slipway s. Laufweg m.

slit v.t. aufschneiden, durchschneiden; aufschlitzen; spalten; ~ s. Riss m.; Spalte f.

sliver s. Holzsplitter m.; v.t. & i. (zer-)spalten, zersplittern.

slobber v.i. geifern; ~ v.t. begeifern.

sloe s. Schlehe f.

slogan s. Wahlparole f.; Schlagwort n.

sloop s. Schaluppe f.

slop v.t. verschütten; ~ s. Krankensuppe f.; **~s** pl. Spülicht n.

slop-basin s. Spülnapf m.

slope s. Abhang m.; Abdachung f.; ~ v.i. abfallen; ~ v.t. abschrägen.

sloping a., ~ly adv. schief, abschüssig.

sloppy a. schmutzig; nachlässig.

slot s. Spalte f., Schlitz m.; *~ machine* (Verkaufs-)Automat m.

sloth s. Trägheit f.; Faultier n.

slothful a., ~ly adv. träge, faul.

slotter, slotting machine s. (mech.) (Senkrecht)Stossmaschine f., Stanzmaschine f.

slouch v.i. den Kopf hängen; schlendern; ~ v.t. ins Gesicht drücken.

slough s. Morast, Sumpf m.; Haut f.; Schorf m.; ~ v.i. sich häuten.

sloven s. Schlumpe f.

slovenly a. & adv. liederlich, schlumpig.

slow a., ~ly adv. langsam, träge; schwerfällig, begriffsstützig; *to be ~*, (Uhr) nachgehen; *~ down* s. Verlangsamung f.; *~ train* s. Bummelzug m.; *~-motion picture* s. Zeitlupenaufnahme f.; *~ down* v.t. verlangsamen.

slow-worm s. Blindschleiche f.

slubber v.t. besudeln; pfuschen.

slug s. Klumpen m.; Hackblei n.; Wegschnecke f.

sluggard *s.* Faulenzer *m.*; ~ *a.* träge.
sluggish *a.*, **~ly** *adv.* langsam, träge.
sluice *s.* Schleuse *f.*; ~ *v.t.* ablassen.
slum *s.* Hintergässchen *n.*; **~s** *pl.* Armeleuteviertel *n.*
slumber *s.* Schlummer *m.*; ~ *v.i.* schlummern.
slump *v.i.* fallen, stürzen; ~ *s.* Kurssturz *m.*; Baisse *f.*
slur *v.t.* besudeln; verleumden; (*mus.*) verschleifen; rasch darüberhingehen; ~ *s.* Fleck *m.*; Vorwurf *m.*; (*mus.*) Bindezeichen *n.*
slush *s.* Schlamm, Matsch *m.*; sentimentale Kitsch *m.*
slut *s.* Schlampe *f.*
sluttish *a.*, **~ly** *adv.* schlampig, schmutzig.
sly *a.*, **~ly** *adv.* schlau; *on the* ~, verstohlenerweise; ~ *digs pl.* Seitenhiebe *m.pl.*
smack *s.* Beigeschmack *m.*; Bischen *n.*; Klaps *m.*; Schmatz *m.*; ~ *v.i.* schmecken; schmatzen, schnalzen; ~ *v.t.* klatschen; prügeln.
small *a.* klein, gering; dünn; ~ *hours*, frühe Morgenstunden *f.pl.*; ~ *s.* dünne Teil *m.*; ~ *of the back*, Kreuz *n.*
small-arms *s.pl.* Handfeuerwaffen *f.pl.*
small-pox *s.* Blattern *f.pl.*
small shot *s.* Schrot *n.*
small-talk *s.* Geplauder *n.*
smart *s.* Schmerz *m.*; ~ *a.*, **~ly** *adv.* schmerzhaft; beissend, scharf; lebhaft; schneidig, fesch; pfiffig; geputzt, elegant; ~ *v.i.* schmerzen; büssen.
smash *s.* Schmiss, Fall *m.*; Bankerott *m.*; ~ *v.t.* zerschmettern.
smattering *s.* oberflächliche Kenntnis *f.*
smear *v.t.* beschmieren; ~ *s.* Fleck *m.*
smell *v.t. & i.r. & st.* riechen; wittern; ~ *s.* Geruch *m.*
smelling-bottle *s.* Riechfläschchen *n.*
smelt *v.t.* (Erz) schmelzen.
smile *v.i.* lächeln; schmunzeln; ~ *s.* Lächeln *n.*
smirch *v.t.* beschmieren.
smirk *v.i.* schmunzeln.
smite *v.t.st.* schlagen, treffen; zerstören; heimsuchen.
smith *s.* Schmied *m.*
smithereens *s.pl.* Stückchen *n.pl.*, Splitter *m.*
smithy *s.* Schmiede *f.*
smitten *a.*, ~ *with a person*, stark verliebt, bezaubert.
smock *s.* Frauenhemd *n.*; Kittel *m.*
smock-frock *s.* Arbeitskittel *m.*
smoke *s.* Rauch *m.*; (*mil.*) Nebel; **~screen** Nebelwand *f.*; ~ *stack* s. Schornstein *m.*; ~ *v.i.* rauchen; *no smoking*, Rauchen verboten!; ~ *v.t.* rauchen; räuchern.
smokeless *a.* rauchlos.

smoker *s.* Raucher, *m.*
smoky *a.* rauchend, rauchig.
smooth *a.*, **~ly** *adv.* glatt, eben; sanft, lieblich; ~ *v.t.* ebnen; polieren; mildern.
smother *v.t.* ersticken.
smoulder *v.i.* schwelen.
smudge *s.* Schmutz, Schmier *m.*; ~ *v.t.* beschmutzen, verschmieren.
smug *a.*, **~ly** *adv.* schmuck, geschniegelt; selbstgefällig.
smuggle *v.t. & i.* schmuggeln.
smuggler *s.* Schmuggler *m.*
smuggling *s.* Schmuggelei *f.*
smut *s.* Russfleck *m.*; Schlüpfrigkeit *f.*; Getreidebrand *m.*; ~ *v.t.* beschmutzen.
smutty *a.*, **~ly** *adv.* russig, schmutzig; brandig (von Gewächsen); unflätig.
snack *s.* Bissen, Imbiss *m.*; ~ *bar s.* Imbissraum *m.*
snaffle *s.* Trense *f.*; ~ *bit*, Trensengebiss *n.*
snag *s.* Knorren *m.*; unerwartete Hindernis *n.*
snail *s.* Schnecke *f.*
snake *s.* Schlange *f.*; ~ *skin s.* Schlangenleder *n.*
snaky *a.* schlangenartig.
snap *v.t. & i.* schnappen, abschnappen; beissen; bissig antworten; ~ *one's fingers*, ein Schnippchen schlagen; ~ *s.* Schnapp *m.*; Biss *m.*; Fang *m.*; Knall *m.*; Schnappschloss *n.*; ~ *a.* plötzlich, überraschend.
snapdragon *s.* (*bot.*) Löwenmaul *n.*
snappish *a.*, **~ly** *adv.* bissig, schnippisch.
snappy *a.*, **~ily** *adv.* schneidig, elegant.
snap-shot *s.* Momentaufnahme *f.*
snare *s.* Schlinge *f.*; ~ *v.t.* verstricken.
snarl *v.i.* knurren.
snatch *v.t.* erschnappen, ergreifen, an sich reissen; ~ *v.i.* haschen; ~ *s.* schnelle Griff *m.*; Ruck, Hui *m.*
sneak *v.i.* kriechen; schleichen; ~ *s.* Schleicher, Kriecher *m.*
sneer *v.i.* hohnlächeln; sticheln; grinsen; ~ *s.* Spott *m.*; Stichel *f.*
sneeze *v.i.* niesen.
snick *v.t.* einschneiden, kerben.
sniff *v.i.* schnüffeln; ~ *s.* Nasevoll *f.*
snigger *v.i.* kichern.
snip *v.t.* schneiden; schnippen; ~ *s.* Schnitt *m.*; Schnitzel *n.*
snipe *s.* Schnepfe *f.*; ~ *v.i.* aus gedeckter Stellung schiessen.
sniper *s.* (*mil.*) Heckenschütze *m.*
snivel *v.i.* winseln; greinen; weinerlich sein.
snivelling *a.* triefnasig; heulend.
snob *s.* Geck *m.*
snobbery *s.* eitle Vornehmtun *n.*
snobbish *a.* vornehmtuend.
snore *v.i.* schnarchen; ~ *s.* Schnarchen *n.*

snort v.i. schnaufen; schnauben.

snout s. Schnauze f.; Rüssel m.

snow s. Schnee m.; ~ v.i. schneien; ~ed up p. verschneit, eingeschneit.

snowball s. Schneeball m.

snowbound a. eingeschneit.

snowdrift s. Schneewehe f.

snowdrop s. Schneeglöckchen n.

snowplough s. Schneepflug m.

snowshow s. Schneeschuh m.

snow-white a. schneeweiss.

snowy a. schneeig; schneeweiss.

snub v.t. zurechtweisen; brüskieren; ~ s. scharfe Rüge f.; Abfuhr f.

snub-nosed a. stumpfnasig.

snuff s. Schnupftabak m.; ~ v.t. schnupfen.

snuff-box s. Schnupftabaksdose f.

snuffers s.pl. Lichtputze f.

snuffle v.i. schnüffeln; näseln.

snug a., ~ly adv. geborgen; anheimelnd, gemütlich, nett.

snuggery s. Privatzimmer n., Bude f.

snuggle v.i. sich anschmiegen.

so adv. & c. so; also, folglich; daher; so and so, so und so.

soak v.t. einsaugen; durchnässen; einweichen; ~ v.i. weich werden, durchziehen; saufen.

soap s. Seife f.; toilet ~, Toilettenseife f.; laundry ~, Waschseife f.; soft ~, Schmierseife; (fig.) Schmus m.; ~ v.t. einseifen.

soap-bubble s. Seifenblase f.

soap-flakes pl. Seifenflocken f.pl.

soapmaker s. Seifensieder m.

soap-suds s.pl. Seifenwasser n.

soapy a. seifig; salbungsvoll.

soar v.i. sich aufschwingen, schweben; in die Höhe gehen.

sob v.i. schluchzen; ~ s. Schluchzen n.

sober a., ~ly adv. nüchtern; besonnen; gesetzt; ~ v.t. ernüchtern; mässigen.

sobriety s. Nüchternheit, Mässigkeit f.

so-called a. sogenannt.

soccer = socker.

sociable a., ~bly adv. gesellig.

social a. gesellschaftlich; gesellig; sozial; ~ s. gesellige Zusammenkunft f.; ~ science, Gesellschaftswissenschaft f.; ~ worker, Fürsorgebeamter m.

socialism s. Sozialismus m.

socialist s. Sozialist m.

socialize v.t. sozialisieren, vergesellschaften.

society s. Gesellschaft f.; Verein m.

sociology s. Soziologie f.

sock s. Socke f.; Einlegesohle f.

socker s. (Association) Fussballspiel n.

socket s. Hülse f.; (Augen-, Zahn-)Höhle f.; (elek.) Steckdose f.

socle s. Sockel m.; Gestell n.

sod s. Rasenstück n.

soda s. Soda f.; ~-water (künstliche) Mineralwasser n.

sodden a. durchweicht; teigig; verdöst.

sodium s. (chem.) Natrium n.; ~ chloride s. Kochsalz n.

soever adv. auch immer.

sofa s. Sofa n.

so far adv. bis jetzt.

soft a., ~ly adv. weich, mürbe; gelind, sanft, zärtlich; leise; einfältig, dumm; ~!, i. gemach! gelassen! sachte!; ~ drinks pl. nichtalkoholische Getränke n.pl.

soften v.t. & i. erweichen; mildern, besänftigen; weich werden.

soft-hearted a. weichherzig.

soft-spoken a. sanftredend.

soggy a. durchweicht, sumpfig.

soil s. Boden m.; Erdreich n.; Flecken m.; Schmutz m.; ~ v.t. besudeln.

sojourn s. Aufenthalt m.; ~ v.i. sich aufhalten.

solace s. Trost m.; ~ v.t. erquicken, lindern, trösten.

solar a. Sonnen...

solder v.t. löten; ~ s. Lot n.

soldier s. Soldat m.

soldiering s. Soldatenleben n.

soldierly a. soldatisch.

soldiery s. Militär n.

sole a., ~ly adv. allein, einzig; bloss; ledig; ~ agent s. (com.) Alleinvertreter m.; ~ s. Sohle f.; Grundfläche f.; Seezunge f.; ~ v.t. besohlen.

solecism s. Sprachfehler m.; Unschicklichkeit f.

solemn a., ~ly adv. feierlich, festlich.

solemnity s. Feierlichkeit f.; Ernst m.

solemnize v.t. feiern.

solicit v.t. (anhaltend) bitten; ansprechen.

solicitation s. Ansuchen, Anliegen n.

solicitor s. Anwalt, Notar.

solicitous a., ~ly adv. besorgt, ängstlich.

solicitude s. Besorgnis f.; Sorgfalt f.

solid a., ~ly adv. fest, gediegen; massiv, gründlich; ernst; echt; solide; ~ tyre, Vollreifen; ~ s. feste Körper m.

solidarity s. Solidarität f.

solidity s. Festigkeit, Dichtheit f.; Gründlichkeit, Echtheit f.

soliloquize v.i. ein Selbstgespräch führen.

soliloquy s. Selbstgespräch n.

solitary a., ~ily adv. einsam; eingezogen; ~ confinement, Einzelhaft f.; ~ s. Einsiedler m.

solitude s. Einsamkeit f.; Einöde f.

solo s. Solo n.

soloist s. (mus.) Soloist m.

solstice s. Sonnenwende f.

soluble a. auflösbar; lösbar.

solution s. Auflösung f.; Lösung f.

solve v.t. lösen; erklären; (be)heben.

solvency s. Zahlungsfähigkeit f.

solvent *a.* zahlungsfähig; ~ *s.* Lösungsmittel *n.*
sombre *a.* dunkel, düster.
some *a.* ein paar, manch; ein bisschen, einige, etliche, irgendein; etwas, ein wenig; ungefähr; ~*body,* jemand, einer; ~*how,* irgendwie; ~*thing,* etwas; ~*time,* einst, vormals; ~*times,* zuweilen; ~*what,* etwas; ~*where,* irgendwo.
somersault *s.* Purzelbaum *m.*
somnambulism *s.* Schlafwandeln *n.*
somnolent *a.* schläfrig.
son *s.* Sohn *m.*; ~-in-law, Schwiegersohn *m.*
sonata *s.* Sonate *f.*
song *s.* Gesang *m.*; Lied *n.*; *for a* ~, spottbillig.
songster *s.* Sänger *m.*
sonnet *s.* Sonett *n.*
sonny *s.* Söhnchen *n.*
sonorous *a.*, ~ly *adv.* resonant.
soon *adv.* bald; früh; gern; *as* ~ *as,* sobald (als).
sooner *adv.* eher, früher; lieber; *no* ~ *than,* kaum.
soonest *adv.* ehestens.
soot *s.* Russ *m.*; ~*ed up a.* verrusst.
sooth *s.* Wahrheit *f.*
soothe *v.t.* besänftigen, lindern.
soothsayer *s.* Wahrsager *m.*
sooty *a.* russig.
sop *s.* eingetunkte Bissen *m.*; (*fig.*) Köder *m.*; ~ *v.t.* eintunken.
sophism *s.* Trugschluss *m.*
sophist *s.* Sophist *m.*
sophistical *a.*, ~ly *adv.* sophistisch.
sophisticate *v.t.* verfälschen, verdrehen.
sophisticated *a.* unecht, überzivilisiert.
sophistry *s.* Spitzfindigkeit *f.*
soporific *a.* einschläfernd.
soprano *s.* Sopran *m.*
sorcerer *s.* Zauberer *m.*
sorceress *s.* Hexe *f.*
sorcery *s.* Zauberei *f.*
sordid *a.*, ~ly *adv.* schmutzig; gemein.
sore *a.* wund; schmerzhaft, empfindlich; ~ *spot,* wunde Punkt; ~ *s.* wunde Stelle *f.*
sorely *adv.* schmerzlich, in hohem Grade.
sorrel *a.* rötlich; ~ *s.* Rotfuchs *m.*; Sauerampfer *m.*
sorrow *s.* Kummer *m.*, Sorge *f.*
sorrowful *a.*, ~ly *adv.* traurig.
sorry *a.*, ~ily *adv.* traurig, betrübt; erbärmlich, armselig; *I am* ~ *for it,* es tut mir leid; *I am sorry*..., leider...; Verzeihung.
sort *s.* Gattung, Sorte, Art *f.*; *out of* ~*s,* verstimmt; ~ *v.t.* sortieren.
sortie *s.* Ausfall *m.*
SOS, SOS message *s.* drahtlose Hilferuf in Seenot.
sot *s.* Trunkenbold *m.*

sottish *a.*, ~ly *adv.* dumm, albern; versoffen.
soul *s.* Seele *f.*
sound *a. & adv.*, ~ly *adv.* gesund, fest, stark, tüchtig; ~ *s.* Schall, Laut, Klang *m.*; Sund *m.*; Sonde *f.*; Schwimmblase (eines Fisches) *f.*; ~-film *s.* Tonfilm *m.*; ~-insulation, Schalldämpfung *f.*; ~ *v.i.* klingen, tönen, lauten; ~ *v.t.* ertönen lassen; sondieren, ausforschen; loten; *to* ~ *the lungs,* die Lungen abhorchen.
sound-box *s.* Schalldose *f.*
sounding-board *s.* Resonanzboden *m.*
soundless *a.* klanglos.
sound-track *s.* (*film*) Tonspur *f.*
soup *s.* Suppe, Fleischbrühe *f.*
sour *a.*, ~ly *adv.* sauer, herb, bitter; mürrisch; ~ *v.t.* sauer machen; (*fig.*) verbittern; ~ *v.i.* sauer werden.
source *s.* Quelle *f.*; Ursprung *m.*; ~ *of supply,* Bezugsquelle *f.*
souse *v.t.* einpökeln.
south *s.* Süden *m.*; ~ *a. & adv.* südlich, gegen Süden.
southern *a.* südlich.
southernmost *a.* südlichst.
southward *adv.* südwärts.
southwester *s.* Südwestwind *m.*; ~, sou'wester *s.* Südwester (Seemannskappe) *m.*
souvenir *s.* Andenken *n.*
sovereign *a.* oberherrlich; höchst; ~ *s.* Landesherr *m.*; Zwanzigschillingstück *n.*
sovereignty *s.* Oberherrschaft *f.*
Soviet *s.* Sowjet *m.*
sow *s.* Sau *f.*; Trog *m.*; ~ *v.t.r. & st.* säen.
sowing machine *s.* Sämaschine *f.*
soya bean, (*Am.*) soy bean *s.* Soyabohne *f.*
spa *s.* Bad *n.*, Badeort *m.*
space *s.* Raum *m.*; Zeitraum *m.*; Weilchen *n.*; Strecke, Frist *f.*; ~ *v.t.* (Druck) sperren; single-~d in Einzeilenstellung (Schreibmaschine); double-~d, in Zweizeilenstellung.
spacious *a.*, ~ly *adv.* geräumig.
spade *s.* Spaten *m.*; ~*s,* Grün, Pik (in der Karte) *n.*
span *s.* Spanne *f.*; Gespann *n.*; Spannweite *f.*; ~ *v.t.* spannen, (aus)messen.
spandrel *s.* (*arch.*) Zwickel *m.*
spangle *s.* Flitter *m.*, Flimmer *m.*; ~ *v.t.* beflittern.
spaniel *s.* Wachtelhund *m.*
spank *v.t.* durchwichsen; klapsen; ~ *v.i.* tüchtig ausschreiten.
spanner *s.* Schraubenschlüssel *m.*; *adjustable* ~, Engländer *m.*
spar *s.* Sparren *m.*; Spiere *f.*; Scheinhieb *m.*; (*min.*) Spat *m.*; ~ *v.i.* boxen, Finten machen.
spare *v.t. & i.* sparen, scheuen; antbehren; (ver)schonen, Nachsicht haben; erübrigen; ~ *a.* sparsam, spärlich; mager;

überzählig; ~ s. Ersatzteil m.; ~-part s.
Ersatzteil m.; ~-room s. Fremden-
zimmer n.; ~-wheel s. Ersatzrad n.
sparing a., ~ly adv. sparsam, spärlich.
spark s. Funke m.; lustige Gesell m.;
Stutzer m.; ~ v.i. Funken sprühen.
sparking-plug (Am.) sparkplug s. (mot.)
Zündkerze f.
sparkle s. Funke m.; ~ v.i. funkeln; perlen
(vom Wein); sprühen; sparkling wine,
Schaumwein m.
sparrow s. Sperling m.; ~-hawk, Sperber
m.
sparse a., ~ly adv. zerstreut, dünn.
spasm s. Krampf·m.
spasmodic a. krampfhaft.
spat s. (kurze) Gamasche f.
spate s. Hochwasser n.; (fig.) Flut f.
spatter v.t. bespritzen; besudeln.
spavin s. (Pferdekrankheit) Spat m.
spawn s. Laich m.; Rogen m.; Brut f.;
~ v.i. laichen; ~ v.t. ausbrüten.
speak v.t. & i.st. sprechen, reden.
speak-easy s. (Am.) illegale Ausschank m.
speaker s. Sprecher, Redner m.; Präsident
(m.) des Unterhauses; (radio) Lautsprecher m.
speaking-tube s. Sprachrohr n.
spear s. Speer, Spiess m., Lanze f.
spearhead s. (mil.) Spitze f.
spearmint s. grüne Minze f.
special a., besonder, eigen; vorzüglich;
~ correspondent, Sonderberichterstatter
m.; ~ diet, Diät f.; ~i pleading, Spitzfindigkeit f.; ~ tra n s. Extrazug,
Sonderzug m.; ~ly adv. besonders.
specialist s. Fachmann, Spezialist m.
speciality, specialty s. Besonderheit,
Eigenheit f.; Sonderfach f.
specialize v.i. (in) als Spezialfach betreiben.
specie s. Metallgeld n.
species s. Art, Gattung f.; Gestalt f.
specific a., ~ally adv. eigen, eigenartig;
bestimmt; spezifisch; ~ gravity, spezifische Gewicht n.
specification s. namentliche Angabe f.;
(Patent-)Beschreibung f.
specify v.t. einzeln angeben.
specimen s. Probe f., Muster n.; Exemplar n.; ~-copy, Frei-, Probeexemplar
n.
specious a., ~ly adv. bestechend; trügerisch.
speck s. Fleck m.; Fleckchen n.; ~ v.t.
flecken, sprenkeln.
speckle s. Fleckchen, Tüpfelchen n.; ~
v.t. flecken, sprenkeln.
spectacle s. Schauspiel n.; Anblick m.;
~s pl. Brille f.; ~-frame, Brillengestell
n.
spectacular a. in die Augen fallend,
pomphaft.

spectator s. Zuschauer m.
spectral a. gespenstig; Spektral...
spectre s. Gespenst n.
spectrum s. Spektrum n.
speculate v.i. nachsinnen, grübeln; spekulieren.
speculation s. Betrachtung f.; Nachsinnen
n.; Spekulation f.
speculative a., ~ly adv. forschend; unternehmend, spekulativ.
speculator s. Denker m.; Spekulant m.
speculum s. (med.) Spiegel m.
speech s. Rede f.; Sprache f.; freedom of
~, Redefreiheit f.; to deliver a ~, eine
Rede halten.
speechday s. Schlussfeier (Schule) f.
speechless a. sprachlos.
speed v.i. sich beeilen, eilen; glücken; ~
v.t. beschleunigen, befördern; to ~ up,
beschleunigen; ~ s. Eile f.; gute Erfolg
m.; Geschwindigkeit f.; ~-limit s.
Höchstgeschwindigkeit f.; ~-boat s.
Schnellboot n.
speedometer s. Geschwindigkeitsanzeiger
m.
speedy a., ~ily adv. eilig, schnell.
spell v.i. & t.r. & st. buchstabieren;
(richtig) schreiben; bedeuten; to ~ out,
entziffern, enträtseln; to ~ out a number, eine Zahl ausschreiben; ~ s.
Zauber m.; Schicht f.; kurze Zeit f.
spell-bound a. (fest)gebannt.
spelling s. Buchstabieren n.; Rechtschreibung f.; ~-book Fibel f.
spelt s. Spelz, Dinkel m.
spencer s. Gaffelsegel n.; Jäckchen n.
spend v.t. & i.st. verwenden; ausgeben;
verschwenden; Aufwand machen; erschöpfen; (Zeit) zubringen.
spendthrift s. Verschwender m.
spent a. erschöpft, kraftlos.
sperm s. Samen m.
spew v.t. ausspeien.
sphere s. Kugel f.; Erd-, Himmelskugel f.;
Bereich, Wirkungskreis m.
spherical a., ~ly adv. kugelförmig.
spice s. Gewürz n.; Anflug, Beigeschmack
m.; ~ v.t. würzen.
spick-and-span adv. herausgeputzt; fun-
kelnageleneu.
spicy a. würzig, gewürzhaft; pikant,
scharf.
spider s. Spinne f.
spigot s. Zapfen, Hahn m.
spike s. Spitze f.; langer Nagel; Kornähre
f.; ~ v.t. festnageln; (ein Geschütz)
vernageln.
spill v.t.r. & st. verschütten, vergiessen.
spin v.t.st. spinnen; wirbeln; ~ v.i. kreiseln, sich drehen.
spinach s. Spinat m.
spinal a. Rückgrat...; ~ chord, Rücken-
mark n.

spindle s. Spindel f.; Stengel m.
spine s. Rückgrat n.; Dorn m.
spineless a. rückgratlos (fig.).
spinner s. Spinner(in) m. (& f.).
spinning-jenny s. Feinspinnmaschine f.; **~-wheel** s. Spinnrad n.
spinster s. ledige Frau, (alte) Jungfer f.
spiral a., **~ly** adv. gewunden, schneckenförmig; **~** s. Schneckenlinie f., Spirale f.; **~** staircase s. Wendeltreppe f.
spire s. (Kirch)turm m., Turmspitze f.; Turm m.
spirit s. Geist m.; Seele f.; Gespenst n.; Lebhaftigkeit, Energie f.; Gemütsart f.; **~s** pl. Lebensgeister m.pl., gute Laune f.; geistige Getränke n.pl.; in high **~s**, munter; in low **~s**, verstimmt; **~** v.t. to **~** away, hinwegzaubern.
spirited a., **~ly** adv. geistreich; lebhaft, mutig, feurig.
spiritism s. Spiritismus m.
spiritless a., **~ly** adv. mutlos.
spirit-level s. Nivellierwage f.
spirit of wine s. Weingeist m.
spiritual a., **~ly** adv. geistig; geistlich.
spiritualism s. Spiritualismus m.
spirt v.t. & i. spritzen.
spiry a. gewunden.
spit v.t. & i.st. spucken; fauchen; aufspiessen; **~** s. Bratspiess m.; schmale Landzunge f.
spite s. Groll m.; Verdruss m.; in **~** of, trotz; **~** v.t. ärgern.
spiteful a., **~ly** adv. boshaft, feindselig.
spitfire s. Brausekopf, Hitzkopf m.
spittle s. Speichel m.
spittoon s. Spucknapf m.
spiv s. verkrachte Existenz f., Schieber m.
splash v.t. bespritzen; **~** s. Kotfleck m.; to make a **~**, Aufsehen erregen.
splash-board s. Spritzbrett n.
splay v.t. bespritzen, ausschrägen; **~** a. auswärts gebogen; **~** s. Ausschrägung f.
spleen s. Milz f.; Milzsucht f.; üble Laune f.
spleeny a. mürrisch, launisch.
splendent, splendid a., **~ly** adv. glänzend, prachtvoll.
splendour s. Glanz m.; Pracht f.
splenetic a. milzsüchtig; übellaunig.
splice v.t. splissen, einfügen.
splinter s. (Bein)Schiene f.; Span, Splitter m.; **~-proof** a. splittersicher; **~** v.t. schienen; splittern.
split v.t.st. spalten; **~** v.i. bersten; zerspringen; **~** s. Spalt, Riss m.; **~** second s. Sekundenbruchteil m.
splutter s. Lärm m.; **~** v.i. herauspoltern; spritzen, sprudeln.
spoil v.t. rauben, plündern; verderben, verwüsten; (Kinder) verziehen; **~** v.i. verderben; **~** s. Beute f.

spoke s. Speiche f.; Sprosse f.
spokesman s. Wortführer m.
spoliation s. Beraubung, Plünderung f.
sponge s. Schwamm m.; **~** v.t. wegwischen; **~** v.i. in sich saugen; schmarotzen; to throw up the **~**, die Flinte ins Korn werfen; **~-bag** s. Schwammsack m.
sponge-cake s. Biskuitkuchen m.
sponger s. Schmarotzer m.
spongy a. schwammig.
sponsor s. Bürge, Pate m.; **~** v.t. (Am.) fördern, organisieren; **~ing** member, förderndes Mitglied n.
spontaneity s. Freiwilligkeit f.
spontaneous a., **~ly** adv. freitätig.
spool s. Spule f.; **~** v.t. spulen.
spoon s. Löffel m.; **~** v.i. Liebeleien treiben.
sporadic a. sporadisch.
spore s. (bot.) Spore f.
sport s. Sport m.; Spiel n.; Scherz, Zeitvertreib m.; (fig.) Spielball m.; **~** v.t. & i. spielen; scherzen, belustigen; zur Schau tragen.
sporting a. Jagd...; sportlich, ritterlich.
sportive a., **~ly** adv. lustig, scherzhaft.
sportsman s. Sportsmann m., Freund des Sports m.; Jäger m.
sportswear s. Sportskleidung f.
spot s. Platz m.; Stelle f.; Stück Land n.; Fleck m.; Schandfleck m.; sofort lieferbar oder zahlbar; **~** v.t. flecken, sprenkeln; genau erkennen; im voraus bestimmen.
spotless a. unbefleckt.
spotlight s. Scheinwerferlicht n.
spotted a. gesprenkelt, getüpfelt; **~** fever, Fleckfieber n.
spotty a. fleckig, sprenklicht; befleckt.
spouse s. Gatte m., Gattin f.; the **~s** pl. die Eheleute.
spout s. Rinne f.; Tülle f.; Wasserstrahl m.; Wasserhose f.; **~** v.t. & i. (aus)spritzen; deklamieren.
sprain v.t. verstauchen; **~** s. Verstauchung f.
sprat s. Sprotte f.
sprawl v.i. sich spreizen, räkeln; (bot.) wuchern.
spray s. Gischt m.; **~** v.t. zerstäuben; (Metall) spritzen.
spread v.t.ir. (v.i. sich) ausbreiten; (be)decken; **~** s. Ausdehnung f.; Verbreitung f.
spree s. Jux m.; Zecherei f.; to have a **~**, sich amüsieren, bummeln.
sprig s. Spross, Sprössling m.; **~s** pl. Reisig n.
sprightly a. lebhaft, munter.
spring v.i.st. springen; entspringen, aufspriessen; entstehen; **~** v.t. sprengen; hervorbringen; jagen, aufstöbern; **~** s.

Sprung *m.*; Leck *n.*; Quelle *f.*; Spring-brunnen *m.*; Frühling *m.*; Springfeder *f.*

springe *s.* Sprenkel *m.*; Schlinge, Dohne *f.*; ~ *v.t.* verstricken.

spring-gun *s.* Selbstschuss *m.*

spring-mattress *s.* Sprungfedermatratze *f.*

spring-steel *s.* (*mech.*) Federstahl *m.*

spring-tide *s.* Springflut *f.*

springy *a.* elastisch, federnd.

sprinkle *v.t. & i.* (be)sprengen; ausstreuen.

sprinkling *s.* Anflug *m.*; Wenig *n.*

sprint *s.* kurze, scharfe Rennen *n.*

sprinter *s.* (*Sport*) Flieger *m.*

sprite *s.* Schrat *m.*; Gespenst *n.*

sprout *v.i.* sprossen; ~ *s.* Sprössling *m.*; Brussels ~s *pl.* Rosenkohl *m.*

spruce *a.*, ~ly *adv.* nett; geputzt; ~ *s.* Rottanne *f.*; ~ *v.t.* (*v.i. sich*) herausputzen.

sprung *a.* gefedert; well-~, gut gefedert.

spry *a.* munter, lebhaft.

spume *s.* Schaum *m.*; ~ *v.i.* schäumen.

spunk *s.* Zunder *m.*; Lunte *f.*; faule Holz *n.*; Lebhaftigkeit *f.*

spur *s.* Sporn, Stachel *m.*; Antrieb *m.*; Ausläufer einer Bergkette *m.*; ~ *v.t.* (auch *fg.*) anspornen; ~ *v.i.* eilen.

spurious *a.*, ~ly *adv.* unecht.

spurn *v.t.* verschmähen; ~ *v.i.* ausschlagen; verschmähen.

spurt *v.i.* spritzen; ~ *s.* plötzliche Anstrengung *f.*, Ruck *m.*

sputter *v.i.* sprudeln; ~ *v.t.* sprudelnd ausstossen; ~ *s.* Gesprudel *n.*

spy *s.* Späher, Spion *m.*; ~ *v.i. & t.* (aus)spähen.

squabble *v.i.* zanken, Händel suchen; ~ *s.* Streit, Wortwechsel *m.*

squad *s.* Rotte, Schar *f.*

squadron *s.* Schwadron *f.*; (*nav.*) Geschwader *n.*; (*avi.*) Staffel *f.*; (*avi.*) ~leader *s.* Staffelkapitän *m.*

squalid *a.* schmutzig.

squall *s.* laute Schrei *m.*; Windstoss *m.*; Bö *f.*; ~ *v.i.* laut schreien.

squalor *s.* Schmutz *m.*

squander *v.t.* verschwenden.

square *a.* viereckig, rechtwinklig; passend; quitt; redlich; ~ *deal*, ehrliche Behandlung; ~ *s.* Viereck, Quadrat *n.*; viereckige Platz *m.*; Feld (Schach) *n.*; Winkelmass *n.*; *10 inches* ~, 10 Zoll im Quadrat; ~ *v.t.* viereckig machen; regeln, anpassen, ausgleichen; (*math.*) ins Quadrat erheben; ~ *v.i.* passen; übereinstimmen; ~ *measures* *pl.* Flächenmasse *n.pl.*

square-built *a.* vierschrötig.

squash *v.t.* zerquetschen; ~ *s.* Brei *m.*, Gedränge *n.*; Fruchtsaft *m.*; ~ (*rackets*) *pl.* ein Ballspiel.

squat *v.i.* kauern, sich ansiedeln; ~ *a.* kauernd; stämmig.

squatter *s.* Ansiedler (*m.*) auf fremdem Boden *m.*

squaw *s.* Indianerweib *m.*

squeak *v.i.* quieken, schreien; ~ *s.* Gequiek *n.*; Schrei *m.*

squeal *v.i.* schreien, winseln.

squeamish *a.*, ~ly *adv.* wählerisch; heikel; empfindlich.

squeeze *v.t.* drücken, pressen, quetschen; ~ *v.i.* sich (durch)drängen; ~ *s.* Druck *m.*; Quetschung *f.*; Gipsabguss *m.*

squelch *v.i.* glucksen.

squib *s.* Frosch (Feuerwerk) *m.*; Spottgedicht *n.*

squint *v.i.* schielen; ~ *a.* schielend.

squint[ing] *s.* Schielen *n.*

squirarchy *s.* Junkerherrschaft *f.*

squire *s.* (*obs.*) Schildknappe *m.*; Landedelmann *m.*; (Land)junker *m.*

squirrel *s.* Eichhörnchen *n.*

squirt *v.t.* spritzen; ~ *s.* Spritze *f.*; Wasserstrahl *m.*

stab *s.* Stich *m.*; Stoss *m.*; Wunde *f.*; ~ *v.t. & i.* erstechen, stechen.

stability *s.* Beständigkeit *f.*, Stabilität *f.*

stabilization *s.* Stabilisierung *f.*; ~ *fund*, Währungsausgleichfonds *m.*

stabilize *v.t.* stabilisieren.

stable *a.* fest, dauerhaft; beständig; stabil (Währung); ~ *s.* Stall *m.*

stack *s.* Schober, Stapel *m.*; (Gewehr-)Pyramide *f.*; ~ *v.t.* aufschichten.

stadium *s.* Stadion *n.*

staff *s.* Stab, Stock *m.*; (General)stab *m.*; Personal *n.*; die fünf Notenlinien *pl.*; ~, *v.t.* mit Personal versehen.

stag *s.* Hirsch *m.*; (Börse) Konzertzeichner *m.*

stage *s.* Gerüst *n.*; Bühne *f.*; Schauplatz *m.*; Etappe *f.*, Stadium *n.*; Stufe *f.*; Poststation *f.*; *to go on the* ~, zur Bühne gehen; ~-direction *s.* Bühnen anweisung *f.*; ~ *v.t.* inszenieren, veranstalten.

stage-box *s.* Proszeniumsloge *f.*

stage-fright *s.* Lampenfieber *n.*

stage-manager *s.* Bühnenleiter *m.*

stage-coach *s.* Postkutsche *f.*

stager *s.* erfahrene Mann, Praktikus *m.*

stagger *v.i.* wanken, taumeln; schwanken; ~ *v.t.* verblüffen; staffeln; ~ed holidays *pl.* gestaffelte Ferien *pl.*; ~ *s.* (*avi.*) Staffelung (der Flügel) *f.*

stagnant *a.* stillstehend, stockend.

stagnate *v.i.* stillstehen, stocken.

stagnation *s.* Stillstand *m.*; Stockung *f.*

staid *a.* gesetzt, ernsthaft.

stain *s.* Flecken *m.*; Beize *f.*; Makel *m.*; ~ *v.t.* beflecken; färben; ~ed *glass*, bunte Glass *n.*, Glasmalerei *f.*

stainless *a.* unbefleckt; rostfrei.

stair *s.* Stufe *f.*; ~s *pl.* Treppe *f.*; ~-carpet *s.* Treppenläufer *m.*

staircase *s.* Treppe *f.*; Treppenhaus *n.*

stairway s. (Am.) Stiege f.
stake s. Pfahl m.; Einsatz (im Spiel) m.; at ~, auf dem Spiele; ~ v.t. aufs Spiel setzen.
stalactite s. Tropfstein m.
stale a. alt, altbacken; schal, geistlos; ~ v.t. alt machen; patt machen.
stalemate s. Patt n.; ~ v.t. patt machen; (fig.) lahmlegen.
stalk s. Stengel, Federkiel m.; gravitätische Schritt m.; ~ v.t. & i. einherschreiten; beschleichen, pirschen.
stalking-horse s. Pferd, hinter dem sich Jäger versteckt; (fig.) Vorwand m.
stall s. Stall m.; Stand m., Box f. (im Stall); Sperrsitz m.; Chorstuhl m.; Krambude f.; ~ v.t. zum Stehen bringen; ~ v.i. steckenbleiben.
stallion s. Hengst m.
stalwart s. stark, mutig; ~ s. Vorkämpfer m.
stamen, stamina s. Staubfäden m.pl.; (fig.) Ausdauer f.
stammer v.i. stammeln, stottern.
stammerer s. Stammler m.
stamp v.t. stampfen; stempeln, prägen; mit einer Marke versehen, (Brief) frankieren; to ~ out, austreten, unterdrücken; ~ s. Stampfe f.; Stempel m.; Gepräge n.; Abdruck m.; Briefmarke f., Marke f.; ~ collector, Briefmarkensammler m.; ~ duty, Stempelsteuer f.; ~ pad, Stempelkissen f.
stampede s. wilde Flucht f.; ~ v.t. in wilde Flucht jagen.
stamper s. Stampfe f.
stanch a., -ly adv. standhaft, fest; sicher; ~ v.t. stillen, hammen.
stand v.t. & i. stehen; stellen; aushalten, sich verhalten; gelten; kosten, zu stehen kommen; zum besten geben; to ~ by, dabeistehen; to ~ for, eintreten für; to ~ up, aufrecht stehen; to ~ up to, aushalten; ~ s. Ständer m.; (phot.) Stativ n.; Stand m.; Gestell, Gerüst n.; ~-camera (phot.) Stativapparat m.
standard s. Standarte f.; Ständer m.; Pfosten m.; Eichmass n.; Masstab m., Regel, Richtschnur f., Norm f.; Münzfuss m.; gold ~, Goldstandard m.; ~ of life, Lebenshaltung f.; ~-lamp s. Stehlampe f.; ~ operating procedure (SOP) (mil.) vorschriftsmässige Verfahren n.; ~ a. musterhaft, normal, klassisch.
standardize v.t. normieren.
standing p. & a. stehend, bleibend, beständig; ~ s. Stand, Platz m.; Rang m.; Dauer f.; Stellung f.; of long (old) ~, von lange her.
standing-order s. Geschäftsordnung f.
standing-room s. Stehplatz m.
standpoint s. Standpunkt m.
stand-still s. Stillstand m.

stand-up a. regelrecht (vom Faustkampf); ~ collar, Stehkragen m.
stanza s. Stanze f.; Strophe f.
staple s. Niederlage f.; Stapelplatz m.; Krampe f.; Heftklammer f.; ~, v.t. mit einer Heftklammer versehen; stapling machine, Heftmaschine f.; staple goods pl. Massenwaren pl.
star s. Stern m.; grosse Schauspieler, Star m.; ~ v.t. & i. besternen; eine Hauptrolle spielen; ~s and stripes, Sternenbanner n.
starboard s. Steuerbord n.
starch s. Stärke (zur Wäsche) f.; Steifheit f.; ~ v.t. stärken.
stare s. starre Blick m.; Staunen n.; ~ v.i. anstarren.
stark a., -ly adv. stark, steif; völlig.
starlight s. Sternenlicht; ~ night, Sternennacht f.
starling s. Star (Vogel) m.; Eisbrecher m. (an Brücke).
starred a. gestirnt.
starry a. sternig; sternhell.
start v.i. auffahren, zurückfahren; (rail.) abgehen; (Sport) starten; anfangen; ~ v.t. aufjagen; stutzig machen; aufwerfen (Fragen); beginnen; (mech.) in Gang bringen, anlassen; (Sport) ablaufen lassen; erschrecken, stören; ~ s. Auffahren, Stutzen n.; Ruck, Stoss m.; Anfall m.; Anwandlung f.; Anlauf m.; Ablauf m. (Rennen); Abfahrt f.; Beginn m.; Vorsprung m.
starter s. Anreger m.; (Sport) Ablasser, Starter m.; (mech.) Anlasser m.; (Rennen) Teilnehmer m.
startle v.t. erschrecken, überraschen.
starvation s. Verhungern n.; ~ wages pl. Hungerlohn m.
starve v.i. Not leiden, verhungern; ~ v.t. verhungern lassen, aushungern.
starveling s. Hungerleider m.
state s. Zustand m.; Stand, Rang m.; Staat m.; Aufwand m.; ~-aided a. staatlich unterstützt; ~-owned a. im Staatsbesitz; lying in ~, Aufbahrung f.; ~ v.t. stellen, festsetzen; dartun, vortragen, erklären, sagen.
stately a. stattlich, prächtig; stolz.
statement s. Angabe, Aussage f.; Überschlag, Bericht m., Angabe f.; ~ of account s. (Rechnungs)auszug m.
state-room s. Luxuskabine f.
statesman s. Staatsmann m.
statesmanlike a. staatsmännisch.
statesmanship s. Regierungskunst f.
statics s.pl. Statik f.
station s. Stand m.; Stelle f., Amt n.; Rang m.; Standort m.; Bahnhof m.; ~s of the cross, Kreuzwegstationen pl.; ~ v.t. hinstellen; (mil.) stationieren.
stationary a. feststehend, beharrend.

stationer s. Schreibwarenhändler m.; ~s Hall, Buchhändlerbörse f.
stationery s. Schreibwaren f.pl.
station-master s. Bahnhofsvorsteher m.
statistic(al) a. statistisch.
statistician s. Statistiker m.
statistics s.pl. Statistik f.
statuary s. Bildhauerkunst f.; Bildhauerarbeit f.; Bildhauer m.
statue s. Bildsäule f.
statuette s. Statuette f.
stature s. Leibesgrösse f.; Wuchs m.
status s. Lage f.; Stand m.
statute s. Satzung f.; Landesgesetz n.; Parlamentsakte f.; ~-law (geschriebene) Landesrecht n.
statutory a. gesetzmässig; ~ corporation, Körperschaft des öffentlichen Rechts; ~ declaration, eidesstattliche Erklärung f.
staunch a. zuverlässig, treu.
stave v.t. to ~ in, den Boden ausschlagen; to ~ off, abwehren; ~ s. Fassdaube f.
stay v.i.st. stillstehen, bleiben, warten; wohnen; ~ v.t. aufhalten, hindern; stützen; (law) einstellen (Verfahren, etc.); stillen (Hunger); ~ s. Aufenthalt m.; Hemmung f.; Stütze f.; (law) Einstellung f.
stayer s. Steher m.
stays s.pl. Korsett n.
stead s. Stelle f.; Platz m.; in his ~, an seiner Stelle; in~ of, statt.
steadfast a., ~ly adv. fest, standhaft.
steady a., ~ily adv. fest, standhaft; beständig; ~ v.t. festmachen, ruhig machen.
steak s. Fleischschnitte f., Schnitzel n.
steal v.t.st. stehlen; ~ v.i. schleichen.
stealth s. Heimlichkeit f.; by ~, verstohlen.
stealthy a. verstohlen, heimlich.
steam s. Dampf m.; ~ v.t. dämpfen; ~ v.i. dampfen.
steam-boat s. Dampfschiff n.
steam-engine s. Dampfmaschine f.
steamer s. Dampfer m.; Dämpfer m.
steam-navigation s. Dampfschiffahrt f.
steam-pressure gauge s. Dampfdruckmesser m.
steam-roller s. Dampfwalze f.
steamship s. Dampfschiff n.
steam-tug s. Schleppdampfer m.
stearin s. Stearin n.
steed s. Streitross n., Ross n.
steel s. Stahl m.; ~ v.t. stählen; ~ cabinet, Stahlschrank m.; ~-engraving s. Stahlstich m.; ~ frame s. Eisenkonstruktion f.; ~ helmet s. Stahlhelm m.; ~ wool s. Stahlwolle f.
steely a. stählern; stahlhart.
steelyard s. Schnellwaage f.
steep a., ~ly adv. jäh, steil; (fam.) übertrieben; (~) hill (up), (mot.) Steigung f.; ~ hill down, starke Gefälle n.; ~ v.t. eintunken, einweichen; to be ~ed in, verstrickt sein in, voll sein von.
steeple s. Kirchturm m.
steeple-chase s. Hindernisrennen n.
steer v.t. & i. steuern; ~ing column s. (mot.) Lenksäule f.; steering wheel s. Steuerrad n.
steerage s. Steuerung f.; Zwischendeck n.; ~-passenger, Zwischendeckpassagier m.
steersman s. Steuermann m.
stellar a. gestirnt, Sternen...
stem s. Stiel, Stengel m.; Stamm m.; Vordersteven m.; ~ v.t. stemmen, ankämpfen; sich widersetzen.
stench s. Gestank m.
stencil s. Schablone f., Schablonenpapier n.
stenographer s. Stenograph m.
stenography s. Stenographie f.
stentorian a. überlaut.
step v.i. schreiten, treten; ~ up v.t. antreiben; to ~ in, sich ins Mittel legen; ~ s. Schritt, Tritt, Gang m.; Fussstapfe f.; Stufe f.; Trittbrett n.; ~ by ~, Schritt für Schritt; to fall into ~ with, in gleichen Schritt fallen mit; to keep ~ with, Schritt halten mit; to take ~s, Schritte tun, Massnahmen ergreifen; ~s pl., ~ ladder s. Trittleiter f.; ~ a. (Bruder, etc.).
steppe s. Steppe f.
stepping-stone s. Steinstufe f.; (fig.) Sprungbrett n.
stereoscope s. Stereoskop n.
stereoscopic a. stereoskopisch.
stereotype s. Stereotyp n.; ~ a. Stereotyp... (typ.); (fig.) abgedroschen, stereotyp; ~ v.t. stereotypieren; unveränderlich festlegen.
sterile a. unfruchtbar.
sterilize v.t. unfruchtbar, keimfrei machen.
sterility s. Unfruchtbarkeit f.
sterilization s. Unfruchtbarmachung f.
sterling s. Sterling (20 Schilling) m.; a pound ~, ein Pfund Sterling; ~ a. echt, zuverlässig.
stern a., ~ly adv. ernst, starr; streng, grausam; ~ s. (nav.) Heck n.
stertorous a. röchelnd, schnarchend.
stethoscope s. Stethoskop n.
stevedore s. Güterpacker m.
stew s. geschmorte Fleisch n.; ~ v.t. schmoren, dämpfen; ~ed fruit, Kompott n.
steward s. Verwalter, Rentmeister m.; Aufwärter (m.) auf Schiffen.
stewardess s. Aufwärterin f.
stewardship s. Amtsführung f.
stick s. Stock, Stecken m.; Stange f.; ~ of

wood, Holzscheit *n*.; ~ *v.t.* stecken, ankleben; *to ~ together*, zusammenleimen; ~ *v.i.* stocken; sich anhängen; *to ~ at nothing*, vor nichts zurückscheuen; *to ~ to*, beharren bei.
stickleback *s*. Stichling *m*.
stickler *s*. Verfechter *m*.; Eiferer *m*.
stick-up *a*. aufrecht stehend.
sticky *a*. klebrig.
stiff *a*., ~ly *adv.* steif; starr; schwierig; teuer; hartnäckig.
stiffen *v.t.* steifen; hartnäckig machen; ~ *v.i.* steif werden, erstarren.
stiffness *s*. Steifheit *f*.
stifle *a*. ersticken.
stigma *s*. Brandmal *n*.; Schande *f*.
stigmatize *v.t.* brandmarken.
stile *s*. Zauntritt *m*.
still *a*. still, ruhig; ~ *adv.* stets, noch, immer noch; ~ *c*. doch, indessen; ~ *v.t.* stillen, beruhigen.
stillbirth *s*. Totgeburt *f*.
still-born *a*. totgeboren.
still-life *s*. (*fig.*) Stilleben *n*.
stilt *s*. Stelze *f*.
stilted *a*. hochtrabend, gespreizt.
stimulant *a*. anreizend; ~ *s*. Reizmittel *n*.
stimulate *v.t.* anspornen, anreizen.
stimulative *a*. anreizend, antreibend.
stimulus *s*. Antrieb, Sporn *m*.; Reizmittel *n*.
stimy, stymie *v.t.* lahmlegen.
sting *v.t.st.* stechen; schmerzen; anstacheln; (*fig.*) kränken; ~ *s*. Stachel *m*.; Stich *m*.; Biss *m*.; Spitze *f*.
stingy *a*., ~ily *adv.* karg, geizig.
stink *v.i.st.* stinken; ~ *s*. Gestank *m*.
stint *s*. Beschränkung *f*.; Mass *n*.; ~ *v.t.* knapp halten; einschränken.
stipend *s*. Besoldung *f*.; Lohn *m*.
stipendiary *a*. besoldet.
stipulate *v.t.* vereinbaren, bedingen; *as ~d*, wie vereinbart.
stipulation *s*. Abrede, Übereinkunft *f*.; Klausel *f*.
stir *v.t.* regen, bewegen; aufrühren, schüren; umrühren; ~ *v.i.* sich regen; aufstehen; ~ *s*. Regung *f*.; Lärm, Aufruhr *m*.; Getümmel *n*.
stirring *a*. aufregend, vielbewegt.
stirrup *s*. Steigbügel *m*.
stitch *v.t. & i.* stechen; heften; säumen; ~ *s*. Stich *m*.; Masche *f*.
stoat *s*. Hermelin *n*.
stock *s*. Stock, Stamm, Klotz *m*.; (Gewehr-)Schaft *m*.; Grundstock *m*.; Vorrat *m*.; Lager *n*.; (*Am.*) Aktie; Aktien *pl*., (Stamm-)Kapital *n*.; Herkunft *f*.; Inventar *n*.; *in ~*, auf Lager; ~ *taking*, Bestandsaufnahme *f*.; ~-*in-trade* *s*. Betriebsvorrat *m*. (auch *fig.*); ~ *a*. ständig; vorrätig; ~ *v.t.* versehen mit; auf Lager haben.

stockade *s*. Staket *n*., Umpfählung *f*.
stockbroker *s*. Börsenmakler *m*.
stock-exchange *s*. (*Fonds-*) Börse *f*.
stock-holder *s*. Aktionär *m*.
stockinet *s*. Trikot *n*.
stocking *s*. Strumpf *m*.
stock-jobber *s*. Börsenmakler *m*.
stockpile *s*. (*Am.*) Vorrat *m*.; ~ *v.t.* einen Vorrat sammeln.
stock-still *a*. unbeweglich.
stocky *a*. stämmig.
stodgy *a*. füllend, unverdaulich; dick.
stoic *s*. Stoiker *m*.
stoical *a*., ~ly *adv.* stoisch, standhaft.
stoicism *s*. Gleichmut *m*.
stoke *v.t.* schüren, heizen.
stoker *s*. Heizer *m*.
stole *s*. Stola *f*.
stolid *a*., ~ly *adv.* dumm, dickhäutig.
stomach *s*. Magen *m*.; (Ess)lust *f*.; Bauch *m*.; ~-*ache*, Bauchweh *n*.; ~ *v.t.* sich gefallen lassen; verschmerzen.
stone *s*. Stein, (Obst-)Kern *m*.; Gewicht (*n*.) von 14 Pfund; ~ *a*. steinern; ~ *v.t.* steinigen; auskernen; *a ~'s throw*, eine kurze Entfernung.
stone-blind *a*. stockblind.
stone-dead *a*. mausetot.
stone-fruit *s*. Steinobst *n*.
stone-mason *s*. Steinmetz *m*.
stone-pine *s*. Pinie *f*.
stony *a*. steinig; steinern; steinhart.
stool *s*. Schemel *m*.; Stuhlgang *m*.
stoop *v.i.* sich bücken; ~ *s*. Bücken *n*.; Herablassung *f*.
stoopingly *adv.* vorwärts geneigt.
stop *v.t.* (ver)stopfen; hemmen, hindern; versperren; (Zahn) füllen; (Zahlungen) einstellen; *to ~ payment on a cheque*, einen Scheck sperren; ~ *v.i.* stillstehen; anhalten; stehenbleiben; aufhören; *to ~ at an hotel*, in einem Hotel absteigen; ~ *s*. Stillstand *m*.; Klappe *f*.; Pause *f*.; Unterbrechung, Hemmung *f*.; Verbot *n*.; Ende *n*.; Haltestelle *f*.; ~!, *i.* halt!
stop-cock *s*. Absperrhahn *m*.
stop-gap *s*. Lückenbüsser *m*.
stopover *s*. (*Am.*) Fahrtunterbrechung *f*.; Aufenthalt (im Bahnhof) *m*.
stoppage *s*. Verstopfung, Hemmung, Zahlungseinstellung *f*.
stopper *s*. Stöpsel *m*.; ~ *v.t.* zustöpseln.
stopping *s*. Zahnfüllung, Plombe *f*.
stop-press *a*. nach Schluss der Redaktion.
stop-watch *s*. Sekundenuhr (*f*.) mit Hemmfeder, Stopuhr *f*.
storage *s*. Lagern, Lagergeld *n*.; ~ *charge*, Lagergebühr *f*.; ~ *battery* *s*. Akkumulator *m*.
store *s*. Vorrat, Proviant *m*.; Fülle *f*.; (*Am.*) Laden *m*.; ~-*room* *s*. Vorratskammer *f*.; *to put in ~*, einlagern; ~*s*, Warenhaus *n*.; Vorräte *m.pl.*; *military*

~s, Kriegsvorräte *pl.*; Magazin *n.*; ~ *v.t.* aufspeichern, (Möbel) einlagern; (Schiff) verproviantieren.

store-house *s.* Lagerhaus *n.*; Schatzkammer *f.*

store-keeper *s.* Magazinaufseher *m.*

storey, story *s.* Stockwerk *n.*

stork *s.* Storch *m.*

storm *s.* Sturm (auch *mil.*) *m.*; Gewitter *n.*; Aufruhr *m.*; ~ *v.t. & i.* (be)stürmen; wüten.

stormy *a.* stürmisch; ungestüm.

story *s.* Geschichte *f.*; Erzählung *f.*; Lüge *f.*; ~-teller *s.* Erzähler *m.*; Flunkerer *m.*

stout *a.*, ~ly *adv.* stark; standhaft, wacker, tapfer; wohlbeleibt; ~ *s.* dunkle Bier *n.*

stove *s.* Ofen *m.*; Treibhaus *n.*

stovepipe *s.* Ofenrohr *n.*

stow *v.t.* stauen; schichten, packen.

stowage *s.* Stauen *n.*; Stauraum *m.*; Packerlohn *m.*

stowaway *s.* blinde Passagier *m.*

straddle *v.i.* sich ausspreizen, sich rittlings setzen.

strafe *v.t.* (*mil.*) bombardieren, angreifen.

straggle *v.i.* herumstreifen; abschweifen; herumliegen; wuchern (von Pflanzen).

straggler *s.* Nachzügler *m.*

straight *a. & adv.*, ~ly *adv.* gerade; unmittelbar, direkt; ~ *on,* ~ *ahead,* geradeaus; *to put* ~, in Ordnung bringen.

straighten *v.t.* gerade, straff machen; *to* ~ *out,* in Ordnung bringen; *to* ~ *up,* aufrichten.

straightforward *a.* geradsinnig, bieder.

strain *v.t.* spannen, strecken; quetschen, durchseihen; anstrengen; verstauchen; übertreiben; ~ *v.i.* sich anstrengen; ~ *s.* Anstrengung *f.*; Spannung *f.*; Inanspruchnahme *f.*; Verstauchung *f.*; Neigung *f.*; Tonart *f.*, Stil, Charakter *m.*; Melodie *f.*; Stamm *m.*, Klasse, Familie *f.*; Art *f.*

strained *p. & a.* gespannt.

strainer *s.* Filtriertrichter *m.*; (Tee)Seiher *m.*

strait *a.*, ~ly *adv.* eng, knapp, genau, streng; schwierig; ~-jacket *s.* Zwangsjacke *f.*; ~ *s.* Enge, *f.*; Meerenge *f.*; ~s *pl.* Verlegenheit, Klemme *f.*

straiten *v.t.* verengen; in Verlegenheit setzen.

straitness *s.* Enge *f.*; Strenge *f.*; Einschränkung *f.*; Verlegenheit *f.*

strand *s.* Strand *m.*; Strähne *f.*; (*fig.*) Ader *f.*; ~ *v.i.* stranden.

strange *a.*, ~ly *adv.* fremd; seltsam.

stranger *s.* Fremde, Ausländer *m.*

strangle *v.t.* erdrosseln.

stranglehold *s.* Würgegriff *m.*

strangles *s.pl.* Druse *f.*

strangulate *v.t.* abschnüren.

strangulation *s.* Erdrosselung *f.*

strap *s.* Riemen, Gurt *m.*; Strippe *f.*; (*mil.*) Achselschnur *f.*; ~-hanger *m.* Stehplatzinhaber (*m.*) in Strassenbahn; ~ *v.t.* mit Riemen fest machen.

strapping *a.* stämmig *f.*

stratagem *s.* Kriegslist *f.*; Schachzug *m.*

strategic *a.* strategisch.

strategist *s.* Stratege *m.*

strategy *s.* Kriegskunst *f.*; List *f.*

stratify *v.t.* schichten.

stratum *s.* Lage, Schicht *f.*

straw *s.* Stroh *n.*; Kleinigkeit *f.*

strawberry *s.* Erdbeere *f.*

straw-cutter *s.* Häckselschneidemaschine *f.*

straw-mattress *s.* Strohsack *m.*

stray *v.i.* irregehen; umherstreifen; ~ *a.* verirrt, verlaufen.

streak *s.* Strich, Streifen *m.*

streaky *a.* streifig; durchwachsen (Speck).

stream *s.* Bach *m.*; Lauf *m.*; ~ *v.i.* strömen, fliessen.

streamer *s.* Wimpel *f.*; (flatternde) Band *n.*; Papierschlange *f.*

streamlined *a.* Stromlinien...

street *s.* Strasse, Gasse *f.*

street arab *s.* obdachlose Junge *m.*

streetcar *s.* (*Am.*) Strassenbahnwagen *m.*

street-lamp *s.* Strassenlaterne *f.*

street vendor *s.* Strassenverkäufer *m.*

strength *s.* Stärke, Kraft *f.*; *on the* ~ *of,* auf Grund von; ~ *report,* (*mil.*) Stärkenachweisung *f.*

strengthen *v.t.* stärken; befestigen; bekräftigen; ~ *v.i.* erstarken.

strenuous *a.*, ~ly *adv.* tapfer, wacker, tätig, eifrig; anstrengend.

stress *s.* Nachdruck *m.*; Gewicht *n.*; Hauptton *m.*; Anspannung *f.*, Druck *m.*; ~ *v.t.* betonen.

stretch *v.t.* (*v.i. sich*) strecken, (aus) dehnen, anstrengen; übertreiben; ~ *s.* Ausdehnung, Strecke *f.*; Überanspannung *f.*; Anstrengung *f.*; *at a* ~, in einem Zuge, ununterbrochen.

stretcher *s.* Streckwerkzeug *n.*; Handschuhweiter *m.*; Tragbahre *f.*; ~-bearer *s.* Krankenträger *m.*

strew *v.t.st.* streuen, bedecken.

stricken *a.* betroffen (von).

strict *a.*, ~ly *adv.* eng; straff; genau; streng; *~ly speaking,* streng genommen.

stricture *s.* Verengung *f.*; Tadel *m.*

stride *s.* (weite) Schritt *m.*; ~ *v.i.st.* schreiten.

strident *a.* kreischend.

strife *s.* Streit *m.*; Wettstreit *m.*

strike *v.t. & i.* schlagen, stossen; treffen; rühren, bewegen; auffallen; (Flage, *f.*) streichen; (Zelt, Lager) abbrechen; (Handel) abschliessen; die Arbeit einstellen, streiken; *to* ~ *a balance,* den Saldo ziehen; *to* ~ *a match,* Zündholz anzünden; *to ~ a mine*, auf eine Mine laufen; *to ~ off, out*, ausstreichen; *to ~ a person off the list*, einen von der Liste streichen; *to ~ a chord*, eine Saite anschlagen; *to ~ up*, (Lied) anstimmen; *~ s.* Arbeitseinstellung *f.*, Streik *m.*; *on ~*, streikend; *~-breaker s.* Streikbrecher *m.*

striker *s.* Streikende *m.*

striking *a.*, *~ly adv.* auffallend, ergreifend; treffend; *~ distance*, Schlagweite *f.*; *~ power*, Schlagkraft *f.*

string *s.* Bindfaden *m.*; Schnur *f.*; Sehne *f.*; Saite *f.*; Reihe *f.*; *~ v.t.* besaiten; aufreihen.

string-band *s.* Streichorchester *n.*

stringency *s.* Strenge *f.*; Knappheit *f.*

stringent *a.* streng; zusammenziehend; bindend.

stringy *a.* faserig.

strip *v.t.* abstreifen; berauben; *~ v.i.* sich auskleiden; *~ s.* Streifen *m.*

stripe *s.* Streifen *m.*; (*mil.*) Tresse *f.*

striped *a.* gestreift.

stripling *s.* Bürschchen *n.*

strive *v.i.st.* streben; streiten.

stroke *s.* Streich, Schlag, Stoss *m.*; Schlag (der Uhr) *m.*; Schlaganfall *m.*; Strich *m.*; Zug, Federstrich *m.*; Kolbenhub *m.*; *~ v.t.* streichen; streicheln.

stroll *v.i.* herumstreifen, herumschlendern; *~ s.* Spaziergang *m.*

strong *a.*, *~ly adv.* stark, kräftig; tüchtig, streng, mundрücklich; *40 men ~*, 40 Mann hoch; *~ drinks pl.* alkoholische Getränke *n.pl.*

strong-box *s.* Geldschrank *m.*

stronghold *s.* Feste *f.*; Bollwerk *n.*

strong-room *s.* Stahlkammer *f.*

strop *s.* Streichriemen *m.*; *~ v.t.* abziehen.

structural *a.*, *~ly adv.* strukturell, organisch.

structure *s.* Bau *m.*; Bauart, Einrichtung *f.*

struggle *v.i.* sich anstrengen; ringen; sich sträuben; *~ v.i.* Sträuben *n.*; Kampf *m.*; Zuckung *f.*; *~ for life*, Kampf (*m.*) ums Dasein.

strum *v.t.* klimpern, schlecht spielen.

strut *v.i.* stolzieren; stolzieren, sich brüsten; (*mech.*) abstreifen; *~ s.* Stützbalken *m.*, Versteifung *f.*

strychnine *s.* Strychnin *f.*

stub *s.* Stumpf, Klotz *m.*; (*Am.*) Kontrollabschnitt *m.*; *~ v.t.* ausroden.

stubble *s.* Stoppel *f.*

stubborn *a.*, *~ly adv.* steif, unbiegsam, hart; standhaft; hartnäckig.

stucco *s.* Stuck *m.*

stud *s.* Knaufnagel *m.*; Knopf, Hemdenknopf *m.*; Ständer *m.*; Gestüt *n.*; *~ v.t.* beschlagen; (*fig.*) besetzen.

stud-book *s.* Zuchtbuch *n.*

student *s.* Student *m.*; Gelehrte *m.*

studied *a.*, *~ly adv.* gelehrt; studiert; absichtlich; erkünstelt.

studio *s.* Atelier *n.*; (*radio*) Senderaum *m.*; (*film*) Aufnahmeatelier *n.*

studious *a.*, *~ly adv.* beflissen, fleissig; bedacht; geflissentlich.

study *s.* Studium *n.*; Studierstube *f.*; Studie *f.*; *~ v.i.* studieren; nachsinnen, sich befleissigen; *~ v.t.* einstudieren; genau untersuchen.

stuff *s.* Stoff *m.*; Zeug *n.*; Gerät *n.*; Unsinn *m.*; Plunder *m.*; *~ v.t.* (aus)stopfen; füllen.

stuffing *s.* Füllung *f.*; Füllsel *n.*

stuffy *a.* dumpfig.

stultify *v.t.* wirkungslos machen (durch ungereimtes Handeln).

stumble *v.i.* stolpern.

stumbling-block *s.* Stein des Anstosses *m.*

stump *s.* Stumpf *m.*; (Zigarren)stummel *m.*; (Zeichnen) Wischer *m.*; *~ v.t.* stampfen; tappen.

stumpy *a.* kurz und dick.

stun *v.t.* betäuben, verdutzen.

stunning *a.* erstaunlich; famos.

stunt *v.t.* am Wachstum hindern; *~ s.* (*sl.*) Kraftanstrengung *f.*; (Zeitung) Werbetrick *m.*; Sensation *f.*

stupefaction *s.* Betäubung *f.*

stupefy *v.t.* betäuben, verblüffen.

stupendous *a.*, *~ly adv.* erstaunlich.

stupid *a.*, *~ly adv.* dumm, albern; langweilig.

stupidity *s.* Dummheit *f.*

stupor *s.* Erstarrung *f.*; Staunen *n.*

sturdy *a.*, *~ily adv.* derb, stark; dreist.

sturgeon *s.* Stör *m.*

stutter *v.i.* stottern.

sty *s.* Schweinestall *m.*

sty(e) *s.* Gerstenkorn (am Auge) *n.*

style *s.* Griffel, Stichel *m.*; Schreibart *f.*, Stil *m.*; Machart, Aufmachung *f.*; Titel *m.*; *~ v.t.* benennen, betiteln.

stylish *a.* elegant, modisch.

stylograph *s.* Tintenfüllstift *m.*

stymie *see* stimy.

styptic *a.* blutstillend; *~ pencil*, Alaunstift *m.*

suasion *s.* Überredung *f.*; *moral ~*, gute Zureden *n.*

suave *a.* mild, sanft; verbindlich.

suavity *s.* Lieblichkeit, Anmut *f.*

subaltern *a.* untergeordnet; *~ s.* Unterbeamte *m.*; Subalternoffizier *m.*

subcaliber *a.* (*mil.*) Kleinkaliber...

sub-committee *s.* Unterausschuss *m.*

subconscious *a.*, *~ly adv.* unterbewusst.

subcontract *s.* Unterkontrakt *m.*

subcontractor *s.* Subkontrahent, Unterlieferant *m.*

subcutaneous *a.* unter der Haut.

subdeacon *s.* Subdiakon *m.*

subdivide v.t. unterteilen.
subdivision s. Unterabteilung f.
subdue v.t. unterwerfen; dämpfen.
sub-editor s. Unterredakteur m.
subheading s. Untertitel m.
subject a. unterworfen, ausgesetzt; zu Grunde liegend; ~ to, vorbehaltlich; ~ to reservations, unter Vorbehalt; ~ s. Untertan m.; Person f.; Gegenstand m., Object n.; Betreff m.; Subjekt n.; ~ index s. Sachregister n.; ~ matter, Gegenstand m., Thema n.
subject v.t. unterwerfen; aussetzen.
subjection s. Unterwerfung f.
subjective a. subjektiv.
subjoin v.t. beifügen.
subjugate v.t. unterjochen.
subjunctive s. (gram.) Konjunktiv m.
sublet v.t. unterverpachten, weitervermieten.
sublicence s. Unterlizenz f; to sublicense v.t. in Unterlizenz vergeben.
sublimate s. (chem.) Sublimat n.
sublime a., ~ly adv. erhaben, hehr, hoch; ~ v.t. veredeln, sublimieren.
sublimity s. Erhabenheit f.
sublunar, sublunary a. irdisch.
submachinegun s. Maschinenpistole f.
submarine a. unterseeisch; ~ s. Unterseeboot n.; ~-pen s. U-boot Bunker m.
submerge v.t. & i. untertauchen; überschwemmen.
submersion s. Untertauchen n.; Überschwemmung f.
submission s. Unterwürfigkeit, Demut, Ergebung f.; Eingabe f.
submissive a., ~ly adv. unterwürfig.
submit v.t. unterwerfen; unterbreiten; ~ v.i. sich fügen.
subnormal a. unternormal.
subordinate a., ~ly adv. untergeordnet; ~ clause, (gram.) Nebensatz m.; ~ s. Untergeordnete, Untergebene m.; ~ v.t. unterordnen.
suborn v.t. (zu falschem Zeugnis) verleiten.
subornation s. Anstiftung f.
subpoena s. Vorladung bei Strafe f.
subscribe v.t. unterschreiben; zeichnen; ~ v.i. abonnieren; einwilligen.
subscriber s. Unterschreiber, Abonnent, m.
subscription s. Unterzeichnung f.; Abonnement n.; (Geld) Beitrag m.; annual ~, Jahresabonnement n.; monthly ~, Monatsabonnement n.; ~ list, Subskriptionsliste, Zeichnungsliste f.; to withdraw one's ~, sein Abonnement aufgeben.
subsection s. Unterabteilung f.
subsequent a. nachfolgend, nachträglich; ~ delivery, Nachlieferung f.; ~ payment, Nachzahlung f.; ~ly adv. nachher.

subservience s. Unterwürfigkeit f.
subservient a. dienlich; unterwürfig.
subside v.i. sinken, abnehmen; aufhören.
subsidiary a. Hilfs..., helfend; ~ company, Tochtergesellschaft f.; ~ subject, Nebenfach n.; ~ s. Gehilfe m.
subsidize v.t. mit Geld unterstützen, subventionieren.
subsidy s. Beisteuer f.; (Hilfs)geld n., Subvention f.
subsist v.i. bestehen, auskommen; ~ v.t. erhalten, ernähren.
subsistence s. Dasein, Bestehen, Auskommen n.; Lebensunterhalt m.; ~ allowance s. Verpflegungsgeld n.; minimum of ~, Existenzminimum n.
subsoil s. Untergrund m.
substance s. Wesen n.; Stoff m., Substanz f.; Hauptinhalt m.; Vermögen n.
substantial a., ~ly adv. wesentlich, wirklich, körperlich; nahrhaft; stark; zahlungsfähig, vermögend.
substantiality s. Wesenheit f.
substantiate v.t. dartun, nachweisen.
substantive s. Hauptwort n.
substitute v.t. setzen an die Stelle von; unterschieben; ~ s. Stellvertreter m.; Ersatzmittel n.; ~ material, Werkstoff m.
substitution s. Stellvertretung, Unterschiebung f.
substratum s. Unterlage, Grundlage f.
substruction s. Unterbau m., Grundlage f.
substructure s. Unterbau m.
subtenant s. Untermieter, Afterpächter m.
subterfuge s. Ausflucht f.
subterranean a. unterirdisch.
subtilize v.t. & i. verfeinern; spitzfindeln, klügeln.
subtitle s. Untertitel m.
subtle a., ~tly adv. fein, schlau.
subtlety s. Schlauheit f., Scharfsinn m.
subtract v.t. abziehen, subtrahieren.
subtraction s. Abziehen n., Subtraktion f.
subtrahend s. (ar.) Subtrahend m.
subtropical a. subtropisch.
suburb s. Vorstadt f.
suburban a. vorstädtisch; ~ traffic, Vorortsverkehr m.; ~ train, Vorortszug m.
subvention s. Hilfsgeld n., Beihilfe f.
subversion s. Umsturz m.
subversive a. umstürzend; ~ activities pl. Wühlarbeit f.
subvert v.t. umstürzen, zerstören.
subway s. unterirdische Gang m.; Unterführung f.; (Am.) Untergrundbahn f.
succeed v.t. & i. nachfolgen; to ~ to an estate, ein Vermögen erben; to ~ to a person, einen beerben; to ~ in doing, gelingen.
success s. Erfolg m., Glück n.
successful a., ~ly adv. erfolgreich.
succession s. Reihenfolge, Folge, Nach

folge *f.*; Erbfolge *f.*; *in ~*, hintereinander, nacheinander; *right of ~*, Erbfolge *f.*; *~ to the throne*, Thronfolge *f.*

successive *a.* einander folgend; **~ly** *adv.* der Reihe nach.

successor *s.* Nachfolger *m.*

succinct *a.*, **~ly** *adv.* gedrängt, bündig.

succour *s.* Hilfe *f.*; Beistand *m.*; (*mil.*) Entsatz *m.*; **~** *v.t.* beistehen.

succulent *a.* saftig.

succumb *v.i.* unterliegen.

such *pn.* solcher, solche, solches; von der Art, so gross; **~** *a.* so ein; **~-like**, dergleichen; **~** *as*, die, welche...; *no ~ thing*, nichts dergleichen.

suck *v.t. & i.* (ein)saugen; pumpen; **~** *s.* Saugen *n.*

sucker *s.* Saugkolben *m.*, Saugrohr *n.*; Wurzelspross *m.*; (*Am.*) Grünschnabel *m.*

sucking-pig *s.* Spanferkel *n.*

sucking-pump *s.* Saugpumpe *f.*

suckle *v.t.* säugen, stillen.

suction *s.* Saugen *n.*; Saug. (.

sudden *a.*, **~ly** *adv.* plötzlich; übereilt, hitzig; *on a ~*, *all of a ~*, plötzlich.

suddenness *s.* Plötzlichkeit *f.*

suds *s.pl.* Seifenwasser *n.*

sue *v.i.* ansuchen; **~** *v.t.* bitten, verklagen; *to ~ for damages*, auf Schadenersatz klagen.

suède *s.* Ziegenleder *n.*

suet *s.* Talg *m.*; Hammelfett *n.*

suffer *v.t. & i.* leiden, ausstehen; Strafe, Schaden leiden; gestatten.

sufferable *a.*, **~bly** *adv.* erträglich; zulässig.

sufferance *s.* Leiden *n.*; Duldung *f.*

suffering *s.* Leiden *n.*

suffice *v.i.* genügen; **~** *v.t.* Genüge leisten, befriedigen.

sufficiency *s.* Genüge *f.*; Auskommen *n.*

sufficient *a.*, **~ly** *adv.* hinlänglich.

suffix *v.t.* anhängen; **~** *s.* Anhängesilbe *f.*

suffocate *v.t.* ersticken.

suffragan *s.* Weihbischof *m.*

suffrage *s.* Wahlstimme *f.*; Beifall *m.*; Stimmrecht *n.*; *universal ~*, allgemeine Wahlrecht *n.*

suffragette *s.* Frauenstimmrechtlerin *f.*

suffuse *v.t.* übergiessen; überziehen.

sugar *s.* Zucker *m.*; *~ tongs pl.* Zuckerzange *f.*; **~** *v.t.* zuckern.

sugar-basin *s.* Zuckerschale *f.*

sugar-cane *s.* Zuckerrohr *n.*

sugar-loaf *s.* Zuckerhut *m.*

sugar-plum *s.* Bonbon *m.*

sugar-refiner *s.* Zuckersieder *m.*

sugar-works *s.pl.* Zuckersiederei *f.*

sugary *a.* zuckerig.

suggest *v.t.* eingeben, beibringen, raten, vorschlagen; einflössen.

suggestion *s.* Eingebung *f.*; Wink *m.*; Rat *m.*, Vorschlag *m.*

suggestive *a.* andeutend; anregend; vielsagend; schlüpfrig.

suicidal *a.* selbstmörderisch.

suicide *s.* Selbstmord *m.*; Selbstmörder *m.*; *to commit ~*, Selbstmord begehen.

suit *s.* Folge *f.*; Farbe (Karte) *f.*; Gesuch *n.*; Prozess *m.*; Anzug *m.*; Bitte *f.*; **~** *v.t.* ordnen; passen; gefallen; geziemen; gut stehen; **~** *v.i.* übereinstimmen.

suitable *a.*, **~bly** *adv.* gemäss, angemessen, schicklich, passend.

suit-case *s.* Handkoffer *m.*

suite *s.* Gefolge *n.*; Hotelsuite *f.*; Zimmereinrichtung *f.*

suiting *s.* Anzugsstoff *m.*

suitor *s.* Bittsteller *m.*; Bewerber, Freier *m.*

sulk *v.i.* zürnen, schmollen.

sulky *a.*, **~ily** *adv.* mürrisch.

sullen *a.*, **~ly** *adv.* düster, verdriesslich.

sully *v.t.* besudeln.

sulphate *s.* schwefelsaure Salz *n.*

sulphide *s.* Sulphid *n.*

sulphur *s.* Schwefel *m.*

sulphuric *a.* Schwefel...; **~** *acid s.* Schwefelsäure *f.*

sulphurous *a.*, **~ly** *adv.* schwef[e]llig.

sulphury *a.* schwefelgelb.

sultan *s.* Sultan *m.*

sultana *s.* Sultanin *f.*; (kernlose) Rosine *f.*, Sultanine *f.*

sultry *a.* schwül.

sum *s.* Summe *f.*; Rechenaufgabe *f.*; *~ total*, Gesamtsumme *f.*; **~** *v.t.* zusammenzählen, rechnen; *to ~ up*, zusammenfassen, (*law*) Beweisaufnahme zusammenfassen.

summarize *v.t.* (kurz) zusammenfassen.

summary *a.*, **~ily** *adv.* summarisch, kurz; **~** *s.* Auszug, kurze Inhaltsangabe *f.*; *~ jurisdiction*, *~ proceedings*, (*law*) Schnellverfahren, beschleunigte Verfahren *n.*

summer *s.* Sommer *m.*; Tragbalken *m.*; *~ time*, Sommerzeit *f.*

summer-house *s.* Gartenhaus *n.*

summit *s.* Gipfel *m.*, Spitze *f.*

summon *v.t.* vorladen, aufrufen; (Kraft) zusammennehmen.

summons *s.* Vorladung *f.*; Aufforderung *f.*

sumptuary *a.* Aufwand(s)...

sumptuous *a.*, **~ly** *adv.* prächtig.

sun *s.* Sonne *f.*

sunburn *s.* Sonnenbrand *m.*

sunburnt *a.* gebräunt, verbrannt.

sundae *s.* Fruchteis *m.*

Sunday *s.* Sonntag *m.*

sunder *v.t.* trennen, absondern.

sun-dial *s.* Sonnenuhr *f.*

sundown *s.* (*Am.*) Sonnenuntergang *m.*

sundry *a.* mehrere, verschiedene; **sundries** *s.pl.* verschiedene Gegenstände *m.pl.*; Nebenausgaben *f.pl.*

sunflower *s.* Sonnenblume *f.*

sun-glasses, sun-spectacles *pl.* Sonnenbrille *f.*

sunken *a.* versunken; (*fig*) eingefallen.

sunny *a.* sonnig.

sunrise *s.* Sonnenaufgang *m.*

sunset *s.* Sonnenuntergang *m.*

sunshade *s.* Sonnenschirm *m.*

sunshine *s.* Sonnenschein *m.*

sun-spot *s.* Sonnenflecken *m.*

sunstroke *s.* Sonnenstich *m.*

sup *v.t.* schlürfen; *v.i.* zu Abend essen.

super *s.* Statist (Theater) *m.*

superabound *v.i.* Überfluss haben.

superabundant *a.*, ~ly *adv.* überreichlich.

superadd *v.t.* hinzufügen.

superaddition *s.* Hinzufügung *f.*

superannuable *a.* pensionsberechtigt.

superannuate *v.t.* als zu alt erklären; pensionieren.

superannuation *s.* Pensionierung *f.*; ~fund, Pensionsfonds *m.*

superb *a.*, ~ly *adv.* prächtig, herrlich.

supercargo *s.* Ladungsaufseher *m.*

supercharger *s.* (*avi.*) Lader, Vorverdichter, Kompressor *m.*

supercilious *a.*, ~ly *adv.* anmassend.

supererogation *s.* Übergebühr *f.*; Mehrleistung *f.*

superficial *a.*, ~ly *adv.* oberflächlich; seicht.

superficies *s.* Oberfläche *f.*

superfine *a.* extrafein, hochfein.

superfluity *s.* Überfluss *m.*

superfluous *a.*, ~ly *adv.* überflüssig.

superhuman *a.* übermenschlich.

superintend *v.t.* die Aufsicht führen.

superintendence *s.* Aufsicht *f.*

superintendent *s.* Inspektor, Aufseher *m.*

superior *a.* höher; grösser; vorzüglich; überlegen; ~ *s.* Obere, Vorgesetzte *m.*; ~ authority, vorgesetzte Behörde *f.*

superiority *s.* Überlegenheit *f.*; Vorrang *m.*; Vorrecht *n.*

superlative *a.*, ~ly *adv.* im höchsten Grade; ~ *s.* Superlativ *m.*

superman *s.* Übermensch *m.*

supernatural *a.*, ~ly *adv.* übernatürlich.

supernumerary *a.* überzählig; ~ *s.* Überzählige *m.*; Figurant *m.*

superscribe *v.t.* überschreiben.

superscription *s.* Überschrift *f.*

supersede *v.t.* verdrängen; abschaffen.

supersession *s.* Ersatz *m.*, Verdrängung *f.*

superstition *s.* Aberglaube *m.*

superstitious *a.*, ~ly *adv.* abergläubisch.

superstructure *s.* Oberbau *m.*

supertax *s.* Steuerzuschlag *m.*

supervene *v.i.* hinzukommen; (plötzlich) eintreten.

supervention *s.* Hinzukommen, plötzliche Eintreten *n.*

supervise *v.t.* beaufsichtigen.

supervision *s.* Aufsicht *f.*

supervisor *s.* Aufseher *m.*

supervisory *a.* Aufsichts...

supine *a.* zurückgelehnt; gleichgültig; ~ *s.* (*gram.*) Supinum *n.*

supper *s.* Abendessen *n.*; *the Lord's* ~, das (heilige) Abendmahl *n.*

supplant *v.t.* verdrängen, ausstechen.

supple *a.*, ~ly *adv.* geschmeidig, biegsam; nachgiebig.

supplement *s.* Ergänzung *f.*; Zusatz, Anhang *m.*; Beilage (Zeitung) *f.*

supplement *v.t.* ergänzen.

supplemental, supplementary *a.* ergänzend; ~ *order*, Nachbestellung *f.*

supplementation *s.* Ergänzung *f.*

suppliant *a.* demütig flehend.

supplicant *a.*, ~ly *adv.* bittend, flehend; ~ *s.* Bittsteller *m.*

supplicate *v.t.* anflehen.

supplication *s.* demütige Bitte *f.*

supplier *s.* Versorger *m.*

supply *v.t.* ersetzen, ergänzen; liefern, versorgen; ~ *s.* Beschaffung *f.*; Zuschuss *m.*; Vorrat *m.*; (*mil.*) Nachschub *m.*; ~-depot *s.* Nachschublager *n.*; ~ *and demand*, Angebot (*n.*) und Nachfrage (*f.*); ~ies *pl.* (*mil.*) Versorgung *f.*; (Parlament) Etat, Haushalt *m.*

support *v.t.* unterstützen; erhalten, ernähren; ertragen; bekräftigen; ~ *s.* Stütze *f.*; Unterstützung *f.*; Unterhalt *m.*; *in* ~ *of*, zum Beweis von.

supporter *s.* Unterstützer *m.*; Gönner *m.*; Verteidiger *m.*; Anhänger *m.*

suppose *v.t.* voraussetzen, vermuten.

supposition *s.* Voraussetzung *f.*

suppress *v.t.* unterdrücken; verhindern.

suppression *s.* Unterdrückung *f.*; Verheimlichung *f.*; Abschaffung *f.*

suppurate *v.i.* eitern.

supremacy *s.* Obergewalt *f.*; Übergewicht, Überlegenheit *f.*

supreme *a.*, ~ly *adv.* höchst, oberst.

surcharge *s.* Überladung *f.*; Überforderung *f.*; Zuschlag (Porto) *m.*, Strafporto *n.*; ~ *v.t.* überladen.

surcingle *s.* Sattelgurt *m.*; Leibgürtel *m.*

sure *a. & adv.*, ~ly *adv.* sicher, gewiss, zuverlässig; *to be* ~, sicher wissen; allerdings, freilich; *to make* ~, sich vergewissern; *for* ~, sicher.

sureness *s.* Sicherheit *f.*

surety *s.* Sicherheit *f.*; Bürge *m.*, Bürgschaft *f.*

surf *s.* Brandung *f.*

surface *s.* Oberfläche *f.*; Flächeninhalt *m.*; ~ *mail* *s.* gewöhnliche Post (nicht Luftpost) *f.*

surfeit *s.* Überladung *f.*; Ekel *m.*; ~ *v.t.* (*v.refl. sich*) überfüllen, überladen.
surge *s.* Woge, Brandung *f.*; ~ *v.i.* wogen; steigen.
surgeon *s.* Wundarzt *m.*, Chirurg *m.*
surgery *s.* Wundarzneikunst, Chirurgie *f.*; (ärztliche) Sprechzimmer *n.*
surgical *a.* chirurgisch, wundärztlich.
surly *a.*, ~ily *adv.* grob, mürrisch.
surmise *v.t.* mutmassen; ~ *s.* Vermutung *f.*
surmount *v.t.* überragen; überwinden.
surname *s.* Zuname *m.*; ~ *v.t.* einen Zunamen geben.
surpass *v.t.* übertreffen.
surplice *s.* Chorhemd *n.*
surplus *s.* Überschuss *m.*; Überrest *m.*; ~ *a.* überzählig, überschüssig.
surprisal, surprise *s.* Überraschung *f.*
surprise *v.t.* überraschen; erstaunen.
surprising *a.*, ~ly *adv.* erstaunlich.
surrender *v.t.* übergeben, überliefern; abtreten; ~ *v.i.* sich ergeben; ~ *s.* Übergabe, Auslieferung *f.*
surreptitious *a.*, ~ly *adv.* erschlichen, verstohlen; ~ *passage*, gefälschte Stelle *f.*
surrogate *s.* Stellvertreter *m.*
surround *v.t.* umgeben, einschliessen.
surroundings *s.pl.* Umgebung *f.*
surtax *s.* Steuerzuschlag *m.*
surveillance *s.* Überwachung *f.*
survey *v.t.* überblicken, besichtigen; ausmessen; ~ *s.* Überblick *m.*; Besichtigung, Vermessung *f.*; Riss, Plan *m.*
surveyor *s.* Inspektor, Bauinspektor, Baurat *m.*; Feldmesser *m.*
survival *s.* Überleben *n.*
survive *v.t.* überleben; ~ *v.i.* übrig bleiben, noch leben, fortleben.
survivor *s.* Überlebende *m.*
susceptibility *s.* Empfänglichkeit *f.*
susceptible *a.* empfänglich; empfindlich.
suspect *v.i.* Verdacht hegen, argwöhnen, besorgen; ~ *v.t.* in Verdacht haben; bezweifeln; ~ *s.* Verdächtige *m.*; *to be* ~, belastet sein.
suspected *a.* verdächtig.
suspend *v.t.* aufhängen; unterbrechen; suspendieren, zeitweise ausschliessen; einstellen; aufschieben; absetzen.
suspenders *pl.* Strumpfhalter *pl.*; (*Am.*) Hosenträger *pl.*
suspense *s.* Ungewissheit *f.*; Spannung *f.*
suspension *s.* Aufhängen *n.*; Aufschub *m.*; Unschlüssigkeit *f.*; Einstellung *f.*; Stillstand *m.*; Suspension *f.*; ~ *of payments*, Zahlungseinstellung *f.*
suspension-bridge *s.* Hängebrücke *f.*
suspicion *s.* Verdacht, Argwohn *m.*; *above* ~, über allen Verdacht erhaben.
suspicious *a.*, ~ly *adv.* argwöhnisch; verdächtig.
sustain *v.t.* stützen; aufrechthalten; helfen; (Verlust) erleiden; behaupten.

sustenance *s.* Unterhalt *m.*
suture *s.* Naht *f.*
suzerain *s.* Oberlehnsherr *m.*
suzerainty *s.* Oberlehnsherrlichkeit *f.*
swab *s.* Kehrwisch *m.*; ~ *v.t.* abschwabbern; kehren, reinigen.
swaddle *v.t.* windeln, wickeln; ~ *s.* Windel *f.*
swaddling-clothes *s.pl.* Windeln *pl.*
swagger *v.i.* stolzieren; prahlen; grosstun; ~ *a.* schneidig.
swain *s.* Bursche *m.*; Schäfer *m.*; Liebste *m.*
swallow *v.t.* (ver)schlucken; verschlingen; ~ *s.* Schwalbe *f.*
swamp *s.* Sumpf *m.*; ~ *v.t.* (in Morast) versenken; überschwemmen.
swan *s.* Schwan *m.*
swank *s.* Grosstuerei *f.*; ~ *v.i.* grosstun, renommieren.
swap = **swop.**
sward *s.* Rasen *m.*
swarm *s.* Schwarm *m.*; Gewimmel *n.*; ~ *v.i.* wimmeln.
swarthy *a.*, ~ily *adv.* schwärzlich, dunkel.
swash *v.i.* plantschen.
swash-buckler *s.* Schwadroneur *m.*
swastika *s.* Hakenkreuz *n.*
swatch *s.* Tuchmuster *n.*
swath *s.* Grasrand, Mähstreifen *m.*
swathe *s.* Wickelband *n.*; ~ *v.t.* einwindeln.
sway *v.t.* schwenken; lenken, regieren; ~ *v.i.* schwanken; Einfluss haben, herrschen; ~ *s.* Schwung *m.*; Ausschlag (der Waage) *m.*; Macht *f.*
swear *v.i.st.* schwören; fluchen; ~ *v.t.* vereidigen; beschwören; ~ *by*, schwören bei; *to* ~ *false*, falsch schwören; *to* ~ *in*, vereidigen.
sweat *s.* Schweiss *m.*; *v.i.r. & ir.* schwitzen; ~ *v.t.* schwitzen; schweissen; (*fig.*) ausbeuten, für Hungerlohn beschäftigen; ~*ed labour*, Schwitzarbeit *f.*
sweater *s.* Sweater *m.*, Wolljacke *f.*
sweep *v.i.ir.* dahinfahren, streifen; ~ *v.t.* fegen, kehren; schleppen; ~ *s.* Zug, Schwung *m.*; Schleppe *f.*; Schornsteinfeger *m.*; flache Landstrich *m.*
sweeping *a.* reissend; weitgreifend; ~s *s.pl.* Kehricht *m.*
sweep-stake *s.* Wettrennlotterie, wo der Gewinner die Einsätze erhält.
sweet *a.*, ~ly *adv.* süss; lieblich; freundlich; ~ *pea*, Edelwicke *f.*; ~ *william*, Bartnelke *f.*; ~ *tooth*, Leckermaul *n.*; ~ *s.* Süssigkeit, Lieblichkeit *f.*; Schätzchen *n.*; ~s *pl.* Zuckerwerk *n.*
sweetbread *s.* Bries *n.*, Kalbsbröschen *n.*
sweeten *v.t.* versüssen; lieblich machen.
sweetheart *s.* Liebchen *n.*
sweetmeats *s.pl.* Zuckerwerk *n.*
sweetness *s.* Süssigkeit, Lieblichkeit *f.*

sweet potato s. Batate f.
sweetroll s. Schnecke (Gebäck) f.
swell v.i.st. schwellen; zunehmen; sich blähen; ~ v.t. aufblasen; vergrössern; ~ s. Anschwellen n.; Erhebung f.; Dünung f.; Stutzer m.; hervorragende Mann m.; ~ a. vorzüglich; aufgedonnert.
swelling s. Geschwulst f.
swelter v.i. lechzen; vor Hitze vergehen.
swerve v.i. abweichen; abschweifen.
swift a. schnell, flüchtig; bereit; ~ s. Turmschwalbe f.
swill v.i. & t. stark trinken; spülen; ~ s. Spülicht n.
swim v.i.st. schwimmen; schwindlig sein; ~ v.t. durchschwimmen; schwemmen.
swimming-bath,   swimming-pool s. Schwimmbad n.
swimmingly adv. ohne Schwierigkeit.
swindle v.t. beschwindeln; erschwindeln; ~ s. Schwindel m.
swindler s. Schwindler m.
swine s. Schwein n. (meist fig.).
swing v.t. schwingen, schaukeln; ~ v.i. sich schwingen; schwanken; eindrehen, sich umdrehen; baumeln; (nav.) schwaien; ~ s. Schwung m.; Schaukel f.; Spielraum m.; Gang m.; in full ~, in vollem Gang; ~-bridge s. Drehbrücke f.; ~ing chair s. Schaukelstuhl m. ~(ing) door, Drehtür f.; ~ing lamp, Hängelampe f.
swingeing a., ~ly adv. ungeheuer.
swing-gate s. Drehtor n.
swingle s. Flachsschwinge f.
swinish a., ~ly adv. schweinisch.
swirl v.i. wirbeln; ~ s. Strudel m.
switch s. Gerte f.; (rail.) Weiche f.; (elek.) Schalter m.; (elek.) ~-gear s. Schaltgerät n.; ~ v.t. hauen; (elek.) (um)schalten; to ~ on, off, andrehen, abdrehen.
switchback,   ~-railway s. Berg-und-Talbahn f.
switch-board s. Schalttafel f., Schaltbrett n.
swivel s. Drehzapfen, Drehring m.; ~-bridge s. Drehbrücke f.; ~-chair s. Drehstuhl m.; ~ v.i. & t. (sich) auf einem Zapfen drehen.
swoon v.i. in Ohnmacht fallen; ~ s. Ohnmacht f.
swoop s. Stoss m.; plötzliche Razzia f.; ~ v.i. & t. herabstossen, herfallen über.
swop s. Tausch m.; ~ v.t. tauschen.
sword s. Schwert n.; Degen m.
sword-belt s. Degenkoppel f.
sword-knot s. Degenquaste f.
swordsman s. Fechter m.
sworn a. beeidigt, vereidigt; ~ to, beschworen.
sybarite s. Geniesser m.

sybaritic(al) a. üppig.
sycamore s. Sykomore f.
sycophant s. Ohrenbläser, Schmeichler m.
syllabic(al) a. silbisch, Silben...
syllabication s. Silbentrennung f.
syllable s. Silbe f.
syllabus s. Lehrplan m.; Prospekt m.
syllogism s. (Vernunft-) Schluss m.
sylph s. Luftgeist m.
symbol s. Sinnbild, Symbol n.; graphische Zeichen n.
symbolical a., ~ly adv. sinnbildlich.
symbolize v.t. sinnbildlich darstellen.
symmetrical a., ~ly adv. ebenmässig.
symmetry s. Ebenmass n.
sympathetic a. mitfühlend; (seelen)verwandt; ~ ink s. unsichtbare Tinte f.; ~ strike s. Sympathiestreik m.
sympathize v.i. mitempfinden; übereinstimmen.
sympathy s. Mitgefühl n.; Sympathie f.
symphony s. Symphonie, Sinfonie f.
symptom s. Anzeichen n.
symptomatic a. bezeichnend.
synagogue s. Synagoge f.
synchronize v.t. gleichgehend machen.
synchronous a. gleichzeitig.
syncopate v.t. (mus.) synkopieren.
syndic s. Syndikus m.
syndicate s. Syndikat n., Konzern m.; Konsortium n.; ~ credit s. Konsortialkredit m.
synod s. Kirchenversammlung f.
synonym s. sinnverwandte Wort n.
synonymous a., ~ly adv. sinnverwandt.
synonymy s. Sinnverwandtschaft f.
synopsis s. kurze Abriss m.
syntax s. Wortfügung f., Syntax f.
synthetic a., ~ally adv. synthetisch, künstlich(hergestellt); ~ material, Werkstoff m.; ~ petrol, künstliche Benzin n.; ~ rubber, künstliche Gummi m.
synthesis s. Synthese f.
syphilis s. Syphilis f.
syphon see siphon.
syringe s. Spritze f.; ~ v.t. einspritzen.
syrup, sirup s. Syrup m.
system s. System, Lehrgebäude n.
systematic(al) a., ~ally adv. systematisch, planmässig.

T

tab s. Lasche f.; Aufhänger m.; Schildchen, Etikett n.; (Am.) Kontrolle f.
tabby a. gewässert; gestreift; moiriert; ~ s. dunkelgrau gezeichnete gestreifte Katze f., Klatschbase, alte Jungfer f.
tabernacle s. Stiftshütte f.; Sakramentshäuschen n.
table s. Tafel f.; Kost f.; Tisch m.;

Tabelle *f.*; ∼ *of equipment*, (*mil.*) Ausrüstungsnachweisung *f.*; ∼ *of organization*, Stärkenachweisung *f.*; ∼ *v.t.* auf den Tisch legen.

tableau vivant *s.* lebende Bild *n.*

table-cloth *s.* Tischtuch *n.*

table-land *s.* Hochebene *f.*

table-linen *s.* Tafelzeug *n.*

tablespoon *s.* Esslöffel *m.*; **∼ful**, Esslöffelvoll *n.*

table-turning *s.* Tischrücken *n.*

tablet *s.* Täfelchen *n.*; Tablette *f.*; Schreibtafel *f.*

tabloid *s.* Tablette *f.*; *in ∼ form*, in kondensierter Form (*fig.*).

taboo *s.* Verruf *m.*; ∼ *a.* verboten; ∼ *v.t.* in Verruf erklären.

tabular *a.* getäfelt; tabellarisch.

tabulate *v.t.* in Tabellen bringen.

tachometer *s.* (*mot.*) Umdrehungsmesser *m.*

tacit *a.*, **∼ly** *adv.* stillschweigend.

taciturn *a.* schweigsam.

taciturnity *s.* Schweigsamkeit *f.*

tack *s.* Stift *m.*; Häkchen *n.*; Zwecke *f.*; (*nav.*) Halse *f.*; Geitau *n.*; (Lavier) Gang *m.*; Richtung *f.*; ∼ *v.t.* anheften, befestigen.

tackle, Takelwerk *n.*; Gerät *n.*; Flaschenzug *m.*; ∼ *v.t.* takeln; in Angriff nehmen.

tact *s.* Feingefühl *n.*; Takt *m.*

tactful *a.*, **∼ly** *adv.* taktvoll.

tactical *a.*, **∼ly** *adv.* taktisch.

tactician *s.* Taktiker *m.*

tactics *s.pl.* Kriegskunst, Taktik *f.*

tactless *a.*, **∼ly** *adv.* taktlos.

tadpole *s.* Kaulquappe *f.*

taffeta *s.* Taft *m.*

taffrail *s.* Heckbord *m.*

tag *s.* Stift *m.*; Senkel *m.*; Zettel *m.*; Anhängsel *n.*; ∼ *v.t.* anheften; anhängen.

tail *s.* Schwanz *m.*; Ende *n.*; Rockschoss *m.*; ∼ *suit*, *tails*, Frack *m.*

tailor *s.* Schneider *m.*; **∼-made**, vom Schneider angefertigt; ∼ *v.t.* & *i.* schneidern.

taint *v.t.* beflecken; verderben; anstecken; verführen; ∼ *s.* Flecken *m.*; Ansteckung *f.*; Verderbnis *f.*

take *v.t.st.* (mit-, an-, ein-, fest-, weg-) nehmen, empfangen; ergreifen; dafürhalten, meinen; bringen; sich gefallen lassen, einstecken; (Feuer) fangen; ∼ *v.i.* gefallen, anschlagen, ansprechen; *it ∼s* (*me*) *three hours*, ich brauche drei Stunden; *to ∼ after*, einem nachgeraten; *to ∼ down*, aufschreiben, zu Protokoll nehmen; *to ∼ in*, betrügen; *to ∼ in a paper*, eine Zeitung bestellen; *to ∼ off*, ausziehen, (Hut) abnehmen; abfliegen; **∼-off** *s.* Abflug *m.*; *to ∼ to*,

Gefallen finden an; *to ∼ to heart*, sich zu Herzen nehmen; *to ∼ for granted*, als erwiesen annehmen; *to ∼ ill*, *amiss*, übelnehmen; *to ∼ into account*, in Betracht ziehen; *to ∼ part in*, teilnehmen an; *to ∼ place*, stattfinden; *to ∼ prisoner*, gefangennehmen; *to ∼ a seat*, Platz nehmen; *to ∼ one's time*, sich Zeit nehmen; *to ∼ an examination*, *test*, eine Prüfung machen.

taker *s.* Abnehmer *m.*

taking *s.* Nehmen *n.*; Einnahme *f.*; ∼ *a.* einnehmend, packend.

talc, talcum *s.* Talk *m.*; **talcum powder** *s.* Körperpuder *m.*

tale *s.* Erzählung *f.*; Märchen *n.*

tale-bearer *s.* Zuträger *m.*

talent *s.* Talent *n.*, Begabung *f.*

talented *a.* talentvoll, begabt.

talk *v.i.* reden, sprechen; schwatzen; ∼ *s.* Gespräch *n.*; Gerücht *n.*

talkative *a.*, **∼ly** *adv.* gesprächig.

talking film, Sprechfilm, Tonfilm *m.*

tall *a.* lang, gross; (*fig.*) geflunkert.

tallboy *s.* Kommode (*f.*) mit Aufsatz.

tallow *s.* Talg *m.*; ∼ *v.t.* einschmieren.

tally *v.t.* einkerben; (*nav.*) anholen; ∼ *v.i.* passen, entsprechen, stimmen; ∼ *s.* Kerbholz *n.*; (Holz)schildchen *n.*; Seitenstück *n.*

tally-ho *i.* hallo!; ∼ *s.* Weidruf *m.*

talon *s.* Kralle, Klaue *f.*

tamarind *s.* Tamarinde *f.*

tambour *s.* Handtrommel *f.*; Stickrahmen; ∼ *v.t.* sticken.

tambourine *s.* Tamburin *n.*

tame *a.*, **∼ly** *adv.* zahm; folgsam; ∼ *v.t.* zähmen; bändigen.

tamper (with) *v.i.* heimlich unterhandeln; sich einmischen; an etwas herumpfuschen.

tam-o'-shanter *s.* Tellermütze *f.*

tan *s.* Lohe *f.*; ∼ *v.t.* lohen, gerben.

tandem *s.* spitzbespannte Wagen *m.*; Tandem *n.*

tang *s.* Seegras *n.*; Nachgeschmack *m.*; Heftzapfen *m.*

tangent *s.* Tangente *f.*

tangerine *s.* Mandarine *f.*

tangible *a.* greifbar, fühlbar.

tangle *v.t.* verwirren, verwickeln; ∼ *s.* Knoten *m.*, Verwicklung *f.*

tank *s.* Wasserbehälter *m.*; Tank *m.*; ∼ *car* *s.* (*rail.*) Kesselwagen, Tankwagen *m.*; ∼ *driver* *s.* (*mil.*) Panzerfahrer *m.*; ∼ *v.i.* tanken.

tankard *s.* Trinkgefäss *n.*; Krug *m.*

tanker *s.* Tankdampfer *m.*

tanner *s.* Lohgerber *m.*; Sixpencestück *n.*

tannery *s.* Gerberei *f.*

tannin *s.* Gerbstoff *m.*

tantalize *v.t.* quälen.

tantamount *a.* gleichwertig.

tantrum s. Wutanfall m., Bock m.
tap s. gelinde Schlag m.; Zapfen m.; Hahn m.; (mech.) Gewindebohrer m.; ~ wrench s. Halter für Gewindebohrer; on ~ angezapft, erhältlich; ~ v.t. klopfen an, abklopfen; anzapfen; (Telegramme) abfangen, Telephon abhören.
tape s. Zwirnband n.; (Sport) Zielband n.; (tel.) Papierstreifen m.; red ~, (fig.) grüne Tuch n., Bürokratie f.
tape-measure s. Bandmass n.
taper s. Wachskerze f.; Wachsstock m.; ~ v.i. spitz zulaufen; ~ v.t.; spitzen; ~ a. spitzig.
tapestry s. gewirkte Tapete f., Gobelin m.
tapeworm s. Bandwurm m.
tapioca s. Tapioka f.
tap-room s. Schenkstube f.
tapster s. Zapfer, Kellner m.
tar s. Teer m.; Matrose m.; ~ v.t. teeren.
tarantula s. Tarantel f.
tardy a., ~ily adv. langsam; träge; spät.
tare s. Wicke f.; (com.) Tara f.; ~ v.t. tarieren.
target s. (Schiess-)Scheibe; (mil., avi.) Ziel n.; ~ date, Termin m.; ~ practice, Scheibenschiessen n.
tariff s. Zolltarif m.; ~-wall s. Zollschranke f.
tarnish v.t. trübe machen; beschmutzen; ~ v.i. den Glanz verlieren.
tarpaulin s. Teertuch n.
tarry a. teerig; ~ v.i. warten; zögern.
tart s. Obsttörtchen n.; ~ a., ~ly adv. herb, sauer.
tartan s. bunt gewürfelte Zeug n.
tartar s. Weinstein m.; Zahnstein m.; Tartar, Tatar m.
tartaric a. Weinstein...; ~ acid s. Weinsäure f.
tartlet s. Törtchen n.
task s. Aufgabe f.; take to ~, zur Rede stellen; ~ v.t. in Anspruch nehmen.
taskmaster s. Zuchtmeister m.
tassel s. Troddel, Quaste f.
taste v.t. & i. kosten, schmecken; versuchen; (fig.) empfinden; ~ s. Probe f.; Geschmack m.; Neigung f.
tasteful a. schmackhaft, geschmackvoll.
tasteless a. geschmacklos.
tasty a. geschmackvoll.
tat see tit.
tatter s. Lumpen m.; ~ v.t. zerlumpen, zerfetzen.
tatterdemalion s. Lumpenkerl m.
tattle v.i. schwatzen; ~ s. Geschwätz n.
tattoo s. Zapfenstreich m.; Tätowierung f.; ~ v.t. tätowieren.
taunt v.t. schmähen, höhnen; ~ s. Hohn, Spott m.
taut a. straff, steif.
tauten v.t. & i. straff machen, sich straffen.

tavern s. Wirtshaus n.; Schenke f.
tawdry a. flitternd; bunt.
tawny a. lohfarbig, falb.
tax s. Steuer, Abgabe f.; ~ v.t. besteuern; belasten; beschuldigen; ~ arrears pl. Steuerschulden pl.; ~ free, steuerfrei; ~ payer s. Steuerzahler m.; ~ collector s. Steuereinnehmer m.; ~ remission, Steuerlass m.; ~ refund, Steuerrückvergütung f.
taxable a. steuerbar.
taxation s. Abschätzung f.; Besteuerung f.; exempt from ~, steuerfrei.
taxi, taxicab s. Autodroschke f.; ~ plane s. Mietflugzeug n.; ~ stand s. Autohaltestelle f.; ~ v.i. im Auto fahren; (avi.) rollen.
taximeter s. Taxameter m.
tea s. Tee m.; high ~, Tee mit Fleisch, etc.; ~ cloth s. Teetischdecke f.; ~ gown s. Hauskleid zum Tee; ~ leaves pl. Teesatz m.; ~ pot s. Teekanne f.; ~ set s. Teeservice n.; ~ shop s. Imbissraum m.; ~ things pl. Teesachen pl.
teach v.t. & i.ir. lehren, unterrichten.
teachable a., ~bly adv. gelehrig.
teacher s. Lehrer m.; Lehrerin f.
teak-wood s. Tiekholz n.
team s. Gespann n.; Mannschaft f.; ~ work, Zusammenspiel n.
teamster s. Frachtfuhrmann m.
ea-party s. Teegesellschaft f.
tear s. Träne f.; ~ v.t.st. reissen, zerren, zerreissen; ~ v.i. wüten; rasen; ~ s. Riss m.; Abnutzung f.
tearing a. zerreissbar; tobend; heftig.
tease v.t. plagen, necken, quälen.
teasel s. Kardendistel f.; Karde f.; ~ v.t. Tuch rauhen.
teaser s. Plagegeist m.; harte Nuss f.
teat s. Brustwarze f.; Saughütchen n.
tea-things s.pl. Teegeschirr n.
tea-tree s. Teestrauch m.
tea-urn s. Teemaschine f.
technical a., ~ly adv. kunstmässig, technisch; Fach...
technical consultant s. Fachberater m.
technicality s. Kunstmässigkeit f.; Fachausdruck m.
technique s. Technik f.; mechanische Fertigkeit f.
technology s. Gewerbekunde f.
teddy-bear s. Teddybär m.
tedious a., ~ly adv. langweilig, lästig.
tedium s. Langweiligkeit f., Überdruss m.
teem v.i. fruchtbar sein; wimmeln (von); strotzen.
teen-ager s. Halbwüchsige m., f.
teens s.pl. Lebensjahre (n.pl.), die auf teen endigen (von 13–19).
teeth s.pl. Zähne m.pl.
teethe v.i. zahnen.
teetotaller s. Abstinenzler m.

telegram s. Drahtnachricht, Depesche f., Telegramm n.
telegraph s. Telegraph m.; ~ v.t. telegraphieren.
telegraphic a. telegraphisch.
telegraphist s. Telegraphist m.
telegraphy s. Telegraphie f.
telephone s. Telephon n., Fernsprecher m.; ~ v.t. & i. telephonieren; ~ box s. Telephonzelle f.; ~-exchange s. Fernsprechamt n.
teleprinter s. Fernschreiber m.
telescope s. Fernrohr n.; ~ v.t. & i. (sich) ineinanderschieben.
telescopic a. teleskopisch.
teletype s. Fernschreiber m., Fernschreiben n.; ~ v.t. fernschreiben.
television s. Fernsehen n.; ~ set s. Fernsehapparat m.
tell v.t. & i.ir. sagen; erzählen, melden, anzeigen; Wirkung tun; zählen; to ~ off, anschnauzen, abfahren lassen.
teller s. Stimmenzähler m.
telling a. durchschlagend, wirkungsvoll.
tell-tale s. Ohrenbläser m.; ~ a. klatschaft; verräterisch.
temerity s. Tollkühnheit f.
temper v.t. vermischen, versetzen; mässigen; (Metall) härten; (Stahl) tempern; ~ s. gehörige Mischung f.; Gemütsstimmung f.; Mässigung f.; üble Laune f.; Härte f.; to keep one's ~, die Ruhe behalten; to lose one's ~, heftig werden.
temperament s. Temperament n.
temperamental a., ~ly adv. temperamentvoll; Temperaments...
temperance s. Mässigkeit f.; Enthaltsamkeit f.
temperate a., ~ly adv. mässig, gemässigt; ruhig, gelassen.
temperature s. Temperatur f.; to have a ~, (leicht) Fieber haben; to take the ~, Temperatur messen, nehmen.
tempered a. gelaunt.
tempest s. Sturm m.; Ungewitter n.
tempestuous a., ~ly adv. stürmisch.
Templar s. Tempelherr m.
temple s. Tempel m.; Schläfe f.
temporal a., ~ly adv. zeitlich; weltlich.
temporary a. zeitweilig, vorläufig; ~ duty, (mil.) zeitweilige Dienst m.
temporize v.i. zögern; die passende Zeit abwarten; hinhalten; Zeit zu gewinnen suchen.
tempt v.t. versuchen, verleiten.
temptation s. Versuchung f.
tempter s. Versucher m.
temptress s. Versucherin f.
ten a. zehn; ~ s. Zehn f.
tenable a. haltbar.
tenacious a. festhaltend, zähe.
tenacity s. Zähigkeit, Beharrlichkeit f.
tenancy s. Pacht m.

tenant s. Pächter, Mieter m.
tenantry s. Pächter m.pl.
tench s. Schleie f.
tend v.t. warten, pflegen; bedienen (Maschine); ~ v.i. abzielen, (zu-) neigen, gerichtet sein; dienen.
tendency s. Richtung, Neigung f.; Zweck m., Tendenz f.
tendentious a. tendentiös.
tender a., ~ly adv. weich, zart; zärtlich, besorgt; teuer; ~ s. Angebot n.; Wärter m.; (rail.) Tender m.; Zahlungsmittel n.; ~ v.t. anbieten; to ~ one's resignation, seine Entlassung beantragen.
tenderness s. Zartheit f.; Zärtlichkeit f.; Sorgfalt f.
tendon s. Sehne, Flechse f.
tendril s. Ranke f., Trieb m.
tenement s. Haus n.; Mietswohnung f.
tenet s. Satz, Grundsatz m.; Lehre f.
tenfold a. zehnfach.
tennis s. Tennisspiel n.; ~ court, Tennisplatz m.
tenon s. Fuge f.; Zapfen m.
tenor s. Inhalt m.; Tenor m.
tense s. (gram.) Zeitform f., Tempus n.; ~ a. gespannt; straff.
tensile a. dehnbar; ~ strength, Zugfestigkeit f.
tension s. Spannung f.
tent s. Zelt n.; Wieke f.
tentacle s. Fühler m.
tentative a. versuchend; ~ s. Versuch m.
tenter-hook s. Spannhaken m.; to be on ~s, wie auf Kohlen sitzen, in Ängsten sein.
tenuity s. Dünne f.; Zartheit f.; Armseligkeit f.
tenuous a. dünn, fein.
tenure s. Besitzrecht n.; Innehaben n.
tepid a., lau, lauwarm.
tergiversation s. Ausflucht, Ausrede f.; Wankelmut m.
term s. Grenze f.; Ausdruck m.; Begriff m.; Termin m., Frist f.; Trimester n.; ~s pl. Preis m.; Bedingungen pl.; prison ~, Strafzeit f.; inclusive ~s pl. Preis, in dem alles einbegriffen ist; in ~s of numbers, in Zahlen ausgedrückt; to come to ~s with, sich einigen mit; to be on good ~s with, mit einem gut stehen; ~ v.t. nennen, benennen.
termagant a. zanksüchtig; tobend; ~ s. Zankteufel m.
terminal a. letzt..., End...; ~ s. Endstück n.; (elek.) Pol, m.
terminate v.t. begrenzen; endigen; ~ v.i. enden.
termination s. Ende n.; Endung f.
terminology s. Terminologie f.
terminus s. Endstation f.
termite s. Termite f.

terrace *s.* Terrasse *f.*; Häuserreihe *f.*
terrain *s.* Gelände *n.*
terrestrial *a.*, ~ly *adv.* irdisch.
terrible *a.*, ~bly *adv.* fürchterlich.
terrier *s.* Terrier *m.*
terrific *a.* fürchterlich.
terrify *v.t.* erschrecken.
territorial *a.* Landes...; ~ *s.* Milizsoldat *m.*; ~ *waters pl.* Hoheitsgewässer *pl.*; *limit of ~ waters*, Hoheitsgrenze *f.*
territory *s.* Gebiet *n.*; Landschaft *f.*
terror *s.* Schrecken *m.*
terrorist *s.* Terrorist *m.*
terse *a.*, ~ly *adv.* glatt; bündig; knapp.
tertian *s.* dreitägige Wechselfieber *n.*
tertiary *a.* tertiär.
tessellated *a.* Mosaik...; gewürfelt.
test *s.* Prüfung, Probe *f.*; (*fig.*) Prüfstein *m.*; ~ *case*, Schulfall, Probefall *m.*; ~ *flight*, Probeflug *m.*; ~ *tube*, Reagensglas *n.*; *to put to the ~*, auf die Probe stellen; ~ *v.t.* prüfen; (*chem.*) untersuchen; *to ~ the heart*, das Herz abklopfen; *to ~ the sight*, das Sehvermögen prüfen.
testament *s.* Testament *n.*, letzte Wille *m.*
testamentary *a.* testamentarisch.
testator *s.* Erblasser *m.*
testatrix *s.* Erblasserin *f.*
testicle *s.* Hode *f.*
testify (to) *v.i.* etwas bezeugen.
testimonial *a.* schriftliche Zeugnis *n.*
testimony *s.* Zeugnis *n.*; *to bear ~*, Zeugnis ablegen.
test paper *s.* Reagenzpapier *n.*; Extemporale *n.*
testy *a.*, ~ily *adv.* mürrisch, reizbar.
tetanus *s.* Starrkrampf *m.*
tetchy *a.* empfindlich.
tether *s.* Spannseil *n.*; (*fig.*) Fähigkeit *f.*, Kraft *f.*; *to be at the end of one's ~*, am Ende seiner Kraft sein; ~ *v.t.* anbinden.
text *s.* Text *m.*; Bibelstelle *f.*
text-book *s.* Leitfaden *m.*; Lehrbuch *n.*
textile *a.* gewebt; Textil...; ~s *pl.* Webwaren *f.pl.*
textual *a.* textgemäss, wörtlich.
texture *s.* Gewebe *n.*, Gefüge *n.*
than *c.* als.
thank *v.t.* danken; ~s *pl.* Dank *m.*
thankful *a.*, ~ly *adv.* dankbar.
thankless *a.* undankbar.
thanksgiving *s.* Danksagung *f.*
that *pn.* jener, jene, jenes; welcher, welche, welches; der, die, das; ~ *c.* dass, damit, weil.
thatch *s.* Dachstroh *n.*; Strohdach *n.*; ~ *v.t.* mit Stroh decken.
thaw *v.t. & i.* tauen; ~ *s.* Tauwetter *n.*
the *art.* der, die, das; den; so, desto; ~ *less*, umsoweniger.
theatre *s.* Theater *s.*; Schauplatz *m.*; ~ *of*

operations, (*mil.*) Operationsgebiet; ~ *of war*, Kriegsschauplatz *m.*
theatrical *a.*, ~ly *adv.* bühnenhaft, theatralisch; ~s *s.pl.* dramatische Vorstellung(en) *f.(pl.).*
thee *pn.* dir, dich.
theft *s.* Diebstahl *m.*
their *pn.* ihr, ihre.
theirs *pn.* ihr, ihre; der, die, das ihrige.
them *pn.pl.* sie, ihnen.
theme *s.* Gegenstand *m.*; Thema *n.*
themselves *pn.pl.* sie selbst, sich (selbst).
then *adv.* dann, alsdann, damals; *now and ~*, dann und wann; ~ *c.* dann, daher, folglich.
thence *adv.* von da, von dort, daher.
thenceforth *adv.* seitdem; von da ab.
theocracy *s.pl.* Gottes-, Priesterherrschaft
theocratic *a.* theokratisch.
theologian *s.* Theologe *m.*
theological *a.*, ~ly *adv.* theologisch.
theology *s.* Theologie *f.*
theorem *s.* Lehrsatz, Grundsatz *m.*
theoretical *a.*, ~ly *adv.* theoretisch.
theorize *v.i.* Theorien aufstellen.
theosophy *s.* Theosophie *f.*
theorist *s.* Theoretiker *m.*
theory *s.* Theorie *f.*; Lehre *f.*
therapeutics *s.pl.* Therapie, Heilkunde *f.*
therapy *s.* Heilverfahren *n.*
there *adv.* da, dort, dahin; hin; ~ *is*, ~ *are*, es gibt, es sind; ~ *about*, daherum; ~ *after*, danach; ~*by*, damit, dadurch; ~*fore*, daher, folglich, also; ~*from*, davon, daraus; ~*in*, darin; ~*of*, davon; ~*on*, darauf, daran; ~*to*, dazu; ~*under*, darunter; ~*upon*, darauf, hierauf; deswegen; ~*with*, damit; ~*withal*, ausserdem, überdies; ~ *you are*, da hast du es!
thermal *a.* Wärme..., Thermal...
thermometer *s.* Thermometer *n.* or *m.*
thermos-flask *s.* Thermosflasche *f.*
these *pn.pl.* diese.
thesis *s.* These *f.*; Dissertation *f.*
they *pn.pl.* sie, diejenigen; man; es.
thick *a. & adv.*, ~ly *adv.* dick, dicht; trübe; häufig; unklar; vertraut; ~ *s.* dicke Ende *n.*; Gewühl *n.*
thicken *v.t.* verdicken, verdichten; vermehren; ~ *v.i.* dick, trübe werden; sich verstärken.
thicket *s.* Dickicht *n.*
thickness *s.* Dicke, Dichtheit *f.*; Lage, Schicht *f.*
thick-set *a.* untersetzt, gedrungen.
thief *s.* Dieb *m.*; Räuber (am Licht) *m.*
thieve *v.i.* stehlen.
thievery *s.* Diebe*rei f.*
thievish *a.*, ~ly *adv.* diebisch.
thigh *s.* Schenkel *m.*; Lende *f.*
thill *s.* Gabeldeichsel *f.*
thimble *s.* Fingerhut *m.*
thin *a.*, ~ly *adv.* dünn; mager, schwach;

spärlich; ~ *paper*, Dünndruckpapier *n*.; ~ *v.t.* verdünnen; lichten.
thine *pn.* dein; der, die, das deinige.
thing *s.* Ding *n.*, Sache *f.*; Geschöpf *n.*; ~s *pl.* Kleider *n.pl.*; Sachen *f.pl.*
think *v.t. & i.ir.* denken, nachdenken; meinen, wofür halten; *to* ~ *over*, überlegen.
thinker *s.* Denker *m.*
thinking *s.* Denken, Dafürhalten *n.*
third degree *s.* (*Am.*) Mittel zur Erpressung von Geständnissen.
thirdly *adv.* drittens.
third party *s.* (*law*) dritte Person *f.*
thirst *s.* Durst *m.*; Begierde *f.*; ~ *v.i.* dursten.
thirsty *a.*, ~ily *adv.* durstig.
thirteen *a.* dreizehn.
thirty *a.* dreissig.
this *pn.* dieser, diese, dies(es); ~ *way!*, hierher!
thistle *s.* Distel *f.*
thither *adv.* dorthin, dahin.
tho' *c.*=though.
thong *s.* Riemen *m.*; Peitschenschnur *f.*
thorax *s.* Brustkasten *m.*
thorn *s.* Dorn, Stachel *m.*
thorny *a.* dornig, stachelig
thorough *a.* gänzlich; gründlich; ~ly *adv.* durch und durch.
thoroughbred *a.* vollblut (Pferd).
thoroughfare *s.* Hauptstrasse *f.*; Durchgang *m.*, Durchfahrt *f.*
thorough-going *a.* gründlich.
thoroughness *s.* Gründlichkeit *f.*
those *pn.pl.* diejenigen, jene.
thou *pn.* du.
though *c.* obgleich; freilich, doch, dennoch; wenn auch; *as* ~, als wenn.
thought *s.* Gedanke *m.*; Meinung *f.*
thoughtful *a.*, ~ly *adv.* gedankenvoll; achtsam, rücksichtsvoll.
thoughtless *a.*, ~ly *adv.* gedankenlos.
thousand *a.* tausend; ~ *s.* Tausend *n.*
thousandfold *a. & adv.* tausendfach.
thraldom *s.* Knechtschaft *f.*
thrall *s.* Sklave *m.*
thrash *v.t.* dreschen; prügeln; ~ *out*, eingehend erörtern.
thrashing *s.* Tracht (*f.*) Prügel.
thread *s.* Faden, Zwirn *m.*; Schraubengang *m.*, Gewinde *n.*; (Reifen) Profil *n.*; ~ *v.t.* einfädeln.
threadbare *a.* fadenscheinig.
threat *s.* Drohung *f.*
threaten *v.t.* drohen; ~*ing letter*, Drohbrief *m.*
three *a.* drei.
threefold *a.* dreifach.
threepence *s.* Dreipencestück *n.*
threepenny bit *s.* Dreipencestück *n.*
three-phase *a.* (*current*) Drehstrom *m.*
threescore *a.* sechzig, Schock *n.*

thresh *see* thrash.
threshold *s.* Türschwelle *f.*
thrice *adv.* dreimal.
thrift *s.* Sparsamkeit *f.*
thriftless *a.* verschwenderisch.
thrifty *a.* sparsam, wirtschaftlich.
thrill *v.t.* durchzucken; ~ *v.i.* beben; schauern; ~ *s.* Schauer *m.*
thriller *s.* Sensationsdrama *n.*; Schmöker *m.*
thrilling *a.* durchdringend; packend.
thrive *v.i.st.* wachsen; gedeihen.
thriving *a.*, ~ly *adv.* gedeihlich, blühend.
throat *s.* Schlund *m.*; Kehle *f.*, Hals *m.*; *to clear one's* ~, sich räuspern.
throb *v.i.* pochen, klopfen; ~ *s.* Klopfen, Schlagen *n.*
throes *s.pl.* Geburtschmerzen*m.pl.*
throne *s.* Thron *m.*
throng *s.* Gedränge *n.*, Schar *f.*; ~ *v.t.* (*v.refl. sich*) drängen.
throstle *s.* Drossel *f.*
throttle *s.* Kehle, Luftröhre *f.*; ~ *v.t.* erdrosseln; (*mech.*) abdrosseln.
throttle-valve *s.* Drosselventil *n.*
through *pr. & adv.* durch, mittels; ~ *carriage*, Kurswagen *m.* (*rail.*); ~ *train* s. durchgehende Zug *m.*; ~ *ticket* *s.* direkte Billet *n.*; *wet* ~, durch und durch nass.
throughout *pr. & adv.* ganz durch; durchaus, überall.
throw *v.t. & i.st.* (hin-, um-) werfen; *to* ~ *off*, von sich werfen, entsagen; *to* ~ *open*, weit öffnen; *to* ~ *out*, verwerfen; *to* ~ *over*, aufgeben; *to* ~ *up*, in die Höhe werfen; aufgeben; ~ *s.* Schlag *m.*; Wurf *m.*
thrush *s.* Drossel *f.*; Mundschwamm *m.*
thrust *v.t. & i.ir.* stossen; schleudern; drücken, pressen; drängen; *to* ~ *upon*, aufdrängen; ~ *s.* Stoss, Stich, Angriff *m.*
thud *s.* dröhnende, dumpfe Schlag *m.*
thug *s.* Raubmörder *m.*
thumb *s.* Daumen *m.*; ~ *v.t.* befingern; ungeschickt handhaben; *under a person's* ~, unter jemandes Gewalt.
thumbscrew *s.* Daumenschraube *f.*
thumbtack *s.* (*Am.*) Reissnagel *m.*
thump *s.* Schlag, Stoss *m.*; ~ *v.t.* schlagen, stossen, puffen.
thumping *a.* sehr gross, kolossal.
thunder *s.* Donner *m.*; ~ *v.t. & i.* donnern.
thunder-bolt *s.* Donnerkeil, Blitz *m.*
thunder-clap *s.* Donnerschlag *m.*
thunderstorm *s.* Gewitter *n.*
thunder-struck *a.* wie vom Donner gerührt.
Thursday *s.* Donnerstag *m.*
thus *adv.* so, also, in solcher Weise.
thwack = whack.
thwart *a.* schräg; ~ *v.a.* durchkreuzen.

thy *pn.* dein, deine.

thyme *s.* Thymian *m.*

thyroid gland *s.* Schilddrüse *f.*

thyself *pn.* du selbst, selbst; dich, dir.

tiara *s.* Tiara *f.*

tibia *s.* Schienbein *n.*

tick *s.* Borg *m.*; Schaflaus *f.*; Ticken *n.*; (Inlett-)Überzug *m.*; on ~, auf Pump; ~ *v.i.* ticken; ~ *off,* anhaken, markieren.

ticket *s.* Zettel *m.*; Billett *n.*, Fahrkarte *f.*; Pfandschein *m.*; (*Am.*) Parteiprogramm *n.*; *to take a* ~, ein Billett lösen; ~ *v.t.* einen Zettel anheften.

ticket-office *s.* Fahrkartenausgabe *f.*

ticking *s.* Drell, Drillich *m.*; Matratzenbezug *m.*

tickle *v.t.* kitzeln.

ticklish *a.* kitzlig; verfänglich.

tidal *a.* Gezeiten..., Flut...

tide *s.* Gezeiten *f.pl.,* Ebbe und Flut *f.*; Flut (*fig.*) *f.*; *the* ~ *turns,* das Blatt wendet sich; *the turning of the* ~, Umschwung *m.*; *to* ~ *over v.t.* hinwegkommen über, überbrücken.

tidiness *s.* Ordnung *f.* Nettigkeit *f.*

tidings *s.pl.* Nachrichten *f.pl.*

tidy *a.,* ~ily *adv.* ordentlich, niedlich, nett; ~ *v.t.* sauber machen, ordnen.

tie *v.t.* binden, knüpfen; verpflichten; (*mus.*) (ver)binden; ~ *up,* zubinden; ~ *down* (*mil.*) (Kräfte) binden; ~ *s.* Knoten *m.*; Kravatte, Halsbinde *f.*; Schleife *f.*; (*mus.*) Bindung *f.*; (*Sport*) Gleichstand *m.*

tiepin *s.* Schlipsnadel, Kravattennadel *f.*

tier *s.* Reihe, Linie *f.*; Rang *m.*

tiff *s.* Zank *m.*; Schmollen *n.*

tiger *s.* Tiger *m.*

tight *a.,* ~ly *adv.* fest, dicht; knapp, eng, straff; genau; betrunken; ~ *corner,* Klemme *f.*; ~ *fitting,* eng anliegend; ~ *rope,* gespannte Seil *n.*

tighten *v.t.* festziehen, schnüren; enger machen.

tights *s.pl.* Trikothosen *pl.*; Trikot *n.*

tigress *s.* Tigerin *f.*

tilde *s.* Tilde *f.*, Wiederholungszeichen *n.*

tile *s.* Ziegel *m.*; Kachel *f.*; ~ *v.t.* mit Ziegeln decken.

tiler *s.* Ziegeldecker *m.*

till *pr.* & *c.* bis; ~ *v.t.* pflügen, ackern; ~ *s.* Ladenkasse *f.*

tillage *s.* Ackern *n.*; Ackerbau *m.*

tiller *s.* Pflüger *m.*; Ruderspinne *f.*

tilt *s.* Zelt *n.*, Plane *f.*; Turnier *n.*; Neigung, Kippe *f.*; ~ *v.t.* stossen, überschlagen; überdecken; ~ *v.i.* turnieren; kippen, umschlagen, schwanken.

tiltyard *s.* Turnierhof *m.*

timber *s.* Bauholz *n.*; ~ *v.t.* zimmern; ~ed house, Fachwerkhaus *n.*

timber-yard *s.* Holzlager *n.*

timbre *s.* Klangfarbe *f.*

time *s.* Zeit *f.*; Zeitmass *n.*; Mal, *n.*; Tempo *n.*, Takt *m.*; *at a* ~, zugleich; *at the same* ~, zugleich, gleichzeitig; *in* ~, rechtzeitig; mit der Zeit; *in no* ~, im Handumdrehen; *behind* ~, verspätet; *what is the* ~?, wieviel Uhr ist es?; *to tell the* ~, sagen, wieviel Uhr es ist; *I am having a good* ~, es geht mir gut; ich amüsiere mich; *I am having a bad* ~, es geht mir schlecht; *high* ~, hohe, höchste Zeit; *to beat* ~, den Takt schlagen; *full-* ~ *a.* ganzzeitlich; *half-* ~ *a.* halbzeitlich; ~ *v.t.* abmessen; Zeit festsetzen für.

time-bomb *s.* Zeitbombe *f.*

time-fuse *s.* Zeitzünder *m.*

time-keeper *s.* Uhr *f.*; Kontrolleur *m.*

time-lens *s.* Zeitlupe *f.*

time-limit *s.* Frist *f.*

time-signal *s.* Zeitzeichen *n.*

timely *a.* & *adv.* (recht)zeitig.

time-piece *s.* Uhr *f.*

time-server *s.* Achselträger *m.*

time-table *s.* Fahrplan *m.*

time-worn *a.* abgenutzt.

timid *a.* furchtsam, schüchtern.

timidity *s.* Furchtsamkeit *f.*

timorous *a.,* ~ly *adv.* furchtsam.

tin *s.* Zinn *n.*; Weissblech *n.*; (Blech-) Büchse (zum Einmachen) *f.*; ~ *v.t.* verzinnen; in Büchsen einmachen.

tincture *s.* Anstrich *m.*; Tinktur *f.*

tinder *s.* Zunder *m.*

tinfoil *s.* Stanniol, Blattzinn *n.*

tinge *v.t.* färben; ~ *s.* Anstrich *m.*

tingle *v.i.* klingen; prickeln.

tin-hat *s.* (*fam.*) Stahlhelm *m.*

tinker *s.* Kesselflicker *m.*; ~ *v.t.* flicken; pfuschen.

tinkle *v.t.* klingen.

tinner *s.* Klempner *m.*

tin-opener *s.* Büchsenöffner *m.*

tinplate *s.* Weissblech *n.*

tinsel *s.* Flittergold *n.*

tint *s.* Farbe *f.*; (Farb-) Ton *m.*, Tönung *f.*; ~ *v.t.* färben; abtönen.

tiny *a.* winzig.

tip *s.* Spitze *f.*; leichte Berührung *f.*; Wink *m.*; Trinkgeld *n.*; ~ *v.t.* bespitzen; antupfen; kippen; Trinkgeld geben; *to* ~ *up,* einen Wink geben.

tipcart *s.* Kippkarren *m.*

tippet *s.* Halskragen *m.*; Pelzkragen *m.*

tipple *s.* berauschende Getränk *n.*; ~ *v.i.* zechen.

tipstaff *s.* Gerichtsdiener *m.*

tipsy *a.* berauscht, benebelt.

tiptoe *s.* Zehenspitze *f.*; ~ *v.i.* auf den Zehenspitzen gehen.

tiptop *a.* ausgezeichnet, hochfein.

tirade *s.* Wortschwall *m.*; Scheltrede *f.*

tire *s.* Kopfputz *m.*; Radreifen *m.*; (Luft-)

reifen *m.*; ~ *v.t. & i.* ermüden; müde werden.

tired *a.* müde; überdrüssig.

tireless *a.* unermüdlich.

tiresome *a.*, **~ly** *adv.* ermüdend, langweilig.

tissue *s.* Gewebe *n.*

tissue-paper *s.* Seidenpapier *n.*

tit *s.* Zitze *f.*; kleine Ding *n.*; Meise *f.*; ~ *for tat,* wie du mir, so ich dir.

titanic *a.* titanisch.

titbit *s.* Leckerbissen *m.*

tithe *s.* Zehnte *m.*; ~ *v.t.* zehnten.

title *s.* Titel *m.*; Name *m.*; Anspruch *m.*, Recht *n.*; ~ *v.t.* benennen.

titled *a.* adelig.

title-deed *s.* Eigentumsurkunde *f.*

title-page *s.* Titelblatt *n.*

titmouse *s.* Meise *f.*

titter *v.i.* kichern; ~ *s.* Kichern *n.*

tittle *s.* Tüttelchen *n.*

tittle-tattle *s.* Geschwätz *n.*

titular *a.* Titular...

to *pr.* zu, nach, an, auf, mit, gegen, für, um, in Ansehung, bis, vor; ~ *adv.* zu; ~ *and fro,* hin und her.

toad *s.* Kröte *f.*

toad-eater *s.* kriechende Schmeichler *m.*

toad-stool *s.* Giftpilz *m.*

toady *s.* niedrige Schmeichler *m.*

toast *v.t.* rösten; wärmen; trinken auf; ~ *s.* geröstete Brotschnitte *f.*; Trinkspruch *m.*

toaster *s.* Rösteisen *n.*

toasting-fork *s.* Röstgabel *f.*

tobacco *s.* Tabak *m.*; **~-pouch** Tabaksbeutel *m.*

tobacconist *s.* Tabakhändler *m.*

toboggan *s.* Rodelschlitten *m.*

tocsin *s.* Sturmglocke *f.*

to-day *adv.* heute.

toddle *v.i.* watscheln; herumschlendern.

toddler *s.* kleine Kind *n.*

to-do *s.* Aufheben *n.*, Lärm *m.*

toe *s.* Zehe *f.*; Vorderhuf *m.*

toffee *s.* Braunzuckerwerk *n.*

together *adv.* zusammen; ~ *with,* samt.

toil *s.* schwere Arbeit, Mühseligkeit *f.*; ~ *v.i.* sich abarbeiten.

toilet *s.* Putztisch *m.*; Toilette *f.*; ~ *paper s.* Klosettpapier *n.*; ~ *requisites pl.* Toilettenartikel *pl.*; ~ *set,* Toilettengarnitur *f.*

toilsome *a.* mühselig, mühsam.

token *s.* Zeichen *n.*; Geschenk *n.*

tolerable *a.*, **~bly** *adv.* leidlich.

tolerance *s.* Duldung *f.*; (*mech.*) zulässige Abweichung *f.*

tolerant *a.* duldsam.

tolerate *v.t.* ertragen, dulden.

toleration *s.* Duldung, Nachsicht *f.*

toll *s.* Zoll *m.*; Läuten *n.*; ~ *v.t.* läuten; Zoll erheben, verzollen.

toll-bar *s.* Schlagbaum *m.*

toll-call *s.* Vorortsferngespräch *n.*

tomato *s.* Tomate *f.*

tomb *s.* Grab, Grabmal *n.*; ~ *stone s.* Grabstein *m.*

tomboy *s.* Wildfang (Mädchen) *m.*

tom-cat *s.* Kater *m.*

tome *s.* Band *m.*, Buch *n.*

tomfool *s.* Narr *m.*

tomfoolery *s.* Narretei *f.*

tommy-gun *s.* Maschinenpistole *f.*

to-morrow *adv.* morgen.

tomtit *s.* Meise *f.*

ton *s.* Tonne (Gewicht: 1016 kg.; Schiffsmass: 40 Kubikfuss) *f.*

tone *s.* Ton, Klang, Laut *m.*; ~ *v.t.* abtönen.

tongs *pl.* Zange *f.*

tonic *a.* tonisch; spannend; stärkend; ~ *s.* Stärkungsmittel *n.*

to-night *adv.* heute abend, heute nacht.

tonnage *s.* Tonnengehalt *m.*, Raumgehalt (Schiff) *m.*

tonsil *s.* Halsdrüse *f.*, Mandel *f.*

tonsilitis *s.* Mandelentzündung *f.*

tonsure *s.* Tonsur *f.*

too *adv.* zu, alizu; gleichfalls, auch.

tool *s.* Werkzeug, Gerät *n.*; (*mech.*) Stahl *m.*; **~-holder,** Stahlhalter *m.*

toot *v.t. & i.* blasen, tuten.

tooth *s.* Zahn *m.*; ~ *v.t.* mit Zähnen versehen.

tooth-ache *s.* Zahnweh *n.*

toothbrush *s.* Zahnbürste *f.*

tooth-filling *s.* Zahnfüllung *f.*

toothless *a.* zahnlos.

toothpaste *s.* Zahnpaste *f.*

tooth-pick *s.* Zahnstocher *m.*

top *s.* Gipfel, Wipfel *m.*; Spitze *f.*; Kreisel *m.*; Haupt *n.*; Obere *s.*; höchste Rang *m.*; (*nav.*) Mars *m.* or *f.*; ~ *a.* oberst, Haupt...; *from ~ to toe,* vom Scheitel bis zur Sohle; ~ *coat s.* (*Am.*) Überzieher *m.*; ~ *floor,* oberste Stockwerk *n.*; ~ *righthand corner,* obere rechte Ecke; ~ *secret a.* ganz geheim, *s.* (*mil.*) geheime Kommandosache; ~ *speed,* Höchstgeschwindigkeit *f.*; ~ *v.i.* sich erheben, hervorstechen; ~ *v.t.* übertreffen.

topaz *s.* Topas *m.*

top-boots *s.pl.* Stulpstiefel *m.pl.*

tope *v.i.* zechen.

toper *s.* Säufer *m.*

top-gallant *s.* Bramsegel *n.*

top-hat *s.* Zylinderhut *m.*

top-heavy *a.* oberlastig.

topic *s.* Gegenstand *m.*, Thema *n.*

topical *a.*, **~ly** *adv.* aktuell.

topmast *s.* Topmast *m.*

topmost *a.* oberst, höchst.

topography *s.* Ortsbeschreibung *f.*

topping *a.* hervorragend.

topple—transport

476

topple v.i. vorwärts fallen, hinstürzen.
torrential a. strömend; reissend.
topsy-turvy adv. das unterste zu oberst.
torch s. Fackel f.; ~-light procession, Fackelzug m.
topsail s. Marssegel n.
torment v.t. peinigen, martern; ~ s. Qual, Marter f.
tormentor s. Peiniger m.
torpedo s. Zitterrochen m.; Torpedo (ge-schoss n.) m.; ~ boat s. Torpedoboot n.; ~(boat) destroyer s. Torpedo(boot)-zerstörer m.; ~ tube s. Lanzierrohr n.
torpid a. starr; betäubt; stumpf.
torpor s. Erstarrung f.; Stumpfsinn m.
torrent s. Giessbach m.; (fig.) Strom m.
torrid a. brennend heiss.
torsion s. Drehung, Windung f.
tort s. (law) schadenersatzpflichtiges Delikt n.
tortoise s. Schildkröte f.
tortoise-shell s. Schildpatt n.
tortuous a. gewunden.
torture s. Folter f.; Marter f.; ~ v.t. foltern, martern.
Tory s. Tory, englische Konservative m.
toss v.t. schleudern; losen; ~ v.i. sich herumwerfen; ~ s. Wurf m.; Aufwerfen n. (einer Münze), Losen n.
tot s. kleine Kind n.; Schlückchen, Gläschen n.
total a., ~ly adv. ganz, gänzlich; ~ s. Gesamtsumme f., Gesamtbetrag m.; ~ v.i. sich belaufen auf; ~ loss, Total-ausfall m.; ~ war, totale Krieg m.
totalisator s. Totalisator m.
totality s. Ganze n., Vollständigkeit f.
tote s.=totalisator.
totter v.i. wanken, wackeln.
touch v.t. (be)fühlen; betreffen; anstossen, rühren, berühren; to ~ up, auffrischen, restaurieren; ~ v.i. sich berühren; sich beziehen; ~ wood! unberufen!; ~ s. Berührung f.; Gefühl n.; Anflug, An-strich m.; (mus.) Anschlag m.; to get in ~ with, sich in Verbindung setzen mit.
touch-and-go, ur sicher, gewagt.
touching a. rührend, treffend; ~ pr. be-treffend, in betreff.
touch-line s. Marklinie f.
touch-stone s. Prüfstein m.
touchy a. empfindlich, reizbar.
tough a., ~ly adv. zähe; hart.
toughen v.t. zähe machen; ~ v.i. zähe werden.
tour s. (Rund-)Reise f.; Ausflug m.; ~ v.t. & i. (be)reisen.
tourist s. Vergnügungsreisende m.; Tour-ist m.; ~ agent, Reiseagent m.; ~ traffic, Fremdenverkehr m.; ~'s ticket, Rund-reisebillet n.
tournament s. Turnier n.
tout v.i. Kunden locken; ~s. Schlepper m.

tow s. Werg n.; Schlepptau n.; ~ v.t. schleppen.
toward=towards.
towards pr. gegen, zu, bis an, entgegen; auf...zu.
towel s. Handtuch n.; ~-horse Handtuch-ständer m.; face-~ Gesichtshandtuch n.; roller ~, Rollhandtuch n.; to ~ one-self v.t. sich mit dem Handtuch abreiben.
towelling s. Handtuchdrell m.
tower s. Turm m.; Zwinger m.; Hort m.; ~ v.i. hoch ragen, sich erheben.
towering a. ragend; heftig.
towing-boat s. Schleppschiff n.
towing-path s. Leinpfad m.
town s. Stadt f.
town-clerk s. Stadtsyndikus m.
town-hall s. Rathaus n.
town-planning s. Städtebau m.
township s. Stadtgemeinde f.
townsman s. Städter, Bürger m.
toy s. Tand m.; Spielzeug n.; ~ v.i. tändeln.
trace s. Spur, Fusstapfe f.; Strang m., Zugseil n.; ~ v.t. nachspüren; zeichnen, entwerfen; abstecken; durchpausen.
traceable a. auffindbar.
tracer-bullet s. Leuchtspurgeschoss n.
tracery s. Masswerk n.
trachea s. Luftröhre f.
tracing s. Durchpausen n.; Pauszeich-nung n.; Aufriss m.; ~-paper s. Paus-papier n.
track s. Spur f.; Fährte f.; Geleise f.; Pfad f.; (Panzer)Kette f.; ~ed vehicles pl. Raupenfahrzeuge pl.; to be on the wrong ~, auf der falschen Fährte sein; ~ v.t. der Spur folgen; to ~ down, auf-spüren.
trackless a. spurlos, pfadlos.
tract s. Strecke f.; Traktat m.
tractable a., ~bly adv. lenksam, folgsam.
traction s. Ziehen n.; Zug m.; ~ engine, Strassenlokomotive f.
tractor s. Traktor m., Zugmaschine f.
trade s. Handel m.; Gewerbe, Geschäft n.; ~ v.i. Handel treiben; (Am.) aus-tauschen; foreign ~, Aussenhandel m.; ~ name, Firmenname m.; ~ price, En-grospreis m.; ~ school, Gewerbeschule f.
trade-mark s. Schutzmarke f.
trader s. Handelsmann, Kaufmann m.
tradesman s. Handwerker m.; ~'s entrance Lieferanteneingang m.
trade(s)-union s. Gewerkschaft f.
trade-unionist s. Gewerkschaftler m.
trade-wind s. Passatwind m.
trading estate s. Industriesiedlung f.
tradition s. Überlieferung f.; Brauch m.
traditional a. überliefert; sagenhaft; her-kömmlich.

traduce *v.t.* verleumden; verdrehen.
traffic *s.* Handel *m.*; Verkehr *m.*; *goods* ~, Güterverkehr *m.*; *passenger* ~, Personenverkehr *m.*; ~ *code*, Verkehrsregeln *pl.*; ~ *indicator*, Autowinker *m.*; ~ *jam*, Verkehrsstockung *f.*; ~ *light*, Verkehrsampel *f.*; ~ *regulation*, Verkehrsregelung *f.*; ~ *sign*, Verkehrszeichen *n.*; ~ *v.i.* Handel treiben.
tragedy *s.* Trauerspiel *n.*
tragic *a.*, ~ally *adv.* tragisch.
tragi-comedy *s.* Tragikomödie *f.*
trail *s.* Spur, Fährte *f.*; Pfad *m.*; ~ *v.t.* nachspüren; schleppen; ~ *v.i.* sich in die Länge ziehen.
trailer *s.* (*mot.*) Anhängewagen *m.*
train *s.* Schweif *m.*; Schleppe *f.*; Reihe *f.*; Gefolge *n.*; (*rail.*) Zug *m.*; ~ *v.t.* ziehen, schleppen; abrichten; ausbilden; trainieren; (Geschütz) richten; ~ *v.i.* sich trainieren.
trainee *s.* in der Ausbildung Stehender, Lehrling *m.*
trainer *s.* Abrichter *m.*; Zureiter *m.*; Sportlehrer *m.*
training *s.* Ausbildung *s.*; *to be under* ~, ausgebildet werden; ~-centre *s.* Ausbildungsstelle *f.*; ~-college *s.* Lehrerseminar *n.*; ~-ship *s.* Schulschiff *n.*
train-oil *s.* Fischtran *m.*
trait *s.* Zug, Strich *m.*
traitor *s.* Verräter *m.*
traitorous *a.*, ~ly *adv.* verräterisch.
traitress *s.* Verräterin *f.*
trajectory *s.* Flugbahn *f.*
tram *s.* ~-car, Strassenbahnwagen *m.*
trammel *s.* Netz, Garn *n.*; Spannriemen *m.*; ~s *pl.* (*fig.*) Bande *n.pl.*; ~ *v.t.* verhindern; fesseln.
tramp *s.* Landstreicher *m.*; Frachtschiff *n.*; ~ *v.i.* & *t.* treten; umherstreifen; trampeln.
trample *v.i.* & *t.* trampeln; *to* ~ *upon*, mit Füssen treten (*fig.*).
tramway, tramroad *s.* Strassenbahn *f.*
trance *s.* Trancezustand *m.*
tranquil *a.* ruhig, gelassen.
tranquillity *s.* Ruhe *f.*
tranquillize *v.t.* beruhigen.
transact *v.t.* abmachen; verrichten.
transaction *s.* Geschäft *n.*; Verhandlung *f.*
transalpine *a.* jenseits der Alpen.
transatlantic *a.* transatlantisch.
transcend *v.t.* übersteigen; übertreffen.
transcendent *a.* vorzüglich.
transcribe *v.t.* abschreiben; übertragen.
transcript, transcription, *s.* Abschrift *f.*; Umschrift *f.*; (*law*) Protokoll *n.*
transept *s.* (Kirche) Kreuzflügel *m.*; ~s *pl.* Querschiff *n.*
transfer *v.t.* übertragen; versetzen, verlegen; (Geld) überweisen; ~ *s.* Über-

tragung *f.*; Überweisung *f.*; Verlegung, Versetzung *f.*; *disciplinary* ~, Strafversetzung *f.*; ~-paper *s.* Umdruckpapier *n.*
transferable *a.* übertragbar.
transfiguration *s.* Verklärung *f.*
transfigure *v.t.* verwandeln; verklären.
transfix *v.t.* durchbohren.
transform *v.t.* umgestalten, verwandeln.
transformation *s.* Verwandlung *f.*
transformer *s.* (*elek.*) Umformer, Transformator *m.*; ~-station, Transformatorenhaus *n.*
transfuse *v.t.* umgiessen; (Blut) übertragen.
transgress *v.t.* überschreiten, verletzen.
transgression *s.* Überschreitung *f.*; Vergehen *n.*
transgressor *s.* Übertreter *m.*
transient *a.*, ~ly *adv.* vergänglich; vorübergehend; (*Am.*) ~ *hotel*, Passantenhotel *n.*; ~ *billets pl.* Passantenquartier *n.*
transit *s.* Durchgang *m.*; (*mil.*) Durchmarsch *m.*; *in* ~, unterwegs, auf dem Transport; ~ *duty*, Durchgangszoll *m.*; ~ *trade*, Durchgangshandel *m.*; ~ *traffic*, Durchgangsverkehr *m.*
transition *s.* Übergang *m.*
transitional *a.* Übergangs...
transitive *a.*, ~ly *adv.* (*gram.*) transitiv.
transitory *a.*, ~ily *adv.* vorübergehend, vergänglich; flüchtig.
translate *v.t.* übersetzen; versetzen.
translation *s.* Übersetzung *f.*
translator *s.* Übersetzer *m.*
transload *v.t.* umladen.
translucent *a.* durchscheinend.
transmarine *a.* überseeisch.
transmigration *s.* Ortswechsel *m.*; ~ *of souls*, Seelenwanderung *f.*
transmissible *a.* übertragbar; vererblich.
transmission *s.* Übertragung *f.*; Übersendung *f.*; (*phys.*) Fortpflanzung; (*mech.*) Transmission.
transmit *v.t.* übersenden, übertragen; (*phys.*) leiten; vererben.
transmitter *s.* (*tel.*, *radio*) Sender *m.*
transmutation *s.* Verwandlung *f.*
transmute *v.t.* umwandeln.
transoceanic *a.* überseeisch.
transom *s.* Querbalken *m.*
transparency *s.* Durchsichtigkeit *f.*
transparent *a.*, ~ly *adv.* durchsichtig.
transpire *v.t.* ausdünsten; ~ *v.i.* schwitzen; verlauten.
transplant *v.t.* verpflanzen.
transplantation *s.* Verpflanzung *f.*
transport *v.t.* befördern, transportieren; hinreissen, entzücken; ~ *s.* Versendung, Beförderung *f.*, Transportschiff *n.*; Transport *m.*; Entzückung *f.*; ~ *charges pl.* Speditionskosten *pl* ; ~

plane, Transportflugzeug *n.*; *Minister of* ~, Verkehrsminister *m.*
transportation *s.* Fortschaffung *f.*; Deportierung *f.*; (*Am.*) Transport *m.*, Transportmittel *n.*
transpose *v.t.* umstellen.
transposition *s.* Umstellung *f.*
tranship *v.t.* umladen.
transhipment *s.* Umladung *f.*, Umschlag *m.*; ~**-harbour**, Umschlagshafen *m.*
transubstantiation *s.* Wesensverwandlung *f.*
transverse *a.*, ~**ly** *adv.* schräg, quer.
trap *s.* Falle *f.*; Klappe *f.*; ~ *v.t.* ertappen; ~**ped** *p.* eingeklemmt.
trap-door *s.* Falltür *f.*
trapeze *s.* Trapez *n.*
trapper *s.* Pelztierfänger *m.*
trappings *s.pl.* Schmuck *m.*
trash *s.* Plunder, Abfall *m.*; (*fig.*) Blech *n.*; Schund *m.*
travail *s.* Last *f.*; Kindeswehen *pl.*
travel *v.i.* reisen; sich bewegen; ~ *v.t.* bereisen; ~ *s.* Reise *f.*; *away on* ~, verreist; ~ *agency*, Reiseagentur *f.*; ~ *goods* (od.) ~ *order* (*mil.*) Reiseartikel *pl.*; ~ *order* (*mil.*) Fahrtbefehl *m.*, Fahrtausweis *m.*; ~*rug* *s.* Reisedecke *f.*
traveller *s.* Reisende, Geschäftsreisende *m.*; ~*s' cheque*, Reisescheck *m.*
travelling bag, Reisetasche *f.*
traverse *s.* Querholz *n.*; (*mech.*) Querstück *n.*, Querträger *m.*, Traverse *f.*; (*fig.*) Querstrich *m.*; Quergang *m.*; ~ *v.t.* durchkreuzen; durchwandern; durchforschen; (durch)queren; *a. & adv.* quer.
travesty *s.* Travestie *f.*; ~ *v.t.* travestieren.
trawl *v.i.* mit einem Schleppnetze fischen.
trawler *s.* Schleppnetzfischerboot *n.*
tray *s.* Tee-, Kaffeebrett *n.*; Koffereinsatz *m.*; **ash-**~ Aschenbecher *m.*
treacherous *a.*, ~**ly** *adv.* verräterisch.
treachery *s.* Verräterei *f.*; Heimtücke *f.*
treacle *s.* Sirup *m.*
tread *v.i. & i.st.* (be)tre(t)en; ~ *s.* Schritt, Tritt *m.*; Lauffläche, Gleitfläche eines Reifens *f.*
treadle *s.* Tretbrett *n.*
tread-mill *s.* Tretmühle *f.*
treason *s.* Verrat *m.*; *high* ~, *capital* ~, Hochverrat *m.*
treasonable *a.*, ~**bly** *adv.* verräterisch.
treasure *s.* Schatz *m.*; ~ *v.t.* aufhäufen; wertschätzen.
treasurer *s.* Schatzmeister *m.*
treasury *s.* Schatzkammer *f.*; Schatzamt *n.*; ~ *bill* *s.* Schatzwechsel *m.*; ~ *bond*, (*Am.*) ~ *certificate*, Schatzanweisung *f.*
treat *v.t. & i.* handeln, behandeln; unterhandeln; freihalten; ~ *s.* Bewirtung *f.*, Schmaus *m.*; Genuss *m.*

treatise *s.* Abhandlung *f.*
treatment *s.* Behandlung *f.*
treaty *s.* Vertrag *m.*
treble *a.* dreifach; ~ *s.* Sopranstimme *f.*; Diskant *m.*; ~ *v.t.* verdreifachen.
tree *s.* Baum *m.*
trefoil *s.* Klee *m.*
trellis *s.* Gitter *n.*; Spalier *n.*
tremble *v.i.* zittern.
tremendous *a.*, ~**ly** *adv.* schrecklich, furchtbar; ungeheuer gross.
tremor *s.* Zittern, Beben *n.*
tremulous *a.* zitternd; flackernd.
trench *s.* (Schützen-) Graben *m.*; ~**-coat**, Wettermantel *m.*
trenchant *a.* schneidend, scharf.
trencher *s.* hölzerne Teller *m.*; ~**-cap** (viereckige) Studentenmütze *f.*
trend *v.i.* gerichtet sein; ~ *s.* Richtung *f.*; Drang *m.*
trepan *s.* Schädelbohrer *m.*; ~ *v.t.* trepanieren.
trepidation *s.* Zittern *n.*, Angst *f.*
trespass *v.i.* übertreten, sich vergehen; unbefugt betreten; ~ *s.* Übertretung *f.*; Eingriff *m.*; unbefugte Betreten *n.*; *action of* ~, (*law*) Besitzstörungsklage *f.*
tress *s.* Haarlocke *f.*; Flechte *f.*
trestle *s.* Bockgestell *n.*
trial *s.* Versuch *m.*; Probe *f.*; Prüfung *f.*; Verhör *n.*, gerichtliche Untersuchung *f.*; ~ *by jury*, Schwurgerichtsverhandlung *f.*; ~ *in absentia*, Verhandlung in Abwesenheit des Angeklagten; *to be on* ~, *to stand* ~ *for*, unter Anklage stehen; *to bring to* ~, vor Gericht stellen; ~ *run*, Probefahrt (Auto) *f.*
triangle *s.* Dreieck *n.*
triangular *a.*, ~**ly** *adv.* dreieckig.
tribal *a.* Stammes...
tribe *s.* Stamm *m.*; Sippe *f.*
tribulation *s.* Trübsal *f.*
tribunal *s.* Richterstuhl, Gerichtshof *m.*
tributary *a.* zinspflichtig; ~ *s.* Nebenfluss *m.*
tribute *s.* Beisteuer *f.*; Tribut *m.*
trice *s.* Augenblick *m.*, Nu *m.* or *n.*
trick *s.* Kniff *m.*; Streich, Betrug *m.*; Eigentümlichkeit *f.*; Kartenstich *m.*; *to play a person a* ~, einem einen Streich spielen; ~ *v.t.* betrügen, anführen.
trickery *s.* Betrügerei, List *f.*
trickle *v.i.* tröpfeln; ~ *s.* Getröpfel *n.*
trickster *s.* Betrüger *m.*
tricky *a.* verschmitzt, heikel.
tricolour *s.* Trikolore *f.*
tricycle *s.* Dreirad *n.*
trident *s.* Dreizack *m.*
tried *a.* erprobt.
triennial *a.*, ~**ly** *adv.* dreijährlich.
trier *s.* Untersucher, Prüfer *m.*
trifle *s.* Kleinigkeit, Lappalie *f.*; Biskuit

(n.) mit Kompott; ~ *v.i.* tändeln, spielen, scherzen.

trifling *a.*, ~ly *adv.* nichtig, geringfügig.

trig *v.t.* hemmen.

trigger *s.* Drücker (am Gewehr) *m.*

trigonometry *s.* Trigonometrie *f.*

trilateral *a.* dreiseitig.

trill *s.* Triller *m.*; ~ *v.t.* trillern.

trilogy *s.* Trilogie *f.*

trim *a.*, ~ly *adv.* in Ordnung; geputzt; niedlich; ~ *s.* Putz, Besatz *m.*; Ausrüstung *f.*; ~ *v.t.* putzen; ausrüsten; stutzen; einfassen; *(nav.)* trimmen; ~ *v.i.* schwanken, unschlüssig sein.

trimmer *s.* *(fig.)* Mitläufer *m.*

trimming *s.* Besatz *m.*; Verzierung *f.*

Trinity *s.* Dreieinigkeit *f.*

trinket *s.* Geschmeide *n.*; Anhängsel *n.*

trip *v.i.* trippeln; einen Ausflug machen; straucheln, fehlen; ~ *v.t. to ~ up*, ein Bein stellen, erwischen; ~ *s.* Fehltritt *m.*; Ausflug *m.*; Reise *f.* (bes. *Am.*).

tripartite *a.* dreiteilig, Dreimächte...; ~ *commission*, Dreierkommission; ~ *pact*, Dreierpakt *m.*

tripe *s.* Kaldaunen (Nahrung) *pl.*; Eingeweide *pl.*; Kitsch, Quatsch *m.*

triphase *a.* dreiphasig; ~ *current*, *(elek.)* Drehstrom *m.*

triple *a.* dreifach; ~ *v.t.* verdreifachen.

triplet *s.* Dreirein *m.*; Drilling *m.*

triplicate *a.* in dreifacher Ausführung; ~ *s.* Triplikat *n.*; *in* ~, in dreifacher Ausführung.

tripod *s.* Dreifuss *m.*; dreifüssige Ständer *m.*

tripos *s.* Schlussprüfung *(f.)* (in Cambridge).

tripping *a.*, ~ly *adv.* hüpfend; munter; strauchelnd.

triptych *s.* Triptychon *n.*

trisyllable *s.* dreisilbige Wort *n.*

trite *a.*, ~ly *adv.* abgedroschen.

triturate *v.t.* zerreiben.

triumph *s.* Triumph, Sieg *m.*; ~ *v.i.* triumphieren; siegen.

triumphant *a.*, ~ly *adv.* triumphierend.

trivial *a.*, ~ly *adv.* alltäglich, platt.

triviality *s.* Plattheit *f.*

trochee *s.* Trochäus *m.*

trolley *s.* Förderkarren *m.*; Handwagen *m.*; Kontaktrolle *(f.)* bei elektrischen Bahnen; ~**-bus**, elektrische Omnibus *m.*; ~ *s.* *(Am.)* Strassenbahn *f.*

trollop *s.* Schlampe, Dirne *f.*

trombone *s.* Posaune *f.*

troop *s.* Haufen *m.*, Schar *f.*; Trupp *m.*; ~ *s pl.* Truppen *f.pl.*; ~ *ship* *s.* Truppentransportschiff *n.*; ~ *training ground*, Truppenübungsplatz *m.*; ~ *v.i.* sich scharen, in Scharen ziehen.

trope *s.* bildliche Ausdruck, Tropus *m.*

trophy *s.* Siegeszeichen *n.*

tropic *s.* Wendekreis *m.*; ~*s*, Tropen *f.pl.*

tropical *a.*, ~ly *adv.* tropisch; bildlich.

trot *v.i.* traben; ~ *s.* Trab, Trott *m.*

troth *s.* Treuegelöbnis *n.*

trotter *s.* Traber *m.*; Fuss *(m.)* eines Tieres.

trouble *v.t.* trüben, stören; beunruhigen; bemühen; quälen; ~ *v.i.* sich kümmern, sich bemühen; ~ *s.* Störung, Unruhe, Sorge *f.*; Kummer, Verdruss *m.*

troublesome *a.*, ~ly *adv.* beschwerlich.

trough *s.* Trog *m.*; Wellental *n.*, Tief *n.*

trounce *v.t.* heruntermachen.

troupe *s.* (Theater) Truppe *f.*

trousering *s.* Hosenstoff *m.*

trousers *pl.* Hosen *pl.*; **trouser-hanger** *s.* Hosenaufhänger *m.*

trousseau *s.* Brautausstattung *f.*

trout *s.* Forelle *f.*

trowel *s.* Kelle *f.*

troy-weight *s.* Gold- und Silber- gewicht *n.*

truant *a.*, ~ly *adv.* müssig, träge; ~ *s.* Schulschwänzer *m.*; Müssiggänger *m.*

truce *s.* Waffenstillstand *m.*

truck *s.* Tausch, Tauschhandel *m.*; Handkarren *m.*; *(rail.)* Güterwagen *m.*; Lore *f.*; *(Am.)* Lastwagen *m.*; ~ *v.t.* Tauschhandel treiben; ~ *system*, Lohnzahlung in Waren statt Geld.

truckle *v.i.* sich unterwerfen, kriechen.

truculent *a.* wild, roh, grimmig.

trudge *v.i.* sich fortschleppen, forttrotten.

true *a.* wahr; echt; treu, aufrichtig, redlich; richtig.

truffle *s.* Trüffel *f.*

truism *s.* Gemeinplatz *m.*

truly *adv.* wirklich, wahrhaftig; aufrichtig; *yours* ~, Ihr ergebener.

trump *s.* Trumpf *m.*; ~ *v.t.* trumpfen; *to* ~ *up*, erdichten.

trumpery *s.* Plunder, Flitter *m.*

trumpet *s.* Trompete *f.*; ~ *v.t.* ausposaunen.

truncate *v.t.* verstümmeln, abkürzen.

truncheon *s.* Knüttel *m.*

trundle *v.t. & i.* rollen, (sich) wälzen; ~ *s.* Rolle, Walze *f.*

trunk *s.* Stamm *m.*; Stumpf *m.*; Rumpf *m.*; Rüssel *m.*; Koffer *m.*; ~ *call*, *(tel.)* Ferngespräch *n.*; ~ *exchange*, Fernamt *n.*

trunk-line *s.* *(rail.)* Hauptlinie *f.*; *(tel.)* Fernleitung *f.*

trunnion *s.* Zapfen *m.*

truss *v.t.* packen; aufbinden; stützen; ~ *s.* Band, Bruchband *n.*; Bündel *n.*; Hängewerk *n.*

trust *s.* Vertrauen *n.*; Kredit *m.*; Obhut, Treuhand *f.*; anvertraute Gut *n.*; (Unternehmer-)Ring, Trust *m.*; *in* ~, zu treuen Händen; *on* ~, auf Treu und

Glauben; *to take on* ~, auf Treu und Glauben hinnehmen; *breach of* ~, Vertrauensbruch *m.*; *position of* ~, Vertrauensstellung *f.*; ~-company, Treuhandgesellschaft *f.*; ~ *v.i. & t.* (ver)trauen, sich verlassen; anvertrauen.

trustee *s.* Treuhänder *m.*; Kurator *m.*; ~ securities *pl.* mündelsichere Werte *m.pl.*

trustful *a.* vertrauensvoll.

trustworthy *a.* vertrauenswürdig.

trusty *a.* treu, zuverlässig.

truth *s.* Wahrheit *f.*; Wirklichkeit *f.*; Wahrhaftigkeit, Redlichkeit, Treue *f.*

truthful *a.* wahrhaftig.

try *v.t.* versuchen, sich bemühen; quälen; untersuchen, probieren, prüfen, verhören; (*law*) Prozess verhandeln; *to* ~ *on*, anprobieren.

trying *a.* schwierig; misslich.

tub *s.* Fass *n.*; Zuber *m.*; Kübel *m.*; Badewanne *f.*

tube *s.* Rohr *n.*, Röhre *f.*; Untergrundbahn *f.*; Schlauch (Fahrrad) *m.*; (*Am.*) Radioröhre *f.*

tuber *s.* Knolle *f.*

tubercle *s.* Knötchen *n.*; Tuberkel *f.*

tuberculosis *s.* Tuberkulose *f.*

tuberculous, tuberkulös.

tubing *s.* Röhrenmaterial *n.*

tubular *a.* röhrenförmig.

tuck *s.* Falte *f.* Umschlag (am Kleid) *m.*; Näschereien *pl.*; ~ *v.t.* aufschürzen; einschlagen, einwickeln.

Tuesday *s.* Dienstag *m.*

tufa, tuff *s.* Tuffstein *m.*

tuft *s.* Büschel *m.* or *n.*; Quaste *f.*; ~ *v.t.* bequasten.

tug *v.t. & i.* ziehen, zerren; ~ *s.* Ziehen, Zerren *n.*; Schlepper *m.*; *seagoing* ~, Hochseeschlepper *m.*; ~ *of war*, Tauziehen *n.*

tuition *s.* Unterricht *m.*; Erziehung *f.*

tulip *s.* Tulpe *f.*

tulle *s.* Tüll *m.*

tumble *v.i.* umfallen, stürzen; sich wälzen; ~ *v.t.* werfen, umwenden; zerknittern; ~ *s.* Fall, Sturz *m.*

tumble-down *a.* baufällig.

tumbler *s.* (fusslose) Trinkglas *n.*

tumid *a.* geschwollen.

tummy *s.* (*fam.*) Magen *m.*

tumour *s.* Geschwulst, Beule *f.*

tumult *s.* Getümmel *n.*; Aufruhr *m.*

tumultuous *a.*, ~ly *adv.* lärmend, aufrührerisch.

tun *s.* Tonne *f.*; Fass *n.*

tunable *a.*, ~bly *adv.* wohlklingendharmonisch.

tune *s.* Ton *m.*; Melodie *f.*; Tonstück *n.*; Stimmung *f.*; *out of* ~, verstimmt; ~ *v.t.* stimmen; (*radio*) einstellen; *tuning dial* *s.* (*radio*) Einstellscheibe *f.*

tuneful *a.* wohlklingend.

tuner *s.* (Klavier-), Stimmer *m.*

tungsten *s.* Wolfram *n.*

tunic *s.* Tunika *f.*; Waffenrock *m.*

tuning-fork *s.* Stimmgabel *f.*

tunnel *s.* Tunnel *m.*

tunny *s.* Thunfisch *m.*

turban *s.* Turban *m.*

turbid *a.*, ~ly *adv.* trübe, dick.

turbine *s.* Kreiselrad *n.*, Turbine *f.*

turbot *s.* Steinbutt *m.*

turbulence *s.* Ungestüm *n.*; Aufruhr *m.*; Verwirrung *f.*

turbulent *a.*, ~ly *adv.* aufrührerisch; stürmisch.

tureen *s.* Suppenschüssel *f.*

turf *s.* Rasen *m.*; Rennbahn *f.*; Pferderennen *n.*

turgid *a.* geschwollen, gedunsen; schwülstig.

turkey *s.* Truthahn *m.*

turkish bath *s.* türkische Bad, Schwitzbad *n.*

turmoil *s.* Unruhe *f.*; Aufruhr *m.*

turn *v.t.* drehen, (um)wenden; drechseln; umlegen; ~ *v.i.* sich (um)drehen; sich verwandeln; werden; umschlagen, verderben; *to* ~ *down*, zurückweisen, ablehnen; (Gas) kleindrehen; *to* ~ *in*, abgeben; *to* ~ *off*, ablenken; abdrehen, ausdrehen; *to* ~ *on*, andrehen; *to* ~ *out*, ausfallen, sich erweisen; hinausreiben; antreten (Waren) herstellen; *to* ~ *over*, übertragen; (um)wenden, durchblättern; (Waren) überstellen; umsetzen (Waren); *please* ~ *over* (PTO), bitte wenden!; *to* ~ *round*, sich herumdrehen; *to* ~ *up*, umwenden; umschlagen; aufschlagen; auftauchen, erscheinen; ~ *s.* Umdrehung, Schwenkung *f.*; Änderung *f.*; Wechsel *m.*; Streich *m.*; Neigung *f.*; Gestalt, Beschaffenheit *f.*; *a good* ~, eine Gefälligkeit *f.*; *it is your* ~, Sie sind an der Reihe; *by* ~s, wechselweise, abwechselnd.

turncoat *s.* Achselträger, Überläufer *m.*

turncock *s.* Wasserröhrenaufseher *m.*

turn-down, ~ collar *s.* (Klapp-) Umlegekragen *m.*

turner *s.* Drechsler *m.*; Eisendreher *m.*

turning *s.* Drechseln, Drehen *n.*; Wendung *f.*; Krümmung *f.*; Querstrasse *f.*

turning-point *s.* Wendepunkt *m.*

turnip *s.* (weisse) Rübe *f.*

turnkey *s.* Schliesser, Gefangenwärter *m.*

turn-out *s.* Gesamtertrag *m.*; Antreten (*n.*) zur Arbeit.

turnover *s.* Umsatz *m.*; ~ *tax*, Umsatzsteuer *f.*

turnpike *s.* Schlagbaum *m.*

turnspit *s.* Bratenwender *m.*

turnstile *s.* Drehkreuz *n.*

turntable *s.* (*rail.*, *radio*) Drehscheibe *f.*

turn-up *s.* Hosenaufschlag *m.*

turpentine *s.* Terpentin *m.*
turpitude *s.* Schändlichkeit *f.*
turquoise *s.* Türkis *m.*
turret *s.* Türmchen *n.*; Panzerturm *m.*
turtle *s.* Turteltaube *f.*; Seeschildkröte *f.*
tusk *s.* Fangzahn *m.*
tussle *s.* Streit *m.*, Rauferei *f.*
tut *i,* ach was!
tutelage *s.* Vormundschaft *f.*; Unmündigkeit *f.*
tutelar(y) *a.* schützend; vormundschaftlich.
tutor *s.* Hauslehrer *m.*; Lehrer *m.*; Vormund *m.*; ~ *v.t.* unterrichten.
tutorial Lehr..., Lehrer...
twaddle *v.i.* schwatzen; ~ *s.* Quatsch *m.*
twain *s.* zwei.
twang *v.i.* schwirren; näseln; ~ *s.* näselnde Aussprache *f.*
tweak *v.t.* zwicken, kneifen.
tweed *s.* Tweed *m.* geköperte Wollzeug *n.*; Halbtuch *n.*
tweezers *s.pl.* Haarzange *f.*
Twelfth-day *s.* Dreikönigsfest *n.*
twelve *a.* zwölf.
twenty *a.* swanzig.
twice *adv.* zweimal, doppelt.
twig *s.* Zweig *m.*; Rute *f.*
twilight *s.* Zwielicht *n.*
twill *s.* geköperte Zeug *n.*; ~ *v.t.* weben, köpern.
twin *s.* Zwilling *m.*; ~-engine(d), *a.* (*avi.*) zweimotorig.
twine *v.t.* drehen, zwirnen; ~ *v.i.* sich verschlingen; ~ *s.* Bindfaden *m.*; Zwirn *m.*; Windung *f.*
twinge *v.t.* zwicken, kneipen; ~ *s.* Stich *m.*
twinkle *v.i.* blinken, blinzeln; ~ *s.* Blick, Wink *m.*; Augenblick *m.*
twinkling *s.* Blinzeln *n.*; Wink, Augenblick *m.*
twirl *v.t.* & *i.* quirlen; wirbeln; ~ *s.* Wirbel *m.*; Schnörkel *m.*
twist *v.t.* (*v.i.* sich) drehen, verdrehen, flechten, spinnen; verzerren; ~ *s.* Geflecht *n.*; Faden *m.*; Maschiŋengarn *n.*; Kautabak *m.*; Windung *f.*
twitch *v.t.* zupfen, zwicken; zucken; ~ *s.* Zupfen, Kneipen *n.*; Krampf *m.*
twitter *v.i.* zwitschern; kichern, zittern; ~ *s.* Gezwitscher *n.*
two *a.* zwei; ~-speed (*mech.*) *a.* mit zwei Gängen; ~-piece suit, zweiteilige Anzug *m.*; *in* ~, entzwei.
twofold *a.* zweifach.
twopence *s.pl.* zwei englische Pfennig *m.pl.*
tympanum *s.* Trommelfell *n.*; Giebelfeld *n.*
type *s.* Urbild *n.*; Vorbild *n.*; Letter *f.*, Schrift *f.*; Typ, Typus *m.*; ~ *v.t.* auf der Schreibmaschine schreiben, tippen.

type-founder *s.* Schriftgiesser *m.*
typescript *s.* Maschinenschrift *f.*; ~ *a.* maschinengeschrieben.
typesetter *s.* (*typ.*) Setzer *m.*
type-write *v.t.* & *i.* mit der Schreibmaschine schreiben, tippen.
typewriter *s.* Schreibmaschine *f.*; ~-ribbon, Schreibmaschinenfarbband *n.*
typhoid *s.* Typhus *m.*
typhoon *s.* Teifun *m.*
typhus *s.* Fleckfieber *n.*
typical *a.*, ~ly *adv.* vorbildlich, typisch.
typist *s.* Maschinenschreiber(in) *m.* (*f.*).
typify *v.t.* charakteristisch darstellen.
typographer *s.* Buchdrucker *m.*
typographic(al) *a.*, ~ly *adv.* typographisch.
tyrannical *a.*, ~ly *adv.* tyrannisch.
tyrannize *v.t.* tyrannisieren.
tyranny *s.* Tyrannei *f.*
tyrant *s.* Tyrann *m.*
tyro *s.* Anfänger *m.*

U

ubiquitous *a.* allgegenwärtig.
ubiquity *s.* Allgegenwart *f.*
udder *s.* Euter *n.*
ugh *i.* scheusslich!, pfui!
ugly *a.* hässlich, ekelhaft.
uhlan *s.* Ulan *m.*
ulcer *s.* Geschwür *n*,.
ulcerate *v.i.* schwären.
ulcerous *a.* geschwürig.
ulster *s.* lange, lose Mantel *m.*
ulterior *a.* jenseitig; weiter, später.
ultimate *a.*, ~ly *adv.* letzt, zuletzt, endlich.
ultimatum *s.* Ultimatum *n.*
ultimo *adv.* vorigen (Monats).
ultra *a.* übermässig; ~ *s.* Extreme *m.*
ultramarine *a.* überseeisch; ~ *s.* Ultramarin *n.*
ultramontane *a.* ultramontan.
ultra shortwave *s.* (*radio*) Ultrakurzwelle *f.*
ultraviolet *a.* ultraviolett.
umbel *s.* Dolde *f.*
umber *s.* Umbra (Farbe) *f.*
umbilical cord *s.* Nabelschnur *f.*
umbrage *s.* Anstoss, Ärger *m.*
umbrageous *a.* schattig, dunkel.
umbrella *s.* Regenschirm, Schirm *m.*; ~ stand, Regenschirmständer *m.*
umlaut *s.* Umlaut *m.*
umpire *s.* Schiedsrichter *m.*
unabashed *a.* unbeschämt; frech.
unabated *a.* unvermindert.
unable *a.* unfähig, unvermögend.
unaccented *a.* unbetont.
unacceptable *a.*, ~bly *adv.* unannehmbar.
unaccommodating *a.* unnachgiebig.

unaccompanied *a.* unbegleitet.
unaccountable *a.*, ~bly *adv.* unverantwortlich; unerklärlich.
unaccustomed *a.* ungewohnt; ungewöhnlich.
unacquainted *a.* unbekannt.
unadjusted *a.* schwebend, unerledigt.
unadorned *a.* schmucklos.
unadulterated *a.* unverfälscht, echt.
unadvisable *a.* nicht ratsam, unklug.
unadvised *a.*, ~ly *adv.* unbedachtsam.
unaffected *a.*, ~ly *adv.* ungerührt; unbeeinflusst; ungekünstelt.
unaided *a.* ohne Hilfe, allein, ununterstützt; (Auge) bloss.
unalloyed *a.* unvermischt.
unalterable *a.*, ~bly *adv.* unveränderlich.
unaltered *a.* unverändert.
unambiguous *a.*, ~ly *adv.* eindeutig.
unanimity *s.* Einmütigkeit *f.*
unanimous *a.*, ~ly *adv.* einmütig.
unanswerable *a.*, ~bly *adv.* unwiderleglich.
unanswered *a.* unbeantwortet.
unappalled *a.* unerschrocken.
unappreciated *a.* unbeachtet.
unapproachable *a.* unerreicht; unzugänglich.
unapt *a.*, ~ly *adv.* untauglich, unpassend.
unarmed *a.* unbewaffnet, wehrlos.
unashamed *a.* schamlos, nicht beschämt.
unasked *a.* ungefordert, ungebeten.
unassailable *a.* unangreifbar.
unassisted *a.* ohne Hilfe, ununterstützt.
unassuming *a.* anspruchslos.
unatoned *a.* ungesühmt.
unattached *a.* unverbunden.
unattainable *a.* unerreichbar.
unattained *a.* unerreicht.
unattempted *a.* unversucht.
unattended *a.* unbeaufsichtigt; unbegleitet.
unattested *a.* unbezeugt, nicht beglaubigt.
unattractive *a.* nicht anziehend, reizlos.
unauthentic *a.* unverbürgt.
unauthorized *a.* unberechtigt.
unavailing *a.* vergeblich, nutzlos.
unavenged *a.* ungerächt.
unavoidable *a.*, ~bly *adv.* unvermeidlich.
unaware (of) *a.* ohne Kenntnis von, unbewusst; ~s *adv.* unversehens.
unawed *a.* nicht eingeschüchtert.
unbalanced *a.* nicht im Gleichgewicht.
unbearable *a.* unerträglich.
unbeaten *a.* unbesiegt, unübertroffen.
unbecoming *a.*, ~ly *adv.* nicht kleidsam; ungeziemend.
unbeknown *a.* ohne Wissen, unbekannt.
unbelief *s.* Unglaube *m.*
unbelievable *a.* unglaublich, unglaubhaft.
unbeliever *s.* Ungläubige *m.*
unbelieving *a.* ungläubig.
unbend *v.t.ir.*; entspannen, nachlassen; schwächen; ~ *v.i.* gemütlich werden.

unbending *a.* unbiegsam; starr.
unbiassed *a.*, ~ly *adv.* vorurteilsfrei.
unbid(den) *a.* ungebeten, freiwillig.
unbind *v.t.st.* losbinden.
unbleached *a.* ungebleicht.
unblemished *a.* unbefleckt, tadellos.
unblest *a.* nicht gesegnet; verrucht.
unblushing *a.* schamlos.
unbolt *v.t.* aufriegeln, öffnen.
unborn *a.* ungeboren.
unbosom *v.t.* (Herz) ausschütten.
unbound *a.* ungebunden.
unbounded *a.* unbegrenzt.
unbridle *v.t.* abzäumen; ~d *a.* zügellos.
unbroken *a.* ungebrochen.
unbuckle *v.t.* aufschnallen.
unburden *v.t.* entlasten.
unbusinesslike *a.* nicht geschäftsmässig; unpraktisch.
unbutton *v.t.* aufknöpfen.
uncalled, uncalled-for *a.* ungerufen; unnötig; unaufgefordert; nicht eingefordert.
uncanny *a.* unheimlich.
uncared-for *a.* vernachlässigt.
unceasing *a.* fortwährend, unaufhörlich.
unceremonious *a.* ungezwungen, einfach.
uncertain *a.*, ~ly *adv.* ungewiss; unzuverlässig.
uncertainty *s.* Ungewissheit *f.*
unchain *v.t.* entfesseln.
unchallenged *a.* unbestritten.
unchanged *a.* unverändert.
unchanging *a.* unveränderlich, bleibend.
uncharitable *a.*, ~bly *adv.* lieblos.
unchaste *a.*, ~ly *adv.* unkeusch.
unchastity *s.* Unkeuschheit *f.*
unchecked *a.* ungehemmt.
unchristian *a.*, ~ly *adv.* unchristlich.
uncivilized *a.* ungesittet.
unclaimed *a.* unverlangt, nicht beansprucht; unbestellbar.
unclasp *v.t.* aufhefteln, loshaken.
uncle *s.* Onkel, Oheim *m.*
unclean *a.*, ~ly *adv.* unrein; unkeusch.
unclouded *a.* unbewölkt; heiter.
uncoil *v.t.* abwickeln.
uncoloured *a.* ungefärbt.
uncombed *a.* ungekämmt.
uncomfortable *a.*, ~bly *adv.* unbehaglich.
uncommon *a.*, ~ly *adv.* ungemein.
uncomplaining *a.* nicht klagend.
uncompromising *a.* unnachgiebig.
unconcern *s.* Gleichgültigkeit *f.*
unconcerned *a.*, ~ly *adv.* gleichgültig; sorglos.
unconditional *a.* bedingunslos.
unconfined *a.*, ~ly *adv.* unbegrenzt.
unconfirmed *a.* unbestätigt.
uncongenial *a.* ungleichartig; nicht zusagend.
unconnected *a.* unverbunden.

unconquerable a., ~bly adv. unüberwindlich.
unconquered a. unbesiegt.
unconscionable a., ~bly adv. gewissenlos; übertrieben.
unconscious a. unbewusst; bewusstlos.
unconsecrated a. ungeweiht.
unconstitutional a. verfassungswidrig.
unconstrained a., ~ly adv. ungezwungen.
uncontaminated a. unbefleckt.
uncontested, uncontradicted a. unbestritten, unwidersprochen.
uncontrollable a., ~bly adv. unbezwingbar, zügellos.
uncontrolled a., ~ly adv. unbeschränkt.
uncontroverted a. unangefochten.
unconventional a. ohne Förmlichkeit.
unconverted a. unbekehrt.
unconvinced a. unüberzeugt.
unconvincing a. nicht überzeugend.
uncork v.t. entkorken.
uncorrected a. unberichtigt.
uncorrupted a. unverdorben.
uncourteous a., ~ly adv. unhöflich.
uncouth a., ~ly adv. ungeschlacht, grob.
uncover v.t. aufdecken; entblössen.
uncritical a. unkritisch.
uncrossed a. ungekreuzt (Scheck).
uncrowned a. ungekrönt.
unction s. Salbung f.; Salbe f.; extreme ~, letzte Ölung f.
unctuous a. ölig, fettig; salbungsvoll.
uncultivated a. unangebaut; ungebildet.
uncurbed a. ungezähmt, ausgelassen.
undamaged a. unbeschädigt.
undated a. ohne Datum.
undaunted a., ~ly adv. unerschrocken.
undeceive v.t. einem die Augen öffnen.
undecided a. unentschieden.
undecipherable a. nicht zu entziffern.
undefaced a. nicht verunstaltet.
undefended a. nicht verteidigt.
undefiled a. unbefleckt, unverdorben.
undefined a. unbestimmt.
undemonstrative a. zurückhaltend, ruhig.
undeniable a., ~bly adv. unleugbar.
undenominational a. keiner Sekte zugehörig, paritätisch.
under pr. & adv. unter; weniger, geringer; unten; ~ age, unmündig.
underbid v.t.st. unterbieten.
undercarriage s. (avi.) Fahrgestell n.
under-clothing s. Unterzeug n.
under-current s. Unterströmung f.
under-cut s. Lende f., Filet n.
underdog s. Unterlegener, schlecht Weggekommener m.
underdone a. nicht gar.
underestimate v.t. unterschätzen; ~ s. Unterschätzung f.
underexposure s. (phot.) Unterbelichtung f.
underfed a. unterernährt.

under-foot adv. unter dem Fusse.
undergo v.t.st. sich unterziehen; ausstehen; erfahren.
undergraduate s. Student m.
underground a. unterirdisch; (rail.) Untergrundbahn f.; ~ (movement), politische Widerstandsbewegung f.
undergrowth s. Unterholz n.
underhand a. & adv. unter der Hand, heimlich; tückisch; (Tennis) Tief...
underlie v.i. zu Grunde liegen.
underline v.t. unterstreichen.
underling s. Untergeordnete m.
undermine v.t. untergraben.
undermost a. unterst.
underneath adv. unten, darunter; ~ pr. unter.
underpaid a. schlecht bezahlt.
underpass s. (Am.) Unterführung f.
underpin v.t. unterbauen; stützen.
underproduction s. Unterproduktion f.
underprop v.t. unterstützen.
underquote v.t. Preis niedriger berechnen.
underrate v.t. unterschätzen.
underscore v.t. (bes. Am.) unterstreichen.
under secretary s. Unterstaatssekretär m.
undersell v.t.ir. unterbieten.
undershot a. unterschlächtig.
undersigned a. unterschrieben; I, the ~, der Unterzeichnete.
undersized a. unter normaler Grösse.
understaffed a. ohne genügendes Personal.
understand v.t. & i.st. verstehen; vernehmen, hören, erfahren.
understanding a. verständig; ~ s. Verstand m.; Einsicht f.; Einverständnis n.; to come to an ~ with, sich verständigen mit; on the ~ that, unter der Voraussetzung, dass.
understate v.t. zu gering angeben.
understatement s. zu massvolle Darstellung f.
understudy s. Ersatzschauspieler (m.).
undertake v.t.st. unternehmen, übernehmen; sich verpflichten, garantieren.
undertaker s. Leichenbestatter m.
undertaking s. Unternehmen n.; feierliche Versprechen n.
undertone s. halbleise Rede; Unterton m.
undervalue v.t. unterschätzen.
underwear s. Unterzeug n.
underwood s. Unterholz n.
underworld s. Unterwelt f.
underwrite v.t.st. (com.) zeichnen; assekurieren.
underwriter s. Versicherer, Assekurant m.
undeserved a., ~ly adv. unverdient.
undeserving a. unwürdig, unwert.
undesigned a., ~ly adv. unvorsätzlich.
undesirable a. unerwünscht.
undetected a. unentdeckt.
undetermined a. unentschieden.

undeterred a. unabgeschreckt.
undeveloped a. unentwickelt.
undigested a. unverdaut.
undignified a. würdelos; unedel.
undiminished a. unvermindert.
undiscerned a., ~ly adv. unbemerkt, unentdeckt.
undiscernible a., ~bly adv. ununterscheidbar, unbemerklich.
undiscerning a. einsichtslos.
undisciplined a. ungeschult; zuchtlos.
undiscovered a. unentdeckt.
undiscriminating a. wahllos.
undisguised a. unverstellt, offen.
undismayed a. unverzagt.
undisputed a. unbestritten.
undisturbed a., ~ly adv. ungestört.
undivided a., ~ly adv. ungeteilt, ganz.
undo v.t.st. aufmachen; auflösen; zerstören; ungeschehen machen.
undoing s. Aufmachen n.; Verderben n.
undoubted a., ~ly adv. unzweifelhaft.
undreamt-of a. ungeahnt.
undress v.t. (v.i. sich) auskleiden; ~ s. Hauskleidung f.; (mil.) Halbuniform f.
undue a. ungebührlich; übermässig.
undulate v.t. & i. Wellen schlagen.
unduly adv. ungebührlich.
undutiful a., ~ly adv. pflichtvergessen.
undying a. unsterblich.
unearned a. nicht erworben, unverdient.
unearth v.t. ausgraben; aufstöbern.
unearthly a. unirdisch, überirdisch.
uneasy a., ~ily adv. unruhig, ängstlich.
uneconomic a., ~ally adv. unwirtschaftlich.
unedifying a. unerbaulich.
uneducated a. unerzogen, ungebildet.
unembarrassed a. nicht verlegen.
unemotional a. temperamentlos.
unemployable a. verwendungsunfähig.
unemployed a. arbeitslos.
unemployment s. Arbeitslosigkeit f.; ~ insurance, Arbeitslosenversicherung f.
unencumbered a. unbelastet; ohne Hypotheken.
unending a. endlos.
unendowed a. nicht dotiert.
unendurable a. unerträglich.
unenterprising a. nicht unternehmend.
unenviable a. nicht beneidenswert.
unequal a., ~ly adv. ungleich; unangemessen; nicht gewachsen.
unequalled a. unvergleichlich, unerreicht.
unequivocal a. unzweideutig.
unerring a., ~ly adv. untrüglich.
unessential a. unwesentlich.
uneven a., ~ly adv. uneben, ungleich; ungerade.
uneventful a. ereignislos.
unexampled a. beispiellos, unerhört.
unexceptionable a., ~bly adv. unverwerflich, tadellos.

unexpected a., ~ly adv. unerwartet.
unexpired a., noch nicht abgelaufen.
unexplained a. unerklärt.
unexplored a. unerforscht.
unfaded a. unverwelkt; unverschossen.
unfading a. unverwelklich; echt.
unfailing a. unfehlbar, gewiss; zuverlässig; unerschöpflich.
unfair a., ~ly adv. nicht unparteiisch; unbillig, unredlich; ~ competition, unlautere Wettbewerb m.
unfaithful a., ~ly adv. untreu.
unfaltering a. nicht schwankend, kühn.
unfamiliar a. ungewöhnt.
unfashionable a., ~bly adv. unmodern.
unfasten v.t. losmachen, losbinden.
unfathomable a., ~bly adv. unergründlich, unermesslich.
unfavourable a., ~bly adv. ungünstig.
unfeeling a. gefühllos.
unfeigned a., ~ly adv. aufrichtig.
unfermented a. ungegoren; ungesäuert.
unfetter v.t. entfesseln.
unfilial a. unkindlich.
unfinished a. unvollendet.
unfit a., ~ly adv. ungeeignet; untauglich; ~ v.t. untüchtig machen.
unfix v.t. losmachen; lösen.
unfixed a. unbefestigt, lose; unstet, unentschieden.
unflagging a. nicht erschlaffend.
unfledged a. nicht flügge.
unflinching a. unerschrocken.
unfold v.t. entfalten; darlegen.
unforeseeable unvorhersehbar.
unforeseen a. unvorhergesehen.
unforgettable a. unvergesslich.
unforgiving a. unversöhnlich.
unforgotten a. unvergessen.
unfortified a. unbefestigt; schwach.
unfortunate a., ~ly adv. unglücklich; leidig.
unfortunately adv. leider.
unfounded a. unbegründet; grundlos.
unfrequented a. unbesucht.
unfriendly a. unfreundlich.
unfrock v.t. entkleiden; der Priesterwürde entsetzen.
unfruitful a., ~ly adv. unfruchtbar.
unfulfilled a. unerfüllt.
unfunded a. (Staatsschuld) nicht konsolidiert, schwebend.
unfurl v.t. aufspannen, entfalten.
unfurnished a. nicht ausgestattet (mit); unmöbliert; entblösst.
ungainly a. plump, ungeschickt.
ungallant a. unhöflich.
ungathered a. ungepflückt; ungesammelt.
ungenerous a. unedel; karg.
ungentle a., ~tly adv. unsanft, grob.
ungentlemanlike eines gentleman unwürdig.
ungentlemanly a. ungebildet; unfein.
ungird v.t.st. losgürten.

unglazed *a.* unglasiert; ohne Fensterscheiben.
ungodly *a.* gottlos.
ungovernable *a.*, ~bly *adv.* unlenksam.
ungracious *a.*, ~ly *adv.* ungnädig; ungünstig; missfällig.
ungrammatical *a.* ungrammatisch.
ungrateful *a.*, ~ly *adv.* undankbar.
ungrounded *a.* nicht stichhaltig.
ungrudging *a.*, ~ly *adv.* gern, ohne Murren.
unguarded *a.*, ~ly *adv.* unbewacht.
unguent *s.* Salbe *f.*
unguided *a.* ungeleitet.
unhallowed *a.* verrucht; ungeweiht.
unhampered *a.* ungehindert.
unhandy *a.* nicht behend, ungeschickt.
unhang *v.t.* abhängen, aushängen.
unhappiness *s.* Unglück *n.*
unhappy *a.*, ~ily *adv.* unglücklich.
unharmed *a.* unversehrt.
unharness *v.t.* abschirren.
unhatched *a.* unausgebrütet.
unhealthy *a.*, ~ily *adv.* ungesund.
unheard *a.* ungehört; ~ of, unerhört.
unheeded *a.* unbeachtet.
unheedful, unheeding *a.* unachtsam.
unheralded *a.* unangekündigt.
unhesitating *a.* ohne Zaudern.
unhewn *a.* unbehauen.
unhindered *a.* ungehindert.
unhinge *v.t.* aus den Angeln heben.
unhistoric *a.*, ~ally *adv.* unhistorisch.
unholy *a.* unheilig, gottlos; verrucht.
unhook *v.t.* loshaken.
unhoped (for) *a.* unverhofft.
unhorse *v.t.* aus dem Sattel heben.
unhuman *a.*, ~ly *adv.* nicht menschlich, überirdisch.
unhurt *a.* unverletzt.
unicorn *s.* Einhorn *n.*
unidentified *a.* nicht identifiziert.
uniform *a.*, ~ly *adv.* einförmig, gleichförmig; ~ *s.* Uniform *f.*
uniformity *s.* Gleichförmigkeit *f.*
unify *v.t.* vereinigen, vereinheitlichen.
unilateral *a.* einseitig.
unimaginable *a.* undenkbar.
unimaginative *a.* phantasielos.
unimpaired *a.* unvermindert; unverletzt.
unimpeded *a.* ungehemmt.
unimportant *a.* unwichtig.
unimproved *a.* unverbessert; unbenutzt (Land).
uninfluenced *a.* unbeeinflusst.
uninformed *a.* ununterrichtet.
uninhabitable *a.* unbewohnbar.
uninhabited *a.* unbewohnt.
uninjured *a.* unverletzt.
uninspired *a.* nicht begeistert.
uninstructed *a.* ununterrichtet.
uninsured *a.* nicht versichert.
unintelligible *a.*, ~bly *adv.* unverständlich.

unintended, unintentional *a.* unbeabsichtigt.
uninteresting *a.* uninteressant.
uninterrupted *a.*, ~ly *adv.* ununterbrochen.
uninvited *a.* uneingeladen.
uninviting *a.* nicht anziehend.
union *s.* Vereinigung *f.*, Anschluss *m.*; Bund *m.*; Verein *m.*; Verband *m.*; Gewerkschaft *f.*; ~-Jack, britische Nationalflagge *f.*
unique *a.* einzigartig.
unison *s.* Einklang *m.*
unit *s.* Einheit *f.*
Unitarian *s.* Unitarier *m.*; ~ *a.* unitarisch.
unite *v.t.* (*v.i. sich*) vereinigen.
unity *s.* Einheit, Eintracht *f.*
universal *a.*, ~ly *adv.* allgemein; allumfassend; Welt...
universality *s.* Vielseitigkeit *f.*
universe *s.* Weltall, Universum *n.*
university *s.* Universität *f.*; ~-man, Akademiker *m.*
univocal *a.* eindeutig.
unjust *a.*, ~ly *adv.* ungerecht.
unjustifiable *a.*, ~bly *adv.* nicht zu rechfertigen; unverantwortlich.
unjustified *a.* nicht gerechtfertigt.
unkempt *a.* ungekämmt.
unkind *a.*, ~ly *adv.* unfreundlich, lieblos.
unknowable *a.* unerkennbar.
unknowing *a.*, ~ly *adv.* unwissend.
unknown *a.* unbekannt.
unlaboured *a.* leicht, fliessend (Stil).
unlace *v.t.* aufschnüren.
unlamented *a.* unbeklagt.
unlatch *v.t.* aufklinken.
unlawful *a.*, ~ly *adv.* ungesetzlich.
unlearn *v.t.* verlernen.
unlearned *a.*, ~ly *adv.* ungelehrt.
unleavened *a.* ungesäuert.
unless *c.* wenn nicht, ausser wenn.
unlettered *a.* ungelehrt.
unlicensed *a.* ohne Konzession.
unlicked *a.* ungeleckt; ungeformt.
unlike *a.*, ~ly *adv.* ungleich, anders als.
unlikelihood *s.* Unwahrscheinlichkeit *f.*
unlikely *a.* & *adv.* unwahrscheinlich.
unlimber *v.t.* abprotzen.
unlimited *a.*, ~ly *adv.* unbegrenzt; unbestimmt.
unlined *a.* ungefüttert; ohne Linien.
unliquidated *a.* unbezahlt.
unlit *a.* unbeleuchtet.
unload *v.t.* abladen.
unlock *v.t.* aufschliessen.
unlooked-for *a.* unerwartet, unvermutet.
unloose *v.t.* lösen, losmachen.
unloving *a.* lieblos.
unlucky *a.* unglücklich.
unmake *v.t.ir.* vernichten.
unman *v.t.* entmannen; entmutigen.
unmanageable *a.* unlenksam, unbändig.

unmanly *a.* unmännlich.
unmannerly *a.* ungesittet, unartig.
unmanufactured *a.* unverarbeitet.
unmarked *a.* unbemerkt; unbezeichnet.
unmarketable *a.* unverkäuflich.
unmarred *a.* unverdorben.
unmarried *a.* unverheiratet, ledig.
unmask *v.t.* (*v.i. sich*) entlarven.
unmatched *a.* unvergleichlich.
unmeaning *a.* nichtssagend.
unmeasured *a.* ungemessen.
unmentionable *a.* nicht zu erwähnen.
unmentioned *a.* nicht erwähnt.
unmerciful *a.*, ~ly *adv.* unbarmherzig.
unmerited *a.* unverdient.
unmethodical *a.* unmethodisch.
unmindful *a.* uneingedenk, sorglos.
unmingled *a.* unvermischt.
unmistakable *a.* unverkennbar.
unmitigated *a.* ungemildert, völlig.
unmodified *a.* unverändert.
unmolested *a.* unbelästigt.
unmotherly *a.* unmütterlich.
unmounted *a.* (Bild) nicht aufgezogen;
(Stein) nicht gefasst.
unmoved *a.* unbewegt; unverändert.
unmusical *a.* unmusikalisch.
unnamed *a.* ungenannt, namenlos.
unnatural *a.*, ~ly *adv.* unnatürlich.
unnecessary *a.* unnötig.
unnerve *v.t.* entnerven, entkräften.
unnoticed *a.* unbemerkt.
unnumbered *a.* ungezählt.
unobjectionable *a.* unverwerflich.
unobservant *a.* unachtsam.
unobserved *a.*, ~ly *adv.* unbeobachtet.
unobstructed *a.* nicht verstopft; ungehindert.
unobtainable *a.* nicht erhältlich; unerreichbar.
unobtrusive *a.* unaufdringlich, bescheiden.
unoccupied *a.* unbesetzt; unbenutzt; un-
bebaut; unbeschäftigt.
unoffending *a.* unschädlich, harmlos.
unofficial *a.* nicht amtlich.
unopened *a.* ungeöffnet.
unopposed *a.* ohne Widerstand.
unorthodox *a.* unorthodox; unüblich.
unpack *v.t.* auspacken; aufmachen.
unpaid *a.* unbezahlt.
unpalatable *a.* unschmackhaft; widrig.
unparalleled *a.* unvergleichlich.
unpardonable *a.*, ~bly *adv.* unverzeihlich.
unparliamentary *a.* unparlamentarisch.
unpatriotic *a.* unpatriotisch.
unpaved *a.* ungepflastert.
unperceived *a.*, ~ly *adv.* unbemerkt.
unperformed *a.* unverrichtet.
unperturbed *a.* nicht beunruhigt.
unpin *v.t.* losheften, abstecken.
unpleasant *a.*, ~ly *adv.* unangenehm.
unpleasantness *s.* Unannehmlichkeit *f.*;
Misshelligkeit *f.*

unpledged *a.* nicht verpflichtet, frei; un-
verpfändet.
unploughed *a.* ungepflügt.
unpoetical *a.*, ~ly *adv.* undichterisch.
unpolished *a.* ungeglättet; ungesittet.
unpolitical *a.* unpolitisch.
unpolluted *a.* unbefleckt.
unpopular *a.* nicht beliebt.
unpopularity *s.* Unbeliebtheit *f.*
unpractical *a.* unpraktisch.
unpractised *a.* ungeübt, unerfahren.
unprecedented *a.* beispiellos, unerhört.
unprejudiced *a.* vorurteilsfrei.
unpremeditated *a.* nicht absichtlich.
unprepared *a.* unvorbereitet.
unprepossessing *a.* nicht einnehmend.
unpretentious *a.* anspruchslos.
unpriced *a.* ohne Preisangabe.
unprincipled *a.* gewissenlos.
unprinted *a.* ungedruckt.
unprivileged *a.* nicht bevorrechtigt.
unprocurable *a.* nicht zu beschaffen.
unproductive *a.* unfruchtbar, unergiebig.
unprofessional *a.* nicht fachmännisch,
gegen die Berufsehre.
unprofitable *a.*, ~ly *adv.* nicht vorteilhaft, uneinträglich, unnütz.
unpromising *a.* nicht viel versprechend.
unpropitious *a.* ungünstig.
unproportioned *a.* unverhältnismässig.
unprotected *a.* unbeschützt.
unproved *a.* ungeprüft; unbewiesen.
unprovided *a.* unversorgt; unvorhergesehen.
unprovoked *a.* unprovoziert, grundlos.
unpublished *a.* nicht veröffentlicht.
unpunctual *a.* unpünktlich.
unpunctuality *s.* Unpünktlichkeit *f.*
unpunished *a.* ungestraft.
unpurified *a.* ungereinigt.
unqualified *a.* nicht fähig, ungeeignet; unberechtigt; uneingeschränkt.
unquenchable *a.* unlöschbar.
unquestionable *a.*, ~bly *adv.* zweifellos.
unquestioned *a.* unbefragt; unbestritten.
unquestioning *a.* bedingungslos, blind.
unquiet *a.*, ~ly *adv.* unruhig, ungestüm.
unravel *v.t.* aufwickeln, entwirren.
unread *a.* ungelesen; unbelesen.
unreadable *a.* nicht lesenswert.
unready *a.*, ~ily *adv.* nicht bereit.
unreal *a.* nicht wirklich.
unrealizable *a.* nicht realisierbar, nicht
verkäuflich.
unreasonable *a.*, ~bly *adv.* unvernünftig;
unbillig, ohne Grund.
unreasoning *a.* blind, vernunftlos.
unreclaimed *a.* nicht zurückgefordert; unangebaut; nicht gebessert.
unrecognizable *a.*, ~ly *adv.* nicht wieder-
zuerkennen.
unreconciled *a.* unversöhnt.
unrecorded *a.* nicht aufgezeichnet.

unredeemed *a.* nicht losgekauft; unerlöst; ungemildert.
unredressed *a.* nicht abgeholfen.
unrefined *a.* ungeläutert.
unreflecting *a.* gedankenlos, unüberlegt.
unregarded *a.* unberücksichtigt.
unregenerate *a.* nicht wiedergeboren, verderbt.
unrelenting *a.* unbeugsam, unerbittlich.
unreliable *a.* unzuverlässig.
unrelieved *a.* ungemildert, ununterbrochen.
unremitting *a.* unablässig, unaufhörlich.
unremunerative *a.* uneinträglich.
unrepentant *a.* reuelos.
unrepining *a.,* ~**ly** *adv.* nicht klagend.
unrequited *a.* unerwidert.
unresented *a.* ungeahndet.
unreserved *a.,* ~**ly** *adv.* nicht vorbehalten; rückhaltlos; nicht numeriert.
unresisting *a.* widerstandslos; wehrlos.
unresolved *a.* unentschlossen.
unrest *s.* Unruhe *f.*
unrestored *a.* nicht wiederhergestellt.
unrestrained *a.* unbeschränkt; zügellos.
unrestricted *a.,* ~**ly** *adv.* uneingeschränkt, unbeschränkt.
unreturned *a.* nicht zurückgegeben; nicht gewählt.
unrevoked *a.* unwiderrufen.
unrewarded *a.* unbelohnt.
unriddle *v.t.* enträtseln.
unrig *v.t.* abtakeln.
unrighteous *a.,* ~**ly** *adv.* ungerecht.
unripe *a.* unreif.
unrivalled *a.* ohne Nebenbuhler.
unroof *v.t.* abdecken (Haus).
unroot *v.t.* entwurzeln.
unruffled *a.* ruhig (vom Meer).
unruly *a.* unlenksam, unbändig.
unsaddle *v.t.* absatteln.
unsafe *a.,* ~**ly** *adv.* unsicher, gefährlich.
unsaid *a.* unerwähnt; widerrufen.
unsalaried *a.* unbesoldet.
unsaleable *a.* unverkäuflich.
unsalted *a.* ungesalzen.
unsanctioned *a.* unbestätigt.
unsanitary *a.* unhygienisch.
unsatisfactory *a.,* ~**ily** *adv.* unzulänglich, unbefriedigend.
unsatisfied *a.* unbefriedigt; unzufrieden.
unsatisfying *a.* unbefriedigend.
unsavoury *a.,* ~**ily** *adv.* unschmackhaft.
unsay *v.t.ir.* sich lossagen, widerrufen.
unscathed *a.* unversehrt.
unschooled *a.* ungeschult.
unscientific *a.* unwissenschaftlich.
unscrew *v.t.* losschrauben.
unscriptural *a.* schriftwidrig.
unscrupulous *a.* gewissenlos; skrupellos.
unseal *v.t.* entsiegeln.
unsearchable *a.,* ~**bly** *adv.* unerforschlich.

unseasonable *a.* unzeitig; unschicklich, unpassend; ~**bly** *adv.* zur Unzeit.
unseat *v.t.* vom Sitze vertreiben, aus dem Sattel heben.
unseconded *a.* nicht unterstützt.
unsecured *a.* (*com.*) ungedeckt, nicht sichergestellt.
unseemly *a.* unziemlich.
unseen *a.* ungesehen, unsichtbar.
unselfish *a.* selbstlos, uneigennützig
unsent *a.* (for) ungerufen.
unserviceable *a.,* ~**bly** *adv.* unnütz.
unsettle *v.t.* umstossen.
unsettled *a.* ungeordnet; unbeständig, unsicher, veränderlich; unbezahlt.
unshackle *v.t.* entfesseln.
unshaken *a.* unerschüttert; fest.
unshaven *a.* nicht rasiert.
unsheltered *a.* unbedeckt; ungeschützt.
unshorn *a.* ungeschoren.
unshrinkable *a.,* ~**ly** *adv.* nicht einlaufend (Stoff).
unshrinking *a.* unverzagt; nicht einlaufend.
unsightly *a.* hässlich.
unsigned *a.* unsigniert, nicht unterzeichnet.
unskilful *a.,* ~**ly** *adv.* ungeschickt, unkundig.
unskilled *a.* unerfahren; ungelernt; ~ *worker,* ungelernte Arbeiter *m.*
unslaked *a.* ungelöscht.
unsociable *a.,* ~**bly** *adv.* ungesellig.
unsocial *a.* unsozial.
unsoiled *a.* unbeschmutzt.
unsold *a.* unverkauft.
unsolicited *a.* unverlangt, ungefordert.
unsolved *a.* ungelöst.
unsophisticated *a.* unverfälscht; unverdorben, natürlich.
unsought *a.* ungesucht.
unsound *a.* ungesund; nicht stichhaltig; verdorben; nicht echt, nicht aufrichtig; *of* ~ *mind,* geisteskrank.
unsounded *a.* unergründet.
unsparing *a.* reichlich; schonungslos.
unspeakable *a.,* ~**bly** *adv.* unsäglich.
unspecified *a.* nicht spezifiziert.
unspent *a.* unerschöpft, unverbraucht.
unspoiled *a.* unverdorben.
unspoken *a.* ungesprochen.
unsportsmanlike *a.* nicht sportsmässig; unweidmännisch.
unspotted *a.* unbefleckt.
unstable *a.* nicht fest, unbeständig.
unstained *a.* unbefleckt; ungefärbt.
unstamped *a.* ungestempelt, ohne Marke.
unsteady *a.,* ~**ily** *adv.* unbeständig, veränderlich, wankelmütig.
unstinted *a.* ungeschmälert, freigebig.
unstirred *a.* unaufgerührt; unaufgeregt.
unstrained *a.* ungezwungen.
unstressed *a.* unbetont.

unstring *v.t.st.* abspannen, lösen.
unstudied *a.* unstudiert; ungekünstelt.
unstuffed *a.* ungefüllt.
unsubdued *a.* ununterjocht.
unsubmissive *a.* widerspenstig.
unsubstantial *a.* unkörperlich; wesenlos.
unsuccessful *a.*, ~ly *adv.* erfolglos.
unsuitable *a.*, ~bly *adv.* nicht passend.
unsuited *a.* nicht passend, ungeeignet.
unsure *a.* unsicher.
unsurpassed *a.* unübertroffen.
unsuspected *a.*, ~ly *adv.* unverdächtig.
unsuspecting *a.* arglos, unbefangen.
unsuspicious *a.* nicht argwöhnisch.
unswayed *a.* unbeeinflusst.
unswerving *a.* unentwegt, standhaft.
unsworn *a.* unvereidigt.
unsymmetrical *a.* unsymmetrisch.
untainted *a.*, ~ly *adv.* unverdorben.
untamed *a.* ungezähmt.
untarnished *a.* ungetrübt.
untasted *a.* ungekostet, unversucht.
untaxed *a.* unbesteuert.
unteachable *a.* ungelehrig.
untempered *a.* ungemildert.
untenable *a.* unhaltbar.
untested *a.* ungeprüft.
unthankful *a.*, ~ly *adv.* undankbar.
unthinkable *a.* undenkbar.
unthinking *a.* gedankenlos, sorglos.
unthought *a.* (of) unvermutet.
unthread *v.t.* ausfädeln.
untidy *a.* unordentlich, unreinlich.
untie *v.t.* aufbinden, lösen.
until *c.* bis; ~ *pr.* bis (an), bis zu.
untilled *a.* ungepflügt.
untimely *a. & adv.* unzeitig, vorschnell.
untinged *a.* nicht gefärbt.
untiring *a.* unermüdet.
unto *pr.* zu, an, bis, bis an.
untold *a.* ungezählt; ungesagt.
untouched *a.* unberührt, ungerührt.
untoward *a.*, ~ly *adv.* eigensinnig; ungeschickt; widrig, ungünstig.
untraceable *a.* unaufspürbar.
untractable *a.* schwer zu behandeln.
untrained *a.* unerzogen, ungebildet; untrainiert.
untrammelled *a.* ungehindert.
untranslatable *a.* unübersetzbar.
untravelled *a.* ungereist; unbereist.
untried *a.* unversucht; unverhört; unerprobt; unerfahren.
untrimmed *a.* ungeschmückt.
untrodden *a.* unbetreten.
untroubled *a.* ungestört, ungetrübt.
untrue *a.* unwahr, falsch.
untruly *adv.* fälschlich.
untrustworthy *a.* unzuverlässig.
untruth *s.* Unwahrheit *f.*
untune *v.t.* verstimmen, verwirren.
untutored *a.* ununterrichtet, ungeschult.
untwine *v.t.* aufwickeln, auftrennen.

untwist *v.t.* aufrebbeln, aufdrehen.
unused *a.* ungebraucht; ungewohnt.
unusual *a.*, ~ly *adv.* ungewöhnlich.
unutterable *a.*, ~bly *adv.* unaussprechlich.
unvaccinated *a.* ungeimpft.
unvalued *a.* ungeschätzt.
unvaried *a.* unverändert.
unvarnished *a.* ungeschminkt.
unvarying *a.* unveränderlich.
unveil *v.t.* entschleiern.
unventilated *a.* ungelüftet; (*fig.*) ununtersucht, unerörtert.
unversed *a.* unbewandert.
unvisited *a.* unbesucht.
unvouched-for *a.* unverbürgt.
unwarlike *a.* unkriegerisch.
unwarrantable *a.*, ~bly *adv.* unverantwortlich, unbefugt.
unwarranted *a.* ungerechtfertigt; unverbürgt.
unwary *a.* unbehutsam.
unwearied *a.* unermüdet; ~ly *adv.* ohne Unterlass.
unweave *v.t.st.* aufweben, ausfasern.
unwedded *s.* unverheiratet.
unweighed *a.* ungewogen; unerworgen.
unwelcome *a.* unwillkommen.
unwell *a.* unwohl, unpässlich.
unwholesome *a.* ungesund.
unwieldy *a.*, ~ily *adv.* schwerfällig, unhandlich.
unwilling *a.* nicht willig; ~ly *adv.* wider Willen.
unwind *v.t.st.* loswinden, abwickeln.
unwise *a.*, ~ly *adv.* unweise, unklug.
unwished *a.* (for) unerwünscht.
unwitting *a.*, ~ly *adv.* unwissentlich.
unwomanly *a.* unweiblich.
unwonted *a.* ungewöhnt; ungewöhnlich.
unworkable *a.* unpraktisch.
unworn *a.* ungetragen.
unworthy *a.*, ~ily *adv.* unwürdig.
unwrap *v.t.* loswickeln.
unwritten *a.* ungeschrieben.
unwrought *a.* unbearbeitet; roh.
unyielding *a.* unnachgiebig, unbeugsam.
unyoke *v.t.* aufjochen, ausspannen.
up *adv. & pr.* auf, aufwärts hinauf; empor, oben; *the second* ~, der zweite von unten; *it is* ~ *to him,* es ist seine Sache; ~ *to date a.* modern, auf der Höhe; ~ *against,* gegen…an.
upbraid *v.t.* vorwerfen, tadeln, schelten.
upbringing *s.* Erziehung *f.*
upgrade *v.t.* (*Am.*) befördern.
upheaval *s.* Erhebung *f.*
upheave *v.t.st.* emporheben.
uphill *a.* bergan; schwierig.
uphold *v.t.st.* aufrecht(er)halten.
upholsterer *s.* Tapezierer *m.*
upkeep *s.* Instandhaltung *f.*
upland *s.* Hochland *n.*; ~ *a.* hoch gelegen.

uplift v.t. emporheben; ~ s. (Am.) seelische Erhebung f.
upon pr. auf, an, bei, nach.
upper a. ober, höher; Ober...; ~ circle s. (theat.) erste Rang m.; ~ leather s. Oberleder n.; down on one's ~s, in zerlumpten Schuhen, heruntergekommen.
uppermost a. höchst, oberst.
uppish a. stolz, anmassend.
uprear v.t. aufrichten.
upright a., ~ly adv. aufrecht, gerade; aufrichtig; ~ s. Ständer m.; ~ size, Hochformat n.
uprising s. (Am.) Aufstand m.
uproar s. Aufruhr m.; heftiges Getöse n.
uproarious a. aufrührerisch, lärmend.
uproot v.t. ausreissen, entwurzeln.
upset v.t. umstürzen; ausser Fassung bringen; ~ stomach, verdorbene Magen m.
upshot s. Ausgang m.; Ergebnis n.
upside s. Oberseite f.; ~ down, das Oberste zu unterst, drunter und drüber.
upstairs adv. oben (im Hause), nach oben.
upstart s. Emporkömmling m.; ~ v.i. auffahren; aufschiessen.
up-train s. Eisenbahnzug (m.) in der Richtung nach London.
upward(s) adv. aufwärts, oben; ~ of, mehr als.
uranium s. Uran n.
urban a. Stadt..., städtisch.
urbane a. höflich, artig, gebildet.
urbanity s. Artigkeit, Höflichkeit f.
urchin s. (kleine) Schelm m.
urethra s. Harnröhre f.
urge v.t. treiben, drängen; reizen; eifrig betreiben; darauf bestehen.
urgency s. Dringlichkeit f.
urgent a., ~ly adv. dringend, heftig.
uric a. Harn...; ~ acid, Harnsäure f.
urine s. Urin, Harn m.
urn s. Urne f.; Teekessel m.
us pn. uns.
usage s. Gebrauch m.; Sitte f.
use s. Gebrauch, Brauch m.; Genuss, Vorteil m.; Verwendung f.; in ~, üblich, gebräuchlich; (of) no ~, unnütz, zwecklos; to make ~ of, Gebrauch machen von; ~ v.t. gebrauchen, sich bedienen; anwenden; gewöhnen; behandeln; ausüben; to ~ up, aufbrauchen; ~ v.i. pflegen, gewohnt sein.
used a. gewöhnt; more widely ~, gebräuchlicher; ~-up, verbraucht.
useful a., ~ly adv. nützlich, dienlich.
usefulness s. Nützlichkeit f.
useless a., ~ly adv. unnütz, unbrauchbar.
usher s. Zeremonienmeister m.; Türhüter m.; ~ v.t. (in), einführen, anmelden.
usual a., ~ly adv. gebräuchlich, üblich.
usufruct s. Nutzniessung f.

usurer s. Wucherer m.
usurious a. wucherisch.
usurp v.t. unrechtmässig an sich reissen.
usurpation s. widerrechtliche Besitzerergreifung, Aneignung f.
usurper, unrechtmässige Machthaber, Inhaber m.
usury s. Wucher m.
utensil s. Gerät, Guschirr n.
uterine a. Gebärmutter...
uterus s. Gebärmutter f.
utilitarian s. Utilitarier m.; ~ a. Nützlichkeits...
utility s. Nützlichkeit f.; Nutzen m.; ~ a. Gebrauchs... (ohne Verschönerung, z.B. ~ shirt, ~ furniture, etc.); public utilities, gemeinnützige Anstalten pl.
utilize v.t. nutzbar machen.
utmost a. äusserst, höchst.
utopian a. utopisch, schwärmerhaft.
utter a. äusserst; gänzlich; ~ v.t. sprechen, äussern.
utterance s. Aussprache f.; Äusserung f.
utterly adv. äusserst, gänzlich, durchaus.
uvula s. Zäpfchen (im Halse) n.
uxorious a. der Gattin zu sehr ergeben.

V

vacancy s. Leere f.; freie Stelle f.
vacant a. leer, erledigt; gedankenarm.
vacate v.t. räumen; (Amt) niederlegen.
vacation s. Räumung f.; Ferien f.pl.
vaccinate v.t. impfen.
vaccination s. Impfung f.
vaccine s. Impfstoff m.
vacillate v.i. wanken; schwanken.
vacuous a. leer; ausdruckslos.
vacuum s. luftleere Raum m.; ~ cleaner, Staubsauger s.; ~ flask s. Thermosflasche f.
vagabond a. umherstreifend; ~ s. Landstricher m.
vagary s. Grille, Laune f.
vagina s. (Mutter-) Scheide f.
vagrancy s. Landstreicherei f.
vagrant s. Landstreicher m.; ~ a. wändernd, unstet.
vague a. unbestimmt, vag; schwankend.
vain a., ~ly adv. leer, nichtig, eitel vergeblich; in ~, vergebens.
vainglorious a. ruhmredig.
vainglory s. Ruhmredigkeit f.
vale s. Tal n.
valediction s. Abschied m.
valedictory a. Abschieds...
valentine s. Liebesbrief (m.) am Valentinstage (14. Februar); (Valentins-) Schatz m.
valet s. Kammerdiener, Lakai m.

valetudinarian *a.* kränklich, siech; **~** *s.* Kranke *m.*

valiant *a.*, **~ly** *adv.* tapfer, brav.

valid *a.*, **~ly** *adv.* rechtskräftig; gültig.

validate *v.t.* gültig machen.

validity *s.* Gültigkeit *f.*; Wert *m.*

valley *s.* Tal *n.*

valorous *a.*, **~ly** *adv.* tapfer.

valour *s.* Tapferkeit *f.*

valuable *a.* schätzbar; kostbar; **~s** *pl.* Wertsachen *f.pl.*

valuation *s.* Schätzung *f.*

value *s.* Wert, Preis *m.*; **~** *v.t.* schätzen, Achtung erweisen; trassieren.

valueless *a.* wertlos.

valuer *s.* Taxator, Schätzer *m.*

valve *s.* Ventil *n.*; Klappe *f.*; (*Radio*) Röhre *f.*

vamp *v.t.* aufstutzen; zusammenstoppeln.

vampire *s.* Vampir *m.*

van *s.* Wanne, Schwinge *f.*; Vorhut *f.*; Möbelwagen *m.*; Packwagen *m.*

Vandalism *s.* Vandalismus *m.*

vane *s.* Wetterfahne *f.*; Schieber (an Instrumenten) *m.*

vanguard *s.* Vorhut *f.*

vanilla *s.* Vanille *f.*

vanish *v.i.* verschwinden, zergehen.

vanity *s.* Eitelkeit, Nichtigkeit *f.*

vanquish *v.t.* besiegen; widerlegen.

vantage *s.* Vorteil *m.*; gute Gelegenheit *f.*; **~-ground** Vorteil (*m.*) des Terrains, überlegene Stellung *f.*

vapid *a.* schal; geistlos.

vaporize *v.i.* verdampfen.

vaporous *a.* dunstig; nebelhaft, nichtig.

vapour *s.* Dunst, Dampf *m.*; Grillen *f.pl.*

variable *a.*, **~bly** *adv.* veränderlich.

variance *s.* Uneinigkeit, Misshelligkeit *f.*; *to be at* **~**, sich widersprechen.

variant *s.* Variante *f.*; **~** *a.* abweichend.

variation *s.* Veränderung *f.*; Verschiedenheit, Abweichung *f.*

varicose veins *pl.* Krampfadern *pl.*

varied *a.* mannigfaltig.

variegate *v.t.* bunt machen.

variety *s.* Mannigfaltigkeit, Abwechslung, Veränderung *f.*; Spielart *f.*; **~** *entertainment*, Varietéaufführung *f.*

various *a.* verschieden; mannigfach.

varnish *s.* Firnis *m.*; Anstrich *m.*; **~** *v.t.* firnissen, lackieren; (*fig.*) bemänteln.

varsity *s.*=**university**.

vary *v.t.* (*u. sich*) verändern; verschieden sein, abweichen.

vascular *a.* (*med.*) Gefäss...

vase *s.* Vase *f.*

vaseline *s.* Vaselin *n.*

vassal *s.* Lehnsmann, Untertan *m.*

vassalage *s.* Lehnsverhältnis *f.*

vast *a.*, **~ly** *adv.* sehr gross, weit.

vastness *s.* ungeheure Grösse *f.*

vat *s.* Fass *n.*; Kufe *f.*

vaticinate *v.t.* weissagen.

vault *s.* Gewölbe *n.*; Gruft *f.*; Sprung *m.*; Tresor *m.*; **~** *v.i.* springen; **~** *v.t.* wölben; **~ing horse**, Pferd (Turnen).

vaunt *v.t.* preisen, loben; **~** *v.i.* prahlen; sich rühmen.

veal *s.* Kalbfleisch *n.*

v-belt *s.* (*mech.*) Keilriemen *m.*

vee *a.* prismenförmig.

veer *v.i.* sich drehen; (*nav.*) (ab)fieren.

vegetable *s.* Pflanze *f.*; (*meist pl.*) Gemüse *n.*; **~** *a.* Pflanzen..., pflanzenartig; **~ fat**, Pflanzenfett *n.*; **~ kingdom**, Pflanzenreich *n.*; **~ oil**, Pflanzenöl *n.*

vegetarian *s.* Vegetarier *m.*

vegetation *s.* Vegetation *f.*

vegetative *a.* grünend; fruchtbar.

vehemence *s.* Heftigkeit *f.*; Eifer *m.*

vehement *a.*, **~ly** *adv.* heftig, ungestüm.

vehicle *s.* Fuhrwerk *n.*; Vermittler, Träger *m.*

vehicular *a.* Fahr...

veil *s.* Schleier *m.*; **~** *v.t.* verschleiern.

vein *s.* Blutader *f.*; Ader (im Holze, etc.) *f.*; Laune, Stimmung *f.*; Metallader *f.*

vellum *s.* feine Pergament *n.*

velocity *s.* Schnelligkeit *f.*

velvet *s.* Samt *m.*; **~** *a.* samten.

velveteen *s.* Plüsch *m.*

venal *a.* feil, käuflich.

venality *s.* Feilheit *f.*; Bestechlichkeit *f.*

vend *v.t.* verkaufen.

vender, vendor *s.* Verkäufer *m.*

vendible *a.* verkäuflich.

veneer *v.t.* fournieren, auslegen; **~** *s.* Fournier *n.*

venerable *a.*, **~bly** *adv.* ehrwürdig.

venerate *v.t.* verehren.

venereal disease *s.* (VD) Geschlechtskrankheit *f.*

vengeance *s.* Rache *f.*

vengeful *a.* rachsüchtig.

venial *a.* verzeihlich; erlaubt; lässlich.

venison *s.* Wildbret *n.*

venom *s.* Gift *n.*

venomous *a.*, **~ly** *adv.* giftig; boshaft.

venous *a.* venös, Venen...

vent *s.* Abfluss *m.*; Abzug *m.*; *to give* **~**, Luft machen; **~** *v.t.* lüften.

ventilate *v.t.* lüften; erörtern.

ventilation *s.* Lüftung *f.*

ventilator *s.* Ventilator, Luftfächer *m.*

ventricle *s.* Höhle *f.*; Herzkammer *f.*

ventriloquist *s.* Bauchredner *m.*

venture *s.* Wagnis *n.*; Unternehmung *f.*; Einsatz *m.*; *at a* **~**, auf gut Glück; **~** *v.i. & t.* wagen.

venturesome *a.*, **~ly** *adv.* verwegen.

venue *s.* Gerichtsstand, zuständige Gerichtshof *m.*; Treffpunkt *m.*

veracious *a.* wahrhaft, aufrichtig.

veracity *s.* Wahrhaftigkeit *f.*

veranda(h) *s.* Veranda *f.*

verb s. Zeitwort n.
verbal a., ~ly adv. mündlich; wörtlich.
verbatim adv. wörtlich.
verbiage s. Wortschwall m.
verbose a. wortreich, weitschweifig.
verdant a. grün, grünend.
verdict s. Geschwornenausspruch m.; Entscheidung f.; Urteil n.
verdigris s. Grünspan m.
verdure s. Grün n.
verge s. Stab m.; Rand m.; Grenze f.; ~ v.i. sich neigen, grenzen, streifen.
verger s. Stabträger, Küster m.
verification s. Bewahrheitung, Bestätigung f.; Nachprüfung f.
verify v.t. beglaubigen, bestätigen.
vermicelli s.pl. Fadennudeln f.pl.
vermilion s. Scharlach m.; Zinnober m.; ~ v.t. rot färben.
vermin s. Ungeziefer n.
vernacular s. Landessprache f.; ~ a. einheimisch, Landes...
vernal a. Frühlings...
vernier s. (mech.) Nonius m.
veronica s. (bot.) Ehrenpreis n.
versatile a., vielseitig; veränderlich.
versatility s. Vielseitigkeit f.
verse s. Vers m.
versed a. bewandert, erfahren.
versification s. Versbau m.
versify v.t. & i. reimen.
version s. Übersetzung f.; Lesart f.; Darstellung f.
versus pr. gegen.
vertebra s. Rückenwirbel m.
vertebral a. Wirbel...
vertebrate s. Wirbeltier m.
vertex s. Scheitelpunkt m.; Spitze f.
vertical a., ~ly adv. senkrecht, lotrecht.
vertigo s. Schwindel m.
very a. wahr, wirklich; echt; völlig; gerade, gar; ~ adv. sehr; the ~ same, genau derselbe; the ~ best, der allerbeste.
Véry-light s. (mil.) Leuchtrakete f.
vesicle s. Bläschen n.
vespers s.pl. Abendgottesdienst m.
vessel s. Gefäss n.; Fahrzeug n., Schiff n.
vest s. Unterjacke f.; Weste f.; ~ v.t. bekleiden; verleihen; to be ~ed in, jemandem zustehen; ~ed interests pl. übermächtige Privatinteressen pl.
vestal s. Vestalin f.
vested p. & a., altbegründet, gesetzlich festgestellt, verbrieft.
vestibule s. Vorhalle f.
vestige s. Spur f.
vestment s. Gewand n.; Anzug m.
vestry s. Sakristei; Gemeindeversammlung f.; ~-men pl. Kirchenälteste m.pl.
vet s. = veterinary.
vetch s. Wicke f.
veteran s. alte Soldat m.; ~ a. erfahren.

veterinary s. Tierarzt m.; ~ a. tierärztlich.
veto s. Verwerfungsrecht n.; Einspruch m.; ~ v.t. Einspruch erheben.
vex v.t. plagen, ärgern; ~ v.i. sich grämen.
vexation s. Plage f.; Verdruss m.
vexatious a., ~ly adv. beschwerlich; ärgerlich; schikanös.
via pr. über.
viaduct s. Bahnbrücke f.
vial s. Flasche, Phiole f.
viands s.pl. Speisen f.pl.
viaticum s. Wegzehrung f.
vibrate v.i. zittern, beben.
vibration s. Schwingung f.
vicar s. Pfarrer m.
vicarage s. Pfarrerstelle f.; Pfarrhaus n.
vicarious a. stellvertretend.
vice s. Laster n.; Fehler, Mangel m.; Schraubstock m.; ~ pr. an Stelle von; ~ (in Zus.) Vize..., Unter...
vice-admiral s. Vizeadmiral m.
vice-chairman s. stellvertretende Vorsitzende m.
vicegerent s. Statthalter, Stellvertreter m.
viceroy s. Vizekönig m.
vice-versa adv. umgekehrt.
vicinity s. Nachbarschaft, Nähe f.
vicious a., ~ly adv. lasterhaft; bösartig (Tier); ~ circle, Zirkelschluss m.
vicissitude s. Wechsel(fall), Umschlag m.
victim s. Opfer n.
victimize v.t. opfern; betrügen, prellen.
victor s. Sieger m.
victorious a., ~ly adv. siegreich.
victory s. Sieg m.
victual v.t. mit Lebensmitteln versorgen.
victualler s. licensed ~, Schankwirt m.
victuals s.pl. Lebensmittel n.pl.
vie v.i. wetteifern.
Vienna steak s. Bulette f.
view s. Aussicht f.; Ansicht f.; Anblick m.; Absicht f.; in ~ of, in Hinblick auf; with a ~ to, mit der Absicht zu...; ~ v.t. besichtigen, betrachten; prüfen.
viewfinder s. (phot.) Sucher m.
viewpoint s. Gesichtspunkt m.
vigil s. Nachtwache f.; Vorabend (m.) eines Festtages.
vigilance s. Wachsamkeit f.
vigilant a., ~ly adv. wachsam.
vigilantes pl.(Am.) Sicherheitsausschuss m.
vigorous a., ~ly adv. kräftig, rüstig.
vigour s. Stärke, Kraft f.; Energie f.
vile a., ~ly adv. schlecht, niedrig.
vilify v.t. erniedrigen, beschimpfen.
villa s. Landhaus n.; Villa f.
village s. Dorf n.
villager s. Dorfbewohner m.
villain s. Schurke m.
villainous a., ~ly adv. niederträchtig.
villainy s. Schändlichkeit, Niederträchtigkeit f.

vindicate *v.t.* verteidigen; beanspruchen.
vindictive *a.* rachsüchtig.
vine *s.* Weinstock *m.*; Rebe, Ranke *f.*
vinegar *s.* (Wein-)Essig *m.*
vine-grower *s.* Weinbauer *m.*
vine-growing *s.* Weinbau *m.*
vinery *s.* Treibhaus für Reben *n.*
vineyard *s.* Weinberg *m.*
vintage *s.* Weinlese *f.*; (Wein)jahrgang *m.*
vintner *s.* Weinhändler *m.*
viol *s.* Bratsche *f.*
viola *s.*, viol *s.* Bratsche *f.*
violate *v.t.* verletzen; schänden.
violation *s.* Verletzung *f.*
violence *s.* Heftigkeit, Gewalt.
violent *a.*, ~ly *adv.* heftig; gewalttätig.
violet *s.* Veilchen *n.*
violin *s.* Violine, Geige *f.*; ~-case *s.* Geigenkasten *m.*
violinist *s.* Violinspieler, Geiger *m.*
violoncello *s.* Cello *n.*, kleine Bassgeige *f.*
viper *s.* Viper, Natter *f.*
virago *s.* Mannweib *n.*
virgin *s.* Jungfrau *f.*
virginity *s.* Jungfräulichkeit *f.*
virile *a.* männlich, kräftig.
virility *s.* Männlichkeit, Mannheit *f.*
virtual *a.*, ~ly *adv.* eigentlich, so gut wie.
virtue *s.* Tugend *f.*; Kraft *f.*; Wert *m.*; *in ~ of*, zufolge; *by ~ of*, kraft.
virtuoso *s.* Virtuose *m.*
virtuous *a.*, ~ly *adv.* tugendhaft, sittsam.
virulence *s.* Bösartigkeit *f.*
virulent *a.*, ~ly *adv.* giftig; bösartig.
virus *s.* (organische) Gift *n.*
visa *s.* Sichtvermerk *m.*, Visum *n.*; ~ *v.t.* visieren, mit Sichtvermerk versehen.
visage *s.* Gesicht *n.*; Anblick *m.*
vis-à-vis *pr.* gegenüber.
viscosity *s.* Zähflüssigkeit *f.*
viscount *s.* Vicomte *m.*
viscountess *s.* Vicomtesse *f.*
viscous *a.* zähflüssig; klebrig.
visibility *s.* Sichtbarkeit *f.*; Sichtigkeit *f.*
visible *a.*, ~bly *adv.* sichtbar.
vision *s.* Sehen *n.*; Erscheinung *f.*
visionary *s.* Träumer, Schwärmer *m.*; ~ *a.* eingebildet; seherhaft.
visit *s.* Besuch *m.*; ~ *v.t.* & *i.* besuchen; besichtigen; heimsuchen.
visitation *s.* Besuch *m.*; Besichtigung *f.*; Heimsuchung *f.*
visiting card *s.* Visitenkarte *f.*
visitor *s.* Besucher *m.*; Sommergast *m.*; ~s' book, Fremdenbuch *n.*; ~s' bureau, Fremdenamt *n.*
visor *s.* Visier *n.*; Maske *f.*; Mützenschirm *m.*
vista *s.* Aussicht *f.*; Baumallee *f.*
visual *a.* Seh..., Gesichts...
visualize *v.t.* sich im Geiste vorstellen; ins Auge fassen.

vital *a.*, ~ly *adv.* Lebens...; unentbehrlich, wesentlich; ~s *s.pl.* edle Teile *m.pl.*
vitality *s.* Lebenskraft *f.*
vitamin(e) *s.* Vitamin *n.*
vitiate *v.t.* verderben, verfälschen.
viticulture *s.* Weinbau *m.*
vitreous *a.* gläsern, glasartig.
vituperate *v.t.* tadeln.
vivacious *a.* munter, lebhaft.
vivacity *s.* Lebhaftigkeit *f.*
viva voce *adv.* mündlich.
vivid *a.*, ~ly *adv.* lebhaft, kräftig.
vivify *v.t.* beleben.
viviparous *a.* lebendige Junge gebärend.
vivisection *s.* Vivisektion *f.*
vixen *s.* Füchsin *f.*; zänkische Weib *n.*
viz *adv.* (statt videlicet) nämlich.
vizier *s.* Wesir *m.*
vocabulary *s.* Wörterverzeichnis *n.*; Wortschatz *m.*
vocal *a.* Stimm..., stimmhaft; Vokal...; ~ chord, Stimmband *n.*
vocalist *s.* Sänger(in) *m.* (& *f.*).
vocation *s.* Neigung *f.*; Beruf *m.*
vocational *a.* Berufs...; ~ guidance *s.* Berufsberatung *f.*
vociferate *v.i.* & *a.* heftig schreien.
vociferous *a.* schreiend, brüllend.
vogue *s.* Mode *f.*
voice *s.* Stimme *f.*; Sprache *f.*; *at the top of one's ~*, aus voller Kehle; ~ *v.t.* äussern.
voiced *a.* stimmhaft.
voiceless *a.* stimmlos.
void *a.* leer; ungültig, nichtig; ~ *s.* Leere *f.*; ~ *v.t.* (aus)leeren; räumen, aufheben; ungültig machen.
volatilize *v.t.* verflüchtigen.
volcanic *a.* vulkanisch.
volcano *s.* Vulkan *m.*
volition *s.* Wollen *n.*
volley *s.* Salve *f.*
volt *s.* Volte *f.*; Volt *n.*
voltage *s.* (elek.) Spannung *f.*
volte-face *s.* Frontwechsel *m.*
voltmeter *s.* (elek.) Voltmesser *m.*
voluble *a.*, ~bly *adv.* beweglich; geläufig; gesprächig.
volume *s.* (Buch) Band *m.*; Masse *f.*; Umfang *f.*; Rauminhalt *m.*; (Radio) Lautstärke *f.*; ~ control, Lautstärkeneinstellung *f.*
voluminous *a.*, ~ly *adv.* umfangreich.
voluntary *a.* freiwillig; absichtlich.
volunteer *s.* Freiwillige *m.*; ~ *v.t.* freiwillig dienen.
voluptuary *s.* Wollüstling *m.*
voluptuous *a.*, ~ly *adv.* wollüstig.
volute *s.* Windung *f.*; Schnecke *f.*
vomit *v.i.* sich erbrechen; ~ *v.t.* ausspeien, auswerfen; ~ *s.* Auswurf *m.*
voracious *a.*, ~ly *adv.* gefrässig, gierig.

voracity s. Gefrässigkeit, Raubsucht f.
vortex s. Wirbel m.
votary s. Geweihte m.; Verehrer m.
vote s. Wahlstimme f.; Beschluss m.; ~ v.t. & i. wählen, stimmen.
voter s. Wähler m.; Abstimmender m.
voting s. Abstimmung f.
votive a. gelobt, Weih...
vouch v.t. bezeugen; verbürgen; ~ v.i. Gewähr leisten.
voucher s. Zeuge m.; Zeugnis n.; Beleg, Schein, Gutschein m.
vouchsafe v.t. verstatten, bewilligen; ~ v.i. geruhen.
vow s. Gelübde, feierliche Versprechen n.; ~ v.t. & i. geloben.
vowel s. Selbstlaut(er), Vokal m.
voyage s. Seereise f.; ~ v.t. & i. bereisen; zur See reisen; ~ out, Ausfahrt, Hinfahrt f.
vulcanize v.t. vulkanisieren.
vulcanite s. Hartgummi n.
vulgar a., ~ly adv. gemein; pöbelhaft; landesüblich; ~ s. Pöbel m.
vulgarity s. Gemeinheit f.
vulgarize v.t. herabwürdigen.
vulnerable a. verwundbar.
vulpine a. fuchsartig.
vulture s. Geier m.

W

wad s. (Watte-) Bausch m.; Ladepfropf m.; ~ v.t. wattieren.
wadding s. Wattierung f.; Watte f.
waddle v.i. watscheln, wackeln.
wade v.t. & i. (durch)waten.
wafer s. Oblate f.; Hostie f.; Eiswaffel f.; ~ v.t. mit Oblate siegeln.
waffle s. Waffel f.
waft v.t. leicht fortbewegen; zuwehen; ~ v.i. schweben; ~ s. Hauch f.
wag v.t. schütteln; wedeln; ~ v.i. wackeln; ~ s. Spassvogel m.
wage s. Lohn m.; ~-earner s. Lohnempfänger m.; ~-tariff s. Lohntarif m.; ~ v.t. to ~ war, Krieg führen.
wager s. Wette f.; ~ v.t. & i. wetten.
wages s.pl. Lohn m.
waggish a., ~ly adv. schalkhaft.
waggle v.i. wackeln, wanken.
wag(g)on s. Wagon, Güterwagen m.
wagtail s. Bachstelze f.
waif s. herrenlose Sache f.; ~s and strays pl. obdachlose Kinder n.pl.
wail v.t. beklagen; ~ v.i. wehklagen; ~ s. Klage f.
wain s. Wagen m.; Charles's ~, der grosse Bär.
wainscot s. Getäfel n.; ~ v.t. täfeln.
waist s. Taille f.; schmalste Stelle f.; (Am.) Damenbluse f.

waistband s. Taillenband n.
waistcoat s. Weste f.
wait v.i. warten; aufwarten; aufpassen; to keep a person ~ing, einen warten lassen; ~ s. Lauer f.; Hinterhalt m.
waiter s. Aufwärter, Kellner m.
waiting-room s. Wartesaal m.
waiting-woman s. Kammermädchen n.
waitress s. Kellnerin f.
waive v.t. aufgeben, verzichten (auf).
wake s., ~ up v.i. & t., st. wachen; aufwachen; aufwecken; ~ s. Wachen n.; Kirmes f.; Kielwasser n.
wakeful a., ~ly adv. wachsam.
waken v.t. aufwecken; ~ v.i. wachen, aufwachen.
walk v.t. & i. (im Schritte) gehen; spazierengehen; im Schritt gehen lassen; ~ s. Gang, Schritt m.; Spaziergang m.; Allee f.; (Schaf-) Weide f.
walker s. Fussgänger, Spaziergänger m.
walking-dress s. Strassenkleid n.
walking-tour s. Fusstour f.
walking wounded a. & s. Gehverwundete m.
walk of life s. Lebensstellung f.
walk-over s. leichte Sieg m.
wall s. Wand, Mauer f.; ~ v.t. ummauern; befestigen.
wallet s. Tasche f., Felleisen n.; Brieftasche f.
wallflower s. (bot.) Goldlack m.; (fig.) Mauerblümchen n.
wallop v.t. prügeln.
wallow v.i. sich wälzen.
wallpaper s. Tapete f.
wall-table s. Wandtafel f.
walnut s. Walnuss f.
walrus s. Walross n.
waltz s. Walzer m.; ~ v.i. walzen.
wan a. blass, bleich.
wand s. Stab m.; Gerte f.
wander v.i. wandern; abschweifen, irre reden.
wane v.i. abnehmen, welken; ~ s. Abnahme f., Verfall m.
want v.t. nötig haben, brauchen, Mangel; haben (an); wollen; wünschen; ~ v.i. mangeln, fehlen; ~ s. Bedürfnis n.; Mangel m.; Not f.
wanting s. Mangel m.; Bedürfnis n.; ~ a. mangelnd, fehlend.
wanton a., ~ly adv. üppig, ausgelassen, mutwillig; zwecklos; liederlich, heil; ~ s. liederliche Person f.; ~ v.i. schäkern, schwärmen.
wantonness s. Mutwille m.; Geilheit f.; Üppigkeit f.; Zwecklosigkeit f.
war s. Krieg m.; ~ v.i. Krieg führen.
warble v.t. & i. wirbeln; trillern.
warbler s. Sänger m.; Singvogel m.
war-blinded a. & s. Kriegsblinde m.
war-bonus s. Kriegszulage f.

war-clause s. Kriegsklausel f.
war-cry s. Kriegsruf, Schlachtruf m.
ward s. Gewahrsam m.; Vormundschaft f.; Stadtbezirk m.; Mündel f.; (Hospital-)Saal m.; ~ v.t. bewachen; abwehren.
warden s. Aufseher m.
warder s. Wächter, Hüter, Wärter m.
wardress s. Gefängniswärterin f.
wardrobe s. Kleiderschrank m.
ward-room s. (nav.) Offiziersmesse f.
wardship s. Vormundschaft f.; Minderjährigkeit f.
ware s. Ware f., Geschirr n.
warehouse s. Warenlager, Magazin n.; ~ clerk s. Lagerist m.; ~ v.t. aufspeichern.
war-effort s. Kriegseinsatz m.
warfare s. Kriegsführung f.; rules of land ~, Landkriegsordnung f.
war guilt s. Kriegsschuld f.
warlike a. kriegerisch, Kriegs...
warm a., ~ly adv. warm; eifrig; feurig, hitzig; ~ v.t. (v.i. sich) erwärmen.
war memorial s. Kriegerdenkmal n.
warmonger s. Kriegshetzer m.
warmth s. Wärme f.; Eifer m.
warn v.t. warnen, ermahnen; ankündigen, wissen lassen.
warning s. Warnung f.; Kündigung f.; Bescheid m.; at a minute's ~, fristlos.
war-office s. Kriegsministerium n.
warp v.i. sich werfen (vom Holz); abweichen; ~ v.t. krümmen; ~ s. Weberkette f.; Krümmung f.
warrant s. Vollmacht f.; Bürgschaft f.; Haftbefehl m.; Lagerschein m.; Gewähr f.; ~ officer, Deckoffizier m.; Feldwebelleutnant m.; ~ v.t. Gewähr leisten, verbürgen, rechtfertigen.
warrantable a., ~bly adv. zu verantworten; billigerweise.
warranty s. Gewährleistung f.; Vollmacht f.; Sicherheit f.
warren s. Kaninchengehege n.
warrior s. Krieger m.
war-risk s. Kriegsrisiko n.
wart s. Warze f.
wary a. vorsichtig; schlau.
wash v.t. & i. (sich) waschen; bespülen; ~ s. Wäsche f.; Wellenschlag m.; Schwemmland n.; Anstrich m.; Tusche f.; Spülwasser n.; ~-basin s. Waschbecken n.; ~-day s. Waschtag m.; ~-house s. Waschhaus n.; ~ out s. Unterspülung f.; ~ tub s. Waschfass n.; ~ up s. Aufwaschen n.; ~ing things pl. Waschzeug n.; ~ing powder s. Waschpulver n.
washable a. waschbar.
wash-bill s. Waschzettel m.
washer s. Wäscher(in) m.(f.); Dichtungsring m.
washerwoman s. Wäscherin f.

washing s. Waschen n.; Wäsche f.
wash(ing)stand s. Waschtisch m.
wasp s. Wespe f.
waspish a., ~ly adv. reizbar, zänkisch.
wastage s. Vergeudung f.
waste v.t. verwüsten, zerstören; verschwenden; ~ v.i. abnehmen; schwinden; ~ a. verwüstet, öde; unnütz; ~ s. Verwüstung f.; Abnahme f.; Auszehrung f.; Einöde f.; Vergeudung f.; Abfall m.; ~ of time, Zeitvergeudung f.; ~ land s. Ödland n.; ~ product s. Abfallprodukt n.; ~ (water) s. Abwasser n.
waste-book s. Kladde f.
wasteful a., ~ly adv. verschwenderisch.
waste-paper s. Makulatur f.; ~ basket, Papierkorb m.
waste-pipe s. Abzugsrohr n.
wastrel s. Tunichtgut m.
watch s. Wache, Wachsamkeit f.; Posten m.; Taschenuhr f.; ~ v.t. bewachen; beobachten; abpassen; ~ v.i. wachen.
watchband, watchbracelet s. Uhrenarmband n.
watch-case s. Uhrgehäuse n.
watchful a., ~ly adv. wachsam.
watchglass s. Uhrglas n.
watch-maker s. Uhrmacher m.
watchman s. Nachtwächter m.
watchstrap s. Lederuhrband m.
watchword s. Losung f.
water s. Wasser n.; to make ~, sein Wasser abschlagen; ~s pl. (Heil) Brunnen m.; ~ v.t. wässern, begiessen, tränken; to ~ milk, Milch pantschen; ~ing-can s. Giesskanne f.
watercart s. Sprengwagen m.
water-closet s. Wasserklosett n.
water-colour s. Aquarell n.
water-colourist s. Aquarellist m.
water-cress s. Brunnenkresse f.
waterfall s. Wasserfall m.
water-fowl s. Wassergeflügel n.
water-gauge s. Wasserstandzeiger m.
water-glass s. Wasserglas n.
watering-place s. Badeort m.
water-level s. Wasserstand m.
water-lily s. Seerose f.
waterlogged a. wasserdurchtränkt.
water-melon s. Wassermelone f.
water-pipe s. Wasserrohr n.
water-proof a. wasserdicht; ~ s. Regenmantel m.
waterman s. Bootsführer m.
water-mark s. Wasserzeichen n.
water-power s. Wasserkraft f.
water-rate s. Wassergeld n.
water-shed s. Wasserscheide f.
water-spout s. Dachtraufe f.
water-supply s. Wasserversorgung f.
water-tight a. wasserdicht.
water-tower s. Wasserturm m.
waterways pl. Wasserstrassen pl.

water-works s. Wasserwerk n.
watery a. wässerig, wasserreich.
watt s. (elek.) Watt n.
wattage s. elektrische Leistung f.
wattle s. Bart (des Hahns) m.; Hürde f.
wave s. Welle, Woge f.; ~ v.i. wogen winken; ~ v.t. schwingen.
wave-band s. (radio) Wellenband n.
wavelength s. (radio) Wellenlänge f.
waver v.i. schwanken.
wavy a. wogend; wellig.
wax s. Wachs n.; Siegellack n.; Ohrenschmalz n.; Schusterpech n.; ~ v.t. wichsen, bohnern.
wax v.i. wachsen, zunehmen; werden.
waxen a. wächsern, Wachs...
waxwork s. Wachsfiguren pl.
waxy a. wachsartig.
way s. Weg m.; Richtung f.; Bahn f.; Art und Weise f.; Verfahren n.; Mittel n.; ~s pl. Benehmen n.; the ~ out, Ausgang m., Ausweg m.; right of ~, Wegerecht n.; by the ~, beiläufig, übrigens; by ~ of excuse, als Entschuldigung; this ~, so, auf diese Weise; this ~ or that, so oder so; to make ~ for, ausweichen; to lead the ~, vorgehen, vorangehen; to lose one's ~, sich verlaufen; to find one's ~, sich zurechtfinden; on his ~, under ~, unterwegs.
way-bill s. Beförderungsschein m.
wayfarer s. Wanderer, Reisende m.
waylay v.t.ir. auflauern, nachstellen.
wayside s. Seite (f.) des Weges; by the ~, am Wege.
wayward a., ~ly adv. eigensinnig.
we pn. wir.
weak a. schwach, schwächlich.
weak current s. (elek.) Schwachstrom m.
weaken v.t. schwächen, entkräften.
weakling s. Schwächling m.
weakly a. & adv. schwächlich.
weakness s. Schwäche, Schwachheit f.
weal s. Glück n.; Wohlfahrt f.
wealth s. Wohlstand m.
wealthy a., ~ily adv. wohlhabend, reich.
wean v.t. entwöhnen; abgewöhnen.
weapon s. Waffe f.; Wehr f.
wear v.t.st. tragen; anhaben; ~ v.i. sich tragen; to ~ off, sich abnutzen, sich verlieren; to ~ out, abtragen; ~ s. Tragen f.; Abnutzung f.; Tracht f.; Anzug m.; ~ and tear, Abnutzung f.; hard ~, starke Beanspruchung f.; to have longer ~, länger halten; resistance to ~, Strapazierfähigkeit f.; ~ing apparel s. Kleidungsstücke pl.
wearisome a., ~ly adv. langweilig, ermüdend.
weary a., ~ily adv. müde, matt; überdrüssig; ~ v.t. ermüden; belästigen; ~ v.i. müde werden.
weasel s. Wiesel n.

weather s. Wetter n.; Witterung f.; ~ bureau s. Wetterwarte f.; ~ outlook, Wetteraussichten pl.; ~ permitting, bei gutem Wetter; ~ v.t. der Luft aussetzen, lüften; widerstehen; umschiffen.
weather-beaten a. abgehärtet; von Wind und Wetter mitgenommen.
weather-cock s. Wetterhahn m.
weather-forecast s. Wetterbericht m.
weatherproof a. wetterfest; ~ v.t. wetterfest machen.
weave v.t. & i.st. weben, flechten.
weaver s. Weber m.
web s. Gewebe n.; Schwimmhaut f.
web-footed a. mit Schwimmfüssen.
wed v.t. & i. heiraten; (fig.) eng verbinden.
wedding s. Hochzeit f.; ~-ring, Trauring m.
wedge s. Keil m.; ~ v.t. (ver)keilen; durchzwängen.
wedlock s. Ehe f.; Ehestand m.
Wednesday s. Mittwoch m.
wee a. winzig, klein.
weed s. Unkraut n.; ~s pl. weibliche Trauerkleider n.pl.; ~ v.t. jäten.
weedy a. voll Unkraut.
week s. Woche f.; to-morrow ~, morgen über acht Tage; yesterday ~, gestern vor acht Tagen.
week-day s. Wochentag m.
week-end s. Wochenende n.
weekly a. & adv. wöchentlich; ~ s. Wochenblatt n.
weep v.i. & t.ir. weinen; beweinen.
weeping-willow s. Trauerweide f.
weevil s. Kornwurm m.
weft s. Gewebe n.; Einschlag m.
weigh v.t. wiegen, wägen, erwägen; schätzen; to ~ out, auswiegen; ~ v.i. wiegen, (nieder)drücken.
weigh-bridge s. Brückenwaage f.
weighing-machine s. Hebelwaage f.
weight s. Gewicht n.; Wucht f.; Schwergewicht n.; Nachdruck m.; ~ v.t. beschweren; to carry ~ with, viel gelten bei; to lose ~, abnehmen.
weighty a., ~ily adv. gewichtig; schwer.
weir s. Wehr n.
weird a. Schicksals...; unheimlich.
welcome a. & i. willkommen; ~ s. Willkomm m.; to bid ~, willkommen heissen; ~ v.t. bewillkommnen; you are ~, (Am.) bitte!
weld v.t. zusammenschweissen.
welfare s. Wohlfahrt f.; ~ officer s. Fürsorgebeamter m.; ~ work s. Fürsorge, soziale Wohlfahrt f.
well s. Quelle f.; Brunnen m.; ~s pl. Heilquelle f.; ~ v.i. quellen; ~ a. & adv. wohl, gut; gesund; leicht; gern; as ~ as, so wohl als auch.
well-appointed a. gut ausgestattet.

well-authenticated a. wohlverbürgt.
well-being s. Wohlsein n.
well-bred a. wohlerzogen, höflich.
well-done a. 'durch' (Braten).
well-groomed a. von gepflegtem Äusseren.
well-nigh adv. beinahe.
well-off, well-to-do a. wohlhabend.
well-wisher s. Gönner, Freund m.
Welsh a. wallisisch; **~-rabbit** s. Käse auf geröstetem Brot m.; **~** v.i. durchbrennen.
welt s. Rand m.; Rahmen m.; **~** v.t. einfassen.
welter v.i. sich wälzen; **~** s. Wirrwarr m.
wen s. Fleischgeschwulst f.
wench s. Mädchen n.; Dirne f.
wend v.i. & t. gehen, (sich) wenden.
werewolf s. Werwolf m.
west s. Westen, Abend m.; **~** a. & adv. westlich.
westerly, western a. westlich.
westerner s. (Am.) Westländer m.
westward a., **~ly** adv. westwärts.
wet a. nass, feucht, regnerisch; **~** paint!, frisch gestrichen!; **~** s. Nässe f.; **~** v.t. nässen, anfeuchten.
wether s. Hammel, Schöps m.
wet-nurse s. Amme f.
whack v.t. tüchtig schlagen, prügeln.
whale s. Walfisch m.
whalebone s. Fischbein n.
whaler s. Walfischfänger m.
whale-oil s. Tran m.
wharf s. Kai m.; Landeplatz m.
wharfage s. Kaigeld n.
wharfinger s. Kaimeister m.
what pn. was; welcher, welches; was für ein; **~...,** teils... teils.
what(so)ever pn. was auch immer.
wheat s. Weizen m.
wheaten a. Weizen...
wheedle v.t. schmeicheln; beschwatzen.
wheel s. Rad, Spinnrad n.; Töpferscheibe f.; (mil.) Schwenkung f.; **~** v.t. (v.i. sich) drehen, rollen; (mil.) schwenken, einschwenken; fahren (v.t.); right **~**!, (mil.) rechts schwenkt!; left **~**!, (mil.) links schwenkt!
wheelbarrow s. Schubkarren m.
wheelchair s. Fahrstuhl, Rollstuhl m.
wheel-wright s. Wagenbauer m.
wheeze v.i. keuchen, schnaufen, röcheln.
whelp s. Junge n.; junge Hund m.; **~** v.i. Junge werfen.
when adv. & c. wenn, wann, da, als; wo.
whence adv. woher, von wo.
where adv. wo, wohin; **~about,** wo herum; worüber; **~s** pl. Aufenthalt m.; **~as,** da, doch, während; **~at,** wobei, woran, worauf; **~by,** wodurch, womit; **~fore,** weshalb, wofür; **~in,** worin; **~into,** worin; **~of,** wovon, woraus; **~on,**

woran, worauf; **~so, ~soever,** wo auch immer; **~to, wozu, worauf; ~upon,** worauf; **~with,** womit; **~withal,** womit auch; **~** s. Nötige n., Mittel n.pl.
wherever adv. wo immer, überall wo.
wherry s. Fährboot n.
whet v.t. wetzen.
whether c. ob.
whetstone s. Wetzstein, Schleifstein m.
whey s. Molken f.pl.
which pn. welcher, welche, welches; wer, was; der, die, das.
which(so)ever pn. welcher auch immer, was auch.
whiff s. Hauch, Paff m.
Whig s. Whig, Liberaler m.
while s. Weile, Zeit, f.; **~** v.t. verbringen, vertreiben.
while, whilst c. indem, während, solange (als).
whim s. Grille f.; Einfall m.; Göpel m.
whimper v.i. winseln.
whimsical a., **~ly** adv. grillenhaft.
whine v.i. weinen, wimmern; **~** s. Gewimmer n.
whip s. Peitsche, Geissel f.; (Parlament) Einpeitscher m.; Aufforderung (f.) an Parteimitglieder im Parlament; **~** v.t. peitschen, geisseln; übernähen; **~** v.i. springen, flitzen; **~ped cream** s. Schlagsahne f., Schlagrahm m.
whip-hand s. Oberhand f.
whippet s. Art Windhund m.
whipping s. Tracht Prügel f.; **~-top,** Kreisel m.
whir(r) v.i. schwirren.
whirl s. Wirbel, Strudel m.; **~** v.t. wirbeln; **~** v.i. herumwirbeln.
whirligig s. Kreisel m.; Karussell n.
whirl-pool s. Strudel, Wirbel m.
whirlwind s. Wirbelwind m.
whisk s. kleine Besen, Wisch m.; Kehrbürste f.; **~** v.t. kehren, wischen; **~** v.i. schwirren, huschen.
whisker s. Backenbart m.
whisky s. Whisky m.
whisper v.t. & i. wispern, flüstern; zuraunen; **~** s. Geflüster n.
whist! i. bst; **~** a. still; **~** s. Whist(spiel) n.
whist-drive s. Whistturnier n.
whistle v.i. & t. pfeifen; **~** s. Pfeifen n.; Pfiff m.; Pfeife f.
whit s. Punkt m.; Kleinigkeit f.; not a **~,** nicht im geringsten.
white a. weiss; bleich; rein; **~** horse, Schimmel m.
whitebait s. Stint m.
white-heat s. Weissglühhitze f.
white-hot a. weissglühend.
white-lead s. Bleiweiss n.
whiten v.t. weissen; bleichen.
whiteness s. Blässe f.; Reinheit f.
whitepaper s. Weissbuch n.

white-wash s. Tünche f.; ~ v.t. weissen, tünchen; weiss waschen.
whither adv. wohin; ~soever, wohin auch.
whiting s. Weissling (Fisch) m.; Kreide f.
whitish a. weisslich, etwas blass.
whitlow s. Nagelgeschwür n.
Whitsunday s. Pfingstsonntag m.
Whitsuntide s. Pfingstzeit f.
whittle v.t. schneiden; schnitzeln.
whiz v.i. zischen, sausen, schwirren; ~ s. Zischen, Sausen n.
who pn. wer; welcher; der, die, das; Who's Who?, Wer ist's?
whoever pn. wer auch (immer); jeder.
whole a. ganz; heil, gesund; ~ number, ganze Zahl f.; ~ s. Ganze n.; on the ~, im Ganzen.
wholehearted a., ~ly adv. mit ganzem Herzen.
wholelength a. in Lebensgrösse f.
whole-meal s. Vollkorn....
wholesale a. Gross..., im grossen, Grosshandels...; ~ s. Grosshandel m.; ~ a. im grossen.
wholesome a., ~ly adv. gesund, heilsam.
wholly adv. gänzlich, völlig.
whoop s. Jagdgeschrei n.
whooping-cough s. Keuchhusten m.
whore s. Hure f.
whorl s. Quirl m.; Windung f.
whortleberry s. Heidelbeere f.
whose pn. dessen, deren; wessen.
whosoever pn. wer auch (immer).
why adv. warum; ~! i. ei! nun, ja, doch.
wick s. Docht m.; Dorf n. (in Zus).
wicked a., ~ly adv. gottlos, verrucht.
wickedness s. Gottlosigkeit, Bosheit f.
wicker s. Weidenzweig m.; ~ a. aus Zweigen geflochten, Korb..., Weiden ...
wickerwork s. Korbflechtwaren pl.; wicker furniture s. Korbmöbel pl.
wicket s. Pförtchen n.; Schalter m.; ~s pl. Tor n. (beim Kricket).
wide a., ~ly adv. weit; breit; fern; sehr; far and ~, weit und breit.
wide-awake s. ganz wach; pfiffig.
widen v.t. (v.i. sich) erweitern.
widespread a. weit verbreitet.
widow s. Witwe f.; ~ v.t. zur Witwe machen.
widowed a. verwitwet.
widower s. Witwer m.
widowhood s. Witwenstand m.
width s. Weite, Breite f.
wield v.t. handhaben; schwingen.
wife s. Frau f.; Weib n.; Ehefrau f.
wifely a. frauenhaft.
wig s. Perücke f.
wight s. Wicht, Kerl m.
wigwam s. Indianhütte f.
wild a., ~ly adv. wild.
wildcat a. schwindelhaft, abenteuerlich.

wilderness s. Wildnis f.
wildfire s. Lauffeuer n.
wile s. List, Tücke f.; Streich m.
wilful a., eigensinnig; vorsätzlich.
will s. Wille m.; Testament n.; ~ v.t.ir. wollen; pflegen; ~ v.i. letzwillig verfügen.
willed a. gesonnen, geneigt.
willing a., ~ly adv. willig; gern.
willingness s. Bereitwilligkeit f.
will-o'-the-wisp, Irrlicht n.
willow s. Weide f.; (mech.) Wolf m.
willy-nilly adv. wohl oder übel.
wilt v.i. welken.
wily a. schlau, verschmitzt.
wimple s. Nonnenhaube f.
win v.t. & i.st. gewinnen; einnehmen; siegen; erobern; to ~ over, gewinnen für.
wince v.i. zucken; zurückfahren.
winch s. Kurbel f.; Winde f., Kran m.
wind s. Wind m.; Atem m.; ~ v.t.st. winden, wickeln; drehen, wenden; to ~ up, aufziehen (Uhr); liquidieren (Geschäfte).
windbag s. (fig.) Schaumschläger m.
windfall s. Fallobst n.; Glücksfall m.
winding s. Windung, Krümmung f.; (elek.) Wickelung f.; ~ a. gewunden; ~-sheet s. Leichentuch n.; ~-stairs s.pl. Wendeltreppe f.
wind-instrument s. Blasinstrument n.
windlass s. Winde f., Haspel m.
windmill s. Windmühle f.
window s. Fenster n.; ~ cleaner s. Fensterputzer m.; ~ dresser s. Schaufensterdekorateur m.; ~ dressing, Schaufensterdekoration f., Aufmachung f.; ~ replacement fabrics pl. Fensterglasersatz m.
windpipe s. Luftröhre f.
windscreen, windshield s. (mot.) Windscheibe f.; ~-wiper s. Scheibenwischer m.
windy a. windig; nichtig.
wine s. Wein m.
wine-bibber s. Weinsäufer m.
wine-press s. Kelter f.
wing s. Flügel m.; Schwinge f.; Kulisse f.; (avi.) Tragfläche f.; (avi.) Geschwader n.; ~-commander s. Geschwaderkommandeur m.; on the ~, im Fluge; ~ v.t. beflügeln; ~ v.i. fliegen.
winged a. geflügelt, schnell.
wink s. Blinzeln n.; ~ v.i. (zu-)blinzeln; ein Auge zudrücken bei.
winner s. Gewinner m.; Sieger m.
winning p. & a. gewinnend, einnehmend; ~ s. Gewinn m.
winnow v.t. schwingen, worfeln; sichten.
winsome a. gefällig, anziehend.
winter s. Winter m.
winterly, wintry a. winterlich.

wipe *v.t.* wischen, wegwischen; abtrocknen; *to ~ out*, (*mil.*) vernichten; *~ s.* Wischen *n.*

wire *s.* Draht *m.*; Drahtnachricht *f.*; *~ v.t.* drahten; *~-brush s.* Drahtbürste *f.*; *~-entanglement s.* Drahtverhau *m.*; *~- netting s.* Drahtgeflecht *n.*; *~-rope s.* Drahtseil *n.*

wiredraw *v.i.* Draht ziehen; (*fig.*) in die Länge ziehen.

wireless *a.* drahtlos; *~ v.i.* funken; *~ s.* Rundfunk *m.*, Radio *n.*; *by ~*, durch Rundfunk; *on the ~*, im Rundfunk, im Radio; *~ message*, Funkspruch *m.*; *~ operator*, Funker *m.*; *~ set*, Radioapparat *m.*; *~ telegraphy*, drahtlose, Funk-telegraphie *f.*; *~ station*, Funkspruchstation *f.*, Radiostation *f.*

wire-puller *s.* Marionettenspieler *m.*; (*fig.*) Drahtzieher *m.*

wire-pulling *s.* heimliche Umtriebe *pl.*

wiry *a.* aus Draht; zäh, sehnig.

wisdom *s.* Weisheit, Klugheit *f.*

wise *a.* weise; verständig, erfahren.

wiseacre *s.* Klugtuer *m.*

wish *v.t. & i.* wünschen; *~ s.* Wunsch *m.*

wishful *a.*, *~ly adv.* wünschend, sehnlich; *~ thinking*, Wunschtraum *m.*

wishy-washy *a.* wässerig; (*fig.*) dünn.

wisp *s.* Bündel *n.*; Wisch *m.*

wistful *a.*, *~ly adv.* sehnsüchtig.

wit *s.* Witz *m.*; Geist *m.*; witzige Kopf *m.*; *to ~*, nämlich, das heisst; *to be at one's ~'s end*, nicht mehr ein und aus wissen.

witch *s.* Heze, Zauberin *f.*

witchcraft *s.* Hexerei *f.*

with *pr.* mit, samt, bei, für, auf, an.

withal *adv.* zugleich, übrigens, auch.

withdraw *v.t.st.* zurücknehmen, zurückziehen; abberufen; (Geld) abheben; *~ v.i.* sich zurückziehen.

withdrawal *s.* Zurückziehung, Zurücknahme *f.*

wither *v.t. & i.* ausdörren, verwelken, vertrocknen, vergehen; vernichten.

withers *s.pl.* Widerrist *m.*

withhold *v.t.st.* zurückhalten; vorenthalten; verhindern.

within *pr.* in, innerhalb, binnen; *~ adv.* drinnen, im Innern.

without *pr.* ausserhalb, vor; ohne; *~ adv.* ausserhalb; draussen.

withstand *v.t.st.* widerstehen.

witness *s.* Zeugnis *n.*; Zeuge *m.*; *~ box*, Zeugenbank *f.*; *to bear ~*, Zeugnis ablegen; *to take the ~ stand*, in den Zeugenstand treten; *~ for the prosecution*, Belastungszeuge *m.*; *~ for the defence*, Entlastungszeuge *m.*; *~ summons*, Zeugenvorladung *f.*; *~ v.t.* bezeugen; zugegen sein, erleben.

witticism *s.* Witz *m.*, Witzelei *f.*

wittingly *adv.* wissentlich, vorsätzlich.

witty *a.*, *~ily adv.* witzig; geistreich.

wizard *s.* Zauberer *m.*

wizened *a.* verschrumpft, vertrocknet.

woad *s.* Waid *m.*

wobble *v.i.* wackeln.

woe *s.* Weh *n.*; *~! i.* weh!

woeful *a.*, *~ly adv.* traurig; erbärmlich.

wolf *s.* Wolf *m.*

wolfish *a.* wölfisch, gefrässig.

wolfram *s.* Wolfram(erz) *n.*

woman *s.* Frau *f.*

womanhood *s.* Weiblichkeit *f.*

womanish *a.*, *~ly adv.* weibisch.

womankind *s.* weibliche Geschlecht *n.*

womanly *a.* weiblich.

womb *s.* Mutterleib, Schoss *m.*

wonder *s.* Wunder *n.*; Verwunderung *f.*; *~ v.i.* sich wundern; gern wissen mögen.

wonderful *a.*, *~ly adv.* wunderbar.

wonder-struck *a.* höchst erstaunt.

wondrous *a.*, *~ly adv.* wunderbar, ausserordentlich.

won't = will not.

wont *s.* Gewohnheit *f.*; *use and ~*, feste Gebrauch *m.*; *~ a.* gewöhnt.

wonted *a.* gewohnt; gewöhnlich.

woo *v.t. & i.* freien, werben; zustreben.

wood *s.* Wald *m.*; Holz *n.*

wood-bine *s.* Geissblatt *n.*

wood-carver *s.* Holzschnitzer *m.*

wood-carving *s.* Holzschnitzerei *f.*

wood-cock *s.* Waldschnepfe *f.*

wood-cut *s.* Holzschnitt *m.*

wooded *a.* holzreich, waldig.

wooden *a.* hölzern; (*fig.*) steif.

wood-engraver *s.* Holzschneider *m.*

wood-land *s.* Waldung *f.*

wood-lark *s.* Heidelerche *f.*

wood-louse *s.* Assel *f.*

woodman *s.* Holzhacker *m.*; Förster *m.*

wood-pecker *s.* Specht *m.*

woodpulp *s.* Holzzellstoff *m.*

wood-ruff *s.* Waldmeister (Pflanze) *m.*

woodshaving *s.* Holzspan *m.*

wood-shed *s.* Holzschuppen *m.*

woodwool *s.* Holzwolle *f.*

woodwork *s.* Holzarbeit *f.*; Holzwerk *n.*; Täfelung *f.*

woodworker *s.* Holzarbeiter *m.*

woody *a.* waldig, holzig.

wooer *s.* Freier, Bewerber *m.*

woof *s.* Einschlag *m.*; Gewebe *n.*

wool *s.* Wolle *f.*

wool-comber *s.* Wollkämmer *m.*

wool-gathering *a.* zerstreut.

woollen *a.* wollen; *~-draper s.* Tuchhändler *m.*; *~s s.pl.* Wollwaren *f.pl.*

woolly *a.* wollig; verworren, unklar.

word *s.* Wort *n.*; Nachricht *f.*; *~ for ~*, Wort für Wort; *in other ~s*, mit anderen Worten; *~ v.t.* in Worte fassen.

wording *s.* Fassung *f.*; Stil *m.*

wordy *a.* wortreich.

work *s.* Arbeit *f.*; Werk *n.*; Getriebe *n.*; Handarbeit *f.*; *hours of* ~, Arbeitsstunden *pl.*; ~-bag, Arbeitsbeutel *m.*, ~-basket, Arbeitskorb *m.*, ~-box, Arbeitskästchen *n.* (Handarbeit); ~-order *s.* Werkstattauftrag *m.*; ~-permit *s.* Arbeitserlaubnis *f.*; ~s *pl.* Fabrik *f.*, Werk *n.*; Getriebe, Werk *n.* (Uhr, Klavier); Schriften *f.pl.*; ~ *v.i.* arbeiten; wirken; gären; funktionieren; ~ *v.t.* bearbeiten; behandeln; arbeiten lassen; in Betrieb haben; bedienen (Handwerkzeug), arbeiten mit; *to* ~ *out*, berechnen; *to* ~ *out at*, kommen auf; *to* ~ *up*, aufarbeiten, verarbeiten.

workable *a.* zu bearbeiten.

workaday *a.* Alltags...

worker *s.* Arbeiter(in) *m.* (*f.*); *heavy* ~, Schwerarbeiter *m.*

workhouse *s.* Armenhaus *n.*

working *a.* Arbeits...; ~ *capacity*, Leistungsfähigkeit *f.*; ~ *capital*, Betriebskapital *n.*; ~-day *s.* Arbeitstag *m.*; ~ *expenses pl.* Betriebsunkosten *pl.*; ~ *hours pl.* Arbeitsstunden *pl.*; ~ *majority*, arbeitsfähige Mehrheit *f.*; ~ *partner*, aktive Teilhaber *m.*

workman *s.* Arbeiter *m.*; ~'s *ticket s.* (*rail*) Arbeiterkarte *f.*

workmanship *s.* Werk *n.*; Arbeit *f.*; Geschicklichkeit *f.*; Stil *m.*

workshop *s.* Werkstatt *f.*

world *s.* Welt *f.*; Erde *f.*; Menge *f.*

worldling *s.* Weltkind *n.*

worldly *a.* weltlich, irdisch; Welt...

world-wide *a.* weitverbreitet.

worm *s.* Wurm *m.*; Gewinde *n.*; ~ *v.t. & i.* wühlen, bohren; sichein schleichen.

worm-eaten *a.* wurmstichig.

wormgear *s.* (*mech.*) Schneckenrad *n.*

wormwood *s.* Wermut *m.*

worn-out *a.* abgenutzt; zerrüttet.

worry *v.t.* würgen, zerren; ängstigen, plagen; ~ *s.* Quälerei *f.*, Sorge *f.*

worse *a. & adv.* schlechter, schlimmer, ärger; *the* ~, desto schlimmer.

worship *s.* Verehrung *f.*; Ehrerbietung *f.*; Gottesdienst *m.*; ~ *v.t. & i.* verehren; anbeten.

worshipful *a.*, ~ly *adv.* ehrwürdig; ehrenfest.

worshipper *s.* Anbeter, Verehrer *m.*; Andächtige *m.*

worst *a. & adv.* schlechtest, schlimmst; ~ *s.* Schlimmste, Ärgste *n.*; *to get the* ~ *of it*, den kürzeren ziehen; *if the* ~ *comes to the* ~, wenn alle Stricke reissen; ~ *v.t.* besiegen.

worsted *s.* Wollgarn, Kammgarn *n.*; ~ *a.* wollen.

wort *s.* Kraut *n.*; (Bier) Würze *f.*

worth *s.* Wert *m.*, Verdienst *n.*; ~ *a.* wert, würdig; ~ *while*, der Mühe wert.

worthless *a.* unwürdig; wertlos.

worthy *a.*, ~ily *adv.* würdig.

would *pret.* von *will*, wollte; würde.

would-be *a.* vorgeblich, Schein...; Gerne...

wound *s.* Wunde *f.*; ~ *v.t.* verwunden.

wraith *s.* Gespenst *n.*

wrangle *v.i.* zanken, streiten; ~ *s.* Zank, Streit *m.*

wrap *v.t.* wickeln, einwickeln.

wrapper *s.* Umschlagetuch *n.*; Hülle *f.*; Kreuzband *n.*; Deckblatt *n.*

wrapping *s.* Verpackung *f.*

wrapping-paper *s.* Packpapier *n.*

wrath *s.* Zorn, Grimm *m.*

wrathful *a.*, *adv.* zornig, grimmig.

wreak *v.t.* rächen; (ver)üben.

wreath *s.* Gewinde *n.*; Flechte *f.*; Locke *f.*; Kranz *m.*; ~ *v.t.* flechten winden, bekränzen; ~ *v.i.* sich ringeln.

wreck *s.* Schiffbruch *m.*; Wrack *n.*; Verwüstung *f.*; Strandgut *n.*; ~ *v.t. & i.* zertrümmern; zum Scheitern bringen; scheitern.

wreckage *s.* Schifftrümmer *pl.*

wren *s.* Zaunkönig *m.*

wrench *v.t.* heftig ziehen, entwinden; verrenken; ~ *s.* Ruck *m.*; Verrenkung *f.*; Schraubenschlüssel *m.*

wrest *v.t.* drehen, zerren; (ent)reissen; verdrehen; ~ *s.* Stimmhammer *m.*

wrestle *v.i.* ringen, kämpfen.

wrestling *s.* Ringkampf *m.*

wretch *s.* Elende *m.*; Schuft *m.*

wretched *a.*, ~ly *adv.* unglücklich, elend.

wriggle *v.i.* sich biegen, sich winden.

wright *s.* Arbeiter *m.*;...macher *m.*

wring *v.t.st.* (*v.i. sich*) winden, ringen; peinigen, bedrücken; auswringen; ~ *s.* Händeringen *n.*

wrinkle *s.* Runzel *f.*; Falte *f.*; Kniff *m.*, Wink *m.*; ~ *v.t.* (*v.i. sich*) runzeln; rümpfen; zerknittern.

wrist *s.* Handgelenk *n.*

wrist-band *s.* Manschette *f.*

wristwatch *s.* Armbanduhr *f.*

writ *s.* Schrift *f.*; Gerichtsbefehl *m.*; Wahlausschreiben *n.*

write *v.t. & i.st.* schreiben; *to* ~ *off*, abschreiben (Schuld); *to* ~ *out*, ausschreiben.

writer *s.* Schriftsteller *m.*

writhe *v.t.* drehen, winden, verdrehen; ~ *v.i.* sich krümmen, sich winden.

writing *s.* Schreiben *n.*; Schrift, Urkunde *f.*; Aufsatz *m.*; Schriftstellerei *f.*; ~-book, Schreibheft *n.*; ~-case, Schreibmappe *f.*; ~-desk, Schreibtisch *m.*; ~-pad, ~-tablet, Schreibblock *m.*; ~-paper, Schreibpapier *n.*; *in* ~, schriftlich.

wrong *a. & adv.*, **~ly** *adv.* unrecht; verkehrt; falsch; *to be ~*, unrecht haben; *~ s.* Unrecht *n.*; Irrtum *m.*; *to put a person in the ~*, einen ins Unrecht setzen; *~ v.t.* unrecht tun, Schaden zufügen; kränken.

wrongful *a.*, **~ly** *adv.* ungerecht.

wrong-headed *a.* verkehrt, starrköpfig.

wroth *a.* zornig.

wrought *p. & a.* gearbeitet; gewirkt; *~ iron*, Schmiedeeisen *n.*

wry *a.*, **~ly** *adv.* krumm, schief, verkehrt.

wry-neck *s.* Wendehals *m.*

X

X-rays *s.pl.* Röntgenstrahlen *m.pl.*; *x-ray tube*, Röntgenröhre *f.*

xylographer *s.* Holzschneider *m.*

Y

yacht *s.* Jacht *f.*; *~ v.i.* mit einer Jacht fahren.

yachtsman *s.* Jachtfahrer *m.*

Yankee *s.* Nordamerikaner *m.*

yard *s.* Hofraum *m.*; englische Elle *f.* (0,914 m.); Rahe *f.*; Werft *f.*

yardstick *s.* Ellenmass *n.*, Ellenstock *m.*

yarn *s.* Garn *n.*; *(fig.)* Erzählung *f.*

yarrow *s.* Schafgarbe (Pflanze) *f.*

yawn *v.i.* gähnen; *~ s.* Gähnen *n.*

ye *pr.* ihr, euch.

yea *adv.* ja, ja doch.

year *s.* Jahr *n.*; *~ by ~*, Jahr um Jahr.

yearbook *s.* Jahrbuch *n.*

yearly *a. & adv.* jährlich.

yearn *v.i.* sich sehnen, verlangen.

yeast *s.* Hefe *f.*

yell *v.i.* gellen, schreien, kreischen; *~ s.* Angstgeschrei, Gellen *n.*

yellow *a.* gelb; *~ fever*, gelbe Fieber *n.*; *~-(h)ammer* *s.* Goldammer *f.*; *~ press*, Massenpresse *f.*; *~ s.* Gelb *n.*

yellowish *a.* gelblich.

yelp *v.i.* kläffen, bellen.

yeoman *s.* Freisasse, Pächter *m.*; *~ of the guard*, Leibgardist *m.*; *~ service*, Hilfe (*f.*) in der Not.

yeomanry *s.* Bauernschaft *f.*; (berittene) Landmiliz *f.*

yes *adv.* ja.

yesterday *adv.* gestern.

yet *c.* doch, dennoch, aber; *~ adv.* noch, sogar; schon; *as ~*, bisher; *not ~*, noch nicht.

yew-tree *s.* Eibe *f.*

yield *v.t.* hergeben; hervorbringen, gestatten; aufgeben, übergeben; abwerfen, einbringen; *~ v.i.* sich ergeben; nachgeben; weichen; *~ s.* Ertrag *m.*

yielding *a.*, **~ly** *adv.* nachgiebig.

yodel *v.i.* jodeln; *~ s.* Jodler *m.*

yoke *s.* Joch *n.*; Paar *n.*; *~ v.t.* zusammenkoppeln.

yokel *s.* dumme Bauer *m.*

yolk *s.* Eidotter *n.*

yon, yonder *a.* jener, jene, jenes; *~ adv.* an jenem Orte, da drüben.

yore *adv.*; *of ~*, ehedem, vormals.

you *pn.* Sie, du, dich, ihr, euch; man, einen.

young *a.* jung; *~ s.* Junge *n.*

youngish *a.* jugendlich.

youngster *s.* junge Bursche *m.*

your *pn.* euer, Ihr, dein.

yours *pn.* euer, eurig, eurige, Ihr, dein, etc.

yourself, yourselves *pn.* euch, euch selbst; ihr selbst, Sie (selbst) etc.

youth *s.* Jugend *f.*; Jüngling *m.*; *~ hostel* *s.* Jugendherberge *f.*

youthful *a.*, **~ly** *adv.* jugendlich.

Yule *s.* Weihnachten *pl.*

Z

zany *s.* Hanswurst *m.*

zeal *s.* Eifer *m.*

zealot *s.* Eiferer, Zelot *m.*

zealous *a.*, **~ly** *adv.* eifrig, warm, innig.

zebra *s.* Zebra *n.*

zenith *s.* Scheitelpunkt, Zenit *m.*

zephir *s.* Zephyr, Westwind *m.*

zero *s.* Null *f.*; Nullpunkt *m.*; *~ hour*, *(mil.)* Nullzeit *f.*, x Uhr.

zest *s.* erhöhte Geschmack, Genuss *m.*; Eifer *m.*

zigzag *s.* Zickzack *n.*

zink *s.* Zink *n.*

zip-fastener *s.* Reissverschluss *m.*

zither *s.* Zither *f.*

zodiac *s.* Tierkreis *m.*

zonal *a.* Zonen...

zone *s.* Gürtel *m.*; Erdstrich *m.*; Gebiet *n.*, Zone *f.*; *~ of the interior* (ZI), *(mil.)* Heimat *n.*; *~ of occupation*, Besatzungszone *f.*; *~ of operations*, Operationsgebiet *n.*

Zoo (=*Zoological Gardens*) *s.* Zoo *m.*

zoological *a.* zoologisch.

zoologist *s.* Zoologe *m.*

zoology *s.* Tierkunde *f.*

zoom *v.i.* Flugzeug hochreissen.

zymotic *a.* Gärungs...; ansteckend; epidemisch.

A List of the more important Geographical Names that differ in the two languages

Abyssinia, Abessinien; Abyssinian, Abessinier, abessinisch.
the Adriatic, das Adriatische Meer.
Ægæan, the ~ Sea, das Ägeische Meer.
Africa, Afrika; African, Afrikaner, afrikanisch.
Aix-la-Chapelle, Aachen.
Albania, Albanien; Albanian, Albanese, albanisch.
Alexandria, Alexandrien.
Algiers, Algier.
the Alps, die Alpen; Alpine, Älpler, Alpen...
Alsace, Elsass; Alsatian, Elsässer, elsässisch.
the Amazon, der Amazonenstrom.
America, Amerika; American, Amerikaner, amerikanisch.
Andalusia, Andalusien; Andalusian, Andalusier, andalusisch.
the Andes, die Anden.
Anglo-Saxon, Angelsachse; angelsächsisch.
the Antilles, die Antillen.
Antioch, Antiochien.
Antwerp, Antwerpen.
the Apennines, die Apenninen.
Arabia, Arabien; Arab, Araber; Arabian, arabisch.
Aragon, Aragonien; Aragonese, Aragonier, aragonisch.
the Ardennes, die Ardennen.
Argentina, Argentinien; Argentine, argentinisch.
Armenia, Armenien; Armenian, Armenier, armenisch.
Asia, Asien; Asiatic, Asiate, asiatisch.
Asia Minor, Kleinasien.
Astrakhan, Astrachan.
Asturias, Asturien; Asturian, Asturier, asturisch.
Athens, Athen; Athenian, Athener, athenisch.
the Atlantic, das Atlantische Meer.
Australia, Australien; Australian, Australier, australisch.
Austria, Österreich; Austrian, Österreicher, österreichisch.
Avon, Avon.
the Azores, die Azoren.

Bale, Basel.
Balearic, the ~ Isles, die Balearen.

Baltic, baltisch.
the Baltic, die Ostsee.
the Barbadoes, die Barbaden Inseln.
Barbary, die Berberei.
Bavaria, Bayern; Bavarian, Bayer, bayrisch.
Belgium, Belgien; Belgian, Belgier, belgisch.
Bengal, Bengalen; Bengali, Bengale bengalisch.
Bessarabia, Bessarabien.
Biscay, Biskaya; Biscayan, Biskayer, biskayisch.
the Black Forest, der Schwarzwald.
the Black Sea, das Schwarze Meer.
Bœotia, Böotien.
Boer, Bur.
Bohemia, Böhmen; Bohemian, Böhme, böhmisch.
Bosnia, Bosnien; Bosnian, Bosnier, bosnisch.
Bothnia, the Gulf of ~, der Bottnische Meerbusen.
Brazil. Brasilien; Brazilian, Brasili(an)er, brasili(ani)sch.
Britain, Great ~, Grossbritannien; British, britisch; Briton, Brite.
Britanny, die Bretagne; Breton, Bretone, bretonisch.
Bruges, Brügge.
Brunswick, Braunschweig.
Brussels, Brüssel.
Bucharia, die Bucharei.
Bulgaria, Bulgarien; Bulgarian, Bulgare, bulgarisch.
Burgundy, Burgund; Burgundian, Burgunder, burgundisch.
Burmah, Birma; Burmese, Birmane, birmanisch.
Byzantium, Byzanz; Byzantine, Byzantiner, byzantinisch.

Cadiz, Cadix, Kadiz.
Caffraria, das Kaffernland.
Caffre (= Kaffir), Kaffer.
Calabria, Kalabrien; Calabrian, Calabrese, Kalabrier, kalabrisch.
California, Kalifornien; Californian, Kalifornier, kalifornisch.
Cameroon, Kamerun.
the Canaries, Canary Islands, die Kanarischen Inseln.
Candian, Kandiot, kretisch.

Caribbee, the ~ Islands, die Karibischen Inseln.
Carinthia, Kärnten.
Carniola, Krain.
the Carpathians, die Karpathen.
Cashmere, Kaschmir.
Caspian, the ~ Sea, das Kaspische Meer.
Castile, Kastilien.
Catalonia, Katalonien; Catalonian, Katalonier, katalonisch.
the Caucasus, der Kaukasus.
Celt, Kelte.
China, China; Chinese, Chinese, chinesisch.
Circassia, Zirkassien; Circassian, Zirkassier, zirkassisch.
Cleves, Kleve.
Cologne, Köln.
Constance, Lake ~, der Bodensee.
Copenhagen, Kopenhagen.
the Cordilleras, die Kordilleren.
Corsican, Korse, korsisch.
Courland, Kurland.
Cossack, Kosak.
Cracow, Krakau.
Crete, Kreta, Kandia; Cretan, Kreter, kretisch.
the Crimea, die Krim.
Croatia, Kroatien; Croatian, Kroate, kroatisch.
Cyprus, Cypern.
Czech, Tscheche.
Czechoslovakia ., die Tschechoslovakei f.

Dalmatia, Dalmatien; Dalmatian, Dalmatiner, dalmatisch.
Dane, Däne; Danish, dänisch.
the Danube, die Donau.
Dauphiny, die Dauphiné.
the Dead Sea, das Tote Meer.
Denmark, Dänemark.
Dunkirk, Dünkirchen.
Dutch, holländisch; the ~, die Holländer; ~man, Holländer.

the East Indies, Ostindien.
Edinburgh, Edinburg.
Egypt, Ägypten; Egyptian, Ägypter, ägyptisch.
England, England; English, englisch; the ~, die Engländer; the ~ Channel, der Ärmelkanal; Englishman, Engländer.
Est(h)onia, Estland; Est(h)onian, Estländer, estnisch.
Europe, Europa; European, Europäer, europäisch.

Flanders, Flandern.
Fleming, Flamländer; Flemish, flämisch.
Florence, Florenz; Florentine, Florentiner, florentinisch.
Flushing, Vlissingen.
France, Frankreich.

Franconia, Franken.
Frankfort, Frankfurt.
French, französisch; the ~, die Franzosen; ~man, Franzose.
Frisian, Friese, friesisch.

Gael, Gäle; Gaelic, gälisch.
Galicia, Galizien; Galician, Galizier, galizisch.
Galilee, Galiläa.
Gascony, die Gascogne; Gascon, Gascogner, gascognisch.
Gaul, Gallien; Gallier.
Geneva, Genf; Genevan, Genevese, Genfer, genferisch.
Genoa, Genua; Genoese, Genuese, genuesisch.
Germany, Deutschland; German, Deutsche, deutsch.
Ghent, Gent.
Greece, Griechenland; Greek, Grieche, griechisch; Grecian, griechisch.
Greenland, Grönland.
the Grisons, Graubünden.
Guelderland, Geldern.
Guelph, Welfe m.

the Hague, der Haag.
Hainault, Hennegau.
Hanover, Hannover; Hanoverian, Hannoveraner, hannöversch.
Hebrew, Hebräer, hebräisch.
the Hebrides, die Hebriden.
Heligoland, Helgoland.
Helvetia, Helvetien, die Schweiz.
Hesse, Hessen; Hessian, Hesse, hessisch.
Hindoo, Hindu.
Hungary, Ungarn; Hungarian, Ungar, ungarisch.

Iceland, Island; Icelander, Isländer; Icelandic, isländisch.
Illyria, Illyrien.
India, Indien; the Indies, Indien; Indian, Inder, indisch.
Ingria, Ingermanland.
Ionia, Ionien; Ionian, Ionier, ionisch.
Ireland, Irland; Irish, irisch; the ~, die Iren, Irländer; Irishman, Ire, Irländer.
Istria, Istrien.
Italy, Italien; Italian, Italiener, italienisch.

Japanese, Japaner, japanisch.
Judea, Judäa.

Kaffir, Kaffer m.

Lapland, Lappland; Lapp, Laplander, Lappe; Lappish, lappländisch.
Latvia, Lettland.
the Lebanon, der Libanon.
the Leeward Isles, die kleinen Antillen.

Leghorn, Livorno.
Leipsic, Leipzig.
Lett, lettisch; the ~, der Lette.
the Levant, die Levante.
Liege, Lüttich.
Lisbon, Lissabon.
Lisle, Lille.
Lithuania, Litauen; Lithuanian, Litauer, litauisch.
Livonia, Livland; Livonian, Livländer, livländisch.
Lombardy, Lombardei; Lombard, Lombarde, lombardisch.
Lorraine, Lothringen.
Louvain, Löwen.
the Low Countries, die Niederlande.
Lucerne, Luzern; the Lake of ~, der Vierwaldstädter See.
Lusatia, die Lausitz; Lusatian, Lausitzer, lausitzisch.
Lyons, Lyon.

Macedonia, Mazedonien; Macedonian, Mazedonier, mazedonisch.
Madeira, Madeira.
Malay, Malaie; malaiisch.
Maltese, Malteser, maltesisch.
Manxman, Bewohner der Insel Man.
the Marches, die Marken.
Marseilles, Marseille.
Mayence, Mainz.
the Mediterranean, das Mittelländische Meer.
Milan, Mailand.
Moldavia, die Moldau.
the Moluccas, die Molukken.
Mongolia, die Mongolei; Mongol, Mongole, mongolisch.
Moor, Maure, Mohr; Moorish, maurisch.
Moravia, Mähren; Moravian, Mähre, mährisch; the Moravian Brethren, die Herrnhuter.
Morocco, Marokko; Moroccan, Marokkaner, marokkanisch.
Moscovy, Moskovien.
Moscow, Moskau.
the Moselle, die Mosel.
Munich, München.

Naples, Neapel; Neapolitan, Neapolitaner, Neapeler, neapolitanisch.
the Netherlands, die Niederlande.
Neu(f)chatel, Neuenburg.
Newfoundland, Neufundland.
Nice, Nizza.
the Nile, der Nil.
Nimeguen, Nimwegen.
Normandy, die Normandie; Norman, Normanne, normannisch.
Norway, Norwegen; Norwegian, Norweger, norwegisch.
Nova Scotia, Neuschottland.

Nubia, Nubien; Nubian, Nubier, nubisch.
Nuremberg, Nürnberg.

Orange, Oranien.
the Orcades or Orkneys, die Orkaden Inseln.
Ostend, Ostende.
Ottoman, the ~ Empire, das Osmanische Reich.
Oxonian, Oxforder.

the Pacific, der Stille Ozean.
the Palatinate, die Pfalz; Palatine, Pfälzer, pfälzisch.
Palestine, Palästina.
Patagonia, Patagonien; Patagonian, Patagonier, patagonisch.
Pennsylvania, Pennsylvanien.
Persia, Persien; Persian, Perser, persisch.
Peruvian, Peruaner, peruanisch.
Piedmont, Piemont; Piedmontese, Piemontese, piemontesisch.
Poland, Polen; Pole, Pole; Polish, polnisch.
Pomerania, Pommern; Pomeranian, Pommer, pommer[i]sch.
Portuguese, Portugiese, portugiesisch.
Prague, Prag.
Prussia, Preussen; Prussian, Preusse, preussisch.
the Pyrenees, die Pyrenäen.

Ratisbon, Regensburg.
Rhenish, rheinisch.
the Rhine, der Rhein.
Rhineland, Rheinland.
Rhodes, Rhodos.
the Rocky Mountains, das Felsengebirge.
Rome, Rom; Roman, Römer, römisch.
R(o)umania, Rumänien; R(o)umanian, Rumäne, rumänisch.
R(o)umelia, Rumelien.
Russia, Russland; Russian, Russe, russisch.

Saracen, Sarazene, sarazenisch.
Sardinia, Sardinien; Sardinian, Sardinier, sardinisch.
Savoy, Savoyen; Savoyard, Savoyarde.
Saxony, Sachsen; Saxon, Sachse, sächsisch.
Scandinavia, Skandinavien; Scandinavian, Skandinavier, skandinavisch.
Scania, Schonen.
the Scheldt, die Schelde.
Scotland, Schottland; Scotch, Scottish, schottisch; the Scotch, Scots, die Schotten; Scotsman, Scot, Schotte.
Serbia, Serbien; Serbian, Serbe, serbisch.
Siberia, Sibirien; Siberian, Sibirier. sibirisch.

Sicily, Sizilien; **Sicilian**, Sizili[an]er, sizili[an]isch.
Silesia, Schlesien; **Silesian**, Schlesier, schlesisch.
Slav, Slave.
Slavonia, Slavonien; **Slavonian**, Slavonier, slavonisch.
the Sound, der Sund.
Spain, Spanien; **Spaniard**, Spanier; Spanish, spanisch.
Spires, Speyer.
Styria, Steiermark; **Styrian**, Steiermärker, stei[e]risch.
Sudetic, the ~ Mountains, die Sudeten.
Swabia, Schwaben; **Swabian**, Schwabe, schwäbisch.
Sweden, Schweden; **Swede**, Schwede; Swedish, schwedisch.
Switzerland, die Schweiz; **Swiss**, Schweizer, schweizerisch.
Syracuse, Syrakus.
Syria, Syrien; **Syrian**, Syr[i]er, syrisch.

the Tagus, der Tajo.
Tangier, Tanger.
Tartary, die Tatarei; **Tartar**, Tatare, tatarisch.
Teuton, Germane, Teutone; **Teutonic**, germanisch.
the Thames, die Themse.
Thermopylæ, die Thermopylen.
Thessaly, Thessalien; **Thessalian**, Thessalier, thessalisch.
Thrace, Thrazien; **Thracian**, Thrazier, thrazisch.
Thuringia, Thüringen; **Thuringian**, Thüringer, thüringisch.
Transylvania, Siebenbürgen.
Trent, Trient.

Treves, Trier.
Troy, Troja; **Trojan**, Trojaner, trojanisch.
Turkey, die Türkei; **Turk**, Türke; Turkish, türkisch.
Tuscany, Toskana; **Tuscan**, Toskaner, toskanisch.
Tyre, Tyrus.
Tyrol, Tirol; **Tyrolese**, Tiroler, tirolisch.

Umbria, Umbrien.
the United States, die Vereinigten Staaten.

Valais, Wallis.
Valtelline, Veltlin.
Vaud, Waadt, Waadtland.
Venice, Venedig; **Venetian**, Venediger, Venezianer, venezianisch.
Vesuvius, der Vesuv.
Vienna, Wien; **Viennese**, Wiener, wienerisch.
the Vistula, die Weichsel.
the Vosges, die Vogesen.

Wallachia, die Wallachei; **Wallachian**, Wallache, wallachisch.
Walloon, Wallone, wallonisch.
Warsaw, Warschau.
Welsh, walisisch; **the ~**, die Waliser.
the West Indies, Westindien; **West Indian**, Westindier, westindisch.
Westphalia, Westfalen; **Westphalian**, Westfale, westfälisch.
Wurtemberg, Württemberg.

Yugoslavia, Jugoslavien.

Zealand, Seeland.
the Zuider Zee, die *or* der Zuidersee.

A List of the more usual Christian Names that differ in the two languages

Adelaide, Adelheid.
Adolphus, Adolf.
Alice, Elschen.
Ambrose, Ambrosius.
Amelia, Amalie.
Andrew, Andreas.
Andy = Andrew.
Ann, Anne, Anna.
Annie, Ännchen.
Anthony, Anton.
Aubr(e)y, Alberich.
Augusta, Auguste.
Augustus, August.
Austin, Augustin.

Baldwin, Balduin.
Barnaby, Barnabas.
Bartholomew, Bartholomäus. Barthel.
Beatrice, Beatrix.
Ben = Benjamin.
Bernard, Bernhard.
Bess, Betsy, Betty = Elizabeth.
Biddy = Bridget.
Bill, Billy = William.
Blanche, Bianka.
Bob, Bobby = Robert.
Bridget, Brigitte.

Caroline, Karoline.
Carrie = Caroline.
Catherine, Katharine.
Cecily, Cäcilie.
Charles, Karl.
Christ, Christus.
Christopher, Christoph.
Cissy = Cecily.
Clement, Klemens.
Clementina, Klementine.
Constance, Konstanze.
Constantine, Konstantin.

Dan = Daniel.
Davy = David.
Dick, Dicky = Richard.
Doll, Dolly = Dorothy.
Dorothy, Dorothea.

Edward, Eduard.
Eleanor, Eleonore.
Eliza = Elizabeth.
Elizabeth, Elisabeth.
Ellen = Eleanor.

Emily, Emilie.
Ernest, Ernst.
Eugene, Eugen.
Eugenia, Eugenie.
Eve, Eva.

Fanny = Frances.
Florence, Florentine.
Frances, Franziska.
Francis, Franz.
Frank = Francis.
Fred = Frederick.
Frederick, Friedrich.

Geoffrey, Gottfried.
George, Georg.
Gerard, Gerhard.
Gerty = Gertrude, Gertrud.
Giles, Ägidius.
Godfrey, Gottfried.
Gregory, Gregor.
Gustavus, Gustav.
Guy, Guido, Veit.

Harriet = Henrietta, Jettchen.
Harry = Henry.
Helen, Helene.
Henrietta, Henriette.
Henry, Heinrich.
Hester = Esther.
Hetty = Henrietta.
Hodge = Roger.
Horace, Horaz.
Hugh, Hugo.
Humphrey, Humfried.

Ignatius, Ignaz.
Isaac, Isaak.

Jack, Johann, Hans.
James, Jakob[us].
Jane, Johanna.
Janet, Hannchen.
Jacqueline, Jakobine.
Jasper, Kaspar.
Jeffrey = Geoffrey.
Jem, Jemmy = James.
Jenny = Jane.
Jeremy, Jeremias.
Jerry = Jeremy.
Jim, Jimmy = James.
Jo, Joe = Joseph.
Joan, Johanna.

Job, Hiob.
John, Johann.
Johnny = John, Hänschen.
Josh = Joshua.
Joshua, Josua.
Joyce, Jodoka.
Julia, Julie.
Juliet, Julchen.

Kate = Catherine, Kätchen.
Kit = Christopher.
Kitty = Kate.

Laurence, Lawrence, Lorenz.
Lenny = Leonard.
Leonard, Leonhard.
Lettice, Lätitia.
Lewis, Ludwig.
Lizzie = Elizabeth, Lieschen.
Loo = Louise.
Louis = Lewis.
Louise, Luise.
Lucy, Luzia.
Luke, Lukas.

Madge = Margaret.
Magdalen, Magdalene.
Maggie, Maggy = Margaret, Gretchen.
Margaret, Margarete.
Margery = Margaret.
Maria, Marie.
Mark, Markus.
Mary, Marie.
Mat = Matthew.
Matilda, Mathilde.
Matthew, Matthäus.
Maud = Magdalen, Lenchen.
Maurice, Moritz.
May = Mary.
Meg = Margaret.
Mike = Michael.
Moll, Molly = Mary.

Nan, Nancy, Nannie = Anne, Nannchen.
Nat = Nathaniel, Nathanael.
Ned, Neddy = Edward.
Nell, Nelly = Helen.
Nicholas, Nikolaus.
Nick = Nicholas.
Noll = Oliver.

Oliver, Olivier.

Pad, Paddy, Pat = Patrick.
Patrick, Patrizius.
Patty = Matilda.
Peg, Peggy = Margaret.
Peter, Petrus, Peter.
Phil = Philip.
Philip, Philippus, Philipp.
Philippa, Philippine.
Pip = Philip.
Poll, Polly = Mary.

Rachel, Rahel.
Ralph, Rudolf.
Randal, Randolf.
Raymond, Raimund.
Reginald, Reinwald.
Reynold, Reinhold.
Richard, Richard.
Robin = Robert.
Roderick, Roderich.
Roger, Rüdiger.
Roland, Rowland, Roland.
Rory = Roderick.
Rose, Rosa, Röschen.
Rupert, Ruprecht.

Sal, Sally = Sarah, Salchen.
Sam = Samuel.
Sandy, Sawney = Alexander.
Solomon, Salomo.
Sophia, Sophy, Sophie.
Stephen, Stephan.
Sue, Suky = Susan.
Susan, Susanna, Susanne, Suschen.

Taffy = David.
Ted, Teddy = Edward.
Theresa, Therese, Theresia.
Tim = Timothy.
Timothy, Timotheus.
Toby = Tobias.
Tom, Tommy = Thomas.
Tony = Anthony.

Valentine, Valentin.
Vitus, Veit.

Walt = Walter, Walter.
Wat = Walter.
Will, Willy = William.
William, Wilhelm.
Winifred, Winfried.

Zachary, Zacharias.

Table of Strong and Irregular Weak Verbs

Present.	Imperfect.	Participle.	Present.	Imperfect.	Participle.
abide	abode	abode	engrave	engraved	engraven*
am	was	been	fall	fell	fallen
arise	arose	arisen	feed	fed	fed
awake	awoke*	awaked	feel	felt	felt
bear	bore	borne, born	fight	fought	fought
beat	beat	beaten	find	found	found
become	became	become	flee	fled	fled
befall	befell	befallen	fling	flung	flung
beget	begot	begotten	fly	flew	flown
begin	began	begun	forbear	forbore	forborne
bend	bent	bent*	forbid	forbade	forbidden
bereave	bereft*	bereft*	forego	forewent	foregone
beseech	besought	besought	foretell	foretold	foretold
bid	bade	bidden	forget	forgot	forgot, for-
bind	bound	bound			gotten
bite	bit	bitten	forgive	forgave	forgiven
bled	bled	bled	forsake	forsook	forsaken
blow	blew	blown	forswear	forswore	forsworn
break	broke	broken	freeze	froze	frozen
breed	bred	bred	get	got	got, gotten
bring	brought	brought	gild	gilt*	gilt*
build	built	built	gird	girt*	girt*
burn	burnt*	burnt*	give	gave	given
burst	burst	burst	go	went	gone
buy	bought	bought	grind	ground	ground
can	could	—	grow	grew	grown
cast	cast	cast	hang	hung*	hung*
catch	caught	caught	have	had	had
chide	chid	chid(den)	hear	heard	heard
choose	chose	chosen	heave	hove*	hove*
cleave	cleft, clove	cleft, cloven	hew	hewed	hewn*
cling	clung	clung	hide	hid	hidden, hid
clothe	clad*	clad*	hit	hit	hit
come	came	come	hold	held	held
cost	cost	cost	hurt	hurt	hurt
creep	crept	crept	keep	kept	kept
cut	cut	cut	kneel	knelt*	knelt*
dare	durst*	dared	knit	knit*	knit*
deal	dealt	dealt	know	knew	known
dig	dug*	dug*	lade	laded	laden*
do	did	done	lay	laid	laid
draw	drew	drawn	lead	led	led
dream	dreamt*	dreamt*	lean	leant*	leant*
drink	drank	drunk	leap	leapt*	leapt*
drive	drove	driven	learn	learnt*	learnt*
dwell	dwelt*	dwelt*	leave	left	left
eat	ate, eat	eaten	lend	lent	lent

Verbs marked * are conjugated in the regular weak form too.

Present.	Imperfect.	Participle.	Present.	Imperfect.	Participle.
let	let	let	slit	slit	slit
lie (liegen)	lay	lain	smell	smelt*	smelt*
light	lit*	lit*	smite	smote	smitten
lose	lost	lost	sow	sowed	sown*
make	made	made	speak	spoke	spoken
may	(*subj.*) might	—	speed	sped	sped
mean	meant	meant	spell	spelt*	spelt*
meet	met	met	spend	spent	spent
melt	melted	molten*	spill	spilt*	spilt*
methinks	methought	—	spin	spun	spun
mow	mowed	mown*	spit	spit	spit
must	(must)	—	split	split	split
ought (*subj.*)	—	—	spread	spread	spread
pay	paid	paid	spring	sprang	sprung
pen (einschliessen)	pent*	pent*	stand	stood	stood
			stave	stove*	stove*
put	put	put	steal	stole	stolen
read	read	read	stick	stuck	stuck
rend	rent	rent	sting	stung	stung
rid	rid, ridded	rid	stink	stank, stunk	stunk
ride	rode	ridden			
ring	rang	rung	strew	strewed	strewn*
rise	rose	risen	stride	strode	stridden
rive	rived	riven	strike	struck	struck (stricken)
run	ran	run			
saw	sawed	sawn*	string	strung	strung
say	said	said	strive	strove	striven
see	saw	seen	strow	strowed	strown
seek	sought	sought	swear	swore	sworn
seethe	seethed	sodden*	sweep	swept	swept
sell	sold	sold	swell	swelled	swollen*
send	sent	sent	swim	swam	swum
set	set	set	swing	swung	swung
shake	shook	shaken	take	took	taken
shall	(*subj.*) should	—	teach	taught	taught
			tear	tore	torn
shape	shaped	shapen*	tell	told	told
shear	shore*	shorn*	think	thought	thought
shed	shed	shed	thrive	throve*	thriven*
shew	shewed	shewn*	throw	threw	thrown
shine	shone	shone	thrust	thrust	thrust
shoe	shod	shod	tread	trod	trod, trodden
shoot	shot	shot			
show	showed	shown*	wake	woke, waked	waked, woke[n]
shred	shred	shred	waylay	waylaid	waylaid
shrink	shrunk, shrank	shrunk, shrunken	wear	wore	worn
			weave	wove	woven
shut	shut	shut	weep	wept	wept
sing	sang	sung	will	would	—
sink	sank	sunk	win	won	won
sit	sat	sat	wind	wound	wound
slay	slew	slain	work	wrought*	wrought*
sleep	slept	slept	wrap	wrapt*	wrapt*
slide	slid	slid	wring	wrung	wrung
sling	slung	slung	write	wrote	written
slink	slunk	slunk			

Verbs marked * are conjugated in the regular weak form too.

List of Abbreviations

A., *Associate*, ausserordentliche Mitglied *n.*

AI, *first class*, erster Klasse, erstklassig.

A.B., *able-bodied*, dienstfähige Matrose *m.*

Abp., *Archbishop*, Erzbischof *m.*

A.C., *ante Christum*, vor Christi Geburt.

a/c, *account*, Rechnung.

A.D., *anno Domini*, im Jahre des Herrn.

A.D.C., *Aide-de-Camp*, Adjutant *m.*

Adm., *Admiral*, Admiral *m.*

A.G., *Adjutant-General*, Generaladjutant *m.*

A.I.C.E., *Associate of the Institute of Civil Engineers.*

a.m., *ante meridiem*, vormittags.

A.R.A., *Associate of the Royal Academy.*

b., *born*, geboren.

B.A., *Bachelor of Arts*, Bakkalaureus der freien Künste.

Bart., *Baronet*, Baronet *m.*

B.C., *before Christ*, vor Christi Geburt; *British Columbia*, Britisch Kolumbia.

B.C.L., *Bachelor of Civil Law*, Bakkalaureus des bürgerlichen Rechts.

B.D., *Bachelor of Divinity*, Bakkalaureus der Theologie.

Beds., *Bedfordshire.*

Berks, *Berkshire.*

B.L., *Bachelor of Letters or Law*, Bakkalaureus der Literatur oder der Rechte.

B.M., *Bachelor of Medicine*, Bakkalaureus der Medizin.

B.Mus., *Bachelor of Music*, Bakkalaureus der Musik.

Bp., *Bishop*, Bischof *m.*

Bros., *brothers*, Gebrüder *pl.*

B.Sc., *Bachelor of Science*, Bakkalaureus der Naturwissenschaften.

Bt., *Baronet m.*

Bucks, *Buckinghamshire.*

C. (*Amer.*), *cent*; *centigrade*, Grad Celsius.

ca., *circa*, etwa.

Cal., *California*, Kalifornien.

Cam., Camb., *Cambridge.*

Cambs., *Cambridgeshire.*

Can., *Canada*, Kanada.

Cant., *Canterbury.*

Capt., *Captain*, Kapitän; Hauptmann, Rittmeister.

C.B., *Companion (of the Order of the) Bath*, Ritter des Bathordens.

C.C., *County Council*, Grafschaftsrat.

C.E., *Civil Engineer*, Ingenieur.

Ches., *Cheshire.*

cg., *centigram*, Zentigramm.

C.I., *Crown of India*, Indischer Kronenorden.

C.I.E., *Companion (of the Order of the) Indian Empire.*

cl., *centilitre*, Zentiliter.

cm., *centimetre*, Zentimeter.

C.M.G., *Companion (of the Order of) St. Michael and St. George.*

C.O., *Colonial Office*, Kolonialamt.

Co., *Company*, Gesellschaft; *County*, Grafschaft.

c/o, *care of*, per Adresse, bei.

C.O.D., *cash on delivery*, zahlbar bei Sicht.

Col., *Colonel*, Oberst.

Col.-Sergt., *Colour-Sergeant*, Fahnenunteroffizier; Feldwebel.

con., *contra*, gegen.

Corn., *Cornwall.*

C.O.S., *Charity Organization Society*, Armenpflegeverband *m.*

cf., *compare*, vergleiche.

C.P.R., *Canadian Pacific Railway.*

C.T.C., *Cyclists' Touring Club*, Radfahrerverein.

cwt., *hundredweight*, Zentner *m.*

d. (*denarius*), *penny* (= 8 Pfennige); *died*, gestorben.

D.C.L., *Doctor of Civil Law*, Doktor des bürgerlichen Rechts.

D.D., *Doctor of Divinity*, Doktor der Theologie.

deg., *degree*, Grad *m.*

disc., *discount*, Abzug *m.*, Rabatt *m.*

D.Litt., *Doctor of Literature*, Doktor der Literatur.

D.L.O., *Dead Letter Office*, Postamt für unbestellbare Briefe.

D.Mus., *Doctor of Music*, Doktor der Musik.

doz., *dozen*, Dutzend *n.*

Dpt., *department*, Abteilung *f.*

Dr., *debtor*, Schuldner *m.*; *Doctor*, Doktor *m.*

D.Sc., *Doctor of Science*, Doktor der Naturwissenschaften.

D.S.O., *Distinguished Service Order*, Verdienstorden *m.*

dwt., *pennyweight* (= $\frac{1}{20}$ Unze

509

E., *east*, Osten *m.*
Ebor., *Eboracum*, York.
e.g., *exempli gratia*, zum Beispiel.
E.I.C., *East India Company.*
esp., *especially*, besonders.
Esq., *Esquire*, Hochwohlgeboren.
etc., *et cetera*, usw.
Exon., *Exonia*, Exeter.
E. & O. E., *errors and omissions excepted*, Irrtum vorbehalten.

F., *Fel ow*, Mitglied *n.*, Ehrenmitglied *n.*
F., *Fahr.*, Fahrenheit.
F.A., *Footbal Association.*
F.B.A., *Fellow of the British Academy.*
F.C.S., *Fellow of the Chemical Society.*
F.G.S., *Fellow of the Geological Society.*
F.L.S., *Fellow of the Linnaean Society.*
f.o.b., *free on board*, frei an Bord.
fo., fol., *folio*, Folio.
foll., *following*, folgend.
F.R.A.S., *Fellow of the Royal Astronomical Society.*
F.R.C.S., *Fellow of the Royal Col ege of Surgeons.*
F.R.G.S., *Fellow of the Royal Geographical Society.*
F.R.S., *Fellow of the Royal Society.*
F.R.S.L., *Fellow of the Royal Society of Literature.*
F.S.A., *Fellow of the Society of Arts* or *Antiquaries.*
ft., *foot, feet*, Fuss.
fth., fthm., *fathom*, Klafter.
fur., *furlong*, Achtelmeile *f.*
F.Z.S., *Fellow of the Zoological Society.*

G.B., *Great Britain*, Grossbritannien.
G.C., *Grand Cross*, Grosskreuz *n.*, e.g.
G.C.B., *Grand Cross of the Bath.*
Gent, *gentleman.*
Geo., *George*, Georg.
G.E.R., *Great Eastern Railway.*
G.L., *Grand Lodge*, Grossloge *f.*
Glos., *Gloucestershire.*
G.P., *General Practitioner*, praktische Arzt *m.*
G.P.O., *General Post Office*, Hauptpostamt *n.*
gs., *guineas*, Guineen *pl.f.*

h., hr., *hour*, Stunde *f.*, **hrs.,** *hours*, Stunden.
Hants., *Hampshire.*
H.B.M., *His* (or *Her*) *Britannic Majesty*, Seine (Ihre) Majestät der König (die Königin) von Grossbritannien.
H.G., *His Grace*, Seine Durchlaucht.
hhd., *hogshead*, Oxhoft *n.*
H.I.H., *His Imperial H ghness*, Seine Kaiserliche Hoheit.

H.M., *H s Majesty*, Seine Majestät.
H.M.I.S., *His Majesty's Inspector of Schools.*
H.M.S., *His Majesty's Ship*, Seiner Majestäts Schiff.
Hon., *Honourable*, Ehrenwert; *Honorary*, Ehren...
h.p., *horse-power*, Pferdestärke *f.*
H.R.H., *His Royal Highness*, Seine Königliche Hoheit.
H.S., *High School*, höhere Schule.
H.S.H., *His Serene Highness*, Seine Durchlaucht.
Hy., *Henry*, Heinrich.

Ia., *Iowa.*
I.C.S., *Indian Civil Service*, Indische Staatsdienst *m.*
i.e., *id est*, das heisst, d.h.
i.h.p., *indicated horse-power*, angezeigte Pferdestärke *f.*
Ill., *Illinois.*
I.L.P., *Independent Labour Party*, Unabhängige Arbeiterpartei *f.*
I.M.S., *Indian Medical Service*, Indische Sanitätsdienst *m.*
in, *inches*, Zoll.
inst., *instant, of the present month*, dieses Monats, d.M.
I.O.U., *I owe you*, ich schulde Ihnen; Schuldschein *m.*
I.S.C., *Indian Staff Corps*, Indischer Generalstab.
ital., *italics*, Kursivdruck *m.*

Jas., *James*, Jakob.
Joe, *Joseph*, Josef.
J.P., *Justice of the Peace*, Friedensrichter *m.*

Kan., *Kansas.*
K.B., *King's Bench*, Oberhofgericht *n.*
K.C., *Knight Commander*, Komtur, Grossmeister *m.*; *King's Counsel*, Justizrat *m.*
K.C.B., *Knight Commander of the Bath.*
K.C.V.O., *Knight of the Royal Victorian Order.*
K.G., *Knight of the Garter*, Ritter des Hosenbandordens.
K.G.C., *Knight of the Grand Cross*, Ritter des Grosskreuzes.
K.G.C.B., *Knight of the Grand Cross of the Bath.*
K.G.F., *Knight of the Golden Fleece*, Ritter des goldenen Vlieses.
Kg., *kilogramme*, Kilogramm *n.*
km., *kilometre*, Kilometer.
Kt., *Knight*, Ritter *m.*
K.S.I., *Knight of the Star of India.*
K.T., *Knight of the Thistle.*
Ky., *Kentucky.*

L., £, *libra*, Pfund (Sterling) *n*.
La., *Louisiana.*
Lancs, *Lancashire.*
Lat., *latitude*, Breite *f*.
lb., *libra*, Pfund *n*.
l.c., *loco citato*, am angeführten Orte; *letter of credit*, Kreditbrief *m*.
L.C.C., *London County Council*, Londoner Stadtrat *m*.
L.C.J., *Lord Chief Justice*, Lord Oberrichter.
Ld., Lord.
L.D.S., *Licentiate in Dental Surgery*, Zahnarzt *m*.
Lieut., Lt., *Lieutenant*, Leutnant *m*.
lit., *literally*, wörtlich.
Litt.D., *Literarum Doctor*, Doktor der Literatur.
Ll.B., *Legum Baccalaureus*, Bakkalaureus der Rechte.
Ll.D., *Legum Doctor*, Doktor der Rechte.
long., *longitude*, Länge *f*.
L.R.C.P., *Licentiate of the Royal College of Physicians.*
L.R.C.S., *Licentiate of the Royal College of Surgeons.*
L.S., *loco sigilli*, an Stelle des Siegels.
L.S.A., *Licentiate of the Society of Apothecaries.*
L.S.D., *librae, solidi, denarii* (*pounds, shillings, pence*).
Ltd., *limited* (*liability company*), Gesellschaft mit beschränkter Haftung.
L.U., *Liberal Unionist.*

m., *masculine*, männlich; *metre*, Meter *m*.; *mile*, Meile *f*.; *minute*, Minute *f*.
M.A., *Master of Arts*, Magister der freien Künste.
Mass., *Massachusetts.*
M.B., *Medicinae baccalaureus*, Bakkalaureus der Medizin.
M.C., *Member of Congress*, Kongressmitglied.
Md., *Maryland.*
M.D., *Medicinae doctor*, Dr. med.
Me., *Maine.*
M.E., *Mining Engineer*, Bergingenieur *m*.
Messrs., *Messieurs*, Herren.
mfd., *manufactured*, angefertigt.
M.F.H., *Master of Foxhounds.*
Mgr., *Monsigneur*, Monsignore.
M.H.R., *Member of the House of Representatives*, Abgeordneter *m*.
M.I.C.E., *Member of the Institute of Civil Engineers.*
Mich., *Michigan.*
Minn., *Minnesota.*
Mis., *Missouri.*
Miss., *Mississippi.*
mo., *month*, Monat.
M.O., *Money Order*, Postanweisung *f*.

Mods., *Moderations*, zweite Universitätsprüfung in Oxford.
mos., *months*, Monate.
M.P., *Member of Parliament*, Parlamentsmitglied.
M.R., *Master of the Rolls*, Staatsarchivar *m*.
M.R.A.S., *Member of the Royal Academy of Sciences.*
M.R.C.C., *Member of the Royal College of Chemistry.*
M.R.C.P., *Member of the Royal College of Physicians.*
M.R.C.S., *Member of the Royal College of Surgeons.*
M.R.C.V.S., *Member of the Royal College of Veterinary Surgeons.*
M.R.G.S., *Member of the Royal Geographical Society.*
M.R.I., *Member of the Royal Institution.*
Mrs., *Mistress*, Frau *f*.
MS., *manuscript*, Handschrift *f*.
M.S., *Master in Surgery.*
m.s., *months after sight*, Monate nach Sicht.
M.Sc., *Master of Science.*
m.s.l., *mean sea level*, mittlere Meeresspiegel *m*.
MSS., *manuscripts*, Handschriften.
Mt., *Mount*, Berg *m*.
Mus.B., *Baccalaureus of Music*, Bakkalaureus der Musik.
Mus.D., *Doctor of Music*, Doktor der Musik.
M.V.O., *Member of the Victorian Order.*

N., *north*, Norden *m*.; *Nitrogen*, Stickstoff *m*.; *neuter*, sächlich.
Na., *Nebraska.*
N.B., *North Britain*, Schottland; *New Brunswick*, Neubraunschweig; *nota bene.*
N.C., *North Carolina*, Nordkarolina.
N.C.U., *National Cyclists' Union*, Nationaler Radfahrerverein *m*.
N.D., *no date*, ohne Jahr.
N.Dak., *North Dakota.*
N.E., *north-east*, Nordost *m*.
Neb., *Nebraska.*
nem-con., *nemine contradicente*, ohne Widerspruch.
net., *netto*, Rein...
NF., *Newfoundland*, Neufundland.
N.H., *New Hampshire.*
N.J., *New Jersey.*
N.N.E., *north-north-east*, Nord-Nordost.
N.N.W., *north-north-west*, Nord-Nordwest.
N.O., *New Orleans.*
no., *numero*, Nummer *f*.
Northumb., *Northumberland.*
nos., *numbers*, Nummern.
Notts., *Nottinghamshire.*

N.S., *Nova Scotia,* Neu-Schottland.
n.s., *not specified,* nicht angegeben.
N.S.P.C.C., *National Society for the Prevention of Cruelty to Children.*
N.S.W., *New South Wales,* Neusüd-wales.
N.U.T., *National Union of Teachers.*
N.W., *north-west,* Nordwest *m.*
N.Y., *New York,* Neuyork.
N.Z., *New Zealand,* Neuseeland.

O., *Ohio; Oxygen,* Sauerstoff.
O. & O., *Oriental & Occidental Steamship Company.*
O.H.M.S., *On Her Majesty's Service,* im Dienste Sr. Majestät; Dienstsache *f.*
O.K., *all correct,* diensttauglich.
O.M., *Order of Merit,* Verdienstorden *m.*
Ont., *Ontario.*
Ore., *Oregon.*
O.T., *Old Testament,* Altes Testament.
Oxon, Oxonia, *Oxfordshire;* Oxford.
O.S.N.C., *Oriental Steam Navigation Company.*
oz., *ounce,* Unze *f.*

p., *page,* Seite *f.*
Pa., *Pennsylvania,* Pennsylvanien.
Pat. *Patrick.*
P. & O., *Peninsular and Oriental Company.*
P.C., *Privy Councillor,* Geheime Rat *m.; police constable,* Schutzmann *m.*
p.c., *postcard,* Postkarte *f.*
per pro, *per procurationem,* in Vertretung.
p.m., *post meridiem,* nachmittags.
P.M.G., *Postmaster-General,* Oberpostdirektor *m.*
p.n., *prom ssory note,* Schuldschein *m.*
P.O., *Post Office,* Postamt *n.*
P.O.O., *Post Office Order,* Postanweisung *f.*
pp., *pages,* Seiten.
P.R.A., *President of the Royal Academy.*
pro tem, *pro tempore,* zeitweilig.
prox., *proximo,* nächsten Monats.
P.R.S., *President of the Royal Society.*
P.S., *Postscript,* Nachschrift *f.*
P.S.N.C., *Pacific Steam Navigation Company.*
pt., *pint,* Pinte *f.*
P.T., *Pupil Teacher,* Lehramts-Aspirant *m.*
Pte., *Private,* Gemeiner (Soldat).
P.T.O., *Please turn over,* bitte umwenden.

Q., *Query,* Frage *f.*
Q.M., *Quartermaster,* Quartiermeister *m.*
Q.M.G., *Quartermaster-General,* General-quartiermeister *m.*

qr., *quarter,* Viertel.
Q.S., *Quarter Sessions,* Gerichtsitzung *f.*
q.t., *quiet,* vertraulich.
qt., *quart,* englisher Quart.
qto., *quarto,* Quartformat *n.*
qu., *query,* Frage *f.*
Que, *Quebec,* Quebeck.

R., *Rex, Regina,* König, Königin.
R.A., *Royal Academy; Royal Academician.*
R.B., *Rifle Brigade,* Schützenbrigade *f.*
R.B.A., *Royal Society of British Artists,* Britische Künstlerverein *m.*
R.C.M., *Royal College of Music.*
R.C.P., *Royal College of Physicians.*
R.C.S., *Royal College of Surgeons.*
rcpt., *receipt,* Quittung *f.*
Regt., *Regiment,* Regiment *n.*
Rev., *Reverend,* Ehrwürden, Hochwürden.
R.G.S., *Royal Geographical Society.*
R.H., *Royal Highness,* Königliche Hoheit.
R.H.A., *Royal Horse Artillery,* Reitende Artillerie *f.*
R.I., *Rhode Island.*
R.M., *Royal Marine,* Königliche Seesoldaten *pl.*
R.M.A., *Royal Marine Artillery.*
R.N., *Royal Navy,* Kgl. Marine *f.*
R.N.R., *Royal Naval Reserve,* Marinereserve *f.*
R.S., *Royal Society,* Kgl. Akademie der (Natur) Wissenschaften.
Rt. Hon., *Right Honourable,* Hochwohlgeboren.
Rt. Rev., *Right Reverend,* Hoch(ehr)würden.
R.U., *Rugby Union,* Rugby-Fussball-Bund *m.*
Rs., *rupees,* Rupien *pl.*
Rx., *tens of rupees.*
R.S.P.C.A., *Society for Prevention of Cruelty to Animals,* Tierschutzverein *m.*
Ry., *railway,* Eisenbahn *f.*

s., *shilling,* Schilling *m.*
S., *south,* Süden *m.; Saint,* Sankt; *Society,* Verein.
S.A., *South Africa,* Südafrika.
Salop, *Shropshire.*
Sarum, *Salisbury.*
S.C., *South Carolina,* Südkarolina.
sc., scil., *scilicet,* nämlich.
Sc.D. = *D.Sc.*
S.D., *South Dakota,* Süddakota.
S.E., *south-east,* Südost *m.*
Sec., *Secretary,* Schriftführer *m.*
Sergt., *Sergeant,* Sergeant *m.*
s.g., *specific gravity,* spezifische Gewicht *n.*

sh., *shilling*, Schilling *m.*
S.P.C.K., *Society for Promoting Christian Knowledge.*
Sq., *Square*, Platz *m.*
S.S., *Saints*, Heilige *pl.*
s.s., *screw steamer*, Schraubendampfer *m.*
S.S., *steamship*, Dampfer *m.*
S.S.E., *south-south-east*, Südsüdost *m.*
S.S.W., *south-south-west*, Südsüdwest *m.*
St., *Saint*, Heilige *m.*; *Street*, Strasse *f.*
Staffs, *Staffordshire.*
ster., stg., *sterling*, Sterling.
Supt., *superintendent*, Oberaufseher *m.*
Surg., *surgery*, Chirurgie *f.*; *surgeon*, Chirurg *m.*

T.C.D., *Trinity College, Dublin.*
Tenn., *Tennessee.*
Tex., *Texas.*
Tho., Thos., *Thomas.*
T.O., *Turn over*, umschlagen.
T.R.H., *Their Royal Highnesses*, Ihre Königlichen Hoheiten *pl.*

U.C., *Upper Canada*, Ober-Kanada.
U.K., *United Kingdom*, Vereinigte Königreich *n.*, Grossbritannien.
ult., *ultimo*, letzten Monats.
U.S., *United States*, Vereinigte Staaten, *n.pl.*
U.S.A., *United States of America*, Vereinigte Staaten von Nordamerika; *United States Army*, Heer (*n.*) der Vereinigten Staaten.
U.S.N., *United States Navy*, Marine (*f.*) der Vereinigten Staaten.
U.T., *Utah Territory.*

v., *vide*, siehe; *verse*, Vers *m.*
V.A., *Victoria and Albert*, Viktoria- und Albert-Orden *m.*

Va., *Virginia.*
V.C., *Victoria Cross*, Viktoriakreuz *n.*; *Vice-Chancellor*, Vizekanzler *m.*; *Vice-Consul*, Vizekonsul *m.*
Ven., *Venerable*, Ehrwürden.
Vet., *veterinary*, Tierarzt.
Vis., *Viscount*, Vicomte *m.*
viz., *videlicet*, nämlich.
V.O., *Victorian Order*, Viktoria-Orden *m.*
vol., *volume*, Band *m.*; **vols.,** *volumes*, Bände *m.pl.*
vv., *verses*, Verse *m.pl.*

W., *west*, Westen *m.*
War., *Warwickshire.*
Wash., *Washington.*
W.C., *water closet*, Abort *m.*; *West Central*, London, W.C.
W.I., *West Indies*, Westindien.
Wis., *Wisconsin.*
Wm., *William*, Wilhelm.
W.N.W., *west-north-west*, West-Nordwest.
W.O., *War Office*, Kriegsministerium *n.*
Worcs., *Worcestershire.*
W.S., *Writer to the Signet*, schottische Rechtsanwalt *m.*
W.S.W., *west-south-west*, West-Südwest.
wt., *weight*, Gewicht *n.*
Wyo., *Wyoming.*

Xmas., *Christmas*, Weihnachten *n.*

yd., *yard*, Yard *n.*
ye (*dhe*)= *the*; γ for Old English þ= *th.*
Y.M.C.A., *Young Men's Christian Association*, Verein (*m.*) christlicher Jünglinge.
Yorks, *Yorkshire.*
Y.W.C.A., *Young Women's Christian Association*, Verein (*m.*) christlicher Jungfrauen.